D1163114

PEARSON ALWAYS LEARNING

The Science of Psychology and Human Behavior

Sixth Custom Edition

Taken from:
Psychology, Eleventh Edition
by Carole Wade, Carol Tavris, and Maryanne Garry

Understanding Psychology, Eleventh Edition
by Charles G. Morris and Albert A. Maisto

Psychological Science, Second Edition
by Mark Krause and Daniel Corts

Mastering the World of Psychology, Fifth Edition
by Samuel E. Wood, Ellen Green Wood, and Denise Boyd

Psychology from Inquiry to Understanding, Third Edition
by Scott O. Lilienfeld, Steven Jay Lynn, Laura L. Namy, and Nancy J. Woolf

Psychology: The Science of Behavior, Seventh Edition
by Neil R. Carlson, Harold Miller, C. Donald Heth, John W. Donahoe, and G. Neil Martin

Cover Art: Courtesy of mopic/123RF.

Taken from:

Psychology, Eleventh Edition
by Carole Wade, Carol Tavris, and Maryanne Garry
Copyright © 2014, 2011, 2008 by Pearson Education, Inc.
New York, New York 10013

Understanding Psychology, Eleventh Edition
by Charles G. Morris and Albert A. Maisto
Copyright © 2016, 2013, 2010 by Pearson Education, Inc.

Psychological Science, Second Edition
by Mark Krause and Daniel Corts
Copyright © 2016, 2014, 2012 by Pearson Education, Inc.

Mastering the World of Psychology, Fifth Edition
by Samuel E. Wood, Ellen Green Wood, and Denise Boyd
Copyright © 2014, 2011, 2008 by Pearson Education, Inc.

Psychology from Inquiry to Understanding, Third Edition
by Scott O. Lilienfeld, Steven Jay Lynn, Laura L. Namy, and Nancy J. Woolf
Copyright © 2014, 2011, 2009 by Pearson Education, Inc.

Psychology: The Science of Behavior, Seventh Edition
by Neil R. Carlson, Harold Miller, C. Donald Heth, John W. Donahoe, and G. Neil Martin
Copyright © 2010, 2007, 1997, 1993, 1990, 1987, 1984 by Pearson Education, Inc.

Pearson Education, Inc., 330 Hudson Street, New York, New York 10013
A Pearson Education Company
www.pearsoned.com

Printed in the United States of America

2 16

000200010272023638

TG/KS

ISBN 10: 1-323-40152-0
ISBN 13: 978-1-323-40152-1

Special thanks to Anthony Bonita, Sarah Casella, Colleen Cullinan, Tanya Douleh, Matthew Jameson, Rebecca Kolb, Jennifer Kuhn, Kristin Marroletti, Eliza McManus, Rachel Petts, Brandon Ring, and Christina Sheerin for their valuable input on the development of this book.

Contents

1 Learning Strategies for Psychology and Beyond: A Different Kind of Beginning 1

By Douglas A. Johnson, Ph.D. and Sophie Rubin, Ph.D.

2 Introduction to the Science of Psychology: Why We Need Both Science and Psychology in Our Lives 19

By Douglas A. Johnson, Ph.D. and Sophie Rubin, Ph.D.

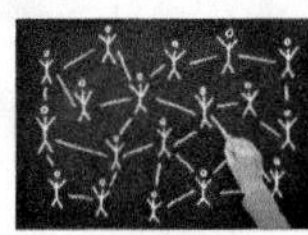

3 How Psychologists Do Research 50

Taken from **Psychology,** *Eleventh Edition by Carole Wade, Carol Tavris, and Maryanne Garry*

4 Evolution, Heredity, and Behavior 85

Taken from **Psychology: The Science of Behavior,** *Seventh Edition by Neil R. Carlson, Harold Miller, C. Donald Heth, John W. Donahoe, and G. Neil Martin*

5 Biology and Behavior 118

Taken from **Mastering the World of Psychology,** *Fifth Edition by Samuel E. Wood, Ellen Green Wood, and Denise Boyd*

6 Body Rhythms and Mental States* 158

Taken from **Psychology,** *Eleventh Edition by Carole Wade, Carol Tavris, and Maryanne Garry*

7 Conditioning Principles and Applications: How the Environment We Live in Shapes Us 192

By Douglas A. Johnson, Ph.D. and Sophie Rubin, Ph.D

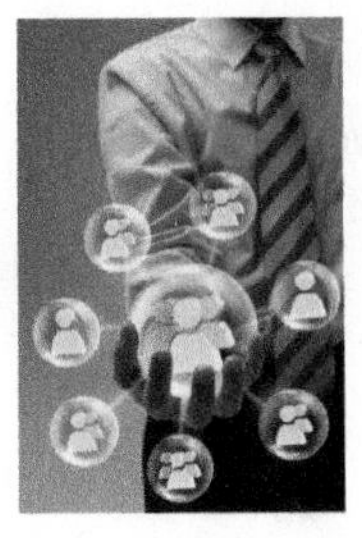

8 Social Psychology 218

By Douglas A. Johnson, Ph.D. and Sophie Rubin, Ph.D.

9 Cognition and Mental Abilities 245

Taken from **Understanding Psychology,** ***Eleventh Edition by Charles G. Morris and Albert A. Maisto***

10 Motivation and Emotion 291

Taken from **Understanding Psychology,** *Eleventh Edition by Charles G. Morris and Albert A. Maisto*

11 Memory 326

Taken from Psychology, *Eleventh Edition by Carole Wade, Carol Tavris, and Maryanne Garry*

12 Development 366

By Douglas A. Johnson, Ph.D. and Sophie Rubin, Ph.D.

13 Health, Stress, and Coping 390

Taken from Psychological Science, *Second Edition by Mark Krause and Daniel Corts*

14 Psychology in the Workplace 426

By Douglas A. Johnson, Ph.D. and Sophie Rubin, Ph.D.

1

Learning Strategies for Psychology and Beyond

A Different Kind of Beginning

BY DOUGLAS A. JOHNSON, PH.D. AND SOPHIE RUBIN, PH.D.

Considering all the studying you may find yourself doing for your classes, you'll want the best study habits possible!

An introductory textbook for any given field of study would normally start off by describing the field and what that field is about. Don't worry, we'll get to that material in the next chapter, but we wanted to start this book off with a slightly different approach. For now, it will be sufficient to note that **psychology** is the discipline that scientifically studies behavior and/or mental processes. As such, it is a large and diverse field that covers many different topics. One topic that is particularly likely to be useful for you is psychology's emphasis on how people learn and gain knowledge, skills, and abilities. This emphasis means that the field of psychology can provide practical tips and strategies to help make you a better student and teach you how to utilize more effective and efficient study techniques. We consider this to be especially important because many students receive little to no specific instruction in self-study strategies, other than a general suggestion to do a large quantity of studying (Adams, Carnine, & Gersten, 1992). Many of the self-study skills students develop in early education are often quite poor, even when the students themselves tend to believe otherwise (Yuksel, 2006). We hope you'll be open to learning some new study habits that can improve your performance or perhaps make your studying more efficient even if you are someone who is already performing well. Keep in mind that many people can perform well even when using poor and inefficient techniques because they overcompensate with huge amounts of excessive study time. Therefore, even if you are an A student, you may still have much to learn from this chapter (and may save yourself a lot of unnecessary time by doing so). While high quality learning will always require a considerable investment of time and there are no effort-free shortcuts, not all self-study strategies are equally effective or efficient. It is quite unlikely you have already acquired the best techniques available or even the best ones suited for you. Given that you may want to start applying these techniques to your learning right away, we decided to cover this material first. Let's start by focusing on why you might need strong study skills to prepare for a potentially demanding course, even if you think you already have a solid understanding of psychology.

THE DEMANDS OF HIGH SCHOOL VERSUS THE DEMANDS OF COLLEGE

College may require some very different things from you than high school in order to reach your goals.

You may feel like you have a good grasp on psychology because you took a class (or classes) on psychology during high school. While having this experience can be quite valuable and may have also been the inspiration that led you to enroll in a college level psychology course, some caution is once again warranted. Your high school psychology class achievements may not necessarily predict your performance in your college psychology class (Rossi, Keeley, & Buskist, 2005). The types of activities and the methods of assessing knowledge can differ quite dramatically between high school and college, a point that isn't always conveyed during freshman orientations. There are at least three key differences between the activities and assessment used in high school and the typical college course (Michael, 2004).

1. **Source of the material to be learned:** In high school, students often learn much, if not most, of the course material through classroom discussions and working on projects (either alone or in groups). This often causes high school students to neglect or completely ignore textbook material and pay minimal attention to teachers. Unlike high school, in most college classes, the bulk of the material to be learned comes from the textbook and lectures. Furthermore, most instructors will expect you to have read the textbook before an exam, and often times before lectures. Students who have come to depend on everything to be completely summarized in class or group discussions often find it difficult to adapt to the new requirements demanded by many college classes.
2. **Basis of grades:** In high school, there is often a very high emphasis placed on attendance and participation in class. This is often reflected in grading

psychology
the discipline that scientifically studies behavior and/or mental processes

Textbooks and grades often get a stronger emphasis in college.

Your time outside of class is critical to your success in class.

practices where students who do poorly on exams can still earn passing class grades because much, if not most, of the class grade is based on attendance and participation. This is less typical in many college classrooms, where exam grades will count for most, if not all, of the student's final course grade. As such, you have to really know the material to do well in the course, not simply engage in frequent activities unrelated to mastery.

3. **Outside of class time requirements:** High school students can often successfully pass their courses with minimal to no work outside of the classroom itself. When homework is assigned, it rarely requires an intense time commitment and can often be successfully ignored in its entirety. The reduced emphasis on examination grading means students are frequently not required to master the material in any depth. The opposite tends to be true in college settings, where a very high time commitment is necessary outside of class in order to do well within the class. It is not uncommon for students to need to put in at least 6–9 hours of study outside of the classroom per class and per week in order to achieve minimally passing grades. Self-study at home is not just an occasional hassle in college settings; it is the main basis of learning.

This transition in demands for learning from high school to college is often difficult for some incoming students to adjust to, even for students who were accustomed to performing quite well in high school. These differences are not true in all classes. For example, many college classes in the fine arts still assign most of the points for projects and in-class activities. However, for a science-based college course such as psychology, the primary requirement is to understand material well enough that you can demonstrate your acquired knowledge, skills, and abilities on an examination.

You May Not Understand Psychology As Well As You Think You Do

Unlike other scientific disciplines such as chemistry or biology, untrained people will often assume they are experts on psychology. This false assumption can originate from many different sources. You may have spent many years watching TV shows, movies, and other types of entertainment that seem "psychological" and this leads you to feel like you have a firm grasp of psychology.

Or perhaps you are the person whom your friends always come to for advice and your friends have told you that your advice is very helpful and insightful. Maybe you have

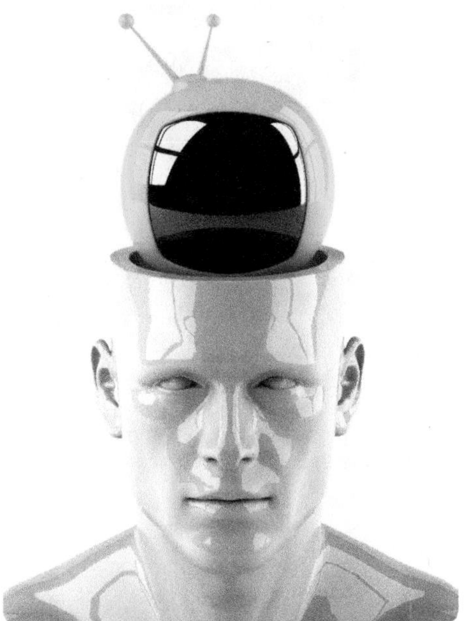
The psychology depicted in popular media is often very different from real psychology.

noticed that you are more attuned to your thoughts and feelings than the average person. It is likely you have spent much of life observing yourself and others, which may have led you to draw conclusions about why people behave the way that they do. While these experiences are meaningful and may have been very valuable to you, it would be a mistake to interpret them as meaning that you understand psychology as a discipline and in enough detail to perform well in a psychology class. You should still be prepared to invest a high degree of time and effort since that discipline may be quite different than your initial understanding.

Psychology is more than simply guessing about why people do what they do.

It is important to note the difference between armchair psychology and scientific psychology. **Armchair psychology** involves trying to understand behavior and mental processes without relying on the psychological literature or scientific research. It often amounts to little more than applying "common sense" to understanding why people do what they do or passively guessing from the sidelines. Armchair psychology is sometimes referred to as popular psychology or "pop" psychology. For example, suppose that a salesperson spent 30 years observing customers and guessing why they acted the way that they did. Even though this is a long time period and observing something firsthand is more valuable than simply guessing, it still isn't true psychology. It is considered armchair psychology because it just involved informal observation, not the methods of science.

This is contrasted with scientific psychology, which requires using the scientific method to actively investigate behavior and mental processes (we'll talk more about science and methodology in the upcoming chapters). This textbook will be primarily an examination of scientific psychology (hence the title of this book). To fully grasp any scientific field, you need to develop an extensive knowledge about what has already been discovered in that field. The main point here is that you are going to need to make significant gains in your knowledge, skills, and abilities before you understand psychology, regardless of the confidence your previous experiences may have given you. This will require good study habits and independent practice using proven self-study skills. There is much to be learned so you will need to study carefully and work hard (don't worry, we think it is worth it).

Different Levels of Understanding

Students sometimes mistake their ability to understand the gist of the material as being equivalent to mastering material, which is sometimes exemplified by comments such as "I know the material, but I just can't pass the exam for some reason." Keep in mind that there may be a big difference between understanding the material well enough to keep up with what is being said in lecture and understanding the material well enough to pass an examination. Depending on your class, you may be required to understand the material at various levels, including definitional/factual, conceptual, and application levels of understanding.

There are many different types of knowledge and understanding.

At a definitional/factual level of understanding, you can simply provide the definition or some fact in response to some question or objective. For example, in response to the question "*What is psychology?*" being able to state "*The discipline that scientifically studies behavior and/or mental processes*" represents the definitional/factual level of understanding. This is an important and fundamental skill that should not be taken lightly or dismissed. After all, it helps to be able to describe what some fact or concept is before one tries to describe what it is not or tries to apply it. Some instructors may require you to provide a definition word-for-word as it was originally described to you or they might ask you to put the definition in your own words. Both are important skills, but putting something in your own words deserves a note of caution: Students will often change the meaning of a definition as they change the words used to describe it. Unfortunately, due to their inexperience with the concepts and principles of a field, they are unaware that they have changed the meaning of the definition and are unable to detect these fundamental differences. For example, imagine that a student unfamiliar with cars learns that a car is defined as "*a vehicle that is capable of carrying people and is powered by combustion.*" Now imagine that the inexperienced student was to define a car in his or her own words. The student may give a definition such as "*metal box that moves.*" While that definition

armchair psychology
an understanding of behavior and mental processes that is not informed by well-conducted research

might seem pretty close to the mark and may even fit certain examples, the inexperienced student may fail to notice something fundamental was lost in translation. To the inexperienced student, "*a vehicle that is capable of carrying people and is powered by combustion*" is equivalent to a "*metal box that moves.*" However, the student definition does not prove that the student can tell the difference between cars and toasters being pulled by a string. To give a more relevant example, when giving the definition of psychology, some students will put the definition in their own words and say something like "*watching people around you to figure out what's happening in their minds*" instead of "*the discipline that scientifically studies behavior and/or mental processes.*" While these are similar definitions, there are some important and fundamental differences between those two definitions that can be difficult for an inexperienced student to understand. If you are learning definitions that are new to you and your instructor is not asking you to put it in your own words, you may want to be very careful about changing the wording too much, if at all, for an examination.

Be careful that when you change the wording of a concept that you don't accidently change the original idea as well.

At a conceptual level of understanding, you should be able to accurately recognize new examples and accurately reject new non-examples of some concept. For example, a student could be asked to classify the following as either psychology or non-psychology: "*Carefully observing and measuring how well children acquire reading skills when taught using phonics or whole word method*" versus "*Sitting on your couch and speculating why people do what they do*" (the first one is classified as an example of psychology, the second one is a non-example of psychology). Understanding the definition of the concept can often be helpful in these cases, especially if the definition suggests the relevant criteria to use when judging examples and non-examples. For example, you could use criteria as a checklist such as:

Checklist when deciding if something is psychology:

1. *does the example involve scientific study?,*
2. *does the example involve behavior or mental processes?, etc.*

The key to conceptual understanding is to be able to pick out the key characteristics/features that underlie all the examples common to the concept (i.e., the critical attributes of the concept) and ignore the characteristics/features that are not relevant in defining the concept (i.e., the variable attributes of the concept). The first statement above meets both of the criteria needed to classify it as an example of psychology, whereas the second statement meets only one of the criteria (speculating is not the same as scientific study). It is possible to achieve conceptual understanding without being able to explicitly state a concept (i.e., "I can recognize it when I see it, but I can't put it in words"), but in most academic settings both levels of understanding will be required of you.

Different tests will measure different types of memory.

An applied level of understanding means you can examine a situation, decide what concept or principle would be most relevant to apply, or determine a solution using one or more concepts/principles. This is both one of the most valued outcomes of education and one of the most difficult skills to acquire. Having a solid grasp of definitional/factual and conceptual understandings can facilitate the application of material you are learning. The most important component to building these different types of understandings is experience, which comes from frequent and active interaction with the material.

Keep in mind that your grade in your coursework is a reflection of understanding of the material, not your intentions or desire to learn. It is critical that you can demonstrate the relevant knowledge, skills, and abilities to others, not just simply have the confidence that you can. Of course, we are not trying to undermine your confidence here. Instead, we would like to focus on providing you with the tools for success in demonstrating your understanding of material. After all, success is one way of building confidence.

Being asked to supply the right answer tends to be harder than recognizing the right answer.

Mnemonics can often be enough of a prompt to help you recall the test item.

recognition measures
assessment techniques that require the individual to accurately make a selection as a result of encountering a familiar option

recall measures
assessment techniques that require an individual to produce a response in the absence of familiar answer choices

mnemonics
acronyms, rhymes, verses, and other simple tactics that aid in the recall of facts and lists

Two Types of Memory Retrieval

Understanding the difference between recognition and recall measures of memory will help you to prepare for tests that might assess memory using either method. **Recognition measures** will require you to accurately identify the answer from various alternatives and is dependent upon selecting a piece of information that was encountered previously. Multiple-choice, true-false, and matching questions typically assess memory through recognition. For example:

Which of the following will scientifically study behavior and/or mental processes?

A: *History*

B: *Physics*

C: *Psychology*

D: *None of the above*

Recall measures will require you to produce information in response to a question that doesn't contain the answer. Fill-in-the-blank, short-answer, and essay questions typically assess memory through recall. For example:

What does psychology study? Please write your answer in the provided space:

____

In general, recognition measures tend to be easier than recall measures (as most students will note on exam days) likely due to increased number of cues and prompts that a recognition measure provides in comparison to a recall measure. This is not just true of exams but life in general, such as when people find it is much easier to recognize the names of people they went to high school with from a list than to simply recall those names without a list (Bahrick, Bahrick, & Wittlinger, 1975). However, recognition measures can potentially still be very difficult, especially if one needs to recognize an example from three very closely related and familiar non-examples (Tiemann & Markle, 1983). As such, you'll want to study the material until you are prepared to produce the correct answer with just minimal prompts (for recall measures) or to accurately pick the correct answer even if there are distracting and similar incorrect options.

Mnemonics As a Retrieval Aid for Some Memory

What can you do if you are being asked to recall information, especially a long list of difficult to remember information? One strategy is the use of **mnemonics**, which are tips to improve recall such as the usage of similar and easy to relate terms, acronyms (words formed from the first letters of other words), and verses. For example, if you were having trouble recalling whether the sympathetic nervous system or parasympathetic nervous system slows down the body's functioning, you might try the mnemonic of remembering that a symphony can excite people (just as the sympathetic nervous system speeds up activity) and that a parachute slows down one's descent (just as the parasympathetic nervous system slows down activity). Symphony and sympathetic are similar enough in spelling and function so that you may find this pairing of terms will aid in your recall, as is the case with parachute and parasympathetic.

Or if you were trying to remember that the five factors in the Big 5 model of personality are openness, conscientiousness, extraversion, agreeableness, and neuroticism, you might use the acronym OCEAN (of course, this requires you to remember that O stands for openness, rather than organization, overcompensating, or originality). If you have trouble remembering the acronym, you might use a verse to help. For example, if you might try to remember the acronym DKPCOFGS for the biological classifications of Domain,

Learning things in sequence can make it harder to recall them later if they are out of order or you are missing any part of the sequence.

Kingdom, Phylum, Class, Order, Family, Genus, and Species. However, DKPCOFGS itself might be difficult to remember, so the verse "Dumb Kids Playing Catch On Freeways Get Squashed" may improve your recall of both the letters and order of those letters.

While mnemonics can be very helpful for examinations specifically when recalling long lists of information, there are important limits to their use. Expert performers rarely make extensive use of mnemonics and these tricks may not necessarily help one to apply material or successfully recognize examples and non-examples. The lesson here is that while it is good to use mnemonics for the occasional list or tricky to remember item, don't become too dependent on them or think they'll solve all your recall problems.

How Sequencing Can Influence Your Recollection

You'll also want to be cautious about **serial learning**, which is the tendency to recall facts in the order in which they were learned. Many students will study material in the order in which it was presented to them via lecture, book, or study objectives. The problem with this is that they become dependent on that same order for recalling that information later. If an examination presents questions in a different order than how material was studied, students will often find their recall is impaired by the different sequencing. Think of how much easier it is to recall the order of the alphabet if you go in sequence (what comes after A, B, C, D, E, F, G, H, I, J, K?) rather than starting somewhere in the middle (what comes after K?).

We tend to more easily remember things at the beginning and end.

A closely related phenomenon is known as the **serial position effect**. The serial position effect is the tendency for items at the beginning and end of a list to be easier to recall than items in the middle. The practical advice to be taken from the concepts of serial learning and serial position effect is this: shuffle the order in which you study material if the examination questions are going to be in a random order. There are exceptions to this since sometimes serial learning is desirable. For example when you are giving a presentation (the first part of your speech always comes first, the second part always comes second, etc.) or you must memorize various developmental stages in psychology in order. Most of the time an assessment won't have a particular order to it, so be sure to shuffle the order in which you study the material.

serial learning
when the recollection of facts is dependent upon the sequence in which those facts are listed

serial position effect
the tendency to more easily recall items at the beginning and end of a sequence

What Research Has to Say about Learning in Your Own Style

A frequent area of concern for many students involves learning style. **Learning style** is typically used to refer to the notion that some students will learn better in one modality than another and therefore they have certain perceptual strengths and weaknesses (Landrum & McDuffie, 2010; Pashler, McDaniel, Rohrer, & Bjork, 2009). An implication of this is that it would be best if the instruction matched a learner's preferred modality because this will make it easier for the learner to absorb information. For example, auditory learners should be taught with lecture or audio recordings, visual learners need large amounts of text and graphic aids, some learners require hands-on instruction, etc. The idea of learning styles is often extended beyond perceptual abilities to include factors such left-brain versus right-brain styles, impulsive versus reflective styles, and many other factors. The notion of learning styles is very well accepted by a large number of both educators and students and is frequently discussed in educational textbooks.

Interestingly, despite such widespread acceptance, there is virtually no experimental evidence to support the idea that differing learning styles are important for learning new material. In fact, there are actually several pieces of evidence contradicting the idea. It is clear that students vary greatly in terms of their readiness, preparation, and interest (i.e., some students have better previous education), but actual research that there are certain *types* of learners (i.e., visual learner, tactile/kinesthetic learner, global learner, etc.) is lacking. This is an example of how commonly held beliefs about our behaviors and mental processes don't necessarily match the reality, a common theme that will emerge many times throughout this textbook. This also illustrates the importance of using the scientific literature to inform our understanding of the world.

Despite the intuitive appeal of learning styles, the research suggests that it would actually be a better investment of time to practice the skills being outlined in this chapter rather than becoming preoccupied with how well your learning style and the instructor's teaching style match. Furthermore, even if a certain learning style was better suited to you (again, the research doesn't support this notion), being able to adapt to different learning situations and demands is an important life skill, especially when you consider that the world outside academics is very unlikely to accommodate your particular learning style. For example, you probably shouldn't tell your new boss that he or she has to provide your

learning style
the idea that certain modalities are better suited for different types of learners

Is it true that certain learning styles are easier for you?

Being able be accurately assess your thinking skills is important for preparation.

training as an oral workshop instead of the company's usual training manual because you are an "auditory learner."

Your Skill at Thinking about Your Thinking

It is important to frequently assess your progress and see if you are in alignment with your goals.

It is also important that you are able to recognize your strengths and weaknesses when it comes to learning new material. The ability to evaluate your own competence in any given area is known as **metacognition**. Hopefully, your confidence in the new material matches your self-assessment. However, research shows that people have a tendency to do the opposite (Kruger & Dunning, 1999). That is, people who are low in competence have a tendency to have higher confidence while those who are high in competence have a tendency to have lower confidence (there are many exceptions, especially in areas with clear feedback). Metacognition can help explain why people's self-assessments often mismatch their confidence level and skill level. When people are unskilled in some area, that means they will also have difficulty in recognizing their shortcomings (i.e., that they lack the necessary metacognition skills). In regards to the material presented in this textbook, people who are inexperienced with psychology will have difficulty recognizing when they misunderstand some psychological concept or principle. Earlier we gave the example of how changing the wording of a definition sometimes also changes the meaning of that definition, but novice students fail to notice the important distinction between the correct and incorrect definitions. Since they do not perceive a misunderstanding on their part, they tend to assume they are doing just fine (which leads to inappropriate confidence).

When people are experienced with psychology, they will find it easier to accurately recognize misunderstanding and shortcomings (i.e., they have better metacognition skills). However, they also tend to focus too much on those shortcomings that are painfully obvious to themselves, leading them to sometimes underestimate their overall skill level and inappropriately reduce their confidence level. This holds for many intellectual areas besides psychology and can help explain why students who are new to a subject matter might have trouble accurately judging how well they are doing.

Make changes to your study behavior early so you don't have to try and dig yourself out of a bad situation.

Seek and Create Feedback on Your Performance

Given the difficulty in accurate self-assessment for areas you are unskilled in, it is important you try to seek feedback on your understanding of material instead of just using your own subjective self-assessment. Completing practice problems, seeking clarification from tutors, or interacting with other students who are high performers can help you obtain better feedback. Furthermore, don't wait for your instructor to calculate your grade in a class in order to figure out how well you are performing. Even if your instructor gives you points instead of grades, you can often still calculate your current grade. Find your instructor's grading scale and convert your earned points to a grade. Use the simple formula of taking all the points you've earned so far, divide it by the total points possible so far in the class and then multiply by 100 to find out your percentage (earned/total points × 100). If you like how well you are doing, then great, keep it up! If you don't like your progress, you need to immediately change your behavior. Changing your intention or desire to do better isn't enough; you have to take immediate action. After all, if you keep doing the same behaviors that you've always done, you are likely to keep getting the same outcomes you've always gotten. If you wait too long to try to change your study behaviors, it may be too late to change the outcome. Even if you can change the outcome, it is not a pleasant experience to try and dig yourself out of the deep hole of negative grades from early in the semester.

metacognition
self-awareness and reflection on one's strengths and weaknesses in thinking, problem-solving, remembering, and other cognitive skills

Many have tried learning during sleep in the past (as seen in this advertisement), but not with much success. *(Source: Image taken from advertisement in* Popular Science, *Feb 1955, p. 22.)*

How Sleep Learning and Baby Geniuses Show That Passive Learning Isn't Real Learning

Psychologists are experts on behaviors and mental processes and there is a very consistent pattern in the research relating to study behaviors and the learning process: *Passive study is a very ineffective method for acquiring knowledge*. You may passively watch a highly educational TV show or movie, but you are unlikely to gain much true learning. As an example, try to list as many facts as you can recall from the last documentary or educational show you saw. Odds are high you'll have trouble listing very many solid facts due to the lack of interaction or rehearsal with the material, even if you felt like you were getting smarter while watching. Throughout time people have always tried to shortcut the learning process and throughout time these shortcuts have failed. The acquisition of complex knowledge requires high amounts of dedicated study.

For example, the idea of a sleep learning effect was very popular many years ago. The hope was that material could be learned by having information presented to people while they slept (you may note that there are still some students who seem to be attempting this in your class). After all, it was argued, children learn a great deal simply by being exposed to language as part of their environment, even if they lack the awareness to understand and process it correctly. Perhaps one could learn a foreign language simply by having it as part of their environment, even if they lacked awareness due to the fact that they were asleep. It was a popular enough idea that articles supporting the technique were written and sleep learning machines were sold to the general public (Sherover, 1950). To quote the materials accompanying one such device (Sweetland, 1956): "During the night while you sleep, the voice from the record penetrates your pillow. Your conscious mind is asleep, but the subconscious mind, which never sleeps, hears every word distinctly." Sounds terrific, right? However, when researchers took steps to monitor brainwaves and ensure people were actually asleep before presenting material, any benefit of sleep learning completely disappeared (Emmons & Simon, 1956). Simply being exposed to material isn't enough for you to learn it (so stay awake in class; your desk probably isn't that comfortable anyhow!). There are clear benefits to getting enough sleep when it comes to learning, but not if you try to do those two activities at the same time.

Another example of a passive attempt to enhance learning and performance occurred more recently and is known as the Mozart Effect. The Mozart Effect involves the reported enhancement of intelligence after being exposed to classical music. Interest in this idea began when researchers found some short-lived improvements in spatial reasoning for college students after having a brief duration of Mozart's music played for them (Rauscher, Shaw, & Ky, 1993; Rauscher & Shaw, 1998). It wasn't long before the media got hold of this research and started discussing how the complexity of classical music must stimulate thinking. Eventually, this possibility was extended from college students to younger people, including babies. When excited parents heard how classical music may help develop the intellect of their children and perhaps give them an early head start in intelligence, a thriving marketplace for intelligence enhancing music products was born. The problem was that very few studies had suggested that a Mozart Effect truly existed and those that did exist were limited to only adults on a few types of tasks. In fact, most research argues for the non-existence of a Mozart Effect at any age (Chabris et al., 1999; Pietschnig, Voracek, & Formann, 2010). Even though the Mozart Effect does not appear to be a real effect, Mozart for infants-type CDs are still sold (often being recommended for babies while they are still in the womb), along with hundreds of other intelligence boosting DVDs, CDs, and downloads for people of all ages.

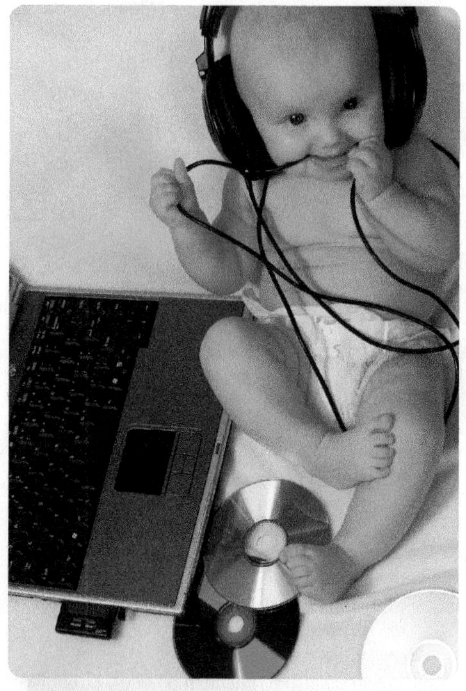

Can music, computer software, or videos make babies smarter?

Both sleep learning and the Mozart Effect tie into a broader point: Despite our strong desire to find a "get smart quick" solution, there is no shortcut to learning and being passively exposed to material will do little to enhance your mental skills. No matter how interesting or inspiring your psychology instructor might be, simply attending lectures and

Unfortunately, there aren't any shortcuts to learning, but some routes to knowledge are easier than others.

You should keeping practicing even after you are accurate . . .

passively listening isn't enough to enable you to master the material (even if you happen to love your psych class or instructor). You need to actively interact with the material: take notes, rehearse the material, study your notes, rehearse the material, study this textbook, rehearse the material, answer any questions or study objectives posed by the instructor, and rehearse the material (if you can't tell, we think frequent rehearsal is important). This will require much persistence on your part, but it is important to work past any initial frustration in order to build a stronger sense of understanding.

Using High Speed Interactions to Build a Smarter You

When students rehearse material, they often study until they have achieved a high level of accuracy and then quit. However, studies show that it is better to engage in **overlearning**, which is continued study past the set criterion. For example, even if you have learned all the study objectives to 100%, you will want to keep studying the material. Research has suggested that overlearning has clear benefits for your retention of material (Driskell, Willism & Copper, 1992). Some educators have dismissed repeated practice as simple "drill and kill." In truth, extensive practice with material is one of the best ways of gaining competence (Anderson, Reder, & Simon, 2000). However, research has also shown that simply obtaining a high degree of accuracy or extended study past full accuracy may not be the best measures of skill mastery. Instead, it is recommended that one attain fluency with the knowledge and skills to be acquired. **Fluency** is when one has reached a level of performance that is both *accurate* and *fast*, so that knowledge, skills, and abilities can be performed automatically and are not lost when they are not being used (Maloney, 1998).

. . . and continue practicing until your performance is without hesitation.

Note that fluency involves going beyond just accuracy alone and involves timing the speed of your performance (unlike overlearning, which does not necessarily emphasize rate or speed). If you watch a sports coach, he or she isn't usually satisfied when players can perform a move correctly or even perform a move correctly many times. Instead, he or she wants the players to perform the movement without error or hesitation (note that stopwatches are familiar items during training). The same holds true with your learning: you need to practice the material not only until you are accurate, but until you can produce the correct answer immediately. If you hesitate, you probably need more practice. True mastery usually refers to fluency with concepts and principles, not just accuracy.

overlearning
continued practice with material even after it appears to be mastered

fluency
when a skill is mastered at such a fast and accurate rate that it is performed automatically and is not lost during non-use

Exams will become easier and less stressful if you practice to fluency.

More complex, higher-level material tends to be easier if you first completely master the basic building blocks.

The Benefits of Fluent Rehearsal

Building your performance to fluency involves a high level of rehearsal, but there are many benefits to this investment of time. One benefit of being able to perform fluently is that distractions are much less likely to interfere with your performance.

Flashcards can often be effective if you use them properly.

One common source of distraction for students is exam day stress. Students are worried about how they will be assessed, testing rooms may be crowded or uncomfortable, and sometimes being monitored produces discomfort. This stress will likely interfere with your test performance if you don't study to fluency, but fluent students tend to find such distraction easy to ignore. Some students will interpret their impaired performance on exam days as a sign that they are simply "bad test-takers," although it is more likely they are "bad test-preparers." By "bad test-preparer," we mean they probably have not studied the material to that high, fluent level of performance and instead quit studying after attaining high accuracy or simply feeling like they understood the "gist" of the material.

Not only is fluency important for passing your current class, but it is important in later courses. It has long been recognized that attaining complex knowledge, skills, and abilities depends first upon learning more basic knowledge, skills, and abilities (Bloom, Engelhart, Furst, Hill, & Krathwohl, 1956). Research has shown that simply studying basic material to accuracy alone will set limits on how much and how easily you can acquire more complex material (Haughton, 1972). However, studying basic material to fluency will make your acquisition of later material go much easier. This may be part of the reason that experts in a field acquire new information about their field more readily than non-experts and why introductory courses can pose a big challenge for many individuals. Given that the later chapters in this book will build upon the earlier chapters and later courses in psychology are likely to build upon the course you are using this book for (if you choose to explore psychology further), it is highly recommended that you begin overlearning the material and studying to fluency right away.

SAFMEDS: A Better Way to Study with Flashcards

There are multiple ways to actively rehearse study material, including the popular use of flashcards. While flashcards can sometimes enhance self-study, not all flashcard methods are created equal. One particularly effective flashcard technique is known as the **SAFMEDS** (pronounced saff-meds) method (Eshleman, 1985; Potts, Eshleman, & Cooper, 1993). It is possible that you have tried traditional flashcards in the past and decided that they don't work for you. The SAFMEDS flashcard technique is different because it is a more systematic approach to studying that can improve mastery and exam performance better than traditional flashcards or simply making outlines and re-reading chapters. Traditional flashcards are often constructed with a wide variety of approaches. Sometimes students will write questions and answers on the same side. It is not uncommon for traditional flashcards to have very long and in-depth answers. In contrast, SAFMEDS study cards are always constructed so that questions or study objectives are on one side and answers are on the other side. These cards can be made using standard index cards or downloadable flashcard programs/applications. It is critical that both sides of the cards are as brief as possible. This will facilitate fast responding (recall that goal of fluency) and allow you to more precisely pinpoint confusing cards that need to be studied more carefully later on. In order to break the material down to its smallest components, it is not uncommon for multiple cards to be dedicated to a single question or study objective. Traditional flashcards often have many irrelevant hints on the front of the cards. Examples of irrelevant hints include circled numbers (student often do this to keep the cards in order or relate the card to a particular objective), highlighting, different color cards or ink being used, smudge marks, unusually large or small lettering, unusually long or brief text on the front, bent corners, or tears. There is a big problem with these irrelevant hints: the learner frequently becomes dependent on these prompts in order to state the correct answers, often without being aware that he or she is doing so. For example, when studying Piaget's stages of cognitive development, a student may come to notice that the card with the question "*What is the first stage of cognitive development?*" on the front side and a bend in the corner has the answer "*sensorimotor*" on the back. After much practice, the learner quickly establishes the relationship of *see bent corner ⟶ say "sensorimotor.*" Of course, the student may not purposely be using the bent corner as a hint, but it may be influencing his or her responding nonetheless.

You may have a tip-of-the-tongue experience if you make some common study mistakes.

Be careful to not become passive when using your study cards.

Unfortunately, when the exam has a test item such as "*Name the first stage of cognitive development,*" the student may find he or she has trouble coming up with the right answer because the hint of a bent corner is missing. As such, the student may experience a **tip-of-the-tongue phenomenon**, where the answer feels like it is very close to being retrieved from memory but the individual still fails to produce it. This phenomenon is sometimes caused during exams when students (who are unknowingly dependent on both relevant and irrelevant prompts) are given the relevant prompt (i.e., the test question) but missing the irrelevant prompt (i.e., the smudge, highlighting, bent corner, etc.). SAFMEDS cards should be created to remove any of these irrelevant hints from the cards so that only the relevant prompts (questions/objectives) influence your learning.

For similar reasons, unusual and exotic words (ex: an unusual last name such as Piaget) should be minimized from the front of cards. For example, you don't want to learn the relationship of *see Piaget ⟶ say "sensorimotor"* since an exam may not use his name in the question. If it is necessary for you to learn the unusual and exotic word, it is recommended that you create multiple versions of the SAFMEDS cards, some with the unusual or exotic word and duplicates with the unusual or exotic word removed. For example, you could have a card with the front stating "*What is Piaget's first stage?*" and another card with the front stating "*What is the first stage of cognitive development?*" with the answer to both cards being "*sensorimotor.*" That way you can be prepared regardless of how the question is phrased on the exam.

The word SAFMEDS is an acronym that stands for Say All Fast a Minute Every Day Shuffle. Each part of that acronym is important, so let's examine each of those parts. The *Say* part emphasizes that you should actually say the answers to your SAFMEDS cards out loud, not just privately think the answer to yourself. The benefit of actually saying the answer, rather than just thinking it, has been established well enough to earn its own label called the **production effect**. When comparing study items that are read aloud versus study items that are studied silently, research has shown a 10%-25% improvement in recollection

SAFMEDS
a flashcard self-study technique that minimizes irrelevant hints, breaks material into small chunks, emphasizes vocal responding, utilizes fast responding with all cards in random order, and has frequent assessment

tip-of-the-tongue phenomenon
the state in which an answer feels as if it is close to being recalled but the person is still unable to produce the required information due to insufficient cues

production effect
an improvement in recall and recognition resulting from saying the material aloud during rehearsal

Both speed and accuracy matter when studying.

for the items that were read aloud (Ozubko, Gopie, & MacLeod, 2012). The act of actually saying the material out loud may help make the information more distinctive and takes advantage of memories associated with physical actions (Ozubko & MacLeod, 2010). The production effect can last for extended periods of time, for a variety of test question types, and can be produced just by writing, typing, or simply mouthing the words without vocalization (MacLeod, 2010). However, writing and typing are less time efficient than simply reading the study material out loud. While silently mouthing the answer to yourself can technically work and may be your only option in crowded or public locations, it is too easy to slip into the bad habit of letting your interactions become passive. For example, many students will start by silently saying the answer, but before long they find themselves simply flipping through cards without committing to an answer before seeing the feedback on the back of the card. Saying the answer out loud forces you to commit to an answer before you reveal the back of the card. Once again, active interaction with the material is best, so say the answer aloud as frequently as you can.

The *All* part refers to the fact that you should practice with the entire deck of SAFMEDS cards, not just a few. Recall the benefits of overlearning material. While it is okay to occasionally pull out and devote some extra practice to a troublesome card, most of the time should be dedicated to learning everything in the deck. The *Fast* part ties into the goal of fluency. Practice with your SAFMEDS cards should be quick and timed, not leisurely paced. If you produce the correct answer but you do so slowly or with hesitation, you should count that card as an error. Fluent outcomes only come from fast and accurate practice. When people report having trouble with material despite making flashcards, one of the most frequent underlying problems is that they didn't practice to the point of fluency.

The *Minute Every Day* part refers to self-monitoring your progress. While your average amount of study time should far exceed one minute per day, you should take a brief timing every day to count up how many cards you had right (fast *and* accurate) and how many you had wrong (inaccurate *or* slow) by placing the cards in different piles during a one minute period. It is okay if you don't complete the entire deck during that one minute, as you are just trying to get a snapshot of your current skills. These brief samples will give you a good idea if you're improving, doing the same, or getting worse across time. Depending on the answer, you may want to keep doing what you've been doing or change your study habits. These frequent samplings will also make it easier to see daily improvements, which can help make studying a more rewarding activity.

Most of us tend to have trouble coming up with accurate time estimates.

Finally, the *Shuffle* part refers to the fact you should very frequently shuffle the order of your cards. Students are often tempted to practice cards in a certain order. Unfortunately, this may lead to serial learning as described earlier and can impair test performance. Instead, shuffle your SAFMEDS cards to prevent this serial learning. The SAFMEDS method can not only help struggling students learn better, it can help high-performing students study more efficiently and therefore save instructional time (Clorfene, Matsumoto, Bergman, Zhang, & Merbitz, 1998).

There are some limits to SAFMEDS: *this technique won't help with your mastery of the material if you don't understand the words you are memorizing.* As mentioned earlier, you should treat definitions like checklists when attempting to classify or generate new examples. If there are parts of that checklist you don't understand, it is important to look up the meaning of those parts. It may also be helpful to create study cards for terms that are unfamiliar to you. If you just blindly memorize the material you may find yourself in trouble when asked to create or recognize a new example of some concept or principle.

Some Difficulties in Time Management and How to Overcome Them

planning fallacy
the tendency to underestimate how much time or money a project will take to complete

Naturally, it will take a fair amount of time to both prepare your study materials and then actually study them. One big obstacle to this is the **planning fallacy**, the tendency of people to underestimate how long it will take to achieve a goal or complete a task (Buehler,

Griffin, & Ross, 1994; Koole & Spijker, 2000; Kruger & Evans, 2004). This fallacy frequently leads to missed deadlines and projects running over budget. For example, the famous Sydney Opera House in Australia was planned to take approximately 6 years at a cost of 7 million dollars to build, but actually took 16 years and 102 million dollars, despite being scaled down from the original plans (Hall, 1980). In regards to schoolwork, the planning fallacy often leads students to frequently underestimate how long it will take them to fully study all the material. Interestingly, we tend to be fairly accurate at making estimates for other people but terrible at estimating our own projects.

Most of us also tend to put off required work until right before the deadline.

Students, like everyone else, also have a strong tendency to procrastinate until right before a deadline (Malott & Trojan, 2008). This double threat of procrastination and planning fallacy often leads to students anxiously trying to cram in as much study as possible right before exam day (or perhaps the morning of the exam) and finding they simply don't have the time they need. The procrastination problem is very common because the motivation to study often doesn't become powerful enough to produce study behavior until the threat of exam day is looming nearby (Michael, 2004). There are other frequent demands and enticing opportunities that can often be very compelling and difficult to put off in favor of studying (especially if we know there are still a few days left before we *really* need to study).

Fortunately, there are several things you can do to remedy these poor time management practices caused by procrastination and the planning fallacy:

1) Unpack the task into smaller sub-task components. For example, try to calculate how long it will take to learn one study objective or read one chapter and then add up those time estimates rather than estimating the entire set of study objectives or all the chapters at once. These bit-by-bit estimates tend to be more accurate than when we try to guess the overall time commitment without individually considering each sub-task.

Breaking a task into smaller pieces can help with better time management.

2) Make a public promise to meet your deadlines and ask a significant other, roommate, friend, or family member to help enforce it. Publicly stated promises tend to be more difficult to break than the private promises we make to ourselves. These commitments are often more effective if you build a reward for meeting or penalty for failing to meet a deadline into your arrangements with other people. For example, make a public commitment with your friend to finish reading chapter 1 before Friday and if you succeed, you get to go to a movie with that friend. Don't give yourself rewards as sympathy for frustration that may occur during studying; give the rewards only for successful completion of goals.

More frequent deadlines can help, especially if you arrange a consequence for meeting (or not meeting) those deadlines.

Textbooks should not be read the same way you read books for entertainment.

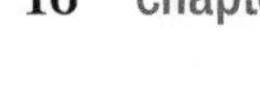

3) Set personal deadlines that occur more frequently than instructor-imposed deadlines, especially if your course has very few deadlines. For example, if an instructor has a test over chapter 1 in 8 days, you should set a personal deadline to read chapter 1 by the end of day 1, another deadline to write out answers to study objectives by the end of day 2, another deadline to create SAFMEDS cards by the end of day 3, etc. (notice this is also an example of breaking a task down to smaller sub-tasks). In general, frequent deadlines that break course material into small and manageable chunks are better than trying to tackle an entire set of requirements all at once.

4) Carefully consider how long similar study requirements took you in the past. Don't fall for the common error of assuming the future will be problem-free or a best case scenario. When reflecting on the past, assume you will experience similar obstacles in the future that derailed your past success. By assuming similar obstacles and building them into your future time estimates, you are more likely to succeed in time management. To be on the safe side, it is a good idea to build in more time than you need because you never know when a new and unpredictable obstacle or obligation may interfere with your study time.

Simply flipping through a text without further study has little value for learning.

APPLYING THE SQ3R METHOD TO STUDYING TEXTBOOKS (INCLUDING THIS ONE)

It is also important to use proper study techniques when reading a textbook. Although many students tend to avoid reading the textbooks they've purchased, it is best to read the textbook material before your instructor gives a lecture as this will save you time and effort in the long run. It will make it easier to understand the lecture and give you the opportunity to focus more carefully on material that you found difficult to understand while reading. Even if you would prefer to just listen to material in class, your instructor is highly likely to expect you to engage in a high level of independent reading (Lei, Bartlett, Gorney, & Herschbach, 2010; Marek & Christopher, 2011; Ryan, 2006). However, **simply skimming a textbook and only reading the bolded key terms does not enhance your understanding or exam performance** (Gurung, 2003). Even the study techniques that are the most popular with students, such as highlighting material or simply re-reading the text have been shown to fail when it comes to remembering the material (Dunlosky, Rawson, Marsh, Nathan, & Willingham, 2013). Learners need to go beyond these common but ineffective techniques.

One important consideration is that you shouldn't read textbooks in the same way you would read a book for entertainment. If you wish to benefit from your textbook, one effective study method is the **SQ3R** method, an acronym that stands for Survey, Question, Read, Recite, and Review. The SQ3R method has been found to improve student performance because the technique facilitates active engagement with the material, which is more effective than passive reading. The SQ3R method has also been found to boost subsequent examination performance in grade school children and college students, including those in introductory psychology classes (Adams, Carnine, & Gersten, 1982; Artis, 2008; Carlston, 2011). This method is primarily aimed at academic textbooks, particularly those with much content to be mastered, such as this textbook and most textbooks in college classrooms (there are exceptions, such as statistics or math textbooks that are designed to primarily have students work through problems rather than read material). The steps of the SQ3R are detailed below:

a note on terms in margins
only reading definitions in margins will not be enough to improve your understanding or exam performance

SQ3R
a technique for studying textbooks that emphasizes surveying, questioning, reading, reciting, and reviewing of material

Step 1 *Survey* the textbook chapter: Read through the headings for each of the sections to find out what is to be learned. Skim through the material to get a sense of how the various topics might be tied together.

Step 2 *Questions* should be developed: If your instructor has supplied you with specific study objectives or questions, review these so you have a sense of what material to pay extra attention to before you begin reading (or attending lecture). If your instructor does not supply objectives or questions, you will need to generate your own objectives. One way to accomplish this is to change the headings into questions. For example, the heading of "*Applying the SQ3R Method to Studying Textbooks (including this one)*" could be changed to a question such as "*How can the SQ3R method be applied to studying a textbook*?" or "*What is the SQ3R method?*" Develop additional questions using your predictions of what the material will cover based on your brief survey of the material in step 1. Questions can also be developed based on your guesses as to why the author or publisher went to the effort of writing the material or developing visual aids such as charts and pictures.

Reading the textbook should also be an active experience.

Step 3 *Read* the material actively: By active reading, we mean that you should try to answer the questions developed in step 2, whether they are instructor-provided or self-generated study objectives and questions. However, do not simply skim the material to find the answers. Read everything and consider how it might relate to and help you understand the objectives. The additional context may help clarify the material you need to learn. Keep in mind that learning is a cumulative effort and often early information must be fully understood before moving on to later information. As such, make sure you understand each section before moving on to the next section. If the material is complex or seems significant, it may require you to read the section slowly or even re-read it a few times before proceeding. Write notes in the margins or on a separate notebook. If you do not understand a particular word being used, look it up using a dictionary or online resource.

College lectures need to be an active experience on your part. Even if you don't ask questions, take notes and pay attention to both what is shown and said.

Step 4 *Recite* the answers you've developed: Write out the answers to all of your questions and organize your notes. Try to think what the answers to the questions might be before looking up the answers to verify if you are correct. This is the point where you should construct SAFMEDS cards or any other study aids you may be using. In many courses, you'll want to be prepared in advance to get further answers or elaboration from lectures. Ideally, you should have completed all 4 of these steps before the lecture occurs. One side note about lectures: Take careful and frequent notes to make the lecture a more active experience. Also keep in mind that information presented on a PowerPoint is often just a talking point for the instructor and may not be intended to be the main point. Pay attention to what he or she is saying and take notes on that; don't just copy down the PowerPoint word-for-word and ignore everything else.

Step 5 *Review* your study materials: Double-check that your answers are accurate. Make sure there aren't any discrepancies between your answers and the textbook/lecture material. If there are, immediately work to resolve the discrepancy by further review or seeking out help from a tutor or high performing peer, if available. Once you are sure of your answers, you will want to repeatedly rehearse the SAFMEDS cards and other study materials. Remember, you need to engage in overlearning and practice until you achieve fluency. This step is where most of your learning will take place and is fairly time consuming, so make sure you allocate sufficient time for it, keeping in mind the pitfalls of procrastination and the planning fallacy.

Use these psychology study tips to meet your goals and begin your journey into psychology!

Final Comments Before Beginning Our Introduction to Psychology

The preceding material is recommended because it has been based on careful psychological research. The techniques have been demonstrated to work, even with students who claim that they already have a study method that "works for them." These techniques have a broad application beyond just your psychology class. We cannot emphasize enough how important it is to commit hard work and time to your courses, even if the course is not part of your intended field of study. Education is an expensive and valuable endeavor. You probably have multiple goals related to your psychology courses and other coursework. It is a good idea to occasionally step back and non-judgmentally evaluate if your study behavior is fitting in with your ultimate goals and values. Are you meeting your goals? If not, evaluate why and ask yourself what you need to do to change this. Not only will improved study techniques help you meet your goals; they can help enrich your courses so that you get more out of your classes and enjoy them more in the long run. It is likely you have invested a great deal for this opportunity and you likely do not want to waste such an opportunity, so apply some careful study techniques to your courses right away!

2

Introduction to the Science of Psychology

Why We Need Both Science and Psychology in Our Lives

BY DOUGLAS A. JOHNSON, PH.D. AND SOPHIE RUBIN, PH.D.

People are always looking for new breakthroughs to help improve their lives or better the life of someone they know. We tend to find ourselves searching for such breakthroughs when life presents us with a difficult challenge. Parents of children diagnosed with autism are presented with many challenges on a daily basis and sometimes find themselves hoping for some new breakthrough. Autism is a disorder that impairs social interaction and communication skills. Some people diagnosed with autism may engage in repetitive behavior and perform the same task over and over again without attempting to speak with others. In some ways, it seems as if they live in a world of their own, cut off from those on the outside. This is a demanding situation for many parents of autistic children who may be frustrated by this lack of interaction and desperately want to hear their child say something meaningful to them. This desperation often leads them on a relentless search for a therapy to help their children communicate with the world around them.

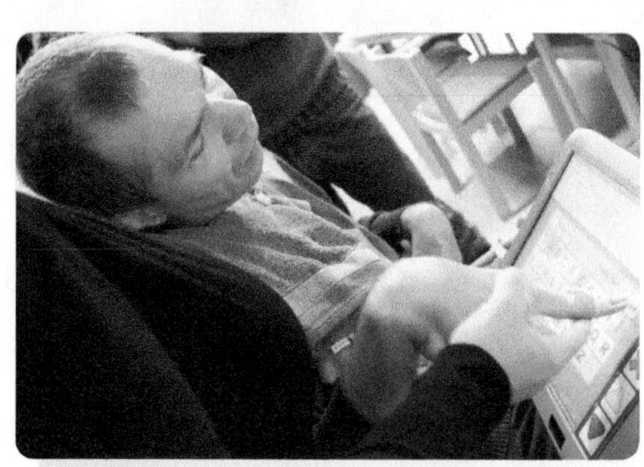

Many therapies offer hope to those in desperate need, but they might do more harm than good.
(Courtesy of Yves Logghe/Associated Press.)

One such therapy called facilitated communication claims to help individuals with limited to no communication skills to suddenly express themselves, usually at a fairly advanced level. The technique requires an individual called a facilitator to help aid the communication of an individual with impaired communication skills. The facilitator will hold the hands or otherwise support the arms of the individual with impaired communication and help him or her type out words on a keyboard. The technique seems to miraculously unlock their communication skills, with newfound levels of expression that appear to be comparable to poets, writers, and advanced students. It is as if these individuals with autism and other disabilities were waiting for years to communicate and we have now discovered the means to allow these hidden and intelligent voices trapped inside to finally be released.

Among all the elation from these dramatic discoveries, there remained one very important question: *Does this therapy actually work?* You can find newsletters filled with testimonials from joyous parents giving their personal stories of success with facilitated communication. Are these stories enough proof for us to invest large amounts of time and money? Even if it doesn't work, does it really matter? After all, these parents seem happy enough. Perhaps the offer of any hope at all may be enough for them to believe in the therapy. Isn't a false hope better than no hope at all?

An example of why real proof matters can be found by examining the case of a young girl named Aislinn Wendrow (Braiser & Wisely, 2011). Aislinn was a 14-year-old girl with autism living in West Bloomfield, not far from Detroit, Michigan. Despite being diagnosed as severely autistic, having the intelligence of a 2 year old, and being unable to communicate, her parents continued to search for a solution and discovered facilitated communication through an education professor. When Aislinn entered high school, her parents insisted the school provide their daughter with this promising communication aid. Aislinn used this aid for many years and seemed to be functioning quite well.

However, accusations began surfacing through these facilitated communications. With the help of the facilitator, the daughter stated that her father had been raping her for years. Additional accusations through facilitated communication were made that the girl's mother ignored this sexual abuse and that her father threatened her life if she confessed to anyone. Unable to ignore such possible wrongdoings, the police arrested the father and placed him in Oakland County Jail. When one is faced with the possibility of a 75 year prison sentence as a child rapist, suddenly the question of if and how the therapy works becomes tremendously important. Was this the story of a false accusation against an innocent couple or a silent victim finally being given the means to confront her abusers? Fortunately for the people involved in this accusation, scientific psychology had studied this very issue (Gorman, Wynne, Morse, & Todd, 2011).

Is facilitated communication a fancy version of a Ouija board?

Many years of careful research into facilitated communication has repeatedly proven that no real communication is actually taking place. It turns out that the facilitator, not the impaired individual, is the one who intentionally or unintentionally does all the communication (Wheeler, Jacobson, Paglieri, & Schwartz, 1993; Mostert, 2010). When the facilitator cannot hear or see what the child is hearing or seeing, the technique fails completely to produce any meaningful communication. For example, if the child is asked a question while the facilitator is wearing earplugs, the typed reply will have nothing to do with the question that was asked. Or if the facilitator is blindfolded while the child is shown pictures, the typed responses will fail to accurately describe those pictures. It is only when the facilitator is aware of the questions that the answers make any sense. If the child was truly the one communicating, it should not matter whether the facilitator was also informed about the question since their role is to aid communication, not actually supply the answers. These facilitators are quite frequently unaware of how much they are controlling the messages being expressed.

In this case, the accusations of abuse were not coming from the young girl at all, but rather from the mind of the facilitator alone. Fortunately for the Wendrow family, psychologists testified in court about the flaws of this therapy. When the judge asked the young girl simple questions that her facilitator could not hear, the young girl's answer made no sense even when the facilitator helped type her responses. For example, the judge asked the young girl (while her facilitator waited outside the courtroom), "What are you holding in your hand right now?" The facilitator then came into the courtroom to help Aislinn type a reply of "I am 14." The young girl failed to answer even one question correctly if the facilitator did not also hear the question. Careful scientific research had saved this family from further harm.

The Wendrow family experienced tremendous suffering due to a fake therapy, highlighting the need for our whole society to become critical consumers. *(Courtesy of Andre J. Jackson/PARS International Corporation.)*

The sad news is that substantial harm from this "therapy" had already been done by time the girl's father was finally released. He had spent 80 days in jail, Aislinn and her brother had been removed from both parents for 106 days, the family had spent $60,000 in legal fees, and many individuals in the community still suspected that there must have been abuse, despite the complete lack of evidence beyond the fraudulent therapy. Even though there have not been any legitimate research studies supporting the use of facilitated communication, the technique still shockingly remains in use in homes and schools today. This suggests that everyone needs to become critical thinkers about psychological issues, not just scientists or psychologists.

What Is Psychology?

Psychology is a broad field with many areas of application. Psychology can help us understand why people make certain choices, how people are capable of both great good and evil, what animal behavior is like and how that relates to human behavior, how our perceptions and knowledge may not be aligned with reality, how memories may become distorted or inaccurate, why people engage in strange or extreme behavior, why people may support a fake therapy long after it has been discredited, and why we perform the normal and routine behaviors seen in everyday life. **Psychology** is defined as the discipline that scientifically studies behavior and/or mental processes. If an area of our lives involves behavior or mental processes, then psychology will have relevance to understanding and improving it.

To better grasp what psychology is, it may be helpful to also talk about what psychology is not.

- Psychology is **not** about simply being very intuitive about the thoughts and feelings of yourself or others.
- Psychology is **not** idle speculation about the causes of behavior or mental activity.
- Psychology is **not** the application of common sense to solve problems.

Scientific psychology helps us better understand ourselves while protecting us from bias.

Psychology is none of these things because these things do not involve scientific study. It is not unusual for people to accuse psychology of being common sense, but there are problems with common sense. People often use the term loosely and apply it even when the knowledge isn't all that common. It does not require careful consideration to say that something is common sense. Most importantly, common sense is often completely wrong. If we look through history, you can find examples of common sense that seem absurd by today's standards. For example, it was once considered common sense that the world was flat, the sun rotated around the earth, women were both intellectually and morally inferior

psychology
the discipline that scientifically studies behavior and/or mental processes

How do we come to know what we know?

to men, surgery should be done without gloves or hand washing, and that certain races preferred to be enslaved.

This is part of the reason why science is incredibly valuable: it can help prevent us from tricking ourselves into thinking we know something that we don't. Science enables us to have a reliable fact checker to compare our possible misinterpretations and misunderstandings against the truth of reality. It doesn't matter how popular or well accepted any given idea is, it should still be tested against the methods of science before we place too much confidence in any idea, belief, or assertion. As history has illustrated, popular ideas, well accepted beliefs, and common sense assertions can be later proven to be completely wrong. Science can help us discover which of our currently held ideas, beliefs, and assertions are incorrect and therefore should be abandoned, as well as which ones are accurate and therefore should be retained. In essence, all knowledge should be open to questioning and consideration. Some knowledge will survive this questioning and some will be discarded. This applies to psychological knowledge just as much as the knowledge from any other scientific discipline.

Evaluating the Sources of Our Knowledge

It is important to consider the source of your knowledge regarding how the world operates. There are several ways in which we can accumulate knowledge. Some things we know because it was told to us by an authority figure. We believe in these things because doctors, police officers, politicians, journalists, parents, and other authorities tell us they are true, such as when mothers tell their children to wear a coat or else they'll catch a cold. This can be valuable because it doesn't require much time on our part and these authority figures often have more expertise than we do. We also believe things simply because we hope they are true and we have an emotional investment in our present knowledge being correct, such as when a smoker believes that cigarettes may kill some people but he or she will be fine. Some things we believe because of social consensus. That is, we believe because everyone else also believes or our peers tell us it is true. We often trust this source of knowledge because it seems unlikely that so many other people could be wrong, such as when we believe a restaurant or nightclub must be good because of the long lines of people waiting to get in or that taking vitamin C helps prevent the common cold because we have heard so many people say so. Sometimes we know things because we applied logic and reason to come up with a sensible explanation that fits with what we know, such as when we reason that something bad must have happened to our friend because he or she stops smiling or joking. Finally, we sometimes know things because we have directly or indirectly observed their occurrence.

In science, the best kind of knowledge is obtained through observation and measurement of our world.

While scientists use all the ways of gaining knowledge mentioned here, observation is considered to be the most valuable. More specifically, a particular type of observation known as empirical evidence is valued. This is more than just casually observing or recalling your personal experiences or recognizing patterns to these experiences. **Empirical evidence** is information gathered by systematic observation and careful measurement. By systematic we are referring to a deliberate and planned series of observations. Careful measurement means we take notes, keep records, or other means of summarizing information. Empirical evidence helps us separate out what we hope is true from what is actually true.

empirical evidence
information about the world that is gathered using systematic observation and careful measurement

Psychology: One of the Hardest of Sciences

Some people talk about psychology as a "soft" science, one with more relaxed standards than other scientific disciplines known as "hard" sciences. The authors of this book would disagree with that suggestion and recommend you think about psychology in the same way you might think of any other natural science such as biology or chemistry. Not only do we consider psychology a hard science, in many ways it is one of the most difficult sciences because of the inherent biases and complexity involved when dealing with people.

We are biased because we have spent so much of our lives informally studying the behavior and mental processes of ourselves and those around us. This lifetime of experience inevitably results in many preconceptions and expectations before we even have our first chance to begin collecting empirical evidence. Our tendency to want to hold onto these preconceptions is usually quite strong, especially since we're studying a subject matter that is quite personal to us. After all, the subject matter in question includes ourselves and those that we care about. We have accumulated an extensive set of ideas and assumptions that we think we "know", unlike other scientific fields where our preconceptions, expectations, and personal investments were probably much less developed before we began our study of those fields. For example, if we believe that boys are more aggressive and girls are more social, we may interpret that an instance of a boy hitting a girl as aggression, but interpret a girl hitting a boy as flirting. It is important for those studying psychology to avoid distorting such observations by striving to minimize assumptions and expectations that may conflict with reality.

Psychology can be tricky because of biases from a lifetime of self-observation.

Psychology is also difficult due to the complexity of behavior and mental processes. Behavior is rarely the result of a single process and is often multiply determined, meaning that several factors will influence the development and maintenance of any particular behavior. An illustration of this can be seen with the **nature vs. nurture debate**. This debate revolves around whether we are products of nature (factors such as evolution, physiology, and biology) or we are products of nurture (factors such as the current situation, social influences, learning history, and culture). In many ways this is a false debate, as our behavior is influenced by both nature and nurture continually interacting with one another (sometimes referred to as **nature through nurture**).

However, parts of this debate remain active in regards to the degree to which nature influences any given behavior and to what degree does nurture influence that same behavior (e.g., is creativity 20% influenced by nature and 80% influenced by nurture?). This is complicated by the fact that the answer to the debate will depend on the behavior and individual in question. Furthermore, we are always trying to answer that question with incomplete information because we do not have complete access to the person's lifetime of learning and experience. Even a simple behavior, such as asking for water, could be seen as a complex interaction between nature and nurture. For example, we need to consider the biological needs and the physiological functioning of the individual, the possible biological and learning components relevant to that person's language, the appropriateness of the

Are we a product of our genes or environment?

The complexity of psychology is both fascinating and challenging.

nature vs. nurture debate
the long-standing debate over whether human behavior and mental processes developed because of inherited or environmental factors

nature through nurture
perspective that behavior and mental processes are the result of the ongoing interaction between inherited and environmental factors

request in the current environment, observations of what others are currently doing, how successful that request has been in the past, etc. Furthermore, there are individual differences in how these influences will interact because each person has a unique learning history and genetic endowment. Even if we had a complete understanding of any particular person, that understanding may not necessarily apply to everyone else. Given that we are trying to understand all human behavior, both simple and complex, this is a very difficult challenge we are charged with. It is why William James, an influential and early psychologist, called psychology "a nasty little subject" (James, 1920).

Should you go with your first instinct or second choice on multiple choice tests?

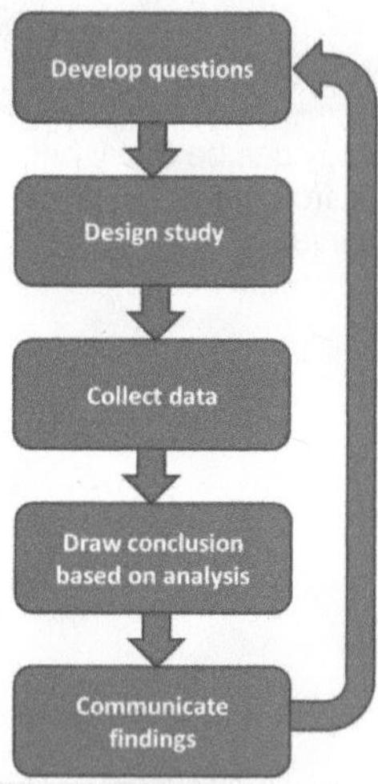

The most important part of science is the process for collecting data.

The first step is to figure out what we want to study.

scientific method
the process by which data is obtained through systematic observation, careful measurement, and experimentation

Making Sense of It All Using the Tools of Science

Fortunately, we have some useful guidelines to help us tackle this "nasty little subject" known as psychology. Namely, we have the scientific method, which helps us safeguard against bias and suggests steps for dealing with the complexity of the task before us. We use the **scientific method** in order to collect that valuable empirical evidence so that we can more accurately know our world with appropriate confidence.

Let's illustrate these steps using a problem that many students encounter on examination day: When you are unsure of an answer on a multiple-choice test, is it best to stick with your first instinct or to switch to the second choice you are considering? Obviously there are times when staying may be in your best interest and other times when changing may be in your best interest, but it would be nice to know which strategy would be best in the long run. That is, will you gain more points overall on an exam if you usually stick with the first choice or if you tend to switch to the second choice?

There are lots of ways you could answer that question. You could seek social consensus and ask other students what they think. Most students would state that it is best to trust your gut and go with your first pick. You could also ask an authority figure such as your instructor. Most college instructors would also recommend going with your initial choice. You could use reason and logic, making an argument such as, "If I'm unsure, it is most likely that my first guess is also my strongest guess since I was first attracted to that choice before that second one distracted me and made me doubt myself. Therefore the first one is most likely correct." You could use emotional hope to decide that the first choice must be right because you usually "go with your gut" and the notion that you might have been wrong all these years and needlessly lost points would be upsetting. Or you could use your own personal observations, where you can more easily remember those times when you changed to a second choice and lost points as a result of that self-doubt.

While all these ways of gathering knowledge may suggest that it is best to stick with your first instinct, none of these involve empirical evidence. As such, you should be cautious about trusting any of these sources of knowledge too much. Let's instead try applying the steps of the scientific method to our original question of whether it is better to stick with or switch answers.

Step 1 *Develop a research question of interest*: First, we need to figure out what we wish to study. Just because common sense or non-empirical knowledge has already supplied us with an answer does not mean that a question is not worth investigating. Our past assumptions have been wrong before, so there is good reason to suspect that our current assumptions might also be incorrect. Often psychologists seek to investigate questions that have obvious, immediate value to society, although occasionally we pursue questions for the sake of knowledge alone. Knowledge for knowledge's sake can also be valuable in broadening our understanding of how the world works and may benefit us in unpredictable ways later on. Returning to our present example, let's begin by phrasing our research question as follows: When a student is undecided between two answer choices, is it a better overall strategy to stay with the initial choice or to change to the other choice?

Step 2 *Design a systematic approach to study the research question*: This is often one of the more difficult steps. There is no single correct way to study a problem and we have many different methods at our disposal. As we design the study, we need to be sure that the selected method will produce evidence relevant to answering our original question. For the current example, we need to first figure out how to determine if a student was undecided between two answer choices. We could ask students to let us know if they have any indecision, but that might be disruptive to the test-taking process and may give us a distorted view of what is going on. We might also look at the eraser marks on the test itself afterwards. Signs of erasing are typically easy to see, although we might still miss a few eraser marks that were really hard to see. It would also fail to find cases where the student decided to stick with the first choice and therefore never made an eraser mark. However, on questions where students changed their mind, we would be able to note the original choice (as shown by the eraser marks) and the final choice. All these approaches have advantages and disadvantages. Other possibilities for investigation exist but they will be imperfect as well. No single approach is likely to fully answer a question, especially if the question is complex.

After figuring out what to study, we need to figure out how to study it.

For the sake of our example, let's decide to pursue the eraser marks to find cases of student indecision. Next, we need to come up with criteria to determine if switching choices helped (changed from incorrect to correct), hurt (changed from correct to incorrect), or had no effect (changed from incorrect to another incorrect option) on the student's exam grade. In this particular case it is relatively simple: we could compare an answer key against the test items with eraser marks and total up the number of times students have been helped, hurt, or unaffected by changing answers.

Step 3 *Collect data according to our study's design*: It is not enough to just think through a problem and speculate about a solution, we need to actually go out and observe the phenomenon according to our plan and take careful measurements. Notice that we are collecting empirical evidence by this point in the process. Occasionally scientists will tweak and alter the original plan in response to their current observations, but most of the time the study is implemented as originally decided. As was the case with the previous step, there is more than one way of accomplishing this step. We could bring students into a lab and observe their test taking behavior or we could go to the classroom itself and observe. We could choose to observe directly, have someone observe for us, record the process, or simply look at the materials afterwards. These details would usually be specified during step 2. For the sake of our example, let's suppose we decided to study about 1,500 students from an actual college classroom and we reviewed the test materials afterwards.

After figuring out how to study the problem, we need to put our plan into action.

Step 4 *Analyze the collected data and draw conclusions*: Even though the collection of empirical evidence is complete with step 3, the scientific method has a few important steps left. You still have to do something with the data even after you have collected it. At this point in the process you have to analyze your collected data and draw an appropriate conclusion. There are multiple ways in which data can be summarized and then analyzed, such as figures, tables, visual inspection of graphs, statistical calculations, etc. Sometimes the lessons to be learned from the analysis are obvious and straightforward; sometimes it requires careful consideration to decide on the implications of the analysis. It is customary to also try to explain how the collected data fits within the larger framework of accumulated knowledge we have gained from past research. As long as the study was designed correctly and the research question was of importance, we can potentially learn something interesting regardless of the final outcome. For example, our present study would be

After we get data, we have to analyze it and figure out what the implications are.

valuable regardless of whether it confirmed or contradicted common sense and/or previous research.

Step 5 *Communicate the findings to the scientific community*: This step is sometimes omitted when writers describe the scientific method, but we think it is important enough to warrant its explicit inclusion. Regardless of how well designed or analyzed the research is, no study is worth much if no one has heard of it. Science is a collaborative activity, in which research methods and results are openly shared across the scientific community. There are many routes for communicating findings of research. One could publish a book, deliver a talk summarizing the research, or submit a poster presentation at a conference. However, the communication method that tends to carry the most weight and importance is publishing the findings in a peer-reviewed journal. We will explain what it means to be peer-reviewed and why it is valuable shortly.

We need to communicate our discoveries so others can plan more research.

Incidentally, the example of research on sticking with or switching examination answers was an actual study conducted by Kruger, Wirtz, and Miller (2005). They pointed out that survey results suggest that most students and instructors believe it is best to go with your first instinct when completing a multiple choice exam. They also analyzed the eraser marks of students in an introductory psychology class. They found that most of the students changed one or more answers on their tests. They also discovered that the majority of students benefited overall by changing their answers, which is the opposite of what people typically believe to be true. The exam scores for 54% of the students benefited from changing their answers; whereas only 19% of students were hurt by changing their answers. The remaining students were neither helped nor hurt by changing their answers (they went from one incorrect answer to another incorrect answer). As we discussed in both this chapter and the previous chapter, this is another example of how our beliefs about behaviors and mental processes may not match reality. It also suggests the importance of the scientific method and why psychological scientists tend to value empirical evidence over other forms of knowledge. Once again, it is our best reality check for when our intuitions and assumptions lead us astray.

We need to replicate results before we place too much confidence in them.

Even after we have collected data on some phenomenon, it is important that we continue to repeat the steps of the scientific method. This ongoing collection of evidence is related to another important concept called replication. **Replication** is the reproduction of a previously obtained result from a research study, preferably by an independent researcher. Sometimes replications are exact, using the exact same procedures to obtain the same outcomes. Sometimes replications are partial, using slightly modified procedures to obtain similar outcomes. It is critical that a finding be replicated before we put too much confidence in any given finding, no matter how well the original research was conducted.

replication
the partial or complete repetition of experimental procedures that results in similar experimental outcomes

Despite the fact that one published research study suggested that it is usually not best to go with your first instinct on a multiple choice test, you should have been cautious before fully accepting that finding. There are several reasons for adopting a cautious nature regarding research findings. First off, no single study explores all aspects of a psychological phenomenon and therefore we are always missing the complete picture when only considering a single study in isolation. The study we described didn't investigate people who may not immediately mark their first choice, but who instead mentally debate between a first and second choice before making any marks. Perhaps observing students pausing at answers and/or asking them about which answers were the ones that they debated with themselves would have yielded a different conclusion. Secondly, even if the researchers did everything correctly, it is possible that the study obtained unusual results. Perhaps there was something unusual about the participants in that study, despite the best attempts of the researchers to select participants in the average range of performance and demographics (it is difficult to know if a participant is "normal" in advance). Maybe due to random chance, the study just happened to have an unusually high percentage of indecisive or intelligent people. If the participants are unusual, then perhaps the results are also unusual and may not apply to the average person. The third reason is the unfortunate fact that sometimes people commit fraud, even among distinguished scientists. While scientific communities are very strict about protecting against fraud and fabrication (this is another reason the scientific method is critical), it sometimes takes time for such unethical behavior to be exposed. In the case of the "first instinct fallacy," these results have been replicated across more than 30 studies using different researchers, participants, tasks, and settings, all coming to the conclusion that it is best to switch to your second answer choice (Benjamin et al, 1984; Kruger, Wirtz, & Miller, 2005). To our knowledge, no studies have demonstrated that going with your first instinct is best and as such, you can have confidence in these findings while simultaneously recognizing that future research may still possibly disprove the past findings.

The Dangerous Impersonators of Science

Thus far we have been discussing what science is, but it is also important to talk about what science is not. One good illustration of this is **pseudoscience**, a set of statements and assertions that appear scientific but are not supported by evidence or based on the scientific method.

Pseudoscience involves the appearance of science, but without the hard work that makes science valuable (pseudo- is the Greek prefix for "false" or "lying"). Pseudoscience is often used to make something appear more credible to others for the purpose of selling some product or service. There are several warning signs you can look for to help you recognize instances of pseudoscience.

Even a bad therapy can occasionally work.

The first warning sign of a possible pseudoscience is the excessive use of anecdotes, testimonials, and personal experience (e.g., "I used this product and it worked great for me!") instead of empirical evidence to back up statements and assertions. There is nothing inherently wrong with anecdotes or personal testimonials. They can help put a personal touch on a phenomenon and help us to better relate to it. However, it is a problem when they are the only source of evidence to support some product or service. A true statement or assertion should be capable of being corroborated by empirical evidence. Both anecdotes and testimonials are accounts of events that do not require any rigorous observation or documentation. As such, they can easily be biased and may not be representative of reality or typical experiences. As the old saying goes, even a broken clock is right twice a day. Similarly, even a broken therapy, theory, or technique can occasionally appear to help people or explain events. Part of the reason the scientific method has steps involving a systematic approach and careful measurement of observations is to guard against potentially misleading anecdotes and personal testimonials.

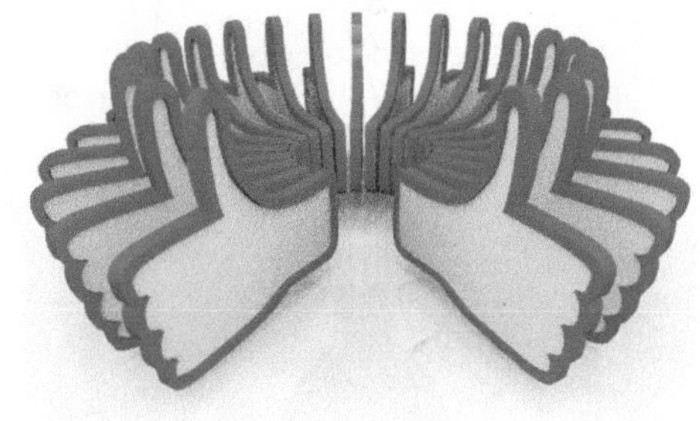

Peer review helps prevent bad science.

The second warning sign of a pseudoscience is the lack of peer review. Peer review is an important hurdle that all reputable research needs to pass and a critical part of the communication element in the scientific method. **Peer review** begins when a scientist submits an article to a peer-reviewed scientific journal. The editor will take the article and send it to other experts in field (i.e., peers), experts who typically have a background related to the topic examined in the article. These experts will review the article to determine its merit by evaluating factors such as whether the design and data collection were sufficient, if the researcher appropriately considered relevant explanations, whether the discussion of how the research fits within the larger body of current knowledge is properly done, and other important issues. Depending on the outcome of the review, the article may be accepted or rejected for publication. In essence, the article must prove its worth prior to being published. While the peer review process is not perfect (sometimes good articles get rejected and sometimes bad articles get printed), it does help provide a filter between the public and claimed findings. This form of quality control protects the general public and the integrity of the field, which is why scientists hold peer-reviewed journals in higher esteem than other type of publications such as popular press books and magazines. Pseudoscience almost never undergoes peer review and as such, there is nothing preventing outlandish

pseudoscience
a set of statements and assertions that appear scientific but are not based on empirical evidence or the scientific method

peer review
when the research or ideas of a scientist or practitioner are professionally evaluated by qualified experts in the field

One of science's greatest virtues is the capacity for self-correction.

and outrageous claims from being made by pseudoscientists, even if there is little to no evidence backing up those claims.

A related third warning sign is the lack of progression or self-correction. One of the biggest contributions of science is that if there are erroneous claims in the scientific literature, there is a built-in mechanism in place to eventually find and eliminate such false evidence or incorrect conclusions. The ongoing collection and replication of empirical evidence and the subsequent communication of these findings to the scientific community means we are continually updating and refining our knowledge base. If anything is incorrect in our knowledge base, these updates will help repair such mistakes. For example, in the last chapter we described the Mozart effect. The initial research findings into this phenomenon suggested a beneficial effect, but later replications and extensions demonstrated this initial conclusion was wrong and eventually the field corrected itself. Our knowledge is never perfect or complete, but it is advancing all the time. This is contrasted with pseudoscience, which often has nothing in place to correct mistaken assumptions. If a mistake or error is made in the claims of a pseudoscience, those claims are likely to remain in place indefinitely. Furthermore, many pseudoscience claims are made in such a way that it is difficult, if not impossible, to disprove those claims even if they aren't actually true. We'll explain this problem more fully when we discuss the importance of falsifiability later in this chapter.

Use of psychological words alone does not make something scientific or trustworthy.

A fourth warning sign of a pseudoscience is the presence of psychobabble. **Psychobabble** is the usage of psychological language and buzzwords that sound technical, scientific, and plausible, but ultimately lack any real meaning or explanation. Once again, there is an attempt to copy the appearance of science within the actual substance of science (similarly related concepts are technobabble and neurobabble for empty jargon involving technology and neurology). For example, an "expert" might state that a young child has concentration issues due to a long-standing subconscious need to express bipolar tendencies. A therapy may claim to restore mental health by normalizing brainwave functioning so that bio-energetic levels return to the ideal range. Some may claim that certain movies excite us by tapping into our reptilian brain and a need to vent suppressed energy. Or you may hear people claim that their behavior wasn't them, but it was their ADD (or whatever disorder is fashionable at the moment). All these statements appear psychological because they use words that the general public associates with psychology, but they don't contain any real explanation. Such language can mislead people into thinking a pseudoscience is more credible than it really is.

The harms of pseudoscience should not be underestimated.

You may be inclined to think that pseudoscience is not a big concern. After all, what's the harm if people choose to believe in a pseudoscience? Shouldn't people be allowed to believe in whatever they want? Aren't these approaches simply trying to explain and solve people's problems, just like psychology does? While this is understandable and rational sounding, it is worthwhile to point out there are some very concerning harms that occur as a result of pseudoscience (Normand, 2008).

One major concern is the direct harm of therapies and techniques supported by pseudoscience. People can and do suffer from pseudoscience in terms of lost income, time, and even life. For example, the pseudoscience of graphology purports to identify personality characteristics, work performance, or aptitude by analyzing a

psychobabble
descriptions and statements about psychology that sound meaningful or scientific but do not provide a useful or accurate explanation of events

person's handwriting. If you write the letter "I" too large, you may be arrogant. If your lettering drifts upward, you may be a positive optimist. Graphology has consistently failed to predict anything useful about people and graphologists do not use the scientific method to support their work (Dean, 1992; Klimoski, 1992). Despite the lack of evidence for graphology, businesses have employed this pseudoscience to screen job applicants and make hiring decisions. As such, qualified individuals have been undeservingly denied work and income.

Besides financial harm, pseudoscience can also directly harm in terms of mental and physical damage. For example, attachment therapy is a pseudoscience that proclaims it can help adopted and foster children better bond with their caregivers. It says that such children often have trouble making new connections due to suppressed emotions involving abandonment. The tragic aspect of this fake treatment is that multiple children have been killed by the techniques of attachment therapy.

Some pseudoscience therapies have been fatal, such as in the case of Candace Newmaker. *(Courtesy of Associated Press.)*

One example of a fatality involved a 10 year old girl named Candace Newmaker, who was killed by the rebirthing technique used in some versions of attachment therapy (Mercer, Sarner, & Rosa, 2003). This technique involved wrapping the young girl in a flannel sheet and demanding she escape the symbolic womb. Supposedly after emerging from this "womb," she would bond with her adoptive mother. This symbolic womb ended up as a death trap for Candace, who suffocated after an extended "therapy" session inside the sheet, despite repeatedly vomiting and begging to be released.

In addition to the direct harm sometimes caused by pseudoscience, another second danger is indirect harm. While some pseudoscience therapies and techniques may not directly hurt the recipients, they frequently prevent people from utilizing therapies and techniques that have an actual benefit. For example, facilitated communication is a pseudoscience therapy that was described at the beginning of this chapter. While facilitated communication doesn't always directly harm the individual (although the parents from the story at the beginning might disagree), it does reliably cause indirect harm because time and money is being wasted on a bogus promise and fraudulent treatment instead of finding a technique or therapy that might actually be beneficial. Perhaps another therapy approach could provide real progress instead of some empty miracle cure destined for failure.

Facilitated communication is just one example of many time wasting and resource consuming pseudoscience therapies. Primal Therapy supposedly unearths the buried pain of childhood, subliminal advertising supposedly convinces

Sometimes effective therapies are denied to us when we choose pseudoscience instead.

people to change their buying habits without awareness, and urine therapy supposedly treats various diseases by getting people to literally drink their own urine (we wish we were making these up). None of these therapies and techniques have produced real improvements, despite the testimonials of their many proponents. People rarely have the luxury of committing resources to all possible therapies and treatments. As such, they have to choose among the available options and by choosing a pseudoscience, people are restricted from obtaining any real help. Unfortunately, these fake therapies and techniques do not advertise themselves as pseudoscience. Even for those who can afford all options, the science and pseudoscience options will frequently contradict one another. As such, one still has to make a choice that might result in losing the opportunity for true progress.

It is important to be a critical thinker in general to avoid exploitation.

A third type of harm worth mentioning is that pseudoscience brings us farther away from our quest to discover the truth about how our world works. Not only is psychology already a huge field with many current applications of practical importance, there are many potential applications that have yet to be discovered. This is why we are steadily and progressively collecting empirical evidence. With these observations, we better understand reality and the psychological functioning of people. Pseudoscience distracts people from this important task and undermines the mission of science. We believe that the scientific method is the best way of illuminating our understanding of the world, as it is based on careful observations of real people doing real things (i.e., it better reflects reality than assumptions, biases, or intuition). Pseudoscience can often confirm our hopes and beliefs whereas scientific psychology may sometimes challenge us in uncomfortable ways, but that does not mean we should choose pseudoscience over science. A comfortable delusion is still a delusion; one that detracts from the truth.

A fourth type of harm is that pseudoscience can make people more vulnerable to exploitation in general. Whenever people accept a pseudoscience as legitimate, they are accepting something without evidence or proof. If that particular pseudoscience doesn't have any harm that is obvious to the person using it, that person is more likely to accept other things without evidence or proof. These include things such as damaging scams and outright hurtful manipulation of others. The more uncritical a person becomes in their acceptance of a particular unproven therapy or technique, the more likely they'll be accepting of any therapy or technique, including the harmful ones.

The Point of It All: What Psychology Is Trying to Analyze and Accomplish

If you agree that a scientific approach to psychology is the best route to proceed, that doesn't mean you will automatically agree with all scientific psychologists or that they even agree with one another. Even when psychology is limited to the scientific branches of the field, there is a wide diversity in perspectives. Psychology has many theoretical perspectives (more on these later) and multiple levels of analysis. If you were interested in understanding why some people seem to be very hardworking and self-determined, you could investigate this observation from many different levels of analysis. You could examine these admirable characteristics at a genetic and chemical level, investigating the genetic makeup and brain chemistry of people typically labeled as highly motivated. You could examine this at the behavioral level, discovering what behavior patterns are typically exhibited by motivated people. The mental level could be examined as well, noting what mental processes are reported by those high in motivation. Hard work and self-determination could also be examined at a societal level, which might involve an analysis of what cultural and broad social influences determine motivation. All these different levels are worthy topics for a psychologist to pursue and each level supplies a slightly different part of the overall picture when trying to understand our behavior and mental processes.

Psychology often examines behavior from many levels and perspectives.

Despite the different perspectives and levels of analysis, all scientific psychologists are committed to achieving the basic goals of psychology: description, prediction, explanation, and control. The goal of *description* refers to attempts to clarify what is happening with the behavior or mental process we are currently interested in. If we were interested in job satisfaction, we would try to detail what behaviors are taken as evidence of job satisfaction. What sort of things do people who are satisfied with their jobs typically say or do? How does this differ from the behaviors of people who are unsatisfied with their jobs? Or if we were trying to describe an eating disorder, we might list common behaviors observed in this disorder. We might list typical thoughts people with eating disorders report having. We might also try to list how common the occurrence of an eating disorder is in a particular country or culture. All of these help meet the goal of description in different ways.

One goal is to be able to describe what a behavior or mental process is like.

Sometimes it isn't enough to just describe what the psychological phenomenon is, we often also want to develop a working *prediction* so we can know when it will happen again. To meet this goal we might collect information on workplace features or personality aspects that are typically associated with job satisfaction. Once we had that information, we could predict whether or not certain types of jobs are likely to have people who are satisfied and what types of people are more likely to be satisfied. Or we might collect information about what cultural or social factors are associated with an eating disorder, which in turn could help us predict the likelihood that someone from a particular culture or social group will develop such a pattern of behavior. However, just because a factor can help predict a psychological phenomenon, it doesn't mean it necessarily causes the phenomenon. For example, your cat may frequently sleep next to you on the couch as you watch TV. As such, we could use the presence of your sleeping cat next to you on the couch to predict your TV watching behavior, but that doesn't mean that the cat caused you to watch TV.

Psychologists often want to know when a behavior or mental process will occur.

Occasionally we are satisfied by simply being able to describe and predict some behavior or mental process, but often we want to achieve more than that. We want to know why the psychological phenomenon happened. In other words, we want to meet the goal of *explanation*. We want to know how job satisfaction is caused, not just what predicts it. What specific features of a workplace or personality actually produce job satisfaction? What specific elements in a culture or upbringing may actually cause an eating disorder? Why do we see job satisfaction or eating disorders in some people but not everyone?

Our final goal is to *control* psychological phenomenon. We want to be able to make the behavior or mental process happen again (or not happen in some cases). We want to modify the world to produce more job satisfaction, to reduce eating disorders, improve interpersonal relationships, promote more efficient learning, minimize hostility, and many more important changes. One of the major values of science is that it has consistently produced real world applications to improve our lives and this value in developing relevant applications extends to psychology as well. The word "control" deserves some extra consideration because many people have a negative reaction to the word itself. Note that the word "control" does not imply anything sinister, malevolent, or exploitive. Instead it is being used in the more traditional scientific meaning of the word, that is, to influence an outcome. By virtue of being in a profession that is dedicated to helping people and improving lives, psychologists are trying to control the behavior and mental processes of others. Terms such as "treatment," "intervention," "therapy," and "modify" all describe methods for controlling the behavior of others. Even the most "hands off" type of practitioners are still trying to influence people (i.e., control them), even if they argue that they are not. It is a noble goal to try to improve the well-being of others, not something to be avoided due to words such as "control" having a negative connotation for certain people.

Much of psychology is dedicated to understanding why a behavior or mental process is happening.

The Use of Theories and Hypotheses to Meet the Goals of Psychology

As psychologists work to meet some or all of the goals of psychology, they often develop various theories. A **theory** is an organized set of facts, assumptions, and principles used to explain how separate observations are related. For example, you may observe that every time the family dog whines at the dinner table, some members of your family give the dog table scraps. You also note that the dog begins whining more frequently at the dinner table. You notice a similar behavior in your little brother. Every time he fusses and cries in the checkout line in the grocery store, your parents give him a candy from the checkout

theory
an organized set of facts, assumptions, and principles used to explain how separate observations are related

One of the most practical benefits of psychology is knowing how to cause a behavior or mental process.

display. Similar to the dog's behavior, you notice your brother's fussing and crying occurs more frequently when in the grocery store. If you decided to systematically take data, you could get enough empirical evidence to accurately describe and predict these behaviors. However, if you want to meet the goal of explanation, you'll probably need a theory. You might come up with a "theory of rewarded misbehavior" that states undesirable behavior that is followed by food or other good outcomes will tend to get worse over time.

Notice that this theory helps relate these separate observations by creating a unifying explanation. Also notice that you have made some assumptions here: you are assuming this theory applies to organisms besides your dog and brother. You are also assuming that the theory applies to items besides food. You need to collect more empirical evidence to see if your assumptions are accurate. However, note that your theory wasn't a blind guess, it was based on multiple observations that you carefully collected. While there isn't a "theory of rewarded misbehavior" in psychology, we do have a somewhat similar and broader theory known as operant conditioning.

The common, everyday language use of the word theory differs greatly from the scientific usage of the word. The everyday meaning of the word theory is treated as being loosely equivalent to a general idea, notion, or guess. Everyday usage of the word often implies that a theory is worth less than an actual fact (embodied by expressions such as "that's just your theory"). The scientific use of the word theory is very different than this and has special value beyond mere guesswork. In many ways, scientific theories can be better than facts because they integrate a large number of facts (such as the separate facts of dog whines, dog gets food, brother fusses, brother gets food, etc.) in a meaningful and useful manner. Since our knowledge of the world is incomplete, sometimes our theories have assumptions built into them to help complete our explanations of observed phenomena, but this does not mean a theory is something trivial that you can easily dismiss.

The word theory has a special meaning in science.

For example, the heliocentric theory of the universe is "just a theory" (this theory states that planets revolve around the sun). Although the heliocentric theory still has the status of a theory, it is well accepted by all scientists and not currently in dispute. However, since all knowledge is considered to be tentative and possibly subject to later revisions (no matter how confident we currently are about the theory), even well-established theories remain as "just theories." Not all theories are as well established as the heliocentric theory, but it does demonstrate that theories are often more substantial than educated guesses.

Many things that are "just theories" are actually very well accepted.

People often confuse the terms theory and hypothesis. A **hypothesis** is a prediction about the relationship between two variables. Unlike a theory, which attempts to integrate known facts, a hypothesis predicts what the facts will be. Hypotheses are often generated during the early stages of developing the research question to be investigated. For example, our earlier example of a "theory of rewarded misbehavior" may lead to a hypothesis such as "I predict that all rewarded behavior will tend to increase, not just misbehavior." As such, you are predicting an outcome, which you would then confirm or disconfirm with empirical evidence. It may be helpful to note that theories are used to explain phenomena using what is currently known, whereas hypotheses are used to predict phenomena regarding what is currently unknown.

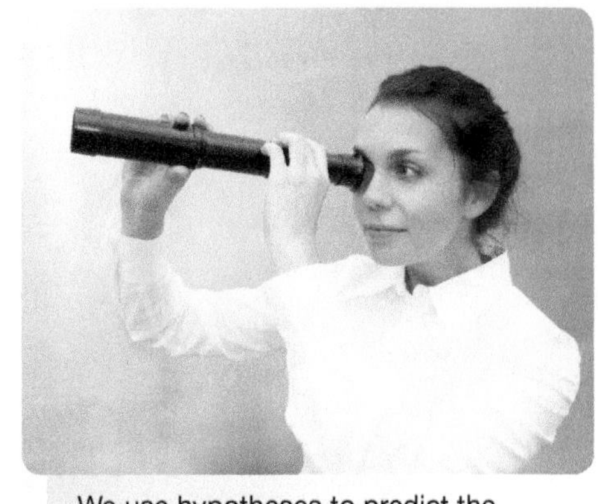
We use hypotheses to predict the relation between variables.

Whatever you discover from research, that new information can be incorporated into the existing theories or may lead to the development of new theories. While much of psychological research is driven by hypotheses, having a hypothesis is not a prerequisite to doing good research. Some of our most important research has been guided by simple curiosity rather than a need to test a particular hypothesis.

It is important that both theories and hypotheses utilize operational definitions. An **operational definition** is a description that precisely details the phenomenon of interest. You can know if your definition was precise enough if two individuals independently observing the same event both agree as to whether or not the phenomenon occurred.

Without an operational definition, contradictions and confusion can arise that are difficult to resolve. This is because the label we use for any particular behavior or mental process may be interpreted differently by different researchers. For example, the label "hyperactivity" could mean many different things. One researcher may interpret hyperactivity in children as referring to a child who runs around frequently. Another researcher may interpret it as referring to a child who quickly switches between different activities. A third researcher may interpret it as referring to a child who is unable to focus on some important task. If the term hyperactivity isn't operationally defined with a precise description or set of guidelines, then each individual researcher may use his or her own personal criteria. When conducting research, this may result in a different conclusion being reached about a therapy that causes children to sit still more frequently (our first researcher would argue that hyperactivity was reduced while the other two researchers may or may not agree due to different definitions). If we agree upfront what hyperactivity means, or at least

It is important to define something precisely enough that we can all agree that we're observing the same thing.

hypothesis
a prediction about the relationship between two variables to be investigated

operational definition
a precise description or set of criteria of the characteristics that will be used for measuring some behavior, mental process, event, or concept

detail the precise criteria being employed in a particular study, we are less likely to be confused. Furthermore, it is important to make sure we are talking about the same things if we ever hope to integrate our knowledge.

Criteria for Evaluating the Worth of a Psychological Theory

The discipline of psychology is rich with multiple theories on every important aspect of human functioning. These theories are often in competition with one another and sometimes they make claims that fundamentally contradict one another. This places us in the difficult position of trying to determine the relative worth of these varying explanations to find the ones that best reflect reality and serve us in meeting the goals of psychology. Below are five guidelines for judging the relative merit of psychological theories (Gilbert & Gilbert, 1991; Poling, Schlinger, Starin, & Blakely, 1990; Schlinger, 1992).

You should avoid using labels for behavior as explanations for behavior.

A Good Psychological Theory is Logically Coherent

As scientific theories are developed within psychology, one criterion for judging their value relates to whether they avoid logical errors such as nominal fallacy or reification. We are highlighting these two errors because they are often seen in psychological explanations from the general public and even experts. **Nominal fallacy** occurs when the term or label created for some phenomenon is then also used as an explanation for that phenomenon. For example, dyslexia is a label for the difficulties some people have in acquiring reading comprehension that isn't caused by visual impairment. Put more briefly, it is the label for someone who has trouble reading. It is common to hear someone remark, "that child *has trouble reading* because he has *dyslexia*." Although this may sound like an explanation, you should keep the definition of dyslexia in mind. Essentially, the person has "explained" the observation by stating, "that child *has trouble reading* because he *has trouble reading*." Nominal fallacies get accepted because they have the appearance of an explanation and people often feel better when a perplexing observation is given a name. Under these circumstances, naming creates the illusion of understanding, when in truth we still remain ignorant of the real causes. Too often, people, even experienced theorists, confuse *descriptions* of phenomena with *explanations* of phenomena (recall that these are two different goals for psychology).

Be careful to not treat abstract ideas such as emotions or mental states as if they were tangible objects.

One of the dangers that nominal fallacies pose for psychology is they often lead to *circular explanations*, in that the cause of behavior is inferred from the behavior itself (i.e., cause and effect are treated as the same thing). For example, we may observe that someone "works hard and persists despite obstacles." We may even label that observed pattern of behavior as "motivation," which leads some people to believe we have now explained that behavior (nominal fallacy). The circular explanation can quickly be exposed when you start looking for the evidence of motivation (effect) and the explanation for the hard work (cause).

- How do you know the person is motivated?
- "They work hard and persist despite obstacles." (effect)
- Why do they work hard and persist despite obstacles?
- "Because they are motivated." (cause)
- How do you know the person is motivated? (the explanation continues running in circles)

You'll see similar problems with other statements about psychological issues, such as "she is sad because she has depression," "he drinks too much because he is an alcoholic," or "they get in fights because they have a stormy relationship." When you translate the "explanation," you often realize that there is no explanation at all in the original statement. In each one of these cases, the information being used for the cause of behavior is the exact same information being used for the effect of behavior. The biggest threats from nominal fallacies and circular explanations are that they can make us feel like we have explained the

nominal fallacy
a reasoning error in which the label for a phenomenon is treated as an explanation for that phenomenon

phenomenon. Such self-satisfaction leads people to stop searching further for an explanation, despite the fact that there is still much work to be done in understanding the phenomenon and pinpointing the real causes of behavior.

It is also important to avoid reification when using terms and concepts in psychology. **Reification** occurs when we treat some abstract idea as if it is something concrete. For example, intelligence is an abstract idea used to represent the acquired knowledge and skills we observe in a person. However, people will frequently treat intelligence as if it is something more concrete, as if you could hold it in your hand or find an actual physical thing in someone's brain (Gould, 1981). You'll hear phrases such as "he has high intelligence" as if intelligence itself was something the person actually has, rather than an intangible, abstract description of a person's skills (or application of such skills). It is possible to apply both a nominal fallacy and reification to the same term. Returning to the example of dyslexia, you may hear people use dyslexia as an explanation for reading difficulties (nominal fallacy) or talk about dyslexia as if it is something a person has, possibly in their brain (reification). Once again, we would be better off searching for actual causes of dyslexia rather than using these non-explanations (Engelmann, 2003).

A Good Psychological Theory Makes Testable Claims That Are Supported by Empirical Evidence

Empirical evidence may be the most important consideration when evaluating a psychological theory. All reputable psychologists must bring data to back up their claims and the claims with the most empirical evidence should be the most convincing. In order for empirical evidence to be collected properly, the claims being made must be testable.

Falsifiability is an important consideration in the testability of a theory or hypothesis. **Falsifiability** refers to the potential of a theory or hypothesis to be refuted or proven false. It is important that all scientific theories and hypotheses be developed in such a way as to be falsifiable. Keep in mind that a theory that meets the falsifiability criterion is not guaranteed to be proven wrong; it just has a possibility of being proven wrong. With falsifiability, it is important to realize that scientists are not necessarily trying to prove everything false, but if a theory is wrong it could be proven to be false.

Theories should be willing to risk the possibility of being proven wrong.

To illustrate why this is important, let's consider a theory that is unfalsifiable. Suppose a friend of yours told you that hidden unicorns exist. He claims to have many direct observations of these unicorns that he has carefully collected over many years. Assuming you take your friend seriously, you ask for details on his "theory of hidden unicorns." He explains that unicorns are horse-like creatures with glowing horns and long golden tails. They hide in forests and as they walk, their long tails completely erase their tracks. Their horns will detect any form of technology and will cause the unicorn to immediately teleport to another part of the forest if any camera or other technology is observing them, no matter how great the distance. In fact, these unicorns are so disdainful of modern technology that you can only see them with your bare eyes and if you are well-attuned to the natural world.

Can we truly prove that unicorns don't exist?

What if your friend is completely wrong and such unicorns really don't exist? How would you prove it to anyone? You could point out that there are no pictures or video of unicorns, but remember the theory states that they teleport away when those technologies are present (even a satellite from space would be useless). You could point out the lack of unicorn tracks, but remember those tails that erase hoof prints. You could spend thousands of hours in the forest and report that you never saw a unicorn, but perhaps that is because the unicorns were elsewhere on those days or perhaps you aren't attuned enough to nature. As such, the theory is unfalsifiable and can never be refuted. However, that doesn't automatically mean that the theory must be true since you failed to disprove it. This is why the burden of proof rests with those making a claim. That is, it is your friend's job to prove that unicorns do exist, not your job to prove that they don't (after all, this may be an impossible task to do even if you are correct).

If the theory is *correct and falsifiable*, the theory will be retained by science. On the other hand, if the theory is both *incorrect and falsifiable*, the scientific method will

reification
when some abstract idea or concept is treated as if it is a concrete or material thing

falsifiability
the potential of a hypothesis or theory to be disconfirmed by empirical evidence

eventually discard it. If the theory meets the falsifiability criterion, we can have confidence that a true theory will stand the test of time for honest and legitimate reasons, unlike an unfalsifiable theory. One past psychological theory that was discarded was phrenology, the idea that aspects of a person's mental abilities lie in different parts of the brain and therefore the size of that part of the brain reflects the person's skill at a particular mental ability. Supporters of phrenology also claimed that these different abilities could be assessed by measuring the shape and bumps of a person's head since the brain's shape would determine the shape of the skull. For example, they would claim that combativeness rested in a part of the brain close to the back of the ear. If you have a slight bump near the back of your ear, you must have an enlarged combative part of the brain and therefore you must be a combative person. Similarly, memory rested in the front, benevolence near the top, self-esteem towards the back of the head, etc. The theory of phrenology was falsifiable and empirical evidence eventually discredited the theory (despite being disproven, phrenology has lingered on for many years as a pseudoscience). A theory that never has the possibility of being proven wrong is a theory that should be discarded immediately. Keep in mind that a theory that can't be proven false with current technology but may be proven incorrect with future technological advancement is still a theory worth considering because the potential for disconfirmation exists. A scientific theory that could be proven false but isn't despite large amounts of collected empirical evidence is the most powerful type of theory. In science we accept that any theory could be falsified at any time, but we put our confidence in the ones that survive the test of time and empirical evidence.

Occam's razor helps cut away the unnecessary theories.

A Good Psychological Theory is Parsimonious

A third criterion for determining the value of psychological theories relates to the principle of *parsimony*. A good theory is parsimonious if simpler explanations have been ruled out before more complicated explanations are considered. This is important because speculation is easy and can quickly generate an endless supply of possible explanations.

For any given set of observations, multiple theories may exist that overlap, contradict, and are redundant with one another, but each one of those theories still has the potential to be correct. A helpful guideline for selecting among these many theoretical offerings is **Occam's razor** (or Ockham's razor), which suggests that the best theory or explanation is the one that best accounts for all the evidence while also making the fewest unconfirmed assumptions. Occam's razor is a guideline used to cut away unnecessary information from our explanations.

It is important to remember that although multiple explanations exist, we should be careful which ones we choose.

Occam's razor
the guideline that states that the best explanation is the one that best accounts for all the evidence while also making the fewest unconfirmed assumptions

To better understand the need for parsimony, suppose for a moment that you noticed that your socks were missing. You could account for this observation by simply stating that you must have misplaced your socks. However, you could also account for this observation by stating that leprechauns must have stolen your socks. Both the misplacement assumption and leprechaun assumption can be used to fully explain why your socks are currently missing. You can confirm that you have misplaced objects such as socks in the past. However, you cannot confirm the existence of leprechauns. Even though both fit the observed data, the leprechaun explanation has more unconfirmed assumptions, making it unnecessarily complex. Occam's razor would suggest that we select the simpler explanation that you must have misplaced the socks.

Alternatively, let's say you were trying to explain how Eye Movement Desensitization and Reprocessing Therapy (EMDR) works. EMDR is used to successfully treat some forms of anxiety disorders by having a client move his or her eyes to follow a therapist's fingers in a safe environment while also imagining traumatic images (Spates & Rubin, 2012). At least three explanations are possible: 1) simply being in a safe environment will eliminate anxiety disorders, 2) repeated exposure to traumatic images in a safe environment weakens the power of those images, or 3) being asked to both track finger movements and visualize images causes a person to split their attention, which helps to reprocess stored memories of trauma. Past research on anxiety disorders suggests that merely being placed in a safe environment will not eliminate anxiety disorders by itself in the long run. Therefore, the first explanation is too simple and must be rejected because it cannot account for all the evidence. Research on anxiety disorders has confirmed that exposure to threatening images or information in safe environments is necessary for the reduction of anxiety disorders. Research on EMDR has also demonstrated that the eye movement aspect of treatment is unnecessary for success and therefore has not confirmed the need to split one's attention. Even though both the second and third explanations can fully account for the evidence, the third explanation contains more unconfirmed assumptions (eye movements split attention and help to reprocess memory) than the second explanation. Occam's razor would suggest that the second is best since it accounts for all the evidence while containing the fewest unconfirmed assumptions. Some people have characterized Occam's razor as "the simplest explanation tends to be the best." However, note that it is not desirable to oversimplify our understanding of events. A complex explanation will be favored by Occam's razor if simpler explanations cannot fit the evidence. Occam's razor not only cuts away unnecessary details, it also cuts away insufficient explanations. Complexity is added when necessary, but it is better to favor the simpler and more parsimonious accounts so long as they fit.

A Good Psychological Theory Has Cohesive Generality

While a theory that is highly specific to a particular set of circumstances can still have value, if an alternative theory can equally explain those specific situations as well as other broader situations, the alternative theory has more value. For example, if you developed a theory that explains why your younger cousin is sometimes aggressive, that theory may have some merit. However, if another theory could explain why young people in general, including your cousin, sometimes become aggressive, that second theory would have more value than the first. If a third theory came along that could explain why people of all ages sometimes become aggressive, this third theory would be even more valuable. As some theories become broader in scope, the various pieces of the theory should fit together in an elegant way, not become a mess of ideas that do not fit well with one another and incoherently change from situation to situation. Furthermore, the theory should integrate well with other established bases of knowledge, including those sciences outside of psychology. That is, the discoveries of psychology should fit well with the discoveries of other natural sciences such as chemistry, biology, and physics.

A Good Psychological Theory Generates Useful Applications

The final criterion for evaluating the worth of a psychological theory relates to its utility. A good theory can be extended outside of academic textbooks and scientific laboratories; it can be put into practice for the benefit of humankind. By developing explanations that help us establish scientific control over the subject matter we are studying, we know how to promote socially desired outcomes and solve the problems we are confronted with. Not all theories have to be immediately useful and the future applications of basic research may be hard to see during the present day. In general, any theory that allows for more precise description, explanation, prediction, and control is also a theory that is likely to translate scientific activity into practical technologies.

Thinking Critically About Psychology and Your World

Critical thinking is one of the most important skills for any psychologist.

The ideas and guidelines we discussed so far not only apply to good scientific practices, but we could also extend our discussion to guidelines that extend more broadly than just scientific conduct. To be more specific, we can consider critical thinking guidelines and their relevance for scientific thinking. Indeed, a good psychologist should also be someone who exercises good critical thinking. Incidentally, the word "exercise" was purposely chosen, because critical thinking requires frequent practice and effort much like physical exercise. **Critical thinking** is not about being negative in your thoughts, but instead involves evaluating the claims of both others and yourself using only well-supported evidence. In

critical thinking
evaluation of all claims (including personal) on the basis of well-supported evidence

You should be willing to question everything, including your own perspective and assumptions.

Our understanding of the world or people is never complete.

The field of psychology has many diverse roots.

addition to the scientific guidelines mentioned previously, we would add the following critical thinking guidelines:

1. *All opinions (or theories) are not created equal*—There is a social rule in our culture that suggests that everyone's thoughts are equal in status or that a compromise to balance two viewpoints is always superior. While this rule may help us get along with one another sometimes, it is also the opposite of critical thinking. When exercising critical thinking, it is important to realize that some opinions or theories have more value than others. Namely, the opinions or theories that are better supported by empirical evidence have more value than those that are unsupported. However, you should be careful when thinking critically and avoid extending negative criticism to the people themselves (even good people can make bad claims). It is possible to be both respectful and critically minded. Also, it is not always easy or straightforward to decide which side is better supported by empirical evidence, especially when the research results are mixed or lacking. As such, there is frequently room left for much debate, but different viewpoints still need to support their opinions or theories with actual evidence. Remember that in both science and everyday life, empirical evidence should always trump unsupported opinions.
2. *Ask questions of everything*—A good critical thinker is always considering the possibility that the established knowledge may be wrong. Every claim should be viewed with a skeptical eye. This is not to say that everything should be rejected. After all, many claims may be accurate. However, a healthy dose of skepticism will help discover new research questions that would not occur to us if we had just blindly accepted claims. Not only should you question the claims themselves, but it is worth questioning the source producing such claims. Is the source trustworthy and credible? Does the source have some financial or personal gain to be achieved by convincing others of the claim? While a conflict of interest does not mean that a claim is wrong, it does suggest we should be a little more cautious in our evaluation of that claim.
3. *Consider that alternative interpretations might be correct*—Not only should you question that the information being presented to you may be wrong, you should simultaneously consider that it may also be right. Note that considering alternative perspectives or interpretations doesn't automatically mean you have to accept those alternatives. However, you should remain open to the possibility that a perspective besides your own may be more accurate. This balance between skepticism and openness was best summarized by James Oberg, who stated that keeping an open mind is admirable, but don't be so open that your brains fall out (Sagan, 1996). Consider all the evidence and how good that evidence may or may not be.
4. *Analyze your personal assumptions and biases*—This is a difficult guideline to follow, as many of us are hesitant to admit to being biased and are sometimes emotionally invested in our assumptions. Everyone in the world has biases, including the best scientists and critical thinkers. The trick is not to eliminate them, as that would be impossible, but to be aware of them and try to minimize them from interfering with your critical thinking. To be biased is part of being human; to be mindful and restrictive of your biases is part of being a critical thinker.
5. *Tolerate a lack of immediate or simple answers*—We do not have a complete understanding of the world. You may have some questions about psychology that cannot presently be answered or are more complex than you would prefer. While this may be frustrating if you are expecting a quick or easy answer, it is important to accept some uncertainty and complexity as we continue to explore various research possibilities. This is good news to those of us who enjoy exploring mysteries and solving puzzles, for there is much work to still

be done. We are discovering new things about our world and ourselves all the time. Part of the basic nature of science is that it draws the best conclusions possible using the available evidence. If the evidence is unavailable, no firm conclusions can be drawn. Furthermore, the conclusions may be revised as new evidence emerges and may become complex. Sometimes this involves tweaking old theories and sometimes it involves adopting a completely new perspective or set of theoretical assumptions (Kuhn, 1962). Uncertainty and continual revision are an inherent part of an ever-expanding empirical knowledge base.

THE EARLY ROOTS OF SCIENTIFIC PSYCHOLOGY

Now that we have outlined many of the important basic concepts to a scientific approach to psychology, it is now time to briefly discuss some of the key figures in history of psychology and the various perspectives they brought with them.

The first individual we will consider is a German psychologist named Wilhelm Wundt (pronounced "voont"). Wundt's important contribution was to introduce scientific methodology and experimentation to psychology. He was the first person to call himself a psychologist and asserted that psychology could be a natural science, much like chemistry, biology, or physics. While people had been interested in understanding human behavior and mental processes long before Wundt, he created the first laboratory to carefully conduct experiments on psychological experiences, such as the internal perceptions people have in reaction to various sights, sounds, and tastes. Wundt and his students focused on cataloging the common reactions to such stimulation in a manner that was as unbiased as possible. For example, researchers in his lab were trained to immediately record reactions to prevent faulty memory or altered judgments from distorting the original perception. Collecting actual data to implement the testing of ideas about our behaviors and thoughts is what began psychology's transition from philosophical musings to the field of scientific inquiry that we see today. The creation of his lab in 1879 is sometimes referred as the birth year of modern psychology. In addition to establishing the first research laboratory in psychology, he also created the first journal dedicated to publishing psychological research. During the 15 years following the establishment of Wundt's laboratory, more than 20 other laboratories would be created around the world, many by Wundt's former students. Although his particular approach to psychology was eventually abandoned, Wundt still remains famous for his stance that psychology must become scientific and is known as the father of experimental psychology.

Wilhelm Wundt (1832–1920). *(Courtesy of INTERFOTO/Alamy.)*

Another influential figure in the early days of scientific psychology was Edward Titchener. Titchener was a British psychologist who studied under Wundt and eventually conducted research in America. He extended and modified Wundt's techniques in order to create the structuralism perspective. **Structuralism** was an attempt to understand the human mind by breaking it down to its basic elements.

Edward Titchener (1867–1927). *(Courtesy of The Granger Collection.)*

Titchener believed that the mind could be broken down into thoughts and sensations, much like physical matter can be broken down into chemical elements (he was clearly influenced by the scientific methods of chemistry and biology. He further reasoned that the thoughts and sensations themselves could be broken down into properties such as intensity and duration.

Titchener used **introspection** to collect data in his lab, which involved people systematically observing their inner sensations and then reporting those observations to others. For example, a participant in Titchener's lab may have heard some sound and then been asked to give a very detailed and lengthy description of the inner sensation they experienced as a result. This was more than standard self-observation; it required many hours of rigorous training to report observations properly. Wundt's study of internal perceptions was a form of introspection as well, but he limited his study to immediate and simple perceptions only, unlike Titchener's attempt to quantify all mental activity. Ultimately, the method

structuralism
a psychological perspective that attempted to study the mind by breaking down mental elements into core components

introspection
a method of data collection that relied on the self-examination and reporting of mental perceptions and sensations

William James (1842–1910). *(Courtesy of Bettmann/Corbis Images.)*

Charles Darwin (1809–1882). *(Courtesy of Michael Nicholson/Corbis Images.)*

of introspection was eventually abandoned because results from both Wundt's and Titchener's labs proved to be too unreliable and subjective. Due to his reliance on introspection to better understand the structures of the mind, Titchener's approach to psychology was abandoned shortly after his death.

William James is another figure famous in the early history of psychology. He was an American originally trained in medicine but was eventually drawn to the study of psychology. His perspective was partially influenced by Charles Darwin's theory of evolution, which sought to describe how adaptations to the environment can explain the origin and diversity of the physical characteristics seen in and across species. These adaptations are passed on over time because they serve an important function in helping the organism better survive and reproduce (Dawkins, 2009). For example, cheetahs progressively evolved over time to develop legs well suited for fast running and capable of capturing prey that are also well suited for fast running. William James took a slightly similar approach to psychology, focusing on how behavior and mental processes are current adaptations to the person's environment. Unlike Wundt and Titchener, James was less interested in the structure of the mind and more interested in the function of the mind. James objected to the efforts of structuralists to break the mental world down into components and instead viewed the mental world as a steady flow of information and experience, which he termed a stream of consciousness. While he did not reject introspection, he did think it was too biased and limited to be solely relied on.

His approach became known as **functionalism**, which sought to describe the purpose of human behaviors, thoughts, and sensations. James found laboratory life boring and therefore focused much less on experimentation in comparison to Wundt and Titchener, concentrating instead on teaching and writing. He is credited as giving the first lectures on the science of psychology and once remarked that the first psychology lecture he ever heard was from his own voice. His textbook, *Principles of Psychology* (1890), became one of the most influential textbooks in the history of psychology.

The structuralism and functionalism schools of thought rarely interacted with one another in a manner other than outright hostility, with both sides being dismissive of the accomplishments of the other side. Wilhelm Wundt argued that William James wasn't really doing true psychology and James retaliated by arguing that Wundt's techniques were just thoughtless and meaningless activities (Fancher, 1996; James, 1904). However, functionalism had at least one thing in common with structuralism: both were eventually abandoned as psychological perspectives. Even though structuralism and functionalism were very different perspectives and are no longer active areas of research or theory, they both had an enormous influence on later perspectives and on the development of psychology as a science. Next we will consider perspectives that are still active today. These perspectives will only be covered briefly here.

Modern Day Psychological Perspectives

One of the current perspectives is the psychodynamic perspective, founded by the neurologist Sigmund Freud. One of the defining features of the **psychodynamic perspective** suggests that people are largely motivated by unconscious forces. Additionally, it is suggested that unobservable mental energies representing instinct, reason, and societal demands frequently conflict with one another and these internal conflicts drive the observable behavior we see people engaging in. In many ways, your observable behaviors would be considered just symptoms of the ongoing mental battles within. Freud and his followers largely ignored science in favor of trying to get into the minds of their patients. As such, it is not surprising that the psychodynamic perspective fails to meet the rigors of science. The theories in this perspective were not based on experimentation, were often defined in ways that were unfalsifiable, and lacked empirical evidence to support them.

Individuals such as the psychiatrist Carl Jung (pronounced "yoong") later extended Freud's ideas. Carl Jung is famous for attempting to divide people into different types of

functionalism
a psychological perspective that attempted to study the mind by emphasizing the purpose that mental activities serve for adapting to one's environment

psychodynamic perspective
a perspective that emphasizes how unconscious forces may underlie observable behavior and how those mental energies interact with one another

Sigmund Freud (1856–1939). *(Courtesy of Corbis Images.)*

Carl Jung (1875–1961). *(Courtesy of Bettmann/Corbis Images.)*

personality and emphasizing the idea of an unconscious awareness shared by all people. Despite the unscientific nature of this perspective, it is still important to the history of psychology because of the large influence that the psychodynamic approach had on the culture's understanding of psychology.

Many common terms in our language, such as regression, denial, and anal retentive, can be traced back to the psychodynamic perspective. Even though this perspective was not founded by psychologists, it is frequently associated with psychology and there are still current psychologists being trained in therapies and techniques derived from the psychodynamic perspective.

A more scientific and modern approach to psychology is the behavioral perspective. This approach was strongly rooted in experimentation and popularized by psychologists John B. Watson and B. F. Skinner. They proposed that psychology could be a study of behavior alone and that most behavior can be explained by examining the person's environment and learning history. Unlike the previously discussed historical figures, who only studied behavior in order to better understand the mind within, the **behavioral perspective** stated that behavior itself was worthwhile for study and could be understood in terms of the behavior and event relations found in the environment. Watson focused on how reflexive behavior to events (e.g., startling in response to a loud noise) could be extended into new types of reactions to events (e.g., startling in response to a furry animal). He tended to avoid an analysis of thoughts and sensations due to the difficulties in observation, as illustrated by the earlier failings of introspection.

John B. Watson (1879–1958). *(Courtesy of Bettmann/Corbis Images.)*

behavioral perspective
the scientific study of psychology asserting that most psychological phenomena can be best understood in terms of the relation between behavior and environment

Skinner spent more time and effort focusing on types of behavior that influence or operate on that surrounding environment (rather than behavior that is only a passive reaction to events). For example, you might push a button on a vending machine. This causes food to be dispensed (i.e., your behavior influenced the environment) and this food makes you more likely to push the button again (i.e., the environment influenced your behavior). Skinner also extended the behavioral perspective to include an analysis of thoughts and sensations. Unlike previous psychologists, Skinner considered thoughts and sensations to simply be more forms of behavior, which should be explained using the same theories and principles that are used to explain other types of behavior (Palmer, 2011). Skinner is responsible for the modern day approach to the behavioral perspective and is frequently ranked as the most influential psychologist of all time (Haggbloom et al., 2002; Korn,

B. F. Skinner (1904–1990). *(Courtesy of Bachrach/Getty Images, Inc.)*

Davis, & Davis, 1991). Although much of the early work in behavioral psychology focused in animal behavior in laboratory settings, modern applications are frequently seen with animals, school children, employees, and adult clients in diverse settings.

Another approach in psychology is the **humanistic perspective**, which was developed as a reaction against the psychodynamic and behavioral perspectives. The humanistic perspective argues that people are inherently good and that psychology should focus on factors such as the search for meaning and the fulfillment of one's potential. In this perspective it is argued that the primary reason we aren't always fulfilled or self-satisfied is because of how the demands of others misalign us with our natural growth. As such, it is best to avoid attempts to control a person too much and to instead allow the individual's free will and self-understanding to find the best path.

Some of the more influential figures in this perspective include Carl Rogers and Abraham Maslow. This perspective has frequently downplayed or ignored scientific research, often including terms that lack an operational definition, and in addition, many humanistic theories are not falsifiable. Although there are some humanistic psychologists who do collect types of empirical research, they argue that the traditional scientific method is best reserved for use in other sciences and those standards should not be applied to psychology. Although the humanistic approach has declined significantly over the years, it has still made a significant impact on therapeutic goal setting, self-help literature, and more recent movements such as positive psychology, which emphasizes a focus on the positive qualities of life rather than disorders and dysfunction.

The **biopsychology perspective** is a perspective that studies the anatomical, physiological, and genetic bases of behavior and mental processes. This psychological approach investigates how the underlying physical structures relate your body with your psychology. The human brain is a complex organ filled with millions of neurons, electrical impulses, hormones, and chemicals that can potentially influence how you behave and think. This perspective often focuses on animal experimentation to better understand how the human brain functions and impacts our learning, memory, emotions, and perceptions.

A closely aligned field is *evolutionary psychology,* which attempts to explain current psychological traits in terms of past adaptations that enabled better survival and reproduction. These successful adaptations would then be passed on through genetic inheritance.

humanistic perspective
a perspective that emphasizes inherent growth, self-determination, and free will

biopsychology perspective
the scientific study of psychology that focuses on how behavior and mental processes are related to physical structures and activity within the body

Carl Rogers (1902–1987). *(Courtesy of Roger Ressmeyer/Corbis Images.)*

Abraham Maslow (1908–1970). *(Courtesy of Bettmann/Corbis Images.)*

If certain physical traits can be passed on through genetics, it is reasonable to suppose psychological traits might also be passed on in the same manner. For example, perhaps aggressive tendencies helped our species to gather food and defend against opponents. This may have enabled those with such tendencies to survive longer and mate, allowing the trait to be passed on. However, this is a relatively young branch of psychology and which specific psychological traits have been inherited is often a source of disagreement.

The **sociocultural perspective** takes a broad view of psychology by examining the effects of societal standards and cultural expectations on the behavior of individuals. This psychological perspective often involves cross-cultural research into the behaviors that are universal and the behaviors that are unique to each culture. For example, a psychologist may study different cultural expectations regarding public displays of affection. In some cultures, such as those of Europe and the United States, it is considered socially appropriate to hug or kiss in public. Other cultures may consider these same behaviors to be taboo or even a criminal offense, such as seen in the culture of India. These different standards influence the behavior and mental processes of the individuals living in these different cultures. A closely related area is social psychology, which utilizes scientific methodology to examine how behaviors and mental processes are influenced by the real or imagined presence of others in regards to phenomena such as conformity, obedience, attitudes, persuasion, and more.

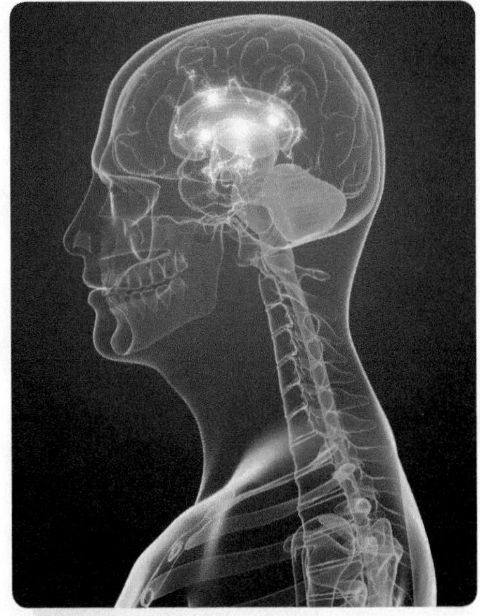

Our brain is one source of influence on our psychology.

The last perspective we will discuss in this chapter is the cognitive perspective. The **cognitive perspective** focuses on human thought and other mental events and infers that unique processes underlie such events. Unlike the psychodynamic perspective, cognitive psychology applies the scientific method to the study of the mind. Unlike the behavioral perspective, the cognitive perspective does not treat thoughts and sensations as simply more examples of behaviors, but instead treats these as fundamentally different from other behaviors and suggests that mental phenomena require a separate analysis from other types of behavior. Unlike the biopsychology perspective, the cognitive perspective typically examines the non-physical aspects of psychology. Common areas of study include attention, memory, perception, expectations, and awareness.

The society and culture we live in affects our psychology.

To illustrate each of the modern perspectives more fully, we will discuss how each perspective might attempt to explain the psychological issue of depression. The psychodynamic perspective might attempt to explain depression as a symptom of some underlying imbalance among your mental energies. While you may report feeling sad, the real problem is some unconscious conflict that may take many hours of intensive therapy to expose. The behavioral perspective might try to explain depression as a set of undesirable behaviors that have been rewarded (perhaps expressions of sadness were followed by sympathy) or desirable behaviors that have failed to be rewarded (perhaps normal interactions have been ignored or punished). As such, it would be important to produce a more desirable relationship between your current situation and your behavior, such as prompting and praising non-depressive behaviors. A humanistic perspective might try to explain depression as a reaction to the demands of others and a failure to live in harmony with your true goals. As such, it may be best to focus on a journey of self-discovery with the aid of a therapist who supports you regardless of what you ultimately choose to do. A biopsychology perspective might suggest that the depression was inherited through genetic factors or is the result of a chemical

Some psychologists focus primarily on mental factors.

sociocultural perspective
the scientific study of psychology that examines how an individual's behavior and mental processes are influenced by the larger society and culture

cognitive perspective
the scientific study of psychology of inferred mental processes that assumes such processes are the primary determinant of behavior

imbalance in the brain. As such, medications may be suggested to counteract the chemical imbalance. The sociocultural perspective may explain depression as a fulfillment of the expectations from one's social group. This perspective may try to isolate sociocultural factors that are common to depression, such as gender roles or prevalence rates in certain cultures. The cognitive perspective on depression may try to address faulty thought processes, such as unrealistic expectations for one's self or the perception of hopelessness. It is not uncommon for some psychologists to combine elements from two or more of these perspectives. The behavioral, biopsychology, sociocultural, and cognitive perspectives represent the major modern approaches to a scientific understanding of psychology, although there is often great diversity even within those perspectives.

THE APPLICATIONS AND OCCUPATIONS OF PSYCHOLOGY

Just as there are many different perspectives in psychology, there are also many different activities and occupations for psychologists. Although the discipline had been around since the late 1800s, it didn't really start to seriously focus on applied concerns until the middle of the 20th century. This was in response to World War II, when psychologists were called upon to analyze new military recruits and to treat soldiers who were suffering mentally. Although psychology is relatively young compared to other sciences, the range of psychological applications to all areas of life has risen dramatically. You will commonly find psychologists working in private practice, universities, colleges, hospitals, and clinics.

You cannot call yourself a psychologist if you only earn a bachelor's degree in psychology. However, that doesn't mean that a bachelor's degree in psychology is a worthless degree or that you are required to get a graduate degree. In fact, less than 30% of psychology undergraduates will continue on as full-time students following the completion of their bachelor's degree (Lan, 2012). Despite only completing a bachelor's degree in psychology, over 90% are employed and earning an average income of $32,000 (unsurprisingly, the average income increases with advanced degrees). Although there aren't many jobs that specifically advertise for an individual possessing a bachelor's in psychology, there are many jobs where research skills and people skills are highly valued. These skills are a major focus in psychology, which makes those trained in psychology quite valuable to employers across a wide variety of jobs. The fact that psychology combines both science and a liberal arts background is one of the biggest selling points for those earning a bachelor's degree in psychology (Kuther, 2012). Despite the variety of jobs well-suited

Psychologists are involved in many different activities and occupations.

to an individual with a bachelor's in psychology, you may still want to become an actual psychologist, not just a person trained in psychology. Below is a sampling of the career options available for those with an advanced degree in psychology. Note that this is not an exhaustive list of all career options and new career options will likely develop in the future.

Experimental Psychologists

Some psychologists are experimental psychologists, who conduct basic research on human behavior, both in laboratories and real life settings. Basic research is research intended to increase our understanding of the world without any immediate or obvious practical benefits (the findings may end up being used at a later time for practical benefits). This is contrasted with applied research, which is conducted to solve some practical problem or produce a financial gain. Most individuals working as experimental psychologists work for universities, governments, and private research companies, conducting basic studies on the effects of drugs, perceptual abilities, memory, thinking, and learning processes.

Educational Psychologists

Educational psychologists focus on how students learn and how to develop better methods for teaching people. They examine how individuals learn at different ages and apply these findings to the educational process. This may entail teacher training, refinement of educational materials, or re-designing school curricula. A closely related profession is school psychologist. These psychologists often focus on the intellectual assessment of children in school settings, including the diagnoses of impairments and delays. The school psychologist may also suggest treatments in response to these diagnoses.

Developmental Psychologists

Developmental psychologists study the physical, social, and cognitive growth of human beings from birth through death. Many developmental psychologists will specialize in a particular age range, such as infancy, childhood, adolescence, adulthood, or the elderly years. Developmental psychologists will work on tasks such as ensuring that toys and educational materials are developmentally appropriate, assessing whether an individual

Although therapy is an important part of psychology, the field is much broader than that.

is progressing at the expected developmental rate, and designing elderly care facilities to handle losses in physical and mental skills.

Forensic Psychologists

Forensic psychologists often work with prisoners or as consultants for the legal system. They provide expert testimony on the strengths and limitations of eyewitness memory, input in the juror selection process, evaluations of defendants and prisoners, expert opinions on parole decisions, mental health treatments and rehabilitation for inmates, development of legal policy, and services that are mandated by the court.

Sports Psychologists

Sports psychologists frequently serve as consultants to improve the performance of athletic teams and individual athletes. This may involve fostering teamwork, managing stress related to sports performance, improving goal achievement, and training athletes in motivational strategies.

Industrial-Organizational Psychologists

Industrial-organizational psychologists work in business settings, finding better ways to select, train, and motivate employees while maintaining their safety and well-being. This will often involve designing measurement and feedback systems, creating training materials, developing and administering personality tests, and suggesting improvements to incentive approaches. Industrial-organizational psychologists frequently work as external consultants for multiple companies or are hired as internal consultants to work as a regular part of a company's staff.

Health Psychologists

Health psychologists attempt to improve the lifestyles of people by promoting more active and healthy choices. This often involves training people in stress management, coping strategies, exercise promotion, relaxation skills, weight management, improving communication of health care professionals, and changing behaviors to support wellness. Not surprisingly, health psychologists are frequently employed by hospitals, although they can be found in other settings as well.

Neuropsychologists

Neuropsychologists study human behavior in relation to the nervous system. This job often entails studying both normal and abnormal functioning. This may take the form of neurological and psychological assessments, research into the biological determinants of behavior, drug research, and diagnosing the extent of brain injuries.

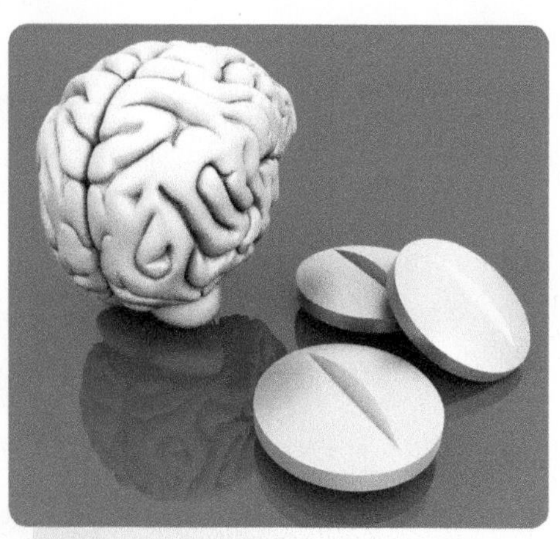

Although it is often confused with psychology, psychiatry involves a very different approach to therapy.

Counseling and Clinical Psychologists

Counseling psychologists help individuals cope with routine life problems and everyday stressors, such as martial problems, grief, and mild anxieties. Clinical psychologists diagnose and treat those with severe mental disorders that interfere with one's ability to function well, such as major depression, phobias, and schizophrenia. You can find counseling and clinical psychologists working in a wide variety of settings including private practice, hospitals, universities, schools, and mental health clinics. Despite the stereotype of psychologists dealing with just mental disorders, we hope you can already begin to see that the field is much broader than that.

While we are on the topic of clinical psychologists, it may be worthwhile to clarify a common point of confusion seen in the general public. Quite frequently, people fail to distinguish between clinical psychologists, psychiatrists, counselors, psychotherapists, and therapists. All of these involve very different types of training and credentials, which frequently results in different viewpoints, methodologies, and treatment approaches. A clinical psychologist is someone with a Ph.D. (or similar doctorate such as Ed.D. or Psy.D.) and has been trained in the application of psychological techniques to mental disorders. A clinical psychologist is most likely to utilize talk therapy or behavior management practices. In the United States, clinical psychologists cannot prescribe medication (with specials exceptions within Louisiana and New Mexico), although most are knowledgeable about medication issues and research.

Critical thinking is necessary so that you can identify a therapist who can actually help.

While psychiatrists also have a doctorate, their degree is an M.D. (medical degree) and involves training in medicine. A psychiatrist is most likely to prescribe medications to treat clients with mental disorders or other life problems. Although both clinical psychologists and psychiatrists frequently treat people with psychological concerns and try to alleviate mental suffering, psychology and psychiatry are very different disciplines involving separate techniques and training. Both "clinical psychologist" and "psychiatrist" are legally regulated terms, meaning that you have to meet certain qualifications to call yourself one of these occupational titles.

By contrast, counselor, psychotherapist, and therapist are unregulated terms in many places and the distinctions between these titles are rarely clear or consistent. As such, anyone can legally advertise themselves as a counselor, psychotherapist, or therapist, regardless of their background, qualifications, or training. This means there are no safeguards against a counselor, psychotherapist, and therapist using an ineffective and possibly harmful therapy. Many pseudoscience approaches are advocated by those calling themselves by one of these labels or some variation of these titles. It is important to check a person's credentials and education; don't be impressed by a fancy sounding occupational title. Once again, critical thinking is important, as you cannot just blindly trust someone calling themselves a counselor, psychotherapist, or therapist.

Should I Pursue a Career or Major in Psychology?

You may be wondering if a career or major in psychology is right for you. Obviously this will be an easier question to answer after you have finished reading this textbook, but we want to offer some early advice to those who are considering this question (it would be good to review this advice again at some point in the future).

Learn More About Options Within Psychology

It is usually a good idea to speak with an academic advisor to learn more about career and class options for psychology. Some universities and colleges will assign students to a specific faculty advisor, whereas other universities and colleges may have an advising office with full-time advising staff (sometimes including advisors who specialize in psychology). Regardless of the advising process at your school, you should seek out advice and feedback from an advisor early and often. They can frequently help you understand the requirements for majoring in psychology, suggest coursework, and may provide suggestions to prepare for transferring to another school or getting into graduate school.

You will get more out of your advisor if you come to an advising appointment prepared with questions and ideas relevant to your future. You may want to read ahead in your textbook or skim through unassigned chapters and other course content. By doing so, you may discover potential interests and career routes that you can then ask your advisor about.

Another way to learn more about options in psychology is to talk to your instructor. You should keep in mind that many instructors have very limited time and probably have many students in their courses and/or assigned as advisees. You will want to show a high level of commitment and motivation for pursuing psychology to increase the odds that the instructor will want to invest extra time and effort towards your concerns. Naturally, the

Advisors and faculty are good options for learning how to further yourself in a career related to psychology.

best way of doing this is by performing well in that instructor's courses. Performing well means getting top grades in your courses, not simply passing. If you want to demonstrate extra commitment to a faculty member, take time and read about the background of that person, including the articles or other works he or she has published. Many departments maintain webpages with information on the faculty and many instructors maintain professional webpages. In the process of researching these resources, you may discover another faculty member who can mentor you or discover a new area of psychology that interests you.

Get Active in the Field of Psychology

One of the simplest ways for becoming active in the field is to participate in psychological research. While serving as a psychology participant is not appropriate for listing on a resume or vita, it does have other valuable benefits. You can begin to learn about the breadth of research that is conducted and get a first-hand look at psychology research methods. If available, serving as a research assistant is even more valuable than participating in research. Likewise, working as a teaching assistant can be equally as valuable and both types of assistant activities look great on a resume or vita.

The process for becoming a research or teaching assistant varies considerably. There may be a formal application process or instructors may simply approach high performing students. It is also reasonable to approach an instructor and indicate your interest in becoming a research or teaching assistant. Once again, it is critical that you perform well in your coursework if you wish to be considered for an assistant position. There are many benefits to working as an assistant: you can gain new skills, develop an enhanced mentoring relationship with a graduate student or faculty member, secure a high-quality letter of recommendation, and build your resume or vita with extra experience and responsibilities. Opportunities to become an assistant can be quite limited and some schools may not even provide this option, so you shouldn't pass up such an opportunity if given the chance.

You can also become more active by joining professional organizations related to psychology, such as the American Psychological Association. There are many professional organizations dedicated to a psychological perspective (such as behavioral psychology) or profession (such as industrial-organizational psychology). Furthermore, there are local professional organizations dedicated to psychology that operate in just a certain state or

Getting experience is an important step if pursuing psychology.

region of the country. Many of these organizations will offer a heavily discounted membership rate for students and joining will give you access to many of their resources. You should also consider attending the conferences put on by these organizations. This is a great way to learn about the cutting edge developments in psychology and possibly meet some new people who share your interests. It is common for these conferences to also offer discounted admission rates for students.

Further Your Knowledge of Psychology Beyond This Textbook

The best way to further your knowledge in psychology is to continue taking courses in psychology, including a variety of elective courses. Not only will this broaden your understanding of psychology, you may discover a new specialization in psychology to pursue as a career. It is not uncommon for a student to completely change career paths and/or majors, perhaps even during his or her senior year, after discovering a new passion in an elective course. Don't be afraid to switch to your new passion, even if it delays your undergraduate progress (keep in mind that you are gaining skills relevant for the rest of your life). Work with an advisor to look at some of the psychology courses you may want to take in the future. This is important because there may be prerequisites to the courses you are interested in, so it is best to plan for those in advance.

Finally, seek out psychology books and articles mentioned in class and this textbook. No single instructor or textbook can cover all the fascinating aspects of psychology, so you should investigate beyond those requirements if you are serious about psychology. One word of caution: your average bookstore is likely to have a large amount of self-help and pop psychology books stocked in the section labeled psychology. Despite the fact that these books sell well to the general public, they rarely represent what real psychologists think or do. Look for the books and articles mentioned in serious textbooks, recommended by your instructor, or listed as a suggestion by professional organizations.

3

How Psychologists Do Research*

---

*Taken from *Psychology*, Eleventh Edition by Carole Wade, Carol Tavris, and Maryanne Garry

Here are four words that make many people nervous: *research, statistics, methods,* and *math.* "What do we have to learn this stuff for?" our students have often lamented. "I'm never going to need it anyway. Let's just cut straight to the findings." In this chapter, we hope to persuade you that of all the stuff you are going to learn in psychology, the information in this chapter may be the most important for protecting yourself from making wrong choices, adopting mistaken beliefs, or coming to wrong conclusions. Consider these claims:

Ask questions. . . Be willing to wonder

- If you want to be a psychologist so that you can help people, why in the world do you need to study statistics and research methods?
- If you hear that TV watching is linked to hyperactivity, can you say which causes which?
- How could you find out whether driving while talking on a cell phone is dangerous?
- Why do psychologists study animals—the nonhuman kind?

- A study reports that testosterone, that famously male hormone, plummets after a man becomes a parent. And the more time he spends caring for his children, the lower his testosterone drops. Do men have to choose between manliness and dadliness?
- Various studies report that playing fast-paced video games such as *Medal of Honor* and *Grand Theft Auto* improves players' cognitive abilities, such as visual attention and speed of response. Moreover, these games have a "transfer effect," improving visual skills in other areas of life. Does this mean that college students now have a legitimate reason to spend more time playing video games?
- A paper in a major psychology journal claims that the results of nine experiments, involving 1,000 college students, found "statistically significant" evidence of extrasensory perception (ESP). The students had to choose which of two curtains on a computer screen had an erotic picture behind it, and they allegedly demonstrated ESP by doing this at a rate that was slightly above chance (Bem, 2011). Stephen Colbert had a lot of fun with this study, as you can imagine. But was it good evidence of ESP?
- Your 9-year-old son is autistic. He lives in his own private world, cut off from normal social interaction. He does not speak, and he rarely looks you in the eye. He has never been able to function in a public school classroom. You hear

Thinking Critically

Examine the evidence

A study reported that testosterone in men drops when they become fathers, and another claimed that playing *Grand Theft Auto* may help children's cognitive abilities. Some people worried that fathering causes a decline in masculinity, and many students happily concluded that video games were beneficial. But how else could these findings be interpreted? Later in this chapter, you will learn the answers.

about a technique called "facilitated communication" (FC), in which children with autism are placed in front of a keyboard while an adult "facilitator" gently places a hand over the child's hand or forearm. The method's proponents claim that children who have never used words before are able to peck out complete sentences, answer questions, and divulge their thoughts. Some children, through their facilitators, have supposedly mastered advanced subjects or have written poetry of astonishing beauty. Should you sign up your child for FC?

By the time you finish this chapter, you will know how to think about these questions and the many others you encounter. Research methods are the tools of the psychological scientist's trade, and understanding them is crucial for everyone who reads or hears about a new program or an "exciting finding" that is said to be based on psychological research. Trying to practice critical thinking or apply psychological findings to your own life without having these tools is like trying to dig a foundation for your house with teaspoons. You could do it, but it will take a *long* time and the result won't be very sturdy. Knowing the difference between claims based on good research and those based on sloppy research or anecdotes can help you make wiser psychological and medical decisions, prevent you from spending money on worthless programs, and sometimes even save lives.

You are about to learn . . .

- the characteristics of an ideal scientist.
- the nature of a scientific theory.
- the secret of a good scientific definition.
- the risk scientists take when testing their ideas.
- why secrecy is a big "no-no" in science.

WHAT MAKES PSYCHOLOGICAL RESEARCH SCIENTIFIC?

When we say that psychologists are scientists, we do not mean they work with complicated gadgets and machines (although some do). The scientific enterprise has more to do with attitudes and procedures than with apparatus (Stanovich, 2010). Here are a few key characteristics of the ideal scientist:

1 **Precision.** Scientists sometimes launch an investigation simply because of a hunch they have about some behavior. Often, however, they start out with a general **theory**, an organized system of assumptions and principles that purports to explain certain phenomena and how they are related. Many people misunderstand what scientists mean by a theory. A scientific theory is not just someone's personal opinion, as in "It's only a theory" or "I have a theory about why he told that lie." Many scientific theories are tentative, pending more research, but others, such as the theory of evolution, are accepted by nearly all scientists.

From a hunch or theory, a psychological scientist derives a **hypothesis**, a statement that attempts to describe or explain a given behavior. Initially, this statement may be quite general, as in, say, "Misery loves company." But before any research can be done, the hypothesis must be made more precise. "Misery loves company" might be rephrased as "People who are anxious about a threatening situation tend to seek out others facing the same threat."

A hypothesis, in turn, leads to predictions about what will happen in a particular situation. In a prediction, terms such as *anxiety* or *threatening situation* are given **operational definitions**, which specify how the phenomena in question are to be observed and measured. "Anxiety" might be defined operationally as a score on an anxiety questionnaire, and

theory
an organized system of assumptions and principles that purports to explain a specified set of phenomena and their interrelationships.

hypothesis
a statement that attempts to predict or to account for a set of phenomena; scientific hypotheses specify relationships among events or variables and are empirically tested.

operational definition
a precise definition of a term in a hypothesis, which specifies the operations for observing and measuring the process or phenomenon being defined.

"threatening situation" as the threat of an electric shock. The prediction might be, "If you raise people's anxiety scores by telling them they are going to receive electric shocks, and then give them the choice of waiting alone or with others who are in the same situation, they will be more likely to choose to wait with others than they would be if they were not anxious." The prediction can then be tested using systematic methods.

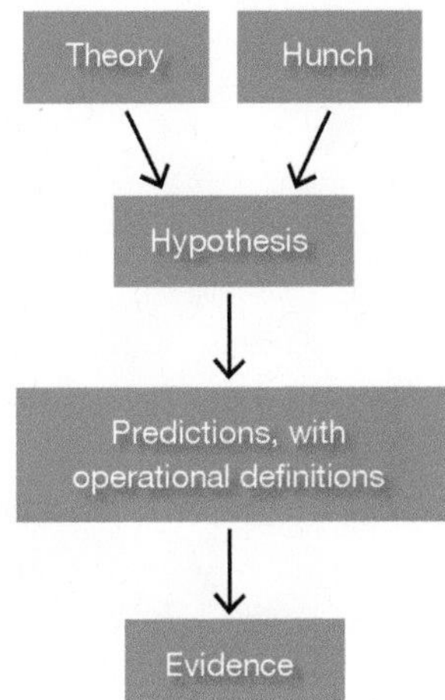

2 Skepticism. Scientists do not accept ideas on faith or authority; their motto is "Show me!" Some of the greatest scientific advances have been made by those who dared to doubt what everyone else assumed to be true: that the sun revolves around the earth, that illness can be cured by applying leeches to the skin, that madness is a sign of demonic possession. In the world of science, skepticism means treating conclusions, both new and old, with caution.

Thus, in the case of facilitated communication, psychological scientists did not simply say, "Wow, what an interesting way to help autistic kids." Rather than accept testimonials about the method's effectiveness, they have done experiments involving hundreds of autistic children and their facilitators (Romanczyk et al., 2003). Their techniques have been simple: They have the child identify a picture but show the facilitator a different picture or no picture at all; or they keep the facilitator from hearing the questions being put to the child. Under these conditions, the child types only what the facilitator sees or hears, not what the child does. This research shows that what happens in facilitated communication is exactly what happens when a medium guides a person's hand over a Ouija board to help the person receive "messages" from a "spirit": The person doing the "facilitating" unconsciously nudges the other person's hand in the desired direction, remaining unaware of having influenced the responses produced (Wegner, Fuller, & Sparrlow, 2003). In other words, facilitated communication is really facilitator communication. This finding is vitally important, because if parents waste their time and money on a treatment that doesn't work, they may never get genuine help for their children, and they will suffer when their false hopes are finally shattered by reality.

"Skepticism" is not simply about debunking some claim, but showing *why* the claim is invalid—so that better methods can replace it. Skepticism and caution, however, must be balanced by openness to new ideas and evidence. Otherwise, a scientist may wind up as shortsighted as the famous physicist Lord Kelvin, who reputedly declared with great confidence at the end of the nineteenth century that radio had no future, X-rays were a hoax, and "heavier-than-air flying machines" were impossible.

3 Reliance on empirical evidence. Unlike plays and poems, scientific theories and hypotheses are not judged by how pleasing or entertaining they are, or by whether they fit our prejudices and preferences. An idea may initially generate excitement because it is plausible or imaginative, but it must eventually be backed by empirical evidence. A collection of anecdotes or an appeal to authority will not do, nor will the intuitive appeal of the idea or its popularity. As Nobel Prize–winning scientist Peter Medawar (1979) once wrote, "The intensity of the conviction that a hypothesis is true has no bearing on whether it is true or not." In 2011, Richard Muller, a prominent physicist who had doubted that global warming was occurring, made headlines when he reported, after a two-year investigation, that temperatures really are rising, and the following year, that human beings are a large part of the reason. Muller had been funded in large measure by two conservative oil billionaires who did not welcome his results. But Muller let the evidence trump politics, as a scientist should.

4 Willingness to make "risky predictions." A related principle is that a scientist must state an idea in such a way that it can be *refuted*, or disproved by counterevidence. This important rule, known as the **principle of falsifiability**, does not mean that the idea *will* be disproved, only that it could be if contrary evidence were to be discovered. In other words, a scientist must risk disconfirmation by predicting not only what will happen but also what will *not* happen. In the "misery loves company" study, the hypothesis would be supported if most anxious people sought each other out, but would be disconfirmed if

principle of falsifiability
the principle that a scientific theory must make predictions that are specific enough to expose the theory to the possibility of disconfirmation; that is, the theory must predict not only what will happen but also what will *not* happen.

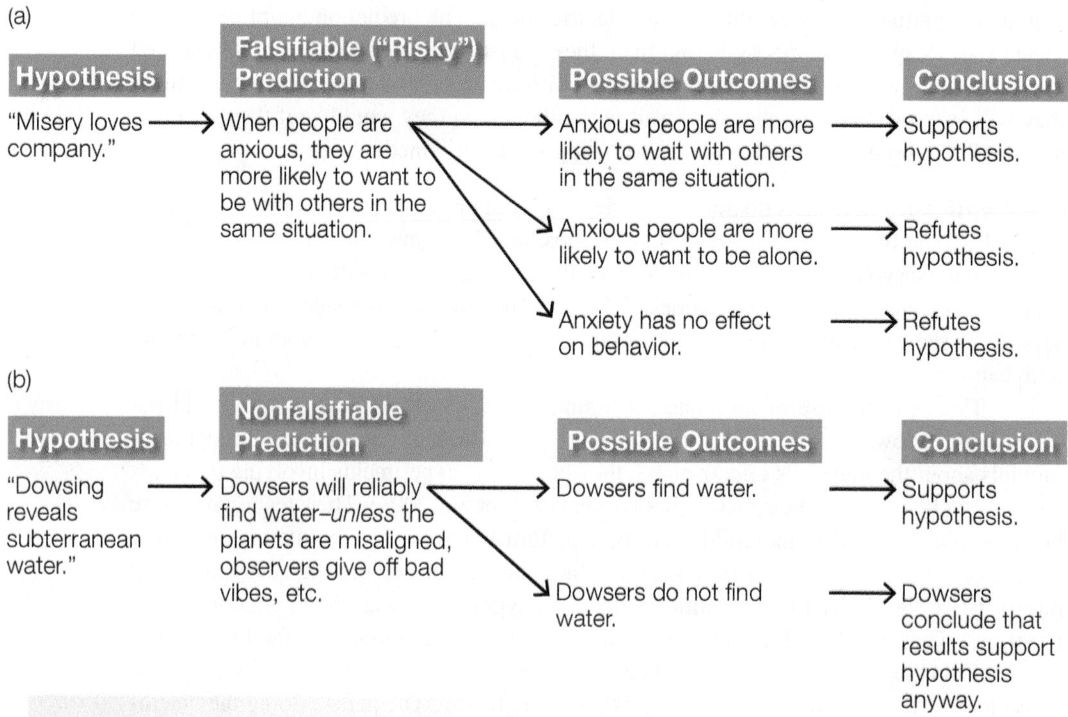

Figure 3.1 The Principle of Falsifiability
The scientific method requires researchers to expose their ideas to the possibility of counterevidence, as in row (a). In contrast, people claiming psychic powers, such as dowsers (who say they can find underground water with a "dowsing rod" that bends when water is present), typically interpret all possible outcomes as support for their assertions, as in row (b). Their claims are therefore untestable.

most anxious people went off alone to sulk and worry, or if anxiety had no effect on their behavior (see Figure 3.1). A willingness to risk disconfirmation forces the scientist to take negative evidence seriously and to abandon mistaken hypotheses.

The principle of falsifiability is often violated in everyday life, because all of us are vulnerable to the **confirmation bias**: the tendency to look for and accept evidence that supports our pet theories and assumptions and to ignore or reject evidence that contradicts our beliefs. If a police interrogator is convinced of a suspect's guilt, he or she may interpret anything the suspect says, even the person's maintenance of innocence, as confirming evidence that the suspect is guilty ("Of course he says he's innocent; he's a liar"). But what if the suspect *is* innocent? The principle of falsifiability compels scientists—and the rest of us—to resist the confirmation bias and to consider counterevidence.

confirmation bias
the tendency to look for or pay attention only to information that confirms one's own belief.

5 Openness. Science depends on the free flow of ideas and full disclosure of the procedures used in a study. Secrecy is a big "no-no"; scientists must be willing to tell others where they got their ideas, how they tested them, and what the results were. They must do this clearly and in detail so that other scientists can repeat, or *replicate*, their studies and verify—or challenge—the findings. Replication is an essential part of the scientific process because sometimes what seems to be a fabulous phenomenon turns out to be only a fluke.

If you think about it, you will see that these principles of good science correspond to the critical-thinking guidelines. Formulating a prediction with operational definitions corresponds to "define your terms." Openness to new ideas encourages scientists to "ask questions" and "consider other interpretations." Reliance on empirical evidence helps scientists avoid the temptation to oversimplify. The principle of falsifiability forces scientists to "analyze assumptions and biases" in a fair-minded fashion. And until their results have been replicated and verified, scientists must "tolerate uncertainty."

Do psychologists and other scientists always live up to these lofty standards? Not always. Being only human, they may put too much trust in their personal experiences, be biased by a conflict of interest when they are funded by private industry, or permit ambition to interfere with openness. Like everyone else, they may find it hard to admit that the evidence does not support their hypothesis; it is far easier to be skeptical about someone else's ideas than about your own (Tavris & Aronson, 2007).

Commitment to one's theories is not in itself a bad thing. Passion is the fuel of progress. It motivates researchers to think boldly and do the exhaustive testing that is often required to support an idea. But passion can also cloud perceptions, causing scientists to misinterpret their own data to confirm what they want to see. Other scientists, motivated by the desire for fame, discovery, or fortune, have even resorted to plagiarism, faking their data, and deceptive methods. That is why science is a communal activity. Scientists are expected to submit their results to professional journals, which send the findings to experts in the field for evaluation before deciding whether to publish them. This process, called *peer review,* is an effort to ensure that the work lives up to accepted scientific standards. Peer review and scientific publication are supposed to precede announcements to the public through press releases, Internet postings, or popular books. The research community acts as a jury, scrutinizing and sifting the evidence, judging its integrity, approving some viewpoints, and relegating others to the scientific scrap heap.

The peer-review process is not perfect, but it does give science a built-in system of checks and balances. Individuals are not necessarily objective, honest, or rational, but science forces them to subject their findings to scrutiny and to justify their claims.

Recite & Review

Recite: Out loud, say as much as you can about these concepts: *theory, hypothesis, operational definition, principle of falsifiability, confirmation bias, replicate,* and *peer review.*

Review: Next, go back and reread this section.

Now take this ***Quick Quiz:***

Can you identify which rule of science was violated in each of the following cases?

1. For nine months after being diagnosed with a treatable form of pancreatic cancer, Steve Jobs refused to have surgery and instead tried to cure himself with carrot juice, fruit, and psychics.
2. Sigmund Freud theorized that all men unconsciously experience "castration anxiety." When his fellow analysts questioned this notion and asked for his evidence, he was amused. He wrote: "One hears of analysts who boast that, though they have worked for dozens of years, they have never found a sign of the existence of the castration complex. We must bow our heads in recognition of ... [this] piece of virtuosity in the art of overlooking and mistaking."

Answers: 1. Jobs did not gather empirical evidence from scientific studies of similarly sick people who were not helped by unusual diets or psychics, nor of those who were helped by the surgery he avoided. **2.** Freud violated the principle of falsifiability. If analysts saw castration anxiety in their patients, Freud was right; but if they failed to see it, they were "overlooking" and "mistaking" it, and Freud was still right. Thus, no possible counterevidence could refute the theory.

You are about to learn . . .

- **how participants are selected for psychological studies, and why it matters.**
- **the methods psychologists use to describe behavior.**
- **the advantages and disadvantages of each descriptive method.**

© S. Harris/www.CartoonStock.com

DESCRIPTIVE STUDIES: ESTABLISHING THE FACTS

Psychologists gather evidence to support their hypotheses by using different methods, depending on the kinds of questions they want to answer. These methods are not mutually exclusive, however. Just as a police detective may rely on DNA samples, fingerprints, and interviews of suspects to figure out "who done it," psychological sleuths often draw on different techniques at different stages of an investigation.

One of the first challenges facing any researcher, no matter what method is used, is to select the participants (sometimes called "subjects") for the study. Ideally, the researcher would prefer to get a **representative sample**, a group of participants that accurately represents the larger population that the researcher is interested in. Suppose you wanted to learn about drug use among first-year college students. Questioning or observing every first-year student in the country would obviously not be practical; instead, you would need to recruit a sample. You could use special selection procedures to ensure that this sample contained the same proportion of women, men, blacks, whites, poor people, rich people, Catholics, Jews, and so on as in the general population of new college students. Even then, a sample drawn just from your own school or town might not produce results applicable to the entire country or even your state.

Plenty of studies are based on unrepresentative samples. The American Medical Association reported, based on "a random sample" of 664 women who were polled online, that binge drinking and unprotected sex were rampant among college women during spring break vacations. The media had a field day with this news. Yet the sample, it turned out, was not random at all. It included only women who volunteered to answer questions, and only a fourth of them had ever taken a spring break trip (Rosenthal, 2006).

A sample's size is less critical than its representativeness. A small but representative sample may yield accurate results, whereas a large study that fails to use proper sampling methods may yield questionable results. But in practice, psychologists and others who study human behavior must often settle for a sample of people who happen to be available—a "convenience" sample—and more often than not, this means undergraduate students. One group of researchers noted that most of these students are WEIRDos—from Western, educated, industrialized, rich, and democratic cultures—and thus hardly representative of humans as a whole. "WEIRD subjects are some of the most psychologically unusual people on the planet," said one of the investigators (Henrich, Heine, & Norenzayan, 2010).

College students, in addition, are younger than the general population. They are also more likely to be female and to have better cognitive skills. Does that matter? It depends. Many psychological processes, such as basic perceptual or memory processes, are likely to be the same in students as in anyone else; after all, students are not a separate species, no matter what they (or their professors) may sometimes think! When considering other topics, however, we may need to be cautious about drawing conclusions until the research can be replicated with nonstudents. Scientists are turning to technology to help them do this. Amazon runs a site called Mechanical Turk, where people across the world do online tasks that computers cannot do, typically for small rewards that they usually convert into Amazon vouchers. Many of the 500,000 registered Turk workers also participate in research, allowing scientists to quickly and cheaply recruit a diverse sample of thousands of people (Buhrmester, Kwang, & Gosling, 2011). One research team was able to analyze the patterns of moods in people's tweets worldwide (Golder & Macy, 2011).

representative sample
a group of individuals, selected from a population for study, which matches the population on important characteristics such as age and sex.

We turn now to the specific methods used most commonly in psychological research. As you read about these methods, you may want to list their advantages and disadvantages so that you will remember them better. Then check your list against the one in Review 3.1 on page 71. We will begin with **descriptive methods**, which allow researchers to describe and predict behavior but not necessarily to choose one explanation over competing ones.

Case Studies

A **case study** (or *case history*) is a detailed description of a particular individual based on careful observation or formal psychological testing. It may include information about a person's childhood, dreams, fantasies, experiences, and relationships—anything that will provide insight into the person's behavior. Case studies are most commonly used by clinicians, but sometimes academic researchers use them as well, especially when they are just beginning to study a topic or when practical or ethical considerations prevent them from gathering information in other ways.

Suppose you want to know whether the first few years of life are critical for acquiring a first language. Can children who have missed out on hearing speech (or, in the case of deaf children, seeing signs) during their early years catch up later on? Obviously, psychologists cannot answer this question by isolating children and seeing what happens. So, instead, they have studied unusual cases of language deprivation.

This picture, drawn by Genie, a young girl who endured years of isolation and mistreatment, shows one of her favorite pastimes: listening to researcher Susan Curtiss playing the piano. Genie's drawings were used along with other case material to study her mental and social development.

One such case involved a 13-year-old girl who had been cruelly locked up in a small room since the age of 1½, strapped for hours to a potty chair. Her mother, a battered wife, barely cared for her, and no one in the family spoke a word to her. If she made the slightest sound, her severely disturbed father beat her with a large piece of wood. When she was finally rescued, "Genie," as researchers called her, did not know how to chew or stand erect and was not toilet trained. She spat on anything that was handy, including other people, and her only sounds were high-pitched whimpers. Eventually, she was able to learn some rules of social conduct, and she began to understand short sentences and to use words to convey her needs, describe her moods, and even lie. But even after many years, Genie's grammar and pronunciation remained abnormal. She never learned to use pronouns correctly, ask questions, produce proper negative sentences, or use the little word endings that communicate tense, number, and possession (Curtiss, 1977, 1982; Rymer, 1993). This sad case, along with similar ones, suggests that a critical period exists for language development, with the likelihood of fully mastering a first language declining steadily after early childhood and falling off drastically at puberty (Pinker, 1994).

Case studies illustrate psychological principles in a way that abstract generalizations and cold statistics never can, and they produce a more detailed picture of an individual than other methods do. In biological research, cases of patients with brain damage have yielded important clues to how the brain is organized. But in most instances, case studies have serious drawbacks. Information is often missing or hard to interpret; no one knows what Genie's language development was like before she was locked up or whether she was born with mental deficits. The observer who writes up the case may have certain biases that influence which facts are noticed or overlooked. The person who is the focus of the study may have selective or inaccurate memories, making any conclusions unreliable (Loftus & Guyer, 2002). Most important, because that person may be unrepresentative of the group the researcher is interested in, this method has only limited usefulness for deriving general principles of behavior. For all these reasons, case studies are usually only sources, rather than tests, of hypotheses.

Many psychotherapists publish individual case studies of their clients in treatment. These can be informative, but they are not equivalent to scientific research and can sometimes be wrong or misleading. Consider the sensational story of "Sybil," whose account of her 16 personalities became a famous book and TV movie, eventually launching an epidemic of multiple personality disorder. Detective work by investigative journalists and other skeptics later revealed that Sybil was not a multiple personality after all; her diagnosis was created in collusion with her psychiatrist, Cornelia Wilbur, who hoped to profit professionally and financially from the story

descriptive methods
methods that yield descriptions of behavior but not necessarily causal explanations.

case study
a detailed description of a particular individual being studied or treated.

Thinking Critically

Don't oversimplify

Case studies are often enormously compelling, which is why talk shows love them. But often they are merely anecdotes. What are the dangers in using case studies to draw general conclusions about human nature?

(Nathan, 2011). Wilbur omitted many facts from her case study of Sybil, such as the vitamin B-12 deficiency that produced Sybil's emotional and physical problems. Wilbur did not disclose that she was administering massive amounts of heavy drugs to her patient, who became addicted to them. And she never informed her colleagues or the public that Sybil had written to her admitting that she did not have multiple personalities.

Be wary, then, of the compelling case histories reported in the media by individuals or by therapists. Often, these stories are only "arguing by anecdote," and they are not a basis for drawing firm conclusions about anything.

Observational Studies

In **observational studies**, a researcher observes, measures, and records behavior, taking care to avoid intruding on the people (or animals) being observed. Unlike case studies, observational studies usually involve many participants. Often, an observational study is the first step in a program of research; it is helpful to have a good description of behavior before you try to explain it.

The primary purpose of *naturalistic observation* is to find out how people or animals act in their normal social environments. Psychologists use naturalistic observation wherever people happen to be—at home, on playgrounds or streets, in schoolrooms, or in offices. In one study, a social psychologist and his students ventured into a common human habitat: bars. They wanted to know whether people in bars drink more when they are in groups than when they are alone. They visited all 32 pubs in a midsized city, ordered beers, and recorded on napkins and pieces of newspaper how much the other patrons imbibed. They found that drinkers in groups consumed more than individuals who were alone. Those in groups did not drink any faster; they just lingered in the bar longer (Sommer, 1977).

Note that the students who did this study did not rely on their impressions or memories of how much people drank. In observational studies, researchers count, rate, or measure behavior in a systematic way, to guard against noticing only what they expect or want to see, and they keep careful records so that others can cross-check their observations. Observers must also take pains to avoid being obvious about what they are doing so that those who are being observed will behave naturally. If the students who studied drinking habits had marched into those bars with camcorders and announced their intentions to the customers, the results might have been quite different.

Get Involved!

A Study of Personal Space

Try a little naturalistic observation of your own. Go to a public place where people voluntarily seat themselves near others, such as a movie theater or a cafeteria with large tables. If you choose a setting where many people enter at once, you might recruit some friends to help you; you can divide the area into sections and give each observer one section to observe. As individuals and groups sit down, note how many seats they leave between themselves and the next person. On average, how far do people tend to sit from strangers? Once you have your results, see how many possible explanations you can come up with.

observational study
a study in which a researcher carefully and systematically observes and records behavior without interfering with the behavior; it may involve either naturalistic or laboratory observation.

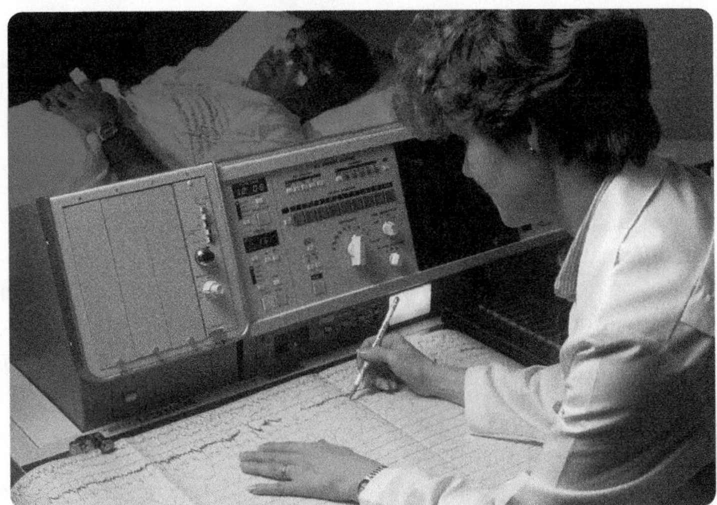

Psychologists using laboratory observation have gathered valuable information about brain and muscle activity during sleep. Psychologists using naturalistic observation have studied how people in crowded places modify their gaze and body position to preserve a sense of privacy.

Sometimes psychologists prefer to make observations in a laboratory setting. In *laboratory observation*, researchers have more control of the situation. They can use sophisticated equipment, determine the number of people who will be observed, maintain a clear line of vision, and so forth. Say you wanted to know how infants of different ages respond when left with a stranger. You might have parents and their infants come to your laboratory, observe them playing together for a while through a one-way window, then have a stranger enter the room and, a few minutes later, have the parent leave. You could record signs of distress in the children, interactions with the stranger, and other behavior. If you did this, you would find that very young infants carry on cheerfully with whatever they are doing when the parent leaves. However, by the age of about 8 months, many children will burst into tears or show other signs of what child psychologists call "separation anxiety."

One shortcoming of laboratory observation is that the presence of researchers and special equipment may cause people to behave differently than they would in their usual surroundings. Further, whether they are in natural or laboratory settings, observational studies, like other descriptive methods, are more useful for describing behavior than for explaining it. The barroom results we described do not necessarily mean that being in a group makes people drink a lot. People may join a group because they are already interested in drinking and find it more comfortable to hang around the bar if they are with others. Similarly, if we observe infants protesting whenever a parent leaves the room, is it because they have become attached to their parents and want them nearby, or have they simply learned from experience that crying brings an adult with a cookie and a cuddle? Observational studies alone cannot answer such questions.

Tests

Psychological tests, sometimes called *assessment instruments*, are procedures for measuring and evaluating personality traits, emotions, aptitudes, interests, abilities, and values. Typically, tests require people to answer a series of written or oral questions. The answers may then be totaled to yield a single numerical score, or a set of scores. *Objective tests*, also called *inventories*, measure beliefs, feelings, or behaviors of which an individual is aware; *projective tests* are designed to tap unconscious feelings or motives.

psychological tests
procedures used to measure and evaluate personality traits, emotional states, aptitudes, interests, abilities, and values.

At one time or another, you no doubt have taken a personality test, an achievement test, or a vocational aptitude test. Hundreds of psychological tests are used in industry, education, the military, and the helping professions, and many tests are also used in research. Some tests are given to individuals, others to large groups. These measures help clarify differences among people, as well as differences in the reactions of the same person on different occasions or at different stages of life. Tests may be used to promote self-understanding, to evaluate psychological treatments and programs, or, in scientific research, to draw generalizations about human behavior. Well-constructed psychological tests are a great improvement over simple self-evaluation, because many people have a distorted view of their own abilities and traits.

One test of a good test is whether it is **standardized**, having uniform procedures for giving and scoring the test. It would hardly be fair to give some people detailed instructions and plenty of time and others only vague instructions and limited time. Those who administer the test must know exactly how to explain the tasks involved, how much time to allow, and what materials to use. Scoring is usually done by referring to **norms**, or established standards of performance. The usual procedure for developing norms is to give the test to a large group of people who resemble those for whom the test is intended. Norms determine which scores can be considered high, low, or average.

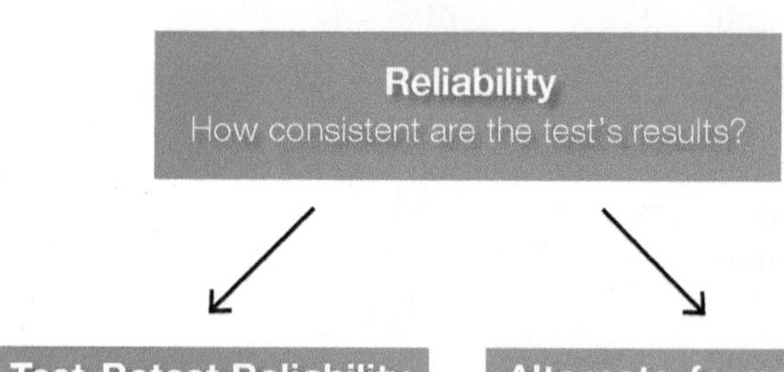

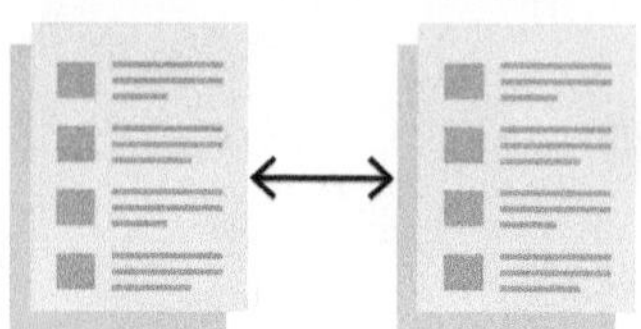

Are scores similar from one session to another?

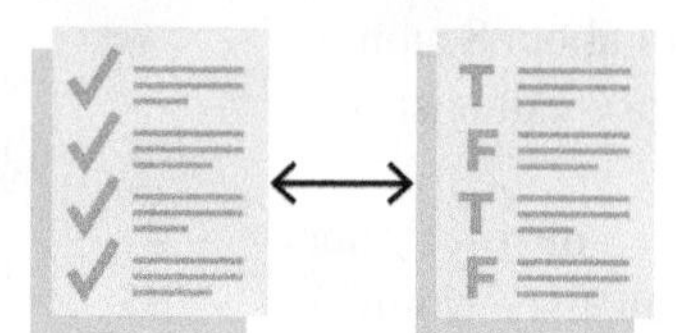

Are scores similar on different versions of the test?

Test construction presents many challenges. For one thing, the test must have **reliability**, producing the same results from one time and place to the next or from one scorer to another. A vocational interest test is not reliable if it says that Tom would make a wonderful engineer but a poor journalist, but then gives different results when Tom retakes the test a week later. Psychologists can measure *test–retest reliability* by giving the test twice to the same group of people and comparing the two sets of scores statistically. If the test is reliable, individuals' scores will be similar from one session to another. This method has a drawback, however: People tend to do better the second time they take a test, after they have become familiar with it. A solution is to compute *alternate-forms reliability* by giving different versions of the same test to the same group on two separate occasions. The items on the two forms are similar in format but are not identical in content. Performance cannot improve because of familiarity with the items, although people may still do somewhat better the second time around because they have learned the procedures expected of them.

To be useful, a test must also have **validity**, measuring what it sets out to measure. A creativity test is not valid if what it actually measures is verbal sophistication. If the items broadly represent the trait in question, the test is said to have *content validity*. If you were testing, say, employees' job satisfaction, and your test tapped a broad array of relevant beliefs and behaviors (e.g., "Do you feel you have reached a dead end at work?" "Are you bored with your assignments?"), it would have content validity. If the test asked only how workers felt about their salary level, it would lack content validity and would be of little use; after all, highly paid people are not always satisfied with their jobs, and people who earn low wages are not always dissatisfied.

Most tests are also judged on *criterion validity,* the ability to predict independent measures, or criteria, of the trait in question. The criterion for a scholastic aptitude test might be college grades; the criterion for a test of shyness might be behavior in social situations. To find out whether your job satisfaction test had criterion validity, you might return a year later to see whether it correctly predicted absenteeism, resignations, or requests for job transfers.

standardize
in test construction, to develop uniform procedures for giving and scoring a test.

norms
in test construction, established standards of performance.

reliability
in test construction, the consistency of scores derived from a test, from one time and place to another.

validity
the ability of a test to measure what it was designed to measure.

Teachers, parents, and employers do not always stop to question a test's validity, especially when the results are summarized in a single, precise-sounding number, such as an IQ score of 115 or a job applicant's ranking of 5. Among psychologists and educators, however, controversy exists about the validity and usefulness of even some widely used tests, including mental tests like the Scholastic Assessment Test (SAT) and standardized IQ tests. A comprehensive review of the evidence from large studies and national samples concluded that mental tests do a good job of predicting intellectual performance (Sackett, Borneman, & Connelly, 2008). But not everyone has access to the opportunities that lead to strong test scores and strong real-world performance. Motivation, study skills, self-discipline, practical "smarts," and other traits not measured by IQ or other mental tests are major influences on success in school and on the job.

Validity
Does the test measure what it was designed to measure?

Content Validity
Do items broadly represent the trait in question?

Criterion Validity
Do the test results predict other measures of the trait?

Behavior 1
Behavior 2
Behavior 3

Criticisms and reevaluations of psychological tests keep psychological assessment honest and scientifically rigorous. In contrast, the pop-psych tests found in magazines, newspapers, and on the Internet usually have not been evaluated for either validity or reliability. These questionnaires have inviting headlines, such as "Which Breed of Dog Do You Most Resemble?" or "The Seven Types of Lover," but they are merely lists of questions that someone thought sounded good.

Surveys

Everywhere you go, someone wants your opinion. Political polls want to know what you think of some candidate. Eat at a restaurant, get your car serviced, or stay at a hotel, and you'll get a satisfaction survey five minutes later. Online, readers and users of any product offer their rating. Whereas psychological tests usually generate information about people indirectly, **surveys** are questionnaires and interviews that gather information by asking people *directly* about their experiences, attitudes, or opinions. How reliable are all these surveys?

Surveys produce bushels of data, but they are not easy to do well. Sampling problems are often an issue, When a talk-radio host or TV personality invites people to send comments about a political matter, the results are not likely to generalize to the population as a whole, even if thousands of people respond. Why? As a group, people who listen to Rush Limbaugh are more conservative than fans of Jon Stewart. Popular polls and surveys (like the one about college women on spring break) also frequently suffer from a **volunteer bias:** People who are willing to volunteer their opinions may differ from those who decline to take part. When you read about a survey (or any other kind of study), always ask who participated. A nonrepresentative sample does not necessarily mean that a survey is worthless or uninteresting, but it does mean that the results may not hold true for other groups.

"Are you (a) contented, (b) happy, (c) very happy, (d) wildly happy, (e) deliriously happy?"

Thinking Critically

Analyze assumptions.

A magazine has just published a survey of its female readers, called "The Sex Life of the American Wife." It reports that "Eighty-seven percent of all wives like to make love in rubber boots." Is the assumption that the sample represents all married American women justified? Is it relevant that the study was funded by a rubber-boot manufacturer? What would be a more accurate title for the survey?

surveys
questionnaires and interviews that ask people directly about their experiences, attitudes, or opinions.

volunteer bias
a shortcoming of findings derived from a sample of volunteers instead of a representative sample; the volunteers may differ from those who did not volunteer.

Yet another problem with surveys, and with self-reports in general, is that people sometimes lie, especially when the survey is about a touchy or embarrassing topic. ("What? Me do that disgusting/illegal/dishonest thing? Never!") In studies comparing self-reports of illicit drug use with urinalysis results from the same individuals, between 30 and 70 percent of those who test positive for cocaine or opiates deny having used drugs recently (Tourangeau & Yan, 2007). The likelihood of lying is reduced when respondents are guaranteed anonymity and allowed to respond in private. Researchers can also check for lying by asking the same question several times with different wording to see whether the answers are consistent. But not all surveys use these techniques, and even when respondents are trying to be truthful, they may misinterpret the survey questions, hold inaccurate perceptions of their own behavior, or misremember the past.

When you hear about the results of a survey or opinion poll, you also need to consider which questions were (and were not) asked and how the questions were phrased. These aspects of a survey's design may reflect assumptions about the topic or encourage certain responses—as political pollsters well know. Many years ago, the famed sex researcher Alfred Kinsey, in his pioneering surveys of sexual behavior, made it his practice always to ask, "*How many times have you* (masturbated, had nonmarital sex, etc.)?" rather than "*Have you ever* (masturbated, had nonmarital sex, etc.)?" (Kinsey, Pomeroy, & Martin, 1948; Kinsey et al., 1953). The first way of phrasing the question tended to elicit more truthful responses than the second because it removed the respondent's self-consciousness about having done any of these things. The second way of phrasing the question would have permitted embarrassed respondents to reply with a simple but dishonest "No."

Technology can help researchers overcome some of the problems inherent in doing surveys. Because many people feel more anonymous when they answer questions on a computer than when they fill out a paper-and-pencil questionnaire, computerized questionnaires can reduce lying (Turner et al., 1998). Participants are usually volunteers and are not randomly selected, but because Web-based samples are often huge, consisting of hundreds of thousands of respondents, they are more diverse than traditional samples in terms of gender, socioeconomic status, geographic region, and age. In these respects, they tend to be more representative of the general population than traditional samples are (Gosling et al., 2004). Even when people from a particular group make up only a small proportion of the respondents, in absolute numbers, they may be numerous enough to provide useful information about that group. Whereas a typical sample of 1,000 representative Americans might include only a handful of Buddhists, a huge Internet sample might draw hundreds.

Internet surveys also carry certain risks, however. It is hard for researchers to know whether participants understand the instructions and the questions and are taking them seriously. Also, many tests and surveys on the Web have never been validated, which is why drawing conclusions from them about your personality or mental adjustment could be dangerous to your mental health! Always check the credentials of those designing the test or survey and be sure it is not just something someone made up at his or her computer in the middle of the night.

Recite & Review

Recite: Say aloud to yourself or a study partner everything you can recall about the use of *representative samples, descriptive methods, case studies, observational studies, psychological testing,* and *surveys.* Include as much detail as possible about each of these methods, including their strengths and weaknesses.

Review: Next, go back and reread this section.

Now take this *Quick Quiz:*

A. Which descriptive method would be most appropriate for studying each of the following topics? (By the way, psychologists have investigated all of them.)

1. Ways in which the games of boys differ from those of girls	**a.** case study
2. Changes in attitudes toward nuclear disarmament after a television movie about nuclear holocaust	**b.** naturalistic observation
3. The math skills of children in the United States versus Japan	**c.** survey
4. Physiological changes that occur when people watch violent movies	**d.** laboratory observation
5. The development of a male infant who was reared as a female after his penis was accidentally burned off during a routine surgery	**e.** test

B. Professor Flummox gives her new test of aptitude for studying psychology to her psychology students at the start of the year. At the end of the year, she finds that those who did well on the test averaged only a C in the course. The test lacks ________.

C. Over a period of 55 years, a British woman snorted large amounts of cocaine, which she obtained legally under British regulations for the treatment of addicts. Yet she appeared to show no negative effects (Brown & Middlefell, 1989). What does this case tell us about the dangers or safety of cocaine?

Answers: A. 1. b **2.** d **3.** e **4.** c **5.** a **B.** Validity (more specifically, criterion validity) **C.** Not much. Snorting cocaine may be relatively harmless for some people, such as this woman, but extremely harmful for others. Also, the cocaine she received may have been less potent than cocaine purchased on the street. Critical thinking requires that we resist generalizing from a single case.

You are about to learn . . .

- **what it means to say that two things, such as grades and TV watching, are "negatively" correlated.**
- **whether a positive correlation between TV watching and hyperactivity means that too much TV makes kids hyperactive.**

CORRELATIONAL STUDIES: LOOKING FOR RELATIONSHIPS

In descriptive research, psychologists often want to know whether two or more phenomena are related and, if so, how strongly. Are students' grade point averages related to the number of hours they spend watching television, playing video games, or texting? To find out, a psychologist would do a **correlational study**.

correlational study
a descriptive study that looks for a consistent relationship between two phenomena.

Measuring Correlations

The word **correlation** is often used as a synonym for "relationship." Technically, however, a correlation is a numerical measure of the *strength* of the relationship between two things. The "things" may be events, scores, or anything else that can be recorded and tallied. In

correlation
a measure of how strongly two variables are related to one another.

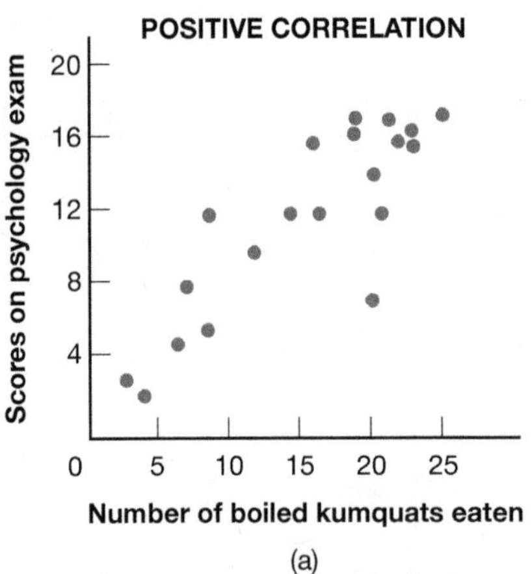

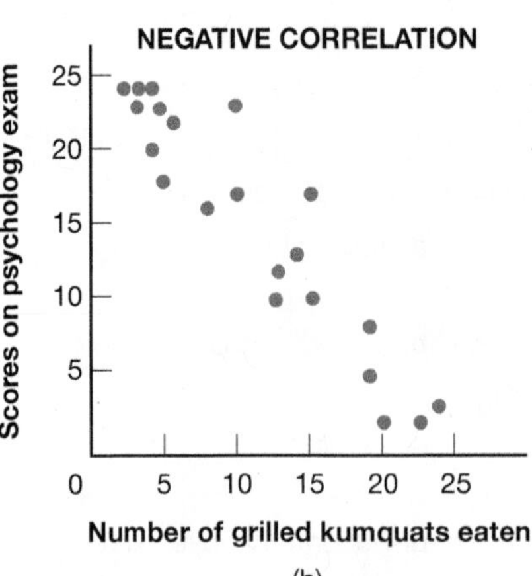

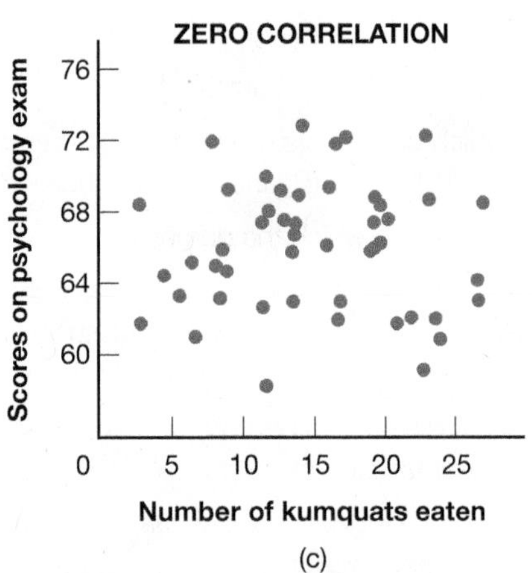

Figure 3.2 Correlations
Graph (a) shows a positive correlation between scores on a psychology test and number of boiled kumquats eaten per month: The higher the score, the higher the number of kumquats. Graph (b) shows a negative correlation between test scores and number of grilled kumquats eaten: The higher the scores, the lower the number of kumquats. Graph (c) shows the reality—a zero correlation between kumquat-eating and test scores.

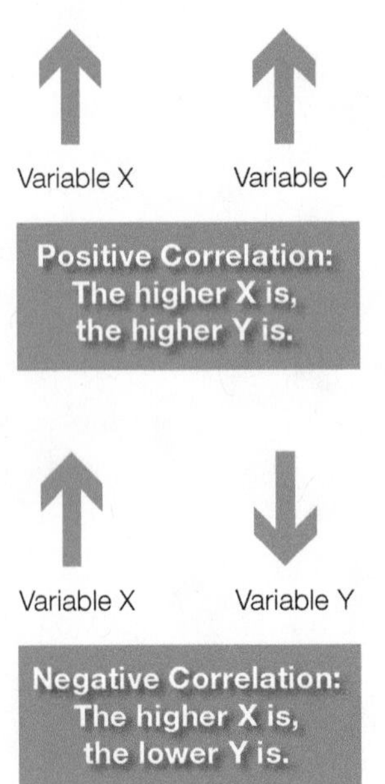

psychological studies, such things are called **variables** because they can vary in quantifiable ways. Height, weight, age, income, IQ scores, number of items recalled on a memory test, number of smiles in a given time period—anything that can be measured, rated, or scored can serve as a variable.

A **positive correlation** means that high values of one variable are associated with high values of the other and that low values of one variable are associated with low values of the other. Height and weight are positively correlated; so are IQ scores and school grades. Rarely is a correlation perfect, however. Some tall people weigh less than some short ones; some people with average IQs are academic superstars and some with high IQs get poor grades. Figure 3.2a shows a positive correlation between scores on a psychology exam and the average number of boiled kumquats eaten per month by students. (Obviously, we made this up.) Each dot represents a student; you can find each student's score by drawing a horizontal line from the person's dot to the vertical axis. You can find the number of kumquats a student ate by drawing a vertical line from the student's dot to the horizontal axis. In general, the more kumquats, the higher the score.

A **negative correlation** means that high values of one variable are associated with *low* values of the other. Figure 3.2b shows a hypothetical negative correlation between scores on a psychology exam and number of *grilled* kumquats eaten per month. In general, the more kumquats eaten, the lower the test score. Here's another more realistic example: In general, the older adults are, the fewer miles they can run. How about hours spent watching TV and grade point averages? You guessed it; they're negatively correlated: Spending lots of hours in front of the television is associated with lower grades (Ridley-Johnson, Cooper, & Chance, 1983). See whether you can think of other variables that are negatively correlated. Remember that a negative correlation tells you that the *more* of one thing, the *less* of another. If no relationship exists between two variables, we say that they are *uncorrelated* (see Figure 3.2c). Shoe size and IQ scores are uncorrelated.

The statistic used to express a correlation is called the **coefficient of correlation**. This number conveys both the size of the correlation and its direction. A perfect positive correlation has a coefficient of +1.00, and a perfect negative correlation has a coefficient of −1.00. Suppose you weighed ten people and listed them from lightest to heaviest, then measured their heights and listed them from shortest to tallest. If the names on the two lists were in exactly the same order, the correlation between weight and height would be +1.00. If the correlation between two variables is +.80, it means that they are strongly related. If the correlation is −.80, the relationship is just as strong, but it is negative. When there is no association between two variables, the coefficient is zero or close to zero.

variables
characteristics of behavior or experience that can be measured or described by a numeric scale.

positive correlation
an association between increases in one variable and increases in another—or between decreases in one and in another.

negative correlation
an association between increases in one variable and decreases in another.

coefficient of correlation
a measure of correlation that ranges in value from −1.00 to +1.00.

Cautions about Correlations

Correlational findings are common in psychology and often make the news. But beware: Many supposed "correlations" reported in the media or on the Internet are based on rumor and anecdote, and turn out to be small or meaningless. Some are merely *illusory correlations*, apparent associations between two things that are not really related. Illusory correlations can create dangerous beliefs and cause great social harm. Claims of an association between autism and vaccination for childhood diseases have alarmed many parents. The supposed culprit was thimerosal, a preservative used in childhood vaccines until 1999, and now contained in trace amounts in only a few. However, no convincing evidence exists that thimerosal is involved in autism. After this preservative was removed from most vaccines, the incidence of autism did not decline, as it would have if thimerosal were to blame. And study after study has failed to find any connection whatsoever (Mnookin, 2011; Offit, 2008). In one major study of all children born in Denmark between 1991 and 1998 (over a half million children), the incidence of autism in vaccinated children was actually a bit *lower* than in unvaccinated children (Madsen et al., 2002). The apparent link between vaccination and autism is almost certainly a coincidence, an illusory correlation, arising from the fact that symptoms of childhood autism are often first recognized at about the same time that children are vaccinated.

You can see why an understanding of correlations matters. In 2009, a special court set up to rule on lawsuits filed by parents of autistic children ruled that the evidence overwhelmingly failed to support an autism–vaccination link. But unfortunately, some parents who believe that vaccines caused their children's autism are resorting to useless and potentially dangerous treatments, such as supplements that remove metals from the body—along with essential minerals necessary for physical and mental development. And rates of measles and whooping cough, which can be fatal, are rising in children whose parents have refused to have them vaccinated.

Even when correlations are meaningful, they can still be hard to interpret, because *a correlation does not establish causation*. It is often easy to assume that if variable A predicts variable B, A must be causing B—that is, making B happen—but that is not necessarily so. A positive correlation has been found between the number of hours that children ages 1 to 3 watch television and their risk of hyperactivity (impulsivity, attention problems, difficulty concentrating) by age 7 (Christakis et al., 2004). Does this mean that watching

Thinking Critically

Consider other interpretations

The number of hours toddlers spend watching TV is correlated with their risk of being hyperactive a few years later. Does that mean TV watching causes hyperactivity problems? Are there other possible explanations for this finding?

TV *causes* hyperactivity? Maybe so, but it is also possible that children with a disposition to become hyperactive are more attracted to television than those disposed to be calm. Or perhaps the harried parents of distractible children are more likely than other parents to rely on TV as a babysitter. It's also possible that neither variable causes the other directly: Perhaps parents who allow their young kids to watch a lot of TV have attention problems themselves and therefore create a home environment that fosters hyperactivity and inattentiveness. Likewise, the negative correlation between TV watching and grades mentioned earlier might exist because heavy TV watchers have less time to study, because they have some personality trait that causes an attraction to TV *and* an aversion to studying, because they use TV as an escape when their grades are low, … you get the idea.

And remember the opening story about testosterone dropping in men who become involved fathers? Many commentators were quick to assume that there was some evolutionary reason for the hormonal decline; perhaps it equips men for bonding to infants. But we think a simpler explanation is in order: When men (and women) are tired because of having many demands on their time from child care and housework, libido flags and sex life slows down. Accordingly, so do hormones. Fatherhood itself probably has little to do with hormones; fatigue does!

The moral: When two variables are associated, one variable may or may not be causing the other.

Recite & Review

Recite: Out loud, tell us everything you can remember about these concepts. Go on … we're listening: *correlation and causation, variables, positive* versus *negative correlation,* and *illusory correlation.*

Review: Next, go back and reread this section.

Now take this ***Quick Quiz:***

A. Identify each of the following as a positive or negative correlation.

1. The higher a male monkey's level of the hormone testosterone, the more aggressive he is likely to be.
2. The older people are, the less frequently they tend to have sexual intercourse.
3. The hotter the weather, the higher the crime rate.

B. Now see whether you can generate two or three possible explanations for each of the preceding findings.

Answers: **A. 1.** positive **2.** negative **3.** positive **B. 1.** The hormone may cause aggressiveness; acting aggressively may stimulate hormone production; or some third factor, such as age or dominance, may influence aggressiveness and hormone production independently. **2.** Older people may have less interest in sex than younger people, have less time, less energy or more physical ailments, or simply lack partners. **3.** Hot temperatures may make people edgy and cause them to commit crimes; potential victims may be more plentiful in warm weather because more people go outside; criminals may find it more comfortable to be out committing their crimes in warm weather than in cold. (Our explanations for these correlations are not the only ones possible.)

You are about to learn . . .

- **why psychologists rely so heavily on experiments.**
- **what control groups control for.**
- **who is "blind" in single- and double-blind experiments, and what they are not supposed to "see."**
- **some special challenges in doing cross-cultural research.**

Experiments: Hunting for Causes

Researchers gain plenty of illuminating information from descriptive studies, but when they want to track down the causes of behavior, they rely heavily on the experimental method. An **experiment** allows a researcher to control and manipulate the situation being studied. Instead of being a passive recorder of behavior, the researcher actively does something that he or she believes will affect people's behavior and then observes what happens. These procedures allow the experimenter to draw conclusions about cause and effect—about what causes what.

Experimental Variables

Imagine that you are a psychologist whose research interest is multitasking. Almost everyone multitasks these days, and you would like to know whether that's a good thing or a bad thing. Specifically, you would like to know whether or not using a handheld cell phone while driving is dangerous, an important question because most people have done so. Talking on a cell phone while driving is associated with an increase in accidents, but maybe that's just for people who are risk takers or lousy drivers to begin with. To pin down cause and effect, you decide to do an experiment.

In a laboratory, you ask participants to "drive" using a computerized driving simulator equipped with an automatic transmission, steering wheel, gas pedal, and brake pedal. The object, you tell them, is to maximize the distance covered by driving on a busy highway while avoiding collisions with other cars. Some of the participants talk on the phone for 15 minutes to a research assistant in the next room about a topic that interests them; others just drive. You are going to compare how many collisions the two groups have. The basic design of this experiment is illustrated in Figure 3.3, which you may want to refer to as you read the next few pages.

The aspect of an experimental situation manipulated or varied by the researcher is known as the **independent variable**. The reaction of the participants—the behavior that the researcher tries to predict—is the **dependent variable**. Every experiment has at least one independent and one dependent variable. In our example, the independent variable is cell phone use (use versus nonuse). The dependent variable is the number of collisions.

Ideally, everything in the experimental situation except the independent variable is held constant, that is, kept the same for all participants. You would not have those in one group use a stick shift and those in the other group drive an automatic, unless shift type were an independent variable. Similarly, you would not have people in one group go through the experiment alone and those in the other perform in front of an audience. Holding everything but the independent variable constant ensures that whatever happens is due to the researcher's manipulation and no other factors. It allows you to rule out other interpretations.

Understandably, students often have trouble keeping independent and dependent variables straight. You might think of it this way: The dependent variable—the outcome of the study—*depends* on the independent variable. When psychologists set up an experiment, they

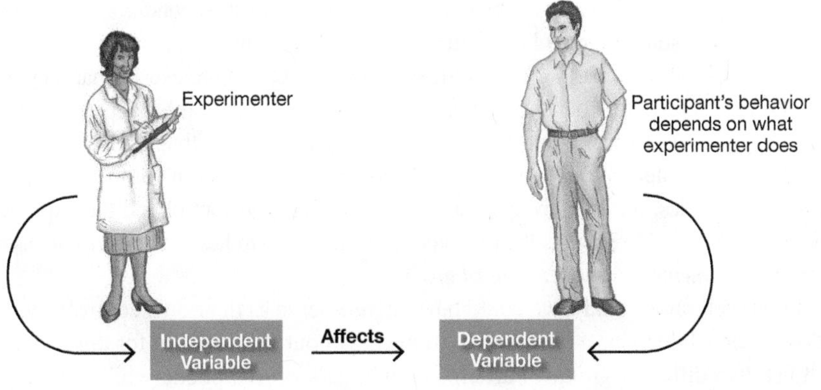

experiment
a controlled test of a hypothesis in which the researcher manipulates one variable to discover its effect on another.

independent variable
a variable that an experimenter manipulates.

dependent variable
a variable that an experimenter predicts will be affected by manipulations of the independent variable.

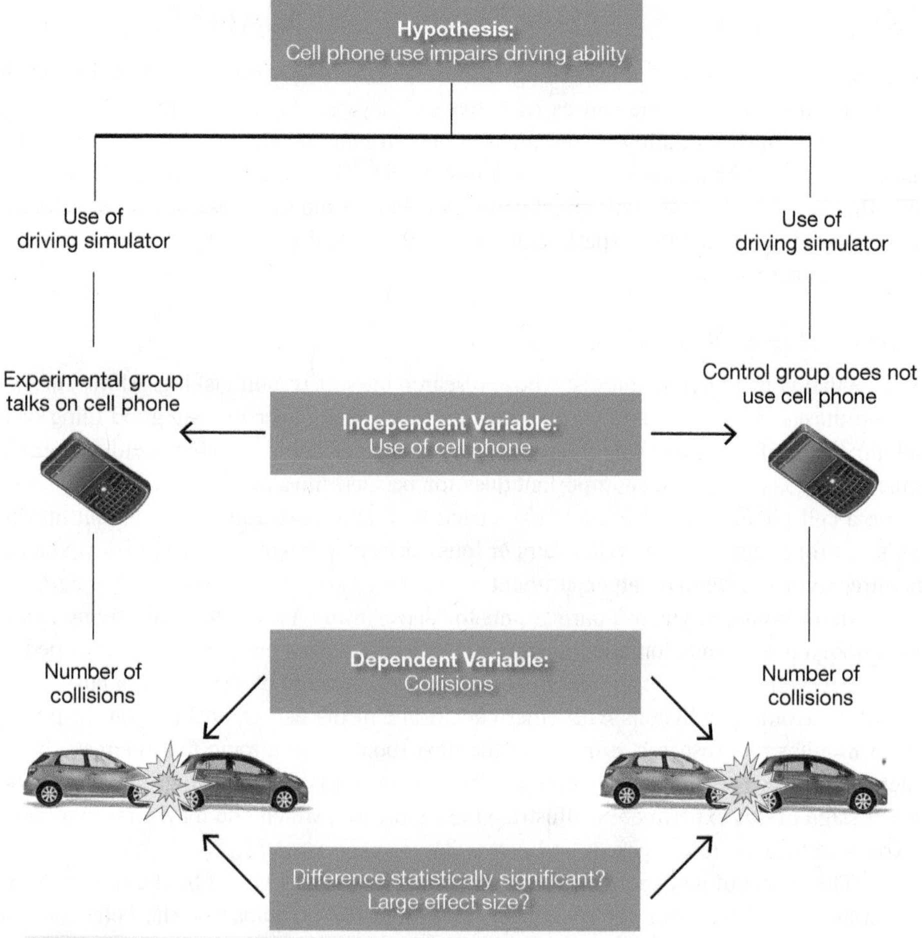

Figure 3.3 Do Cell Phone Use and Driving Mix?
The text describes this experimental design to test the hypothesis that talking on a cell phone while driving impairs driving skills and leads to accidents.

think, "If I do X, the people in my study will do Y." The "X" represents the independent variable; the "Y" represents the dependent variable:

Most variables may be either independent or dependent, depending on what the experimenter wishes to find out. If you want to know whether eating chocolate makes people nervous, then the amount of chocolate eaten is the independent variable. If you want to know whether feeling nervous makes people eat chocolate, then the amount of chocolate eaten is the dependent variable.

Experimental and Control Conditions

Experiments usually require both an experimental condition and a comparison, or **control condition**. In the control condition, participants are treated exactly as they are in the experimental condition, except that they are not exposed to the same treatment or manipulation of the independent variable. Without a control condition, you cannot be sure that the behavior you are interested in would not have occurred anyway, even without your manipulation. In some studies, the same people can be used in both the control and the experimental conditions; they are said to serve as their own controls. In other studies, participants are assigned to either an *experimental group* or a *control group*.

control condition
in an experiment, a comparison condition in which participants are not exposed to the same treatment as in the experimental condition.

In our cell phone study, we could have drivers serve as their own controls by having them drive once while using a cell phone and once without a phone. But for this illustration, we will use two different groups. Participants who talk on the phone while driving make

Thinking Critically

Consider other interpretations

You have developed a new form of therapy that you believe cures anxiety. Sixty-three percent of the people who go through your program improve. What else, besides your therapy, could account for this result? Why shouldn't you rush out to open an anxiety clinic?

up the experimental group, and those who just drive along silently make up the control group. We want these two groups to be roughly the same in terms of average driving skill. It would not do to start out with a bunch of reckless roadrunners in the experimental group and a bunch of tired tortoises in the control group. We also probably want the two groups to be similar in age, education, driving history, and other characteristics so that none of these variables will affect our results. One way to accomplish this is to use **random assignment** of people to one group or another, perhaps by randomly assigning them numbers and putting those with even numbers in one group and those with odd numbers in another. If we have enough participants in our study, individual characteristics that could possibly affect the results are likely to be roughly balanced in the two groups, so we can safely ignore them.

Sometimes researchers use different groups or conditions within their experiment. In our cell phone study, we might want to examine the effects of short versus long phone conversations, or conversations on different topics—say, work, personal matters, and *very* personal matters. In that case, we would have more than one experimental group to compare with the control group. In our hypothetical example, though, we'll just have one experimental group, and everyone in it will drive for 15 minutes while talking about whatever they wish.

This description does not cover all the procedures that psychological researchers use. In some kinds of studies, people in the control group get a **placebo**, a fake treatment or sugar pill that looks, tastes, or smells like the real treatment or medication, but is phony. If the placebo produces the same result as the real thing, the reason must be the participants' expectations rather than the treatment itself. Placebos are critical in testing new drugs, because of the optimism that a potential "miracle cure" often brings with it. Medical placebos usually take the form of pills or injections that contain no active ingredients. (To see what placebos revealed in a study of Viagra for women's sexual problems, see Figure 3.4.)

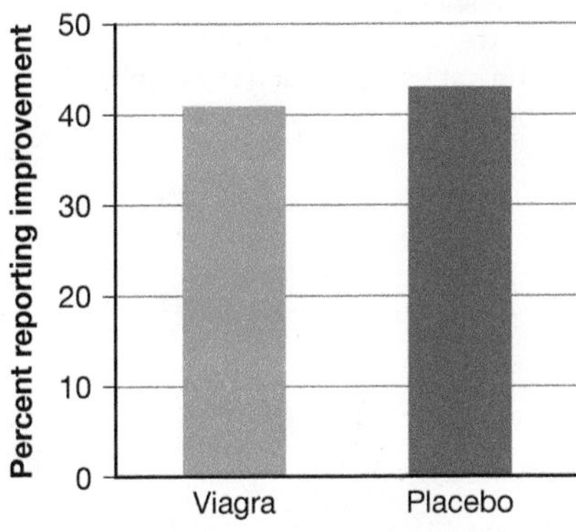

Figure 3.4 Does Viagra Work for Women?
Placebos are essential to determine whether people taking a new drug improve because of the drug or because of their expectations about it. In one study, 41 percent of women taking Viagra said their sex lives had improved. That sounds impressive, but 43 percent taking a placebo pill also said their sex lives had improved (Basson et al., 2002).

Control groups, by the way, are also crucial in many nonexperimental studies. For example, some psychotherapists have published books arguing that girls develop problems with self-esteem and confidence as soon as they hit adolescence. But unless the writers have also tested or surveyed a comparable group of teenage boys, we cannot know whether low self-esteem is a problem unique to girls or is just as typical for boys.

Experimenter Effects

Because their expectations can influence the results of a study, participants should not know whether they are in an experimental or a control group. When this is so (as it usually is), the experiment is said to be a **single-blind study**. But participants are not the only ones who bring expectations to the laboratory; so do researchers. And researchers' expectations, biases, and hopes for a particular result may cause them to inadvertently influence the participants' responses through facial expressions, posture, tone of voice, or some other cue.

Many years ago, Robert Rosenthal (1966) demonstrated how powerful such **experimenter effects** can be. He had students teach rats to run a maze. Half of the students were told that their rats had been bred to be "maze bright," and half were told that their rats had been bred to be "maze dull." In reality, there were no genetic differences between the two groups of rats, yet the supposedly brainy rats actually did learn the maze more quickly, apparently because of the way the students were handling and treating them. If

random assignment
a procedure for assigning people to experimental and control groups in which each individual has the same probability as any other of being assigned to a given group.

placebo
an inactive substance or fake treatment used as a control in an experiment or given by a medical practitioner to a patient.

single-blind study
an experiment in which participants do not know whether they are in an experimental or a control group.

experimenter effects
unintended changes in study participants' behavior due to cues that the experimenter inadvertently conveys.

In *Alice in Wonderland*, the Cheshire cat understood the power of a smile. Whenever the cat vanished, it left its smile behind.

an experimenter's expectations can affect a rodent's behavior, reasoned Rosenthal, surely they can affect a human being's behavior, and he went on to demonstrate this point in many other studies (Rosenthal, 1994). Even an experimenter's friendly smile or cold demeanor can affect people's responses.

Get Involved!

The Power of a Smile

Prove to yourself how easy it is for experimenters to affect the behavior of a study's participants by giving off nonverbal cues. As you walk around campus, quickly glance at individuals approaching you and either smile or maintain a neutral expression; then observe the other person's expression. Try to keep the duration of your glance the same whether or not you smile. You might record the results as you collect them instead of relying on your memory. Chances are that people you smile at will smile back, whereas those you approach with a neutral expression will do the same. What does this tell you about the importance of doing double-blind studies?

One solution to the problem of experimenter effects is to do a **double-blind study**. In such a study, the person running the experiment, the one having actual contact with the participants, also does not know who is in which group until the data have been gathered. Double-blind procedures are essential in drug research. Different doses of a drug (and whether it is the active drug or a placebo) are coded in some way, and the person administering the drug is kept in the dark about the code's meaning until after the experiment. To run our cell phone study in a double-blind fashion, we could use a simulator that automatically records collisions and have the experimenter give instructions through an intercom so he or she will not know which group a participant is in until after the results are tallied.

Think back now to the opening story on the alleged benefits of video games. Most of the studies that reported such benefits suffered from basic mistakes of experimental design. The experimental and control groups were not comparable: Often, the cognitive performances of expert gamers were compared with those of nongamers, who had no experience. The studies were not blind: Players knew they were chosen to participate precisely because they were expert gamers, an awareness that could have influenced their performance and motivation to do well. And the researchers knew which participants were in the experimental and control groups, knowledge that might have affected the participants' performance (Boot, Blakely, & Simons, 2011).

Because experiments allow conclusions about cause and effect, and because they permit researchers to distinguish real effects from placebo effects, they have long been the method of choice in psychology. However, like all methods, the experiment has its limitations. Just as in other kinds of studies, the participants are typically college students and may not always be representative of the larger population. Moreover, in an experiment, the researcher designs and sets up what is often a rather artificial situation, and the participants try to do as they are told. For this reason, many psychologists have called for more **field research**, the careful study of behavior in natural contexts such as schools and the workplace (Cialdini, 2009). Suppose you want to know whether women are more "talkative" than men. If you just ask people, most will say "sure women are!," as the stereotype suggests. A field study would be the best way to answer this question, and indeed such a study has been done. The participants wore an unobtrusive recording device as they went about their normal lives, and the researchers found no gender differences at all (Mehl et al., 2007).

Every research method has both its strengths and its weaknesses. Did you make a list of each method's advantages and disadvantages, as we suggested earlier? If so, compare it now with the one in Review 3.1.

double-blind study
an experiment in which neither the people being studied nor the individuals running the study know who is in the control group and who is in the experimental group until after the results are tallied.

field research
descriptive or experimental research conducted in a natural setting outside the laboratory.

Review 3.1 Research Methods in Psychology: Their Advantages and Disadvantages		
Method	**Advantages**	**Disadvantages**
Case study	Good source of hypotheses. Provides in-depth information on individuals. Unusual cases can shed light on situations or problems that are unethical or impractical to study in other ways.	Vital information may be missing, making the case hard to interpret. The person's memories may be selective or inaccurate. The individual may not be representative or typical.
Naturalistic observation	Allows description of behavior as it occurs in the natural environment. Often useful in first stages of a research program.	Allows researcher little or no control of the situation. Observations may be biased. Does not allow firm conclusions about cause and effect.
Laboratory observation	Allows more control than naturalistic observation. Allows use of sophisticated equipment.	Allows researcher only limited control of the situation. Observations may be biased. Does not allow firm conclusions about cause and effect. Behavior may differ from behavior in the natural environment.
Test	Yields information on personality traits, emotional states, aptitudes, and abilities.	Difficult to construct tests that are reliable and valid.
Survey	Provides a large amount of information on large numbers of people.	If sample is nonrepresentative or biased, it may be impossible to generalize from the results. Responses may be inaccurate or untrue.
Correlational study	Shows whether two or more variables are related. Allows general predictions.	Usually does not permit identification of cause and effect.
Experiment	Allows researcher to control the situation. Permits researcher to identify cause and effect and to distinguish placebo effects from treatment effects.	Situation is artificial, and results may not generalize well to the real world. Sometimes difficult to avoid experimenter effects.

Culture and Research

Doing good research is demanding enough, but the challenges are multiplied when psychologists venture into societies other than their own to learn which attitudes, behaviors, and traits are universal and which are specific to particular groups. Here are three major concerns that arise in cross-cultural research:

1 **Methods and sampling.** Right off the bat, researchers must worry about how one language translates into another. Speakers of English know that "Mary had a little lamb" means she owned one, not that she gave birth to it, ate it, or had an affair with it. But that's not clear from the words alone! Further, sometimes the term for a concept or emotional experience that is central in one culture (say, the Chinese concept of "filial piety," honoring your ancestors) may have no exact linguistic equivalent in another. In doing cross-cultural research, scientists must also be sure that their samples are similar in all important ways except for ethnicity or nationality. Otherwise, what seems like a cultural difference may really be a difference in education, crowding, or some other noncultural factor.

2 **Stereotyping.** When researchers describe average differences across societies, they may be tempted to oversimplify their findings, which can lead to stereotyping. Of course, cultural rules do make Nigerians different, on average, from Australians and Cambodians different from Italians. Yet, within every society, individuals vary according to their temperaments, beliefs, and learning histories.

(continued)

The challenge is to understand average cultural differences without implying that everyone in Culture A is as different from everyone in Culture B as chocolate is from cheese.

3 Reification. To *reify* means to regard an intangible process, such as a feeling, as if it were a literal object. When people say, "I have a lot of anger buried in me," they are treating anger as if it were a thing that sits inside them like a kidney, when in fact it is a cluster of mental and physical reactions that come and go. In cultural psychology, reification—treating "culture" as a thing instead of a collection of beliefs and traditions—can lead to circular reasoning, as in "Country A attacks its neighbors because it has a warlike culture, and we know it is a warlike culture because it attacks its neighbors." This is like telling a man with a leg injury that he can't walk because he's lame (Lonner & Malpass, 1994). Cultural psychologists must therefore identify not only the average differences in traits and behaviors across cultures but also the underlying mechanisms that account for them. They ask *why* Country A is "warlike," and why it changed from being peaceful (Matsumoto & Yoo, 2006).

Doing good cross-cultural research is therefore difficult, requiring the right methods and the ability to interpret them critically. But the results are essential for a deeper, more accurate understanding of human behavior in all its rich variety.

Recite & Review

Recite: Tell someone (even if that someone is you) all that you remember about these concepts: experiment, independent and dependent variables, control condition, random assignment, and field research.
Review: Next, go back and reread this section.

Now take this ***Quick Quiz:***

A. Name the independent and dependent variables in studies designed to answer the following questions:

1. Whether sleeping after learning a poem improves memory for the poem
2. Whether the presence of other people affects a person's willingness to help someone in distress
3. Whether listening to heavy metal makes people aggressive

B. Identify three special challenges in doing cross-cultural research.

C. On a TV show, Dr. Blitznik announces a fabulous new program she calls chocolate immersion therapy (CIT). "People who spend one day a week doing nothing but eating chocolate are soon cured of eating disorders, depression, and poor study habits," claims Dr. Blitznik. What should you find out about CIT before signing up?

Answers: A. 1. Opportunity to sleep after learning is the independent variable; memory for the poem is the dependent variable. **2.** The presence of other people is the independent variable; willingness to help others is the dependent variable. **3.** Exposure to heavy metal is the independent variable; aggressive behavior is the dependent variable. **B.** Problems in methodology (e.g., translation problems) and sampling; stereotyping; reification of culture when explaining results. **C.** Some questions to ask: Is there research showing that people who went through CIT did better than those in a control group who did not have the therapy or who had a different therapy—say, broccoli immersion therapy? If so, how many people were studied? How were they selected, and how were they assigned to the therapy and nontherapy groups? Did the person running the experiment know who was getting CIT and who was not? How long did the "cures" last? Has the research been peer-reviewed? Has it been replicated?

You are about to learn . . .

- why averages can be misleading.
- how psychologists can tell whether a finding is impressive or trivial.
- why some findings are significant statistically yet unimportant in practical terms.
- how psychologists can combine results from many studies of a question to get a better overall answer.

Evaluating the Findings

If you are a psychologist who has just done an observational study, a survey, or an experiment, your work has just begun. Once you have some results in hand, you must do three things with them: (1) describe them, (2) assess how reliable and meaningful they are, and (3) figure out how to explain them.

Descriptive Statistics: Finding Out What's So

Let's say that 30 people in the cell phone experiment talked on the phone, and 30 did not. We have recorded the number of collisions for each person on the driving simulator. Now we have 60 numbers. What can we do with them?

The first step is to summarize the data. The world does not want to hear how many collisions each person had. It wants to know how the the cell phone group did as a whole compared to the control group. To provide this information, we need numbers that sum up our data. Such numbers, known as **descriptive statistics**, are often depicted in graphs and charts.

A good way to summarize the data is to compute group averages. The most commonly used type of average is the **arithmetic mean**, which is calculated by adding up all the individual scores and dividing the result by the number of scores. We can compute a mean for the cell phone group by adding up the 30 collision scores and dividing the sum by 30. Then we can do the same for the control group. Now our 60 numbers have been boiled down to 2. For the sake of our example, let's assume that the cell phone group had an average of 10 collisions, whereas the control group's average was only 7.

We must be careful, however, about how we interpret these averages. It is possible that no one in our cell phone group actually had 10 collisions. Perhaps half the people in the group were motoring maniacs and had 15 collisions, whereas the others were more cautious and had only 5. Perhaps almost all the participants in the group had 9, 10, or 11 collisions. Perhaps the number of accidents ranged from 0 to 15. The mean does not tell

descriptive statistics
statistical procedures that organize and summarize research data.

arithmetic mean
an average that is calculated by adding up a set of quantities and dividing the sum by the total number of quantities in the set.

Most people assume that "on average" means "typically"—but sometimes it doesn't! Averages can be misleading if you don't know the extent to which events deviated from the statistical mean and how they were distributed.

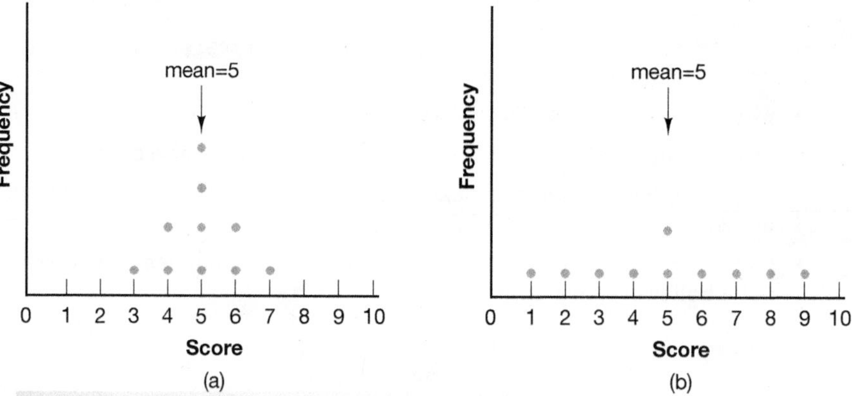

Figure 3.5 Same Mean, Different Meaning
In both distributions of scores, the mean is 5, but in (a), the scores are clustered around the mean, whereas in (b), they are widely dispersed, so the standard deviations for the distributions will be quite different. In which distribution is the mean more "typical" of all scores?

us about such variability in the participants' responses. For that, we need other descriptive statistics. The **standard deviation** tells us how clustered or spread out the individual scores are around the mean; the more spread out they are, the less "typical" the mean is. (See Figure 3.5.) Unfortunately, when research is reported in the news, you usually hear only about the mean.

Inferential Statistics: Asking "So What?"

At this point in our study, we have one group with an average of 10 collisions and another with an average of 7, a difference of 3 collisions. Should we break out the champagne? Hold a press conference? Call our mothers?

Better hold off. Perhaps if one group had an average of 15 collisions and the other an average of 1, we might get excited. But rarely does a psychological study hit you between the eyes with a sensationally clear result. In most cases, the difference between the two groups is due simply to chance. Despite all our precautions, perhaps the people in the cell phone group just happened to be a little more accident-prone, and their extra 3 collisions had nothing to do with talking on the phone.

To find out how impressive the data are, psychologists use **inferential statistics**. These statistics do not merely describe or summarize the data; they permit a researcher to draw *inferences* (conclusions based on evidence) about how meaningful the findings are. Like descriptive statistics, inferential statistics involve the application of mathematical formulas to the data.

Historically, the most commonly used inferential statistics have been **significance tests**, which tell researchers how likely it is that their result occurred by chance. (We have given you the general meaning; statisticians use a more technical one.) Suppose that in the real world, people who talk on cell phones have no more collisions than people who do not. How likely, then, would you be to obtain the difference you found (or an even larger one) between the experimental group and the control group? If that likelihood is quite low, we reject the hypothesis that there is no difference in the real world, and we say that our result is *statistically significant*. This means there is a good probability that the difference we got in our study is real.

Psychologists consider a result to be significant if it would be expected to occur by chance only rarely, and "rarely" usually means 5 or fewer times in 100 repetitions of the study. We would then say that the result is significant at the .05 level, or $p < .05$, where p stands for probability and .05 is referred to as the *p value*. If, however, the significance test shows that the p value is greater than .05, many researchers would have little confidence in the study's result, although they might still want to do further research to confirm their judgment.

standard deviation
a commonly used measure of variability that indicates the average difference between scores in a distribution and their mean.

inferential statistics
statistical procedures that allow researchers to draw inferences about how statistically meaningful a study's results are.

significance tests
statistical tests that show how likely it is that a study's results occurred merely by chance.

Statistically significant results allow psychologists to make general predictions about human behavior: "Talking on a cell phone while driving increases people's risk of accidents." But these predictions do not tell us with any certainty what a *particular* person will do in a particular situation. Probabilistic results are typical in all of the sciences, not just psychology. Medical research can tell us that the odds are high that someone who smokes will get lung cancer, but because many variables interact to produce any particular case of cancer, research cannot tell us for sure whether Aunt Bessie, who smokes two packs a day, will come down with the disease.

Today, a growing number of psychologists and other researchers also report their results by using a statistical formula that creates a **confidence interval**. The mean from a particular sample will almost never be exactly the same value as the true mean in the population; instead, it will probably be a little higher or a little lower. A confidence interval draws a range a little higher and lower than the sample mean to help depict where the true mean probably lies (Fidler & Loftus, 2009). As Figure 3.6 shows, if you repeated your study over and over, you would produce a different sample mean and confidence interval each time. But notice something interesting: Although none of the means in each study (the green circles) is exactly the same as the population mean (the straight vertical line), most of the confidence intervals (CIs) contain the true mean. In fact, if you repeated your study over and over, 95 percent of the CIs would contain the true mean, although you would occasionally produce a rogue CI (the gray bars) (Cumming, 2012). So do you see the problem with drawing strong conclusions on the basis of any one study?

Figure 3.6 Confidence Intervals across Repeated Studies

By the way, many studies similar to our hypothetical one have confirmed the dangers of talking on a cell phone while driving. In one study, cell phone users, whether their phones were handheld or hands-free, were as impaired in their driving ability as intoxicated drivers were (Strayer, Drews, & Crouch, 2006). Because of such research, some states have made it illegal to drive while holding a cell phone to your ear. Others are considering making any cell phone use by a driver illegal.

Interpreting the Findings

The last step in any study is to figure out what the findings mean. Trying to understand behavior from uninterpreted findings is like trying to become fluent in Swedish by reading a Swedish–English dictionary. Just as you need the grammar of Swedish to tell you how the words fit together, psychologists need hypotheses and theories to explain how the facts that emerge from research fit together.

Choosing the Best Explanation.

Sometimes it is hard to choose between competing explanations of a finding. Does cell phone use disrupt driving by impairing coordination, by increasing a driver's vulnerability to distraction, by interfering with the processing of information, by distorting the driver's perception of danger, or by some combination of these or other factors? Several explanations may fit the results equally well, which means that more research will be needed to determine the best one.

In a real study of cell phone use while driving, a participant "drives" in a high-tech driving simulator.

Sometimes the best interpretation of a finding does not emerge until a hypothesis has been tested in different ways. Although the methods we have described tend to be appropriate for different questions (see Review 3.2 on page 76), sometimes one method can be used to confirm, disconfirm, or extend the results obtained with another. If the findings of studies using various methods converge, researchers have greater reason to be confident about them. If the findings conflict, researchers must modify their hypotheses or investigate further.

confidence interval
a statistical measure that provides, with a specified probability, a range of values within which a population mean is likely to lie.

Here is an example. When psychologists compare the mental test scores of young people and old people, they usually find that younger people outscore older ones. This type of research, in which different groups are compared at the same time, is called **cross-sectional**:

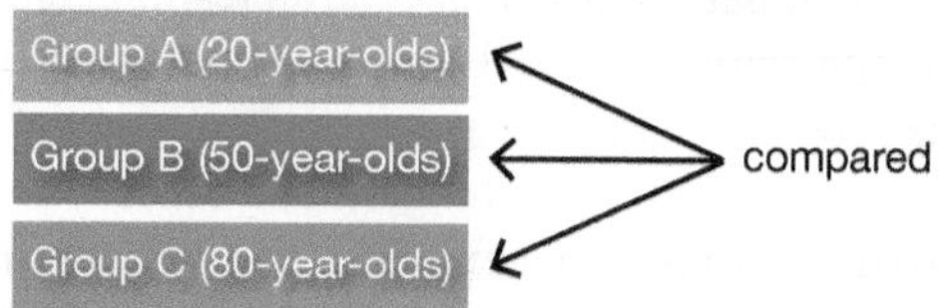

But **longitudinal studies** can also be used to investigate mental abilities across the life span. In a longitudinal study, the same people are followed over a period of time and are reassessed at regular intervals:

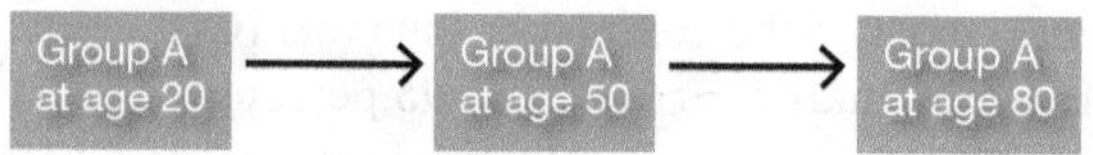

cross-sectional study
a study in which people (or animals) of different ages are compared at a given time.

longitudinal study
a study in which people (or animals) are followed and periodically reassessed over a period of time.

In contrast to cross-sectional studies, longitudinal studies find that as people age, they sometimes perform as well as they ever did on certain mental tests. A *general* decline in ability may not occur until people reach their 70s or 80s. Why do results from the two types of

Review 3.2 Psychological Research Methods Contrasted

Psychologists may use different methods to answer different questions about a topic. This table shows some ways in which the methods described in this chapter can be used to study different questions about aggression. Sometimes, however, two or more methods can be used to investigate the same question, and findings based on one method may extend, support, or disconfirm findings based on another.

Method	Purpose	Example
Case study	To understand the development of aggressive behavior in a particular individual; to formulate research hypotheses about the origins of aggressiveness	Developmental history of a serial killer
Naturalistic observation	To describe the nature of aggressive acts in early childhood	Observation of hitting, kicking, etc., during free-play periods in a preschool
Laboratory observation	To find out whether aggressiveness in pairs of same-sex and different-sex children differs in frequency or intensity	Observation through a one-way window of same-sex and different-sex pairs of preschoolers; pairs must negotiate who gets to play with an attractive toy that has been promised to each child
Test	To compare the personality traits of aggressive and nonaggressive people	Administration of personality tests to violent and nonviolent prisoners
Survey	To find out how common domestic violence is in the general population	Questionnaire asking anonymous respondents (in a sample representative of the population) about the occurrence of slapping, hitting, etc., in their homes
Correlational study	To examine the relationship between aggressiveness and television viewing	Administration to college students of a paper-and-pencil test of aggressiveness and a questionnaire on number of hours spent watching TV weekly; computation of correlation coefficient
Experiment	To find out whether high air temperatures elicit aggressive behavior	Arrangement for individuals to "shock" a "learner" (actually a confederate of the experimenter) while seated in a room heated to either 72°F or 85°F

studies conflict? Probably because cross-sectional studies measure generational differences; younger generations tend to outperform older ones in part because they are better educated or are more familiar with the tests used. Without longitudinal studies, we might falsely conclude that all types of mental ability inevitably decline with advancing age.

Judging the Result's Importance.

Sometimes psychologists agree on the reliability and meaning of a finding but not on its ultimate relevance for theory or practice. Part of the problem is statistical. Traditional tests of significance continue to be used in the majority of psychological studies, which is why we have described them here, but these tests have important drawbacks (Cumming, 2012; Cumming et al., 2007; Erceg-Hurn & Mirosevich, 2008). A result may be statistically significant yet be small and of little consequence in everyday life because the independent variable does not explain most of the variation in people's behavior. Moreover, *p* values don't guarantee that other researchers (or even the same researchers) will be able to obtain a similar effect if they run their study again; in fact, *p* values can vary considerably from one replication to another (Cumming, 2012). That is why so many "findings" that make the news don't pan out in later studies. Remember the ESP study that we mentioned at the start of this chapter? Because the results were just barely statistically significant, the paper was published in an academic journal, which appalled many psychological scientists (Alcock, 2011). As one statistician noted, the article did not show that ESP exists; rather, it showed why a reliance on *p* values produces too many results that are just flukes (in Miller, 2011).

To gain better protection against spurious, unsubstantial results, many psychology journals now encourage or require the use of alternate methods and statistics. One is to use statistical procedures that reveal the **effect size**. Think of effect sizes as similar to measuring how much something weighs: Regardless of what you're weighing, 100 pounds is weightier than 10 pounds. Effect sizes, then, help us to understand how important—how weighty—an effect is. One such measure tells us how much of the variation in the data the independent variable accounts for. If it explains 5 percent of the variation, it's not very powerful, even if the result is statistically significant; if it explains 40 percent, it's very impressive.

A popular set of statistical techniques called **meta-analysis** provides an especially good way to measure the overall "weight" of a finding, because it combines data from a number of related studies instead of assessing each study's results separately. A single result based on a small sample may be just a coincidence; meta-analysis comes to the rescue, assessing the effect of some independent variable across all the studies in the analysis. This approach is important because rarely does one study prove anything, in psychology or any other field. That is why you should be suspicious of headlines that announce a sudden major scientific breakthrough based on a single study. Breakthroughs do occur, but they are rare.

Consider the gender gap in math achievement, which persists in some nations although not in others. Is it largely due to a "natural" male superiority in math, or to gender differences in educational and professional opportunities in the sciences? A meta-analysis of studies across 69 nations, representing nearly 500,000 students ages 14 to 16, found that although boys have more positive attitudes toward math than girls do, average effect sizes in actual mathematics achievement are very small. Moreover, *national* effect sizes show considerable variability; that is, a male–female math gap is wider in some countries than in others. The most powerful predictors of that cross-national variation were whether boys and girls were equally likely to be enrolled in school; the percentage of women in research jobs; and women's representation in their nation's government (Else-Quest, Hyde, & Linn, 2010).

Another approach, growing in popularity among scientists in medicine and other fields as well as psychology, is based on **Bayesian statistics**, named for the eighteenth-century English minister who developed it (Dienes, 2011; McGrayne, 2011). Bayesian statistics involve a formula that takes prior knowledge into consideration when evaluating any finding. In the case of ESP, "prior knowledge" of physics and biology suggests no known or possible mechanism for this phenomenon. And in fact, when a team of mathematical

effect size
an objective, standardized way of describing the strength of the independent variable's influence on the dependent variable.

meta-analysis
a set of techniques for combining data from a number of related studies to determine the explanatory strength of a particular independent variable.

Bayesian statistics
statistics that involve a formula for calculating the likelihood of a hypothesis being true and meaningful, taking into account relevant prior knowledge.

psychologists reassessed the ESP paper using Bayes' formula, they concluded that the data actually support the hypothesis that ESP does *not* exist (Wagenmakers et al., 2011).

One writer nicely summarized the Bayesian approach as the "yeah, right" effect. If a study finds that eating blueberry muffins reduces the risk of heart disease by 90 percent or that a treatment cures drug addiction in a week, a Bayesian's reaction would be to evaluate that finding against what can be observed in the real world, and the result would have to pass the "yeah, right" test of plausibility (Carey, 2011). A team of researchers compared p values, effect sizes, and Bayes factors as measures of statistical evidence, using 855 published findings (Wetzels et al., 2011). They found that although p values and Bayes factors almost always agreed about which hypotheses were better supported by the data, the measures often disagreed about the strength of this support. In many cases, the Bayes analysis showed that the result was only anecdotal.

The Bayesian approach is still controversial, and arguments continue about how precisely to quantify "prior knowledge," which can vary from strong empirical evidence to more subjective estimates. But its importance is growing among the statistical methods of science.

Recite & Review

Recite: Major scientific breakthrough: Reciting what you've read helps! So go ahead and recite everything you know about these concepts: *arithmetic mean, standard deviation, statistical significance, confidence intervals, effect size, meta-analysis*, and *Bayesian analysis.*

Review: Next, go back and reread this section.

Now take this ***Quick Quiz:***

A. Check your understanding of the descriptive–inferential distinction by placing a check in the appropriate column for each phrase:

	Descriptive statistics	Inferential statistics
1. Summarize the data	______	______
2. Give likelihood that a result occurred by chance	______	______
3. Include the mean	______	______
4. Give measure of statistical significance	______	______
5. Tell you whether to call your mother about your results	______	______
6. Examine a confidence interval around the sample mean	______	______

B. If a researcher studies the same group over many years, the study is said to be ________.

C. Suppose a researcher wants to know about the effects on memory of energy drinks. Unfortunately, in the 45 studies that have examined this question, the results vary. What statistical method might be used to determine whether the relationship between energy drinks and memory is strong or weak?

D. On the Internet, you read about a "Fantastic Scientific Breakthrough in Treating Shyness." Why should you be cautious about this announcement?

Answers: A. 1. descriptive **2.** inferential **3.** descriptive **4.** inferential **5.** inferential **6.** inferential **B.** longitudinal **C.** meta-analysis **D.** Scientific progress usually proceeds gradually, not all at once. And besides, anyone can post a claim on the Internet, so you will want to ask, "What's the original source of this claim? What is the 'science' behind that alleged breakthrough? How was shyness defined, and what was the method of treating it? How was success defined and measured?"

You are about to learn . . .

- why psychologists sometimes lie to people taking part in their studies.
- why psychologists study nonhuman animals.

Keeping the Enterprise Ethical

Because rigorous research methods are the very heart of science, psychologists spend considerable time discussing and debating their procedures for collecting and evaluating data. And they are also concerned about the ethical principles governing research and practice. In colleges and universities, a review committee must approve all studies and be sure they conform to federal regulations. In addition, the American Psychological Association (APA) has a code of ethics that all members must follow. Even people who are not members of the APA, whether working in the United States or around the world, often follow the code in their research. The code of ethics is subject to frequent reexamination. In 2009, after vehement debate about psychologists' participation in the interrogation of suspected terrorists being held at Guantanamo prison, APA members voted to prohibit psychologists from working in any capacity in an institution that violates international law or the U.S. Constitution.

The Ethics of Studying Human Beings

The APA code calls on psychological scientists to respect the dignity and welfare of the people they study. Participants must enter a study voluntarily and must know enough about it to make an intelligent decision about taking part, a doctrine known as **informed consent**. Researchers must also protect participants from physical and mental harm, and if any risk exists, they must warn them in advance and give them an opportunity to withdraw at any time.

The policy of informed consent sometimes clashes with an experimenter's need to disguise the true purpose of the study. In such cases, if the purpose were revealed in advance, the results would be ruined because the participants would not behave naturally. In social psychology especially, a study's design sometimes calls for an elaborate deception. For example, a confederate of the researcher might pretend to be having a seizure. The researcher can then find out whether bystanders—the uninformed participants—will respond to a person needing help. If the participants knew that the confederate was only acting, they would obviously not bother to intervene or call for assistance.

"So! How is everybody today?"

Sometimes people have been misled about procedures that are intentionally designed to make them angry, guilty, ashamed, or anxious so that researchers can learn what people do when they feel this way. In studies of embarrassment and anger, people have been made to look clumsy in front of others, have been called insulting names, or have been told they were incompetent. In studies of dishonesty, participants have been entrapped into cheating and have then been confronted with evidence of their guilt. The APA code requires that participants be thoroughly debriefed when the study is over and told why deception was necessary. In addition to debriefing, the APA's ethical guidelines require researchers to show that any deception is justified by a study's potential value and to consider alternative procedures.

informed consent
the doctrine that anyone who participates in human research must do so voluntarily and must know enough about the study to make an intelligent decision about whether to take part.

Psychologists sometimes use animals to study learning, memory, emotion, and social behavior. On the left, John Boitano and Kathryn Scavo observe a swimming rat as it learns the location of platforms in a pool of dark water. On the right, Frans de Waal observes a group of chimpanzees socializing in an outdoor play area.

The Ethics of Studying Animals

Ethical issues also arise in animal research. Animals are used in only a small percentage of psychological studies, but they play a crucial role in some areas. Usually they are not harmed (as in research on mating in hamsters, which is definitely fun for the hamsters), but sometimes they are (as when rats brought up in deprived or enriched environments are sacrificed so that their brains can be examined for any effects). Psychologists study animals for many reasons:

- *To conduct basic research on a particular species.* For example, researchers have learned a great deal about the unusually lusty and cooperative lives of bonobo apes.
- *To discover practical applications.* For example, behavioral studies have shown farmers how to reduce crop destruction by birds and deer without resorting to their traditional method—shooting the animals.
- *To clarify theoretical questions.* For example, we might not attribute the longer life spans of women solely to lifestyle factors and health practices if we discover that a male–female difference exists in other mammals as well.
- *To improve human welfare.* For example, animal studies have helped researchers develop ways to reduce chronic pain, rehabilitate patients with neurological disorders, and understand the mechanisms underlying memory loss and senility.

In recent decades, some psychological and medical scientists have been trying to find ways to do their research without using animals at all, by using computer simulations or other new technologies. When animals are essential to research, the APA's ethical code includes comprehensive guidelines to ensure their humane treatment. Federal laws governing the housing and care of research animals—particularly our closest relatives, the great apes—are stronger than they used to be; no future research can be done on apes unless it is vital to human welfare and cannot be conducted with other methods. Moreover, thanks to a growing understanding of animals' instinctive, social, and cognitive needs—even in so-called "lower" species like the lab rat—many psychological scientists have changed the way they treat them, which improves their research as well as the animals' well-being (Patterson-Kane, Harper, & Hunt, 2001).

The difficult task for scientists is to balance the benefits of animal research with an acknowledgment of past abuses and a compassionate concern for the welfare of species other than our own.

Now you are ready to explore more deeply what psychologists have learned about human psychology. The methods of psychological science, as we will see repeatedly in the remainder of the book, have overturned some deeply entrenched assumptions about the way people think, feel, act, and adapt, and have yielded information that greatly improves human well-being. These methods illuminate our human errors and biases and enable us to seek knowledge with an open mind. Biologist Thomas Huxley put it beautifully. The essence of science, he said, is "to sit down before fact as a little child, be prepared to give up every preconceived notion, follow humbly wherever and to whatever abyss nature leads, or you shall learn nothing."

Taking Psychology with You

Lying with Statistics

We have seen that statistical procedures are indispensable tools for assessing research. But in the real world, statistics can be manipulated, misrepresented, and even made up by people hoping to promote a particular political or social agenda. That is why an essential part of critical and scientific thinking is learning not only how to use statistics correctly but also how to identify their misuse.

A primary reason for the misuse of statistics is "innumeracy" (mathematical illiteracy). In *Damned Lies and Statistics*, Joel Best (2001) told of a graduate student who copied this figure from a professional journal: "Every year since 1950, the number of American children gunned down has doubled." Sounds scary, right? But if that claim were true, then by 1987, the number of children gunned down would have surpassed 137 billion, more than the total human population throughout history; and by 1995, the annual number of victims would have been 35 *trillion!*

"Statistics don't lie; people do—or, more likely, they misrepresent or misinterpret what the numbers mean. When statistics are used correctly, they can expose unwarranted conclusions and protect us from our biases and blind spots."

Where did this wildly inaccurate number come from? The author of the original article misrepresented a statistic from the Children's Defense Fund (CDF), which in 1994, claimed that "The number of American children killed each year by guns has doubled since 1950." Notice the difference: The CDF was saying that there were twice as many deaths in 1994 as in 1950, not that the number had doubled every year.

We don't want you to distrust all statistics. Statistics don't lie; people do—or, more likely, they misrepresent or misinterpret what the numbers mean. When statistics are used correctly, they neither confuse nor mislead. On the contrary, they can expose unwarranted conclusions, promote clarity and precision, and protect us from our biases and blind spots. You need to be careful, though. Here are a few things you can do when you hear that "2 million people do this" or "one out of four people are that":

Ask how the number was computed. Suppose someone on your campus gives a talk about a hot social issue and cites some big number to show how serious and widespread the problem is. You should ask how the number was calculated. Was it based on government data, such as the census? Did it come from just one small study or from a meta-analysis of many studies? Or is it pure conjecture?

Ask about base rates and absolute numbers. If we tell you that the *relative risk* of getting ulcers is increased by 300 percent in college students who eat a bagel every morning (relax, it isn't!), that sounds pretty alarming, but it does not tell you much. You would need to know how many students get ulcers in the first place, and then how many bagel-eating students get ulcers. If the "300 percent increased risk" is a jump from 100 students in every thousand to 300 students, then you might reasonably be concerned. If the number shifts from one in every thousand to three in every thousand, that is still a 300 percent increase, but the risk is very small and could even be a random fluke. Many health findings are presented in ways that increase worry and even panic, as an increased relative risk of this or that. What you want to know is the *absolute risk*, what the actual, absolute numbers show. They may be quite trivial (Bluming & Tavris, 2009; Gigerenzer et al., 2008).

Ask how terms were defined. If we hear that "one out of every four women" will be raped at some point in her life, we need to ask: How was rape defined? If women are asked if they have ever experienced any act of unwanted sex, the percentages are higher than if they are asked specifically whether they have been forced or coerced into intercourse.

(*continued*)

Similarly, although far more women are raped by men they know than by strangers, many women do not define acts of date rape or acquaintance rape as "rape."

Always, always look for the control group. If an experiment does not have a control group, then, as they say in New York, "fuhgeddaboudit." The kinds of "findings" often reported without a control group tend to be those promoting a new herbal supplement, treatment, or self-improvement program. People are motivated to justify any program or treatment in which they have invested time, money, or effort. Further, thanks to the placebo effect, people's expectations of success are often what helps them, not the treatment itself. This is why testimonials don't provide a full or accurate picture of a medication's or treatment's benefits or harms. It's like the bartender who says to the customer, "Why are you waving your arms around like that?" And the customer says, "It keeps the gerbils away." "But there aren't any gerbils here," the bartender says. "See?" says the customer, "it works!" All the arm waving in the world won't substitute for a good study.

Be cautious about correlations. We said this before, but we'll say it again: With correlational findings, you usually cannot be sure what's causing what. A study reported that teenagers who listened to music five or more hours a day were eight times more likely to be depressed than those who didn't listen that often (Primack et al., 2011). Does listening to music make you depressed? A more likely explanation is that being depressed causes teenagers to tune out and listen to music, as they don't have the mental energy to do much else. "At this point, it is not clear whether depressed people begin to listen to more music to escape, or whether listening to large amounts of music can lead to depression, or both," said the lead researcher.

The statistics that most people like best are usually the ones that support their own opinions and prejudices. Unfortunately, bad statistics, repeated again and again, can infiltrate popular culture, spread like a virus on the Internet, and become difficult to eradicate. The information in this chapter will get you started on telling the difference between numbers that are helpful and those that mislead or deceive. In future chapters, we will give you other information to help you think critically and scientifically about popular claims and findings that make the news.

Summary

WHAT MAKES PSYCHOLOGICAL RESEARCH SCIENTIFIC?

- Research methods provide a way for psychologists to separate well-supported conclusions from unfounded belief. An understanding of these methods can also help people think critically about psychological issues and become astute consumers of psychological findings and programs.
- The ideal scientist states hypotheses and predictions precisely, is skeptical of claims that rest solely on faith or authority, relies on empirical evidence, resists the *confirmation bias* and complies with the *principle of falsifiability*, and is open about methods and results so that findings can be *replicated*. The public nature of science and the process of *peer review* give science a built-in system of checks and balances.

DESCRIPTIVE STUDIES: ESTABLISHING THE FACTS

- In any study, the researcher would ideally like to use a *representative sample*, one that is similar in composition to the larger population that the researcher wishes to describe. But in practice, researchers must often use "convenience" samples, which typically means college undergraduates. In the study of many topics, the consequences are minimal, but in other cases, conclusions about "people in general" must be interpreted with caution.
- *Descriptive methods* allow psychologists to describe and predict behavior but not necessarily to choose one explanation over others. Such methods include case studies, observational studies, psychological tests, and surveys, as well as correlational methods.
- *Case studies* are detailed descriptions of individuals. They are often used by clinicians and can also be valuable in exploring new research topics and addressing questions that would otherwise be difficult to study. But because the person under study may not be representative of people in general, case studies are typically sources rather than tests of hypotheses.
- In *observational studies*, researchers systematically observe and record behavior without interfering in any way with the behavior. *Naturalistic observation* is used to find out how animals and people behave in their natural environments. *Laboratory observation* allows more control and the use of special equipment; behavior in the laboratory, however, may differ in certain ways from behavior in natural contexts.
- *Psychological tests* are used to measure and evaluate personality traits, emotional states, aptitudes, interests, abilities, and values. A good test is one that has been *standardized*, is scored using established *norms*, and is both *reliable* and *valid*. Critics have questioned the reliability and validity of even some widely used tests.

- *Surveys* are questionnaires or interviews that ask people directly about their experiences, attitudes, and opinions. Unrepresentative samples and *volunteer bias* can influence the generalizability of survey results. Findings can also be affected by the fact that respondents sometimes lie, misremember, or misinterpret the questions. Technology and use of the Internet can help psychologists minimize some of these problems, but they also introduce some new methodological challenges. People should be cautious about tests they take on the Internet because not all of them meet scientific standards.

CORRELATIONAL STUDIES: LOOKING FOR RELATIONSHIPS

- In descriptive research, studies that look for relationships between phenomena are known as *correlational*. A *correlation* is a measure of the strength of a positive or negative relationship between two variables and is expressed by the *coefficient of correlation*. Many correlations reported in the media or on the Internet are based on rumor and anecdote and are not supported by data. Even when a correlation is real, it does not necessarily demonstrate a causal relationship between the variables.

EXPERIMENTS: HUNTING FOR CAUSES

- Experiments allow researchers to control the situation being studied, manipulate an *independent variable*, and assess the effects of the manipulation on a *dependent variable*. Experimental studies usually require a comparison or control condition and often involve random assignment of participants to *experimental and control groups*. In some studies, those in the control group receive a *placebo*, or fake treatment. *Single-blind and double-blind procedures* can be used to prevent the expectations of the participants or the experimenter from affecting the results.

- Because experiments allow conclusions about cause and effect, they have long been the method of choice in psychology. However, like laboratory observations, experiments create a special situation that may call forth behavior not typical in other environments. Many psychologists, therefore, have called for more *field research*.

EVALUATING THE FINDINGS

- Psychologists use *descriptive statistics*, such as the *arithmetic mean* and the *standard deviation*, to summarize data. They use *inferential statistics* to find out how impressive the data are. *Significance tests* tell the researchers how likely it is that the results of a study occurred merely by chance. The results are said to be *statistically significant* if this likelihood is very low. Statistically significant results allow psychologists to make predictions about human behavior, but, as in all sciences, probabilistic results do not tell us with any certainty what a particular person will do in a given situation.

- Choosing among competing interpretations of a finding can be difficult, and care must be taken to avoid going beyond the facts. Sometimes the best interpretation does not emerge until a hypothesis has been tested in more than one way, as by using both *cross-sectional* and *longitudinal* methods.

- Statistical significance does not always imply real-world importance because the amount of variation in the data accounted for by the independent variable may be small. Therefore, many psychologists are now turning to other measures. *Confidence intervals* help researchers evaluate where the real population mean is likely to be if they could repeat their study over and over. The *effect size* is an objective, standardized way of describing the strength of the independent variable's influence on the dependent variable. *Meta-analysis* is a procedure for combining data from many related studies to determine the overall strength of an independent variable. *Bayesian statistics* take prior knowledge into account in assessing the likelihood that a finding is true and meaningful.

KEEPING THE ENTERPRISE ETHICAL

- The APA's ethical code requires researchers to obtain the *informed consent* of anyone who is participating in a study or experiment, protect them from harm, and warn them in advance of any risks. Many studies require deceptive procedures. Concern about the morality of such procedures has led to guidelines to protect participants.

- Psychologists study animals to gain knowledge about particular species, discover practical applications of psychological principles, study issues that cannot be studied with human beings for practical or ethical reasons, clarify theoretical questions, and improve human welfare. Debate over the use of animals in research has led to more comprehensive regulations governing their treatment and care.

TAKING PSYCHOLOGY WITH YOU

- Statistics help scientists understand the complexities of behavior, but statistics can also be misrepresented and misused. Critical thinkers should ask how numbers were calculated, look at percentages that provide *absolute* risk rather than *relative* risk, ask how terms were defined, make sure there was a control group, and be cautious about inferring a cause from a correlation.

Key Terms

theory (p. 52)
hypothesis (p. 52)
operational definition (p. 52)
principle of falsifiability (p. 53)
confirmation bias (p. 54)
replicate (p. 54)
peer review (p. 55)
representative sample (p. 56)
descriptive methods (p. 57)
case study (p. 57)
observational study (p. 58)
naturalistic observation (p. 58)
laboratory observation (p. 59)
psychological tests (p. 59)
standardization (p. 60)
norms (p. 60)
reliability (p. 60)
test–retest reliability (p. 60)
alternate-forms reliability (p. 60)
validity (p. 60)
content validity (p. 60)
criterion validity (p. 60)
surveys (p. 61)
volunteer bias (p. 61)
correlational study (p. 63)
correlation (p. 63)
variables (p. 64)
positive correlation (p. 64)
negative correlation (p. 64)
coefficient of correlation (p. 64)
illusory correlations (p. 65)
experiment (p. 67)
independent variable (p. 67)
dependent variable (p. 67)
control condition (p. 68)
experimental and control groups (p. 68)
random assignment (p. 69)
placebo (p. 69)
single-blind study (p. 69)
experimenter effects (p. 69)
double-blind study (p. 70)
field research (p. 70)
descriptive statistics (p. 73)
arithmetic mean (p. 73)
standard deviation (p. 74)
inferential statistics (p. 74)
significance tests (p. 74)
statistical significance (p. 74)
p value (p. 74)
confidence interval (p. 75)
cross-sectional study (p. 76)
longitudinal study (p. 76)
effect size (p. 77)
meta-analysis (p. 77)
Bayesian statistics (p. 77)
informed consent (p. 79)
relative versus absolute risk (p. 81)

Evolution, Heredity, and Behavior*

*Taken from *Psychology: The Science of Behavior,* Seventh Edition by Neil R. Carlson, Harold Miller, C. Donald Heth, John W. Donahoe, and G. Neil Martin

John Harold Johnson Sr., founder of *Ebony* magazine.

Prologue
A Favored Son?

John Harold Johnson died at the young age of 25. He died from a disease called sickle-cell anemia. Sickle-cell anemia is a disorder in which the red-blood cells that carry oxygen to the body become curved and sticky. Normally, red-blood cells are flat and smooth and pass readily through even small blood vessels. However, because of the change in shape caused by sickle-cell anemia some of the red-blood cells become stuck in the smaller blood vessels. This produces a painful condition with widespread damage to the body's organs. The disease is known to run in families. But John's parents and his sister did not have the disease. How could John have sickle-cell anemia? In addition, his entire family is long-lived. John's father, for whom he was named, died recently at the age of 87 and—at this writing—his mother and sister are still alive. Moreover, John Jr.'s family was not only long-lived but highly accomplished. His father rose from a poor background to found ***Ebony*** magazine and several other companies. In fact, he was the first African American listed among Forbes' 400 wealthiest Americans. His mother and his sister were also achievers. His mother suggested the name for the magazine and his sister now runs the publishing company that her father founded. John Jr. seems truly a favored son by virtue of both the environments of his ancestors and his personal environment. How could John Jr. not be among the "fittest"?

More generally, how could such a potentially devastating disease remain in the human family if its effects were so terrible? Would not "survival of the fittest" eliminate the disease from the human population? The answers to these puzzling questions, and many others, are provided by Darwin's principle of natural selection when coupled with the biological mechanisms that implement it—genetics.

THE DEVELOPMENT OF EVOLUTIONARY SCIENCE

When we come upon a story like that of John Harold Johnson, Jr., we are puzzled. He seems to have had every advantage of birth and fortune and, yet, he died at a young age from a disease that runs in families. Charles Darwin was also struck by similarly puzzling observations and he searched for some way to make sense of them. Later in life, he reflected upon his achievements as follows: "My mind seems to have become a kind of machine for grinding general laws out of large collections of facts" (1888, p. 139). How did Darwin come upon his "large collection of facts"?

The Voyage of the *Beagle*

As a young man, Darwin had few scholarly interests. He spent much of his time hiking around the English countryside, examining rock formations, and shooting small game. Uncertain about what to do with his life, he began to study religion at Christ's College, Cambridge. He considered becoming a country parson—a fairly common occupation for upper-class Englishmen with undefined interests. However, in 1831, Darwin was introduced by a mutual acquaintance to Captain Robert Fitz Roy, an officer in the royal navy. Fitz Roy was looking for someone to serve as an unpaid naturalist and traveling companion during a five-year voyage on the *HMS Beagle*. The *Beagle*'s mission was to explore and survey the coast of South America and to make worldwide nautical observations that would benefit the British navy. After overcoming his father's objections, Darwin volunteered for the voyage.

During the voyage, Darwin observed the animals and plants of South America, Australia, South Africa, and the islands of the Pacific, South Atlantic, and Indian oceans. These included most notably the Galapagos Islands off the west coast of South America. Darwin spent most of his time collecting specimens of plants, objects of various sorts, and animals (most of which he shot, continuing his boyhood habit). He did not form his theory of evolution through natural selection while at sea, although he was struck by the tremendous diversity among seemingly related animals. He interpreted this diversity as being consistent with the doctrine of *essentialism*. Essentialism, which can be traced to the Greek philosopher Plato, views all living things as belonging to fixed classes or "kinds." Each class is thought to have unchanging characteristics that reflect the essential quality of each species and separate each species from others (Mayr, 2001).

Charles Darwin (1809–1882)

The Origin of Species

Darwin returned to England in 1836 and began to sift through his collections, comparing the similarities and differences of the creatures he had found. He carefully reviewed the work of earlier naturalists. His own grandfather, Erasmus Darwin, had speculated about evolution but was unable to account for how the changes came about. Darwin also became interested in the process of **artificial selection,** a practice in which animal breeders selectively mated animals, with the goal of producing offspring that possessed desirable characteristics. Using artificial selection, breeders selectively mated sheep that grew heavier wool coats, cows that produced more abundant milk, and birds that had more beautiful plumage. For example, a pigeon fancier who wanted to produce a pigeon with beautiful plumage would examine the available variation in his colony and permit only the most beautiful birds to mate with one another. When this process was repeated over generations, the plumage of the population of birds in the colony became more pleasing. The factors that produced beautiful plumage were, in some unknown way, passed from one generation to the next. Darwin was intrigued with artificial selection and, in fact, had bred pigeons himself. (See Figure 4.1.) He speculated that if artificial selection could produce different varieties, perhaps some naturally occurring process would have a similar effect.

Another year and a half passed before Darwin's naturalistic observations and knowledge of artificial selection bore fruit. Darwin recalled the event in his autobiography:

> I happened to read for amusement Malthus on *Population,* and being well prepared to appreciate the struggle for existence which everywhere goes on from long continued observation of plants and animals, it at once struck me that under these

Figure 4.1 Varieties of pigeons that have been produced through artificial selection. (a) Wild rock pigeon. This type is believed to be the ancestor of each of the other breeds of pigeons shown here. (b) Blue grizzle frillback. (c) English pouter. (d) Indian fantail.

artificial selection
procedure that differentially mates organisms to produce offspring with specific characteristics

> circumstances favorable variations would tend to be preserved, and unfavorable ones to be destroyed. The result would be the formation of a new species. (Darwin, 1888/1950, p. 54)

What struck Darwin was the idea of **natural selection.** Malthus had proposed that populations increase in size faster than the resources required to sustain them and that, as a consequence, competition for resources occurs. Darwin recognized that differences among individuals competing for the same resources would inevitably favor some over others. An individual that possessed characteristics that benefited its survival would be more likely to live longer and thereby produce more offspring. If the characteristics of the more frequently reproducing individuals were heritable (that is, could be passed from one generation to the next), then natural selection would have the same effect as artificial selection but without anyone doing the selecting.

Darwin came to this realization in September 1838, but he did not publish his ideas until 20 years later. Why did he wait so long? Among other things, he devoted considerable time to gathering supportive evidence. He took great pains to develop a clear and coherent case for his account. He examined his specimens from the voyage of the Beagle, studied current research and theory in the natural sciences, conducted his own research on artificial selection, and tested out his ideas with close scientific colleagues whom he often met at a pub in London.

Darwin might have been even slower to publish his theory if another naturalist, Alfred Wallace, had not independently come up with the same idea. In 1858, Alfred Wallace—while suffering from a bout of fever in the Spice Islands—read the same book by Malthus that had inspired Darwin. Wallace also recognized that the natural environment, through its effect on differential reproduction, could be the source of evolutionary change. Unlike Darwin, however, Wallace quickly wrote up the idea and sent the paper to—of all people—Charles Darwin! Darwin was already known from his published work on related subjects. Wallace had also discovered the principle by which the natural environment could accomplish the same result as artificial selection.

Darwin and Wallace each presented their separate works before a scientific society—the Linnean Society in London. A few months thereafter, Darwin published the massive book on which he had been working for over 20 years. He described the book as an "abstract" of his ideas. Darwin's "abstract," which we know today as *On the Origin of Species* (1859), ran to 500 pages. It established both his priority in developing the principle of natural selection and his careful accumulation of evidence to support the principle.

Discovering the Mechanisms of Heredity

With natural selection, Darwin and Wallace had identified a process by which the environment selected from among varying individuals those characteristics that most benefited survival (*positive selection*), eliminated those that most harmed survival (*negative selection*), and maintained those that permitted survival (*stabilizing selection*). But what exactly was passed on from one generation to the next? Male and female pigeons with beautiful plumage passed on their fertilized eggs, not their plumage. Something in the fertilized egg had to contain the potential for developing beautiful plumage in the offspring. Moreover, this "something" must be passed on from one generation to the next if the final state of plumage is to be realized. What was this "something"?

Darwin did not know what the "something" was. He made a guess that the various organs of the body each contributed to the egg certain substances, which he called *gemmules*. A blending of these gemmules was then proposed to determine the characteristics of the offspring. Soon after he made his guess, however, the Scottish engineer Fleeming Jenkin demonstrated mathematically that a favorable gemmule from a parent would be so "diluted" by the presence of other gemmules that a blending theory of heredity could never support evolution. In a population of interbreeding organisms, a rare favorable gemmule would be overwhelmed by the presence of the more numerous other gemmules. In short, Darwin had a persuasive account of the contribution of variation and selection to evolution, but he had no explanation for the accumulation of these changes. And, the accumulation of changes was

natural selection
process whereby the environment differentially favors organisms with characteristics that affect survival and production of offspring

necessary to produce the diversity and complexity of life. Darwin betrayed the fact that he was a human being as well as a scientist when he disparaged Jenkin's analysis in a letter to a friend: "Be cautious in trusting mathematicians." Darwin had rejected the messenger and tried to ignore the message. Because Darwin did not know what was transmitted from one generation to the next, most scientists did not accept his account of evolution through natural selection until over 70 years later. What changed their minds?

The belated recognition of Gregor Mendel's work on heredity was the key. Mendel was a monk who had conducted breeding experiments using peas in his monastery garden. Pea plants vary in their characteristics—the color of the seed (yellow or green), the shape of the seed (wrinkled or smooth), and so on. He found that the characteristics of plants in successive generations were not blends of the characteristics from prior generations, as Darwin's gemmule theory supposed. Instead, the frequency with which a given characteristic appeared in the next generation of peas revealed that (a) the "factors" were passed to descendents *unchanged* (b) each parent contributed one such factor to each offspring, and (c) a factor was passed on even when it was sometimes not expressed in the offspring. Thus Mendel's experiments indicated that what was passed from one generation to the next was not a blend of gemmules but an unchanged set of factors. Mendel's factors are now called **genes** (to be discussed in more detail later in this chapter). Darwin's blending account of how characteristics were passed from one generation to the next was replaced by Mendel's *particulate* account. Mendel published the results of his experiments in a scientific journal in 1866—only seven years after Darwin's *On the Origin of Species.* However, Mendel's results did not become generally known until the early 1900s, well after Darwin's death in 1882. Darwin had died unaware of findings that were crucial to the acceptance of evolution through natural selection. Given Mendel's findings, most biologists began to accept Darwin's account of evolution when the principle of natural selection was integrated with the burgeoning science of genetics in the 1930s. This integration of natural selection with genetics is known as the *Modern Synthesis* in biology (e.g., Dobzhansky, 1937).

The Three Components of Evolution through Natural Selection

Darwin's account of **biological evolution** describes how changes take place in the characteristics of a population of organisms over time. This account stands as the primary explanatory principle of the origin, diversity, and complexity of life. It is the unifying theme of all biology. Evolution through natural selection is now understood as the result of repeated cycles of a three-component process that acts across the generations: variation, selection, and retention.

Variation

The term ***variation*** reflects Darwin's observation that each living organism is unique—each differs somewhat from every other, even others within the same species. Before Darwin, scientists focused on the ways that members of the same species were alike—the essential features that all individuals presumably shared with the group. Individual differences were merely a nuisance that obscured the essential features of the group. After Darwin, individual differences moved to center stage. Similarities among individuals were seen as abstractions that might be useful for some purposes (for example, classification), but not fundamental to the evolutionary process. Variation between individuals provides the raw material upon which natural selection acts. Variation is the source of whatever new arises from repeated cycles of the evolutionary process because natural selection can act only on characteristics that already exist. Variation is undirected in the sense that the conditions that affect variation are different from those that affect selection (Campbell, 1974).

Selection

The second component of the evolutionary process is *natural selection.* **Selection** by the environment favors (or disfavors) some variants over others. By the environment, we include not only the physical environment but also the organic environment—members of

gene
unit of heredity, inferred from Mendel's experiments

biological evolution
changes in characteristics over successive generations due to natural selection and mutation

variation
first component of evolution: individual members of a species differ from one another

selection
second component of evolution, provides direction to the process

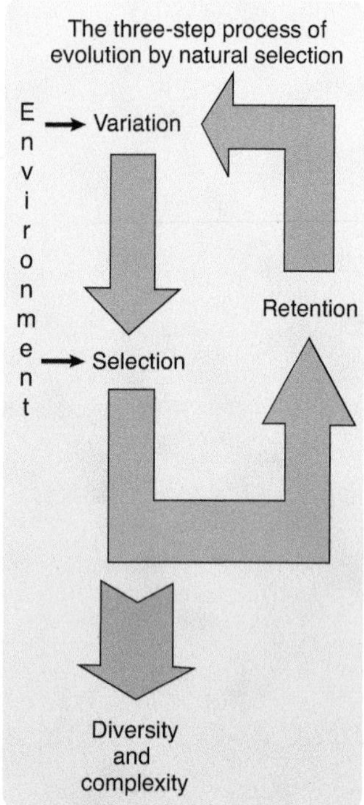

Figure 4.2 The three-step process of evolution by natural selection.
Initial differences in characteristics provide the variation on which natural selection operates within a given environment. Individuals whose characteristics favor reproductive fitness in that environment are more likely to survive. The individual's genes are retained when they are passed to the next generation and contribute to the variation on which subsequent selections operate. Over repeated cycles of this process, diverse and complex species can emerge.

the same and different species that are competing for resources. Selection confers to the evolutionary process whatever direction it appears to have. The direction is toward an ever closer adaptation to the demands of the environment in which the individual organism finds itself. The more constant the environment, the more specialized are the various species that are competing for the resources of that environment (Mittelbach et al., 2007). But the environment is rarely constant, so the direction of evolution is not constant. Because there are many different environments, evolution is not directed toward any particular end. The diversity of life arises from the diversity of environments. These environments range from the extremes of the hot sulphur springs of Yellowstone Park (Ward et al.,1998) to the arctic cold of sea ice (Mock & Thomas, 2005), both of which contain life. Only to the extent that future environments share features in common with past environments does evolution through natural selection make us adapted to future environments.

Retention

The third component, **retention,** is necessary if the evolution of complex organisms is to occur. Selected variations must accumulate to produce complexity. Mendel's research demonstrated the particulate nature of heredity and allowed even rare genes to endure and have the possibility of affecting distant generations. Variation provides the raw material on which selection operates. But, unless the selected variations are retained and contribute to the pool of variations on which later selections operate, evolution cannot take place. Figure 4.2 summarizes the three-component process of evolution through natural selection. Henceforth, we refer to Darwin's approach to the explanation of complexity as **selectionism.**

retention
third component of evolution: the favored variations are retained through heredity

selectionism
explanation of complex outcomes as the cumulative effect of the three-component process identified by Darwin

Natural Selection and Behavior

Natural selection affects function (behavior) as well as structure. In fact, the effects of natural selection on structure and function are closely related: Unless a structure is used in a way that benefits survival of the population, the genes affecting that structure cannot be naturally selected. Consider the complex structure of the eye. Light-sensitive structures have independently evolved at least ten different times in the history of life, all selected by the same physical properties of light. In fact, the light-sensitive compounds in the retina may be traced to compounds that permit photosynthesis in plants. (*Photosynthesis* is the process whereby plants use energy from light to make sugars and starch.) Thus, the beginnings of vision are found in the quest for food. If the eye did not provide information that guided behavior, such as food-seeking, the various components of the eye would never have been selected. Natural selection has also favored the formation of neural circuits that govern the function of the eye as well as its structure. When an object enters the periphery of vision, the eye rapidly moves to focus on that object. In the history of the human population, individuals who immediately attended to moving objects were more likely to behave adaptively—to avoid predators, to dodge projectiles, to greet approaching members of the group, and so on. Individuals who behaved in these ways were more likely to survive to the age of reproduction and to pass on their genes to their offspring. Among those genes are those that benefit both the structure and function of the eye.

Acceptance of Evolution through Natural Selection

Today, natural selection is the central unifying principle of biology from molecules to man. Moreover, Darwin's account of how selection processes produce the richness of life provides a natural-science-based account of how diverse and complex phenomena arise in other fields. The repeated action of the process—whether acting through physical, chemical, or biological means—can yield complex outcomes. The evolution of a solar system of planets from an initial swirling mass of randomly moving particles is but one example. Selection is provided by gravity and retention by physical processes such as friction and adhesion. As a cumulative result of these processes, the swirling particles coalesce into one or more central stars with planets possibly orbiting about them. (For more general treatments of selectionism, see Sober, 1984 and Donahoe, 2003.) Darwin gave us a way by which complex phenomena may emerge as the product of the repeated action of relatively simple processes.

Although evolution through natural selection is very generally accepted within science, it remains controversial in some segments of society. This is particularly true in the United States. A recent survey was taken in which people were asked to respond to the following statement: "Human beings, as we know them, developed from earlier species of animals." Approximately 80% of respondents in Europe and Japan regarded this statement as true, but only 40% of respondents in the United States—5% less than a survey conducted 20 years earlier (see Figure 4.3). When given the statement "Evolution is absolutely false," only 10% of Europeans agreed whereas 33% of U.S. respondents did. As Figure 4.3 shows,

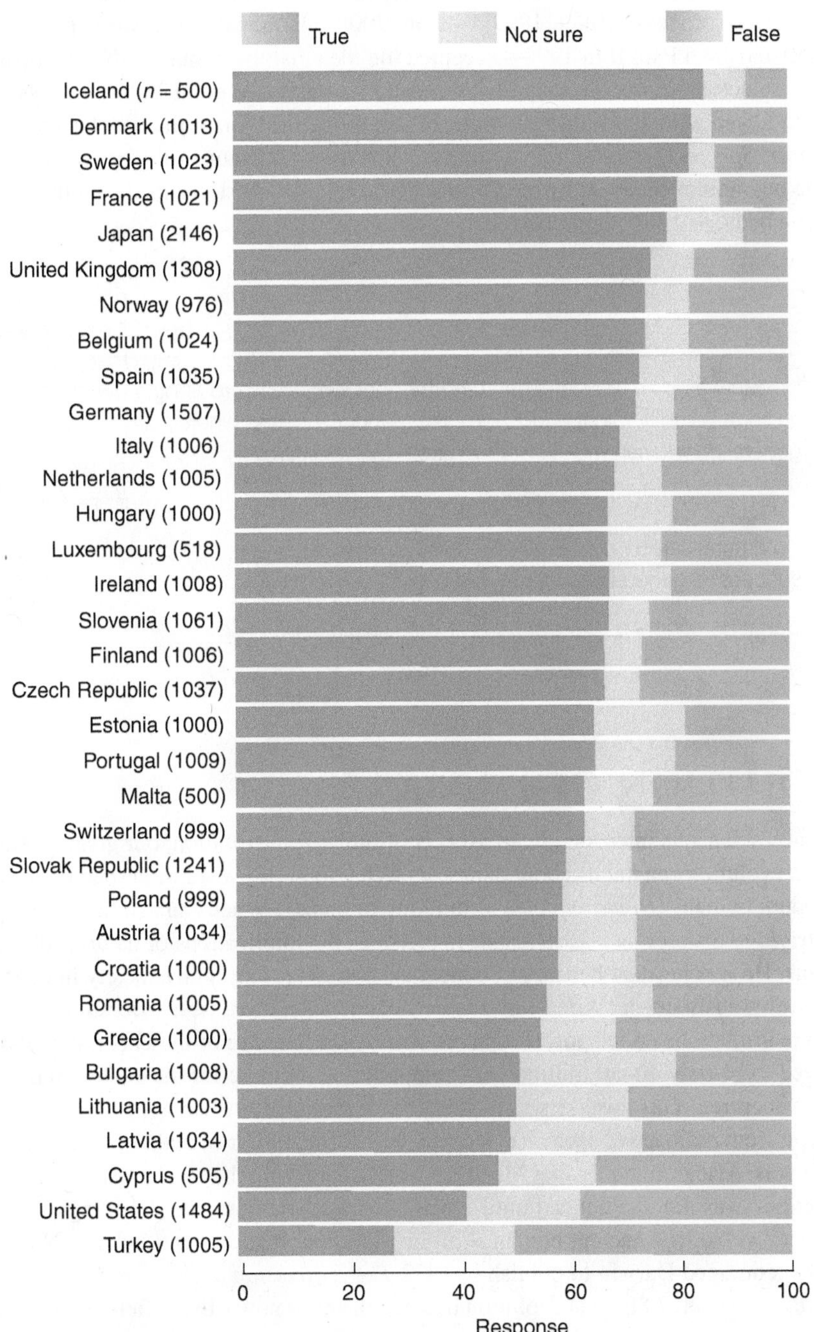

Figure 4.3 The response of people in different countries to the statement "Human beings, as we know them, developed from earlier species of animals." Responses of "True" are shown in green, "Not sure" in tan, and "False" in orange. *(From Miller, Scott, & Okamoto, 2006. Science, 313, 765.)*

only respondents in Turkey were less receptive to evolution. What accounts for this difference between respondents in the United States and many industrialized nations? The analysis of other survey data indicates that the difference is primarily due to the greater prevalence of persons who believe that the founding documents of their religion have implications for science as well as for morality—whether Christianity in the United States or Islam in Turkey (Miller, Scott, & Okamoto, 2006). Recent rulings of the federal court in the United States have upheld the need to maintain the mutual independence of science and religion (Jones, 2005).

There is no necessary conflict between religion and evolution, however. For many religious scientists, an all-knowing deity would appreciate that natural selection could produce the diversity and complexity of life, including human life, without the need to "oversee" the process (Miller, 1999; Couzin, 2008). As an example, two popes—Pius XII in 1950 and John Paul II in 1996—accepted the idea that the human body may result from natural selection. However, they also believed that at some point in the process humans were endowed with a nonphysical spirit by the deity. Darwin, at the conclusion of *On the Origin of Species,* said something similar: "There is grandeur in this view of life. From simple beginnings breathed by the Creator endless forms most beautiful and most wonderful have been, and are being evolved."

Questions to Consider

1. Darwin was obviously intelligent and thought long and hard about how retention through heredity might occur. Why did Mendel succeed where Darwin failed? What general conclusion might be drawn from this example?
2. Could evolution occur with only variation and selection? Explain your answer.
3. Do natural selection and genetics always produce greater complexity over successive generations? If not, why not?
4. Can a person be a scientist and still hold religious beliefs?

EVOLUTION OF HUMANS

Although science is interested in all aspects of biological evolution, our greatest interest is in what evolution can tell us about ourselves. What light does evolution shed on the origins of modern humans (*Homo sapiens,* or thinking humans)? When Darwin first published *On the Origin of Species* he was reluctant to consider the implications of natural selection for humans. He was hesitant because of concerns about its reception by society in general and by his religiously devout wife Emma in particular. Also, there were scientific issues about possible limitations on the power of natural selection. The age of the Earth was mistakenly believed to be only 40–50 million years old, not enough time for the evolution of humans to have occurred. This mistake was made because radioactivity had not yet been discovered and heat from radioactive decay had slowed the cooling of Earth, making it appear younger than it was. Also, remember that Mendel's work identifying the mechanisms of heredity—the genes—was not appreciated until much later. Nevertheless, other findings such as the discovery of the first ancient human skull in 1856 (much later identified as a Neanderthal skull) encouraged Darwin to publish in 1872 *The Expression of the Emotions in Man and Animals*. The study of human evolution had begun and is now a lively field of investigation.

Human Origins

Because chimpanzees are our closest *living* relatives, some uncritical observers mistakenly believe that evolution holds that chimpanzees turned into humans. However, evolutionary change does not take place in this manner. Instead, evolution holds that chimpanzees and humans shared a common ancestor at some point in the distant past, and that this ancestor was neither a chimpanzee nor a human. Chimpanzees *never* evolved into humans. Evolution proceeds as the branching of a tree or bush, not in a straight-line fashion. What is sought are related species that can be ordered in time.

Methods for Studying Human Evolution

The study of human evolution focuses on whatever remains of those species that lie along the branches that ultimately led to modern humans. These lingering remains include **fossils** as well as any signs of the culture of our predecessors, such as tools. What endures from the past are those few things that can withstand the ravages of time—the effects of chemical and physical degradation. Bones, particularly teeth and the large bones of the skull and legs, are most apt to endure. What also endures, when we are particularly fortunate, is the genetic material (**DNA,** an acronym for deoxyribonucleic acid) that has been protected within those bones. Bones, occasional DNA, and stone implements are the primary sources of information about our ancestors.

When these relics from the past are found, how can we order them in time? Which came earlier and which came later? Several independent methods are available to determine the time at which fossils were deposited. First, *relative* measures of time are provided by the *morphology* (form) of the fossil. Fossils that differ by small amounts were probably deposited at similar times because large evolutionary changes did not have enough time to occur. Most importantly, *systematic* changes in morphology are noted. In the case of human-related fossils, the skull shows progressively smaller brow ridges and less protrusion of the lower face. The leg and ankle bones show progressively better adaptation for walking on two legs (**bipedalism**). And, the fingers, thumbs, and the bones of the wrist are progressively better adapted for grasping. Second, several *absolute* measures of time help determine when a fossil was deposited. Animals breathe in small amounts of a naturally occurring radioactive form of carbon (C^{14}) while they are living, Once death has occurred and breathing stops, C^{14} is no longer inspired and begins to decay at a known and constant rate. The amount of C^{14} that remains in the fossil can help determine its age. **Carbon dating** thus provides an estimate of the time when the fossil was deposited. Counting the changes in the DNA between two fossils provides another measure. A small change is taken as evidence that a small amount of time has elapsed. The interpretation of both C^{14}

fossil
remains of an animal or plant found in the Earth

DNA
deoxyribonucleic acid. Molecule resembling a twisted ladder whose sides are connected by rungs of pairs of nucleotides (adenine, thymine, guanine, and cytosine)

bipedalism
habitually walking upright on two legs

carbon dating
method to determine the age at which an organism lived by measuring the amount of radioactive carbon (C^{14})

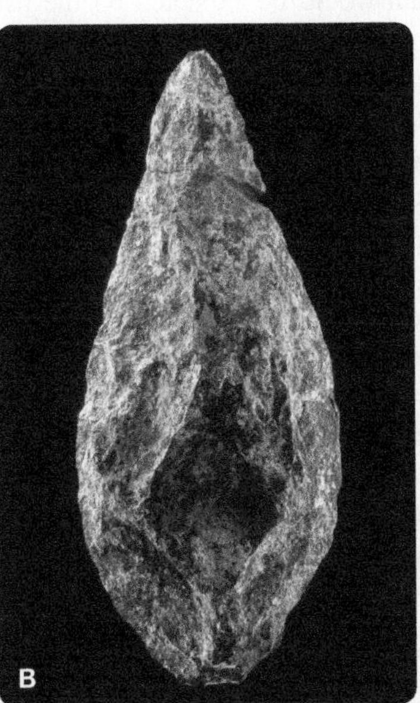

Stone hand-axe tools of hominids: Africa-only hominids: A. Slightly modified stone core; **Out-of-Africa Hominids:** B. *Homo erectus:* Modified stone core; C. *Homo neanderthalis and sapiens:* Highly modified stone core with sharpened edges.

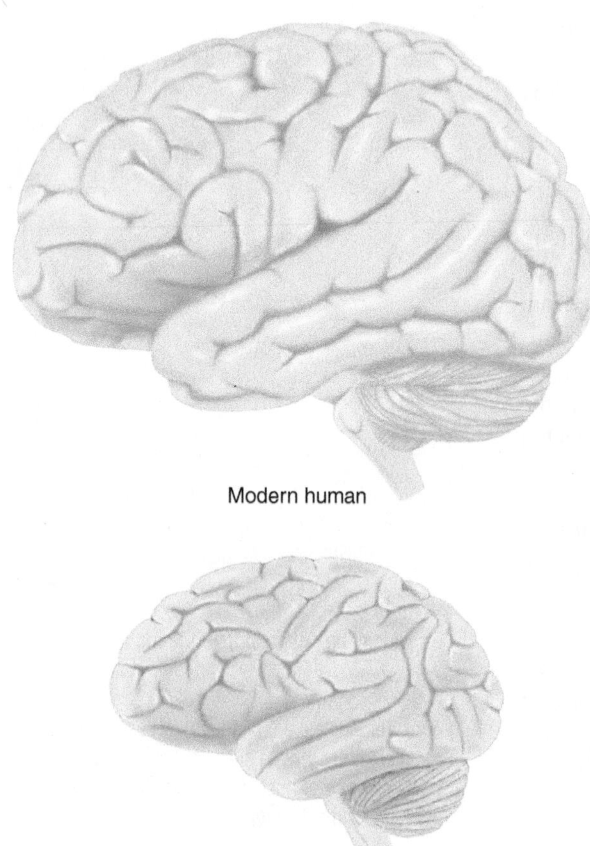

Figure 4.4 Side views of the brains of a chimpanzee and a modern human.
The average chimpanzee brain weighs about 300 grams, while the average human brain weighs about 1,500 grams.
(Adapted from Balter, 2007, Science, 315, 1209.)

and DNA is complicated, however (for example, Friderun & Cummins, 1996). Carbon dating can be influenced by changes in the amount of C^{14} in the atmosphere when the organism was alive and changes in the DNA molecule may not occur at a constant rate. That is, the so-called *molecular clock* may not "tick" at the same rate for all time and for all species. Although uncertainties remain, the course of evolution that is revealed by morphology, carbon dating, and changes in DNA has generally converged on a common order of events in human evolution and a common estimate of the time at which these events occurred.

Course of Human Evolution

The two branches of the tree of life that ultimately led to humans and chimps diverged over 7 million years ago. In spite of the vast time that separates our two species, numerous resemblances remain. Figure 4.4 shows a side view of the brains of a chimp and a human. The similarities in their gross appearances are apparent in spite of the large differences in size. The chimp brain has an average volume of only about 370 cm^3 whereas the comparable figure for humans is 1,500 cm^3. This difference in volume of the brain amounts to many millions in the total number of neurons. The behavior of chimps and humans also shows similarities. Chimps and humans both live in social groups and use tools to aid their survival. (A *tool* is any fabricated object that facilitates the behavior of the user.) In fact, chimpanzees have recently been observed to break off a slender straight branch from a tree, strip it of bark, sharpen its end, and then use the sharpened stick to spear small prey animals that sleep in the hollows of trees (Pruetz & Bertolani, 2007).

Genetic tests that compare the DNA of chimps and humans also reflect their common ancestry. About 99% of the DNA involved in the production of proteins is identical in chimps and humans (King & Wilson, 1975)! However, about 98% of the total human genome is not involved in protein production. The rest of the DNA molecule determines when and how much of the protein is produced. These genes are known as **regulatory genes.** It is with respect to regulatory genes that humans and chimps most differ (Demuth et al., 2006; Cohen, 2007a). As an example, in a region of the DNA molecule that regulates neural development there are over 60 times more differences between humans and chimpanzees than would be expected on the basis of chance alone (Pollard et al., 2007). The importance of these regions is indicated by the finding that over 110,000 of the human-specific regions of DNA have remained unchanged over evolutionary time (Prabhakar et al., 2006; Balter, 2007). If these regions were not important, chance factors in heredity would have produced many more changes. Also, there are more multiple copies of genes in humans than in chimps (Pennisi, 2006). The proteins of which chimps and humans are made are much alike, but they are assembled differently. A shack and a mansion can be built of the same materials, but the amount of material and how it is put together make all the difference.

The branching line that leads to modern humans began in East Africa over 4 million years ago according to the fossil record and, perhaps, as long as 6 million years ago according to the molecular clock. The primates that fall along the human line are called **hominids.** Their main distinguishing feature is that they habitually walk on two legs, that is, they are *bipedal*. Among the factors that likely led to the natural selection of upright walking were standing on branches to reach other branches in our more distant tree-dwelling ancestors (Thorpe, Holder, & Crompton, 2007) and carrying slowly maturing offspring who were unable to walk during the first months of life. Whatever the selecting factors, the most important benefit of bipedal walking was to free the forelimbs from the responsibility of locomotion. Now the forelimbs, and in particular the hands, could come into contact with different selecting environments that favored manual dexterity. When the forelimbs are devoted to locomotion, the ability to manipulate objects is of little use.

regulatory genes
genes that govern genes that code for proteins

hominids
the genus of bipedal apes ancestral to humans

These early hominids had brains whose size increased over the next 2 million years from 350 to almost 500 cm^3(a volume of about 2 cups). This produced a brain that was larger than that of chimpanzees, but still much smaller than that of modern humans. (Because the soft tissue of the brain does not fossilize, brain size is estimated by determining the volume of the interior of the skull.) The height of these ancestors also tended to increase over evolutionary time. Early hominids were less than 5 feet tall. Other changes took place as well. The finger bones became less curved and the thumbs increased in length, which increased manual dexterity. From examining the materials surrounding these fossils, early hominids lived primarily in woodlands and later in grasslands. From examining their teeth, the diet consisted of fruits, seeds, and roots obtained through foraging. There is no evidence from the fossil record that these early hominids ever migrated out of Africa. Technically, these early hominids generally fall in the genus *Australopithecus* (ape from the south). (For a comprehensive overview of the course of human evolution, go to http://www.becominghuman.org/.)

Beginning some 2 million years ago, hominids were sufficiently changed by natural selection to be classified in a new genus, *Homo* (human). This is the genus that ultimately includes modern humans. At the beginning of this period, the brain volume is estimated at 650 cm^3 and the height at just above 5 feet. With time, both measures progressively increased to the present values of 1,500 cm^3 and 175 cm (5 feet, 9 inches). Members of the genus *Homo* ate a varied diet that included for the first time meat, a rich source of protein. These species also became progressively better adapted for bipedal locomotion, as judged by changes in the form of their hips, knees, and ankles as well as the placement of the head on the neck. Other changes occurred in the general proportions of the body (the relative lengths of the arm and leg) and in the form of the face (less sloping of the forehead and less protrusion of the lower face). The first members of the genus *Homo* remained in Africa, but later species migrated out of Africa to the Middle East, Asia, Europe, Oceania, and lastly the Americas (Spoor et al., 2007). The three widely migrating species of *Homo* were *H. erectus* (standing man), *H. neanderthalis* (Neanderthal man, named for the valley in Germany where their fossils were first found), and *H. sapiens* (thinking man). Only *H. sapiens*—our species—remains. (See Figure 4.5 for reconstructions of the skulls of a hominid that remained in Africa and three species of hominids that migrated out of Africa.) *H. erectus* became extinct after 1.5 million years, surviving for some 400,000 years. *H. neanderthalis* became extinct only 25,000 years ago, with its last outpost in southern Spain near Gibraltar (Finlayson et al., 2006). *H. sapiens* has thus far endured 200,000 years. Our species overlapped with *H. neanderthalis* in southern Europe for about 10,000 years (Grine et al., 2007).

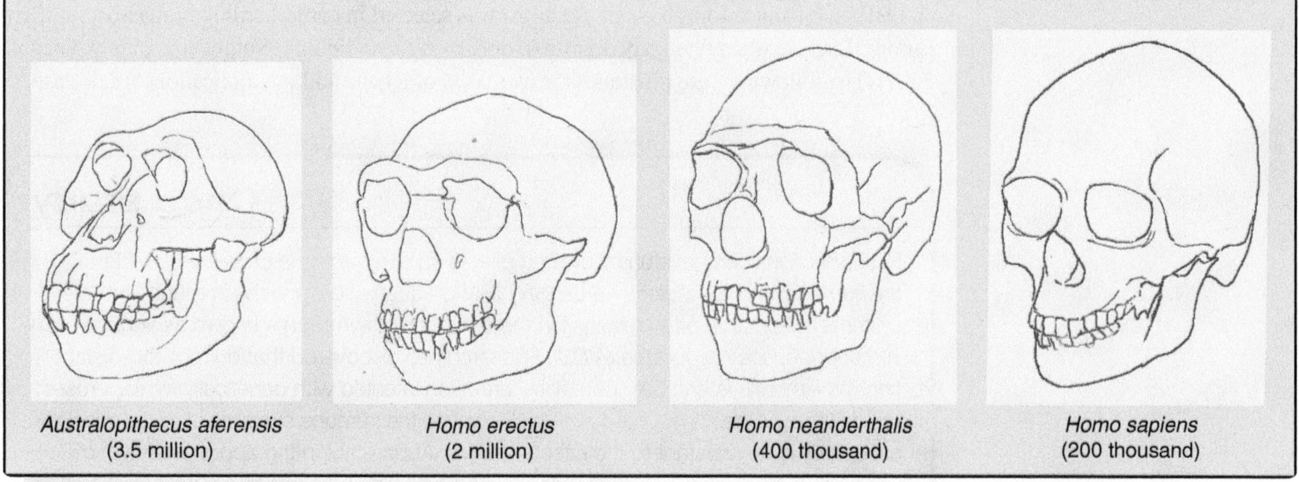

Figure 4.5 Drawings of the partially reconstructed skulls of three hominids of the genus *Homo* that migrated out of Africa—*H. erectus, H. neanderthalis,* and *H. sapiens.*

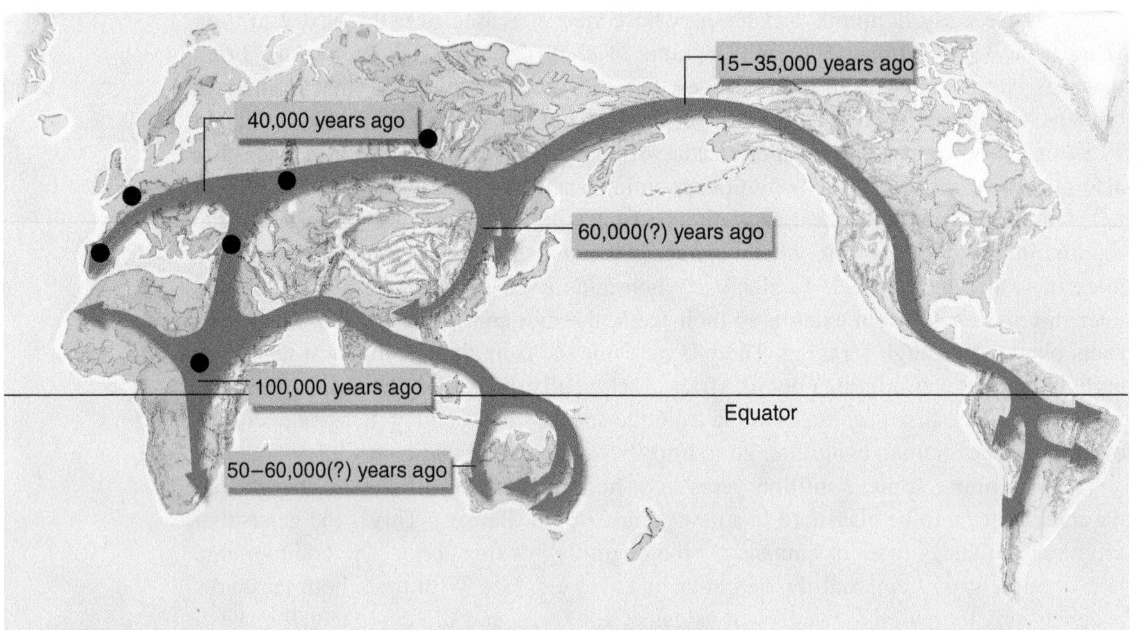

Figure 4.6 Migrations of two species of humans (*Homo*) out of Africa.
The black dots show the locations where Neanderthal (*H. neanderthalis*) fossils have been found. The green lines show some of the migratory paths taken by modern humans (*H. sapiens*) based on dated fossil remains. The dates are the approximate times of arrival of *H. sapiens* in each region.

(See Figure 4.6 for the extent of dispersion of *H. neanderthalis* and possible migratory routes of *H. sapiens* out of Africa as reflected by the fossil record; see also Li et al., 2008.) Whether interbreeding occurred between *H. sapiens* and *H. neandethalis* is a matter of current debate (Noonan et al., 2006; Pennisi, 2007). *H. sapiens* is now more widely distributed than any other animal species in the history of Earth. Reminders of our evolutionary origins remain, however. Modern-day astronauts in the frigid shadows of the mountains of the moon preserve in their space suits the warm and moist microenvironment of our African beginnings.

We should not regard ancestral hominid species as entirely alien to ourselves. They made tools of progressively greater complexity by carving wooden implements and shaping stones into hammers and cutters. They tamed fire and made clothing. By 50,000 years ago, they crafted representational art and jewelry and they buried their dead. Moreover, our species has continued to evolve. In addition to genetic changes that counter diseases such as malaria and HIV, a tolerance to milk sugar (lactose) was selected in cattle-herding humans of northern Europe. Lactose was previously digestible only by nursing infants (Voight et al., 2006; Gibson, 2007). The following case illustrates the evolution of a gene and its implications for disease.

Case study

Past selections can have unanticipated effects on survival in the present. Consider the *human immunodeficiency virus (HIV)*. HIV gradually weakens the immune systems of humans, often resulting in the collection of symptoms known as *acquired immunodeficiency syndrome (AIDS)*. Research has discovered that our not-too-distant cousins—monkeys and chimpanzees—are often infected with genetically similar viruses, *simian immune-deficient viruses (SIVs)*. However, the immune systems of these species are usually quite resistant to the effects of SIVs. Apparently, in the approximately 7 million years since chimpanzees and humans shared a common ancestor, natural selection has favored the survival of chimpanzees whose genes resisted the effects of the virus. It is believed that SIV, in either its original or a slightly altered form, was introduced into the human population through eating monkey and chimpanzee meat (so-called "bushmeat"). HIV infection first arose in Africa, perhaps as long as 50 years ago, but became recognized in the United States only in the 1980s. In southern Africa, 20% of the human population is now infected by the virus. The availability of modern forms of transportation has spread HIV rapidly and widely (Cohen, 2007b).

A recent discovery has revealed that some populations of humans are relatively resistant to the virus. These are humans who trace their ancestry to Northern European populations that were devastated during the Middle Ages by the bacterium that caused bubonic plague (the Black Death) (Galvani & Slatkin, 2003; cf. Kolata, 1998). During the 14th century, and at regular intervals thereafter, roughly one-third of the human population of Europe was killed by the Black Death. Those individuals who survived selection by the plague bacterium had immune reactions that combated the infection. It now appears that these same immune reactions resist infection and progression of the AIDS virus. The plague bacterium and the HIV virus both attack the same group of white-blood cells. As a result, the genes that benefit the immune response to bubonic plague also benefit the immune response to HIV. Over 10% of the ancestors of Northern Europeans have at least one copy of this gene, but only about 5% of Southern Europeans and almost no Africans, American Indians, or Asians. Clearly, it was not the "purpose" of natural selection by the plague bacterium to make Northern Europeans resistant to a viral infection that they would not encounter for 600 years!

Natural selection is locked in a perpetual dance with the environment, but the environment is always in the lead. The course of selection depends utterly on the environment. If the selecting environment is relatively constant or changes gradually, the process of natural selection effectively adapts us to the environment. The process appears to display purpose, but this is shown to be an illusion when the selecting environment changes rapidly with slowly reproducing species such as our own (Skinner, 1966; Sober, 1984). In sub-Saharan Africa, over 2 million people have already been killed by the HIV virus. Natural selection is again at work: A gene has been detected that is becoming increasingly duplicated in the African population and the products of this gene appear to confer some resistance to HIV (Bahcall, 2005; Julg & Goebel, 2005).

Questions to Consider

1. From what you know about how evolution works, do you think that *H. erectus* evolved into *H. neanderthalis*, and then *H. neanderthalis* evolved into *H. sapiens*?
2. If humans evolved in the way that evolutionary science indicates, does that in any way diminish the accomplishments of our species?

Heredity, Genetics, and Evolution

Recall that Darwin was not aware of Mendel's work on the breeding of pea plants. Therefore, he did not know how the effects of selection were retained. Mendel's work demonstrated that the units of heredity were transmitted in discrete form, now known as *genes*. A deeper knowledge of genetics is required if we are to better understand the evolution of our own species and the implications of natural selection for human behavior. **Genetics** is the scientific discipline that investigates the structure and functions of genes and their role in the transmission of the selecting effects of the environment from one generation to the next (Suzuki et al., 1989). Genetics is concerned with how **heredity**—genetic make-up—affects the behavioral as well as the structural characteristics of organisms.

genetics
study of the hereditary structures of organisms (genes)

heredity
sum of the traits inherited from one's parents

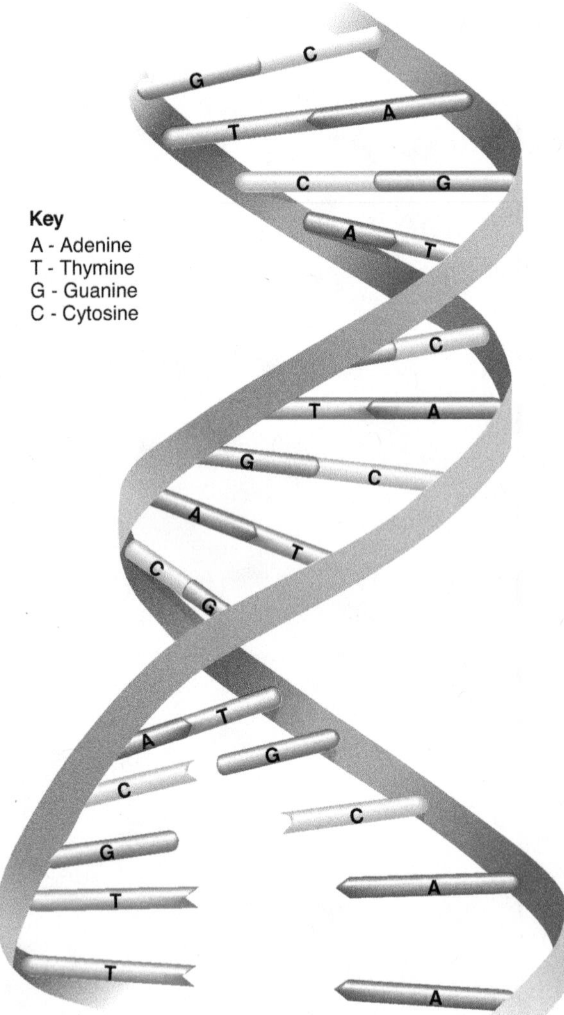

Figure 4.7 The structure and composition of DNA. DNA resembles a twisted ladder whose sides are composed of molecules of sugar and phosphate and whose rungs are made up of combinations of four nucleotide bases: adenine, thymine, guanine, and cytosine. Genes are segments of DNA that direct the synthesis of proteins and enzymes according to the particular sequences of nucleotide bases they contain. In essence, genes serve as "recipes" for the synthesis of these proteins and enzymes, which regulate the cellular and other physiological processes of the body, including those responsible for behavior.

(Based on Watson, J. D. (1976). Molecular biology of the gene. Menlo Park: Benjamin.)

Basic Principles of Genetics

Heredity is transmitted by genetic material called *DNA*. DNA is composed of strands of sugar and phosphate. The two strands are interconnected by pairs of four nucleotides—adenine paired with thymine and guanine paired with cytosine. The order in which the nucleotides occur determines the function of the gene. The structure of DNA was discovered by James Watson and Francis Crick in 1953. How they made their discovery is described in a fascinating (and controversial) book by Watson, *The Double Helix* (1968).

The DNA molecule is shaped like a twisted ladder. Sugar and phosphate form the sides of the ladder; the nucleotides form the rungs. (See Figure 4.7.) A gene is a specific sequence of nucleotides at a particular location along the DNA molecule. Some genes are composed of a short sequence of nucleotides, whereas others contain longer sequences. Regardless of their length, the sequence of nucleotides directs the synthesis of a protein molecule. Protein synthesis is guided by single-stranded molecules called **RNA** (ribonucleic acid). Through the mediation of RNA, different genes *code* the production of different proteins. The proteins, in turn, make up the structure of the body and its organs. The total set of genetic material in a species is known as the **genome.** In 1990, geneticists began an effort to determine the entire genome for our species. This work—known as The Human Genome Project—was essentially completed in 2003. It was discovered that the number of different protein-coding genes in humans was approximately 25,000. Many geneticists were surprised because this is only about twice as many genes as the common housefly (The Genome Sequencing Consortium, 2001).

Genes

Genes may be viewed as "recipes" for protein synthesis. Genes influence our physical and behavioral development in only one way—through the proteins they enable. Proteins are strings of amino acids, arranged in a chain. The order of amino acids within the string is specified by the sequence of nucleotides in the DNA molecule. A sequence of three nucleotides specifies a particular amino acid.

Strictly speaking, *there are no genes for behavior,* only for the protein-based physical structures and physiological processes that affect behavior. For example, if we were interested in the genetic basis of learning, we would look for genes that affect the synthesis of proteins that influence learning. Evidence from behavioral and pharmacological studies indicates that one of the substances in the brain that affects learning is dopamine (Schultz, 2001). We might be tempted to call the gene that affected dopamine a "learning" gene. However, this gene affects dopamine, not learning, and dopamine has other effects as well. For example, dopamine affects the contractions of smooth muscle in the stomach and intestines.

Genes also specify proteins that affect the synthesis of other proteins. These proteins are called **enzymes.** A faulty enzyme-specifying gene may produce serious physiological and behavioral problems. In addition to genes within the six-foot-long DNA molecule, large stretches consist of replications of genes and so-called "junk" DNA. Junk DNA does not provide a template for protein synthesis and for that reason is known as a *noncoding DNA*. Evidence increasingly indicates that noncoding sequences play a critical role. They contain regulatory genes that govern protein synthesis by protein-coding genes and thereby affect evolution, including human evolution (Greally, 2007).

RNA
single-stranded nucleic acid that is involved in several functions within the cell

genome
total set of genetic material of an organism

enzymes
proteins that regulate processes that occur within cells—organic catalysts

Chromosomes and Meiosis

Genes are located on *chromosomes*. (A few genes are also located in an intracellular structure called *mitochondria*. Mitochondria are important for energy production within the cell and are thought originally to have come from independent organisms that were incorporated into

Focus on

Frontiers in Evolutionary Research

A critical challenge for natural selection is to explain not merely how the evolution of species occurred through genetic mechanisms but how the genetic mechanisms themselves were selected in the first place. How did purely physiochemical processes produce a molecule that was capable of replicating itself, albeit imperfectly? Imperfect replication is required to produce the variation upon which selection processes could operate. Science has yet to meet this challenge, but it remains an active area of research. What is known is that the process began quite early in the history of earth. Evidence of life has been found only one billion years after the formation of the Earth 4.5 billion years ago (Eiler, 2007).

Scientists are studying several nonmutually exclusive possibilities for the origin of self-replicating molecules. Perhaps energy from lightning, volcanism, or sunlight acted on chemicals present in the atmosphere or surface of the early earth. These various compounds might through chance interactions, produce a self-replicating molecule (Lorsch & Szostak, 1996). Another possibility is that pre-existing compounds interacted with undersea volcanism or with the clays of the early Earth to produce a self-replicating molecule (Gallori, Biondi, & Branciamore, 2006). Still another possibility is that various organic molecules were brought to the Earth by extraterrestrial objects such as comets and that these contained compounds from which molecular evolution began. In 2006, NASA's Project Stardust successfully returned a capsule to Earth that collected particles from the tail of a comet. These particles gave indirect evidence of organic materials. Francis Crick, the co-discoverer with James Watson of the DNA molecule, once conjectured that Earth may have been seeded with DNA molecules by an alien species (Crick at al., 1976). Whatever the origins of the compounds from which molecular evolution began, single-stranded RNA appears to have been selected before double-stranded DNA. Life began with an "RNA world" (Ma & Yu, 2006).

For an evolutionary account of complexity to prevail Darwin (1859) said, "If it could be demonstrated that any complex organ existed which could not possibly have been formed by numerous, successive, slight modifications, my theory would absolutely break down." The same requirement applies at the molecular level. For molecular evolution to occur, each change in nucleotides that produces a different protein must be beneficial, or at least neutral. A recent experiment nicely illustrates that natural selection applies equally well at the molecular level.

A population of bacteria was exposed to penicillin, an antibiotic that kills many bacteria. From prior work, it was known that changes in five pairs of nucleotides in a particular gene were necessary for a bacterium to have resistance to penicillin. Mathematically, there are 120 possible combinations of sequences by which these five pairs could be changed to reach the resistant state. However, when successive generations of bacteria were exposed to penicillin, resistance developed along only a very few of the mathematically possible sequences. This was because only a very few of the sequences produced intermediate states that benefited or permitted the survival of the bacteria. Natural selection occurs at the molecular level, but it is constrained by the same Darwinian principles that operate at the level of organisms. (For a description of a long-term study of molecular evolution, see Elena & Lenski, 2003.)

cells in a mutually beneficial relation. Because mitochondrial DNA is passed along from only the mother, mitochondrial DNA has played in important role in tracing human evolution.) **Chromosomes** are threadlike structures of DNA that are found in the nucleus of every cell. Within the cell, chromosomes come in pairs. We inherit 23 individual chromosomes from each parent, making a total of 23 pairs. For 22 pairs of chromosomes, the DNA molecules are of corresponding types. Thus, we have two genes for each protein, one from each pair of chromosomes. The chromosomes with corresponding genes are called **autosomes.** The remaining pair consists of the **sex chromosomes.** This pair contains genes that affect characteristics that differ between males and females. In females, the two sex chromosomes have corresponding genes and are known as *X* chromosomes. In males, one of the chromosomes does not provide completely corresponding genes and is the *Y* chromosome. Thus the sex chromosomes for females are *XX* and for males *XY*. The Y chromosome has also played an important role in tracing human evolution because only males possess and pass on its DNA.

chromosomes
paired rod-like structures in the nucleus of a cell; contain genes

autosomes
the 22 pairs of chromosomes that are not sex chromosomes

sex chromosomes
X or Y chromosomes that contain genes affecting sexual development

sexual reproduction
production of offspring by combining the germ cells of a male and female

germ cells
reproductive cells, a collective term for the sperm and ovum taken together; have only one member of each pair of chromosome

meiosis
process of cell division by which germ cells are produced

Sexual Reproduction

Sexual reproduction occurs with the union of a *sperm*, which carries genes from the male, and an *ovum* (egg), which carries genes from the female. The sperm and ovum are collectively known as **germ cells.** Germ cells differ from all other cells in the body (*somatic cells*) in two ways. First, they contain only one chromosome from each of the 23 pairs of chromosomes. All somatic cells contain 23 *pairs* of chromosomes. Sperm and ova are produced by a process called **meiosis** in which the 23 pairs of chromosomes from each parent separate into two groups, with only one member of each pair joining each group. The cell

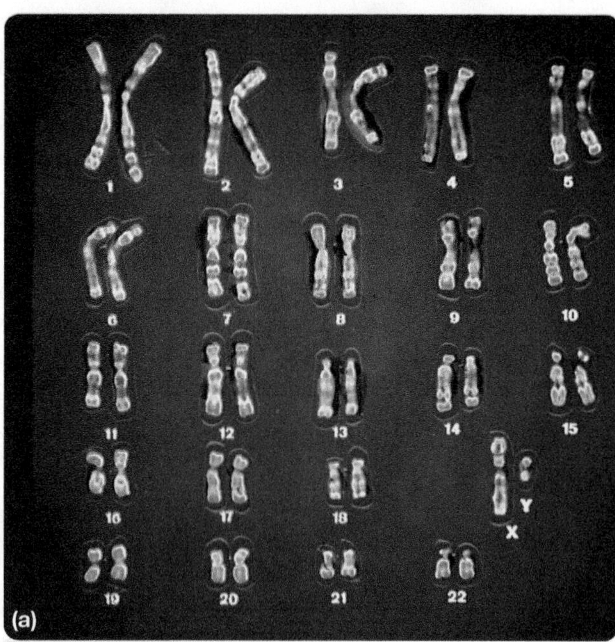

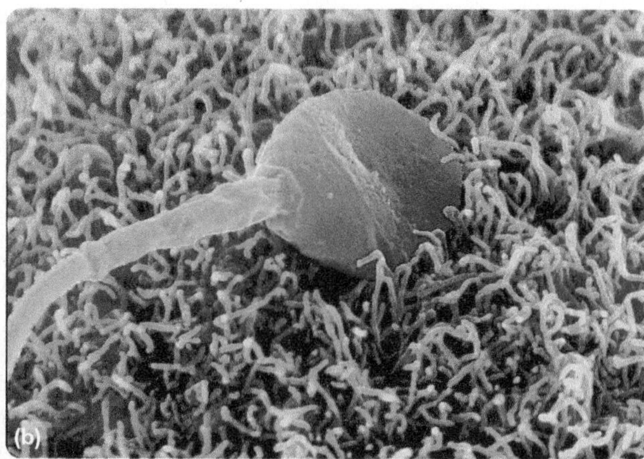

(a) Human chromosomes. The presence of a Y chromosome indicates that the sample came from a male. (b) Fertilization—a human sperm cell penetrating an egg.

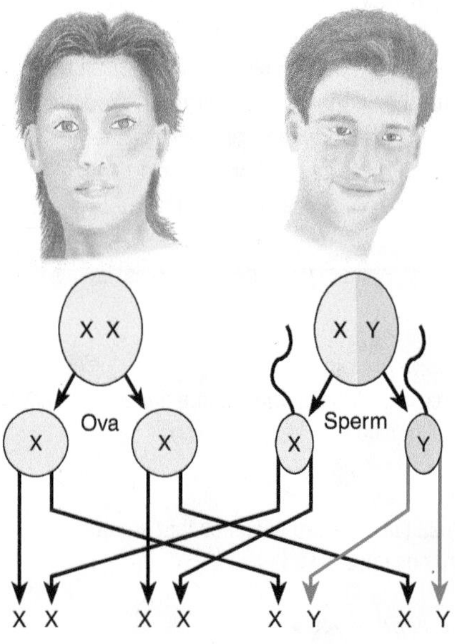

Figure 4.8 Determination of sex. The sex of human offspring depends on whether the sperm that fertilizes the ovum carries an X or a Y chromosome.

then divides into two cells, each containing 23 *individual* chromosomes. The assignment of a chromosome to a group is a random process. A single individual can produce 2^{23} (8,388,608) different germ cells. Second, during meiosis corresponding portions of paired chromosomes may be interchanged. This produces a recombination of genes and adds still greater variation to the reproduction process. Because the union of a particular sperm with an ovum is also variable, the fertilized egg can produce 8,388, 608 × 8,388, 608 (70,368, 774,177,664) different possible offspring! Parenthood is a gamble, but one that all sexually reproducing species must accept if the species is to continue.

Only identical twins are genetically identical. Identical twins occur when a single ovum divides into two independent cells *after* it has been fertilized by a single sperm. This gives rise to two identical fertilized eggs. Fraternal twins occur when a female produces two ova, each of which is fertilized by a different sperm. Fraternal twins are no more alike genetically than any two siblings, but they do share a common uterine environment.

The sex of the offspring is affected by the sex chromosomes. Females produce only ova with *X* chromosomes. Each ovum contains an *X* chromosome in addition to 22 autosomes. Males produce sperm cells with either an *X* or a *Y* chromosome. Each sperm cell contains either an X or a Y chromosome in addition to 22 autosomes. Thus, the sex of offspring is determined by the presence of a Y chromosome in the sperm. Changes in the sexual development of the fetus and adult are affected by the Y chromosome. (See Figure 4.8.)

Dominant and Recessive Traits

Although each of the 22 pairs of autosomes contains corresponding pairs of genes, the members of the pair need not be identical. A given gene comes in different forms called **alleles.** (*Allele* comes from the Greek *allo* "other," as does the word "alias.") Consider eye color. The pigment found in the iris of the eye is produced by a particular pair of genes. If corresponding genes from each parent are the same allele, then the gene combination is called *homozygous* (from the Greek *homo*, "same," and *zygon*, "yolk"). However, if the parents contribute different alleles, the gene combination is said to be *heterozygous* (from the Greek *hetero*, "different"). The character or trait produced by the pair of genes depends

allele
alternative forms of the same gene for a trait

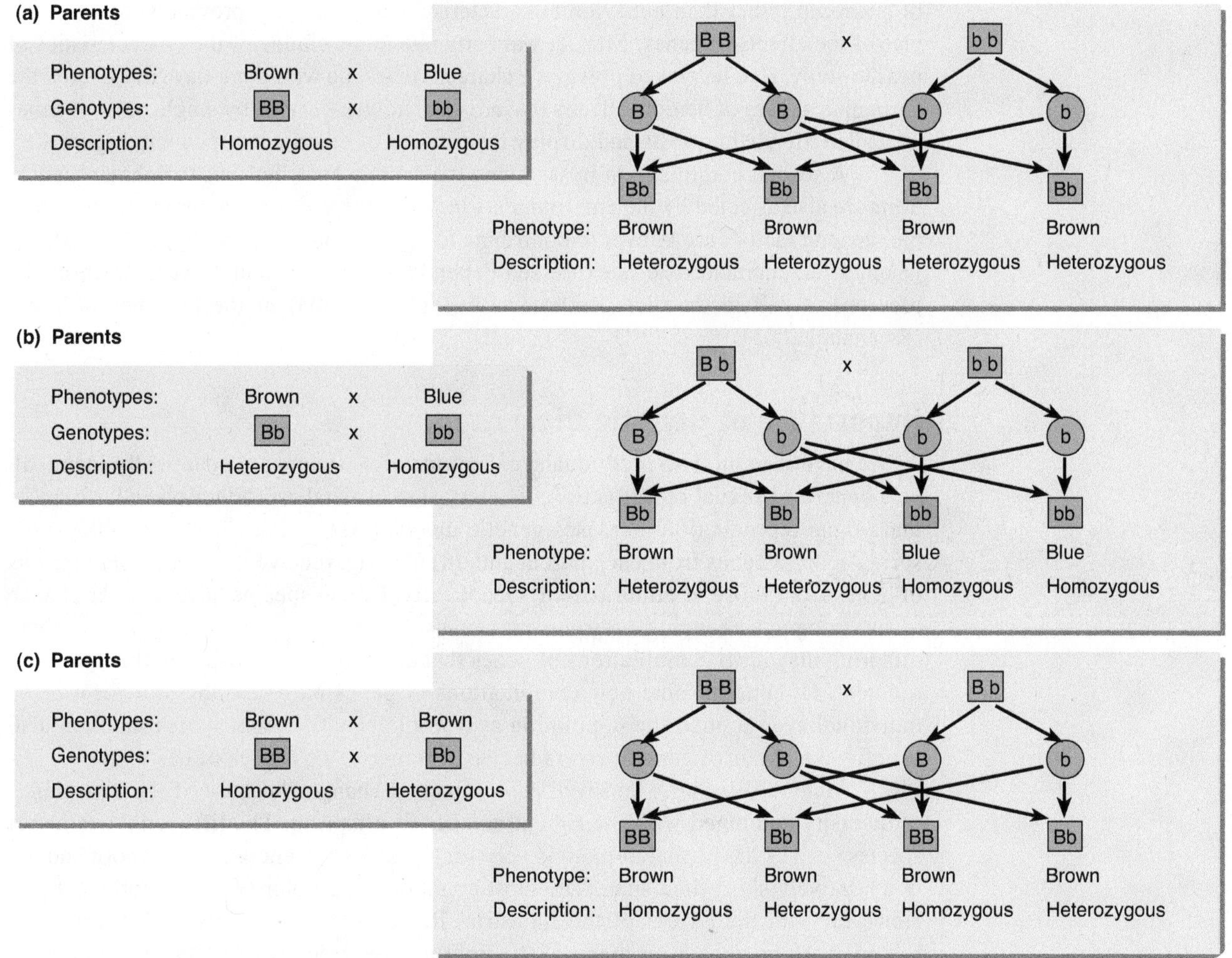

Figure 4.9 Patterns of inheritance for eye color.
(a) If one parent is homozygous for the dominant eye-color gene (BB) and the other parent is homozygous for the recessive eye-color gene (bb), then all of their children will be heterozygous for eye color (Bb) and will have brown eyes. (b) If one parent is heterozygous (Bb) and the other parent is homozygous recessive (bb), then each child will have a 50 percent chance of being heterozygous (brown eyes) and a 50 percent chance of being homozygous recessive (eye colors other than brown). (c) If one parent is homozygous dominant (BB) and the other parent is heterozygous (Bb), then each child will have a 50 percent chance of being homozygous for the dominant eye color (BB) and a 50 percent chance of being heterozygous (Bb)—and in either case will have brown eyes.

on the particular gene combination. Some alleles are **dominant.** For dominant alleles, the character that is expressed requires the presence of only that allele. Thus the character is expressed whether the gene is present on one or both chromosomes. When characters are expressed, the relevant genes are said to affect the organism's **phenotype,** or appearance. Other alleles are **recessive.** For recessive alleles, *both* chromosomes must contain the same allele for the character to be expressed. When a character is not expressed but the genes for that character are present, those genes are said to affect only the **genotype.** Recall the case of John Harold Johnson, Jr. The sickle-cell gene is a recessive gene. It was not expressed in the phenotype of either parent because each had only one copy of the recessive allele. The fertilized egg that produced John Jr. unfortunately had two sickle-cell alleles. (For another example of dominant and recessive genes, see Figure 4.9.) The sickle-cell gene affected John Jr.'s phenotype whereas it affected only the genotypes of his parents and sister.

The genetic contributions to behavior are usually more complex than the simple dominant-recessive relation of sickle-cell anemia. Characteristics—especially behavioral characteristics—are usually affected by many genes, not just a single pair. Such characteristics are said to be under **polygenic control.** Examples of polygenic characteristics include human intelligence and personality. In this chapter, we generally use examples

dominant allele
a trait that is exhibited when only one allele is present, a trait expressed in heterozygous cells

phenotype
the appearance or behavior of an organism; outward expression of the genotype

recessive allele
a trait that is expressed only when both alleles of a gene are the same, a trait expressed homozygous cells

genotype
the genetic makeup of an organism

polygenic control
characteristic affected by more than one gene, as with most behavior

of structural rather than behavioral characteristics because they provide simpler examples of the effects of genes. Mendel was fortunate in his choice of the characteristics of peas to study. Had he picked polygenic characteristics, he would not have discovered the particulate nature of heredity. Traits that are discretely expressed by single pairs of genes are called **Mendelian traits** and display the patterns of inheritance shown in Figure 4.9.

A second complication in assessing the genetic contributions to behavior is that traits are also affected by the environments in which the genes are expressed. For example, genetic factors are known to contribute to high-blood pressure (hypertension), but whether the characteristic is expressed depends on environmental events such as the presence of salt in the diet (Barlassina & Taglietti, 2003) or the presence of stress (Rosmand, 2005).

Importance of Genetic Diversity

As we have seen, no two individuals, except identical twins, are genetically identical. One benefit of sexual reproduction, in contrast to asexual reproduction as in fungi, is that sexual reproduction increases genetic diversity (see West-Eberhard, 2005). Offspring acquire genes from each parent and, in so doing, receive different *combinations* of genes from those of either parent. Genetically diverse species have a better chance of surviving in a changing environment because when the environment changes, some offspring may have combinations of genes that allow them to prosper in the new environment. Of course, some new combinations of genes may be unhelpful for a given individual even though the population as a whole benefits. Sexual reproduction also benefits the repair of genetic errors because there are two copies of each gene.

Many insects have survived environmental changes because of the advantages of diversity combined with their great number of offspring. The lifespan of an insect species such as the peppered moth is very short and many generations are born and die in a relatively short time span. The most common wing color of these moths is light. However, with the advent of the Industrial Revolution in the early 1900s, tree bark became dark from soot on many of the light-colored trees where these moths rested. Because a light-colored moth on a dark background is more visible to predating birds, the lighter colored variety was eaten more frequently than their darker cousins. Over time, the darker variety became more numerous. The latent capacity of the peppered-moth genome to produce a darker wing color ensured that the species survived this change in environment (Dawkins, 1996). Rapidly reproducing species can change their nature when nature changes. In the case of the peppered moth, we may take some comfort that the lighter variety is again becoming more numerous as pollution lessens (Grant & Wiseman, 2002).

Sex-Linked Traits

If an allele on the X chromosome is not paired with a corresponding allele on the Y chromosome, a trait affected by a recessive allele on the X chromosome can be expressed. Thus, males are more likely than females to express the traits of recessive genes because males have only XY, whereas females have XX sex chromosomes. Females have two chances of getting the dominant allele, whereas males have only one. Genes that are found on the sex chromosomes give rise to **sex-linked traits.** Hemophilia is a deleterious recessive allele. In hemophilia, clotting of the blood is delayed after an injury. Even a minor cut or a bruise may take a long time to clot. Because females have two X chromosomes, they may carry one allele for hemophilia but still have normal blood clotting because the dominant allele is present on the other X chromosome. A female fetus in which both X chromosomes have the allele for hemophilia does not survive. Males, however, have only a single X chromosome. If they have the recessive gene on the X chromosome that they received from their mother, they have the hemophilic phenotype. Hemophilia is an example of a sex-linked trait.

Mendelian traits
traits showing a dominant, recessive, or sex-linked pattern of inheritance. Mendelian traits are not polygenic

sex-linked traits
traits affected by genes located on the sex chromosomes

The light and dark varieties of peppered moth are shown on trees with light-colored bark (left) and with dark-colored bark. Note the differences in the visibility of the two varieties on the different backgrounds.

Some sex-related genes express themselves in both sexes and are called *sex-influenced genes*. For example, male pattern baldness develops when men inherit one or both alleles for baldness, but is seldom seen in women in either case. This is because the expression of male pattern baldness is affected by male sex hormones, which occur at much lower levels in women.

Mutations and Chromosomal Aberrations

Changes in the genome can be produced by processes other than recombination of segments of chromosomes during meiosis. Two other sources of genetic diversity are mutations or chromosomal aberrations. **Mutations** are chance alterations in the sequence of nucleotides within a single gene. Although most mutations are harmful, they may produce genes that are beneficial in some environments. Mutations occur either spontaneously during normal biological processes or as the result of external factors such as high-energy radiation. That is why dentists and physicians cover the reproductive organs with a lead apron when taking X-rays.

Hemophilia provides one of the most famous examples of mutation. Although hemophilia has appeared many times in human history, it had particularly far-reaching effects when a spontaneous mutation was passed among the royal families of nineteenth-century Europe. Through genealogical analysis, researchers have discovered that this particular mutation arose with Queen Victoria (1819–1901) of England. She was the first in her family line to bear affected children—two daughters who were carriers of the gene and one afflicted son. The tradition that nobility married only other nobility allowed the mutant gene to spread rapidly throughout the royal families of Europe, most notably to the royal family of Russia. The son of Nicholas II, the last Tsar of Russia, had hemophilia. He and his entire family were killed at the outset of the Russian Revolution.

The second type of genetic change, **chromosomal aberration,** refers to changes in part of a chromosome (for example, deletion of a gene) or in the total number of chromosomes (for example, failure of paired chromosomes to separate during meiosis). A disorder caused by a chromosomal aberration—in this case, a partial deletion of genetic material in chromosome 5—is the *cri-du-chat syndrome*. Infants who have this syndrome have gastrointestinal, cardiac, and intellectual problems and make crying sounds that resemble a cat's mewing (hence the syndrome's name, "cry of the cat"). The severity of the syndrome is determined by the amount of genetic material that is missing. Early special education can reduce, although not eliminate, difficulties in self-care and communication. Even severe behavioral deficits with a known genetic basis, such as cri-du-chat syndrome, can be modified by experience. A much more common and less severe example is the impairment of visually guided behavior caused by myopia (near-sightedness). This is readily overcome by wearing prescription eyeglasses.

mutation
alterations in the nucleotides within a single gene. Can occur spontaneously or from experimental manipulation

chromosomal aberration
displacement or deletion of genes within chromosomes, or a change in the number of chromosomes

Genetic Disorders

Some genes decrease an organism's viability—its ability to survive. These "killer genes" are more common than one might think, but they are almost always recessive. When a child inherits a healthy allele from one parent and a lethal allele from the other, the lethal gene is not expressed. A few lethal genetic disorders are dominant, however, and usually express themselves in spontaneous abortions.

There are a number of human genetic disorders. Several of the more common ones with intellectual and other behavioral effects are described below.

Down's syndrome

Down's syndrome (named after the British physician John Langdon Down) is caused by a chromosomal aberration in which there is an extra 21st chromosome. When an ovum is formed during meiosis, the 21st pair of chromosomes fails to separate, and then, when the ovum is fertilized, the sperm provides a third 21st chromosome. People with Down's syndrome have various degrees of impaired physical, psychomotor, and cognitive development. The frequency of Down's syndrome increases with the age of the mother, especially when the father is older as well (Rischer & Easton, 1992; Fisch et al., 2003). About 40% of all Down's syndrome children are born to women over 40. Because Down's syndrome is caused by a chromosomal aberration, it is not heritable.

Huntington's disease

Huntington's disease (previously known as *Huntington's chorea;* named after the American physician George Huntington) is caused by a dominant lethal gene. However, the lethal gene is not expressed until the afflicted person is between 30 and 40 years of age. Before that time, functioning appears essentially normal. With the onset of the disease, certain portions of the brain degenerate. This produces progressive mental and physical deterioration. Because the onset of Huntington's disease occurs after sexual maturity, this lethal gene can pass unrecognized from parent to child. Perhaps the best known case of Huntington's disease is that of Woody Guthrie, the author of the folk song "This land is your land, this land is my land." There is now a test to determine if a person will be afflicted with the disease, but Woody Guthrie's son, the folk singer Arlo Guthrie, decided not to take the test. Fortunately, Arlo did not inherit the lethal gene from his father.

Phenylketonuria (PKU)

Phenylketonoria (PKU) is a recessive trait. Infants who are homozygous for the gene cannot break down phenylalanine, an amino acid found in many high-protein foods. As a result, blood levels of phenylalanine increase, which cause brain damage and impairment of intellectual functioning. There is now a test for the disease that is routinely given to newborns. Newborns who test homozygous for this recessive gene are placed on a low-phenylalanine diet shortly after birth. When the diet is carefully followed, brain development is normal. Again, environment and genes interact to produce the expressed characteristics of the organism (that is, the *phenotype*).

Down's syndrome
chromosomal aberration consisting of an extra 21st chromosome. Produces varying physical and behavioral impairment

Huntington's disease
genetic disorder caused by a dominant lethal gene that produces progressive mental and physical deterioration after adulthood (also known as Huntington's chorea)

phenylketonuria (PKU)
genetic disorder caused by recessive genes that impair ability to break down phenylalanine; can cause mental retardation if untreated

Questions to Consider

1. Eye color is inherited. How could you account for the fact that you and a sibling have different eye colors since you have the same parents?
2. Given what you now know about genetics, is it likely that there could be a single gene for such complex characteristics as intelligence or personality?
3. Does the fact that a characteristic is heritable mean that the behavior it affects cannot be changed?

Heredity and Human Behavior

Even casual observation reveals that people differ from one another. However, it may be surprising to learn that humans are genetically much less diverse than other primates. For example, we show less genetic diversity than our closest living relative, the chimpanzee (Strachan & Read, 1999). Nevertheless, each of us possesses unique combinations of genes and lives in uniquely different environments. We vary in size and shape, in personality and intelligence, and in artistic and athletic abilities to name but a few. To what extent are these differences due to genetic differences?

Answering this question is difficult. First, if we want to determine experimentally whether a difference is due to one variable, we must change only that variable while holding all others constant. But, we cannot vary the heredity of humans while holding their environments constant. Nor can we vary their environments while holding their heredity constant. Thus, for humans, the experimental procedures normally used to determine the effect of a variable can only be approximated, and not fully implemented. And, even if experiments of this sort were possible with humans, we would not conduct them for ethical reasons. Another difficulty is that the effects of heredity and environment interact: If we manipulate the value of one variable and hold the other variables constant, the effect of the manipulated variable may depend on the specific values of the variables we hold constant. If the other variables are held constant at a different value, the manipulated variable might have a different effect. For example, manipulating a gene known to affect high blood pressure might have little effect when the environment was held constant with little salt. We might then incorrectly conclude that the gene had no effect on blood pressure. Keeping such complications in mind, what has research revealed about the role of genetic and environmental differences in human behavior?

Heritability

The degree to which genes affect a characteristic in a given environment is called **heritability.** Heritability is a statistical measure based on correlations. It measures the amount of variation in a trait that is due to naturally occurring genetic differences among individuals in that population. Heritability varies from 0.0 (no effect of genetic differences) to 1.0 (complete genetic determination). The measure reflects the variation of a trait in a *population* of individuals; it does not indicate the contribution of genetic factors to the characteristics of any one individual. Statistical procedures can be applied to humans because these procedures are observational and do not involve direct manipulation of variables. Darwin's cousin Francis Galton (1869) began the use of correlations to study heritability in humans. A second, and complementary, approach to assessing heritability is **behavior genetics.** Behavior genetics uses experimental methods in which genetic variables are manipulated by the researcher and the effects of these manipulations on behavior are measured. Clearly, behavior genetics is largely restricted to the study of the nonhuman animals, but the results of such studies can be used to interpret the behavior of humans.

Experimental Procedures for Studying Genetic Influences

Animal breeders have used artificial selection for many years, but laboratory methods have been employed to study the relation between heredity and behavior for only about 100 years. Most behavioral traits are continuously varying characteristics that are polygenic and the various genes may well be located on different chromosomes. These polygenic traits are **nonmendelian traits.** Polygenic traits play an important role in human evolution (Carroll, 2003) and methods for their study are described shortly.

Artificial Selection

Artificial selection involves selective breeding within a population of organisms. Using these procedures, the heritability of many characteristics, or traits, has been demonstrated in nonhuman animals. These traits include such things as aggression, docility, alcohol preference, running speed, and mating behavior.

heritability
variation in a trait due to genetic factors, varies from 0.0 to 1.0

behavior genetics
the study of how genes affect behavior

nonmendelian trait
characteristic when alleles do not have a dominant-recessive relation

Tryon's selective breeding study showed that a rat's ability to learn how to navigate a maze was affected by genetic factors.

Perhaps the best known example of artificial selection is a study of maze learning in rats conducted by Robert Tryon (1940). Tryon began with an unselected population of rats and had them learn to run a maze for food. As you might imagine, some rats learned the correct path with few errors and some with many errors. Tryon interbred those rats that learned with the fewest errors with their kind and interbred the rats that learned with the most errors with their kind. The offspring of this artificial-selection procedure then learned the maze. Successive generations of offspring were, in turn, interbred in the same manner.

After a number of generations of artificial selection, the maze performance of the two groups did not overlap. (See Figure 4.10.) It is important to note that the two groups did not differ on their first attempt at the maze, but that the difference emerged during learning. The artificial-selection procedure had produced two groups of rats that learned the correct path at different rates.

You should not conclude that the differences in maze performance indicated that their behavior could be affected only by genetic factors. For example, Cooper and Zubek (1958) showed that differences in maze performance were virtually eliminated when "maze-bright" and "maze-dull" groups of rats were both stimulated by rearing them in enriched environments (cages containing geometric objects such as tunnels, ramps, and blocks). Differences were also eliminated when Tryon's maze-bright rats were raised in impoverished environments (cages containing only food and water). Thus, the effects of the genetic differences depended on the environments in which the genes were expressed. It would also be a mistake to conclude that Tryon's two groups differed in some more general respect such as "intelligence" or "ability to learn." Tryon's "dull" rats learned a task that required escape from water faster than the "bright" rats (Searles, 1949, see McClearn, 1963 for a review). General effects of selection can be expected only if the selecting environments are very diverse, such as the widely differing challenges that humans and many other species have faced over evolutionary time.

Molecular Genetics

Molecular genetics uses powerful techniques to directly manipulate genes and their expression. Molecular genetics studies genes at the level of DNA and then relates differences in genes to the structure and behavior of the organism. Perhaps its greatest accomplishment to date has been to determine essentially the entire sequence of nucleotides in the human genome.

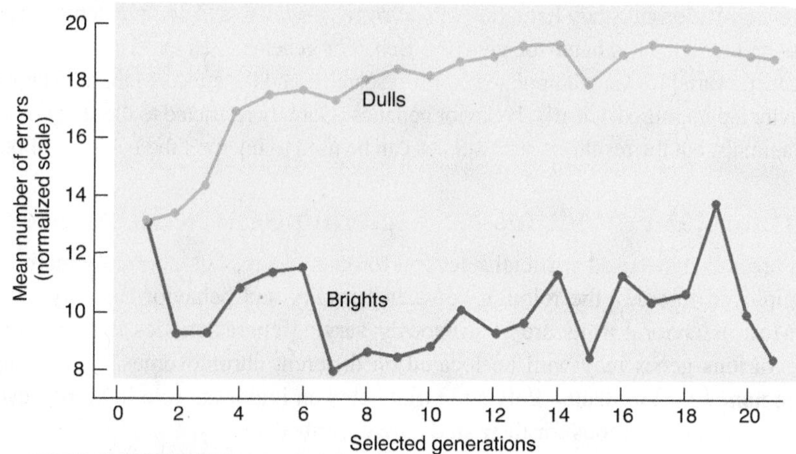

Figure 4.10 Results from Tryon's 1940 artificial breeding research of rats' ability to learn a maze.

Within a few generations, differences in the rats' ability to negotiate the maze became distinct.

(Adapted from Tryon, R. C. (1940). Genetic differences in maze-learning ability in rats. Yearbook of the National Society for the Study of Education, 39, 111–119.)

molecular genetics
the study of genetics at the level of the DNA molecule

One of the techniques for studying the effects of genes at the molecular level is **knockout mutations.** Molecular biologists have developed methods that directly affect the gene by damaging genes with radiation or by inserting nucleotides that prevent the expression of a gene. This produces what is called a *knockout mutation*. In one such study with rats, the gene that was knocked out is normally expressed in a part of the brain known to be important for spatial learning in humans. When this gene was knocked out in rats, they were impaired in their ability to learn to swim to the location of a slightly submerged platform on which they could rest (Nakazawa et al., 2003). By examining the changes in performance after a gene has been knocked out, clues are obtained about the function of the gene.

Research with identical twins has provided psychology with information about the role of heredity in behavior traits.

The methods of molecular biology can also be combined with artificial selection to study the effects of genes on behavior. For example, a biochemically detectable change can be produced in a genetically inactive portion of a chromosome. This change then becomes a **genetic marker** for those genes that are nearby on the chromosome. When artificial selection produces a change in behavior, as in maze performance in Tryon's experiment, the genetic markers can be examined to see if different artificially selected groups vary in the frequency or placement of the genetic marker. If the groups differ, then the genes that are responsible for the difference must lie nearby on the chromosome. By using multiple markers on different chromosomes, the chance of finding the locations of relevant genes is increased. As an example, this technique has been used to isolate the location of a gene that affects exploratory behavior in fruit-fly larvae (Osborne et al., 1997).

Table 4.1 Comparison of Concordance Rates between Monozygotic (MZ) and Dizygotic (DZ) Twins for Various Traits

	Concordance	
Trait	MZ	DZ
Blood type	100%	66%
Eye color	99	28
Mental retardation	97	37
Measles	95	87
Idiopathic epilepsy	72	15
Schizophrenia	69	10
Diabetes	65	18
Identical allergy	59	5
Tuberculosis	57	23

Source: Table 7.4, p. 161 from *Concepts of Genetics,* 2nd ed. by William S. Klug and Michael R. Cummings. Copyright © 1986 by Scott, Foresman and Company. Reprinted by permission of Pearson Education, Inc.

Correlation Methods for Studying the Effects of Genes

Human behavior cannot be subjected to the experimental procedures of artificial selection and molecular genetics, such as knockouts and gene-marking. Nevertheless, much has been learned about the effects of genes on human behavior through correlation methods. In correlation methods, individuals with naturally occurring differences in behavior are examined to determine if differences in genetic variables are related to (correlated with) the behavior. With humans, we cannot manipulate the genetic make-up (the genotype), but we can observe their behavior (the phenotype). In addition, we can analyze the sequences of nucleotides to see if they are correlated with the phenotype. Such research with humans requires their informed consent.

Concordance research

Concordance research takes advantage of the fact that identical twins have identical genes. Recall that identical twins, technically *monozygotic (MZ) twins*, arise from a single fertilized ovum, or zygote. The zygote divides into two genetically identical cells that develop independently thereafter. Fraternal twins, technically *dizygotic (DZ) twins*, arise from the fertilization of two different ova by two different sperm. If genes affect behavior, then MZ twins should be more alike than DZ twins, or than other siblings raised in similar environments.

Two individuals are said to be *concordant* for a trait if both express that same trait. If only one of the two individuals expresses the trait, then they are said to be *discordant* for the trait. In these terms, MZ twins should be more often concordant than other pairs of individuals because they are more genetically similar. As shown in Table 4.1, MZ twins are indeed concordant for many traits. For example, the physical characteristic of blood type has a heritability of 1.0 and is highly concordant in MZ twins but less so in DZ twins. Environmental similarity as well as genetic similarity also affects concordance. Note the lower concordance of MZ twins for schizophrenia, which is a behavioral characteristic, than for blood type. The lower concordance reflects the contribution of environmental as well as genetic factors to schizophrenia. The concordance rate of DZ twins for schizophrenia is 10%, which is above what would be expected from a disease that occurs in only about 1% of the general population. This indicates the contribution of genetic as well as environmental facts to schizophrenia.

knockout mutations
experimentally induced genetic sequence preventing gene expression

genetic marker
a known nucleotide sequence that occurs at a particular location on a chromosome

concordance research
studies the similarity of traits between twins, especially identical twins. Twins are concordant if they exhibit the same phenotype

In research described in later chapters, studies compare the performance of MZ and DZ twins on other behavior. These studies show that genetic factors can also affect cognitive skills such as the scores on intelligence tests (Bouchard & McGue, 1981), personality traits such as extroversion (the tendency to be outgoing), language ability, and certain psychological disorders such as schizophrenia and mental retardation (Bouchard & Propping, 1993).

Segregation Analysis

Segregation analysis is another correlation method that is used to assess genetic contributions to human behavior. Although behavioral geneticists cannot insert a genetic marker in humans, they can identify specific regions of chromosomes and correlate the presence or absence of these regions with behavioral phenotypes. These identified regions are made up of nucleotide sequences that are relatively constant. Behavior geneticists use the information from concordances and kin relations to search for traits that show strong genetic influences. The chromosomes are then examined to see if any of the various markers is differentially associated—*segregated*—with the behavioral trait. If some markers are segregated between the behavioral phenotypes, then the critical genes lie on or near the marker. Additional work in molecular biology can then be directed toward those regions of the chromosome to identify the precise gene.

The potential power of segregation analysis is illustrated in a study of a particular language deficit. The deficit is a widespread difficulty in the articulation of words, especially in the formation of grammatical word endings—for instance, forming the past tense of regular verbs by adding *-ed* as in "walk" and "walk*ed*" (Enard et al., 2002). Three generations of a family were known to have this particular language disorder. One gene on the seventh chromosome, designated by the letters FOXP2, showed a mutation that was unique to those members of the family who had the language disorder. The mutation was not seen in a large sample of unrelated individuals who did not show the language-disorder phenotype. This finding strongly suggests that a normally functioning FOXP2 gene affects the fine articulatory movements that make refined speech possible (Pinker, 2001). An especially intriguing result arose as a byproduct of this work. When the map of the human genome was compared to analogous genetic sequences in other primates, it was found that the FOXP2 gene had changed quite rapidly after humans diverged from the great apes (Enard et al., 2002). Based on the rate at which mutations are thought to occur, the estimated date at which the modern human form of FOXP2 emerged was within the last 200,000 years of human evolution. However, for reasons noted earlier in the study of heritability of maze learning in rats, it is simplistic to think that the FOXP2 gene is a "language gene" because the gene also affects other behavior.

Questions to Consider

1. Given what you know about how heritability is determined, would the heritability of skin color be different in the United States, Scandinavia, and Africa?
2. What problems would be faced in determining the genetic basis (if any) of human characteristics such as aggression?

segregation analysis
correlational method to identify sections of chromosomes that are the same for individuals expressing a common trait

evolutionary psychology
branch of psychology studying how human behavior is affected by evolution

Evolution and Human Behavior

Evolution through natural selection has affected not only the structure of humans but their behavior as well. In this final major section of the chapter, we consider some of the implications of natural selection for human behavior. The field of psychology that studies the effect of natural selection on behavior is called **evolutionary psychology**

(Buller, 2005). Work in this field began with research on animals in biology, which focused on the implications of evolution for social behavior. Sexual and parenting behavior were of greatest interest because both directly affect reproductive fitness.

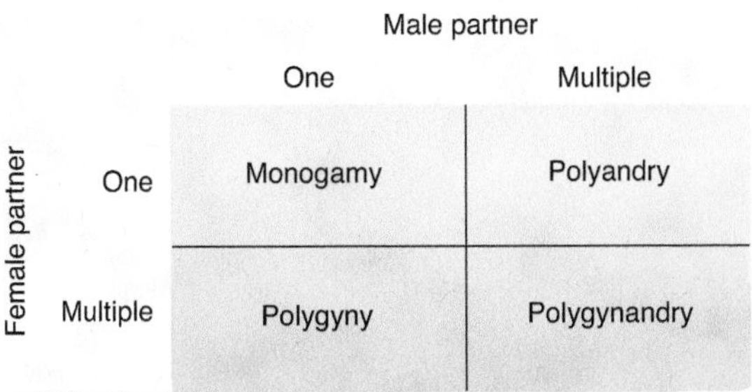

Figure 4.11 Reproductive strategies. Different numbers of males mating with different numbers of females yield the four reproductive strategies of monogamy, polygyny, polyandry, and polygynandry.

Sociobiology

Sociobiology is the study of genetic influences on social behavior (Wilson, 1975). Typically, sociobiologists observe and perform experiments on the social behavior of nonhuman animals and then explore the implications of those findings for the social behavior of humans. Thus sociobiology involves experimentation to determine the adaptiveness of a given social behavior and then uses those findings to interpret behavior in the natural environment.

Reproductive and parenting behavior have been the primary focus of sociobiological research. Much of this work has been concerned with **reproductive strategies**—the various systems of mating and rearing offspring.

Reproductive Strategies

Of the various reproductive strategies, our culture sanctions only **monogamy,** the mating of one female and one male. If offspring result from mating, the culture endorses sharing responsibility for raising the child. However, different reproductive strategies occur in different species and cultures—including our own (Barash, 1982). Three additional classes of reproductive strategy are possible. (See Figure 4.11.) **Polygyny** involves one male mating with more than one female; *polyandry* involves one female mating with more than one male; and *polygynandry* involves several females mating with several males. (*Poly* refers to many, *and* to male, and *gyn* to female.) We consider only monogamy and polygyny because they are the predominant reproductive strategies in humans.

Different reproductive strategies arise from important sex differences in the resources that each parent invests in conceiving and rearing offspring (Trivers, 1972). **Parental investment** refers to the time, physical effort, and risks to life involved in procreating, nurturing, and protecting offspring. From an evolutionary perspective, individuals who make a greater investment in parenting should be more discriminating when choosing a mate and, in turn, should be more sought after as mates.

Among humans, polygyny is a common reproductive strategy, especially in cultures in which some men have much greater resources available to them than others do—as in Africa and portions of the Middle East and Asia (Kanazawa & Still, 2001). Monogamy is the most common reproductive strategy in Western culture (Badcock, 1991). In fact, even though it is not sanctioned by Western culture, men especially engage in polygynous mating practices. In the United States, for example, 25% of men but only 15% of women are estimated to engage in extramarital sexual relations (Laumann et al., 1994). Polygynous practices are especially common with humans who have reproductively beneficial traits such as wealth or power. Think of the multiple alliances of "captains of industry" and "movie stars."

Sexual Selection

Competition for mates can lead to **sexual selection,** that is, natural selection for traits that are characteristic of a particular sex, such as appearance, body size, or behavioral patterns. Elaborate displays of the peacock's tail feathers are preferred by peahens because such displays are correlated with the general health and vigor of the male. These characteristics—if heritable—favor the survival of the peahen's chicks. In the developed world, physically attractive women are generally those with a low *waist-to-hip ratio (WHR),* reflecting a greater deposition of fat on the buttocks and hips than the waist. A preference for women with low WHR is consistent with the evolutionary argument that mates are selected for their health and fitness to reproduce. However, such preferences are not universal. A study by Yu and Shepard (1998) compared the preferences for women of American men and men of the Matsigenka people in southeast Peru. These Peruvian men live in an isolated village and have not been exposed to the mass media of Western civilization. Whereas

sociobiology
the study of genetic influences on social behavior, especially in animals

reproductive strategies
evolutionary effects on systems of mating and rearing offspring; these need not be conscious strategies

monogamy
mating strategy of one female with one male

polygyny
mating strategy of one male with more than one female

parental investment
resources that parents expend in procreating and nurturing offspring

sexual selection
preference for traits that are differentially expressed in the two sexes, for example, body size

Large male elephant seals are more successful in competing for females than are smaller males. But is there a point at which larger size could become maladaptive?

Western men prefer women with low WHR, the Matsigenka men preferred women with high WHR. Perhaps being overweight in this isolated Peruvian society was associated with coming from a relatively prosperous family that was—in turn—correlated with a favorable genetic endowment. Researchers who study the sexual preferences of men in other agricultural societies have found a similar pattern. They speculate that "the more subsistence-oriented a society is, and the more energetically expansive women's work, the more men will find fatter women attractive" (Marlowe & Wetzman, 2001). Indeed, an article posted on BBC News (July 19, 2007) quotes a husband from the Efik tribe in Africa who said that he sends his wife to a special fattening room where "I add rice and beans and more meat and fish to make her more huge and big to maintain the stature you want your woman to be." His wife added, "When you are fat, it makes you look healthy. People respect you. People honor you. Wherever you go, they say, 'Your husband feed you fine.'" It is clear that sexual preferences are not influenced by natural selection alone.

Polygyny is a common reproductive strategy among mammals (including humans). The costs associated with reproduction are generally much less for males than females. Females have fewer opportunities than males to reproduce because they produce only one ovum or a few ova periodically, whereas males can produce numerous sperm at relatively frequent intervals. Thus, females can bear only a limited number of offspring in a lifetime, regardless of the number of males with whom they mate. In contrast, males are limited in their reproductive success only by the number of females that they can impregnate. Perhaps the most dramatic example of this difference is illustrated by King Ismail of Morocco, who reportedly fathered 1,056 children (Young, 1998)! Females also carry the fertilized ovum in their bodies during a long gestation period. This requires diverting a major portion of their own metabolic resources to nourishing the fetus. Because they carry the fertilized ovum, females also assume the risks that accompany pregnancy and childbirth. The contributions of males to reproduction can be quite minimal—sperm and the time for mating. Once offspring are born, females often continue to devote some of their metabolic resources to the infant by nursing it.

Females in polygynous species invest especially heavily in their offspring because the male is shared with other females. As a result, females are usually quite selective in their mates. They mate with males who possess such traits as physical size, strength, and aggressiveness. This selectivity often benefits the adaptation of both the female and her progeny. The offspring of such males will tend to possess the same adaptively significant attributes as the father and thus will be more likely to eventually win their own quests for mating privileges. Also, her female offspring will more likely be attracted to the same male attributes. To the extent that such preferences are heritable, the net effect is that the genes of the mother will have greater representation in future generations than will genes of females who mate with males having less adaptive traits. Of course, which traits are adaptive depend on the environment. For example, for humans in developed countries the intelligence of men would likely be more adaptive than their strength.

Monogamy is also common among humans. In general, monogamy occurs in species whose environments favor the contributions of both parents to the survival of offspring. In these environments, reproductive fitness benefits more from sharing parental duties than from exclusive care by one parent. For example, a fox must provide food, milk, and protection for its offspring. A single female attempting to fulfill all of these responsibilities would put the pups at risk. Hunting would be difficult with the pups straggling along, but leaving the pups behind would risk predation. The reproductive strategy exhibited by foxes is that both parents hunt and protect the cubs. By jointly caring for the pups, both male and female foxes enhance the chance that their offspring will survive and reproduce. Thus, the parental genes will more likely be represented in the next generation.

Although both males and females in monogamous species share parenting responsibilities, females generally continue to have greater parental investment in the offspring. Many of the reasons for greater female investment endure—the limited opportunity for mating, the cost of pregnancy, and so on. As a result, very few monogamous species, including our own, are exclusively monogamous. In fact, there is a strong tendency in most monogamous species toward patterns of reproductive behavior and parental investment that approximate polygynous species (Tavris & Sadd, 1977; Badcock, 1991; Hyde & Oliver, 2000; Shackelford & Weekes-Shackelford, 2004). Of course, learning and culture, as well as the genetic legacy of the ancestral environment, affect reproductive and mating behavior in humans. The advent of effective contraception has reduced the relation between mating and child-bearing; in addition, increased opportunities for education and employment for women undoubtedly increasingly affect human reproductive strategies. Contemporary culture does not measure reproductive success only by the number of children, but also by the quality of the children's lives as well as those of their parents. Most people have the biological capacity to produce a larger number of children, but many choose not to do so.

Altruism

Altruistic behavior involves self-sacrifice, as when parents risk their own survival by defending their young against predators or by feeding their young in times of scarcity. If individuals behave in a manner that is a cost to themselves but a benefit to others, then that behavior is said to be *altruistic*. Altruistic behavior is of particular interest because it seems to conflict with the layman's conception of "survival of the fittest." If natural selection favors traits that benefit survival, then how could behavior that reduces survival of the individual ever be selected? And yet, abundant examples of altruism exist even among nonhuman animals.

Consider the honeybee that sacrifices its life on behalf of its hive mates when it stings an intruder, or the prairie dog that gives alarm calls that warn other prairie dogs of a predator but increases its own chances of being preyed upon. Examples of altruistic behavior abound in humans. In its most extreme form, human altruism is demonstrated when persons risk their lives to save the lives of others. How can such self-sacrifice be understood? More important for present purposes, how can evolution interpret such behavior?

The evolutionary explanation of altruistic behavior is based on the following insight: It is the survival of the *genes,* not the individual who carries those genes, that is of central concern to natural selection. An individual's genes are held partially in common with all those with whom that individual is genetically related. For example, each parent shares 50% of his or her genes with each offspring—on the average half of the offspring's genes come from the mother and half from the father. Thus parents who disadvantage themselves to the benefit of their children are, in fact, benefiting their own genes! The geneticist William D. Hamilton (1964, 1970) realized that, strictly speaking, natural selection does not favor reproductive success but **inclusive fitness**—the reproductive success of individuals with whom we share genes as well as ourselves. Note that the evolutionary account of altruism does not assume that there is any conscious appreciation of the genetic consequences of altruism.

In confirmation of inclusive fitness, experiments have determined that altruistic behavior is more apt to occur when the organism that benefits is genetically related to organism that pays the cost. Bees and other social insects, such as termites, are among the most altruistic species because their special genetic relationship causes them to share a particularly high number of genes in common. Birds make alarm calls upon sighting a hawk, but only if their *relatives* are near, not otherwise (Wilson, 1975). In general, altruistic behavior most benefits close relatives such as parents, siblings, grandparents, and grandchildren. The closer the family relation, the greater the genetic overlap among the individuals involved. Such biologic favoritism toward relatives is called **kin selection** (Mayr, 2001).

Not all instances of altruistic behavior can be understood in terms of kin selection. What about altruism between unrelated individuals? Could this also be affected by genetic variables? The evolutionary biologist Trivers (1971) identified an additional genetic source of altruism. This type of altruism is known as **reciprocal altruism.** Reciprocal altruism occurs when genetically unrelated persons engage in behavior that reduces their fitness at the moment but may increase their fitness in the longer term. For example, one individual may share his food with another now and the other may, in turn, share his food later. Thus each individual has increased his own fitness by an altruistic act because the likelihood is increased that each will pass his genes to the next generation.

altruistic behavior
behavior benefiting another organism at an apparent cost to the individual who executes the action

inclusive fitness
total reproductive success of those with whom the individual has genes in common, e.g., siblings

kin selection
selection that favors altruistic acts toward individuals with whom one has genes in common

reciprocal altruism
altruism in which one individual benefits another when it is likely that the other will return the benefit at a later time

Reciprocal altruism is the biological version of the Golden Rule—"Do unto others as you would have them do unto you." However, the biological version is not as generous as the Golden Rule. To increase reproductive fitness, altruistic behavior must carry a low risk to the altruist and a high benefit to the recipient. The lower the cost to the altruist, the more likely the altruistic act will benefit the altruist's fitness. If the altruist is not likely ever to benefit by a reciprocal action from the recipient, the fitness of the altruist is decreased. Finally, the altruist and the recipient must be able to recognize each other; otherwise, the behavior cannot be reciprocated. Does this genetic analysis of the conditions required for reciprocal altruism help explain why people are more likely to follow the Golden Rule in small communities than in big cities? Does this analysis help explain why people are especially good at facial recognition? Again, cultural factors and individual experience both play a role in reciprocal altruism, but genetic factors are a part of the story.

Evolutionary Psychology

Evolutionary psychology applies evolutionary thinking to the full range of human behavior (Buss, 2007; Buss et al., 1998). However, it is much more difficult to experimentally assess the effects of a given behavior on reproductive fitness in humans. As a result, efforts to understand human behavior in terms of evolutionary considerations must often be indirect and sometimes border on reasoning by analogy (Cornell, 1997; Roney, 1999). What is clear is that although natural selection undoubtedly affects human behavior—especially reproductive and parenting behavior—cultural factors also play an important role. Consider the effects of differences in parental investment on the sexual behavior of men and women. We have already seen that the preference for monogamous as contrasted with polygynous mating strategies depends on the equality of distribution of resources among men in the society. Other factors, such as the availability of effective methods of contraception, also undoubtedly affect mating strategies. In addition, it is often difficult to distinguish behavior that is a byproduct of selection for some other characteristic from behavior that has actually been an object of selection (Roney, 1999).

Evaluating Evolutionary Psychology

Evolutionary psychology has been controversial among psychologists, social scientists, and the general public. Several objections have been raised by its critics, often based on an incomplete understanding of the field. One objection has been that human behavior is too complex to be understood by natural selection alone. However, no evolutionary psychologist would ever make this claim. Social behavior—indeed all behavior—is the concerted effect of both the ancestral environment, as reflected in our genes, and our individual experience, as reflected in our nervous systems. To claim that evolution has *something* to say about human behavior is not to claim that evolution has *everything* to say. Another objection has been that evolutionary psychology is based on simplistic analogies between the behavior of nonhuman animals and humans. It is true that experimental work has been largely restricted to nonhumans, but experimental work is necessarily limited in any science that deals with human behavior. Care must always be taken when applying findings from other animals to humans—or, for that matter, from any one species to another.

We are encouraged to seek commonalities in the behavior of humans and other species by the fact of evolution—that all species are related to each other through branching descent—and the fact of selection—that all species have been subjected to selection by a partially common environment. The words of Edward O. Wilson, the "father" of sociobiology are to the point.

> The purpose of sociobiology is not to make crude comparisons between animal species or between animals and men. . . . Its purpose is to develop general laws of the evolution and biology of social behavior, which might then be extended in a disinterested manner to the study of human beings. . . . To devise a naturalistic description of human social behavior is to note a set of facts for further investigation, not to pass a value judgment

> or to deny that a great deal of the behavior can be deliberately changed if individual societies wish. . . . Human behavior is dominated by culture in the sense that the greater part, perhaps all, of the variation between societies is based on differences in cultural experiences . . . To understand the evolutionary history . . . is to understand in a deeper manner the construction of human nature, to learn what we really are and not just what we hope we are, as viewed through the various prisms of our mythologies. (Wilson, in Barash, 1982, pp. xiv–xv)

The criticisms of evolutionary accounts of human behavior are specific examples of general reservations that have been raised about natural selection as a basis for understanding the diversity and complexity of life. Before Darwin, these phenomena seemed beyond the reach of a natural-science explanation. After Darwin, the *possibility* of a natural-science explanation of life appeared. Repeated cycles of variation, selection, and retention promised an account that appealed only to processes that could be known through the methods of science.

Today, natural selection is the central unifying principle of biology and is playing an increasing role in psychology in the form of evolutionary psychology (Caporael, 2001; see also Lickliter & Honeycutt, 2003). Darwin's account of how selection processes produced the diversity and complexity of life is seen as a general approach to the explanation of the emergence of order and complexity in many fields. The repeated action of physical, chemical, biological, and behavioral processes—each of which could be subjected to independent scrutiny in the laboratory—may yield complex outcomes as their emergent product. (For more general treatments of selectionism, see Dennett, 1995; Mayr, 2000; and Donahoe, 2003.) Darwin has identified a means whereby complex phenomena in many fields can be understood as products of the repeated action of variation, selection, and retention. Through the selecting effect of the environment, order emerges naturally.

One general criticism of selectionism is that the complete sequence of events in the evolutionary process is not known. When complex electronic circuits are developed through a selection process, we can examine each step in the sequence and assure ourselves that the circuits came about through the cumulative effects of selection (Mead, 1989). However, when naturally occurring processes are studied, only glimpses of the entire sequence are usually visible. In the evolution of our species, for example, we see only a tooth here, a leg bone there. Darwin recognized the incompleteness of our knowledge of all of the steps in any natural process. Commenting on the meagerness of the fossil record, he remarked, ". . . we are confessedly ignorant; nor do we know how ignorant we are" (Darwin, 1859). The fossil record is now much more complete than when Darwin made his comments, but our knowledge remains imperfect. Faced with imperfect knowledge, science seeks to fill in the gaps rather than abandoning the effort. All the gaps in the course of evolution may never be filled, but none will be filled unless we seek them. Recent fossil discoveries have identified transitional forms between birds and the dinosaurs that were their ancestors (Prum, 2003) and between land-dwelling creatures and their aquatic ancestors (Daeschler, Shubin, & Jenkins, Jr., 2006). We now know much more about the evolutionary process from the fossil and molecular records.

A second general criticism of selectionism is that it undermines our uniqueness, and even our worth, as a species. Consider the sociobiological account of altruism. We prefer to think of ourselves as selfless individuals who help others out of the goodness of our hearts. Sociobiology suggests that altruism is, at least in part, a selfish act that is undertaken because it benefits the survival of our genes. But is this not a kind of selflessness? It is our genes that benefit and not us as individuals. And, most importantly, knowledge of evolution through natural selection opens the possibility of undoing the effects of those prior selections that once benefited the population as a whole but are now a burden for the individual. Through **genetic engineering** and other applications of our increasing knowledge of natural selection, we can implement *counter-selections*. Counter-selections seek to change our present environment so that we minimize the otherwise untoward effects of selection by the ancestral environment. Consider adult-onset diabetes, in which the effectiveness of insulin to store excess glucose as fat is diminished. Evolutionary research indicates that this was an adaptive response in the history of our species: It increased survival in

genetic engineering
procedures intended to alter an organism's genes to produce a more favorable phenotype

environments with intermittent food shortages. Knowing the origin of diabetes, more effective treatment regimens can now be formulated (Watve & Yajnik, 2007). Again, knowledge of evolution helps us understand and counter an effect of natural selection. If counter-selections are done wisely, is this not testimony to the uniqueness and worth of our species (Campbell, 1976)?

Culture

Culture is the sum of socially transmitted knowledge, customs, and behavior patterns that is common to a particular group of people. Culture is a means—in addition to natural selection—by which the environment of one generation can affect the behavior of the next generation. Culture insures that the skills acquired by one generation are transmitted to the next generation. The changes wrought by culture occur much more rapidly than those produced by natural selection. No account of human behavior is complete without considering the effects of both evolution (the genetic legacy of the ancient past) and culture (the learned legacy of the more recent past). Although cultural influences are much more pronounced in humans than other species, some evidence of cultural transmission can be found in other social species. For example, if a chimpanzee acquires a skill, such as operating a device to secure food while separated from its group, when the trained chimp returns to the group, other individuals in the group rapidly acquire that same skill through observing the first chimp (White, Horner, & de Waal, 2005). Without cultural transmission, the group might never have acquired the skill.

By understanding how behavior developed through evolution by natural selection and through acculturation by learning, we can understand how our behavior has become adapted to the environments of the past and present. More importantly, by understanding natural selection and learning, we can better design environments that permit us not only to survive in the present but also to attain our goals in the future.

Questions to Consider

1. Does the fact that social behavior is affected by natural selection through genetic mechanisms have any implications for the concept of personal responsibility or for our legal system?
2. Suppose a child is in a dangerous situation. From an evolutionary perspective alone, should a parent risk his or her own life to rescue the child? Would your answer depend on the number of children the parent already had? Would it depend on the age of the parent?

Epilogue
A Favored Gene, Not a Favored Individual

As we have seen, natural selection operates on the level of *populations*, not of individuals. On the average, those members of the population having characteristics that favor the survival of their offspring are more likely to have their genes survive into the next generation. However, there is no guarantee that any one individual with favorable characteristics will survive and reproduce. George Washington was an individual with clearly admirable characteristics—he was a physical specimen possessed of both courage and intelligence. However, he left no offspring. To better understand the implications of the selection process for the individual, let us return to the case of that seemingly favored son John Harold Johnson, Jr. Sickle-cell anemia is now known to be caused by a gene that does not produce the disease when present in a single copy. However, as Mendel's work demonstrated, each offspring receives *two* copies of most genes—one from each parent. By chance, John Jr. received one sickle-cell gene from his father and one from his mother. But, because each parent had only one copy of the gene,

culture
socially transmitted knowledge, customs, and behavior of a group of people

they did not express the disease. Thus, knowledge of genetics lets us understand how John Jr. could have sickle-cell anemia even though his parents and sibling did not.

That leaves the question of how to account for the persistence of the sickle-cell gene in the human population. Why has such a potentially lethal genetic disease continued to plague humanity? Here, natural selection, not genetics, provides the answer. The sickle-cell gene is found primarily in people who trace their ancestry to populations that previously lived around the Mediterranean. In that region, humans have long co-existed with an insect called the *Anopheles mosquito.* This mosquito obtains the proteins needed to produce its eggs from human blood and, in the process of biting humans to get the blood, injects them with the parasite that causes malaria. The parasite then reproduces inside red-blood cells and, from time-to-time, releases more parasites from the infected cells. In so doing, the infected blood cells are destroyed. The destruction of these cells produces the symptoms of malaria—chills, anemia (due to insufficient oxygen), and, not uncommonly, death. When blood vessels in the brain and other organs become clogged with the debris of the destroyed cells, those organs are damaged. Even today, almost two out of every 100 children under four years of age die of malarial infection in countries such as Angola and Sierra Leone.

What does the prevalence of malaria in John Jr.'s ancestors have to do with the persistence of the sickle-cell gene? The sickle-cell gene was selected in this ancestral population of humans because one copy of the gene causes only those few red-blood cells that were initially infected by the parasite to sickle. These few misshapen cells are then removed by the spleen and the parasite dies. Parents with only one copy of the gene are thus more likely to live long enough to have children and only one out of every four of their children will be unlucky enough to receive two copies of the gene. Thus the *population* of humans in this region benefits from the persistence of the sickle-cell gene. On the average, two out of every four children receive immunity from malaria because they have only a single copy of the gene, one child remains susceptible to malaria because he has no copy of the gene, and one child suffers sickle-cell anemia because he receives two copies. Thus, on the average, the sickle-cell gene benefits the survival of the population as a whole: Twice as many offspring benefit as lose from the continued existence of the gene. Individuals such as John Harold Johnson, Jr. pay a heavy price as the legacy of that long-ago benefit. In the environment of the United States, infection by the malarial parasite is almost nonexistent. The introduction of insecticides into the environment has eliminated the prior benefit of the sickle-cell gene, but its cost remains.

The unfortunate case of John Harold Johnson, Jr. teaches us two general and important lessons about evolution through natural selection. First, the adaptations arising from natural selection are understandable on the level of *populations* of individuals, not on the level of the individual. Although it is individuals who live or die, who reproduce or not, it is the effect of their fate on the *population* that determines the course of natural selection. John Jr. died because the genes that he carried benefited the population of which his ancestors were members. The second lesson that John Jr. teaches us is that *past* environments determine the effects of natural selection on the individual. To the extent that the present is like the past, we are well adapted. However, when the present differs from the past—as in John Jr.'s case—the illusion is shattered. Strictly speaking, natural selection "prepares" us to live in the past. It is only to the extent that past environments resemble later environments that we are adapted to the present and the future.

At first glance, evolution through natural selection seems a simple idea: If the environment favors the survival of organisms having some characteristic, then that characteristic—if heritable—becomes more common over successive generations. The complex implications of natural selection emerge only upon closer examination. As the philosopher of biology David Hull commented, "Evolution is so simple, anyone can misunderstand it." Natural selection occurs in one environment, but its effects are felt in later environments. If the later environments are similar to the environment in which the characteristic was selected, then the population is adapted to the later environments. If the later environments differ from the ancestral environment, then the illusion of adaptation is shattered. Natural selection is only as far-sighted as the environment is constant. As observed in Ecclesiastes of the Old Testament, "the race is . . . [not necessarily] . . . to the swift, the battle to the strong, or favor to men of skill. Time and chance happeneth to them all."

Summary

THE DEVELOPMENT OF EVOLUTIONARY SCIENCE

Charles Darwin observed the diversity of life during his voyage around the world in the naval ship *HMS Beagle*. On his return to England, he carried out additional observations and experiments on artificial selection. On the basis of this work, Darwin proposed that the diversity of life came about because the environment favored the survival of some organisms over others. Organisms with favored characteristics had a greater chance of surviving and producing offspring. The result of this natural-selection process was that the favored characteristics became more numerous over successive generations with different organisms becoming adapted to the different environments in which they lived.

For life to become more complex, the characteristics that were favored by natural selection had to be passed from one generation to the next. Only in that way could favored characteristics accumulate and lead to complex organisms. Darwin did not know how this happened, After his death Mendel's work on the breeding of peas was discovered and provided the answer. Mendel's work began the science of *genetics.* His work showed that the factors we now call genes were passed unchanged from one generation to the next. Thus favored characteristics could add up over time and life could become more complex under the guidance of the selecting environment.

Evolution through natural selection requires three components—*variation*, *selection*, and *retention*. Variation is required for evolutionary change. It provides the differences in characteristics that selection can favor or disfavor. Selection is the result of differential reproduction of those organisms whose characteristics benefit the survival of themselves and, ultimately, their offspring. Retention allows the favored characteristics to be passed to the next generation by genetic mechanisms, thus permitting the effects of selection to accumulate.

For religious reasons, some people in the United States and elsewhere do not accept evolution through natural selection, especially with regard to the origin of humans. Natural selection is most clearly seen at the level of *populations* of individuals, not at the level of each individual. Natural selection affects the behavior of *organisms* as well as their structures: The effect of a structure on reproductive fitness depends on how that structure is used. As an example, the beautiful feathers of a peacock's tail do not affect his reproductive fitness unless he displays the feathers when he sights a peahen and the display is favored by the peahen. Natural selection increases adaptation in the present environment only to the extent that the selecting environments of the past are like those of present.

EVOLUTION OF HUMANS

Human evolution can be traced through changes in *fossils*, by methods such as *carbon dating* and DNA analysis, and by the *molecular clock* through counting *nucleotide exchanges.* Using these techniques *hominids* (*bipedal* apes) first came on the scene some 4 to 6 million years ago in southeastern Africa. For about 2 million years, our hominid ancestors remained in Africa, becoming larger and progressively more proficient bipedal walkers and more skillful users of their hands. These hominids are classified in a new genus, *Homo,* when the size of their brains increased to about twice that of present-day chimpanzees and tool-making became more proficient. Species of this genus began to move out of Africa about 2 million years ago in three major, successive partially overlapping waves, first *H. erectus*, then *H. neanderthalis*, and finally *H. sapiens*. They spread across much of Europe, Africa, Asia, and Oceania and, finally, *H. sapiens* came to the Americas. Only the last of these species remains—our own.

HEREDITY, GENETICS, AND EVOLUTION

The sequence of *nucleotides* within a *gene* controls the synthesis of proteins, which in turn make up the structure of the body. Genes are found on *chromosomes*, each of which usually contains thousands of genes. We inherit 23 individual chromosomes from each parent. The genetic endowment of individuals is a *recombination* of the genes of their parents. The recombination of genes produces tremendous genetic diversity. Genetic diversity provides the variation upon which natural selection operates and increases the possibility of adapting to changing environmental conditions.

The expression of a gene depends on several factors, whether it is a *dominant* or a *recessive* gene, how it interacts with other genes (*polygenic* traits), whether the sex of the individual is male or female, and how the environment under which that individual lives interacts with the gene. *Mutations* and *chromosomal aberrations* can change genes and alter their expression. For example, *hemophilia*, which decreases the ability of blood to clot, is the result of a mutation. *Down's syndrome*, which impairs mental development, is the result of a chromosomal aberration.

Behavior genetics is the study of how genes influence behavior. Psychologists and other scientists use both experimental methods, such as *artificial selection*, and *correlation methods*, such as *concordance* rates in *identical-twin* studies, to investigate the relation between genes and behavior.

HEREDITY AND HUMAN BEHAVIOR

The contributions of heredity and environment to human behavior are difficult to study because we cannot use experimental procedures to manipulate one variable while holding all others constant. However, experimental procedures such as *artificial selection* and *molecular knockouts* can be used with nonhuman animals and it clear from this work that genetic variables affect behavior. With humans, correlation procedures can be used to determine the *heritability* of a characteristic, that is, the proportion of the total variation in a characteristic that can be attributed to genetic influences. *Concordance research* and *segregation analysis* can also be used with humans because these methods do not manipulate either the environment or genes, but merely observe the relation between the presence of a gene and the occurrence of a behavior.

EVOLUTION AND HUMAN BEHAVIOR

Evolutionary psychology is concerned with the contribution of natural selection to human behavior and seeks to identify the adaptiveness of behavior. *Sociobiology* is the part of the field that studies those aspects of social behavior in animals and humans that are related to *reproductive* and *parental behavior* because this behavior is most directly affected by natural selection. Different *reproductive strategies* have evolved because of sex differences in the *parental investment* in procreation and child-rearing. Because of greater female parental investment, *polygynous* and *monogamous* reproductive strategies are most common in humans.

Altruism is an important topic of study because it presents an intriguing scientific puzzle. Why should natural selection favor a characteristic that could lower one's own reproductive success while increasing the reproductive success of others? Sociobiology provides two principal answers to this question—*inclusive fitness* and *reciprocal altruism*.

Evolutionary psychology has been criticized on several grounds, principally that environmental factors play a greater role than genetic factors in human behavior. It attempts to understand human behavior in an evolutionary context, not to justify that behavior. By appreciating the effect of the ancestral environment on current behavior, culture can devise *counter-selections* that change those aspects of behavior that are regarded as unhelpful.

Key Terms

allele (p. 100)
altruistic behavior (p. 111)
artificial selection (p. 87)
autosomes (p. 99)
behavior genetics (p. 105)
biological evolution (p. 89)
bipedalism (p. 93)
carbon dating (p. 93)
chromosomal aberration (p. 103)
chromosomes (p. 99)
concordance research (p. 107)
culture (p. 114)
DNA (p. 93)
dominant allele (p. 101)
Down's syndrome (p. 104)
enzymes (p. 98)
evolutionary psychology (p. 108)
fossil (p. 93)
gene (p. 89)
genetic engineering (p. 113)
genetic marker (p. 107)
genetics (p. 97)
genome (p. 98)
genotype (p. 101)
germ cells (p. 99)
heredity (p. 97)
heritability (p. 105)
hominids (p. 94)
Huntington's disease (p. 104)
inclusive fitness (p. 111)
kin selection (p. 111)
knockout mutations (p. 107)
meiosis (p. 99)
Mendelian traits (p.102)
molecular genetics (p. 106)
monogamy (p. 109)
mutation (p. 103)
natural selection (p. 88)
nonmendelian trait (p. 105)
parental investment (p. 109)
phenotype (p. 101)
phenylketonuria (PKU) (p. 104)
polygenic control (p. 101)
polygyny (p. 109)
recessive allele (p. 101)
reciprocal altruism (p. 111)
regulatory genes (p. 94)
retention (p. 90)
RNA (p. 98)
segregation analysis (p. 108)
selection (p. 89)
selectionism (p. 90)
sex chromosomes (p. 99)
sex-linked traits (p. 102)
sexual reproduction (p. 99)
sexual selection (p. 109)
sociobiology (p. 109)
variation (p. 89)

Suggestions for Further Reading

Wilson, D. S. (2007). *Evolution for everyone: How Darwin's theory can change the way we think about our lives*. New York: Delacorte Press.

A reader-friendly introduction to Darwin's ideas and their implications for our lives.

Dawkins, R. (1986). *The blind watchmaker*. New York: W. W. Norton and Company.

A very well-written discussion of the far-reaching implications of Darwinian thinking. One reviewer of the book commented: "Readers who are not outraged will be delighted."

Darwin, C. (1859). *On the origin of species by means of natural selection*. London: Murray.

Darwin's original presentation of evolution through natural selection. A must-read for any serious student of evolution that will disabuse many of their erroneous preconceptions of his ideas.

Plomin, R., DeFries, J. C., McClearn, G. E., & McGuffin, P. (2001). *Behavioral genetics* (4th ed.). New York: Worth Publishers.

A comprehensive and technical presentation of current research in behavioral genetics.

Wilson, E. O. (1975). *Sociobiology: The new synthesis*. Cambridge, MA: Harvard University Press.

The seminal work in the field of sociobiology—a well-written, graduate-level text.

Buss, D. M. (2007). *Evolutionary psychology: The new science of the mind.* Boston: Allyn & Bacon.

A comprehensive presentation of the field.

5

Biology and Behavior

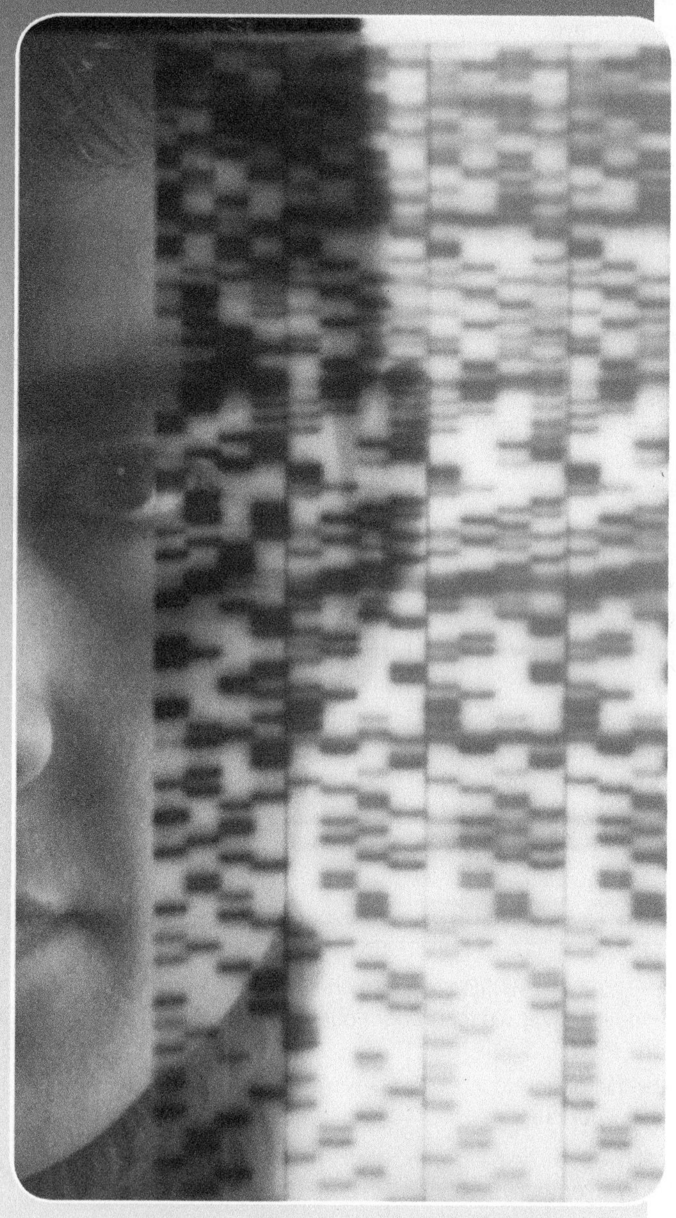

---

*Taken from *Mastering the World of Psychology,* Fifth Edition by Samuel E. Wood, Ellen Green Wood, and Denise Boyd

Think About It

Interpreting others' facial expressions is such a commonplace task that we usually do it without thinking about it. But your eyes can sometimes fool you. See if you can figure out which of the faces below is the happier of the two (Jaynes, 1976).

Which face did you say was the happier one? Your answer probably depended on whether you are right- or left-handed. You see, the brain tends to assign some tasks to the right side of the brain and others to the left. These assignments are correlated to some degree with handedness. For instance, if you are right-handed, you tend to use the right side of the brain to interpret emotions. Since the right side of the brain controls the left side of the body, you would use the left side of people's faces to make inferences about their emotional states (Abbott, Cumming, Fidler, & Lindell, 2012). Consequently, even though the faces in the drawing are mirror images, right-handed people tend to see the face on the left as the happier one. Left-handers display the opposite pattern. They rely on the left side of the brain to interpret emotions, and because the left side of the brain controls the right side of the body, they usually judge the face on the right to be the happier one.

How the brain divides functions between its left and right halves is just one of many interesting things about the biological foundations of behavior and mental processes that you will read about in this chapter. We will tell you much more about the brain and nervous system, and we will introduce you to the endocrine system. You will also read about genetics. Pay close attention to the information in this chapter.

Discovering the Mysteries of the Nervous System

How do we know what we know about the nervous system? Until quite recently, researchers had few techniques for directly studying it. Scientists relied on case studies of people in whom an injury to a specific part of the system, a *lesion*, had led to specific changes in behavior to identify the functions associated with the various parts of the system. For instance, because severe injuries to the back of the head were observed to result in visual problems, researchers were able to infer that the back of the brain was involved in vision. By the mid-19th century, researchers began making great strides in understanding the nervous system thanks to the availability of more powerful microscopes that enabled them to directly examine the nervous system tissues of deceased humans and animals. Today, scientists continue to use both case studies and microscopic tissue studies to answer questions about the nervous system. But since the early 20th century, researchers have also been able to observe the living brain in action. How do they do this? Through a variety of tools and imaging techniques, researchers are able to observe different parts of the brain and their functions. Exactly what the researcher is trying to study determines which tool or technique works best.

The EEG and the Microelectrode

5.1 What does the electroencephalogram (EEG) reveal about the brain?

In 1924, Austrian psychiatrist Hans Berger invented the electroencephalograph, a machine that records the electrical activity occurring in the brain. This electrical activity, detected by electrodes placed at various points on the scalp and amplified greatly, provides the power to drive a pen across paper, producing a record of brain-wave activity called an **electroencephalogram (EEG).**

electroencephalogram (EEG) (ee-lek-tro-en-SEFF-uh-lo-gram) A record of brain-wave activity made by a machine called the electroencephalograph

A computerized EEG imaging technique shows the different levels of electrical activity occurring every millisecond on the surface of the brain (Gevins et al., 1995). It can

(a)

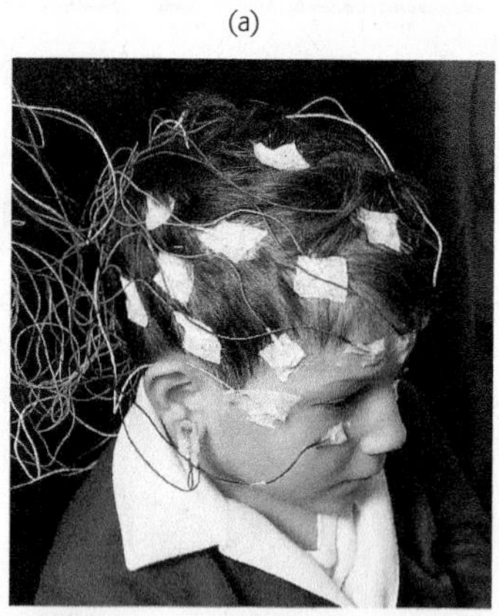

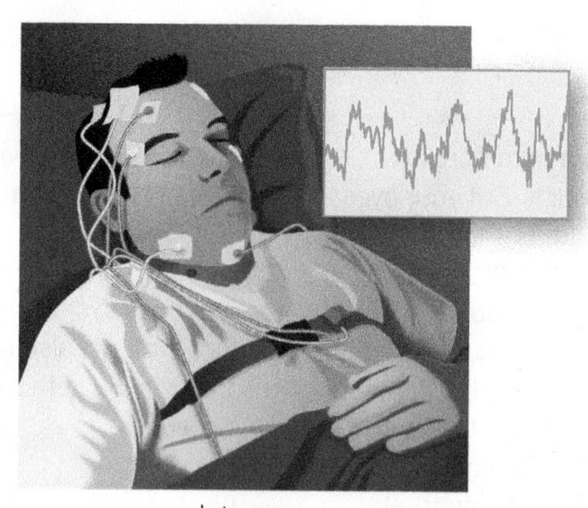

beta wave

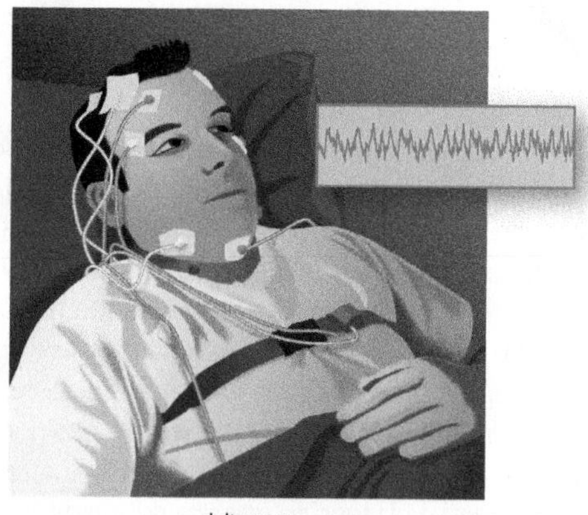

delta wave

The electroencephalograph, or EEG, uses electrodes placed on the scalp to amplify and record electrical activity in the brain, as shown in (a). An EEG typically measures brain waves while the person is awake and asleep, because the characteristics of the brain's electrical activity vary across sleeping and waking states, as shown in (b) and (c).

show an epileptic seizure in progress and can be used to study neural activity in people with schizophrenia, Alzheimer's disease, sleep disorders, and other neurological problems.

Although the EEG is able to detect electrical activity in different areas of the brain, it cannot reveal what is happening in individual neurons. However, the **microelectrode** inserted directly into the brain can. A microelectrode is a wire so small that it can be inserted near or into a single neuron without damaging it. Microelectrodes can be used to monitor the electrical activity of a single neuron or to stimulate activity within it. They are used in *intracranial electroencephalograms* (iEEG) that enable neurologists to pinpoint the precise neuronal origin of seizures in individuals who have epilepsy (Rummel et al., 2013).

5.2 How do researchers use imaging techniques to study the nervous system?

Imaging Techniques

Since the early 1970s, a number of techniques that provide scientists and physicians with images of the brain's structures have become available. For example, a person undergoing a **CT scan (computerized axial tomography)** of the brain is placed inside a large, doughnut-shaped structure where an X-ray tube encircles the entire head. The tube rotates in a complete circle, shooting X-rays through the brain as it does so. A series of computerized, cross-sectional images reveal the structures within the brain as well as abnormalities and injuries, including tumors and evidence of old or more recent strokes.

MRI (magnetic resonance imaging), which became widely available in the 1980s, produces clearer and more detailed images without exposing people to potentially dangerous X-rays (Potts, Davidson, & Krishman, 1993). MRI can be used to find abnormalities in the central nervous system and in other systems of the body. Although the CT scan and MRI do a remarkable job of showing what the brain looks like both inside and out, they cannot reveal what the brain is doing. But other technological marvels can.

Several techniques capture images of both brain structures and their functions. The oldest of these techniques, the **PET scan (positron-emission tomography)** has been used since the mid-1970s to identify malfunctions that cause physical and psychological disorders. For example, researchers have found that patterns of glucose metabolism in the brains of individual with autism differs from that of people who do not have this condition (Brasic & Kao, 2011). PET scanning has also been used to study normal brain activity. A PET scan maps the patterns of blood flow, oxygen use, and glucose consumption (glucose is the food of the brain). It can also show the action of drugs and other biochemical substances in the brain and other bodily organs (Farde, 1996).

A technique that became available in the 1990s, **functional MRI (fMRI)**, uses magnetic impulses to create images of brain structures and functions. It has several important advantages over PET: (1) it requires no injections (of radioactive or other material);

microelectrode
A small wire used to monitor the electrical activity of or stimulate activity within a single neuron

CT scan (computerized axial tomography)
A brain-scanning technique that uses a rotating, computerized X-ray tube to produce cross-sectional images of the structures of the brain

MRI (magnetic resonance imaging)
A diagnostic scanning technique that produces high-resolution images of the structures of the brain

PET scan (positron-emission tomography)
A brain-imaging technique that reveals activity in various parts of the brain, based on patterns of blood flow, oxygen use, and glucose consumption

functional MRI (fMRI)
A brain-imaging technique that reveals both brain structure and brain activity more precisely and rapidly than PET

(2) it can identify locations of activity more precisely than PET can; and (3) it can detect changes that take place in less than a second, compared with about a minute for PET ("Brain Imaging," 1997).

Still other imaging devices are now available. SQUID (superconducting quantum interference device) shows brain activity by measuring the magnetic changes produced by the electric current that neurons discharge when they fire. Another imaging marvel, MEG (magnetoencephalography), also measures such magnetic changes and shows neural activity within the brain as rapidly as it occurs, much faster than PET or fMRI. A new kind of MRI, diffusion tensor imaging (DTI), enables researchers to examine individual neuron bundles. These new techniques enable researchers and clinicians to identify the exact locations of brain lesions and malfunctions associated with conditions such as epilepsy, strokes, Alzheimer's disease, and multiple sclerosis with greater precision and speed than the older imaging techniques do.

Brain-imaging techniques have helped neuroscientists accumulate an impressive store of knowledge about brain functions such as memory (Logothetis, 2008). Studies using these imaging techniques have also shown that, to varying degrees, the structures and functions of the brain differ in people who have serious psychological disorders from those who do not. In addition, imaging techniques have revealed where and how drugs affect the brain (Gorman, 2007). Some neuroscientists have experimented with combining virtual reality with fMRI to study how the brain responds to situations and environments that would be impossible to observe using conventional imaging techniques (Wiederhold & Wiederhold, 2008). For example, virtual reality therapy is useful for treating phobias such as fear of flying. By using fMRI monitoring in conjunction with virtual reality treatments that simulate real-world situations that trigger phobic responses, researchers can determine how the brain processes such treatments. The information that researchers obtain the fMRI helps them improve the effectiveness of virtual reality interventions.

Remember It

1. The CT scan and MRI are used to produce images of the ______________ of the brain.
2. The ______________ reveals the electrical activity of the brain by producing a record of brain waves.
3. A ______________ scan reveals brain activity and function, rather than the structure of the brain.
4. A newer imaging technique called ______________ reveals both brain structure and brain activity.

The Neurons and the Neurotransmitters

Earlier we mentioned that 19th-century researchers used microscopes to study the nervous system tissues of deceased humans and animals. These studies led to the discovery of the specialized cells that conduct impulses through the nervous system, the **neurons**. In the early 20th century, the invention of the microelectrode allowed researchers to study the connections between neurons. These studies revealed the existence of chemicals that are essential to nervous system functioning. These chemicals, the **neurotransmitters**, can facilitate or inhibit the transmission of impulses from one neuron to the next. Working together, neurons and neurotransmitters convey messages within the nervous system and from the nervous system to other parts of the body.

neuron
(NEW-ron) A specialized cell that conducts impulses through the nervous system

neurotransmitters
Specialized chemicals that facilitate or inhibit the transmission of impulses from one neuron to the next

5.3 What does each part of the neuron do?

The Structure of the Neuron

All of our thoughts, feelings, and behavior can ultimately be traced to the activity of neurons. Afferent (sensory) neurons relay messages from the sense organs and receptors—eyes, ears, nose, mouth, and skin—to the brain or spinal cord. Efferent (motor) neurons convey signals from the central nervous system to the glands and the muscles, enabling the body to move. Interneurons, thousands of times more numerous than motor or sensory neurons, carry information between neurons in the brain and between neurons in the spinal cord.

Although no two neurons are exactly alike, nearly all are made up of three important parts: the cell body, the dendrites, and the axon. The **cell body**, or *soma,* contains the nucleus and carries out the metabolic, or life-sustaining, functions of a neuron. Branching out from the cell body are the **dendrites**, which look much like the leafless branches of a tree (*dendrite* comes from the Greek word for "tree"). The dendrites are the primary receivers of signals from other neurons, but the cell body can also receive signals directly.

The **axon** is the slender, tail-like extension of the neuron that sprouts into many branches, each ending in a bulbous **axon terminal**. Signals move from the axon terminals to the dendrites or cell bodies of other neurons and to muscles, glands, and other parts of the body. In humans, some axons are short—only thousandths of an inch long. Others can be as long as a meter (39.37 inches)—long enough to reach from the brain to the tip of the spinal cord, or from the spinal cord to remote parts of the body. Figure 5.1 shows the structure of a neuron.

Glial cells are specialized cells in the brain and spinal cord that support the neurons. They are smaller than neurons and make up more than one-half the volume of the human brain. Glial cells remove waste products, such as dead neurons, from the brain by engulfing and digesting them, and they handle other manufacturing, nourishing, and cleanup tasks. Glial cells in the spinal cord are also involved in pain sensations that are associated with damaged nerves (Gwak, Kang, Unabia, & Hulsebosch, 2012).

5.4 How do neurons transmit messages through the nervous system?

Communication between Neurons

Remarkably, the billions of neurons that send and receive signals are not physically connected. The axon terminals are separated from the receiving neurons by tiny, fluid-filled gaps called *synaptic clefts*. The **synapse** is the junction where the axon terminal of a sending (presynaptic) neuron communicates with a receiving (postsynaptic) neuron across the synaptic cleft. It is estimated that one cubic centimeter of the cerebral cortex, the brain's outer covering, contains as a trillion synapses (Drachman, 2005). A single neuron may also form thousands of synapses with other neurons (Drachmann, 2005). If neurons aren't connected, how do they communicate with one another?

A small but measurable electrical impulse is present every time you move or have a thought. As the impulse travels down the axon, the permeability of the cell membrane (its capability of being penetrated or passed through) changes. In other words, the membrane changes in a way that makes it easier for molecules to move through it and into the cell. This process allows ions (electrically charged atoms or molecules) to move into and out of the axon through ion channels in the membrane.

Body fluids contain ions, some with positive electrical charges and others with negative charges. Inside the axon, there are normally more negative than positive ions. When at rest (not firing), the axon membrane carries a negative electrical potential of about –70 millivolts (–70 thousandths of a volt) relative to the fluid outside the cell. This slight negative charge is referred to as the neuron's **resting potential**.

When an impulse reaches a neuron, ion channels begin to open in the cell membrane of the axon at the point closest to the cell body, allowing positive ions to flow into the axon (see Figure 5.2 on p. 124). This inflow of positive ions causes the membrane potential to change abruptly, to a positive value of about +50 millivolts (Pinel, 2000). This sudden reversal of the resting potential, which lasts for about 1 millisecond (1 thousandth of a second), is the **action potential**. Then, the ion channels admitting positive ions close, and other ion channels open, forcing some positive ions out of the

cell body
The part of a neuron that contains the nucleus and carries out the metabolic functions of the neuron

dendrites
(DEN-drytes) In a neuron, the branch-like extensions of the cell body that receive signals from other neurons

axon
(AK-sahn) The slender, tail-like extension of the neuron that transmits signals to the dendrites or cell body of other neurons and to muscles, glands, and other parts of the body

axon terminal
Bulbous end of the axon where signals move from the axon of one neuron to the dendrites or cell body of another

glial cells
(GLEE-ul) Specialized cells in the brain and spinal cord that support neurons, remove waste products such as dead neurons, and perform other manufacturing, nourishing, and cleanup tasks

synapse
(SIN-aps) The junction where the axon terminal of a sending neuron communicates with a receiving neuron across the synaptic cleft

resting potential
The slight negative electrical potential of the axon membrane of a neuron at rest, about –70 millivolts

action potential
The sudden reversal of the resting potential, which initiates the firing of a neuron

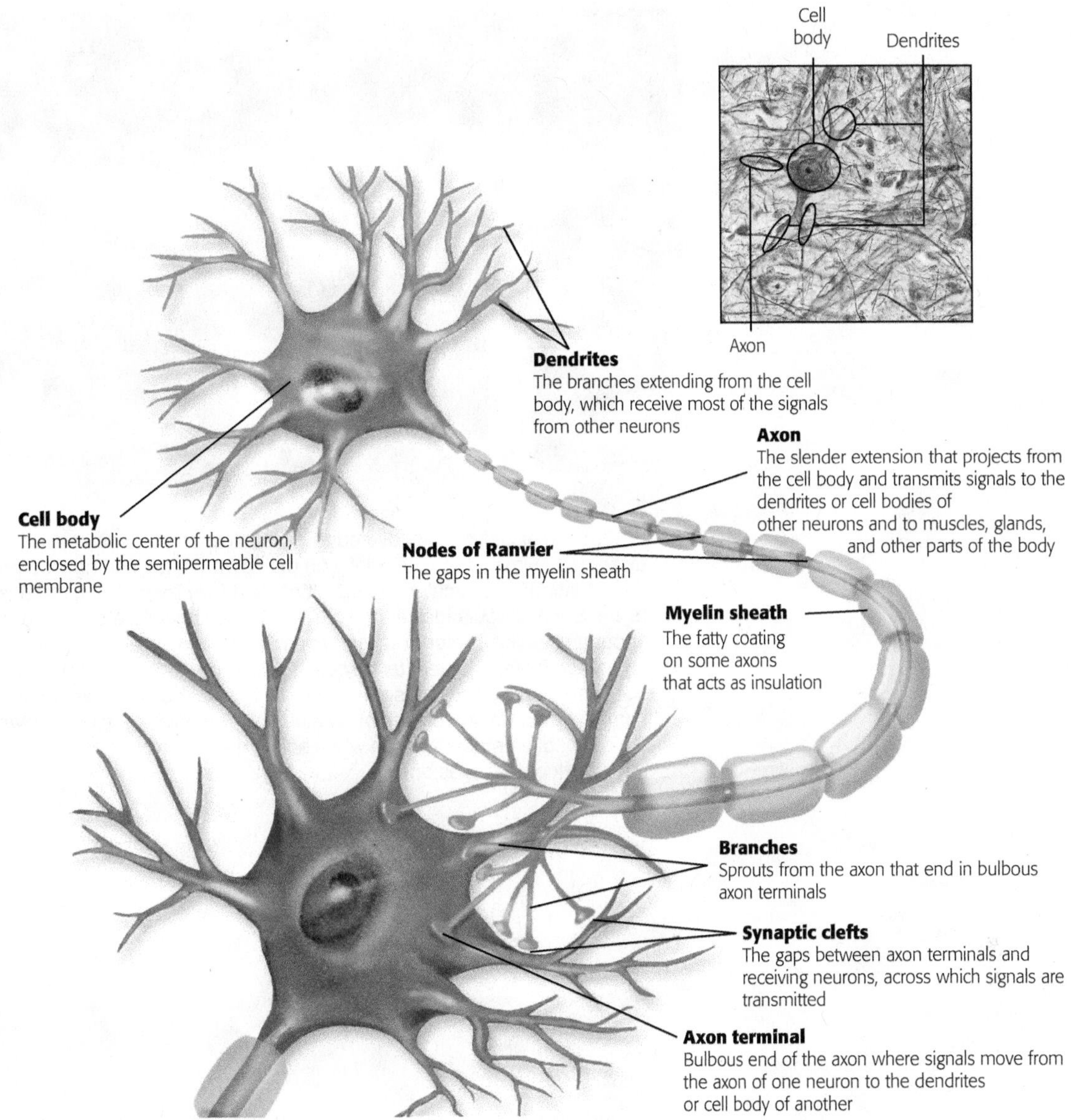

Figure 5.1 The Structure of a Typical Neuron
A typical neuron has three important parts: (1) a cell body, which carries out the metabolic functions of the neuron; (2) branched fibers called dendrites, which are the primary receivers of the impulses from other neurons; and (3) a slender, tail-like extension called an axon, the transmitting end of the neuron, which sprouts into many branches, each ending in an axon terminal. The photograph shows human neurons greatly magnified.

axon. As a result, the original negative charge, or resting potential, is restored. The opening and closing of ion channels continues, segment by segment, down the length of the axon, causing the action potential to move along the axon (Cardoso de Mello & Sabbatini, 2000). The action potential operates according to the "all-or-none" law—a neuron either fires completely or does not fire at all. Immediately after a neuron fires, it enters a *refractory period,* during which it cannot fire again for 1 to 2 milliseconds. But even with these short resting periods, neurons can fire hundreds of times per second.

If a neuron only fires or does not fire, how can we tell the difference between a very strong and a very weak stimulus? In other words, what is the neurological distinction between feeling anxious about being disciplined by your boss for being late to work and running for your life to avoid being the victim of a criminal attacker? The answer lies in the number of neurons firing at the same time and their rate of firing. A weak stimulus may cause relatively few neurons to fire, while a strong stimulus may trigger thousands of neurons to fire at the same time. Also, a weak stimulus may be signaled by neurons firing very slowly; a stronger stimulus may incite neurons to fire hundreds of times per second.

In 1786, Luigi Galvani discovered that electrical stimulation caused the muscles of dissected animals to move briefly on their own. These findings led proponents of "reanimation" to speculate that a jolt of electricity might bring dead organisms back to life. Such speculations inspired Mary Shelley to write a shocking (at the time) novel about a scientist, Victor Frankenstein, who developed a procedure for reanimating human corpses, *Frankenstein: The Modern Prometheus*, first published in 1818. Although scientists have known for some time that the link between electricity and life is far more complex than the advocates of reanimation imagined, Shelley's powerful message about the moral dilemmas that arise when science enables humankind to grant and withhold the "spark of life" lives on.

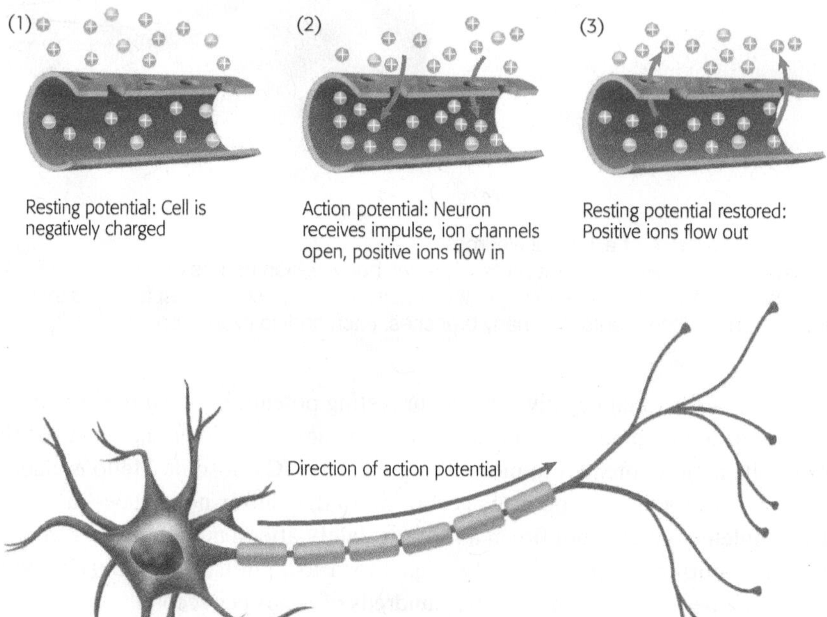

Figure 5.2 The Action Potential
The action potential moves down the axon to the axon terminals.
Source: Adapted from Lilienfeld, Lynn, Namy, & Wolf (2009).

Impulses travel at speeds from about 1 meter per second to approximately 100 meters per second (about 224 miles per hour). The most important factor in speeding the impulse on its way is the **myelin sheath**—a white, fatty coating wrapped around most axons that acts as insulation. If you look again at Figure 5.1 (p. 123), you will see that the coating has numerous gaps, called *nodes of Ranvier*. The electrical impulse is retriggered or regenerated at each node (or naked gap) on the axon. This regeneration makes the impulse up to 100 times faster than impulses in axons without myelin sheaths. Damage to the myelin sheath causes interruptions in the transmission of neural messages. In fact, the disease multiple sclerosis (MS) involves deterioration of the myelin sheath, resulting in loss of coordination, jerky movements, muscular weakness, and disturbances in speech.

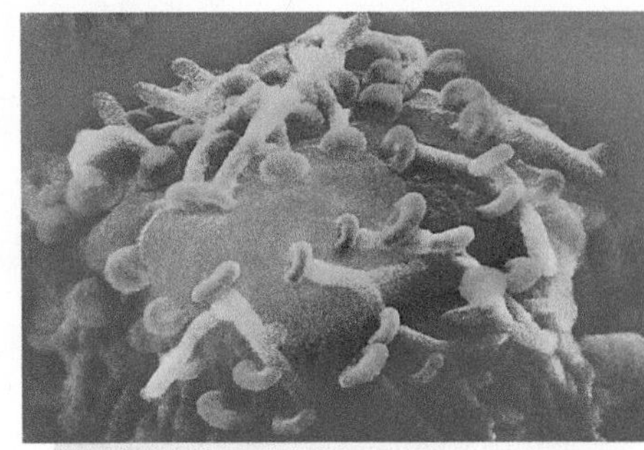

This scanning electron micrograph shows numerous axon terminals (the orange, button-shaped structures) that could synapse with the cell body of the neuron (shown in green).

Neurotransmitters

5.5 How do neurotransmitters work?

Once a neuron fires, how does it get its message across the synaptic cleft and on to another neuron? Inside the axon terminal are many small, sphere-shaped containers with thin membranes called *synaptic vesicles,* which hold the neurotransmitters. (*Vesicle* comes from a Latin word meaning "little bladder.") When an action potential arrives at the axon terminal, synaptic vesicles move toward the cell membrane, fuse with it, and release their neurotransmitter molecules. This process is shown in Figure 5.3.

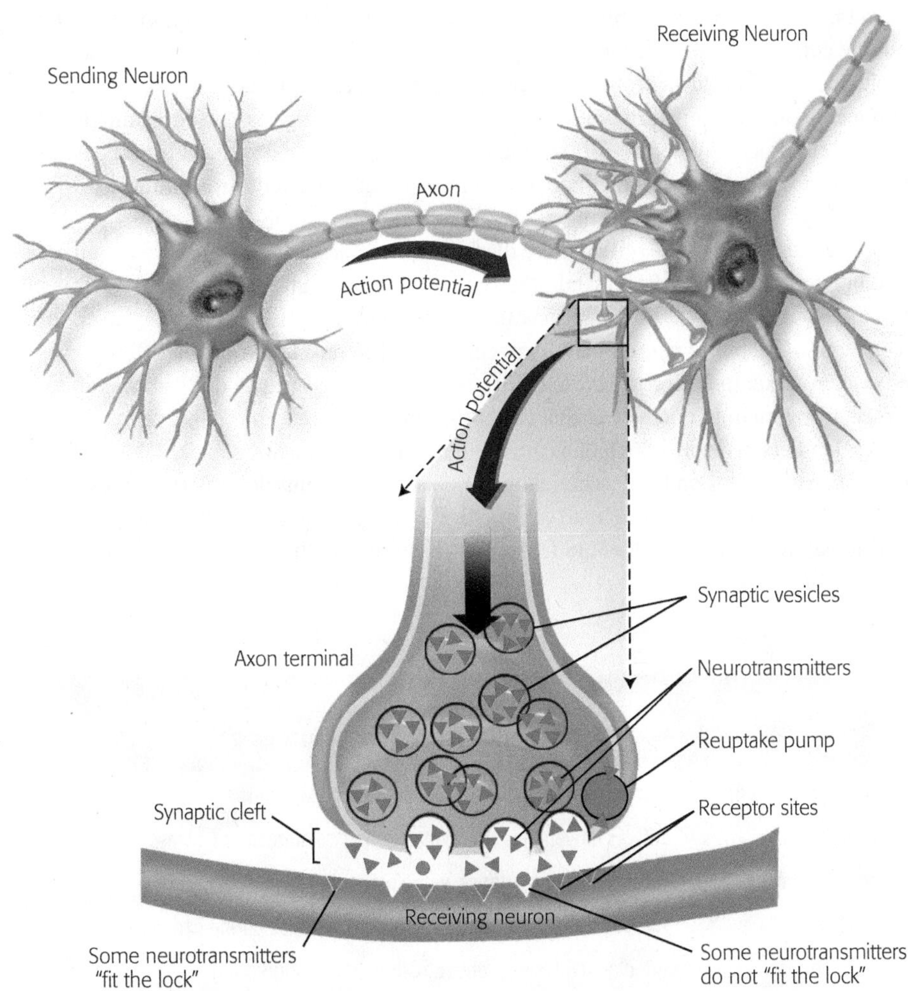

Figure 5.3 Synaptic Transmission
Sending neurons transmit their messages to receiving neurons by electrochemical action. When a neuron fires, the action potential arrives at the axon terminal and triggers the release of neurotransmitters from the synaptic vesicles. Neurotransmitters flow into the synaptic cleft and move toward the receiving neuron, which has numerous receptors. The receptors will bind only with neurotransmitters whose molecular shapes match their enclosed volumes. Neurotransmitters influence the receiving neuron to fire or not to fire.

myelin sheath
(MY-uh-lin) The white, fatty coating wrapped around some axons that acts as insulation and enables impulses to travel much faster

Once released, neurotransmitters do not simply flow into the synaptic cleft and stimulate all the adjacent neurons. Each neurotransmitter has a distinctive molecular shape, as do **receptors**, which are protein molecules on the surfaces of dendrites and cell bodies. In other words, each receptor is somewhat like a lock that only certain neurotransmitter keys can unlock. However, the binding of neurotransmitters with receptors is not as fixed and rigid a process as keys fitting locks or jigsaw puzzle pieces interlocking. Receptors on neurons are somewhat flexible; they can expand and contract their enclosed volumes. And neurotransmitters of different types can have similar shapes. Thus, two different neurotransmitters may compete for the same receptor. The receptor will admit only one of the competing neurotransmitters—the one that fits it best. A receptor may receive a certain neurotransmitter sometimes but not receive it in the presence of a better-fitting neurotransmitter.

The neurotransmitter acetylcholine helps you process new information by facilitating neural transmissions involved in learning.

When neurotransmitters bind with receptors on the dendrites or cell bodies of receiving neurons, their action is either excitatory (influencing the neurons to fire) or inhibitory (influencing them not to fire). Because a single receiving neuron may have synapses with thousands of other neurons at the same time, it will always be subject to both excitatory and inhibitory influences from incoming neurotransmitters. For the neuron to fire, the excitatory influences must exceed the inhibitory influences by a sufficient amount (the threshold).

You may wonder how the synaptic vesicles can continue to pour out neurotransmitters, yet maintain a ready supply so that the neuron can respond to continuing stimulation. First, the cell body of the neuron is always working to manufacture more of the neurotransmitter. Second, unused neurotransmitters in the synaptic cleft may be broken down into components and reclaimed by the axon terminal to be recycled and used again. Third, by an important process called **reuptake**, the neurotransmitter is taken back into the axon terminal, intact and ready for immediate use. This terminates the neurotransmitter's excitatory or inhibitory effect on the receiving neuron.

Researchers have identified more than 100 chemical substances that are manufactured in the brain, spinal cord, glands, and other parts of the body and may act as neurotransmitters (Purves et al., 2011). Table 5.1 lists the major neurotransmitters. As you look over the table, keep in mind that neurotransmitters can serve different functions in different parts of the body. For example, *acetylcholine* (Ach) exerts excitatory effects on the skeletal muscle fibers, causing them to contract so that the body can move. But it has an inhibitory effect on the muscle fibers in the heart, which keeps the heart from beating too rapidly. Thus, when you run to make it to class on time, acetylcholine helps your leg muscles contract quickly, while simultaneously preventing your heart muscle from pumping so rapidly that you pass out. The differing natures of the receptors on the receiving neurons in the two kinds of muscles cause

receptors
Protein molecules on the surfaces of dendrites and cell bodies that have distinctive shapes and will interact only with specific neurotransmitters

reuptake
The process by which neurotransmitters are taken from the synaptic cleft back into the axon terminal for later use, thus terminating their excitatory or inhibitory effect on the receiving neuron

Table 5.1 Major Neurotransmitters and Their Functions

Neurotransmitter	Functions
Acetylcholine (Ach)	Affects movement, learning, memory, REM sleep
Dopamine (DA)	Affects movement, attention, learning, reinforcement, pleasure
Norepinephrine (NE)	Affects eating, alertness, wakefulness
Epinephrine	Affects metabolism of glucose, energy release during exercise
Serotonin	Affects mood, sleep, appetite, impulsivity, aggression
Glutamate	Active in areas of the brain involved in learning, thought, and emotion
GABA	Facilitates neural inhibition in the central nervous system
Endorphins	Provide relief from pain and feelings of pleasure and well-being

these opposite effects. Acetylcholine also plays an excitatory role in stimulating the neurons involved in learning new information. So, as you are reading this text, acetylcholine is helping you understand and store the information in your memory.

Drugs influence the nervous system through their action on neurotransmitters. For instance, responses to cocaine involve the neurotransmitters *dopamine* and *glutamate* (Fasano et al., 2009). Moreover, you will learn that researchers have discovered links between neurotransmitter functioning and several psychological disorders. For example, researchers suspect that the neurotransmitter *dopamine* plays a role in attention-deficit/hyperactivity disorder (ADHD) (Volkow et al., 2009).

Remember It

1. The branchlike extensions of neurons that act as the *primary* receivers of signals from other neurons are the ________________.
2. ________________ support neurons, supplying them with nutrients and carrying away their waste products.
3. The ________________ is the junction where the axon of a sending neuron communicates with a receiving neuron.
4. When a neuron fires, neurotransmitters are released from the synaptic vesicles in the ________________ into the ________________.
5. The ________________ potential is the firing of a neuron; the ________________ potential is the state in which the cell membrane is relatively impermeable.
6. Receptor sites on the receiving neuron receive only neurotransmitter molecules whose ________________ is similar to theirs.
7. The neurotransmitter called ________________ keeps the heart from beating too fast.
8. ________________ affects eating habits by stimulating the intake of carbohydrates.
9. ________________ are neurotransmitters that act as natural painkillers.

The Human Nervous System

Now that you understand how the cells of the nervous system function, you're ready to learn more about how the system is organized. As you can see in Figure 5.4, there are two major divisions in the system. You'll be happy to learn that it's easy to remember the difference between the two. The **peripheral nervous system (PNS)** includes all of the nerves (i.e., bundles of neurons) that are not encased in bone, that is, all of the neural tissue that lies outside your skull and backbone. The function of these tissues is to transmit messages to and from the body and brain. The **central nervous system (CNS)** includes all of the neural tissues inside the skull and backbone. In other words, the CNS is made up of the spinal cord and brain.

5.6 What are the structures and functions of the peripheral nervous system?

The Peripheral Nervous System

What makes your heart pound and palms sweat when you watch a scary movie? Such reactions are the result of signals from the brain's limbic system and other structures that regulate emotions to the peripheral nervous system. The peripheral nervous system (PNS) is made up of all the nerves that connect the central nervous system to the rest of the body. It has two subdivisions: the somatic nervous system and the autonomic nervous system, which is further divided into the sympathetic nervous system and parasympathetic nervous system.

peripheral nervous system (PNS) (peh-RIF-er-ul) The nerves connecting the central nervous system to the rest of the body

central nervous system (CNS) The part of the nervous system comprising the brain and the spinal cord

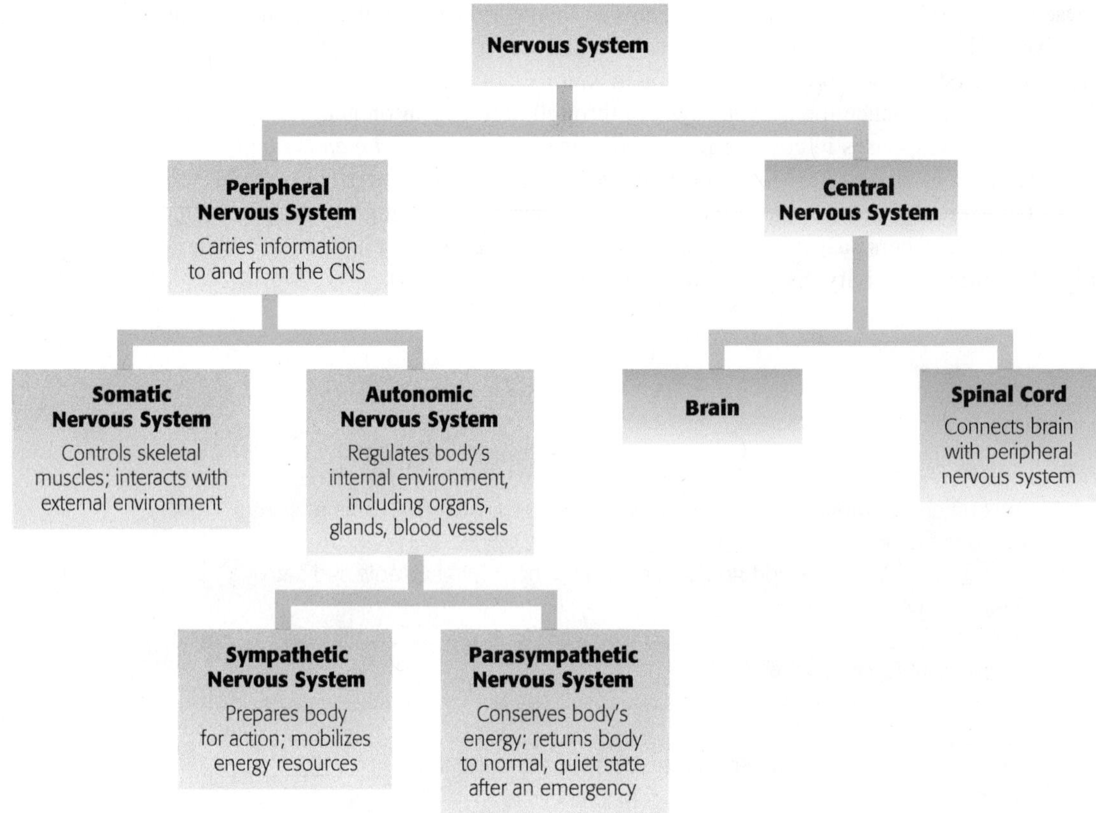

Figure 5.4 The Human Nervous System
The nervous system is divided into two parts: the peripheral nervous system and the central nervous system. The diagram shows the relationships among the parts of the nervous system and provides a brief description of the functions of those parts.

The *somatic nervous system* consists of (1) all the sensory nerves, which transmit information from the sense receptors—eyes, ears, nose, tongue, and skin—to the central nervous system, and (2) all the motor nerves, which relay messages from the central nervous system to all the skeletal muscles of the body. In short, the nerves of the somatic nervous system make it possible for you to sense your environment and to move, and they are primarily under conscious control.

The *autonomic nervous system* operates without any conscious control or awareness on your part. It transmits messages between the central nervous system and the glands, the cardiac (heart) muscle, and the smooth muscles (such as those in the large arteries and the gastrointestinal system), which are not normally under voluntary control. This system is further divided into two parts—the sympathetic and the parasympathetic nervous systems.

Any time you are under stress or faced with an emergency, the **sympathetic nervous system** automatically mobilizes the body's resources, preparing you for action. This physiological arousal produced by the sympathetic nervous system was named the *fight-or-flight response* by Walter Cannon (1929, 1935). If an ominous-looking stranger started following you down a dark, deserted street, your sympathetic nervous system would automatically go to work. Your heart would begin to pound, your pulse rate would increase rapidly, your breathing would quicken, your digestive system would nearly shut down, and the blood flow to your skeletal muscles would be enhanced. These reactions would make all of your bodily resources ready to handle the emergency.

sympathetic nervous system
The division of the autonomic nervous system that mobilizes the body's resources during stress and emergencies, preparing the body for action

parasympathetic nervous system
The division of the autonomic nervous system that brings the heightened bodily responses back to normal following an emergency

Once the emergency is over, the **parasympathetic nervous system** brings these heightened bodily functions back to normal. As a result of its action, your heart stops pounding and slows to normal, your pulse rate and breathing slow down, and your digestive system resumes its normal functioning. As shown in Figure 5.5 the sympathetic and parasympathetic

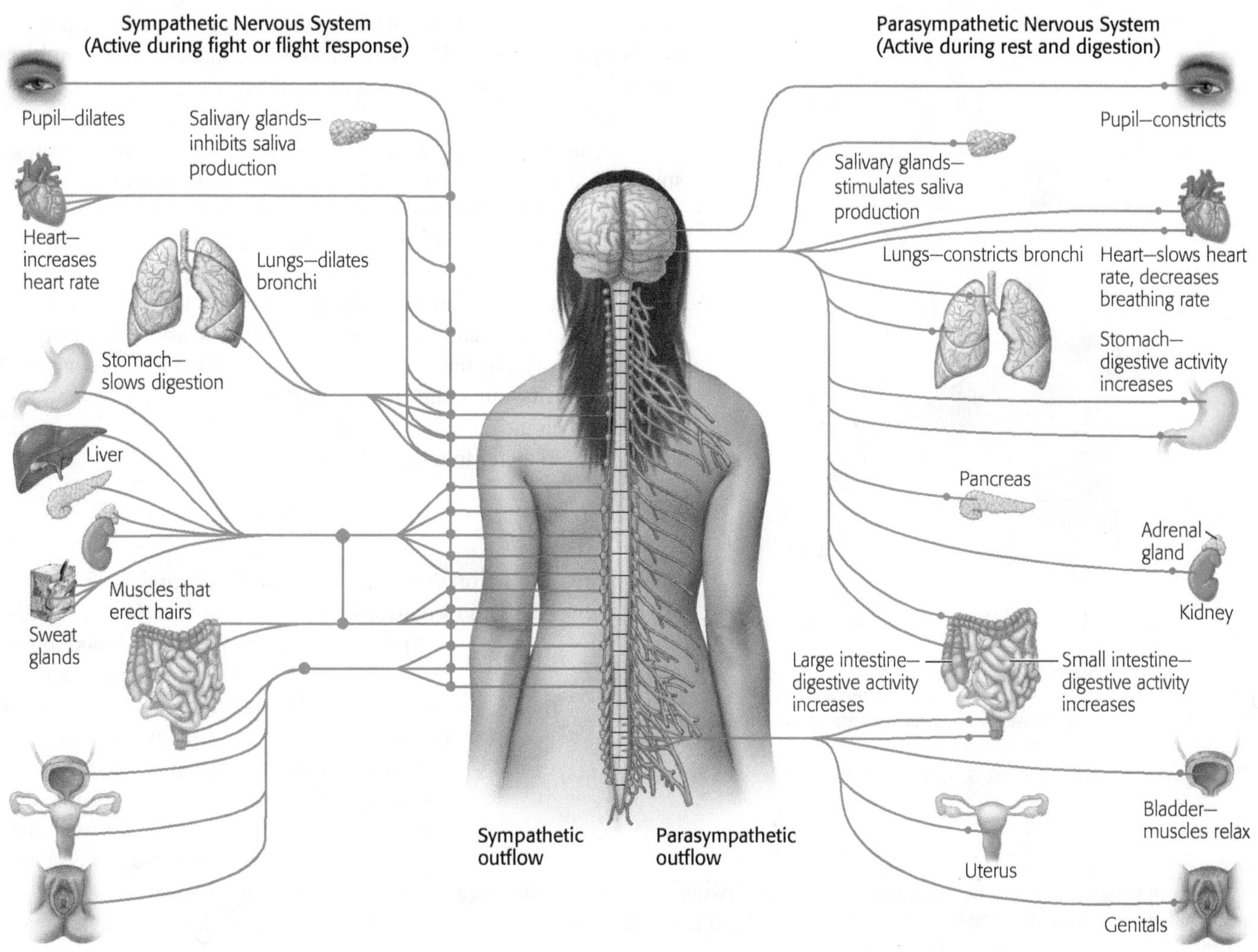

Figure 5.5 The Autonomic Nervous System
The autonomic nervous system consists of (1) the sympathetic nervous system, which mobilizes the body's resources during emergencies or stress, and (2) the parasympathetic nervous system, which brings the heightened bodily responses back to normal afterward. This diagram shows the opposite effects of the sympathetic and parasympathetic nervous systems on various parts of the human body.
Source: Lilienfeld, Lynn, Namy, & Woolf (2009).

branches act as opposing but complementary forces in the autonomic nervous system. Their balanced functioning is essential for health and survival.

The Central Nervous System

5.7 What are the structures and functions of the central nervous system?

As we noted earlier, the central nervous system includes the spinal cord and the brain. The spinal cord is the link between the peripheral nervous system and the brain. As you will see, the brain itself includes several different components, each of which has distinctive functions.

The Spinal Cord

The **spinal cord** can best be thought of as an extension of the brain. A cylinder of neural tissue about the diameter of your little finger, the spinal cord reaches from the base of the brain, through the neck, and down the hollow center of the spinal column. It is protected by bone and also by spinal fluid, which serves as a shock absorber. The spinal cord literally

spinal cord
An extension of the brain, from the base of the brain through the neck and spinal column, that transmits messages between the brain and the peripheral nervous system

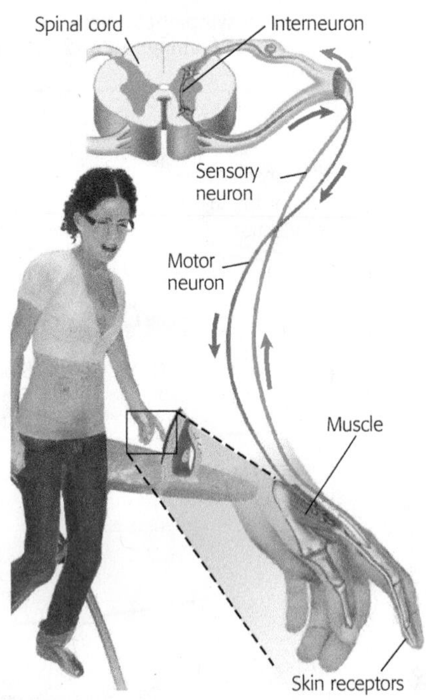

Figure 5.6 The Spinal Reflex
The sequence that begins with a sensory stimulus (such as touching something hot) and ends with a behavioral response (withdrawing the hand) involves sensory neurons, interneurons, and motor neurons.
Source: Adapted from Lilienfeld, S., Lynn, S., Namy, L., & Woolf, N. (2009).

links the body with the brain. It transmits messages between the brain and nerves in other parts of the body. Thus, sensory information can reach the brain, and messages from the brain can be sent to the muscles, the glands, and other parts of the body.

Although the spinal cord and the brain usually function together, the spinal cord can act without help from the brain to protect the body from injury. A simple withdrawal reflex triggered by a painful stimulus—touching a hot iron, for example—involves three types of neurons (see Figure 5.6). Sensory neurons in your fingers detect the painful stimulus and relay this information to interneurons in the spinal cord. These interneurons activate motor neurons that control the muscles in your arm and cause you to jerk your hand away. All this happens within a fraction of a second, without any involvement of your brain. However, the brain quickly becomes aware and involved when the pain signal reaches it. At that point, you might plunge your hand into cold water to relieve the pain.

The Hindbrain

Brain structures are often grouped into the *hindbrain,* the *midbrain,* and the *forebrain,* as shown in Figure 5.7 (p. 131). The structures of the **hindbrain** control heart rate, respiration, blood pressure, and many other vital functions. The part of the hindbrain known as the **brainstem** begins at the site where the spinal cord enlarges as it enters the skull. The brainstem handles functions that are so critical to physical survival that damage to it is life threatening. The **medulla** is the part of the brainstem that controls heartbeat, breathing, blood pressure, coughing, and swallowing. Fortunately, the medulla handles these functions automatically, so you do not have to decide consciously to breathe or remember to keep your heart beating.

Above the medulla and at the top of the brainstem is a bridgelike structure called the **pons** that extends across the top front of the brainstem and connects to both halves of the cerebellum. The pons plays a role in body movement and even exerts an influence on sleep and dreaming.

Extending through the central core of the brainstem into the pons is another important structure, the **reticular formation**, sometimes called the *reticular activating system* (RAS) (refer to Figure 5.7). The reticular formation plays a crucial role in arousal and attention (Gadea et al., 2004). For example, a driver may be listening intently to a radio program when, suddenly, a car cuts in front of her. In response, the reticular formation blocks the sensory information coming from the radio and fixes the driver's attention on the potential danger posed by the other driver's action. Once the traffic pattern returns to normal, the reticular formation allows her to attend to the radio again, while continuing to monitor the traffic situation.

The reticular formation also determines how alert we are. When it slows down, we doze off or go to sleep. But thanks to the reticular formation, important messages get through even when we are asleep. This is why parents may be able to sleep through a thunderstorm but will awaken to the slightest cry of their baby.

The **cerebellum** is critically important to the body's ability to execute smooth, skilled movements (Spencer et al., 2003). It also regulates muscle tone and posture. Furthermore, it has been found to play a role in motor learning (Orban et al., 2009). It coordinates the series of movements necessary to perform many simple activities such as walking in a straight line or touching your finger to the tip of your nose—without conscious effort. For people who have damage to their cerebellum or who are temporarily impaired by too much alcohol, such simple acts may be difficult or impossible to perform.

hindbrain
A link between the spinal cord and the brain that contains structures that regulate physiological functions, including heart rate, respiration, and blood pressure

brainstem
The structure that begins at the point where the spinal cord enlarges as it enters the brain and handles functions critical to physical survival. It includes the medulla, the reticular formation, and the pons

medulla
(muh-DUL-uh) The part of the brainstem that controls heartbeat, blood pressure, breathing, coughing, and swallowing

pons
The bridgelike structure that connects the medulla and the cerebellum

reticular formation
A structure in the brainstem that plays a crucial role in arousal and attention and that screens sensory messages entering the brain

cerebellum
(sehr-uh-BELL-um) The brain structure that helps the body execute smooth, skilled movements and regulates muscle tone and posture

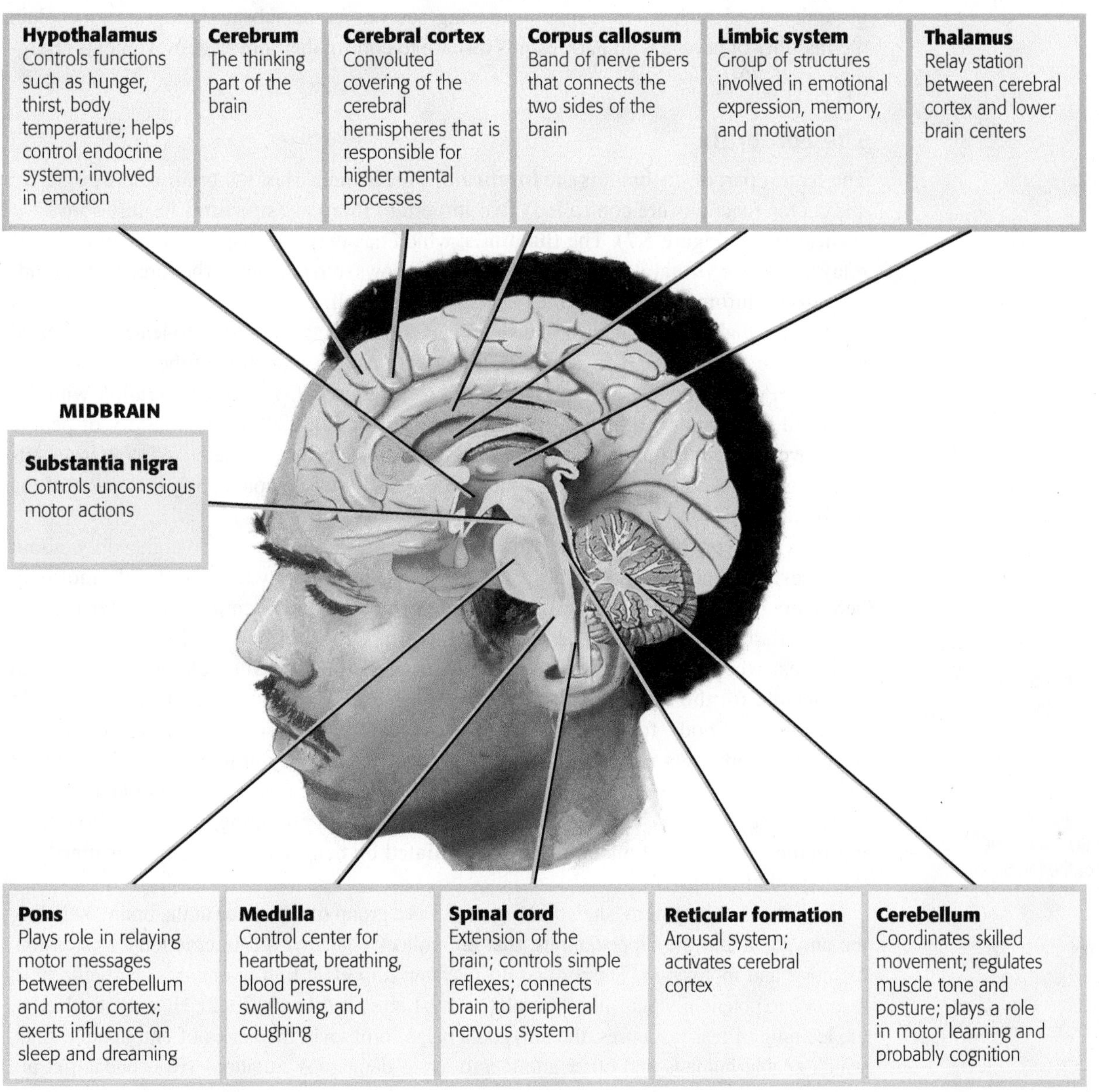

Figure 5.7 Major Structures of the Human Brain
This drawing shows some of the major structures of the brain with a brief description of the function of each. The brainstem contains the medulla, the reticular formation, and the pons.

The Midbrain

As shown in Figure 5.7, the **midbrain** lies between the hindbrain and the forebrain. The structures of this brain region act primarily as relay stations through which the basic physiological functions of the hindbrain are linked to the cognitive functions of the forebrain. For example, when you burn your finger, the physical feeling travels through the nerves of your hand and arm, eventually reaching the spinal cord, resulting in the reflexive action of dropping a pot. From there, nerve impulses are sent through the midbrain to the forebrain, where they are interpreted ("Next time, I'll remember to use a potholder!").

midbrain
Area that contains structures linking the physiological functions of the hindbrain to the cognitive functions of the forebrain

substantia nigra
(sub-STAN-sha NI-gra)
The structure in the midbrain that controls unconscious motor movements

The **substantia nigra** is located in the midbrain. This structure is composed of the darkly colored nuclei of nerve cells that control our unconscious motor actions. When you ride a bicycle or walk up stairs without giving your movements any conscious thought, the nuclei of the cells that allow you to do so are found in the substantia nigra. Research suggests that the defects in dopamine-producing neurons in the substantia nigra may explain the inability of people with Parkinson's disease to control their physical movements (Bergman et al., 2010).

The Forebrain

The largest part of the brain is the **forebrain**. This is the part of the brain where cognitive and motor functions are controlled. Two important forebrain structures lie just above the brainstem (see Figure 5.7). The **thalamus**, which has two egg-shaped parts, serves as the relay station for virtually all the information that flows into and out of the forebrain, including sensory information from all the senses except smell.

The thalamus, or at least one small part of it, affects our ability to learn new verbal information (Soei, Koch Schwarz, & Daum, 2008). Another function of the thalamus is the regulation of sleep cycles, which is thought to be accomplished in cooperation with the pons and the reticular formation (Saper, Scammell, & Lu, 2005). The majority of people who have had acute brain injury and remain in an unresponsive "vegetative" state have suffered significant damage to the thalamus, to the neural tissue connecting it to parts of the forebrain, or to both (Young, 2009).

The **hypothalamus** lies directly below the thalamus and weighs only about 2 ounces. It regulates hunger, thirst, sexual behavior, and a wide variety of emotional behaviors. The hypothalamus also regulates internal body temperature, starting the process that causes you to perspire when you are too hot and to shiver to conserve body heat when you are too cold. It also houses the biological clock—the mechanism responsible for the timing of the sleep/wakefulness cycle and the daily fluctuation in more than 100 body functions (Wirz-Justice, 2009). Because of the biological clock, once your body gets used to waking up at a certain time, you tend to awaken at that time every day—even if you forget to set your alarm. The physiological changes in the body that accompany strong emotion—sweaty palms, a pounding heart, a hollow feeling in the pit of your stomach—are also initiated by neurons concentrated primarily in the hypothalamus.

The **limbic system**, shown in Figure 5.8 is a group of structures in the brain, including the amygdala and the hippocampus, that are collectively involved in emotional expression, memory, and motivation. The **amygdala** plays an important role in emotion, particularly in response to potentially punishing stimuli (Murty, Labar, & Adcock, 2012). Heavily involved in the learning of fear responses, the amygdala helps form vivid memories of emotional events, which enable humans and other animals to avoid dangerous situations (Roozendaal, et al., 2008).

The **hippocampus** is an important brain structure of the limbic system (see Figure 5.8). If your hippocampal region—the hippocampus and the underlying cortical areas—were destroyed, you would not be able to store any new personal or cognitive information, such as that day's baseball score or the phone number of the person you met at dinner (Wirth et al., 2003). Yet, memories already stored before the hippocampal region was destroyed would remain intact.

The hippocampus also plays a role in the brain's internal representation of space in the form of neural "maps" that help us learn our way about in new environments and remember where we have been (Wilson & McNaughton, 1993). A widely cited study of taxi drivers in London revealed that their posterior (rear) hippocampus was significantly larger than that of participants in a control group who did not have extensive experience navigating the city's streets (Maguire et al., 2000). In fact, the more experience a taxi driver had, the larger that part of the hippocampus was. This study shows that the posterior hippocampus is important for navigational ability and that experience strongly influences its functioning.

forebrain
The largest part of the brain where cognitive functions as well as many of the motor functions of the brain are carried out

thalamus
(THAL-uh-mus) The structure, located above the brainstem, that acts as a relay station for information flowing into or out of the forebrain

hypothalamus
(HY-po-THAL-uh-mus) A small but influential brain structure that regulates hunger, thirst, sexual behavior, internal body temperature, other body functions, and a wide variety of emotional behaviors

limbic system
A group of structures in the brain, including the amygdala and hippocampus, that are collectively involved in emotional expression, memory, and motivation

amygdala
(ah-MIG-da-la) A structure in the limbic system that plays an important role in emotion, particularly in response to unpleasant or punishing stimuli

hippocampus
(hip-po-CAM-pus) A structure in the limbic system that plays a central role in the storing of new memories, the response to new or unexpected stimuli, and navigational ability

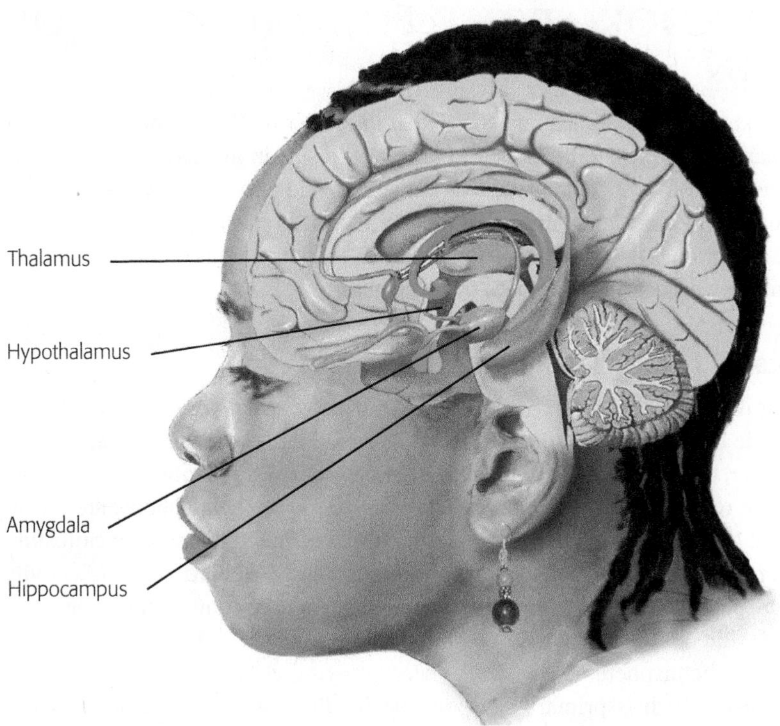

Figure 5.8 The Principal Structures in the Limbic System
The amygdala plays an important role in emotion; the hippocampus is essential in the formation of new memories.

Finally, the *cerebral cortex* is the forebrain structure that is responsible for the functions we usually associate with the word *brain*. It is the wrinkled, gray covering of the *cerebrum*, or the thinking part of the brain. In the next section, you will read about the cerebrum in more detail.

Remember It

1. The ______________ and ______________ make up the central nervous system.
2. Internal body temperature is regulated by the ______________.
3. The ______________ is associated with emotions, and the ______________ is involved in memory and learning.
4. The ______________ serves as a relay station for most sensory information.
5. The ______________ consists of the pons, medulla, and reticular formation.
6. Coordinated body movements are controlled by the ______________.
7. The ______________ nervous system connects the brain and spinal cord to the rest of the body.
8. The ______________ nervous system mobilizes the body's resources during times of stress.
9. The ______________ nervous system restores the body's functions to normal once a crisis has passed.

A Closer Look at the Thinking Part of the Brain

5.8 What are the components of the cerebrum?

Researchers have known for more than a century that the majority of the functions that distinguish the human species from others, such as language, reside in the part of the forebrain known as the *cerebrum*. Modern techniques, such as the EEG and the CT and MRI scans, have enabled researchers to localize many important functions, such as planning and logic, to specific parts of the cerebrum. They have also learned a great deal about the communication that goes on between the two sides and four lobes of the cerebrum.

cerebrum
(seh-REE-brum) The largest structure of the human brain, consisting of the two cerebral hemispheres connected by the corpus callosum and covered by the cerebral cortex

cerebral hemispheres
(seh-REE-brul) The right and left halves of the cerebrum, covered by the cerebral cortex and connected by the corpus callosum; they control movement and feeling on the opposing sides of the body

corpus callosum
(KOR-pus kah-LO-sum) The thick band of nerve fibers that connects the two cerebral hemispheres and makes possible the transfer of information and the synchronization of activity between the hemispheres

cerebral cortex
(seh-REE-brul KOR-tex) The gray, convoluted covering of the cerebral hemispheres that is responsible for the higher mental processes of language, memory, and thinking

Components of the Cerebrum

If you could peer into your skull and look down on your brain, what you would see would resemble the inside of a huge walnut. Like a walnut, which has two matched halves connected to each other, the **cerebrum** is composed of two **cerebral hemispheres**—a left and a right hemisphere resting side by side (see Figure 5.9). The two hemispheres are physically connected at the bottom by a thick band of nerve fibers called the **corpus callosum**. This connection makes possible the transfer of information and the coordination of activity between the hemispheres. In general, the right cerebral hemisphere controls movement and feeling on the left side of the body; the left hemisphere controls the right side of the body.

The cerebral hemispheres have a thin outer covering about 1/8 inch thick called the **cerebral cortex**, which is primarily responsible for the higher mental processes of language, memory, and thinking. The presence of the cell bodies of billions of neurons in the cerebral cortex gives it a grayish appearance. Thus, the cortex is often referred to as *gray matter*. Immediately beneath the cortex are the white myelinated axons (referred to as *white matter*) that connect the neurons of the cortex with those of other brain regions. Research suggests that the amount of gray matter is positively correlated with intelligence in humans (Taki et al., 2012). In other words, the more gray matter you have, the higher your scores on intelligence tests are likely to be.

In humans, the cerebral cortex is very large—if it were spread out flat, it would measure about 2 feet by 3 feet, about the size of a large poster board you might have used

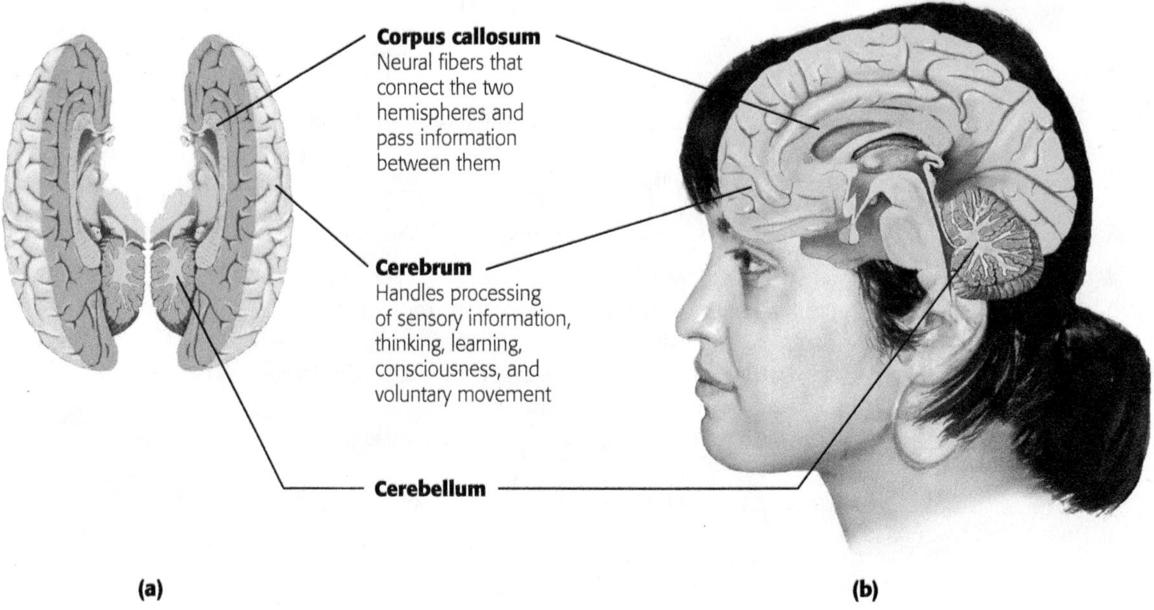

Figure 5.9 Two Views of the Cerebral Hemispheres
(a) The two hemispheres rest side by side like two matched halves, physically connected by the corpus callosum. (b) An inside view of the right hemisphere.

for a project in your school days. Because the cortex is roughly three times the size of the cerebrum itself, it does not fit smoothly around the cerebrum. Rather, it is arranged in numerous folds or wrinkles, called *convolutions*. About two-thirds of the cortex is hidden from view in these folds. The cortex of less intelligent animals is much smaller in proportion to total brain size and, therefore, is much less convoluted. The cerebral cortex contains three types of areas: (1) sensory input areas, where vision, hearing, touch, pressure, and temperature register; (2) motor areas, which control voluntary movement; and (3) **association areas**, which house memories and are involved in thought, perception, and language.

Finally, the brain assigns different functions to different regions of the cerebral cortex. The first functional division involves the left and right sides of the cortex. The second involves areas known as the *lobes*—the front (frontal), top (parietal), side (temporal), and back (occipital) of the cortex. As you read about the various neurological divisions of labor in the next two sections, keep in mind that all parts of the brain are in communication with one another at all times. Consequently, everything we do involves the coordination of neural activity in several areas of the brain at once.

5.9 What are the specialized functions of the left and right cerebral hemispheres?

The Cerebral Hemispheres

We all know that some people are right-handed and others are left-handed. As discussed in the *Explain It* (p. 136), handedness is neurologically based. Consequently, discussions in the media about the differences between "right-brained" and "left-brained" people might seem to make sense. However, there is no scientific basis for the notion that hemisphere dominance varies across individuals in the same way that hand preference does. In everyone's brain, the right and left hemispheres are in constant contact with one another, thanks to the corpus callosum (shown in Figure 5.9 on p. 134). But research has shown that some **lateralization** of the hemispheres exists; that is, each hemisphere is specialized to handle certain functions. Let's look at the specific functions associated with the left and right hemispheres.

The Left Hemisphere

The **left hemisphere** handles math, logic, analytical thought, and most of the language functions, including speaking, writing, reading, speech comprehension, and comprehension of written information (Hellige, 1990; Long & Baynes, 2002). Many of these functions have specific regions of the left hemisphere devoted to them. For instance, the sounds and meanings associated with spoken language are processed in different areas of the left hemisphere (Poldrack & Wagner, 2004).

The left hemisphere coordinates complex movements by directly controlling the right side of the body and by indirectly controlling the movements of the left side of the body. It accomplishes this by sending orders across the corpus callosum to the right hemisphere so that the proper movements will be coordinated and executed smoothly. (Remember that the cerebellum also plays an important role in helping coordinate complex movements.)

The Right Hemisphere

The **right hemisphere** is generally considered to be the hemisphere more adept at visual–spatial relations. Also, the auditory cortex in the right hemisphere appears to be far better able to process music than the left (Zatorre, Belin, & Penhune, 2002). When you arrange your bedroom furniture or notice that your favorite song is being played on the radio, you are relying primarily on your right hemisphere.

The right hemisphere also augments the left hemisphere's language-processing activities. For example, it produces verbal associations characteristic of creative thought and uses of language (Kounios et al., 2008). Consider this well-known phrase from President John F. Kennedy's inaugural address, a type of expression known as a *parallelism*:

Ask not what your country can do for you, but what you can do for your country.

association areas
Areas of the cerebral cortex that house memories and are involved in thought, perception, and language

lateralization
The specialization of one of the cerebral hemispheres to handle a particular function

left hemisphere
The hemisphere that controls the right side of the body, coordinates complex movements, and, in most people, handles most of the language functions

right hemisphere
The hemisphere that controls the left side of the body and, in most people, is specialized for visual-spatial perception

Explain It

Why Are Most People Right-Handed?

Scientists have searched for an answer to this question for more than a century and have yet to find a definitive answer. In your own thinking about the matter, you have probably concluded that there are three possibilities:

- Handedness is completely determined by genes.
- Handedness is completely determined by learning.
- Handedness is determined by both genes and learning.

If you are drawn to the first hypothesis, consider the finding that only 82% of identical twins, whose genotypes (genetic makeup) are identical, have the same hand preference (Klar, 2003). If handedness were completely determined by genes, then identical twins' phenotypes (actual characteristics) would always be the same for handedness. Therefore, handedness cannot be entirely explained as a function of our genes. Does this mean that handedness is determined by learning? Not necessarily.

The learning hypothesis cannot explain why handedness appears very early in infancy, long before children are exposed to formal instruction that requires them to use one hand or the other (Rönnqvist & Domellöf, 2006). Moreover, the proportions of left-handers and right-handers in the human population have been about the same for thousands of years (Hopkins & Cantalupo, 2004). In fact, these proportions are evident even in the skeletons of humans who died long before writing was invented as well as Neanderthals (Steele & Mays, 1995; Volpato et al., 2012).

The key to understanding the evidence on handedness is to adopt the view that both genes and learning are at work in the development of hand preferences, but not in the way that you might expect. In most of us, right-handedness is completely determined by our genes, but in a few of us handedness, whether left or right, is influenced by learning. Sound confusing? To clarify, here is the most current thinking on the genetics of handedness.

Researchers suspect that right-handedness is determined by a single dominant gene, *R* (Francks et al., 2003). If an individual receives a copy of *R* from one or both parents, then she will be right-handed. The frequency of *R* in the human population is extremely high, scientists believe, because it is tied to the genes that support left-lateralization of language function in the brain. (Remember, the left side of the brain controls the right side of the body.) It makes sense that motor functions are linked to language, experts claim, because producing language requires activity in both the language centers and motor cortex of the brain. Putting both on the same side of the brain facilitates the rapid development of neural connections between the two without having to go through the slowly developing membrane between the two hemispheres (corpus callosum). But what happens to the relatively small proportion of humans who do not receive a copy of *R* from either parent?

The dominant gene for right-handedness, *R*, is complemented by a recessive gene, *r* (Francks et al., 2007). You might think that the phenotype of an individual who receives a copy of *r* from both parents would include left-handedness, but, in reality, the phenotype that is associated with *rr* is *non-handedness.* In individuals with the *rr* genotype, learning shapes handedness. Because most people are right-handed, and the tools that humans have developed for use in fine motor activities (e.g., scissors) favor righties, there is a considerable amount of cultural pressure on those who lack innate handedness, those with the genotype *rr*, to become right-handed. Nevertheless, some of them do develop left-handedness. Why?

Researchers believe that other genes come into play as well. Specifically, if a person possesses genes that cause language functions to lateralize to her right rather than her left cerebral hemisphere, then she is also likely to be left-handed. Here again, the lateralization of handedness follows the lateralization of language function. To make matters more complicated, in 2007, scientists discovered a gene that pushes us in the direction of left-handedness when we receive it from our fathers. When we get the gene from our mothers, it seems to have no influence on hand dominance (Francks et al., 2007).

Finally, although genetics appears to play a complex, but important, role in the development of hand preferences, the capacity of individuals to adapt to severe injuries to or the loss of the dominant hand demonstrates the adaptability of the brain with regard to motor functions. Thus, as the trait of hand preference illustrates, nature and nurture are often linked in complex ways. Remember this the next time you are involved in a debate with someone about whether a given trait is *either* genetic *or* learned.

Writers employ parallelisms because the echoing of the first part of the expression in the second engages the listener's attention. The writer's right hemisphere is the one that judges whether the parallelism succeeds at this goal while simultaneously conveying the speaker's message as accurately as possible. To experience an effect of the specialization of the cerebral hemispheres, try your hand at the *Try It* in the next page.

As you read earlier, the left hemisphere processes the linguistic aspects of speech. However, researchers have found that the processing of natural language involves an interaction between the two halves of the brain in which the right hemisphere carries out a number of critical functions (Berckmoes & Vingerhoets, 2004). One such function is the comprehension of idiomatic expressions, such as "She let the cat out of the bag." The right hemisphere also processes causal links between statements such as "I fell off my bicycle yesterday. My knee is killing me" (Mason & Just, 2004). The right hemisphere also responds to the emotional message conveyed by another's tone of voice (LeDoux, 2000). Reading and interpreting nonverbal behavior, such as gestures and facial expressions, is another right hemisphere task (Hauser, 1993; Kucharska-Pietura & Klimkowski, 2002). For example, the subtle clues that tell us someone is lying (such as excessive blinking or lack of eye contact) are processed in the right hemisphere (Etcoff et al., 2000). Figure 5.10 summarizes the functions associated with the left and right hemispheres.

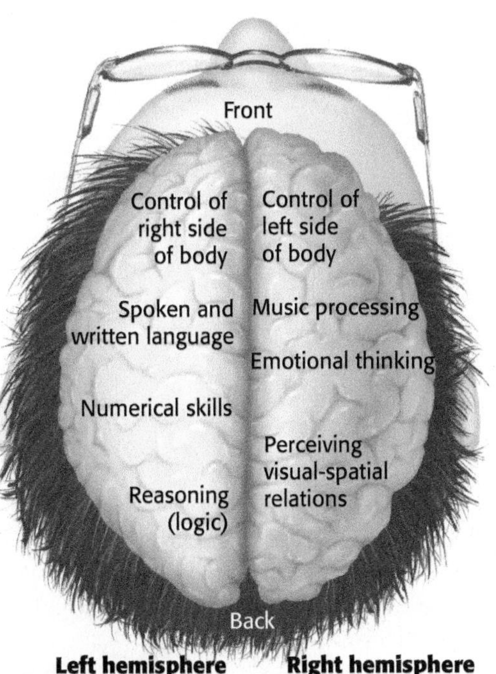

Figure 5.10 Lateralized Functions of the Brain
Assigning functions to one hemisphere or the other allows the brain to function more efficiently.
Source: Based on Gazzaniga (1983).

The Split Brain

A great deal of knowledge about lateralization has been gained from studies involving individuals in whom the corpus callosum is absent or has been surgically modified. Many such individuals have had their corpus callosum severed in a drastic surgical procedure called the **split-brain operation**. Neurosurgeons Joseph Bogen and Philip Vogel (1963) found that people with severe epilepsy, who had frequent and uncontrollable grand mal seizures, could be helped by surgery that severed their corpus callosum, rendering communication between the two hemispheres impossible. The operation decreases the frequency of seizures in two-thirds of such people and causes minimal loss of cognitive functioning or change in personality (Washington University School of Medicine, 2003).

Research with split-brain patients by Roger Sperry (1964) and colleagues Michael Gazzaniga (1970, 1989) and Jerre Levy (1985) expanded knowledge of the unique capabilities of the individual hemispheres. Sperry (1968) found that when the

Try It

A Balancing Act

Get a meter stick or yardstick. Try balancing it vertically on the end of your left index finger, as shown in the drawing. Then try balancing it on your right index finger. Most people are better with their dominant hand—the right hand for right-handers, for example. Is this true for you?

Now try this: Begin reciting the ABCs out loud as fast as you can while balancing the stick with your left hand. Do you have less trouble this time? Why should that be? The right hemisphere controls the act of balancing with the left hand. However, your left hemisphere, though poor at controlling the left hand, still tries to coordinate your balancing efforts. When you distract the left hemisphere with a steady stream of talk, the right hemisphere can orchestrate more efficient balancing with your left hand without interference.

split-brain operation
A surgical procedure, performed to treat severe cases of epilepsy, in which the corpus callosum is cut, separating the cerebral hemispheres

brain was surgically separated, each hemisphere continued to have individual and private experiences, sensations, thoughts, and perceptions. However, most sensory experiences are shared almost simultaneously because each ear and eye has direct sensory connections to both hemispheres.

Sperry's research, for which he won a Nobel Prize in medicine in 1981, revealed some fascinating findings. In Figure 5.11, a split-brain patient sits in front of a screen that separates the right and left fields of vision. If an orange is flashed to the right field of vision, it will register in the left (verbal) hemisphere. If asked what he saw, the patient will readily reply, "I saw an orange." Suppose that, instead, an apple is flashed to the left visual field and is relayed to the right (nonverbal) hemisphere. The patient will reply, "I saw nothing."

Why could the patient report that he saw the orange but not the apple? Sperry (1964, 1968) maintains that in split-brain patients, only the verbal left hemisphere can report what it sees. In these experiments, the left hemisphere does not see what is flashed to the right hemisphere, and the right hemisphere is unable to report verbally what it has viewed. But did the right hemisphere actually see the apple that was flashed in the left visual field? Yes,

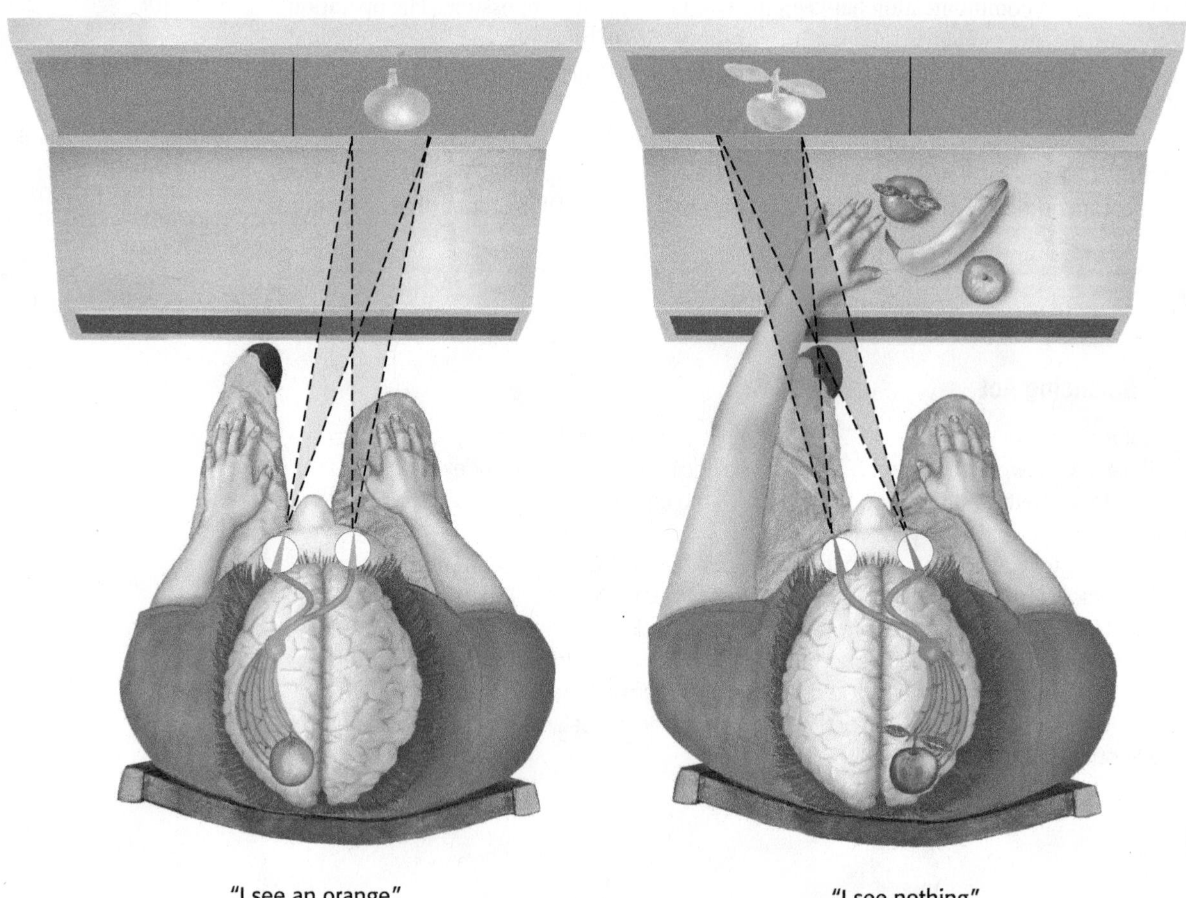

Figure 5.11 Testing a Split-Brain Person
Using special equipment, researchers are able to study the independent functioning of the hemispheres in split-brain patients. In this experiment, when a visual image (an orange) is flashed on the right side of the screen, it is transmitted to the left (talking) hemisphere. When asked what he sees, the split-brain patient replies, "I see an orange." When an image (an apple) is flashed on the left side of the screen, it is transmitted only to the right (nonverbal) hemisphere. Because the split-brain patient's left (language) hemisphere did not receive the image, he replies, "I see nothing." But he can pick out the apple by touch if he uses his left hand, proving that the right hemisphere "saw" the apple.
Source: Based on Gazzaniga, M. (1983).

because with his left hand (which is controlled by the right hemisphere), the patient can pick out from behind a screen the apple or any other object shown to the right hemisphere. The right hemisphere knows and remembers what it sees just as well as the left, but unlike the left hemisphere, the right cannot name what it has seen. (In these experiments, images must be flashed for no more than 1/10 or 2/10 of a second so that the subjects do not have time to refixate their eyes and send the information to the opposite hemisphere.)

The Four Cerebral Lobes

5.10 Which functions are associated with each of the four lobes of the cerebral cortex?

Each of the cerebral hemispheres has four further divisions. These divisions, or *lobes*, are named for the skull bones to which they are adjacent, the *frontal*, *parietal*, *occipital*, and *temporal* bones (see Figure 5.12). Each lobe is responsible for a different set of functions.

The Frontal Lobes: Prefrontal Cortex

Have you ever thought about how many tasks your brain is doing at once when you read a textbook? Your brain is simultaneously translating the letters on the page into words, pulling up the information from memory needed to comprehend them, monitoring how well you understand what you are reading, giving you instructions to go back and reread when needed, and making judgments about what might be on your next exam. All of this activity takes place in your **frontal lobes**, the largest of the brain's lobes (see Figure 5.12 on p. 140). Thanks to the **prefrontal cortex**, the part of the frontal lobes that coordinates multiple functions to serve cognitive goals, a function called *executive processing*, you experience all of these tasks as a unified whole instead of a collection of fragmentary, disconnected activities (Moss et al., 2011). Imaging studies suggest that individuals who have difficulty with cognitive functions such as problem solving display a different, less efficient pattern of prefrontal cortex activation than people who do not have such problems do (Ashkenazi, Rosenberg-Lee, Tenison, & Menon, 2012).

The prefrontal cortex also contributes to personality functioning (DeYoung et al., 2010). People who experience damage to the prefrontal cortex can lose the ability to control impulses, modulate emotions, and anticipate the consequences of their behavior. One of the best known cases involving this type of damage, that of the unfortunate railroad construction worker Phineas Gage, took place on September 13, 1848. Twenty-five-year-old Gage was using dynamite to blast rocks and dirt out of the pathway of the railroad tracks he was helping to lay that would connect the east and west coasts of the United States by rail. Suddenly, an unplanned explosion sent a 3-foot-long, 13-point metal rod under his left cheekbone and out through the top of his skull. Much of the brain tissue in his prefrontal cortex was torn away, and he was rendered unconscious for a few minutes. A few weeks later, Gage appeared to be fully recovered. However, prior to the accident, Gage had been an easygoing fellow. Afterward, he was rude and impulsive. His changed personality cost him his job, and he lived out the rest of his life as a circus sideshow exhibit (adapted from Harlow, 1848).

Frontal Lobes: Motor Cortex

The **motor cortex** is the frontal lobe region that coordinates voluntary body movements. The right motor cortex controls movement on the left side of the body, and the left motor cortex controls movement on the right side of the body. In 1937, Canadian neurosurgeon Wilder Penfield applied electrical stimulation to the motor cortex of conscious human patients undergoing neurosurgery. He then mapped the primary motor cortex in humans. The parts of the body that are capable of the most finely coordinated movements, such as the fingers, lips, and tongue, have a larger share of the motor cortex. Movements in the lower parts of the body are controlled primarily by neurons at the top of the motor cortex, whereas movements in the upper body parts (face, lips, and tongue) are controlled mainly by neurons near the bottom of the motor cortex. For example, when you wiggle your right big toe, the movement is produced mainly by the firing of a cluster of brain cells at the top of the left motor cortex.

frontal lobes
The largest of the brain's lobes, which contain the motor cortex, Broca's area, and the frontal association areas

prefrontal cortex
The part of the frontal lobes directly behind the forehead that controls executive processing, the coordination of multiple brain activities in pursuit of cognitive goals

motor cortex
The strip of tissue at the rear of the frontal lobes that controls voluntary body movement and participates in learning and cognitive events

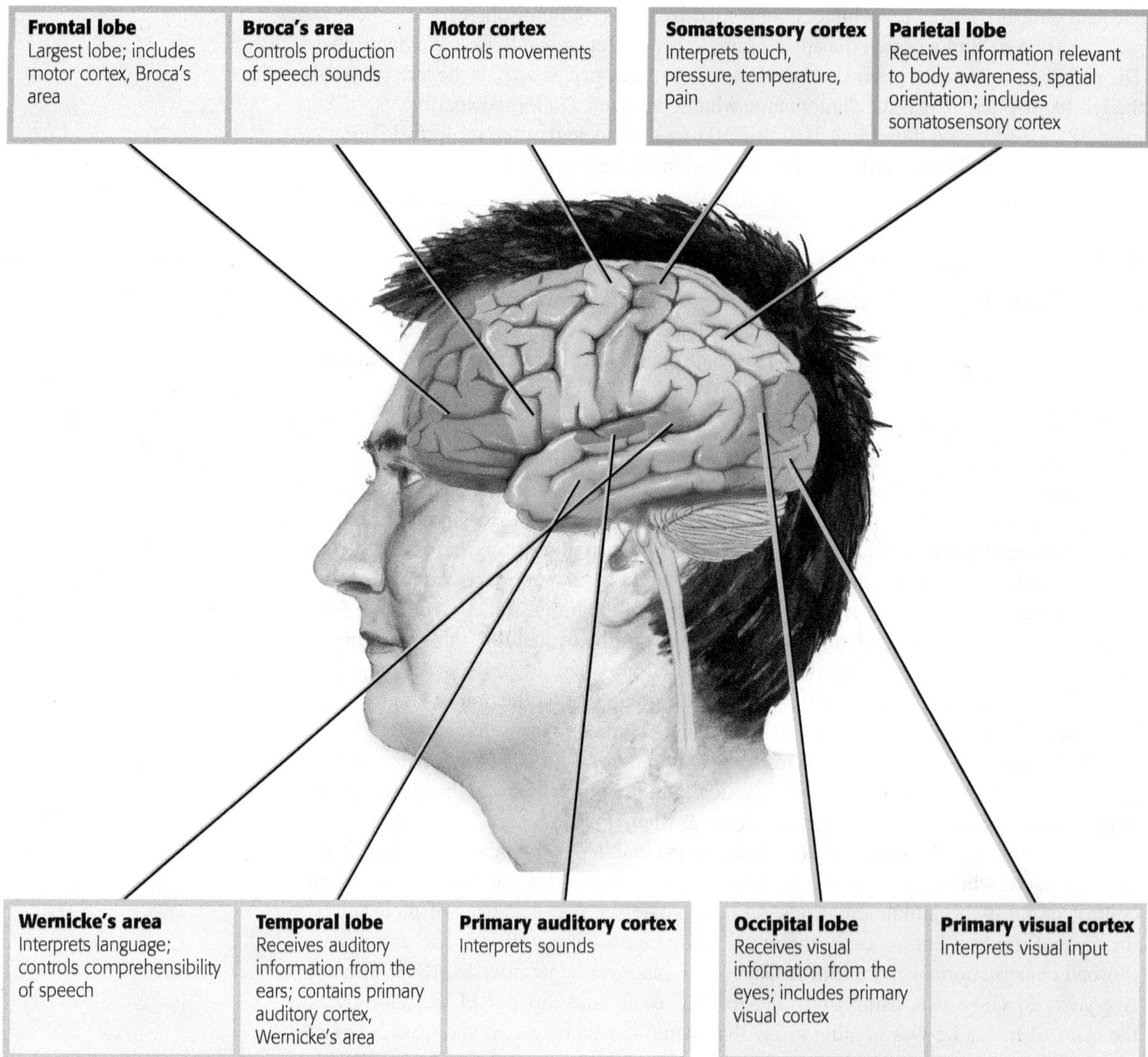

Figure 5.12 The Four Lobes of the Cerebral Cortex
This illustration of the left cerebral hemisphere shows the four lobes: (1) the frontal lobe, including the motor cortex and Broca's area; (2) the parietal lobe, with the somatosensory cortex; (3) the occipital lobe, with the primary visual cortex; and (4) the temporal lobe, with the primary auditory cortex and Wernicke's area.

How accurately and completely does Penfield's map account for the control of body movement? Although it may be useful in a broad sense, more recent research has shown that there is not a precise one-to-one correspondence between specific points on the motor cortex and movement of particular body parts. Motor neurons that control the fingers, for example, play a role in the movement of more than a single finger. In fact, the control of movement of any single finger is handled by a network of neurons that are widely distributed over the entire hand area of the motor cortex (Sanes & Donoghue, 2000).

Frontal Lobes: Broca's Area

In 1861, physician Paul Broca performed autopsies on two patients—one who had been totally without speech and another who could say only four words (Jenkins et al., 1975). Broca found that both individuals had damage in the left hemisphere, slightly in front of the part of the motor cortex that controls movements of the jaw, lips, and tongue. He concluded that the site of left hemisphere damage he identified through the autopsies was the part of the brain responsible for speech production, now called **Broca's area** (refer to Figure 5.12). Broca's area is involved in directing the pattern of muscle movement required to produce speech sounds.

If Broca's area is damaged as a result of head injury or stroke, **Broca's aphasia** may result. **Aphasia** is a general term for a loss or impairment of the ability to use or understand language, resulting from damage to the brain (Kirshner & Jacobs, 2008). Characteristically, patients with Broca's aphasia know what they want to say but can speak very little or not at all. If they are able to speak, their words are produced very slowly, with great effort, and are poorly articulated.

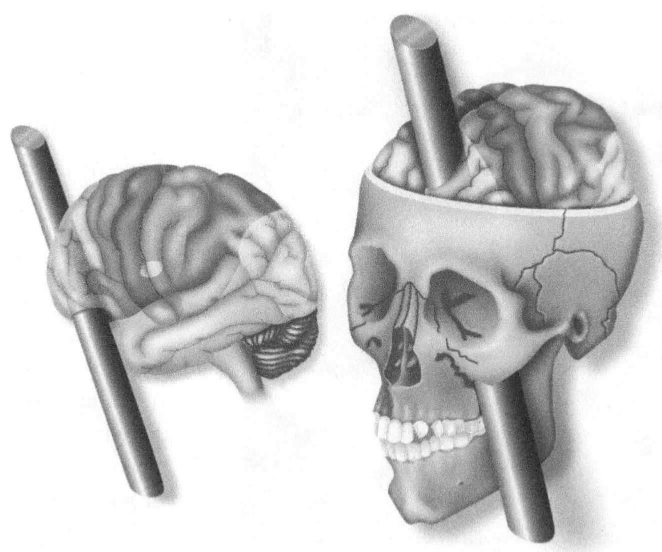

The skull of Phineas Gage is on display at the Warren Anatomical Museum at Harvard University. As you can see, the tamping rod tore through his frontal lobes leaving him with an altered personality.

The Parietal Lobes

The **parietal lobes** lie directly behind the frontal lobes, in the top middle portion of the brain (refer back to Figure 5.12). The parietal lobes are involved in the reception and processing of touch stimuli. The front strip of brain tissue in the parietal lobes is the **somatosensory cortex**, the site where touch, pressure, temperature, and pain register in the cerebral cortex (Purves et al., 2011). Thesomatosensory cortex also makes you aware of movement in your body and the positions of your body parts at any given moment.

The two halves of the somatosensory cortex, in the left and right parietal lobes, are wired to opposite sides of the body. Also, cells at the top of the somatosensory cortex govern feeling in the lower extremities of the body. If you drop a brick on your right foot, the topmost brain cells of the left somatosensory cortex will fire and register the pain sensation. (*Note:* This is *not* a *Try It!*) The large somatosensory areas are connected to sensitive body parts such as the tongue, lips, face, and hand, particularly the thumb and index finger.

Other parts of the parietal lobes are responsible for spatial orientation and sense of direction—for example, helping you to retrace your path when you take a wrong turn. The hippocampus cooperates with these parts of the parietal lobes in performing such functions, as the study of London taxi drivers discussed on page 132 indicates (Maguire et al., 2000). Association areas in the parietal lobes also house memories of how objects feel against the human skin, a fact that explains why we can identify objects by touch. People with damage to these areas could hold a computer mouse, a CD, or a baseball in their hand but not be able to identify the object by touch alone.

The Occipital Lobes

Behind the parietal lobes at the rear of the brain lie the **occipital lobes**, which are involved in the reception and interpretation of visual information (refer to Figure 5.12). At the very back of the occipital lobes is the **primary visual cortex**, the site where vision registers in the cortex.

Each eye is connected to the primary visual cortex in both the right and the left occipital lobes. Look straight ahead and draw an imaginary line down the middle of what you see. Everything to the left of the line is referred to as the left visual field and registers in the right visual cortex. Everything to the right of the line is the right visual field and registers in the left visual cortex. A person who sustains damage to one half of the primary visual cortex will still have partial vision in both eyes because each eye sends information to both the right and the left occipital lobes.

The association areas in the occipital lobes are involved in the interpretation of visual stimuli. They hold memories of past visual experiences and enable us to recognize what is familiar among the things we see. That's why the face of a friend stands out in a crowd of unfamiliar people. When these areas are damaged, people can lose the ability to

Broca's area
(BRO-kuz) The area in the frontal lobe, usually in the left hemisphere, that controls the production of speech sounds

Broca's aphasia
(BRO-kuz uh-FAY-zyah) An impairment in the physical ability to produce speech sounds or, in extreme cases, an inability to speak at all; caused by damage to Broca's area

aphasia
(uh-FAY-zyah) A loss or impairment of the ability to use or understand language, resulting from damage to the brain

parietal lobes
(puh-RY-uh-tul)The lobes that contain the somatosensory cortex (where touch, pressure, temperature, and pain register) and other areas that are responsible for body awareness and spatial orientation

somatosensory cortex
(so-MAT-oh-SENS-or-ee) The strip of tissue at the front of the parietal lobes where touch, pressure, temperature, and pain register in the cerebral cortex

occipital lobes
(ahk-SIP-uh-tul) The lobes that are involved in the reception and interpretation of visual information; they contain the primary visual cortex

primary visual cortex
The area at the rear of the occipital lobes where vision registers in the cerebral cortex

Because the left hand of a professional string player like Boyd Tinsley of the Dave Matthews Band must rapidly and accurately execute fine movements and slight pressure variations, it is not surprising that these musicians have an unusually large area of the somatosensory cortex dedicated to the fingers of that hand.

identify objects visually, although they will still be able to identify the same objects by touch or through some other sense.

The Temporal Lobes

The **temporal lobes**, located slightly above the ears, are involved in the reception and interpretation of auditory stimuli. The site in the cortex where hearing registers is known as the primary auditory cortex. The **primary auditory cortex** in each temporal lobe receives sound inputs from both ears. Injury to one of these areas results in reduced hearing in both ears, and the destruction of both areas causes total deafness.

Adjacent to the primary auditory cortex in the left temporal lobe is **Wernicke's area**, which is the language area involved in comprehending the spoken word and in formulating coherent written and spoken language (refer to Figure 5.12). When you listen to someone speak, the sound registers first in the primary auditory cortex. The sound is then sent to Wernicke's area, where the speech sounds are unscrambled into meaningful patterns of words.

Wernicke's aphasia is a type of aphasia resulting from damage to Wernicke's area. Although speech is fluent and words are clearly articulated, the actual message does not make sense to listeners (Kirshner & Hoffmann, 2012). The content may be vague or bizarre and may contain inappropriate words, parts of words, or a gibberish of nonexistent words. One Wernicke's patient, when asked how he was feeling, replied, "I think that there's an awful lot of mung, but I think I've a lot of net and tunged in a little wheat duhvayden" (Buckingham & Kertesz, 1974). People with Wernicke's aphasia are not aware that anything is wrong with their speech. Thus, this disorder is difficult to treat.

The remainder of the temporal lobes consists of the association areas that house memories and are involved in the interpretation of auditory stimuli. For example, the association area where your memories of various sounds are stored enables you to recognize the sounds of your favorite band, a computer booting up, your roommate snoring, and so on. There is also a special association area where familiar melodies are stored.

We've covered all of the various parts of the brain and their respective functions unique to all humans, but are all human brains the same? In the next section, we'll look at the ways our brains may or may not be different.

temporal lobes
The lobes that are involved in the reception and interpretation of auditory information; they contain the primary auditory cortex, Wernicke's area, and the temporal association areas

primary auditory cortex
The part of each temporal lobe where hearing registers in the cerebral cortex

Wernicke's area
(VUR-nih-keys) The language area in the left temporal lobe involved in comprehending the spoken word and in formulating coherent speech and written language

Wernicke's aphasia
Aphasia that results from damage to Wernicke's area and in which the person's speech is fluent and clearly articulated but does not make sense to listeners

Remember It

1. The band of fibers connecting the left and right cerebral hemispheres is the ______________.
2. When you listen to a person talk, you most likely process her words in your ______________ hemisphere.
3. You process facial expressions in your ______________ hemisphere.
4. The split-brain operation is sometimes performed to cure ______________.
5. ______________ is to speech production as ______________ is to speech understanding.
6. The primary auditory cortex is found in the ______________ lobe, while the primary visual cortex is located in the ______________ lobe.
7. A person with brain damage who has problems regulating emotion most likely has an injury to the ______________ lobe.
8. The sense of touch is associated with the ______________ lobe.

AGE, GENDER, AND THE BRAIN

How many adults express concern that the moon might be following them? It is likely that you have never heard an adult express such a concern. Nevertheless, it is one of several irrational worries that are frequently expressed by preschoolers. Nowadays, most people have heard something about the link between brain development and such differences in children's and adults' thinking. And it is common to hear people attribute the cognitive deficits displayed by some elderly people to deterioration of their brains. Likewise, interest never seems to wane in the idea that men's and women's brains process information differently. What is the evidence regarding these popular notions about age and gender differences in the brain?

The Ever-Changing Brain

5.11 How does the brain change across the lifespan?

When do you think the brain reaches full maturity? The answer to this question might surprise you. In fact, the brain grows in spurts from conception until well into adulthood (Chamley, Carson, & Sandwell, 2005). In childhood and adolescence, many of these spurts are correlated with major advances in physical and intellectual skills, such as the acquisition of fluency in language that happens around age 4 for most children. Each growth spurt also seems to involve a different brain area. For example, the spurt that begins around age 17 and continues into the early 20s mainly affects the frontal lobes, where the abilities to plan and to control one's emotions are located. Differences between teens and adults in these abilities may be due to this growth spurt. Changes in brain function are influenced by several development processes.

Synapses develop as a result of the growth of both dendrites and axons. This process, known as *synaptogenesis,* occurs in spurts throughout the life span. Each spurt is followed by a period of **pruning**, the process through which the developing brain eliminates unnecessary or redundant synapses. The activity of neurotransmitters within the synapses also varies with age. For example, acetylcholine is less plentiful in the brains of children than in the brains of teens and adults. This difference may help explain age differences in memory and other functions influenced by this excitatory neurotransmitter.

The process of *myelination,* or the development of myelin sheaths around axons, begins prior to birth but continues well into adulthood. For example, the brain's association areas are not fully myelinated until age 12 or so (Tanner, 1990). And the reticular formation, which regulates attention, isn't fully myelinated until the mid-20s (Spreen et al., 1995). Thus, differences in myelination may account for differences between children and adults in processing speed, memory, and other functions.

Some degree of hemispheric specialization is present very early in life. Language processing, for example, occurs primarily in the left hemisphere of the fetal and infant brain, just as it does in the adult brain (Chilosi et al., 2001; de Lacoste et al., 1991). Other functions, such as spatial perception, aren't lateralized until age 8 or so. Consequently, children younger than age 8 exhibit much poorer spatial skills than do older children (Roberts & Bell, 2000). For instance, children younger than 8 have difficulty using maps and distinguishing between statements such as *It's on your left* and *It's on my left.*

The brain's **plasticity**—its capacity to adapt to changes such as brain damage—is maintained throughout life. This plasticity allows synapses to strengthen and reorganize their interconnections when stimulated by experience and practice as the *Try It* on page 144 demonstrates. Plasticity is greatest in young children within whom the hemispheres are not yet completely lateralized. However, researchers have found that the correction of hearing defects in late-middle-aged adults results in changes in all the areas of the brain that are involved in sound perception (Fallon, Irvine, & Shepherd, 2008). Moreover, the brains of these individuals appear to develop responses to sounds in areas in which the brains of people with normal hearing do not.

pruning
The process through which the developing brain eliminates unnecessary or redundant synapses

plasticity
The capacity of the brain to adapt to changes such as brain damage

Try It

Mirror Tracing

For this activity, you will need a mirror, some way to stand the mirror up, a pencil, and two pieces of lined paper. First, write the word PSYCHOLOGY in block letters two lines high five times working from the top of the paper to the bottom, as shown below:

PSYCHOLOGY
PSYCHOLOGY
PSYCHOLOGY
PSYCHOLOGY
PSYCHOLOGY

Next, prop up the mirror at the top of the paper so that it is at a right angle to the paper as shown below:

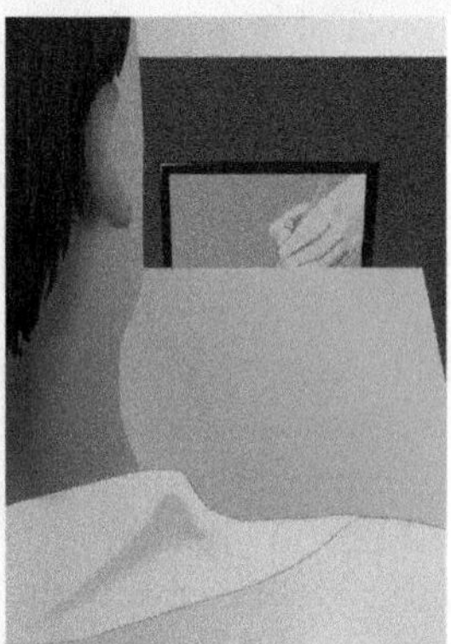

Now comes the difficult part. Looking only at the images of the paper and your hand in the mirror, trace the letters. If you can't resist looking at your hand as you write, hold the second piece of paper in your other hand so that it blocks your view and forces you to look in the mirror. When you're finished tracing, determine your error rate by counting the number of times your tracings deviate from the letters' lines and curves. Repeat the exercise four more times, recording your error rate for each trial.

If you're like most people, you will find that your error rate declines somewhat from the first to the fifth trial. Why? At first, the task is extremely difficult, because interpretations of visual information that are produced by the visual cortex in the occipital lobes guide the actions of the frontal lobes' motor cortex. In the mirror image, the effects of your movements are the opposite of what years of experience with handwriting have led your visual cortex to expect. As a result, it must acquire a new set of expectations that apply to mirror image movements before it can effectively guide your motor cortex. Each time you practice the task, you are providing your visual cortex with the information it needs to create these new expectations. (Practice makes perfect!) This activity demonstrates that, no matter how much we have practiced a particular skill, some degree of neural plasticity remains.

Despite the retention of some degree of plasticity, the brain is subject to the physical effects of aging. For example, the brain both gains and loses synapses throughout life. At some point in adulthood, however, losses begin to exceed gains (Huttenlocher, 1994). Brain weight begins to decline around age 30 (Raz et al., 2006). Age-related deficits due to the loss of brain weight are common. For example, shrinkage of the cerebellum causes elderly people tend to experience problems with balance, they become less steady on their feet, and their gait is affected.

In addition, the health of the heart and blood vessels often deteriorates as adults get older. With this deterioration comes an increased risk of **stroke**, an event in the cardiovascular system in which a blood clot or plug of fat blocks an artery and cuts off the blood supply to a particular area of the brain. Strokes cause brain damage that can range from mild to severe. Some survivors have long-term intellectual and physical impairments. However, physical therapy can help most of them recover at least partial motor functions, providing yet another example of the brain's plasticity (Bruno-Petrina, 2009).

Gender Differences in the Brain

5.12 How do the brains of men and women differ?

Throughout development, the brains of males and females differ to some degree. However, these differences and their possible links to behavior have been most thoroughly researched among adults. One such difference involves gender differences in the distribution of gray and white matter and gray matter. Generally, the more white matter there is in an area of the brain, the more neural communication there is in it. Thus, that the brains of men have a higher proportion of white matter than do the brains of women may be relevant to understanding gender differences in cognitive functioning (Gur et al., 1999). Moreover, men have a lower proportion of white matter in the left brain than in the right brain. In contrast, in women's brains, the proportions of gray matter and white matter in the two hemispheres are equivalent. Such findings have led some neuropsychologists to speculate that gender differences in the distribution of gray and white matter across the two hemispheres may explain men's superior performance on right-hemisphere tasks such as mental rotation of geometric figures. Likewise, women's superior abilities in the domain of emotional perception may be attributable to the fact that they have more gray matter than men do in the right hemisphere where information about emotions is processed (Gur et al., 2002).

Other research has revealed that some tasks stimulate different parts of the brain in men and women. For example, imaging studies have shown that men process navigational information, such as that needed to find the way out of a maze, in the left hippocampus. By contrast, women who are engaged in the same task use the right parietal cortex and the right frontal cortex (Gron et al., 2000). Similarly, studies show that men and women use different areas of the brain when searching for the location of a sound (Lewald, 2004).

What is the meaning of these gender differences in the brain? The short answer is that scientists won't know for certain until a great deal more research is done. Moreover, studies that look for links between these brain differences and actual behavior are needed before any conclusions can be drawn regarding the possible neurological bases for gender differences in behavior.

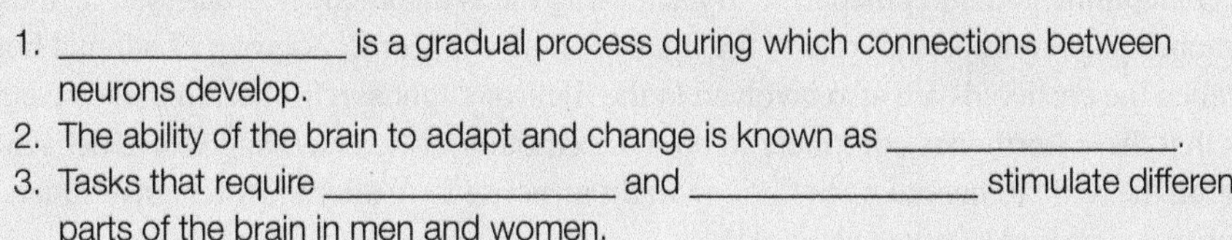

Remember It

1. _______________ is a gradual process during which connections between neurons develop.
2. The ability of the brain to adapt and change is known as _______________.
3. Tasks that require _______________ and _______________ stimulate different parts of the brain in men and women.

stroke
An event in the cardiovascular system in which a blood clot or plug of fat blocks an artery and cuts off the blood supply to a particular area of the brain

Beyond the Nervous System

The body has two additional systems that influence how we function both physically and psychologically. The glands of the *endocrine system* exert their influences by producing, secreting, and regulating *hormones*. By contrast, in some cases, information encoded in our *genes* affects us from the moment of conception; in others, the influences of the genes appear later in life or depend on input from the environment.

5.13 What are the functions of the glands of the endocrine system?

The Endocrine System

Most people think of the reproductive system when they hear the word *hormones*. Or they may associate hormones with particular physical changes, such as those of puberty, pregnancy, or menopause. However, these substances regulate many other physical and psychological functions, and their influence reaches far beyond the reproductive system.

The **endocrine system** is a series of ductless glands, located in various parts of the body, that manufacture and secrete the chemical substances known as **hormones**, which are manufactured and released in one part of the body but have an effect on other parts of the body. Hormones are released into the bloodstream and travel throughout the circulatory system, but each hormone performs its assigned job only when it connects with the body cells that have receptors for it. For instance, in women, the ovaries and adrenal glands produce *progesterone* for which there are receptor sites in the reproductive tissues of women's bodies. Some of the same chemical substances that are neurotransmitters act as hormones as well—norepinephrine and vasopressin, to name two. Figure 5.13 shows the glands in the endocrine system and their locations in the body.

The **pituitary gland** rests in the brain just below the hypothalamus and is controlled by it (see Figure 5.13). The pituitary is considered to be the "master gland" of the body because it releases the hormones that activate, or turn on, the other glands in the endocrine system—a big job for a tiny structure about the size of a pea. The pituitary also produces the hormone that is responsible for body growth (Howard et al., 1996). Too little of this powerful substance will make a person a dwarf; too much will produce a giant.

The **pineal gland** lies deep within the brain. Its function is to produce and regulate the hormone *melatonin*. This hormone regulates sleep and wakefulness. Deficiencies are associated with jet lag and other disturbances of the sleep/wakefulness cycle.

The **thyroid gland** rests in the front, lower part of the neck just below the voice box (larynx). The thyroid produces the important hormone thyroxine, which regulates the rate at which food is metabolized, or transformed into energy. The **parathyroid glands** are attached to the left and right lobes of the thyroid. Parathyroid hormone (PTH) is involved in the absorption of calcium and magnesium from the diet and regulates the levels of these minerals in the bloodstream. Dysfunctions of the parathyroid are also linked to depression and memory loss (Kim & Makdissi, 2009).

The **thymus gland**, produces hormones such as thymosin that are needed for the production of specialized white blood cells that circulate throughout the body and destroy microorganisms that can cause diseases. When the body is threatened by one of these invaders, the thymus gland signals the body to produce more of these cells. The **pancreas** regulates the body's blood sugar levels by releasing the hormones insulin and glucagon into the bloodstream. In people with diabetes, too little insulin is produced. Without insulin to break down the sugars in food, blood-sugar levels can get dangerously high.

The two **adrenal glands**, which rest just above the kidneys (as shown in Figure 5.13), produce epinephrine and norepinephrine. By activating the sympathetic nervous system, these two hormones play an important role in the fight-or-flight syndrome. A group of adrenal hormones called the corticoids are also involved in the fight-or-flight syndrome. Animal research suggests that these hormones contribute to both the emotion of rage and aggressive behavior by signaling the brain to maintain the fight-or-flight response long after the threat that initiated the response has passed (Kruk et al., 2004).

endocrine system
(EN-duh-krin) A system of ductless glands in various parts of the body that manufacture hormones and secrete them into the bloodstream, thus affecting cells in other parts of the body

hormone
A chemical substance that is manufactured and released in one part of the body and affects other parts of the body

pituitary gland
The endocrine gland located in the brain that releases hormones that activate other endocrine glands as well as growth hormone; often called the "master gland."

pineal gland
The endocrine gland that secretes the hormone that controls the sleep/wakefulness cycle

thyroid gland
The endocrine gland that produces thyroxine and regulates metabolism

parathyroid glands
The endocrine glands that produce PTH, a hormone that helps the body absorb minerals from the diet

thymus gland
The endocrine gland that produces hormones that are essential to immune system functioning

pancreas
The endocrine gland responsible for regulating the amount of sugar in the bloodstream

adrenal glands
(ah-DREE-nal) A pair of endocrine glands that release hormones that prepare the body for emergencies and stressful situations and also release corticoids and small amounts of the sex hormones

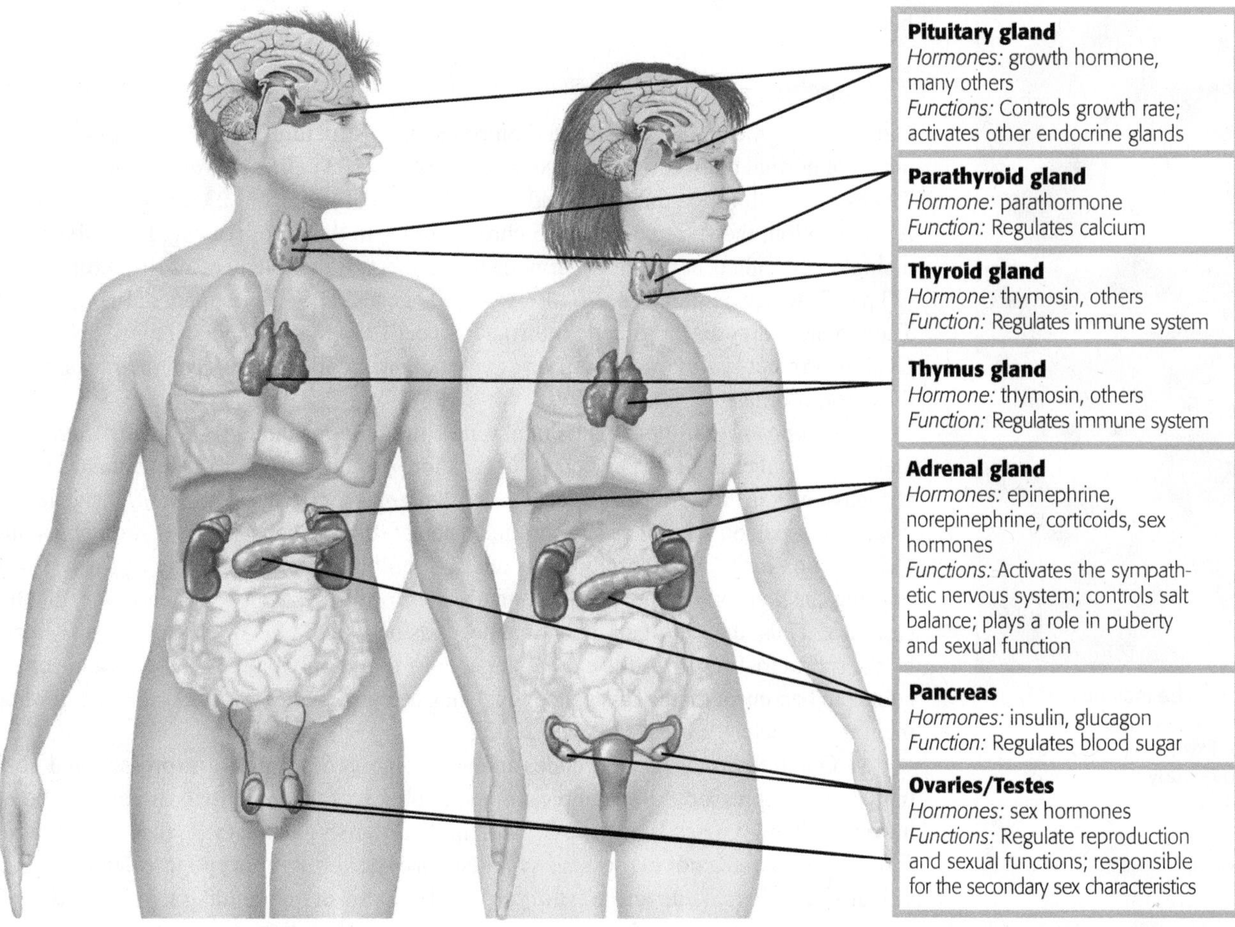

Figure 5.13 The Endocrine System
The endocrine system is a series of glands that manufacture and secrete hormones. The hormones travel through the circulatory system and have important effects on many bodily functions.

The adrenals also produce small amounts of sex hormones. However, the **gonads**—the ovaries in females and the testes in males—have the primary responsibility for these hormones (refer to Figure 5.13). Activated by the pituitary gland, the gonads release the sex hormones that make reproduction possible and that are responsible for the secondary sex characteristics—pubic and underarm hair in both sexes, breasts in females, and facial hair and a deepened voice in males. Androgens, the male sex hormones, influence sexual motivation. Estrogen and progesterone, the female sex hormones, help regulate the menstrual cycle. Although both males and females have androgens and estrogens, males have considerably more androgens, and females have considerably more estrogens.

Genes and Behavioral Genetics

5.14 How does heredity affect physical and psychological traits?

You may have heard of the Human Genome Project, a 13-year enterprise spearheaded by the U.S. Department of Energy and devoted to mapping the entire human genetic code. Remarkably, in April 2003, only 50 years after scientists James Watson and Francis Crick discovered the structure of DNA (of which genes consist), the international team of scientists involved in the project announced that they had achieved their goal (U.S. Department of Energy, 2009). Of course, you received your own genetic code from your parents.

gonads
The ovaries in females and the testes in males; endocrine glands that produce sex hormones

This child's phenotype includes curly hair. What can you infer about her genotype? How likely is it that neither of her parents has curly hair?

genes
The segments of DNA that are located on the chromosomes and are the basic units for the transmission of all hereditary traits

chromosomes
Rod-shaped structures in the nuclei of body cells, which contain all the genes and carry all the genetic information necessary to make a human being

genotype
An individual's genetic makeup

phenotype
An individual's actual characteristics

dominant–recessive pattern
A set of inheritance rules in which the presence of a single dominant gene causes a trait to be expressed but two genes must be present for the expression of a recessive trait

polygenic inheritance
A pattern of inheritance in which many genes influence a trait

multifactorial inheritance
A pattern of inheritance in which a trait is influenced by both genes and environmental factors

But just how do the chemical messages that make up your genes affect your body and your behavior?

The Mechanisms of Heredity

Genes are segments of DNA located on rod-shaped structures called **chromosomes**. The nuclei of normal body cells, with two exceptions, have 23 pairs of chromosomes (46 in all). The two exceptions are the sperm and egg cells, each of which has 23 single chromosomes. At conception, the sperm adds its 23 chromosomes to the 23 of the egg. From this union, a single cell called a *zygote* is formed; it has the full complement of 46 chromosomes (23 pairs), which contain about 20,000 to 25,000 genes (U.S. Department of Energy, 2012). These genes carry all the genetic information needed to make a human being. The Human Genome Project is aimed at identifying the functions of all the genes and their locations on the chromosomes.

Twenty-two of the 23 pairs of chromosomes are matching pairs, called *autosomes,* and each member of these pairs carries genes for particular physical and mental traits. The chromosomes in the 23rd pair are called *sex chromosomes* because they carry the genes that determine a person's sex. The sex chromosomes of females consist of two X chromosomes (XX); males have an X chromosome and a Y chromosome (XY). The egg cell always contains an X chromosome. Half of a man's sperm cells carry an X chromosome, and half carry a Y. Thus, the sex of an individual depends on which type of chromosome is carried by the sperm that fertilizes the egg. A single gene found only on the Y chromosome causes a fetus to become a male. This gene, which has been labeled Sry, orchestrates the development of the male sex organs (Capel, 2000).

Our individual genetic codes include some genes that are expressed and some that are not expressed. For example, some people carry the gene for a disease but do not have the disorder associated with it. To help distinguish genetic traits that are expressed from those that are not expressed, scientists use the term **genotype** to refer to an individual's genetic makeup and **phenotype** to refer to his or her actual traits. Thus, if a person carries the gene for a disease but does not have it, the disease is part of her genotype but not part of her phenotype. The *Apply It* feature on page 149 outlines some situations in which you might consider genetic counseling. Scientists still do not fully understand all of the factors that govern the expression of genes. However, a few of the rules that determine which aspects of an individual's genotype are expressed in her phenotype have been well established by research.

Many traits are influenced by complementary gene pairs, one from the sperm and the other from the egg. In most cases, these gene pairs follow a set of inheritance rules known as the **dominant–recessive pattern**. The gene for curly hair, for example, is dominant over the gene for straight hair. Thus, a person having one gene for curly hair and one for straight hair will have curly hair, and people with straight hair have two recessive genes.

Several neurological and psychological characteristics are associated with dominant or recessive genes. Hand preference appears to follow the dominant recessive pattern, although in a somewhat complex way, as discussed in the *Explain It* feature on page 136. However, most of the traits of interest to psychologists follow more complex inheritance patterns.

In **polygenic inheritance**, many genes influence a particular characteristic. For example, skin color is determined by several genes. When one parent has dark skin and the other is fair skinned, the child will have skin that is somewhere between the two. Many polygenic characteristics are subject to **multifactorial inheritance**; that is, they are influenced by both genes and environmental factors. For instance, a man's genes may allow him to reach a height of 6 feet, but if he suffers from malnutrition while still growing, his height may not reach its genetic potential. Both intelligence and personality are believed to be polygenic and multifactorial in nature. In addition, many psychological disorders are both polygenic and multifactorial (Leonardo & Hen, 2006; McMahon et al., 2010).

Sex-linked inheritance involves the genes on the X and Y chromosomes. In females, the two X chromosomes function pretty much like the autosomes: If one carries

Apply It

Should You Consult a Genetic Counselor?

The purpose of genetic counseling is to estimate individuals' risk of having a child with a genetic disorder or of developing an inherited disorder themselves. If you have relatives who have such disorders, you may have wondered whether you should seek genetic counseling. Such counseling can be helpful to just about anyone, but there are a few situations in which professionals advise that genetic counseling is especially important.

Birth Defects and Inherited Diseases of Childhood

As you may know, prenatal testing can identify many birth defects and genetic disorders before a child is born. However, experts say that screening for such risks should be done prior to conception if any of the following applies to you or your partner (Brundage, 2002):

- You or your partner has previously had a child with a birth defect (e.g., spina bifida) or an inherited disorder (e.g., phenylketonuria).
- There is someone in your or your partner's family who displayed an unexplained developmental delay or disability (i.e., visual or hearing impairment, mental retardation) early in life.
- You or your partner belongs to an ethnic group in which there is a particularly high incidence of a specific inherited disorder (e.g., African Americans: sickle cell disease; European Jews: Tay-Sachs disease; Caucasians: cystic fibrosis; people of Greek, Middle Eastern, or North African descent: thalassemia).

Adult-Onset Genetic Disorders

Genetic counselors suggest that you seriously consider genetic counseling if anyone in your family has ever been diagnosed with one of these adult-onset genetic disorders:

- Huntington disease
- Myotonic muscular dystrophy
- Amyotrophic lateral sclerosis (ALS, Lou Gehrig disease)
- Schizophrenia

Hereditary Cancers

If someone in your family has been diagnosed with cancer, then genetic counseling can be helpful in determining your own risk of developing the disease. According to the Massey Cancer Center at Virginia Commonwealth University (2006), the following types of family histories are especially indicative of a need for genetic counseling:

- A family history of multiple cases of the same or related types of cancers
- One or more relatives with rare cancers
- Cancers occurring at an earlier age of onset than usual (for instance, under the age of 50 years) in at least one member
- Bilateral cancers (two cancers that develop independently in a paired organ, i.e., both kidneys or both breasts)
- One or more family members with two primary cancers (two original tumors that develop in different sites)
- Eastern European Jewish background

Multifactorial Disorders

Many chronic health conditions are attributable to a combination of genetic and lifestyle factors. While there are no genetic tests for these disorders, a genetic counselor can analyze your family history and help you determine your risk of developing one or more of them. A genetic counselor can also advise you as to the degree to which lifestyle changes might enable you to avoid some of the effects of a disorder that you have seen diminish the quality of life of one of your family members. Thus, you may want to seek genetic counseling if anyone in your family has been diagnosed with one or more of these multifactorial disorders:

- Adult-onset diabetes
- Hypertension
- Glaucoma
- Heart disease
- Rheumatoid arthritis
- Disorders of the endocrine system (e.g., hypothyroidism, pancreatitis)
- Autoimmune disorders (e.g., lupus, multiple sclerosis)
- Liver or kidney disease
- Depression
- Parkinson disease
- Alzheimer's disease

Making the Decision

Even if these checklists have led you to the conclusion that you should consult a genetic counselor, you may find it difficult to confront the possibility that you or your child may have to deal with a serious health problem. Such feelings are common among individuals whose family members have one of the conditions previously described. However, researchers have found that people who are uninformed about their personal genetic vulnerability actually tend to overestimate their chances of developing an inherited disorder (Quaid et al., 2001; Tercyak et al., 2001). Thus, genetic counseling will help you formulate a realistic assessment of your own personal risks and will also enable you to develop a plan for coping with them if a genetic disorder is likely to be in your future.

a harmful gene, the other usually has a gene that offsets its effects. In males, however, if the single X chromosome carries a harmful gene, there is no offsetting gene on the Y chromosome because it is very small and carries only the genes needed to create the male body type. Consequently, disorders caused by genes on the X chromosome occur far more often in males than in females. For example, one fairly common sex-linked disorder is *red-green color blindness*. About 5% of men have the disorder, but fewer than 1% of women have it (Mather, 2006). About 1 in every 4,000 males and 1 in every 8,000 females have a far more serious sex-linked disorder called *fragile-X syndrome*, which can cause mental retardation (Jewell & Buehler, 2011).

Behavioral Genetics

Behavioral genetics is a field of research that investigates the relative effects of heredity and environment—nature and nurture—on behavior (Loehlin, 2009). In twin studies, behavioral geneticists study identical twins (monozygotic twins) and fraternal twins (dizygotic twins) to determine how much they resemble each other on a variety of characteristics (Johnson, Turkheimer, Gorresman, & Bouchard, 2009). Identical twins have exactly the same genes because a single sperm of the father fertilizes a single egg of the mother, forming a cell that then splits and forms two human beings—"identical copies." In the case of fraternal twins, two separate sperm cells fertilize two separate eggs that happen to be released at the same time during ovulation. Fraternal twins are no more alike genetically than any two siblings born to the same parents.

Twins who are raised together, whether identical or fraternal, have similar environments. If identical twins raised together are found to be more alike on a certain trait than fraternal twins raised together, then that trait is assumed to be more influenced by heredity. But if the identical and fraternal twin pairs do not differ on the trait, then that trait is assumed to be influenced more by environment.

In adoption studies, behavioral geneticists study children adopted shortly after birth. Researchers compare the children's abilities and personality traits to those of their adoptive parents and those of their biological parents. This strategy allows researchers to disentangle the effects of heredity and environment.

Because heredity and environment work together to influence so many of the variables of interest to psychologists.

Remember It

1. The endocrine glands secrete ______________ directly into the ______________.
2. The ______________ gland acts as a "master gland" that activates the others.
3. Blood sugar levels are regulated by the ______________ through the release of ______________ and ______________.
4. Sex hormones are produced by both the ______________ and the ______________.
5. The ______________ is the gland responsible for maintaining balanced metabolism.
6. A ______________ gene will not be expressed if the individual carries only one copy of it.
7. Characteristics that are affected by both genes and environment are said to be ______________.
8. ______________ is the field of research that investigates the relative effects of heredity and environment on behavior.

behavioral genetics
A field of research that uses twin studies and adoption studies to investigate the relative effects of heredity and environment on behavior

Looking Back

One of the many things you learned about the nervous system in this chapter is that adaptability is one of its important features. For instance, as the case of Phineas Gage illustrates, many areas of the adult brain are irrevocably committed to certain functions, leaving us with a more vulnerable but more efficient brain than we had as children. Nevertheless, even in the face of devastating injury, the brain may continue to function. The complementary functions of excitatory and inhibitory neurotransmitters enable our brains to respond appropriately to different kinds of situations. Individuals who have split-brain surgery function quite well in everyday life; only in certain kinds of tasks do they show any effects from the loss of interhemispheric communication. When we need to react to an emergency, our endocrine and peripheral nervous systems collaborate to produce the temporary burst of energy we need. Finally, although a few characteristics and diseases are fully determined by our genes, most of our psychological traits are shaped by both heredity and environment.

Summary

DISCOVERING THE MYSTERIES OF THE NERVOUS SYSTEM (PP. 119–121)

5.1 What does the electroencephalogram (EEG) reveal about the brain? (pp. 119–120)

An electroencephalogram (EEG) is a record of brain-wave activity. It can reveal an epileptic seizure and can show patterns of neural activity associated with learning disabilities, schizophrenia, Alzheimer's disease, sleep disorders, and other problems.

Key Terms

electroencephalogram (EEG), p. 119
microelectrode, p. 120

5.2 How do researchers use imaging techniques to study the nervous system? (pp. 120–121)

Both the CT scan and MRI provide detailed images of brain structures. The PET scan reveals patterns of blood flow, oxygen use, and glucose metabolism in the brain. It can also show the action of drugs in the brain and other organs. PET scan studies show that different brain areas are used to perform different tasks. Functional MRI (fMRI) can provide information about brain function and structure more precisely and more rapidly than a PET scan. Two more recently developed technologies, SQUID and MEG, measure magnetic changes to reveal neural activity within the brain as it occurs.

Key Terms

CT scan (computerized axial tomography), p. 120
MRI (magnetic resonance imagery), p. 120
PET scan (positron-emission tomography), p. 120
functional MRI (fMRI), p. 120

THE NEURONS AND THE NEUROTRANSMITTERS (PP. 121–127)

5.3 What does each part of the neuron do? (p. 122)

The cell body carries out metabolic functions. The dendrites receive messages from cell bodies and other neurons. The axon transmits messages to the dendrites and cell bodies of other neurons and to the muscles, glands, and other parts of the body. Glial cells support neurons' vital functions.

Key Terms

neuron, p. 121
neurotransmitters, p. 121
cell body, p. 122
dendrites, p. 122
axon, p. 122
axon terminal, p. 122
glial cells, p. 122

5.4 How do neurons transmit messages through the nervous system? (pp. 122–125)

The action potential, the primary means by which the brain and body communicate with one another via the nervous system, is the sudden reversal (from a negative to a positive value) of the resting potential on the cell membrane of a neuron; this reversal initiates the firing of a neuron. A strong stimulus will cause many more neurons to fire and to fire much more rapidly than a weak stimulus will.

Key Terms

synapse, p. 122
resting potential, p. 122
action potential, p. 122
myelin sheath, p. 125

5.5 How do neurotransmitters work? (pp. 125–127)

Neurotransmitters are chemicals released into the synaptic cleft from the axon terminal of the sending neuron. They cross the synaptic cleft and bind to receptors on the receiving neuron, influencing the cell to fire or not to fire. Neurotransmitters work by speeding up, slowing down, or blocking messages between neurons. Drugs affect the nervous system by altering or mimicking neurotransmitters. Some neurotransmitters contribute to psychological disorders.

Key Terms

receptors, p. 126
reuptake, p. 126

THE HUMAN NERVOUS SYSTEM (PP. 127–134)

5.6 What are the structures and functions of the peripheral nervous system? (pp. 127–129)

The peripheral nervous system includes all of the nerves that connect the various parts of the body to the central nervous system. The somatic subdivision governs voluntary control of the body; the autonomic subdivision governs involuntary processes. Within the autonomic subdivision, the sympathetic nervous system mobilizes the body's resources during emergencies or during stress, and the parasympathetic nervous system brings the heightened bodily responses back to normal after an emergency.

Key Terms

peripheral nervous system, p. 127
central nervous system, p. 127
sympathetic nervous system, p. 128
parasympathetic nervous system, p. 128

5.7 What are the structures and functions of the central nervous system? (pp. 129–133)

The spinal cord transmits information from the body to the brain and from the brain to the body. The hindbrain contains the cerebellum, which regulates movement, muscle tone, and posture. The brainstem contains the medulla, which controls vital functions; the reticular formation, which controls arousal and attention; and the pons, which connects the two halves of the cerebellum. The substantia nigra, a structure in the midbrain, controls unconscious motor actions, such as riding a bicycle. The structures of the forebrain include (1) the thalamus, the relay station for information flowing into and out of the brain; (2) the hypothalamus, which regulates hunger, thirst, sexual behavior, internal body temperature, and emotional behaviors; (3) the limbic system, including the amygdala and the hippocampus, which is involved in emotional expression, memory, and motivation. The cerebrum is also part of the forebrain.

Key Terms

spinal cord, p. 129
hindbrain, p. 130
brainstem, p. 130
medulla, p. 130
pons, p. 130
reticular formation, p. 130
cerebellum, p. 130
midbrain, p. 131
substantia nigra, p. 131
forebrain, p. 132
thalamus, p. 132
hypothalamus, p. 132
limbic system, p. 132
amygdala, p. 132
hippocampus, p. 132

A CLOSER LOOK AT THE THINKING PART OF THE BRAIN (pp. 134–142)

5.8 What are the components of the cerebrum? (pp. 134–135)

The cerebral hemispheres are connected by the corpus callosum and covered by the cerebral cortex, which is primarily responsible for higher mental processes such as language, memory, and thinking.

Key Terms

cerebrum, p. 134
cerebral hemispheres, p. 134
corpus callosum, p. 134
cerebral cortex, p. 134
association areas, p. 135

5.9 What are the specialized functions of the left and right cerebral hemispheres? (pp. 135–139)

The left hemisphere controls the right side of the body, coordinates complex movements, and handles most of the language functions, including speaking, writing, reading, and understanding the written and the spoken word. The right hemisphere controls the left side of the body. It is specialized for visual–spatial perception, the interpretation of nonverbal behavior, and the recognition and expression of emotion.

Key Terms

lateralization, p. 135
left hemisphere, p. 135
right hemisphere, p. 135
split-brain operation, p. 137

5.10 Which functions are associated with each of the four lobes of the cerebral cortex? (pp. 139–142)

The frontal lobes contain (1) the motor cortex, which controls voluntary motor activity; (2) Broca's area, which functions in speech production; and (3) the frontal association areas, which are involved in thinking, motivation, planning for the future, impulse control, and emotional responses. The somatosensory cortex, where touch, pressure, temperature, and pain register, is in the parietal lobes. The occipital lobes receive and interpret visual information. The temporal lobes contain (1) the primary auditory cortex, where hearing registers in the cortex; (2) Wernicke's area, which processes the spoken word and formulates coherent speech and written language; and (3) the temporal association areas, which interpret auditory stimuli.

Key Terms

frontal lobes, p. 139
prefrontal cortex, p. 139
motor cortex, p. 139
Broca's area, p. 141
Broca's aphasia, p. 141
aphasia, p. 141
parietal lobes, p. 141
somatosensory cortex, p. 141
occipital lobes, p. 141
primary visual cortex, p. 141
temporal lobes, p. 142
primary auditory cortex, p. 142
Wernicke's area, p. 142
Wernicke's aphasia, p. 142

AGE, GENDER, AND THE BRAIN (pp. 143–145)

5.11 How does the brain change across the lifespan? (pp. 143–151)

The brain grows in spurts, each of which is followed by a period of pruning of unnecessary synapses. The activity of neurotransmitters within the synapses also varies with age. Few neurons are myelinated at birth, but the process of myelination continues into the adult years. Language appears to be lateralized very early in life, but other functions, such as spatial perception, aren't fully lateralized until age 8 or so. Aging eventually leads to a reduction in the number of synapses.

Key Terms

pruning, p. 143
plasticity, p. 143
stroke, p. 145

5.12 How do the brains of men and women differ? (p. 145)

Men's brains have a lower proportion of white matter in the left than in the right brain; women have equal proportions of gray and white matter in the two hemispheres. Some tasks tap different areas in men's brains than they do in the brains of women.

BEYOND THE NERVOUS SYSTEM (pp. 146–151)

5.13 What are the functions of the glands of the endocrine system? (pp. 146–147)

The pituitary gland releases hormones that control other glands in the endocrine system and also releases a growth hormone. The thyroid gland produces thyroxine, which regulates metabolism. The pancreas produces insulin and glucagon and regulates blood sugar levels. The adrenal glands release epinephrine and norepinephrine, which prepare the body for emergencies and stressful situations; these glands also release corticoids and small amounts of the sex hormones. The gonads are the sex glands, which produce the sex hormones and make reproduction possible.

Key Terms

endocrine system, p. 146
hormone, p. 146
pituitary gland, p. 146
pineal gland, p. 146
thyroid gland, p. 146
parathyroid glands, p. 146
thymus gland, p. 146
pancreas, p. 146
adrenal glands, p. 146
gonads, p. 147

5.14 How does heredity affect physical and psychological traits? (pp. 147–151)

Some genetic traits follow the dominant–recessive pattern in which pairs of genes control their manifestation. Others involve multiple genes (polygenic), and still others depend on the combined effects of genes and environmental factors (multifactorial). Behavioral geneticists use twin studies to examine the relative effects of heredity and environment on behavior as well as adoption and family studies. Such studies suggest that both intelligence and personality are polygenic and multifactorial.

Key Terms

genes, p. 148
chromosomes, p. 148
genotype, p. 148
phenotype, p. 148
dominant–recessive pattern, p. 148
polygenic inheritance, p. 148
multifactorial inheritance, p. 148
behavioral genetics, p. 150

Study Guide

SECTION ONE: CHAPTER REVIEW

Discovering the Mysteries of the Nervous System (pp. 119–121)

1. A(n) ______________________ requires that electrodes be placed on a person's scalp, while a(n) ____________ requires that microelectrodes be inserted directly into the brain.

2. The CT scan and MRI are used to
   a. show the amount of activity in various parts of the brain.
   b. produce images of the brain's structures.
   c. measure electrical activity in the brain.
   d. observe neural communication at synapses.

3. Which of the following reveals the electrical activity of the brain by producing a record of brain waves?
   a. electroencephalogram
   b. CT scan
   c. PET scan
   d. MRI

4. Which of the following reveals brain structures, but not brain activity?
   a. CT scan
   b. EEG
   c. PET scan
   d. fMRI

5. Which of the following reveals both brain structure and brain activity?
   a. MRI
   b. PET scan
   c. fMRI
   d. CT scan

The Neurons and the Neurotransmitters (pp. 121–127)

6. The branchlike extensions of neurons that act as receivers of signals from other neurons are the
   a. dendrites.
   b. axons.
   c. neurotransmitters.
   d. cell bodies.

7. _________ support neurons, supplying them with nutrients and carrying away their waste products.

8. The junction where the axon of a sending neuron communicates with a receiving neuron is called the
   a. reuptake site.
   b. receptor site.
   c. synapse.
   d. axon terminal.

9. When a neuron fires, neurotransmitters are released from the synaptic vesicles in the _________ terminal into the synaptic cleft.
   a. dendrite
   b. cell body's
   c. receptor
   d. axon

10. The (resting, action) potential is the firing of a neuron that results when the charge within the neuron becomes more positive than the charge outside the cell membrane. The (resting, action) potential is the slight negative charge of the neuron.

11. Receptor sites on the receiving neuron
    a. receive any available neurotransmitter molecules.
    b. receive only neurotransmitter molecules of specific shapes.
    c. can only be influenced by neurotransmitters from a single neuron.
    d. are located only on the dendrites.

12. The neurotransmitter called *acetylcholine* is involved in
    a. memory.
    b. motor function.
    c. rapid eye movement during sleep.
    d. all of the above

13. _________ is a neurotransmitter that may be associated with ADHD.

14. _________ are neurotransmitters that act as natural painkillers.

15. Responses to cocaine involve the neurotransmitters _________ and _________.

16. The _________ nervous system connects the central nervous system to the rest of the body.
    a. central
    b. peripheral
    c. somatic
    d. autonomic

17. The _________ nervous system mobilizes the body's resources during times of stress; the _________ nervous system brings the heightened bodily responses back to normal when the emergency is over.
    a. somatic; autonomic
    b. autonomic; somatic
    c. sympathetic; parasympathetic
    d. parasympathetic; sympathetic

The Human Nervous System (pp. 127–133)

18. Match the brain structure with its description.
    ____ (1) connects the brain with the peripheral nervous system
    ____ (2) controls heart rate, breathing, and blood pressure
    ____ (3) consists of the medulla, the pons, and the reticular formation
    ____ (4) influences attention and arousal
    ____ (5) coordinates complex body movements
    ____ (6) serves as a relay station for sensory information flowing into the brain

____ (7) controls unconscious movements

a. medulla
b. spinal cord
c. reticular formation
d. thalamus
e. cerebellum
f. brainstem
g. substantia nigra

19. The hypothalamus regulates all the following *except*
a. internal body temperature.
b. coordinated movement.
c. hunger and thirst.
d. sexual behavior.

20. The part of the limbic system primarily involved in the formation of memories is the (amygdala, hippocampus).

21. The __________ is associated with emotions, and the __________ is involved in memory.

A Closer Look at the Thinking Part of the Brain (pp. 134–142)

22. What is the thick band of fibers connecting the two cerebral hemispheres?
a. cortex
b. corpus callosum
c. cerebrum
d. motor cortex

23. The outer covering of the cerebrum is the
a. cerebral cortex.
b. cortex callosum.
c. myelin sheath.
d. white matter.

24. Match the lobes with the brain areas they contain.
____ (1) primary auditory cortex
____ (2) primary visual cortex
____ (3) motor cortex
____ (4) somatosensory cortex

a. frontal lobes
b. parietal lobes
c. occipital lobes
d. temporal lobes

25. Match the specialized area with the appropriate description of function.
____ (1) hearing registers
____ (2) vision registers
____ (3) touch, pressure, and temperature register
____ (4) voluntary movement
____ (5) thinking, motivation, impulse control

a. primary visual cortex
b. motor cortex
c. association areas
d. auditory cortex
e. somatosensory cortex

26. Match the hemisphere with the specialized abilities usually associated with it.
____ (1) visual–spatial skills
____ (2) speech
____ (3) recognition and expression of emotion
____ (4) musical perception
____ (5) mathematics

a. right hemisphere
b. left hemisphere

27. Which of these statements is *not* true of the split-brain operation?
a. It is used on people with severe epilepsy.
b. It provides a means of studying the functions of the individual hemispheres.
c. It causes major changes in intelligence, personality, and behavior.
d. It makes transfer of information between hemispheres impossible.

Age, Gender, and the Brain (pp. 143–145)

28. Synaptic development (synaptogenesis) involves growth of
a. dendrites.
b. axons.
c. both dendrites and axons.

29. One developmental process that contributes to differences in processing speed between children and adults is __________.

30. Men have a lower proportion of __________ __________ in the left hemisphere than in the right.

31. Navigational tasks stimulate (different, the same) areas of the brain in men and women.

32. As adults get older, brain weight (increases, decreases).

33. As adults get older, the risk of brain damage from __________ increases.

Beyond the Nervous System (pp. 146–151)

34. Match the endocrine gland with the appropriate description.
____ (1) keeps body's metabolism in balance
____ (2) acts as a master gland that activates the other glands
____ (3) regulates the blood sugar
____ (4) makes reproduction possible
____ (5) releases hormones that prepare the body for emergencies
____ (6) regulates sleep

a. pituitary gland
b. adrenal glands
c. gonads
d. thyroid gland
e. pancreas
f. pineal gland

35. A __________ gene will not be expressed unless an individual carries two copies of it.

36. Characteristics that are affected by both genes and environment are said to be
a. polygenic.
b. dominant.
c. recessive.
d. multifactorial.

37. Researchers use __________ and __________ to examine the effects of heredity and environment.

SECTION TWO: LABEL THE BRAIN

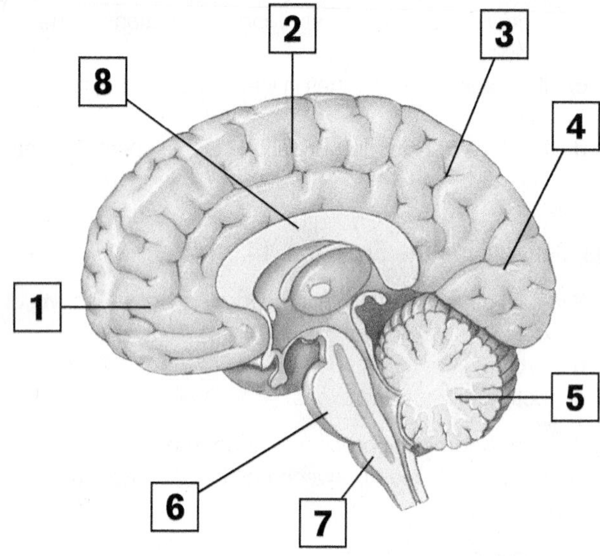

Identify each of the numbered parts in the brain diagram.

1. __________
2. __________
3. __________
4. __________
5. __________
6. __________
7. __________
8. __________

SECTION THREE: COMPREHENSIVE PRACTICE TEST

1. Phineas Gage changed from a polite, dependable, well-liked railroad foreman to a rude and impulsive person who could no longer plan realistically for the future after he suffered serious damage to his
   a. occipital lobe.
   b. frontal lobe.
   c. medulla.
   d. cerebellum.
2. A researcher interested in getting information about the brain's activity based on the amount of oxygen and glucose consumed should use a(n)
   a. MRI.
   b. EEG.
   c. PET scan.
   d. CT scan.
3. Functional MRI (fMRI) reveals both brain structure and brain activity. (true/false)
4. Afferent is to efferent as
   a. sensory is to sensation.
   b. sensation is to perception.
   c. motor is to sensory.
   d. sensory is to motor.
5. __________ plays an important role in regulating mood, sleep, impulsivity, aggression, and appetite.
   a. Dopamine
   b. Norepinephrine
   c. Acetylcholine
   d. Serotonin
6. Neurons can conduct messages faster if they have
   a. an axon with a myelin sheath.
   b. a positive resting potential.
   c. more than one cell body.
   d. fewer dendrites.
7. The electrical charge inside a neuron is about –70 millivolts and is known as the __________ potential.
   a. action
   b. refractory
   c. resting
   d. impulse
8. The main divisions of the nervous system are the __________ and the __________ systems.
   a. somatic; autonomic
   b. central; peripheral
   c. brain; spinal cord
   d. sympathetic; parasympathetic
9. The structure that is located above the brainstem and serves as a relay station for information flowing into or out of the forebrain is the
   a. pituitary gland.
   b. hypothalamus.
   c. thalamus.
   d. hippocampus.
10. The structure that is located in the brainstem and is important for basic life functions such as heartbeat and breathing is the
    a. pons.
    b. medulla.
    c. hypothalamus.
    d. amygdala.
11. The __________ is sometimes referred to as the body's thermostat because it controls temperature, hunger, thirst, and emotional behaviors.
    a. corpus callosum
    b. pituitary gland
    c. cerebellum
    d. hypothalamus
12. The lobe that contains the primary visual cortex is the
    a. parietal lobe.
    b. occipital lobe.
    c. temporal lobe.
    d. frontal lobe.
13. The primary motor cortex is located in the __________ lobe.
    a. frontal
    b. occipital
    c. temporal
    d. oculo-visual
14. The pituitary gland, known as the master gland, is part of the __________ system.
    a. somatic
    b. peripheral nervous
    c. endocrine
    d. central nervous
15. The __________ nervous system controls skeletal muscles and allows the body to interact with the external environment.
    a. autonomic
    b. parasympathetic
    c. sympathetic
    d. somatic
16. Damage to Broca's area will result in a type of aphasia that impairs one's ability to produce speech sounds. (true/false)
17. The prefrontal cortex is involved in all of the following functions *except*
    a. controlling heart beat and respiration
    b. impulse control
    c. personality
    d. coordination of multiple brain functions to accomplish cognitive goals
18. __________ __________ isn't lateralized to the right hemisphere until age 8 or so.

19. Women are more likely than men to process navigational tasks in the __________ __________ __________ and __________ __________ __________.

20. Red-green color blindness is caused by a defective gene on the __________.

Section FOUR: Critical Thinking

1. Much of the brain research you have read about in this chapter was carried out using animals. In many studies, it is necessary to euthanize animals to study their brain tissues directly. Many people object to this practice, but others say it is justified because it advances knowledge about the brain. Prepare arguments to support both of the following positions:
   a. The use of animals in brain research projects is ethical and justifiable because of the possible benefits to humankind.
   b. The use of animals in brain research projects is not ethical or justifiable on the grounds of possible benefits to humankind.

SECTION FIVE: Application Essays

1. How would your life change if you had a massive stroke affecting your left hemisphere? How would it change if the stroke damaged your right hemisphere? Which stroke would have the greater effect on the quality of your life, and why?
2. Imagine that your parent has been diagnosed with diabetes, and you are worried about whether the disease is hereditary. What would a genetic counselor be able tell you about your risk of developing it?

6

Body Rhythms and Mental States*

*Taken from *Psychology*, Eleventh Edition by Carole Wade, Carol Tavris, and Maryanne Garry

Ask questions. . . be willing to wonder

- If you didn't know what time it was, would your body?
- Why do we need to sleep—and dream?
- Can hypnotized people be made to do things against their will?
- Why can a glass of wine make a person feel happy and excited on one occasion but tired and depressed on another?

In Lewis Carroll's immortal story *Alice's Adventures in Wonderland,* the ordinary rules of everyday life keep dissolving in a sea of logical contradictions. First, Alice shrinks to within only a few inches of the ground; then she shoots up taller than the treetops. The strange antics of Wonderland's inhabitants make her smile one moment and shed a pool of tears the next. "Dear dear!" muses the harried heroine. "How queer everything is today! . . . I wonder if I've been changed in the night? Let me think: *Was* I the same when I got up this morning? I almost think I can remember feeling a little different. But if I'm not the same, the *next* question is, 'Who in the world am I?' Ah, *that's* the great puzzle!"

In a way, we all live in a sort of Wonderland. For much of our lives, we reside in a realm where the ordinary rules of logic and experience are often suspended: the dream world of sleep. Throughout the day, mood, alertness, efficiency, and *consciousness* itself—our awareness of ourselves and the environment—are in perpetual flux, sometimes shifting as dramatically as Alice's height. Sometimes we are hyperalert and attentive to our own feelings and everything around us; at other times, we daydream or go on "automatic pilot." Sometimes we speak as though our minds are separate from us; we say, "My mind is playing tricks on me," but who is the "me" watching your mind play those tricks, and who is it that's being tricked? If you say that your brain stores events or registers emotions, who is the "you" that is "using" that brain?

One way to understand consciousness is to study how it changes over time. Starting from the assumption that mental and physical states are as intertwined as sunshine and shadow, psychologists, along with other scientists, are exploring the links between fluctuations in subjective experience and changes in brain activity and hormone levels. They have come to view changing states of consciousness as part of the rhythmic ebb and flow of experience over time. Dreaming, traditionally classified as a state of consciousness, is also related to a 90-minute cycle of brain activity.

Examining a person's ongoing rhythmic cycles is like watching a video of consciousness. Studying the person's distinct states of consciousness is more like looking at separate photos. In this chapter, we will first run the video, to see how functioning and consciousness vary predictably over time. Then we will zoom in on one specific snapshot, the world of dreams, and examine it in some detail. Finally, we will turn to two techniques that "retouch" or alter the video: hypnosis and the use of recreational drugs.

You are about to learn. . .

- how biological rhythms affect our physiology and performance.
- why you feel out of sync when you fly across time zones or change shifts at work.
- why some people get the winter blues.
- how culture and learning affect reports of "PMS" and estimates of its incidence.

Biological Rhythms: The Tides of Experience

The human body goes through dozens of ups and downs in physiological functioning over the course of a day, a week, and a year, changes that are known as **biological rhythms**. A biological clock in our brains governs the waxing and waning of hormone levels, urine volume, blood pressure, and even the responsiveness of brain cells to stimulation.

biological rhythm
a periodic, more or less regular fluctuation in a biological system; it may or may not have psychological implications

Biological rhythms are typically in tune with external time cues, such as changes in clock time, temperature, and daylight, but many rhythms continue to occur even in the absence of such cues; they are **endogenous**, or generated from within.

Circadian rhythms are biological rhythms that occur approximately every 24 hours. The best-known circadian rhythm is the sleep–wake cycle, but hundreds of others affect physiology and performance. Body temperature fluctuates about 1 degree centigrade each day, peaking, on average, in the late afternoon and hitting a low point, or trough, in the wee hours of the morning. Other rhythms occur less frequently than once a day—say, once a month, or once a season. In the animal world, seasonal rhythms are common. Birds migrate south in the fall, bears hibernate in the winter, and marine animals become active or inactive, depending on bimonthly changes in the tides. Some seasonal and monthly rhythms also occur in humans. In both men and women, testosterone peaks in the autumn and dips in the spring (Stanton, Mullette-Gillman, & Huettel, 2011), and in women, the menstrual cycle occurs roughly every 28 days. Other rhythms occur more frequently than once a day, many of them on about a 90-minute cycle. In humans, these include physiological changes during sleep, and (unless social customs intervene) stomach contractions, hormone levels, susceptibility to visual illusions, verbal and spatial performance, brain-wave responses during cognitive tasks, and daydreaming (Escera, Cilveti, & Grau, 1992; Klein & Armitage, 1979; Kripke, 1974; Lavie, 1976).

With a better understanding of our internal tempos, we may be able to design our days to take better advantage of our bodies' natural tempos. Let's take a closer look at how these rhythms operate.

Circadian Rhythms

Circadian rhythms evolved in plants, animals, insects, and human beings as an adaptation to the many changes associated with the rotation of the earth on its axis, such as changes in light, air pressure, and temperature.

In most societies, clocks and other external time cues abound, and people's circadian rhythms become tied to them, following a strict 24-hour schedule. Therefore, to identify endogenous rhythms, scientists isolate volunteers from sunlight, clocks, environmental sounds, and all other cues to time. Some hardy souls have spent weeks isolated in underground caves; usually, however, participants live in specially designed rooms equipped with audio systems, comfortable furniture, and temperature controls. Free of the tyranny of a timepiece, a few of these people have lived a "day" that is much shorter or longer than 24 hours. If allowed to take daytime naps, however, most soon settle into a day that averages 5 to 10 minutes longer than 24 hours (Duffy et al., 2011). For many people, alertness, like temperature, peaks in the late afternoon and falls to a low point in the very early morning (Lavie, 2001).

The Body's Clock

Circadian rhythms are controlled by a biological clock, or overall coordinator, located in a tiny cluster of cells in the hypothalamus called the **suprachiasmatic nucleus (SCN)**. Neural pathways from special receptors in the back of the eye transmit information to the SCN and allow it to respond to changes in light and dark. The SCN then sends out messages that cause the brain and body to adapt to these changes. Other clocks also exist, scattered around the body, but for most circadian rhythms, the SCN is regarded as the master pacemaker.

The SCN regulates fluctuating levels of hormones and neurotransmitters, and they in turn provide feedback that affects the SCN's functioning. During the dark hours, one hormone regulated by the SCN, **melatonin**, is secreted by the pineal gland, deep within the brain. Melatonin induces sleep. When you go to bed in a darkened room, your melatonin

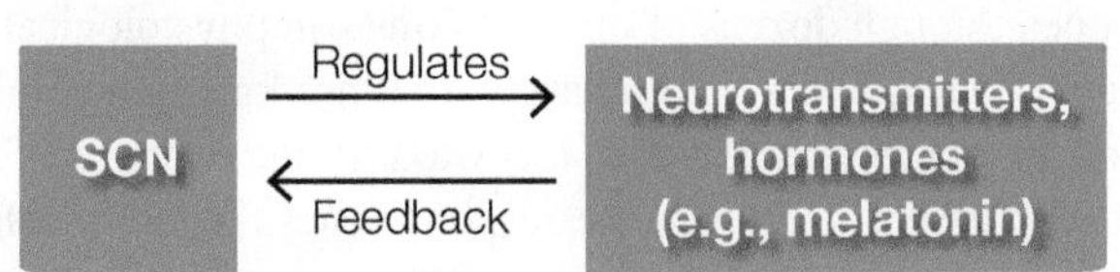

endogenous
generated from within rather than by external cues

circadian [sur-CAY-dee-un] rhythm
a biological rhythm with a period (from peak to peak or trough to trough) of about 24 hours; from the Latin *circa*, "about," and *dies*, "a day"

suprachiasmatic [soo-pruh-kye-az-MAT-ick] nucleus (SCN)
an area of the brain containing a biological clock that governs circadian rhythms

melatonin
a hormone secreted by the pineal gland; it is involved in the regulation of circadian rhythms

Stefania Follini (left) spent four months in a New Mexico cave (above), 30 feet underground, as part of an Italian study on biological rhythms. Her only companions were a computer and two friendly mice. In the absence of clocks, natural light, or changes in temperature, she tended to stay awake for 20 to 25 hours and then sleep for 10. Because her days were longer than usual, when she emerged she thought she had been in the cave for only two months.

level rises; when light fills your room in the morning, it falls. Melatonin, in turn, appears to help keep the biological clock in phase with the light–dark cycle (Haimov & Lavie, 1996; Lewy et al., 1992).

Melatonin treatments have been used to regulate the disturbed sleep–wake cycles of blind people who lack light perception and whose melatonin production does not cycle normally (Sack & Lewy, 1997).

Travel can be exhausting, and jet lag makes it worse.

When the Clock Is Out of Sync

Under normal conditions, the rhythms governed by the SCN are in phase with one another. Their peaks may occur at different times, but if you know when one rhythm peaks, you can predict fairly well when another will. It's a little like knowing the time in London if you know the time in New York. But when your normal routine changes, your circadian rhythms may be thrown out of phase. Such **internal desynchronization** often occurs when people take airplane flights across several time zones. Sleep and wake patterns usually adjust quickly, but temperature and hormone cycles can take several days to return to normal. The resulting jet lag affects energy level, mental skills, and motor coordination (Sack, 2010).

Internal desynchronization also occurs when workers must adjust to a new shift. Efficiency drops, the person feels tired and irritable, accidents become more likely, and sleep disturbances and digestive disorders may occur. For police officers, emergency-room personnel, airline pilots, truck drivers, and operators of nuclear power plants, the consequences can be a matter of life and death. Night work itself is not necessarily a problem: With a schedule that always stays the same, even on weekends, people often adapt. However, many swing- and night-shift assignments are made on a rotating basis, so a worker's circadian rhythms never have a chance to resynchronize.

Some scientists hope eventually to help rotating-shift workers and travelers crossing time zones adjust more quickly by using melatonin, drugs, or other techniques to "reset the clock" (Revell & Eastman, 2005), but so far these techniques do not seem ready for prime time. Giving shift workers melatonin sometimes helps and sometimes does not; stimulant drugs can improve attention but don't eliminate physical fatigue; and although short naps

internal desynchronization
a state in which biological rhythms are not in phase with one another

"IF WE EVER INTEND TO TAKE OVER THE WORLD, ONE THING WE'LL HAVE TO DO IS SYNCHRONIZE OUR BIOLOGICAL CLOCKS."

on the job increase alertness, many employers do not like the idea of paying people to sleep (Kolla & Auger, 2011). When a pilot in Nevada was unable to contact a napping air traffic controller at 2 a.m., scientists butted heads with government officials about who was to blame. "There should be sanctioned on-shift napping. That's the way to handle night-shift work," said one neuroscientist. But the Federal Aviation Administration still bans the practice, while calling for more data.

One reason a simple cure for desynchronization has so far eluded scientists may be that circadian rhythms can be affected by illness, stress, exercise, drugs, mealtimes, and many other factors. Also, circadian rhythms differ greatly from person to person. There truly are morning people ("larks") and evening people ("owls"). Scientists call your identity as a lark or owl your "chronotype." Genetic influences may contribute to chronotypes, although early attempts to find "chronotype genes" have proven difficult to replicate (Chang et al., 2011; Osland et al., 2011). Moreover, your chronotype may change as you age: Adolescents are more likely than children and older adults to be owlish (Biss & Hasher, 2012), which may be why many teenagers have trouble adjusting to school schedules. You may be able to learn about your own personal pulses through careful self-observation, and you may want to try putting that information to use when planning your daily schedule.

Get Involved!

Measuring Your Alertness Cycles

For at least three days, except when you are sleeping, keep an hourly record of your mental alertness level, using this five-point scale: 1 = extremely drowsy or mentally lethargic, 2 = somewhat drowsy or mentally lethargic, 3 = moderately alert, 4 = alert and efficient, 5 = extremely alert and efficient. Does your alertness level appear to follow a circadian rhythm, reaching a high point and a low point once every 24 hours? Or does it follow a shorter rhythm, rising and falling several times during the day? Are your cycles the same on weekends as during the week? Most important, how well does your schedule mesh with your natural fluctuations in alertness?

Moods and Long-Term Rhythms

According to Ecclesiastes, "To every thing there is a season, and a time for every purpose under heaven." Modern science agrees: Long-term cycles have been observed in everything from the threshold for tooth pain to conception rates. Folklore holds that our moods follow similar rhythms, particularly in response to seasonal changes and, in women, menstrual changes. But do they?

Does the Season Affect Moods?

Clinicians report that some people become depressed during particular seasons, typically winter, when periods of daylight are short, a phenomenon that has come to be known as **seasonal affective disorder (SAD)**. This condition is relatively uncommon and is not recognized as an official disorder in the leading diagnostic manual used by clinicians (Rosenthal, 2009). During the winter months, SAD patients report feelings of sadness, lethargy, drowsiness, and a craving for carbohydrates. To counteract the effects of sunless days, physicians and therapists often treat SAD patients with phototherapy, having them sit in front of bright fluorescent lights at specific times of the day, usually early in the morning. In some cases, they have also begun prescribing antidepressants and other drugs.

seasonal affective disorder (SAD)
a controversial disorder in which a person experiences depression during the winter and an improvement of mood in the spring

Unfortunately, much of the research on the effectiveness of light treatments has been flawed; a review of 173 published studies found that only 20 had a proper design and suitable controls (Golden et al., 2005). But a meta-analysis of the data from those

This woman reads and drinks tea for at least 15 minutes in front of what she calls her "happy light," which she uses for seasonal depression.

20 studies did throw some light on the subject, so to speak. When people with SAD were exposed to either a brief period (e.g., 30 minutes) of bright light after waking or to light that slowly became brighter, simulating the dawn, their symptoms were in fact reduced. Light therapy even helped people with mild to moderate *non*seasonal depression (Pail et al., 2011).

SAD may occur in people whose circadian rhythms are out of sync; in essence, they have a chronic form of jet lag (Lewy et al., 2006). Or they may also have some abnormality in the way they produce or respond to melatonin (Wehr et al., 2001). They may produce too much daytime melatonin in the winter, or their morning levels may not fall as quickly as other people's. However, it is not clear why light therapy also appears to help some people with nonseasonal depression. True cases of SAD may have a biological basis, but if so, the mechanism remains uncertain. Keep in mind, too, that for many people who get the winter blues, the reason could be that they hate cold weather, are physically inactive, do not get outside much, or feel lonely during the winter holidays.

Thinking Critically

Examine the evidence

Many women say they become more irritable or depressed premenstrually, and PMS remedies line the shelves of drugstores. But what does the evidence show about PMS? How might attitudes and expectations affect reports of emotional symptoms? What happens when women report their daily moods and feelings to researchers without knowing that menstruation is being studied?

Does the Menstrual Cycle Affect Moods?

Controversy has persisted about another long-term rhythm, the female menstrual cycle, which occurs, on average, every 28 days. During the first half of this cycle, an increase in the hormone estrogen causes the lining of the uterus to thicken in preparation for a possible pregnancy. At midcycle, the ovaries release a mature egg, or ovum. Afterward, the ovarian sac that contained the egg begins to produce progesterone, which helps prepare the uterine lining to receive the egg. Then, if conception does not occur, estrogen and progesterone levels fall, the uterine lining sloughs off as the menstrual flow, and the cycle begins again. The interesting question for psychologists is whether these physical changes cause emotional or intellectual changes, as folklore and tradition would have us believe.

Most people nowadays seem to think so. They are often surprised to learn that it was not until the 1970s that a vague cluster of physical and emotional symptoms associated with the days preceding menstruation—including fatigue, headache, irritability, and depression—was packaged together and given a label: *premenstrual syndrome ("PMS")* (Parlee, 1994). Since then, most laypeople, doctors, and psychiatrists have assumed, uncritically, that many women "suffer" from PMS or from its supposedly more extreme and debilitating version, "premenstrual dysphoric disorder" (PMDD). What does the evidence actually show?

Culture and PMS

The story of PMS illustrates the close interconnection between bodily changes and cultural norms, which help determine how a person's bodily symptoms are labeled and interpreted (Chrisler & Caplan, 2002). PMS symptoms have been reported most often in North America, western Europe, and Australia. But with the rise of globalization and the influence of worldwide drug marketing, reports of such symptoms are increasing in places where they were previously not reported, from Mexico (Marvan, Diaz-Erosa, & Montesinos, 1998) to Saudi Arabia (Rasheed & Al-Sowielem, 2003). In most tribal cultures, however, PMS is virtually unknown; the concern has been with menstruation itself, which is often considered "unclean." And in some cultures, women say they have physical symptoms but not emotional symptoms: Women in China report fatigue, water retention, pain, and cold (American women rarely report cold), but not depression or irritability (Yu et al., 1996).

Hormones do influence all of us, of course, as do many other internal processes. In some cases, hormonal abnormalities or sudden hormonal changes can make women ***and*** men feel depressed, listless, irritable, or "not themselves." Yet even in cultures where PMS symptoms are most commonly reported, few women are likely to undergo personality shifts solely because of their hormones. Testosterone doesn't make men violent.

Many women do have ***physical*** symptoms associated with menstruation, including cramps, breast tenderness, and water retention. Naturally, these physical symptoms can make some women feel grumpy, just as pain or discomfort can make men feel grumpy. But ***emotional*** symptoms such as irritability and depression are pretty rare, affecting fewer than 5 percent of women predictably over their cycles (Brooks-Gunn, 1986; Reid, 1991; Walker, 1994).

Then why do so many women think they have PMS, a predictable "syndrome"? One possibility is that they tend to notice feelings of depression or irritability when these moods happen to occur premenstrually but overlook times when such moods are ***absent*** premenstrually. Or they may label symptoms that occur before a period as PMS ("I am irritable and cranky; I must be getting my period") and attribute the same symptoms at other times of the month to a stressful day or a low grade on an English paper ("No wonder I'm irritable and cranky; I worked really hard on that paper and only got a C"). A woman's perceptions and recall of her own emotional ups and downs can also be influenced by cultural attitudes and myths about menstruation. Yet most clinicians diagnose PMS on the basis of women's retrospective reports, and some studies have encouraged biases in the reporting of premenstrual and menstrual symptoms by using questionnaires with gloomy titles such as "Menstrual Distress Questionnaire."

To get around these problems, some psychologists have polled women about their psychological and physical well-being without revealing the true purpose of the study (e.g., AuBuchon & Calhoun, 1985; Chrisler, 2000; Gallant et al., 1991; Hardie, 1997; Parlee, 1982; Slade, 1984; Walker, 1994). Using double-blind procedures, they have had women report symptoms for a single day and have then gone back to see what phase of the menstrual cycle the women were in; or they have had women keep daily records over an extended period of time. Some studies have also included a control group that is usually excluded from research on hormones and moods: men!

In one such study, men and women filled out a symptom questionnaire that made no mention of menstruation (Callaghan et al., 2009). The proportion of men who met the criteria for "premenstrual dysphoric disorder," a presumably more extreme version of PMS, did not differ significantly from the proportion of women who did so! In another study, women and men rated their moods every day for 70 days for what they thought was a straightforward study of mood and health (McFarlane, Martin, & Williams, 1988). After the 70 days were up, the women then recalled their average moods for each week and phase of their menstrual cycle. In their daily reports, women's moods fluctuated less over the menstrual cycle than over days of the week. (Mondays, it seems, are tough for most of us.) Moreover, women and men reported similar emotional symptoms and number of mood swings at any time of the month, as you can see in Figure 6.1. But in their retrospective reports, women ***recalled*** feeling more angry, irritable, and depressed in the premenstrual and menstrual phases than they had reported in their daily journals, showing that their retrospective reports were influenced by their expectations and their belief that PMS is a reliable, recurring set of symptoms.

Other investigations have confirmed that most women do not have typical PMS symptoms even when they firmly believe that they do (Hardie, 1997; McFarlane & Williams, 1994). For example, women often say they cry more premenstrually than at other times, but they are usually wrong. A study of Dutch women who kept "crying diaries" found no association at all between crying and phase of the menstrual cycle (van Tilburg, Becht, & Vingerhoets, 2003).

The really important question is whether the phase of the menstrual cycle a woman is in affects her ability to work, think, study, do brain surgery, run for office, or run a business.

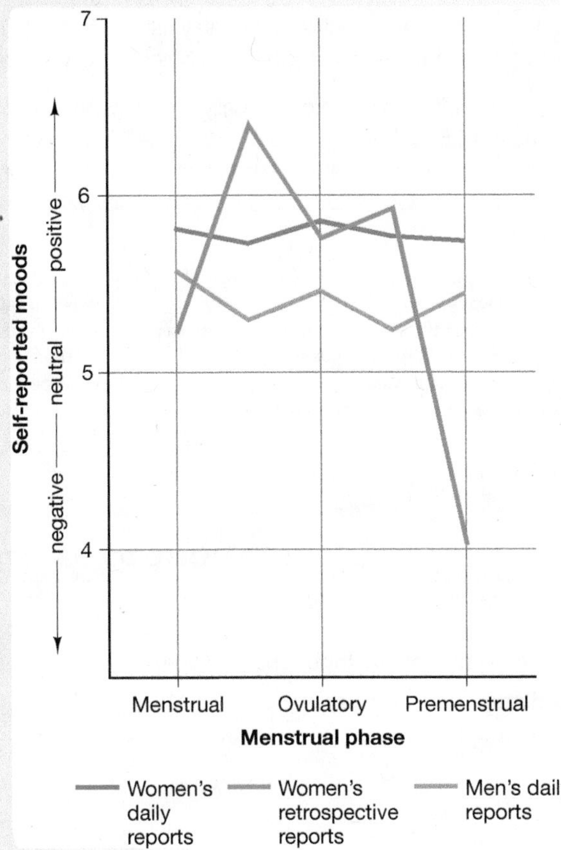

Figure 6.1 Mood Changes in Men and Women
In a study that challenged popular stereotypes about PMS, college women and men recorded their moods daily for 70 days without knowing the purpose of the study. At the end of the study, the women thought their moods had been more negative premenstrually than during the rest of the month (green line), but their daily diaries showed otherwise (blue line). Both sexes experienced only moderate mood changes, and there were no significant differences between women and men at any time of the month (McFarlane, Martin, & Williams, 1988).

In the laboratory, women tend to be faster on tasks such as reciting words quickly or sorting objects manually before and after ovulation, when their estrogen is high (e.g., Saucier & Kimura, 1998). But phase of the menstrual cycle is unrelated to work efficiency, problem solving, grades, college exam scores, creativity, or any other behavior that matters in real life (Earl-Novell & Jessop, 2005; Golub, 1992; Richardson, 1992). In the workplace, men and women report similar levels of stress, well-being, and ability to do the work required of them—and it doesn't matter whether the women are premenstrual, menstrual, postmenstrual, or nonmenstrual (Hardie, 1997).

In sum, the body provides only the clay for our symptoms and feelings. Learning and culture mold that clay by teaching us which symptoms are important or worrisome, and which are not. Whether we are male or female, the impact of most of the changes associated with our biological rhythms depends on how we interpret and respond to them.

"You've been charged with driving under the influence of testosterone."
For both sexes, the hormonal excuse rarely applies.

Recite & Review

Recite: It's time to say out loud everything you can remember about *biological rhythms, endogenous cues, circadian rhythms,desynchronization, seasonal affective disorder,* and *PMS.*

Review: Next, go back and read this section again.

Now take this ***Quick Quiz:***

1. The functioning of the biological clock governing circadian rhythms is affected by the hormone _________.
2. Jet lag occurs because of _________.

3. For most women, the days before menstruation are reliably associated with (a) depression, (b) irritability, (c) elation, (d) creativity, (e) none of these, (f) a and b.

4. A researcher tells male subjects that testosterone usually peaks in the morning and that it probably causes hostility. She then asks them to fill out a "HyperTestosterone Syndrome Hostility Survey" in the morning and again at night. Based on your knowledge of menstrual-cycle findings, what do you think her study will reveal? How could she improve her study?

Answers: 1. melatonin **2.** internal desynchronization **3.** e **4.** Because of the expectations that the men now have about testosterone, they may be biased to report more hostility in the morning. It would be better to keep them in the dark about the hypothesis and to measure their actual hormone levels at different points in the day, because individuals vary in their biological rhythms. Also, a control group of women could be added to see whether their hostility levels vary in the same way that men's do. Finally, the title on that questionnaire is pretty biased. A more neutral title, such as "Health and Mood Checklist," would be better.

You are about to learn. . .

- **the stages of sleep.**
- **what happens when we go too long without enough sleep.**
- **how sleep disorders disrupt normal sleep.**
- **the mental benefits of sleep.**

THE RHYTHMS OF SLEEP

Perhaps the most perplexing of all our biological rhythms is the one governing sleep and wakefulness. Sleep, after all, puts us at risk: Muscles that are usually ready to respond to danger relax, and senses grow dull. As the British psychologist Christopher Evans (1984) once noted, "The behavior patterns involved in sleep are glaringly, almost insanely, at odds with common sense." Then why is sleep such a profound necessity?

The Realms of Sleep

Let's start with some of the changes that occur in the brain during sleep. Until the early 1950s, little was known about these changes. Then a breakthrough occurred in the laboratory of physiologist Nathaniel Kleitman, who at the time was the only person in the world who had spent his entire career studying sleep. Kleitman had given one of his graduate students, Eugene Aserinsky, the tedious task of finding out whether the slow, rolling eye movements that characterize the onset of sleep continue throughout the night. To both men's surprise, eye movements did occur but they were rapid, not slow (Aserinsky & Kleitman, 1955). Using the electroencephalograph (EEG) to measure the brain's electrical activity, these researchers, along with another of Kleitman's students, William Dement, were able to correlate the rapid eye movements with changes in sleepers' brain-wave patterns (Dement, 1992). Adult volunteers were soon spending their nights sleeping in laboratories, while scientists measured changes in their brain activity, muscle tension, breathing, and other physiological responses.

As a result of this research, today we know that during sleep, periods of **rapid eye movement (REM)** alternate with periods of fewer eye movements, or *non-REM (NREM) sleep*, in a cycle that recurs every 90 minutes or so. The REM periods last from a few minutes to as long as an hour, averaging about 20 minutes in length. Whenever they begin, the pattern of electrical activity from the sleeper's brain changes to resemble that of alert wakefulness. Non-REM periods are themselves divided into distinct stages, each associated with a particular brain-wave pattern (see Figure 6.2 on the next page).

rapid eye movement (REM) sleep
sleep periods characterized by eye movement, loss of muscle tone, and vivid dreams

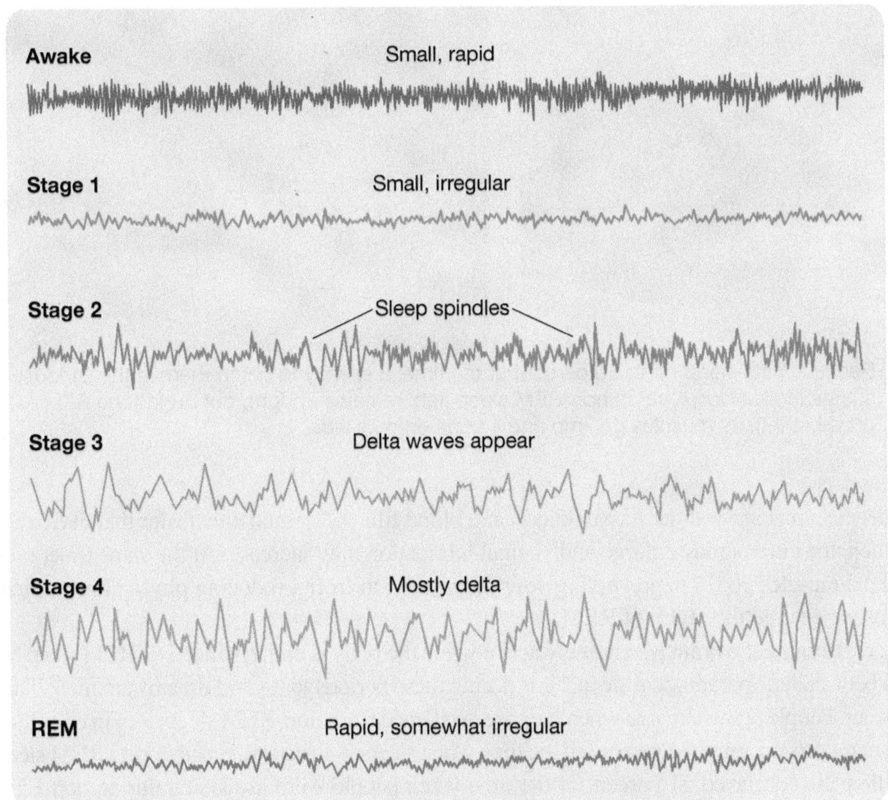

Figure 6.2 Brain-Wave Patterns during Wakefulness and Sleep
Most types of brain waves are present throughout sleep, but different ones predominate at different stages.

When you first climb into bed, close your eyes, and relax, your brain emits bursts of *alpha waves*. Compared to brain waves during alert wakefulness, on an EEG recording alpha waves have a somewhat slower rhythm (fewer cycles per second) and a somewhat higher amplitude (height). Gradually, these waves slow down even further, and you drift into the Land of Nod, passing through four stages, each deeper than the previous one:

Stage 1. Your brain waves become small and irregular, and you feel yourself drifting on the edge of consciousness, in a state of light sleep. If awakened, you may recall fantasies or a few visual images.

Stage 2. Your brain emits occasional short bursts of rapid, high-peaking waves called *sleep spindles*. Minor noises probably won't disturb you.

Stage 3. In addition to the waves that are characteristic of Stage 2, your brain occasionally emits *delta waves*, very slow waves with very high peaks. Your breathing and pulse have slowed down, your muscles are relaxed, and you are hard to waken.

Stage 4. Delta waves have now largely taken over, and you are in deep sleep. It will probably take vigorous shaking or a loud noise to awaken you. Oddly, though, if you walk in your sleep, this is when you are likely to do so. No one yet knows what causes sleepwalking, which occurs more often in children than adults, but it seems to involve unusual patterns of delta-wave activity (Bassetti et al., 2000).

This sequence of stages takes about 30 to 45 minutes. Then you move back up the ladder from Stage 4 to 3 to 2 to 1. At that point, about 70 to 90 minutes after the onset of sleep, something peculiar happens. Stage 1 does not turn into drowsy wakefulness, as one might expect. Instead, your brain begins to emit long bursts of very rapid, somewhat irregular waves. Your heart rate increases, your blood pressure rises, and your breathing gets faster and more irregular. Small twitches in your face and fingers may occur. In men, the penis may become

Because cats sleep up to 80 percent of the time, it is easy to catch them in the various stages of slumber. A cat in non-REM sleep (left) remains upright, but during the REM phase (right), its muscles go limp and it flops onto its side.

somewhat erect as vascular tissue relaxes and blood fills the genital area faster than it exits. In women, the clitoris may enlarge and vaginal lubrication may increase. At the same time, most skeletal muscles go limp, preventing your aroused brain from producing physical movement. You have entered the realm of REM.

Because the brain is extremely active while the body is entirely inactive, REM sleep has also been called "paradoxical sleep." It is during these periods that vivid dreams are most likely to occur. People report dreams when they are awakened from non-REM sleep, too; in one study, dream reports occurred 82 percent of the time when sleepers were awakened during REM sleep, but they also occurred 51 percent of the time when people were awakened during non-REM sleep (Foulkes, 1962). Non-REM dreams, however, tend to be shorter, less vivid, and more realistic than REM dreams, except in the hour or so before a person wakes up in the morning.

Thinking Critically

Consider other interpretations

In a state between sleeping and waking, some people have thought they've seen a ghost or a visitor from space in their bedroom—a pretty scary experience. What other explanation is possible?

Occasionally, as the sleeper wakes up, a curious phenomenon occurs. The person emerges from REM sleep before the muscle paralysis characteristic of that stage has entirely disappeared, and becomes aware of an inability to move. About 30 percent of the general population has experienced at least one such episode, and about 5 percent have had a "waking dream" in this state. Their eyes are open, but what they "see" are dreamlike hallucinations, most often shadowy figures. They may even "see" a ghost or space alien sitting on their bed or hovering in a hallway, a scary image that they would regard as perfectly normal it if were part of a midnight nightmare. Instead of saying, "Ah! How interesting! I am having a waking dream!" some people interpret this experience literally and come to believe they have been visited by aliens or are being haunted by ghosts (Clancy, 2005; McNally, 2003).

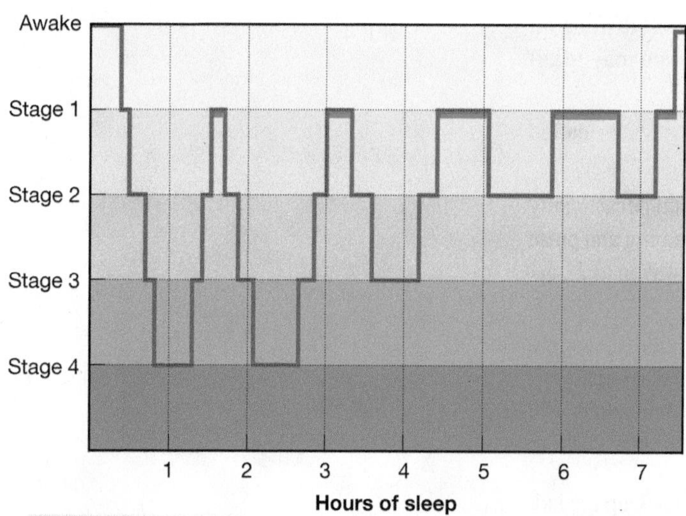

Figure 6.3 A Typical Night's Sleep for a Young Adult
In this graph, the thin horizontal red bars represent time spent in REM sleep. REM periods tend to lengthen as the night wears on, but Stages 3 and 4, which dominate during non-REM sleep early in the night, may disappear as morning approaches.

REM and non-REM sleep continue to alternate throughout the night. As the hours pass, Stages 3 and 4 tend to become shorter or even disappear, and REM periods tend to get longer and closer together (see Figure 6.3). This pattern may explain why you are likely to be dreaming when the alarm clock goes off in the morning. But the cycles are far from regular. An individual may bounce directly from Stage 4 back to Stage 2 or go from REM to Stage 2 and then back to REM. Also, the time between REM and non-REM is highly variable, differing from person to person and also within any given individual.

If you wake people up every time they lapse into REM sleep, nothing dramatic will happen. When finally allowed to sleep normally, however, they will spend a longer time than usual in the REM phase, and it will be hard to rouse them. Electrical brain activity associated with REM may burst through into non-REM sleep and even into wakefulness, as if the person is making up for something he or she had been deprived of. Some researchers have proposed that this "something" is connected with dreaming, but that idea has problems. For one thing, in rare cases, brain-damaged patients have lost the capacity to dream, yet they continue to show the normal sleep

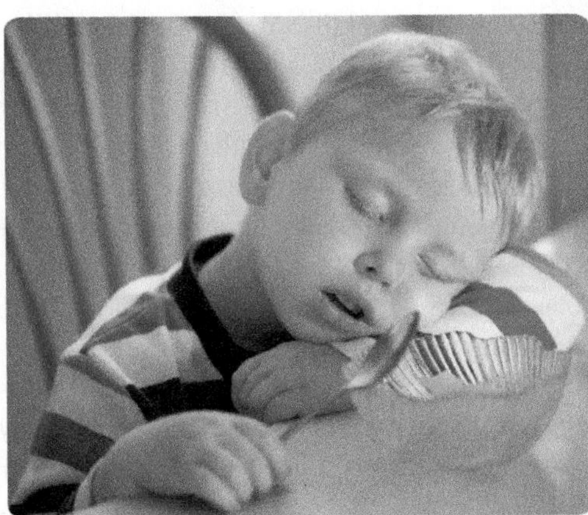

Whatever your age, sometimes the urge to sleep is irresistible, especially because in fast-paced modern societies, many people—even young children—do not get as much sleep as they need.

stages, including REM (Bischof & Bassetti, 2004). Moreover, nearly all mammals experience REM sleep, but many theorists doubt that rats or moles have the cognitive abilities required to construct what we think of as dreams. REM is clearly important, but it must be for reasons other than dreaming, as we will see.

Why We Sleep

Generally speaking, sleep appears to provide a time-out period, so that the body can eliminate waste products from muscles, repair cells, conserve or replenish energy stores, strengthen the immune system, and recover abilities lost during the day. When we do not get enough sleep, our bodies operate abnormally. Hormone levels necessary for normal muscle development and immune system functioning decline (Leproult, Van Reeth, et al., 1997).

Although most people can still get along reasonably well after a day or two of sleeplessness, sleep deprivation that lasts for four days or longer becomes uncomfortable and soon becomes unbearable. In animals, forced sleeplessness leads to infections and eventually to death, and the same seems to be true for people. In one tragic case, a 51-year-old man abruptly began to lose sleep. After sinking deeper and deeper into an exhausted stupor, he developed a lung infection and died. An autopsy showed that he had lost almost all the large neurons in two areas of the thalamus that have been linked to sleep and hormonal circadian rhythms (Lugaresi et al., 1986).

The Mental Consequences of Sleeplessness

Sleep is also necessary for normal mental functioning. Chronic sleep deprivation increases levels of the stress hormone cortisol, which may damage or impair brain cells that are necessary for learning and memory (Leproult, Copinschi, et al., 1997). Also, new brain cells may either fail to develop or may mature abnormally (Guzman-Marin et al., 2005). Perhaps in part because of such damage, after the loss of even a single night's sleep, mental flexibility, attention, and creativity all suffer. After several days of staying awake, people may even begin to have hallucinations and delusions (Dement, 1978).

Of course, sleep deprivation rarely reaches that point, but people do frequently suffer from milder sleep problems. According to the National Sleep Foundation, about 10 percent of adults are plagued by difficulty in falling or staying asleep. The causes of their insomnia include worry and anxiety, psychological problems, physical problems such as arthritis, and irregular or overly demanding work and study schedules. In addition, many drugs interfere with the normal progression of sleep stages—not just the ones containing caffeine, but also alcohol and some tranquilizers. The result can be grogginess and lethargy the next day.

Another cause of daytime sleepiness is **sleep apnea**, a disorder in which breathing periodically stops for a few moments, causing the person to choke and gasp. Breathing may cease hundreds of times a night, often without the person knowing it. Sleep apnea is seen most often in older males and overweight people but also occurs in others. It has several causes, from blockage of air passages to failure of the brain to control respiration correctly. Over time, it can cause high blood pressure and irregular heartbeat; it may gradually erode a person's health, and is associated with a shortened life expectancy (Young et al., 2008).

With **narcolepsy**, an even more serious disorder that often develops in the teenage years, an individual is subject to irresistible and unpredictable daytime attacks of sleepiness lasting from 5 to 30 minutes. The cause is not well understood, but the disorder has been associated with reduced amounts of a particular brain protein, possibly brought on by an autoimmune problem, a viral infection, or genetic abnormalities (Kornum, Faraco, & Mignot, 2011; Lin, Hungs, & Mignot, 2001; Mieda et al., 2004). When the person lapses into sleep, he or she is likely to fall immediately into the REM stage. Some people with narcolepsy experience an unusual symptom called *cataplexy*, which brings on the paralysis of REM sleep although they are still awake; as a result, they may suddenly drop to the floor. Cataplexy is often triggered by laughing excitedly, but it can sometimes be induced by telling a joke or even having an orgasm (Overeem et al., 2011).

Other disorders also disrupt sleep, including some that cause odd or dangerous behavior. In **REM behavior disorder**, the muscle paralysis associated with REM sleep does not occur, and the sleeper (usually an older male) becomes physically active, often acting out a dream without any awareness of what he is doing (Randall, 2012; Schenck & Mahowald, 2002). If he is dreaming about football, he may try to "tackle" a piece of furniture; if he is dreaming about a kitten, he may try to pet it. Other people may consider this disorder amusing, but it is no joke; sufferers may hurt themselves or others, and they have an increased risk of later developing Parkinson's disease and dementia (Postuma et al., 2008).

However, the most common cause of daytime sleepiness is the most obvious one: simply not getting enough sleep. Some people do fine on relatively few hours, but most adults need more than six hours for optimal performance, and many adolescents need ten. In the United States, drowsiness is involved in 100,000 vehicle accidents a year, causing 1,500 road deaths and 71,000 injuries. Sleep deprivation also leads to accidents and errors in the workplace, a concern especially for first-year doctors doing their medical residency.

The driver of this truck crashed when he apparently fell asleep at the wheel. Thousands of serious and fatal vehicle accidents occur each year because of driver fatigue.

sleep apnea
a disorder in which breathing briefly stops during sleep, causing the person to choke and gasp and momentarily awaken

narcolepsy
a disorder involving sudden and unpredictable daytime attacks of sleepiness or lapses into REM sleep

REM behavior disorder
a disorder in which the muscle paralysis that normally occurs during REM sleep is absent or incomplete, and the sleeper is able to act out his or her dreams

Although federal law limits work hours for airline pilots, truck drivers, and nuclear-plant operators, in many states, medical residents often still work 24- to 30-hour shifts (Landrigan et al., 2008).

Don't doze off as we tell you this, but lack of sleep has also been linked to reduced alertness in school and lower grades. In 1997, a high school in Minneapolis changed its start time from 7:20 a.m. to 8:30 a.m. Teachers watched in surprise as students became more alert and—according to their parents—"easier to live with" (Wahlstrom, 2010). Since then, many other school districts in the United States and other countries have followed suit by starting school later in the morning (Vedaa et al., 2012). Children and teenagers who start school later sleep more, have improved mood, are able to pay more attention in class, and get better test scores; teenage drivers even have fewer car accidents (Fallone et al., 2005; Vorona et al., 2011).

Late hours or inadequate sleep won't do anything for your grade point average. Daytime drowsiness can interfere with reaction time, concentration, and the ability to learn.

The Mental Benefits of Sleep

Just as sleepiness can interfere with good mental functioning, a good night's sleep can promote it, and not just because you are well rested. In a classic study conducted nearly a century ago, students who slept for eight hours after learning lists of nonsense syllables retained them better than students who went about their usual business (Jenkins & Dallenbach, 1924). For years, researchers attributed this result to the lack of new information coming into the brain during sleep, information that could interfere with already-established memories. Today, however, most believe that sleep is a crucial time for **consolidation**, in which synaptic changes associated with recently stored memories become durable and stable (see Chapter 11).

One theory is that while we are sleeping, the neurons that were activated during the original experience are reactivated, promoting the transfer of memories from temporary storage in the hippocampus to long-term storage in the cortex and thus making those changes more permanent (Born & Wilhelm, 2012). During sleep, consolidation seems to target important information that we know we might need later. When researchers had people learn new information and then let them sleep, those who were told before sleeping that they would later be taking a memory test did better on it than those who did not know about the upcoming test (Wilhelm et al., 2011). Sleep seems to strengthen many kinds of memories, including the recollection of events, locations, facts, and emotional experiences, especially negative ones (see Figure 6.4).

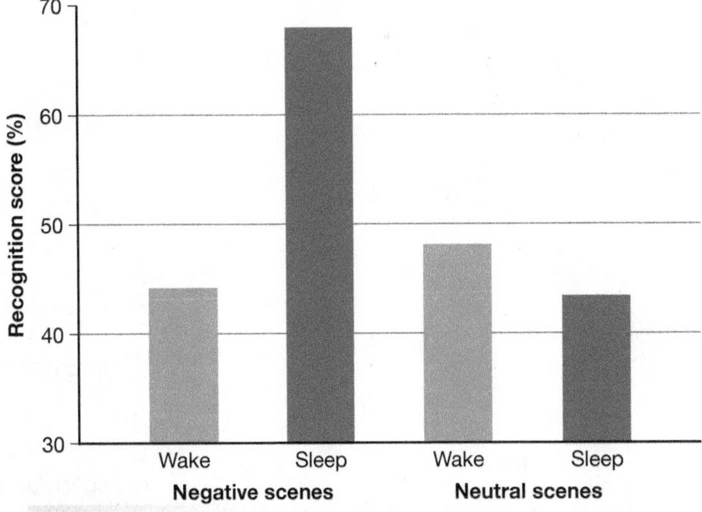

Figure 6.4 Sleep and Consolidation in Memory
When college students studied neutral scenes (e.g., an ordinary car) and emotionally negative scenes (e.g., a car totaled in an accident), sleep affected how well they later recognized the objects in the scenes. Students who studied the scenes in the evening and then got a night's sleep before being tested did better at recognizing emotional objects than did those who studied the scenes in the morning and were tested after 12 hours of daytime wakefulness (Payne et al., 2008).

Memory consolidation is most closely associated with the slow waves of neural activity that occur during stages 3 and 4 of sleep. In one study, while scientists taught people the locations of several matching pairs of cards (a memory game), they also presented the scent of roses. Later, some people were exposed to the smell of roses again during slow-wave sleep, REM sleep, or when they were awake. Exposure to the smell during slow-wave sleep, but not REM or wakefulness, improved people's memories for the card locations (Rasch et al., 2007). But REM sleep does seem to be related to some improvements in learning and memory (Mednick et al., 2011). When people or animals learned a perceptual task and were allowed to get normal REM sleep, their memory for the task was better the next day, even when they had been awakened during non-REM periods. When they were deprived of REM sleep, however, their memories were impaired (Karni et al., 1994). Thus, both periods of sleep seem to be important for consolidation, and scientists are now trying to determine their respective roles (Born & Wilhelm, 2012).

If sleep enhances memory, perhaps it also enhances problem solving, which relies on information stored in memory. To find out, German researchers gave volunteers a math test that required them to use two mathematical rules to generate one string of numbers

consolidation
The process by which a memory becomes durable and stable

from another and to deduce the final digit in the new sequence as quickly as possible. The volunteers were not told about a hidden shortcut that would enable them to calculate the final digit almost immediately. One group was trained in the evening and then got to snooze for eight hours before returning to the problem. Another group was also trained in the evening but then stayed awake for eight hours before coming back to the problem. A third group was trained in the morning and stayed awake all day, as they normally would, before taking the test. Those people who got the nighttime sleep were nearly three times likelier to discover the hidden shortcut as those in the other two groups (Wagner et al., 2004).

Sleep, then, seems essential in memory and problem solving. The underlying biology appears to involve not only the formation of new synaptic connections in the brain but also the weakening of connections that are no longer needed (Donlea, Ramanan, & Shaw, 2009; Gilestro, Tononi, & Cirelli, 2009). In other words, we sleep to remember, but we also sleep to forget, so that the brain will have space and energy for new learning. Remember that the next time you are tempted to pull an all-nighter. Even a quick nap may help your mental functioning and increase your ability to put together separately learned facts in new ways (Lau, Alger, & Fishbein, 2011; Mednick et al., 2002). Sleep on it.

Recite & Review

Recite: Consolidate your memory for the previous material by saying out loud everything you can about *REM* versus *non-REM sleep,* the stages of sleep, the consequences of sleeplessness, *sleep apnea, narcolepsy, REM behavior disorder*, and the role of sleep in memory *consolidation*.

Review: Next, go back and read this section again.

Now take this ***Quick Quiz:***

A. Match each term with the appropriate phrase:

1. REM periods	**a.** delta waves and sleepwalking
2. alpha	**b.** irregular brain waves and light sleep
3. Stage 4 sleep	**c.** relaxed but awake
4. Stage 1 sleep	**d.** active brain but inactive muscles

B. Sleep is necessary for normal (a) physical and mental functioning, (b) mental functioning but not physical functioning, (c) physical functioning but not mental functioning.

C. *True or false:* Most people need more than six hours of sleep a night.

D. *True or false:* Only REM sleep has been associated with dreaming and memory consolidation.

Answers: A. 1. d 2. c 3. a 4. b B. a C. true D. false

You are about to learn. . .

- **about Freud's theory that dreams are the "royal road to the unconscious."**
- **how dreams might be related to your current problems and concerns.**
- **how dreams might be related to ordinary daytime thoughts.**
- **how dreams could be caused by meaningless brain-stem signals.**

Exploring the Dream World

Every culture has its theories about dreams. In some cultures, dreams are believed to occur when the spirit leaves the body to wander the world or speak to the gods. In others, dreams are thought to reveal the future. A Chinese Taoist of the third century B.C. pondered the possible reality of the dream world. He told of dreaming that he was a butterfly flitting about. "Suddenly I woke up and I was indeed Chuang Tzu. Did Chuang Tzu dream he was a butterfly, or did the butterfly dream he was Chuang Tzu?"

For years, researchers believed that everyone dreams, and indeed most people who claim they never have dreams will report them if they are awakened during REM sleep. However, as we noted earlier, a few rare individuals apparently do not dream at all (Pagel, 2003; Solms, 1997). Most but not all of them have suffered some brain injury.

In dreaming, the focus of attention is inward, though occasionally an external event, such as a wailing siren, can influence the dream's content. While a dream is in progress, it may be vivid or vague, terrifying or peaceful. It may also seem to make perfect sense—until you wake up and recall it as illogical, bizarre, and disjointed. Although most of us are unaware of our bodies or where we are while we are dreaming, some people say that they occasionally have **lucid dreams**, in which they know they are dreaming and feel as though they are conscious (LaBerge & Levitan, 1995). A few even claim that they can control the action in these dreams, much as a scriptwriter decides what will happen in a movie.

Why do the images in dreams arise at all? Why doesn't the brain just rest, switching off all thoughts and images and launching us into a coma? Why, instead, do we spend our nights taking a chemistry exam, reliving an old love affair, flying through the air, or fleeing from dangerous strangers or animals in the fantasy world of our dreams?

In popular culture, many people still hold to Freudian psychoanalytic notions of dreaming. Freud (1900/1953) claimed that dreams are "the royal road to the unconscious" because our dreams reflect unconscious conflicts and wishes, often sexual or violent in nature. The thoughts and objects in these dreams, he said, are disguised symbolically to make them less threatening: Your father might appear as your brother, a penis might be disguised as a snake or a cigar, or intercourse with a forbidden partner might be expressed as a train entering a tunnel.

Most psychologists today accept Freud's notion that dreams are more than incoherent ramblings of the mind and that they can have psychological meaning, but they also consider psychoanalytic interpretations of dreams to be far-fetched. No reliable rules exist for interpreting the unconscious meaning of dreams, and there is no objective way to know whether a particular interpretation is correct. Nor is there any convincing empirical support for most of Freud's claims. Psychoanalytic interpretations are common in popular books and on the Internet, but they are only the writers' personal hunches. Even Freud warned against simplified "this symbol means that" interpretations; each dream, said Freud, must be analyzed in the context of the dreamer's waking life. Not everything in a dream is symbolic; sometimes, he cautioned, "A cigar is only a cigar."

Anxiety dreams are common throughout life.

Dreams as Efforts to Deal with Problems

One modern explanation of dreams holds that they reflect the ongoing *conscious* preoccupations of waking life, such as concerns over relationships, work, sex, or health (Cartwright, 1977; Hall, 1953a, b). In this *problem-focused approach* to dreaming, the symbols and metaphors in a dream do not disguise its true meaning; they convey it. Psychologist Gayle Delaney once told of a woman who dreamed she was swimming underwater. The woman's 8-year-old son was on her back, his head above the water. Her husband was supposed to take a picture of them, but for some reason he wasn't doing it, and she was starting to feel as if she were going to drown. To Delaney, the message was obvious: The woman was "drowning" under the responsibilities of child care and her husband wasn't "getting the picture" (in Dolnick, 1990).

lucid dreams
dreams in which the dreamer is aware of dreaming

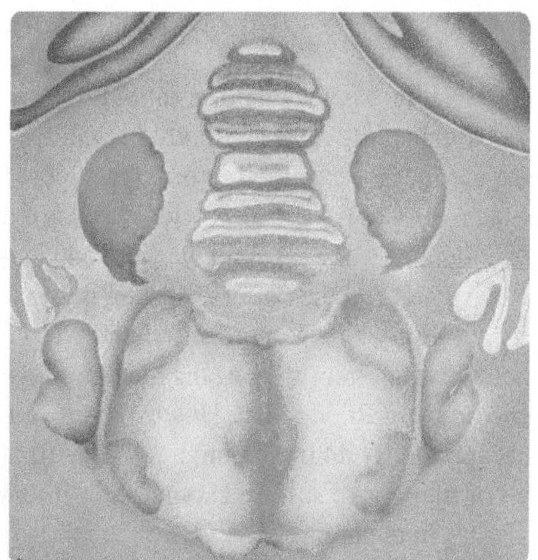

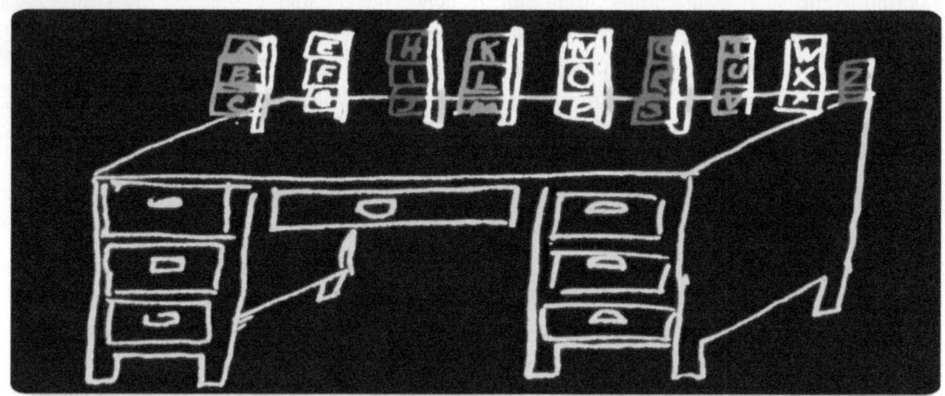

These drawings from dream journals show that the images in dreams can be either abstract or literal. In either case, the dream may reflect a person's concerns, problems, and interests. The two fanciful paintings at the top represent the dreams of a person who worked all day long with brain tissue, which the drawings rather resemble. The desk was sketched in 1939 by a scientist to illustrate his dream about a mechanical device for instantly retrieving quotations—an early desktop computer!

The problem-focused explanation of dreaming is supported by findings that dreams are more likely to contain material related to a person's current concerns than chance would predict (Domhoff, 1996). Among college students, who are often worried about grades and tests, test-anxiety dreams are common: The dreamer is unprepared for or unable to finish an exam, or shows up for the wrong exam, or can't find the room where the exam is being given. (Sound familiar?) For their part, instructors sometimes dream that they have left their lecture notes at home, or that their notes contain only blank pages so they have nothing to say. Traumatic experiences can also affect people's dreams. In a cross-cultural study in which children kept dream diaries for a week, Palestinian children living in neighborhoods under threat of violence reported more themes of persecution and violence than did Finnish or Palestinian children living in peaceful environments (Punamaeki & Joustie, 1998).

Some psychologists believe that dreams not only reflect our waking concerns but also provide us with an opportunity to resolve them. According to Rosalind Cartwright (2010), in people suffering from the grief of divorce, recovery is related to a particular pattern of dreaming: The first dream of the night often comes sooner than it ordinarily would, lasts longer, and is more emotional and story-like. Depressed people's dreams tend to become less negative and more positive as the night wears on, and this pattern, too, predicts recovery (Cartwright et al., 1998). Cartwright concluded that getting through a crisis or a rough period in life takes "time, good friends, good genes, good luck, and a good dream system."

Dreams as Thinking

Like the problem-focused approach, the *cognitive approach* to dreaming emphasizes current concerns, but it makes no claims about problem solving during sleep. In this view, dreaming is simply a modification of the cognitive activity that goes on when we are awake. In dreams, we construct reasonable simulations of the real world, drawing on the same kinds of memories, knowledge, metaphors, and assumptions about the world that we do when we are not sleeping (Antrobus, 1991, 2000; Domhoff, 2003; Foulkes, 1999). Thus, the content of our dreams may include thoughts, concepts, and scenarios that may or may not be related to our daily problems. We are most likely to dream about our families, friends, studies, jobs, worries, or recreational interests—topics that also occupy our waking thoughts.

In the cognitive view, the brain is doing the same kind of work during dreams as it does when we are awake; indeed, parts of the cerebral cortex involved in perceptual and cognitive processing during the waking hours are highly active during dreaming. The difference is that when we are asleep we are cut off from sensory input and feedback from the world and our bodily movements; the only input to the brain is its own output. Therefore, our dreaming thoughts tend to be more unfocused and diffuse than our waking ones—unless we're daydreaming. Our brains show similar patterns of activity when we are night dreaming as when we are daydreaming—a finding that suggests that nighttime dreaming, like daydreaming, might be a mechanism for simulating events that we think (or fear) might occur in the future (Domhoff, 2011).

The cognitive view predicts that if a person could be totally cut off from all external stimulation while awake, mental activity would be much like that during dreaming, with the same hallucinatory quality. The cognitive approach also predicts that as cognitive abilities and brain connections mature during childhood, dreams should change in nature, and they do. Toddlers may not dream at all in the sense that adults do. And although young children may experience visual images during sleep, their cognitive limitations keep them from creating true narratives until age 7 or 8 (Foulkes, 1999). Their dreams are infrequent and tend to be bland and static, and are often about everyday things ("I saw a dog; I was sitting"). But as they grow up, their dreams gradually become more and more intricate and story-like.

Dreams as Interpreted Brain Activity

A third modern approach to dreaming, the **activation–synthesis theory**, draws heavily on physiological research, and aims to explain not why you might dream about a test when you are about to take one, but why you might dream about being a cat that turns into a hippo that plays in a rock band. Often dreams just don't make sense; indeed, most are bizarre, illogical, or both. According to the activation–synthesis explanation, first proposed by psychiatrist J. Allan Hobson (1988, 1990), these dreams are not "children of an idle brain," as Shakespeare called them. They are largely the result of neurons firing spontaneously in the pons (in the lower part of the brain) during REM sleep. These neurons control eye movement, gaze, balance, and posture, and they send messages to sensory and motor areas of the cortex responsible during wakefulness for visual processing and voluntary action.

According to this view, the signals originating in the pons have no psychological meaning in themselves. But the cortex tries to make sense of them by *synthesizing,* or integrating, them with existing knowledge and memories to produce some sort of coherent interpretation. This is just what the cortex does when signals come from sense organs during ordinary wakefulness. The idea that one part of the brain interprets what has gone on in other parts, whether you are awake or asleep, is consistent with many modern theories of how the brain works.

When neurons fire in the part of the brain that handles balance, for instance, the cortex may generate a dream about falling. When signals occur that would ordinarily produce running, the cortex may manufacture a dream about being chased. Because the signals from the pons occur randomly, the cortex's interpretation—the dream—is likely to be incoherent and

ACTIVATION–SYNTHESIS THEORY OF DREAMS

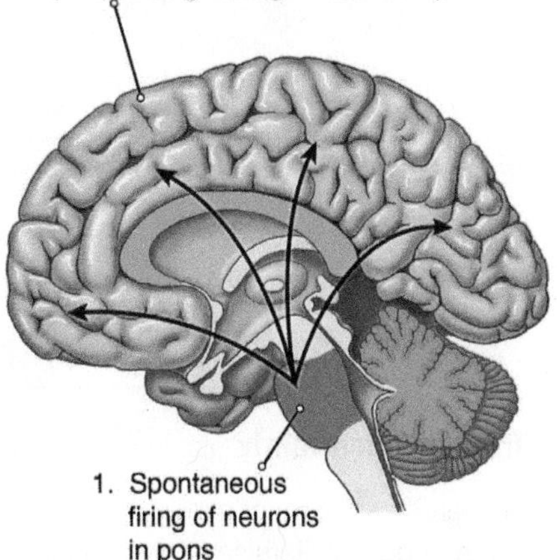

activation–synthesis theory
the theory that dreaming results from the cortical synthesis and interpretation of neural signals triggered by activity in the lower part of the brain

confusing. And because the cortical neurons that control the initial storage of new memories are turned off during sleep, we typically forget our dreams upon waking unless we write them down or immediately recount them to someone else.

Since Hobson's original formulation, he and his colleagues have refined and modified this theory (Hobson, Pace-Schott, & Stickgold, 2000; Hobson et al., 2011). The brain stem, they say, sets off responses in emotional and visual parts of the brain. At the same time, brain regions that handle logical thought and sensations from the external world shut down. These changes could further account for the fact that dreams are often emotionally charged, hallucinatory, and illogical.

Get Involved!

Keep a Dream Diary

It can be fun to record your dreams. Keep a notebook or a recorder by your bedside. As soon as you wake up in the morning (or if you awaken during the night while dreaming), record everything you can remember about your dreams, even short fragments. After you have collected several dreams, see which theory or theories discussed in this chapter seem to best explain them. Do your dreams contain any recurring themes? Do you think they provide any clues to your current problems, activities, or concerns? (By the way, if you are curious about other people's dreams, you can find lots of them online at www.dreambank.net.)

In sum, in this view, wishes do not cause dreams; brain mechanisms do. Dream content, says Hobson (2002), may be "as much dross as gold, as much cognitive trash as treasure, and as much informational noise as a signal of something." But that does not mean dreams are *always* meaningless. Hobson (1988) has argued that the brain "is so inexorably bent upon the quest for meaning that it attributes and even creates meaning when there is little or none to be found in the data it is asked to process." By studying these attributed meanings, you can learn about your unique perceptions, conflicts, and concerns—not by trying to dig below the surface of the dream, as Freud would, but by examining the surface itself. Or you can relax and enjoy the nightly entertainment that dreams provide.

Evaluating Dream Theories

How are we to evaluate these attempts to explain dreaming? All three modern approaches account for some of the evidence, but each one also has its drawbacks.

Are dreams a way to solve problems? It seems pretty clear that some dreams are related to current worries and concerns, but skeptics doubt that people can actually solve problems or resolve conflicts while sound asleep (Blagrove, 1996; Squier & Domhoff, 1998). Dreams, they say, merely give *expression* to our problems. The insights into those problems that people attribute to dreaming could be occurring after they wake up and have a chance to think about what is troubling them.

The activation–synthesis theory has also come in for criticism (Domhoff, 2003). Not all dreams are as disjointed or as bizarre as the theory predicts; in fact, many tell a coherent, if fanciful, story. Moreover, the activation–synthesis approach does not account well for dreaming that goes on outside of REM sleep. Some neuropsychologists emphasize different brain mechanisms involved in dreams, and many believe that dreams do reflect a person's goals and desires.

Finally, the cognitive approach to dreams is promising, but some of its claims remain to be tested against neurological and cognitive evidence. At present, however, it is a leading contender because it incorporates many elements of other theories and fits what we currently know about waking cognition and cognitive development.

Thinking Critically

Tolerate uncertainty

Researchers dream of explaining dreams, and some popular writers say they can tell you what yours mean. But at present, we cannot be sure about the function and meaning of dreams. Do all dreams have hidden meanings? Are all dreams due to random firing of brain cells? Is dreaming all that different from our waking thoughts?

Perhaps it will turn out that different kinds of dreams have different purposes and origins. We all know from experience that some of our dreams seem to be related to daily problems, some are vague and incoherent, and some are anxiety dreams that occur when we are worried or depressed. But whatever the source of the images in our sleeping brains may be, we need to be cautious about interpreting our own dreams or anyone else's. A study of people in India, South Korea, and the United States showed that individuals are biased and self-serving in their dream interpretations, accepting those that fit in with their preexisting beliefs or needs, and rejecting those that do not. For example, they will give more weight to a dream in which God commands them to take a year off to travel the world than one in which God commands them to take a year off to work in a leper colony. And they are more likely to see meaning in a dream in which a friend protects them from attackers than one in which their romantic partner is caught kissing that same friend (Morewedge & Norton, 2009). Our biased interpretations may tell us more about ourselves than do our actual dreams.

Recite & Review

Recite: No, it's not a dream: It's time for you to say everything you can remember about *lucid dreams*, Freud's ideas about dreams, and the differences between three modern theories of dreaming.

Review: Next, read this section again.

Now see if you can dream up the correct answers to this ***Quick Quiz:***

In his dreams, Andy is a child crawling through a dark tunnel looking for something he has lost. Which theory of dreams would be most receptive to each of the following explanations?

1. Andy recently found a valuable watch he had misplaced.
2. While Andy was sleeping, neurons in his pons that would ordinarily stimulate parts of the brain involved in leg-muscle movements were active.
3. Andy has repressed an early sexual attraction to his mother; the tunnel symbolizes her vagina.
4. Andy has broken up with his lover and is working through the emotional loss.

Answers: 1. the cognitive approach (the dreamer is thinking about a recent experience) 2. the activation-synthesis theory 3. psychoanalytic theory 4. the problem-focused approach

You are about to learn. . .

- **common misconceptions about what hypnosis can do.**
- **the legitimate uses of hypnosis in psychology and medicine.**
- **two ways of explaining what happens during hypnosis.**

The Riddle of Hypnosis

For many years, stage hypnotists, "past-lives channelers," and some psychotherapists have been reporting that they can "age regress" hypnotized people to earlier years or even earlier centuries. Some therapists claim that hypnosis helps their patients accurately retrieve long-buried memories, and a few even claim that hypnosis has helped their patients recall alleged abductions by extraterrestrials. What are we to make of all this?

Thinking Critically

Analyze assumptions and biases

Is it hypnosis that enables the man stretched out between two chairs to hold the weight of the man standing on him, without flinching? This audience assumes so, but the only way to find out whether hypnosis produces unique abilities is to do research with control groups. It turns out that people can do the same thing even when they are not hypnotized.

Hypnosis is a procedure in which a practitioner suggests changes in the sensations, perceptions, thoughts, feelings, or behavior of the subject (Kirsch & Lynn, 1995). The hypnotized person, in turn, tries to alter his or her cognitive processes in accordance with the hypnotist's suggestions (Nash & Nadon, 1997). Hypnotic suggestions typically involve performance of an action ("Your arm will slowly rise"), an inability to perform an act ("You will be unable to bend your arm"), or a distortion of normal perception or memory ("You will feel no pain," "You will forget being hypnotized until I give you a signal"). People usually report that their response to a suggestion feels involuntary, as if it happened without their willing it.

To induce hypnosis, the hypnotist typically suggests that the person being hypnotized feels relaxed, is getting sleepy, and feels the eyelids getting heavier and heavier. In a singsong or monotonous voice, the hypnotist assures the subject that he or she is sinking "deeper and deeper." Sometimes the hypnotist has the person concentrate on a color or a small object, or on certain bodily sensations. People who have been hypnotized report that the focus of attention turns outward, toward the hypnotist's voice. They sometimes compare the experience to being totally absorbed in a good movie or favorite piece of music. The hypnotized person almost always remains fully aware of what is happening and remembers the experience later unless explicitly instructed to forget it. Even then, the memory can be restored by a prearranged signal.

Because hypnosis has been used for everything from parlor tricks and stage shows to medical and psychological treatments, it is important to understand just what this procedure can and cannot achieve. We will begin with a general look at the major findings on hypnosis; then we will consider two leading explanations of hypnotic effects.

The Nature of Hypnosis

Since the late 1960s, thousands of articles on hypnosis have appeared. Based on controlled laboratory and clinical studies, most psychological scientists agree that hypnosis is not a mystical trance or strange state of consciousness. Indeed, some worry that thinking of hypnosis in those ways, as a kind of dark art, has interfered with our understanding of it (Posner & Rothbart, 2011). Although scientists disagree about what exactly hypnosis is, they generally agree on the following points (Kirsch & Lynn, 1995; Nash, 2001; Nash & Nadon, 1997):

1 **Hypnotic responsiveness depends more on the efforts and qualities of the person being hypnotized than on the skill of the hypnotist.** Some people are more responsive to hypnosis than others, but why they are is unknown. Surprisingly, such susceptibility is unrelated to general personality traits such as gullibility, trust, submissiveness, or conformity (Nash & Nadon, 1997). And it is only weakly related to the ability to become easily absorbed in activities and the world of imagination (Council, Kirsch, & Grant, 1996; Green & Lynn, 2010; Nash & Nadon, 1997).

hypnosis
a procedure in which the practitioner suggests changes in a subject's sensations, perceptions, thoughts, feelings, or behavior

2 **Hypnotized people cannot be forced to do things against their will.** Like drunkenness, hypnosis can be used to justify letting go of inhibitions ("I know this looks silly, but after all, I'm hypnotized"). Hypnotized individuals may even comply with a suggestion to do something that looks embarrassing or dangerous. But the person is choosing to turn responsibility over to the hypnotist and to cooperate with the hypnotist's

suggestions (Lynn, Rhue, & Weekes, 1990). Hypnotized people will not do anything that actually violates their morals or constitutes a real danger to themselves or others.

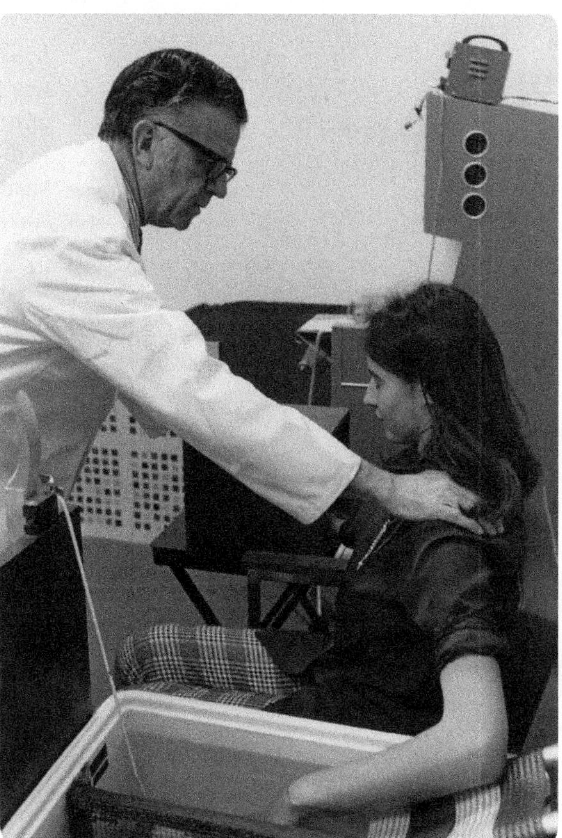

A person whose arm is immersed in ice water ordinarily feels intense pain. But Ernest Hilgard, a pioneer in hypnosis research, discovered that when hypnotized people are told the pain will be minimal, they report little or no discomfort and seem unperturbed.

3 **Feats performed under hypnosis can be performed by motivated people without hypnosis.** Hypnotized subjects sometimes perform what seem like extraordinary mental or physical feats, but hypnosis does not actually enable people to do things that would otherwise be impossible. With proper motivation, support, and encouragement, the same people could do the same things even without being hypnotized (Chaves, 1989; Spanos, Stenstrom, & Johnson, 1988).

4 **Hypnosis does not increase the accuracy of memory.** In rare cases, hypnosis has been used successfully to jog the memories of crime victims, but usually the memories of hypnotized witnesses have been completely mistaken. Although hypnosis does sometimes boost the amount of information recalled, it also increases *errors*, perhaps because hypnotized people are more willing than others to guess, or because they mistake vividly imagined possibilities for actual memories (Dinges et al., 1992; Kihlstrom, 1994). Because pseudomemories and errors are so common in hypnotically induced recall, many scientific societies around the world oppose the use of "hypnotically refreshed" testimony in courts of law.

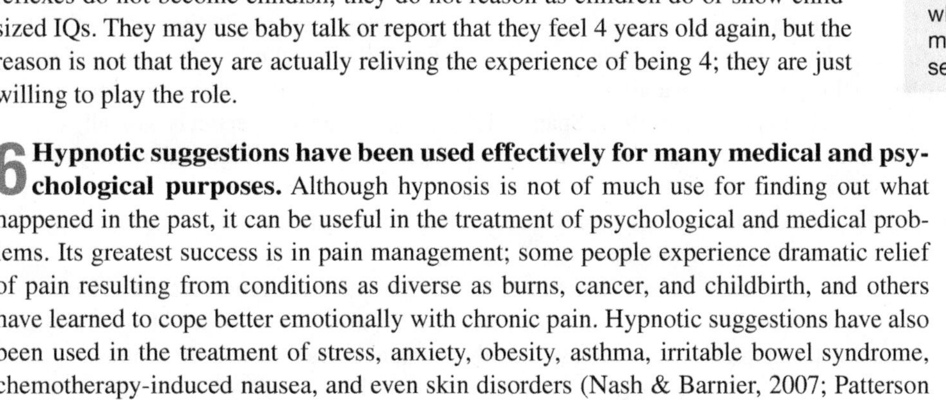

5 **Hypnosis does not produce a literal reexperiencing of long-ago events.** Many people believe that hypnosis can be used to recover memories from as far back as birth. When one clinical psychologist who uses hypnosis in his own practice surveyed over 800 marriage and family therapists, he was dismayed to find that more than half agreed with this common belief (Yapko, 1994). But it is just plain wrong. When people are regressed to an earlier age, their mental and moral performance remains adultlike (Nash, 1987). Their brain-wave patterns and reflexes do not become childish; they do not reason as children do or show child-sized IQs. They may use baby talk or report that they feel 4 years old again, but the reason is not that they are actually reliving the experience of being 4; they are just willing to play the role.

6 **Hypnotic suggestions have been used effectively for many medical and psychological purposes.** Although hypnosis is not of much use for finding out what happened in the past, it can be useful in the treatment of psychological and medical problems. Its greatest success is in pain management; some people experience dramatic relief of pain resulting from conditions as diverse as burns, cancer, and childbirth, and others have learned to cope better emotionally with chronic pain. Hypnotic suggestions have also been used in the treatment of stress, anxiety, obesity, asthma, irritable bowel syndrome, chemotherapy-induced nausea, and even skin disorders (Nash & Barnier, 2007; Patterson & Jensen, 2003).

Theories of Hypnosis

Over the years, people have proposed many explanations of what hypnosis is and how it produces its effects. Today, two competing theories predominate.

Dissociation Theories

One leading approach was originally proposed by Ernest Hilgard (1977, 1986), who argued that hypnosis, like lucid dreaming and even simple distraction, involves **dissociation**, a split in consciousness in which one part of the mind operates independently of the rest of consciousness. In many hypnotized people, said Hilgard, most of the mind is subject to hypnotic suggestion, but one part is a *hidden observer*, watching but not participating. Unless given special instructions, the hypnotized part remains unaware of the observer.

dissociation
a split in consciousness in which one part of the mind operates independently of others

Hilgard attempted to question the hidden observer directly. In one procedure, hypnotized volunteers had to submerge an arm in ice water for several seconds, an experience that is normally excruciating. They were told that they would feel no pain, but that the unsubmerged hand would be able to signal the level of any hidden pain by pressing a key. In this situation, many people said they felt little or no pain—yet at the same time, their free hand was busily pressing the key. After the session, these people continued to insist that they had been pain-free unless the hypnotist asked the hidden observer to issue a separate report.

A contemporary version of this theory holds that during hypnosis, a dissociation occurs between two systems in the brain: the system that processes incoming information about the world, and an "executive" system that controls how we use that information. In hypnosis, the executive system turns off and hands its function over to the hypnotist. That leaves the hypnotist able to suggest how we should interpret the world and act in it (Woody & Bowers, 1994; Woody & Sadler, 2012).

DISSOCIATION THEORIES OF HYPNOSIS

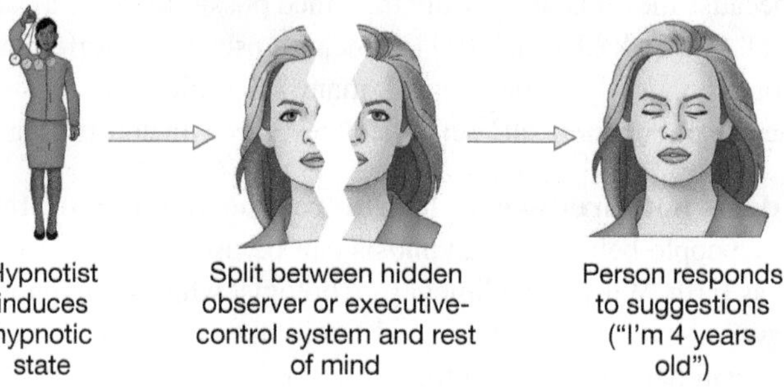

The Sociocognitive Approach

The second major approach to hypnosis, the *sociocognitive explanation*, holds that the effects of hypnosis result from an interaction between the social influence of the hypnotist (the "socio" part) and the abilities, beliefs, and expectations of the subject (the "cognitive" part) (Kirsch, 1997; Sarbin, 1991; Spanos, 1991). The hypnotized person is basically enacting a role. This role has analogies in ordinary life, where we willingly submit to the suggestions of parents, teachers, doctors, therapists, and television commercials. In this view, even the "hidden observer" is simply a reaction to the social demands of the situation and the suggestions of the hypnotist (Lynn & Green, 2011).

The hypnotized person is not merely faking or playacting, however. A person who has been instructed to fool an observer by faking a hypnotic state will tend to overplay the role and will stop playing it as soon as the other person leaves the room. In contrast, hypnotized subjects continue to follow the hypnotic suggestions even when they think they are not being watched (Kirsch et al., 1989; Spanos et al., 1993). Like many social roles, the role of "hypnotized person" is so engrossing and involving that actions required by the role may occur without the person's conscious intent.

SOCIOCOGNITIVE THEORIES OF HYPNOSIS

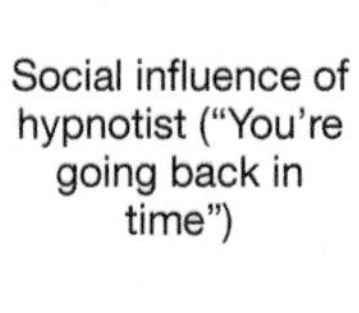

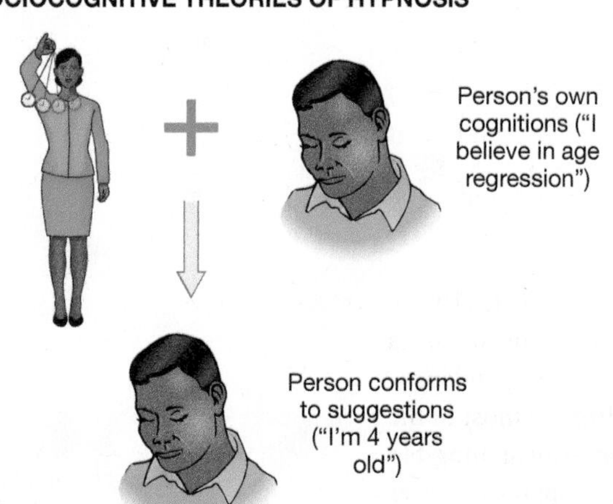

Sociocognitive views explain why some people under hypnosis have reported spirit possession or "memories" of alien abductions (Clancy, 2005; Spanos, 1996). Suppose a young woman goes to a therapist or hypnotist seeking an explanation for her loneliness, unhappiness, nightmares, puzzling symptoms (such as waking up in the middle of the night in a cold sweat), or the waking dreams we described earlier. A therapist who already believes in alien abduction may use hypnosis, along with subtle and not-so-subtle cues about UFOs, to shape the way the client interprets her symptoms.

The sociocognitive view can also explain apparent cases of past-life regression. In a fascinating program of research, Nicholas

Spanos and his colleagues (1991) directed hypnotized Canadian university students to regress past their own births to previous lives. About a third of the students (who already believed in reincarnation) reported being able to do so. But when they were asked, while supposedly reliving a past life, to name the leader of their country, say whether the country was at peace or at war, or describe the money used in their community, the students could not do it. (One young man, who thought he was Julius Caesar, said the year was 50 A.D. and he was emperor of Rome. But Caesar died in 44 B.C. and was never crowned emperor, and dating years as A.D. or B.C. did not begin until several centuries later.) Not knowing anything about the language, dates, customs, and events of their "previous life" did not deter the students from constructing a story about it, however. They tried to fulfill the requirements of the role by weaving events, places, and people from their *present* lives into their accounts, and by picking up cues from the experimenter.

The researchers concluded that the act of "remembering" another self involves the construction of a fantasy that accords with the rememberer's own beliefs and also the beliefs of others—in this case, those of the authoritative hypnotist.

Thinking Critically

Consider other interpretations

Under hypnosis, Jim describes the chocolate cake at his fourth birthday, and Joan remembers a former life as a twelfth-century French peasant. But lemon cake was served at Jim's party and Joan can't speak twelfth-century French. What explanation best accounts for these vivid but incorrect memories?

Biology and Hypnosis

Debates over what hypnosis really is and how it works have intensified as scientists have begun using technology to study this mysterious phenomenon. We have known for some time from EEG studies that alpha waves are common when a person is in a relaxed hypnotic state. This is not surprising, because alpha waves are associated with relaxed wakefulness. Brain scans, however, permit a more detailed and useful picture of what is going on in the brain of a hypnotized person.

red
yellow
green
blue
red
blue
yellow
green
blue
red

One study that used both fMRI and event-related potentials (ERP) showed that hypnosis can reduce conflict between two mental tasks (Raz, Fan, & Posner, 2005). The researchers gave participants the Stroop Test, which is often used to study what happens when color perception conflicts with reading. You look at words denoting colors (*blue, red, green, yellow . . .*), with some of the letters printed in the corresponding color (e.g., ***red*** printed in red) and others in a different color (e.g., ***red*** printed in blue). It is a lot harder to identify the color of the ink a word is printed in when the word's meaning and its color are different. To see what we mean, try identifying as quickly as you can the color of the words in the adjacent illustration. It's pretty hard, right?

In the study, hypnotized participants were told that later, after they were no longer hypnotized, they would see words from the Stroop Test on a computer screen but the words would seem like strings of meaningless symbols—like "characters in a foreign language that you do not know." During the test, highly suggestible people were faster and better at identifying the clashing colors the words were printed in than people who were less suggestible; in fact, the "Stroop effect" virtually disappeared. Apparently, the easily hypnotized people were literally not seeing the color words; they were seeing only gibberish. Moreover, during the task, they had reduced activity in a brain area that decodes written words and in another area toward the front of the brain that monitors conflicting thoughts. Because of the suggestions made during hypnosis, they were able to pay less attention to the words themselves during the task and thus were able to avoid reading them. They could focus solely on the color of the ink.

Various regions of the brain also change when people are hypnotized and lying in a PET scanner. In one study, highly hypnotizable people, under hypnosis, were able to visually drain color from a drawing of red, blue, green, and yellow rectangles, or to see color when the same drawing was presented in gray tones. When they were told to see color in the gray drawing, their brains showed activation in areas associated with color perception; when they were told to see gray in the colored drawing, the same areas had decreased activation (Kosslyn et al., 2000).

What do findings like these mean for theories of hypnosis? The fact that hypnosis can affect patterns of activity in the brain gives encouragement to those who believe that hypnosis is a special state, different from elaborate role-playing or extreme concentration. Others feel that it is too soon to draw any conclusions from this research about the mechanisms or nature of hypnosis. *Every* experience alters the brain in some way; hypnosis is no exception, however it may work. Moreover, suggestion can reduce the Stroop effect in highly suggestible people even *without* hypnosis (Raz et al., 2006). In fact, highly suggestible people can even hallucinate color without hypnosis (McGeown et al., 2012).

Further work may tell us whether or not there is something special about hypnosis. But whatever the outcome of this debate, all hypnosis researchers agree that hypnosis does not cause memories to become sharper or allow early experiences to be replayed with perfect accuracy. The study of hypnosis is teaching us much about human suggestibility, the power of imagination, and the way we perceive the present and remember the past.

Recite & Review

Recite: We'd like to plant a suggestion in your mind that you say aloud what you know about *hypnosis,* hypnotic susceptibility, *dissociation theories* of hypnosis, the *sociocognitive approach* to hypnosis, and the biology of hypnosis.

Review: You are not getting sleepy . . . you are not getting sleepy . . . so reread this section.

Now take this ***Quick Quiz:***

A. True or false:

1. A hypnotized person is usually aware of what is going on and remembers the experience later.
2. Hypnosis gives us special powers that we do not ordinarily have.
3. Hypnosis reduces errors in memory.
4. Hypnotized people play no active part in controlling their behavior and thoughts.
5. According to Hilgard, hypnosis is a state of consciousness involving a "hidden observer."
6. Sociocognitive theorists view hypnosis as mere faking or conscious playacting.

B. Some people believe that hypnotic suggestions can bolster the immune system and help a person fight disease, but the findings have been mixed, and many studies have been flawed (Miller & Cohen, 2001). One therapist dismissed these concerns by saying that a negative result just means that the hypnotist isn't skilled enough. As a critical thinker, can you spot what is wrong with his reasoning?

Answers: A. 1. true **2.** false **3.** false **4.** false **5.** true **6.** false **B.** The therapist's argument violates the principle of falsifiability. If a result is positive, he counts it as evidence. But if a result is negative, he refuses to count it as counterevidence ("Maybe the hypnotist just wasn't good enough"). With this kind of reasoning, there is no way to tell whether the hypothesis is right or wrong.

You are about to learn. . .

- **the major types of psychoactive drugs.**
- **how psychoactive drugs affect the brain.**
- **how people's prior drug experiences, expectations, and mental sets influence their reactions to drugs.**

CONSCIOUSNESS-ALTERING DRUGS

In Jerusalem, hundreds of Hasidic men celebrate the completion of the annual reading of the holy Torah by dancing for hours in the streets. For them, dancing is not a diversion; it is a path to religious ecstasy. In South Dakota, several Lakota (Sioux) adults sit naked in the darkness and crushing heat of a sweat lodge; their goal is euphoria, the transcendence of pain, and connection with the Great Spirit of the Universe. In the Amazon jungle, a young man training to be a shaman, a religious leader, takes a whiff of hallucinogenic snuff made from the bark of the virola tree; his goal is to enter a trance and communicate with animals, spirits, and supernatural forces.

These three rituals, seemingly quite different, are all aimed at release from the confines of ordinary consciousness. Because cultures around the world have devised such practices, some writers believe they reflect a human need, one as basic as the need for food and water (Siegel, 1989). William James (1902/1936), who was fascinated by

All cultures have found ways to alter consciousness. The Maulavis of Turkey (left), the famous whirling dervishes, spin in an energetic but controlled manner to achieve religious rapture. People in many cultures meditate (center) as a way to quiet the mind and achieve spiritual enlightenment. And in some cultures, psychoactive drugs are used for religious or artistic inspiration, as in the case of the Huichol Indians of western Mexico, one of whom is shown here harvesting hallucinogenic mushrooms.

alterations in consciousness, would have agreed. After inhaling nitrous oxide ("laughing gas"), he wrote, "Our normal waking consciousness, rational consciousness as we call it, is but one special type of consciousness, whilst all about it, parted from it by the filmiest of screens, there lie potential forms of consciousness entirely different." But it was not until the 1960s, as millions of people began to seek ways to deliberately produce *altered states of consciousness*, that researchers became interested in the psychology, as well as the physiology, of psychoactive drugs. The filmy screen described by James finally began to lift.

Classifying Drugs

A **psychoactive drug** is a substance that alters perception, mood, thinking, memory, or behavior by interacting with the biochemistry of brain and body. Around the world and throughout history, the most common ones have been nicotine, alcohol, marijuana, mescaline, opium, cocaine, peyote—and, of course, caffeine. The reasons for taking psychoactive drugs have varied: to alter consciousness, as part of a religious ritual, for recreation, to decrease physical pain or discomfort, and for psychological escape.

In Western societies, a whole pharmacopeia of recreational drugs exists, and new ones, both natural and synthetic, emerge every few years. Most of these drugs can be classified as *stimulants, depressants, opiates,* or *psychedelics,* depending on their effects on the central nervous system and their impact on behavior and mood (see Review 6.1). Here we describe only their physiological and psychological effects.

psychoactive drugs
drugs capable of influencing perception, mood, cognition, or behavior

Review 6.1 Some Psychoactive Drugs and Their Effects

Class of Drug	Type	Common Effects	Some Results of Abuse/Addiction
Amphetamines **Methamphetamine** **MDMA (Ecstasy)***	Stimulants	Wakefulness, alertness, raised metabolism, elevated mood	Nervousness, headaches, loss of appetite, high blood pressure, delusions, psychosis, heart damage, convulsions, death
Cocaine	Stimulant	Euphoria, excitation, feelings of energy, suppressed appetite	Excitability, sleeplessness, sweating, paranoia, anxiety, panic, depression, heart damage, heart failure, injury to nose if sniffed
Nicotine (tobacco)	Stimulant	Varies from alertness to calmness, depending on mental set, setting, and prior arousal; decreases appetite for carbohydrates	*Nicotine:* heart disease, high blood pressure, impaired circulation, erectile problems in men, damage throughout the body due to lowering of a key enzyme *Tar (residue from smoking cigarettes):* lung cancer, emphysema, mouth and throat cancer, many other health risks
Caffeine	Stimulant	Wakefulness, alertness, shortened reaction time	Restlessness, insomnia, muscle tension, heartbeat irregularities, high blood pressure
Alcohol (1 to 2 drinks)	Depressant	Depends on setting and mental set; tends to act like a stimulant because it reduces inhibitions and anxiety	
Alcohol (several/many drinks)	Depressant	Slowed reaction time, tension, depression, reduced ability to store new memories or to retrieve old ones, poor coordination	Blackouts, cirrhosis of the liver, other organ damage, mental and neurological impairment, psychosis, death with very large amounts
Tranquilizers (e.g., Valium); barbiturates (e.g., phenobarbital)	Depressants	Reduced anxiety and tension, sedation	Increased dosage needed for effects; impaired motor and sensory functions, impaired permanent storage of new information, withdrawal symptoms; possibly convulsions, coma, death (especially when taken with other drugs)
Opium, heroin, morphine, codeine, codone-based pain relievers	Opiates	Euphoria, relief of pain	Loss of appetite, nausea, constipation, withdrawal symptoms, convulsions, coma, possibly death
LSD, psilocybin, mescaline, Salvia divinorum	Psychedelics	Depending on the drug: Exhilaration, visions and hallucinations, insightful experiences	Psychosis, paranoia, panic reactions
Marijuana	Mild psychedelic (classification controversial)	Relaxation, euphoria, increased appetite, reduced ability to store new memories, other effects depending on mental set and setting	Throat and lung irritation, possible lung damage if smoked heavily

* Ecstasy also has psychedelic properties.

1 ***Stimulants*** **speed up activity in the central nervous system.** They include nicotine, caffeine, cocaine, amphetamines, methamphetamine (meth), and MDMA (Ecstasy, which also has psychedelic properties). In moderate amounts, stimulants produce feelings of excitement, confidence, and well-being or euphoria. In large amounts, they can make a person anxious, jittery, and hyperalert. In very large doses, they may cause convulsions, heart failure, and death.

stimulants
drugs that speed up activity in the central nervous system

Amphetamines are synthetic drugs taken in pill form, injected, smoked, or inhaled. Methamphetamine is structurally similar to amphetamine and is used in the same ways; it comes in two forms, as a powder or in a freebase (purified) form, as a crystalline solid. Cocaine is a natural drug, derived from the leaves of the coca plant. Rural workers in Bolivia and Peru chew coca leaf every day without apparent ill effects. In North America, the drug is usually inhaled, injected, or smoked in the freebase form known as *crack* (because of the cracking sound it makes when smoked). These methods provide more rapid access to the blood and therefore the brain, giving the drug a more immediate, powerful, and dangerous effect than when coca leaf is chewed. Amphetamines, methamphetamine, and cocaine make users feel charged up but do not actually increase energy reserves. Fatigue, irritability, and depression may occur when the effects of these drugs wear off.

2 ***Depressants*** **slow down activity in the central nervous system.** They include alcohol, tranquilizers, barbiturates, and most of the common chemicals that some people inhale to try to get high. Depressants usually make a person feel calm or drowsy, and they may reduce anxiety, guilt, tension, and inhibitions. These drugs enhance the activity of GABA, the neurotransmitter that inhibits the ability of neurons to communicate with each other. In large amounts, depressants may produce insensitivity to pain and other sensations. Like stimulants, in very large doses they can cause irregular heartbeats, convulsions, and death.

People are often surprised to learn that alcohol is a central nervous system depressant. In small amounts, alcohol has some of the effects of a stimulant because it suppresses activity in parts of the brain that normally inhibit impulsive behavior, such as loud laughter and clowning around. In the long run, however, it slows down nervous system activity. Like barbiturates and opiates, alcohol can produce anesthesia, which is why people may pass out (if they don't throw up first) when they drink excessively. Over time, alcohol damages the liver, heart, and brain. Extremely large amounts of alcohol can kill by inhibiting the nerve cells in brain areas that control breathing and heartbeat. Every so often, a news report announces the death of a college student who had large amounts of alcohol "funneled" into him as part of an initiation or drinking competition. On the other hand, *moderate* drinking—an occasional drink or two of wine, beer, or liquor—is associated with a variety of health benefits, including a reduced risk of heart attack and stroke, and antidiabetic effects (Brand-Miller et al., 2007; Mukamal et al., 2003; Reynolds et al., 2003).

3 ***Opiates*** **relieve pain.** They include opium, derived from the opium poppy; morphine, a derivative of opium; heroin, a derivative of morphine; synthetic drugs such as methadone; and codeine and codone-based pain relievers such as oxycodone and hydrocodone. These drugs work on some of the same brain systems as endorphins do, and some have a powerful effect on the emotions. When injected, opiates can enhance the transmission of dopamine, and so produce a *rush*, a sudden feeling of euphoria. They may also decrease anxiety and motivation. Opiates are highly addictive and in large amounts can cause coma and even death.

Marijuana was once regarded as a mild and harmless sedative, but its image changed in the 1930s, when books and movies began to warn about the dire consequences of "reefer madness."

4 ***Psychedelic drugs*** **disrupt normal thought processes,** such as the perception of time and space. Sometimes they produce hallucinations, especially visual ones. Some psychedelics, such as lysergic acid diethylamide (LSD), are made in the laboratory. Others, such as mescaline (from the peyote cactus), *Salvia divinorum* (from an herb native to Mexico), and psilocybin (from certain species of mushrooms), are natural substances. Emotional reactions to psychedelics vary from person to person and from one time to another for any individual. A "trip" may be mildly pleasant or unpleasant, a mystical revelation or a nightmare. For decades, research on psychedelics languished because of a lack of funding, but a few clinical researchers are now exploring their potential usefulness in psychotherapy, the relief of psychological distress, the treatment of anxiety disorders, and end-of-life distress (Griffiths et al., 2008). In a pilot study in which moderate doses of psilocybin were administered to 12 patients facing death from advanced-stage cancer, the drug significantly reduced their anxiety and despair (Grob et al., 2011).

Some commonly used drugs fall outside these four classifications, combine elements of more than one category, or have uncertain effects. One is *marijuana*, which is smoked or, less commonly, eaten in foods such as brownies; it is the most widely used illicit drug in North America and Europe. Some researchers classify it as a psychedelic, but others feel that its chemical makeup and its psychological effects place it outside the major classifications. The main active ingredient in marijuana is tetrahydrocannabinol (THC), derived from the hemp plant, *Cannabis sativa.* In some respects, THC appears to be a mild stimulant, increasing heart rate and making tastes, sounds, and colors seem more intense. But users often report reactions ranging from mild euphoria to relaxation or even sleepiness.

depressants
drugs that slow activity in the central nervous system

opiates
drugs, derived from the opium poppy, that relieve pain and commonly produce euphoria

psychedelic drugs
consciousness-altering drugs that produce hallucinations, change thought processes, or disrupt the normal perception of time and space

Some researchers believe that heavy smoking of the drug (which is high in tar) may increase the risk of lung damage (Barsky et al., 1998; Zhu et al., 2000). In moderate doses, it can interfere with the transfer of information to long-term memory and impair coordination and reaction times, characteristics it shares with alcohol. In large doses, it can cause hallucinations and a sense of unreality. However, a meta-analysis found only a small impairment in memory and learning among long-term users versus nonusers, less than what typically occurs in users of alcohol and other drugs (Grant et al., 2003). And there have been zero deaths reported from the use of marijuana.

Cannabis has been used therapeutically for nearly 3,000 years and is one of the fundamental herbs of traditional Chinese medicine. Its benefits have been affirmed in contemporary medicine as well. It reduces the nausea and vomiting that often accompany chemotherapy treatment for cancer and AIDS treatments; it reduces the physical tremors, loss of appetite, and other symptoms caused by multiple sclerosis; it reduces pain; it helps reduce the frequency of seizures in some patients with epilepsy; it helps clear arteries; and it alleviates the retinal swelling caused by glaucoma (Aggarwal et al., 2009; Ben Amar, 2006; Grinspoon & Bakalar, 1993; Steffens et al., 2005).

The Physiology of Drug Effects

Psychoactive drugs produce their effects by acting on brain neurotransmitters, the chemical substances that carry messages from one nerve cell to another. A drug may increase or decrease the release of neurotransmitters at the synapse; prevent the reuptake (reabsorption) of excess neurotransmitter molecules by the cells that have released them; or interfere with the receptors that a neurotransmitter normally binds to. Figure 6.5 shows how one drug, cocaine, increases the amount of norepinephrine and dopamine in the synapse by blocking the reuptake of these neurotransmitters following their release. Cocaine, like other drugs, also increases the availability of serotonin (Rocha et al., 1998).

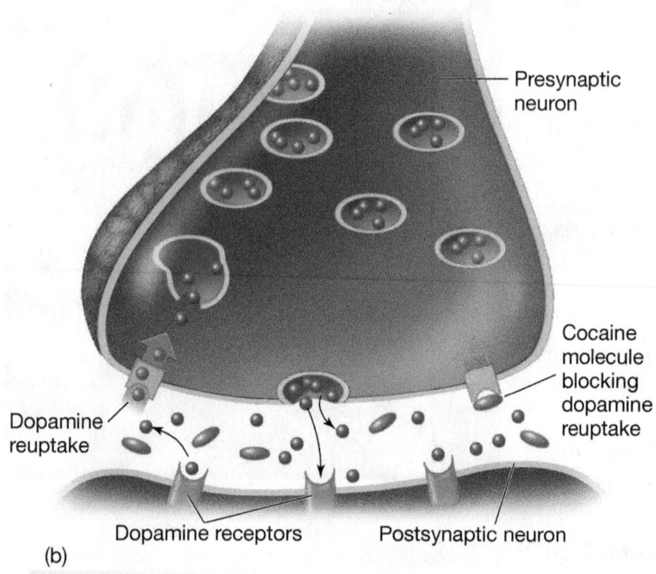

Figure 6.5 Cocaine's Effect on the Brain
Cocaine blocks the brain's reuptake of dopamine and norepinephrine so that synaptic levels of these neurotransmitters rise. The result is overstimulation of certain brain receptors and a brief euphoric high. Then, when the drug wears off, a depletion of dopamine may cause the user to "crash" and become sleepy and depressed.

These biochemical changes affect cognitive and emotional functioning. Alcohol activates the receptor for GABA, the inhibitory neurotransmitter found in virtually all parts of the brain. Because GABA is so prevalent and modulates the activity of other neurotransmitter systems, alcohol can affect many behaviors. Just a couple of drinks can affect perception, response time, coordination, and balance, despite the drinker's own impression of unchanged or even improved performance. Alcohol also affects memory, possibly by interfering with the work of serotonin. Information stored before a drinking session remains intact during the session but is retrieved more slowly (Haut et al., 1989). Consuming small amounts does not seem to affect *sober* mental performance, but even occasional binge drinking—usually defined as five or more drinks on a single occasion—impairs later abstract thought. Binge-drinking college students often have impaired executive functioning: They are less able to hold on to, and work with, verbal information (Parada et al., 2012). In other words, a Saturday night binge is potentially more disabling than a daily drink.

As for other recreational drugs, there is little evidence that *light* or *moderate* use can damage the human brain enough to affect cognitive functioning, but nearly all researchers agree that heavy or frequent use is another matter. In one study, heavy users of methamphetamine had damage to dopamine cells and performed more poorly than other people on tests of memory, attention, and movement, even though they had not used the drug for at least 11 months (Volkow et al., 2001).

Under some conditions, the repeated use of some psychoactive drugs can lead to **tolerance**: Over time, more and more of the drug is needed to produce the same effect. When habitual heavy users stop taking a drug, they may suffer severe physical **withdrawal** symptoms, which, depending on the drug, may include nausea, abdominal cramps, sweating, muscle spasms, depression, disturbed sleep, and intense craving for more of the drug.

tolerance
increased resistance to a drug's effects accompanying continued use

withdrawal
physical and psychological symptoms that occur when someone addicted to a drug stops taking it

The Psychology of Drug Effects

People often assume that the effects of a drug are automatic, the inevitable result of the drug's chemistry. But reactions to a psychoactive drug involve more than the drug's chemical properties. They also depend on a person's experience with the drug, individual characteristics, environmental setting, and mental set:

> **Thinking Critically**
>
> **Consider other interpretations**
>
> One person takes a drink and flies into a rage. Another has a drink and mellows out. What qualities of the user rather than the drug might account for this difference?

1 **Experience with the drug refers to the number of times a person has taken it.** When people try a drug—a cigarette, an alcoholic drink, a stimulant—for the first time, their reactions vary markedly, from unpleasant to neutral to enjoyable. Reactions to a drug may become increasingly positive once a person has used a drug for a while and has become familiar with its effects.

2 **Individual characteristics include body weight, metabolism, initial state of emotional arousal, personality characteristics, and physical tolerance for the drug.** Women generally get drunker than men on the same amount of alcohol because women are smaller, on average, so they get a higher proportionate dose of alcohol in each drink; their bodies also metabolize alcohol differently (Fuchs et al., 1995). Asians are more likely than Anglos to have a genetic variation that prevents alcohol from being metabolized normally and leads to the accumulation of a toxic substance, acetaldehyde. As a result, they tend to have adverse reactions to even small amounts of alcohol, which can cause severe headaches, facial flushing, and diarrhea (Cloninger, 1990). For individuals, a drug may have one effect after a tiring day and a different one after a rousing quarrel, or the effect may vary with the time of day because of circadian rhythms that affect various neurotransmitters. And some differences among individuals in their responses to a drug may be due to their personality traits. When people who are prone to anger and irritability wear nicotine patches, dramatic bursts of activity occur in the brain while they are working on competitive or aggressive tasks. These changes do not occur, however, in more relaxed and cheerful people (Fallon et al., 2004).

"Oh, that wasn't me talking. It was the alcohol talking."

3 **"Environmental setting" refers to the context in which a person takes the drug.** A person might have one glass of wine at home alone and feel sleepy, but have three glasses of wine at a party and feel full of energy. Someone might feel happy and calm drinking with good friends, but fearful and nervous drinking with strangers. In an early study of reactions to alcohol, most of the drinkers became depressed, angry, confused, and unfriendly. Then it dawned on the researchers that anyone might become depressed, angry, confused, and unfriendly if asked to drink bourbon at 9:00 a.m. in a bleak hospital room, which was the setting for the experiment (Warren & Raynes, 1972).

4 **"Mental set" refers to a person's expectations about the drug's effects and reasons for taking it.** Some people drink to become more sociable, friendly,

The motives for using a drug, expectations about its effects, and the setting in which it is used all contribute to a person's reactions to the drug. That is why drinking alone to drown your sorrows is likely to produce a different reaction than bingeing during a competitive game of beer pong.

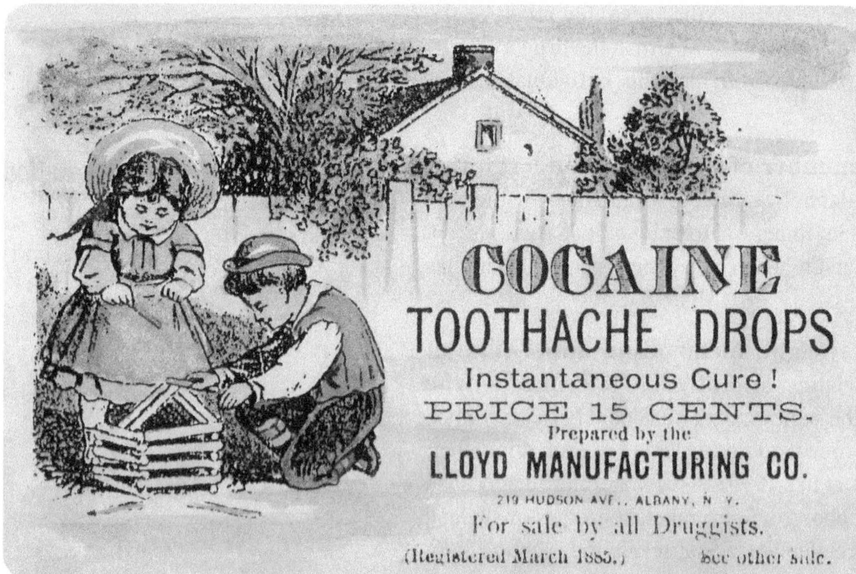

Attitudes about drugs vary with the times. Cigarette smoking was once promoted as healthy and glamorous. And before it was banned in the United States in the 1920s, cocaine was widely touted as a cure for everything from toothaches to timidity. It was used in teas, tonics, throat lozenges, and even soft drinks (including, briefly, Coca-Cola, which derived its name from the coca plant).

or seductive; some drink to try to reduce feelings of anxiety or depression; and some drink to have an excuse for abusiveness or violence. Addicts abuse drugs to escape from the real world; people living with chronic pain may use the same drugs to function in the real world. The motives for taking a drug greatly influence its effects.

Expectations can sometimes have a more powerful effect than the chemical properties of the drug itself. In several imaginative studies, researchers compared people who were drinking liquor (vodka and tonic) with those who *thought* they were drinking liquor but were actually getting only tonic and lime juice. (Vodka has a subtle taste, and most people could not tell the real and phony drinks apart.) The experimenters found a *"think–drink" effect:* Men behaved more belligerently when they thought they were drinking vodka than when they thought they were drinking plain tonic water, regardless of the actual content of the drinks. And both sexes reported feeling sexually aroused when they thought they were drinking vodka, whether or not they actually got vodka (Abrams & Wilson, 1983; Marlatt & Rohsenow, 1980).

None of this means that alcohol and other drugs are merely placebos. Psychoactive drugs, as we have seen, have physiological effects, many of them extremely potent. But by understanding the psychological factors involved in drug use, we can think more critically about the ongoing national debate over which drugs, if any, should be legal. In "Taking Psychology with You," we discuss some points to consider as you decide what your own position is on this issue.

Recite & Review

Recite: Say aloud everything you can about *psychoactive drugs (stimulants, depressants, opiates, psychedelics, marijuana), withdrawal, tolerance,* and psychological influences on drug reactions, including *environmental setting* and *mental set.*

Review: Next, reread this section.

Now take this ***Quick Quiz:***

A. Name the following:

1. Three stimulants used illegally

2. Two drugs that interfere with the formation of new long-term memories

(continued)

3. Three types of depressant drugs
4. A legal recreational drug that acts as a depressant in the central nervous system
5. Four factors that influence a person's reactions to a psychoactive drug

B. A bodybuilder who has been taking anabolic steroids says the drugs make him more aggressive. What are some other possible interpretations?

Answers: A. 1. cocaine, amphetamines, and methamphetamine **2.** marijuana and alcohol **3.** barbiturates, tranquilizers, and alcohol **4.** alcohol **5.** prior experience with the drug; the person's physical, emotional, and personality traits; the person's mental set; and the environmental setting **B.** The bodybuilder's increased aggressiveness could be due to his expectations (a placebo effect); bodybuilding itself may increase aggressiveness; the culture of the bodybuilding gym may encourage aggressiveness; other influences in his life or other drugs he is taking may be making him more aggressive; or he may only think he is more aggressive, and his behavior may contradict his self-perceptions.

As we have seen in this chapter, changes in consciousness and body rhythms are not only interesting in themselves; they also show us how our expectations and explanations of our own mental and physical states affect what we do and how we feel. Research on SAD and PMS, the purposes of sleep, the meaning of dreams, the nature of hypnosis, and the dangers and benefits of drugs has done much to dispel many popular but mistaken ideas about these topics. And the scientific scrutiny of biological rhythms, dreaming, hypnotic suggestion, and drug-induced states has deepened our understanding of the intimate relationship between body and mind.

Taking Psychology with You

The Drug Debate

Because the consequences of drug *abuse* are so devastating to individuals and to society, people often have trouble thinking critically about drug laws and policies: Which drugs should be legal, which should be illegal, and which should be "decriminalized" (that is, not made legal, but not used as a reason for arresting and jailing their users)? At one extreme, some people cannot accept evidence that their favorite drug—be it caffeine, nicotine, alcohol, or marijuana—might have harmful effects. At the other extreme, some cannot accept the evidence that their most hated drug—be it alcohol, morphine, marijuana, or the coca leaf—might not be dangerous in all forms or amounts and might even have some beneficial effects. Both sides often confuse potent drugs with others that have only subtle effects and confuse light or moderate use with heavy or excessive use.

"No one has ever died from smoking marijuana, but tobacco use contributes to 24 times the number of deaths from all illegal forms of drug use combined."

Once a drug is declared illegal, many people assume it is deadly, even though some legal drugs are more dangerous than illegal ones. Addiction to prescription painkillers and sedatives used for recreational rather than medical purposes has risen dramatically among teenagers and adults. Nicotine, which of course is legal, is as addictive as heroin and cocaine, which are illegal. No one has ever died from smoking marijuana, but tobacco use contributes to between 400,000 and 500,000 deaths in the United States every year, 24 times the number of deaths from all illegal forms of drug use combined, and worldwide it is the largest single cause of preventable deaths (Brandt, 2007). Yet most people have a far more negative view of marijuana, heroin, and cocaine than of nicotine and prescription painkillers.

Emotions run especially high in debates over marijuana. Heavy use has some physical risks, just as heavy use of any drug does. However, a review of studies done between 1975 and 2003 failed to find any compelling evidence that marijuana causes chronic mental or behavioral problems in teenagers or young adults. The researchers observed that cause and effect could just as well work in the other direction; that is, people with problems could be more likely to abuse the drug (Macleod et al., 2004).

Because marijuana has medical benefits, Canada, Spain, Italy, Portugal, Israel, Austria, Finland, the Netherlands, and Belgium have either decriminalized it or made it legally available for patients who demonstrate a medical need for it. In the United States, 17 states and the District of Columbia (as of 2012) have approved the medical use of marijuana; in other states, possession of any amount of pot remains illegal, and punishment for first offenses ranges from a few years in prison to life imprisonment without parole. In many states, a person who has been convicted of marijuana possession cannot later get food stamps or welfare, which even convicted rapists and murderers are entitled to.

At one end of the spectrum, many people remain committed to the eradication of all currently illegal drugs. At the other end, some people think that all recreational drugs should be legalized

(*continued*)

or decriminalized. In between lie a range of possible strategies. One is to develop programs to reduce or at least delay drug use by young teens, because multiple drug use before age 15 increases the risk of drug dependence, criminal activity, and other problems in adulthood (Odgers et al., 2008). Another approach would legalize narcotics for people who are in chronic pain and marijuana for recreational and medicinal use, but would ban tobacco and most hard drugs. And in a third approach, instead of punishing or incarcerating people who use drugs, society would regulate where drugs are used (never at work or when driving, for example), provide treatment for addicts, and educate people about the benefits and hazards of particular drugs.

Where, given the research findings, do you stand in this debate? Which illegal psychoactive drugs, if any, do you think should be legalized? Can we create mental sets and environmental settings that promote safe recreational use of some drugs, minimize the likelihood of drug abuse, and permit the medicinal use of beneficial drugs? What do you think?

Summary

BIOLOGICAL RHYTHMS: THE TIDES OF EXPERIENCE

- *Consciousness* is the awareness of oneself and the environment. Changing states of consciousness are often associated with *biological rhythms*—periodic fluctuations in physiological functioning. These rhythms are typically tied to external time cues, but many are also *endogenous*, generated from within even in the absence of such cues. *Circadian* fluctuations occur about once a day; other rhythms occur less frequently or more frequently than that.
- When people live in isolation from all time cues, they tend to live a day that is slightly longer than 24 hours. Circadian rhythms are governed by a biological clock in the *suprachiasmatic nucleus (SCN)* of the hypothalamus. The SCN regulates and, in turn, is affected by the hormone *melatonin,* which is responsive to changes in light and dark and which increases during the dark hours. When a person's normal routine changes, the person may experience *internal desynchronization,* in which the usual circadian rhythms are thrown out of phase with one another. The result may be fatigue, mental inefficiency, and an increased risk of accidents.
- Some people experience depression every winter in a pattern that has been labeled *seasonal affective disorder (SAD)*. The causes of SAD, which is relatively uncommon, are not yet clear. They may involve biological rhythms that are out of phase and/or an abnormality in the secretion of melatonin, although there can also be other, nonbiological causes. Light treatments can be effective.
- Another long-term rhythm is the menstrual cycle, during which various hormones rise and fall. Well-controlled, double-blind studies on *PMS* do not support claims that emotional symptoms are reliably and universally tied to the menstrual cycle. Overall, women and men do not differ in the emotional symptoms they report or in the number of mood swings they experience over the course of a month. As we saw in "Culture and PMS," culture has a major impact on the experience and reporting of PMS symptoms.
- Expectations and learning affect how both sexes interpret bodily and emotional changes. Few people of either sex are likely to undergo dramatic monthly mood swings or personality changes because of hormones.

THE RHYTHMS OF SLEEP

- During sleep, periods of *rapid eye movement (REM)* alternate with *non-REM sleep* in approximately a 90-minute rhythm. Non-REM sleep is divided into four stages on the basis of characteristic brain-wave patterns. During REM sleep, the brain is active, and there are other signs of arousal, yet most of the skeletal muscles are limp; vivid dreams are reported most often during REM sleep. Some people have had "waking dreams" when they emerge from REM sleep before the paralysis of that stage has subsided, and occasionally, people have interpreted the resulting hallucinations as real.
- Sleep is necessary not only for bodily restoration but also for normal mental functioning. Many people get less than the optimal amount of sleep. Some suffer from insomnia, *sleep apnea, narcolepsy,* or *REM behavior disorder,* but the most common reason for daytime sleepiness is probably a simple lack of sleep. When schools begin the school day later, children and teenagers tend to get more sleep, have improved mood, and do better on tests.
- Sleep may contribute to the consolidation of memories and subsequent problem solving. These benefits have been associated most closely with slow-wave sleep, but also with REM sleep.

EXPLORING THE DREAM WORLD

- Dreams are sometimes recalled as illogical and disjointed. Some people say they have *lucid dreams* in which they know they are dreaming.
- Freud thought that dreams allow us to express forbidden or unrealistic wishes and desires that have been forced into the unconscious part of the mind and disguised as symbolic images. But there is no objective way to verify Freudian interpretations of dreams and no convincing support for most of his claims.
- Three modern theories of dreaming emphasize the connections between dreams and waking thoughts. The *problem-focused approach* holds that they express current concerns and may even help us solve current problems and work through emotional issues, especially during times of crisis. The *cognitive approach* holds that they are simply a modification of the cognitive activity that goes on when we are awake. The difference is that during sleep we are cut off from sensory input from the world and our bodily movements, so our thoughts tend to be more diffuse and unfocused. The *activation–synthesis theory* holds that dreams occur when the cortex tries to make sense of, or interpret, spontaneous neural firing initiated in the pons. The resulting synthesis of these signals with existing knowledge and memories results in a dream.

- All of the current theories of dreams have some support, and all have weaknesses. Some psychologists doubt that people can solve problems during sleep. The activation–synthesis theory does not seem to explain coherent, story-like dreams or non-REM dreams. The cognitive approach is now a leading contender, although some of its specific claims remain to be tested.

THE RIDDLE OF HYPNOSIS

- *Hypnosis* is a procedure in which the practitioner suggests changes in a person's sensations, perceptions, thoughts, feelings, or behavior, and the person tries to comply. Although hypnosis has been used successfully for many medical and psychological purposes, people hold many misconceptions about what it can accomplish. It cannot force people to do things against their will, confer special abilities that are otherwise impossible, increase the accuracy of memory, or produce a literal reexperiencing of long-ago events.
- A leading approach to understanding hypnosis is that it involves *dissociation,* a split in consciousness. In one version of this approach, the split is between a part of consciousness that is hypnotized and a *hidden observer* that watches but does not participate. In another version, the split is between an executive-control system in the brain and other brain systems responsible for thinking and acting.
- Another leading approach, the *sociocognitive explanation,* regards hypnosis as a product of normal social and cognitive processes in which the hypnotized person's expectations and beliefs combine with the desire to comply with the hypnotist's suggestions. In this view, hypnosis is a form of role-playing; the role is so engrossing that the person interprets it as real. Sociocognitive processes can account for the apparent age and past-life "regressions" of people under hypnosis and their reports of alien abductions.
- As we saw in "Biology and Hypnosis," several techniques are providing more information about what happens in the brain during hypnosis, but they are not able to distinguish between the dissociation and sociocognitive explanations.

CONSCIOUSNESS-ALTERING DRUGS

- In all cultures, people have found ways to produce *altered states of consciousness. Psychoactive drugs* alter cognition and emotion by acting on neurotransmitters in the brain. Most psychoactive drugs are classified as *stimulants, depressants, opiates,* or *psychedelics,* depending on their central nervous system effects and their impact on behavior and mood. However, some common drugs, such as marijuana, straddle or fall outside these categories.
- When used frequently and in large amounts, some psychoactive drugs can damage neurons in the brain and impair learning and memory. Their use may lead to *tolerance,* in which increasing dosages are needed for the same effect, and *withdrawal* symptoms if a heavy user tries to quit. But certain drugs, such as alcohol and marijuana, are also associated with some health benefits when used in moderation.
- Reactions to a psychoactive drug are influenced not only by its chemical properties but also by the user's prior experience with the drug, individual characteristics, environmental setting, and mental set—the person's expectations and motives for taking the drug. Expectations can be even more powerful than the drug itself, as shown by the *"think–drink" effect.*

TAKING PSYCHOLOGY WITH YOU

- People often find it difficult to distinguish drug use from drug abuse, heavy use from light or moderate use, and a drug's legality or illegality from its potential dangers and benefits.

Key Terms

consciousness (p. 159)
biological rhythm (p. 159)
endogenous (p. 160)
circadian rhythm (p. 160)
suprachiasmatic nucleus (SCN) (p. 160)
melatonin (p. 160)
internal desynchronization (p. 161)
seasonal affective disorder (SAD) (p. 162)
premenstrual syndrome (p. 164)
rapid eye movement (REM) sleep (p. 166)
non-REM (NREM) sleep (p. 166)
alpha waves (p. 167)
sleep spindles (p. 167)
delta waves (p. 167)
sleep apnea (p. 170)
narcolepsy (p. 170)
cataplexy (p. 170)
REM behavior disorder (p. 170)
consolidation (p. 171)
lucid dream (p. 173)
problem-focused approach to dreams (p. 173)
cognitive approach to dreams (p. 175)
activation–synthesis theory of dreams (p. 175)
hypnosis (p. 178)
dissociation (p. 179)
hidden observer (p. 179)
sociocognitive explanation of hypnosis (p. 180)
altered states of consciousness (p. 183)
psychoactive drug (p. 183)
stimulants (p. 184)
depressants (p. 185)
opiates (p. 185)
psychedelics (p. 185)
tolerance (p. 186)
withdrawal (p. 186)
"think–drink" effect (p. 189)

7

Conditioning Principles and Applications

How the Environment We Live in Shapes Us

BY DOUGLAS A. JOHNSON, PH.D. AND SOPHIE RUBIN, PH.D

> I remember the rage I used to feel when a prediction went awry. I could have shouted at the subjects of my experiments, "Behave, damn you! Behave as you ought!" Eventually I realized that the subjects were always right. They always behaved as they should have behaved. It was I who was wrong. I had made a bad prediction.
>
> *Walden Two (pg. 271)*

The Philosophy of Behaviorism

The quote above is taken from T.E. Frazier, a character from B.F. Skinner's only fictional novel. Skinner, a renowned psychologist, was using Frazier's character to describe his own early frustrations in the laboratory. Skinner would carefully design experiments for rats to be tested on, only to find the rats wouldn't perform as he expected. After many failures, he recalled yelling at the rats in desperation, pleading with them to behave as they ought. Of course, yelling at rats did not produce results. He began to wonder if he had been looking at the problem incorrectly. He reasoned that rats always behave in ways that seem natural for them. If nothing was wrong with the rats, perhaps something else was responsible for the failed predictions. Skinner then began to look at redesigning the environments the rats were put in. These changes in the environment led to reliable changes in the rats' behavior. Suddenly, the behavior of the rats became predictable, but only if one focused on altering the environment rather than altering the rats themselves. What had been unpredictable chaos now became orderly patterns of behavior.

B.F. Skinner (1904–1990). *(Courtesy of Everett Collection Inc./Alamy.)*

Now, it may seem odd that a distinguished scientist such as B.F. Skinner would be yelling at rats for not doing what they're supposed to, but it isn't that different from what most people do on a regular basis. Parents are frustrated with their children, wondering why they don't just clean their rooms and do their chores as they are supposed to. Employers endlessly urge employees to do various job tasks, wondering why they don't just work harder and more carefully as they are supposed to. Teachers lament the performance of their students, wondering why they procrastinate and don't put more effort into their studies. One of Skinner's early realizations was that blaming the person (or rat) doesn't lead to productive change and that it is more effective to see how the environment around people can be altered to produce desirable behavior. Rather than blame the children, employees, and students, it might be more pragmatic to simply look to the environments of these individuals.

This notion that the external environment is a critical consideration in modifying and understanding our emotions, thoughts, personality, language, self-control, problem-solving, awareness, creativity, and social behavior helped lay the groundwork for the behaviorism philosophy. This philosophy, developed and refined by behaviorists such as John B. Watson and B.F. Skinner, states that behavior is a subject matter worthy of its own field of study. Prior to this philosophy, most psychologists only considered behavior to be important as a way of studying what's going on in the mind or psyche. Behavior was only relevant as a sign or symptom for examining what was happening in the mind. The behavioral philosophy was a strong contrast to this because it did not just consider behavior to be a mere symptom or indication of some other underlying process. Instead, the behavior itself could be a complex and rich subject matter. According to behaviorists, it is a subject matter so complex and rich that an entire science dedicated to behavior alone can be justified. This does not deny the existence or devalue the worth of other subject matters and methods, such as studying the influence of genetics. The behavioral perspective simply considers those to be separate disciplines.

One of the lessons a behavioral approach teaches us is that we shouldn't focus all our effort simply on blaming the individual.

Stimuli, Responses, and Behavioral Relations

Before getting too far into the behavioral perspective, it would be helpful to define two fundamental terms: stimulus and response. A **stimulus** is any change in the environment that influences an organism (i.e., any living creature, including humans) by activating one of the sense receptors. Environment is defined quite broadly; it could refer to the physical world around you, the social interactions around you, or even stimulation from within your skin, such as your own physical sensations and thoughts. Stimuli (the plural of stimulus) could

stimulus
any change in the environment that can influence an organism by activating one of the sense receptors

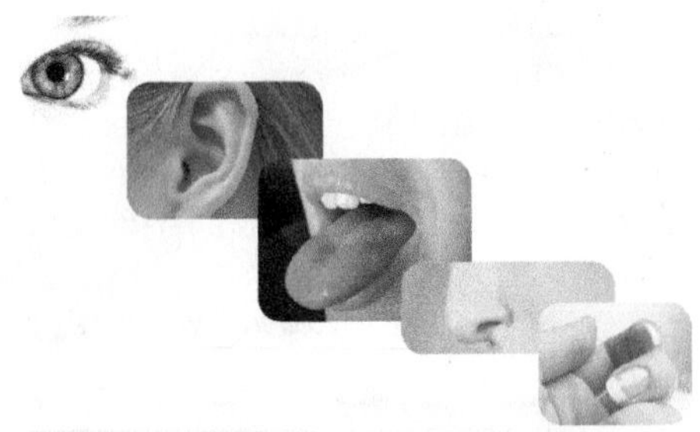

Our responses to various stimuli is a critical aspect of the behavioral approach.

include environmental changes such as the sight of a friend approaching, the sound of your name being called, the taste of a good meal, an unpleasant smell, a feeling of nausea, the sensation of being off balance, and many other examples. As long as you can sense it, it would qualify as a stimulus.

A **response** is any action performed by the organism. This could be as simple as one of your glands secreting some sweat or as complex as you trying to think of a novel solution to an unsolved problem. Essentially, a response is anything you say or do. By the way, behaviorists do not make a distinction between the terms "response" and "behavior".

The behavioral perspective led to the development of the field of study known as behavior analysis. Despite the name, people in this field are not very concerned about behavior in isolation. Behavior analysts study *behavioral relations*, or how stimuli and behavior relate to and influence one another. Behavior described out of context has very little meaning to behavior analysts because they focus less on the *form* of behavior (i.e., what does it look like) and more on the *function* that the behavior serves (i.e., why is this behavior happening). Of particular interest is how these behavioral relations influence *learning,* defined as a relatively permanent change in behavior as a result of experience. The process of creating such learning is known as conditioning. An important milestone in the study of behavioral relations occurred when a scientist began investigating the digestive process in dogs, as we'll discuss next.

Ivan Pavlov (1849–1936). *(Courtesy of Hulton-Deutsch Collection/Corbis Images.)*

Ivan Pavlov and Respondent Conditioning

Around the beginning of the 20th century, a Russian scientist by the name of Ivan Pavlov had devoted decades of his life to a careful analysis of physiology, with much of it focusing on the digestive system. He was a skilled researcher and his studies into gastrointestinal physiology eventually won him the Nobel Prize in 1904. Despite the rewards and recognition that had come from this line of work, he discovered a new and curious phenomenon he eventually considered so important that, at the age of 52, he abandoned the study of physiology and digestion in order to pursue this discovery for the remaining 34 years of his life. His detailed explanations of this discovery would lead Pavlov to become one of the most famous figures in psychology (Babkin, 1949; Hunt, 2007).

The discovery started with a simple but confusing occurrence. Pavlov had been using dogs to study digestion and he placed his research assistants in charge of feeding these dogs. While running experiments, Pavlov observed that many of the dogs began producing stomach acid before food actually reached the stomach. He also noted this typically occurred when the dogs could see the assistants in charge of feedings. While this phenomenon must have been confusing and aggravating to a researcher initially only interested in physiology, Pavlov came to realize that he could not fully explain physiological processes without also understanding the psychology relevant to such processes. This realization led to the study of **respondent conditioning** (also known as classical conditioning or Pavlovian conditioning). A stimulus that does not produce a response is called a **neutral stimulus** (NS). Respondent conditioning is a form of learning which involves the pairing of a neutral stimulus with another stimulus that already causes a response, until the neutral stimulus becomes a **conditioned stimulus** that can elicit (i.e., bring forth or cause) a similar response, known as a **conditioned response**. When a stimulus causes a response due to a pairing history, it is called a conditioned stimulus (CS). The response caused by a conditioned stimulus is called a conditioned response (CR).

response
any action performed by the organism

respondent conditioning
the repeated pairing of two stimuli resulting in a previously neutral stimulus becoming a conditioned stimulus

neutral stimulus (NS)
a detectable change in the environment that does not produce a response

conditioned stimulus (CS)
a detectable change in the environment that produces a response due to a learning history in which stimuli had been paired together

conditioned response (CR)
the response of an organism that is elicited by a conditioned stimulus

Pavlov's Conditioning Experiments

Pavlov quickly realized that conducting experiments involving the visual presentation of research assistants and the observation of stomach acid would be very difficult. To make experimentation easier, he simplified his procedures and inserted a small tube into the cheek of the dogs. Whenever the dogs would salivate, the saliva would be collected via the tube so that it could be precisely measured (much easier than observing stomach acid!). Instead of just using visual stimuli (e.g., sight of the research assistant), he often employed a variety of sounds, the best known was his use of a bell (Goodwin, 2008). His experimental procedure was as follows:

First, Pavlov would ring a bell for a dog with no special training history (that is, who was new to experiments like these). Unsurprisingly, the dog would not salivate to the sound of the bell alone, meaning that the bell would be considered a neutral stimulus (NS). On separate occasions Pavlov would put meat powder in the dog's mouth. The dog would predictably and immediately salivate because dogs are biologically hardwired for this reflexive relationship (i.e., salivating is a necessary step in the natural digestive process). Any stimulus that causes a response without training is an **unconditioned stimulus** (US). Any reflexive reaction to an unconditioned stimulus is called an **unconditioned response** (UR). This means that the meat powder in the mouth is an unconditioned stimulus and the salivating is an unconditioned response. So far, nothing particularly noteworthy has occurred in the absence of training or conditioning.

PRE-CONDITIONING BEHAVIORAL RELATIONS:

Bell (NS) ⃠→ Salivating

Meat powder (US) ⟶ Salivating (UR)

After we have witnessed the natural, unconditioned relations, we can now create a new relationship. Pavlov accomplished this by repeatedly pairing the bell (NS) and the meat powder (US). It was important to do this multiple times, as a single pairing would not be effective. It was also important to present the bell first and then immediately follow it with the meat powder. Also note that the pairing of two stimuli is the critical element, not the pairing of stimuli and responses (it would be a technical language faux pas to say that a stimulus and response were paired). Even though the focus is on pairing stimuli, the salivation would still be occurring because of the pre-existing unconditioned relationship between the meat powder (US) and salivation (UR).

CONDITIONING PROCEDURE:

Bell (NS) / Meat powder (US) ⟶ Salivating (UR)

Finally, as a result of this conditioning history, a new behavioral relation emerges and the status of the bell changes. The previously neutral stimulus now has the power to elicit salivating independently. The bell would now be labeled as a conditioned stimulus and the salivating would be labeled as a conditioned response.

POST-CONDITIONING BEHAVIORAL RELATION:

Bell (CS) ⟶ Salivating (CR)

Note that even though we labeled "salivating" as an unconditioned response earlier, we are now labeling it as a conditioned response. Recall the earlier point about behavior and context: how we label the response depends upon what stimulus elicited it. You cannot classify "salivating" in isolation; you must know what stimulus produced it. Also note that by definition, conditioned stimuli always elicit conditioned responses (CS ⟶ CR) and unconditioned stimuli always elicit unconditioned responses (US ⟶ UR). It would not make sense to say that a CS elicited a UR or that a US elicited a CR. Make sure your stimuli and responses match!

This simple discovery had profound implications. A completely new behavioral relation had emerged from the simplest of techniques. It was a behavioral relation that would appear bizarre and nonsensical if you were unaware of the conditioning history (i.e.,

unconditioned stimulus (US)
a detectable change in the environment that produces a response (i.e., a natural reflex) without any learning on the part of the organism

unconditioned response (UR)
the response of an organism that is elicited by an unconditioned stimulus

How did learning in dogs help us better understand the psychology of humans?

how previous stimuli have been paired together to create new responses). This experiment helps shed light on many acquired behaviors, not just for dogs, but for humans and other animals as well. Although Pavlov recognized the importance of this finding, it would take another individual by the name of John B. Watson to use this idea to establish a new branch of psychology.

Watson's Establishment of Behaviorism

At the time John B. Watson began studying psychology, it was a field characterized by subjective and unreliable methods such as introspection (see Chapter 2). Pavlov's techniques strongly appealed to Watson, who saw this as a way for psychology to become a true science (Buckley, 1989; Cohen, 1979). He decided to create a new approach to psychology, one that would focus on observable behavior and rigorous methodology. He also saw the greater implications of Pavlov's discovery and began to champion respondent conditioning as a way to understand nearly all of human behavior and change behavior in whichever way was desired. One of the most famous quotes from Watson is the following:

John B. Watson (1878–1958). *(Courtesy of Bettmann/Corbis Images.)*

> Give me a dozen healthy infants, well-formed, and my own specified world to bring them up in and I'll guarantee to take any one at random and train him to become any type of specialist I might select-doctor, lawyer, artist, merchant-chief and, yes, even beggar-man and thief, regardless of his talents, penchants, tendencies, abilities, vocations, and race of his ancestors. I am going beyond my facts and I admit it, but so have the advocates of the contrary and they have been doing it for many thousands of years.
>
> John B. Watson, Behaviorism (p. 104)

Many have used this quote to argue that Watson, and behaviorism as a whole, went too far. Indeed, it does make a very bold claim that seems to deny the influence of biology on behavior. Watson self-admittedly overstated his case and did not actually deny the relevance of genetics, having spent several years studying instinctive behavior in infants and birds. Watson was also controversial for denying the importance of studying consciousness, which had been the bread and butter of psychologists since Wilhelm Wundt formed the first scientific laboratory to study psychology. For Watson, the methodology for studying consciousness was far too imprecise and unreliable. He did not deny the existence of such phenomena and even spent time trying to scientifically investigate private thinking (which he believed to be just silent movement of the vocal muscles), but he did seriously question whether these topics belonged in a proper science. His strict adherence to observable methods later earned his particular brand of behaviorism the name of *methodological behaviorism*.

However, Watson needed to show the world how his approach was better. Drooling dogs weren't enough to persuade the world at large. He needed to demonstrate respondent conditioning in human behavior. Human drooling wouldn't be any better though; he needed a topic that would be of great interest to psychologists and the average person. Fortunately, he created such a demonstration with a little boy he nicknamed Albert B. (Beck, Levinson, & Irons, 2009).

Are you afraid of rats? Respondent conditioning might help you understand why.

Little Albert and the Development of a Conditioned Phobia

Watson and his research assistant, a student by the name of Rosalie Rayner, wanted to demonstrate whether an irrational fear could be explained using respondent conditioning. To test this, they worked with an eleven-month-old boy in what became known as the "Little Albert" experiments. Initially, Watson and Rayner would place a white rat near Albert. The young child showed no fear to this rat, instead reacting with curiosity. As such, the white rat was a neutral stimulus in regards to fear for Albert (you may want to review the section on Pavlov one more time to help keep all these stimuli and responses straight). As with nearly all infants, a sudden loud noise would reliably produce a fearful reaction in Albert. To demonstrate this, Watson banged a hammer against a steel bar just behind Albert's head. Albert would immediately start crying and showing other signs of fear in response to this loud noise. This meant that the loud noise was an unconditioned stimulus and the fear reaction was an unconditioned response for Albert.

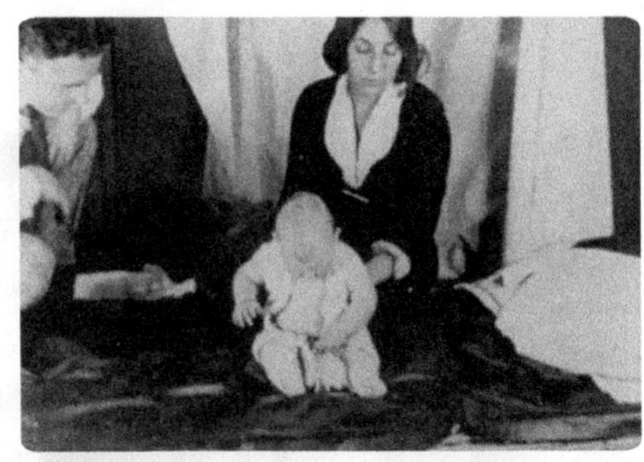

Before conditioning Albert showed no fear of white rats or other animals such as dogs and rabbits. *(Courtesy of Archives of the History of American Psychology.)*

PRE-CONDITIONING BEHAVIORAL RELATIONS FOR LITTLE ALBERT:

White rat (NS) ⊘→ Fearful response

Loud noise (US) ⟶ Fearful response (UR)

Next, Watson and Rayner proceeded to condition a new behavioral relation. Similar to the pairing procedure Pavlov used, they would consistently pair the sight of the white rat (NS) with a sudden loud noise (US). They would place the white rat in front of Albert and would then immediately bang the hammer against the steel bar. This was repeated several times.

CONDITIONING PROCEDURE FOR LITTLE ALBERT:

White rat (NS) / Loud noise (US) ⟶ Fearful response (UR)

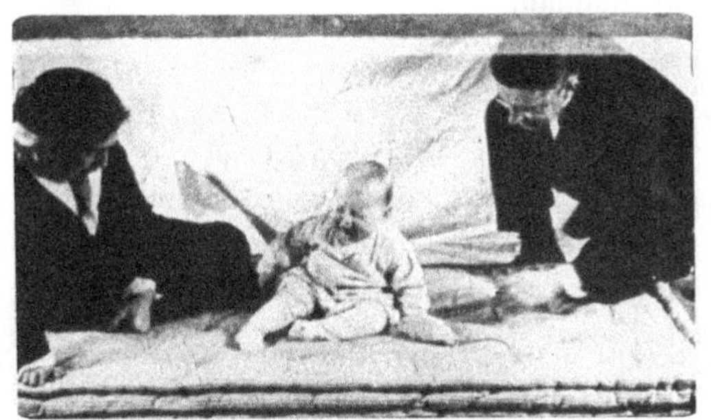

After the white rate was paired with a frightening noise, Albert developed a conditioned fear of the rat itself and would try to escape the rat. *(Courtesy of Professor Ben Harris, University of New Hampshire.)*

Finally, to demonstrate that the conditioning had been successful, Watson and Rayner would expose Albert to the white rat in silence (i.e., without the presentation of the loud noise). Despite the fact the loud, fear-eliciting sound was not in the current environment, Albert still reacted in terror to this little rat he had earlier been curious about. Upon seeing the rat, Albert would struggle to get away from the rat, instantly crying and whimpering. Even though the rat itself was not dangerous, Albert had acquired a strong irrational fear of it. In other words, the rat had become a conditioned stimulus, which could now elicit a conditioned response of fear. This was in direct conflict with other explanations at the time as to why phobias develop, such as the Freudian approach that suggested phobias were the result of repressed conflicts in the psyche. If the sound of dentist drill alone causes you fear, then you should understand Little Albert's fear all too well.

POST-CONDITIONING BEHAVIORAL RELATION FOR LITTLE ALBERT:

White rat (CS) ⟶ Fearful response (CR)

Stimulus Generalization and Discrimination of Respondent Relations

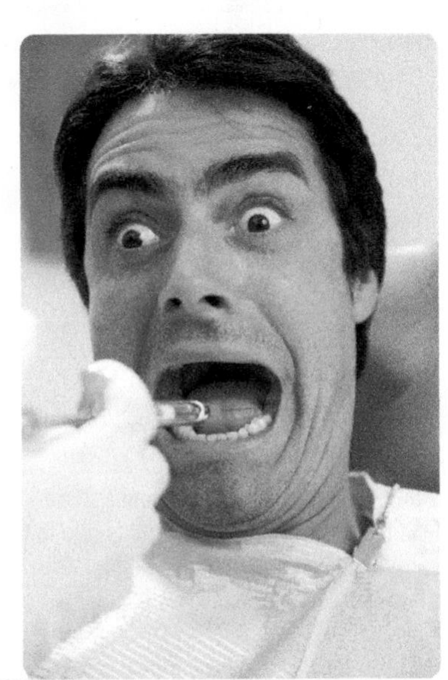

How might Watson explain why people are afraid of the sound of a dentist drill or the sight of a dentist office?

Watson and Rayner decided to test how extensive Little Albert's newly acquired fear was by presenting a variety of other similar stimuli. They brought out a white rabbit and immediately Little Albert exhibited a similar fear reaction (whimpering, crying, crawling away, etc.) to the one he had shown with the white rat. Dogs and fur coats also caused Little

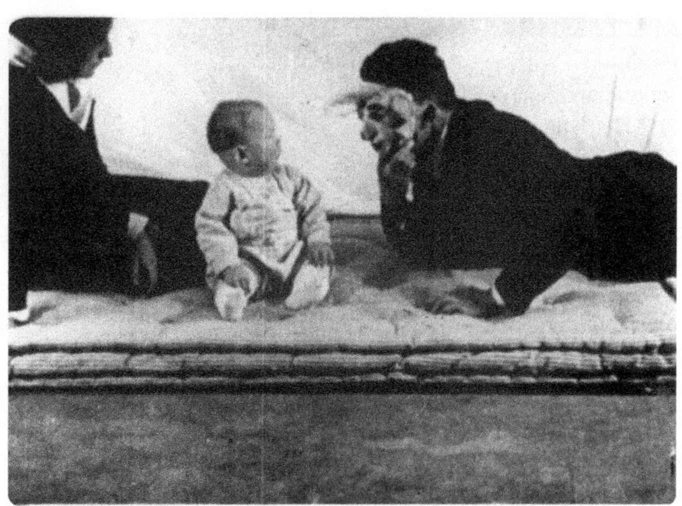
Albert's fear generalized beyond the original pairings. In this picture he is fearful of a mask with a white beard. *(Courtesy of Professor Ben Harris, University of New Hampshire.)*

Albert strong distress. Even something as simple as a Santa Claus mask terrified Albert, even though Albert had previously enjoyed the mask. Note that Little Albert's fear had spread to objects that had never been paired with a loud noise or any other frightening stimuli. Their physical similarity to the white rat was enough to cause Albert terror. This is known as **stimulus generalization**, in which a stimulus not involved in the original conditioning causes a similar reaction as the original stimulus due to some similarity between the stimuli.

One implication of stimulus generalization is that respondent relationships can emerge without direct pairing. Another implication is that unusual and unexpected reactions without any obvious direct training may have simply occurred via stimulus generalization. As the old proverb states, "a cat bitten once by a snake dreads even rope." This can help explain the development of phobias that at first glance, seem to develop out of nowhere.

The opposite of stimulus generalization is discrimination. Note that Little Albert did not become fearful of everything in the experiment. In the absence of white, fuzzy stimuli Albert's fear response would not occur. This tendency to respond to some stimuli but not others is called **stimulus discrimination**. More precisely, stimulus discrimination is when a conditioned response occurs in the presence of a conditioned stimulus but not in the presence of other dissimilar stimuli.

Respondent conditioning can also work by pairing a neutral stimulus with a conditioned stimulus.

Higher-Order Conditioning

In the previous examples, a neutral stimulus (NS) was paired with an unconditioned stimulus (US) in order to create a new conditioned stimulus (CS). Respondent conditioning doesn't always require an unconditioned stimulus, as seen with *higher-order conditioning*. Higher-order conditioning is a type of respondent conditioning in which an already effective conditioned stimulus (CS^1) is paired with a neutral stimulus to create a second conditioned stimulus (CS^2). Let's return to Pavlov's experiments briefly. Suppose that the dogs had already been trained to salivate (CR) to the sound of a bell (CS^1). We could extend this conditioning by repeatedly pairing a neutral stimulus, such as orange light, with the sound of the bell. As a result, the orange light by itself would also become a conditioned stimulus (CS^2) that elicits salivation.

BEFORE HIGHER-ORDER CONDITIONING:

Orange light (NS) ⊘ Salivating

Bell (CS^1) ⟶ Salivating (CR)

DURING HIGHER-ORDER CONDITIONING:

Orange light (NS) / Bell (CS^1) ⟶ Salivating (CR)

AFTER HIGHER-ORDER CONDITIONING:

Orange light (CS^2) ⟶ Salivating (CR)

stimulus generalization (respondent)
a conditioned response that becomes more likely in the presence of one stimulus due to the similarity between that stimulus and another stimulus involved in original conditioning

stimulus discrimination (respondent)
a conditioned response that occurs in the presence of a conditioned stimulus but not in the presence of other dissimilar stimuli

Extinction of Respondent Relations

Life would be quite difficult if every new association we acquired was permanent. Imagine if someone had to spend the rest of life frightened of a white rat simply because it was paired with a loud noise. Combine that process with stimulus generalization and higher-order conditioning and we might find ourselves fearful of everything in existence! Or perhaps, we would begin drooling to every light and sound that went off! The passage of time is not enough to eliminate this type of learning, as people will display conditioned responses to stimuli they haven't encountered for many years. Fortunately, there are some procedures to undo this learning. Watson and Rayner never got a chance to remove Albert's fear to a white rat as they had intended since Albert's mother moved away with him.

However, if they had been given the opportunity, it would have been fairly simple to remove the fearful relation. They would simply have to present the white rat multiple times alone, in a safe context absent of the loud noise. At first, Albert would respond with fear (CR) but after enough presentations, the white rat would lose its power to elicit fear and once again become a neutral stimulus. This procedure is known as **respondent extinction**.

This procedure is effective with any respondent relationship. For example, if Pavlov wished to undo the conditioning he had created with his dogs, he would only need to repeatedly present the bell in the absence of meat powder. After a sufficient number of trials, the dogs would no longer salivate to the sound of a bell.

Spontaneous Recovery

There are often times when it may appear that extinction is complete, only to have the conditioned response occur once again. This is known as spontaneous recovery. For example, after extinguishing a response such as salivating to the sound of a bell, the response may suddenly appear again out of nowhere. However, this simply indicates that the extinction process wasn't fully complete. After some additional presentations of the conditioned stimulus alone, then the response will be fully extinguished.

Counterconditioning and Little Peter

Respondent conditioning is not the only way to eliminate a conditioned response, as demonstrated by an experiment by Mary Cover Jones, a former student of Watson. Jones came into contact with a three-year-old boy named Peter, who had a conditioned fear of rabbits similar to Little Albert's fear of rats. However, unlike Albert, Peter's fear was not purposely created and Jones had an opportunity to eliminate it. She accomplished this by using **counterconditioning**, a procedure where a conditioned stimulus is paired with another stimulus that elicits an incompatible response, that is, a response that cannot occur at the same time.

If you have a phobia of rabbits, maybe you should pair rabbits with delicious cookies!

Mary Cover Jones reasoned that food would produce a pleasant reaction in Peter and that Peter would be unable to experience both pleasant and fearful reactions simultaneously. Therefore, she would present the feared rabbit and then quickly present some food afterwards. Initially, she would bring out the rabbit, only to have Peter begin crying. She also would give Peter cookies, which he would quickly eat and appeared quite happy. The counterconditioning consisted of bringing out the rabbit for Peter and then immediately bringing him some cookies as well. Peter was unable to feel fear from the rabbit and joy from the cookies at the same time. She continued this process until Peter's fear decreased and eventually ceased. Peter's love of cookies had won out and long-standing, irrational fear of rabbits had finally been cured! This basic procedure has been incorporated into a technique known as systematic desensitization and used to treat a wide range of fears and phobias, which we'll talk about more in later chapters.

respondent extinction
when a conditioned stimulus becomes neutral again due to repeated presentations of the conditioned stimulus In the absence of the stimulus it was originally paired with

counterconditioning
when a conditioned stimulus loses the ability to elicit a conditioned response due to repeated pairings with another stimulus that elicits an incompatible response

Respondent Conditioning and Advertising

John Watson was a controversial figure not only because of his work in psychology, but also because of issues in his personal life. For example, he conducted experiments on the effects of whiskey on dart throwing during the prohibition era. However, his biggest personal controversy involved Rosalie Rayner, the student whom he worked with on the Little Albert experiment. His work with Rayner eventually culminated in a romantic affair, much to the distress of Watson's wife and the president of the university Watson worked at (who was already uncomfortable with Watson's research on alcohol). Unwilling to stop the affair, Watson ended up divorcing from his wife and was forced to resign from the university. Although he ended up eventually marrying Rayner, the scandal resulted in Watson being unable to secure an academic position anywhere in the country.

Still in the need of an income, Watson turned to applying his respondent conditioning techniques to advertising, with much success. Although he wasn't the first to introduce psychology to marketing, his emphasis on research and experimentation still had a strong impact. During this period of time, the Queen of Romania and Queen of Spain were popular and well-liked public figures. While working on an advertisement campaign for Ponds Cold and Vanishing Cream, Watson decided to use respondent conditioning to make the product more desirable to the general public. He persuaded these popular royalty figures to appear in advertisements proclaiming the virtues of the cosmetic products (Cohen, 1979).

Why is this young woman eating a burger? To better convince you by using the power of respondent conditioning, of course! *(Courtesy of J. Vespa/WireImage/ Getty Images, Inc.)*

BEFORE ADVERTISING:

Cosmetic product (NS) ⃠→ Pleasant feelings

Popular celebrity (CS^1) ⟶ Pleasant feelings (CR)

DURING ADVERTISING:

Cosmetic product (NS) / Popular celebrity (CS^1) ⟶ Pleasant feelings (CR)

AFTER ADVERTISING:

Cosmetic product (CS^2) ⟶ Pleasant feelings (CR)

After this respondent-based advertising, much of the general public felt more positive towards this particular brand of cosmetics, which in turn influenced their purchasing habits. Watson continued to apply psychological principles to other products such as baby powder and coffee with success. Later researchers have confirmed similar benefits of using respondent conditioning to alter preference. For example, Smith and Engel (1968) showed men one of two automobile advertisements: one featuring an attractive female model and one without the model. Although the car was exactly the same in both advertisements, the men who saw the ad with the model rated the car as faster and better designed than the men who saw the other advertisement. In other words, the pleasant feelings the men had for the attractive female model extended to the car itself, even though the model had nothing to do with the car. Interestingly, the men insisted that the presence of the woman had no influence on their ratings. This illustrates an important point about conditioning: awareness or rationality are not required for respondent conditioning to work. We often find ourselves liking or disliking something or someone for reasons we may not fully understand. This is why advertisements constantly pair products with fun people, cute animals, funny babies, attractive celebrities, and popular events that may have nothing in common with the product being sold.

Why might people be angry with the weather forecaster for the weather?

How Respondent Conditioning Might Influence Our Attitudes

Where do our attitudes and feelings about certain topics come from? Why might we feel more comfortable around certain people and situations and less comfortable with other people and situations? Why do some of us irrationally favor certain groups or are unfairly prejudiced against other groups? Part of this may be due to careful consideration of events/people and thoughtful reflections about their merits or lack of merits. However, much of the time, we often develop strong feelings without much thought or consideration. We may dislike the weather forecasters because they keep predicting freezing rain and snow, even though they don't control the weather. We may love someone who brings us good news, even though that person isn't actually responsible for that news. All we may know is "I just like them" or "I feel uncomfortable around those people," without quite knowing why those attitudes developed or wishing to have such feelings.

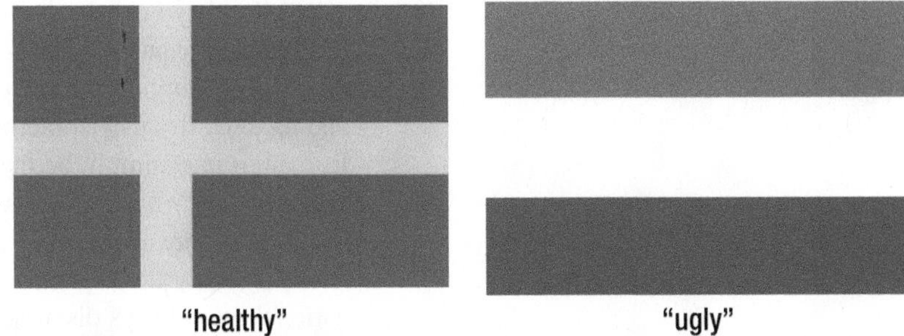

Staats and Staats paired certain nationalities with evaluative words.

Staats and Staats (1958) conducted a study designed to examine how these attitudes and feelings may develop. In their experiment, adult participants were presented with a large number of words in both spoken and visual form. From the perspective of the participants, the words appeared to have no discernible pattern. However, there was a pattern: every time the labels "Swedish" or "Dutch" were presented visually, a word with positive or negative evaluative meaning was presented in spoken form. For some participants, the sight of the word Swedish was consistently paired with positive words such as "sweet" and "healthy," whereas the sight of the word Dutch was consistently paired with negative words such as "ugly" and "bitter." For other participants, Swedish was paired with negative words and Dutch with positive words (this was done to ensure no inherent bias towards either nationality). Other nationalities were also presented, but they were not consistently paired with words of any particular meaning.

The results clearly demonstrated that this simple procedure changed how people felt about these nationalities. The participants found themselves feeling more positive towards Swedish people and more negative towards Dutch people, for reasons they couldn't explain (or opposite feelings for the reversed conditions). Many years later, Kuykendall and Keating (1990) replicated these findings, this time using the countries Brazil and Turkey. They found similar results and further asked participants to rate the economic conditions in those countries. When Brazil had been paired with positive words, participants rated Brazil as having favorable economic conditions. When Brazil had been paired with negative words, participants rated Brazil as having unfavorable economic conditions. Perceptions of the richness or poorness of Turkey were similarly influenced. Again, participants were unaware

Our attitudes and preferences may be determined by simple pairings with positive or negative words.

How we feel about certain groups may depend on what those groups have been paired with. *(Courtesy of Shutterstock and iStockphoto.com.)*

as to why they held these positive or negative attitudes. Thus the pairing procedure went beyond simple and general feelings but also affected judgments of financial conditions.

The implication is that our attitudes and judgments about other countries, races, and nationalities may sometimes have little to do with evidence or well-supported reasons. Instead, it may simply be the case that preference and prejudice arises due to respondent conditioning. We may form a negative attitude towards certain races or groups of people if those people are always portrayed in television in a negative context (e.g., criminals, terrorists, etc.), regardless of whether or not such a feeling was deserved. Conversely, if a certain nationality is always discussed favorably by your family (i.e., paired with positive words), you may feel favorably predisposed towards that nationality. Later studies have continued to support the idea that awareness is not necessary for attitudes to be conditioned (Olson & Fazio, 2002). These findings also suggest that to overcome undesirable prejudice and attitudes, we may need to make sure the people who are judged negatively appear in desirable contexts to ensure a better pairing history.

Behavioral Drug Tolerance

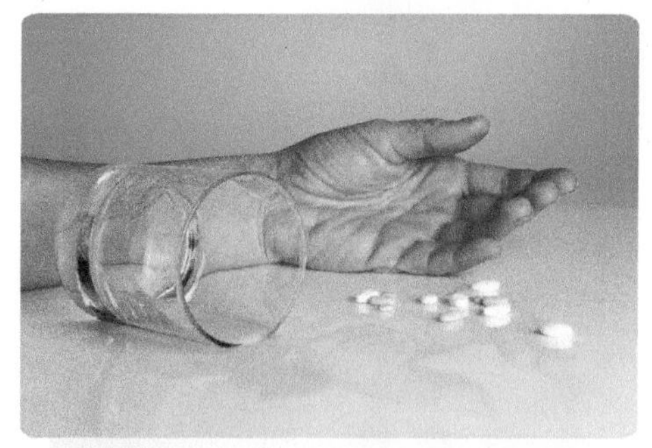
Why would a normal quantity of a drug suddenly become deadly? *(Courtesy of iStockphoto.)*

Shepard Siegel (1989) described the unusual case of an addict named E.C. This addict lived at home with her mother and was a regular user of heroin, a fact she kept hidden from her mother. In order to cover up her drug habit, she always woke up much earlier than her mother, turned on water in the bathroom (pretending to take a shower), and then injected the heroin while in the bathroom. One day, as she was following her normal routine and injecting her usual amount of heroin, her mother had woken up earlier than usual and began impatiently knocking at the door. Despite the unusual surprise of her mother pounding on the door, E.C. continued to inject the heroin and soon found she could not breathe. The worried mother eventually broke down the door, only to find her daughter suffering from an overdose. Thankfully, the daughter was rushed to hospital and barely survived to tell the story. This example brings up an important question: why did E.C. suffer an overdose? She was a long-term drug user who was injecting her usual amount of drugs. Why did an overdose occur this time but not the previous times? The answer may have been something as simple as the sounds in her environment, which we will illustrate through respondent conditioning next.

Development of Situational Specific Tolerance

When someone takes a drug, it has two effects. First is the drug effect, by which the drug produces its intended chemical effect (e.g., euphoria from heroin). The second is a compensatory response, in which the body tries to offset the drug effects and maintain homeostasis (i.e., the range of normal functioning for the body). These compensatory responses are frequently in the opposite direction of the effects of the drug, with the end result being that the body approaches a balanced state of homeostasis. For instance, cocaine will speed up a person's heart rate (the drug effect), but the body's compensatory response will work in opposition by slowing down the heart rate to return the body to a more normal state. Eventually, the body begins to anticipate the drug effects and begin producing a compensatory response prior to the administration of the drug (at this point, tolerance begins to occur).

Your body will try to remain in balance by working against the effects of drugs you take.

These compensatory responses can be conditioned so that they are specific to only certain environments. That is, these compensatory responses are caused by conditioned stimuli that have a history of being paired with drugs. Accordingly, these conditioned compensatory responses do not occur in different environments (i.e., those environments without a history of drug administration). In the example above, a quiet bathroom environment was conditioned to cause a compensatory response in E.C. When E.C.'s mother began knocking on the door, the stimulus conditions were changed so that her environment became sufficiently different. No longer was E.C. in her usual quiet bathroom with the gentle sound of softly running water. Now she found herself in a very noisy bathroom filled with constant knocking sounds. This very different set of circumstances no longer elicited the compensatory responses, meaning that E.C. now experienced the full effect of the heroin with nothing to counterbalance it, resulting in her near fatal overdose.

BEFORE ADDICTION:

Quiet bathroom (NS) $\not\longrightarrow$ Compensatory response

Heroin (US) ⟶ Compensatory response (UR)

CONDITIONING AS DRUG USE CONTINUES:

Quiet bathroom (NS) / Heroin (US) ⟶ Compensatory response (UR)

AFTER EXPERIENCE WITH DRUG:

Quiet bathroom (CS) ⟶ Compensatory response (CR)

ON DAY THAT E.C.'S MOTHER INTERRUPTED HER NORMAL ROUTINE BY CONSTANTLY KNOCKING:

Noisy bathroom (NS) $\not\longrightarrow$ Compensatory response

This possibility has been repeatedly confirmed with animal studies (Melchior, 1990; Siegel, 1982; 2005, Siegel & Ramos, 2002; Vila, 1989). In these studies, an animal such as a rat is given progressively larger and larger quantities of some drug in the presence of some randomly selected stimulus, such as a buzzing sound or red light. Over time, these animals develop a strong tolerance for these drugs, presumably because their bodies are reacting with a large degree of compensatory responding to offset the drug effects. However, this tolerance is situational specific, meaning it only occurs in the presence of the arbitrary stimulus. When that arbitrary stimulus is removed, many of the animals experience a fatal overdose (due to a lack of compensatory responding), despite only being given their normal dosage of drugs. Just like with E.C., a change in stimulus conditions changes the way they experience the drug in a very dangerous way.

Edward Thorndike and his Puzzle Boxes

John B. Watson came to believe that nearly all behavior could be explained by respondent conditioning and he attempted to trace back to the original pairing histories for a wide variety of human behaviors. In essence, his view stated that most of your behavior is constantly being elicited by the endless supply of everyday stimuli that precedes it. In many ways, the behavior is not necessary to the conditioning process; all that matters is that the right stimuli are paired together. Around the same time Watson was forming the tenets of behaviorism, a graduate student by the name of Edward Thorndike was doing pioneering work with cats and custom-made boxes that introduced puzzles for the cats to solve. His research ended up becoming the most famous dissertation in psychology (an impressive feat to accomplish before one even graduates!).

Edward Thorndike (1874–1947). *(Courtesy of Bettmann/Corbis Images.)*

Thorndike's dissertation with puzzle boxes did not quite fit within Watson's new framework (although Watson and Thorndike did admire each other's work). Thorndike would place hungry cats inside these boxes and had food outside of the box, just out of reach. Naturally, these cats were highly motivated to escape the box and get the food. Initially, their behavior consisted of a random pattern of bites, scratches, and meows. In this process of engaging in a feline temper tantrum, the cats would often accidently hit a level or switch Thorndike had built into the box. This resulted in a door on the box immediately opening, providing the cat with a most satisfying new situation.

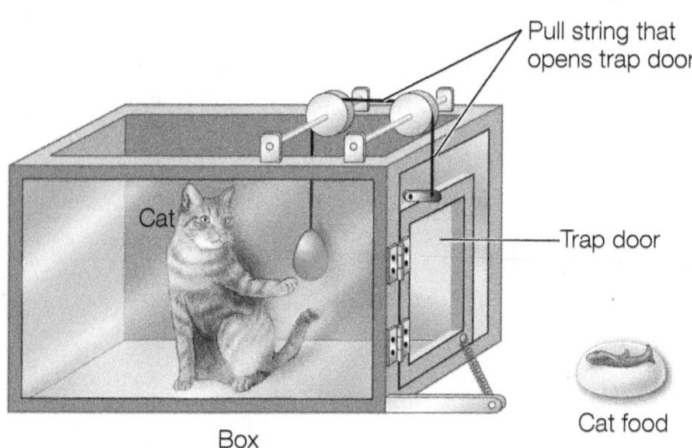

Edward Thorndike developed the law of effect by studying cats in puzzle boxes. *(Courtesy of Pearson Education, Inc.)*

Thorndike would place the cat back in the box. Again, the cat would engage in seemingly random trial-and-error behavior until the door opened. Thorndike noted that over time, the cats spent less time in the box and seemed to be learning the trick faster. Soon, the cats would immediately hit the switch or lever to escape the box within seconds, so fast that the behavior appeared to be "stamped in". Thorndike termed this learning as the **law of effect**, in which any response that produces a satisfying state of affairs would become more likely when placed in the same situation again.

It is difficult to explain this change in behavior using respondent conditioning. The pairing of stimuli preceding behavior did not seem critical to the process; rather it was the consequent stimuli (i.e., escape and food) following behavior that seemed most important. Furthermore, the behavior of the cats was instrumental in producing an effect. It was not simply being produced by stimuli, instead the behavior itself was a critical component in producing the change in stimulus conditions. However, Thorndike's definition of this process was vague, as there is no easily agreed upon standard for a "satisfying state of affairs." Two different people might observe the same situation and disagree as to whether it was satisfying or not. Furthermore, Thorndike's writing did not revolutionize the field like Watson's did, partially because he stopped pursuing such experimental work early in his career. It would take a later psychologist by the name of B.F. Skinner (whom we discussed at the beginning of this chapter) to popularize this notion of control by consequences and to create a more detailed analysis of this type of conditioning.

B.F. Skinner and the Founding of Operant Conditioning

Although B.F. Skinner considered himself a behaviorist much like John Watson, his approach to behavior had many important differences. For one thing, Watson considered thoughts and other mental activities to be outside the bounds of a proper science due to their subjective and elusive nature. Skinner, on the other hand, thought any science that excluded these phenomena would be woefully incomplete. Skinner, however, differed from cognitive and other mentalistic psychologists in that he considered such thoughts and mental activities as simply more examples of behavior to be explained using the same principles that explained all other behavior. Furthermore, Skinner considered it more effective to search for causes of behavior in the surrounding environment rather than spending too much time dwelling on the world within our skin (i.e., genetics and mental processes). As stated before, this is not the same as denying the existence of internal events, but rather looking for cause and effect relationships elsewhere. In fact, Skinner considered the study of genetics and neuroscience to be very important disciplines in their own right.

Skinner believed that consequences for behavior were the most important determinant of why we do what we do.

Skinner also differed from Watson regarding the importance placed on consequences. According to Skinner, the consequences of behavior were critical to understanding behavioral relationships. Skinner's approach to behaviorism was more far-reaching than Watson's and he chose the label *radical behaviorism* to clarify that he was proposing a departure from earlier forms of behaviorism. Skinner did not disregard the essential ideas of Pavlov and Watson, but rather his approach was radical because of its inclusion of covert and private behaviors in the analysis of behavior (i.e., thoughts and feelings). This new form of behaviorism did not exclude respondent conditioning or differ from the basic philosophy of building a science based on behavior alone. Modern behavior analysis has much more in common with Skinner's approach than Watson's, although respondent conditioning is still considered an important type of learning. Skinner did more to advance the behavioral perspective than any other individual and therefore it is his name that most psychologists associate with behaviorism. Also important is Skinner's updated version of the law of effect, known as **operant conditioning**. An *operant* is any behavior that produces an effect upon the environment. Thorndike's cats demonstrated this because their behavior

operant conditioning
the probability that a behavior is increased or decreased depending on the consequences that have followed that behavior

operated upon the puzzle box to produce the effect of an open door. Unlike the law of effect, operant conditioning is more precisely defined. Quite simply, operant conditioning involves the change in the likelihood of behavior occurring again due to the consequences that have followed that behavior.

There are three main principles involved in operant conditioning: reinforcement, punishment, and operant extinction. The relationship between behavior, preceding events, and consequent events is known as a *contingency*, also known as an ABC relation (*A*ntecedents, *B*ehavior, and *C*onsequences). Let's take a simple example of driving through an intersection. The relation between antecedents, behaviors, and consequences influence the probability of any given behavior, such as driving your car through an intersection. If the light is red (antecedent) and you press the accelerator (behavior), the possible outcome is that another car will hit you or the police will give you a traffic ticket (consequence). This contingency lowers the probability that you will drive through intersections when the light is red. If the light is green (antecedent) and you press the accelerator (behavior), the possible outcome is that you will get to continue moving forward without an accident or ticket (consequence). This contingency raises the probability that you will drive through intersections when the light is green.

Consequences that strengthen our behavior are known as reinforcers

The Principle of Reinforcement

The first principle to be discussed is **reinforcement**, which involves a change in stimuli following behavior, which results in an increased probability of that behavior occurring in the future.

In regards to Thorndike's puzzle boxes, when the cats began pressing a lever more often in the future as a result of the door opening, this was an example of reinforcement. Also important is the concept of **reinforcer**, which is the stimulus that strengthens the responding.

Returning to Thorndike's cats, the sight of an open door and access to food was the reinforcer. This immediately followed the behavior of lever pressing and increased the likelihood that the cat would press the lever again. A similar concept is that of reward, although reinforcer and reward do have different meanings. A *reward* is something pleasant given in return for some desired action. A reward does not have to strengthen behavior in order to be called a reward, even though that is often the intent. For example, while writing a paper someone could give you a "Good Writer's Award," which may be a piece of paper with a ribbon on it. Even though this is considered a reward, it may not necessarily change your behavior. Therefore, the award could not be called a reinforcer. By definition, reinforcers will strengthen (or increase) behavior, otherwise they are not labeled as reinforcers. If you did not begin writing more papers, the "Good Writer's Award" would be a reward, but not a reinforcer. If you did start writing more papers as a result of the award, then the award would be both a reinforcer and a reward.

Token economies deliver gold stars, points, money, and other tokens for good behavior. These are later exchanged for something of value. *(Courtesy of iStockphoto.)*

Reinforcers can be either *primary* (also called unlearned or unconditioned) or *secondary* (also called learned or conditioned). Primary reinforcers typically satisfy some biological needs, such as food, water, warmth, oxygen, etc. Secondary reinforcers can be any number of possible stimuli, such as praise, good grades, money, and hobbies. Secondary reinforcers are created by pairing stimuli with other reinforcers (similar to the development of a CS). As a result, every individual has a set of reinforcers that is unique to him or her. This is why you should be careful about making assumptions about what will be reinforcing for other people. After all, what may reinforce your behavior may not necessarily reinforce someone else's behavior. The only way to be sure whether something works as a reinforcer is to test it out and observe its effect on behavior.

One example of reinforcement is the use of *token economies*. A token (points, plastic chips, stars, slips of paper, etc.) is a reinforcer that can be accumulated and then later exchanged for another reinforcer. In a token economy, tokens can be earned for engaging in various desired behavior. For example, a child could earn gold stars for making his bed, reading books, mowing the lawn, or flossing. The number of gold stars earned may depend

reinforcement
following some behavior of interest there is a change in stimulus conditions (i.e., some stimulus is presented or removed) and the behavior of interest then *increases* in future frequency

reinforcer
the stimulus that follows a behavior and increases the future frequency of that behavior

upon the difficulty and/or importance of the behavior. Approximately once per week, the child may trade in his gold stars for various desired items and activities, such as a video game or trip to the mall. Token economies have been incredibly successful with children, adults with mental disorders, and normal adults. In fact, money is the most commonly used token reinforcer and is valuable due to its ability to be accumulated and exchanged later for other reinforcers.

Although token economies have frequently been successful when carefully applied, they have also been a source of controversy. This is particularly true when vulnerable populations are involved, such as those in group homes and mental institutions. Critics argue such techniques involve cruelly withholding items and activities from individuals who are at the mercy of authority figures. In essence, they are arguing people have a right to comforts such a preferred foods, televisions, and choice of activities. On the other side, proponents of token economies argue that in the rest of the world, we do not often get access to these things unless we earn them. If the goal of therapy is to normalize an individual's behavior, then they should have similar demands as the rest of us (Skinner, 1978). Furthermore, these token economies often produced more positive interactions between staff and clients. Sadly, prior to the introduction of token economies, care often tended to be a custodial approach in which staff and clients only briefly interacted. While the argument was never fully resolved, changes in institutional rules and policies often eliminated the use of these successful programs.

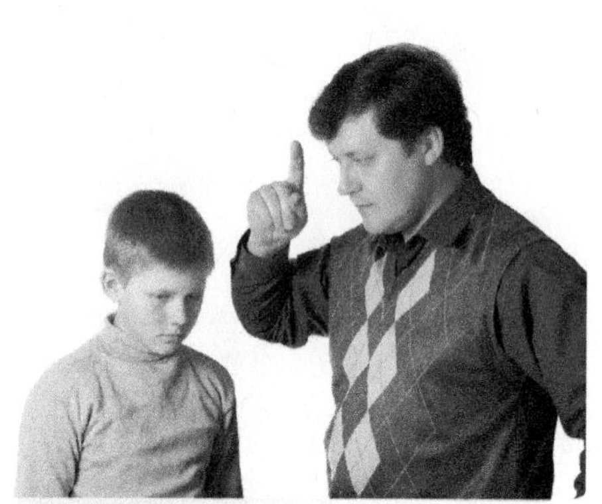

Consequences can also weaken behavior. *(Courtesy of iStockphoto.)*

THE PRINCIPLE OF PUNISHMENT

Punishment is very much the same principle as reinforcement, except for one key difference. Both reinforcement and punishment involve consequences following operant behavior and influence the future frequency of that behavior. However, whereas reinforcement <u>increases</u> the future probability of behavior, punishment <u>decreases</u> the future probability of behavior. **Punishment** is defined as a change in stimulus conditions following some behavior that results in that behavior decreasing in future frequency.

Time out needs to be carefully and appropriately used if you want to be successful. *(Courtesy of SW Productions/* Design Pics/Corbis Images.)

punishment
following some behavior of interest there is a change in stimulus conditions (i.e., some stimulus is presented or removed) and the behavior of interest then <u>decreases</u> in future frequency

punisher
the stimulus that follows a behavior and decreases the future frequency of that behavior

Similar to a reinforcer, there is a concept known as a punisher. Again, it mirrors the effect of a reinforcer, except for the key difference in its effect on future behavior. **Punishers** are stimuli that always follow behavior and decrease the future frequency of the behavior that they follow.

Unfortunately, there is a tendency in our culture to rely too heavily on punishment, yelling at children who fail to follow directions, sending misbehaving kids to the principal's office, criticizing employees who fall short of standards, and jailing citizens who break laws. People sometimes confuse punishment with revenge, harshly dealing with those who violate our rules and then using this principle to justify their actions. Punishers do not necessarily have to be severe to be effective. In fact, behavior analysts try to minimize the usage of punishment and will only use the minimal amount necessary (Van Houten et al., 1988). If punishment is used too much, the recipient will only learn to avoid the person who delivers the punishment (such as children or employees who hide when the teacher or boss is coming).

An example of the use of punishment is *time out*, a behavior management technique that is frequently misunderstood. With time out, undesired behavior is immediately followed by removal from a reinforcing situation. If a young girl hits her baby brother at the dinner table, her parents may immediately send the girl to her room. If this young girl hits her baby brother less often in the future, then you know this time out worked as punishment. You need to be cautious though, because as with reinforcement, you should not assume you have delivered a punisher until you assess its effect on behavior. Suppose that the young girl above actually loves being in her room or hates the dinner table. In that case, sending her to her room may actually reinforce her behavior and result in her hitting her brother more often! In order for <u>time out</u> to be effective as punishment, <u>time in</u> must be reinforcing. As a rule of thumb, time out should be kept brief, as a few minutes is typically effective and you want to give the person frequent opportunities to engage in the desired behavior, not just sit in time out doing nothing.

Much like reinforcers, punishers can be primary or secondary. Primary punishers tend to be related to events that are biological in nature, such as pain stimulation or extreme temperatures. Secondary punishers are acquired by being paired with other punishing events. Common examples include criticism, embarrassment, and loss of possessions.

When used carefully and sensibly, punishment of undesired behavior can be extremely effective, especially when combined with reinforcement for desired behavior. Mike Maloney (1998) describes how he implemented reinforcement and punishment to get children in his classroom to study harder. He would monitor his classroom and when he caught children studying attentively, he placed a single piece of candy in a cup for them. However, one child still could not seem to focus. Maloney waited until the child looked away from his schoolwork and then he immediately took a candy from the child's cup and ate it. The child's eyes widened and then went straight back to his assignment. Maloney had successfully punished the child's behavior of looking away from his schoolwork. Note that this situation was made more effective by including reinforcement for good behavior, not just punishing poor behavior.

The Principle of Operant Extinction

Punishment isn't the only way to reduce behavior with operant conditioning. Behavior can be weakened by withholding consequences, as with **operant extinction**. In this case, behavior that has historically been followed by reinforcement now has the maintaining reinforcer withheld.

Consider this scenario: In high school, there may have been certain topics, such as a favorite music group, that you and your friends frequently discussed. Mentioning this music group reliably resulted in attention and approval from your friends, which reinforced your verbal behavior in regards to this topic. However, when you move away to college, your new peers do not share your interests in music. Every time you bring up your favorite music group to these people, they ignore it. The result is that the attention and approval you used to receive is now being withheld. The likely effect of this is that you'll talk about this music group less often over time, perhaps never mentioning them again to your college friends. This is because your behavior underwent operant extinction. Many instances of lost interests and reduced performance can be traced to reinforcement being withheld.

Different Types of Reinforcement and Punishment

Most psychologists further classify reinforcement into two different types: positive reinforcement and negative reinforcement. These terms often causes students a great deal of confusion, so you need to be careful. The terms positive and negative are used in the mathematical sense and have nothing to do with value judgments. That is, **positive reinforcement** involves the addition (+) of a stimulus following a response and **negative reinforcement** involves the subtraction (-) of a stimulus following a response. Both types of reinforcement increase the future frequency of behavior.

After giving an answer in class (behavior of interest), the teacher may tell you "good job" (stimulus being presented). If you then answer questions <u>more often</u>, this would be an example of positive reinforcement. In the morning your unpleasant alarm clock begins sounding. Therefore you hit the snooze button (behavior of interest) and the annoying sound immediately stops (stimulus being removed). If you begin hitting the alarm <u>more often</u> in the future, then this would be an example of negative reinforcement. Note that negative reinforcement is a good thing, as it typically involves the removal of undesirable things from your life. Despite the word "negative," you would be unwise to turn down an offer of negative reinforcement!

A similar distinction can be made with punishment. Once again, the terms positive or negative only refer to the presentation and removal of a stimulus and have nothing to do

operant extinction
following some behavior of interest there is no change in stimulus conditions (i.e., the reinforcer is withheld) and the behavior of interest then <u>decreases</u> in future frequency

positive reinforcement
following some behavior of interest a stimulus is immediately presented and the behavior of interest then <u>increases</u> in future frequency

negative reinforcement
following some behavior of interest a stimulus is immediately removed and the behavior of interest then <u>increases</u> in future frequency

with the "goodness" or "badness" of that stimulus. If after telling a bad joke (behavior of interest) someone may say "you're a jerk" (stimulus being presented). This would be an example of **positive punishment** if you then tell that joke less often in the future. If after hitting the wrong button on your computer (behavior of interest) all of your files are deleted (stimulus being removed) and therefore you then hit that button less often in the future, that would be an example of **negative punishment**.

Again, it is worth noting that negative reinforcement always strengthens behavior, despite the use of the word "negative." Similarly, positive punishment always weakens behavior, despite the use of the word "positive." Not all psychologists agree that it is sensible that talk about a logical distinction between these types of reinforcement and punishment (see Michael, 2004 for a discussion of this topic). Further adding to the confusion is the fact that some psychologists will distinguish between positive and negative reinforcement, but may not distinguish between positive and negative punishment. Nonetheless, it is in your best interest to be familiar with all the distinctions. Reinforcement always strengthens behavior and punishment always weakens behavior. Again, the qualifiers of "positive" and "negative" are only referring to whether the behavior change was due to adding or removing something from the environment.

As our circle of friends change, so might our likes and dislikes.

Stimulus Control in Operant Conditioning

Although consequences play a starring role in operant behavior, antecedent stimuli (stimuli that occur prior to the behavior) play a significant part as well. Antecedent stimuli that are associated with the availability or non-availability of reinforcement for responding will influence the probability that a response will occur. Let's return to the example we discussed earlier in which talking about your favorite music group was extinguished. Using that example, let's suppose you then run into your old high school buddies and the topic of this music group comes up. Once again, you begin receiving plenty of attention and approval (i.e., reinforcers) for talking about this group. When you return to your college friends, they once again ignore your mention of the band, so once again you stop talking about the band. Most likely you will reliably begin talking about the band when your high school friends show up (one antecedent condition) and stop talking about the band when your college friends show up (a different antecedent condition). This is an example of **stimulus control**, in which antecedent stimuli influence the probability of an operant behavior, such as the presence or absence of certain people, due to reinforcement that has or has not occurred in the presence of those antecedents. Note that the consequences for behavior are still of critical importance (whether your friends give or withhold attention and approval), unlike what we saw in respondent conditioning.

Can pigeons become art critics? Watercolor by Christy Freeman. *(Christy Freeman at http://www.christyfreeman.com http://www.christyfreeman.com/Pigeon.html. Courtesy of Christy Freeman.)*

Specifically, the stimulus that is associated with reinforcement for responding is known as a *discriminative stimulus* (abbreviated as S^D). The stimulus that is associated with extinction for responding is known as an *S-delta* (abbreviated as S^Δ). Being able to respond differently to S^Ds and S^Δs is a type of stimulus control called *stimulus discrimination*. The example above can be diagrammed like this:

S^D (presence of high school friends): Behavior (talk about music band) ⟶ Reinforcement (approval, attention)

S^Δ (presence of college friends): Behavior (talk about music band) ⟶ Extinction (no approval or attention)

Another example of stimulus control can be seen in an experiment by Watanabe, Sakamoto, and Wakita (1995). In their study they taught pigeons to accurately classify paintings as being done by either Monet or Picasso. Their complex skills arose from a simple procedure: in the presence of a Monet painting, pigeons were reinforced for pecking a key that indicated Monet, while in the presence of a Picasso painting they were reinforced for pecking a key that indicated Picasso.

positive punishment
following some behavior of interest a stimulus is immediately presented and the behavior of interest then decreases in future frequency

negative punishment
following some behavior of interest a stimulus is immediately removed and the behavior of interest then decreases in future frequency

stimulus control
behavior that becomes more or less probable in the presence of an antecedent condition due to that behavior being reinforced or extinguished in the presence of that antecedent condition

In addition to stimulus discrimination, *stimulus generalization* also plays a role in stimulus control. With stimulus generalization, the responding occurs in the presence of a new stimulus because that stimulus is similar to another stimulus that is correlated with reinforcement for responding. Please note an area of possible confusion: respondent conditioning also involves stimulus discrimination and stimulus generalization with similar effects, but the procedures involved are different for operant conditioning. In operant conditioning, the provision of consequences is critical to producing these effects, unlike respondent conditioning.

Imagine you begin a new job and your fellow employees are very similar looking to your high school friends whom share your love of music. You may find yourself beginning to discuss your beloved band once again, even though these employees haven't reinforced that behavior yet. In the case of the art critic birds mentioned above, they became so good that they could easily and accurately classify examples of artwork that had never been directly trained on, such as works by other impressionist and cubist artists. Such stimulus generalization shows that even simple birds can acquire complex conceptual behavior.

Schedules of Reinforcement

If you've ever been to a casino, it is likely you've seen gamblers who seem to be obsessively trapped. They will spend days, weeks, months, and even years chasing big wins. Occasionally they hit jackpot, but in the long run "the house always wins" (those luxurious accommodations at casinos have to come from somewhere) and the gamblers lose more than they will ever gain. If you watch people long enough, you begin to appreciate why some people refer to the gambling area of casinos as the "pit," as many people seem endlessly stuck there. Why do people give away money in a system that rarely favors the player? Why is it so hard for the addicted gambler to just walk away? The frequency with which reinforcement is delivered may help us answer those questions.

Skinner originally began investigating schedules of reinforcement simply because he ran short of food pellets by accident. *(Courtesy of Everett Collection Inc./Alamy.)*

When a reinforcer is delivered after every single time someone engages in a behavior, we are using *continuous reinforcement*. Reinforcers do not have to necessarily be delivered after every instance of behavior in order to be effective. In fact, *intermittent reinforcement*, in which a reinforcer is delivered for only some responses, actually produces behavior that is more resistant to the effects of extinction than continuous reinforcement. This is why the gambling behavior of people who only win occasionally can remain strong. B.F. Skinner discovered this quite by accident, when he ran short of food pellets and was forced to deliver a reinforcer only occasionally to the rats he was working with (some of the best discoveries are unintended). He soon found out that his rats worked even harder than before, despite receiving fewer pellets overall. In collaboration with Charles Ferster, Skinner meticulously analyzed different reinforcement delivery schedules and they discovered that reliable patterns of behavior could be predicted by varying aspects of reinforcer delivery (Ferster & Skinner, 1957). We cover a few of the more commonly discussed schedules below.

Ratio Schedules

With ratio schedules, the delivery of reinforcement depends upon the number of responses emitted. There are two main variations of this: fixed-ratio (FR) schedules and variable-ratio (VR) schedules. With fixed-ratio, reinforcement follows after a specific number of responses have occurred. For example, in a FR-5 schedule, a reinforcer is delivered immediately after the person has responded 5 times.

Schedules of reinforcement can make gambling difficult to quit.

With variable-ratio, reinforcement follows after an average number of responses have occurred. For example, in a VR-10 schedule, after the person has responded an average of 10 times a reinforcer is delivered (the actual response requirements may be 2, 3, 7, 9, 13, 26 or some other combination; note that these numbers average out to 10). Much like a casino slot machine, you never quite know which behavior will pay off in a near-win or actual win, but it will happen eventually if you play enough (assuming you have any money left!).

Interval Schedules

With interval schedules, the delivery of reinforcement depends upon responding following the passage of time. There are two main variations of this: fixed-interval (FI) schedules and variable-interval (VI) schedules. With fixed-interval, reinforcement follows the first response that occurs after a specific passage of time. For example, in a FI-5 minutes schedule, the first response that occurs after 5 minutes will be reinforced.

With variable-interval, reinforcement follows the first response that occurs after an average amount of time has passed. For example, in a VI-10 minute schedule, the first response that occurs after an average of 10 minutes has passed will be reinforced (the actual number of minutes may be 2, 3, 7, 9, 13, 26 or some other combination; note that these times average out to 10 minutes). From the perspective of the organism, both variable schedules are more unpredictable and therefore tend to produce higher rates of responding (after all, you don't know when your behavior will pay off).

Using Shaping to Create a New Response

Shaping involves using closer and closer steps to reach our goals.

Sometimes we can strengthen a behavior simply by waiting for it to occur and then providing reinforcement, similar to how Thorndike simply had to wait for his cats to perform the correct response. Other times we may wish to strengthen some behavior in a person, but they never perform the behavior, no matter how patient we are. This poses a difficulty because we cannot reinforce a behavior that never occurs. Fortunately, we can reinforce *successive approximations* to gradually produce the target behavior. A successive approximation is the most similar behavior to the target behavior that the organism does at least occasionally.

For example, a new mother may wish to hear her young child say "mommy." Initially, the infant never says "mommy," which makes it impossible for the mother to reinforce this non-existent behavior. However, the infant does possess the successive approximation of saying "muh" as part of the infant's normal babbling. Therefore, every time the infant says "muh," the mother provides lots of attention and excitation, which is likely to reinforce the infant's behavior. Now that the infant says "muh" very frequently and at some point accidently says "muh-muh." This is a new successive approximation, which the mother reinforces with more attention and excitement. Critically, the mother also stops reinforcing utterances of "muh," resulting in "muh-muh" becoming more common and "muh" alone becoming less common. This is the essence of **shaping**.

As the mother continues to differentially reinforce closer and closer steps to "mommy" the infant's behavior changes in the desired direction. This type of shaping can occur even if the mother isn't intentionally reinforcing behavior. Just like respondent conditioning, operant conditioning does not require awareness, rationality, or intentional action. In fact, parents can unintentionally use shaping to create undesired behaviors as well, such as slowly shaping up louder and louder tantrums in children by attending to louder and louder screams and extinguishing quieter ones.

shaping
the creation of a new behavior by reinforcing successive approximations (progressively closer steps) to the desired behavior and extinguishing previous approximations to the desired behavior

The Legacy of B.F. Skinner

Skinner's conceptualization of operant conditioning had a lasting influence on the field of psychology. Skinner was also an active and ambitious scientist, applying his ideas to a wide range of human affairs, including the design of cultures based on reinforcement, the development of instructional machines (Skinner was one the earliest people to fully recognize the potential of computer-based instruction), education, language development, and

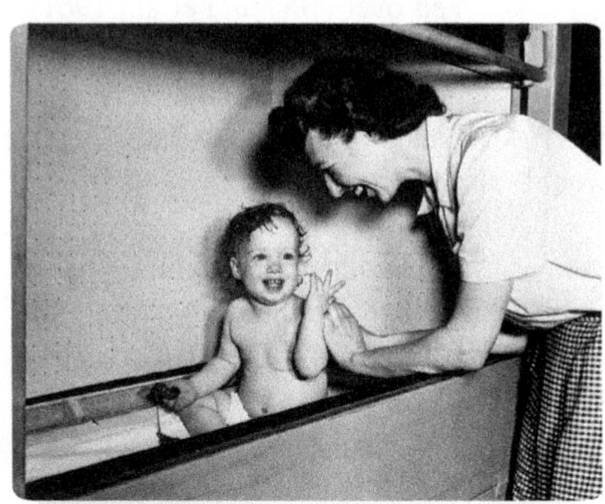

This photo depicts Skinner's daughter with her mother. Skinner designed new crib called an Air Crib to reduce discomfort for his daughter and make care easier . . . *(Courtesy of Bettmann/ Corbis Images.)*

. . . but many people wrongly believed Skinner was doing something much more drastic and evil to his daughters (note: this is not Skinner's daughter in this picture). *(Photo by Fox Photos/ Getty Images at http://www.telegraph.co.uk/ travel/picturegalleries/6021785/Londoners-Througha-Lens.html?image=3. Courtesy of Fox Photos/Getty Images, Inc.)*

other complex behavior. He also disagreed with the direction many other theorists pursued, which earned him many critics and enemies. For example, he designed an Air Crib for his infant daughters to reduce discomfort for his children and simplify child rearing (which was very different from the boxes he used to study animals). Traditional cribs often require many clothes and blankets to keep babies warm. Skinner's Air Crib controlled the temperature and humidity in the baby's sleeping area. This meant the babies wouldn't feel too hot or cold, could move around easily without being restricted by excessive clothing/blankets, and there would be less laundry for parents. However, critics used this as an opportunity to accuse Skinner of neglecting his daughters, treating them as laboratory rats, and/or keeping them locked away in some evil box. Rumors still abound today that one of Skinner's daughters went crazy, sued her father, and committed suicide, a myth still disputed by both of Skinner's daughters (who grew up well-adjusted and happy). Over 14 years after her father's death, Skinner's daughter Deborah was still countering such rumors in an article entitled "I was not a lab rat" (Skinner-Buzan, 2004).

Skinner also made many people uncomfortable due to his choice of words. He often spoke of "manipulating behavior" and "controlling responses." His use of these terms was strictly scientific. After all, science is all about manipulating variables and controlling experiments. Skinner insisted on applying scientific techniques to human affairs, for which he was sometimes characterized by others as a sinister and devious dictator (Chomsky, 1971). However, Skinner saw it as unethical to not try and improve human conditions with the powerful science he had helped develop. He continued his dedication to bettering humankind for his entire life and received awards such as the Humanist of the Year Award from the American Humanist Society and the Lifetime Achievement Award from the American Psychological Association for these efforts.

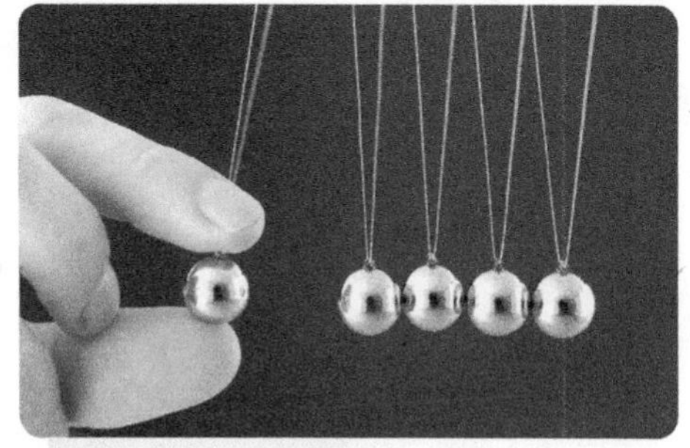

For Skinner "control" simply referred to cause and effect relationships.

Beyond Skinner

Observational Learning

Just as Skinner greatly expanded the scope of Watson's behaviorism, others have wished to expand the scope of Skinner's behaviorism. Albert Bandura was one such person when

Many psychologists after Skinner wanted to put a stronger focus on mental events and how they might be unique from other forms of behavior.

he proposed a new type of learning called *observational learning* (also called vicarious conditioning). His famous demonstration of this involved a Bobo doll, which was an inflatable plastic clown toy with sand in the bottom, so that it would repeatedly sit upright even if knocked over (Bandura et al., 1961). In this experiment, children would watch an adult model engage in either aggressive actions against Bobo or non-aggressive actions. That is, sometimes the adult would repeatedly punch, kick, and throw Bobo in the presence of children. Other times the adult would calmly play with puzzles and Tinkertoys in the presence of children.

The interesting part of the experiment is what children did after the adults left, when the child believed they were alone and unobserved (in truth they were being monitored through a one-way mirror). Children who had witnessed aggressive actions became aggressive themselves: punching, kicking, and throwing Bobo as they had just observed the adult doing earlier. Children who had witnessed non-aggressive actions became non-aggressive themselves: calmly playing with various toys as they had just observed the adult doing earlier. The children learned to imitate whatever they had seen.

Bandura argued this was different than operant conditioning because the children acquired a new behavior without reinforcement. Traditional behaviorists would argue that this observational learning is just another type of operant conditioning, pointing out that children and adults are regularly reinforced for imitating in general, and that reinforcement can be infrequent and effective (as illustrated by intermittent reinforcement schedules). Regardless, Bandura's study has profound implications, particularly in regards to violence portrayed in entertainment. This remains a controversial topic, with the two sides arguing over the artistic freedom and choice in entertainment versus the violent impact on children and the culture at large. The research in this area is often difficult to interpret, as children who watch violent shows do tend to be more aggressive, but their aggressive tendencies may have attracted them to television rather than being caused by television (as stated in previous chapters, correlation does not prove causation). In essence, it is difficult to know if watching violence causes aggression or if aggression causes the watching of violence.

Bandura's research also suggested that not only observations of models mattered, but observations of the consequences received by the models also mattered. Children tended not to imitate the aggressive actions of adults if they saw those adults receive punishment for being aggressive. Children became even more likely to imitate if they observed the adults being rewarded for their actions. Accordingly, Bandura attached a great deal of importance to the expectation of reinforcement or punishment, not just the consequences themselves.

Bandura's work suggests that we behave the way we do by imitating others. *(Courtesy of Albert Bandura, PhD.)*

Latent Learning

Edward Tolman proposed another kind of learning in the absence of reinforcement, which he termed *latent learning*. Latent learning is any kind of learning that occurs in the absence of any obvious immediate changes in behavior. In the classic experiment, Tolman and Honzik (1930) trained three groups of rats to complete mazes: a) a group that received food at the end, b) a group that never received food, and c) a group that received no food initially but then began receiving food on the 11th day of the experiment. The group that never received food made many errors and showed little learning, which may not be surprising considering the lack of reinforcement. The group that always received food made few errors and showed much learning, also not so surprising.

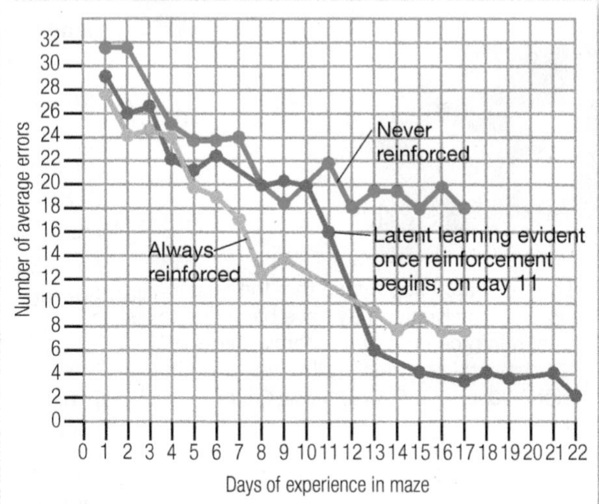

Despite not receiving reinforcement during their first 10 days in the maze, one group of rats showed latent learning. (Psychology: From Inquiry to Understanding, *2nd edition, by Lilienfeld, Lynn, Namy, & Woolf.)*

What was surprising was the behavior of the group that didn't receive food until the 11th day. Within just a couple of days after reinforcement being introduced, that group performed similarly to the group that had been receiving reinforcement all along. This suggested that some form of learning must have been taking place in the absence of reinforcement during those first 10 days, although the effects were neither large or robust (Donahoe & Palmer, 1994). Therefore, reinforcement may not be essential for learning to occur, even if it is essential for observable changes in behavior. According to Tolman, this also suggested that the rats did not simply learn a sequence of turns, but instead developed a *cognitive map* of the maze. This mental representation of the maze explained why the rats learned to reach the food so quickly after it was introduced. Some have suggested that this is a fundamental flaw to reinforcement theory since learning occurred without reward, although it is worth noting that Skinner and later behavior analysts never argued that reinforcement was necessary for new behaviors to be acquired (Jensen, 2006; Skinner, 1950). Furthermore, it is to be expected that an organism such as a rat will engage in exploratory behaviors rather than simply sit still. It is likely that such exploration that results in the discovery of new areas and avoidance of dead ends in the maze is a source of reinforcement itself, albeit not as powerful a reinforcer as food. This interpretation suggests that reinforcement may have always been present in Tolman's maze, even on trials when food wasn't presented.

Insight Learning

Another challenge to the behavioral perspective came from Wolfgang Köhler (1925), who strongly disagreed with Thorndike's model of trial and error learning and instead proposed *insight learning* as an alternative type of learning. With insight learning, new behavior will suddenly emerge seemingly out of nowhere, as though the idea just popped into someone's mind. During World War I, Köhler became stuck on an island full of native chimpanzees for 4 months.

In Köhler's experiments, chimpanzees appeared to learn through flashes of insight. *(Courtesy of Superstock.)*

Deciding to take advantage of a bad situation, Köhler wanted to demonstrate insight learning with a native chimpanzee he named Sultan. Sultan was placed in a cage with a banana suspended from the ceiling, out of Sultan's reach, as well as several boxes scattered on the ground. Sultan spent some time unsuccessfully jumping at the banana, looking frustrated, and then eventually had what appeared to be an "aha" moment. He immediately grabbed the boxes, stacked them underneath the banana, and then climbed the boxes to reach his desired banana. This particular sequence of behaviors had never been taught before or reinforced; it appeared as though some important cognitive change just suddenly developed. However, Köhler did not describe Sultan's past learning history in detail (and could not, given that Sultan was a wild chimpanzee), so it is difficult to know how much of Sultan's behavior came from insight and how much came from past learning. Furthermore, the chimpanzees shared cages, so observational learning is also possible.

Many years later Epstein et al. (1984) replicated Köhler's experiment, this time using pigeons instead of chimpanzees. Just like with Sultan, the pigeon's cage had a banana

Later research suggested that the results obtained by Köhler may have been due to past reinforcement of the components of a behavioral sequence rather than insight alone. *(Courtesy of Baxley Media Group.)*

near the ceiling and out of reach (this banana was small and plastic). If the pigeon pecked the banana it would immediately be given food. The cage also featured a box that was not underneath the banana. Epstein's pigeons behaved exactly like Sultan. They attempted to jump at the banana without success (the experimental setup prevented them from getting food by flying up to peck the banana). The pigeons would then suddenly begin to push the box with their beak until the box was underneath the banana. They would then quickly jump on the box and peck the banana to earn a treat. This was a very unusual sequence of behaviors for a bird, given that they usually get food by flying around and pecking off the ground below them, not climbing boxes and pecking upward.

Unlike Köhler, Epstein et al. did carefully describe the learning histories of their pigeons. Those pigeons had been separately taught three skills earlier: 1) Climbing a box, 2) Pecking a banana, and 3) Pushing boxes in a particular direction. The researchers discovered that if a pigeon lacked training on even one of those three component skills, then the insightful behavior would never occur. Even though the new behavioral sequence of climbing the box to reach the banana was not directly trained, that does not mean it emerged out of nowhere. Rather, it required several previously learned skills being recombined in a novel way. Therefore, insight still requires certain skills and reinforcement of those skills. If one was not aware of the previous history, it may appear as though the behavior came from a flash of insight or other mental event, as Köhler believed many years prior. Other replications have similarly shown that the more experience with the task the animal has, the more likely it is they will develop an "insightful" solution for a new variation of that task (Windholz & Lamal, 1985).

B.F. Skinner used operant conditioning to teach pigeons to guide missiles during World War II. Painting by Anton van Dalen. *(Courtesy of Anton van Dalen.)*

Modern Days Applications of Operant Conditioning

Early work on operant conditioning was firmly rooted in experimental work conducted in the laboratory using careful and precise methodology. However, as early as the 1950s, scientists began looking for ways to apply these new findings to everyday concerns (Rutherford, 2009). Modern day implementation of applied behavior analysis has relevance for any situation calling for behavior to be influenced. Several applications are outlined below.

Operant Conditioning in Animal Training

Given that much of the early work in operant conditioning was conducted using rats and pigeons, it is not surprising that one of the most obvious applications of behavior analysis is to the area of animal learning. One of Skinner's early experiments was Project Pigeon, in which he training pigeons to guide missiles during World War II. At the time, current missile technology was very inaccurate and the military was interested in projects that could minimize the risk to their soldiers (risks to the pigeons seemed to be less concerning). Interestingly, the project actually worked, with the pigeons successfully guiding the missiles to their targets. Despite the accuracy of the pigeons, their services were never put to use because the military commanders were not willing to seriously entertain the idea of pigeon pilots. Skinner also used shaping to teach pigeons to play ping-pong with one another, although in this case he was happy to not be taken too seriously.

Operant conditioning has made animal training more effective and humane. *(Source: Photo courtesy of Douglas A. Johnson.)*

Operant conditioning has also had a dramatic effect on animal training in zoos and amusement parks (Markowitz, 1982; Ramirez, 1999; Sutherland, 2006). Prior to implementation of behavioral techniques, much of animal training was characterized by forcing animals into tricks by the use of whips, sticks, and other brutal tools. Reinforcement-based strategies such as the popular clicker training method have now replaced such earlier coercion. Through careful shaping, dolphins learn to perform acrobatic jumps on command, elephants gently hold their feet up for grooming, and monkeys will present their arms so veterinarians can draw blood samples.

Scientists have successfully trained rats to detect tuberculosis and landmines.

Such animal training can benefit owners of domestic animals too, giving us better ways of training dogs to walk loosely on a leash, cats to come when called, and fish to perform tricks (Pryor, 1999). Other applications include training service dogs to help people with various perceptual and motor impairments. One research team even trained giant African rats to detect the presence of tuberculosis (TB) in humans (Poling et al., 2010). To accomplish this, the researchers simply gave the rats bananas every time they sniffed samples containing TB. After a few months of careful training, the rats became capable of deciding whether or not a person had TB, and it was more accurate than traditional detection methods (the rats were cheaper too).

Treatment of Mental Disorders

Respondent and operant conditioning techniques are frequently used to treat a variety of mental disorders, reducing signs of mood disorders, anxiety, and even schizophrenia (Hayes & Smith, 2005; Salzinger, 1973; Wong, 2006). In fact, most non-biological treatments that are successful involve some component of behavioral conditioning. For example, exposure treatments based on extinction have successfully eliminated fears and phobias and social skills training that teach one how to secure new sources of reinforcement have eliminated crippling depression. We'll discuss these techniques in more detail in later chapters.

Long-standing fears and phobias can be reduced through behavioral conditioning.

Contingency management (i.e., changing the relationship between antecedents, behaviors, and consequences) has successfully treated substance abuse disorders even where other methods have failed (Higgins, Silverman, & Heil, 2008). For example, many addicts have trouble finding employment, in part due to their status as felony offenders. Under these circumstances, job seeking behaviors are being extinguished while drug use behaviors are still being reinforced by the experience of feeling high. Under those conditions, it is not surprising that many recovering addicts have great difficulty in staying clean. Some behavior analysts have used token economies to remedy this by actually hiring the addicts to do work for them! If the recovering addicts showed up to work clean (no drugs in their system), they were allowed to work and earn money (reinforcement). If the recovering addicts showed up to work and failed the drug test, they were not allowed to work that day (punishment), although they could come back the next day. Furthermore, the amount of money they earned increased over time in an effort to combat the fact that it is harder to stay clean over a long period of time than a short time period. This employment was not just pure charity; the former addicts generated enough profit that researchers could afford to hire even more recovering addicts.

Behavior Analysis Goes to Work

These conditioning techniques aren't just relevant to animals or those suffering with disorders, they also apply to adults in everyday life. One example of this is a type of business psychology known as *organizational behavior management (OBM)*, which is the application of operant conditioning techniques to business and industry (Johnson, Redmon, & Mawhinney, 2001; O'Brien, Dickinson, & Rosow, 1982). It has been said that "people don't quit the job, they quit their boss." Many management strategies do not promote desired employee performance, including common techniques such as employee-of-the-month, infrequent performance appraisals, promoting the wrong people, and paying for time rather than performance (Abernathy, 1996; Daniels, 2009; Johnson & Dickinson,

Behavioral analysis has been applied to a diverse number of settings, including the workplace. *(Courtesy of Wiley Miller/ Universal Uclick.)*

Psychologists have used the ABCs of behavior analysis (antecedents, behaviors, and consequences) to improve educational techniques.

2010). As such, OBM frequently strives to teach managers better ways of objectively monitoring and rewarding productive employee performance.

By using operant conditioning, behavior analysts have increased productivity and profits, reduced accidents and injuries, promoted better relationships between employers and employees, and decreased absenteeism and turnover (Braksick, 2007; Geller, 2001). For example, researchers working with a manufacturing company implemented feedback, goal setting, and reinforcement in an effort to promote safe behavior. As a result, lost time due to accidents decreased by 93%, greatly contributing to the safety and well-being of employees (Sulzer-Azaroff et al., 1990). Despite the added time and cost of monitoring employees and implementing reinforcement, the company experienced a net savings of over $55,000 per year due to reduced lost time and worker's compensation.

Behavioral Strategies for Improving Education

If you recall the story from the beginning of the chapter, one of the lessons of behavior analysis is "don't blame the rat." It seems fitting to close this chapter with the same lesson. Many have taken this mantra and applied it to instruction, changing the saying to "don't blame the learner." Instead of focusing on what possible impairment or lack of motivation that the learner may or may not have, behavior analysts have concentrated on altering the classroom contingencies and the quality of instruction. When behavioral techniques have been applied they have been enormously successful in improving the rate and amount that children and adults learn (Engelmann, 2007; Moran & Malott, 2004). *Project Follow Through*, the largest and most expensive educational experiment ever funded by the federal government, clearly demonstrated that behavior-based educational methods produced the greatest gains in basic education skills, complex cognitive skills, and improved self-esteem in children from diverse backgrounds (Watkins, 1997). For example, Morningside Academy in Seattle uses behavioral techniques to help children progress at twice the rate of traditional education, even in deficit skill areas of children labeled with learning disabilities and ADHD (Johnson & Street, 2004).

Improving Athletic Performance Through Behaviorism

Behavior analysis can be used to improve coaching behaviors and athletic performance, a specialization known as *behavioral sports psychology* (Martin, 2003). Behavioral principles can be applied to the coaching process by explicitly identifying the precise behaviors to be executed, developing a specific plan to manage contingencies through monitoring and rewards, distinguishing between novel athletic behaviors and maintaining pre-existing skills, and creating appropriate goals (Martin & Lumsden, 1987). For example, behavior analysts have used weekly and daily goals, recording of skating behaviors, and feedback during weekly meetings to motivate speed skaters and increase their performance during practice by 25% (Wanlin, Hrycaiko, Martin, & Mahon, 1997). Similar success stories have been seen with swimming, gymnastics, basketball, football, figure skating, pole vaulting, and golf (Martin & Thomson, 2011). These studies have addressed sports applications such as fitness training, acquisition of new skills, reduction of errors and excessive nervousness, self-talk enhancement strategies, and increasing concentration.

Synthesis: The Intersection of Biology and Behaviorism

Given how much attention the field of behavior analysis has given to acquisition of behaviors through conditioning, it may not surprising that some individuals have suggested that the behavioral perspective denies the relevance of any other factors, such as biology or genetics (Pinker, 2002). This suggestion is sometimes phrased as the "black box" issue, with behavior analysts supposedly only accepting the possibility of variables going in and out of the body or mind (i.e., the black box), with no consideration of the inner workings of the body or mind itself.

This is a significant misinterpretation of the behavioral perspective and is commonly seen in psychology textbooks. However, the truth is that there has never been a notable behavior analyst who accepted that organisms contain nothing interesting inside themselves. The behavioral perspective has long accepted and supported the biological perspective, including its strong focus on the inner workings of the brain and body (Morris, Lazo, & Smith, 2004). It is not uncommon to find a textbook assert that John B. Watson thought that all behavior was learned. However, Watson himself would have disagreed with this notion. Given that unconditioned responses are unlearned reactions to environmental stimuli, it follows that many important behaviors can be attributed to evolutionary inheritance (a biological process) rather than a learning history.

Some writers have incorrectly labeled behaviorism as a "black box" psychology.

B.F. Skinner did not object to an analysis of the world within the skin (i.e., our underlying anatomy and physiology) and even criticized Watson for neglecting genetic factors (Skinner, 1959). Furthermore, he suggested that there was no true boundary between observable public behavior and internal private behavior (Skinner, 1953). It is self-evident that organisms are not just empty vessels and these two famous behaviorists were well aware of this fact. Behavior analysts will often state that thoughts, emotions, and sensation can be best understood as bodily events that are physical in nature. A behavioral explanation requires neuroscience to understand the inner workings of the "black box" and for a complete analysis of human behavior (Skinner, 1989).

What behaviorism discarded was the inference that there are unique, mental constructions that mediate the process between the stimulus and the behavior. For example, a rat may see a light turn on and then process this information before finally pressing a lever. The "processing of information" step in the analysis is a unique, mental construction that has never been directly observed. Behavior analysts would argue that this step is unnecessary for describing, predicting, understanding, or controlling the behavior of the rat (or any other organism). Using Occam's razor as a guideline, it may be better to suggest that the events within our skin follow the same rules and principles as observable events. Alternatively, it would also be helpful to collect direct observations using the advancements of neuroscience instead of relying on unconfirmed assumptions. As Skinner (1974, p. 233) stated, "The organism is, of course, not empty, and it cannot be adequately treated simply as a black box, but we must carefully distinguish between what is known about what is inside and what is merely inferred."

The intervening physiology that occurs between stimulus and behavior is important because behavior change is accompanied by changes in the nervous system. The behavioral perspective also suggested the importance and relevance of genetics by pointing out that the ability to be reinforced by certain events is a genetically inherited trait itself (MacCorquodale, 1970; Skinner, 1983). Variability is another inherited trait that was produced by evolutionary forces, as an organism that can produce many different types of behavior is an organism more likely to survive long enough to reproduce. Natural selection favored species that displayed variability at birth and then behavioral contingencies favored certain behaviors to be strengthened or weakened through the lifetime of each individual member of the species. As such, there are at least two levels of selection and retention operating on every organism: natural selection for genetic traits and behavioral conditioning for new behavior patterns (Donahoe & Palmer, 1994).

Behaviorism and neuroscience have great potential for complementing one another, as both disciplines deal with physical events, just at different levels of analysis. As technological innovations allow for greater precision in neuroscience, the connection between biological and behavioral functioning can be better elaborated upon. Neither behavior analysis nor neuroscience requires the other discipline to justify its existence and both can operate as self-contained fields, but our understanding will be enhanced if we understand and consider both perspectives. Much of this research is ongoing and is attempting to identify the neurological correlates of various behaviors and physiological bases of reinforcement, punishment, and extinction (Silva, Gonçalves, & Garcia-Mijares, 2007).

8

Social Psychology

BY DOUGLAS A. JOHNSON, PH.D. AND SOPHIE RUBIN, PH.D.

A Dangerous Waiting Room

What could compel you to sit in a room filling with dangerous smoke?

Imagine that you are invited to an interview to discuss some of the problems that students experience while in college. You show up to this interview and the secretary at the desk asks you to go to the waiting room and fill out a questionnaire. You are busy filling out the seemingly endless pages of this lengthy questionnaire when something unusual begins to happen. White smoke begins to fill the room from a small vent in the wall. Smoke continues to flood the room and becomes so thick that it is difficult to see. You find yourself needing to wave away the smoke in order to even see the words on the questionnaire. You begin coughing and rubbing your eyes. Clearly, something very wrong and potentially dangerous is occurring. Do you continue sitting there waiting for a possible death by fire or do you take action?

You may think the answer is obvious, but in truth the real answer is that it may depend on the social world around you. If you were seated in this room alone, you would probably do something about the worrisome smoke right away. However, as Latané and Darley (1968) discovered when they conducted research involving this very scenario, if there were just two other people in that waiting room, people were quite likely to continue to sit there and place their lives at risk by doing nothing. The two other people in the waiting room were also filling out questionnaires and were not any better equipped to judge the danger that the smoke may be warning about. When people were alone, the vast majority of them would leave the room to report the smoke and investigate the danger. However, when joined by two other people who continued to fill out their questionnaires, 90% of people would sit in the smoke filled room, possibly waiting for death to claim them along with these two strangers (who were actually actors told to remain calm beforehand).

What is it about the presence of other people that could make us put our own personal safety at risk? For no apparent rational reason, the participants in this study would decide that the smoke must not be dangerous when they saw other people acting calm. How much of an impact do our fellow social creatures have on our behavior? To better answer that question, we now turn to the study of social psychology.

Other people can have a profound effect on behavior.

The Influence of the Social World around Us

Social psychology is the study of how the presence of other people, whether real or imagined, influences the common reactions of individual people. Unlike sociology, social psychology typically analyzes individual reactions rather than broad cultural or societal behavior patterns. Experiments in social psychology can be traced as far back as the late 1800s, when Norman Triplett (1897) discovered that people performed a task (in this case, winding a fishing reel) faster when someone else was around rather than when they were alone. This phenomenon became known as **social facilitation**, in which the presence of other people enhances our performance on simple tasks and tasks we are well practiced with. Note that social facilitation only extends to familiar or easy tasks; the presence of others disrupts our performance with difficult and unfamiliar tasks. As such, you may ride a bicycle faster when other bicyclists are around (a simple and likely familiar task), but may have trouble working out the solution to a new math problem when others are staring at you (difficult and unfamiliar task).

social psychology
the study of how the presence of other people, whether real or imagined, influences the reactions of individuals

social facilitation
the enhancement of performance on simple or well-practiced tasks when we are aware of the presence of others

Having others around can facilitate the improvement of one's performance.

Sometimes the Best Way to Get Along is to Go Along

While in a competitive environment, group pressure might drive us to better ourselves. However, group pressure can often have a different effect. Instead of trying to exceed the performance of our peers, sometimes we just try to blend in with the rest of the group, an effect known as conformity. **Conformity** involves changing one's beliefs or behaviors to match that of the larger group as a result of social pressure. An early study conducted by Muzafer Sherif (1935) can help illustrate the power of conformity.

To understand Sherif's research, you need to first understand a visual illusion known as the *autokinetic effect*. To create this effect, we need two ingredients: 1) a person placed in a completely dark room with no visible features (so dark that one could not even see inches in front of him or her) and 2) a single pinpoint of light that does not move. Although the light may not be moving, that dark environment will create an illusion in which the person falsely perceives the light to be moving around (this phenomenon can occur if you stare at a single star in a pitch black setting). Muzafer Sherif took advantage of this illusion during a three-stage experiment.

Are your judgments easily swayed by others?

During the first stage, Sherif placed participants alone in the completely dark room, turned on the single point of light, and then asked participants how much the point of light moved. Although the true answer should be "not at all," thanks to the illusion all participants reported some movement. The movement estimates varied greatly between individuals and individuals often disagreed with themselves initially ("a few inches…, no wait, six inches, no three inches…"). As this first stage continued, participants would eventually settle on a consistent answer.

During the second stage, participants would once again be asked to provide estimates of light movement, except this time the participants were placed in the dark room in groups of three people. Once again, the room was so dark they couldn't see anything (or each other), but they could hear one another. As they spoke their estimates aloud, their initial answers inevitably disagreed with one another. However, as this second stage continued, a group average began to emerge. By the time this second stage ended, all of the participants had conformed to a single answer. Although they had the option to stick with the answer they had given during the first stage, they eventually caved to the pressure and went along with the group.

Asch's research was an early demonstration on how difficult it can be to resist group pressure.

Sherif then held a third and final stage. Once again, the participants were placed in the dark room and asked to estimate the movement of light. However, during this third stage they were once again alone in the room. The main question arising from this last stage was to find out whether the participants would return to the estimates they had been giving during the first stage or would they provide the estimates that they had conformed to during the second stage. Reliably, the answers that they had agreed upon during the second stage were given once again during the third stage, even though the participants no longer had peers around to judge them. Conformity had exerted enough pressure that its effect continued even after social pressure was removed.

As compelling as Sherif's research might seem, there are problems with saying that it offers conclusive proof of the power of conformity. This is because Sherif's experimental task was ambiguous; the movement of the light was very difficult to judge. The judgments of the participants depended upon an inconsistent illusion since the light never truly moved (recall that the participants even disagreed with themselves during that first stage). Given that they probably had no true commitment to their original answers during the first stage, it may not be very meaningful that they changed their answers when confronted with alternative answers from other members of their group. The best demonstration of conformity would involve someone giving an answer that he or

conformity
the change in an individual's behavior to match that of the larger group as a result of perceived social pressure

she obviously knows is false. In this scenario, there would be a change in behavior to match the group's behavior despite knowledge that the group is wrong. Such a test of true conformity would be demonstrated by the research of Solomon Asch (1951).

Placing One Correct Person against Several Incorrect People

To understand Solomon Asch's research, it may be helpful to imagine yourself in the role of one of his participants: You are minding your own business when someone approaches you and states that a psychological experiment on visual discrimination is about to begin. This person says that they are short one person and asks if you want to join the group. You agree to this and follow the person to a group of people already waiting outside of a door for the experiment to start. There are nine people in this group if you include yourself. A man who appears to be the experimenter arrives and lets everyone into the room containing a row of chairs. By the time you get inside the room, only one seat is available since you arrived last and ended up in the back of the crowd, so you take a seat in the second to last spot in the row. The experimenter stands before you and explains that this visual discrimination task involves several cards that will be presented one pair at a time. On the right card will be three lines of different lengths and numbered 1, 2, or 3. On the left card will be a single comparison line that matches one of the lines on the right card (see the sample picture on this page). Your job is simple: State which of the three lines on the right matches the line on the left. There is no ambiguity or illusion at work here.

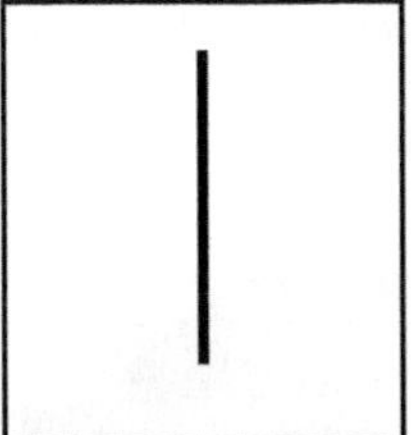

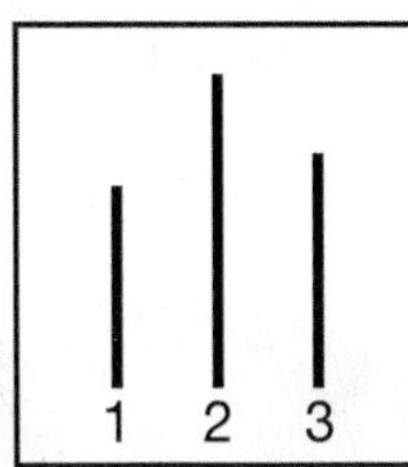

Asch's participants simply had to match line lengths while resisting the pressure of an incorrect large group.

The first set of cards is presented and clearly line "3" matches. The seven people seated before you all say "3." You agree by also stating "3," as does the person seated after you. The second set of cards is presented. This time line "1" clearly matches. You and everyone else in the group agree once again. So far, this is turning out to be a pretty simple "visual" experiment.

The third set of cards is presented and the correct answer is clearly "2," but the first person in the row says "1." This is a strange and obvious mistake because the "1" is nearly an inch shorter than the comparison line. How could he make such a simple error? But then the second person also says "1." You take another look at the cards and line "2" still clearly appears to be a match. The third person then says "1." Everyone seems so casual and calm. How can they all be so wrong? The fourth, fifth, sixth, and seventh person all say "1." It is now your turn. Do you say "1" like everyone else is doing or do you say "2" and go with your original answer that you think is correct? In other words, do you cave to the group pressure or do you remain committed to the answer you think is correct? As this experiment continues through all the sets of cards, the group will continue to be unanimously wrong and in disagreement with the visual evidence right before you. Can you maintain your independence against this incorrect group?

Many of Asch's participants went along with the group and some even came to doubt their own perception.

If Asch's research is any indication, it will prove incredibly difficult for you to avoid conformity. Why was the group so consistently wrong? Those eight incorrect individuals were actually members of the research team only pretending to be normal participants, a role known as a **confederate**. These confederates were instructed by Asch to begin making errors so that he could observe the effect on the one naïve or real participant who wasn't aware of the true nature of the experiment. In Asch's classic experiment conducted with regular American college students, approximately 26% of participants were completely independent, resisting the group pressure on every set of cards that the group was unanimously wrong about. However, 74% conformed at least once and some of these participants conformed on nearly every set.

Even those who remained independent still felt the group pressure to conform. These participants were often embarrassed about their disagreements ("why must I always disagree?") and never outright said the majority of people were wrong. Instead they gave gentler disagreements such as "they have their point of view, I have mine." When directly asked about whether the group was wrong, some of them even conceded that the group might actually be right ("everyone else is probably correct, but they could be wrong"). They exhibited a **minority slowness effect**, in which people with dissenting views often state their views much slower than people belonging to the position of the majority.

confederate
a member of the research team that the real participants of a study believes is a fellow participant

minority slowness effect
the tendency of people with minority views to express their viewpoints more slowly when in the presence of the majority

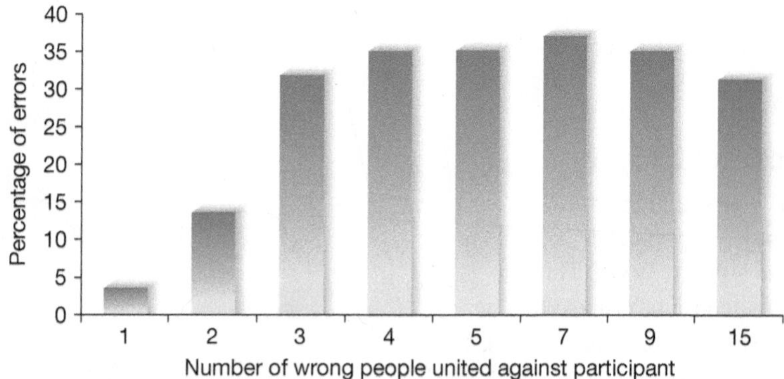

It is relatively easy to resist the pressure from 1 or 2 people, but once we are pitted against larger numbers it becomes more difficult to resist. The graph here shows that conformity rose sharply when the incorrect but unanimous majority had 3 or more people and increases in the number of people in that majority did not have much of an effect. *(Based on data from Asch, 1955)*

Among those who conformed, many reported being aware that their private thoughts were not aligned with the rest of the group and that it just felt easier to go along. Some of them were even convinced that something must be wrong with their perception and that the group must actually be correct ("there's no way that many people could be wrong, so it must be me"). That is, they not only outwardly conformed to the group pressure, but they also privately accepted the group as correct. Furthermore, Asch discovered it didn't take many people to create a strong sense of group pressure. A unanimous but incorrect group of at least 3 people was enough to bring forth the full force of conformity. In fact, the addition of more people did not greatly change the rates of conformity.

Explaining Why Conformity is So Difficult to Resist

As always, it is important to avoid circular reasoning. Conformity is a label that describes the phenomenon whereby people change their behavior or beliefs to be similar to the behaviors or beliefs of the group. The label itself is a description and not an explanation as to why people conform. That is, it would be a mistake to say Asch's participants gave wrong answers (description) because of conformity (label for description). In essence, that isn't any different than saying Asch's participants *changed their behavior to match others* because of *changing their behavior to match others*. So what does account for the behaviors we are calling instances of conformity? Another experimental variation by Solomon Asch may help provide an answer. In this variation he inverted the procedures of the classic experiment. Recall that in the classic experiment, there were 8 confederates who purposely gave wrong answers and 1 naïve participant whose answers were natural or genuine. In Asch's inverted experiment, there was only 1 confederate who purposely gave wrong answers and 16 naïve participants giving natural answers. How did those 16 unsuspecting people react to the one confederate who was continually out of sync with the majority? Not very kindly! The naïve majority openly mocked and laughed at the single independent person. Such disdain and ridicule is likely to function as punishment for nonconforming behavior. We may learn to conform as a general strategy for avoiding social punishers because we have learned there are unpleasant social consequences for nonconformity.

There can be unpleasant social consequence for not conforming.

Culture can play a big role in determining the social values and behaviors.

A student of Solomon Asch's later discovered that conformity is a worldwide phenomenon while replicating Asch's conformity study in other countries (Milgram, 1961). He discovered that the majority of people would conform to group pressure on the same visual discrimination task regardless of the country he travelled to. This does not mean that country or culture is irrelevant. Although all countries showed conformity, the rates of conformity varied across countries. For example, participants in France tended to conform much less frequently than participants in Norway. In general, cultures that tend to be high in **collectivism** (the value of giving priority to group goals over individual goals) tend to demonstrate higher rates of conformity than cultures that tend to be high in **individualism** (the value of giving priority to individual goals over group goals). This difference in conformity may be due to the fact that collectivistic cultures tend to emphasize relations among others and maintaining harmony, whereas individualistic cultures tend to emphasize individual personalities and achievement. For example, employees from cultures that emphasize collectivism tend to express more concern for the well-being of their fellow workers, whereas employees from cultures that emphasize individualism tend to express more concern for the performance of the individual business (Finkelstein, 2012). Research has also found that people from individualistic cultures are more likely

collectivism
a cultural set of values that emphasize the importance of relationships and unity among the members of a social group

individualism
a cultural set of values that emphasize the importance of self-reliance and self-interest among the members of a social group

to confront someone regarding their complaints with a service or product while people from collectivistic cultures are more likely to simply stop using the service or product in order to avoid confronting another person about their dissatisfaction (Chapa, Hernandez, Wang, & Skalski, 2014).

The research on conformity has profound implications for all aspects of live involving group decisions, from the board rooms to the juries of the legal system.

Conformity Applied to the World around Us

Understanding how people might change due to group pressure has many significant practical implications. For example, in the United States much of the legal system depends upon the decision making of people placed in groups. Research by Kalven and Zeisel (1966) found that the verdict favored by the majority of jurors on the first vote will end up as the verdict by all members on the final vote over 90% of the time. Although a minority of jurors might initially disagree, by the end they will typically agree with the majority. Conformity could also have implications for safety. Would a lone individual stand against a unanimous mob if someone's safety was in danger? Again, the odds are not favorable. For example, in another replication of Asch's conformity experiment, the experimenter suggested that there may be life endangering consequences for providing false answers (Milgram, 1961). Specifically, he told participants that the information regarding their visual perceptions would be used to design safety signals for airplanes. In other words, if participants did not give honest answers, airplanes would be poorly designed and this could endanger lives. This warning did not produce any statistically significant reductions in conformity. Even when participants were given the opportunity to write down their answers rather than say their answers aloud (so disagreements would be private and unknown to the group), the participants still went along with the incorrect answers of the group that they had just heard.

Research on conformity can give us clues on overcoming group pressure.

The findings of conformity research should not be viewed too harshly or despairingly. Although conformity can sometimes produce negative effects, it can produce positive effects as well. If a crowd of people is running away and screaming from some threat, it may not be in our best interest to decide to exert some independence and stand still during this dangerous situation. Conforming to the behavior of the group may be beneficial in other ways besides the avoidance of negative consequences. We often figure out how to survive strange situations by imitating those around us who may be more familiar with the rules. Other people often have skills we may lack and by following the lead of others, we may learn a new trick or two. When traveling to a foreign country, standard greetings may differ (handshake versus a nod or a bow) and it would be a good idea to imitate those around us.

Even when conformity is undesirable, Solomon Asch's research provides reasons to be optimistic. In another experimental variation, Asch once again pitted 1 naïve participant against an incorrect majority. Except this time there would be a single confederate that also disagreed with the group. Having a single partner side with the naïve participant against the majority had a dramatic effect in reducing the conformity of the naïve participant.

Norms tell us how to navigate the social world by informing us of what is appropriate and expected.

Understanding the Rules for Surviving the Social World

Conformity often involves changing one's behavior to adhere to what is considered normal for the environment we find ourselves in. We often infer the rules by observing how others act and then we conform to match everyone else. In social psychology, the term for a rule regarding how we are supposed to act is known as a social norm. **Social norms** are the expected standards or rules for behaviors and beliefs that are established and enforced by the social group. These rules for what is considered normal may not necessarily be explicitly stated rules for behavior. Instead, they may be learned because they are enforced by social rewards for adhering to group expectations and social punishers for deviating from group expectations, such as when you receive an approving nod or judgmental scowl for your actions. Social norms determine your conduct almost everywhere you go. The easiest way to obtain proof of these norms is to violate the rules (or just imagine violating them). How would people react if you decided to sit on the floor of an uncrowded bus rather than the

social norms
the expectations and rules for how most people are supposed to behave that are established and enforced by the social group

Some social norms can be as simple as "you should return favors."

seat? How would people react if you decided to stand only one inch away from a stranger's nose while having an everyday conversation? How would people react if you decided to hop and skip to class and work every day? Mostly likely, you can imagine some strong social consequences for such unusual behavior. You may not run into legal trouble for engaging in these behaviors, but the social trouble would probably quickly end these deviations. For many of us, simply thinking about such violations may be enough to make us slightly uncomfortable or laugh at the absurdity of even considering the idea. Furthermore, imagine if you saw someone else engaging in those actions and how you would react. Most likely you can imagine yourself providing some of those negative social consequences when observing people breaking these rules. Upon reflection you will probably realize how much your actions are controlled by the social group and how much you function as a member of that same group by controlling the actions of other members.

Sometimes deciphering the norms of the social community is as simple as observing others ("I'll do what they're doing"), while at other times we have to work out the rules we're supposed to conform to ("I'm new here, what might others do?"). As time, settings, and people change, these social rules will also change. The social norms of 1800s are very different than the social norms of the 2000s and the social norms of North America may be very different than the social norms of the Middle East (as travelers of the world soon discover when they find their usual actions are suddenly out of place). Social norms often determine the appropriate way to dress, talk, act, and interact with others. We are expected to adhere to these rules even when it is inconvenient or undesirable. For example, the **norm of reciprocity** dictates that it is appropriate to pay back a favor that someone has done for us. This holds true even if we never requested or even wanted the favor in the first place. In an experiment by Regan (1971), participants received a favor from a confederate. Specifically, the confederate entered the room and gave the participant a soft drink as a favor, even though the participant never requested this drink. Later on the confederate would ask the participant to purchase some raffle tickets. Participants who had received the soft drink purchased a greater number of raffle tickets than participants who never received the prior favor. They even spent more money on the raffle tickets than the confederate had spent to purchase the drink! Of course, such a norm can be used for exploitation, so you may want to be cautious the next time you are offered something for "free."

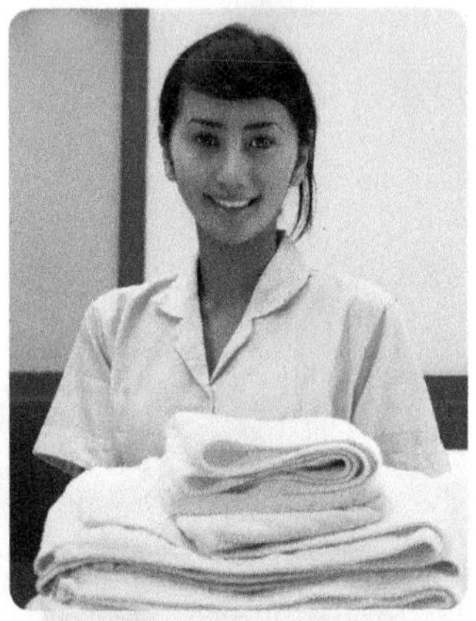
Group pressure can be used to produce socially desirable outcomes.

Conforming to social norms can also be used to produce positive new behaviors. For example, Goldstein, Cialdini, and Griskevicius (2008) took advantage of social norms to increase towel reuse in hotels. Many hotels have tried to encourage guests to reuse towels in order to conserve water. Standard approaches involve simply asking guests to reuse their towels or to provide guests with information about the importance of environmental conservation. In this study, the researchers took advantage of the fact that social norms require us to observe the local habits and customs when travelling ("when in Rome, do as the Romans do"). They concluded that a sign with the typical message about contributing to environmental conservation only resulted in about 37% of guests reusing their towels. However, when researchers left a sign in the hotel room stating that most guests in the hotel reuse their towels (i.e., the norm is to reuse one's towel), suddenly nearly 50% of guests began reusing their towels. Just like the opening story when people sat in a smoke filled room because that's what everyone else was doing, people in these rooms reused their towels because that's what the other guests were doing.

norm of reciprocity
the social norm that dictates that it is appropriate and expected to pay back a favor even when it is inconvenient or that the favor was unrequested

compliance
the change in an individual's behavior in order to fulfill a request from another person

The Social Science of Persuasion

Of course, social forces can do much more than lead to conformity. Sometimes our behavior can change simply because another person asked us to. When social psychologists study this type of behavior change, it is called **compliance**, the act of changing one's behavior to adhere to the request of another person. To better understand how social psychologists study compliance in general, let's turn to another example involving environmental conservation.

A Sweet Deal Loses Some of Its Appeal

This example involves a study conducted by Pallak, Cook, and Sullivan (1980). In this study the researchers approached various households and asked the residents to reduce their natural gas usage in order to assist with environmental conservation efforts. Although the residents agreed to the effort, their actual fuel consumption was not changed by these conservation appeals.

Next, the researchers tried a different tactic. They approached the homeowners and once again asked them to reduce energy usage. Furthermore, they offered to publicize the names of the residents in the newspaper, advertising these people as conscientious and green-friendly citizens. After some time had passed, the researchers checked the energy usage at the households and discovered that the publicity incentive had worked: the residents were now saving natural gas. However, the researchers then went to the households and told them that they would no longer be able to give them the previously promised publicity. What effect did yanking away this promise have on their fuel consumption? It actually caused them to conserve *even more* fuel.

There are a variety of techniques to increase the odds someone will comply with a request.

The researchers had taken advantage of a compliance strategy called the low-ball technique. The **low-ball technique** involves several steps: 1) Get agreement to the desired request under good conditions, 2) allow enough time to pass for the person to consider various reasons why compliance is a good idea, and 3) then making the same request again, but with some attractive features removed or unattractive features added (the low-ball). In the above example, the researchers first got the homeowners to agree to save fuel in order to get free publicity (step 1). Presumably, the homeowners thought of other good reasons to conserve fuel besides the publicity, such as lowered energy bills and improved self-esteem (step 2). Finally, when the researchers took away the publicity offer, the homeowners had already come up with other reasons to maintain their compliance with the request (step 3).

The low-ball technique involves making a deal worse after the person has already committed to it.

A classic example of the low-ball technique involves car sales. The prospective buyer finds a car at an unusually good price. If it wasn't for the price, the person wouldn't have even considered purchasing the car. The car salesperson meets with the customer, who agrees to purchase the car (step 1). While the salesperson is busy drawing up paperwork, speaking with the sales manager, and other time consuming tasks, the buyer begins thinking of other reasons he or she likes the car (step 2). Perhaps the car gets good gas mileage, has a high-tech navigation system, or simply comes in a color the buyer likes. Around this time the salesperson returns and apologizes because the advertised price cannot be given ("it was an error" or "my manager told me I can't give it away at that price"). Even though the attractive price is no longer present, the buyer still agrees to purchase the car for all the other reasons that he or she thought of (step 3). Remember that the buyer wouldn't have even considered the car without the initial low price, but now he or she is buying it despite the low price no longer being part of the deal.

A good price may not always be what it seems.

As the definition indicates, sometimes unattractive features are added in a low-ball technique rather than attractive features being removed. To illustrate this, let's consider the difficulties with scheduling early morning appointments. As you might imagine, few students are interested in participating in research that is conducted at 7 a.m. In a study by Cialdini, Cacioppo, Bassett, and Miller (1978), the researchers asked a sample of students if they would participate that early in the morning and only 24% agreed. The researchers then switched to a low-ball approach with a different group of prospective participants. Rather than inform students of the early time immediately, they first got agreement to simply participate and then waited a bit before letting them know about that unsavory little scheduling detail. Under those conditions, 95% of the students agreed to participate and even more impressively, they still showed up at 7 a.m. on the scheduled day.

low-ball technique
a compliance technique in which an initial request is accepted and then that same request is made again after some time has passed but with attractive features removed or unattractive features added

Asking for Just a Little Bit More

Note the one common element of these low-ball examples: they all involve making the targeted request upfront and then making that targeted request again under slightly worse conditions. Other compliance techniques may involve a slightly different approach. An

Another persuasion strategy involves starting with a small request and then building to a larger request.

example of this is the **foot-in-the-door technique**, which starts with a small request that is a variation of the ultimate target request before eventually making the target request. For example, imagine that you wanted to get people to put a "drive carefully" sign in their front yard. Let's also say that this sign is poorly made and rather large. It is large enough and ugly enough that it would block the view of the person's house and make their property look unappealing. What do you think your odds are of being successful with making a request like this in a nice neighborhood?

Freedman and Fraser (1966) posed this very request to people and, not surprisingly, got very little compliance (83% said *no*). So they next tried the foot-in-the-door approach. With this compliance technique, they first approached the homeowners and asked if they could simply put a 3-inch sign on their door that said "be a safe driver." Nearly everyone agreed to such a minor request. However, the tiny sign wasn't the true target for compliance. After getting compliance for the 3-inch sign, the researchers came back a few weeks later and asked the homeowners to put the huge and ugly sign on the lawn. This time the results were very different from the previous attempt to post the large sign; nearly all of them agreed to this request that would normally be rejected (76% said *yes*).

Failure as a Compliance Strategy

Another compliance technique reverses this sequence of requests by starting with a request that is larger than what is ultimately desired before moving on to the true target request. This technique, known as the **door-in-the-face technique**, begins with a request that is designed to be large and quite likely to be rejected. After that initial rejection (the door is slammed in the person's face, so to speak), the person makes another request that is smaller and seemingly more reasonable when compared to the initial request. Under these conditions, the second request has a higher probability of acceptance. A clever experiment by Cialdini et al. (1975) illustrates the effectiveness of this technique. The researchers approached students on a university campus and pretended to be employees with the local County Youth Counseling Program. Their target request was to have these students agree to volunteer to chaperone children on release from the Juvenile Detention Center. Specifically, the individuals were being asked to take these young criminals to the zoo for *two hours once* without any pay or other type of reward. Naturally, the vast majority of people who were asked right off the bat to comply with the burdensome request refused (interesting side note: almost 17% actually agreed!).

Compliance can also be achieved by purposefully making an unreasonable request that will be rejected and then "retreating" to a more reasonable sounding request.

In order to implement the door-in-the-face techniques, the researchers approached another group of students and this time asked for a larger request first. Specifically, they asked the students to spend *two hours per week for at least two years* working at the County Juvenile Detention Center without pay or any other reward. Nearly everyone refused this huge commitment (another interesting side note: a couple of students actually said yes!). After having this multi-year request rejected, the researchers then asked these same students if they would at least be willing to chaperone the criminal juveniles to the zoo for *two hours once*. Under these conditions, 50% of students agreed to volunteer, nearly three times the percentage of people who agree when the target request is asked first.

Compliance Technique	Initial Request	How the Request Is Changed
Low-ball	Actual desired goal	Request of the desired goal is made again, but under worse conditions
Foot-in-the-door	Smaller than the desired goal	The request gets progressively larger until the desired goal is reached
Door-in-the-face	Larger than the desired goal	The request gets progressively smaller until the desired goal is reached

foot-in-the-door technique
a compliance technique in which an initial small request is accepted followed by a larger request

door-in-the-face technique
a compliance technique in which an initial large request is rejected followed by a smaller request

Compliance techniques can get people to agree to requests they would normally refuse.

Compliance techniques can be applied to everyday life.

Many students confuse these three compliance techniques, so let's use an example to contrast them with one another. Let's suppose you wanted to get four of your friends (Denise, Frank, Lacey, and Luke) to help you *load dozens of heavy boxes onto a truck* next Saturday as you move to a new home. You know they said no the other week when someone else made a similar request of them and you really need their help, so you decide to try some of this social psychology stuff to increase the odds they'll say yes to you.

You call Frank and ask if he could come over on Saturday and help load one or two of the heavier boxes onto the truck. On that day after he finishes putting two boxes on the truck, you say "since you're already here, could you help with these other boxes too?" Eventually he is helping you load dozens of boxes onto the truck. You call Lacey and ask her if she would be willing to help you load a dozen or so boxes. She agrees to do this and at some point in the conversation you mention, "oh, by the way, the boxes are really heavy, are you sure you want to still help?" to which she still says yes. While talking to Denise, you ask her if she would help you spend a couple of days packing up your belongings, loading the boxes, and unloading the boxes. Denise declines your unreasonable request, at which point you say "well, could you at least help load the boxes on Saturday?" She agrees to this second request that is much more modest. Finally, you call Luke and say "will you help me load a dozen or so heavy boxes onto a truck this Saturday? I'll spring for beer and pizza if you help." Luke says yes and eventually you say, "Oh, I just remembered that I

Technique to Get Friends to Help You *Load Dozens of Heavy Boxes onto a Truck*	Initial Request	How the Request Is Changed
Low-ball examples	Load dozens of heavy boxes onto a truck while getting pizza and beer (request is accepted) or Load dozens of boxes onto a truck (request is accepted)	Same request with attractive feature removed: Load dozens of heavy boxes onto a truck, *but without pizza and beer* (Luke) or Same request with unattractive feature added: Load dozens of boxes onto a truck that *happen to also be heavy* (Lacey)
Foot-in-the-door example	Help load *one or two* of the heavier boxes onto the truck (request is accepted)	Request is made larger: Help load *all* of the heavy boxes onto the truck (Frank)
Door-in-the-face example	Spend a couple of days packing up your belongings, loading the boxes, and unloading the boxes (request is rejected)	Request is made smaller: *At least* help load dozens of heavy boxes onto a truck (Denise)

need to pay a deposit on the new place. I won't have enough to pay for the beer and pizza. Can you still help anyhow?" Luke still agrees to help you.

Note that the low-ball was used with both Lacey and Luke, foot-in-the-door was used with Frank, and door-in-the-face was used with Denise. All of them involved the same final target request, but different techniques were used to reach that ultimate goal.

The Authoritative Power Held by Both Wise Leaders and Cruel Tyrants

Most people have been socialized to be very compliant to the orders of an authority figure.

Sometimes you don't need to be so clever to get compliance; sometimes the blunt tool of authority is enough to get people to comply. In fact, complying with the orders of authority figures is a very common social norm. Although older demonstrations of the power of authority exist (Landis, 1924), the most famous demonstration involved research conducted in the early 1960s by Stanley Milgram (1974). Although Milgram spent time being mentored by Solomon Asch and replicating Asch's conformity experiments, he found himself trying to find a subject of even greater social significance. He hit upon such a subject while thinking about World War II. How could someone like Adolf Hitler get an entire country to commit the horrible atrocities seen during the Holocaust? Could Nazi Germany be recreated elsewhere? Could Americans obey evil commands of their leaders the same way Germans obeyed the evil commands of Hitler? Ultimately, he conducted a series of experiments exploring the nature of **obedience** to an authority figure. Among these series of experiments, two experiments in particular are better known than the other experiments. The first one (experiment 1) is well known because it was published first as a standalone article in 1963. The second one (experiment 5) was published as part of a full length book and may be best known because Milgram also videotaped a replication of that experiment. As such, this latter experiment is the one that will be described in depth.

Milgram's Research into Obedience

Stanley Milgram, pictured above, is famous for his research into obedience. *(Courtesy of Al Satterwhite/CPI Syndication.)*

Due to the ingenuity of his procedures, it is important to describe Milgram's experimental setup in detail. First, Milgram needed to recruit people to participate in his study so he placed an advertisement in the local newspaper. The advertisement indicated that this was a study on the nature of memory, that only one hour of the individual's time would be required, and there would be a generous payment for participation (including carfare). His ad also explicitly stated that no experience was needed and that he was interested in people from all types of educational and occupational backgrounds. Milgram was able to secure a very diverse set of individuals interested in working as participants in this memory study because of the lucrative offer and openness of the criteria for participation. It is worth noting that Milgram did not seek participants who were unusually compliant, aggressive, or sadistic. Ordinary and average people responded to the newspaper advertisement. When people arrived to participate in the experiment, they would show up two at a time and be greeted by the experimenter wearing a gray lab coat. The experimenter presented himself as the person in charge while acting both stern and confident.

To help you understand the situation confronting these participants, pretend you are one of these two participants. The other participant introduces himself to you as "Mr. Wallace." He seems like a nice enough fellow with a big smile. The experimenter proceeds to write a check out to both you and Mr. Wallace. He explains that the money is yours for showing up and you can both keep it regardless of what happens. The experimenter continues to explain the study in more detail to both of you. He notes, as the ad had indicated, that this is a study on memory. He further explains there are several aspects of memory we still don't understand, including the effect of punishment on newly learned material. For instance, what is the effect of weak or strong punishment on memory? Does it matter who is learning the material or who is administering the punishment? As such, this is why people such as you and Mr. Wallace are here because the two of you can add variety to the

obedience
compliance with the direct orders given by an authority figure

types of learners and teachers under study. The experimenter also points to a machine on a nearby table, explaining that it can administer different levels of electric shock punishment so that the effects of strong and weak punishment can be examined.

He asks both of you to draw pieces of paper from the palm of his hand to decide who will be the learner and who will be the teacher. Mr. Wallace draws first and tells you that his paper says "learner." You are now assigned the role of teacher by default. With the roles of *learner* and *teacher* finally assigned, Mr. Wallace is taken to the room next door. He sits in a chair with a multiple choice device so he can provide answers to questions about some new material he has just learned. His arms are strapped down to prevent unnecessary movement and electrodes are on placed on him so he can receive the shock punishment in case he makes any mistakes. Mr. Wallace nervously mentions that he has a heart condition, but the experimenter assures him everything will be fine.

You and the experimenter return to the other room where the shock machine is located. It has many switches on it to deliver different intensities of electrical shock. It starts at 15 volts and goes all the way up to 450 volts and each switch adds an additional 15 volts. Your job is to shock Mr. Wallace for his first mistake at 15 volts, second mistake at 30 volts, third mistakes at 45 volts, and so forth. The experimenter even gives you a 45 volt shock so you can empathize with the pain Mr. Wallace may experience (it hurts, by the way). You sit down in your chair in front of the machine and the experimenter sits in the corner behind you. At this point, the experimenter indicates that the memory part of the experiment is ready to begin.

Initially, Mr. Wallace makes no mistakes and your job as the teacher is to simply say "correct." However, Mr. Wallace starts making errors and you are told to deliver a shock for each mistake and the shock needs to be stronger each time. As this process continues and the shocks get stronger for every mistake, Mr. Wallace starts to make painful noises in the other room. As it continues, he begins to loudly complain and eventually demands to be let out of the experiment. If you continue increasing the voltage, his complaints will turn into screams. Through the wall you hear him beg and demand to be set free.

"Mr. Wallace" (the victim in Milgram's obedience research). *(Courtesy of Bob McDonough.)*

As part of the experiment, Milgram's participants were introduced to a shock machine to be used in "studying memory." *(Courtesy of The Chronicle of Higher Education.)*

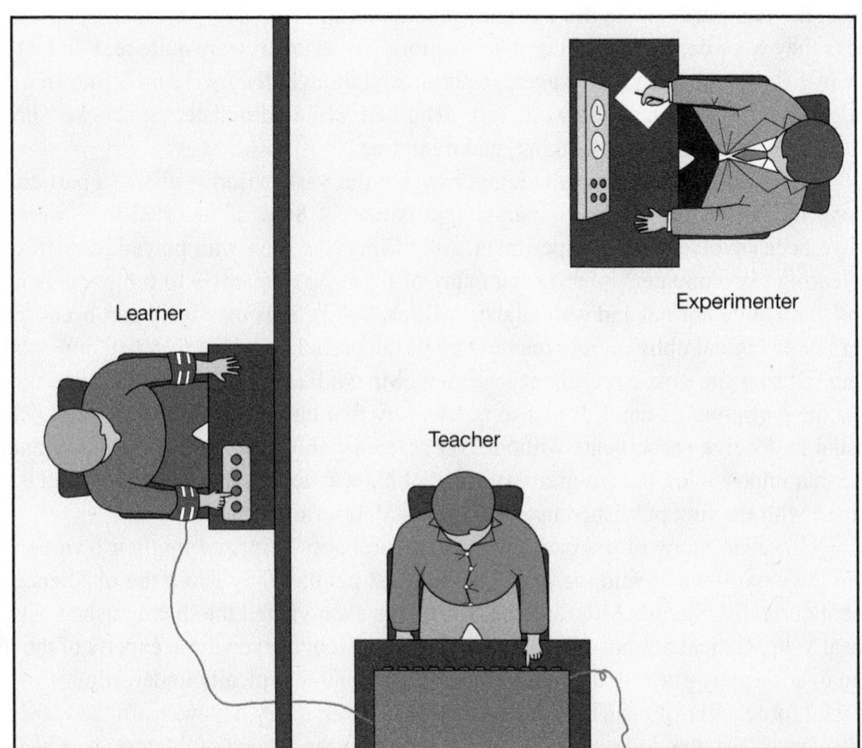

The basic setup of the Milgram experiment involved a learner/victim, teacher/subject, and experimenter/authority figure.

He starts panicking about how his heart is bothering him. At some point Mr. Wallace will fall silent, presumably unconscious or dead. Silent answers will be considered incorrect answers and therefore shocks will need to be administered. No matter what Mr. Wallace or you say in protest, the experimenter will always insist you keep delivering those dangerous electrical shocks to the helpless victim in the other room. Now we arrive at the true purpose of the experiment: How far will you go before you stop obeying the authority figure? What factors make you more or less likely to break away from obeying the person in command?

Milgram's Findings about Obedience

Participants were typically obedient, even over the protests of the victim and their own morality. *(Courtesy of Alexandra Milgram.)*

Milgram's "shocking" discovery was that most people would go the full distance and found it incredibly difficult to disobey authority. That is, 65% showed complete obedience, going all the way to the maximum voltage of 450 volts and repeatedly delivering this dangerous voltage even after Mr. Wallace had screamed and begged them to stop, possibly dying in the process (when Mr. Wallace falls silent, teachers are instructed to continue providing shocks). Less than 18% of the participants stopped after 150 volts (at this point Mr. Wallace yelled that his heart was bothering him and he wanted out of the experiment). The commands of the authority figure typically outweighed the pain of Mr. Wallace and the participant's personal moral objections.

At this point, it is important to highlight several deceptions involved in this experiment. First, despite the advertisement, this was not a study of memory. The cover story about memory was just so that Milgram could study obedience without the participants knowing the true purpose. Second, Mr. Wallace was a research confederate and was only pretending to be a real participant. The drawing to assign roles was rigged to guarantee Mr. Wallace was always the learner and the real participant was the teacher. Finally, with the exception of the sample shock given to the teacher at the beginning, none of the electric shocks were actually given to learners. Mr. Wallace was never in any danger and never experienced any pain. All of his protests were actually pre-recorded and played when he slipped out of his restraints when he was left alone and unmonitored in the other room. Of course, the real participants did not know about any of these deceptions and believed the shocks they were delivering during this "memory" experiment were quite real. In fact, on a scale of 1 (low) to 14 (high), the average participant thought they were inflicting an intense pain of 12. These participants were very disturbed while administering shocks, showing signs of sweating, groaning, shaking, and trembling.

Fortunately, the stress was temporary for the vast majority of these participants. Among the fully obedient participants, approximately 84% of reported they were glad to have been involved in the experiment. Alan Elms (the man who played the part of the unrelenting experimenter) interviewed many of these participants 3 to 6 months later and found them to be normal and well adjusted (Elms, 2008). This may be in part because Milgram felt an ethical obligation to reassure all of the participants that they had done nothing wrong. During the post-experiment interview, Mr. Wallace himself would come out and shake the participant's hand. It is also noteworthy that back in the early 1960s it was not unusual to deceive participants without ever revealing the hoax (today's ethical standards make that impossible), but Milgram went out of his way to debrief participants and is even credited with the first published use of the term "debriefing."

During the obedience experiment, many of the participants experienced high stress from the desire to stop harming another person coming in conflict with the orders of the authority figure.

However, many of the participants were probably surprised by their own conduct. When the experimental setup is described to most people, they guess the obedience outcome incorrectly. Stanley Milgram and Alan Elms even visited the distinguished psychiatrists at Yale Medical School and were delighted to discover even these experts of the mind failed to accurately guess at the results. The general public typically underestimates what a powerful force authority can be in our society. However, every day we learn there are good consequences for obeying authorities (e.g., following the advice of doctors) and bad consequences for not obeying authorities (e.g., not listening when the police say "pull over"). In fact, society would not function very well if we did not heed the orders of authority figures and this may help explain why obedience to authority developed as a social norm. Unfortunately, our experiences with situations where obedience to authority is desirable can generalize to situations where obedience to the authority figures is harmful, such as following the orders of pseudoscience practitioners (see Chapter 2) or corrupt public officials.

Another reason it was so difficult for participants to break away from the authority figure in Milgram's experiment relates to one of the compliance techniques we discussed earlier. Recall that the experimenter simply asked participants to only deliver a 15 volt shock for the first mistake. This is a fairly minor request with virtually no harm (recall that the teacher-participant received a 45 volt shock himself and did not run away in pain). Every single participant complied with this request. Then the experimenter required just a little more: 30 volts for the second mistake, 45 volts for the third mistake, etc. This pattern of "just 15 more volts" continued until the participant was entrapped into eventually delivering lethal shocks. Once again, the foot-in-the-door technique demonstrates that one can succeed in obtaining compliance with fairly extreme demands when first starting with minor requests that are likely to lead to compliance. In fact, not a single participant quit during the first 5 switches (15–75 volts).

Obeying authority figures should not be viewed as inherently bad.

Obedience beyond Milgram's Research

Milgram's experiment challenged common sense regarding how people behave and attracted a large number of criticisms. Among the criticisms are that the situation was irrelevant to real life applications (how often are you asked to electrocute someone during education?), that the results were just a product of the 1960s (that people today are much wiser and/or less compliant), that Milgram's participants figured out that the whole thing was fake (that they were simply playing along), or that all we learned from Milgram is how obedient/ horrible people are. Let's take a look at each of these criticisms.

Regarding the notion that the lessons from Milgram's experiment have little relevance to real life scenarios, it is worth remembering that even though there were some artificial features of the situation, the conflict the participants felt between their desire to stop hurting someone else and the desire to fulfill the orders of the authority figure was very real (remember that participants were observed sweating, groaning, and trembling). Furthermore, studies by other researchers in real life settings have corroborated Milgram's basic finding. For example, in a study conducted with real nurses working in an actual hospital, Hofling, Brotzman, Dalrymple, Graves, and Pierce (1966) discovered that if an unfamiliar doctor ordered the nurses to deliver a fatal dose of a drug, that 95% of the nurses would administer the drug (the drug was fake and the patients were not in true danger, but the nurses did not know that), although in interviews most nurses incorrectly believed that they would resist such an order. Furthermore, many people regularly do disagreeable and morally questionable things in their daily jobs simply because the boss orders them to, such as an employee of the electric company turning off a family's power during a harsh winter (Blass, 2004).

Uncritical and blind obedience can have disastrous, even fatal, outcomes.

Replications of Milgram's study demonstrate that obedience has not decreased over time. Obedience studies with experimental procedures similar to Milgram's have been conducted in the 1980s and 2000s and have found nearly identical results (Burger, 2008; Meeus & Raaijmakers, 1995). Given the large number of people in Milgram's research and subsequent replications, it is not very plausible that such a large number of participants were simply faking their reactions. One noteworthy replication of Milgram's study used actual shocks on the victims (a puppy) and found that 77% of people were fully obedient in causing legitimate pain to a helpless victim (Sheridan & King, 1972).

Milgram's findings on obedience holds relevance for today's society.

How to Create and End Obedience

The idea that the only lesson to be learned from Milgram's study is that people are all disturbingly obedient is a profound misinterpretation of the results from his research. The true lesson of Milgram's research is a better understanding of the powerful influence that situational variables can have on our behavior. Even though only a couple of his

Whether or not a person obeys is determined by more factors than simply being given an order.

obedience studies are well known, recall that Milgram conducted a series of experiments. During these experiments, he discovered that the rates of obedience could be dramatically changed depending upon the situation that the participant was subjected to. Milgram's research gives us a better understanding of the variables that create obedience and therefore it also provides us with the knowledge of how to combat undesirable instances of obedience.

As other experiments by Milgram demonstrate, rates of obedience can increase or decrease depending on the situation. Obedience decreased the closer people were to the victim, especially if they had to make physical contact with that person. Milgram also discovered that if the symbols of authority are taken away, obedience will dramatically decrease. In one experiment Milgram made a small change that involved removing the lab coat from the person giving orders. Under those conditions, most people ignore the plainly dressed experimenter. Another experiment demonstrated that authority can also be used to prevent harm. When a learner demanded to be shocked despite his heart condition (the explanation being that it would be too damaging to his pride if he couldn't endure the shocks), people would instead obey the experimenter who ordered that the dangerous experiment be stopped.

Milgram's last two obedience experiments yielded some of the most interesting results. In one of these, the real participant worked with a partner (a confederate) as part of a team of teachers. The experimenter would demand the team deliver shocks. The real participant never pushed the button but instead relayed these orders to his partner who would do the actual button pushing. This was meant to simulate an experience in which a person is only a small part of the obedience process, such as when an individual helps fulfill orders while working for a harmful company or corrupt bureaucracy. In this situation, when the participants were only a small part of a larger system, obedience rose to 92.5%. In regards to the Milgram's original intent to better understand the events of World War II, it is worth noting that is wasn't Adolf Hitler himself who directly carried out abuses during the Holocaust. Instead the Holocaust required the obedience of a much larger network of people in which many of the individuals only contributed a small degree of harm.

Obedience research also provides hints on how to resist harmful authority figures.

The other experiment also required the participant to work as part of a team of teachers, except there were three teachers in this experiment (one naïve participant and two confederates). As usual, the experimenter demanded that electric shocks be delivered. However, at some point in the experiment the two confederate teachers would refuse. Note that this placed the participant in a conflict between two powerful social norms: conformity and obedience. The norm of conformity would pressure the participants to stop delivering the shocks (most of the other people in the room are now refusing to push the button) while the norm of obedience to authority would pressure the participants to continue with the shocks (since the experimenter is still giving demands to push the button). Under these conditions conformity wins out, with obedience decreasing to just 10%. It appears that harmful authority figures can be easily resisted if there are a few other people willing to take a stand with you.

Knowing Your Role in the Social World

As evidenced by the previous research, social norms can exert a powerful influence on our behavior. A related concept known as social roles can also potentially influence behavior just as strongly. **Social roles** refer to group expectations about how particular people are supposed to behave. These roles are often related to certain situations or jobs. For example, if you were to hear sudden and unexpected gunfire, the social norm may be to run away. However, the rules would change if you were assigned the social role of a police officer. Individuals in that specific role would be expected to investigate the gunfire, even as the broader norm sent everyone else in the opposite direction of gunfire. Any police officer

social role
the expectations and rules for how particular people are supposed to behave that are established and enforced by the social group

who chose to flee the scene with the crowd would then have to face some very negative social consequences from society. Social roles are not always based on occupations. For example, some social roles are based on gender, such as the fact that every society has expectations for how men and women are supposed to act. Of course, gender roles have shifted throughout history and depend on cultural context (women of the 1950's were likely to be homemakers whereas today, women make up a large percentage of the workforce). Some roles might come and go depending on the social context. It might be considered normal for someone to act afraid when they hear noises in a dark and unfamiliar environment. However, if that individual has currently been assigned the social role of parent (i.e., his or her child is watching), then it would suddenly not be appropriate for the person in that current social role to act afraid anymore.

Social roles are the rules for how specific people are supposed to act.

Social Roles and the Stanford Prison Experiment

One of the most famous experiments involving social roles is the Stanford Prison Experiment (Zimbardo, Haney, Banks, & Jaffe, 1973; Zimbardo, 2007). For this study, Philip Zimbardo wanted to see what effect being randomly assigned the role of either prisoner or prison guard for two weeks would have on participants. The researchers built an artificial prison in the basement of the Psychology Department at Stanford University, complete with prison bars and a sign labeled "Stanford County Prison." Zimbardo recruited participants by placing advertisements in the local newspapers and was able to attract approximately 100 interested individuals (it probably helped that the study offered a rather generous payment for participation). The researchers screened out anyone with previous arrests or medical / mental problems. After spending time conducting psychological assessments, they were able to identify 24 well-adjusted and average people to participate in the study. About half participated as guards and about half participated as prisoners.

Those given the prisoner role would soon find out their assignments when they were literally arrested by actual police officers in order to help immerse these participants in the prisoner experience before being brought to the mock prison. When they arrived at the fake prison, the prisoners were stripped of their clothing and given gowns to wear without any undergarments. Their assigned prison number was stitched into the gown and they were given nylon caps to wear on their heads. The guards were given uniforms composed of khaki clothing, sunglasses, whistles, and batons. Neither group was given much direction on how to behave since the researchers wanted the expectations from the assigned social roles to determine their behavior, not obedience with directions from the researchers. However, Zimbardo did hold an orientation for the guards in which he did tell them to maintain order and to never use physical force to get compliance. He also suggested that they could use boredom or frustration as tools for maintaining order.

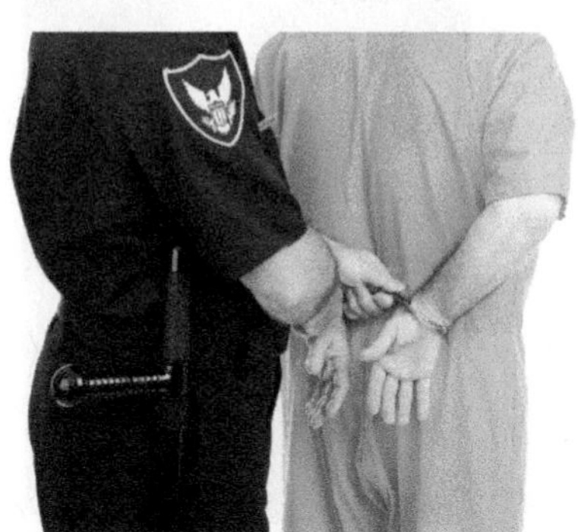

How might your behavior be influenced if you were assigned the role of guard or prisoner?

During the first day of "imprisonment," the participants who were assigned the role of prison guard began acting as they thought guards were supposed to act: authoritative and commanding. The guards informed the prisoners that they would not be using their names and instead referred to them by their assigned prison numbers only. The participants who were assigned the role of prisoner began mocking the guards and their attempt to look tough and in control. In turn, the guards began barking orders such as demands for pushups and jumping jacks to exert control. The demands slowly became insensible, including demands that the prisoners call out their assigned numbers by singing them. The use of absurd demands was purposeful by the guards with the message being that they were in charge and the prisoners were supposed to obey even if the order didn't make sense.

After a few days, the Stanford Prison Experiment felt more like a prison than an experiment.

Although the prisoners had initially rebelled, the guards organized together to break up disruptions. As punishment for the mockery and insubordination, the guards forced the prisoners to scrub walls, floors, and even toilets without protective gloves. They also made them engage in physical exercise for extended durations. The prisoner blankets were pulled through underbrush until they became full of burrs and stickers (which the prisoners had to spend time pulling out if they want to sleep with a blanket). The guards took shifts and to keep the prisoners sleep deprived, they would pound on their cells with their batons to wake them constantly throughout the night. Despite Zimbardo's original instructions, the guards often resorted to physical force to get prisoners to comply with their commands. As one of the guards put it, "I found myself taking on the guard role, I didn't apologize for it; in fact, I became quite bossier. The prisoners were getting quite rebellious and I wanted to punish them for breaking up our system." (Zimbardo, 2007, p. 60). One of the prisoners met with Zimbardo to complain about the behavior of the guards, but Zimbardo, caught up in playing the role of a prison superintendent, acted unsympathetic to these complaints. This prisoner then became panicky after this interaction and complained to the other prisoners that he wasn't allowed out of the experiment-prison.

The behavior of the guards in the Stanford Prison Experiment quickly became abusive.

By the third and fourth day, a remarkable shift in attitude had gradually begun to emerge. None of the guards or prisoners felt like they were acting like the guards and prisoners from movies that they had been previously taking their cues from. Everyone stopped using words like "experiment," "simulation," or "participant" and they began to feel like they were actually guards and prisoners. As the people within the walls of "Stanford County Prison" internalized the expectations of these roles, their behaviors continued to fulfill the role requirements. The guards became a mixture of aggressive, abusive, and rule enforcing types and they all worked together to maintain the prison. The prisoners became emotional, depressed and compliant. Although everyone could technically still quit the experiment at this point, no one tried to because the prison felt too real (one simply does not quit prison). Both a visiting prison chaplain and a former inmate visited and confirmed the realism of the prison setting.

The prison experiment had to be ended early because of the escalating abuse.

As the experiment continued, the behaviors began taking on disturbing new patterns. The guards continually harassed the prisoners and screamed at them for any perceived failure. The guards regularly handcuffed the prisoners, put them in ankle chains, and even put bags on their heads. Some of the guards even humiliated the prisoners by forcing them to expose their genitals and to engage in simulated sex acts. The prisoners even turned on one another, urging non-compliant prisoners to simply do what they are told (perhaps due to becoming tired of group punishments that occurred when any single individual caused trouble). The prisoners all passively accepted their treatment. The experiment had clearly gone too far and should have been terminated earlier, but everyone involved was so caught up in their roles that even those in charge forgot their ethical obligations as university researchers.

On the fifth evening of the experiment, Zimbardo brought his girlfriend, a social psychologist named Christina Maslach, to view the prison "experiment." Unlike the other people involved, she had no assigned role that she was expected to adhere to. Furthermore, she had not spent several days becoming accustomed to the slow but cumulative changes in behavior that had been occurring (note the relevance of the foot-in-the-door concept). This allowed her to see these prison horrors for what they truly were and she demanded that Zimbardo end the experiment. After several hours of arguing, Zimbardo finally realized he had made the error of conforming to the role of the prison superintendent. Returning to his role of researcher, he decided to put an early end to the experiment the next morning, just six days after it had begun.

What lessons can be learned from research such as the Stanford Prison Experiment?

In less than one week, simply being assigned a role of guard or prisoner had created a dramatic change in this small group of individuals. Prior to the experiment, these two groups were as similar as they could be (recall the extensive screening that the researchers had conducted). During the experiment the guards and prisoners appear drastically different from one another. After the experiment, all these people returned to their normal ways of behaving, with no long-term mood disturbances being reported. Even the cruelest of the guards showed no sadistic or antisocial tendencies outside of the Stanford Prison Experiment.

Extensions of the Stanford Prison Experiment

The actions that occurred during the Stanford Prison Experiment would be difficult to replicate given that this study crossed several ethical boundaries. Nonetheless, there are similar studies that corroborate the basic features. Lovibond, Mithiran, and Adams (1979) placed participants into different types of prison simulations. When the people assigned the role of guard were instructed that security was of paramount importance and to be formal with the prisoners, the relationship between the guards and prisoners quickly became hostile, much like in the Stanford Prison Experiment. When the role of guard came with a different set of expectations, such as allowing inmates to have self-respect or to keep the prisoners actively engaged in the smooth running of the prison, the relations between the two sets of roles became significantly less hostile. In another study, Orlando (1973) created a psychiatric ward and randomly assigned people the role of either staff or patient. The people assigned the role of patient appeared to conform to the role and developed emotional symptoms (anxiety, depression) beyond what is likely attributable to simple playacting. In 2004, many of the circumstances of the Stanford Prison Experiment were replicated in real life during the Abu Ghraib Prison scandal. American prison guards committed many crimes while placed in charge of Iraqi prisoners. These guards were asked to obtain military intelligence from these prisoners, but were given very little direction on how to accomplish this task. Prior to and after their arrest and conviction for their crimes, many of these guards displayed no evidence of sadism or abuse in their jobs or daily life. However, during the prison scandal, the prisoners were physically harmed and sexually tortured, had bags placed over the heads, were dragged around by a leash, and forced to comply with intensely stressful and meaningless orders. In essence, many of the same behaviors seen in the Stanford Prison Experiment were seen in real world setting of Abu Ghraib prison.

Individuals such as Zimbardo have argued that the real life tortures that occurred in the Abu Ghraib prison scandal can be traced back to processes similar to what was seen in the Stanford Prison Experiment. *(Courtesy of Associated Press.)*

Despite the fame of the Stanford Prison Experiment, it is not above criticism. Zimbardo was not an objective observer in his research, but instead actively played a part and this may have influenced the results. It is possible the participants were only doing what they thought the researchers wanted to see (Gray, 2013), even though the guards violated the few rules that the researchers had originally established. It is also questionable the extent to which Zimbardo actually directed the behavior of guards versus simply letting the social role determine their behavior (Prescott, 2005). Whether or not the Stanford Prison Experiment represents a real prison environment is also debatable, given that real prisons do not typically involve prisoners being forbidden from using their actual names or having bags placed over their heads. Furthermore, the participants weren't actually guards or prisoners, but were instead conforming to the stereotypes they held about how prisoners or guards are supposed to behave. Their reactions to perceived stereotypes are still noteworthy given that many people hired as real guards or arrested as real prisoners would also have the same stereotypes initially. Regardless of these criticisms, the Stanford Prison Experiment stands as a dramatic illustration of what can happen when ordinary people are put in extraordinary circumstances.

Who or what do we credit/blame for the actions of people?

How Do We Explain the Kindness and Cruelty Seen in the Social World?

The startling outcomes of research such as the Stanford Prison Experiment and Milgram's obedience studies have often led people to wonder how such behavior can be explained. Generally speaking, there are two broad types of explanations or attributions that can be made: **dispositional attributions** and **situational attributions**. A dispositional attribution states that the cause of behavior is related to some internal factor, such as genetics, traits, or inherent personality characteristic. A situational attribution states that the cause of behavior is related to some external factor, such as the environment or learning history.

dispositional attribution
assigning the cause of an individual's behavior as being generated from some internal factor such as genetics, traits, or inherent personality characteristic

situational attribution
assigning the cause of an individual's behavior as being generated from some external factor such as the surrounding environment or learning history

Let's consider the following scenario: Suppose you observed various individuals studying to become ministers. These people should be well aware of the Biblical story about the Good Samaritan, in which a member of the Samaritan religion takes the time to help an injured man who is near death and from a rival religion. The story portrays the helpful Samaritan positively and is meant to inspire people towards charitable acts. You observe these seminary students as they travel outside and their paths cross with a man slumped in a doorway. This man is coughing and groaning with his eyes closed and his head down. His actions clearly indicate that he is in need of help. The preceding scenario actually occurred in a study by Darley and Batson (1973). The situation confronting these seminary students represented a terrific opportunity for them to implement the lessons learned from the tale of the Good Samaritan. However, 60% of those individuals chose to ignore that man's need for help and even stepped directly over this victim on their way to somewhere else.

There is a strong tendency for people to locate the causes of behavior as originating from within the person only.

In terms of attributions, how do you explain the actions of these people? For those who helped, it would not be uncommon to hear observers attribute the reasons for their behavior to being "charitable," "kind-hearted," or some other positive label. For those who failed to help, it would not be surprising if the reasons were attributed to "insensitivity," "callousness," or some other negative label. The common factor among the answers typically given is that they involve dispositional factors. Whether it is "charitableness" or "callousness," the credit or blame is generally laid upon something inside the person. Situational factors are typically not considered, even where they are obvious. This tendency to assign the cause of behavior to dispositional factors while ignoring situational factors is called the **fundamental attribution error**. Examples of this can be seen when we attribute academic success to natural intelligence, an angry conversation to a hot-headed person, and failure to meet deadlines to laziness without considering the environmental factors that could influence one to do well in school, start yelling at others, or miss deadlines.

The fundamental attribution error is considered an error because the environment does play an important role in determining behavior, even though the average individual ignores it in their explanations. In fact, a situational factor was the only factor that would predict helping behavior in the Darley and Batson study. Specifically, some of the seminary students had been told that they were late to their next appointment and that they needed to hurry, while other seminary students were told to take their time to the next appointment. When the students were in a hurry, only 10% helped the victim. When the students were not in a hurry, 63% of them helped the victim.

It is often difficult for us to recognize external influences as an important cause of our own behavior and the behavior of others. In the "causal stream" of events, we are often being pushed and pulled by the situational factors around us.

Of course, situational factors such as these are often invisible to us. We don't see the person being told to hurry or we are unaware of their unique learning history. In the absence of such information, it is all too easy to infer that something inside the person was responsible for their behavior. Inferring a personality defect, trait, attitude, or other disposition can be done instantly and without effort, whereas trying to understand situational factors may require time and effort. Furthermore, many people tend to view the world in terms of types: that there are good types of people and bad types of people. Part of this perspective typically involves seeing good people being driven by good dispositions and bad people being driven by bad dispositions. However, evidence suggests that this perspective is simplistic and that people can vary in their goodness and badness in response to the demands of the social situation.

The fundamental attribution error also varies by culture. Societies high in individualism, such as Western cultures, are more likely to attribute causality to dispositions rather than situations, even when situational influences are obvious. Societies high in collectivism, such as Eastern cultures, tend to show the fundamental attribution error only when situational factors are not salient (Choi, Nisbett, & Norenzayan, 1999). This may be because of the pronounced emphasis on connections in collectivism which causes members to look for the relation between the person's actions and surrounding circumstances. Individualistic cultures tend to emphasize actions independent of the circumstances, which may orient people towards dispositional explanations and away from situational explanations.

fundamental attribution error
the excessive tendency when explaining an individual's behavior to assign the causes of behavior to dispositional factors while ignoring or downplaying the situational factors

This tendency to emphasize dispositions and to ignore situations is part of the reason why people often incorrectly guess the outcome of Milgram's obedience research and are surprised by the behaviors seen in the Stanford Prison Experiment. People who are unaware of the fundamental attribution error often presume that the dispositional factors of Milgram's teachers should exert more power than the situational factors of the experiment or that the dispositions of the guards should prevent any cruelty in the Stanford Prison Experiment. In contrast, the obedience research and the Stanford Prison Experiment offer compelling evidence on why situational influence should not be underestimated. Note that the individuals in both studies were ordinary people from normal backgrounds. In fact, they were screened to ensure they were normal and psychologically healthy before the experiments. Before being placed in the experimental situation, they behaved normally. While being placed in the experimental situation, the average person engaged in disturbing behavior. After being removed from those situations, their behavior returned to normal.

Social psychology research provides strong evidence of how much our behavior can change as the situation changes.

Although Milgram's and Zimbardo's research primarily provides strong evidence regarding the role of situational influence, it is important to avoid simplistic interpretations of the results. Milgram did not obtain 100% obedience in any of the studies he conducted (recall that Milgram conducted a series of experiments). In the one film Milgram made of his obedience research, the first participant to appear on camera steadfastly refuses the orders to continue the shocks. The guards and prisoners of the Stanford Prison Experiment weren't completely equal in the behaviors they displayed. Although many of the guards were abusive in the Stanford Prison Experiment, some of the guards simply did their jobs without actively harming the prisoners. The fact that most people changed their behavior in these situations highlights the importance of situational influence and should not be easily dismissed.

The Interaction between the Person and the Situation

As always, critical thinking about these issues is required. It is overly simplistic to blame the situation or the person. Instead, both factors can come into play and may interact with one another. For example, this may be the case when a person's *current disposition* developed from past *situations* they have experienced (situations determine the disposition) or that people with certain *dispositions* will seek out certain *situations* (dispositions determine the situation). For instance, people may become prone to violence (dispositional) due to a history of situations in which violent behavior was reinforced (situational) or that aggressive people (dispositional) may purposely look for opportunities in which aggression is encouraged (situational).

The Consequence of Labels

One of the general lessons from the Stanford Prison Experiment is that labels can change how people think and act and that some labels may even carry severe consequences. Sometimes we place labels upon an entire group of people. A **stereotype** is a belief about the characteristics of a group and is applied to most individuals from that group. Stereotypes can range from positive (African-Americans are good at sports, French people are good lovers, Southern people are friendly) to negative (Irish people are drunks, Arabs are terrorists, women can't drive) and may not reflect reality. Regardless of their accuracy, stereotypes, like social roles, carry expectations from the social world and the labelled member of that group is often aware of these expectations. Such expectations from our social world may help or hinder us. Consider the phenomenon of **stereotype threat**, in which an individual's performance on a task may be *harmed* when confronted with a stereotype regarding the group they are a member of. Also relevant is the concept of **stereotype boost**,

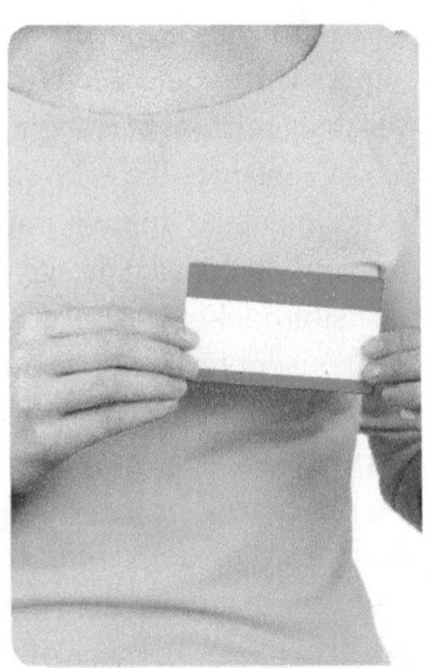
The labels we attach to ourselves can be an important influence on how we act.

stereotype
a positive or negative belief about the characteristics of a group of people

stereotype threat
the disruption in an individual's performance that may occur when one is made aware of a negative stereotype regarding the group that he or she belongs to

stereotype boost
the enhancement in an individual's performance that may occur when one is made aware of a positive stereotype regarding the group that he or she belongs to

Having a stereotype attached to your culture can have a detrimental effect on how you perceive yourself.

in which an individual's performance on a task may be *helped* when confronted with a stereotype regarding the group they are a member of. This suggests African-American people may dance better than usual when confronted with the stereotype of "black people have a good sense of rhythm" whereas Caucasians may dance worse than usual when confronted with the stereotype of "white people can't dance."

Each of us belongs to multiple groups and stereotype threat/boost suggests that our performance may get better or worse depending on which group stereotype we are currently made aware of. An insightful illustration of this is provided by research from Shih, Pittinsky, and Ambady (1999). In regards to mathematics, common stereotypes in American culture include the notion that Asians are good at math and that women are bad at math (Benbow, 1988; Hedges & Nowell, 1995; Steen, 1987). Therefore, the researchers decided to study Asian-American women to see the differential effect of stereotypes on their math skills. The researchers obtained a very difficult math test to give to these participants, one in which it would be normal to only get about half the questions correct. The researchers then subtly made some of the Asian-American women think about their ethnic group, while making others think about their gender. Specifically, some participants were given a survey that asked questions such as "whether their parents or grandparents spoke any languages other than English" and "how many generations of their family had lived in America." Another group of participants were given a survey that asked questions such as "whether they lived on or off campus" and "whether their floors were coed or single sex."

Stereotypes and other types of labels may lead certain groups of people to be mistreated or avoided.

For the Asian-American women who were made to think about the Asian aspect of their identity, their performance on the math test was higher than usual (54% correct) due to stereotype boost. For the Asian-American women who were made to think about the female aspect of their identity, their performance on the math test was lower than usual (43% correct) due to stereotype threat. Despite possessing the same overall identity, their performance changed depending on what stereotype was currently brought to their attention.

Dehumanization and Aggression

Not only can behavior change due to the labels we are given, we may also treat others differently due to the labels they have received. Take, for example, research conducted by Bandura, Underwood, and Fromson (1975). Much like Milgram's obedience studies, this study involved the delivery of fake shocks. Specifically, the participants were asked to serve as supervisors of a three-member team involved in bargaining decisions. The participant-supervisor would be in another room watching these teams and was periodically told that the team had made a poor decision. When such mistakes occurred, the participant-supervisors would need to deliver a shock and were allowed to choose any shock intensity for the punishment (ranging from 1-mild to 10-painful shock).

People feel more comfortable causing harm when the victims have been labeled as less than human.

Besides the fake shocks, the researchers used another important deception in this experiment. At some point during the process, they pretended to "accidently" leave on a microphone, allowing the participant-supervisors to overhear the researchers discuss the decision-making team members (and future shock victims). Some of these participant-supervisors heard the team members described as "perceptive and understanding" while others heard the team members described as "animalistic and rotten." Even though the participants were only supposed to deliver shocks based on errors, not on the personality characteristics of the victim, the overheard labels had a strong influence on the intensity of shock they delivered. The group described with dehumanizing terms received a shock intensity that more than doubled the intensity delivered to the group that was described in positive terms. In other words, the participants were able to justify a higher level of aggression and mistreatment simply because they heard a negative label about that group of individuals. This has significant implications for the stereotypes and labels being applied to many groups of people. Many of the worst actions taken against certain groups often involved the use of dehumanizing and derogatory labels. History provides many examples, such as Jews being described as vermin (followed by the murder of 6 million Jews by Nazi Germans during the 1930s), Chinese being described as mere things rather than people (followed by the murder of about 300,000 Chinese by Japanese soldiers during the 1930s), Vietnamese being described as gooks (followed by 500 civilians being killed by American soldiers in 1968 during the My Lai massacre alone), and Tutsi of Rwanda being described as cockroaches (followed by 1 million Tutsi being killed by Hutu neighbors in 1994). Mistreatment, it seems, is easier to conduct when the victims are described as somehow inferior.

Breaking the Social World into Us and Them

The labels given to members of certain groups can not only evoke mistreatment, they may also foster a sense of *us versus them.* In other words, labels can create the presence of in-groups and out-groups. An **in-group** is a group of people who feel like they belong together and have a common identity. An **out-group** is a group of people outside the in-group who are seen as inherently different from the in-group. Once in-groups and out-groups are formed, there is a strong tendency for members of the in-group to perceive the members of out-group as threatening and to become hostile to those in the out-group. It is also common to see **in-group bias** (the tendency to favor members of the in-group) and **out-group homogeneity** (the tendency to see everyone else as similar). When such a mindset is adopted, the in-group is seen as diverse (we're all unique individuals) and the out-group as lacking diversity (all those other people are all the same).

Robbers Cave Experiment

The Robbers Cave experiment (Sherif, Harvey, White, Hood, & Sherif, 1961) provides evidence on the power of in-groups and out-groups. This experiment was led by Muzafer Sherif (the same person whose conformity study was discussed at the beginning of this chapter) and involved boys around 12 years of age at a summer camp (Sherif observed them by pretending to be the camp janitor). Upon arrival to the summer camp, the researchers split the boys into two different cabins and let them chose their own names. The two groups picked the names Eagles and Rattlers for themselves. This simple step was enough to create in-groups and out-groups. Soon enough, the Eagles decided the Rattlers were no good and the Rattlers also saw the Eagles as worthless. The hostility intensified when the researchers introduce competitive games between the Eagles and Rattlers. Open name-calling (the out-group was full of "cheaters" and "stinkers") and fighting broke out. Rival cabins were raided and their possessions were stolen. The researchers attempted to end the aggression by having the boys participate in non-competitive group activities, such as

Divisions between people will sometimes be created by how we identify ourselves.

Mere exposure to others may not be enough to overcome long-standing hostility and division.

in-group
a group of people that feel like they belong together and share some common identity

out-group
a group of people outside of the person's perceived social group that is seen as being inherently different from members of the in-group

in-group bias
the tendency for people to reliably favor members of the in-group and to reject members of the out-group

out-group homogeneity
the tendency to perceive members of an out-group as lacking diversity or distinction among each other

holding picnics and movie nights together. Unfortunately, the hatred ran too deep, with all these activities being cut short by continued fighting. Once the in-group/out-group identity was developed, simply being in proximity of each other was enough to create war in the summer camp.

Fortunately, the researchers did eventually devise a solution to end the violence: expose the boys to activities in which they could only be successful if they cooperated. For instance, during a road trip with the boys, the researchers pretended that the camp truck had broken down. Only if the Eagles and Rattlers pushed the truck together would it start again. Any fights or attempts for one group to push the truck alone meant failure and that everyone would be stuck on the roadside. In another instance, the researchers pointed out that a fun movie was available for rent, but neither cabin could afford it on their own. Only by working together and combining their money would any fun occur. As these cooperative activities continued, the behavior of the boys changed. The hostility was slowly replaced by kindness. Some of the Eagles began to see the Rattlers as their good friends and vice-versa. The Robbers Cave experiment had successfully demonstrated how to both engineer and eliminate hostility.

Having common goals that can only be solved through cooperation is a useful strategy for uniting groups.

Promoting Cooperation between Hostile Parties

An extension of the Robbers Cave experiment can be seen with the **jigsaw strategy** (Aronson, 2000). This strategy was originally developed for newly desegregated classrooms. From the 1840s until the 1960s, it was legal in many states to separate grade schools and universities by race and to establish white-only or black-only school systems. When desegregation was first legally mandated, the government began to force Caucasians and African-Americans into contact with one another, sometimes by busing children from one neighborhood to another. Unfortunately, the initial results from forced contact were not promising. As predicted by in-group and out-group categories, the students of both races were typically hostile to one another and disruptions in the classroom were a common occurrence.

Psychologists implemented the jigsaw strategy to overcome many of these concerning clashes. The essence of this strategy is to assign group work to the students. Within each group, every student is assigned a critical part of the project and is responsible for teaching their fellow group members about their particular part. Each student needs the other students for their unique contribution to the project. For example, a group may be assigned to do a report on the country of Sweden. One student is assigned to research the economy of Sweden, another assigned to research the politics of Sweden, and so forth. Each student is trained on their piece of the project by the teacher or a group of peers assigned the same task (e.g., all the students responsible for understanding Sweden's economy get together). If the students don't cooperate, the project will be a failure. Each student needs help from the others and every student is a necessary part for the success of the group. When the jigsaw strategy was implemented in desegregated schools, hostility between races sharply decreased (Aronson, 2004). The jigsaw strategy continues to be used today for any group setting in which one wants to promote cooperation and improve relations among groups.

Although danger can occur between groups (and can be solved by a careful application of psychological principles), danger can also occur by simply being a member of a single group. We will discuss several examples of this in the next section.

jigsaw strategy
a technique for promoting cooperation through group projects in which each group member is uniquely assigned a critical part of the project and every member's contribution is necessary for the success of the overall project

group polarization
the tendency for an individual's thinking to become more extreme and intense over time due to the exclusive exposure to a group of people with similar thoughts

The Hazards of Being Just another Face in the Crowd

A phenomenon that can occur by simply being a member of a group is known as **group polarization**. Group polarization is the tendency for individuals of a group to become more extreme in their thinking after discussions with other group members holding similar thoughts, beliefs, and attitudes (Isenberg, 1986). This sharp change in their thinking is unlikely to have occurred if the individual wasn't surrounded by like-minded individuals and we naturally tend to seek out and surround ourselves with like-minded people. Although all the individual members may be quite moderate in their initial beliefs, those beliefs tend to become progressively less moderate until eventually most members of the group become extremists. For example, a person with slightly Democratic or Republican beliefs may commit to their views even more after attending political conventions. Additionally, thanks to the internet that offers unlimited connections with people worldwide, it is becoming easier to find others who hold the same values as us, which in turn may create more extreme viewpoints than previously possible (Sia, Tan, & Wei, 2002). People are particularly susceptible to this effect if they rarely expose themselves to challenging viewpoints. While being committed to a particular viewpoint isn't necessarily a bad thing ("It's good to recycle!"), it can become problematic when such ideas are harmful to begin with (recall the dehumanizing labels discussed earlier in the chapter and the related human suffering).

Being surrounded by like-minded people may create extreme viewpoints, especially if one is never challenged by alternative perspectives.

The Other Person Can Do the Hard Work

Another potential hazard of being in groups is that group members may contribute less than they would individually, also known as **social loafing**. Researchers have demonstrated this phenomenon with a variety of tasks. For example, Latané, Williams, & Harkins (1979) describe research by Ringelmann in which participants were asked to pull a rope as hard as they can. Even though everyone should be putting in their strongest effort at all times, people tended to slack off on the task as more people were added to the group. Individuals exerted twice as much force pulling the rope when they were by themselves as compared to when people were in groups of eight. You may have observed others or yourself putting in less-than-your-best effort when placed in a group project as opposed to individual projects in school. One likely explanation for this is that when you work alone, your individual effort can be evaluated more precisely and consequently, your success is more likely to be rewarded and your failure is more likely to be punished. When working in groups, this may not be true. Individual successes and failures may be lost in combined averages of the group's overall success and/or failure. To some degree, this can be eliminated when an individual is evaluated based on his or her particular contribution to a project instead of the group being graded as a whole.

Individual efforts tend to be reduced in team settings.

Decreasing Your Sense of Individuality

When working/belonging to certain types of group settings, some people may feel like they lose their sense of identity or individuality. **Deindividuation**, involves a loss of individuality that results in reduced fear of evaluation and an increased tendency to engage in destructive behaviors. When you do not feel like you will be individually recognized, it is easy to also feel like your behaviors won't be punished. The way large groups can easily and quickly transform into a rioting mob has sometimes been attributed to deindividuation.

This loss of self-awareness can be achieved in many ways besides simply being a faceless member of a crowd. Anything that makes your individual identity less noticeable, such as uniforms or disguises, can promote deindividuation. Zimbardo (1969) demonstrated this in research in which participants were asked to deliver shocks to someone in another room. Like many of the other social psychology studies we've discussed, the shocks were not real, unbeknownst to the people pushing the shock button. One group of participants was given hoods and large coats to conceal their identities, whereas the other group wore normal clothes with name tags. The anonymous group held down the shock button twice as long as the group who were easily identified. Deindividuation suggests a possible explanation for why individuals interacting in online and anonymous environments may engage in nasty comments and harmful competition (see the comments section of any news website for many examples).

People find it easier to violate social norms when they lose their sense of individuality.

social loafing
the reduction in individual effort that occurs when individuals are placed in group

deindividuation
a decrease in the awareness of one's individuality that results in a reduced fear of evaluation and promotes disinhibited behavior

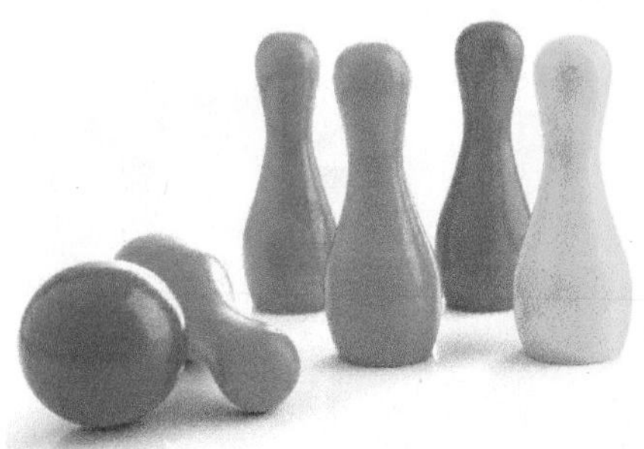

Crowds can inhibit individual help during emergency situations.

Crowd Size and Helping Others

Groups and crowds may also inhibit helping behavior that we would normally provide. In fact, as the size of a crowd increases, the probability of a victim receiving help may actually decrease. This reduction in the likelihood of helping people due to the presence of others has been called the **bystander effect**. One of the most dramatic illustrations of the bystander effect was the murder of Catherine "Kitty" Genovese back in 1964. Kitty Genovese was a young woman on her way home from work when she was suddenly attacked by a stranger. She ran to her apartment building and even made it to the stairwell in her building when her attacker caught up with her. She was stabbed repeatedly and sexually assaulted for approximately 30 minutes before dying in that stairwell. As disturbing as her end was, it wasn't the most shocking aspect of the ordeal. The reason this particular murder became famous was because approximately 30-40 of her neighbors witnessed or overheard this event without helping. Although the exact number of witnesses and their reactions remains a source of debate (Manning, Levine, & Collins, 2007), it is clear that a large number of her neighbors heard her repeated screams for help and did nothing. These seemingly kind and normal people couldn't even be bothered to anonymously call the police. Even though Kitty's case may be one of the famous instances of crowds passively watching someone else get hurt and possibly killed, it is hardly the only occurrence of the bystander effect.

A dangerous situation may be interpreted as safe if other people are acting calm.

Many were quick to suggest that the witnesses of such events are simply apathetic (recall the concept of fundamental attribution error) and to propose that such indifference to the suffering of others is commonplace in modern society, especially in big cities. Despite the intuitive appeal of such simple explanations, researchers remained interested in the possibility of alternative explanations. Although it is easy to sometimes forget, one should keep in mind that the term bystander effect is just a label for non-helpfulness in crowds; it does not explain such behavior. Some important considerations is that emergency situations are sometimes ambiguous ("is that person screaming for help or screaming for another reason?") and we don't want to be embarrassed by providing unwanted help. Imagine the embarrassment you would feel if you rushed into a room to save someone only to discover that their screams came from being tickled too long.

It is also possible that this might be another instance of conformity: we don't see anyone else reacting as if an emergency is occurring, so we don't react as if an emergency is occurring. Recall the opening story of this chapter involving a smoke filled room. In that research, Latané and Darley (1968) discovered that people sitting by themselves would leave the room and report the dangerous smoke. However, when two other people were in the room, the participants typically interpreted the danger as non-dangerous because the other people didn't seem to be reacting as if it was dangerous. Interestingly, two of the participants independently decided that the smoke must actually be truth gas being piped into the room as they completed the questionnaire (strangely, this interpretation didn't seem to disturb them). When alone, such unusual or non-dangerous interpretations did not occur; smoke always meant danger when one is alone.

One effect of being in a group is that it can feel like the responsibility for acting is split among all the group members.

Researchers such as Latané and Nida (1981) have suggested that another factor might be responsible for the bystander effect, such as **diffusion of responsibility**. That is, when we are placed in a crowd, our individual responsibility is reduced and we may assume that someone else will or has already taken action. As a result, we either take no action or we are slower than usual to provide help. Imagine that you are the sole witness of a car accident. Under those circumstances, the responsibility is completely on your shoulders to help because no one else is watching the emergency. However, if you are in a group of 4 people, you may feel like only 25% of the burden for taking action falls upon you. You may also assume that one of those three other witnesses will do something. Unfortunately, those other witnesses may be thinking and feeling the same way, resulting in the group as a whole failing to act or acting too slowly. The larger the group, the less personally responsible each individual member will feel.

bystander effect
the reduction in the likelihood of a victim to receive help as the number of witnesses increases

diffusion of responsibility
the increase in the perception of shared responsibility and the corresponding reduction in the perception of individual responsibility that occurs as the size of a group increases and results in individuals assuming other people will take or have taken action

Darley and Latané (1968) illustrated diffusion of responsibility by placing people in an emergency situation. For this study they brought in various New Yorkers to discuss their personal stories about living in the big city. The researchers told the participants that they would be placed in individual rooms to minimize any embarrassment, but that they could hear each other through an automated microphone and intercom system that allowed one person to speak for two minutes at a time. These participants were told that the researchers would not be listening to these conversations, but the participants would be able to hear each other. When the experiment and the conversations begin, one individual begins to speak with a hesitant sounding voice and reports that exams sometimes scare him because he has a history of seizures. He is terrified that someday stress will trigger one of his seizures and he will die. As the microphone alternates between rooms, other people continue to tell their stories for a few minutes at a time.

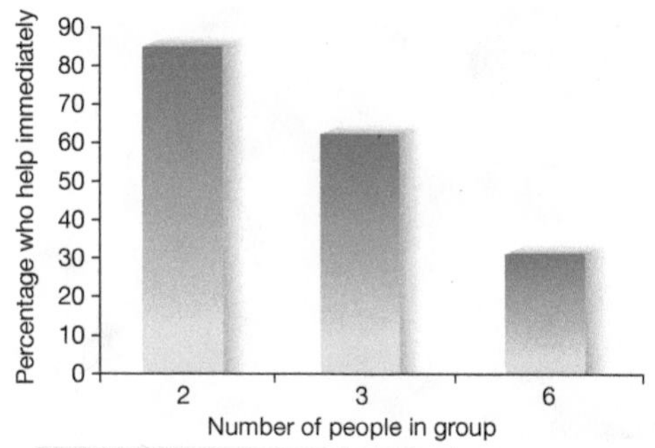

As this data illustrates, the probability of someone taking action decreases as the group gets larger. *(Based on data from Darley and Latané, 1968)*

During everyone's second turn, the nervous man speaks once again. Although he is somewhat calm at first, his voice gets louder and stranger. Then over the intercom the following is heard:

> "I-er-um-I think I-I need-er-if-if could-er-er-somebody er-er-er-er-er-er-er give me a little-er-give me a little help here because-er-I-er-I'm-er-er-h-h-having a-a-a real problem-er-right now and I-er-if somebody could help me out it would-it would-er-er s-s-sure be-sure be good … because-er-there-er-er-a cause I-er-I-uh-I've got a-a one of the-er-sei——er-er-things coming on and-and-and I could really-er-use some help so if somebody would-er-give me a little h-help-uh-er-er-er-er-er c-could somebody-er-er-help-er-uh-uh-uh (choking sounds) …. I'm gonna die-er-er-I'm …gonna die-er-help-er-er-seizure-er- [chokes, then quiet]." (Darley and Latané, 1968, p. 379)

There is no ambiguity here: this person has clearly said he is having a seizure, sounds like he is in serious trouble, and has repeatedly asked for immediate help. The question this experiment is asking concerns whether or not the witnesses will help and how long it will take for them to provide that help. The dying man is actually a confederate pretending to have a seizure, but none of the participants know this fact. Note that conformity cannot influence behavior in this situation, as the witnesses cannot see what others are doing (recall they overhear the man's plea for help while in individual rooms) and cannot even ask others if they are helping (the microphone is stuck on the dying man's room).

As predicted by diffusion of responsibility, the likelihood of helping behavior by the witnesses during this emergency was heavily influenced by the number of witnesses. When people were placed in groups of two (the dying man and a single witness), 100% of participants helped and 85% of those people didn't even wait for the dying man's plea to end. They immediately went to check on the man or to search for someone else who could help. When people were placed in groups of six (the dying man and five witnesses), only 31% helped before the dying man's plea ended. Not only were people in these circumstances slower to help, 38% of the participants never helped at all (the researchers waited a full six minutes before giving up). These people simply sat there alone, waiting for someone else to come along and tell them what was happening. Any inherent personality characteristics or other dispositional factors did not predict who would help. The biggest determinant of behavior was whether or not they were in a small group or large group. The non-helping people certainly didn't appear uncaring about the dying man. In fact, their first response upon the researchers entering the room was typically to ask if the other person was okay. They clearly cared about the other person, but they failed to help for reasons they themselves didn't understand. When asked if the presence of other people influenced their behavior, all the participants reliably denied that the other witnesses had anything to do with their actions (even though the data clearly indicated otherwise).

Sources of influence in our world are often invisible to us.

Using Social Psychology Principles to Engineer a Better World for Everyone

Once again, by understanding the social factors that cause people to behave in undesirable ways, we can also gain insight on the ways to promote desirable behaviors. For example, by understanding that the bystander effect occurs when people feel less individually

By understanding how our social world works, we are left with options for engineering a better future.

responsible, we can promote strategies that limit diffusion of responsibility. If you find yourself in a situation in which you needed help from a group of witnesses, do not call out to everyone for help. Instead, pick an individual in the crowd and say "you there, I need your help" or something similar. By directly singling out that individual (and assigning them the social role of "helper"), you have now placed the responsibility solely on his or her shoulders, thus undoing any diffusion. Thomas Moriarty (1975) demonstrated this by having a woman leave her purse or radio unguarded. A confederate would pretend to be a thief and steal the valuables in front of a crowd of witnesses. Under normal circumstances, the crowd would simply watch the theft occur. However, if the woman simply said "would you watch my things?" to a stranger in the crowd (thus placing the responsibility on a single person), that stranger would reliably intervene and attempt to stop the potentially dangerous thief.

The research in this chapter suggests that people are not inherently bad or good, but rather they react to the social and situational influences around them. Much like when Skinner discovered that blaming a rat was an unproductive method for improving performance (see the beginning of Chapter 7, "Conditioning Principles and Applications"), much of the research in this chapter suggests that it is once again unproductive to simply blame the person. It is a more productive endeavor to study and grasp the psychological principles responsible for behavior. In this way, we can promote desirable social behaviors by engineering the world around us to encourage those behaviors.

9

Cognition and Mental Abilities

*Taken from *Understanding Psychology*, Eleventh Edition by Charles G. Morris and Albert A. Maisto

In his book, *Seeing Voices: A Journey Into the World of the Deaf*, Oliver Sacks (2000) described an 11-year-old boy who entered a school for the deaf without any language skills. He also appeared to have no sense of his past and was unable to plan for the future. He lived only in the present and was able to deal only with concrete things. He simply couldn't think about things in the abstract.

As Sacks suggests, language and thought are intertwined. We find it difficult to imagine one without the other, and we consider both part of what it means to be human. Psychologists use the term **cognition** to refer to all the processes that we use to acquire and apply information. We have already considered the cognitive processes of perception, learning, and memory. In this chapter, we focus on three cognitive processes that we think of as characteristically human: thinking, problem solving, and decision making. We also discuss two mental abilities that psychologists have tried to measure: intelligence and creativity.

ENDURING ISSUES in Cognition and Mental Abilities

The "Enduring Issues" in this chapter are highlighted in four prominent places. We will encounter the diversity–universality theme when we explore the differences and similarities in the way people process information and again when we discuss exceptional abilities. We make two additional references to the enduring issues as we discuss the stability–change of intelligence test scores over time, and again when we explore how measures of intelligence and performance sometimes vary as a function of expectations and situations (*Person–Situation*).

BUILDING BLOCKS OF THOUGHT

What are the three most important building blocks of thought?

When you think about a close friend, you may have in mind complex statements about her, such as "I'd like to talk to her soon" or "I wish I could be more like her." You may also have an image of her—probably her face, but perhaps the sound of her voice as well. Or you may think of your friend by using various concepts or categories such as *woman, kind, strong, dynamic,* and *gentle.* When we think, we make use of all these things—language, images, and concepts—often simultaneously. These are the three most important building blocks of thought.

Language

What steps do we go through to turn a thought into a statement?

Human **language** is a flexible system of symbols that enables us to communicate our ideas, thoughts, and feelings. Joseph, the deaf boy described at the beginning of this chapter, had great difficulty communicating because he knew no languages. Although all animals communicate with each other, language is unique to humans (MacWhinney, 2005).

One way to understand language is to consider its basic structure. Spoken language is based on units of sound called **phonemes**. The sounds of *t, th,* and *k,* for instance, are all phonemes in English. By themselves, phonemes are meaningless and seldom play an important role in helping us to think. But phonemes can be grouped together to form words, prefixes (such as *un-* and *pre-*), and suffixes (such as *-ed* and *-ing*). These meaningful combinations of phonemes are known as **morphemes**—the smallest meaningful units in a language. Unlike phonemes, morphemes play a key role in human thought. They can represent important ideas such as "red" or "calm" or "hot." The suffix *-ed* captures the idea of "in the past" (as in *visited* or *liked*). The prefix *pre-* conveys the idea of "before" or "prior to" (as in *preview* or *predetermined*).

We can combine morphemes to create words that represent quite complex ideas, such as *pre-exist-ing, un-excell-ed, psycho-logy.* In turn, words can be arranged to form sentences

cognition
the processes whereby we acquire and use knowledge

language
a flexible system of communication that uses sounds, rules, gestures, or symbols to convey information

phonemes
the basic sounds that make up any language

morphemes
the smallest meaningful units of speech, such as simple words, prefixes, and suffixes

For example, English has only three words for lightness: white (or light), black (or dark), and gray. Yet English speakers can discriminate hundreds of levels of visual intensity (Baddeley & Attewell, 2009). Moreover, experience and thought actually influence language. For example, the growth of personal computers and the Internet has inspired a vocabulary of its own, such as *gigabyte, CPU, smartphone,* and *blogs.* In short, people create new words when they need them.

Psychologists have not dismissed the Whorf hypothesis altogether, but rather have softened it, recognizing that language, thought, and culture are intertwined (Chiu, Leung, & Kwan, 2007). Experience shapes language; and language, in turn, affects subsequent experience (K. Fiedler, 2008). This realization has caused us to examine our use of language more carefully, as we will see in the next section.

Is Language Male Dominated?

Does language contribute to gender stereotyping?

The English language has traditionally used masculine terms such as *man* and *he* to refer to all people—female as well as male. Several studies suggest that this affects the way English speakers think. Hyde (1984) discovered that the use of "he" or "she" to describe a factory worker affected how children assessed the performance of male and female workers. Children who heard workers described by the masculine pronoun "he" rated female workers poorly; those who heard workers identified by the pronoun "she" judged female workers most positively; and the ratings of children who heard gender-neutral descriptions of workers fell in between those of the two other groups.

More recent research has focused on the unconscious, automatic nature of gender stereotyping and language (Palomares, 2004; Parks & Roberton, 2004). In an experiment requiring men and women to respond rapidly to gender-neutral and gender-specific pronouns, both sexes responded more quickly to stimuli containing traditional gender stereotypes (e.g., nurse/she) than to stimuli containing nontraditional ones (e.g., nurse/he). This occurred even among participants who were explicitly opposed to gender stereotyping (Banaji & Hardin, 1996).

As we have seen, language, cognition, and culture are interrelated in a complex fashion, each contributing to how people communicate, think, and behave. However, as we noted at the beginning of this chapter, non-humans do communicate with one another. The nature of communication and cognition in non-human animals is a topic to which we will now turn.

Quiz Questions

1. Cross-cultural studies indicate that people from different cultures with very different languages nonetheless perceive and are able to think about such things as colors in very similar ways even if their language contains no words for these things. These data ______ Whorf's theory.
   a. neither contradict nor support
   b. support
   c. contradict
   d. validate

2. Which of the following statements is consistent with Whorf's linguistic-relativity hypothesis?
   a. Thoughts are limited to the words in the language that a person speaks.
   b. People create new words when they need them to capture new experiences.
   c. Hopi speakers see great differences between planes and dragonflies even though their language labels the two similarly.
   d. Language has little influence on thought.

3. With regard to Whorf's Linguistic Relativity Hypothesis, psychologist have
   a. found overwhelming support for the hypothesis, confirming its application across a wide variety of cultures.
   b. completely dismissed the hypothesis as false and misleading.
   c. not completely dismissed it, but have softened it, recognizing that language, thought, and culture are intertwined.
   d. found it only applies when comparing very different cultural groups.

NON-HUMAN LANGUAGE AND THOUGHT

Can scientists learn what is on an animal's mind?

The Question of Language

What kind of communication and language do other animals use?

The forms of animal communication vary widely. Honeybees enact an intricate waggle dance that tells their hive mates not only exactly where to find pollen, but also the quality of that pollen (Biesmeijer & Seeley, 2005). Humpback whales perform long, haunting solos ranging from deep bass rumblings to high soprano squeaks. The technical term for such messages is **signs**, general or global statements about the animal's *current* state. But fixed, stereotyped signs don't constitute a language. The distinguishing features of language are *meaningfulness* (or semantics), *displacement* (talking or thinking about the past or the future), and *productivity* (the ability to produce and understand new and unique words and expressions). Using these criteria, as far as we know, no other species has its own language.

For more than two decades, however, Francine Patterson (Bonvillian & Patterson, 1997; F. G. Patterson, 1981) used American Sign Language with a lowland gorilla named Koko. By age 5, Koko had a working vocabulary of 500 signs—similar to a 5-year-old deaf child using sign language, though far lower than a hearing, speaking child's vocabulary of 1,000–5,000 words. In her mid-20s, Koko signed about her own and her companions' happy, sad, or angry emotions. Most interesting, Koko referred to the past and the future (displacement). Using signs *before* and *later, yesterday* and *tomorrow* appropriately, she mourned the death of her pet kitten and expressed a desire to become a mother. More recently, John Pilley has taught a border collie named "Chaser" to understand more than 1,000 words. Chaser also understands simple sentences such as "to ball take Frisbee" and recognizes that command means something different from "to Frisbee take ball." (Pilley, 2013; Pilley & Hinzman, 2013; Pilley & Reid, 2011).

Critics suggest that researchers such as Patterson may be reading meaning and intentions into simple gestures. To reduce the ambiguity of hand signs, other researchers have used computer keyboards to teach and record communications with apes (Rumbaugh, 1977; Rumbaugh & Savage-Rumbaugh, 1978); to document behavior with and without humans on camera; and also to study another ape species, bonobos. Most impressive—and surprising—was a bonobo named Kanzi (Savage-Rumbaugh & Lewin, 1994). Initially in the lab, Kanzi was adopted by an older female who lacked keyboard skills. Some months later, Kanzi, who had been accompanying his "mother" to lessons but who was not receiving formal training, was learning keyboard symbols and spoken English on his own—much as children do.

That non-human great apes can learn signs without intensive training or rewards from human trainers is clear. Whether they can grasp the deep structure of language is less clear. Moreover, at best, apes have reached the linguistic level of a 2- to 2-1/2-year-old child. Critics see this as evidence of severe limitations, whereas others view it as an extraordinary accomplishment.

signs
stereotyped communications about an animal's current state

Professor Sue Savage-Rumbaugh and Kanzi. Savage-Rumbaugh continued Kanzi's naturalistic education through social interaction during walks outside. Kanzi now understands spoken English and more than 200 keyboard symbols. He responds to completely new vocal and keyboard requests and uses the keyboard to make requests, comment on his surroundings, state his intentions, and—sometimes—indicate what he is thinking about.

Animal Cognition

Do some animals think like humans?

As we have seen, language is only one of the building blocks of thought. Without language, can non-humans nonetheless think? The question is particularly difficult to answer because psychologists have only recently developed techniques for learning how other animals use their brains and for identifying the similarities and differences between human and non-human thought.

Numerous studies indicate that other animals have some humanlike cognitive capacities (Herrmann, Hernández-Lloreda, Call, Haer, & Tomasello, 2010; Kluger, 2010; Patton, 2008–2009; Tomasello & Herrmann, 2010).

Parrots, for example, are exceptionally good vocal mimics. But do parrots know what they are saying? According to Irene Pepperberg (2000, 2007), Alex, an African gray parrot, did. Alex could count to 6; identify more than 50 different objects; and classify objects according to color, shape, material, and relative size. Pepperberg contends that rather than demonstrating simple mimicry, the parrot's actions reflected reasoning, choice, and, to some extent, thinking.

Other researchers have taught dolphins to select which of two objects is identical to a sample object—the basis of the concepts *same* and *different* (Herman, Uyeyama, & Pack, 2008)—and to respond accurately to numerical concepts such as *more* and *less* (Jaakkola, Fellner, Erb, Rodriguez, & Guarino, 2005). What's more, rhesus and capuchin monkeys can learn the concept of *numeration,* or the capacity to use numbers, and *serialization,* or the ability to place objects in a specific order based on a concept (Terrace, Son, & Brannon, 2003; A. A. Wright & Katz, 2007). In short, humans are not unique in their ability to form concepts, one of the building blocks of thought.

But do chimps, dolphins, and parrots know what they know? Do non-human animals have a *sense of self?* George Gallup (1985, 1998) noticed that after a few days' exposure, captive chimpanzees began making faces in front of a mirror and used it to examine and groom parts of their bodies they had never seen before. To test whether the animals understood that they were seeing themselves, Gallup anesthetized them and painted a bright red mark above the eyebrow ridge and on the top of one ear. The first time the chimps looked at the mirror after awakening, they reached up and touched the red marks, presumably recognizing themselves.

Since Gallup's initial study, hundreds of researchers have used the mirror test and more recently live video displays with many other animals. So far, only seven non-human species—chimpanzees, bonobos (formerly called "pygmy chimpanzees"), orangutans, dolphins, elephants, magpies, and less frequently, gorillas—have been shown to have self-awareness (Bard, Todd, Bernier, Love, & Leavens, 2006; Boysen & Himes, 1999; Gallup, 1985; Heschl & Burkart, 2006; Prior, Schwarz, & Güntürkün, 2008; Vauclair, 1996). For that matter, even human infants do not demonstrate mirror-recognition until 18 to 24 months of age.

If chimpanzees possess self-awareness, do they understand that others have information, thoughts, and emotions that may differ from their own? Observational studies suggest they do have at least a limited sense of other-awareness. One measure of other-awareness is *deception.* For example, if a chimpanzee discovers a hidden store of food and another chimpanzee happens along, the first may begin idly grooming himself. Presumably, the first chimpanzee recognizes that the second (a) is equally interested in food, and (b) will interpret the grooming behavior as meaning there is nothing interesting nearby. Both in the wild and in captive colonies, chimpanzees frequently practice deception in matters of food, receptive females, and power or dominance.

So far, we have been talking about *what* humans and non-humans think about. As we will see in the next section, cognitive psychologists are equally interested in *how* people use thinking to solve problems and make decisions.

Quiz Questions

1. Among non-humans, great apes (such as bonobos, chimpanzees, and orangutans):
   a. can learn signs without intensive training.
   b. require rewards from human trainers in order to learn signs.
   c. cannot use computer key-boards to communicate with their trainers.
   d. have been shown to reach the linguistic level of a 5 or 6 year-old human child.
2. Research has shown clearly that:
   a. only humans have the ability to form concepts.
   b. some non-human animals can grasp the deep structure of language.
   c. several non-human species have self-awareness.
   d. non-humans can use images to think.
3. When you visit the zoo, you notice a chimpanzee using a mirror to groom itself. This is a sign of:
   a. modeling.
   b. numeration.
   c. displacement.
   d. self-awareness.

Figure 9.2 Figure for Problem 1.

Problem Solving

What are three general aspects of the problem-solving process?

Solve the following problems:

Problem 1 You have three measuring spoons. (See **Figure 9.2.**) One is filled with 8 teaspoons of salt; the other two are empty, but have a capacity of 2 teaspoons each. Divide the salt among the spoons so that only 4 teaspoons of salt remain in the largest spoon.

Most people find this problem easy. Now try solving a more complex problem. (The answers to all of the problems are at the end of this chapter.)

Problem 2 You have three measuring spoons. (See **Figure 9.3.**) One (spoon A) is filled with 8 teaspoons of salt. The second and third spoons are both empty. The second spoon (spoon B) can hold 5 teaspoons, and the third (spoon C) can hold 3 teaspoons. Divide the salt among the spoons so that spoon A and spoon B each have exactly 4 teaspoons of salt and spoon C is empty.

Figure 9.3 Figure for Problem 2.

Most people find this problem much more difficult than the first one. Why? The answer lies in interpretation, strategy, and evaluation. Problem 1 is considered trivial because interpreting what is needed is easy, the strategies for solving it are simple, and the steps required to move closer to a solution can be verified effortlessly. Problem 2, by contrast, requires some thought to interpret what is needed; the strategies for solving it are not immediately apparent; and the steps required to see actual progress toward the goal are harder to evaluate. These three aspects of problem solving—interpretation, strategy, and evaluation—provide a useful framework for investigating this topic.

Interpreting Problems

Why is representing the problem so important to finding an effective solution?

The first step in solving a problem is called **problem representation**, which means interpreting or defining the problem. It is tempting to leap ahead and try to solve a problem just as it is presented, but this impulse often leads to poor solutions. For example, if your business is losing money, you might define the problem as deciphering how to cut costs. But by defining the problem so narrowly, you have ruled out other options. A better representation of this problem would be to figure out ways to boost profits—by cutting costs, by increasing income, or both. Problems that have no single correct solution and that require a flexible, inventive approach call for **divergent thinking**—or thinking that involves generating many different possible answers. In contrast, **convergent thinking** is thinking that narrows its focus in a particular direction, assuming that there is only one solution (or at most a limited number of right solutions).

To see the importance of problem representation, consider the next two problems.

Problem 3 You have four pieces of chain, each of which is made up of three links. (See **Figure 9.4.**) All links are closed at the beginning of the problem. It costs 2 cents to open a link and 3 cents to close a link. How can you join all 12 links together into a single, continuous circle without paying more than 15 cents?

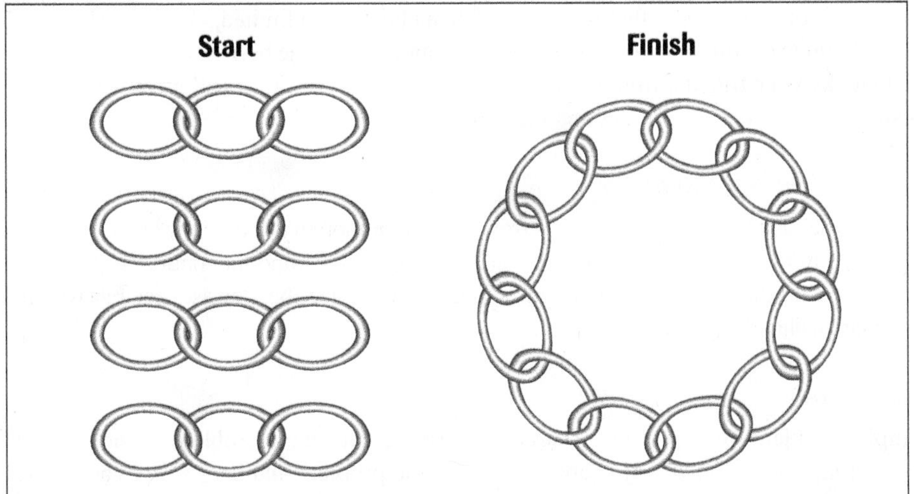

Figure 9.4 Figure for Problem 3.

problem representation
the first step in solving a problem; it involves interpreting or defining the problem

divergent thinking
thinking that meets the criteria of originality, inventiveness, and flexibility

convergent thinking
thinking that is directed toward one correct solution to a problem

Problem 3 is difficult because people assume that the best way to proceed is to open and close the end links on the pieces of chain. As long as they persist with this "conceptual block," they will be unable to solve the problem. If the problem is represented differently, the solution is obvious almost immediately, (See Answer Key at the end of this chapter for solutions.)

If you have successfully interpreted Problem 3, give Problem 4 a try.

Problem 4 A monk wishes to get to a retreat at the top of a mountain. He starts climbing the mountain at sunrise and arrives at the top at sunset of the same day. During the course of his ascent, he travels at various speeds and stops often to rest. He spends the night engaged in meditation. The next day, he starts his descent at sunrise, following the same narrow path that he used to climb the mountain. As before, he travels at various speeds and stops often to rest. Because he takes great care not to trip and fall on the way down, the descent takes as long as the ascent, and he does not arrive at the bottom until sunset. Prove that there is one place on the path that the monk passes at exactly the same time of day on the ascent and on the descent.

This problem is extremely difficult to solve if it is represented verbally or mathematically. It is considerably easier to solve if it is represented visually, as you can see from the explanation that appears at the end of this chapter. Interestingly, Albert Einstein relied heavily on his powers of visualization to understand phenomena that he would later describe by using complex mathematical formulas. This great thinker believed his extraordinary genius resulted in part from his skill in representing problems visually.

Another aspect of successfully representing a problem is deciding to which category the problem belongs. In fact, gaining expertise in any field consists primarily of increasing your ability to represent and categorize problems so that they can be solved quickly and effectively. Star chess players, for example, can readily categorize a game situation by comparing it with various standard situations stored in their long-term memories (Huffman, Matthews, & Gagne, 2001; A. J. Waters, Gobet, & Leyden, 2002). This strategy helps them interpret the current pattern of chess pieces with greater speed and precision than a novice chess player can.

Implementing Strategies and Evaluating Progress

Why are heuristics usually better for solving problems than is trial and error?

Once you have properly interpreted a problem, the next steps are to select a solution strategy and evaluate progress toward your goal. A solution strategy can be anything from simple trial and error, to information retrieval based on similar problems, to a set of step-by-step procedures guaranteed to work (called an algorithm), to rule-of-thumb approaches known as heuristics.

Trial and Error

Trial and error is a strategy that works best when choices are limited. For example, if you have only three or four keys to choose from, trial and error is the best way to find out which one unlocks your friend's front door. In most cases, however, trial and error wastes time because there are many different options to test.

Information Retrieval

One approach is to retrieve information from long-term memory about how such a problem was solved in the past. Information retrieval is an especially important option when a solution is needed quickly. For example, pilots simply memorize the slowest speed at which a particular airplane can fly before it stalls.

Algorithms

Complex problems require complex strategies. An **algorithm** is a problem-solving method that guarantees a solution if it is appropriate for the problem and is properly carried out. For example, to calculate the product of 323 and 546, we multiply the numbers according to the rules of multiplication (the algorithm). If we do it accurately, we are guaranteed to get the right answer.

algorithm
a step-by-step method of problem solving that guarantees a correct solution

Heuristics

Because we don't have algorithms for every kind of problem, we often turn to **heuristics**, or rules of thumb. Heuristics do not guarantee a solution, but they may bring it within reach.

A very simple heuristic is **hill climbing**: We try to move continually closer to our goal without going backward. At each step, we evaluate how far "up the hill" we have come, how far we still have to go, and precisely what the next step should be. On a multiple-choice test, for example, one useful hill-climbing strategy is first to eliminate the alternatives that are obviously incorrect.

Another problem-solving heuristic is to create **subgoals,** which involves breaking a problem into smaller, more manageable pieces that are easier to solve individually than the problem as a whole. Consider the problem of the Hobbits and the Orcs.

Problem 5 Three Hobbits and three Orcs are on the bank of a river. They all want to get to the other side, but their boat will carry only two creatures at a time. Moreover, if at any time the Orcs outnumber the Hobbits, the Orcs will attack the Hobbits. How can all the creatures get across the river without danger to the Hobbits?

You can find the solution to this problem by thinking of it in terms of a series of subgoals. What has to be done to get just one or two creatures across the river safely, temporarily leaving aside the main goal of getting everyone across? We could first send two of the Orcs across and have one of them return. That gets one Orc across the river. Now we can think about the next trip. It's clear that we can't then send a single Hobbit across with an Orc, because the Hobbit would be outnumbered as soon as the boat landed. Therefore, we have to send either two Hobbits or two Orcs. By working on the problem in this fashion—concentrating on subgoals—we can eventually get everyone across.

Once you have solved Problem 5, try Problem 6, which is considerably more difficult. (The answers to both problems are at the end of the chapter.)

Problem 6 This problem is identical to Problem 5, except that there are five Hobbits and five Orcs, and the boat can carry only three creatures at a time.

Subgoals are often helpful in solving a variety of everyday problems. For example, a student whose goal is to write a term paper might set subgoals by breaking the project into a series of separate tasks: choosing a topic, doing research, writing the first draft, editing, and so on. Even the subgoals can sometimes be broken down into separate tasks: Writing the first draft might break down into the subgoals of writing the introduction, describing the position to be taken, supporting the position with evidence, drawing conclusions, writing a summary, and writing a bibliography. Subgoals make problem solving more manageable because they free us from the burden of having to "get to the other side of the river" all at once.

One of the most frequently used heuristics, called **means-end analysis**, combines hill climbing and subgoals. Like hill climbing, means-end analysis involves analyzing the difference between the current situation and the desired end, and then doing something to reduce that difference. But in contrast to hill climbing—which does not permit detours away from the final goal in order to solve the problem—means-end analysis takes into account the entire problem situation. It formulates subgoals in such a way as to allow us temporarily to take a step that appears to be backward in order to reach our goal in the end. One example is the pitcher's strategy in a baseball game when confronted with the best batter in the league. The pitcher might opt to walk this batter intentionally even though doing so moves away from the major subgoal of keeping runners off base. Intentional walking might enable the pitcher to keep a run from scoring and so contribute to the ultimate goal of winning the game. This flexibility in thinking is a major benefit of means-end analysis.

But means-end analysis also poses the danger of straying so far from the end goal that the goal disappears altogether. One way of avoiding this situation is to use the heuristic of **working backward**. Start at the end goal and work backwards through the steps of the solution.

heuristics
rules of thumb that help in simplifying and solving problems, although they do not guarantee a correct solution

hill climbing
a heuristic, problem-solving strategy in which each step moves you progressively closer to the final goal

subgoals
intermediate, more manageable goals used in one heuristic strategy to make it easier to reach the final goal

means-end analysis
a heuristic strategy that aims to reduce the discrepancy between the current situation and the desired goal at a number of intermediate points

working backward
a heuristic strategy in which one works backward from the desired goal to the given conditions

Obstacles to Solving Problems

How can a "mental set" both help and hinder problem solving?

Many factors can either help or hinder problem solving. One factor is a person's level of motivation, or emotional arousal. Generally, we must generate a certain surge of excitement to motivate ourselves to solve a problem, yet too much arousal can hamper our ability to find a solution. (See Chapter 10, "Motivation and Emotion.")

Another factor that can either help or hinder problem solving is **mental set**—our tendency to perceive and to approach problems in certain ways. A mental set can be helpful if we have learned operations that can legitimately be applied to the present situation. In fact, much of our formal education involves learning useful mental sets. But sets can also create obstacles, especially when a novel approach is needed. The most successful problem solvers can choose from many different mental sets and can also judge when to change sets or when to abandon them entirely.

One type of mental set that can seriously hinder problem solving is called **functional fixedness**. Consider **Figure 9.5.** Do you see a way to mount the candle on the wall? If not, you are probably stymied by functional fixedness. (The solution to this problem appears at the end of the chapter.) The more you use an object in only one way, the harder it is to see new uses for it and to realize that an object can be used for an entirely different purpose. See "Applying Psychology: Becoming a More Skillful Problem Solver," for techniques that will improve your problem-solving skills.

Because creative problem solving requires generating original ideas, deliberate strategies don't always help. Solutions to many problems rely on insight, often a seemingly

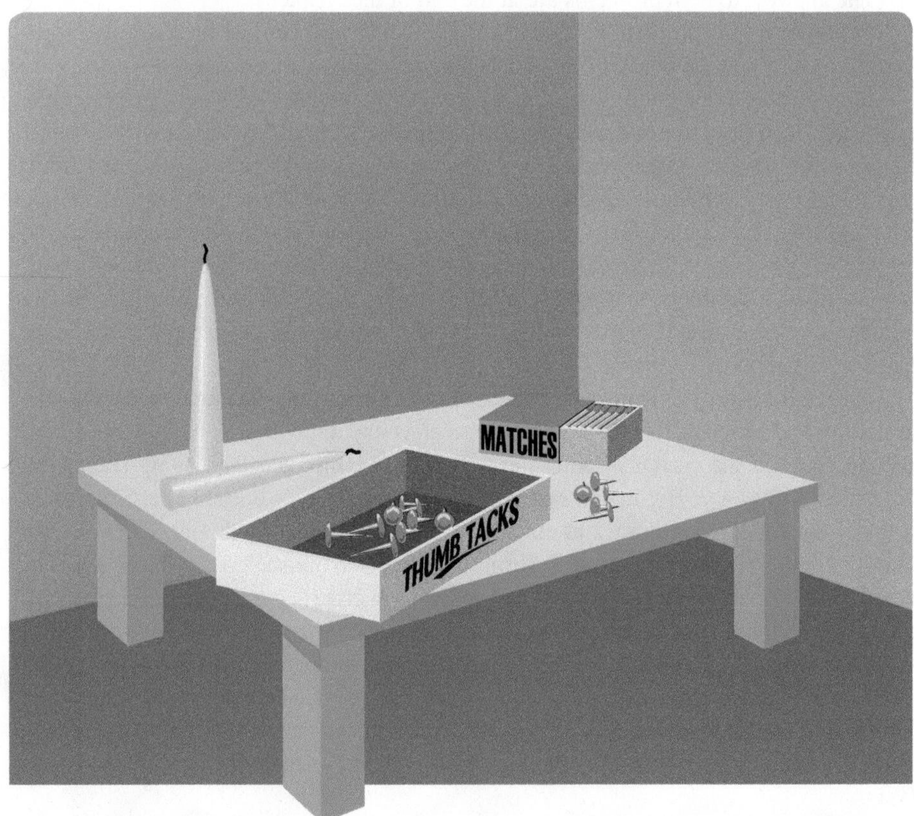

Figure 9.5 To test the effects of functional fixedness, participants might be given the items shown on the table and asked to mount a candle on the wall. See Figure 9.12 for a solution.

mental set
the tendency to perceive and to approach problems in certain ways

functional fixedness
the tendency to perceive only a limited number of uses for an object, thus interfering with the process of problem solving

Applying Psychology

Becoming a More Skillful Problem Solver

Even the best problem solvers occasionally get stumped, but you can do some things that will help you find a solution. These tactics encourage you to discard unproductive approaches and find strategies that are more effective.

1. **Eliminate poor choices.** When we are surer of what won't work than what will, the *tactic of elimination* can be very helpful. After listing all the possible solutions you can think of, discard all the solutions that seem to lead in the wrong direction. Now, examine the list more closely. Some solutions that seem to be ineffective may turn out to be good on closer examination.
2. **Visualize a solution.** If you are stumped by a problem, try using visual images. For example, in the Hobbit and Orc problems, draw a picture of the river, and show the Hobbits and Orcs at each stage of the solution as they are ferried across. Drawing a diagram might help you grasp what a problem calls for, but you also can visualize mentally.
3. **Develop expertise.** We get stumped on problems because we lack the knowledge to find a quick solution. Experts not only know more about a particular subject but also organize their information in larger "chunks" that are extensively interconnected, much like a cross-referencing system in a library.
4. **Think flexibly.** Striving to be more flexible and creative is an excellent tactic for becoming a better problem solver. This will help you avoid *functional fixedness* or prevent a *mental set* from standing in the way of solving a problem.

arbitrary flash "out of the blue." Psychologists have only recently begun to investigate such spontaneous problem-solving processes as insight and intuition, but research indicates that such "mental breakthroughs" are likely to occur only when we widen our scope of attention from a few obvious but incorrect alternatives to more diverse possible solutions (B. Bower, 2008). This conclusion is supported by neuroimaging, which reveals that insight is generally preceded by periods of increased electrical activity in the frontal regions of the brain involved in *suppressing* unwanted thoughts (Kounios et al., 2008; Qiu, Li, Jou, Wu, & Zhang, 2008).

The value of looking for new ways to represent a difficult problem cannot be overstressed. Be open to potential solutions that at first seem unproductive. The solution may turn out to be more effective, or it may suggest related solutions that will work. This is the rationale behind the technique called **brainstorming**: When solving a problem, generate a lot of ideas before you review and evaluate them.

Thinking Critically About . . .

Solving Problems

Think for a moment of the last time you were confronted with a difficult problem.

1. What types of thinking or reasoning did you use to deal with that problem?
2. Having read this portion of the chapter, would you respond differently if you were faced with a similar problem? If so, what would you do differently?
3. You are headed for Mount Rushmore, and you can see it from a distance. You have no map. What is the best problem-solving strategy you can use to get there, and why?

brainstorming
a problem-solving strategy in which an individual or a group produces numerous ideas and evaluates them only after all ideas have been collected

Quiz Questions

1. The first step in solving a problem effectively is to:
   a. conduct a means-end analysis.
   b. eliminate functional fixedness.
   c. create a representation of the problem.
   d. decide on using either an algorithm or heuristic strategy.
2. An algorithm is a:
   a. problem- solving method which, if appropriate, guarantees a solution.
   b. "rule of thumb" that helps to simplify a problem.
   c. classification which permits generalization and discrimination among objects.
   d. noncompensatory decision making model.
3. In taking a multiple choice test, you first read the question and try to develop an answer. Then you check to see if your answer is one of the choices. If it's not, you try to eliminate any obviously wrong alternatives, and finally try to find the best answer from among those that remain. This problem solving strategy is an example of:
   a. an algorithm.
   b. a heuristic.
   c. top-down processing.
   d. functional fixedness.
4. Failing to see that a wrench can also be used to hammer a nail is an example of:
   a. reproductive thinking.
   b. learned helplessness.
   c. positive transfer.
   d. functional fixedness.
5. Mental sets can present obstacles to problem solving because:
   a. the best solution to a particular problem may call for a novel approach.
   b. they rely on hill-climbing.
   c. they rarely work with real-life problems.
   d. they take too much time.

DECISION MAKING

How does decision making differ from problem solving?

Decision making is a special kind of problem solving in which we already know all the possible solutions or choices. The task is not to come up with new solutions, but rather to identify the best available one. This process might sound fairly simple, but sometimes we have to juggle a large and complex set of criteria as well as many possible options. For example, suppose that you are looking for an apartment among hundreds available. A reasonable rent is important to you, but so are good neighbors, a good location, a low noise level, and cleanliness. If you find an inexpensive, noisy apartment with undesirable neighbors, should you take it? Is it a better choice than a more expensive, less noisy apartment in a better location? How can you make the best choice?

Compensatory Decision Making

How would you go about making a truly logical decision?

compensatory model
a rational decision-making model in which choices are systematically evaluated on various criteria

The logical way to make a decision is to rate each of the available choices on all the criteria you are using, arriving at some overall measure of the extent to which each choice matches your criteria. For each choice, the attractive features can offset or compensate for the unattractive features. This approach to decision making is therefore called a **compensatory model**.

Table 9.1 Compensatory Decision Table for Purchase of a New Car				
	Price (weight = 4)	Gas mileage (weight = 8)	Service record (weight = 10)	Weighted Total
Car 1	5 (20)	2 (16)	1 (10)	(46)
Car 2	1 (4)	4 (32)	4 (40)	(76)
Ratings: 5 = excellent; 1 = poor				

Table 9.1 illustrates one of the most useful compensatory models applied to a car-buying decision. The buyer's three criteria are weighted in terms of importance: price (not weighted heavily), gas mileage, and service record (both weighted more heavily). Next, each car is rated from 1 (poor) to 5 (excellent) on each of the criteria. Car 1 has an excellent price (5) but relatively poor gas mileage (2) and service record (1); and Car 2 has a less desirable price but fairly good mileage and service record. Each rating is then multiplied by the weight for that criterion (e.g., for Car 1, the price rating of 5 is multiplied by the weight of 4, and the result is put in parentheses next to the rating). Finally, the ratings in parentheses are totaled for each car. Clearly, Car 2 is the better choice: It is more expensive, but that disadvantage is offset by its better mileage and service record and these two criteria are more important than price to this particular buyer.

Although most people would agree that using such a table is a good way to decide which car to buy, at times people will abandon the compensatory decision-making process in the face of more vivid anecdotal information. For example, if a friend had previously bought Car 2 and found it to be a lemon, many people will choose Car 1 despite Car 2's well-thought-out advantages. Moreover, as we will see in the next section, it is often not possible or desirable to rate every choice on all criteria. In such situations people typically use heuristics that have worked well in the past to simplify decision making, even though they may lead to less-than-optimal decision making.

Decision-Making Heuristics

How can heuristic approaches lead us to make bad decisions?

Research has identified a number of common heuristics that people use to make decisions. We use the **representativeness** heuristic whenever we make a decision on the basis of certain information that matches our model of the typical member of a category.

Another common heuristic is **availability**. In the absence of full and accurate information, we often base decisions on whatever information is most readily available, even though this information may not be accurate or complete.

Yet another heuristic, closely related to availability, is **confirmation bias**—the tendency to notice and remember evidence that supports our beliefs and to ignore evidence that contradicts them (Bower, 2013). For example, individuals who believe that AIDS is something that happens to "other people" (homosexual men and intravenous drug users, not middle-class heterosexuals) are more likely to remember articles about rates of HIV infection in these groups or in third-world countries than articles about AIDS cases among people like themselves (Fischhoff & Downs, 1997). Convinced that HIV is not something that they personally need to worry about, they ignore evidence to the contrary.

A related phenomenon is our tendency to see *connections* or *patterns of cause and effect* where none exist. For example, many parents strongly believe that sugar can cause hyperactivity in children and that arthritis pain is related to weather—despite research evidence to the contrary. The list of commonsense beliefs that persist in the face of contrary evidence is long (Redelmeier & Tversky, 2004).

representativeness
a heuristic by which a new situation is judged on the basis of its resemblance to a stereotypical model

Framing

Does the way information is presented affect decisions?

Numerous studies have shown that subtle changes in the way information is presented can dramatically affect the final decision. A classic study (McNeil, Pauker, Sox, & Tversky, 1982) illustrates how **framing** can influence a medical decision. In this study, experimental participants were asked to choose between surgery and radiation therapy to treat lung cancer. However, the framing of the information they were provided was manipulated. In the *survival frame,* participants were given the statistical outcomes of both procedures in the form of survival statistics, thus emphasizing the 1- and 5-year survival rates after treatment. In the *mortality frame,* the participants were given the same information, presented (or framed) according to death rates after 1 year and after 5 years. Although the actual number of deaths and survivors associated with each procedure was identical in both the survival and mortality frames, the percentage of participants who chose one procedure over another varied dramatically *depending on how the information was framed.* Probably most surprising was that this framing effect was found even when 424 experienced radiologists served as the research participants!

Explaining Our Decisions

How do we explain to ourselves the decisions we make?

Hindsight

Whether a choice is exceptionally good, extraordinarily foolish, or somewhere in between, most people think about their decisions after the fact. The term **hindsight bias** refers to the tendency to view outcomes as inevitable and predictable after we know the outcome, and to believe that we could have predicted what happened, or perhaps that we did. For example, physicians remember being more confident about their diagnoses when they learn that they were correct than they were at the time of the actual diagnoses (Roese & Vohs, 2012). However, this can lead to overconfidence, which in turn can lead to poor decision making in the future (Arkes, 2013).

"If Only"

At times, everyone imagines alternatives to reality and mentally plays out the consequences. Psychologists refer to such thoughts about things that never happened as **counterfactual thinking**—in which thoughts are counter to the facts. Counterfactual thinking often takes

availability
a heuristic by which a judgment or decision is based on information that is most easily retrieved from memory

confirmation bias
the tendency to look for evidence in support of a belief and to ignore evidence that would disprove a belief

framing
the perspective from which we interpret information before making a decision

hindsight bias
the tendency to see outcomes as inevitable and predictable after we know the outcome

counterfactual thinking
thinking about alternative realities and things that never happened

Quiz Questions

1. Julio's girlfriend gets a speeding ticket, and he blames himself, saying, "If only I hadn't let her borrow my car." His thinking is an example of ________.
   a. compensatory decision making.
   b. counterfactual thinking.
   c. confirmation bias.
   d. framing.
2. When deciding where to go on vacation, you decide you want a place where you can relax, a place that is warm, and a place that you can reach inexpensively. You rate each of the available choices on those criteria to determine which choice is the best match. What kind of decision-making model are you using?
   a. Compensatory.
   b. Non-compensatory.
   c. Framing.
   d. The availability heuristic.

3. You are driving down the highway at the posted speed limit. After a while you mention to your passenger, "It sure looks like everyone is either going slower or faster than the speed limit. Hardly anyone seems to be going the same speed as I am." In fact, most of the cars on the highway are also traveling at the speed limit. Your erroneous conclusion is most likely due to:
   a. hindsight bias.
   b. mental set.
   c. the availability heuristic.
   d. framing.
4. People who believe that global warming is not happening are more likely to read and remember articles that cast doubt on global warming. This is an example of:
   a. framing.
   b. the availability heuristic.
   c. the representativeness heuristic.
   d. confirmation bias.

the form of "If only" constructions, in which we mentally revise the events or actions that led to a particular outcome: "If only I had studied harder"; "If only I had said no"; "If only I had driven straight home." It is tempting to think that such imaginary, after-the-fact thinking, is of no value. However, research shows that under some circumstances counterfactual thinking can play a constructive role helping one to regulate behavior, learn from mistakes, and improve future performance (Epstude & Roese, 2008).

MULTITASKING

is multitasking efficient?

With the advent of the digital age, multitasking has become a way of life. We listen to iPods while jogging, program our TiVo while watching a movie, e-mail and surf the Web simultaneously, and follow the directions of a GPS while driving and talking to a passenger in a car. Fortunately, our brains appear reasonably well equipped for at least some multitasking. The prefrontal cortex governs goal-directed behavior and suppresses impulses, also enables us to mentally toggle between separate tasks with relative ease (Jäncke, Brunner, & Esslen, 2008; Modirrousta & Fellows, 2008).

Is multitasking really efficient? Research indicates that if the tasks are dissimilar and the person is an experienced multitasker and is intelligent, multitasking can be effective up to a point. But in general, research has shown that multitasking often slows down thinking, decreases accuracy, and in some cases increases stress (Bühner, König, Pick, & Krumm, 2006; Clay, 2009; Kinney, 2008; Mark, Gudith & Klocke, 2008; J. S. Rubinstein, Meyer, & Evans, 2001). Moreover, despite a commonly held belief that young people are more adept at multitasking than older adults, research that compared 18- to 21-year-olds to 35- to 39-year-olds found the negative effects of multitasking were generally more pronounced in the younger group (Westwell, 2007).

Perhaps nowhere is the impact of multitasking more important than when driving a car (Strayer & Drews, 2007). It makes no difference if the conversations are hands-free or hands-on (Pogue, 2013). The mental challenge of carrying on a conversation has been shown to cause drivers to miss seeing much of what is around them (Strayer et al., 2013). For example, while talking on a "hands-free" cell phone, braking time is slowed and attention to events in the peripheral visual field is reduced. Even when the participants in one study were specifically instructed to give more attention to driving than the extraneous task, or were well practiced at multitasking, driving performance was adversely affected by multitasking (J. Levy & Pashler, 2008; J. Levy, Pashler, & Boer, 2006).

Texting while driving is even worse. One British study using 17- to 24-year-old participants found that texting while driving reduced braking time by 35%, which was much worse than the effect of alcohol or marijuana. Steering control while texting was reduced 91%, compared to a 35% reduction under the influence of marijuana (RAC Foundation, 2008). Once again it makes no difference if you are texting by hand or hands-free by voice. Mental distraction is the same in both cases and response times increase equally (Yager, 2013). Research such as this has prompted Professor David Meyer, a noted researcher in the area of multitasking, to conclude that "If you're driving while cell-phoning, then your performance is going to be as poor as if you were legally drunk" (Hamilton, 2008).

Quiz Questions

1. Which of the following is consistent with the results of research on multitasking?
   - **a.** Talking on a hands-free phone is safer than talking on a hand-held phone.
   - **b.** In one research study, the negative effects of multitask-ing were more pronounced among 35- to 39-year-olds compared to 18- to 21-year-olds.
   - **c.** Multitasking often slows down thinking, decreases accuracy, and in some cases increases stress.
   - **d.** Texting while driving is safer than driving under the influence of alcohol.
2. Which of the following statements about multitasking is true?
   - **a.** While drivers are talking on a "hands-free" cell phone, braking time is slowed and awareness of events in the peripheral visual field is reduced.
   - **b.** Research shows that multitasking has no effect on driving performance if the drivers are experienced and proficient at multitasking.
   - **c.** Drivers who are told to pay more attention to driving than to extraneous tasks drive just as safely as drivers who are not multitasking.
   - **d.** Our brains are poorly equipped for multitasking.

INTELLIGENCE AND MENTAL ABILITIES

What types of questions are used to measure intelligence?

In many societies, one of the nicest things you can say is "You're smart"; and one of the most insulting is "You're stupid." Intelligence is so basic to our view of human nature that any characterization of a person that neglects to mention that person's intelligence is likely to be considered incomplete. Although psychologists have studied intelligence almost since psychology emerged as a science, they still struggle to understand this complex and elusive concept. In the next few sections, you may come to appreciate the difficulty of their task. Toward that end, we begin by asking you some questions intended to measure intelligence:

1. Describe the difference between *laziness* and *idleness*.
2. Which direction would you have to face so that your right ear would be facing north?
3. What does *obliterate* mean?
4. In what way are an hour and a week alike?

5. Choose the lettered block that best completes the pattern in the following figure.

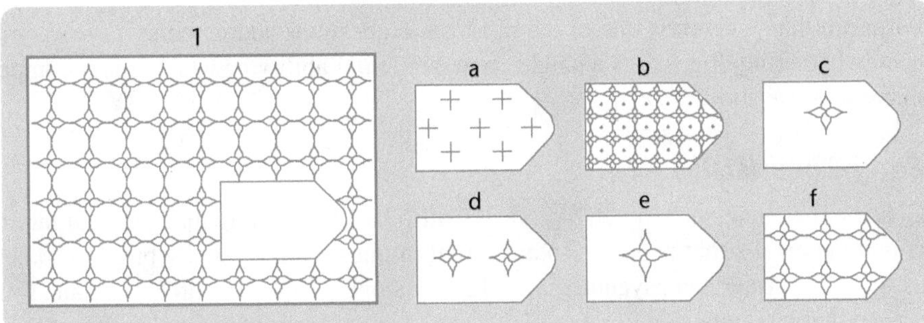

6. If three pencils cost 25 cents, how many pencils can you buy for 75 cents?
7. Select the lettered pair that best expresses a relationship similar to that expressed in the original pair:

   Crutch: Locomotion:

   a. paddle: canoe

   b. hero: worship

   c. horse: carriage

   d. spectacles: vision

   e. statement: contention
8. Decide how the first two items in the following figure are related to each other. Then find the one item at the right that goes with the third item in the same way that the second item goes with the first.

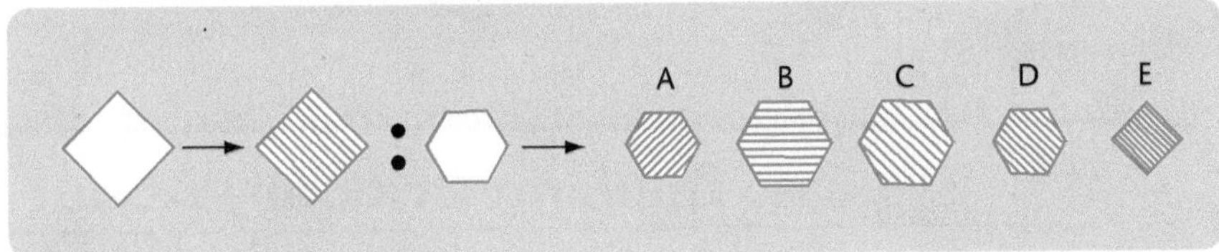

9. For each item in the following figure, decide whether it can be completely covered by using some or all of the given pieces without overlapping any.

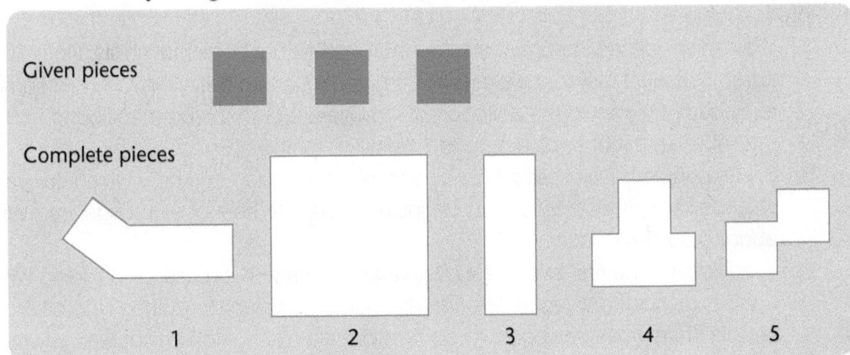

These questions were taken from various tests of **intelligence**, or general mental ability. (The answers appear at the end of the chapter.) We will discuss intelligence tests later in this chapter. But first, let's consider some historical and contemporary theories of intelligence.

intelligence
a general term referring to the ability or abilities involved in learning and adaptive behavior

Theories of Intelligence

What are some of the major theories of intelligence?

For more than a century, one of the most basic questions addressed by psychologists has been whether intelligence is a single, general mental ability or whether it is composed of many separate abilities.

Early Theorists

Charles Spearman, an early 20th-century British psychologist, maintained that intelligence is quite general—that people who are bright in one area are usually bright in other areas as well. The American psychologist L. L. Thurstone disagreed with Spearman. Thurstone argued that intelligence is composed of seven distinct kinds of mental abilities (Thurstone, 1938): *spatial ability, memory, perceptual speed, word fluency, numerical ability, reasoning, and verbal meaning.* Unlike Spearman, Thurstone believed that these abilities are relatively independent of one another. Thus, a person with exceptional spatial ability (the ability to perceive distance, recognize shapes, and so on) might lack word fluency.

Contemporary Theorists

Contemporary psychologists have considerably broadened the concept of intelligence and how it can best be measured. For example, Robert Sternberg (2009) has proposed a triachic theory of intelligence, which proposes that intelligence involves mental skills (analytical intelligence), insight and creative adaptability (creative intelligence), and environmental responsiveness (practical intelligence).

Another contemporary theory of intelligence is the **theory of multiple intelligences** advanced by Howard Gardner and his associates at Harvard (J.-Q. Chen, Moran, & Gardner, 2009). Gardner, like Thurstone, believes that intelligence is made up of several distinct abilities, each of which is relatively independent of the others.

Thinking Critically About . . .

Multiple Intelligences

Gardner's theory clearly includes abilities not normally included under the heading of intelligence.

1. We earlier defined intelligence as general intellectual or mental ability. Do you agree that all of Gardner's facets of intelligence fit that definition? Should some be excluded? Or should the definition of intelligence perhaps be modified to include them? What might such a modified definition look like?
2. Some people have excellent "color sense"—they seem to know which colors go well together. Should this ability be included as one aspect of intelligence? What about rhyming ability?
3. In answering the first two questions, what criteria did you use for deciding which abilities to include as aspects of intelligence and which to exclude? Do other people share your viewpoint, or do their criteria differ? How might you go about deciding which viewpoints have most merit?

theory of multiple intelligences
Howard Gardner's theory that there is not one intelligence, but rather many intelligences, each of which is relatively independent of the others

emotional intelligence
according to Goleman, a form of intelligence that refers to how effectively people perceive and understand their own emotions and the emotions of others, and can regulate and manage their emotional behavior

Finally, Daniel Goleman (1997) has proposed a theory of **emotional intelligence**, which refers to how effectively people perceive and understand their own emotions and the emotions of others and can manage their emotional behavior. Five traits are generally recognized as contributing to emotional intelligence.

Summary Table Comparing Gardner's, Sternberg's, and Goleman's Theories of Intelligence

Gardner's multiple intelligences	Sternberg's triarchic intelligence	Goleman's emotional intelligence
Logical–mathematical	Analytical	
Linguistic		
Spatial	Creative	
Musical		
Bodily-kinesthetic		
Interpersonal	Practical	Recognizing emotions in others and managing relationships
Intrapersonal		Knowing yourself and motivating yourself with emotions
Naturalistic		

- ***Knowing one's own emotions.*** The ability to monitor and recognize our own feelings. This is of central importance to self-awareness and all other dimensions of emotional intelligence.
- ***Managing one's emotions.*** The ability to control impulses, to cope effectively with sadness, depression, and minor setbacks, as well as to control how long emotions last.
- ***Using emotions to motivate oneself.*** The capacity to marshal emotions toward achieving personal goals.
- ***Recognizing the emotions of other people.*** The ability to read subtle, nonverbal cues that reveal what other people really want and need.
- ***Managing relationships.*** The ability to accurately acknowledge and display one's own emotions, as well as being sensitive to the emotions of others.

The "**Summary Table**" reviews the contemporary theories described here. These theories shape the content of intelligence tests and other measures that evaluate the abilities of millions of people. We consider these next.

Intelligence Tests

What kinds of intelligence tests are in use today?

The Stanford–Binet Intelligence Scale

The first test developed to measure intelligence was designed by two Frenchmen, Alfred Binet and Théodore Simon. The test, first used in Paris in 1905, was designed to identify children who might have difficulty in school.

The first *Binet–Simon Scale* consisted of 30 tests arranged in order of increasing difficulty. With each child, the examiner started with the easiest tests and worked down the list until the child could no longer answer questions. A well-known adaptation of the Binet–Simon Scale, the *Stanford–Binet Intelligence Scale,* was prepared at Stanford University by L. M. Terman, first published in 1916 and updated repeatedly since then. The current Stanford–Binet Intelligence Scale is designed to measure four virtually universal abilities related to traditional views of intelligence: *verbal reasoning, abstract/visual reasoning, quantitative reasoning,* and *short-term memory.* The Stanford–Binet is best suited for children, adolescents, and very young adults. Questions 1 and 2 on page 000 were drawn from an early version of the Stanford–Binet.

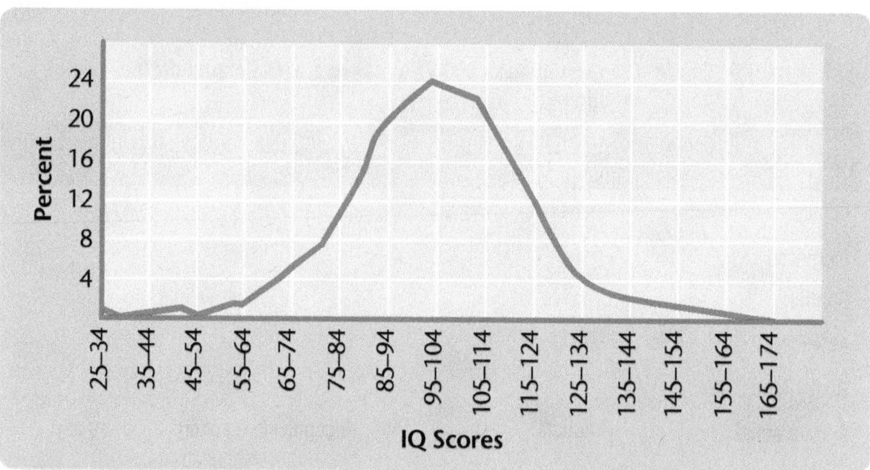

Figure 9.6 The Approximate Distribution of IQ Scores in the Population. Note that the greatest percentage of scores fall around 100. Very low percentages of people score at the two extremes of the curve.

Terman also introduced the now famous term **intelligence quotient (IQ)** to establish a numerical value of intelligence, setting the score of 100 for a person of average intelligence. **Figure 9.6** shows an approximate distribution of IQ scores in the population.

The Wechsler Intelligence Scales

The most commonly used individual test of intelligence for adults is the **Wechsler Adult Intelligence Scale—Fourth Edition (WAIS-IV)**, originally developed in the late 1930s by psychologist David Wechsler. The Stanford–Binet emphasizes verbal skills, but Wechsler believed adult intelligence consists more of the ability to handle life situations than to solve verbal and abstract problems.

The WAIS-IV assesses verbal comprehension, perceptual reasoning, working memory, and processing speed. Scores on all four of those indices can be combined to give a *Full-Scale IQ*. Scores on just the first two indices can be combined to give a *General Ability Index*. Questions 3, 4, and 9 on page 000 resemble questions on the WAIS-IV. Wechsler also developed a similar intelligence test for use with school-age children. Like the WAIS-IV, the **Wechsler Intelligence Scale for Children—Fourth Edition (WISC-IV)** yields a Full-Scale IQ score as well as scores for verbal comprehension, perceptual reasoning, working memory, and processing speed.

Group Tests

With the Stanford–Binet, the WAIS-IV, and the WISC-IV, an examiner takes a single person to an isolated room, spreads the materials on a table, and spends from 60 to 90 minutes administering the test. The examiner may then take another hour or so to score the test according to detailed instructions in a manual. This is a time-consuming, costly operation. Moreover, under some circumstances the examiner's behavior can influence the score. For these reasons, test makers have devised **group tests**, which a single examiner can administer to many people at once. Instead of sitting across the table from a person who asks you questions, you receive a test booklet that contains questions for you to answer in writing within a certain amount of time.

Group tests have some distinct advantages over individualized tests. They eliminate bias on the part of the examiner, answer sheets can be scored quickly and objectively, and it is possible to collect data from large numbers of test takers. But group tests also have

intelligence quotient (IQ)
a numerical value given to intelligence that is determined from the scores on an intelligence test on the basis of a score of 100 for average intelligence

Wechsler Adult Intelligence Scale—Fourth Edition (WAIS-IV)
an individual intelligence test developed especially for adults

Wechsler Intelligence Scale for Children—Fourth Edition (WISC-IV)
an individual intelligence test developed especially for school-age children

group tests
written intelligence tests administered by one examiner to many people at one time

some distinct disadvantages. The examiner is less likely to notice whether a person is tired, ill, or confused by the directions. People who are not used to being tested tend to do less well on group tests than on individual tests. Questions 5 through 9 on page 000 are drawn from group tests.

Performance and Culture-Fair Tests

To perform well on the intelligence tests that we have discussed, people must be proficient in the language in which the test is given. How, then, can we test non-native English speakers in English-speaking countries? Psychologists have designed two general forms of tests for such situations: performance tests and culture-fair tests.

Performance tests consist of problems that minimize or eliminate the use of words. One of the earliest performance tests, the *Seguin Form Board,* is essentially a puzzle. The examiner removes specifically designed cutouts, stacks them in a predetermined order, and asks the person to replace them as quickly as possible. A more recent performance test, the *Porteus Maze,* consists of a series of increasingly difficult printed mazes. People trace their way through the maze without lifting the pencil from the paper. Such tests require the test taker to pay close attention to a task for an extended period and continuously to plan ahead in order to make the correct choices.

Culture-fair tests, like performance tests, minimize or eliminate the use of language. But they also try to downplay skills and values—such as the need for speed—that vary from culture to culture. In the *Goodenough–Harris Drawing Test,* for example, people are asked to draw the best picture of a person that they can. Drawings are scored for proportions, correct and complete representation of the parts of the body, detail in clothing, and so on. An example of a culture-fair item from the *Progressive Matrices* is Question 5 on page 267. This test consists of 60 designs, each with a missing part. The person is given six to eight possible choices to replace the part.

Biological Measures of Intelligence

Thus far we have considered psychological measures of intelligence. However, numerous efforts have been made to assess intelligence using biological measures (Deary, Penke, & Johnson, 2010; Tang et al., 2010). Beginning early in the 20th century, psychologists attempted to correlate brain size with intelligence. The correlations were very weak but always positive, suggesting a slight relation between the two. More recently, investigators have compared the sizes and metabolic functioning of such brain structures as the cerebellum and hippocampus, revealing small but significant differences among the brains of people with different forms of intellectual disability (Lawrence, Lott, & Haier, 2005). Other researchers have found modest relationships between intelligence and the electrical response of brain cells to stimulation (Stelmack, Knott, & Beauchamp, 2003).

To date, no known biological measure of intelligence approaches the accuracy of psychological tests, but findings such as these suggest that measures of intelligence may someday involve a biological component.

What Makes a Good Test?

What are some important characteristics of a good test?

How can we tell whether intelligence tests will produce consistent results no matter when they are given? And how can we tell whether they really measure what they claim to measure? Psychologists address these questions by referring to a test's *reliability* and *validity.* Issues of reliability and validity apply equally to all psychological tests, not just to tests of mental abilities.

performance tests
intelligence tests that minimize the use of language

culture-fair tests
intelligence tests designed to eliminate cultural bias by minimizing skills and values that vary from one culture to another

Reliability

By **reliability**, psychologists mean the dependability and consistency of the scores that a test yields. How do we know whether a test is reliable? The simplest way to find out is to give the test to a group and then, after a while, give the same people the same test again. If they obtain similar scores each time, the test is said to have high *test-retest reliability*. For example, **Table 9.2** shows the IQ scores of eight people tested 1 year apart using the same test. Although the scores did change slightly, none changed by more than six points.

But there's a problem. How do we know that people have not simply remembered the answers from the first testing and repeated them the second time around? To avoid this possibility, psychologists prefer to give two equivalent tests, both designed to measure the same thing. If people score the same on both forms, the tests are considered reliable. One way to create alternate forms is to split a single test into two parts—for example, to assign odd-numbered items to one part and even-numbered items to the other. If scores on the two halves agree, the test has **split-half reliability**.

These methods of testing reliability can be very effective. But psychological science demands more precise descriptions than "very reliable" or "fairly reliable." Psychologists express reliability in terms of **correlation coefficients**, which measure the relation between two sets of scores. If test scores on one occasion are absolutely consistent with those on another occasion, the correlation coefficient is 1.0. If there is no relationship between the scores, the correlation coefficient is zero. In Table 9.2, where there is a very close, but not perfect, relationship between the two sets of scores, the correlation coefficient is .96.

How reliable are intelligence tests? In general, people's IQ scores on most intelligence tests are quite stable (Meyer et al., 2001). Performance and culture-fair tests are somewhat less reliable. However, as we've discussed, scores on even the best tests vary somewhat from one day to another.

Validity

Do intelligence tests really measure "intelligence"? When psychologists ask this question, they are concerned with test validity. **Validity** refers to a test's ability to measure what it has been designed to measure. How do we know whether a given test actually measures what it claims to measure?

One measure of validity is known as **content validity**—whether the test contains an adequate sample of the skills or knowledge that it is supposed to measure. Most widely used intelligence tests seem to measure at least some of the mental abilities that we think of as part of intelligence. These include planning, memory, understanding, reasoning,

reliability
ability of a test to produce consistent and stable scores

split-half reliability
a method of determining test reliability by dividing the test into two parts and checking the agreement of scores on both parts

correlation coefficients
statistical measures of the degree of association between two variables

validity
ability of a test to measure what it has been designed to measure

content validity
refers to a test's having an adequate sample of questions measuring the skills or knowledge it is supposed to measure

Table 9.2 IQ Scores on the Same Test Given 1 Year Apart

Person	First Testing	Second Testing
A	130	127
B	123	127
C	121	119
D	116	122
E	109	108
F	107	112
G	95	93
H	89	94

Enduring Issues

Stability–Change *Test Reliability and Changes in Intelligence*

If a person takes an intelligence test on Monday and obtains an IQ score of 90, and then retakes the test on Tuesday and scores 130, clearly something is amiss. But what? People vary from moment to moment and day to day. Changes in health and motivation can affect test results even with the most reliable tests. And although IQ scores tend to be remarkably stable after the age of 5 or 6 (Deary, Pattie, & Starr, 2013), intellectual ability does sometimes change dramatically—for better or worse. One person's mental ability may decline substantially after a mild head injury; another person's scores on intelligence tests may rise after years of diligent study.

Since scores on even the best tests vary somewhat from one day to the next, many testing services now report a person's score along with a range of scores that allows for variations. For example, a score of 110 might be reported with a range of 104–116. This implies that the true score is most likely within a few points of 110, but almost certainly does not fall lower than 104 or higher than 116.

concentration, and the use of language. Although they may not adequately sample all aspects of intelligence equally well, they at least seem to have some content validity.

Another way to measure a test's validity is to see whether a person's score on that test closely matches his or her score on another test designed to measure the same thing. The two different scores should be very similar if they are both measures of the same ability. Most intelligence tests do this well: Despite differences in test content, people who score high on one test tend to score high on others. However, this outcome doesn't necessarily mean that the two tests actually measure intelligence. Conceivably, they could both be measuring the same thing, but that thing might not be intelligence. To demonstrate that the tests are valid measures of intelligence, we need an independent measure of intelligence against which to compare test scores. Determining test validity in this way is called **criterion-related validity**. Ever since Binet invented the intelligence test, the main criterion against which intelligence test scores have been compared has been school achievement. Even the strongest critics agree that IQ tests predict school achievement very well (Groth-Marnat, 2009).

Criticisms of IQ Tests

What is it about IQ tests, then, that makes them controversial? As you might guess from our earlier discussion of theories of intelligence, one source of disagreement and criticism concerns their content. Since psychologists disagree on the very nature of intelligence, it follows that they will disagree on the merits of particular tests of intelligence.

That said, there is general agreement among psychologists that at the least, intelligence tests measure the ability to take tests. This fact could explain why people who do well on one IQ test also tend to do well on other tests. And it could also explain why intelligence test scores correlate so closely with school performance since academic grades also depend heavily on test-taking ability.

Apart from predicting academic grades, how useful are intelligence tests? IQ tests also tend to predict success after people finish their schooling. People with high IQ scores tend to enter high-status occupations: Physicians and lawyers tend to have higher IQs than truck drivers and janitors. Critics point out, however, that this pattern can be explained in various ways. For one thing, because people with higher IQs tend to do better in school, they stay in school longer and earn advanced degrees, thereby opening the door to high-status jobs. Moreover, children from wealthy families generally grow up in environments that encourage academic success and reward good performance on tests (Blum, 1979; Ceci

criterion-related validity
validity of a test as measured by a comparison of the test score and independent measures of what the test is designed to measure

& Williams, 1997). In addition, they are more likely to have financial resources for post-graduate education or advanced occupational training, as well as family connections that pave the way to occupational success. Still, higher grades and intelligence test scores do predict occupational success and performance on the job (Kuncel, Hezlett, & Ones, 2004; Mcquillan, 2007; Ree & Earles, 1992).

Goleman's concept of emotional intelligence is specifically intended to predict success in the real world. Since this is a relatively new concept, researchers have only begun to evaluate it. However, some studies have shown promising results. For example, one study found that students with higher emotional intelligence scores adapted better socially and academically at school (Mestre, Guil, Lopes, Salovey, & Gil-Olarte, 2006). As you might expect, the ability to manage and regulate one's emotions is also important to success in the workplace (Cherniss & Goleman, 2001; Druskat, Sala, & Mount, 2006).

Though some investigators argue that emotional intelligence is no different from abilities that are already assessed by more traditional measures of intelligence and personality (M. Davies, Stankov, & Roberts, 1998; Waterhouse, 2006), the theory of emotional intelligence continues to gain support from psychological research (Mayer, Salovey, & Caruso, 2008). It has captured the attention of managers and others responsible for hiring, promoting, and predicting the performance of people in the workplace (Salovey, 2006; Yu & Yuan, 2008). In addition, recent research on emotional intelligence is advancing our understanding of the factors that contribute to the development of some forms of mental illness (Malterer, Glass, & Newman, 2008).

Enduring Issues

Person–Situation *Tracking the Future*

Tracking, the practice of assigning students who "test low" to special classes for slow learners, can work to the student's disadvantage if the test results do not reflect the student's true abilities. However, the opposite mistake may sometimes work to the student's advantage: A student of mediocre ability who is identified early on as above average may receive special attention, encouragement, and tutoring that would otherwise have been considered "wasted effort" on the part of teachers. Thus, intelligence test scores can set up a self-fulfilling prophecy, so that students defined as slow become slow, and those defined as quick become quick. In this way, intelligence tests may not only predict achievement but also help determine it (R. Rosenthal, 2002).

Another major criticism of intelligence tests is that their content and administration do not take into account cultural variations and, in fact, discriminate against minorities. High scores on most IQ tests require considerable mastery of standard English, thus biasing the tests in favor of middle- and upper-class White people. Moreover, White middle-class examiners may not be familiar with the speech patterns of lower income African American children or children from homes in which English is not the primary language, a complication that may hamper good test performance (Sattler, 2005). In addition, certain questions may have very different meanings for children of different social classes.

Although some investigators argue that the most widely used and thoroughly studied intelligence tests are not unfairly biased against minorities (Gottfredson, 2009), others contend that a proper study of cultural bias has yet to be made (E. Hunt & Carlson, 2007). Clearly, the issue of whether tests are unfair to minorities will be with us for some time.

Quiz Questions

1. "In terms of content, an intelligence test should cover all seven primary abilities equally." This statement best expresses the attitude of ________ towards intelligence tests.
   a. Sternberg.
   b. Thurstone.
   c. Goleman.
   d. Spearman.
2. A friend of yours says, "Everyone has different talents and abilities. Some people are really good at math but just kind of average at everything else. Other people are really good at music or athletics or dancing but can't add two numbers to save their lives. Just because you have an ability in one area doesn't mean you're talented at other things." Your friend's view of abilities most closely matches which of the following theorists discussed in this section of the chapter?
   a. Goleman.
   b. Spearman.
   c. Gardner.
   d. Binet.
3. Margaret is trying to create a 10-item intelligence test. She compares scores from her test to scores on the Stanford–Binet test in an attempt to determine her test's:
   a. validity.
   b. reliability.
   c. standard scores.
   d. standard deviation.
4. Unlike the Stanford–Binet Intelligence Test, the Wechsler Adult Intelligence Scale also measures:
   a. creativity.
   b. verbal skills.
   c. academic achievement in several areas.
   d. the ability to handle life situations.
5. Which of the following pieces of information about a test would be most relevant in determining the reliability of the test?
   a. People's scores on two alternate forms of the test are virtually identical.
   b. The test can be administered properly without extensive training of test administrators.
   c. The test scores are normally distributed in a large and representative standardization sample.
   d. Experts agree that each question in the test is an appropriate question for the test.

Heredity, Environment, and Intelligence

What determines individual differences in intelligence?

To what extent is intelligence inherited and to what extent is it the product of the environment? Sorting out the importance of each factor as it contributes to intelligence is a complex task.

Heredity

Why are twin studies useful in studying intelligence?

"The Biological Basis of Behavior," scientists can use studies of identical twins to measure the effects of heredity in humans. Twin studies of intelligence begin by comparing the IQ scores of identical twins who have been raised together. As **Figure 9.7** shows, the correlation between their IQ scores is very high. In addition to identical genes, however, these twins grew up in very similar environments: They shared parents, home, teachers, vacations, and probably friends, too. These common experiences could explain their similar IQ scores. To check this possibility, researchers have tested identical twins who were separated early in life—generally before they were 6 months old—and raised in different families. As Figure 9.7 shows, even when identical twins are raised in different families, they tend to have very similar intelligence test scores; in fact, the similarity is much greater than that between non-twin siblings who grow up in the *same* environment.

These findings make a strong case for the heritability of intelligence, though as we pointed out earlier twin studies do not constitute "final proof." However, other evidence also demonstrates the role of heredity (Deary, Johnson, & Houlihan, 2009; Kovas et al., 2013; Plomin et al., 2013). For example, adopted children have been found to have IQ scores that are more similar to those of their *biological* mothers than to those of the mothers who are raising them. Do psychologists, then, conclude that intelligence is an inherited trait and that environment plays little, if any, role?

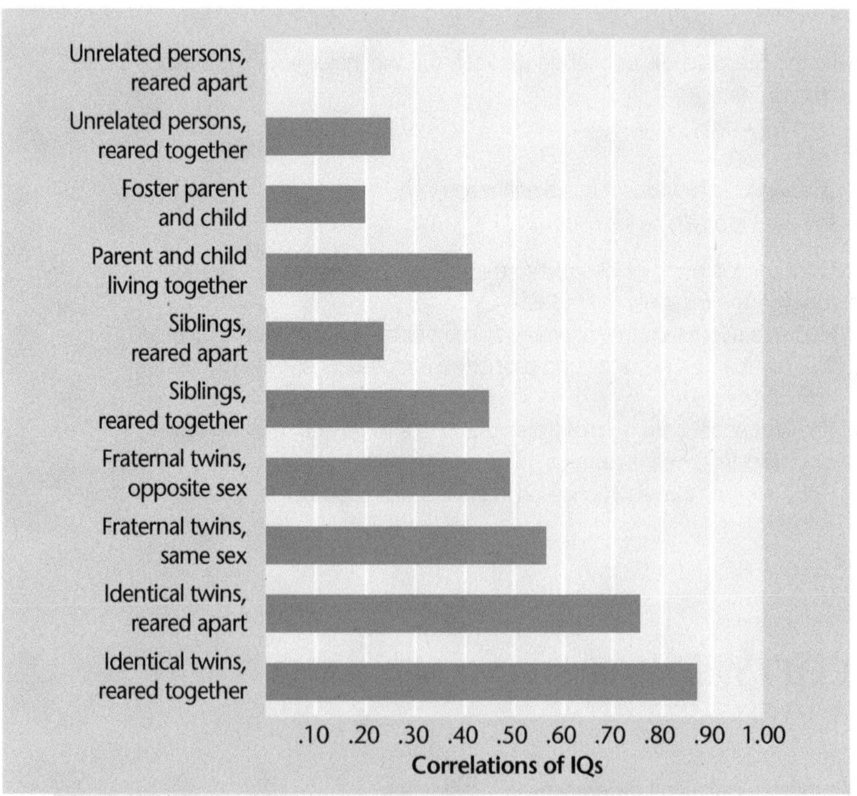

Figure 9.7 Correlations of IQ Scores and Family Relationships.
Identical twins who grow up in the same household have IQ scores that are almost identical to each other. Even when they are reared apart, their scores are highly correlated.

Source: (Erlenmeyer-Kimling & Jarvik, (1963)).

Environment

What have we learned from early intervention programs about the influence of the environment on intellectual development?

Probably no psychologist denies that genes play a role in determining intelligence, but most believe that genes provide only a base or starting point. Each of us inherits a certain body build from our parents, but our actual weight is greatly determined by what we eat and how much we exercise. Similarly, although we inherit certain mental capacities, their development depends on what we see around us as infants, how our parents respond to our first attempts to talk, what schools we attend, which books we read, which television programs we watch—even what we eat (Sternberg & Grigorenko, 2001; Nisbett, 2009). For example, recent evidence indicates that the role of heredity varies with social economic status: In impoverished families, it appears to have little or no bearing on intelligence; in affluent families, its influence appears to be stronger (Bates, Lewis, & Weiss, 2013; Tucker-Drob, Briley, & Harden, 2013). Evidence also shows that the effect of heredity increases from early childhood to middle childhood and into adulthood (Brant et al., 2013; Briley & Tucker-Drob, 2013; Lyons et al., 2009). One explanation for these facts is that bright people and people from more affluent backgrounds are more likely to seek out positive learning experiences, and those experiences in turn stimulate their cognitive development (Kan, Wicherts, Dolan, & van der Maas, 2013; Tucker-Drob, Briley, & Harden, 2013).

Environment affects children even before birth, such as through prenatal nutrition (Protzko, Aronson, & Blair, 2013). During infancy, malnutrition can lower IQ scores by an average of 20 points (Stock & Smythe, 1963). Conversely, vitamin supplements can increase young children's IQ scores, possibly even among well-nourished children (D. Benton & Roberts, 1988; Schoenthaler, Amos, Eysenck, Peritz, & Yudkin, 1991).

Quite by chance, psychologist H. M. Skeels found evidence in the 1930s that IQ scores among children also depend on environmental stimulation. While investigating orphanages for the state of Iowa, Skeels observed that the children lived in very overcrowded wards and that the few adults there had almost no time to play with the children, to talk to them, or to read them stories. Many of these children were classified as "subnormal" in intelligence. Skeels followed the cases of two girls who, after 18 months in an orphanage, were sent to a ward for women with severe intellectual disabilities. Originally, the girls' IQs were in the range of disability, but after a year on the adult ward, as if by magic, their IQs had risen to normal (Skeels, 1938). Skeels regarded this fact as quite remarkable—after all, the women with whom the girls had lived were themselves severely retarded. When he placed 13 other "slow" children as houseguests in such adult wards, within 18 months their mean IQ rose from 64 to 92 (within the normal range)—all apparently because they had had someone (even someone of below-normal intelligence) to play with them, to read to them, to cheer them on when they took their first steps, and to encourage them to talk (Skeels, 1942). During the same period, the mean IQ of a group of children who had been left in orphanages dropped from 86 to 61. Thirty years later, Skeels found that all 13 of the children raised on adult wards were self-supporting, their occupations ranging from waiting on tables to real-estate sales. Of the contrasting group, half were unemployed, four were still in institutions, and all of those who had jobs were dishwashers (Skeels, 1966). Later studies have reinforced Skeels's findings on the importance of intellectually stimulating surroundings as well as the importance of good nutrition (Capron & Duyme, 1989).

Intervention Programs: How Much Can We Boost IQ?

In 1961, the Milwaukee Project set out to learn whether intervening in a child's family life could offset the negative effects of cultural and socioeconomic deprivation on IQ scores (Garber & Heber, 1982; Heber, Garber, Harrington, & Hoffman, 1972). The average score of the 40 pregnant women in the study was less than 75 on the Wechsler scale. Women in the control group received no special education or training; those in the experimental group were sent to school, given job training, and instructed in child care, household management, and personal relationships.

After the babies were born, the research team shifted their focus to them. For 6 years, the children whose mothers received special training spent most of each day in an infant-education center, where they were fed, taught, and cared for by paraprofessionals. The children whose mothers received no special training did not attend the center. Ultimately the children in the experimental group achieved an average IQ score of 126, 51 points higher than their mothers' average scores. In contrast, the average score of the children in the control group was 94. Thus, this landmark study supported the notion that intervention may indeed counter the negative effects of cultural and socioeconomic deprivation on IQ scores.

Head Start, the nation's largest intervention program, began in 1965. Since its inception, Head Start has provided comprehensive services to more than 25 million children and their families through child care, education, health, nutrition, and family support (National Head Start Association, 2008). Focusing on preschoolers between the ages of 3 and 5 from low-income families, the program has two key goals: to provide children with educational and social skills before they go to school, and to provide information about nutrition and health to both the children and their families. Head Start involves parents in all its aspects, from daily activities to administration of the program itself.

Some studies evaluating the long-term effects of Head Start have found that it boosts cognitive and language abilities (W. S. Barnett, 1998; Wasik, Bond, & Hindman, 2006; Zhai, 2008; Zigler & Styfco, 2008). However, the congressionally mandated *Head Start Impact Study* found much more modest benefits (Puma, Bell, Cook, & Hyde, 2010). Specifically, that study concluded that access to Head Start does have a positive impact on children's preschool experiences in some areas but almost all of those advantages faded by the end of the first grade. Thus, it is questionable whether Head Start provides any appreciable, long-term, practical benefits.

Overall, the effectiveness of early intervention appears to depend on the quality of the particular program (S. L. Ramey, 1999; C. T. Ramey & Ramey, 2007; Zigler & Styfco, 1993). Intervention programs that have clearly defined goals—that include reading interactively with the children, that explicitly teach such basic skills as counting, naming colors, language development, and writing the alphabet; and that take into account the broad context of human development, including health care and other social services—achieve the biggest and most durable gains (Protzko, Aronson, & Blair, 2013).

The IQ Debate: A Useful Model

How can the study of plants help us to understand the relationship between heredity and environment?

Both heredity and environment have important effects on individual differences in intelligence, but is one of these factors more important than the other? A useful analogy comes from studies of plants. Suppose that you grow one group of randomly assigned plants in enriched soil, and another group in poor soil. The enriched group will grow to be taller and stronger than the nonenriched group; the difference between the two groups in this case is due entirely to differences in their environment. *Within* each group of plants, however, differences among individual plants are likely to be primarily due to genetics, because all plants in the same group share essentially the same environment. Thus, the height and strength of any single plant reflects both heredity *and* environment.

Similarly, group differences in IQ scores might be due to environmental factors, but differences among people *within* groups could be due primarily to genetics. At the same time, the IQ scores of particular people would reflect the effects of both heredity *and* environment. Robert Plomin, an influential researcher in the field of human intelligence, concludes that "the world's literature suggests that about half of the total variance in IQ scores can be accounted for by genetic variance" (Plomin, 1997, p. 89). This finding means that environment accounts for the other half.

The Flynn Effect

An interesting side note to this discussion is the fact that IQ scores have *gone up* in the population as a whole. Because James Flynn (1984, 1987) of the University of Otago in New Zealand was the first to report this finding, it is often called the *Flynn Effect.* In his original research, Professor Flynn gathered evidence showing that, between 1932 and 1978, intelligence test scores rose about three points per decade. More recently, by pulling together data from five nations (Britain, Netherlands, Israel, Norway, and Belgium) Flynn (1999, 2012) has shown that the average increase in IQ may be as high as six points per decade. Consistent with this result is a finding by Flieller (1999) that children today between the ages of 10 and 15 years display significant cognitive advancement compared with children of the same age tested 20 and 30 years ago. And, as Neisser (1998) points out, accompanying this general increase in IQ scores is a decrease in the difference in intelligence scores between Blacks and Whites.

Although the Flynn Effect has many possible explanations, none of them seem to account entirely for the magnitude of the effect (Sundet, Borren, & Tambs, 2008). Rather than getting smarter, maybe people are simply getting better at taking tests. Environmental factors, such as improved nutrition and health care, may also contribute to this trend (Teasdale & Owen, 2005). Some psychologists have suggested that the sheer complexity of the modern world is responsible (Schooler, 1998). For example, the proliferation of televisions, computers, and video games could be contributing to the rise in IQ scores (Greenfield, 1998; Neisser, 1998).

Mental Abilities and Human Diversity: Gender and Culture

Do culture and gender influence mental abilities?

Gender

In 1974, psychologists Eleanor Maccoby and Carol Jacklin published a review of psychological research on gender differences. They found no differences between males and females in most of the studies they examined. However, a few differences did appear in cognitive abilities: Girls tended to display greater verbal ability, and boys tended to exhibit stronger spatial and mathematical abilities. Largely as a result of this research, gender

Thinking Critically About . . .

The Flynn Effect

Flynn and others have found that IQ scores are rising, but what does this really mean? As Flynn (1999) points out, it is hard to see how genes could account for so rapid an increase in IQ. Clearly, some aspect of the environment must account for most or all of the increase in IQ scores.

1. Of the possible explanations mentioned in the text, which seem to you to be most likely? Why? How might you go about determining whether one explanation is better than another?
2. Do you think IQ scores will continue to rise? Is your position on that question related to your answer to the first question?
3. Does a rise in IQ test scores necessarily mean that there has been a comparable increase in intelligence? Why or why not?

differences in verbal, spatial, and mathematical abilities became so widely accepted that they were often cited as one of the established facts of psychological research.

A closer examination of the research literature, including more recent work, indicates that while gender differences in some math and verbal skills exist, they are relatively small and often concentrated in very specific skills. For example, an analysis of 242 studies involving more than a million people showed no difference between men and women in mathematical ability (Lindberg, Hyde, Petersen, & Linn, 2010). While girls do appear to display stronger verbal skills than boys, female superiority is generally only found when the assessment of verbal skill includes writing. Conversely, boys tend to outperform girls primarily on measures of visual-spatial skill (Halpern et al., 2007). Interestingly, the advantage males have over females in visual-spatial ability has been detected in infants as young as 3–5 months (D. S. Moore & Johnson, 2008; Quinn & Liben, 2008). Men also differ from women in another way: They are more likely than women to fall at the extremes of the mathematical intelligence range (Ceci & Williams, 2010; Halpern et al., 2007; Wai, Cacchio, Putallaz, & Makel, 2010). Conversely, women outnumber men at the very high end of the scale when it comes to verbal reasoning and writing ability (Wai et al., 2010).

What should we conclude from these findings? First, cognitive differences between males and females appear to be restricted to specific cognitive skills. Scores on tests such as the Stanford–Binet or the WAIS reveal no overall gender differences in general intelligence (Halpern, 1992). Second, gender differences typically are small (Skaalvik & Rankin, 1994). Third, we do not know whether the differences that do exist are a result of biological or cultural factors (Hyde & Mezulis, 2002). Finally, one extensive review of the literature concluded that "There is no single factor by itself that has been shown to determine sex differences in science and math. Early experience, biological constraints, educational policy, and cultural context each have effects, and these effects add and interact in complex and sometimes unpredictable ways" (Halpern et al., 2007, p. 41).

Culture

For years, U.S. media have been reporting an achievement gap, especially in math, between American and Asian students. Recent media reports suggest even broader differences.

Psychological research tells us something about the causes of these achievement gaps. Two decades ago, a team of researchers led by the late Harold Stevenson (1924–2005) began to study the performance of first- and fifth-grade children in American, Chinese, and Japanese elementary schools (Stevenson, Lee, & Stigler, 1986). At that time, the American students at both grade levels lagged far behind the other two countries in math and came in second in reading. A decade later, when the study was repeated with a new group of fifth-graders, the researchers discovered that the American students performed even worse than they had earlier. In 1990, the research team also studied the original first-graders from all three cultures, now in the eleventh grade. The result? The American students retained their low standing in mathematics compared with the Asian students (Stevenson, 1992, 1993; Stevenson, Chen, & Lee, 1993).

The next question was, Why? Stevenson's team wondered whether cultural attitudes toward ability and effort might, in part, explain the differences. To test this hypothesis, the researchers asked students, their parents, and their teachers in all three countries whether they thought effort or ability had a greater impact on academic performance. From first through eleventh grade, American students on the whole disagreed with the statement that "everyone in my class has about the same natural ability in math." In other words, the Americans thought that "studying hard" has little to do with performance. Their responses appear to reflect a belief that mathematical skill is primarily a function of innate ability. American mothers expressed a similar view. Moreover, 41% of the American eleventh-grade teachers thought "innate intelligence" is the most important factor in mathematics performance. By contrast, Asian students, parents, and teachers believed that effort and "studying hard" determine success in math.

Thinking Critically About . . .

International Comparisons of School Achievement

1. Do you agree or disagree with the conclusions of Stevenson and his colleagues that cultural attitudes may account for some of the academic performance differences between American students and students from other countries? What additional evidence might provide support for your position?
2. If you were to research this topic today, would you do things differently than Stevenson's team did? Are there any other factors that might account for the differences in achievement that you would investigate? What specific questions would you ask of the parents, students, and teachers? What additional information about the school systems would you collect?
3. Given the results of this research, what specific steps would you take to improve the academic performance of American children?

Such culturally influenced views of the relative importance of effort and innate ability may have profound consequences for the way that children, their parents, and their teachers approach the task of learning. Students who believe that learning is based on natural ability see little value in working hard to learn a difficult subject. By contrast, students who believe that academic success comes from studying are more likely to work hard. Indeed, even the brightest students will not get far without making an effort. Although many Americans no doubt believe in the value of effort and hard work, our widespread perception that innate ability is the key to academic success may be affecting the performance of U.S. students.

In short, while Stevenson's research confirms the existence of significant differences in student performance across various cultures, the evidence suggests that these differences reflect cultural attitudes toward the importance of ability and effort, rather than an underlying difference in intelligence across the cultures.

Hunt (2012, 2013) has investigated a much broader range of countries. He has compared cognitive ability in modern industrial and post-industrial societies (such as the United States, Canada, and Japan) versus pre-industrial societies (such as countries in sub-Saharan Africa). His research has shown that there are substantial differences in cognitive skills between those two kinds of countries and that the differences can be attributed in large part to the same environmental factors that affect cognitive abilities within a country: nutrition, pollution, home environment, educational opportunities, attitudes, and motivation.

Extremes of Intelligence

What do psychologists know about the two extremes of human intelligence: very high and very low?

The average IQ score on intelligence tests is 100. Nearly 70% of all people have IQs between 85 and 115, and all but 5% of the population have IQs between 70 and 130. In this section, we focus on people who score at the two extremes of intelligence—those with an intellectual disability and those who are intellectually gifted.

Intellectual Disability

Intellectual disability (previous known as mental retardation) encompasses a vast array of mental deficits with a wide variety of causes, treatments, and outcomes. The American Psychiatric Association (2013) defines intellectual disability as a significant deficit in general

intellectual disability
condition of significantly subaverage intelligence combined with deficiencies in adaptive behavior, originating during the developmental period

intellectual functioning, accompanied by significant limitations in adaptive behavior. The definition also specifies that the onset of symptoms must originate during the developmental period. (A person of any age may be diagnosed with intellectual disability, but their symptoms must have originated during the developmental period.) There are also various degrees of intellectual disability (mild, moderate, severe, and profound), based principally on the severity of the individual's limitations in adaptive functioning. (See **Table 9.3.**)

It is important to recognize that a low IQ is not sufficient for diagnosing intellectual disability. The person must also be unable to perform the daily tasks needed to function independently (Rust & Wallace, 2004). A person who is able to live independently, for example, is not considered to have an intellectual disability even if his or her IQ may be extremely low. To fully assess individuals and to place them in appropriate treatment and educational programs, mental health professionals need information on physical health and on emotional and social adjustment (Borthwick-Duffy, 2007).

Some people with intellectual disabilities exhibit remarkable abilities in highly specialized areas, such as numerical computation, memory, art, or music (Pring, Woolf, & Tadic, 2008; Treffert & Wallace, 2002). Probably the most dramatic and intriguing examples involve *savant performance* (Boelte, Uhlig, & Poustka, 2002; L. K. Miller, 2005). Savant performances include mentally calculating large numbers almost instantly, determining the day of the week for any date over many centuries, and playing back a long musical composition after hearing it played only once.

What causes intellectual disability? In most cases, the causes are unknown—especially in cases of mild intellectual disability, which account for nearly 90% of all intellectual disability. When causes can be identified, most often they stem from a wide variety of genetic, environmental, social, nutritional, and other risk factors (A. A. Baumeister & Baumeister, 2000; Moser, 2004).

About 25% of cases—especially the more severe forms of intellectual disability—appear to involve genetic or biological disorders. Scientists have identified more than 100 forms of intellectual disability caused by single defective genes (Plomin, 1997). One is the genetically based disease *phenylketonuria,* or *PKU,* which occurs in about one person out of 25,000. In people suffering from PKU, the liver fails to produce an enzyme necessary for early brain development. Fortunately, placing a PKU baby on a special diet can prevent intellectual disability from developing (Merrick, Aspler, & Schwarz, 2005; Widaman, 2009). In the disorder known as *Down syndrome,* which affects 1 in 600 newborns, an extra 21st chromosome is the cause. Down syndrome, named for the physician who first described its symptoms, is marked by mild to severe intellectual disability.

Biologically caused intellectual disability can be moderated through education and training (C. T. Ramey, Ramey, & Lanzi, 2001). The prognosis for those with no underlying physical causes is even better. People whose intellectual disability is due to a history of

Table 9.3 Levels of Intellectual Disability

Severity Level	Attainable Skill Level
Mild	People may be able to function adequately in society and learn skills comparable to a sixth-grader, but they need special help at times of unusual stress.
Moderate	People profit from vocational training and may be able to travel alone. They learn on a second-grade level and perform skilled work in a sheltered workshop under supervision.
Severe	People do not learn to talk or to practice basic hygiene until after age 6. They cannot learn vocational skills but can perform simple tasks under supervision.
Profound	Constant care is needed. Usually, people have a diagnosed neurological disorder.

SOURCE: Based on APA, *DSM-5*, 2013.

social and educational deprivation can respond dramatically to appropriate interventions. Today, the majority of children with physical or intellectual disabilities are educated in local school systems (Doré, Wagner, Doré, & Brunet, 2002), in *inclusion* arrangements (Kavale, 2002) (previously known as *mainstreaming*), which help these students to socialize with their nondisabled peers. The principle of mainstreaming has also been applied successfully to adults with intellectual disability, by taking them out of large, impersonal institutions and placing them in smaller community homes that provide more normal life experiences (I. Brown, Buell, Birkan, & Percy, 2007).

Giftedness

At the other extreme of the intelligence scale are "the gifted"—those with exceptional mental abilities, as measured by scores on standard intelligence tests. As with intellectual disability, the causes of **giftedness** are largely unknown.

The first and now-classic study of giftedness was begun by Lewis Terman and his colleagues in the early 1920s. They defined giftedness in terms of academic talent and measured it by an IQ score in the top 2 percentile (Terman, 1925). The study involved 1,528 children whose average IQ score was 151. More recently, some experts have sought to broaden the definition of giftedness beyond that of simply high IQ (L. J. Coleman & Cross, 2001; Csikszentmihalyi, Rathunde, & Whalen, 1993; Subotnik & Arnold, 1994). One view is that giftedness is often an interaction of above-average general intelligence, exceptional creativity, and high levels of commitment. Various criteria can identify gifted students, including scores on intelligence tests, teacher recommendations, and achievement test results. School systems generally use diagnostic testing, interviews, and evaluation of academic and creative work (Sattler, 1992). These selection methods can identify students with a broad range of talent, but they can miss students with specific abilities, such as a talent for mathematics or music (Cramond & Kim, 2008). This is important because research suggests that most gifted individuals display special abilities in only a few areas. "Globally" gifted people are rare (Achter, Lubinski, & Benbow, 1996; Lubinski & Benbow, 2000; Olzewski-Kubilius, 2003; Winner, 1998, 2000).

A common view of gifted people is that they have poor social skills and are emotionally maladjusted. However, research does not support this stereotype (J. Richards, Encel, & Shute, 2003; Robinson & Clinkenbeard, 1998). Indeed, one review (Janos & Robinson, 1985) concluded that "being intellectually gifted, at least at moderate levels of ability, is clearly an asset in terms of psychosocial adjustment in most situations" (p. 181). Many people who are profoundly gifted (the top 0.01% in mathematical and verbal reasoning) in childhood have been shown to go on to occupy critical leadership positions and to make extraordinary contributions to society throughout early adulthood (Kell, Lubinski, & Benbow, 2013).

Enduring Issues

Diversity–Universality *Not Everyone Wants to Be Special*

Because gifted children sometimes become bored and socially isolated in regular classrooms, some experts recommend that they be offered special programs (Olzewski-Kubilius, 2003). Special classes for the gifted would seem to be something the gifted themselves would want, but this is not always the case. Special classes and special schools can separate gifted students from their friends and neighbors. And stereotypes about the gifted can mean that, once identified as gifted, the student is less likely to be invited to participate in certain school activities, such as dances, plays, and sports. Gifted students also sometimes object to being set apart, labeled "brains," and pressured to perform beyond the ordinary. Many but not all gifted students welcome the opportunities offered by special programs.

giftedness
refers to superior IQ combined with demonstrated or potential ability in such areas as academic aptitude, creativity, and leadership

Quiz Questions

1. Imagine that an adoption agency separates identical twins at birth and places them randomly in very different kinds of homes. Thirty years later, a researcher discovers that the pairs of twins have almost identical scores on IQ tests. Which of the following conclusions is most consistent with that finding?
   a. Heredity has a significant effect on intelligence.
   b. Environment has a significant effect on intelligence.
   c. Heredity provides a starting point, but environment primarily determines our ultimate intelligence.
   d. Because the twins were placed in very different environments, it's not possible to draw any conclusions.
2. Ten-year-old John has a very low IQ score. Which of the following would you need to know before you could determine whether John should be diagnosed as suffering from intellectual disability?
   a. Whether he suffered from malnutrition before birth.
   b. Whether he has a genetic defect in the X chromosome.
   c. Whether he can perform the daily tasks needed to function independently.
   d. Whether his score on the Stanford–Binet Intelligence Scale is below 90.
3. A researcher reports that children today score significantly higher on intelligence tests compared with children of the same age tested 20 and 30 years ago. These findings:
   a. are contrary to the Flynn Effect.
   b. are consistent with the Flynn Effect.
   c. demonstrate the unreliability of intelligence tests.
   d. demonstrate the importance of heredity as a determinant of intelligence.
4. Which of the following statements about gender differences in mental abilities is true based on the most recent evidence?
   a. An analysis of 242 studies involving more than a million people showed no difference between men and women in mathematical ability.
   b. Males display stronger verbal skills than females.
   c. Females outperform males on measures of visual-spatial skill.
   d. Scores on intelligence tests such as the Stanford–Binet or the WAIS reveal significant gender differences in general intelligence.

Any discussion of giftedness inevitably leads to the topic of creativity. The two topics are, indeed, closely related, as we shall see in the next section.

CREATIVITY

What is creativity?

Creativity is the ability to produce novel and socially valued ideas or objects ranging from philosophy to painting, from music to mousetraps (Sternberg, 2012). As we saw earlier in this chapter, Sternberg included creativity and insight as important elements in human intelligence. Most IQ tests, however, do not measure creativity, and many researchers would argue that intelligence and creativity are not the same thing.

creativity
the ability to produce novel and socially valued ideas or objects

Intelligence and Creativity

How is creativity related to intelligence?

The photograph at the opening of this chapter is of Dame Kathleen Timpson Ollerenshaw. She was certainly intelligent: she earned a DPhil from Oxford University in mathematics. She was also highly creative. At the age of 68 she published a paper that showed how to solve the Rubik's cube in the fewest moves. Her crowning achievement in mathematics was a book that she published at the age of 85, in which she described a way to construct a whole class of mathematical "magic squares."

It is tempting to conclude from examples such as Dame Ollerenshaw that creativity and intelligence are related. However, early studies typically found little or no relationship between creativity and intelligence (for example, Getzels & Jackson, 1962; Wing, 1969), but these studies were concerned only with bright students. Perhaps creativity and intelligence are indeed linked, but only until IQ reaches a certain threshold level, after which higher intelligence isn't associated with higher creativity. There is some evidence for this *threshold theory* (Barron, 1963; Yamamoto & Chimbidis, 1966). However, other studies have failed to provide support (Preckel, Holling, & Wiese, 2006) finding instead that the relationship between intelligence and creativity is best understood only when the individual facets of intelligence and creativity (such as musical or artistic) are considered (K. H. Kim, 2008; Sligh, Conners, & Roskos-Ewoldsen, 2005). Creative people are often *perceived* as being more intelligent than less creative people who have equivalent IQ scores. But this may be the result of other characteristics that creative people share. For instance, research has shown that creative people also tend to score high on measures of *extraversion*—a personality trait reflecting gregariousness, assertiveness, and excitement seeking (Furnham & Bachtiar, 2008; Furnham, Batey, Anand, & Manfield, 2008).

In general, creative people are *problem finders* as well as problem solvers. The more creative people are, the more they like to work on problems that they have set for themselves. Creative scientists (such as Charles Darwin and Albert Einstein) often work for years on a problem that has sprung from their own curiosity (Gruber & Wallace, 2001). Also, "greatness" rests not just on "talent" or "genius"; such people also have intense dedication, ambition, and perseverance (Stokes, 2006).

Recent research has confirmed what many of us have experienced: when solving a problem that requires creative thinking, it pays to focus on an undemanding task that lets your mind wander. For reasons that are not yet understood, the irrelevant thoughts that occur as your mind wanders serve to facilitate creative problem solving (Baird et al., 2012). Finally, creativity is also influenced by external factors. One line of research has shown that individuals are more creative when put into disorderly, "messy" environments (Vohs, Redden, & Rahinel, 2013).

Creativity Tests

Can creativity be measured?

Measuring creativity poses special problems (Cramond & Kim, 2008; Naglieri & Kaufman, 2001; Runco, 2008). Because creativity involves original responses to situations, questions that can be answered *true* or *false* or *a* or *b* are not good measures. More open-ended tests are better. Instead of asking for one predetermined answer to a problem, the examiner asks the test takers to let their imaginations run free. Scores are based on the originality of a person's answers and often on the number of responses as well.

In one such test, the *Torrance Test of Creative Thinking,* people must explain what is happening in a picture, how the scene came about, and what its consequences are likely to be. In the *Christensen–Guilford Test,* they are to list as many words containing a given letter as possible, to name things belonging to a certain category (such as "liquids that will burn"), and to write four-word sentences beginning with the letters RDLS—"Rainy days look sad, Red dogs like soup, Renaissance dramas lack symmetry." One of the most widely used creativity tests, S. A. Mednick's (1962) *Remote Associates Test (RAT),* asks people to relate three apparently unrelated words. For example, a test taker might relate the stimulus words *poke*, *go*, and *molasses* using the word *slow:* "Slowpoke, go slow, slow as molasses." In the newer *Wallach and Kogan Creative Battery,* people form associative groupings. For instance, children are asked to "name all the round things you can think of" and to find similarities between objects, such as between a potato and a carrot.

Although people who do not have high IQs can score well on the Wallach and Kogan test, the Torrance test seems to require a reasonably high IQ for adequate performance. This finding raises the question of which of these tests is a valid measure of creativity. In general, current tests of creativity do not show a high degree of validity (Baer, 2008; Clapham, 2004), so measurements derived from them must be interpreted with caution.

As with intelligence, there is considerable interest in identifying the neural mechanisms that underlie creative thinking, but to date the results have been discouraging. One recent, comprehensive review of the literature concludes that creativity as a whole is not clearly associated with any particular brain area. The authors point out that "It is hard to believe that creative behavior, in all its manifestations, from carrying out exquisitely choreographed dance moves, to scientific discovery, constructing poems, and coming up with ingenious ideas of what to do with a brick, engages a common set of brain areas or depends on a limited set of mental processes" (Dietrich & Kanso, 2010, p. 845). Whether there are brain areas associated with *specific kinds* of creativity remains to be seen.

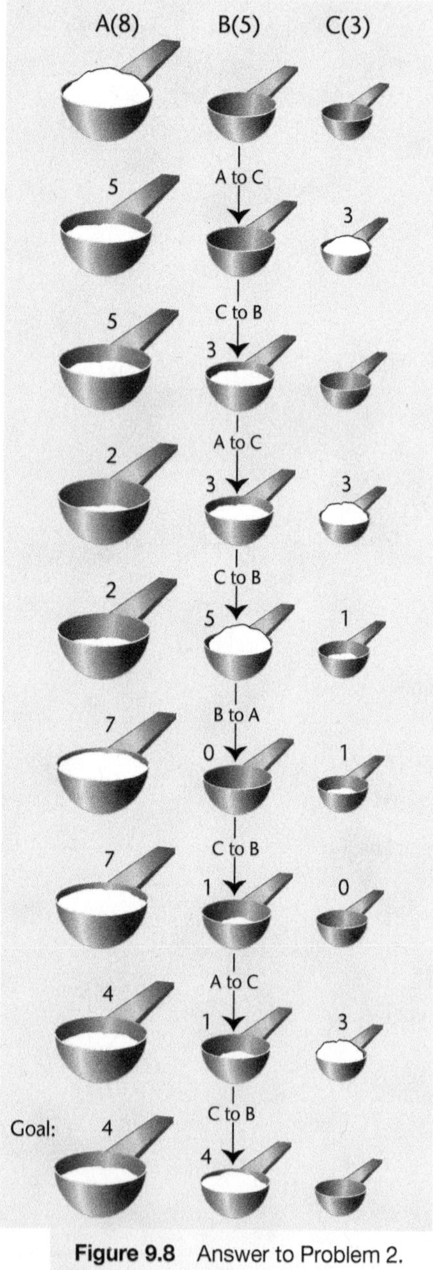

Figure 9.8 Answer to Problem 2.

ANSWERS TO PROBLEMS IN THE CHAPTER

Problem 1 Fill each of the smaller spoons with salt from the larger spoon. That step will require 4 teaspoons of salt, leaving exactly 4 teaspoons of salt in the larger spoon.

Problem 2 As shown in **Figure 9.8,** fill spoon C with the salt from spoon A (now A has 5 teaspoons of salt and C has 3). Pour the salt from spoon C into spoon B (now A has 5 teaspoons of salt, and B has 3). Again fill spoon C with the salt from spoon A. (This leaves A with only 2 teaspoons of salt, while B and C each have 3.) Fill spoon B with the salt from spoon C. (This step leaves 1 teaspoon of salt in spoon C, while B has 5 teaspoons, and A has only 2.) Pour all of the salt from spoon B into spoon A. (Now A has 7 teaspoons of salt, and C has 1.) Pour all of the salt from spoon C into spoon B, and then fill spoon C from spoon A. (This step leaves 4 teaspoons of salt in A, 1 teaspoon in B, and 3 teaspoons in C.) Finally, pour all of the salt from spoon C into spoon B. (This step leaves 4 teaspoons of salt in spoons A and B, which is the solution.)

Problem 3 Take one of the short pieces of chain shown in **Figure 9.9,** and open all three links. (This step costs 6 cents.) Use those three links to connect the remaining three pieces of chain. (Hence, closing the three links costs 9 cents.)

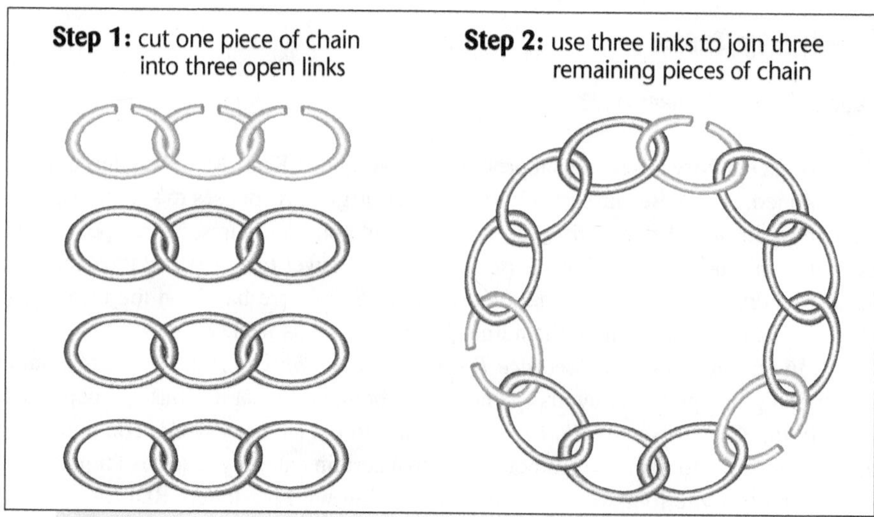

Figure 9.9 Answer to Problem 3.

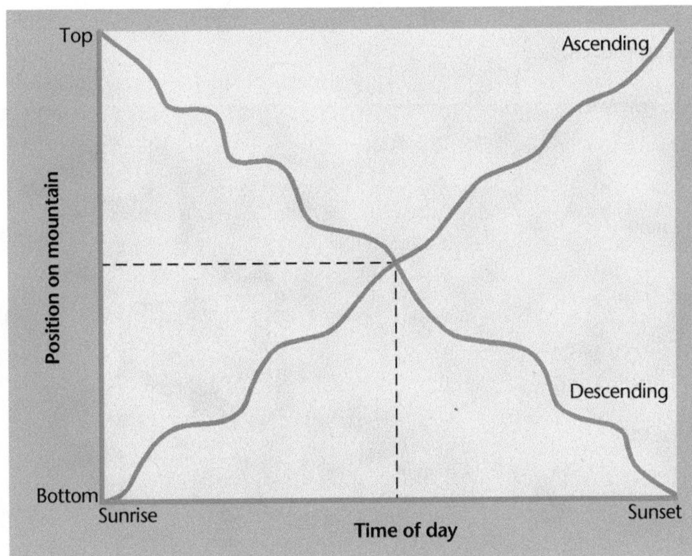

Figure 9.10 Answer to Problem 4.

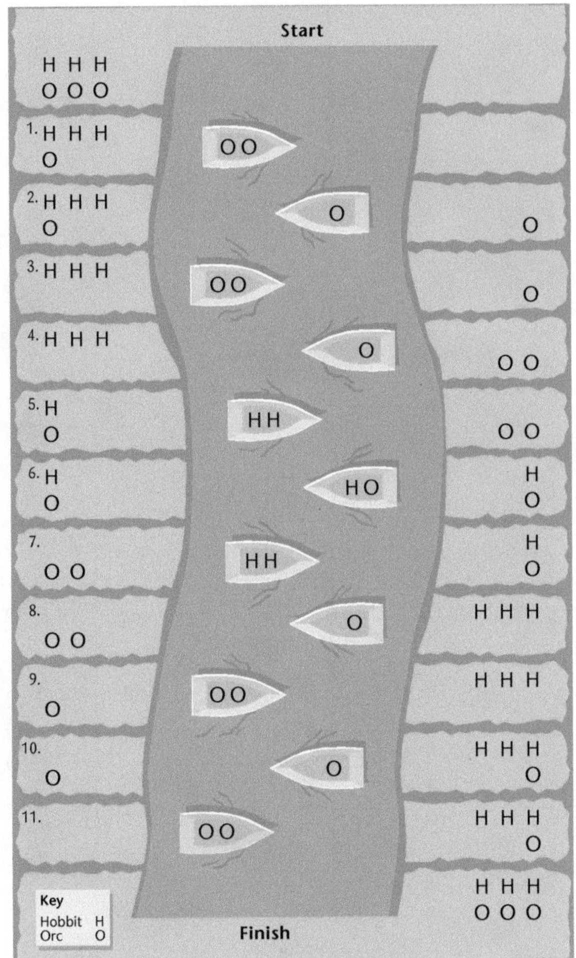

Figure 9.11 Answer to Problem 5.

Problem 4 One way to solve this problem is to draw a diagram of the ascent and the descent, as in **Figure 9.10.** From this drawing, you can see that indeed there is a point that the monk passes at exactly the same time on both days. Another way to approach this problem is to imagine that there are two monks on the mountain; one starts ascending at 7 A.M., while the other starts descending at 7 A.M. on the same day. Clearly, sometime during the day the monks must meet somewhere along the route.

Problem 5 This problem has four possible solutions, one of which is shown in **Figure 9.11.**

Problem 6 There are 15 possible solutions to this problem, of which this is one: First, one Hobbit and one Orc cross the river in the boat; the Orc remains on the opposite side while the Hobbit rows back. Next, three Orcs cross the river; two of those Orcs remain on the other side (making a total of three Orcs on the opposite bank) while one Orc rows back. Now three Hobbits and one Orc row the boat back. Again, three Hobbits row across the river, at which point all five Hobbits are on the opposite bank with only two Orcs. Then, one of the Orcs rows back and forth across the river twice to transport the remaining Orcs to the opposite side.

Answers to Intelligence Test Questions

1. *Idleness* refers to the state of being inactive, not busy, unoccupied; *laziness* means an unwillingness or a reluctance to work. Laziness is one possible cause of idleness, but not the only cause.
2. If you face west, your right ear will face north.
3. *Obliterate* means to erase or destroy something completely.
4. Both an hour and a week are measures of time.
5. Alternative (f) is the correct pattern.
6. Seventy-five cents will buy nine pencils.
7. Alternative (d) is correct. A crutch is used to help someone who has difficulty with locomotion; spectacles are used to help someone who has difficulty with vision.
8. Alternative D is correct. The second figure is the same shape and size but with diagonal cross-hatching from upper left to lower right.

9. Figures 3, 4, and 5 can all be completely covered by using some or all of the given pieces.

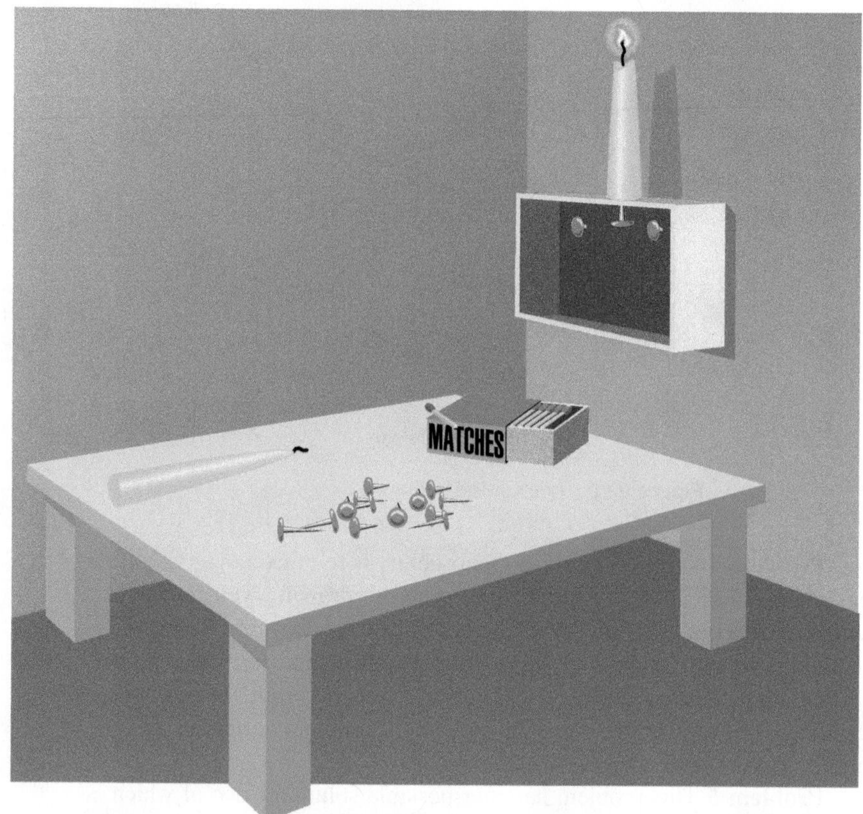

Figure 9.12 Solution to Figure 9.5.
In solving the problem given in Figure 9.5, many people have trouble realizing that the box of tacks can also be used as a candleholder, as shown here.

Writing Assignment

Provide real-world examples for the following types of intelligences as theorized by Gardner: verbal/linguistic, body-kinesthetic (movement), and logical/mathematical. Explain why each example represents one of the types of intelligence. Present some of the arguments critics have offered against Gardner's research.

Quiz Questions

1. You are discussing creativity and intelligence with a friend who says, "Those are two different things. There"s no relationship between being intelligent and being creative." Based on what you have learned in this chapter, which of the following would be the most accurate reply?
   a. "There is a relationship between intelligence and creativity but it is complex, and is understood only when the individual facets of intelligence and creativity are taken into account."
   b. "That's true for people with IQ scores below about 100, but above that point, intelligence and creativity tend to go together".

- **c.** "You're right. There is no evidence of a relationship between creativity and intelligence."
- **d.** "That's apparently true only among very bright people. For most people, creativity and intelligence tend to go together."

2. A test of creativity asks "What word is related to each of the following words? Blue Cottage Cake"
   - **a.** Christensen–Guilford Test.
   - **b.** Torrance Test of Creative Thinking.
   - **c.** Remote Associates Test.
   - **d.** Wallach and Kogan Creative Battery.

Review

BUILDING BLOCKS OF THOUGHT

What are the three most important building blocks of thought? The three most important building blocks of thought are language, images, and concepts. As we think, we use words, sensory "snapshots," and categories that classify things.

What steps do we go through to turn a thought into a statement? **Language** is a flexible system of symbols that allows us to communicate ideas to others. When we express thoughts as statements, we must conform to our language's rules. Every language has rules indicating which sounds (or **phonemes**) are part of that particular language, how those sounds can be combined into meaningful units (or **morphemes**), and how those meaningful units can be ordered into phrases and sentences (rules of **grammar**). To communicate an idea, we start with a thought and then choose sounds, words, and phrases that will express the idea clearly. To understand the speech of others, the task is reversed.

What role do images play in thinking? **Images** are mental representations of sensory experiences. Visual images in particular can be powerful aids in thinking about the relationships between things. Picturing things in our mind's eye can sometimes help us solve problems.

How do concepts help us to think more efficiently? **Concepts** are categories for classifying objects, people, and experiences based on their common elements. Without the ability to form concepts, we would need a different name for every new thing we encounter. We draw on concepts to anticipate what new experiences will be like. Many concepts are "fuzzy," lacking clear-cut boundaries. Therefore we often use **prototypes,** mental models of the most typical examples of a concept, to classify new objects.

LANGUAGE, THOUGHT, AND CULTURE

How do language, thought, and culture influence each other? According to Benjamin Whorf's **linguistic relativity hypothesis,** thought is greatly influenced by language. But critics contend that thought and experience can shape and change a language as much as a language can shape and change thought.

Does language contribute to gender stereotyping? Some evidence indicates that the use of "man" and "he" to refer to all people affects the way that English speakers think. Referring to doctors, college professors, bankers, and executives by the generic "he" may contribute to the gender stereotyping of these respected occupations as appropriate for men but not for women. In contrast, referring to secretaries and housekeepers as "she" may reinforce the stereotype that those occupations are appropriate for women, not men.

NON-HUMAN LANGUAGE AND THOUGHT

Can scientists learn what is on an animal's mind? What kind of communication and language do other animals use? Non-human animals communicate primarily through **signs:** general or global statements about the animal's current state. Using the distinguishing features of language, which include semantics, displacement, and productivity as criteria, no other species has its own language, although chimpanzees have been taught to use American Sign Language.

Do some animals think like humans? Research indicates that some animals have humanlike cognitive capacities, such as the ability to form concepts and to reason. Apes have demonstrated sophisticated problem-solving skills. However, only chimpanzees, bonobos, and orangutans consistently show signs of self-awareness.

PROBLEM SOLVING

What are three general aspects of the problem-solving process? Interpreting a problem, formulating a strategy, and evaluating progress toward a solution are three general aspects of the problem-solving process. Each in its own way is critical to success at the task.

(Continued)

Does the way information is presented affect decisions? Why is representing the problem so important to finding an effective solution? Problem representation—defining or interpreting the problem—is the first step in problem solving. We must decide whether to view the problem verbally, mathematically, or visually; and to get clues about how to solve it we must categorize it. Some problems require **convergent thinking,** or searching for a single correct solution, while others call for **divergent thinking,** or generating many possible solutions. Representing a problem in an unproductive way can block progress completely.

Why are heuristics usually better for solving problems than is trial and error? Selecting a solution strategy and evaluating progress toward the goal are also important steps in the problem-solving process. A solution strategy can range from trial and error, to information retrieval based on similar problems, to a set of step-by-step procedures guaranteed to work (an **algorithm**), to rule-of-thumb approaches known as **heuristics.** An algorithm is often preferable over trial and error because it guarantees a solution and does not waste time. But because we lack algorithms for so many things, heuristics are vital to human problem solving. Some useful heuristics are **hill climbing,** creating **subgoals, means-end analysis,** and **working backward.**

How can a "mental set" both help and hinder problem solving? A **mental set** is a tendency to perceive and approach a problem in a certain way. Although sets can enable us to draw on past experience to help solve problems, a strong set can also prevent us from using essential new approaches. One set that can seriously hamper problem solving is **functional fixedness—**the tendency to perceive only traditional uses for an object. One way to minimize mental sets is the technique of **brainstorming** in which an individual or group collects numerous ideas and evaluates them only after all possible ideas have been collected.

DECISION MAKING

How does decision making differ from problem solving? Decision making is a special kind of problem solving in which all possible solutions or choices are known. The task is not to come up with new solutions, but rather to identify the best one available based on whatever criteria are being used.

How would you go about making a truly logical decision? The logical way to make a decision is to rate each available choice in terms of weighted criteria and then to total the ratings for each choice. This approach is called a **compensatory model** because heavily weighted attractive features can compensate for lightly weighted unattractive ones.

How can heuristic approaches lead us to make bad decisions? Heuristics can save a great deal of time and effort, but they do not always result in the best choices. Errors in judgment may occur based on the **representativeness** heuristic, which involves making decisions based on information that matches our model of the "typical" member of a category. Other examples are overreliance on the **availability** heuristic (making choices based on whatever information we can most easily retrieve from memory, even though it may not be accurate) and the **confirmation bias** (the tendency to seek evidence in support of our existing beliefs and to ignore evidence that contradicts them).

Does the way information is presented affect decisions? How do we explain to ourselves the decisions we make? **Framing,** or perspective in which a problem is presented, can also affect the outcome of a decision. And regardless of whether a decision proves to be good or bad, we often use **hindsight bias,** which refers to our tendency to view outcomes as inevitable or predictable after we know the outcome to "correct" our memories so that the decision seems to be a good one. **Counterfactual thinking** involves revisiting our decisions by considering "what if" alternatives.

MULTITASKING

Contrary to what many people believe, multitasking often results in reduced speed, decreased accuracy, and increased stress. Numerous studies have shown that driving is particularly affected by multitasking. Talking on a cell phone or texting while driving may be as bad as driving legally drunk.

INTELLIGENCE AND MENTAL ABILITIES

What types of questions are used to measure intelligence? Psychologists who study **intelligence** ask what intelligence entails and how it can be measured. To accomplish this, they use a variety of questions to assess general knowledge, vocabulary, arithmetic reasoning, and spatial manipulation.

What are some of the major theories of intelligence? Intelligence theories fall into two categories: those that argue in favor of a "general intelligence" that affects all aspects of cognitive functioning, and those that say intelligence is composed of many separate abilities, in which a person will not necessarily score high in all. Spearman's theory of intelligence is an example of the first category. Thurstone's theory is an example of the second category, as are Sternberg's **triarchic theory of intelligence** and Gardner's **theory of multiple intelligences.** Goleman's theory of **emotional intelligence** emphasizes skill in social relationships and awareness of others' and one's own emotions.

What kinds of intelligence tests are in use today? The *Binet–Simon Scale,* developed in France by Alfred Binet and Theodore Simon, was adapted by Stanford University's L. M. Terman to create a test that yields an **intelligence quotient (IQ),** the *Stanford–Binet Intelligence Scale.* The **Wechsler Adult Intelligence Scale** and the **Wechsler Intelligence Scale for Children** provide scores for several different kinds of mental abilities as well as an overall IQ score. In contrast to these individual intelligence tests, **group tests** of intelligence are administered by one examiner to many people at a time. Alternatives to traditional IQ tests include **performance tests** of mental abilities that exclude the use of language and **culture-fair tests** that reduce cultural bias in a variety of ways.

What are some important characteristics of a good test? **Reliability** refers to the ability of a test to produce consistent and stable scores. Psychologists express reliability in terms of **correlation coefficients,** which measure the relationship between two sets of scores. **Validity** is the ability of a test to measure what it has been designed to measure. **Content validity** exists if a test contains an adequate sample of questions relating to the skills or knowledge it is supposed to measure. **Criterion-related** validity refers to the relationship between test scores and whatever the test is designed to measure. In the case of intelligence, the most common independent measure is academic achievement. Although the reliability of IQ tests is seldom questioned, their validity is questioned. Critics charge that these tests assess a very limited set of mental skills and that some tests may be unfairly biased against minority groups. Also, poor school performance may be the result of, rather than caused by, low test scores. Finally, although IQ tests tend to predict occupational success and performance on the job after college, they are not ideally suited to that important task. New tests are being developed to address these concerns.

HEREDITY, ENVIRONMENT, AND INTELLIGENCE

What determines individual differences in intelligence? Why are twin studies useful in studying intelligence? Although there has been extended debate about the extent to which heredity and environment contribute to IQ, studies comparing the IQ scores of identical and fraternal twins raised in the same and different families indicate that approximately 50% of differences in intelligence are due to genetics and the other half due to differences in environment, including education.

What have we learned from early intervention programs about the influence of the environment on intellectual development? With such a sizable percentage of the differences in IQ scores being attributable to the environment and education, many psychologists are strongly in favor of compensatory education programs for young children from disadvantaged homes. Two such programs are the Milwaukee Project and Head Start. Although they may not boost IQ scores greatly in the long run, such programs do seem to have significant educational benefits.

How can the study of plants help us to understand the relationship between heredity and environment? Plants grown in rich soil under ideal environmental conditions generally do better than plants grown in poor soil under less than ideal conditions, thus showing the importance of environment. But differences between plants grown under the same environmental conditions demonstrate the importance of heredity. Similarly, individual differences in human intelligence reflect both the genetic and environmental factors. However, psychologists cannot yet account for the fact that IQ scores on the whole are increasing (the Flynn Effect).

Do culture and gender influence mental abilities? While males and females do not differ in general intelligence, females do tend to have slightly stronger verbal skills, while males tend to have slightly stronger visual-spatial skills. Research indicates that these differences emerge in early infancy. As for cultural differences, research does not support the notion that people from certain cultures have a natural tendency to excel at academic skills.

What do psychologists know about the two extremes of human intelligence: very high and very low? The IQs of nearly 70% of the population fall between 85 and 115; and all but 5% have IQs between 70 and 130. **Intellectual disability** and **giftedness** are the two extremes of intelligence. About 25% of cases of intellectual disability can be traced to biological causes, including Down syndrome, but causes of the remaining 75% are not fully understood; nor are the causes of giftedness. Gifted people do not necessarily excel in all mental abilities.

CREATIVITY

What is creativity? **Creativity** is the ability to produce novel and socially valued ideas or objects.

How is creativity related to intelligence? The threshold theory holds that a minimum level of intelligence is needed for creativity, but above that threshold level, higher intelligence doesn't necessarily make for greater creativity. Apparently factors other than intelligence contribute to creativity.

Can creativity be measured? Creativity tests are scored on the originality of answers and, frequently, on the number of responses (demonstrating divergent thinking). Some psychologists question how valid these tests are, however.

Test Yourself

1. Images and concepts are:
   a. required by perception but not by sensation.
   b. necessary in problem solving but not in decision making.
   c. two of the most important building blocks of thought.
   d. required by perception but not by sensation.

2. The smallest meaningful units in a language are:
   a. holophrases.
   b. morphemes.
   c. surface structures.
   d. phonemes.

(Continued)

3. An image differs from a concept in that:
   a. an image retains some of the sensory qualities of experiences, whereas a concept is abstract.
   b. an image is very abstract, whereas a concept is concrete.
   c. an image is abstract, whereas a concept retains some of the sensory qualities of experiences.
   d. an image is a perceptual experience, whereas a concept is a cognitive product.

4. The best or most typical model of a concept is called a(n):
   a. phoneme.
   b. exclusive representation.
   c. image.
   d. prototype.

5. In contrast to a problem that requires divergent thinking, a problem that requires convergent thinking:
   a. involves time.
   b. has only one or a very few solutions.
   c. is more creative.
   d. involves more than one person.

6. Your car is not operating correctly. The mechanic opens the hood and says "We've been seeing lots of cars recently with fouled plugs or dirty fuel filters. Let's start there and see if that's your problem, too." The mechanic is using:
   a. a heuristic.
   b. an algorithm.
   c. a compensatory decision model.
   d. a noncompensatory decision model.

7. A TV repair person comes to fix your broken TV. The repair person proceeds to test every circuit board in order until the person finds the one that doesn't work. The person's problem-solving strategy is an example of:
   a. hill climbing.
   b. prototype formulation.
   c. an algorithm.
   d. means-end analysis.

8. Unlike algorithms, heuristics:
   a. lead away from a solution to almost any problem.
   b. guarantee a solution.
   c. cannot be used in every possible problem situation.
   d. do not guarantee a solution.

9. Which of the following is an example of functional fixedness?
   a. Using a book to secure an uneven table leg.
   b. Not realizing that a dime can serve as a screwdriver.
   c. Forgetting the uses for a tool we once owned.
   d. Being able to learn how to use a screwdriver.

10. If you have properly weighted the various criteria and correctly rated each alternative in terms of each criterion, then you have used what type of decision-making model?
   a. Trial and error model.
   b. Heuristic model.
   c. Compensatory model.
   d. Noncompensatory model.

11. Studies have shown that "hands-free" cell phone use while driving:
   a. may be as dangerous as driving while intoxicated.
   b. is far less dangerous for younger drivers than for older drivers.
   c. has little impact on driving as long as the driver remembers to pay more attention to driving than the conversation.
   d. has no detrimental impact on driving ability as long as the driver is an experienced and well-practiced multitasker.

12. The Stanford–Binet, WAIS-IV, and WISC-IV intelligence tests are normally administered:
   a. only to children.
   b. to small groups of 3 or 4 people simultaneously.
   c. in a test booklet that can be given to large numbers of people simultaneously.
   d. by a trained examiner to only one person at a time.

13. Students who get high scores on the Fictitious Achievement Test (FAT) also get high ratings on achievement from teachers, get higher course grades, and have fewer school absences. These data indicate that the FAT has:
   a. high alternate forms reliability.
   b. high criterion-related validity.
   c. high content validity.
   d. a high level of standardization.

14. Which of the following statements about intellectual disability is accurate?
   a. Nearly 90% of all people with intellectual disability are classified as mild.
   b. Genetic and biological disorders account for the majority of intellectual disabilities.
   c. Biologically caused intellectual disability cannot be moderated through education or training.
   d. Many of the people diagnosed with intellectual disability function independently.

15. Two important features of creative people are that they
   a. excel at art or music but are poor at science.
   b. are perceived as less intelligent and more irresponsible than other people.
   c. excel at art or music but are poor at math.
   d. take risks and like to work on problems that they invent themselves.

10

Motivation and Emotion*

Enduring Issues in Motivation and Emotion

*Taken from *Understanding Psychology*, Eleventh Edition by Charles G. Morris and Albert A. Maisto

Classic detective stories are usually studies of motivation and emotion. At the beginning, all we know is that a murder has been committed: After eating dinner with her family, sweet old Amanda Jones collapses and dies of strychnine poisoning. "Now, why would anyone do a thing like that?" everybody wonders. The police ask the same question, in different terms: "Who had a motive for killing Miss Jones?" In a good mystery, the answer is "Practically everybody."

There is, for example, the younger sister—although she is 75 years old, she still bristles when she thinks of that tragic day 50 years ago when Amanda stole her sweetheart. And there is the next-door neighbor, who was heard saying that if Miss Jones's poodle trampled his peonies one more time, there would be consequences. Then there is the spendthrift nephew who stands to inherit a fortune from the deceased. Finally, the parlor maid has a guilty secret that Miss Jones knew and had threatened to reveal. All four suspects were in the house on the night of the murder, had access to the poison (which was used to kill rats in the basement), and had strong feelings about Amanda Jones. All of them had a motive for killing her.

In this story, motivation and emotion are so closely intertwined that drawing distinctions between them is difficult. However, psychologists do try to separate them. A **motive** is a specific need or desire that arouses the organism and directs its behavior toward a goal. All motives are triggered by some kind of stimulus: a bodily condition, a cue in the environment, or a feeling.

Emotion refers to the experience of feelings such as fear, joy, surprise, and anger. Like motives, emotions also activate and affect behavior, but it is more difficult to predict the kind of behavior that a particular emotion will prompt. If a man is hungry, we can be reasonably sure that he will seek food. If, however, this same man experiences a feeling of joy or surprise, we cannot know with certainty how he will act.

The important thing to remember about both motives and emotions is that they push us to take some kind of action whether or not we are aware of it. We do not need to think about feeling hungry to make a beeline for the refrigerator. Similarly, we do not have to realize that we are afraid before stepping back from a growling dog. Moreover, the same motivation or emotion may produce different behaviors in different people. Ambition might motivate one person to go to law school and another to join a crime ring. Feeling sad might lead one person to cry alone and another to seek out a friend. On the other hand, the same behavior might arise from different motives or emotions: You may go to a movie because you are happy, bored, or lonely. In short, the workings of motives and emotions are very complex.

In this chapter, we will first look at some specific motives that play important roles in human behavior. Then we will turn our attention to emotions and the various ways they are expressed. We begin our discussion of motivation with a few general concepts.

ENDURING ISSUES in Motivation and Emotion

The heart of this chapter concerns the ways in which motives and emotions affect behavior and are affected by the external environment (*Person–Situation*). While discussing those key issues, we will explore the question of whether motives and emotions are inborn or acquired (*Nature–Nurture*) and whether they change significantly over the life span (*Stability–Change*). We will also consider the extent to which individuals differ in their motives and emotions (*Diversity–Universality*) and the ways in which motives and emotions arise from and, in turn, affect biological processes (*Mind–Body*).

PERSPECTIVES ON MOTIVATION

How can you use intrinsic and extrinsic motivation to help you succeed in college?

Instincts

Early in the 20th century, psychologists often attributed behavior to **instincts**—specific, inborn behavior patterns characteristic of an entire species. In 1890, William James

motive
specific need or desire, such as hunger, thirst, or achievement, that prompts goal-directed behavior

emotion
feeling, such as fear, joy, or surprise, that underlies behavior

instincts
inborn, inflexible, goal-directed behaviors that are characteristic of an entire species

compiled a list of human instincts that included hunting, rivalry, fear, curiosity, shyness, love, shame, and resentment. But by the 1920s, instinct theory began to fall out of favor as an explanation of human behavior for three reasons: (1) Most important human behavior is learned; (2) human behavior is rarely rigid, inflexible, unchanging, and found throughout the species, as is the case with instincts; and (3) ascribing every conceivable human behavior to a corresponding instinct explains nothing (calling a person's propensity to be alone an "antisocial instinct," for example, merely names the behavior without pinpointing its origins).

drive
state of tension or arousal that motivates behavior

drive-reduction theory
states that motivated behavior is aimed at reducing a state of bodily tension or arousal and returning the organism to homeostasis

Drive-Reduction Theory

An alternative view of motivation holds that bodily needs (such as the need for food or the need for water) create a state of tension or arousal called a **drive** (such as hunger or thirst). According to **drive-reduction theory**, motivated behavior is an attempt to reduce this unpleasant state of tension in the body and to return the body to a state of **homeostasis**, or balance. When we are hungry, we look for food to reduce the hunger drive. When we are tired, we find a place to rest.

According to drive-reduction theory, drives can generally be divided into two categories. **Primary drives** are unlearned, are found in all animals (including humans), and motivate behavior that is vital to the survival of the individual or species. Primary drives include hunger, thirst, and sex. **Secondary drives** are acquired through learning. For instance, no one is born with a drive to acquire great wealth, yet many people are motivated by money.

Arousal Theory

Drive-reduction theory is appealing, but it cannot explain all kinds of behavior. It implies, for example, that once drives are reduced, people will do little. They would literally have no motivation. Yet this is obviously not the case. People work, play, do Sudoku puzzles, and do many other things for which there is no known drive that needs to be reduced.

Thinking Critically About . . .

Primary Drives

Primary drives are, by definition, unlearned. But learning clearly affects how these drives are expressed: We learn how and what to eat and drink.

1. Given that information, how might you design a research study to determine what aspects of a given drive, say hunger, are learned and which are not?
2. What steps would you take to increase the likelihood that your results apply to people in general and not just to a small sample of people?
3. Would you have to rely on self-reports or could you directly observe behavior?

Arousal theory suggests that each of us has an optimum level of arousal that varies over the course of the day and from one situation to another. According to this view, behavior is motivated by the desire to maintain the optimum level of arousal for a given moment. Sometimes, as envisioned in drive-reduction theory, that may call for reducing the level of arousal. But other times, behavior appears to be motivated by a desire to increase the state of arousal. For example, when you are bored, you may turn on the television, take a walk, or check for text messages.

homeostasis
state of balance and stability in which the organism functions effectively

primary drives
unlearned drive, such as hunger, that are based on a physiological state

secondary drives
learned drives, such as ambition, that are not based on a physiological state

arousal theory
theory of motivation that proposes that organisms seek an optimal level of arousal

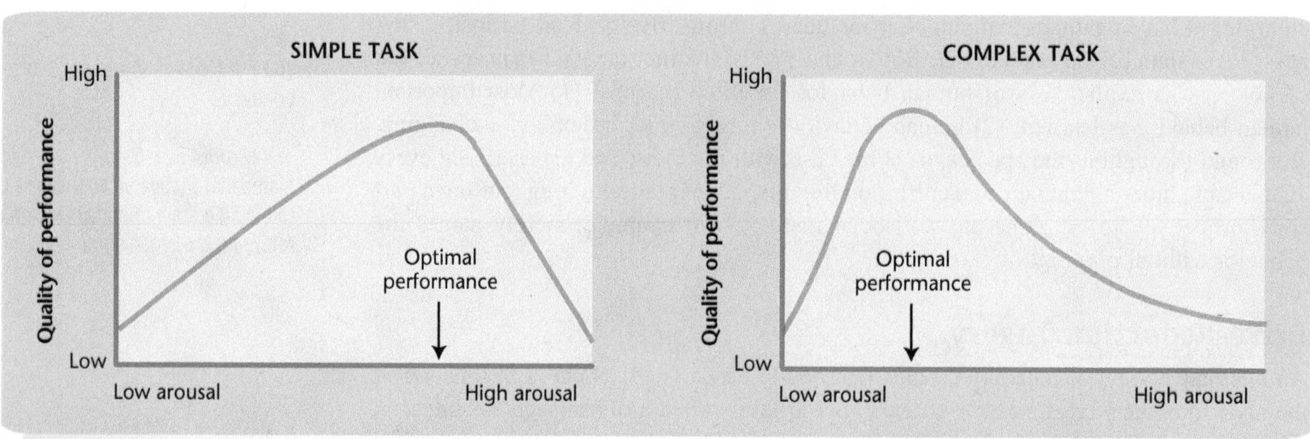

Figure 10.1 The Yerkes–Dodson law.
A certain amount of arousal is needed to perform most tasks, but a very high level of arousal interferes with the performance of complicated activities. That is, the level of arousal that can be tolerated is higher for a simple task than for a complex one.
Source: After Hebb, 1955.

Interestingly, overall level of arousal affects performance in different situations but psychologists agree that there is no "best" level of arousal necessary to perform all tasks (Gray, Braver, & Raichle, 2002). Rather, it is largely a question of degree. The **Yerkes–Dodson law** puts it this way: The more complex the task, the lower the level of arousal that can be tolerated without interfering with performance (Yerkes & Dodson, 1908/2007). Thus, to perform optimally on a simple task, you may need to increase your level of arousal. Conversely, you may need to reduce your level of arousal to perform well on a complex task. (See **Figure 10.1.**)

Enduring Issues

Nature–Nurture *The Evolutionary Basis of Arousal Seeking*

Some evolutionary theorists argue that sensation seeking may have an evolutionary basis. For example, Cosmides and Tooby (2000) propose that risk-taking behavior may have played an important adaptive role for our ancestors by providing them with opportunities to develop successful strategies to deal with potentially dangerous situations. Those who took risks, and who were thereby better equipped to cope with danger and turmoil in their environment, improved their social status and sexual competitiveness more than those who did not (Ermer, Cosmides, & Tooby, 2008).

Arousal theory has some advantages over drive-reduction theory, but neither one can readily account for some kinds of behavior. For example, many people today participate in activities that are stimulating in the extreme: rock climbing, skydiving, bungee jumping, kitesurfing, and hang gliding. Such thrill-seeking activities do not seem to be drive-reducing and do not seem to be done in pursuit of an optimal level of arousal. Zuckerman (2007a) accounts for such activities by suggesting that *sensation seeking* is itself a basic motivation, at least some aspects of which are inherited and neurologically based (Joseph, Liu, Jiang, Lynam, & Kelly, 2009; Zuckerman, 2009). In general, high-sensation seekers, compared to low-sensation seekers, are more likely to

- prefer dangerous sports (Eachus, 2004; Gomà-i-Freixanet, Martha, & Muro, 2012; Zuckerman, 2007b);

Yerkes–Dodson law
states that there is an optimal level of arousal for the best performance of any task; the more complex the task, the lower the level of arousal that can be tolerated before performance deteriorates

- choose vocations that involve an element of risk and excitement (Zuckerman, 2006);
- smoke, drink heavily, gamble, and use illicit drugs (Barrault & Varescon, 2013; Ersche, Turton, Pradhan, Bullmore, & Robbins, 2010; Gurpegui et al., 2007); engage in unsafe driving (Bachoo, Bhagwanjee, & Govender, 2013; S. L. Pedersen & McCarthy, 2008);
- have more sexual partners and engage in more varied and dangerous sexual activities (Berg, 2008; Cohen, 2008; Oshri, Tubman, Morgan-Lopez, Saavedra, & Csizmadia, 2013); and
- be classified in school as delinquent or hyperactive (though not more aggressive) (Ang & Woo, 2003; Modecki, 2008).

Intrinsic and Extrinsic Motivation

Some psychologists further distinguish between intrinsic and extrinsic motivation. **Intrinsic motivation** refers to motivation provided by an activity itself. Children climb trees, finger paint, and play games for no other reason than the fun they get from the activity itself. In the same way, adults may solve crossword puzzles, play a musical instrument, or tinker in a workshop largely for the enjoyment they get from the activity. **Extrinsic motivation** refers to motivation that derives from the consequences of an activity. For example, a child may do chores not because he enjoys them but because doing so earns an allowance, and an adult who plays a musical instrument may do so to earn some extra money.

Whether behavior is intrinsically or extrinsically motivated can have important consequences (Deci & Ryan, 2008). For example, if parents offer a reward to their young daughter for writing to her grandparents, the likelihood of her writing to them when rewards are no longer available may actually decrease. One analysis of some 128 studies that examined the effect of extrinsic rewards on the behavior of children, adolescents, and adults found that when extrinsic rewards are offered for a behavior, intrinsic motivation and sense of personal responsibility for that behavior are likely to decrease, at least for a short time (Deci, Koestner, & Ryan, 1999, 2001). However, unexpected (as opposed to contractual) rewards do not necessarily reduce intrinsic motivation, and positive feedback (including praise) may actually increase intrinsic motivation (Reiss, 2005). For example, one study showed that rewarding small children for eating vegetables they initially disliked resulted in the children consuming more of those vegetables and reporting that they liked them more (Cooke, 2011).

A Hierarchy of Motives

Humanistic psychologist Abraham Maslow (1954) arranged motives in a hierarchy, from lower to higher. The lower motives spring from physiological needs that must be satisfied. As we move higher in Maslow's **hierarchy of needs**, the motives have more subtle origins: the desire to live as safely as possible, to connect meaningfully with other human beings, and to make the best possible impression on others. Maslow believed that the highest motive in the hierarchy is self-actualization—the drive to realize one's full potential. According to Maslow's theory, higher motives emerge only after the more basic ones have been largely satisfied: A person who is starving doesn't care what people think of her table manners.

Within each level on Maslow's Hierarchy of Needs pyramid, try and think about your own needs and which need is the most important to you.

Maslow's model offers an appealing way to organize a wide range of motives into a coherent structure. But recent research challenges the universality of his views. In many societies, people live on the very edge of survival, yet they form strong and meaningful social ties and possess a firm sense of self-esteem (E. Hoffman, 2008; Wubbolding, 2005). As a result of such research findings, many psychologists now view Maslow's model with

intrinsic motivation
a desire to perform a behavior that stems from the enjoyment derived from the behavior itself

extrinsic motivation
a desire to perform a behavior to obtain an external reward or avoid punishment

hierarchy of needs
a theory of motivation advanced by Maslow holding that higher order motives involving social and personal growth only emerge after lower level motives related to survival have been satisfied

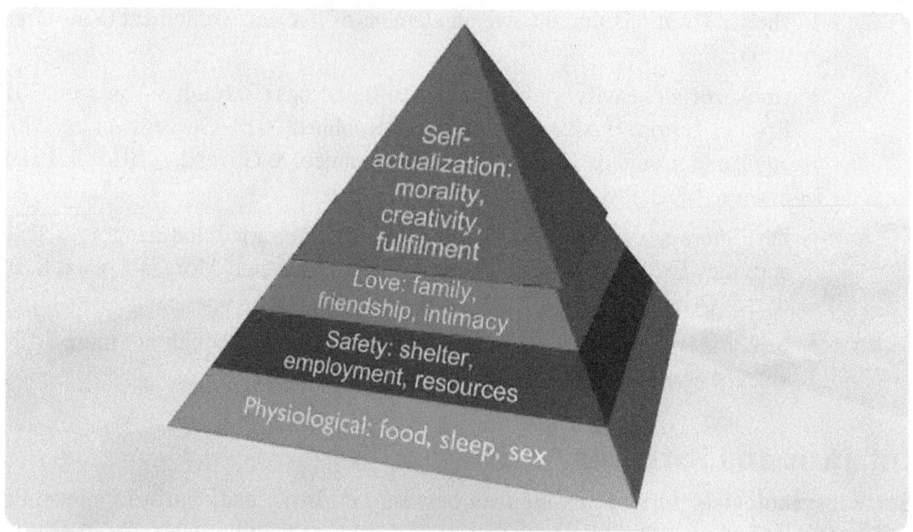

"Maslow's Hierarchy of Needs"

a measure of skepticism although it continues to be a convenient way to think of the wide range of human motives.

We have reviewed some basic concepts about motivation. With these concepts in mind, we now turn our attention to specific motives.

Quiz Questions

1. You are home alone and have nothing to do. You find yourself walking around. You look for something to read, but nothing seems quite right. Then you check to see if anything interesting is on TV, but again nothing seems worth watching. Finally, you decide to go jogging. This kind of motivated behavior that increases the state of arousal is a problem for:
   a. the instinct theory of motivation.
   b. the Yerkes–Dodson law.
   c. the drive-reduction theory of motivation.
   d. any theory of motivation.
2. While you are working on a complex task, your boss stops by your desk and says, "You've only got 10 more minutes to finish that up. It's really important that it be done right. I know you can do it and I'm depending on you." When you complain that he's making you nervous and your performance will suffer, he replies, "I'm just trying to motivate you." Which of the following does your boss apparently not understand?
   a. Drive-reduction theory.
   b. Homeostasis.
   c. Extrinsic motivation.
   d. The Yerkes–Dodson law.
3. The theory that motivated behavior is focused on reducing bodily tension is called:
   a. homeostasis.
   b. drive-reduction theory.
   c. the Yerkes-Dodson law.
   d. arousal theory.
4. A state of tension brought on by biological needs is referred to as:
   a. a drive.
   b. homeostasis.
   c. stimulus.
   d. intrinsic motivator.
5. According to which theory of motivation, do higher motives such as self-esteem, only emerge after lower motives such as physiological needs have been satisfied?
   a. Secondary Drive Theory.
   b. Arousal Theory.
   c. Hierarchy of Needs Theory.
   d. Drive-reduction Theory.

Hunger and Thirst

Why do people usually get hungry at mealtime?

When you are hungry, you eat. If you don't eat, your need for food will increase but your hunger will come and go. Moreover, shortly after lunch when you have no need for further food, if you pass a bakery and smell the baked goods, you may crave a donut or a scone. In other words, the psychological state of hunger is not the same as the biological need for food, although that need often sets the psychological state in motion.

Thirst also is stimulated by both internal and external cues. Internally, thirst is controlled by two regulators that monitor the level of fluids inside and outside the cells. But we may also become thirsty just seeing a TV commercial featuring people savoring tall, cool drinks in a lush, tropical setting. Even what we thirst for can be influenced by what we see. One study showed, for example, that women watching a movie with commercials advertising sweetened soda were more likely to consume soda during movie breaks than where women who viewed commercials advertising water (Koordeman, Anschutz, van Baaren, & Engels, 2010).

Biological and Emotional Factors

How can external cues influence our desire to eat?

Early research identified two regions in the hypothalamus that served as a kind of "switch" that turned eating on or off. When one of these centers was stimulated, animals began to eat; and when it was destroyed, the animals stopped eating to the point of starvation. When the second region was stimulated, animals stopped eating; when it was destroyed, animals ate to the point of extreme obesity. However, recent studies have challenged this simple "on–off" explanation for the control of eating by showing that a number of other areas of the brain are also involved in regulating food intake including regions of the cerebrum, amygdala, the insula, and the spinal cord (Garavan, 2010; Sternson, Betley, & Cao, 2013; Siep et al., 2009).

How do these various areas of the brain know when to stimulate hunger? It turns out that the brain monitors the blood levels of **glucose** (a simple sugar used by the body for energy), fats, carbohydrates, and the hormone *insulin.* (See **Figure 10.2.**) Changes in the levels of these substances signal the need for food. In addition, fat cells within our body produce the hormone **leptin**, which travels in the bloodstream and is sensed by the hypothalamus. High levels of leptin signal the brain to reduce appetite, or to increase the rate at which fat is burned.

The brain also monitors the amount of food that you have eaten. Specialized cells in the stomach and the upper part of the small intestine sense the volume of food in the digestive system. When only a small quantity of food is present, these cells release a hormone called **ghrelin** into the bloodstream. Ghrelin travels to the brain where it stimulates appetite and focuses our thoughts and imagination on food (Faulconbridge, 2008; Langlois et al., 2011).

But, as we noted earlier, the biological need for food is not the only thing that can trigger the experience of hunger. For example, a single night of sleep deprivation can leave one feeling hungry by increasing ghrelin levels and decreasing leptin levels (Schmid, Hallschmid, Jauch-Chara, Born, & Schultes, 2008). Moreover, the mere sight, smell, or thought of food causes an increase in insulin production, which, in turn, lowers glucose levels in the body's cells, mirroring the body's response to a physical need for food (Logue, 2000; van der Laan, de Ridder, Viergever, & Smeets, 2011). Thus, the aroma from a nearby restaurant may serve as more than an **incentive** to eat; it may actually cause the body to react as though there is a real biological need for food. Most Americans eat three meals a day at fairly regular intervals. Numerous studies with both humans and animals have

glucose
a simple sugar used by the body for energy

leptin
a hormone released by fat cells that reduces appetite

ghrelin
a hormone produced in the stomach and small intestines that increases appetite

incentive
external stimulus that prompts goal-directed behavior

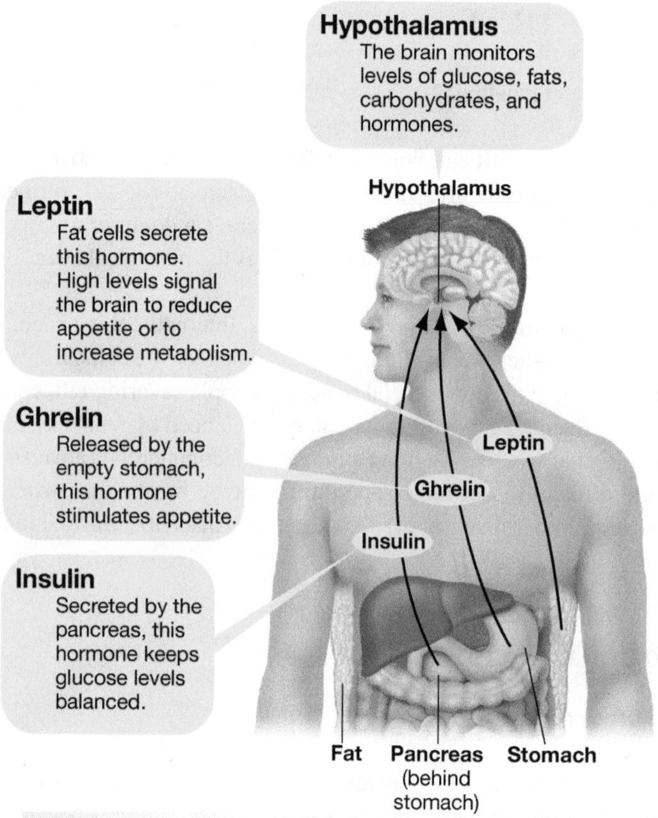

Figure 10.2 Physiological Factors Regulating Appetite and Body Weight.
A variety of chemical messengers interact to stimulate and suppress appetite. Among these are insulin, leptin, and ghrelin.

shown that regularly eating at particular times during the day leads to the release at those times of the hormones and neurotransmitters that cause hunger (Woods, Schwartz, Baskin, & Seeley, 2000). In other words, we get hungry around noon partly because the body "learns" that if it's noon, it's time to eat.

Enduring Issues

Diversity–Universality *Hunger and Eating*

The hunger drive is tied to emotions in complex ways. Some people head for the refrigerator whenever they are depressed, bored, anxious, or angry. Others lose all interest in food at these times and complain that they are "too upset to eat." One student studying for an important exam spends as much time eating as reading; another student studying for the same exam lives on coffee until the exam is over. Under emotionally arousing conditions, what one person craves may turn another person's stomach.

What people eat when they are hungry also varies greatly as a result of learning and social conditioning. Although most Americans will not eat horsemeat, it is very popular in several European countries. Yet many Americans consume pork, which violates both Islamic and Jewish dietary laws. In some parts of South Asia, Africa, and China, people consider monkey brains a delicacy. And in Cambodia, fried tarantulas are popular and cheap!

Eating Disorders and Obesity

How can you tell if someone is suffering from anorexia nervosa or bulimia?

Anorexia Nervosa and Bulimia Nervosa

"When people told me I looked like someone from Auschwitz [the Nazi concentration camp], I thought that was the highest compliment anyone could give me." This confession comes from a young woman who as a teenager suffered from a serious eating disorder known as **anorexia nervosa**. She was 18 years old, 5 feet 3 inches tall, and weighed 68 pounds. This young woman was lucky. She managed to overcome the disorder and has since maintained normal body weight. Many others are less fortunate. In fact, researchers have found that over 10% of the young women with anorexia nervosa die as a result of the disorder, one of the highest fatality rates for psychiatric disorders affecting young females (Birmingham, Su, Hlynsky, Goldner, & Gao, 2005; Huas, 2011).

The following symptoms are used in the diagnosis of anorexia nervosa (American Psychiatric Association, 2013):

- Intense fear of becoming obese, which does not diminish as weight loss progresses.
- Disturbance of body image (for example, claiming to "feel fat" even when emaciated).
- Refusal to maintain body weight at or above a minimal normal weight for age and height.

Approximately 1% of all adolescents suffer from anorexia nervosa; about 90% of these are White upper- or middle-class females (Bulik et al., 2006).

Anorexia is frequently compounded by another eating disorder known as **bulimia nervosa** (Herpertz-Dahlmann, 2009). The following criteria are used for its diagnosis (American Psychiatric Association, 2013):

- Recurrent episodes of binge eating (rapid consumption of a large amount of food, usually in less than 2 hours) accompanied by a lack of control while eating during the episode.
- Recurrent inappropriate behaviors to try to prevent weight gain, such as self-induced vomiting or misuse of laxatives.
- Binge eating and compensatory behaviors occurring at least once a week for three months.
- Body shape and weight excessively influencing the person's self-image.
- Occurrence of the just-mentioned behaviors at least sometimes in the absence of anorexia.

Approximately 1 to 2% of all adolescent females suffer from bulimia nervosa, though some evidence suggests this number may be decreasing (Keel, Heatherton, Dorer, Joiner, & Zalta, 2006). Once again, the socioeconomic group at highest risk for bulimia is upper–middle- and upper-class women.

Although anorexia and bulimia are much more prevalent among females than males (Gleaves, Miller, Williams, & Summers, 2000; S. Turnbull, Ward, Treasure, Jick, & Derby, 1996), many more men are affected by these disorders than was once suspected (Gila, Castro, & Cesena, 2005). Both men and women with eating disorders are preoccupied with body image, but men are not necessarily obsessed with losing weight (Ey, 2010; Ousley, Cordero, & White, 2008). For example, a related phenomenon called **muscle dysmorphia** appears to be on the increase among young men (Olivardia, 2007;

anorexia nervosa
a serious eating disorder that is associated with an intense fear of weight gain and a distorted body image

bulimia nervosa
an eating disorder characterized by binges of eating followed by self-induced vomiting

muscle dysmorphia
a disorder generally seen in young men involving an obsessive concern with muscle size

Woodruff, 2014). Muscle dysmorphia is an obsessive concern with one's muscle size. Men with muscle dysmorphia, many of whom are well muscled, are nonetheless distressed at their perceived puniness, and spend an inordinate amount of time fretting over their diet and exercising to increase their muscle mass (Murray, Rieger, Karlov, & Touyz, 2013; C. G. Pope, Pope, & Menard, 2005).

Little is known about the factors that contribute to eating disorders among men (Crosscope-Happel, 2005), though research has shown that muscle dysmorphia is associated with low self-esteem and having been bullied as a child (Boyda & Shevlin, 2011; Wolke & Sapouna, 2008). We know considerably more about the factors that contribute to eating disorders in women (Garner & Magana, 2006). On one hand, mass media promote the idea that a woman must be thin to be attractive. In addition, women with bulimia commonly have low self-esteem, are hypersensitive to social interactions, and are more likely to come from families where negative comments are often made about weight (Crowther, Kichler, Sherwood, & Kuhnert, 2002; Zonnevylle-Bender et al., 2004). Many also display clinical depression or obsessive–compulsive disorder and have engaged in self-injurious behaviors such as cutting themselves (Herpertz-Dahlmann, 2009). Finally, there is growing evidence that genetics plays a significant role in both anorexia nervosa and bulimia nervosa (Helder & Collier, 2011; Slof-Op't Landt et al., 2013).

Anorexia and bulimia are notoriously hard to treat, and there is considerable disagreement on the most effective approach to therapy (G. T. Wilson, Grilo, & Vitousek, 2007; Yager, 2008). However, research suggests multimodal treatment approaches that draw upon nutritional counseling, individual therapy, family therapy, cognitive–behavioral therapy, and mindful mediation may be most effective (Herpertz-Dahlmann & Salbach-Andrae, 2009; Lenz, Taylor, Fleming, & Serman, 2014).

Unfortunately, some psychologists doubt that we can ever eliminate eating disorders in a culture bombarded with the message that "thin is in" (Fairburn, Cooper, Shafran, & Wilson, 2008). Regrettably, in many developing countries such as Taiwan, Singapore, and China, where dieting is becoming a fad, eating disorders, once little known, are now becoming a serious problem (H. Chen & Jackson, 2008).

Obesity and Weight Control

According to the U.S. Surgeon General, obesity is the most pressing health problem in America (Office of the Surgeon General, 2007). *Obesity* refers to an excess of body fat in relation to lean body mass, while *overweight* refers to weighing more than a desirable standard, whether from high amounts of fat or being very muscular. Obesity has increased by more than 50% during the past decade, with more than two-thirds of Americans being either overweight or obese. In contrast to anorexia nervosa and bulimia nervosa, obesity is more prevalent among Black women than among White women (Y. C. Wang, Colditz, & Kuntz, 2007).

Even more disturbing, the rate of obesity among young people has more than tripled since 1980, with over 9 million overweight adolescents in America today. (See **Figure 10.3**). This problem is particularly serious since overweight children and adolescents are more likely to become overweight adults who are at an increased risk for serious diseases like hypertension, cardiovascular disease, diabetes, and sleep apnea (American Heart Association, 2009).

Many factors contribute to overeating and obesity (Hebebrand & Hinney, 2009). As stated above, many people inherit a tendency to be overweight (Frayling et al., 2007; Ramadori et al., 2008). Neuroimaging studies suggest part of this problem may stem from an inherited tendency in some people to become addicted to compulsive eating (similar to the genetic predisposition toward drug and alcohol addiction). As a result of this predisposition, these individuals are more vulnerable to cravings triggered by food cues in their environment, and less responsive to their body's internal signaling of satiety (Leutwyler-Ozelli, 2007).

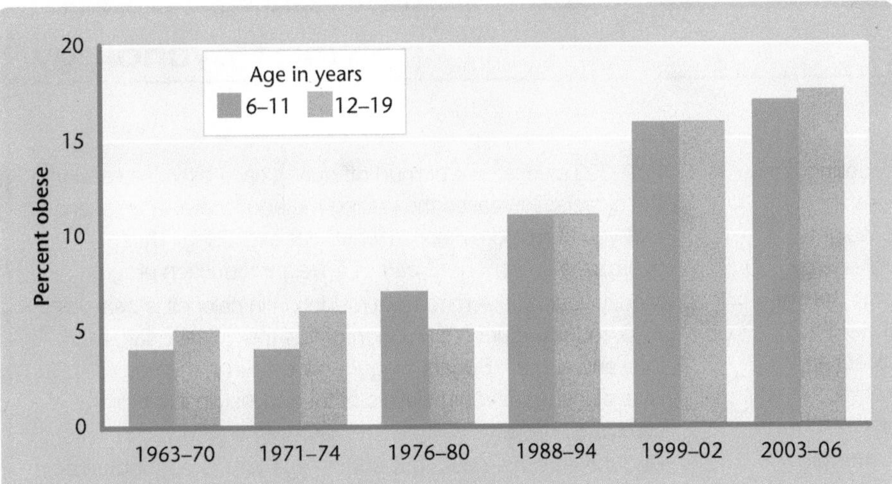

Figure 10.3 Rising Obesity Among American Youth.
The number of overweight children and adolescents has increased sharply in recent years. From 1980 to 2002, the percentage of overweight adolescents tripled. This trend is particularly disturbing since overweight children and adolescents are likely to become overweight adults, placing them at increased risk for cardiovascular disease, hypertension, and diabetes.

Source: CDC/NCHS, NHES, and NHANES.

Notes: Excludes pregnant women starting with 1971–74. Pregnancy status not available for 1963–65 and 1966–70. Data for 1963–65 are for children 6–11 years of age; data for 1966–70 are for adolescents 12–17 years of age, not 12–19 years.

Eating habits established during childhood are also important because they determine the number of fat cells that develop in the body and that number remains fairly constant throughout life. Dieting during adulthood only decreases the amount of fat each cell stores; it doesn't reduce the total number of fat cells (Spalding et al., 2008).

A sedentary lifestyle also contributes to obesity (Lee & Mattson, 2013). Children in the United States today are more likely to watch television and play video games than to play soccer or hockey; and many adults lack adequate physical activity, too. Abundant opportunities and encouragement to overeat in American culture also play a role. Several studies have shown that many obese people eat more than half their calories at night (Mieda, Williams, Richardson, Tanaka, & Yanagisawa, 2006). Portion size has also increased in recent years, as has the constant availability of food from vending machines and fast-food restaurants.

Adding to the medical difficulties accompanying obesity, overweight people often face ridicule and discrimination resulting in significant economic, social, and educational loss (Sikorski, Luppa, Brähler, König, & Riedel-Heller, 2012). For example, overweight women have reported lowered self-confidence owing to victimization in school and at work because of their weight (C. Johnson, 2002; Rothblum, Brand, Miller, & Oetjen, 1990). Obese male lawyers earn less than male lawyers of normal weight (Saporta & Halpern, 2002). Even children who are overweight are often the object of unrelenting and cruel bullying (Browne, 2012), display increased rates of behavior problems, including aggression, lack of discipline, immaturity, anxiety, low self-esteem, and depression when compared with their normal-weight peers (Ward-Begnoche et al., 2009; Q. Yang & Chen, 2001).

With all of the problems associated with being overweight, many people are constantly trying to lose weight. There are no quick fixes to weight loss, but the suggestions in "Applying Psychology: The Slow (but Lasting) Fix for Weight Gain" can help people lose weight and keep it off.

Applying Psychology

The Slow (but Lasting) Fix for Weight Gain

The study of hunger and eating has led to some compelling insights into the problem of weight control. It appears that our bodies are genetically "set" to maintain a certain weight by means of neural networks that monitor and control energy homeostasis (Levin, 2010). According to this **set point theory**, if you consume more calories than you need for that weight, your metabolic rate will increase. As a result, you will feel an increase in energy that will prompt you to be more active, thereby burning more calories. If, however, you eat fewer calories than are needed to maintain your weight, your metabolic rate will decrease; you will feel tired and become less active, thereby burning fewer calories. This mechanism was no doubt helpful during the thousands of years that our species lived literally hand to mouth, but it is less helpful where food is abundant, as in modern industrialized nations.

An implication of our current understanding of hunger and weight regulation is that a successful weight-control program must be long term and must work with, rather than against, the body's normal tendency to maintain weight. On the basis of studies of the hunger drive and the relationship between eating and body weight, here are our recommendations for weight control:

1. First, check with your doctor before you start. People want quick fixes, so they often go overboard on dieting or exercise, sometimes with disastrous consequences. Make sure your weight loss program will be safe.
2. Increase your body's metabolism through regular exercise. The most effective metabolism booster is 20–30 minutes of moderate activity several times a week. Although only about 200–300 calories are burned off during each exercise session, the exercise increases the resting metabolic rate. This means that you burn more calories when not exercising. Thus, exercise is an important part of a weight reduction program.
3. Modify your diet. A moderate reduction in calories is beneficial. Also, reduce your consumption of fats (particularly saturated fats) and sugars. Sugars trigger an increase in the body's level of insulin; and high levels of fat and insulin in the blood stimulate hunger.
4. Reduce external cues that encourage you to eat undesirable foods. The mere sight or smell of food can increase the amount of insulin in the body, thus triggering hunger. Many people find that if they do their grocery shopping on a full stomach, it is easier to resist the temptation to buy junk foods.
5. Set realistic goals. Focus at least as much on preventing weight gain as on losing weight. If you must lose weight, try to shed just one pound a week for 2 or 3 months. After that, concentrate on maintaining that new, lower weight for several months before moving on to further weight loss.
6. Reward yourself—in ways unrelated to food—for small improvements. Use some of the behavior-modification techniques. Reward yourself not only for each pound of weight lost but also for each day or week that you maintain that weight loss. And remember, numerous studies have shown that losing weight is much easier than keeping weight off (T. Mann et al., 2007). The only way you can keep the weight off is by continuing to adhere to a reasonable diet and exercise plan.

set point theory
a theory that our bodies are genetically predisposed to maintaining a certain weight by changing our metabolic rate and activity level in response to caloric intake

Quiz Questions

1. You are on your way out to a play, and you notice that you are hungry. While you are watching the play, you no longer feel hungry. But when the play is over, you notice that you are hungry again. This demonstrates that:
   a. the biological need for food causes hunger.
   b. the primary drives are unlearned and are essential to survival of the individual or species.
   c. if you are distracted, primary drives will decrease but not secondary drives.
   d. the hunger does not necessarily correspond to a biological need for food.

2. You've noticed that when you are hungry, eating a carrot doesn't satisfy you, but eating a chocolate bar does. This is probably because the chocolate bar, to a greater extent than the carrot:
   a. increases the amount of glucose in your bloodstream, which in turn reduces hunger.
   b. reduces your biological need for food.
   c. is an extrinsic motivator.
   d. serves as an incentive.
3. Rachael has an intense fear of obesity, a disturbed body image, eats very little food resulting in weight well below normal minimums. She is likely to be suffering from:
   a. bulimia nervosa.
   b. anorexia nervosa.
   c. muscle dysmorphia.
   d. ghrelin in her bloodstream.
4. Which of the following is NOT one of the substances found in the bloodstream that are involved in regulating food intake?
   a. Leptin.
   b. Ghrelin.
   c. Glucose.
   d. Insula.
5. Anorexia nervosa and bulimia nervosa:
   a. only affect females.
   b. respond quickly to behavioral therapy.
   c. are very difficult to treat.
   d. respond quickly to cognitive therapy.

SEX

How is the sex drive different from other primary drives?

Sex is the primary drive that motivates reproductive behavior. Like the other primary drives, it can be turned on and off by biological conditions in the body as well as by environmental cues. The human sexual response is also affected by social experience, sexual experience, nutrition, emotions, and age. In fact, just thinking about, viewing, or having fantasies about sex can lead to sexual arousal in humans (Bogaert & Fawcett, 2006). Sex differs from other primary drives in one important way: Hunger and thirst are vital to the survival of the individual, but sex is vital only to the survival of the species.

Biological Factors

How well do we understand the biology of the sex drive?

Biology clearly plays a major role in sexual motivation. At one time, the level of hormones such as **testosterone**—the male sex hormone—was believed to *determine* the male sex drive. Today, scientists recognize that hormonal influences on human sexual arousal are considerably more complex (Gades et al., 2008). While moment-to-moment fluctuations in testosterone levels are not directly linked to sex drive, *baseline* levels of testosterone are associated with the frequency of sexual behavior and satisfaction (Persky, 1978). In addition, research has shown that just thinking about sex can increase testosterone levels in women (Goldey & van Anders, 2010) and that testosterone supplements can increase the sex drive in women (Bolour & Braunstein, 2005). However, unlike lower animals, whose sexual activity is tied to the female's reproductive cycle, humans are capable of sexual arousal at any time.

Many animals secrete substances called *pheromones* that promote sexual readiness in potential partners. Some evidence suggests that humans, too, secrete pheromones, in the sweat glands of the armpits and in the genitals, and that they may influence

testosterone
the primary male sex hormone

Thinking Critically About . . .

The Sex Drive

The sex drive is said to have no survival value for the individual; its only value is the survival of the species. Suppose that humans were capable of reproducing, but no longer had a sex drive. How would life be different? In answering that question, would it help to collect data on people alive today who, for one reason or another, have lost their sex drive? Are there ways in which information from such people might not be useful to you?

human sexual attraction (Boulkroune, Wang, March, Walker, & Jacob, 2007; Hummer & McClintock, 2009). The brain exerts a powerful influence on the sex drive, too. In particular, the limbic system and the insula, located deep within the brain, are involved in sexual excitement (Balfour, 2004; Bianchi-Demicheli & Ortigue, 2007).

The biology of sexual behavior is better understood than that of the sex drive itself. Sex researchers William Masters and Virginia Johnson long ago identified a **sexual response cycle** that consists of four phases: *excitement, plateau, orgasm,* and *resolution* (W. H. Masters & Johnson, 1966). In the *excitement phase,* the genitals become engorged with blood. In the male, this causes erection of the penis; in the female, it causes erection of the clitoris and nipples. This engorgement of the sexual organs continues into the *plateau phase,* in which sexual tension levels off. During this phase, breathing becomes more rapid and genital secretions and muscle tension increase. During *orgasm,* the male ejaculates and the woman's uterus contracts rhythmically; and both men and women experience some loss of muscle control. Following orgasm males experience a *refractory period,* which can last from a few minutes to several hours, during which time they cannot have another orgasm. Women do not have a refractory period, and may, if stimulation is reinitiated, experience another orgasm almost immediately. The *resolution phase* is one of relaxation in which muscle tension decreases and the engorged genitals return to normal. Heart rate, breathing, and blood pressure also return to normal.

Cultural and Environmental Factors

How does culture influence sexual behavior?

Although hormones and the nervous system do figure in the sex drive, human sexual motivation, especially in the early stages of excitement and arousal, is much more dependent on experience and learning than on biology.

What kinds of stimuli activate the sex drive? It need not be anything as immediate as a sexual partner. The sight of one's lover, as well as the smell of perfume or aftershave lotion, can stimulate sexual excitement. Soft lights and music often have an aphrodisiac effect. One person may be unmoved by an explicit pornographic movie but aroused by a romantic love story, whereas another may respond in just the opposite way. Ideas about what is moral, appropriate, and pleasurable also influence our sexual behavior. Finally, as shown in **Figure 10.4,** one global survey of reported sexual activity indicated the rate at which couples have sex varies dramatically around the world (Durex Global Sex Survey, 2005). This survey also revealed that the frequency of sexual activity varies by age, with 35- to 44-year-olds reporting to have sex an average of 112 times a year, 25- to 34-year-olds having sex an average of 108 times per year, and 16- to 20-year-olds having sex 90 times annually.

sexual response cycle
the typical sequence of events, including excitement, plateau, orgasm, and resolution, characterizing sexual response in males and females

Gender equality is also an important cultural factor in how much people report enjoying their sex lives (Petersen & Hyde, 2010). For example, heterosexual couples living in countries where women and men hold equal status are the most likely to report that their sex lives are emotionally and physically satisfying. Conversely, both men and women in countries where men traditionally are more dominant report the least satisfying sex lives (Harms, 2006).

Nation	Annual frequency of sex
Japan	44
India	74
Indonesia	76
Taiwan	87
Sweden	91
China	95
Ireland	96
Israel	99
Germany	103
Spain	104
Italy	105
Canada	107
Australia	107
United States	112
United Kingdom	117
France	119
Greece	137

Figure 10.4 Annual Frequency of Sexual Behavior Around the World.

A global survey of reported sexual activity indicates the frequency that couples have sex varies dramatically by country.

Source: http://www.durex.com/cm/gss2005result.pdf. Used with permission of Durex.com.

Patterns of Sexual Behavior Among Americans

Contrary to media portrayals of sexual behavior in publications like *Playboy* or TV shows like *Sex in the City,* which depict Americans as oversexed and unwilling to commit to long-term relationships, research indicates that most people are far more conservative in their sex lives. One carefully designed study (Michael, Gagnon, Laumann, & Kolata, 1994) of 3,432 randomly selected people between the ages of 18 and 59 revealed the following patterns in the sexual activity of American men and women:

- About one-third of those sampled had sex twice a week or more, one-third a few times a month, and the remaining third a few times a year or not at all.
- The overwhelming majority of respondents did not engage in kinky sex. Instead, vaginal intercourse was the preferred form of sex for over 90% of those sampled. Watching their partner undress was ranked second, and oral sex, third.
- Married couples reported having sex more often—and being more satisfied with their sex lives—than did unmarried persons (see also Waite & Joyner, 2001).
- The average duration of sexual intercourse reported by most people was approximately 15 minutes.
- The median number of partners over the lifetime for males was 6 and for females 2 (17% of the men and 3% of the women reported having sex with over 20 partners).
- About 25% of the men and 15% of the women had committed adultery.

Extensive research has also documented at least four significant differences in sexuality between American men and women: Men are more interested in sex than are women; women are more likely than men to link sex to a close, committed relationship; aggression, power, dominance, and assertiveness are more closely linked to sex among men than among women; and women's sexuality is more open to change over time (Lykins, Meana, & Strauss, 2008; Peplau, 2003). However, it is important to point out that gender differences in sexuality are smallest in nations that have gender equality, suggesting many of the observed differences in sexuality between men and women are based in culture (Petersen & Hyde, 2011).

Sexual Orientation

What are the arguments for and against a biological explanation of homosexuality?

Sexual orientation refers to the direction of an individual's sexual interest. What determines sexual orientation? This issue has been argued for decades in the form of the classic nature-versus-nurture debate. Those on the nature side hold that sexual orientation is rooted in biology and is primarily influenced by genetics (LeVay, 2011). They

sexual orientation
refers to the direction of one's sexual interest toward members of the same sex, the other sex, or both sexes

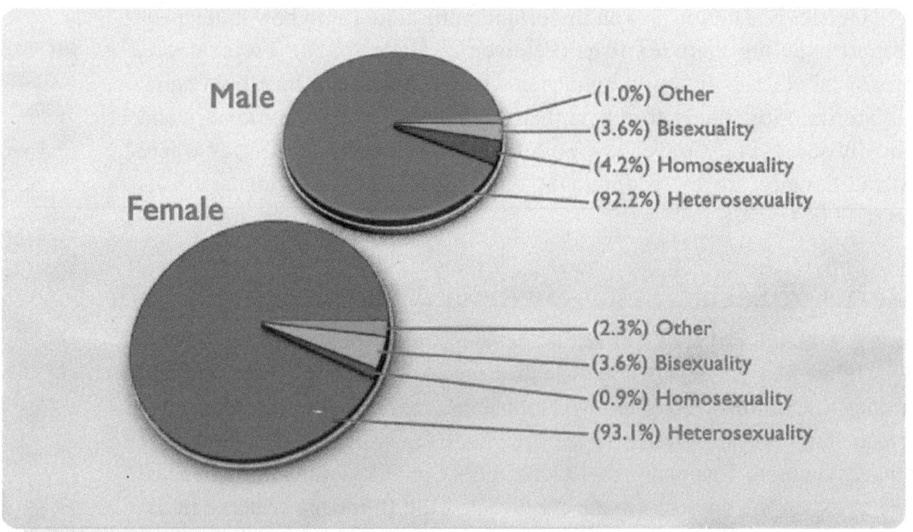

"Sexual Orientation"

point out that homosexual men and women generally know before puberty that they are "different" and often remain "in the closet" regarding their sexual orientation for fear of recrimination (Lippa, 2005). Evidence from family and twin studies shows a higher incidence of male homosexuality in families with other gay men (Camperio-Ciani, Corna, & Capiluppi, 2004), and a higher rate of homosexuality among men with a homosexual twin even when the twins were raised separately (LeVay & Hamer, 1994). The nature position also derives support from studies revealing anatomical and physiological differences between the brains of homosexual and heterosexual men (Fitzgerald, 2008; M. Hines, 2004, 2010; LeVay, 1991). In addition, research has shown that the brains of gay and lesbian people respond to sexual pheromones like the brains of heterosexual people of the opposite gender (Berglund, Lindström, & Savic, 2006; Savic, Berglund, & Lindström, 2007). Finally, if homosexuality is primarily the result of early learning and socialization, children raised by gay or lesbian parents should be more likely to become homosexual. Research, however, has clearly demonstrated that this is not the case (C. J. Patterson, 2000).

Among other animals, homosexual activity occurs with some degree of regularity. For instance, among pygmy chimpanzees, about 50% of all observed sexual activity is between members of the same sex. In zoos, sexual activity between members of the same sex has been observed in several species including penguins and koalas bears. Even male giraffes commonly entwine their necks until both become sexually stimulated. And among some birds, such as greylag geese, homosexual unions have been found to last up to 15 years (Bagemihl, 2000; Driscoll, 2008).

Homosexual activity is common among animals. For example, male giraffes often engage in extreme necking, entwining, and rubbing, becoming sexually aroused as they do.

Those on the nurture side argue that sexual orientation is primarily a learned behavior, influenced by early experience and largely under voluntary control. They find support for their position from cross-cultural studies that show sexual orientations occurring at different frequencies in various cultures.

Regardless of the origin of homosexuality, the general consensus among medical and mental health professionals is that heterosexuality and homosexuality both represent normal expressions of human sexuality, and that there is no convincing evidence that sexual orientation can be changed by so-called "*reparative*" or "*conversion therapy*" (American Psychological Association, 2011; Panozzo, 2013).

Quiz Questions

1. Rebecca has just "come out" to her friend Charles, telling him that she is a lesbian. She says she has known since she was a child that she was different from other girls because she was never attracted to boys, and she has concluded that this is just the way she is meant to be. Charles's reaction, however, is negative. He suggests that Rebecca just isn't trying hard enough and that counseling could help her learn new patterns of attraction. Rebecca is expressing the ________ view of homosexual orientation, while Charles's response demonstrates the ________ view.
   a. nurture; nature
   b. nature; nurture
   c. interventionist; interactionist
   d. interactionist; interventionist
2. You are reading an article in the newspaper when you come across the following statement: "The extent to which a male is interested in sex is determined by the level of the hormone testosterone at that moment." Which of the following would be an accurate response, based on what you have learned in this chapter?
   a. "That's true, but testosterone is a pheromone, not a hormone."
   b. "That would be true only for adolescent and young adult males, not older adults."
   c. "Actually, there is very little relationship between moment-to-moment levels of testosterone and sex drive in males."
   d. "That's true, but only during the excitement phase of the sexual response cycle."
3. The global survey of sexual behavior reveals that:
   a. the rate at which couples have sex is relatively constant across cultures.
   b. 25-34 year olds engage in more sex per year than any other group.
   c. 35-44 year olds have less sex per year than any other age group.
   d. the rate at which couples have sex varies dramatically around the world.
4. One carefully designed study of over 3,000 randomly selected people between the ages of 18 and 59 revealed the following pattern in the sexual activity of American men and women.
   a. About half of those surveyed had sex three times a week or more.
   b. Married couples reported having sex more often—and being more satisfied with their sex lives—than did unmarried persons.
   c. Less than 10% of those surveyed reported having sex a few times a year or not at all.
   d. The majority of people surveyed reported they preferred some form of kinky sex compared to vaginal intercourse.
5. Which phase of the sexual response cycle is followed by a "refractory period" in males?
   a. Orgasm.
   b. Resolution.
   c. Excitement.
   d. Plateau.

Other Important Motives

How are stimulus motives different from primary drives?

stimulus motives
unlearned motives, such as curiosity or contact, that prompts us to explore or change the world around us

So far, we have moved from motives that depend on biological needs (hunger and thirst) to a motive that is far more sensitive to external cues—sex. Next, we consider motives that are even more responsive to environmental stimuli. These motives, called **stimulus motives**, include *exploration, curiosity, manipulation,* and *contact.* They push us to investigate and often to change our environment. Finally, we will turn our attention to the motives of *aggression, achievement,* and *affiliation.*

Exploration and Curiosity

What motives cause people to explore and change their environment?

Where does that road go? What is in that dark little shop? Answering these questions has no obvious benefit: You do not expect the road to take you anywhere you need to go or the shop to contain anything you really want. You just want to know. Exploration and curiosity are motives sparked by the new and unknown and are directed toward no more specific goal other than "finding out." They are not unique to humans. The family dog will run around a new house, sniffing and checking things out, before it settles down to eat its dinner. Even rats, when given a choice, will opt to explore an unknown maze rather than run through a familiar one.

Psychologists disagree about the nature of curiosity, its causes, and even how to measure it (Kashdan & Silvia, 2009). William James viewed it as an emotion; Freud considered it a socially acceptable expression of the sex drive. Others have seen it as a response to the unexpected and as evidence of a human need to find meaning in life. We might assume that curiosity is a key component of intelligence, but research has failed to confirm that hypothesis. Curiosity has been linked to creativity (Kashdan & Fincham, 2002). Interestingly, people who score high on novelty-seeking tests have a reduced number of dopamine receptors, suggesting curiosity and exploration may arise from a need for increased dopamine stimulation (Golimbet, Alfimova, Gritsenko, & Ebstein, 2007; Zald et al., 2008).

Manipulation and Contact

Is the human need for contact universal?

Why do museums have "Do Not Touch" signs everywhere? It is because the staff knows from experience that the urge to touch is almost irresistible. Unlike curiosity and exploration, manipulation focuses on a specific object that must be touched, handled, played with, and felt before we are satisfied. Manipulation is a motive limited to primates, who have agile fingers and toes. In contrast, the need for *contact* is more universal than the need for manipulation. Furthermore, it is not limited to touching with the fingers—it may involve the whole body. Manipulation is an active process, but contact may be passive.

In a classic series of experiments, Harry Harlow demonstrated the importance of the need for contact (Harlow, 1958; Harlow & Zimmerman, 1959). Newborn baby monkeys were separated from their mothers and given two "surrogate mothers." Both surrogate mothers were the same shape, but one was made of wire mesh and had no soft surfaces. The other was cuddly—layered with foam rubber and covered with terry cloth. Both surrogate mothers were warmed by means of an electric light placed inside them, but only the wire-mesh mother was equipped with a nursing bottle. Thus, the wire-mesh mother fulfilled two physiological needs for the infant monkeys: the need for food and the need for warmth. But baby monkeys most often gravitated to the terry-cloth mother, which did not provide food. When they were frightened, they would run and cling to it as they would to a real mother. Because both surrogate mothers were warm, the researchers concluded that the need for closeness goes deeper than a need for mere warmth. The importance of contact has also been demonstrated with premature infants. Low-birth-weight babies who are held and massaged gain weight faster, are calmer, and display more activity than those who are seldom touched (Hernandez-Reif, Diego, & Field, 2007; Weiss, Wilson, & Morrison, 2004).

"Harlow's Monkeys"

Aggression

Is aggression a biological response or a learned one?

Human **aggression** encompasses all behavior that is intended to inflict physical or psychological harm on others. Intent is a key element of aggression. Accidentally hitting a pedestrian with your car is not an act of aggression—whereas deliberately running down a person would be.

Judging from the statistics (which often reflect underreporting of certain types of crimes), aggression is disturbingly common in this country. According to the *FBI's Uniform Crime Reports,* more than 1.2 million violent crimes were reported in the United States in 2011. These crimes included more than 14,800 murders, more than 84,000 forcible rapes, 354,000 robberies, and more than 760,000 aggravated assaults (Federal Bureau of Investigation, 2012).

Why are people aggressive? Freud considered aggression an innate drive, similar to hunger and thirst, that builds up until it is released. In his view, one important function of society is to channel the aggressive drive into constructive and socially acceptable avenues, such as sports, debate, and other forms of competition. If Freud's analysis is correct, then expressing aggression should reduce the aggressive drive. Research shows, however, that under some circumstances, venting one's anger is more likely to increase than to reduce future aggression (Bushman, 2002; Schaefer & Mattei, 2005).

Another view holds that aggression is a vestige of our evolutionary past that can be traced to defensive behaviors characteristic of our ancestors (G. S. McCall & Shields, 2008). According to this view, the potential for aggression became hard-wired in the human brain, since it served an important adaptive function that enabled our ancestors to effectively compete for food and mates (Wallner & Machatschke, 2009).

Frustration also plays an important role in aggression. However, frustration does not always produce aggression. For example, if frustration doesn't generate anger, aggression is unlikely (Berkowitz & Harmon-Jones, 2004). Moreover, people react to frustration in different ways: some seek help and support, others withdraw from the source of frustration, some become aggressive, and some choose to escape into drugs or alcohol. Finally, there is some evidence that frustration is most likely to cause aggression in people who

aggression
behavior aimed at doing harm to others; also, the motive to behave aggressively

have learned to be aggressive as a means of coping with unpleasant situations (R. E. Tremblay, Hartup, & Archer, 2005).

One way we learn aggression is by observing aggressive models, especially those who get what they want (and avoid punishment) when they behave aggressively. For example, in contact sports, we often applaud acts of aggression. In professional hockey, fistfights between players may elicit as much fan fervor as does goal scoring.

But what if the aggressive model does not come out ahead or is even punished for aggressive actions? Observers usually will avoid imitating a model's behavior if it has negative consequences. As children who viewed aggressive behavior learned aggressive behavior, regardless of whether the aggressive model was rewarded or punished. The same results were obtained in a study in which children were shown films of aggressive behavior. Children who saw the aggressive model being punished were less aggressive than those who saw the aggressive model rewarded, but both groups of children were more aggressive than those who saw no aggressive model at all. These data are consistent with research showing that exposure to cinematic violence of any sort causes a small to moderate increase in aggressive behavior among children and adolescents (J. P. Murray, 2008). Indeed, one large-scale meta-analysis of 136 studies that were conducted in several different countries found clear evidence that playing violent video games was associated with increased aggressive behavior and decreased empathy and prosocial behavior (Anderson et al., 2010).

Aggression and Culture

Further evidence that aggression is learned can be seen in the cultural variations that exist for handling of aggression (Lansford & Dodge, 2008; Triandis, 1994). For example, cultures as diverse as the Semai of the Malaysian rain forest, the Tahitian Islanders of the Pacific, the Zuni and Blackfoot nations in North America, the Pygmies of Africa, and the residents of Japan and the Scandinavian nations place a premium on resolving conflicts peacefully. Most of these are *collectivist* societies that emphasize the good of the group over the desires of the individual. Members of collectivist societies are more likely to seek compromise or to withdraw from a threatening interaction because of their concern for maintaining group harmony. In contrast, cultures such as the Yanomanö of South America, the Truk Islanders of Micronesia, and the Simbu of New Guinea encourage aggressive behavior, particularly among males. Members of these *individualist* societies are more likely to follow the adage "Stand up for yourself." Actually, we need not travel to exotic, faraway lands to find such diversity. Within the United States, such subcultures as Quakers, the Amish, the Mennonites, and the Hutterites have traditionally valued nonviolence and peaceful coexistence. This outlook contrasts markedly with individualist attitudes and practices in mainstream American culture.

Are males naturally more aggressive than females? Research suggests that both biology and culture encourage aggression in boys more than in girls. Adults often look the other way when two boys are fighting, sending the message that violence is an acceptable way to settle disputes.

Gender and Aggression

Across cultures and at every age, males are more likely than females to behave aggressively. Three studies that reviewed more than 100 studies of aggression concluded that males are more aggressive than females both verbally (i.e., with taunts, insults, and threats) and, in particular, physically (i.e., with hitting, kicking, and fighting) (Bettencourt & Miller, 1996; Eagly & Steffen, 1986; Hyde, 1986). These gender differences tend to be greater in natural settings than in controlled laboratory settings (Hyde, 2005a) and appear to be remarkably stable (Arsenio, 2004; Knight, Fabes, & Higgins, 1996). Indeed, even historical data that go back to 16th-century Europe show that males committed more than three times as many violent crimes as females (L. Ellis & Coontz, 1990).

Is the origin of gender difference in aggression biological or social? The answer is not simple. On the one hand, certain biological factors appear to contribute to aggressive behavior. As high levels of testosterone are associated with aggressiveness. At the same time, our society clearly tolerates and even encourages greater aggressiveness in boys than in girls (Sommers-Flanagan, Sommers-Flanagan, & Davis, 1993). For example, we are more likely to give boys toy guns and to reward them for behaving aggressively; girls are more likely than boys to be taught to feel guilty for behaving aggressively or to expect parental disapproval for their aggressive behavior. The most accurate conclusion seems to be that, like most of the complex behaviors that we have reviewed, gender differences in aggression undoubtedly depend on the interaction of nature and nurture (Green, 1998; Verona, Joiner, Johnson, & Bender, 2006).

Achievement

Is being highly competitive important to high achievement?

Climbing Mount Everest, sending rockets into space, making the dean's list, rising to the top of a giant corporation—all these actions may have mixed underlying motives. But in all of them there is a desire to excel. It is this desire for achievement for its own sake that leads psychologists to suggest that there is a separate **achievement motive**. Perhaps not surprisingly, achievement motivation is correlated with measures of life satisfaction, success in life, and quality of life. Research also confirms that parental support for achievement is directly correlated with achievement motivation in children (Acharya & Joshi, 2011).

From psychological tests and personal histories, psychologists have developed a profile of people with high achievement motivation. These people are fast learners. They relish the opportunity to develop new strategies for unique and challenging tasks. Driven less by the desire for fame or fortune than by the need to live up to a high, self-imposed standard of performance (M. Carr, Borkowski, & Maxwell, 1991), they are self-confident, willingly take on responsibility, and do not readily bow to outside social pressures. They are energetic and allow few things to stand in the way of their goals.

Affiliation

How do psychologists explain the human need to be with other people?

Generally, people have a need for affiliation—to be with other people. The **affiliation motive** is likely to be especially strong when people feel threatened (Rofe, 1984). *Esprit de corps*—the feeling of being part of a sympathetic group—is critical among troops going into a battle, just as a football coach's pregame pep talk fuels team spirit. Both are designed to make people feel they are working for a common cause or against a common foe. Moreover, being in the presence of someone who is less threatened or fearful can reduce fear and anxiety. For example, patients with critical illnesses tend to prefer being with healthy people, rather than with other seriously ill patients or by themselves (Rofe, Hoffman, & Lewin, 1985). In the same way, if you are nervous on a plane during a bumpy flight, you may strike up a conversation with the calm-looking woman sitting next to you.

Some have argued that our need for affiliation has an evolutionary basis (Buss, 2006). In this view, forming and maintaining social bonds provided our ancestors with both survival and reproductive benefits. Social groups can share resources such as food and shelter, provide opportunities for reproduction, and assist in the care of offspring. Children who chose to stay with adults were probably more likely to survive (and ultimately reproduce) than those who wandered away from their groups. Thus, it is understandable that people in general tend to seek out other people.

achievement motive
the need to excel, to overcome obstacles

affiliation motive
the need to be with others

Recently, neuroscientists have shown how various hormones, including oxytocin and dopamine, are released during times of stress prompting us to build social bonds (Carter, 2005). Not surprisingly, these same hormones also play an important role in romantic attachments and the formation of parental bonds to children (Leckman, Hrdy, Keverne, & Carter, 2006).

Quiz Questions

1. Susan scores high on tests of achievement motivation. Which of the following would you LEAST expect to be true of her?
   a. She seldom deviates from methods that have worked for her in the past.
   b. She has a strong desire to live up to high, self-imposed standards of excellence.
   c. She is a fast learner who willingly takes on responsibility.
   d. She is self-confident and resists outside social pressures.
2. You are watching a children's TV show in which the "bad guys" eventually are punished for their aggressive behavior. Your friend says, "It's a good thing the bad guys always lose. Otherwise, kids would learn to be aggressive from watching TV shows like this." You think about that for a minute and then, on the basis of what you have learned in this chapter, you reply:
   a. "You're right. Seeing aggressors punished for their actions is a good way to reduce the amount of aggressiveness in children."
   b. Seeing an aggressor punished for their aggression only reduces aggressive behavior in boys, it has little effect on girls."
   c. "Actually, seeing an aggressor punished for his or her actions leads to more aggression than seeing no aggression at all."
   d. "Aggression is an instinctual response to frustration, so it really doesn't matter what children see on TV. If they are frustrated, they will respond with aggression."
3. Which of the following has been linked with creativity?
   a. Achievement motivation.
   b. Aggression.
   c. Affiliation.
   d. Curiosity.
4. Joseph is flying on an airplane for the first time in his life and is somewhat frightened. According to what you read, which of the following motives is likely to be strengthened during the flight?
   a. Aggression.
   b. Affiliation.
   c. Curiosity.
   d. Exploration.
5. Research confirms that having the opportunity to vent one's anger:
   a. is the best way for a person to reduce the likelihood of future aggression.
   b. has no impact on the likelihood of future aggression.
   c. explains why members of individualist cultures have a reduced tendency to be aggressive.
   d. is more likely to increase than to reduce future aggression.

EMOTIONS

How many basic emotions are there?

Ancient Greek rationalists thought that emotions, if not held in check, would wreak havoc on higher mental abilities such as rational thought and decision making. In his classic book, *The Expression of Emotions in Man and Animals* (1872/1965), Charles Darwin argued that emotional expression in man evolved by natural selection to serve an adaptive and communicative function (Hess & Thibault, 2009). Many early psychologists, too, often viewed emotions as a "base instinct"—a vestige of our evolutionary heritage that needed to be repressed.

More recently, psychologists have begun to see emotions in a more positive light. Today, they are considered essential to survival and a major source of personal enrichment and resilience (Tugade & Fredrickson, 2004).

Emotions are linked to variations in immune function and, thereby, to disease. And emotions may also influence how successful we are (Goleman, 1997; Goleman, Boyatzis, & McKee, 2002). It is clear, then, that if we are going to understand human behavior, we must understand emotions. Unfortunately, that task is easier said than done. As you will soon see, even identifying how many emotions there are is difficult.

Basic Emotions

Are there basic emotions that all people experience regardless of their culture?

Many people have attempted to identify and describe the basic emotions experienced by humans (Cornelius, 1996; Schimmack & Crites, 2005). Some years ago, Robert Plutchik (1927–2006), for example, proposed that there are eight basic emotions: *fear, surprise, sadness, disgust, anger, anticipation, joy,* and *acceptance* (Plutchik, 1980). Each of these emotions helps us adjust to the demands of our environment, although in different ways. Fear, for example, underlies flight, which helps protect animals from their enemies; anger propels animals to attack or destroy. According to Plutchik's model, different emotions may combine to produce an even wider and richer spectrum of experience. Occurring together, anticipation and joy, for example, yield optimism; joy and acceptance fuse into love; and surprise and sadness make for disappointment. Within any of Plutchik's eight categories, emotions also vary in intensity.

Because of the differences in emotions from one culture to another, the tendency now is to distinguish between primary and secondary emotions. Primary emotions are those that are evident in all cultures, contribute to survival, associated with a distinct facial expression, and evident in non-human primates. Secondary emotions are those that are not found in all cultures. They may be thought of as subtle combinations of the primary emotions.

Attempts to identify primary emotions have generally used cross-cultural studies (Jenkins & Andrewes, 2012; Matsumoto, Olide, Schug, Willingham, & Callan, 2009). For example, one group of researchers asked participants from 10 countries to interpret photographs depicting various facial expressions of emotions (Ekman et al., 1987). The percentage of participants from each country who correctly identified the emotions

Enduring Issues

Diversity–Universality *Are Emotions Universal?*

Some scientists challenge Plutchik's model, noting that it may apply only to the emotional experience of English-speaking people. Anthropologists report enormous differences in the ways that other cultures view and categorize emotions. Some languages, in fact, do not even have a word for "emotion." Languages also differ in the number of words that they have to name emotions. English includes over 2,000 words to describe emotional experiences, but Taiwanese Chinese has only 750 such descriptive words. One tribal language has only seven words that can be translated into categories of emotion. Some cultures lack words for "anxiety" or "depression" or "guilt." Samoans have just one word encompassing love, sympathy, pity, and liking—all distinct emotions in our own culture (Frijda, Markam, & Sato, 1995; Russell, 1991).

ranged from 60% to 98%. The researchers used this and other evidence to argue for the existence of 6 primary emotions—*happiness, surprise, sadness, fear, disgust,* and *anger.* Notice that love is not included in this list. Although Ekman did not find a universally recognized facial expression for love, many psychologists nevertheless hold that love is a primary emotion (Hendrick & Hendrick, 2003; Sabini & Silver, 2005). Its outward expression, however, may owe much to the stereotypes promoted by a culture's media (Fehr, 1994). In one study in which American college students were asked to display a facial expression for love, the participants mimicked the conventional "Hollywood" prototypes such as sighing deeply, gazing skyward, and holding their hand over their heart (Cornelius, 1996).

Theories of Emotion

What is the relationship among emotions, biological reactions, and thoughts?

In the 1880s, the American psychologist William James formulated the first modern theory of emotion. The Danish psychologist Carl Lange reached the same conclusions. According to the **James–Lange theory**, stimuli in the environment (say, seeing a large growling dog running toward us) cause physiological changes in our bodies (accelerated heart rate, enlarged pupils, deeper or shallower breathing, increased perspiration, and goose bumps), and emotions arise from those physiological changes. The emotion of *fear,* then, would simply be the almost instantaneous and automatic awareness of physiological changes.

"Theories of Emotion"

There is some supporting evidence for this theory (R. J. Davidson, 1992; Prinz, 2008), but if you think back to the biology of the nervous system, you should be able to identify a major flaw in the James–Lange theory. Recall that sensory information about bodily changes flows to the brain through the spinal cord. If bodily changes are the source of emotions, then people with severe spinal cord injuries should experience fewer and less intense emotions, but this is not the case (Cobos, Sánchez, Pérez, & Vila, 2004). Moreover, most emotions are accompanied by very similar physiological changes. Bodily changes, then, do not cause specific emotions and may not even be necessary for emotional experience.

Recognizing these facts, the **Cannon–Bard theory** holds that we mentally process emotions and physically respond simultaneously, not one after another. When you see the dog, you feel afraid *and* your heart races at the same time.

Cognitive Theories of Emotion

Cognitive psychologists have taken Cannon–Bard's theory a step further. They argue that our emotional experience depends on our perception of a situation (Lazarus, 1991; C. Phelps, Bennett, & Brain, 2008; Scherer, Schorr, & Johnstone, 2001). According to the **cognitive theory** of emotion, the situation gives us clues as to how we should interpret our state of arousal. One of the first theories of emotion that took into account cognitive processes was advanced by Stanley Schachter and Jerome Singer (1962; 2001). According to Schachter and Singer's *Two-Factor Theory of Emotion,* when we see a bear, there are indeed bodily changes; but we then use information about the situation to tell us how to respond to those changes. Only when we *cognitively* recognize that we are in danger do we experience those bodily changes as fear.

James–Lange theory
states that stimuli cause physiological changes in our bodies, and emotions result from those physiological changes

Cannon–Bard theory
states that the experience of emotion occurs simultaneously with biological changes

cognitive theory
states that emotional experience depends on one's perception or judgment of a situation

Challenges to Cognitive Theory

A direct challenge to the cognitive theory claims that emotions can be experienced without the intervention of cognition (C. E. Izard,1971, 1994). According to this view, a situation such as separation or pain provokes a unique pattern of unlearned facial movements and body postures that may be completely independent of conscious thought. When information about our facial expressions and posture reaches the brain, we automatically experience the corresponding emotion. According to Carroll Izard, then, the James–Lange theory was essentially correct in suggesting that emotional experience arises from bodily reactions. But Izard's theory stresses facial expression and body posture as crucial to the experience of emotion, whereas the James–Lange theory emphasized muscles, skin, and internal organs.

While considerable evidence supports the view that facial expressions influence emotions (Ekman, 2003; Soussignan, 2002), a growing body of research also indicates that the most accurate recognition of emotional expression occurs when the expresser and receiver are from the same cultural group (Jack, Caldara, & Schyns, 2011; Young & Hugenberg, 2010). Exactly how the unlearned and learned components of emotional expression are communicated and recognized is the topic we turn to now.

Quiz Questions

1. Ralph believes that if you're feeling depressed, you should smile a lot and your depression will fade away. His view is most consistent with:
   a. the Schachter–Singer theory.
   b. the James–Lange theory.
   c. the Cannon–Bard theory.
   d. Izard's theory.
2. You are on a camping trip when you encounter a bear. You get butterflies in your stomach, your heart starts racing, your mouth gets dry, and you start to perspire. A psychologist who takes the cognitive perspective on emotion would say:
   a. "Seeing the bear caused the physical changes, which in turn caused you to experience fear."
   b. "Seeing the bear caused you to experience fear, which in turn caused all those physical changes."
   c. "Seeing the bear caused the physical changes. When you realized they were caused by the bear, you experienced fear."
   d. "Seeing the bear caused the physical changes and the emotion of fear at the same time."
3. Sandra and Diego are from different cultures. The facial expression of emotion they are least likely to correctly identify in each other is:
   a. anger.
   b. love.
   c. happiness.
   d. surprise.
4. Primary emotions:
   a. are evident in all cultures.
   b. are not evident in non-human primates.
   c. are not associated with a distinct facial expression.
   d. do not contribute to survival.
5. Charles Darwin held that:
   a. emotions are adaptive but interfere with an organism's ability to communicate effectively.
   b. emotions serve an adaptive and communicative function.
   c. emotions are generally not adaptive, but do enhance an organism's ability to communicate.
   d. the communication of emotion is a distinctly human trait.

COMMUNICATING EMOTION

What is the most obvious signal of emotion?

Sometimes you are vaguely aware that a person makes you feel uncomfortable. When pressed to be more precise, you might say, "You never know what she is thinking." But you do not mean that you never know her opinion of a film or what she thought about the last election. It would probably be more accurate to say that you do not know what she is feeling. Almost all of us conceal our emotions to some extent, but usually people can tell what we are feeling. Although emotions can often be expressed in words, much of the time we communicate our feelings nonverbally. We do so through, among other things, voice quality, facial expression, body language, personal space, and explicit acts.

Voice Quality and Facial Expression

What role can voice and facial expression play in expressing emotion?

If your roommate is washing the dishes and says acidly, "I *hope* you're enjoying your novel," the literal meaning of his words is quite clear, but you probably know very well that he is not expressing a concern about your reading pleasure. He is really saying, "I am annoyed that you are not helping to clean up." Similarly, if you receive a phone call from someone who has had very good or very bad news, you will probably know how she feels before she has told you what happened. In other words, much of the emotional information we convey is not contained in the words we use, but in the way those words are expressed (Gobl & Chasaide, 2003).

Among nonverbal channels of communication, facial expressions seem to communicate the most specific information (Horstmann, 2003). Hand gestures or posture can communicate general emotional states (e.g., feeling bad), but the complexity of the muscles in the face allows facial expressions to communicate very specific feelings (e.g., feeling sad, angry, or fearful). Many facial expressions are innate, not learned. Individuals who are born blind use the same facial expressions of emotion as do sighted persons to express the same emotions (Matsumoto & Willingham, 2009). Moreover, most animals share a common pattern of muscular facial movements. For example, dogs, tigers, and humans all bare their teeth in rage, and research has shown that the same pattern of facial muscles is used to display emotions among most primates, including monkeys, chimpanzees, and humans (Waller, Parr, Gothard, Burrows, & Fuglevand, 2008). Psychologists who take an evolutionary approach believe that facial expressions served an adaptive function, enabling our ancestors to compete successfully for status, to win mates, and to defend themselves (Tooby & Cosmides, 2008).

How the Brain Reads the Face

What parts of the brain are responsible for interpreting facial expressions?

Scientists have known for quite some time that activity in brain circuits centering on the amygdala and insula are critical for the release of emotions (Schafe & LeDoux, 2002; Philip Shaw et al., 2005). The amygdala and insula also appear to play an important role in our ability to correctly interpret facial expressions (Adolphs, 2008; Jehna et al., 2011). Interestingly, some of the underlying brain processes that are used to interpret facial expression take place so quickly (less than 1/10 of a second), it is unlikely that they are consciously driven (Adolphs, 2006).

Adolphs and his colleagues (Adolphs, Tranel, Damasio, & Damasio, 1994) reported the remarkable case of a 30-year-old woman (S. M.) with a rare disease that caused nearly complete destruction of the amygdala. Although S. M. could correctly identify photographs of familiar faces with 100% accuracy, and easily learned to recognize new faces, she had great difficulty recognizing fear and discriminating between different emotions, such as happiness and surprise. More recent research has also shown that people with amygdala damage have trouble "reading faces" (Adolphs, Baron-Cohen, & Tranel, 2002; Adolphs & Tranel, 2003). For example, some patients with severe depressive disorder have an impaired ability to accurately judge another person's facial expression of emotion, and this impairment contributes to their difficulty in interpersonal functioning (Surguladze et al., 2004). In addition, some researchers have suggested that abnormalities in the brain circuits associated with the amygdala can, in some cases, make it difficult for people to perceive threat accurately and that, in turn, can lead to unprovoked violence and aggression (R. J. Davidson, Putnam, & Larson, 2000; Marsh & Blair, 2008).

Body Language, Personal Space, and Gestures

How can posture, personal space, and mimicry affect the communication of emotion?

Body language is another way that we communicate messages nonverbally. How we hold our back, for example, communicates a great deal. When we are relaxed, we tend to stretch back into a chair; when we are tense, we sit more stiffly with our feet together.

The distance we maintain between ourselves and others is called *personal space.* This distance varies depending on the nature of the activity and the emotions felt. If someone stands closer to you than is customary, that proximity may indicate either anger or affection; if farther away than usual, it may indicate fear or dislike. The normal conversing distance between people varies from culture to culture. Two Swedes conversing would ordinarily stand much farther apart than would two Arabs or Greeks.

Explicit acts, of course, can also serve as nonverbal clues to emotions. A slammed door may tell us that the person who just left the room is angry. If friends drop in for a visit and you invite them into your living room, that is a sign that you are probably less at ease with them than with friends whom you invite to sit down with you at the kitchen table. Gestures, such as a slap on the back, an embrace, whether people shake your hand briefly or for a long time, firmly or limply, also tell you something about how they feel about you.

You can see from this discussion that nonverbal communication of emotions is important. However, a word of caution is needed here. Although nonverbal behavior may offer a clue to a person's feelings, it is not an *infallible* clue. Laughing and crying can sound alike, yet crying may signal sorrow, joy, anger, or nostalgia—or that you are slicing an onion. Moreover, as with verbal reports, people sometimes "say" things nonverbally that they do not mean. We all have done things thoughtlessly—turned our backs, frowned when thinking about something else, or laughed at the wrong time—that have given offense because our actions were interpreted as an expression of an emotion that we were not, in fact, feeling.

Many of us overestimate our ability to interpret nonverbal cues. For example, in one study of several hundred "professional lie catchers," including members of the Secret Service, government lie detector experts, judges, police officers, and psychiatrists, every group except for the psychiatrists rated themselves above average in their ability to tell whether another person was lying. Only the Secret Service agents managed to identify the liars at a better-than-chance rate (Ekman & O'Sullivan, 1991).

Sometimes we use *mimicry* to help us understand what others are feeling. Research confirms that during the course of conversation, people often mimic each other's accents, gestures, postures, and facial expressions (McIntosh, 2006; Ponari, Conson, D'Amico, Grossi, & Trojano, 2012). Not surprisingly, research has shown that spontaneous mimicry makes conversations flow more smoothly, helps people feel closer to one another, and fosters friendship (Kobayashi, 2007). In addition, as described previously, because specific emotions are tied to behaviors, and in particular specific facial expressions, mimicking the facial expressions of other helps us to emphasize, or literally feel what another person is feeling (Stel, Van Baaren, & Vonk, 2008). However, even the use of mimicry doesn't overcome our tendency to being deceived. For example, research has also shown that mimicry may actually reduce our accuracy to judge another person's emotions if the person expressing the emotion is purposely trying to be deceptive. In other words, when we mimic a person who is attempting to mislead us, mimicry diminishes our ability to detect that they are trying to deceive us (Stel, van Dijk, & Olivier, 2009).

Gender and Emotion

Are men less emotional than women?

Men are often said to be less emotional than women. But do men feel less emotion, or are they simply less likely to express the emotions they feel? And are there some emotions that men are more likely than women to express?

Research sheds some light on these issues. In one study, when men and women saw depictions of people in distress, the men showed little emotion, but the women expressed feelings of concern (Eisenberg & Lennon, 1983). However, physiological measures of emotional arousal (such as heart rate and blood pressure) showed that the men in the study were actually just as affected as the women were. The men simply inhibited the expression of their emotions, whereas the women were more open about their feelings. Emotions such as sympathy, sadness, empathy, and distress are often considered "unmanly," and traditionally, in Western culture, boys are trained from an early age to suppress those emotions in public (L. Brody & Hall, 2000). The fact that men are less likely than women to seek help in dealing with emotional issues (Komiya, Good, & Sherrod, 2000) is probably a result of this early training. (See **Figure 10.5.**)

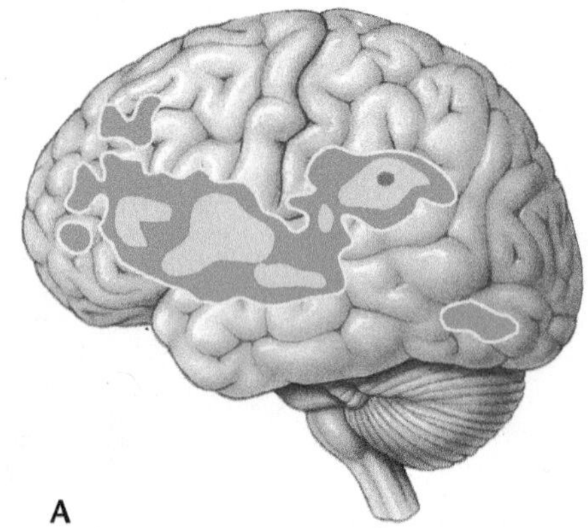
A

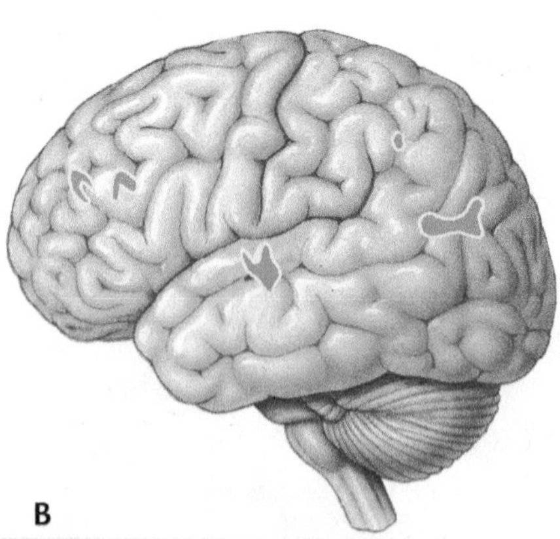
B

Figure 10.5 Emotion and brain activity in men and women.
When asked to think of something sad, women (A) generate more activity in their brains than men (B) (Carter, 1998).

Men and women are also likely to react with very different emotions to the same situation (Gomez, Gunten, & Danuser, 2013). For example, being betrayed or criticized by another person will elicit anger in males, whereas females are more likely to feel hurt, sad, or disappointed (L. Brody & Hall, 2000; Fischer, Rodriguez-Mosquera, van-Vianen, & Manstead, 2004). And, when men get angry, they generally turn their anger outward, against other people and against the situation in which they find themselves. Women are more likely to see themselves as the source of the problem and to turn their anger inward, against themselves. These gender-specific reactions are consistent with the fact that men are four times more likely than women to become violent in the face of life crises; women, by contrast, are much more likely to become depressed.

Men and women also differ in their ability to interpret nonverbal cues of emotion. In particular, women and young girls are more skilled than men or young boys at decoding the facial expressions of emotion (Bosacki & Moore, 2004; Hall & Matsumoto, 2004). Perhaps not surprisingly, research has also shown that men are more likely than women to misperceive friendliness as sexual interest; interestingly, they are also more likely to perceive sexual interest as friendliness (Farris, Treat, Vikden, & McFall, 2008).

How can we explain these gender differences? One possibility is that because women tend to be the primary caregivers for preverbal infants, they need to become more attuned than men to the subtleties of emotional expressions. Some psychologists have even suggested that this skill may be genetically programmed into females. Consistent with this evolutionary perspective, research has shown that male and female infants express and self-regulate emotions differently (McClure, 2000; Weinberg, Tronick, Cohn, & Olson, 1999).

Thinking Critically About . . .

Nonverbal Communication of Emotion

Some people are clearly better than others at reading and sending emotional messages. The question is, why? How might you determine

1. if differences in these skills are learned or inherited?
2. the kinds of learning experiences that produce high skills?
3. whether it is possible to teach the skills?

Another explanation of gender differences in emotional sensitivity is based on the relative power of women and men. Because women historically have occupied less powerful positions, they may have felt the need to become acutely attuned to the emotional displays of others, particularly those in more powerful positions (namely, men). This idea is supported by evidence that, regardless of gender, followers are more sensitive to the emotions of leaders than vice versa (Aries, 2006; Judith Hall, Bernieri, & Carney, 2006).

Culture and Emotion

How can culture influence the way we express emotion?

Does where we live affect wh. we feel? And if so, why? For psychologists, the key issue is how cultures help shape emotional experiences.

Some researchers have argued that across cultures, peoples, and societies, the face looks the same whenever certain emotions are expressed; this phenomenon is known as the *universalist* position. In contrast, other researchers support the *culture–learning* position, which holds that members of a culture learn the appropriate facial expressions for emotions. These expressions, then, can differ greatly from one culture to the next. Which view is more accurate?

As we saw earlier, Ekman and his colleagues have concluded from cross-cultural studies that at least six emotions are accompanied by universal facial expressions: happiness, sadness, anger, surprise, fear, and disgust. Carroll Izard (1980) conducted similar studies in England, Germany, Switzerland, France, Sweden, Greece, and Japan with similar results. These studies seem to support the universalist position: Regardless of culture, people tended to agree on which emotions others were expressing facially. However, this research does not completely rule out the culture–learning view. Because the participants

Enduring Issues

Mind–Body *Holding Anger In*

People who frequently feel anger and hostility may be at a serious health risk if they don't allow themselves to express and learn to regulate their anger (Carrère, Mittmann, Woodin, Tabares, & Yoshimoto, 2005). In a study that tracked a group of women over 18 years, researchers found that those scoring high on hostility were three times more likely to die during the course of the study than those who scored low (Julius, Harburg, Cottington, & Johnson, 1986). However, this higher level of risk applied only to participants who said they got angry in many situations but did not vent their anger. Other participants who reported frequent bouts of anger, which they expressed, were in the same low-risk group as those who said they rarely or never felt angry.

were all members of developed countries that likely had been exposed to one another through movies, magazines, and tourism, they might simply have become familiar with the facial expressions seen in other cultures. A stronger test was needed that reduced or eliminated this possibility.

Such a test was made possible by the discovery of several contemporary cultures that had been totally isolated from Western culture for most of their existence. Members of the Fore and the Dani cultures of New Guinea, for example, had their first contact with anthropologists only a few years before Ekman's research took place. They provided a nearly perfect opportunity to test the universalist/culture–learning debate. If members of these cultures gave the same interpretation of facial expressions and produced the same expressions on their own faces as did people in Western cultures, there would be much stronger evidence for the universality of facial expressions of emotion. Ekman and his colleagues presented members of the Fore culture with three photographs of people from outside their culture and asked them to point to the picture that represented how they would feel in a certain situation. For example, if a participant was told "Your child has died, and you feel very sad," he or she would have the opportunity to choose which of the three pictures most closely corresponded to sadness. The results indicated very high rates of agreement on facial expressions of emotions (Ekman & Friesen, 1971; Ekman, Sorenson, & Friesen, 1969). Moreover, when photographs of the Fore and Dani posing the primary emotions were shown to college students in the United States, the same high agreement was found (Ekman & Friesen, 1975). This finding suggests that at least some emotional expressions are inborn and universal.

If this is true, why are people so often confused about the emotions being expressed by people in other cultures? It turns out that the answer is not simple. Part of the explanation involves **display rules**. Display rules concern the circumstances under which it is appropriate for people to show emotion. Display rules differ substantially from culture to culture (Matsumoto, Yoo, & Chung, 2010; Safdar et al., 2009). In a study of Japanese and American college students, the participants watched graphic films of surgical procedures, either by themselves or in the presence of an experimenter. The students' facial expressions were secretly videotaped as they viewed the films. The results showed that when the students were by themselves, both the Japanese and the Americans showed facial expressions of disgust, as expected. But when the participants watched the films in the presence of an experimenter, the two groups displayed different responses. American students continued to show disgust on their faces, but the Japanese students showed facial expressions that were more neutral, even somewhat pleasant (Ekman, Friesen, & Ellsworth, 1972). Why the sudden switch? The answer in this case appears to lie in the different display rules of the two cultures. The Japanese norm says, "Don't display strong negative emotion in the presence of a respected elder" (in this case, the experimenter). Americans typically don't honor this display rule; hence, they expressed their true emotions whether they were alone or with someone else.

Writing Assignment

Imagine you are walking alone late at night and hear footsteps behind you. Think about your emotional reaction to this situation. Consider the major theories of emotion: James–Lange theory, Cannon–Bard theory, and Schacter–Singer's Two-Factor theory of emotion. From the perspective of these major theories of emotion, describe how each would predict the sequence of events that would occur as you experience a reaction to this situation.

display rules
culture-specific rules that govern how, when, and why expressions of emotion are appropriate

However, display rules don't tell the whole story. In a comprehensive review of the literature, Elfenbein and Ambady (2002, 2003) have demonstrated that differences in language, familiarity, majority or minority status within a culture, cultural learning, expressive style, and a number of other factors may also account for the fact that "we understand emotions more accurately when they are expressed by members of our own cultural or subcultural group" (p. 249). Since research indicates that learning to correctly identify emotions of people from a different culture contributes to intercultural adjustment (Yoo, Matsumoto, & LeRoux, 2006), further research in this area is important as the nations of the world become increasingly interdependent and multicultural.

Quiz Questions

1. Which of the following would probably be best at "reading" nonverbal emotional cues?
   a. An older woman.
   b. An older man.
   c. A young man.
   d. They would all be equally accurate since gender is not related to the ability to understand nonverbal cues to emotion.
2. You are studying gender differences in emotion. You show men and women various films of people in distress. On the basis of what you have read in this chapter, you would predict that the men will show ________ amount of physiological arousal, and __________ emotional expression as the women.
   a. a greater; less
   b. the same; less
   c. a smaller; less
   d. the same; the same
3. Spontaneous mimicry:
   a. is almost always insulting when used during a conversation.
   b. is a type of display rule.
   c. has been shown to make conversations flow more smoothly.
   d. can interrupt the smooth flow of an otherwise normal conversation.
4. People with damage to their ________, may have difficulty reading the facial expressions of others.
   a. amygdala
   b. corpus callosum
   c. prefrontal regions
   d. thalamus
5. Male and female infants:
   a. express and self-regulate emotions identically until they learn from adults to act differently.
   b. do not express and self-regulate emotions.
   c. display no differences in terms of emotional sensitivity or expression.
   d. express and self-regulate emotions differently.

Review

PERSPECTIVES ON MOTIVATION

- ***How can you use intrinsic and extrinsic motivation to help you succeed in college?*** The idea that motivation is based on **instincts** was popular in the early 20th century but since has fallen out of favor. Human motivation has also been viewed as an effort toward **drive reduction** and **homeostasis,** or balance in the body. Another perspective, reflected in **arousal theory,** suggests behavior stems from a desire to maintain an optimum level of arousal. Motivational inducements or incentives can originate from within **(intrinsic motivation)** or from outside **(extrinsic motivation)** the person. The effects of intrinsic motivation are greater and longer-lasting.
- Abraham Maslow suggested human motives can be arranged in a **hierarchy of needs,** with primitive ones based on physical needs positioned at the bottom and higher ones such as self-esteem positioned toward the top. Maslow believed that the higher motives don't emerge until the more basic ones have been met, but recent research challenges his view.

HUNGER AND THIRST

- ***Why do people usually get hungry at mealtime? How can external cues influence our desire to eat?*** Hunger is regulated by several centers within the brain. These centers are stimulated by receptors that monitor blood levels of **glucose,** fats, and carbohydrates as well as the hormones **leptin** and **ghrelin.** Hunger is also stimulated by **incentives** such as cooking aromas and by emotional, cultural, and social factors.
- ***How can you tell if someone is suffering from anorexia nervosa or bulimia?*** Eating disorders, particularly **anorexia nervosa** and **bulimia nervosa,** are more prevalent among females than among males. They are characterized by extreme preoccupation with body image and weight. **Muscle dysmorphia** is a disorder generally seen among young men involving an obsession with muscle size leading to inordinate worry about diet and exercise. Another food-related problem, obesity, affects millions of Americans. Obesity has complex causes and negative consequences particularly for obese children, who are likely to have health problems as adults.

SEX

- ***How is the sex drive different from other primary drives?*** Sex is a primary drive that gives rise to reproductive behavior essential for the survival of the species.
- ***How well do we understand the biology of the sex drive?*** Although hormones such as **testosterone** are involved in human sexual responses, they don't play as dominant a role as they do in some other species. In humans, the brain exerts a powerful influence on the sex drive as well. The human **sexual response cycle,** which differs somewhat for males and females, has four stages—excitement, plateau, orgasm, and resolution.
- ***How does culture influence sexual behavior?*** Experience and learning affect preferences for sexually arousing stimuli. What is sexually attractive is also influenced by culture. Research suggests a more conservative pattern of sexual behavior in the United States than is portrayed in popular media.
- ***What are the arguments for and against a biological explanation of homosexuality?*** People with a heterosexual orientation are sexually attracted to members of the opposite sex; those with a homosexual orientation are sexually attracted to members of their own sex. It is likely that both biological and environmental factors play a role in explaining homosexuality.

OTHER IMPORTANT MOTIVES

- ***How are stimulus motives different from primary drives?*** Stimulus motives are less obviously associated with the survival of the organism or the species, although they often help humans adapt to their environments. **Stimulus motives,** such as the urge to explore and manipulate things, are associated with obtaining information about the world.
- ***What motives cause people to explore and change their environment?*** A gap in understanding may stimulate curiosity, motivating us to explore and, often, to change our environment.
- ***Is the human need for contact universal?*** Another important stimulus motive in humans and other primates is to seek various forms of tactile stimulation. The importance of contact has been demonstrated in non-human animal studies as well as in premature human infants.
- ***Is aggression a biological response or a learned one?*** Any behavior intended to inflict physical or psychological harm on others is an act of **aggression.** Some psychologists see aggression as an innate drive in humans that must be channeled to constructive ends, but others see it more as a learned response that is greatly influenced by modeling, norms, and values. Aggression differs markedly across cultures, supporting the latter view. Males generally are more inclined than females to strike out at others and commit acts of violence.

This gender difference probably stems from an interaction of nature and nurture.

- ***Is being highly competitive important to high achievement?*** People who display a desire to excel, to overcome obstacles, and to accomplish difficult things well and quickly score high in **achievement motive.** Although hard work and a strong desire to master challenges both contribute to achievement, excessive competitiveness toward others can actually interfere with achievement.
- ***How do psychologists explain the human need to be with other people?*** The **affiliation motive,** or need to be with other people, is especially pronounced when we feel threatened or anxious. Affiliation with others in this situation can counteract fear and bolster spirits.

EMOTIONS

- ***How many basic emotions are there? Are there basic emotions that all people experience regardless of their culture?*** Robert Plutchik's circular classification system for **emotions** encompasses eight basic emotions. But not all cultures categorize emotions this way. Some lack a word for emotion; others describe feelings as physical sensations. Cross-cultural research by Paul Ekman argues for the universality of at least six emotions—happiness, surprise, sadness, fear, disgust, and anger. Many psychologists add **love** to this list.
- ***What is the relationship among emotions, biological reactions, and thoughts?*** According to the **James–Lange theory,** environmental stimuli can cause physiological changes; and emotions then arise from our awareness of those changes. In contrast, the **Cannon–Bard theory** holds that emotions and bodily responses occur simultaneously. A third perspective, the **cognitive theory** of emotion, contends that our perceptions and judgments of situations are essential to our emotional experiences. Without these cognitions we would have no idea how to label our feelings. Not everyone agrees with this view, however, because emotions sometimes seem to arise too quickly to depend on mental evaluations. Counter to the cognitive view, C. E. Izard argues that certain inborn facial expressions and body postures are automatically triggered in emotion-arousing situations and are then "read" by the brain as particular feelings.

COMMUNICATING EMOTION

- ***What is the most obvious signal of emotion? What role can voice and facial expression play in expressing emotion?*** People express emotions verbally through words, tone of voice, exclamations, and other sounds. Facial expressions are the most obvious nonverbal indicators of emotion.
- ***What parts of the brain are responsible for interpreting facial expressions?*** The amygdala and insula play an important role in our ability to correctly interpret facial expressions. Abnormalities in these brain circuits may be a factor in depression and unprovoked aggression.
- ***How can posture and personal space communicate emotion?*** Other indicators involve body language—our posture, the way we move, our preferred personal distance from others when talking to them, our degree of eye contact. Explicit acts, such as slamming a door, express emotions, too. People vary in their skill at reading these nonverbal cues.
- ***Are men less emotional than women?*** Research confirms some gender differences in expressing and perceiving emotions. For instance, when confronted with a person in distress, women are more likely than men to express emotion, even though the levels of physiological arousal are the same for the two sexes. Also, being betrayed or criticized elicits more anger in men, versus more disappointment and hurt in women. Women are generally better than men at reading other people's emotions: decoding facial expressions, body cues, and tones of voice. This skill may be sharpened by their role as caretakers of infants and their traditional subordinate status to men.
- ***How can culture influence the way we express emotion?*** Regardless of a person's cultural background, the facial expressions associated with certain basic emotions appear to be universal. This finding contradicts the culture-learning view, which suggests facial expressions of emotion are learned within a particular culture. This is not to say that there are no cultural differences in emotional expression, however. Overlaying the universal expression of certain emotions are culturally varying **display rules** that govern when it is appropriate to show emotion—to whom, by whom, and under what circumstances. Other forms of nonverbal communication of emotion vary more from culture to culture than facial expressions do.

Test Yourself

1. Which of the following is a primary drive?
   a. Activity.
   b. Sex.
   c. Aggression.
   d. Contact.
2. You are home alone, and find nothing to do. You decide to go jogging. This kind of motivated behavior that attempts to increase the level of arousal is a problem for:
   a. any theory of motivation.
   b. the homeostasis theory of motivation.
   c. your glucose levels.
   d. the drive reduction theory of motivation.
3. According to Maslow, the desire to make the best we can out of ourselves corresponds to ____ whereas the desire to deal as best we can with other human beings corresponds to ____.
   a. self actualization needs; belongingness needs
   b. safety needs; esteem needs
   c. self-actualization needs; esteem needs
   d. esteem needs; safety needs
4. According to the Yerkes–Dodson Law, performance on simple tasks is optimal when emotional arousal is ____; for complex tasks optimal performance occurs when emotional arousal is ____.
   a. low; low
   b. high; high
   c. high; low
   d. low; high
5. A medium-sized salad didn't satiate your hunger, but a chocolate bar did. This is probably because the chocolate bar:
   a. raised the glucose level in your bloodstream more than the salad.
   b. raised the insulin level in your bloodstream more than the salad.
   c. lowered the glucose level in your bloodstream more than the salad.
   d. lowered the insulin level in your bloodstream more than the salad.
6. Thirst is controlled by:
   a. the level of fluids inside the body's cells.
   b. the level of fluids in the stomach.
   c. the level of fluids outside the body's cells.
   d. the balance between the level of fluids outside the body's cells and the level of fluids inside the body's cells.
7. Which of the following is not a symptom of anorexia nervosa?
   a. Intense fear of becoming obese, which does not diminish as weight loss progresses.
   b. Disturbance of body image.
   c. Recurrent episodes of binge eating.
   d. Refusal to maintain body weight at or above a minimal normal weight for age and height.
8. Sex differs from the other primary drives in that:
   a. sex is vital to the survival of the individual whereas the other primary drives are not.
   b. the other primary drives are vital to the survival of the individual, but sex is vital only to the survival of the species.
   c. it is not affected by experience or learning.
   d. it can be affected by experience or learning.
9. The general consensus among medical and mental health professionals regarding homosexuality is:
   a. that "reparative therapy" is usually effective for individuals who have a strong network of social support.
   b. that because it has never been observed in other species, it is a behavior unique and distinct to only the human species.
   c. that children raised by gay or lesbian parents have an increased probability of being homosexual.
   d. that there is no convincing evidence that sexual orientation can be changed by "reparative" or "conversion therapy."
10. In a series of famous experiments, Harry Harlow presented newborn monkeys with "surrogate" mothers of two types. Which of the following choices represents an important conclusion that was drawn from these experiments?
    a. When stressed, newborn primates are most powerfully drawn to a source of contact comfort and warmth.
    b. When stressed, newborn primates are most powerfully drawn to their source of nourishment.
    c. Newborn primates cannot survive without their real mothers; newborns given surrogate mothers would not eat any food and subsequently died.
    d. When stressed, newborn primates are powerfully drawn towards their peers.
11. Which of the following is true of individuals who are high in achievement motivation?
    a. They are not competitive.
    b. They are slow learners.
    c. They have high self-imposed standards of performance.
    d. They have a strong tendency to be conformists.
12. The affiliative motive is often aroused when:
    a. stimulation is simple.
    b. people feel threatened.
    c. primary drives are met.
    d. people feel self-confident.
13. Which of the following emotions does not appear to have a universally recognized outward expression?
    a. Anger.
    b. Happiness.
    c. Sadness.
    d. Love.

14. "We feel sorry because we cry, angry because we strike, afraid because we tremble." These words are most likely to have been spoken by which theorist?
    a. Cannon.
    b. Schachter.
    c. Plutchik.
    d. James.
15. In the presence of teachers or authority figures, Japanese students show fewer facial expressions of negative emotion than American students. However, when teachers or authority figures are not present, Japanese and American students show similar facial expressions of emotion. This is an example of:
    a. basic emotional differences between what Japanese and American students experience.
    b. Japanese students paying more attention to their teachers and authority figures than American students.
    c. display rules.
    d. the physiological difference in emotional expression between Japanese and American cultures.

Memory*

11

*Taken from *Psychology*, Eleventh Edition Eleventh Edition by Carole Wade, Carol Tavris, and Maryanne Garry

Ask questions. . . be willing to wonder

- Is everything that ever happened to us stored in the brain?
- What strategies can help us remember better?
- Why can't we remember events from our first two years?
- Do people repress traumatic memories?

Jennifer Thompson swore to herself that she would never, *ever* forget the face of her rapist, a man who climbed through the window of her apartment and assaulted her brutally. During the attack, she made an effort to memorize every detail of his face, looking for scars, tattoos, or other identifying marks. When the police asked her if she could identify the assailant from a book of mug shots, she picked one that she was sure was correct, and later she identified the same man in a lineup. After a jury heard her eyewitness testimony, Ronald Cotton was convicted and sentenced to prison for two life terms. A few years later, evidence surfaced that the real rapist might have been another man, a convict named Bobby Poole. A judge ordered a new trial, where Jennifer Thompson looked at both men face to face and once again said that Ronald Cotton was the man who raped her. Cotton was sent back to prison.

Eleven years later, DNA evidence completely exonerated Cotton and just as unequivocally implicated Poole, who confessed to the crime. Thompson was devastated. She told friends and family that she was absolutely sure that she had correctly identified the man who raped her and stolen her soul, and just as sure that her real rapist was a man she had never seen in her life. She was wrong on both counts. Jennifer Thompson decided to meet Cotton and apologize to him personally. Amazingly, they were both able to put this tragedy behind them and become friends. Nevertheless, she wrote, she still lives with the anguish of knowing that her mistake had cost him years of liberty. And she could not even imagine the tragedy if her mistaken identification had been in a case that resulted in his execution.

Eyewitness testimony is an important and necessary part of the legal system, yet Ronald Cotton's case is not that unusual. As you will see later in this chapter, many wrongfully convicted people have ended up in prison because of an eyewitness's inaccurate

Thinking Critically

Ask questions.

Ronald Cotton (left) was convicted of rape solely on the basis of eyewitness testimony. He spent 11 years in prison until DNA evidence established that he could not have committed the crime and that the real rapist was Bobby Poole (right). In thinking about cases in which an eyewitness provides the only evidence against a suspect, a critical thinker would ask: How accurate is eyewitness testimony, even when the witness is the victim? How trustworthy are our memories, even of traumatic events? Psychological scientists have learned some startling answers, as this chapter will show.

memory. That raises a difficult question: In the absence of corroborating evidence, should a witness's confidence in his or her testimony be sufficient for establishing guilt? Much is at stake in our efforts to answer this question: getting justice for crime victims and also avoiding the false conviction of defendants who are innocent.

And what about the rest of us? When should we trust our own memories and when should we be cautious about doing so? We all forget things that happened; do we also "remember" things that never happened? Are memory malfunctions the exception to the rule or are they commonplace? If memory is not always reliable, what does that tell us about the story we "remember" so clearly of our own lives? How can we hope to understand the past?

You are about to learn . . .

- **why memory does not work like a camera—and how it does work.**
- **why errors can creep into our memories of even surprising or shocking events.**
- **why having a strong emotional reaction to a remembered event does not mean that the memory is accurate.**

Reconstructing the Past

Memory refers to the capacity to retain and retrieve information, and also to the structures that account for this capacity. Human beings are capable of astonishing feats of memory. Most of us can easily remember the tune of our national anthem, how to use an ATM, the most embarrassing experience we ever had, and hundreds of thousands of other bits of information. Memory confers competence; without it, we would be as helpless as newborns, unable to carry out even the most trivial of our daily tasks. Memory also gives us our sense of who we are, for if we are not the sum of our recollections, then who are we? Our very identity depends on our memories, which is why we feel so threatened when others challenge them. Individuals and cultures alike rely on a remembered history for a sense of coherence and meaning. Memory gives us our past and guides our future.

What would life be like if you could never form any new memories? That's what happens to older people who are suffering from dementia, and it also sometimes happens to younger people who have brain injuries or diseases. We introduced Henry Molaison, whose case is the most intensely studied in the annals of medicine (Corkin, 1984; Corkin et al., 1997; Hilts, 1995; Milner, 1970; Ogden & Corkin, 1991). In 1953, when Henry, known in the scientific literature as H. M., was 27, surgeons made a last-ditch effort to cure his unrelenting, uncontrollable epileptic seizures by removing his hippocampus, most of his amygdala, and a portion of his temporal lobes. The operation did achieve its goal: Henry's seizures became milder and could be controlled by medication. But his memory had been affected profoundly: He could no longer remember new experiences for much longer than 15 minutes. Facts, songs, stories, and faces all vanished like water down the drain. He would read the same magazine over and over without realizing it; he could not recall the day of the week, the year, or even his last meal.

Henry still loved to do crossword puzzles and play bingo, skills he had learned long before the operation. And he remained cheerful, even though he knew he had memory problems. He would occasionally recall an unusually emotional event, such as the assassination of someone named Kennedy, and he sometimes remembered that both of his parents were dead. But according to Suzanne Corkin, who studied H. M. extensively, these "islands of remembering" were the exceptions in a vast sea of forgetfulness. This good-natured man felt sad that he could never make friends because he could never remember anyone, not even the scientists who studied him for decades. He always thought he was much younger than he really was, and he was unable to recognize a photograph of his own face; he was stuck in a time warp from the past.

After he died in 2008 at age 82, one neuroscientist said that H. M. gave science the ultimate gift: his memory (Ogden, 2012). He also taught neuroscientists a great deal about the biology of memory; before his surgery, scientists did not realize the important role played by the hippocampus. We will meet H. M. again at several points in this chapter.

The Manufacture of Memory

People's descriptions of memory have always been influenced by the technology of their time. Ancient philosophers compared memory to a soft wax tablet that would preserve anything imprinted on it. Later, with the advent of the printing press, people began to describe memory as a gigantic library, storing specific events and facts for later retrieval. Today, many people compare memory to a digital recorder or video camera, automatically capturing every moment of their lives.

Popular and appealing though this belief about memory is, it is utterly wrong. Not everything that happens to us or impinges on our senses is tucked away for later use. Memory is selective. If it were not, our minds would be cluttered with mental junk: the temperature at noon on Thursday, the price of milk two years ago, a phone number needed only once. Moreover, remembering is not at all like replaying a recording of an event. It is more like watching a few unconnected clips and then figuring out what the rest of the recording must have been like.

One of the first scientists to make this point was the British psychologist Sir Frederic Bartlett (1932). Bartlett asked people to read lengthy, unfamiliar stories from other cultures and then tell the stories back to him. As the volunteers tried to recall the stories, they made interesting errors: They often eliminated or changed details that did not make sense to them, and they added other details from their own culture—details that made the story more sensible to them. Memory, Bartlett concluded, must therefore be largely a *reconstructive* process. We may reproduce some kinds of simple information by rote, said Bartlett, but when we remember complex information, our memories are distorted by previous knowledge and beliefs. Since Bartlett's time, hundreds of studies have supported his original idea, showing that it applies to all sorts of memories.

If these happy children remember this birthday party later in life, their constructions may include information picked up from family photographs, videos, and stories. And they will probably be unable to distinguish their actual memories from information they got elsewhere.

In reconstructing their memories, people often draw on many sources. Suppose that someone asks you to describe one of your early birthday parties. You may have some direct memory of the event, but you may also incorporate information from family stories, photographs, or home videos, and even from accounts of other people's birthdays and reenactments of birthdays on television. You take all these bits and pieces and build one integrated account. Later, you may not be able to distinguish your actual memory from information you got elsewhere—a phenomenon known as **source misattribution**, or sometimes *source confusion* (Johnson, Hashtroudi, & Lindsay, 1993; Mitchell & Johnson, 2009).

A dramatic instance of reconstruction once occurred with H. M. (Ogden & Corkin, 1991). After eating a chocolate Valentine's Day heart, H. M. stuck the shiny red wrapping in his shirt pocket. Two hours later, while searching for his handkerchief, he pulled out the paper and looked at it in puzzlement. When a researcher asked why he had the paper in his pocket, he replied, "Well, it could have been wrapped around a big chocolate heart. It must be Valentine's Day!" But a short time later, when she asked him to take out the paper again and say why he had it in his pocket, he replied, "Well, it might have been wrapped around a big chocolate rabbit. It must be Easter!" Sadly, H. M. *had* to reconstruct the past; his damaged brain could not recall it in any other way. But those of us with normal memory abilities also reconstruct, far more often than we realize.

source misattribution
the inability to distinguish an actual memory of an event from information you learned about the event elsewhere

Of course, some shocking or tragic events—such as earthquakes, a mass killing, an assassination—do hold a special place in memory. So do some unusual, exhilaratingly

happy events, such as learning that you just won a lottery. Years ago, these vivid recollections of emotional and important events were labeled *flashbulb memories,* to capture the surprise, illumination, and seemingly photographic detail that characterize them (Brown & Kulik, 1977). Some flashbulb memories can last for years. In a Danish study, older people who had lived through the Nazi occupation of their country in World War II retained accurate memories, for decades, of the day that the radio announced liberation (Berntsen & Thomsen, 2005). Sometimes, events that are unsurprising can also produce memories with the characteristics of flashbulbs—vivid, emotion-laden images—if they have significant personal or national consequences: the expected resignation of President Nixon after the Watergate scandal, the beginning of the Gulf War in 1991, and a student's first year of college (Talarico, 2009; Tinti et al., 2009).

Yet even flashbulb memories are not always complete or accurate. People typically remember the *gist* of a startling, emotional event they experienced or witnessed, but when researchers question them about their memories over time, errors creep into the details, and after a few years, some people even forget the gist (Neisser & Harsch, 1992; Talarico & Rubin, 2003). Just one day after the 2001 attacks on the World Trade Center and the Pentagon, researchers asked college students when they had first heard the news of the attacks, who had told them the news, and what they had been doing at the time. They also asked the students to report details about a mundane event from the days immediately before the attacks, to allow a comparison of ordinary memories with flashbulb ones. The students were retested at various intervals, up to eight months later. Over time, the vividness of the flashbulb memories and the students' confidence in these memories remained higher than for the everyday memories. Their confidence, however, was misplaced. The details the students reported became less and less consistent (and equally inconsistent) for *both* types of memories (Talarico & Rubin, 2003).

Even with flashbulb memories, then, facts tend to get mixed with fiction. Remembering is an active process, one that involves not only dredging up stored information but also putting two and two together to reconstruct the past. Sometimes, unfortunately, we put two and two together and get five.

The Conditions of Confabulation

Because memory is reconstructive, it is subject to **confabulation**—confusing an event that happened to someone else with one that happened to you, or coming to believe that you remember something that never really happened. Such confabulations are especially likely under certain circumstances (Garry et al., 1996; Hyman & Pentland, 1996; Mitchell & Johnson, 2009):

1 You have thought, heard, or told others about the imagined event many times. Suppose that at family gatherings you keep hearing about the time that your uncle Sam got so angry at a party that he began pounding the wall with a hammer, with such force that the wall collapsed. The story is so colorful that you can practically see it unfold in your mind. The more you think about this event, the more likely you are to believe that you actually were there and that it happened as you "remember" it, even if you were sound asleep in another house. This process has been called *imagination inflation,* because your own active imagination inflates your belief that the event really occurred as you assume it did (Garry & Polaschek, 2000). Even merely explaining how a hypothetical childhood experience *could* have happened inflates people's confidence that it really did. Explaining an event makes it seem more familiar and thus real (Sharman, Manning, & Garry, 2005).

2 The image of the event contains lots of details that make it feel real. Ordinarily, we can distinguish imagined events from real ones by the amount of detail we recall; memories of real events tend to contain more details. But the longer you think about an imagined event, the more likely you are to embroider those images with details—what

confabulation
confusion of an event that happened to someone else with one that happened to you, or a belief that you remember something when it never actually happened

your uncle was wearing, the crumbling plaster, the sound of the hammer—and these added details will persuade you that you really do remember the event and aren't just confusing other people's reports with your own experience (Johnson et al., 2011).

3 The event is easy to imagine. If imagining an event takes little effort (as does visualizing a man pounding a wall with a hammer), then we are especially likely to think that a memory is real rather than false. In contrast, when we must make an effort to form an image of an experience, a place we have never seen, or an activity that is utterly foreign to us, we use our cognitive effort as a cue that we are merely imagining the event or have heard about it from others.

As a result of confabulation, you may end up with a memory that feels emotionally, vividly real to you and yet is false (Mitchell & Johnson, 2009). This means that your feelings about an event, no matter how strong they are, do not guarantee that the event really took place. Consider again our Sam story, which happens to be true. A woman we know believed for years that she had been present as an 11-year-old child when her uncle destroyed the wall. Because the story was so vivid and upsetting to her, she felt angry at him for what she thought was his mean and violent behavior, and she assumed that she must have been angry at the time as well. Then, as an adult, she learned that she was not at the party at all but had merely heard about it repeatedly over the years. Moreover, Sam had not pounded the wall in anger, but as a joke, to inform the assembled guests that he and his wife were about to remodel their home. Nevertheless, our friend's family has had a hard time convincing her that her "memory" of this event is entirely wrong, and they are not sure she believes them yet.

As the Sam story illustrates, and as laboratory research verifies, false memories can be as stable over time as true ones (Roediger & McDermott, 1995). There's just no getting around it: Memory is reconstructive.

In the 1980s, Whitley Strieber published *Communion*, in which he claimed to have had encounters with nonhuman beings, possibly aliens from outer space. An art director designed this striking image for the cover. Ever since, many people have assumed that this is what an extraterrestrial must look like, and some have imported the image into their own confabulated memories of alien abduction.

Recite & Review

Recite: Reconstruct what you just read and say what you can remember about why memory is *reconstructive,* and about *source misattribution, flashbulb memories,* and *confabulation.*

Review: Next, go back and read this section again.

Now take this ***Quick Quiz:***

1. Memory is like (a) a wax tablet, (b) a giant file cabinet, (c) a video camera, (d) none of these.
2. *True or false:* Because they are so vivid, flashbulb memories remain perfectly accurate over time.
3. Which of the following confabulated "memories" might a person be most inclined to accept as having really happened to them, and why? (a) getting lost in a shopping center at the age of 5, (b) taking a class in astrophysics, (c) visiting a monastery in Tibet as a child, (d) being bullied by another kid in the fourth grade

Answers: 1. d **2.** false **3.** a and d, because they are common events that are easy to imagine and that contain a lot of vivid details. It would be harder to induce someone to believe that he or she had studied astrophysics or visited Tibet because these are rare events that take an effort to imagine.

You are about to learn . . .

- **how memories of an event can be affected by the way someone is questioned about it.**
- **why children's memories and testimony about sexual abuse cannot always be trusted.**

Memory and the Power of Suggestion

The reconstructive nature of memory helps the mind work efficiently. Instead of cramming our brains with infinite details, we can store the essentials of an experience and then use our knowledge of the world to figure out the specifics when we need them. But precisely because memory is so often reconstructive, it is also vulnerable to suggestion—to ideas implanted in our minds after the event, which then become associated with it. This fact raises thorny problems in legal cases that involve eyewitness testimony or people's memories of what happened, when, and to whom.

The Eyewitness on Trial

Without the accounts of eyewitnesses, many guilty people would go free. But, as Jennifer Thompson learned to her sorrow, eyewitness testimony is not always reliable. Lineups and photo arrays don't necessarily help, because witnesses may simply identify the person who looks most like the perpetrator of the crime (Wells & Olson, 2003). As a result, some convictions based on eyewitness testimony, like that of Ronald Cotton, turn out to be tragic mistakes.

Eyewitnesses are especially likely to make mistaken identifications when the suspect's ethnicity differs from their own. Because of unfamiliarity with other ethnic groups, the eyewitness may focus solely on the ethnicity of the person they see committing a crime ("He's black"; "She's white"; "He's an Arab") and ignore the distinctive features that would later make identification more accurate (Levin, 2000; Meissner & Brigham, 2001).

In a program of research spanning nearly four decades, Elizabeth Loftus and her colleagues have shown that memories are also influenced by the way in which questions are put to the eyewitness and by suggestive comments made during an interrogation or interview. In one classic study, the researchers showed how even subtle changes in the wording of questions can lead a witness to give different answers. Participants first watched short films depicting car collisions. Afterward, the researchers asked some of them, "About how fast were the cars going when they hit each other?" Other viewers were asked the same question, but with the verb changed to *smashed, collided, bumped,* or *contacted.* Estimates of how fast the cars were going varied, depending on which word was used. *Smashed* produced the highest average speed estimates (40.8 mph), followed by *collided* (39.3 mph), *bumped* (38.1 mph), *hit* (34.0 mph), and *contacted* (31.8 mph) (Loftus & Palmer, 1974).

Misleading information from other sources also can profoundly alter what witnesses report. Consider what happened when students were shown the face of a young man who had straight hair, then heard a description of the face supposedly written by another witness—a description that wrongly said the man had light, curly hair (see Figure 11.1). When the students reconstructed the face using a kit of facial features, a third of their reconstructions contained the misleading detail, whereas only 5 percent contained it when curly hair was not mentioned (Loftus & Greene, 1980). In real life, misleading information about a perpetrator's appearance can reduce an eyewitness's ability to identify the real perpetrator later in a lineup (Zajac & Henderson, 2009).

Does the number of eyewitnesses affect a person's susceptibility to misleading information? In a study of this question, people first watched a video of a simulated crime and later read three eyewitness reports about the crime, each report containing the same misleading claim—such as about the location of objects, the thief's actions, or the name on the side of the suspect van. One group was told that a single person wrote all three reports, whereas another group was told that each report was written by a different person. It made no difference; a single

Thinking Critically

Analyze assumptions and biases.

On TV crime shows, witnesses often identify a criminal from a lineup or a group of photos. But these methods can mislead real witnesses, who may wrongly identify a person simply because he or she resembles the actual culprit more closely than the other people standing there or in the photos do. Based on psychological findings, many law enforcement agencies are now using better methods, such as having witnesses look at photos of suspects one at a time without being able to go back to an earlier one.

Figure 11.1 The Influence of Misleading Information
In a study described in the text, students saw the face of a young man with straight hair and then had to reconstruct it from memory. On the left is one student's reconstruction in the absence of misleading information about the man's hair. On the right is another person's reconstruction of the same face after exposure to misleading information that mentioned curly hair (Loftus & Greene, 1980).

witness's report proved to be as influential as the reports of three different witnesses. Such is the power of a single witness's voice (Foster et al., 2012).

Leading questions, suggestive comments, and misleading information affect people's memories not only for events they have witnessed but also for their own experiences. Researchers have successfully used these techniques to induce people to believe they are recalling complicated events from early in life that never actually happened, such as getting lost in a shopping mall, being hospitalized for a high fever, being harassed by a bully, getting in trouble for playing a prank on a first-grade teacher, or spilling punch all over the mother of the bride at a wedding (Hyman & Pentland, 1996; Lindsay et al., 2004; Loftus & Pickrell, 1995; Mazzoni et al., 1999). When people were shown a phony Disneyland ad featuring Bugs Bunny, about 16 percent later recalled having met a Bugs character at Disneyland (Braun, Ellis, & Loftus, 2002). In later studies, the percentages were even higher. Some people even claimed to remember shaking hands with the character, hugging him, or seeing him in a parade. But these memories were impossible, because Bugs Bunny is a Warner Bros. creation and would definitely be rabbit non grata at Disneyland!

Children's Testimony

The power of suggestion can affect anyone, but its impact on children who are being questioned about possible sexual or physical abuse is especially worrisome. How can adults determine whether a young child has been sexually molested without influencing what the child says? The answer is crucial. Throughout the 1980s and 1990s, accusations of child abuse in daycare centers skyrocketed. After being interviewed by therapists and police investigators, children were claiming that their teachers had molested them in the most terrible ways: hanging them in trees, raping them, and even forcing them to eat feces. Although in no case had parents actually seen the daycare teachers treating the children badly, although none of the children had complained to their parents, and although none of the parents had noticed any symptoms or problems in their children, the accused teachers were often sentenced to many years in prison.

Thanks largely to research by psychological scientists, the hysteria eventually subsided and people were able to assess more clearly what had gone wrong in the way children had been interviewed in these cases. Today we know that although children, like adults, can

Thinking Critically

Don't oversimplify.

Some people claim that children's memories of sexual abuse are always accurate; others claim that children cannot distinguish fantasy from reality. How can we avoid either–or thinking on this emotional issue? Is the question "Are children's memories accurate?" even the right one to ask?

remember many things accurately, they can also be influenced by an interviewer's leading questions, suggestions, or pressure to report certain information (Ceci & Bruck, 1995). Moreover, in the courtroom, the style of questions put to children under cross-examination often leads them to be highly inaccurate (O'Neill & Zajac, 2012). The question to ask, therefore, is not "Can children's memories be trusted?" but "Under what conditions are children apt to be suggestible, and to report that something happened to them when in fact it did not?"

The answer, from many experimental studies, is that a child is more likely to give a false report when an interviewer strongly believes that the child has been molested and then uses suggestive techniques to get the child to reveal molestation (Bruck, 2003). Interviewers who are biased in this way seek only confirming evidence and ignore discrepant evidence and other explanations for a child's behavior. They reject a child's denial of having been molested and assume the child is "in denial." They use techniques that encourage imagination inflation ("Let's pretend it happened!") and that blur reality and fantasy in the child's mind. They pressure or encourage the child to describe terrible events, badger the child with repeated questions, tell the child that "everyone else" said the events happened, or use bribes and threats (Poole & Lamb, 1998).

A team of researchers analyzed the actual transcripts of interrogations of children in the first highly publicized sexual abuse case in the United States, the McMartin preschool case (which ended in a hung jury). Then they applied the same suggestive techniques in an experiment with preschool children (Garven et al., 1998). A young man visited children at their preschool, read them a story, and handed out treats. The man did nothing aggressive, inappropriate, or surprising. A week later, an experimenter questioned the children individually about the man's visit. She asked children in one group leading questions ("Did he bump the teacher? Did he throw a crayon at a kid who was talking?" "Did he tell you a secret and tell you not to tell?"). She asked a second group the same questions but also applied influence techniques used by interrogators in the McMartin and other daycare cases: telling the children what "other kids" had supposedly said, expressing disappointment if answers were negative, and praising the children for making allegations.

In the first group, children said "Yes, it happened" to about 17 percent of the false allegations about the man's visit. And in the second group, they said "yes" to the false allegations suggested to them a whopping 58 percent of the time. As you can see in Figure 11.2, the 3-year-olds in this group, on average, said "yes" to over 80 percent of the false allegations, and the 4- to 6-year-olds said "yes" to over half of the allegations. Note that the interviews in this study lasted only 5 to 10 minutes, whereas in actual investigations, interviewers often question children repeatedly over many weeks or months.

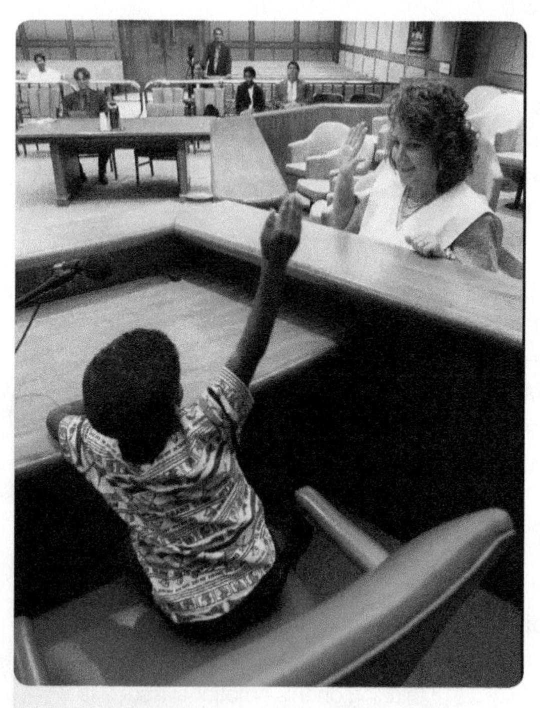

Children's testimony is often crucial in child sexual abuse cases. Under what conditions do children make reliable or unreliable witnesses?

Many people believe that children cannot be induced to make up experiences that are truly traumatic, but psychologists have shown that this assumption, too, is wrong. When schoolchildren were asked for their recollections of an actual sniper incident at their school, many of those who had been absent from school that day reported memories of hearing shots, seeing someone lying on the ground, and other details they could not possibly have experienced directly. Apparently, they had been influenced by the accounts of the children who had been there (Pynoos & Nader, 1989). Indeed, rumor and hearsay play a big role in promoting false beliefs and memories in children, just as they do in adults (Principe et al., 2006).

As a result of such findings, psychologists have been able to develop ways of interviewing children that reduce the chances of false reporting. If the interviewer says, "Tell me the reason you came to talk to me today," and nothing more, most actual victims will disclose what happened to them (Bruck, 2003). The interviewer must not assume that the child was molested, must avoid leading or suggestive questions, and must understand that children do not speak the way adults do. Young children often drift from topic to topic, and their words may not be the words adults would use (Poole & Lamb, 1998). One little girl being interviewed thought her "private parts" were her elbows!

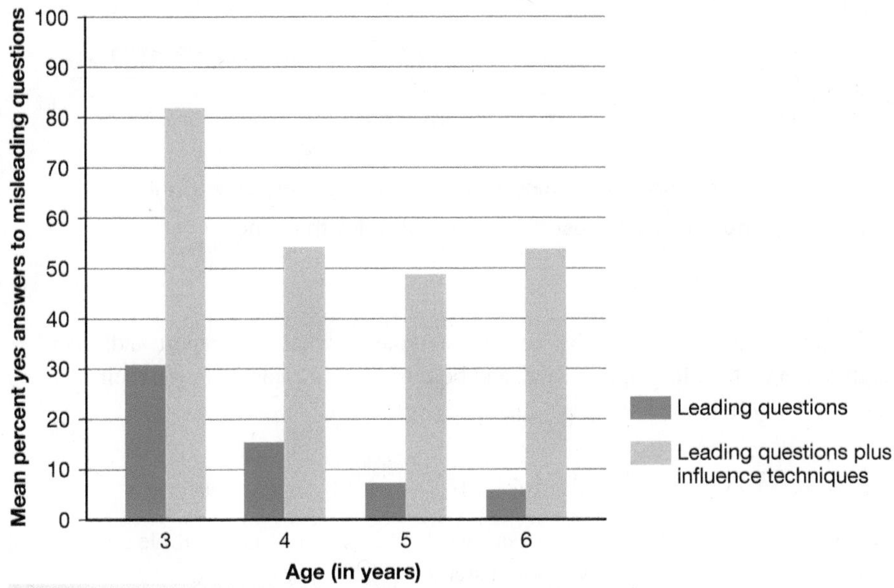

Figure 11.2 Social Pressure and Children's False Allegations
When researchers asked 3-year-olds leading questions about events that had not occurred—such as whether a previous visitor to their classroom had committed aggressive acts—nearly 30 percent said that yes, he had. This percentage declined among older children. But when the researchers used influence techniques taken from actual child-abuse investigations, most of the children agreed with the false allegation, regardless of their age (Garven et al., 1998).

Recite & Review

Recite: Here's a suggestion: Tell someone—anyone—out loud what you remember about the influence of misleading information on people's reports of an event, and about conditions that increase suggestibility in children.

Review: Next, go back and read this section again.

Now take this ***Quick Quiz:***

1. *True or false*: Mistaken identifications are more likely when a suspect's ethnicity differs from that of the eyewitness, even when the witness feels certain about being accurate.
2. Research suggests that the best way to encourage truthful testimony by children is to (a) reassure them that their friends have had the same experience, (b) reward them for saying that something happened, (c) scold them if you believe they are lying, (d) avoid leading questions.
3. Two decades ago, hundreds of people in psychotherapy began claiming that they could recall long-buried memories of having taken part in satanic rituals involving animal and human torture and sacrifice. Yet the FBI was unable to confirm any of these reports. Based on what you have learned so far, how might you explain such "memories"?

Answers: **1.** true **2.** d **3.** Therapists who uncritically assumed that satanic cults were widespread may have asked leading questions and otherwise influenced their patients. Patients who were susceptible to their therapists' interpretations may have then confabulated and "remembered" experiences that did not happen, borrowing details from fictionalized accounts or from other troubling experiences in their lives. The result was source misattribution and the patients' mistaken conviction that their memories were real.

You are about to learn . . .

- why multiple-choice test items are generally easier than short-answer or essay questions.
- whether you can know something without knowing that you know it.
- why the computer is often used as a metaphor for the mind.

In sum, children, like adults, can be accurate in what they report and, also like adults, they can distort, forget, fantasize, and be misled. As research shows, their memory processes are only human.

In Pursuit of Memory

Now that we have seen how memory *doesn't* work—namely, like an infallible recording of everything that happens to you—we turn to studies of how it *does* work.

Measuring Memory

Conscious, intentional recollection of an event or an item of information is called **explicit memory**. It is usually measured using one of two methods. The first method tests for **recall**, the ability to retrieve and reproduce information encountered earlier. Essay and fill-in-the-blank exams require recall. The second method tests for **recognition**, the ability to identify information you have previously observed, read, or heard about. The information is given to you, and all you have to do is say whether it is old or new, or perhaps correct or incorrect, or pick it out of a set of alternatives. The task, in other words, is to compare the information you are given with the information stored in your memory. True–false and multiple-choice tests call for recognition.

Recognition tests can be tricky, especially when false items closely resemble correct ones. Under most circumstances, however, recognition is easier than recall. Recognition for visual images is particularly impressive. If you show people 2,500 slides of faces and places, and later you ask them to identify which ones they saw out of a larger set, they will be able to identify more than 90 percent of the original slides accurately (Haber, 1970).

The superiority of recognition over recall was once demonstrated in a study of people's memories of their high school classmates (Bahrick, Bahrick, & Wittlinger, 1975). The participants, ages 17 to 74, first wrote down the names of as many classmates as they could remember. Recall was poor; even when prompted with yearbook pictures, the youngest people failed to name almost a third of their classmates, and the oldest failed to name most of them. Recognition, however, was far better. When asked to look at a series of cards, each of which contained a set of five photographs, and to say which picture in each set showed a

explicit memory
conscious, intentional recollection of an event or of an item of information

recall
the ability to retrieve and reproduce from memory previously encountered material

recognition
the ability to identify previously encountered material

Get Involved!

Recalling Rudolph's Friends

You can try this test of recall if you are familiar with the poem that begins "'Twas the Night Before Christmas" or the song "Rudolph the Red-Nosed Reindeer." Rudolph had eight reindeer friends; name as many of them as you can. After you have done your best, turn to the Get Involved exercise on page 337 for a recognition test on the same information.

former classmate, recent graduates were right 90 percent of the time—and so were people who had graduated 35 years earlier. The ability to recognize names was nearly as impressive.

Sometimes, information encountered in the past affects our thoughts and actions even though we do not consciously or intentionally remember it, a phenomenon known as **implicit memory** (Schacter, Chiu, & Ochsner, 1993). To get at this subtle sort of memory, researchers must rely on indirect methods instead of the direct ones used to measure explicit memory. One common method, **priming**, asks you to read or listen to some information and then tests you later to see whether the information affects your performance on another type of task.

Suppose that you read a list of words, some of which began with the letters *def* (such as *define, defend,* or *deform*). Later, if you were asked to complete word fragments (such as *def-*) with the first word that came to mind, you would be more likely to complete the fragments so they turned into words from the list than if you had never seen the list—even if you could not remember the original words very well (Richardson-Klavehn & Bjork, 1988; Roediger, 1990). That is, the words on the list have "primed" (made more available) your responses on the word-completion task. Priming isn't limited to words; priming people with unusual sentence constructions causes them to adopt those constructions a week later (Kaschak et al., 2011). Fragments of pictures can also act as primes. In one study, people briefly saw fragments of drawings depicting objects and animals. Then, *17 years later*, they were mailed the same fragments and also fragments of new drawings, with a request to name what the fragments depicted. Even when people couldn't remember having been in the original experiment, they identified the primed objects much better than the new objects (Mitchell, 2006). These studies show that people know more than they think they know—and that they can know it for a very long time.

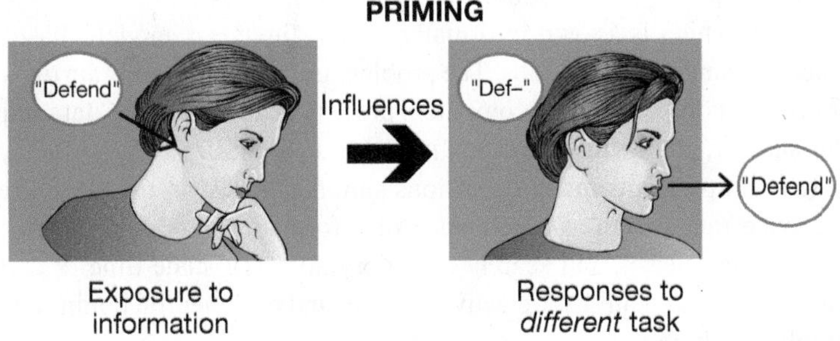

Another way to measure implicit memory, the **relearning method**, or *savings method,* was devised by Hermann Ebbinghaus (1885/1913) in the nineteenth century. The relearning method requires you to relearn information or a task that you learned earlier. If you master it more quickly the second time around, you must be remembering something from the first experience.

Get Involved!

Recognizing Rudolph's Friends

If you took the recall test in the Get Involved exercise on page 336, now try a recognition test. From the following list, see whether you can identify the correct names of Rudolph the Red-Nosed Reindeer's eight reindeer friends. The answers are at the end of this chapter—but no fair peeking!

Blitzen	Dander	Dancer	Masher
Cupid	Dasher	Prancer	Comet
Kumquat	Donder	Flasher	Pixie
Bouncer	Blintzes	Trixie	Vixen

Which was easier, recall or recognition? Can you speculate on the reason?

implicit memory
unconscious retention in memory, as evidenced by the effect of a previous experience or previously encountered information on current thoughts or actions

priming
a method for measuring implicit memory in which a person reads or listens to information and is later tested to see whether the information affects performance on another type of task

relearning method
a method for measuring retention that compares the time required to relearn material with the time used in the initial learning of the material

Models of Memory

Although people usually refer to memory as a single faculty, as in "I must be losing my memory" or "He has a memory like an elephant's," the term *memory* actually covers a complex collection of abilities and processes. If a video camera is not an accurate metaphor for capturing these diverse components of memory, what metaphor would be better?

Many cognitive psychologists liken the mind to an information processor, along the lines of a computer, though more complex. They have constructed *information-processing models* of cognitive processes, liberally borrowing computer-programming terms such as *input, output, accessing,* and *information retrieval.* When you type something on your computer's keyboard, a software program encodes the information into an electronic language, stores it on a hard drive, and retrieves it when you need to use it. Similarly, in information-processing models of memory, we *encode* information (convert it to a form that the brain can process and use), *store* the information (retain it over time), and *retrieve* the information (recover it for use). In storage, the information may be represented as concepts, propositions, images, or *cognitive schemas*, mental networks of knowledge, beliefs, and expectations concerning particular topics or aspects of the world.

In most information-processing models, storage takes place in three interacting memory systems. A *sensory register* retains incoming sensory information for a second or two, until it can be processed further. *Short-term memory (STM)* holds a limited amount of information for a brief period of time, perhaps up to 30 seconds or so, unless a conscious effort is made to keep it there longer. *Long-term memory (LTM)* accounts for longer storage, from a few minutes to decades (Atkinson & Shiffrin, 1968, 1971). Information can pass from the sensory register to short-term memory and in either direction between short-term and long-term memory, as illustrated in Figure 11.3.

This model, which is known informally as the "three-box model," has dominated research on memory since the late 1960s. The problem is that the human brain does not operate like your average computer. Most computers process instructions and data sequentially, one item after another, and so the three-box model has emphasized sequential operations. In contrast, the brain performs many operations simultaneously, in parallel. It recognizes patterns all at once rather than as a sequence of information bits, and it perceives new information, produces speech, and searches memory all at the same time. It can do these things because millions of neurons are active at once, and each neuron communicates with thousands of others, which in turn communicate with millions more.

parallel distributed processing (PDP) model a model of memory in which knowledge is represented as connections among thousands of interacting processing units, distributed in a vast network, and all operating in parallel. Also called a *connectionist model*

Because of these differences between human beings and machines, some cognitive scientists prefer a **parallel distributed processing (PDP)** or *connectionist* model. Instead of representing information as flowing from one system to another, a PDP model represents the contents of memory as connections among a huge number of interacting processing units, distributed in a vast network and all operating in parallel—just like the neurons of

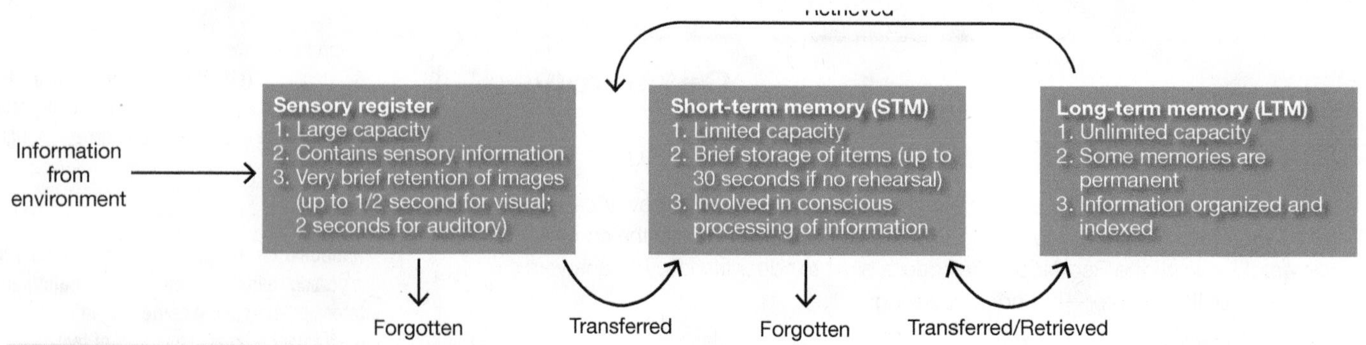

Figure 11.3 Three Memory Systems
In the three-box model of memory, information that does not transfer out of the sensory register or short-term memory is assumed to be forgotten forever. Once in long-term memory, information can be retrieved for use in analyzing incoming sensory information or performing mental operations in short-term memory.

the brain (McClelland, 1994, 2011; Rumelhart, McClelland, & the PDP Research Group, 1986). As information enters the system, the ability of these units to excite or inhibit each other is constantly adjusted to reflect new knowledge.

In this chapter, we emphasize the three-box model, but keep in mind that the computer metaphor that inspired it could one day be as outdated as the metaphor of memory as a camera.

Recite & Review

Recite: To find out how well you've encoded and stored the preceding material, retrieve it by saying out loud everything you can about *recall, recognition, explicit* versus *implicit memory, priming,* the *relearning method*, and models of memory.

Review: Next, go back and read this section again.

Now take this ***Quick Quiz:***

1. Alberta solved a crossword puzzle a few days ago. She no longer recalls the words in the puzzle, but while playing a game of Scrabble, she unconsciously tends to form words that were in the puzzle, showing that she has _________ memories of some of the words.
2. The three basic memory processes are _________, storage, and _________.
3. Do the preceding two questions ask for recall, recognition, or relearning? (And what about *this* question?)
4. One objection to traditional information-processing theories of memory is that, unlike most computers, the brain performs many independent operations _________.

Answers: 1. implicit **2.** encoding, retrieval **3.** The first two questions both measure recall; the third question measures recognition **4.** simultaneously, or in parallel

You are about to learn . . .

- **how the three "boxes" in the three-box model of memory operate.**
- **why short-term memory is like a leaky bucket.**
- **why a word can feel like it's "on the tip of your tongue."**
- **the difference between "knowing how" and "knowing that."**

The Three-Box Model of Memory

The information model of three separate memory systems—sensory, short-term, and long-term—remains a leading approach because it offers a convenient way to organize the major findings on memory, does a good job of accounting for these findings, and is consistent with the biological facts about memory. Let us now peer into each of the "boxes."

The Sensory Register: Fleeting Impressions

In the three-box model, all incoming sensory information must make a brief stop in the **sensory register**, the entryway of memory. The sensory register includes a number of

sensory register
a memory system that momentarily preserves extremely accurate images of sensory information

separate memory subsystems, as many as there are senses. Visual images remain in a visual subsystem for a maximum of a half second. Auditory images remain in an auditory subsystem for a slightly longer time, by most estimates up to two seconds or so.

The sensory register acts as a holding bin, retaining information in a highly accurate form until we can select items for attention from the stream of stimuli bombarding our senses. It gives us a moment to decide whether information is extraneous or important; not everything detected by our senses warrants our attention. And the identification of a stimulus on the basis of information already contained in long-term memory occurs during the transfer of information from the sensory register to short-term memory.

Information that does not quickly go on to short-term memory vanishes forever, like a message written in disappearing ink. That is why people who see an array of 12 letters for just a fraction of a second can only report 4 or 5 of them; by the time they answer, their sensory memories are already fading (Sperling, 1960). The fleeting nature of incoming sensations is actually beneficial; it prevents multiple sensory images—"double exposures"—that might interfere with the accurate perception and encoding of information.

Short-Term Memory: Memory's Notepad

Like the sensory register, **short-term memory (STM)** retains information only temporarily—for up to about 30 seconds by many estimates, although some researchers think that the maximum interval may extend to a few minutes for certain tasks. In short-term memory, the material is no longer an exact sensory image but is an encoding of one, such as a word or a phrase. This material either transfers into long-term memory or decays and is lost forever.

If the visual sensory register did not clear quickly, multiple images might interfere with the accurate perception and encoding of memory.

Victims of brain injury demonstrate the importance of transferring new information from short-term memory into long-term memory. H. M. was able to store information on a short-term basis; he could hold a conversation and his behavior appeared normal when you first met him. Yet, for the most part, he could not retain explicit information about new facts and events for longer than a few minutes. His terrible memory deficits involved a problem in transferring explicit memories from short-term storage into long-term storage. With a great deal of repetition and drill, patients like H. M. can learn some new visual information, retain it in long-term memory, and recall it normally (McKee & Squire, 1992). But usually information does not get into long-term memory in the first place.

The Leaky Bucket

People such as H. M. fall at the extreme end on a continuum of forgetfulness, but even those of us with normal memories know from personal experience how frustratingly brief short-term retention can be. We look up a telephone number, and after dialing it we find that the number has vanished from our minds. We meet someone and two minutes later find

short-term memory (STM)
in the three-box model of memory, a limited-capacity memory system involved in the retention of information for brief periods; it is also used to hold information retrieved from long-term memory for temporary use

Get Involved!

Your Sensory Register at Work

In a dark room or closet, swing a flashlight rapidly in a circle. You will see an unbroken circle of light instead of a series of separate points. The reason: The successive images remain briefly in the sensory register.

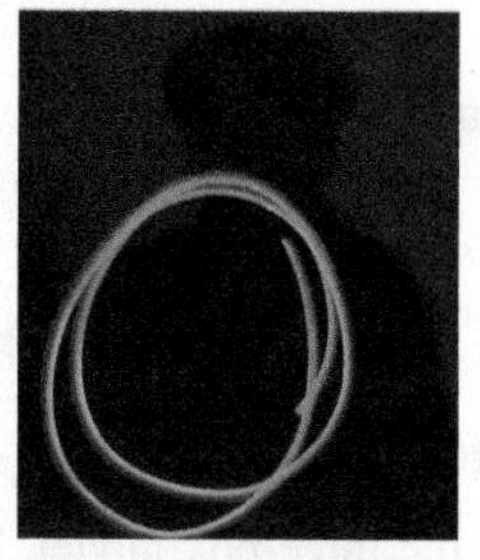

ourselves groping for the person's name. Is it any wonder that short-term memory has been called a "leaky bucket"?

According to most memory models, if the bucket did not leak it would quickly overflow, because at any given moment, short-term memory can hold only so many items. Years ago, George Miller (1956) estimated its capacity to be "the magical number 7 plus or minus 2." Conveniently, 5-digit zip codes and 7-digit telephone numbers fall in this range (at least in the United States); 16-digit credit card numbers do not. Since then, estimates of STM's capacity have ranged from 2 items to 20, with one estimate putting the "magical number" at 4 (Cowan, 2001; Cowan et al., 2008). Everyone agrees, however, that the number of items that short-term memory can handle at any one time is small.

Given the limits on short-term memory, how do we remember the beginning of a spoken sentence until the speaker reaches the end? After all, most sentences are longer than just a few words. Most information-processing models of memory propose that we bind small bits of information into larger units, or **chunks**. The real capacity of STM, it turns out, is not a few bits of information but a few chunks (Gilchrist & Cowan, 2012). A chunk can be a word, a phrase, a sentence, or even an image, and it depends on previous experience. For most Americans, the number 1776 is one chunk, not four, but 1840 is four chunks—unless you're from New Zealand, in which case 1840 is one chunk. (In that year, the British Crown and native Maori chiefs signed a treaty that became New Zealand's founding document.) A chunk can be visual: If you know football, when you see a play unfolding, you might see a single chunk of information—say, a wishbone formation—and be able to remember it. If you do not know football, you will see only a field full of players, and you probably won't be able to remember their positions when you look away.

But even chunking cannot keep short-term memory from eventually filling up. Information that will be needed for longer periods must be transferred to long-term memory or it will be displaced by new information and spill out of the bucket. Particularly meaningful items may transfer quickly, but other information will usually require more processing—unless we do something to keep it in STM for a while, as we will discuss shortly.

These card players are having a great time using their working memories.

Working Memory

In the original three-box model, short-term memory functioned basically as a container for temporarily holding on to new information or information retrieved from long-term memory. But this view did not account for the sense of effort we feel when trying to solve a problem. Does $2 \times (3 + 5) / 4 = 4$? Solving that problem feels as though we are not simply holding on to information but also *working* with it, which is why psychologists today think that STM is really part of a **working memory** system. STM keeps its job as a temporary holding bin, but another more active part—an "executive"—controls attention, focusing it on the information we need for the task at hand and warding off distracting information (Baddeley, 1992, 2007; Engle, 2002). In the previous algebra problem, your working memory must contain the numbers and instructions for operating on them, and also carry out those operations and retain the intermediate results from each step.

People who do well on tests of working memory tend to do well on intelligence tests and on tasks requiring complex cognition and the control of attention, such as understanding what you read, following directions, taking notes, playing bridge, learning new words, estimating how much time has elapsed, and many other real-life tasks (Broadway & Engle, 2011). When they are engrossed in challenging activities that require their concentration and effort, they stay on task longer, and their minds are less likely than other people's to wander (Kane et al., 2007).

The ability to bring information from long-term memory into short-term memory or to use working memory is not disrupted in patients like H. M. They can do arithmetic, relate

chunk
a meaningful unit of information; it may be composed of smaller units

working memory
in many models of memory, a cognitively complex form of short-term memory; it involves active mental processes that control retrieval of information from long-term memory and interpret that information appropriately for a given task

events that predate their injury, and do anything else that requires retrieval of information from long-term into short-term memory. Their problem is with the flow of information in the other direction, from short-term to long-term memory.

Long-Term Memory: Memory's Storage System

The third box in the three-box model of memory is **long-term memory (LTM)**. The capacity of long-term memory seems to have no practical limits. The vast amount of information stored there enables us to learn, get around in the environment, and build a sense of identity and a personal history.

Organization in Long-Term Memory

Because long-term memory contains so much information, it must be organized in some way, so that we can find the particular items we are looking for. One way to organize words (or the concepts they represent) is by the *semantic categories* to which they belong. *Chair*, for example, belongs to the category *furniture*. In a study done many years ago, people had to memorize 60 words that came from four semantic categories: animals, vegetables, names, and professions. The words were presented in random order, but when people were allowed to recall the items in any order they wished, they tended to recall them in clusters corresponding to the four categories (Bousfield, 1953). This finding has been replicated many times.

Evidence on the storage of information by semantic category also comes from cases of people with brain damage. In one such case, a patient called M. D. appeared to have made a complete recovery after suffering several strokes, with one odd exception: He had trouble remembering the names of fruits and vegetables. M. D. could easily name a picture of an abacus or a sphinx, but he drew a blank when he saw a picture of an orange or a carrot. He could sort pictures of animals, vehicles, and other objects into their appropriate categories, but did poorly with pictures of fruits and vegetables. On the other hand, when M. D. was *given* the names of fruits and vegetables, he immediately pointed to the corresponding pictures (Hart, Berndt, & Caramazza, 1985). Apparently, M. D. still had information about fruits and vegetables, but his brain lesion prevented him from using their names to get to the information when he needed it, unless someone else provided the names. This evidence suggests that information in memory about a particular concept (such as *orange*) is linked in some way to information about the concept's semantic category (such as *fruit*).

Culture affects the encoding, storage, and retrieval of information in long-term memory. Navajo healers, who use stylized, symbolic sand paintings in their rituals, must commit to memory dozens of intricate visual designs, because no exact copies are made and the painting is destroyed after each ceremony.

Indeed, many models of long-term memory represent its contents as a vast network of interrelated concepts and propositions (Anderson, 1990; Collins & Loftus, 1975). In these models, a small part of a conceptual network for *animals* might look something like the one in Figure 11.4. The way people use these networks, however, depends on experience and education. In rural Liberia, the more schooling children have, the more likely they are to use semantic categories in recalling lists of objects (Cole & Scribner, 1974). This makes sense, because in school, children must memorize a lot of information in a short time, and semantic grouping can help. Unschooled children, having less need to memorize lists, do not cluster items and do not remember them as well. But this does not mean that unschooled children have poor memories. When the task is one that is meaningful to them, such as recalling objects that were in a story or a village scene, they remember extremely well (Mistry & Rogoff, 1994).

We organize information in long-term memory not only by semantic groupings but also in terms of the way words sound or look. Have you ever tried to recall some name, phrase, or word that just escaped you? Nearly everyone experiences these *tip-of-the-tongue (TOT) states*, which occur across many languages and cultures; users of sign language call them "tip of the finger" states (Thompson, Emmorey, & Gollan, 2005). Scientists value them as a sort of slow-motion video of memory processes (A. Brown, 2012). People in a TOT state tend to come up with words that resemble the right one in sound, meaning, or form (e.g., number of syllables) before finally recalling the one they're searching for, which indicates that information in long-term memory is organized in those terms (R. Brown &

long-term memory (LTM)
in the three-box model of memory, the memory system involved in the long-term storage of information

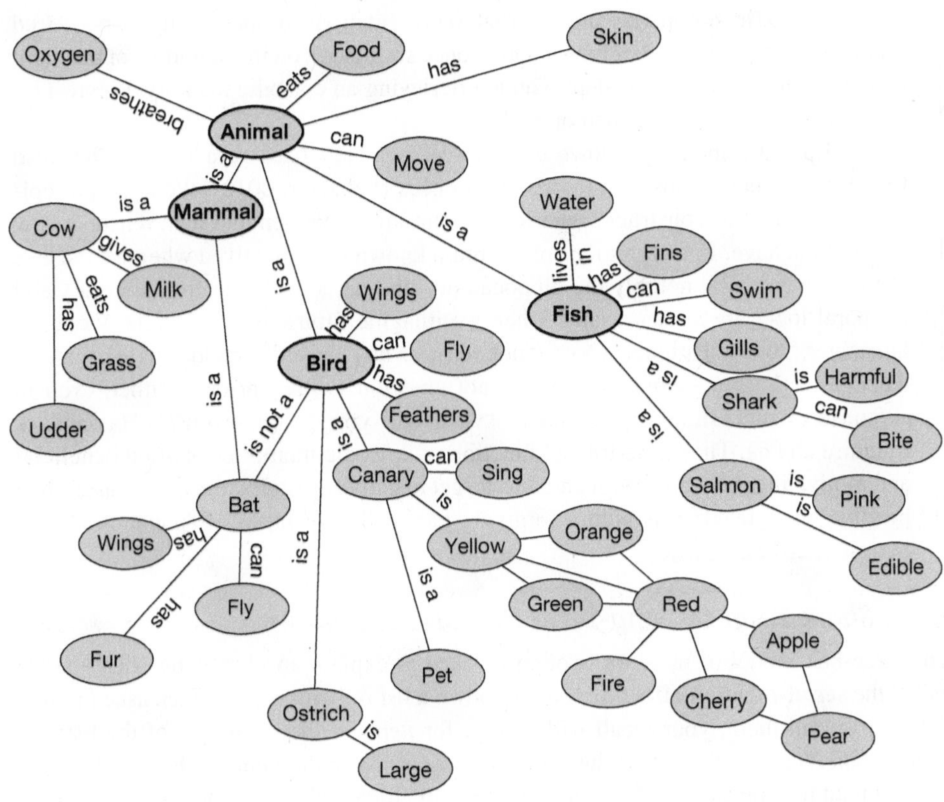

Figure 11.4 Part of a Conceptual Grid in Long-Term Memory
Many models of memory represent the contents of long-term semantic memory as an immense network or grid of concepts and the relationships among them. This illustration shows part of a hypothetical grid for *animals*.

McNeill, 1966). For the name *Kevin* they might say, "Wait, it starts with a K and has two syllables . . . Kenny? Kerran? . . . "

Information in long-term memory may also be organized by its familiarity, relevance, or association with other information. The method used in any given instance probably depends on the nature of the memory; you would no doubt store information about the major cities of Europe differently from information about your first date. To understand the organization of long-term memory, then, we must know what kinds of information can be stored there.

The Contents of Long-Term Memory

Most theories of memory distinguish skills or habits ("knowing how") from abstract or representational knowledge ("knowing that"). **Procedural memories** are memories of knowing how to do something—comb your hair, use a pencil, solve a jigsaw puzzle, knit a sweater, or swim. Many researchers consider procedural memories to be implicit, because once skills and habits are learned well, they do not require much conscious processing. **Declarative memories** involve knowing that something is true, as in knowing that Ottawa is the capital of Canada; they are usually assumed to be explicit.

Declarative memories come in two varieties: semantic memories and episodic memories (Tulving, 1985). **Semantic memories** are internal representations of the world, independent of any particular context. They include facts, rules, and concepts—items of general knowledge. On the basis of your semantic memory of the concept *cat,* you can describe a cat as a small, furry mammal that typically spends its time eating, sleeping, prowling, and staring into space, even though a cat may not be present when you give this description, and you probably won't know how or when you first learned it.

procedural memories
memories for the performance of actions or skills ("knowing how")

declarative memories
memories of facts, rules, concepts, and events ("knowing that"); they include semantic and episodic memories

semantic memories
memories of general knowledge, including facts, rules, concepts, and propositions

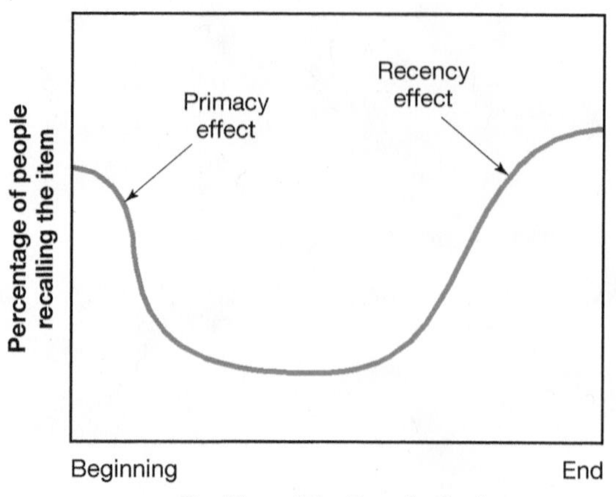

Figure 11.6 The Serial-Position Effect.
When people try to recall a list of similar items immediately after learning it, they tend to remember the first and last items best and the ones in the middle worst.

Episodic memories are internal representations of personally experienced events. When you remember how your cat once surprised you in the middle of the night by pouncing on you as you slept, you are retrieving an episodic memory. Figure 11.5 summarizes these kinds of memories.

Episodic memory allows us to travel not only backward in time, but also forward, to imagine possible future experiences (Schacter, 2012). We mine our episodic memories to construct scenarios of what might happen and then rehearse how we might behave. In fact, regions of the brain known to be involved when we retrieve personal memories, notably the hippocampus and parts of the prefrontal cortex and temporal lobe, are also activated when we imagine future events (Addis, Wong, & Schachter, 2007). Patients who cannot retrieve any episodic memories because of damage to the hippocampus often cannot envision future episodes either, even in response to such simple questions as "what will you do tomorrow?" (Hassabis & Maguire, 2007). The "time-travel" function of episodic memories is often beneficial and motivating, because people tend to forget negative episodic memories faster than positive ones, leaving us with a forgiving past and rosy future (Szpunar, Addis, & Schacter, 2012).

From Short-Term to Long-Term Memory: A Puzzle

The three-box model of memory is often invoked to explain an interesting phenomenon called the **serial-position effect**. If you are shown a list of items and are then asked immediately to recall them, your recall will be best for items at the beginning of the list (the *primacy effect*) and at the end of the list (the *recency effect*); the items in the middle of the list will tend to drop away (Bhatarah, Ward, & Tan, 2008; Johnson & Miles, 2009). If we plot the results, we see a U-shaped curve as shown in Figure 11.6. A serial-position effect occurs when you meet a lot of people at a party and find you can recall the names of the first few and the last few, but almost no one in between.

Primary and recency effects apparently occur for different reasons. Primacy effects happen because the first few items in a list are rehearsed many times and so are

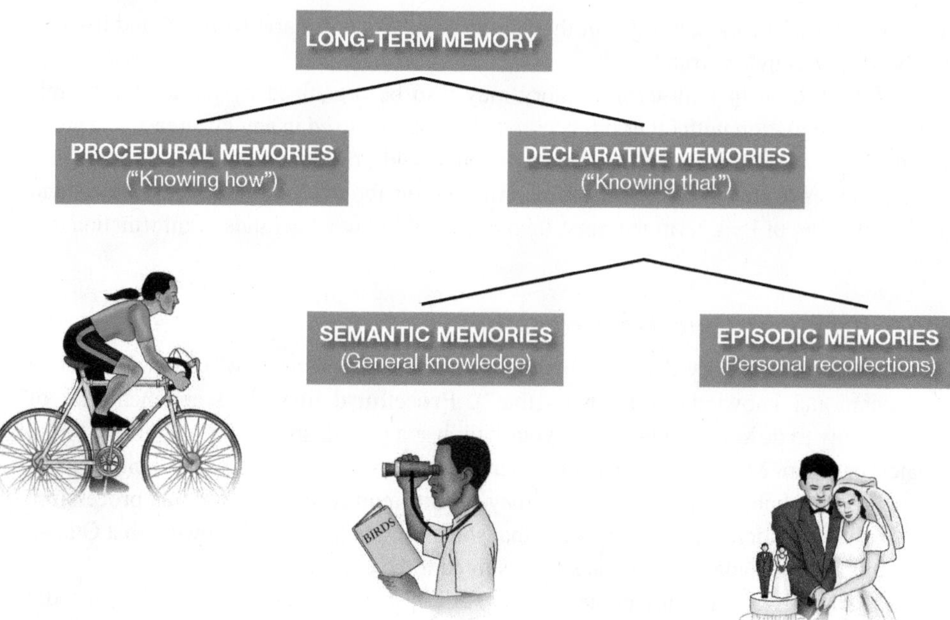

Figure 11.5 Types of Long-Term Memories
This diagram summarizes the distinctions among long-term memories. A procedural memory might be of learning how to ride a bike; a declarative memory might be knowing that Ottawa is the capital of Canada. Can you come up with your own examples of each memory type?

episodic memories
memories of personally experienced events and the contexts in which they occurred

serial-position effect
the tendency for recall of the first and last items on a list to surpass recall of items in the middle of the list

likely to make it to long-term memory and remain memorable. Recency effects occur because at the time of recall, they are plucked out of short-term memory, where they are still sitting. The items in the middle of a list are not so well retained because by the time they get into short-term memory, it is already crowded with the first few items. As a result, middle items often drop out of short-term memory before they can be stored in long-term memory. Indeed, a functional MRI study found that recognition memory for words early in a list activated areas in the hippocampus associated with retrieval from long-term memory, but recognition for words that came near the end of the list did not (Talmi et al., 2005).

The problem with this explanation is that the recency effect sometimes occurs even after a considerable delay, when the items at the end of a list should no longer be in short-term memory (Davelaar et al., 2004). Moreover, the serial position effect can occur not just with semantic memories but also episodic ones—memories of past personal experiences, such as the soccer games you played in over the last season. The serial-position curve, therefore, remains something of a puzzle.

Recite & Review

Recite: To find out whether this section made its way into long-term memory, say out loud everything you can about the *sensory register, short-term memory, chunking, working memory, long-term memory, procedural memory, declarative memory (semantic* and *episodic),* and the *serial-position effect.*

Review: Next, go back and read this section again.

Now take this ***Quick Quiz:***

1. The ________ holds images for a fraction of a second.
2. For most people, the abbreviation *USA* consists of ________ informational chunk(s).
3. Suppose you must memorize a long list of words that includes *desk, pig, gold, dog, chair, silver, table, rooster, bed, copper,* and *horse.* If you can recall the words in any order you wish, how are you likely to group these items in recall? Why?
4. When you roller-blade, are you relying on procedural, semantic, or episodic memory? How about when you recall the months of the year? Or when you remember falling while roller-blading on an icy January day?
5. If a child is trying to memorize the alphabet, which sequence should present the greatest difficulty: *abcdefg, klmnopq,* or *tuvwxyz*? Why?

Answers: 1. sensory register **2.** one **3.** *Desk, chair, table,* and *bed* will probably form one cluster; *pig, dog, rooster,* and *horse* a second; and *gold, silver,* and *copper* a third. Concepts tend to be organized in long-term memory in terms of semantic categories, such as *furniture, animals,* and *metals.* **4.** procedural; semantic; episodic **5.** *klmnopq,* because of the serial-position effect.

You are about to learn . . .

- **some of the changes that occur in the brain when you store a short-term versus a long-term memory.**
- **where memories for facts and events are stored in the brain.**
- **which hormones can improve memory.**

THE BIOLOGY OF MEMORY

We have been discussing memory solely in terms of information processing, but what is happening in the brain while all of that processing is going on?

Changes in Neurons and Synapses

Forming a memory involves chemical and structural changes at the level of synapses, and these changes differ for short-term memory and long-term memory.

In short-term memory, changes within neurons temporarily alter their ability to release neurotransmitters, the chemicals that carry messages from one cell to another. Evidence comes from studies with sea snails, sea slugs, and other organisms that have small numbers of easily identifiable neurons (Kandel, 2001; Kandel & Schwartz, 1982). These primitive animals can be taught simple conditioned responses, such as withdrawing or not withdrawing parts of their bodies in response to a light touch. When the animal retains the skill for only the short term, the neuron or neurons involved temporarily show an increase or decrease in readiness to release neurotransmitter molecules into a synapse.

In contrast, long-term memory involves lasting structural changes in the brain. To mimic what they think happens during the formation of a long-term memory, researchers apply brief, high-frequency electrical stimulation to groups of neurons in the brains of animals or to brain cells in a laboratory culture. In various areas, especially the hippocampus, this stimulation increases the strength of synaptic responsiveness, a phenomenon known as **long-term potentiation** (Bliss & Collingridge, 1993; Whitlock et al., 2006). Certain receiving neurons become more responsive to transmitting neurons, making synaptic pathways more excitable.

Long-term potentiation probably underlies many and perhaps all forms of learning and memory. Both calcium and the neurotransmitter glutamate seem to play a key role in this process, causing receiving neurons in the hippocampus to become more receptive to the next signal that comes along (Lisman, Yasuda, & Raghavachari, 2012). It is a little like increasing the diameter of a funnel's neck to permit more flow through the funnel. In addition, during long-term potentiation, dendrites grow and branch out, and certain types of synapses increase in number (Greenough, 1984). At the same time, in another process, some neurons become *less* responsive than they were previously (Bolshakov & Siegelbaum, 1994).

Most of these changes take time, which probably explains why long-term memories remain vulnerable to disruption for a while after they are stored—why a blow to the head may disrupt new memories even though old ones are unaffected. Memories must therefore undergo a period of **consolidation**, or stabilization, before they "solidify." Consolidation can continue for weeks in animals and for several years in human beings. And memories probably never completely solidify. The very act of remembering previously stored memories can make them unstable again. A new round of consolidation often then sweeps up new information into the old memory, remolding it (Schiller & Phelps, 2011). In Chapter 6, we discuss the probable role of sleep in ensuring consolidation of new information.

Where Memories are Made

Scientists have used electrodes, brain-scan technology, and other techniques to identify the brain structures responsible for the formation and storage of specific types of memories. The amygdala is involved in the formation, consolidation, and retrieval of memories of fearful and other emotional events (Buchanan, 2007). Areas in the frontal lobes of the brain are especially active during short-term and working-memory tasks (Goldman-Rakic, 1996; Mitchell & Johnson, 2009). The prefrontal cortex and areas adjacent to the hippocampus in the temporal lobe are also important for the efficient encoding of pictures and words.

But it is the hippocampus that has the starring role in many aspects of memory. It is critical to the formation of long-term declarative memories ("knowing that"); as we have seen in the case of H. M., damage to this structure can cause amnesia for new facts

long-term potentiation
a long-lasting increase in the strength of synaptic responsiveness, thought to be a biological mechanism of long-term memory

consolidation
the process by which a long-term memory becomes durable and relatively stable

and events. The hippocampus is also critical in recalling past experiences (Pastalkova et al., 2008).

A team of researchers has identified how neurons in the hippocampus may become involved in specific memories. They implanted electrodes into the brains of 13 people about to undergo surgery for severe epilepsy. (This is standard procedure because it enables doctors to pinpoint the location of the brain activity causing the seizures.) As the patients were being prepped, they watched a series of 5- to 10-second film clips of TV shows such as *Seinfeld* or *The Simpsons*, or of animals and landmarks. The researchers recorded which neurons in the hippocampus were firing as the patients watched; for each patient, particular neurons might become highly active during particular videos and respond only weakly to others. After a few minutes, the patients were asked to recall what they had seen. They remembered almost all of the clips, and as they recalled each one, the very neurons that had been active when they first saw it were reignited (Gelbard-Sagiv et al., 2008).

The formation and retention of procedural memories (memory for skills and habits) seem to involve other brain structures and pathways. In work with rabbits, Richard Thompson (1983, 1986) showed that one kind of procedural memory—a simple, classically conditioned response to a stimulus, such as an eye blink in response to a tone—depends on activity in the cerebellum. Human patients with damage in the cerebellum are incapable of this type of conditioning (Daum & Schugens, 1996).

The formation of declarative and procedural memories in different brain areas could explain a curious finding about patients like H. M. Despite their inability to form new declarative memories, with sufficient practice such patients can acquire new procedural memories that enable them to solve a puzzle, read mirror-reversed words, or play tennis—even though they do not recall the training sessions in which they learned these skills. Apparently, the parts of the brain involved in acquiring new procedural memories have remained intact. These patients also retain some implicit memory for verbal material, as measured by priming tasks, suggesting that the brain has separate systems for implicit and explicit tasks. As Figure 11.7 shows, this view has been bolstered by brain scans, which reveal differences in the location of brain activity when ordinary people perform explicit or implicit memory tasks (Reber, Stark, & Squire, 1998; Squire et al., 1992).

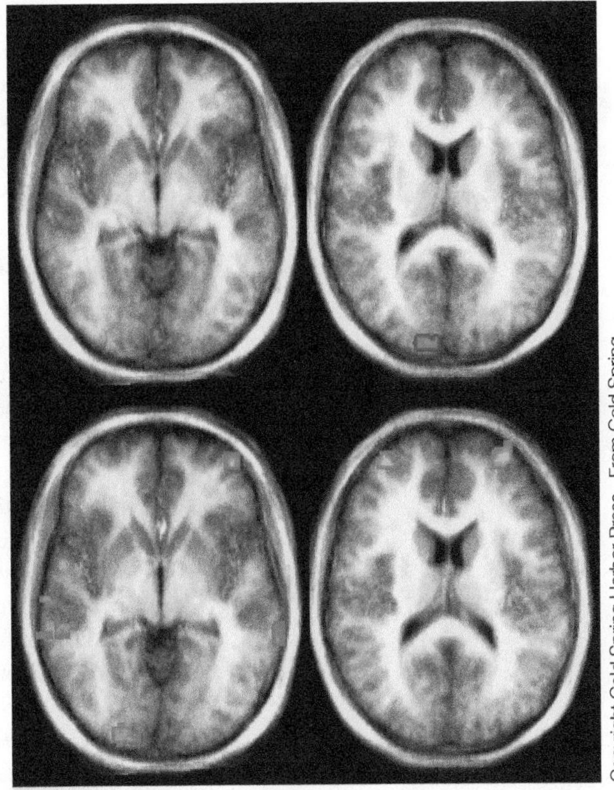

Figure 11.7 Brain Activity in Explicit and Implicit Memory
As these composite functional MRI scans show, patterns of brain activity differ depending on the type of memory task involved. When people had an explicit memory for dot patterns they had seen earlier, areas in the visual cortex, temporal lobes, and frontal lobes (indicated by orange in the lower photos) were more active. When people's implicit memories were activated, areas in the visual cortex (blue in the upper photos) were relatively inactive (Reber, Stark, & Squire, 1998).

The brain circuits that take part in the *formation* and *retrieval* of long-term memories, however, are not the same as those involved in long-term *storage* of those memories. Although the hippocampus is vital for the formation and retrieval of memories, the storage of memories eventually becomes the responsibility of the cerebral cortex (Battaglia et al., 2011). In fact, memories may be stored in the same cortical areas that were involved in the original perception of the information. When people remember pictures, visual parts of the brain become active; when people remember sounds, auditory areas become active, just as they did when the information was first perceived (Nyberg et al., 2000; Thompson & Kosslyn, 2000).

The typical "memory" is a complex cluster of information. When you recall meeting a man yesterday, you remember his greeting, his tone of voice, how he looked, and where he was. Even a single concept, such as *shovel*, includes a lot of information about its length, what it's made of, and what it's used for. These different pieces of information are probably processed separately and stored at different locations that are distributed across wide areas of the brain, with all the sites participating in the representation of the event or concept as a whole. The hippocampus may somehow bind together the diverse aspects of a memory at the time it is formed, so that even though these aspects are stored in different cortical sites, the memory can later be retrieved as one coherent entity (Squire & Zola-Morgan, 1991).

Review 11.1 shows the structures that we have discussed and summarizes some of the memory-related functions associated with them. But we have given you just a few small nibbles from the smorgasbord of findings now available. Neuroscientists hope that someday they will be able to describe the entire stream of events in the brain that occur from the moment you say to yourself "I must remember this" to the moment you actually do remember . . . or find that you can't.

Hormones, Emotion, and Memory

Have you ever smelled fresh cookies and recalled a tender scene from your childhood? Do you have a vivid memory of seeing a particularly horrifying horror movie? Emotional memories such as these are often especially intense, and the explanation resides partly in our hormones.

Hormones released by the adrenal glands during stress and emotional arousal, including epinephrine (adrenaline) and norepinephrine, can enhance memory. If you give people a drug that prevents their adrenal glands from producing these hormones, they will remember less about emotional stories they heard than a control group will (Cahill et al., 1994). Conversely, if you give animals norepinephrine right after learning, their memories will improve. The link between emotional arousal and memory makes evolutionary sense: Arousal tells the brain that an event or piece of information is important enough to encode and store for future use.

However, extreme arousal is not necessarily a good thing. When animals or people are given very high doses of stress hormones, their memories for learned tasks sometimes suffer instead of improving; a moderate dose may be optimal (Andreano & Cahill, 2006). Two psychologists demonstrated the perils of high stress and anxiety in a real-life setting: the Horror Labyrinth of the London Dungeon (Valentine & Mesout, 2009). The labyrinth is a maze of disorienting mirrored walls set in Gothic vaults. As visitors walk through it, they hear strange noises and screams, and various alarming things suddenly appear, including a "scary person"—an actor dressed in a dark robe, wearing makeup to appear scarred and bleeding. Volunteers wore a wireless heart-rate monitor as they walked through the labyrinth, so that their stress and anxiety levels could be recorded. The higher their stress and anxiety, the less able they were to accurately describe the "scary person" later, and the fewer correct identifications they made of him in a lineup.

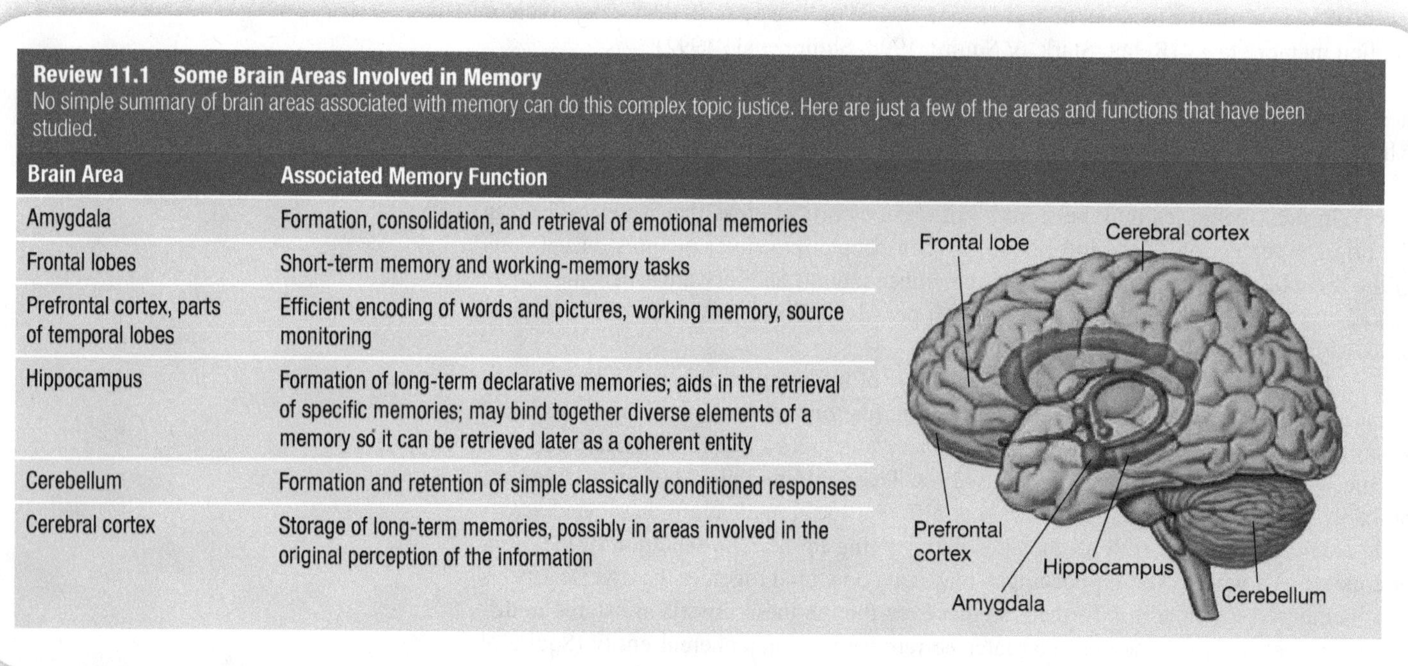

Review 11.1 Some Brain Areas Involved in Memory

No simple summary of brain areas associated with memory can do this complex topic justice. Here are just a few of the areas and functions that have been studied.

Brain Area	Associated Memory Function
Amygdala	Formation, consolidation, and retrieval of emotional memories
Frontal lobes	Short-term memory and working-memory tasks
Prefrontal cortex, parts of temporal lobes	Efficient encoding of words and pictures, working memory, source monitoring
Hippocampus	Formation of long-term declarative memories; aids in the retrieval of specific memories; may bind together diverse elements of a memory so it can be retrieved later as a coherent entity
Cerebellum	Formation and retention of simple classically conditioned responses
Cerebral cortex	Storage of long-term memories, possibly in areas involved in the original perception of the information

Such effects on memory do not matter much at an amusement attraction, but they can have serious consequences when crime victims, police officers, and combat soldiers must recall details of a highly stressful experience, such as a shootout or the identity of an enemy interrogator. Even highly trained soldiers have great difficulty in correctly identifying their captors (Morgan et al., 2007). The unintended effects of misleading suggestions, combined with the effects of extreme stress on memory, mean that we should be especially cautious about how investigators gather intelligence information from captured suspected terrorists (Loftus, 2011).

Assuming that adrenal hormones do not become *too* high, how might these hormones enhance storage of information in the brain? One possibility is that norepinephrine affects glutamate receptors on the surfaces of nerve cells, increasing the strength of incoming signals (Hu et al., 2007; McGaugh, 1990). Another is that adrenal hormones cause the level of glucose (a sugar) to rise in the bloodstream, and from there the glucose can readily enter the brain. Once in the brain, glucose may enhance memory either directly or by altering the effects of neurotransmitters. If so, increasing the amount of glucose available to the brain should enhance memory. Indeed, this "sweet memories" effect does occur both in aged rats and mice and in human beings. In one encouraging study, healthy older people fasted overnight, drank a glass of lemonade sweetened with either glucose or saccharin, and then took two memory tests. The saccharin-laced drink had no effect on their performance, but lemonade with glucose greatly boosted their ability to recall a taped passage 5 or 40 minutes after hearing it (Manning, Hall, & Gold, 1990).

Before you reach for a candy bar, you should know that the effective dose of glucose is narrow; too much can impair cognitive functioning instead of helping it. The "sweet memories" effect also depends on your metabolism, what you have eaten that day, and the level of glucose in your brain before you ingest it. In this area, as in others in the biology of memory, we have much to learn. No one knows yet exactly how the brain stores information, how different memory circuits link up with one another, or how a student is able to locate and retrieve information at the drop of a multiple-choice item.

Recite & Review

Recite: Let's see what your memory has consolidated. Say out loud everything you can about brain changes during short-term memory, *long-term potentiation, consolidation,* the importance of the *hippocampus,* the long-term storage of memories, and hormonal influences on memory.

Review: Next, go back and read this section again.

Now take this ***Quick Quiz:***

1. Is long-term potentiation associated with (a) increased responsiveness of certain receiving neurons to transmitting neurons or (b) a decrease in receptors on certain receiving neurons?
2. The cerebellum has been associated with __________ memories; the hippocampus has been associated with __________ memories.
3. *True or false:* Hormone research suggests that if you want to remember well, you should be as relaxed as possible while learning.
4. After reading about glucose and memory, should you immediately start gulping down lemonade? Why or why not?

Answers: **1.** a **2.** procedural, declarative **3.** false **4.** You should not pig out on sugar yet. You do not know what amount might be effective for you, given your metabolism, brain levels of glucose, and dietary habits. And you need to consider the health risks of consuming sugary foods with lots of calories and little nutritional value.

You are about to learn . . .

- why memory tricks, although fun, are not always useful.
- how memory can be improved, and why rote methods are not the best strategy.

How We Remember

In everyday life, people who want to give their powers of memory a boost sometimes use **mnemonics** [neh-MON-iks], formal strategies and tricks for encoding, storing, and retaining information. (Mnemosyne, pronounced neh-MOZ-eh-nee, was the ancient Greek goddess of memory.) Some mnemonics take the form of easily memorized rhymes (e.g., "Thirty days hath September/April, June, and November . . ."). Others use formulas (e.g., "Every good boy does fine" for remembering which notes are on the lines of the treble clef in musical notation). Still others use visual images or word associations. They may also reduce the amount of information by chunking it, which is why many companies use words for their phone numbers instead of unmemorable numbers.

"YOU SIMPLY ASSOCIATE EACH NUMBER WITH A WORD, SUCH AS 'TABLE' AND 3,476,029."

Some stage performers with amazing recall rely on far more complicated mnemonics. We are not going to spend time on them here, though, because for ordinary memory tasks, such tricks are often no more effective than rote repetition, and sometimes they are actually worse (Wang, Thomas, & Ouellette, 1992). Most memory researchers do not use such mnemonics themselves (Hébert, 2001). After all, why bother to memorize a grocery list using a fancy mnemonic when you can write down what you need to buy?

Well, then, what does work? We introduced you to the Nine Secrets of Learning. Many of those secrets are based on well-established principles of memory that help us encode and store information so that it sticks in our minds and will be there when we need it.

Effective Encoding

Our memories, as we have seen, are not exact replicas of experience. Sensory information is summarized and encoded as words or images almost as soon as it is detected. When you hear a lecture, you may hang on every word (we hope you do), but you do not memorize those words verbatim. You extract the main points and encode them.

To remember information well, you have to encode it accurately in the first place. With some kinds of information, accurate encoding takes place automatically, without effort. Think about where you usually sit in your psychology class. When were you last there? You can probably provide this information easily, even though you never made a deliberate effort to encode it. But many kinds of information require *effortful encoding:* the plot of a novel, the procedures for assembling a cabinet, the arguments for and against a proposed law. To retain such information, you might have to select the main points, label concepts, or associate the information with personal experiences or with material you already know. Experienced students know that most of the information in a college course requires effortful encoding, otherwise known as studying. The mind does not gobble up information automatically; you must make the material digestible.

Rehearsal

An important technique for keeping information in short-term memory and increasing the chances of long-term retention is *rehearsal*, the review or practice of material while you are learning it. When people are prevented from rehearsing, the contents of

mnemonics
strategies and tricks for improving memory, such as the use of a verse or a formula

their short-term memories quickly fade (Peterson & Peterson, 1959). You are taking advantage of rehearsal when you look up a phone number and then repeat it over and over to keep it in short-term memory until you no longer need it. And when you can't remember a phone number because your phone always remembers it for you, you are learning what happens when you *don't* rehearse!

A poignant demonstration of the power of rehearsal once occurred during a session with H. M. (Ogden & Corkin, 1991). The experimenter gave H. M. five digits to repeat and remember, but then she was unexpectedly called away. When she returned after more than an hour, H. M. was able to repeat the five digits correctly. He had been rehearsing them the entire time.

When actors learn a script, they do not rely on maintenance rehearsal alone. They also use elaborative rehearsal and deep processing, analyzing the meaning of their lines and associating their lines with imagined information about the character they are playing.

Short-term memory holds many kinds of information, including visual information and abstract meanings. But most people, or at least most hearing people, seem to favor speech for encoding and rehearsing the contents of short-term memory. The speech may be spoken aloud or to oneself. When people make errors on short-term memory tests that use letters or words, they often confuse items that sound the same or similar, such as *d* and *t*, or *bear* and *bare*. These errors suggest that they have been rehearsing verbally.

Some strategies for rehearsing are more effective than others. **Maintenance rehearsal** involves merely the rote repetition of the material. This kind of rehearsal is fine for keeping information in STM, but it will not always lead to long-term retention. A better strategy if you want to remember for the long haul is **elaborative rehearsal**, also called *elaboration of encoding* (Cermak & Craik, 1979; Craik & Tulving, 1975). Elaboration involves associating new items of information with material that has already been stored or with other new facts. It can also involve analyzing the physical, sensory, or semantic features of an item.

Get Involved!

Pay Attention!

It seems obvious, but often we fail to remember because we never encoded the information in the first place. Which of these Lincoln pennies is the real one? (The answer is at the end of this chapter.) If you are an American, you have seen zillions of pennies, yet you will probably have trouble recognizing the real one because you have never paid close attention to and encoded the details of its design (Nickerson & Adams, 1979). If you are not an American, try drawing the front of one of your most common coins and then check to see how well you did. Again, you're likely to have trouble remembering the details.

maintenance rehearsal
rote repetition of material in order to maintain its availability in memory

elaborative rehearsal
association of new information with already stored knowledge and analysis of the new information to make it memorable

Suppose that you are studying the concept of working memory. Simply memorizing the definition is unlikely to help much. But if you can elaborate the concept, you are more likely to remember it. The word *working* should remind you that working memory is involved in tasks that require effort and attention. And what benefits do effort and attention bring? Yes, that is why working memory is related to the ability to concentrate, resist distraction, and solve problems. Many students try to pare down what they are learning to the bare essentials, but knowing more details about something makes it more memorable; that is what elaboration means.

A related strategy for prolonging retention is **deep processing**, or the processing of meaning (Craik & Lockhart, 1972). If you process only the physical or sensory features of a stimulus, such as how the word *hypothalamus* is spelled and how it sounds, your processing will be shallow even if it is elaborated. If you recognize patterns and assign labels to objects or events ("*Hypo* means 'below,' so the *hypo*thalamus must be *below* the thalamus"), your processing will be somewhat deeper. If you fully analyze the meaning of what you are trying to remember (perhaps by encoding the functions and importance of the hypothalamus), your processing will be deeper yet. *Shallow processing* is sometimes useful; when you memorize a poem, for instance, you will want to pay attention to (and elaborately encode) the sounds of the words and the patterns of rhythm in the poem and not just the poem's meaning. Usually, though, deep processing is more effective. That is why, if you try to memorize information that has little or no meaning for you, the information may not stick.

Retrieval Practice

Many students think that the way to remember course material is simply to study it once thoroughly, or maybe twice, so they can retrieve the correct answers on an exam. Unfortunately, within just a few weeks or months after the exam, some of those answers will have vanished like steam on a bathroom mirror. *Retrieval practice,* the repeated retrieval of an item of information from memory, is necessary if a memory is to undergo consolidation and remain available for a long time. After all, that's the goal of learning.

In a college course, a good way to ensure retrieval practice is to take short quizzes after you have learned some material but before the big exam. In a series of experiments in which students learned words in foreign languages, once a student had learned a word it was (1) repeatedly studied but dropped from further testing, (2) repeatedly tested but dropped from further studying, or (3) dropped from studying and testing. To the surprise of the students themselves, studying after learning had no effect on their subsequent ability to recall the foreign words. But repeated *testing,* which caused them to repeatedly retrieve the words from memory, had a large benefit (Karpicke, 2012; Karpicke & Roediger, 2008). So when your professors and your textbook authors want to keep quizzing you, it's only for your own good!

HOW TO REMEMBER BETTER

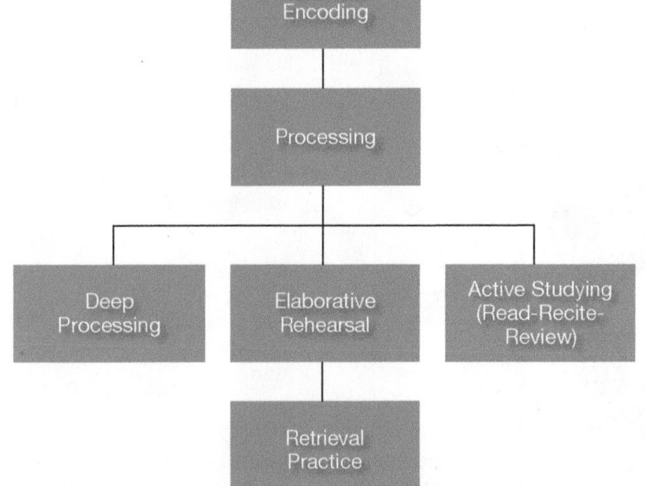

Remembering the Secrets of Learning

The very first "secret of learning" to use the 3R method—read, recite, review—and we've helped you do that by building it into every one of our quizzes in this book. Now might be a good time to go back and—you guessed it!—*review* the other secrets. They work because they encourage you to process deeply, to use your imagination, to use elaborative rehearsal, to test yourself, and to think about what you are hearing or reading. And they all have something important in common: They teach you to be an active rather than a passive learner. Your memory isn't a sponge that simply soaks up whatever is poured on it. Memory requires you to transform new information into something you can understand, use, . . . and remember.

deep processing
in the encoding of information, the processing of meaning rather than simply the physical or sensory features of a stimulus

Recite & Review

Recite: Remember Secret #1 and say out loud everything you can remember about *effortful encoding, maintenance* versus *elaborative rehearsal, deep* versus *shallow processing, retrieval practice,* and *mnemonics.*

Review: Next, go back and read this section again.

Perhaps mnemosyne will help you answer this ***Quick Quiz:***
Camille is furious with her history professor. "I read the chapter three times, but I still failed the exam," she fumes. "The test must have been unfair." What's wrong with Camille's reasoning, and what are some other possible explanations for her poor performance, based on principles of critical thinking and what you have learned so far about memory?

Answers: Camille is reasoning emotionally and is not examining the assumptions underlying her explanation. Perhaps she relied on automatic rather than effortful encoding, used maintenance instead of elaborative rehearsal, and used shallow instead of deep processing when she studied. Perhaps she didn't try to actively retrieve and recall the material while studying. She may also have tried to encode everything instead of being selective.

You are about to learn . . .

- **why remembering everything might not be an advantage.**
- **the major reasons we forget even when we'd rather not.**
- **why most researchers are skeptical about claims of repressed and "recovered" memories.**

Why We Forget

Have you ever, in the heat of some deliriously happy moment, said to yourself, "I'll never forget this, never, *never,* NEVER"? Do you find that you can more clearly remember saying those words than the deliriously happy moment itself? Sometimes you encode an event, you rehearse it, you analyze its meaning, you tuck it away in long-term storage, and still you forget it. Is it any wonder that most of us have wished, at one time or another, for a "photographic memory"?

Actually, having a perfect memory is not the blessing that you might suppose. The Russian psychologist Alexander Luria (1968) once told of a journalist, S., who could reproduce giant grids of numbers both forward and backward, even after the passage of 15 years. To accomplish his astonishing feats, he used mnemonics, especially the formation of visual images. But you should not envy him, for he had a serious problem: He could not forget even when he wanted to. Along with the diamonds of experience, he kept dredging up the pebbles. Images he had formed to aid his memory kept creeping into consciousness, distracting him and interfering with his ability to concentrate. At times he even had trouble holding a conversation because the other person's words would set off a jumble of associations. Eventually, S. took to supporting himself by traveling from place to place, demonstrating his mnemonic abilities for audiences.

Or consider two modern cases: Brad Williams and Jill Price both have extraordinary memories and have offered scientists the opportunity to study their abilities. When given any date going back for decades, they are able to say instantly what they were doing, what day of the week it was, and whether anything of great importance happened on that date. Mention November 7, 1991, to Williams, and he says (correctly), "Let's see; that would be around when [basketball star] Magic Johnson announced he had HIV. Yes, a Thursday. There was a big snowstorm here the week before." Neither Williams nor Price uses mnemonics or can say where their accurate memories come from. Although Williams and his family regard his abilities as a source of amusement, Price describes her nonstop recollections as a mixed blessing (Parker, Cahill, & McGaugh, 2006). The phenomenon of constant, uncontrollable recall, she wrote, is "totally exhausting. Some have called it a gift, but I call it a burden. I run my entire life through my head every day and it drives me crazy!!!"

Paradoxically, then, forgetting is adaptive: We need to forget some things if we wish to remember efficiently. Piling up facts without distinguishing the important from the trivial is just confusing. Nonetheless, most of us forget more than we want to and would like to know why.

In the early days of psychology, in an effort to measure pure memory loss independent of personal experience, Hermann Ebbinghaus (1885/1913) memorized long lists of nonsense syllables, such as *bok, waf,* or *ged,* and then tested his retention over a period of several weeks. Most of his forgetting occurred soon after the initial learning and then leveled off (see Figure 11.8a). Generations of psychologists adopted Ebbinghaus's method of studying memory, but his method did not tell them much about the kinds of memories that people care about most.

A century later, Marigold Linton decided to find out how people forget real events rather than nonsense syllables. Like Ebbinghaus, she used herself as a subject, but she charted the curve of forgetting over years rather than days. Every day for 12 years she recorded on a 4- by 6-inch card two or more things that had happened to her that day. Eventually, she accumulated a catalog of thousands of discrete events, both trivial ("I have dinner at the Canton Kitchen: delicious lobster dish") and significant ("I land at Orly Airport in Paris"). Once a month, she took a random sampling of all the cards accumulated to that point, noted whether she could remember the events on them, and tried to date the events. Linton (1978) expected the kind of rapid forgetting reported by Ebbinghaus. Instead, as you can see in Figure 11.8b, she found that long-term forgetting was slower and proceeded at a much more constant pace, as details gradually dropped out of her memories.

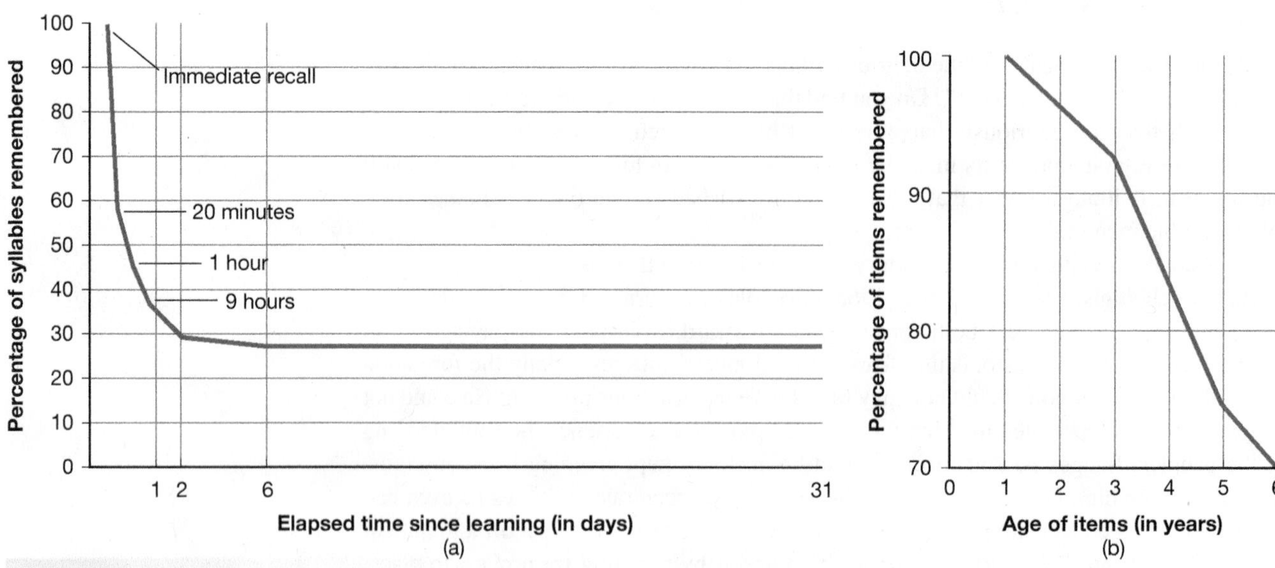

Figure 11.8 Two Kinds of Forgetting Curves
Hermann Ebbinghaus, who tested his own memory for nonsense syllables, found that his forgetting was rapid at first and then tapered off (a). In contrast, when Marigold Linton tested her own memory for personal events over a period of several years, her retention was excellent at first, but then it fell off at a gradual but steady rate (b).

Of course, some memories, especially those that mark important transitions, are more memorable than others. But why did Marigold Linton, like the rest of us, forget so many details? Psychologists have proposed five mechanisms to account for forgetting: decay, replacement of old memories by new ones, interference, cue-dependent forgetting, and psychological amnesia brought on by repression.

Decay

One commonsense view, the **decay theory**, holds that memories simply fade with time if they are not accessed now and then. We have already seen that decay occurs in sensory memory and that it occurs in short-term memory as well unless we keep rehearsing the material. However, the mere passage of time does not account so well for forgetting in long-term memory. People commonly forget things that happened only yesterday while remembering events from many years ago. Indeed, some memories, both procedural and declarative, can last a lifetime. If you learned to swim as a child, you will still know how to swim at age 30, even if you have not been in a pool or lake for 22 years. We are also happy to report that some school lessons have great staying power. In one study, people did well on a Spanish test some 50 years after taking Spanish in high school, even though most had hardly used Spanish at all in the intervening years (Bahrick, 1984). Decay alone cannot entirely explain lapses in long-term memory.

Motor skills, which are stored as procedural memories, can last a lifetime; they rarely decay.

decay theory
the theory that information in memory eventually disappears if it is not accessed; it applies better to short-term than to long-term memory

Replacement

Another theory holds that new information entering memory can wipe out old information, just as rerecording on an audiotape or videotape will obliterate the original material. In a study supporting this view, researchers showed people slides of a traffic accident and used leading questions to get them to think that they had seen a stop sign when they had really seen a yield sign, or vice versa (see Figure 11.9). People in a control group who were not misled in this way were able to identify the sign they had actually seen. Later, all the participants were told the purpose of the study and were asked to guess whether they had been misled. Almost all of those who had been misled continued to insist that they had *really, truly* seen the sign whose existence had been planted in their minds (Loftus, Miller, & Burns, 1978). The researchers interpreted this finding to mean that the subjects had not just been trying to please them and that people's original perceptions had been erased by the misleading information.

Figure 11.9 The Stop-Sign Study
When people who saw a car with a yield sign (left) were later asked if they had seen "the stop sign" (a misleading question), many said they had. Similarly, when those shown a stop sign were asked if they had seen "the yield sign," many said yes. These false memories persisted even after the participants were told about the misleading questions, suggesting that misleading information might have erased their original mental representations of the signs (Loftus, Miller, & Burns, 1978).

Interference

A third theory holds that forgetting occurs because similar items of information interfere with one another in either storage or retrieval; the information may get into memory and stay there, but it becomes confused with other information. Such interference, which occurs in both short- and long-term memory, is especially common when you have to recall isolated facts such as names, addresses, passwords, and area codes.

Suppose you are at a party and you meet someone named Julie. A little later you meet someone named Judy. You go on to talk to other people, and after an hour, you again bump into Julie, but by mistake you call her Judy. The second name has interfered with the first. This type of interference, in which new information interferes with the ability to remember old information, is called **retroactive interference**:

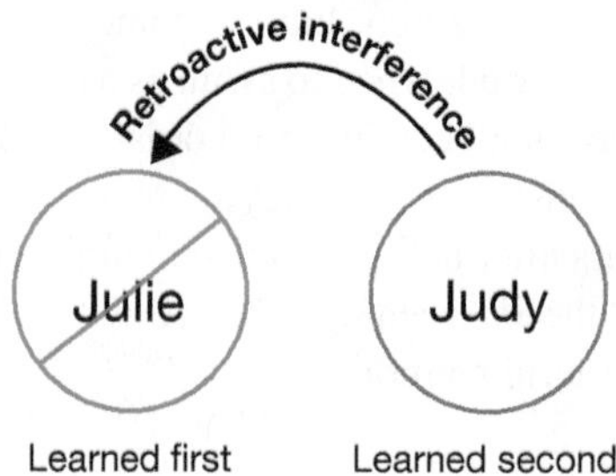

Retroactive interference is illustrated by the story of an absentminded professor of ichthyology (the study of fish) who complained that whenever he learned the name of a new student, he forgot the name of a fish. But whereas with replacement, the new memory erases the old and makes it irretrievable, in retroactive interference the loss of the old memory is sometimes just temporary. With a little concentration, that professor could probably recall his new students and his old fish.

Because new information is constantly entering memory, we are all vulnerable to the effects of retroactive interference, or at least most of us are. H. M. was an exception; his memories of childhood and adolescence were unusually detailed, clear, and unchanging. H. M. could remember actors who were famous when he was a child, the films they were in, and who their costars had been. He also knew the names of friends from the second grade. Presumably, these early declarative memories were not subject to interference from memories acquired after the operation, for the simple reason that H. M. had not acquired any new memories.

Interference also works in the opposite direction. Old information (such as the foreign language you learned in high school) may interfere with the ability to remember current information (such as the new language you are trying to learn now). This type of interference is called **proactive interference**:

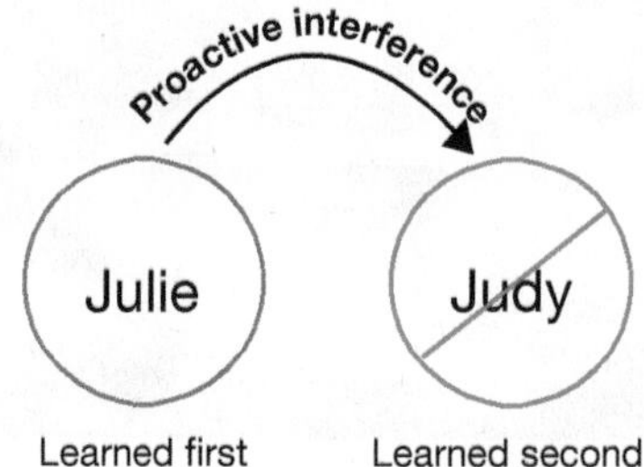

Over a period of weeks, months, and years, proactive interference may cause more forgetting than retroactive interference does, because we have stored up so much information that can potentially interfere with anything new.

retroactive interference
forgetting that occurs when recently learned material interferes with the ability to remember similar material stored previously

proactive interference
forgetting that occurs when previously stored material interferes with the ability to remember similar, more recently learned material

Cue-Dependent Forgetting

Charlie Chaplin's film *City Lights* provides a classic illustration of state-dependent memory. After Charlie saves a drunken millionaire's life, the two spend the rest of the evening carousing. But the next day, after sobering up, the millionaire fails to recognize Charlie and gives him the cold shoulder. Then, once again, the millionaire gets drunk, and once again greets Charlie as a pal. (Note: Your memory will be best if you are sober during both encoding and recall!)

Often, when we need to remember, we rely on *retrieval cues*, items of information that can help us find the specific information we're looking for. If you are trying to remember the last name of an actor you saw in an old film, it might help to know the person's first name or a movie the actor starred in.

When we lack retrieval cues, we may feel as if we are lost in the mind's library. In long-term memory, this type of memory failure, called **cue-dependent forgetting**, may be the most common type of all. Willem Wagenaar (1986), who, like Marigold Linton, recorded critical details about events in his life, found that within a year he had forgotten 20 percent of those details; after five years, he had forgotten 60 percent. Yet when he gathered cues from witnesses about ten events that he thought he had forgotten, he was able to recall something about all ten, which suggests that some of his forgetting was cue dependent.

Cues that were present when you learned a new fact or had an experience are apt to be especially useful later as retrieval aids. That may explain why remembering is often easier when you are in the same physical environment as you were when an event occurred: Cues in the present context match those from the past. Ordinarily, this overlap helps us remember the past more accurately. But it may also help account for the eerie phenomenon of *déjà vu,* the fleeting sense of having been in *exactly* the same situation that you are in now (*déjà vu* means "already seen" in French). Some element in the present situation, familiar from some other context that you cannot identify—even a dream, a novel, or a movie—may make the entire situation seem so familiar that it feels like it happened before (Brown, 2004). In other words, déjà vu may be a kind of mistaken recognition memory. Similar feelings of familiarity can actually be produced in the laboratory. When something about newly presented words, shapes, or photographs resembles elements of stimuli seen previously, people report that the new words, shapes, or photographs seem familiar even though they can't recall the original ones (Cleary, 2008).

In everyday situations, your mental or physical state may act as a retrieval cue, evoking a **state-dependent memory**. If you were afraid or angry at the time of an event, you may remember that event best when you are once again in the same emotional state (Lang et al., 2001). Your memories can also be biased by whether or not your current mood is consistent with the emotional nature of the material you are trying to remember, a phenomenon known as **mood-congruent memory** (Bower & Forgas, 2000; Buchanan, 2007; Fitzgerald et al., 2011). You are more likely to remember happy events, and forget or ignore unhappy ones, when you are feeling happy than when you are feeling sad. Likewise, you are apt to remember unhappy events better and remember more of them when you are feeling unhappy, which in turn creates a vicious cycle. The more unhappy memories you recall, the more depressed you feel, and the more depressed you feel, the more unhappy memories you recall . . . so you stay stuck in your depression and make it even worse (Joormann & Gotlib, 2007; Wenzel, 2005).

The Repression Controversy

A final theory of forgetting is concerned with **amnesia**, the loss of memory for important personal information. Amnesia most commonly results from organic conditions such as brain disease or head injury, and is usually temporary. In *psychogenic amnesia*, however, the causes of forgetting are psychological, such as a need to escape feelings of embarrassment, guilt, shame, disappointment, or emotional shock. Psychogenic amnesia begins immediately after the precipitating event, involves massive memory loss including loss of personal identity, and usually ends suddenly, after just a few weeks. Despite its frequent portrayal in films and novels, it is quite rare in real life (McNally, 2003).

cue-dependent forgetting
the inability to retrieve information stored in memory because of insufficient cues for recall

state-dependent memory
the tendency to remember something when the rememberer is in the same physical or mental state as during the original learning or experience

mood-congruent memory
the tendency to remember experiences that are consistent with one's current mood and overlook or forget experiences that are not

amnesia
the partial or complete loss of memory for important personal information

Psychologists generally accept the notion of psychogenic amnesia. *Traumatic amnesia*, however, is far more controversial. Traumatic amnesia allegedly involves the burying of specific traumatic events for a long period of time, often for many years. When the memory returns, it is supposedly immune to the usual processes of distortion and confabulation, and is recalled with perfect accuracy. The notion of traumatic amnesia originated with the psychoanalytic theory of Sigmund Freud, who argued that the mind defends itself from unwelcome and upsetting memories through the mechanism of **repression**, the involuntary pushing of threatening or upsetting information into the unconscious.

Most memory researchers reject the argument that a special unconscious mechanism called "repression" is necessary to explain either psychogenic or traumatic amnesia (Rofé, 2008). Richard McNally (2003) reviewed the experimental and clinical evidence and concluded, "The notion that the mind protects itself by repressing or dissociating memories of trauma, rendering them inaccessible to awareness, is a piece of psychiatric folklore devoid of convincing empirical support." The problem for most people who have suffered disturbing experiences is not that they cannot remember, but rather that they cannot forget: The memories keep intruding. There is no case on record of anyone who has repressed the memory of being in a concentration camp, being in combat, or being the victim of an earthquake or a terrorist attack, although details of even these horrible experiences are subject to distortion and fading over time, as are all memories.

Further, repression is hard to distinguish from normal forgetting. People who seem to forget disturbing experiences could be intentionally keeping themselves from retrieving their painful memories by distracting themselves whenever a memory is reactivated. Or they may be focusing consciously on positive memories instead. Perhaps, understandably, they are not rehearsing unhappy memories, so those memories fade with time. Perhaps they are simply avoiding the retrieval cues that would evoke the memories. But a reluctance to think about an upsetting experience is not the same as an *inability* to remember it (McNally, 2003).

Thinking Critically

Consider other interpretations

How should critical thinkers evaluate someone's claim that they repressed memories of bizarre, traumatic experiences that went on for years, and only remembered what happened decades later, in therapy? What other explanations can account for these apparent memories?

The debate over traumatic amnesia and repression erupted into the public arena in the 1990s, when claims of recovered memories of sexual abuse began to appear. Many women and some men came to believe, during psychotherapy, that they could recall long-buried memories of having been sexually victimized for many years, often in bizarre ways. For therapists who accepted the notion of repression, such claims were entirely believable (Brown, Scheflin, & Whitfield, 1999; Herman, 1992). But most researchers today believe that almost all of these memories were false, having been evoked by therapists who were unaware of the research we described earlier on the power of suggestion and the dangers of confabulation (Lindsay & Read, 1994; McNally, 2003; Schacter, 2001). By asking leading questions, and by encouraging clients to construct vivid images of abuse, revisit those images frequently, and focus on emotional aspects of the images, such therapists unwittingly set up the very conditions that encourage confabulation and false memories.

Since the 1990s, accusations based on "recovered memories" have steadily declined and many accusers have reconciled with their families (McHugh et al., 2004). Yet the concept of repression lingers on. Many of its original proponents have turned to the term "dissociation" to account for memory failures in traumatized individuals, the idea being that upsetting memories are split off (dissociated) from everyday consciousness. But reviews of the research have found no good evidence that early trauma causes such dissociation (Giesbrecht et al., 2008; Huntjens, Verschuere, & McNally, 2012).

Of course, it is obviously possible for someone to forget a single unhappy or deeply unpleasant experience and not recall it for years, just as going back to your elementary school might trigger a memory of the time that you did something embarrassing in front of your whole class. How then should we respond to an individual's claim to have recovered memories of years of traumatic experiences that were previously "repressed"? How can we distinguish true memories from false ones?

repression
in psychoanalytic theory, the selective, involuntary pushing of threatening or upsetting information into the unconscious

Clearly, a person's recollections are likely to be trustworthy if corroborating evidence is available, such as medical records, police or school reports, or the accounts of other people who had been present at the time. But in the absence of supporting evidence, we may have to tolerate uncertainty, because a person might have a detailed, emotionally rich "memory" that feels completely real but that has been unintentionally confabulated (Bernstein & Loftus, 2009). In such cases, it is important to consider the content of the recovered memory and how it was recovered.

Thus, given what we know about memory, we should be skeptical if the person says that he or she has memories from the first year or two of life; as we will see in the next section, this is not possible, physiologically or cognitively. We should be skeptical if, over time, the person's memories become more and more implausible; for instance, the person says that sexual abuse continued day and night for 15 years without ever being remembered and without anyone else in the household ever noticing anything amiss. We should also be skeptical if a person suddenly recovers a traumatic memory as a result of therapy or after hearing about supposed cases of recovered memory in the news or reading about one in a best-selling autobiography. And we should hear alarm bells go off if a therapist used suggestive techniques, such as hypnosis, dream analysis, "age regression," guided imagery, and leading questions, to "recover" the memories. These techniques are all known to increase confabulation.

Recite & Review

Recite: Make sure you don't have amnesia for the preceding material by reciting out loud everything you can about the *decay theory, replacement* of old information, *retroactive interference, proactive interference, cue-dependent forgetting, state-dependent memory, mood-congruent memory, amnesia,* and *repression.*

Review: Next, go back and reread this section.

Now take this ***Quick Quiz:***

1. Wilma has been a long-time fan of the country singer Tim McGraw. Recently she met an interesting guy named Tom McGraw, but she keeps calling him Tim. Why?
2. When a man at his 20th high school reunion sees his old friends, he recalls incidents he thought were long forgotten. Why?
3. What mechanisms other than repression could account for a person's psychogenic amnesia?

Answers: 1. proactive interference **2.** The sight of his friends provides retrieval cues for the incidents. **3.** The person could be intentionally avoiding the memory by using distraction or focusing on positive experiences; failure to rehearse the memory may be causing it to fade; or the person may be avoiding retrieval cues that would evoke the memory.

You are about to learn . . .

- **why the first few years of life are a mental blank.**
- **why human beings have been called the storytelling animal.**

AUTOBIOGRAPHICAL MEMORIES

For most of us, our memories about our own experiences are by far the most fascinating. We use them to entertain ("Did I ever tell you about the time . . . ?") and to connect with others ("Remember that time we . . . ?"). We analyze them to learn more about who we are. We modify and embellish them to impress others, and some people even publish them.

Childhood Amnesia: The Missing Years

A curious aspect of autobiographical memory is that most adults cannot recall any events from earlier than age 2; and even after that, memories are sketchy at best until about age 6 (Hayne & Jack, 2011). A few people can vaguely recall significant events that occurred when they were as young as 2 years old, such as the birth of a sibling, but not earlier ones (Fivush & Nelson, 2004; Usher & Neisser, 1993). As adults, we cannot remember taking our first steps, or uttering our first halting sentences. We are victims of **childhood amnesia** (sometimes called *infantile amnesia*).

Thinking Critically

Avoid emotional reasoning.

Many people get upset at the idea that their earliest experiences are lost to memory and angrily insist that memories from the first two years must be accurate. How can research help us think clearly about this issue?

Childhood amnesia is disturbing to many people, so disturbing that some adamantly deny it, claiming to remember events from the second or even the first year of life. But like other false memories, these are merely reconstructions based on photographs, family stories, and imagination. The "remembered" event may not even have taken place. Swiss psychologist Jean Piaget (1952) once reported a memory of nearly being kidnapped at the age of 2. Piaget remembered sitting in his pram, watching his nurse as she bravely defended him from the kidnapper. He remembered the scratches she received on her face. He remembered a police officer with a short cloak and white baton who finally chased the kidnapper away. But when Piaget was 15, his nurse wrote to his parents confessing that she had made up the entire story. Piaget noted, "I therefore must have heard, as a child, the account of this story . . . and projected it into the past in the form of a visual memory, which was a memory of a memory, but false."

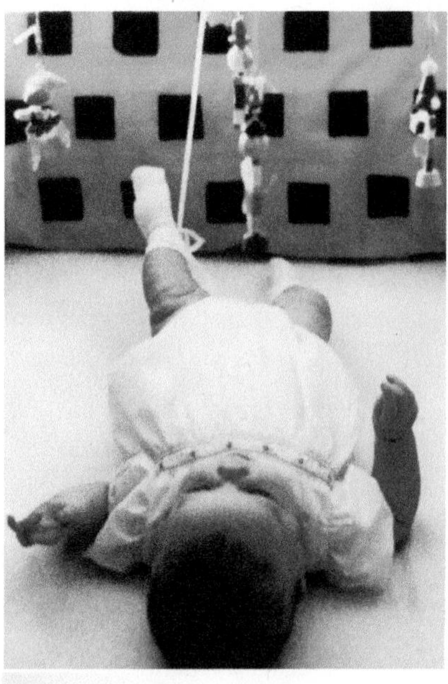

This infant, whose leg is attached by a string to a colorful mobile, will learn within minutes to make the mobile move by kicking it. She may still remember the trick a week later, an example of procedural memory (Rovee-Collier, 1993). However, when she is older, she will not remember the experience itself; she will fall victim to childhood amnesia.

Of course, we all retain procedural memories from the toddler stage, when we first learned to use a fork, drink from a cup, and pull a wagon. We also retain semantic memories acquired early in life: the rules of counting, the names of people and things, knowledge about objects in the world, words and meanings. Moreover, toddlers who are only 1 to 2 years old often reveal nonverbally that they remember past experiences (for example, by imitating something they saw earlier); and some 4-year-olds can remember experiences that occurred before age 2½ (Bauer, 2002; McDonough & Mandler, 1994; Tustin & Hayne, 2010). What young children do not do well is encode and retain their early episodic memories—memories of particular events—and carry them into later childhood or adulthood. They cannot start doing this consistently until about age 4½ (Fivush & Nelson, 2004).

Freud thought that childhood amnesia was a special case of repression, but memory researchers today think that repression has nothing to do with it, and they point to better explanations:

1 **Brain development.** The prefrontal cortex, and other parts of the brain involved in the formation or storage of events, are not well developed until a few years after birth (McKee & Squire, 1993; Newcombe, Lloyd, & Balcomb, 2012). In addition, the brains of infants and toddlers are busily attending to all the new experiences of life, but this very fact makes it difficult for them to focus on just one event and shut out everything else that's going on—the kind of focus necessary for encoding and remembering (Gopnik, 2009).

2 **Cognitive development.** Before you can carry memories about yourself with you into adulthood, you have to have a self to remember. The emergence of a self-concept usually does not take place before age 2 (Howe, Courage, & Peterson, 1994). In addition, the cognitive schemas used by preschoolers are very different from those used by older children and adults. Only after acquiring language and starting school do children form schemas that contain the information and cues necessary for recalling earlier experiences (Howe, 2000). Young children's limited vocabularies and language skills also prevent them from narrating some aspects of an experience to themselves or others. Later, after their linguistic abilities have matured, they still cannot use those abilities to recall earlier, preverbal memories, because those memories were not encoded linguistically (Simcock & Hayne, 2002).

childhood (infantile) amnesia
the inability to remember events and experiences that occurred during the first two or three years of life

3 **Social development.** Preschoolers have not yet mastered the social conventions for reporting events, nor have they learned what is important to others. As a result, they focus on the routine aspects of an experience rather than the distinctive ones that will

provide retrieval cues later, and they encode their experiences far less elaborately than adults do. Instead, they tend to rely on adults' questions to provide retrieval cues ("Where did we go for breakfast?" or "Who did you go trick-or-treating with?"). This dependency on adults may prevent them from building up a stable core of remembered material that will be available later on (Fivush & Nelson, 2005). But as children get older, their conversations with parents help them develop their own autobiographical memories, and thus play an important role in ending childhood amnesia (Reese, Jack, & White, 2010).

Nonetheless, our first memories, even when they are not accurate, may provide useful insights into our personalities, current concerns, ambitions, and attitudes toward life. What are *your* first memories—or, at least, what do you think they are? What might they tell you about yourself?

Memory and Narrative: The Stories of Our Lives

The communications researcher George Gerbner once observed that human beings are unique because we are the only animal that tells stories—and lives by the stories we tell. This view of human beings as the "storytelling animal" has had a huge impact in cognitive psychology. The *narratives* we compose to simplify and make sense of our lives have a profound influence on our plans, memories, love affairs, hatreds, ambitions, and dreams.

Thus we say, "I have no academic motivation because I flunked the third grade." We say, "Let me tell you the story of how we fell in love." We say, "When you hear what happened, you'll understand why I felt entitled to take such cold-hearted revenge." These stories are not necessarily fictions; rather, they are attempts to organize and give meaning to the events of our lives. But because these narratives rely heavily on memory, and because memories are reconstructed and are constantly shifting in response to current needs, beliefs, and experiences, our autobiographies are also, to some degree, works of interpretation and imagination. Adult memories thus reveal as much about the present as they do about the past.

When you construct a narrative about an incident in your life, you have many choices about how to do it. The spin you put on a story depends on who the audience is; you are apt to put in, leave out, understate, and embellish different things depending on whether you are telling about an event in your life to a therapist, your boss, or friends on Facebook. Your story is also influenced by your purpose in relating it: to convey facts, entertain, or elicit sympathy. As a result of these influences, distortions are apt to creep in, even when you think you are being accurate. And once those distortions are part of the story, they are likely to become part of your memory of the events themselves (Marsh & Tversky, 2004).

Your culture also affects how you encode and tell your story. American college students live in a culture that emphasizes individuality, personal feelings, and self-expression. Their earliest childhood memories reflect that fact: They tend to report lengthy, emotionally elaborate memories of events, memories that focus on—who else?—themselves. In contrast, Chinese students, who live in a culture that emphasizes group harmony, social roles, and personal humility, tend to report early memories of family or neighborhood activities, conflicts with friends or relatives that were resolved, and emotionally neutral events (Wang, 2008).

Once you have formulated a story's central theme ("My father never liked us"; "My partner was always competing with me"), that theme may then serve as a cognitive schema that guides what you remember and what you forget (Mather, Shafir, & Johnson, 2000). Teenagers who have strong and secure attachments to their mothers remember previous quarrels with their moms as being less intense and conflicted than they reported at the time, whereas teenagers who have more ambivalent and insecure attachments remember such quarrels as being worse than they were (Feeney & Cassidy, 2003). A story's theme

"And here I am at two years of age. Remember? Mom? Pop? No? Or how about this one. My first day of school. Anyone?"

may also influence our judgments of events and people in the present. If you have a fight with your lover, the central theme in your story about the fight might be negative ("He was a jerk") or neutral ("It was a mutual misunderstanding"). This theme may bias you to blame or forgive your partner long after you have forgotten what the conflict was about (McGregor & Holmes, 1999). You can see that the spin you give a story is critical, so be careful about the stories you tell!

Recite & Review

Recite: It's time to say out loud everything you can about *childhood amnesia* and the influence of *narratives* in autobiographical memory.

Review: Next, go back and read this section again.

Now take this ***Quick Quiz:***

1. A friend of yours claims to remember her birth, her first tooth, and her first birthday party. She is most likely to be (a) lying, (b) confabulating, (c) repressing, (d) revealing wishful thinking, (e) accurately remembering.
2. Give three explanations for childhood amnesia (be specific).
3. Why are the themes in our life stories so important?

Answers: 1. b, d. **2.** the immaturity of certain brain structures, making it difficult for very young children to focus attention, encode, and remember; cognitive factors such as immature cognitive schemas, lack of linguistic skills, and lack of a self-concept; lack of knowledge of social conventions for encoding and reporting events **3.** They guide what we remember and forget about our personal pasts, and affect our judgments of events and people.

If you have been reading this chapter actively, you should be able to recall the many factors that can trip you up when you call upon your memory to add a plot twist to your life story, to remember a fact, or to idly daydream about a past event: confabulation, source misattribution, poor encoding and rehearsal strategies, interference, inadequate retrieval cues, suggestibility, and narrative biases. By now, therefore, you should not be surprised that memory can be as fickle as it can be accurate. As cognitive psychologists have shown repeatedly, we are not merely actors in our personal life dramas; we also write the scripts.

Taking Psychology with You

Memory and Myth

Psychological research is having a significant impact on people's ability to think critically about memory. Most notably, awareness of the fallibility of memory is growing among police, interrogators, prosecutors, and judges. The case of Ronald Cotton, described at the start of this chapter, is far from unique. When psychological scientists examined 40 cases in which wrongful conviction had been established beyond a doubt, they found that 90 percent of those cases had involved a false identification by one or more eyewitnesses (Wells et al., 1998). Of course, not all eyewitness testimony is erroneous. But the potential for errors in identification shows how important it is to gather evidence carefully, ensure adequate legal representation for defendants, conduct police interviews using proper procedures, reduce pressure on witnesses, and obtain a DNA analysis whenever possible.

Inspired by the Innocence Project at the Cardozo School of Law in New York City, grassroots organizations of lawyers and students have been successfully challenging questionable convictions. Since the early 1990s, these efforts have led to the exoneration of nearly 300 innocent people in the United States, some of whom had been condemned to death. One man in Illinois, who had been on death row for 16 years, was just hours from execution when a group of Northwestern University journalism students produced evidence that another man had committed the crime. Other investigative projects around the world have produced similar accomplishments.

How would you feel if your testimony resulted in the conviction of an innocent person? Would you, like Jennifer Thompson, be able to admit your mistake, or would you, as most people do, cling more stubbornly than ever to the accuracy of your memory? Thompson learned from personal experience what you have learned from this chapter: Eyewitnesses can and do make mistakes; ethnic differences can increase these mistakes; even memories for shocking or traumatic experiences are vulnerable to distortion and influence by others; and our confidence in our memories is not a reliable guide to their accuracy. To this day, Thompson and Cotton have made it their personal goal to educate the public and the criminal-justice system, so that the mistake she made will be less likely to be repeated in the future. The subtitle of their book, *Picking Cotton,* is "Our memoir of injustice and redemption" (Thompson-Cannino, Cotton, & Torneo, 2009).

After Ronald Cotton was exonerated of the rape of Jennifer Thompson, the two became friends. Thompson says she has lived with constant anguish because of her mistaken identification.

Human memory has both tremendous strengths and tremendous weaknesses. Because our deepest sense of ourselves relies on our memories, this is a difficult truth to accept. It is so much easier to give in to emotional reasoning ("I just feel that my memory is absolutely, 100 percent true!") and not consider other explanations ("Could my brother's account of that family quarrel be more accurate than mine?"). But if we can do so, we will be able to respect the great power of memory and at the same time retain humility about our capacity for error, confabulation, and self-deception.

Summary

RECONSTRUCTING THE PAST

- Unlike a digital recorder or video camera, human memory is highly selective and is *reconstructive*: People add, delete, and change elements in ways that help them make sense of information and events. They often experience *source misattribution,* the inability to distinguish information stored during an event from information added later. Even vivid *flashbulb memories* tend to become less accurate or complete over time.
- Because memory is so often reconstructive, it is subject to *confabulation,* the confusion of imagined events with actual ones. Confabulation is especially likely when people have thought, heard, or told others about the imagined event many times and thus experience *imagination inflation,* the image of the event contains many details, or the event is easy to imagine. Confabulated memories can feel vividly real yet be false.

MEMORY AND THE POWER OF SUGGESTION

- The reconstructive nature of memory also makes memory vulnerable to suggestion. Eyewitness testimony is especially vulnerable to error when the suspect's ethnicity differs from that of the witness, when leading questions are put to witnesses, or when witnesses are given misleading information.
- Like adults, children often remember the essential aspects of an event accurately but can also be suggestible, especially when responding to biased interviewing by adults—when they are asked questions that blur the line between fantasy and reality, are asked leading questions, are told what "other kids" had supposedly said, and are praised for making false allegations.

IN PURSUIT OF MEMORY

- The ability to remember depends in part on the type of performance called for. In tests of *explicit memory* (conscious recollection), *recognition* is usually better than *recall.* In tests of *implicit memory,* which is measured by indirect methods such as *priming* and the *relearning method,* past experiences may affect current thoughts or actions even when these experiences are not consciously remembered.
- In *information-processing models,* memory involves the *encoding, storage,* and *retrieval* of information. The *three-box model* proposes three interacting systems: the sensory register, short-term memory, and long-term memory. Some cognitive scientists prefer a *parallel distributed processing (PDP)* or *connectionist* model, which represents knowledge as connections among numerous interacting processing units, distributed in a vast network and all operating in parallel. But the three-box model continues to offer a convenient way to organize the major findings on memory.

(Continued)

THE THREE-BOX MODEL OF MEMORY

- In the three-box model, incoming sensory information makes a brief stop in the *sensory register,* which momentarily retains it in the form of sensory images.
- *Short-term memory (STM)* retains new information for up to 30 seconds by most estimates (unless rehearsal takes place). The capacity of STM is extremely limited but can be extended if information is organized into larger units by *chunking.* Early models of STM portrayed it mainly as a bin for the temporary storage of information, but many models now envision it as a part of a more general *working-memory* system, which includes an "executive" that controls the retrieval of information from long-term memory and focuses on information needed for the task being performed. Working memory permits us to control attention, resist distraction, and therefore maintain information in an active, accessible state.
- *Long-term memory (LTM)* contains an enormous amount of information that must be organized to make it manageable. Words (or the concepts they represent) are often organized by semantic categories. Many models of LTM represent its contents as a network of interrelated concepts. The way people use these networks depends on experience and education. Research on *tip-of-the-tongue (TOT) states* shows that words are also indexed in terms of sound and form.
- *Procedural memories* ("knowing how") are memories for how to perform specific actions; *declarative memories* ("knowing that") are memories for abstract or representational knowledge. Declarative memories include *semantic memories* (general knowledge) and *episodic memories* (memories for personally experienced events). Episodic memories allow us to retrieve past events in order to imagine the future.
- The three-box model is often invoked to explain the *serial-position effect* in memory, but although it can explain the *primacy effect,* it cannot explain why a *recency effect* sometimes occurs after a considerable delay.

THE BIOLOGY OF MEMORY

- Short-term memory involves temporary changes within neurons that alter their ability to release neurotransmitters, whereas long-term memory involves lasting structural changes in neurons and synapses. *Long-term potentiation,* an increase in the strength of synaptic responsiveness, seems to be an important mechanism of long-term memory. Neural changes associated with long-term potentiation take time to develop, which helps explain why long-term memories require a period of *consolidation.*
- The amygdala is involved in the formation, consolidation, and retrieval of emotional memories. Areas of the frontal lobes are especially active during short-term and working-memory tasks. The prefrontal cortex and parts of the temporal lobes are involved in the efficient encoding of words and pictures. The hippocampus plays a critical role in the formation and retrieval of long-term declarative memories. Other areas, such as the cerebellum, are crucial for the formation of procedural memories. Studies of patients with amnesia suggest that different brain systems are active during explicit and implicit memory tasks. The long-term storage of declarative memories possibly takes place in cortical areas that were active during the original perception of the information or event. The various components of a memory are probably stored at different sites, with all of these sites participating in the representation of the event as a whole.
- Hormones released by the adrenal glands during stress or emotional arousal, including epinephrine and norepinephrine, enhance memory. These adrenal hormones cause the level of glucose to rise in the bloodstream, and glucose may enhance memory directly or by altering the effects of neurotransmitters. But very high hormone levels can interfere with the retention of information; a moderate level is optimal for learning new tasks.

HOW WE REMEMBER

- *Mnemonics* can enhance retention, but for ordinary memory tasks, complex memory tricks are often ineffective or even counterproductive.
- To remember material well, we must encode it accurately in the first place. Some kinds of information, such as material in a college course, require *effortful,* as opposed to automatic, encoding. Rehearsal of information keeps it in short-term memory and increases the chances of long-term retention. *Elaborative rehearsal* is more likely to result in transfer to long-term memory than is *maintenance rehearsal,* and *deep processing* is usually a more effective retention strategy than *shallow processing. Retrieval practice* is necessary if a memory is going to be consolidated, and therefore last and be available for a long time. The *read-recite-review strategy* encourages active learning and produces better results than simply reading and rereading material.

WHY WE FORGET

- Forgetting can occur for several reasons. Information in sensory and short-term memory appears to *decay* if it does not receive further processing. New information may erase and replace old information in long-term memory. *Proactive* and *retroactive interference* may take place. *Cue-dependent forgetting* may occur when *retrieval cues* are inadequate. The most effective retrieval cues are those that were present at the time of the initial experience. A person's mental or physical state may also act as a retrieval cue, evoking a *state-dependent memory.* We tend to remember best those events that are congruent with our current mood (*mood-congruent memory*).
- *Amnesia,* the forgetting of important personal information, usually occurs because of disease or injury to the brain. *Psychogenic amnesia,* which involves a loss of personal identity

and has psychological causes, is rare. *Traumatic amnesia,* which allegedly involves the forgetting of specific traumatic events for long periods of time, is highly controversial, as is *repression,* the psychodynamic explanation of traumatic amnesia. Because these concepts lack good empirical support, psychological scientists are skeptical about their validity and about the accuracy of "recovered memories." Critics argue that many therapists, unaware of the power of suggestion and the dangers of confabulation, have encouraged false memories of victimization.

AUTOBIOGRAPHICAL MEMORIES

- Most people cannot recall any events from earlier than the age of 2. The reasons for such *childhood amnesia* include the immaturity of certain brain structures, making it difficult for very young children to focus attention, encode, and remember; cognitive factors such as immature cognitive schemas, lack of linguistic skills, and lack of a self-concept; and lack of knowledge of social conventions for encoding and reporting events.
- A person's *narrative* "life story" organizes the events of his or her life and gives them meaning.

TAKING PSYCHOLOGY WITH YOU

- DNA evidence has exonerated many men who were falsely convicted of rape and murder, making the public and the criminal-justice system more aware of the limitations of eyewitness testimony and the fallibility of memory.

Key Terms

memory (p. 328)
reconstructive memory (p. 329)
source misattribution (p. 329)
flashbulb memories (p. 330)
confabulation (p. 330)
imagination inflation (p. 330)
leading questions (p. 334)
explicit memory (p. 336)
recall (p. 336)
recognition (p. 336)
implicit memory (p. 337)
priming (p. 337)
relearning method (p. 337)
information-processing models (p. 338)
encoding, storage, and retrieval (p. 338)
cognitive schemas (p. 338)
three-box model (p. 338)
parallel distributed processing (PDP) model (p. 338)
sensory register (p. 339)
short-term memory (STM) (p. 340)
chunks (p. 341)
working memory (p. 341)
long-term memory (LTM) (p. 342)
semantic categories (p. 342)
tip-of-the-tongue (TOT) state (p. 342)
procedural memories (p. 343)
declarative memories (p. 343)
semantic memories (p. 343)
episodic memories (p. 344)
serial-position effect (p. 344)
primacy and recency effects (p. 344)
long-term potentiation (p. 346)
consolidation (p. 346)
mnemonics (p. 350)
effortful versus automatic encoding (p. 350)
maintenance rehearsal (p. 351)
elaborative rehearsal (p. 351)
deep processing (p. 352)
shallow processing (p. 352)
retrieval practice (p. 352)
read-recite-review strategy (p. 352)
decay theory (p. 355)
retroactive interference (p. 356)
proactive interference (p. 356)
retrieval cues (p. 357)
cue-dependent forgetting (p. 357)
déjà vu (p. 357)
state-dependent memory (p. 357)
mood-congruent memory (p. 357)
amnesia (p. 357)
psychogenic amnesia (p. 357)
traumatic amnesia (p. 358)
repression (p. 358)
childhood (infantile) amnesia (p. 360)
narratives (p. 361)

Answers to the Get Involved exercises on pages 336 and 337: Rudolph's eight friends were Dasher, Dancer, Prancer, Vixen, Comet, Cupid, Donder, and Blitzen.
Answer to the Get Involved exercise on page 351: The real penny is the left one in the bottom row.

12

Development

BY DOUGLAS A. JOHNSON, PH.D. AND SOPHIE RUBIN, PH.D.

The Long Journey through the Changes of Life

Development is a lifelong journey involving many psychological milestones.

As we progress through life, numerous challenges and milestones await us. Understanding how we grow and mature as we strive to meet the opportunities of life falls within the scope of developmental psychology. **Developmental psychology** is the study of the progressive and cumulative changes that occur throughout the lifespan, starting with birth and ending with death. Understanding the developmental process requires an analysis of the mutual contributions of both maturation and experience to a person's development. **Maturation** refers to the genetically directed growth of an organism. As always, it is important to remember that both nature (i.e., maturation) and nurture (i.e., experience) contribute to psychology. The study of development can encompass changes across many different domains, including physical, emotional, social, cognitive, and moral development, as well as the interactions between these various domains.

As with all aspects of psychology, it is critical that we collect data to support our theories and our understanding of the world. Developmental phenomena often present new challenges because we are not looking at just a snapshot of human functioning, but rather, we are examining changes that progress across entire lifetimes. As such, certain research designs are particularly well-suited to this challenge and worth exploring before we discuss the developmental processes themselves.

Research Designs for Developmental Psychology

One method for analyzing developmental changes is to employ a cross-sectional design. **Cross-sectional designs** sample one aspect of behavior across people of many different ages at a single point in time. Essentially, a cross-sectional design treats age as if it was an independent variable, looking at how various ages are associated with certain psychological characteristics. Imagine that you wanted to study the progression of social relationships throughout the lifetime. A researcher could analyze the average number of friendships being maintained, family members being interacted with, romantic relationships being pursued, etc. The researcher could also analyze the quality of these various social relations. To conduct this study using a cross-sectional design, the researcher might collect social relationship data from some 5-year-olds. The researcher would also collect the same data from 10-year-olds, 15-year-olds, 20-year-olds, etc. (the specific ages to be sampled can vary). The researcher could then compare the obtained data on typical social relationships from the various age groups in order to make inferences about the progression of social relationships across time.

One threat to research conducted with cross-sectional designs is the possibility of cohort effects. **Cohort effects** are the influences on development related to a particular historical context. For example, imagine if a cross-sectional study discovered that people in their 60s and 70s tend to be especially frugal with money. One interpretation of this finding may be that as people grow older, they become more cautious with money. However, an alternative explanation of this finding relates to cohort effects. Perhaps the elderly people that the researchers studied are also people who grew up during a time period when the economic conditions were quite difficult. It may be the case that this particular generation is thrifty with money because of their experience with a harsh financial recession, as opposed to the possibility that all people naturally become more frugal as they enter their 60s and 70s.

developmental psychology
the study of progressive and cumulative changes that occur across the lifespan

maturation
the genetically determined changes in development that occur relatively independent of the environment

cross-sectional design
a research design that compares the behavior of different age groups at the same point in time

cohort effect
a type of confounding variable in which behavior is influenced by a particular historical context rather than the standard developmental sequence

With cross-sectional designs, many people of different ages are compared at once.

A second alternative explanation is that perhaps education on topics such as accounting has grown progressively worse over the years or that people born after the computer age rely exclusively on software for their mathematical decisions, leading younger generations to be poor managers of money as compared to previous generations. A third or fourth alternative explanation could easily be generated and the possibility of cohort effects cannot be readily removed from cross-sectional designs, although this does not automatically mean that all results produced by cross-sectional designs are inherently confounded.

Another design frequently used in developmental research is the longitudinal design. A **longitudinal design** measures the behavior of a selected group of individuals across many points in time. This time period could last a few months or span several decades. The distinguishing element is that the progression of behavior change is continually measured with the same people. If a researcher wanted to study the development of social relationships using a longitudinal design, he or she might study the relationships maintained by a group of 5-year-olds. Next the researcher might study that same group of people five years later, then again ten years later, etc. While cohort effects are minimized with longitudinal designs, the design is not without its own set of drawbacks. One significant challenge for this type of design is reliably collecting data from the same people without them exiting the research due to attrition. **Attrition** involves participants disappearing from the research measurement for any number of reasons, including participants simply deciding to withdraw, researchers being unable to locate the participants, or even death of the participants. This problem can be somewhat lessened if the attrition is random, meaning that the loss of participants is fairly evenly distributed amongst the different types of participants. The final size of the sample may be smaller, but it is possible for small samples to still be representative. An even more problematic issue is the potential for **selective attrition**, whereby only certain types of participant data are lost over time. For example, imagine if only the participants with lower household incomes disappeared from a research study. There are a number of reasons why something like this could happen, such as parents who are forced to work multiple minimum wage jobs and simply do not have time to bring their children to be studied by researchers, or families who can no longer afford to pay their phone bills, thus preventing the researchers from calling them to schedule times to meet. This selective attrition means only certain types of participants are being studied, which reduces the representativeness of the sample and threatens the final conclusions of the research. In our example, it may be problematic if only households of higher socioeconomic status are being studied because we are trying to make broad

longitudinal design
a research design that compares the behavior of the same group of individuals at different points in time over an extended time period

attrition
the loss of participants during the data collection stage of a research study

selective attrition
the loss of a particular type or demographic of participants during the data collection stage of a research study

With longitudinal designs, the same people are compared at different stages of their lives.

statements about the development of all people, regardless of the family income. Finally, by their very nature, longitudinal designs are time intensive, requiring researchers to invest long periods of time before anything noteworthy can be reported.

It may be worth noting that the design logic of cross-sectional studies is similar to between-group designs (studies including different people at the same point in time) and the logic of longitudinal studies is similar to within-subjects designs (studies including the same people across different points in time), but the variable being "manipulated" is the age of participants, rather than some other independent variable. However, it is also important to recognize that age is not a proper independent variable, since nothing is being actively manipulated by researchers and the mere passage of time does not cause developmental changes (Gewirtz & Peláez-Nogueras, 1992). Although using age as a variable may have predictive power since physical changes and learning both take place over time, it would be a mistake to treat age itself as if it causes those changes. Even in the case of maturation, it is the physical development that causes changes in the person, not the passing of time itself. Nonetheless, both cross-sectional and longitudinal designs have yielded rich descriptive data to help us establish patterns regarding common developmental sequences and therefore predict age appropriate outcomes.

As with all research designs, developmental methodology poses challenges for researchers to overcome.

Early Physical Development

The chronicle of human development begins with fertilization. It is during fertilization that a zygote is created. A **zygote** is the initial cell that is formed when a sperm fuses with an ovum. This zygote contains the entire genetic code for an individual and this code will have many subtle and profound influences on that individual's later development. Just a few hours after the start of its existence, the zygote has already begun the process of dividing and replicating itself. This process will eventually change the zygote from a single cell into a complex and organized arrangement of trillions of integrated cells that are prepared for the world at large. How this arrangement finally manifests itself depends upon how that initial genetic code interacts with many environmental influences. Despite the subsequent emergence of trillions of cells, each one of those cells will still retain the original genetic code found in that initial zygote.

Approximately three weeks after conception, the process of rapid cellular development has produced enough differences that the zygote is now given the new name of **embryo**. Unlike the cellular division seen with the zygote during the first two weeks, the

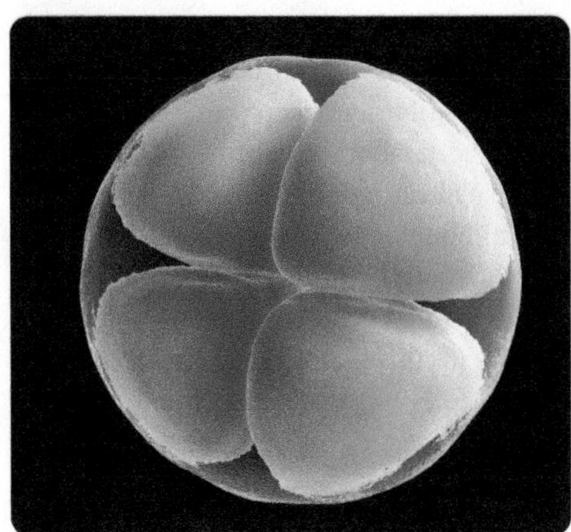
All human life starts off as a humble zygote.

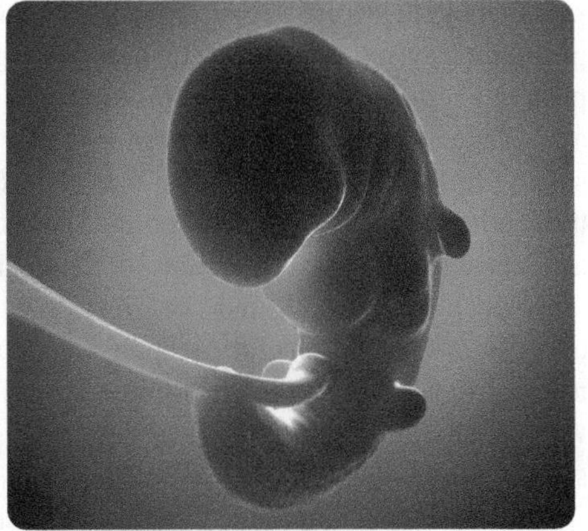
During the embryotic stage, clearly distinct cells begin to form.

zygote
the initial cell that is formed during the first two weeks after fertilization

embryo
the organism possessing specialized cells that emerge during the third and eighth weeks of prenatal development

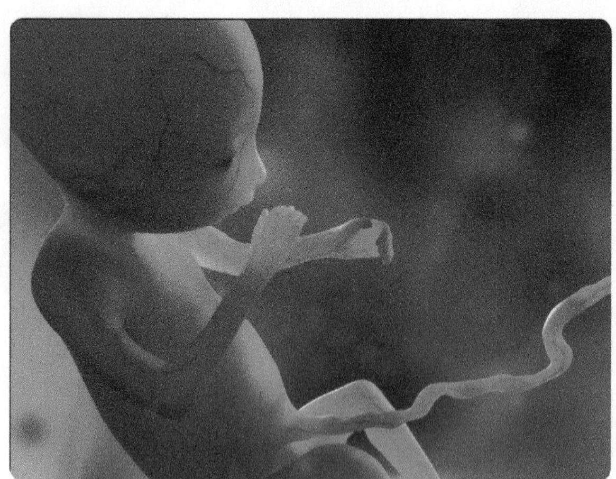
The fetus develops rapidly, but this progression can be irreversibly damaged by harmful agents.

newly emerging cells of the embryo are not simply duplications of each other. Instead, they now begin to differentiate from one another and major physical structures such as the heart and nervous system can be seen in the embryo. Around the ninth week, the embryo develops into a **fetus**, as all of the major body structures have emerged and those structural systems become more specialized and developed. During this stage of development, motor behavior finally emerges and the fetus can show some responsiveness to environmental stimuli. For example, one study (DeCasper & Spence, 1986) had pregnant women read the story *The Cat in the Hat* aloud to their developing fetuses. These babies displayed signs of prenatal (i.e., before birth) learning because they exhibited a preference for *The Cat in the Hat* over other stories following birth, However, it isn't until about 22 weeks when viability becomes possible. **Viability** refers to the potential for a fetus to survive outside of the uterus with special medical care.

As stated before, environmental influences begin to have an impact early in life, even during prenatal development. Unfortunately, some of these influences can be damaging to the normal development process and result in birth defects. For example, **teratogens** are external agents that impair prenatal development and cause physical or behavioral abnormalities. Examples of teratogens include infections, drugs, malnutrition, and maternal emotional states. An illustration of the effect of teratogens can be seen with fetal alcohol syndrome. **Fetal alcohol syndrome** refers to the physical and mental abnormalities that occur when the mother consumes alcohol during pregnancy (Jones & Smith, 1973). Alcohol can damage the brain during prenatal development, culminating in intellectual disabilities after birth. Although the syndrome's name emphasizes the fetal stage, brain development can be negatively impacted at any point during pregnancy. Beyond brain-related deficits, children with fetal alcohol syndrome also experience deficiencies in growth and abnormalities in facial features.

Basic Reflexes

Human beings are not born as blank slates, but rather as creatures whose initial skill set leaves them well positioned to acquire a myriad of subsequent abilities. Imagine how difficult it would be to learn new skills if there were no initial behaviors to be reinforced or shaped by the environment. Furthermore, our chances of survival would be very low if we had to be taught how to breathe, blink, or swallow food. Instead, human beings are genetically prepared with a host of **reflexes**, which are defined as untaught behaviors that occur in response to certain environmental stimuli. Although many of these behaviors may seem fairly simple, they are also the basic skills upon which later and more complex skills are built.

Interestingly, while we are born with many reflexes that we then keep for the rest of our lives (e.g., sneezing or coughing in response to an irritant, jerking one's leg in response to a tap to the knee), there are also some reflexes that are temporary in duration. These **primitive reflexes** are automatic reactions that all healthy babies possess, but are not seen in children or adults (also known as infantile or newborn reflexes). One example of a primitive reflex is the *rooting reflex*, in which the infant will orient his or her head towards a light touch on the cheek or corner of the mouth. The temporary survival value of the rooting reflex may be seen when one considers that such responding helps an infant find the mother's nipple in order to obtain nourishment, although such rooting would have no advantage in finding nourishment for adults. In fact, the rooting reflex does not occur when other people are not around (i.e., infants do not root if they accidently touch their own cheek) and the strength of the response is influenced by levels of hunger (i.e., an infant will not root in response to a touch on the cheek if he or she is not hungry). Similar survival value related to nourishment may be seen in the *sucking reflex*, in which infants naturally suck at stimulation near their mouths.

With the *palmar grasp reflex*, an infant will close his or her fingers with firm pressure if the palm of his or her hand is touched. Such a reflex not only aids in grasping but may also serve to produce affectionate and caretaking responses from people around the

fetus
the organism possessing all of the major body structures after the ninth week during prenatal development

viability
the potential for a fetus to survive outside of the uterus with special medical care

teratogens
external agents that can cause lasting harm to a developing embryo or fetus

fetal alcohol syndrome
a disorder caused by the consumption of alcohol during prenatal development, resulting in intellectual disabilities and abnormal growth

reflex
an automatic and unlearned response to environmental stimuli

primitive reflexes
reflexes that are present in infancy but disappear with maturation

infant—something essential for the survival of babies. Infants also display the *Babinski reflex* (also known as the plantar reflex), in which they will extend their toes outward and then curl the toes back in response to a stroke or light brushing on the bottom of the foot. Similar to the grasping reflex, evolutionary psychologists suspect that the Babinski response may have developed to aid the infant in grabbing onto the caregiver or to help an infant with stabilization. The *Moro reflex* can be demonstrated when the infant experiences a sudden loss of support (i.e., experiences a sense of falling), after which the infant will immediately spread out his or her arms and then retract them all while arching his or her back. Crying often accompanies this response. Evolutionary psychologists have proposed that this reflex aided in survival by allowing the infant to brace for a fall while also making it easier for a caregiver to grab on to a falling infant. All of these primitive reflexes are examples of respondent behaviors (refer back to the chapter on Conditioning Principles and Applications). With the rooting reflex, the touch to the cheek is an unconditioned stimulus that elicits the unconditioned response of orienting. With the Babinski reflex, the unconditioned stimulus is a stroke to the bottom of the foot and the unconditioned response is the fanning and curling of the toes. If these responses begin to occur in response to other types of stimuli, they can no longer be considered reflexes. For example, when an infant orients in the direction of the mother in response to her voice because that voice has been paired with touches to the cheek, rather than a touch to the cheek alone, we can say that respondent conditioning has occurred. When an infant orients in the direction of a mother because it often results in the consequence of attention, then we can say that operant conditioning has occurred. To summarize, humans are born with an array of reflexes, some of which will exist for a lifetime and others which will disappear shortly after birth. Reflexes can be expanded into new behaviors via the processes of respondent and operant conditioning. Additionally, when species are born with genetically programmed traits or behaviors it may be wise to take an evolutionary perspective and consider the survival value of these behaviors. These reflexes may have had survival value for infants by increasing the odds of remaining physically attached to caregivers, especially in the presence of threatening stimuli. Furthermore, many of these reflexes may also increase the chances of survival by encouraging caregivers to respond with affection to an infant's positive attempts to interact. When an infant possesses the reflex past the point where it should have disappeared, or when the reflex is absent or delayed, this can be an important indicator of neurological impairment or developmental delay among other potential problems.

Infants are prepared for the world with an inborn set of reflexes.

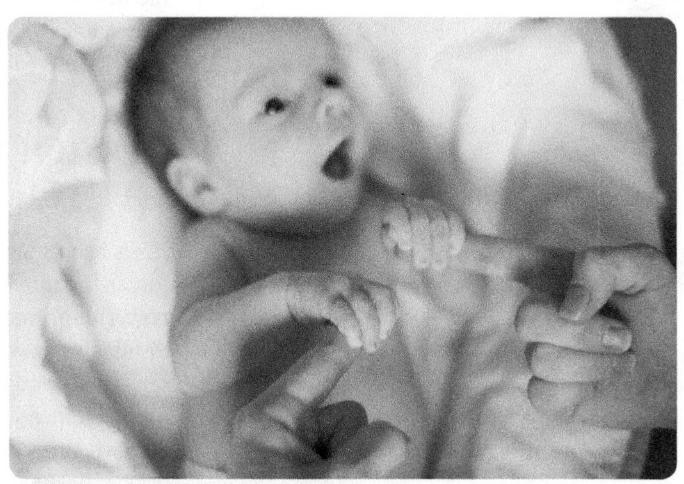

Many of the inborn reflexes disappear with age.

Early Brain Growth

Although all of the major brain structures are in place at birth and a host of reflexes are available, this does not mean that brain development is finished. Far from it, as the brain continues to change and remold itself in response to experience for the remainder of a person's life (Toga, Thompson, & Sowell, 2006; Rubia, 2013). New synaptic connections are created in a process known as **synaptogenesis** as the person encounters new experiences and adapts to the surrounding world. However, shortly after birth the brain undergoes an incredibly rapid transformation that far exceeds any subsequent development (Huttenlocher, 1984; Huttenlocher & Dabholkar, 1997). This critical period of unparalleled brain development involves billions of new synapses being rapidly formed between neurons. The brain becomes much more interconnected as the newborn interacts with environmental stimuli and learns how things work. In other words, babies are born ready for a diverse set of circumstances and then immediately begin customizing themselves in response to the world they are given. Furthermore, through **synaptic pruning**, weak connections between neurons are lost during early childhood if the environment does not support their maintenance. In fact, adults have fewer synaptic connections than infants due to this infantile

synaptogenesis
the development of connections between neurons within the nervous system

synaptic pruning
the elimination of connections between neurons that are not supported by learning or other environmental factors

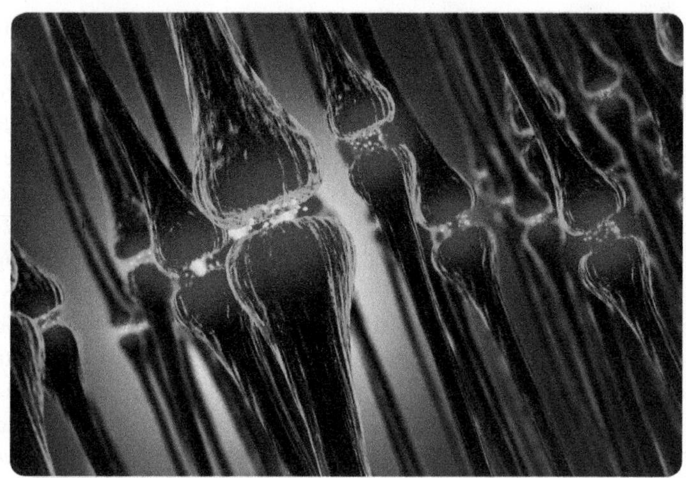

An explosive growth in synapses occurs early in infancy.

explosion of new connections followed by a continual process of pruning. Taken together, this means that environmental experience can have either a positive or negative impact on the development of the brain. In support of this, research has shown that being raised in environments devoid of normal experiences can result in profound and lasting neurological impairments (Nelson, Bos, Gunnar, & Sonuga-Barke, 2011).

Socioemotional Development between Children and Caregivers

It has been suggested that attentive caregivers quickly develop into a powerful social reinforcer for infants (Bijou & Baer, 1965). If you can imagine how often mothers deliver powerful primary reinforcers such as food, water, and pain reduction to infants, it is easy to imagine how the mother would quickly develop into a powerful secondary and social reinforcer. As a result, infants engage in a variety of behaviors that increase their proximity to the mother since her mere presence has now been established as a form of reinforcement. It turns out that infants also appear to have a preference for their mother's voice even as early as 1–2 days after being born. One research study illustrated that infants could not only recognize their mother's voice right away but would learn to engage in behaviors that produced her voice (DeCasper & Fifer, 1980). In this study, a nonnutritive nipple was attached to an apparatus that could measure the amount of time infants spent sucking. The authors were able to demonstrate that infants would suck more when hearing a tape of their mother reading a Dr. Seuss book (*To Think That I Saw it on Mulberry Street*) versus that of another female voice reading the same book.

It has also been demonstrated that within the first year of life, children engage in a behavior known as **social referencing**. That is, they look to significant caregivers for emotional cues regarding how they should behave during novel situations. Emotional cues could include facial expressions, tone of voice, and other types of body language. Several studies have illustrated that infants learn to react with approach behaviors when the mother is smiling or displaying signs of joy. Similarly, infants learn to react with avoidant behavior when the mother is displaying negative cues. For example, if a stranger enters a room and the mother is seen smiling and laughing, the infant is likely to respond by orienting in the direction of the stranger, smiling, etc. If the mother grimaces, frowns, or acts scared, the infant is likely to respond by crying and looking away (Pelaez, Virues-Ortega, & Gewirtz, 2012; Sorce, Emde, Campos, Klinnert, 1985). This pattern of social referencing is not limited to interactions with strangers and occurs in many novel situations. Social referencing is also not limited to mothers but is most likely to occur with caregivers who are established secondary reinforcers.

social referencing
a pattern of behavior in which infants and children encounter an unfamiliar situation or person and base their emotional responses upon the emotional responses being modeled by caregivers

Infants are surrounded by a rich world full of verbal stimuli and this experience with the verbal world can help direct the underlying rapid neuronal growth. The more exposure that babies have with a particular language, the easier it becomes for them to later distinguish the basic units of sound used in that language. Even before children can speak, they demonstrate distinct reactions to the human speech around them. Infants show preference for their caregiver's voice, as well as a preference for normal conversations over random sounds. Furthermore, babies prefer certain types of conversation, such as parentese (a more precise version of "baby talk"). **Parentese** involves the use of exaggerated intonation, simplified grammar, and brief sentences that are frequently repeated (e.g., "Who's the smartest baby? Who's the smartest baby? YOU ARE! THAT'S WHO!"). The clarity of parentese may facilitate the acquisition of language for babies and foster more powerful attachments between caregivers and their children. **Attachment** is defined here as the bond that is formed between a caregiver and the infant. Said another way, when a child a) engages in behavior that increases their proximity to a caregiver, b) frequently references that caregiver, or c) obtains a sense of security while in the caregiver's presence, we can say that the child has formed an attachment to that particular individual.

Attachment isn't automatic, but it does develop early.

Despite popular views on attachment, research shows that attachment is not achieved instantly, but rather develops over time and through experience with caregivers. As evidence of this, newborn babies show minimal preference for their caregivers. Infants as young as 3 months old can be passed between different people with little fuss or negative reactions. Although some infant preference for the mother does exist at birth, this preference is low in intensity. Overall, infants tend to be indiscriminately responsive to all people in their social world.

However, by 6 months of age, a strong change in infant behavior is evident. By this point in time, most infants have developed a strong attachment to their caregivers and show the first signs of significant distress when separated. The distress that young children experience when apart from their caregivers is labeled **separation anxiety** and provides evidence for the existence of a strong attachment. As mentioned earlier in the chapter, significant caregivers are likely to develop into powerful conditioned reinforcers and infants will even engage in behaviors that increase their proximity to them. It is not surprising that when these powerful conditioned reinforcers are absent, emotional behavior such as crying will occur. It is also not surprising that infants will engage in behaviors that result in reuniting with their caregiver since those behaviors are likely to have been reinforced in the past. Think of an infant crying and screaming in a crib as a result of the mother leaving the room. Now imagine the difficulty the mother experiences as she listens to the sounds of her baby and the likelihood that she will quickly return. Upon her return, the baby is calmed. The end of the screaming and crying is a reinforcer for the mother and the return of the mother is a reinforcer for the infant (Gewirtz & Peláez-Nogueras, 1992). Eventually the emotional displays characteristic of separation anxiety subside by the end of the second or third year, but the bonds may be powerful enough to continue for the rest of the person's life.

One sign of a strong attachment is the fact that infants protest when separated from their caregivers.

Theories of Attachment

To better understand the modern psychological view on attachment, it may be helpful to look back to the time period between the 1920s and 1950s. During this time period, there were notable public figures arguing that parents, especially mothers, should not become overly attached to their children. Emotional displays and physical interaction were argued to have a devastating effect on the development of a young child and nothing more was needed for proper attachment than to simply feed children. That is, children feel attached to mothers simply because those mothers were paired with food sources. Some of this sentiment can be traced to the book *Psychological Care of Infant and Child* (1928) by notable behaviorist John B. Watson. Within these pages, Watson offered up bold advice such as:

> "There is a sensible way of treating children. Treat them as though they were young adults. Dress them, bathe them with care and circumspection. Let your behavior always

parentese
a style of speech involving exaggerated intonation, simplified grammar, and repeated brief sentences

attachment
the strong emotional bond that forms between children and caregivers

separation anxiety
the normal presentation of fear or distress when infants are separated from their caregivers

Many years ago experts actually warned against close emotional attachment!

The surrogate mothers from Harlow's research have become one of the most iconic images in psychology. *(Courtesy of The LIFE Picture Collection/Getty Images.)*

be objective and kindly firm. Never hug and kiss them, never let them sit on your lap. If you must, kiss them once on the forehead when they say good night. Shake hands with them in the morning. Give them a pat on the head if they have made an extraordinarily good job of a difficult task. Try it out. In a week's time you will find how easy it is to be perfectly objective with your child and at the same time kindly. You will be utterly ashamed of the mawkish, sentimental way you have been handling it."

Watson's writings at the time influenced how many people viewed psychology and made many people question their own parenting practices. It is important to note that Watson's characterization of motherly love as a "dangerous instrument" was based more on his personal convictions and the common cultural norms of the 1920s, rather than any empirical evidence (the book was published many years after Watson had essentially been exiled from academia for personal issues). Many individuals incorrectly portrayed Watson as the defining voice of modern behaviorism, even though notable behaviorists such as B.F. Skinner disagreed with Watson's conclusions (Skinner regularly played with his daughters, both of whom developed into normal and well-adjusted adults). Skinner's disagreements were deep enough that he split off from Watson to invent his own version of behaviorism in the 1940s. Even Watson himself later came to regret his writings on the subject of parenting (Watson, 1936). Nonetheless, Watson's outlandish assertions spurred on subsequent researchers such as Harry Harlow and John Bowlby as they tried to prove that Watson's mechanistic worldview of attachment was flawed. Perhaps science could prove there was more to effective parenting and socialization than simply feeding one's children.

In a series of studies, Harry Harlow and his colleagues studied the behavior of baby rhesus monkeys in an attempt to discover the fundamental ingredients for attachment. For these experiments he constructed two artificial monkey "mothers." These mothers were made of wire mesh wrapped into the shape of a cylinder and had wooden heads mounted on the top. One of these surrogate mothers was labeled the "cloth mother" because it was covered with soft terrycloth, whereas the other surrogate mother was labeled the "wire mother" because it had no soft covering over the wire structure. Across different experimental manipulations, Harlow would alternate which mother provided nourishment (via a food bottle attached to the surrogate). He also arranged for some of the infant monkeys to have access to both mothers and other monkeys to have access to only one of the mothers.

Despite the different experimental arrangements, one consistent pattern emerged from all the research: the young monkeys reliably preferred the cloth mother and showed little to no attachment to the wire mother (Harlow & Harlow, 1962). When frightened, the monkey would always run towards the cloth mother for security. Even when the wire mother was the only one to provide food, the monkey would quickly get food from the wire mother and then return to the cloth mother for all other interactions. For those monkeys raised exclusively by the wire mother, these infants grew up to become fearful, antisocial, and underweight. They consumed as much milk as normal infant monkeys, but suffered digestive issues that appeared to be a result of psychological stress. Harlow would also completely isolate some of the monkeys from both mothers, as well as any type of additional social contact. These monkeys would spend up to a year in what he termed "pits of despair," cut off from all social interactions and the opportunity to form any type of attachment. The monkeys that emerged from these pits were psychologically disturbed and Harlow was unsuccessful in his later attempts to rehabilitate them. Despite the frequent association between Harlow and words like "love" and "attachment," it is worth noting that his experiments would be considered highly unethical by today's standards and such extreme circumstances would be prohibited in modern psychological research.

Harlow's research made it clear that nourishment alone was insufficient to explain attachment. This is not to say that feeding is irrelevant for attachment, but that nourishment is not the only factor relevant for the emergence of normal attachment. One of the findings that Harlow is best remembered for is his demonstration that contact comfort is a critical primary reinforcer and key variable for normal development. **Contact comfort** refers to the positive physical and emotional responses resulting from the stimulation

contact comfort
positive physical and emotional responses caused by soft tactile stimulation

Contact comfort is an essential ingredient for the development of normal and healthy attachment.

of soft touching. Although it can be provided from surrogates wrapped in terrycloth, it is more commonly experienced when caregivers physically interact with infants. Harlow's research had many profound implications for the care of infants. For example, many orphanages and hospitals began requiring staff to physically interact with infants, rather than simply feed them. His research also suggested that normal development can occur even in the absence of the biological parents, an important discovery for adoptive caregivers. Contact comfort is also a powerful source of reinforcement and subsequent research has shown that early infant behavior can be reinforced by simple touches alone (Peláez-Nogueras et al., 1996). Researchers have also investigated the effects of contact comfort on hospitalized infants who were born prematurely. After these preterm infants were provided with 15-minute massages three times per day, they demonstrated a 21–47% improvement in weight gain and were discharged from hospitals an average of six days earlier in comparison to hospitalized infants who did not regularly receive contact comfort (Field, Diego, & Hernandez-Reif, 2010).

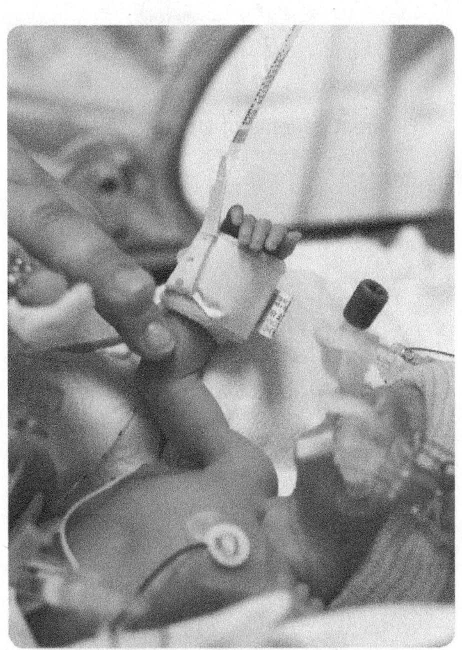

Contact comfort has even been used as a form of therapy for preterm infants.

Since the simple "feeding only" view of attachment was disproved by Harlow, some researchers began to investigate alternative explanations for attachment. One researcher named John Bowlby was impressed with Harlow's discoveries and how contact comfort appeared to be an unlearned basis for the development of attachment (Bowlby, 1982). This led Bowlby to propose a biological system for the development of attachment. Bowlby focused on two general patterns of behavior: signaling behaviors and approach behaviors. *Signaling behaviors* are actions that the infant can take to bring the caregiver closer to the infant, such as smiling, cooing, and crying. *Approach behaviors* are actions that the infant can take to bring the infant closer to the caregiver, such as clinging or reaching towards the caregiver. Bowlby believed that such behaviors were genetically inherited and these biologically driven actions created strong emotional bonds. He further argued that adults are biologically programmed to react favorably to the signaling and approach behaviors of infants. After all, there would be no survival value if adults did not react to crying in a protective manner or if adults pushed away clingy infants. Bowlby believed that survival required reciprocal bonding behaviors.

These signaling and approach behaviors begin to develop new functions over time beyond their original biological functions. For example, an infant that originally cried for purely biological reasons (hunger) may eventually learn to cry for other reasons (to get a favorite toy). Crying becomes a more complex emotional response with each subsequent experience. Bowlby also proposed that the outcomes from these behaviors results in the creation of an internal representation of how the world works. In other words, these early experiences create a template for a subsequent understanding of what to expect from the social world. For example, an infant whose caregiver

Our basic biological reflexes evolve into something more complex over time.

Different patterns of attachment can emerge between caregivers and their children.

does not reliably respond to his or her signaling behaviors may eventually become a child or adult who views the world in general as unreliable. Even though attachment may be biological in origin, its manifestation can vary greatly due to each individual's unique experience.

Bowlby's views guided much of the subsequent research on attachment, including the work of Mary Ainsworth (Ainsworth & Bowlby, 1991; Bowlby, 1988). She is best known for developing the *Strange Situation* test to measure caregiver-child attachment patterns and demonstrating the variety of attachment patterns. The Strange Situation involved a series of trials through which the child (typically at about 1 year of age) witnessed the primary caregiver and a stranger both entering and exiting an observation room. As such, the child was sometimes left alone, sometimes left with just the stranger, sometimes left with just the caregiver, and sometimes left with both the stranger and caregiver. Whether the child responds with comfort or distress to these various circumstances is the basis for assessing the particular type of attachment between that caregiver and child.

Ainsworth originally classified attachment into one of three styles: secure, avoidant, and resistant (a fourth style was added later). Most of the children she tested fell into the *secure* style, in which the child treats the caregiver as a safe base from which he or she can explore the world. These children will explore and interact with strangers when the caregiver is present. These children also display separation anxiety when the caregiver leaves but quickly calm down and appear reassured when their caregiver returns. Although the child may leave the caregiver's immediate presence, he or she will often check back to make sure that the caregiver is still available. Not only are securely attached children more emotionally stable, they also tend to perform better on tasks related to competence and confidence.

Avoidant attachment is an insecure style in which the child appears indifferent to the presence or absence of the caregiver. If the child does explore, he or she will do so without checking back with the caregiver. In contrast, the *resistant* attachment style characterizes a pattern in which the child appears frequently distressed, even when the caregiver is present. These children are less likely to explore and may excessively cling to the caregiver. Such children display even greater distress when the caregiver departs, but unlike the secure style, these children will remain highly distressed upon the caregiver's return and require an extended period of time to calm down.

Later researchers added a fourth category to Ainsworth's classification called *disorganized* attachment. With this style of attachment, children show a mixed pattern of behavior and may even appear confused about whether they should approach or avoid the caregiver. For example, they may approach the caregiver while looking in a different direction. Overall, there is not a standard behavior pattern for children in the disorganized classification, unlike the previous three classification styles.

Attachment can be influenced by a number of factors. Research has shown that different attachment styles can be shaped by operant conditioning (Gewirtz & Peláez-Nogueras, 1987). For example, it is likely that infant behavior can be shaped, maintained, reinforced, or punished due to patterns of caregiver response. Think back to the example given earlier in this chapter where an infant cries and the mother quickly returns. In this scenario involving caregiver response, the behavior of both the infant and mother are reinforced. With other caregiver-child pairs, alternative patterns of response may occur such as when an infant cries but the mother does not return or returns only intermittently. It is possible that we are observing the outcomes of such historical patterns of interaction when we assess child behavior during the Strange Situation. The quality of the general environment has also been found to be related to attachment, with severe early deprivation being associated with insecure forms of attachment (Colvert et al., 2008). Parenting skills have also been found to be predictive of attachment outcomes in that caregiver neglect and depression is associated with the development of insecure attachment (Tomlinson, Cooper, & Murray, 2005).

Infant Temperaments

temperament
the characteristic pattern of behavior that appears early in infant development

Attachment can also be influenced by the child's temperament. **Temperament** refers to the infant's typical pattern of responsiveness and the degree of emotional expressiveness

Although quite young, infants already seem to have their own style and personality.

(Thomas & Chess, 1977). Many new parents are quick to discover their baby already has a unique style of interaction. Some are fussy and cry frequently whereas others are calm and adaptable. Babies with temperaments that are difficult to deal with are also babies whose behavior may inhibit the attachment process. Although many theorists have thought of temperaments as purely genetic in origin, there is evidence that temperaments can be influenced by both prenatal and postnatal environmental factors (Davis et al., 2007; Morris et al., 2002; Susman, Schmeelk, Ponirakis, & Gariepy, 2001). There are three basic classifications of infant temperament: easy, difficult, and slow-to-warm-up.

Babies classified as having *easy* temperaments have positive moods and adapt well to new situations. Reactions to new experiences tend to involve emotions that are of low to moderate intensity. In contrast, babies with *difficult* temperaments have negative moods and adapt poorly to new situations. Their reactions to uncomfortable situations tend to be very intense and they often avoid new experiences. *Slow-to-warm-up* temperaments are somewhat in between these two reactions. Slow-to-warm-up temperaments react poorly to change, but these reactions tend to be of a low intensity. Many babies (approximately 35%) display temperaments that are too inconsistent to be placed into one of these three categories.

Parenting Styles

The social and emotional development of children is strongly influenced by their caregivers and others in their home environment. One clear source of influence is the parenting style used with children. Diana Baumrind (1991; 1993) classified parenting styles according to one of four types: authoritative, authoritarian, permissive, and neglectful.

Authoritative parenting is characterized by a high degree of interpersonal warmth and control. Parents using this style often set high and clear expectations for their children, but tend to be forgiving if these expectations are not met. Although these parents may be forgiving, there are rules regarding proper conduct and there are clear and immediate consequences for breaking the rules. Consequences that are administered by these parents are typically nonphysical and these parents also tend to talk to their children more about the nature of their behavior and the rationale for the punishment. These parents tend to be both responsive and demanding. This parenting style tends to produce well-adjusted children who know what is expected of them thanks to clear rules and consequences. These children are likely to go on to become well-liked by others and high in self-determination.

Different parenting strategies have been shown to produce different emotional and social outcomes for later in life.

Authoritarian parenting is characterized by a low degree of interpersonal warmth, but a high degree of control. These parents issue many commands and demands and have clear rules regarding proper conduct. They have high expectations for their children and often rely heavily on punishment when children fail to meet their demands. The type of consequence administered is often physical in nature (spanking, etc.). They tend to be unresponsive to the needs of their children and show little love or support. In fact, this parent may interact with their child very little other than to issue a command or provide a consequence. This is not to say that this parent doesn't feel affection for their child, only that it is not evident by their behavior. Children raised by this parenting style often have difficulty with their emotions and are less skilled in social interactions. They tend to be fearful and unfriendly.

Permissive parenting involves a high degree of interpersonal warmth, but a low degree of control. These parents are very accepting of their children and responsive to their needs, but place little to no demands upon them. They could be considered very lenient or accommodating. The consequence for the child's misbehavior is typically nonexistent or ineffective (attempts to reason or negotiate). When this type of parent does attempt to provide consequences, it is usually after the child's behavior has gotten "out of control." In other words, the child has a long history of engaging in some problematic behavior that has gone unpunished. Attempts to intervene successfully at this point are unlikely if the parent has no history of acting with authority or intentionally arranging for consequences to be delivered. The relationship that these parents have with their child often resembles the relationships that they have with their fellow adults. It is common for children raised in this style to have difficulty with impulse control and emotional regulation. They tend to be aggressive when things don't go their way and may have difficulty maintaining friendships as a result.

Finally, *neglectful* parenting involves both low interpersonal warmth and low control. These parents utilize an uninvolved and detached approach to their children and therefore are neither responsive nor demanding. They appear to be uncaring and uninvolved. The children often grow up to be demanding of others and have difficulty complying with rules.

Socioemotional Development Over the Lifetime

Erik Erikson believed that life was a series of social conflicts that ultimately determine who we become.

Unlike the previous theorists on social and emotional development, Erik Erikson (1968) believed that this developmental process continued well beyond infancy and childhood. Furthermore, he emphasized relationships both within and outside of child-caregiver interactions. Erikson proposed eight psychosocial developmental stages that begin with infancy and continue until the elderly years. At each of these stages, the individual faces a **psychosocial crisis** that provides an opportunity for possible growth or obstruction. Erikson believed that failure to resolve these conflicts in a satisfactory manner will have a negative impact on the person's social development for the rest of his or her life span. According to Erikson, it is during the first four childhood stages that most of the future adult personality is formed. The conflicts of his eight stages are detailed below:

psychosocial crisis
a developmental conflict involving the relationship between an individual and the social environment

- Trust vs. mistrust (0–1 years): Infants will learn that they can depend on others or that the social world is unfriendly and unreliable. Similar to Bowlby's theories, this is one of Erikson's most fundamental stages because it creates a basic template for all future social interactions. Both Bowlby and Erikson were psychoanalysts (Erikson was trained by Sigmund Freud's daughter; he never obtained a formal academic degree) and psychoanalytic theory places a strong emphasis on how adult personality and functioning are cemented by childhood experience.
- Autonomy vs. shame (1–3 years): As children begin walking and talking, they are given newfound access to their surroundings. During this stage children

will learn to either feel confident or doubtful due to their newfound sources of autonomy. This outcome depends in large part on whether or not caregivers support or mock these attempts at exploration.

- Initiative vs. guilt (3–6 years): Children begin to develop a sense of planning or avoidance of responsibility. The child will either feel confident or ashamed about choices such as dressing oneself. Once again, caregivers play a role in this outcome depending on whether they encourage or dismiss the emerging independence.
- Industry vs. inferiority (6–11 years): The regular academic tasks being demanded of children in this age range will result in a self-concept where they see themselves as intellectual successes or failures. The formal schooling education will provide a basis for the person to compare his or her intellectual achievements against the achievements of peers.
- Identity vs. role confusion (12–18 years): Identity crises emerge as teenagers struggle to gain a personal sense of identity and what they hope to gain from life. For Erikson, it was critical that individuals select their own identities. If pushed too hard to select an identity by either parents or peers, the person will have a lasting sense of role confusion.
- Intimacy vs. isolation (18–40 years): As one enters early adulthood, the individual attempts to establish friendships and intimate relationships of lasting value.
- Generativity vs. stagnation (40–64 years): As part of middle adulthood, the individual must learn to contribute something of lasting value to the next generation (e.g., raising children, crafting sources of inspiration, etc.) or to be content with complacency.
- Integrity vs. despair (65+ years): During the last adulthood stage, the person learns a sense of satisfaction or regret over the decisions in previous stages.

Cognitive Development

Although John Bowlby and Erik Erikson were strongly influential in regard to socioemotional development, the person most associated with the study of cognitive development is Jean Piaget. Similar to Bowlby and Erikson, Piaget thought that the external world was also reflected through internal representations that are altered as one interacts with the world. Piaget believed that mental knowledge consisted of cognitive **schemas**, which are mental structures that integrate incoming information into meaningful networks. For example, a child may have a schema for a ball and this mental representation informs the child's expectations. If the child hears "look at that ball," he or she may begin looking for something small and bouncy that is made for throwing. Schemas can also be developed for certain strategies to interact with the world. For example, once you have developed a schema or plan of action for one interaction, such as purchasing an item online (i.e., click the item, put it into an online cart, checkout to purchase and enter shipping information), now you are better prepared for subsequent interactions (i.e., you know what to expect when going to a new online store for the first time).

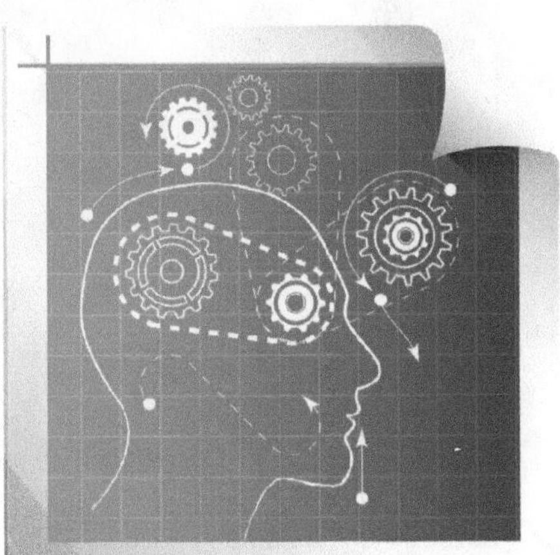
Jean Piaget believed we developed mental representations of the world and how it works.

Piaget argued that children naturally wish to maintain a balance between what they understand and what they encounter (Piaget, 1952). When a new encounter does not match what is already represented by the individual's schemas, this sense of balance is disrupted. Piaget proposed that schemas develop and become more elaborate over time through two basic processes to restore balance: assimilation and accommodation. **Assimilation** involves the incorporation of new experiences into one's existing cognitive schemas. The child's schema of "ball" may have been originally based upon rubber balls, but it becomes more elaborate when a tennis ball is discovered for the first time. Now the child may learn that while all balls can be thrown, some of them are red and rubbery while others are yellow

schema
mental representations that organize knowledge and provide a framework for thinking about the world

assimilation
the process of absorbing new experience into existing schemas

Piaget also believed that new information often presents a challenge to our previous ways of thinking.

and fuzzy. Eventually the child may come to learn that balls come in a variety of colors and textures. Likewise, the child will assimilate new information regarding their schema for cats when they discover that these creatures come in all sorts of shapes and sizes beyond the characteristics of their family pet.

Accommodation involves both the modification of existing schemas and the creation of new schemas in response to experiences that cannot be incorporated into the existing structures. For example, a child unfamiliar with fruit may encounter an orange for the first time and try to throw it like a ball. The parent stops the child and explains, "No, oranges are not for playing. Oranges are for eating." A child may need to change his or her "ball" schema to exclude "oranges," but accommodation will also result in the creation of a new schema for "oranges" or "fruit" in general. Similarly, the child learns that ferrets and raccoons are not new examples of "kitty," despite some physical similarities to cats and this child must create new categories for these new discoveries. Through regular encounters with new experiences, one's mental network becomes more complex with newly emerging schemas and increased sophistication of prior schemas.

According to Piaget, not only do we undergo this continual process of refining and updating our knowledge, but cognitive development transitions through four basic stages as we get older. These four stages progress due to natural growth combined with the elaboration of one's internal schemas. He argued that our first period of cognitive development is the *sensorimotor stage*, which begins at birth and continues until approximately the age of two. This stage is characterized by very limited cognitive thoughts and an understanding of the world that is restricted to only experiences coming from the direct stimulation of one's sense receptors and personal motor movements. In other words, the child cannot comprehend the world unless it is being directly experienced at that very moment. The lack of object permanence is often used as evidence for this type of thinking in the sensorimotor stage. **Object permanence** refers to the realization that objects and people continue to exist independent of a person perceiving them. A classic illustration of this is to select an object that a child has a strong level of interest in (i.e., the child orients or reaches towards it) and then to hide it from the child's view. An older child who understands object permanence will engage in behaviors to try to locate the missing object. For younger children who lack an understanding of object permanence, they will react as if the object has been wiped away from existence and will engage in no efforts to find the absent object. Piaget considered mastery of object permanence to be the beginning of true thought. The ability to think about objects that are not currently within one's direct perception is likely a fundamental skill in being able to understand symbolism and other complex skills.

Piaget's cognitive stages of development are among psychology's most well-known theories. *(Courtesy of Farrell Grehan/Corbis.)*

Realizing that missing objects still exist is one of the first cognitive achievements of life.

Around age 2, children enter the *preoperational stage* of cognitive development and remain in that stage until about age 7. During this stage of development, children become capable of symbolic thinking. They are able to treat one stimulus as a representation of another stimulus (e.g., pretending that a small block is a car). Although symbolic thinking is clearly an important milestone, most descriptions of the preoperational stage tend to focus on the limitations of children during this time period. One critical limitation is the tendency of children to focus on only a single aspect of a stimulus, to the exclusion of other potentially relevant

accommodation
the process of altering existing schemas and creating new schemas in response to unfamiliar experiences

object permanence
the understanding that objects continue to exist even when they are not being directly perceived

aspects, a phenomenon known as **centration**. For example, a child may become concerned that her friend has more potato chips than she does. To fix this situation, she smashes her chips so that she now has the most chips. Note that the child is concentrating too much on one aspect, the quantity of potato chips, to the point of excluding other relevant aspects such as the size of those chips. The classic illustration involves a demonstration with liquid and two containers, one that is tall and narrow and one that is short and wide. In front of the child, the exact same quantity of liquid is poured into both containers. A preoperational child is likely to believe that the tall container contains more liquid (even if the liquid is poured from one container to the other) because of centration. The child is focusing too much on the salient height of the liquid to the exclusion of other relevant properties.

The understanding of symbolism is another early achievement.

Another limitation is the tendency to engage in **egocentrism**, which is the inability to take another person's perspective. The classic illustration of this is the three mountain task (Piaget & Inhelder, 1969). In this task, a miniature model of three mountains is placed on a table in front of a child. The three mountains in the model all look different from one another (i.e., snow on one, a house on another, a cross on the third). A doll is placed at various points around the table that differ from the child's viewpoint. The child is then asked to select from a series of photographs the picture that presents the point of view of the doll ("what do you think the doll saw?"). A child engaging in egocentric thought will consistently choose a picture representing the child's view of the mountains rather than the doll's view.

Young children also have difficulty seeing the world from another person's perspective.

From approximately age 7 to age 12, Piaget believed children entered the *concrete operations stage* of cognitive development. During this stage several important logical skills emerge, such as reversibility and conservation. **Reversibility** refers to the ability to mentally work backwards and an understanding that a stimulus whose appearance has changed can be returned to its previous appearance (or at least one can imagine it reversing), presuming nothing has been added or taken away. A child who observes toothpaste being put on a toothbrush can imagine the toothpaste being pulled off the brush and back into the tube if he or she grasps reversibility. Regarding the liquid and two containers task mentioned earlier, if liquid was transferred from the short container to the tall container, a child who understood reversibility would also understand that the liquid could return to its original short appearance despite the fact that the liquid currently looks tall. If a stack of coins was knocked into a flat pile, someone who understood reversibility would also understand that those coins can return to their original stacked appearance. If a rope was cut in front of a child, it may not be possible to physically repair it, but a child could still demonstrate reversibility if he or she could mentally imagine the process reversing and the rope becoming whole again.

If the child has mastered **conservation**, he or she will further understand that the liquid and coins have essentially remained the same. That is, despite their new appearance, they can not only return to the previous appearance (i.e., reversibility), but they are currently the same stimulus. There is some fundamental property that is carried across the varying appearances. With conversation the child will realize that the liquid remains the same as it is poured into different containers and that a cut rope is still essentially the same object, despite the fact it is currently two pieces instead of its previous one.

As part of the fourth and final stage, the *formal operations stage* begins around age 12 and continues for the rest of the life span. Capstone skills such as abstract reasoning emerge, which allow individuals to think logically about hypothetical situations and

centration
the tendency to focus on only a single salient aspect of a stimulus to the exclusion of other important aspects

egocentrism
a pattern of thinking characterized by the inability to take other perspectives

reversibility
the mental ability to reverse a series of steps and return a stimulus to its previous state

conservation
the understanding that a stimulus can remain the same despite some changes to its physical appearance

To grasp conservation, children must understand that a shift in appearance does not necessarily change the existence of a stimulus.

The potential for abstract thought is one of Piaget's final developmental milestones.

The impact of culture on learning and cognitive milestones should not be underestimated. *(Bottom image courtesy of Jerry Redfern/Getty Images.)*

to reason about ideas never directly experienced. For example, it becomes possible to think about abstract issues such as philosophy and ideals, despite the fact that they have never experienced these issues in a direct or concrete manner.

Despite the huge influence of Piaget's theories on developmental psychology, there are many shortcomings of his approach. One shortcoming is that Piaget often underestimated the cognitive ability of young children (Flavell, 1992). Furthermore, Piaget's research largely consisted of testing the skills of children and interviewing them about their thinking. While such research may produce detailed descriptions of behavior, the explanation for why these behaviors occur still remains absent. Piaget did not use experimental methodology to discover causal relationships. For example, note that schemas are completely inferred and speculative; at no point did Piaget directly observe a schema through experimental observations. Finally, his theories neglected the role of culture and education in cognitive development, a criticism echoed by the next researcher to be discussed.

Cultural Influences on Cognitive Development

Lev Vygotsky was a developmental psychologist who, much like Piaget, studied the cognitive skills of children. However, Vygotsky believed that Piaget's emphasis on internal structures and natural development was misplaced. Vygotsky suggested instead that social and cultural influences play a strong role in cognitive development and that development cannot be understood without a consideration of these factors. One of Vygotsky's biggest contributions to developmental psychology was to draw attention to the effects of sociocultural factors on learning.

zone of proximal development
a stage of development during which a learner cannot quite perform a task independently but can perform it if given supplemental help

Vygotsky also pointed to the importance of other people for progressing development to a level slightly above one's current readiness. He referred to a zone of proximal development to support this idea. The **zone of proximal development** refers to the tasks that a child cannot accomplish independently, but can still learn to complete with some assistance. In other words, the child either a) lacks fluency with the skills for independent performance and/or b) has some, but not all, of the basic skills needed for independent success. Success at this stage is often achieved with the help of **scaffolding**, which is the social support provided to learners. Scaffolding can take the form of hints, encouragement, or reminders and is intended to aid someone to complete a task within their zone of proximal development. These antecedent aids for performance are gradually faded away until the child is able to reliably perform without the supplemental social support. Imagine a child who is learning to ride a bicycle for the first time. Initially, training wheels, extra prompts, and encouragement from adults are needed, but gradually these can be reduced as the child gains the necessary skills.

Moral Development

In the process of cognitive development, it would not be surprising if learning to reason about issues such as morality was included in this growth. Piaget outlined how cognitive processes might lead to moral guidelines and Vygotsky emphasized how cultural standards detail moral codes for children. However, the developmental psychologist most associated with the development of morality was Lawrence Kohlberg, who examined morality in much greater depth than did either Piaget or Vygotsky. Inspired by Piaget, Kohlberg proposed a series of stages by which development can be classified.

Lawrence Kohlberg was interested in better understanding the types of ethical and moral reasoning that people use and how these develop over time.

Kohlberg outlined three basic levels of moral development, each with two stages (thus six stages in total). The first level of moral reasoning is the *preconventional level*, which contains stages 1 and 2. Within this level, morality is determined by the standards of others in regard to one's own personal welfare. In other words, morality is essentially a code for minimizing discomfort or maximizing comfort. For example, in Stage 1 (obedience), morality consists of complying with other people's requests in order to avoid punishment. The physical consequences of one's actions determine the degree to which those actions are considered good or bad. In Stage 2 (individualism), morality consists of simply acting in accordance with one's self-interests to gain rewards. This may coincide with helping others, but only to the extent that such actions simultaneously satisfy one's personal needs. Any act of altruism comes from the basic notion of "you scratch my back, I'll scratch yours" rather than a sense of loyalty or justice. The preconventional level of moral development is typical of most children's moral reasoning.

During the first level of moral reasoning, morals are primarily determined out of self-interest.

The second level of moral reasoning is the *conventional level*, which contains Stages 3 and 4 and involves an internalization of the standards of others, regardless of one's personal welfare. Morality revolves around maintaining the social bonds with other people and fulfilling one's social duty. In Stage 3 (interpersonal relationships), morality is determined by getting along with those people in your immediate social group. Conformity to the expectations of others and maintenance of those standards is emphasized. In Stage 4 (social order), morality is essentially the same as the rules of society and therefore the social group has now been extended to include all of society, not just one's immediate set of contacts. Legal justice and maintaining order for the good of society are emphasized during this stage. The conventional level usually does not emerge until the teenage years or later, if at all.

The third level of moral reasoning is the *postconventional level*, which Kohlberg considered the highest level of moral development. In this level, morality consists of recognizing that some morals may conflict with personal and societal standards. In Stage 5 (individual rights), morality includes a recognition that laws are important, but those laws may need to be changed in order to respect the values and beliefs of other people. Rules

scaffolding
supplemental support that is provided to a learner and then gradually removed as independence emerges

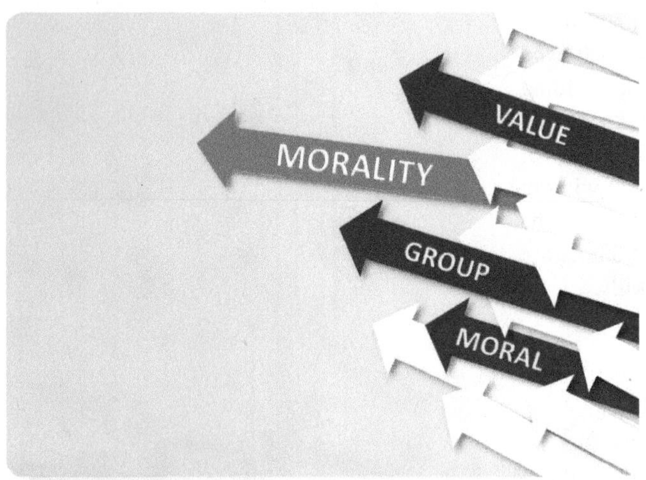

By the final stage of moral reasoning, morals may emerge that transcend self-interest and the rules of society.

are important, but society should agree with these rules rather than blindly follow them. In other words, the social group at both the interpersonal and societal level may conflict with morality, rather than define morality. According to the reasoning of stage 5, one must both follow the law and work to change the law when it fails to protect the greater moral standards. In Stage 6 (universal principles), moral reasoning is based on the premise that there are universal principles of morality that transcend the self, society, and established standards. In this stage, one must follow moral principles even if they violate legal regulations. Kohlberg believed that it was uncommon for people to reach the postconventional level of moral development and that stage 6 reasoning was particularly rare.

Kohlberg classified the development of morality by proposing hypothetical scenarios and asking the person to judge the appropriate moral response. The reasoning that people used to reach their conclusions was more important than the final conclusions themselves. For example, Kohlberg posed a scenario called "Heinz Steals the Drug," which is as follows:

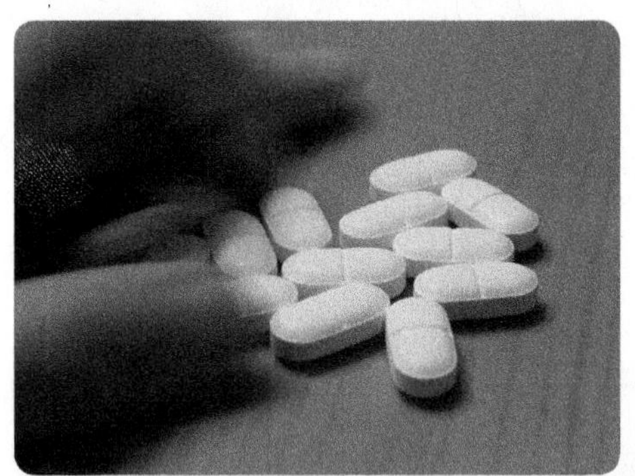
What reasoning would you use in deciding whether or not the drug should have been stolen?

> "In Europe, a woman was near death from a special kind of cancer. There was one drug that the doctors thought might save her. It was a form of radium that a druggist in the same town had recently discovered. The drug was expensive to make, but the druggist was charging ten times what the drug cost him to make. He paid $200 for the radium and charged $2,000 for a small dose of the drug.
>
> The sick woman's husband, Heinz, went to everyone he knew to borrow the money, but he could only get together about $ 1,000 which is half of what it cost. He told the druggist that his wife was dying and asked him to sell it cheaper or let him pay later. But the druggist said: 'No, I discovered the drug and I'm going to make money from it.' So Heinz got desperate and broke into the man's store to steal the drug for his wife. Should the husband have done that?" (Kohlberg, 1963)

The level of morality was not classified based on whether or not the people agreed or disagreed with the husband's decision, but rather the reasons they gave for their agreement or disagreement. For example, if the person said Heinz *should* steal the drug because he would be more miserable with the death of his wife than the misery that might come from going to prison, this response would indicate preconventional morality. However, if the person said Heinz *should not* steal the drug because he might be put in prison and prison is a terrible place to live, this response would also indicate preconventional morality. Note that the reasoning for both decisions, regardless of whether it was an agreement or disagreement, was based on the idea of minimizing personal discomfort.

Similarly, if someone said that Heinz *should* steal the drug because people have the right to choose life over profits, then this would indicate postconventional morality. If the person said that Heinz *should not* steal the drug because other sick people might also need that drug and their lives have as much value as his wife's life, then this would also indicate postconventional morality. With both decisions, the reasoning involved a notion that there are standards more important than self or society.

Although Kohlberg's theory of moral development has been influential, some caution is important when interpreting his theory. One consideration is the fact that Kohlberg's method of assessing morality was based on verbal behavior regarding morality, rather than moral behavior itself. That is, what people say about hypothetical situations may not reflect how they would actually behave if put in those situations firsthand. The progression of individual morality to Kohlberg's later stages may also have less to do with a change in one's moral outlook and more to do with the fact that people become more verbally sophisticated over time (Sanders, Lubinski, & Benbow, 1995). For example, a young adult's moral motivation may have never progressed beyond the avoidance of punishment, but his or her reasoning is now elaborately described in terms of promoting social good. Younger children may simply have difficulty in verbalizing such lofty ideals due to the current limits in their language skills. Furthermore, these descriptions of moral behavior do not tell us much about how moral behavior is created or maintained.

Development During Adolescence and Young Adulthood

With a few exceptions, it is worth noting that most theories of development focus strongly on childhood and may even ignore any post-childhood development. The idea that there may be a stage between childhood and adulthood did not even exist until the early 1900s when the concept of adolescence was introduced. However, it has since become recognized that many great changes continue after the beginning of puberty. **Puberty** refers to the rapid change in physical development that culminates in sexual maturity. It also marks the beginning of adolescence and a time period of many psychological developments.

Development continues past childhood into adolescence and adulthood.

Despite the prevalence of stereotypes regarding rebellious teenagers and their bewildered parents, most parents maintain a healthy relationship with their teenagers (Steinberg & Morris, 2001). However, a stable relationship with parents does not change the fact that many teenagers still feel the need to establish an identity independent of their parents. Some have gone as far as to say that during this time period peers exert more influence on development than do parents (Harris, 1995), although this conclusion remains in dispute (Galambos, Barker, & Almeida, 2003). Regardless of whether or not it is valid, this claim is not quite the same as stating that the parents are irrelevant. Recall that different outcomes in emotional and social wellbeing are associated with different parenting styles. Even if peers did exert a stronger influence during teenage years, the previous parenting still helped to create the current adolescent and how he or she socializes with others (Degner & Dalege, 2013).

Although physical development has reached full maturity by age 18 and many of the traditional theories imply that the developmental process is complete by adulthood, it is common for young adults to report that they feel as though their early 20s is a period of great change and adjustment. This developmental pattern is significant enough that this time period has been labeled emerging adulthood (Arnett, 2004). **Emerging adulthood** is the stage during ages 18 to 25 in which people often feel like they have matured past their childhood and teenage years, but still do not feel like they are fully committed to an adult's roles and responsibilities. Life choices and future aspirations are still undergoing frequent change as people find themselves sampling different aspects of the world, such as trying out new disciplines to major in, beliefs, orientations, politics, and perspectives. It is also a period of considerable overlap, where young adults may feel the independence of working or going to college full-time, but also feel the dependence on parents who still help with some bills. They may also feel capable of making a large number of decisions independently, but still turn to their parents for advice with unfamiliar situations.

Many people in college feel like they are in the emerging adulthood stage as they struggle to adjust to their new role as a young adult.

Development During Middle and Late Adulthood

Although middle adulthood is not characterized by as many dramatic and frequent changes as the stages within childhood and adolescence, change still continues. However, some of the most well-known changes in adulthood may have little basis in reality. For example, two troubling periods of adulthood are referred to as the midlife crisis and empty nest syndrome. A *midlife crisis* refers to the popular notion that as adults reach the midpoint of their lives, they experience great regret due to the missed opportunities of their youth. However, research shows that the majority of adults do not experience a midlife crisis (Wethington, 2000). Similarly, *empty nest syndrome*, the phenomenon where parents

puberty
rapid changes in physical development that culminate in sexual maturity

emerging adulthood
transitional period during which young adults gradually take on roles and responsibilities characteristic of full adulthood

Some of the supposed stages of adulthood are less common than popularly assumed.

Unfortunately, some developmental changes involve the loss of skills as we get older.

experience depression upon their children growing up and departing home, seems to be more of the exception rather than the rule. Research suggests that the departure of children typically has positive effects on the well-being of parents and opens new opportunities (Bouchard, 2014). As such, the adult challenges of midlife crisis and empty nest syndrome appear to be more myth than reality.

Due to advances in medicine and improvements in living conditions, the average lifespan of human beings continues to increase. As such, the number of elderly people has also increased, which has brought with it a growing concern for the difficulties associated with advanced aging. For example, many elders suffer from **dementia**, which is the loss of cognitive abilities related to memory, language, and attention. This decline in skills can be quite disturbing to the impaired individuals and may produce other behavioral problems such as verbal outbursts, frequent repetition of demands, agitation, and physical aggression. It has been reported that such behavioral problems can account for nearly half of resident behaviors in nursing homes (Burgio et al., 2002). Unfortunately, the use of restraints has been a common staff reaction to these nursing home problems (Baker, Hanley, & Mathews, 2006), particularly the use of chemical restraints (i.e., drugging residents into compliance).

Psychological treatments based on conditioning theory have been proposed as an alternative to physical and chemical restraints and has been successfully used to promote independent living while reducing dysfunction in elderly individuals (Buchanan, Christenson, Houlihan, & Ostrom, 2011). Dementia cannot be cured at the present time and developing new behaviors is quite difficult, but much progress can be made in retaining current skills and minimizing further loss. One such treatment involves the use of external memory aids such as memory wallets. A memory wallet is a book of pages containing pictures and photographs that are meaningful to the person (such as a picture of the person's pet, childhood house, former workplace, preferred hobby, etc.) and prompt the person to begin speaking about the picture. These memory wallets greatly increase the individual's ability to recall information and spontaneously

dementia
a brain disease involving the decline of cognitive abilities related to memory, language, and attention

hold conversations. Recall can also be improved through spaced retrieval. *Spaced retrieval* uses shaping to gradually increase the delay between information and the successful recall of that information (e.g., the person is asked to remember after 5 seconds, then after 10 seconds, then after 30 seconds, etc.).

Using behavior management with nursing staff can have a huge impact on elderly behavior. Many staff members are in a hurry and will simply do things for residents to save time. Unfortunately, this also reduces the independent skills of residents, which is concerning because loss of independence often leads to shortened lifespans in the elderly. Staff may also engage in "elderspeak" by talking down to these older adults as if they were children (e.g., "sweetie, eat your breakfast," "honey, don't worry your little head," etc.), which can be frustrating for these individuals who are still fully aware that they are adults (Buchanan, Christenson, Houlihan, & Ostrom, 2011). Behavior analysts have successfully used staff training to eliminate these inappropriate interactions and replace them with more appropriate therapeutic skills. Research has shown that staff training can improve memory, decrease aggression, and promote independence of nursing home residents without requiring additional staff time or changes in medication (Baker, Hanley, & Mathews, 2006; Dixon, Baker, & Sadowski, 2011).

Behavioral treatments have been successful in improving the conditions of old age.

The Stages of Death and Dying

Of course, all things must come to an end. To better understand how people react to the news of an impending death, Elisabeth Kübler-Ross (1969) interviewed approximately 200 people diagnosed with a terminal illness. Like many of the theories within developmental psychology, she outlined a series of stages that people progress through. The first stage is *denial*, in which people are in shock and may even conclude that the diagnosis must be wrong. The second stage is *anger* due to resentment of others who remain healthy or young. The third stage is *bargaining*, in which the person tries to negotiate a longer life in exchange for good behavior. The fourth stage is *depression*, during which people struggle with and despair over the inescapable end. The fifth and final stage is *acceptance*, in which people contemplate the meaning of life without fear.

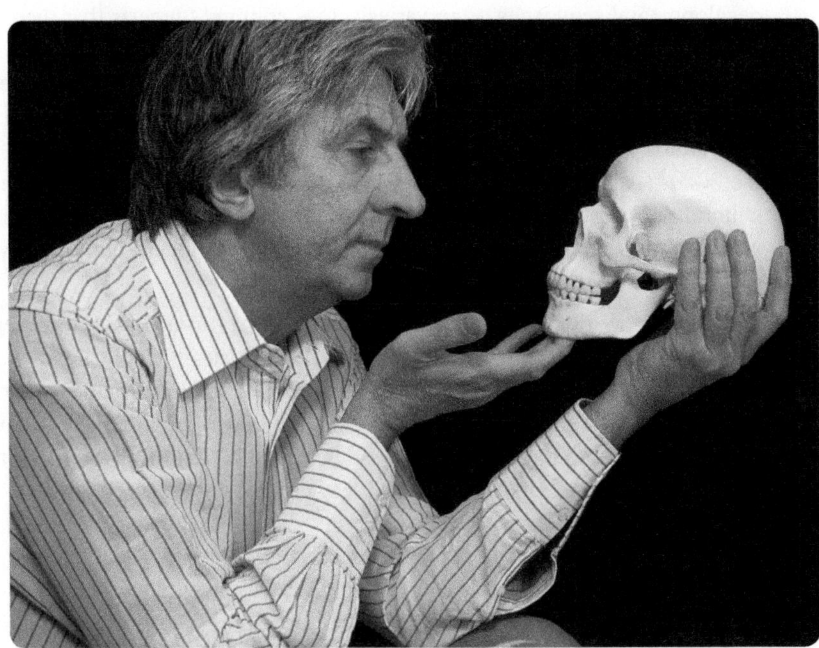

Elisabeth Kübler-Ross proposed a set of stages we go through as we cope with the news of death.

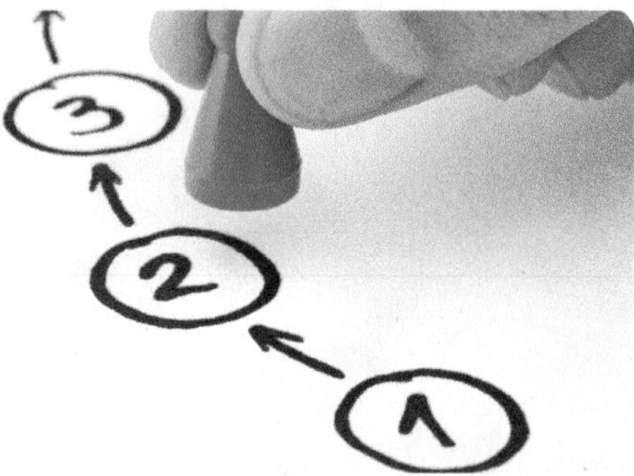

Critical thinking is important when evaluating all theories, including popular stage-based theories.

Critical Considerations with Stage-Based Theories

As you may have noticed throughout this chapter, most of the theories of developmental psychology fit an "ages-and-stages" approach, in which certain characteristic behaviors are expected by particular chronological ages. As we watch people rapidly progress through the same series of steps, it is easy to assume an inherent developmental sequence. However, some problems and cautions are warranted with taking an ages-and-stages approach.

1. Despite the richness of detail and ingenuity shown in many of the stage-based theories, most of them still remain at the descriptive level. While description is important and one of the basic goals of psychology, it paints an incomplete picture by itself. To fully explain behavior, we should understand not only its *form* (i.e., what it looks like), but also its *function* (i.e., why it occurs). Unfortunately, most stage theories of development neglect the function of behavior. Knowing that most children operate at the preconventional level of morality does not explain why children reason in this manner. Discovering that egocentrism is a common thought pattern between age 2 and 7 does not explain why egocentrism occurs or why it eventually disappears. Furthermore, although there may be common standards by which people progress, staged-oriented approaches can sometimes lead people to forget that there remains considerable variability among individuals.
2. Many stage-based theories imply or outright endorse a purely maturational approach (i.e., biologically determined progression) to development, which may cause us to overlook important cultural and learning factors. Abstract reasoning often emerges around age 12 and some have interpreted this to mean that we are biologically hardwired to reason abstractly at this age (much like puberty emerges due to biological factors). However, this interpretation ignores the fact that 12-old-years are also exposed to similar educational experiences around this age and may have been taught similar past lessons at this point in their lives (i.e., experience with basic skills may open the possibility for the emergence of more complex skills). The fact that the timing of developmental sequences often varies across cultures suggests that there may be a strong learning component to development (Hopkins & Westra, 1989; Pumariega & Joshi, 2010). Likewise, the fact that developmental sequences change across time periods also suggests that there is more to development than biology alone. For example, emerging adulthood wasn't proposed until the 2000s (Arnett, 2000) and many of Erikson's theories seem to reflect the cultural values of the 1950s and 1960s (e.g., the notion that relationships are solidified between ages 18 and 40 does not reflect a modern culture in which dating later in life has become more common).
3. Most stage theories focus exclusively on the behavior and therefore neglect the sociocultural and learning contexts that may cause or contribute to such behavior. Again, being able to predict what people are likely to do at a particular age is not the same as understanding why people engage in those behaviors at that age. Note that many of the theories presented in this chapter described the behaviors of infants and children, but omitted how caregivers and other relevant people may have prompted or reinforced those behaviors. Simply stating that infants cry when separated from caregivers ignores what the caregiver may have been doing before and after the crying event. It also ignores the standards that particular culture may have regarding infant crying. As other

Development should not be seen as separate from the lessons we learn from the surrounding world.

chapters have noted, these contextual variables can exert a strong influence on the probability of behavior. Part of the problem may be that many theorists mistakenly treat age as a causal variable (Gewirtz & Peláez-Nogueras, 1992; Schlinger, 1992). When this happens, many people stop searching for the true causal variables. As noted earlier, behavior is caused by changes in bodily and environmental stimuli, not the simple passage of time alone.

Disentangling Nature vs. Nurture Once Again

It is important to remember that development involves an interaction between nature and nurture. From a slightly different perspective, it may be reasonable to state that development is a reciprocal process between our personal selves and our experiences. The developing person may seek out certain experiences, but those experiences also change the developing person (i.e., we select the environment while the environment also selects us). Furthermore, it is important to note that physical, emotional, social, cognitive, and moral development are not always separate processes and these forms of development frequently overlap and interact with one another. For example, our physical development may influence how others treat us (people react differently to different appearances), which in turn may influence our social development. Social factors also play a role in cognitive development and moral reasoning may depend upon the development of certain cognitive skills.

Although psychological theories often present development as separate processes, in practice human development is a series of overlapping and interactive growth.

13

Health, Stress, and Coping*

*Taken from *Psychological Science*, Second Edition by Mark Krause and Daniel Corts

Behavior and Health

Should body weight be a basis for how much tax people pay? Some politicians, hospital administrators, and other members of society advocate a "fat tax"—taxing individuals for any excess weight, or for nonessential food items that contribute to being overweight. Sugary soft drinks contribute hundreds of calories to our daily diet without providing any nutrition, and do little to leave a person feeling full and satisfied. So, like cigarettes, should additional taxes be attached to these products for the same reasons that cigarettes are so heavily taxed? Some healthcare providers are pursuing such a plan. State employees in Alabama who were obese had once been directed to lose weight by year's end or face increased monthly health insurance costs. On one hand, this may sound like blatant discrimination and focusing on just one of many economic burdens associated with obesity. On the otherhand, there is a parallel precedent for fat tax plans—namely, the massive taxes on cigarettes that serve to discourage smoking and help cover the costs of treating smoking-related illnesses. In this section, we examine different factors that affect our mental and physical well-being, and also consider the extent to which physical health is based on psychological processes such as choosing and deciding.

To what degree do you believe your behavior affects your health? Each day we make choices that shape our physical and mental health. We decide what to eat and what to avoid eating, whether to exercise or be inactive. The choices people make about their career paths similarly influence health. Workplace stress levels for air traffic controllers are quite different from those experienced by librarians. The numerous and complex connections between behavior and health certainly have created an important niche for *health psychologists*, who study both positive and negative impacts that our behavior and decisions have on health, survival, and well-being.

The need for health psychologists has increased considerably over the 20th century, as most premature deaths today are attributable to lifestyle factors (see Table 13.1). A century ago, people in the United States were likely to die from influenza, pneumonia, tuberculosis, measles, and other contagious diseases. Advances in medicine have served to keep these conditions under much better control. Instead, people are now much more likely to die from tobacco use, alcohol use, obesity, and inactivity. In fact, the Center for Disease Control (CDC) estimates that the top five causes of death in the United States each year (accounting for about two-thirds of all deaths—around 900,000) are from diseases or accidents related to behavior. Further, estimates indicate that lifestyle changes could have prevented 20% to 40% of those (CDC, 2014; Yoon et al., 2014).

Smoking

Smoking cigarettes causes life-shortening health problems including lung, mouth, and throat cancer; heart disease; and pulmonary diseases such as emphysema. The life expectancy of the average smoker is at least 10 years shorter than that of a nonsmoker. The costs in lives and money attributable to smoking are massive, as shown in Table 13.2. Despite the starkly ominous figures, an estimated 22% (69 million) of US adults smoke cigarettes (USDHHS, 2014).

Obesity

You have likely heard of the "freshman 15"—the supposed number of pounds traditional-aged college students can expect to gain during their first year of school. This is often attributed to increased food intake, decreased physical activity, and, for many

Table 13.1 Estimated Annual Deaths in the United States Due to Behavior-Related Risk Factors
This table presents the estimated number of deaths annually in the United States due to specific behavior-related risk factors such as diet, exercise, and tobacco and alcohol use. To put this in context, there are between 2.4 million and 2.5 million deaths in the United States each year (CDC, 2009a; USDHHS, 2014). The 330,800 male deaths related to tobacco use represent over 13% of all deaths in the United States each year.

Risk Factor	Male	Female	Total
Tobacco use[1]	330,800	225,000	555,800
High blood pressure	164,000	231,000	395,000
Overweight and obesity	114,000	102,000	216,000
High blood sugar	102,000	89,000	190,000
High LDL cholesterol	60,000	53,000	113,000
Alcohol use	45,000	20,000	64,000

Source: Based on Danaei, G., Ding, E. L., Mozafarian, D., Taylor B, & Rehm J. (2009). The preventable causes of death in the United States: Comparative risk assessment of dietary, lifestyle, and metabolic risk factors. PLoS Med, 6(4), e1000058. doi: 10.1371/journal. pmed.1000058

[1]USDHHS, 2014

students, increased levels of alcohol consumption. In reality, the 15-pound estimate is actually inflated, but there is an element of truth to the saying: Those male and female students who gain weight during their early college career put on an average of 6 pounds (Gropper et al., 2009).

Six pounds is not a lot of weight—but habits formed during any period of time, freshman year or otherwise, can be difficult to break. If the habits persist, the student will almost certainly be overweight (if not obese) by graduation. Obesity is defined by **body mass index (BMI)**, *a statistic commonly used for estimating a healthy body weight that factors in an individual's height:* Overweight is a BMI over 25 and obese is a BMI of 30 or more. Obesity is associated with numerous detrimental health consequences, such as cardiovascular disease, diabetes, osteoarthritis (degeneration of bone and cartilage material), and some forms of cancer. Weight is gained because of a positive energy balance, meaning that too many calories come in and not enough are expended. Obviously, overeating can lead to obesity. But why might a 6-foot-tall male weigh 170 pounds while enjoying massive amounts of food and a relatively inactive lifestyle, while another person of similar height and lifestyle weighs in at 200 pounds? Several factors explain this phenomenon, including biological and social variables.

Table 13.2 Health Costs of Tobacco Use

- Tobacco use causes an estimated 5 million deaths worldwide each year.
- Cigarette smoking is the leading preventable cause of death in the United States.
- One in five US deaths is due to cigarette smoking.
- Smoking does not just harm adults—and estimated 1,000 infants die in the United States annually due to smoking-related prenatal conditions and sudden infant death syndrome.
- Cigarette smoking is costly: The United States loses an estimated $150 billion in lost work productivity and $132 billion in adults healthcare expenses each year.

Source: Based on Centers for Disease Control and Prevention (CDC). (2009b). Retrieved June 20, 2011, from http://www.cdc.gov/tobacco/data_statistics/fact_sheets/fast_facts/index.htm; USDHHS, 2014

Working the Scientific Literacy Model

Media Exposure and Smoking

If smoking is so dangerous, why do people do it? This is a perplexing question not only for psychologists, but also for many smokers. One reason may be the exposure young people have to other people who smoke: parents, friends, and even characters on television and in the movies.

What do we know about media influences on smoking?

Many different factors influence whether someone becomes a smoker, including family and local culture, personality characteristics, and socioeconomic status. Thus, people may smoke because they associate it with valued traits or societal roles, such as attractiveness, rebelliousness, and individualism. Each day, approximately 2,000 adolescents in the United States try their first cigarette, and many become full-time smokers (Heatherton & Sargent, 2009). An important question that health psychologists grapple with concerns the societal factors that lead young people to smoke. Here we will focus on a single influence: exposure to smoking in movies and entertainment. Although smoking in films has declined over the past couple of decades, there are still numerous widely popular movies in which characters smoke (Sargent & Heatherton, 2009).

How can science help us analyze the effects of smoking in movies?

To what extent does smoking in movies contribute to adolescent smoking? To find out, researchers conducted a random-digit-dialing survey of 6,522 US adolescents from all major geographic regions and socioeconomic groups. The adolescents reported their age and indicated whether they smoked, and identified whether they had seen specific popular movies that featured smoking. The more exposure the adolescents had to movies that featured smoking, the more likely they were to have tried it (see Figure 13.1). This relationship persisted even after the researchers controlled for socioeconomic status, personality, and parental and peer influences on smoking (Heatherton & Sargent, 2009). Although this study showed a clear correlation linking smoking in movies and adolescent smoking, it did not explain why this correlation exists.

It appears that how people identify with smokers may influence their decision to smoke. An experimental study showed that adolescents who had positive responses to a protagonist who smoked were much more likely to associate smoking with their own identities. This relationship was observed in both adolescents who already smoked and even those who did not smoke (Dal Cin et al., 2007).

Can we critically evaluate this evidence?

It is hard to establish that watching movie stars smoke cigarettes causes adolescents to smoke, even though the studies reviewed

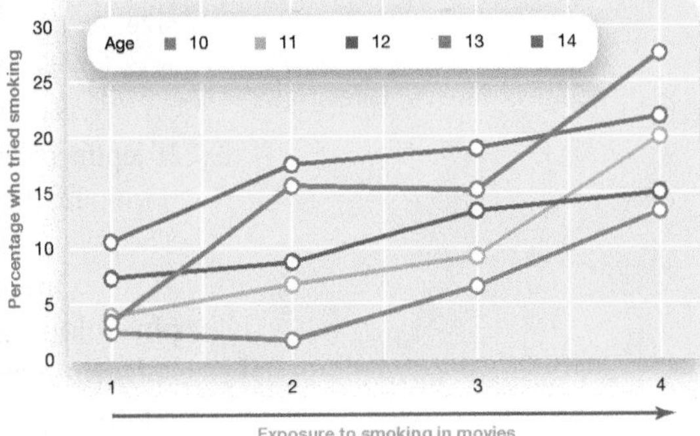

Figure 13.1 Smoking and the Movies
The more 10- to 14-year-olds view smoking in movies, the more likely they are to smoke (Heatherton & Sargent, 2009).

here suggest that it does. When researchers tracked the amount of smoking featured in popular movies from 1990 to 2007, they found that as the incidence of smoking in movies rose, smoking among adolescents increased after a short period of time. Likewise, when smoking in movies decreased, a decline in adolescent smoking followed (Sargent & Heatherton, 2009). However, the problem with these correlations is that multiple explanations could be put forth for why they exist. Perhaps the truth is the other way around: People who are already willing to smoke might be more attracted to movies that feature smoking.

Why is this relevant?

Tobacco-related illness imposes a major societal burden in terms of lost work productivity and rising healthcare costs. As the research shows, cigarette smoking in movies is just one of many influences on smoking behavior. Of course, it may be one influence that could be easier to control than, say, peer pressure. With scientific research in hand, advocacy groups such as Smoke Free Movies and the National Association of Attorneys General have a sound basis for arguing against smoking in movies—especially those that adolescents are likely to watch.

There is some good news related to smoking rates. The prevalence of smoking in the United States declined steadily since the 1990s (CDC, 2010d). State and local laws are reducing the risks posed by secondhand smoke exposure by banning smoking in many public places—especially restaurants and public buildings. As mentioned at the beginning of the section, steep taxes applied to unhealthy products such as tobacco also act as a deterrent against their use. Not only does such a policy tend to reduce the number of smokers (a 10% increase in cigarette price reduces cigarette consumption by an estimated 3% to 5%; USDHSS, 2012), but it also raises funds for healthcare and anti-smoking campaigns. A related issue to consider concerns the rise of e-cigarettes and potential health risks associated with their use (Lerner et al., 2015).

Biological Factors

Twin, family, and adoption studies all suggest that genes account for between 50% and 90% of the variation in body weight (Maes et al., 1997). Genetic factors influence body type, metabolism, and other physiological processes that contribute to body weight and size. At the molecular level, the gene LEP (for "leptin") is associated with obesity. **Leptin** *is a hormone released by fat cells and inhibits hunger by binding to receptors located on organs, tissues, and also the hypothalamus, which is involved in regulating hunger.* If leptin receptors, which are coded by the LEP gene, are not sufficiently sensitive to the hormone, then the individual may fail to recognize that food intake is no longer necessary. The result is overeating and obesity.

One hypothesis about obesity begins with the idea that genes contribute to a physiological **set point**, *a mechanism that maintains body weight around a physiologically programmed level.* The set point is not an exact number of pounds, but rather a relatively small range encompassing 10% to 20% of one's weight. Your initial set point is controlled by genetic mechanisms, but your actual weight can be modified by environmental factors—namely, what and how much you eat. According to set point theory, if someone gains 10% of his body weight (e.g., increasing from 150 to 165 pounds) his set point would make a corresponding shift upward—the body acts as though its normal weight is now 165 pounds. Metabolism slows correspondingly, such that additional energy expenditure is now required to take the weight off. This may explain why people who gain extra weight may shed a few pounds with relative ease, but find it overwhelmingly difficult to continue losing or even maintaining their weight once they reach an initial goal.

In addition to set point, another relevant influence on weight loss is simply individual differences in physical activity. Specifically, people who gain weight expend less energy in their normal day-to-day activities (Weinsier et al., 2002). Thus, the difficulty with losing the weight may be related to lower activity levels. Both changes in set point and reduced activity levels make it increasingly difficult to shed pounds.

Social Factors

Sociocultural influences, including family, peers, and media exposure greatly influence what we eat. Food advertisements trigger eating—after watching a commercial for buttery microwave popcorn, you have probably found yourself rummaging around in the kitchen in search of that last bag you hope is still there. If your popcorn supply is depleted, you are still far more likely to snack after watching commercials about food (Harris et al., 2009). Researchers have found that children who see food commercials while watching a 30-minute cartoon program consume 45% more snack food than do children who view nonfood commercials. The researchers estimated that this difference could lead to an additional 10 pounds of extra weight gained each year (Harris et al., 2009). Also, increased incidences of overweight and obesity occur disproportionately among children who grow up in poverty (Lipling et al, 2012), where low-cost, high-fat diets are commonplace. An attempt to ban fast-food restaurants in South Los Angeles had no impact on obesity (Sturm & Hattori, 2015).

The cost of health care rises with body mass index. Questions over who is responsible for paying these costs have generated heated debates. Should a person who is overweight or obese be obligated to pay more tax toward health care to offset the higher cost of his or her care? Before answering, consider the fact that healthcare costs also rise because of diseases that have little to do with lifestyle. Also, research on employment statistics indicates that workers who are overweight or obese are paid less than thin colleagues with similar qualifications—a finding that has led economists to suggest that the disparity in wage earnings is about equal to the size of the difference in medical costs incurred by thin versus overweight and obese people (Bhattacharya & Bundorf, 2005).

The Sedentary Lifestyle

Modern conveniences have reduced the amount of physical activity required of most people. Many jobs involve very little physical activity, and home entertainment has evolved into activities that typically require nothing more than sitting and, often, snacking. Such pleasurable activities can easily replace exercise. Many children and adolescents are indoctrinated into this lifestyle from their early years. In turn, childhood obesity rates have risen drastically, accompanied by the availability of an even greater variety of sedentary activities, such as video games. Researchers have found that the amount of time that children spend playing sedentary video games or watching TV is positively correlated with levels of obesity, but recent evidence suggests active video games—such as those that involve dancing—might actually be a good way to break sedentary habits (Ferrar & Golley, 2015; Mitre et al., 2011).

Now that you have read about numerous variables that influence health, you may be wondering about which ones you can control versus those that you cannot. Complete the activity in Table 13.3 to evaluate your own beliefs about health.

Psychosocial Influences on Health

The environments where we work, live, and play and the people with whom we interact influence both our physical and mental health. College dormitories are a prime example, especially in the fall of each academic year. Frequently, dormitory space is overbooked,

Table 13.3 The Health Locus of Control Scale

Each of the following items is a belief statement about your health with which you may agree or disagree. Beside each statement is a scale that ranges from strongly disagree (1) to strongly agree (6). For each item, circle the number that represents the extent to which you agree or disagree with that statement. Please make sure that you answer every item and that you circle only one number per item. This is a measure of your personal beliefs; obviously, there are no right or wrong answers.

Item	Strongly Disagree				Strongly Agree	
1. If I get sick, it is my own behavior that determines how soon I get well again.	1	2	3	4	5	6
2. No matter what I do, if I am going to get sick, I will get sick.	1	2	3	4	5	6
3. I am in control of my health.	1	2	3	4	5	6
4. Most things that affect my health happen to me by accident.	1	2	3	4	5	6
5. When I get sick, I am to blame.	1	2	3	4	5	6
6. Luck plays a big part in determining how soon I will recover from an illness.	1	2	3	4	5	6
7. The main thing that affects my health is what I myself do.	1	2	3	4	5	6
8. My good health is largely a matter of good fortune.	1	2	3	4	5	6
9. If I take care of myself, I can avoid illness.	1	2	3	4	5	6
10. No matter what I do, I'm likely to get sick.	1	2	3	4	5	6
11. If I take the right actions, I can stay healthy.	1	2	3	4	5	6
12. If it's meant to be, I will stay healthy.	1	2	3	4	5	6

First, add up the total of your circled responses for the odd-numbered items only: ______

Now add up the total of your circled responses for the even-numbered items only: ______

Here is how you should interpret your scores: The first scale based on odd-numbered items measures the degree to which you believe you have control over your own health. The average of this scale in the original study was 24.1, with higher values indicating a greater sense of control over one's health. The second scale based on even-numbered items measures the degree to which you believe chance is involved in your health. Again, higher scores indicate a greater sense that luck is involved, and the average in the original study was 15.1.

Source: Adapted from "Development of the Multidimensional Health Locus of Control (MHLC) Scales" by K. A. Wallston, B. S. Wallston, & R. DeVellis (1978), *Health Education & Behavior, 6*(1), 160–170.

leaving some students without an established living space, and forcing people to live in cramped conditions. Single rooms may be converted into doubles, and "suites" may appear where there had been none. Perhaps not surprisingly, these conditions lend themselves to the increased spread of influenza and other viruses amid a fairly stressed group of individuals. In addition, these conditions affect the way that individuals interact with one another.

Years ago, psychologists compared students who lived in well-designed dormitory arrangements versus those living in improvised and poorly designed conditions. The crowded, poorly designed accommodations caused students to lose their sense of control over whom they could interact with or avoid. The researchers found that students living in the stressful environment were less socially interactive with strangers, had difficulty with working in small groups, and gave up more easily in a competitive game (Baum & Valins, 1977). The students living in the less than ideal conditions seemed to feel helpless, which in turn affected how they interacted with others. For most students, better accommodations await them at home, and larger spaces open up at the end of the semester. However, for many living with very low incomes, the stresses of poor housing may be permanent.

Poverty and Discrimination

Health and wealth increase together. People who live in affluent communities not only enjoy better access to health care, but also have a greater sense of control over their environments and have the resources needed to maintain a desired lifestyle. People who experience poverty, discrimination, and other social stressors have higher incidences of depression, anxiety, and other mental health problems (Tracy et al., 2008). The lack of control associated with life in poverty continues a negative cycle compromising human health and well-being.

Furthermore, health problems are magnified by stress. Heart disease is prevalent in socioeconomically disadvantaged populations, and children who experience adverse socioeconomic circumstances are at greater risk for developing heart disease in adulthood (Fiscella et al., 2009; Saban et al., 2014). This relationship likely reflects the compound effects of stress; and a poorer diet is often found among individuals residing in communities of low socioeconomic status.

People who are of low socioeconomic status are at increased risk for poor health. Numerous factors, including limited access to health care, stress, poor nutrition, and discrimination, collectively place children growing up in these communities at greater risk for developing health problems.

Discrimination is another stressor that can compromise physical and mental health, and is particularly problematic because it is often uncontrollable and unpredictable. Being a target of prejudice and discrimination is linked to increased blood pressure, heart rate, and secretions of stress hormones, which when experienced over long periods of time compromise physical health. For example, when people perceive that they are the targets of racism, their blood pressure remains elevated throughout the day, and it recovers poorly during sleep (Brondolo et al., 2008; Steffen et al., 2003). Discrimination also puts people at greater risk for engaging in unhealthy behaviors such as smoking and substance abuse (Bennett et al., 2005; Landrine & Klonoff, 1996). Finally, discrimination, or even the perception of discrimination, can put the body on sustained alert against threats. The stress response that this state elicits can have negative, long-term effects on physical health.

Family and Social Environment

Our close, interpersonal relationships impact our health. Isolation not only brings about great subjective discomfort, but also has negative influences on physical health (Cacioppo & Cacioppo, 2014). It is even estimated that chronic loneliness is as great a risk to premature death as obesity (Holt-Lunstad, Smith, & Layton, 2010). **Social resilience**, *the ability to keep positive relationships and endure and recover from social isolation and life stressors*, can protect individuals from negative health consequences of loneliness (Cacioppo, Reis, & Zautra, 2011).

Married people and couples in long-term partnerships are less likely to feel isolated (though it is incorrect to assume married people do not experience loneliness). There are long-term health benefits to the committed. Individuals in heterosexual marriages tend to live longer and have better mental and physical health than do unmarried adults. Married couples enjoy the benefits of social support, combined resources, and they tend to have better health habits (Kiecolt-Glaser & Newton, 2001; Stessman et al., 2014). Of course, marriage can also be a considerable source of stress. Married couples who are experiencing ongoing problems with their relationship tend to experience more health problems, especially among women and older adults (Liu & Waite, 2014). On the whole, it appears that marriage might be healthy for heterosexual adults, but less is known about same-sex marriages because of the limited time since the first states began to recognize them. However, some researchers expect to see similar health benefits in both direct and indirect ways. For example, research has already shown improvements in mental health (Hatzenbuehler et al., 2012; Wright et al., 2013). Indirectly, same-sex benefits from employers means more people are covered by health insurance and can take advantage of medically related tax benefits (Gonzales, 2014).

Social Contagion

You have almost surely found yourself eating food simply because others around you were doing so, even if you were not actually hungry. The simple presence of other people is a puzzling social influence on our behavior—easy to observe, but challenging to explain. Social scientists have discovered an even more puzzling pattern of behaviors spreading among individuals. Body weight seems to spread socially, and not just the pound or so gained from packing in extra food at a birthday party just because others around you were also eating. Body weight changes can spread widely among individuals within social groups. Fluctuations can go in either direction—weight may increase or decrease. The same even appears to happen with smoking—either starting or quitting. It may be that many of our health and lifestyle choices are influenced by what others around us are doing.

Social contagion in the dorms. Your college roommate may influence your GPA more than you know—for better or for worse. At Dartmouth College, students are randomly assigned to their dorm rooms rather than matched on various characteristics, as is customary at many schools. This practice makes Dartmouth's roommate pairs a diverse mixture. Professor Bruce Sacerdote (2001) found that GPA levels are influenced by one's roommate. Students with high GPAs elevate the GPAs of their lower-scoring roommates, and vice versa.

These phenomena are examples of **social contagion**, *the often subtle, unintentional spreading of a behavior as a result of social interactions*. Social contagion of body weight, smoking, and other health-related behaviors have been documented in the Framingham Heart Study. The National Heart Institute began this ongoing study in 1948 to track 15,000 residents of Framingham, Massachusetts. Participants made regular visits to their doctors, who recorded important health statistics such as heart rate, body weight, and other standard physical measures. Scientists working with the Framingham data noticed that over time, clusters of people from this study group became increasingly similar in certain characteristics—such as body weight increases or decreases, starting or quitting smoking, and even levels of happiness (Christakis & Fowler, 2007, 2008; Fowler & Christakis, 2008). Upon closer inspection, researchers found that these clusters were not just similar in terms of health, they included groups of friends and acquaintances. It was as though the behaviors spread in the same way a virus would. Although genetic factors certainly do influence our health, this work seems to show just how powerful social factors can be.

Social networking sites like Facebook greatly extend the reach of social contagion beyond that of our immediate neighbors and peers. One innovative study found that people who posted glum messages about rainy weather (likely with pictures to prove it) in turn elicited negative emotional status updates from Facebook friends who were actually having sunny days (Coviello et al., 2014).

Journal prompt

Social Contagion:

Have you experienced social contagion in action? Describe an example or two of social contagion that you have experienced. Try to think of one example in which a healthy behavior spread in contagious fashion, and one example of an unhealthy behavior.

Summary

Now that you have read this section you should:

KNOW . . .

- ***The key terminology related to health psychology:***

body mass index (BMI) (p. 392)
leptin (p. 394)
set point (p. 394)
social contagion (p. 398)
social resilience (p. 397)

UNDERSTAND . . .

- ***How genetic and environmental factors influence obesity.*** Twin and adoption studies indicate that inheritance plays a strong role as a risk factor for obesity (or, for that matter, as a predictor of healthy body weight). Furthermore, environmental influences on weight gain are abundant. Cultural, family, and socioeconomic factors influence activity levels and diet, even in very subtle ways, such as through social contagion.

APPLY . . .

- ***Your knowledge to exert more control over your own health.*** As you learned in this section, health is influenced by multiple factors. Some of these might be beyond our control, while others we have some measure of control over. The experience of discrimination, for example, is not something that one individual can expect to control because the injustice is perpetrated by someone else. For those factors that we have greater measure of control over, having a sense of control over our health can lead to improved outcomes. The activity Locus of Control and Health in Table 13.3 provided an opportunity to measure the degree to which you feel that your own behaviors affect mental and physical health.

EVALUATE . . .

- ***Whether associating with people who smoke leads to smoking in adolescents.*** Correlational trends certainly show that smoking in popular movies is positively related to smoking among adolescents (e.g., increased exposure is related to increased incidence of smoking). Controlled laboratory studies suggest a cause-and-effect relationship exists between identification with story protagonists who smoke and smoking behavior by young viewers.

Quick Quiz

KNOW . . .

1. __________ is a hypothesized mechanism that serves to maintain body weight around a physiologically programmed level.
   a. BMI
   b. Set point
   c. Obesity
   d. A sedentary lifestyle
2. Which psychological term refers to the often subtle, unintentional spreading of a behavior as a result of social interactions?
   a. Health psychology
   b. Social contagion
   c. Discrimination
   d. Observational learning

UNDERSTAND . . .

3. Which of the following factors is not related to a person's weight?
   a. Exposure to food advertisements
   b. Sedentary lifestyle
   c. Genetics and set point
   d. All of these are related to weight.

APPLY . . .

4. To avoid gaining weight during the freshman year of college, a person should do all of the following except:
   a. Increase physical activity.
   b. Decrease caloric intake.
   c. Increase alcohol intake.
   d. Be aware of the new stressors the individual will face.

ANALYZE . . .

5. Which of the following statements is the best evidence that viewing smoking in movies plays a causal (rather than correlational) role in influencing people's perception of smoking and willingness to try smoking?
   a. Long-term trends show that increased or decreased incidence of smoking by adolescents follows increases or decreases in rates of smoking in movies.
   b. The more adolescents smoke, the more smoking occurs in movies.
   c. Advertisements for smoking occur more frequently, along with smoking by film actors.
   d. Adolescent smoking occurs at roughly the same rate regardless of how smoking is depicted in films.

Stress and Illness

The frustration and embarrassment of choking under pressure is undeniable. Whether the stakes are a championship title or gaining admission to a preferred college, a sudden, inexplicable shift to subpar performance can be devastating. According to psychologist Sian Beilock, the culprit in such cases may be the negative effects that stress has on working memory—the short-term capacity to hold and manipulate information. Calculating a 15% tip for a bill of $43.84 at a restaurant, or while the pizza delivery person waits, requires working memory processes. The pressure of your date or the pizza delivery person looking on impatiently may result in your appearing either foolishly generous or cheap.

Beilock has conducted experiments on how stress affects the cognitive resources needed for problem solving. For example, in one study, research volunteers were asked to solve math problems. Some were told that if they solved the problems correctly, they would earn money for themselves as well as for a partner they were paired with; if they did not perform well, both the volunteer and the partner would lose money. Beilock and her colleagues have found that this type of pressure draws resources away from the working memory processes needed for success (Beilock, 2010; Maloney et al., 2014). Stressful thoughts readily occupy working memory space and cause the unfortunate experience of choking under pressure. Stress, both good and bad, is a part of everyday life for most people, and here we look at how it affects the brain and rest of the body, and how individuals cope with stress

On any given day, we are likely to experience frustration, conflict, pressure, and change. All of these experiences, and others as well, involve stress. **Stress** *is a psychological and physiological reaction that occurs when perceived demands exceed existing resources to meet those demands.*

Stress refers to both events (stressors) and experiences in response to these events (the stress response). Stressors can take a wide variety of forms, such as single events (giving a speech, getting into a minor car accident) and chronic events (illness, marital problems, ongoing job-related challenges).

We can probably all agree that events such as car accidents and relationship troubles are stressful. However, psychologists have discovered that any two individuals may react very differently even if they have experienced the same stressful event. To explain why and how people differ, psychologists Richard Lazarus and Susan Folkman developed a cognitive appraisal theory of stress (Lazarus & Folkman, 1984). Here, the term *appraisal* refers to the cognitive act of assessing and evaluating the potential threat and demands of an event, and these appraisals occur in two steps. First, the individual perceives a potential threat and initiates a *primary appraisal* by asking herself, "Is this a threat?" If the answer is no, then she will not experience any stress; but if the answer is yes, she will experience a physiological stress reaction (perhaps a racing heart and sweaty palms) as well as an emotional reaction (perhaps anxiety and fear). As these events unfold, the *secondary appraisal* begins—she must determine how to cope with the threat. During secondary appraisal, she may determine that she knows how to cope with the stressor or that the stressor goes beyond her ability to cope.

Life changes are a major source of stress, whether they bring about positive or negative emotions. Also, whether something is stressful varies by degree. Psychologists have actually ranked stressful events according to their magnitude, as can be seen in the Social Readjustment Rating Scale in Table 13.4 (Holmes & Rahe, 1968). The highest-stress events include death of a spouse and divorce, while holidays and traffic tickets occupy the lower end of the spectrum. According to the psychologists who developed this scale, as the points in the left column of Table 13.4 accumulate, a person's risk for becoming ill increases. For example, 300 or more points put people at significant risk for developing heart problems and infections. As we will see, our stress responses are closely linked to numerous physiological systems, such as cardiovascular and immune system functioning.

Life-stress experiences for adults will not necessarily generalize across all age groups. Recognizing this fact, some psychologists have focused specifically on what is stressful to college students. The right-hand column of Table 13.4 ranks stressful events reported by college students.

Some level of stress can actually be helpful—without it, motivation to perform can decline. Conversely, as Sian Beilock and many other psychologists have shown, too much stress taxes cognitive resources, resulting in poorer performance. Task complexity is an important factor to consider when it comes to describing the relationship between stress and performance. Generally speaking, higher levels of arousal facilitate solving relatively simple problems, while complex tasks are better performed under lower levels of arousal (see Figure 13.2). Evaluate your own stress experiences by completing the activity in Table 13.5.

An event like this involves a primary appraisal phase in which the individual assesses the level of stress caused by the accident. Even though it was a minor collision; his stomach may feel like it is in a knot and he may begin to worry about the consequences. As the stress sets in, his secondary appraisal may help him cope if he remembers that he has insurance to cover the damage, he considers that nobody was injured, and remembers how his parents have always been supportive and understanding.

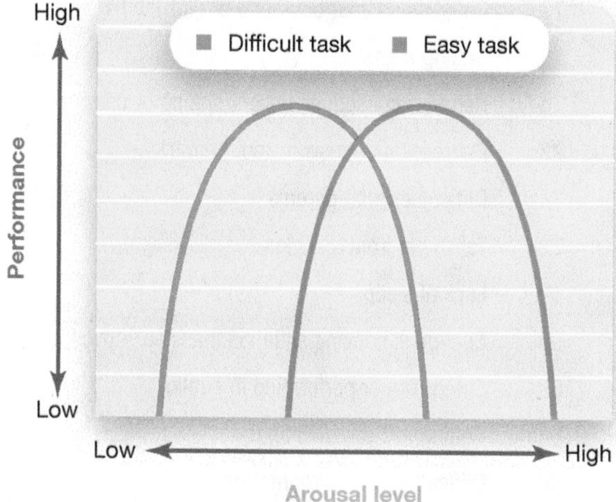

Figure 13.2 Arousal and Performance
Performance is related to at least two critical factors—the difficulty of the task and the level of arousal/stress while they are being performed. For easy tasks, moderately high arousal helps; for difficult tasks, lower levels of arousal are optimal.

Table 13.4 Life Stress Inventories for the General Adult Population and for College Students

Original Social Readjustement Rating Scale (Holmes & Rahe, 1967)		A Life Stress Inventory Applicable to College Students (Renner & Mackin, 1998)	
Rating	**Item**	**Rating**	**Item**
100	Death of a spouse	100	Being raped
73	Divorce	100	Finding out that you are HIV-positive
65	Marital separation	98	Being accused of rape
63	Jail term	97	Death of a close friend
63	Death of a close family member	96	Death of a close family member
53	Personal injury or illness	94	Contracting a sexually transmitted disease (other than AIDS)
50	Marriage	91	Concerns about being pregnant
47	Fired at work	90	Finals week
45	Marital reconciliation	90	Concerns about your partner being pregnant
45	Retirement	89	Oversleeping for an exam
44	Change in health of family member	89	Flunking a class
40	Pregnancy	85	Having a boyfriend or girlfriend cheat on you
39	Sex difficulties	85	Ending a steady dating relationship
39	Gain of new family member	85	Serious illness in a close friend or family member
39	Business readjustment	84	Financial difficulties
38	Change in financial state	83	Writing a major term paper
37	Death of close friend	83	Being caught cheating on a test
36	Change to different line of work	82	Drunk driving
35	Change in number of arguments with spouse	82	Sense of overload in school or work
31	*Mortgage exceeding $10,000	80	Two exams in one day
30	Foreclosure of mortgage or loan	77	Cheating on your boyfriend or girlfriend
29	Change in responsibilities at work	76	Getting married
29	Son or daughter leaving home	75	Negative consequences of drinking or drug use
29	Trouble with in-laws	73	Depression or crisis in your best friend
28	Outstanding personal achievement	73	Difficulties with parents
26	**Wife begins or stops work	72	Talking in front of a class
26	Begin or end school	69	Lack of sleep
25	Change in living conditions	69	Change in housing situation (hassles, moves)
24	Revision of personal habits	69	Competing or performing in public
23	Trouble with boss	68	Getting in a physical fight
20	Change in work hours or conditions	66	Difficulties with a roommate
20	Change in residence	65	Job changes (applying, new job, work hassles)
20	Change in schools	65	Declaring a major or concerns about future plans
19	Change in recreation	62	A class you hate
19	Change in church activities	61	Drinking or use of drugs

(Continued)

Table 13.4 Life Stress Inventories for the General Adult Population and for College Students *(Continued)*

Original Social Readjustement Rating Scale (Holmes & Rahe, 1967)		A Life Stress Inventory Applicable to College Students (Renner & Mackin, 1998)	
Rating	**Item**	**Rating**	**Item**
18	Change in social activities	60	Confrontations with professors
17	Mortgage or loan less than $10,000*	58	Starting a new semester
16	Change in sleeping habits	57	Going on a first date
15	Change in number of family get-togethers	55	Registration
15	Change in eating habits	55	Maintaining a steady dating relationship
13	Vacation	54	Commuting to campus or work, or both
12	Christmas	53	Peer pressures
11	Minor violations of the law	53	Being away from home for the first time
	Total	52	Getting sick
		52	Concerns about your appearance
		51	Getting straight A's
		48	A difficult class that you love
		47	Making new friends, getting along with friends
		47	Fraternity or sorority rush
		40	Falling asleep in class
		20	Attending an athletic event (e.g., football games)
			Total

*today, of course, this figure would be much higher

**modern-day inventories such as this would indicate "spouse or partner," rather than "wife"

To reiterate the definition of this term, stress occurs when perceived demands exceed the resources we believe we have to cope with the demands. In either case, our bodies have evolved important physiological and neural mechanisms to regulate our responses to stress.

Physiology of Stress

Stress involves distinct feelings and sensations when they are relatively brief, such as giving an oral presentation in class, as well as when they are chronic such as the cumulative effect of a challenging school year. Walter Cannon, an early researcher of stress, noted that the physical responses to stressors were somewhat general, despite the fact that stress can

Table 13.5 How Stressed Are You? Apply the life stress inventory to your own experiences and compare overall scores with others.
To complete this activity, refer to the values next to each stressful event listed in the right column of Table 13.4. Add up the numbers that apply to your experiences to compute your total stress score. After you have done so, see below to compare your computed averages from a college student sample.
Renner and Mackin (1998) gathered data on a sample of 257 undergraduate college students using the same instrument (range: 17–45 years; mean: 19.75 years). They reported an average stress score of 1,247 (standard deviation: 441), with scores ranging from 182 to 2,571. How did you compare with their sample?

come from a variety of sources that may be biological, cognitive, or social in nature. Cannon described this general reaction as a *fight-or-flight response*, a set of physiological changes that occur in response to psychological or physical threats.

Hans Selye (1956) looked beyond the immediate fight-or-flight response and saw the unfolding of a larger pattern of responding to stress. He named this pattern the **general adaptation syndrome (GAS)**—*a theory of stress responses involving stages of alarm, resistance, and exhaustion.* As GAS illustrates, a stressful event, such as a mild shock if you see a rat, or a pop quiz if you are a college student, first elicits an *alarm* reaction. Alarm consists of your recognition of the threat and the physiological reactions that accompany it. As the stressful event continues, the second part of this adaptive response, known as *resistance*, is characterized by coping with the event (freezing for the rat, and for you gathering your thoughts and mentally preparing for the quiz). The third and final stage is *exhaustion*—the experience depletes your physical resources and your physiological stress response declines.

Since the work of Cannon and Selye, psychologists have further uncovered the highly complex physiological interactions that occur during and after stress. In their search, two key pathways have been identified: the autonomic pathway and the HPA axis, which we discuss next.

The Stress Pathways

You can likely attest to the fact that stress involves your whole body. During stressful times the heart races, palms get sweaty, and the stomach feels like it is tied in a knot. These sensations are the result of activity in the *autonomic pathway*, which originates in the brain and extends to the body where stress can be felt in the form of tension, nervousness, and arousal. Recall that the nervous system consists of the central nervous system (brain and spinal cord) and the peripheral nervous system, which includes the autonomic nervous system. In response to stress, the hypothalamus stimulates a group of sympathetic nervous system cells called the *adrenal medulla* (located within the adrenal glands) to release epinephrine and norepinephrine, which then trigger bodily changes associated with the fight-or-flight response (see Figure 13.3).

Another physiological system involved in the stress response is the **hypothalamic–pituitary–adrenal (HPA) axis**, *a neural and endocrine circuit that provides communication between the nervous system (the hypothalamus) and the endocrine system (pituitary and adrenal glands).* Think of the HPA axis as a series of steps supporting the body's stress response. When you perceive that you are in a stressful situation, the hypothalamus releases a substance called corticotrophin-releasing factor, which stimulates the pituitary gland to release adrenocorticotrophic hormone. This hormone in turn stimulates the release of **cortisol**, *a hormone secreted by the adrenal cortex that prepares the body to respond to stressful circumstances.* For example, cortisol may stimulate increased access to energy stores or lead to decreased inflammation (immune system activity). In summary, both the sympathetic nervous system (through the release of epinephrine and norepinephrine) and the HPA axis (through the release of cortisol) function to prepare us to respond to stress.

Oxytocin: To Tend and Befriend

Not all stress responses are about fighting or fleeing; in fact, some have the opposite effect. Stress sometimes leads people to seek close contact and social support, a phenomenon known as the *tend and befriend response* (Taylor, 2002; von Dawans et al., 2012). This reaction may be promoted by the release of **oxytocin**, *a stress-sensitive hormone that is typically associated with maternal bonding and social relationships.* Oxytocin influences social bonding in both males and females, but women seem to rely more on this particular physiological adaptation to cope with stress (Taylor, 2006).

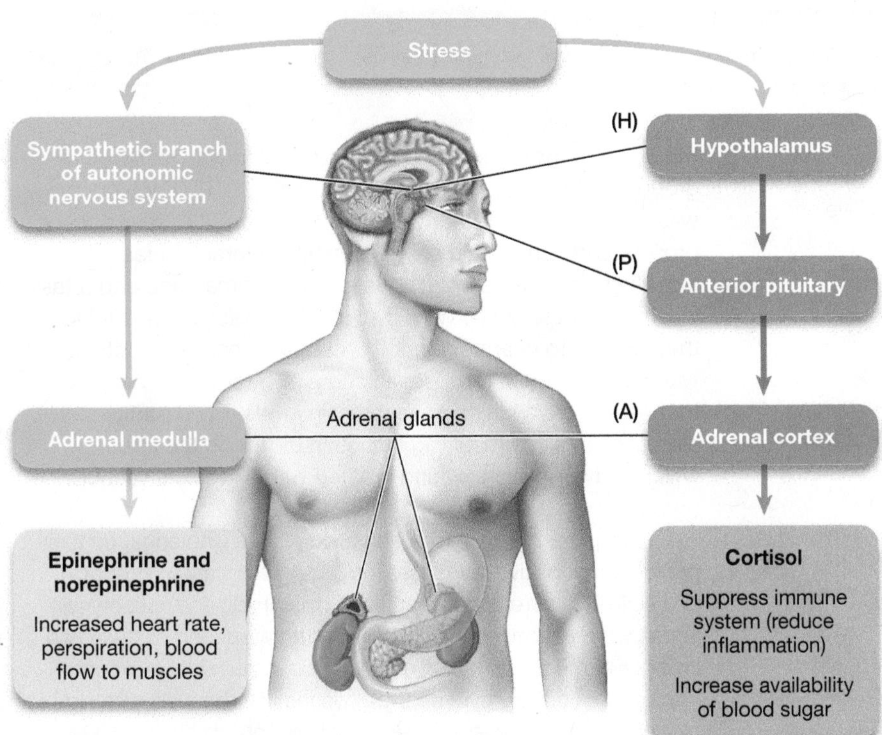

Figure 13.3 Stress Pathways of the Body
The stress pathways of the body include the autonomic nervous system and the HPA axis. Both systems converge on the adrenal glands. The autonomic response involves stimulation of the adrenal medulla of the sympathetic nervous system, resulting in the release of epinephrine and norepinephrine—chemicals that stimulate the fight-or-flight response. Activity of the HPA axis results in stimulation of the adrenal cortex, which releases cortisol into the bloodstream.

This unique stress response for females is thought to have evolutionary significance. For females of many species, the responsibility to avoid harm and protect offspring under stressful circumstances has likely survival advantages over fighting or running away.

Stress, Immunity, and Illness

Stress and physical health are closely related. The immune system, which is responsible for protecting the body against infectious disease, has complex connections with the nervous system, including the stress response systems just discussed (Maier & Watkins, 1998). **Psychoneuroimmunology** *is the study of the relationships among the immune system, behavior, and nervous system functioning*. You have likely had the unfortunate experience of getting sick in the midst of a period of high stress. In fact, in one sense of the word, final exams may be unhealthy. In one investigation, medical students provided blood samples during the term and again during the final exam period. Analysis of these blood samples showed suppressed immune responses during the high-stress period at the end of the term (Kiecolt-Glaser, 1984). This is not an isolated phenomenon; dozens of experimental and correlational studies have shown, for example, that stress predicts whether people will succumb to the cold virus (Cohen et al., 1998). Another issue that health psychologists have explored is the relationship between intimate relationships and physical health.

Working the Scientific Literacy Model

Relationships and Health

Social relationships can be a major source of both positive and negative stress. Given the links between stress and health, it seems reasonable to ask: How do our personal relationships relate to health?

What do we know about relationships and health?

Weddings, holidays, and family and class reunions can bring great joy and closeness, yet can be very stressful. Friendships and romantic relationships can involve negative stress when there is conflict or disagreement, or when individuals feel misunderstood or disregarded. Periods of social distress can distract someone from work, school, and other daily activities. In addition, this type of stress can even affect how the body responds to illness or injury.

Oxytocin, and another hormone called *vasopressin*, are involved in social behavior and bonding. We previously discussed the role of oxytocin in moderating stress responses, primarily in females. People with high vasopressin levels also tend to report better relationship quality with their spouses (Walum et al., 2008). Interestingly, both of these hormones also interact with the immune system, specifically to reduce inflammation.

How can science explain connections between relationships and health?

These observations suggest the possibility that oxytocin and vasopressin might be related to better physical health in the context of close social relationships. A common, if not surprising method for measuring immunity and health is to see how quickly people recover from a minor wound. In one study, the effect of marital stress on wound healing was tested in a group of 37 married couples (Gouin et al., 2010). Each couple was asked to sit together with no other couples or researchers present and complete a series of marital interaction tasks, including a discussion of the history of their marriage and a task in which both spouses were instructed to discuss something they wished to change about themselves. These interactions were videotaped and the researchers also took blood samples to measure oxytocin and vasopressin levels. Each participant also consented to receiving a suction blister on the forearm, which is a very minor wound created with a medical vacuum pump.

During the marital interaction tasks, those who engaged their partner with positive responses including acceptance, support, and self-disclosure had higher levels of oxytocin and vasopressin. Those who responded with hostility, withdrawal, and distress had lower levels (Figure 13.4). In addition, the suction blister wounds healed more quickly over an 8-day period in individuals with high oxytocin and vasopressin levels. (Suction wounds heal to 100% within 12 days.)

The health-promoting effects of oxytocin are also evident from placebo-controlled studies. In another experiment, married couples were given either an intranasal solution of oxytocin or a placebo. The couples then engaged in discussion about conflict within their marriage. Those who received a boost of oxytocin showed more positive, constructive behavior during their discussion compared to couples in the placebo group. The researchers also measured cortisol levels from saliva samples obtained from each individual. Those in the oxytocin group had lower cortisol levels compared to couples in the placebo group (Ditzen et al., 2009).

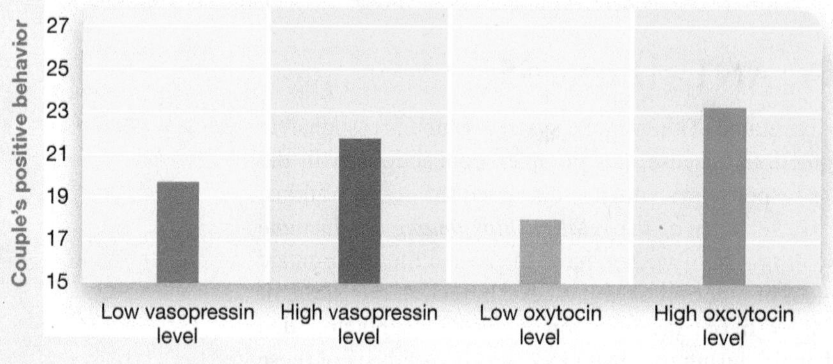

Figure 13.4 Relationship Quality Is Related to Physiological Responses
Higher oxytocin and vasopressin levels are associated with positive social interactions between married couples.

Can we critically evaluate this evidence?

It might be tempting to conclude that a boost of oxytocin or vasopressin could be the key to marital happiness, stress reduction, and physical health. Although the studies you just read about are related to these important qualities, it is important to avoid oversimplifying what their results mean. Claims that supplemental oxytocin can make anyone happier and better at love, marriage, sex, and even "mind reading" should be looked at with skepticism. Advertisements for such products are not hard to find. However, scientists are still in the relatively early stages of learning how oxytocin and vasopressin affect social behavior in humans, and how they are related to immune system function (Gouin et al., 2010; Macdonald & Macdonald, 2010).

Why is this relevant?

Although these studies were conducted with married couples, the physiological and physical healing benefits of close, positive social relationships extend to romantic relationships, friendships, and family. Procedures for healing physical injury currently focus on repair to damaged areas and preventing infection from setting in. In addition to these critical steps, it appears that managing psychological stress is also important for facilitating recovery from wounds (Gouin & Kiecolt-Glaser, 2011).

Journal prompt

Oxytocin:

Oxytocin levels are elevated in couples who show positive responses to each other while dealing with a stressful event. Levels are lower in couples who show negative behavior toward one another. One might conclude that high oxytocin levels cause couples to behave more lovingly toward each other. Explain how this relationship could be correlational, rather than causally related.

Coronary Heart Disease

High stress levels increase risk of **coronary heart disease**—*a condition in which plaques form in the blood vessels that supply the heart with blood and oxygen, resulting in restricted blood flow*. A nine-year study of 12,000 healthy males found that those experiencing chronic stress with their families or at work were 30% more likely to die from coronary heart disease than were men who were not chronically stressed (Matthews & Gump, 2002). Coronary heart disease begins when injury and infection damage the arteries of the heart. This damage triggers the inflammatory response by the immune system—white blood cells travel to affected areas in an attempt to repair the damaged tissue. These cells gather cholesterol and form dangerous plaques, which can rupture, break off, and block blood flow. So how does stress fit into this picture? Stress causes an increased release of molecules that cause inflammation, leading to heart complications (Segerstrom & Miller, 2004).

Does someone need a hug? Psychologists have conducted controlled experimental studies confirming that social support, including receiving hugs, reduces susceptibility to the common cold (Cohen et al., 2015).

Stress influences heart functioning in other, indirect ways as well. For example, stress influences the decisions we make at the grocery store and in trips to the kitchen—decisions that can impact health. Seeking out food in response to stress puts people at increased risk for developing health problems, particularly if the stress is frequent and the food is of poor quality. However, as we learned earlier, males and females differ in how they handle stress. In one study, psychologists offered male research participants snacking options of healthy foods (peanuts and grapes) or unhealthy options (M&Ms and potato chips) while they were given an unsolvable anagram puzzle (stressful) or a solvable anagram (non-stressful). Perhaps counter to what you might predict, men in the no-stress condition ate more junk food than did the men who were stressed by the unsolvable anagram (Zellner et al., 2007). This finding contrasts with the tendencies of female participants—in a similar experiment, women ate more junk food when stressed (Zellner et al., 2006).

An unsolvable anagram is an acute stressor that is easy to leave behind. By comparison, job, family, and other potential sources of stress are much more challenging to manage. So how do real-life chronic stressors affect eating? Chronic stress leads to greater consumption of calorie-rich, less-healthy foods—which likely fits with your own experiences. Why do we turn to tasty, calorie-rich foods when stressed? The answer may seem obvious—it's called "comfort food" for a reason. Stress actually alters the physiological pathways that lead us to food. Evolution has equipped us with a tendency to increase food intake under times of stress. Recall that when the HPA axis is stimulated under stressful circumstances it releases cortisol. Researchers now think that this stress response leads us to regard calorie-rich food as more rewarding than when we are not stressed (Adam & Epel, 2007; Pool et al., 2014).

AIDS

Acquired immune deficiency syndrome (AIDS) is a disease caused by infection with the human immunodeficiency virus (HIV). This disease saps the immune system's ability to fight off infections, to such an extent that even conditions that are relatively harmless to most of the population can be devastating to an individual with AIDS. Patients in industrialized countries with more medical options have a better prognosis than those living in impoverished areas. Retroviral therapies have greatly increased the longevity, health, and overall quality of life of patients. However, living with HIV can bring many forms of stress, and the release of cortisol can even further dampen the ability to fend off infection. Therefore, researchers are exploring how psychological interventions such as relaxation training may be incorporated into HIV treatment (Jones et al, 2013)

Cancer

Researchers are finding numerous links between psychosocial factors and cancer progression (Lutgendorf et al., 2013). Several factors, such as the type of cancer and an individual's age, account for why some people rapidly succumb to cancer while others are able to beat it. In addition, stress levels affect the progression of cancer. Why is this? It appears that norepinephrine supports cancer cell growth, and that cortisol magnifies this effect. Hormones from the autonomic nervous system stimulate cells that reside in tumors, which ultimately results in growth and proliferation of these masses (Antoni, 2013). Thus, when someone experiences stress, the autonomic nervous system and HPA axis naturally respond, but their reactions compromise how well the individual can fight the disease.

For many people, stress levels can be changed and the course of a disease such as cancer can be slowed. For example, individuals who have undergone assertiveness training and learn anger management techniques show reduced autonomic responses and hormonal activity associated with the HPA axis (Antoni et al., 2007). Also, those who are optimistic and cope by using humor and keeping a positive outlook (and thus experience less stress) show physiological benefits such as greater immune response (Lutgendorf et al., 2007).

Psychologists are finding that the stress–illness relationship is a very complex one, involving numerous physiological systems. Also, the effects of mental stress on physical functioning are diverse. Recall that stress can come in a variety of forms—at the very least, we can divide it into acute and chronic variations. It appears that stress also has dual influences on immunity. Acute stressors tend to activate the immune system, whereas chronic exposure to stress generally causes suppression of the immune system (Segerstrom & Miller, 2004).

Stress, Personality, and Illness

How people handle and cope with stress often depends on their personality. First consider your own responses to a common stressful event. Imagine you have a one-hour break between classes, during which you need to get lunch and also visit one of your professors across campus. When you arrive at your professor's office, you see a line of other students awaiting their turn, and the current occupant is blathering on and on about something completely unrelated to schoolwork. How would you tend to react in this situation? Would you become agitated, angry, resentful, and fidgety? Or would you be more inclined to strike up a conversation with others in line to help pass the time? Your answer will likely depend on various factors—but each of us tends to have a common style of responding to stressful events.

Personality characteristics and stress coping skills are also related to long-term health, as well as recovery from illness. **Type A personality** *describes people who tend to be impatient and worry about time, and are easily angered, competitive and, highly motivated.* In contrast, **Type B personality** *describes people who are more laid back and characterized by a patient, easygoing, and relaxed disposition* (Friedman & Rosenman, 1974). The concept of Types A and B did not originate in psychology. Rather, cardiologists suspected that people who were prone to stress had poorer physical health. They identified these individuals as Type A, and their studies revealed that people who fall in the Type A category are far more likely to have heart attacks than are Type B people. This initial finding has been replicated many times, though the correlation between levels of Type A characteristics and coronary heart disease is only moderate. Other factors, not just how a person copes with stress, may further elevate the risk of coronary heart disease. People who have a Type A personality also engage in behaviors that compromise physical health, such as

Myths in Mind

Stress and Ulcers

People typically associate ulcers—open sores in the lining of the esophagus, stomach, and small intestine—with people working in high-stress jobs, such as police officers or air traffic controllers. The belief that stress causes people to develop ulcers is widespread. In actuality, most ulcers are caused by a bacterium, *Helicobacter pylori*, which can cause inflammation of the lining of various regions of the digestive tract. This bacterium is surprisingly common, and approximately 10% to 15% of people who are exposed to it will develop an ulcer resulting from inflammation. Thus, stress does not cause ulcers, although it can worsen their symptoms. Also, smoking, alcohol, pain relievers, and a poor diet—anything that can irritate the digestive system—increases problems associated with ulcers.

Contrary to popular belief, chronic stress, like that experienced by air traffic controllers, will not cause a stomach ulcer.

drinking large quantities of alcohol, smoking, and sleeping less than people with a Type B personality. Thus, numerous correlated factors may explain the relationship between Type A personality and risk of coronary heart disease.

The distinction between Types A and B personalities has not satisfied all behavioral scientists and physicians. Being quick to anger is a characteristic of Type A individuals, but so is being hyper-motivated to succeed at work. Perhaps there is something more specific about personality that increases one's risk for developing heart disease. More recent research has shown that people who are prone to hostility and anger are at greater risk for developing coronary heart disease (Razzini et al., 2008). Other personality characteristics linked to coronary heart disease include anxiety and depression.

Outlook on life seems to influence physical health as well. People who are optimistic tend to have a positive outlook on life and have a constructive way of explaining the causes of everyday events. Pessimists have a more negative perception of life and tend to see the glass as half-empty. Optimism is correlated with better physical health than pessimism. For example, optimists have lower incidence of cardiovascular problems such as congestive heart failure and stroke (Kim et al., 2014; Kim et al., 2011). Pessimism can even compromise health when it comes to viral responses. Women who tend toward pessimism and test positive for the HPV virus (a papilloma virus known to cause cervical cancer) have lower counts of white blood cells that fight disease than do optimistic women with the HPV virus. If stressed, pessimistic women run a greater risk of developing cervical cancer (Antoni et al., 2006).

Summary

Now that you have read this section you should:

KNOW . . .

The key terminology associated with stress and illness:

coronary heart disease (p. 407)
cortisol (p. 404)
general adaptation syndrome (GAS) (p. 404)
hypothalamic–pituitary–adrenal (HPA) axis (p. 404)
oxytocin (p. 404)
psychoneuroimmunology (p. 405)
stress (p. 400)
Type A personality (p. 409)
Type B personality (p. 409)

UNDERSTAND . . .

- ***The physiological reactions that occur under stress.*** When a person encounters a stressor, the hypothalamus stimulates the sympathetic nervous system to act, triggering the release of epinephrine and norepinephrine from the adrenal medulla. This reaction is often referred to as the fight-or-flight response. Another part of the stress response system is the HPA axis, in which the hypothalamus stimulates the pituitary gland to release hormones that in turn stimulate the adrenal cortex to release cortisol, which prepares the body to deal with stressful situations.
- ***How the immune system is connected to stress responses.*** Cortisol suppresses the immune system, leaving people more vulnerable to illness and slowing recovery time from illness and injury.

APPLY . . .

- ***A measure of stressful events to your own experiences.*** An important take home message from this section is that stress has a cumulative effect, and, depending on the amount and the nature of the stressors, as well as personality characteristics, stress can negatively affect both short- and long-term health. Taking an inventory of what is causing stress can help you sort out the different stressors, and also evaluate those that you can and cannot control. This is an important step to stress management. The activity How Stressed Are You? (Table 13.5) offers one way to look at your own stressors.

ANALYZE . . .

- ***The claim that ulcers are caused by stress.*** Ulcers are damaged areas of the digestive tract often caused by infection with the bacterium Helicobacter pylori. Stress and other factors, such as diet and alcohol consumption, can worsen the condition of ulcers, but stress alone does not cause them.

Quick Quiz

KNOW . . .

1. Which of the following is not a component of Selye's general adaptation syndrome?
   - **a.** Resistance
   - **b.** Alarm
   - **c.** Flight
   - **d.** Exhaustion

UNDERSTAND . . .

2. A major difference between the tend and befriend stress response and the responses mediated by the autonomic pathway and the HPA axis is that:
   - **a.** the tend and befriend response involves cortisol activity.
   - **b.** men are more likely to express the tend and befriend response.
   - **c.** the tend and befriend response facilitates care for offspring and others in a social group.
   - **d.** the tend and befriend response is a negative stress reaction, whereas the autonomic pathway and HPA axis responses are positive reactions.

3. How are the stress response and immune systems related?
   - **a.** Illness is a cause a stress, but not the other way around.
   - **b.** The two systems are physiologically separate, but by coincidence are sometimes activated at the same time.
   - **c.** They are both controlled by the same brain regions.
   - **d.** Increased stress levels directly impact the functioning of the immune system.

APPLY . . .

4. What is a sound recommendation for managing stress among hospital patients?
   - **a.** Reduce stress, and therefore cortisol release, as much as possible.
   - **b.** Introduce a mild amount of stress so that the HPA-axis can prime the immune system.
   - **c.** Offer oxytocin inhalers to induce relaxation in patients.
   - **d.** Allow people to attain their preferred level of stress (equal to what they would experience outside of the hospital).

ANALYZE . . .

5. Researchers have concluded that the actual cause of ulcers is __________
   - **a.** stress.
   - **b.** bacterial infection.
   - **c.** genetics.
   - **d.** poor diet.

COPING AND WELL-BEING

What is the best way to cope with a personal disaster, such as losing your job? Writing about how the event makes you feel may not seem like a priority, but according to psychologist James Pennebaker, it may be one of the best strategies for coping and regaining the emotional resources needed to move on. Pennebaker, a leading researcher on the psychological benefits of writing, decided to intervene when a local computing and electronics firm laid off 60 workers. All he asked the workers to do was to write. But their instructions on how to write were different: Half the volunteers were randomly assigned to write about their "deepest thoughts and feelings surrounding the job loss, and how their lives, both personal and professional, had been affected" (Spera et al., 1994, p. 725). In contrast, the control group members were told to write about their plans for the day and how they planned to find another job, which is much less personal and emotional. After a month of weekly 20-minute writing sessions, the group members who were writing about their emotions were getting hired much more frequently than the control group members. This was a double-blind, randomized study, so the differences between the groups can be traced to the writing. Similar methods have been used in Pennebaker's studies of first-year college students, people grieving the loss of a loved one, and other groups experiencing stressful transitions. The result was the same each time—group members who wrote meaningful narratives of their emotions and thoughts came out ahead, not just in terms of mental health, but also physically and in terms of their performance at work or school.

In this section, we will present some widely used solutions for coping with stress and behavioral methods that can help improve mental and physical health. We will also discuss some topics that might be less familiar, but may prove useful in how you cope with stress and negative events. Finally, we will discuss how stress and successful coping are closely related to our sense of control.

COPING

Equally important to understanding how stress works is learning how to cope with it. **Coping** *refers to the processes used to manage demands, stress, and conflict.* Some of us approach a problem or stressor, such as large monetary debt or a setback at work, by taking a problem-solving approach. In other words, we cope by defining the problem and working toward a solution. However, not all stressors are brought about by problems that have identifiable solutions. For example, emotional coping is probably better suited to dealing with an issue such as the loss of a loved one. Neither style of coping is superior to the other—the two are often combined and their suitability depends on the nature of the problem (Folkman & Lazarus, 1980).

Not all coping techniques actually help; some may simply replace one problem with another. For example, some people turn to alcohol or drugs to temporarily avoid feelings of stress, and some turn to food. Ice cream, chocolate, and salty snacks are popular—but probably unhealthy—methods of coping. In this section, we will examine the major ways of coping by focusing first on the positive approaches, and then on some of the negative ways that people cope.

Positive Coping Strategies

Psychology has a bit of a reputation for focusing on the negative, including how damaging stress can be. But psychologists also study what makes people thrive, even in the face of extreme stress. This area of study, known as **positive psychology**, *uses scientific methods to study human strengths and potential.* Research in this area has identified numerous adaptive and constructive ways in which people cope with problems; these strategies produce meaningful solutions to stressful problems or, at the very least, healthy ways of living with them.

Optimism *is the tendency to have a favorable, constructive view on situations and to expect positive outcomes.* The effectiveness of optimism for coping with stress is particularly evident in studies of freshmen adjusting to their first semester of college. Students who were optimistic by nature experienced relatively low levels of stress and depression and were also proactive in seeking out peers for support and companionship. Overall, their adjustment to college was better than the adjustment of those students who were pessimistic in nature (Brissette et al., 2002). People who are optimistic in the face of adversity are better able to approach problems from various angles and come up with constructive solutions. Some evidence also indicates that they are more physiologically equipped to deal with stress than are pessimists. Optimists are better protected against cardiovascular illnesses than pessimists (Kim et al., 2011; Kim et al., 2014), and optimism is associated with quicker recovery following acute coronary problems such as heart attacks (Ronaldson et al., 2015).

Coping is also influenced by **resilience**, *the ability to effectively recover from illness or adversity*. Individuals differ in their ability to bounce back from events such as disaster, disease, or major loss. Resilient people tend to have one or more factors stacked in their favor. Financial and social resources, opportunities for rest and relaxation, and other positive life circumstances contribute to resiliency. Even so, amazing stories of resiliency can be found among individuals living with unimaginable stress. Thus, personality and emotional characteristics are also important contributors to resiliency in the face of adversity. One amazing example is that of Victor Frankl, an early- and mid-20th-century Austrian psychiatrist. Frankl was already an influential physician and therapist when he, his wife, and family were forced into concentration camps during World War II. Frankl found himself in the role of helping people adjust to life in the concentration camp. He encouraged others to tap into whatever psychological resources they had left to cope with very bleak circumstances. Frankl not only helped others find resiliency, but also became more aware of his own resiliency as he had to find meaning in his own circumstances. Eventually Frankl's wife and parents were deported to different concentration camps, where they were murdered. Despite his own enormous losses, Frankl continued helping others to cope and find solace under the worst of circumstances (Frankl, 1959).

Psychologists have long focused on the negative outcomes of stress, but stories such as Frankl's demonstrate that stress and trauma can also lead people to recognize and use positive qualities. In fact, psychologists describe the phenomenon of **posttraumatic growth**, *the capacity to grow and experience long-term positive effects in response to negative events* (Calhoun & Tedeschi, 2013). It happens in response to events such as automobile accidents, sexual and physical assault, combat, and severe and chronic illnesses. Individuals who experience posttraumatic growth often report feeling a greater sense of vulnerability, yet over time develop an increased inner strength. They also report finding greater meaning and depth in their relationships, a greater sense of appreciation for what they have, and an increased sense of spirituality.

Posttraumatic growth is not an alternative reaction to posttraumatic stress. Rather, the two conditions occur together. Clinicians recognize that the growth occurs during the process of coping with stress, not because of the event itself. Clinical psychologists trained in working with trauma victims help facilitate the growth process, and assist individuals in finding the interpersonal and social resources needed for healing.

Biofeedback, Relaxation, and Meditation

As you have been reading this chapter, your circulatory system has been pumping blood and maintaining blood pressure, your lungs have been breathing in air, and your digestive system may have been working on a recent meal, all without the tiniest bit of conscious effort. Certainly you can hold your breath for a moment using conscious effort, but can you hold your heartbeat? Change your blood pressure? If you are like most of us, you cannot control all of these autonomic functions, but that does not mean it is impossible.

Biofeedback involves the use of physiological monitoring, which allows the patient to see and sometimes hear the output of his or her physiological reactions.

Biofeedback *is a therapeutic technique involving the use of physiological recording instruments to provide feedback that increases awareness of bodily responses.* The psychologists who developed this technique believed that by seeing or hearing a machine's representation of bodily processes, people could gain awareness of stress responses and bring them under voluntary control. For example, a patient with chronic stress could use feedback on his blood pressure, heart rate, and tension of his facial muscles to monitor and,

Meditation is practiced in many cultures, often for the purposes of promoting psychological well-being, health, and stress reduction.

possibly, control his stress responses. As you can imagine, this ability would have very useful applications to clinical psychology. However, after some promising findings, the excitement over biofeedback has subsided, in part because it was found that simple relaxation techniques were just as useful.

Many people find great benefit in using *relaxation* and *meditation* techniques to cope with stress and life's difficult periods. Relaxation and meditation techniques are designed to calm emotional responses as well as physiological reactions to stress. People frequently regard meditation as either a religious or new-age ritual—something that takes years of practice from which only "experts" can benefit. This is hardly an accurate summary of meditation. There are different types of meditation, two of which are (1) *mindfulness*, which involves attending to all thoughts, sensations, and feelings without attempting to judge or control them, and (2) *concentrative*, in which the individual focuses on breathing and a specific thought or sensation, such as an image or a repeated sound (Cahn & Polich, 2006). Meditation is most successful when performed in a quiet environment, when the person assumes a relaxed position (but not sufficient to support napping), and when he or she remains passive except for mindfulness activity or focusing attention.

Brain imaging work may take us a step closer to actually visualizing the connections between mind and body. A complex form of meditation called *integrated mind–body training* was developed from traditional Chinese medicine; it involves a combination of mindfulness with traditional meditative practices. This probably sounds mystical and beyond scientific scrutiny. However, Chinese scientists conducted brain scans on students who practiced integrated mind–body training. Over the course of the training, the students' brains appeared to develop an increased ability to control bodily physiology. A region of the midfrontal cortex called the *anterior cingulate* was particularly relevant; this area is involved in various aspects of processing reward and emotion. In this study, activity within the anterior cingulate was associated with the participants' increased control over parasympathetic nervous system responses. The increased parasympathetic activity accounted for the heightened sense of relaxation experienced while meditating. This result was not found in students who engaged in a simpler relaxation technique that did not involve integrating mind–body interactions (Tang et al., 2009). Thus, scientific studies of meditation appear to confirm its health benefits, and are also bringing us closer to understanding precisely how the nervous system is linked with other bodily processes, such as the immune system (Morgan et al., 2014).

Religion and spirituality

Many people use religion and spiritual inspiration as their primary coping mechanism during stressful situations, both large and small. They may use any combination of religious practices, depending on the specific nature of the faith: prayer, meditation, religious counseling, and social support from family and congregations. All of these efforts can provide strength and comfort during difficult times, but they may also be associated with greater overall happiness. Psychologists have become increasingly curious about the possible health benefits associated with religion and spirituality. Numerous studies indicate that people who are religious and are actively engaged with religious practices do, in fact, live a bit longer than do people who are less religious or nonreligious (McCullough et al., 2000).

A hasty interpretation of these results might lead one to conclude that religion causes people to live longer—that the experiences of prayer and church going lead to the greater longevity. However, the studies in this area actually produce correlational, not experimental, data—psychologists cannot randomly assign people to be religious or not. Consequently, we must consider alternative explanations. For example, lifestyle factors are also at play. People of Muslim, Jewish, or Christian faith are more likely to engage in healthy behaviors, including wearing seatbelts, visiting the dentist, and avoiding consumption of alcohol and cigarette smoking (reviewed in McCullough & Willoughby, 2009). Religions also tend to have negative views of criminal activity, drug abuse, and risky sexual behavior. Thus the increased longevity is probably related to the greater self-control and self-regulation that are characteristic of many religious belief systems.

Generally, people who are religious show greater well-being and lower levels of depression (Smith et al., 2003). The determination of whether religion protects people from depression depends on the point of view taken, however. People who cope with problems using positive aspects of religion (e.g., viewing stressors with kindness or collaborating with others in solving problems) are less prone to depression than religious people who adopt negative appraisals of their problems and concerns, such as viewing problems as a result of God's punishment (Ano & Vasconcelles, 2005; McCullough & Willoughby, 2009).

Negativity and Pessimism

Adversity elicits a wide range of emotions and reactions. **Negative affectivity** *refers to the tendency to respond to problems with a pattern of anxiety, hostility, anger, guilt, or nervousness*. We occasionally might hear of someone who deals with a difficult breakup by socially withdrawing from others, becoming angry and resentful, and oftentimes growing hostile enough to threaten and harass the other person with phone calls, repeated texting, or spreading of rumors. Although the anger and upset feelings are perfectly normal reactions, clearly these hostile behaviors are a negative and destructive way of coping. However, for some individuals, this manner of dealing with adversity is consistent, and occurs across a broad number of situations, even ones that are trivial by comparison to a breakup.

Related to negative affectivity is what psychologists refer to as **pessimistic explanatory style**, *which is the tendency to interpret and explain negative events as internally based and as a constant, stable quality* (Burns & Seligman, 1989). The pessimism even bubbles to the surface when events occur beyond one's personal control, such as a natural disaster or war. It is certainly evident in common events as well—for example, a laid-off employee who struggles to find a job may attribute the problem to his perceived inability to network properly or because he is simply doomed to failure. In addition, individuals with a pessimistic explanatory style are at risk for health problems due to stress and increased inflammation (Bennett et al., 2012; Roy et al., 2010). Notably, pessimism appears to have long-term consequences on health. Researchers at the Mayo Clinic administered personality tests assessing optimism and pessimism to patients who came into the clinic for general medical issues during the 1960s. Thirty years later, the data on optimism and pessimism were compared to patient survival, and the researchers found a 19% increase in mortality risk in people who were consistently pessimistic (Maruta et al., 2000). Perhaps a good attitude does more than help individuals cope emotionally with illness; perhaps it actually helps them overcome it. To get a sense of how you cope with stress, see the activity in Table 13.6.

Table 13.6 How Do You Cope with Stress? Complete the scale below, which was designed to measure optimistic versus pessimistic coping styles.

Item	Strongly Disagree		Neutral	Strongly Agree	
1. In uncertain times, I usually expect the best.	0	1	2	3	4
2. If something can go wrong for me, it will.	4	3	2	1	0
3. I always look on the bright side of things.	0	1	2	3	4
4. I'm always optimistic about my future.	0	1	2	3	4
5. I hardly ever expect things to go my way.	4	3	2	1	0
6. Things never work out the way I want them to.	4	3	2	1	0
7. I'm a believer in the idea that "every cloud has a silver lining."	0	1	2	3	4
8. I rarely count on good things happening to me.	4	3	2	1	0
	Now add up the total of the numbers you circled: ______				

Source: Scheier, M. F., & Carver, C. S. (1985). Optimism, coping, and health: Assessment and implications of generalized outcome expectancies. *Health Psychology, 4*(3), 219–247. doi:10.1037/0278-6133.4.3.219

Perceived Control

As Dr. Pennebaker's story from the beginning of this section illustrates, the most stressful of circumstances are the ones that people have little or no control over. For example, children who reside in abusive homes have no control over their circumstances, nor do the victims of natural disasters. Each situation can result in people acquiring a sense that their behavior has little effect on external events.

Laboratory experiments have demonstrated the negative impact that a lack of control has on health and behavior. A classic example comes from work on avoidance learning in dogs conducted in the 1960s by Martin Seligman and his colleagues (Seligman & Maier, 1967; see Figure 13.5). In this study, dogs were exposed to an avoidance learning procedure in which they were placed in a chamber with an electric grid on the floor of one side, where the shock was delivered, and a panel that the dogs could jump over to reach a "safe" zone where there was no shock. Some dogs learned that if a dimming light preceded the shock, they could quickly jump to the safe zone, avoiding the shock altogether. Another group of dogs was first conditioned to the light stimulus paired with an inescapable shock. These dogs were then placed in the avoidance chamber, but did not attempt to avoid the shock when the light dimmed. Rather, they would lie down, whine, and appear resigned to receive the shock. This finding was described as **learned helplessness**—*an acquired suppression of avoidance or escape behavior in response to unpleasant, uncontrollable circumstances.*

Learned helplessness has been offered as an explanation for how people with depression tend to view the world. People with depression are prone to hold beliefs that their actions have no influence on external events, and that their environment and circumstances dictate outcomes. To some extent these beliefs may be true, but when generalized to just about any situation, they can negatively affect mental and physical well-being. The parallels to Seligman's work are rather clear. In some circumstances, humans and some nonhuman species will simply endure pain rather than initiate ways to avoid or escape it.

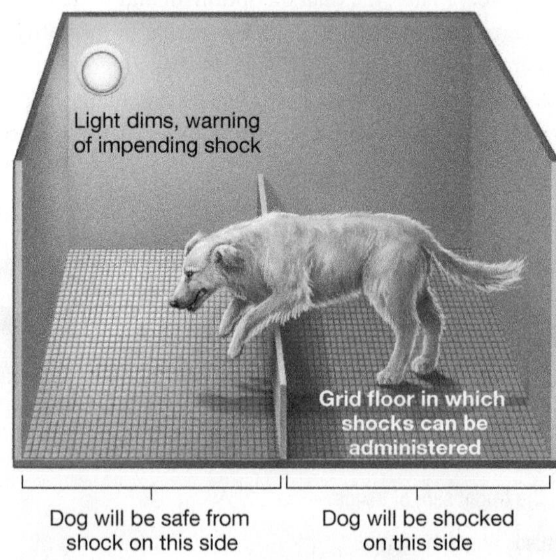

Figure 13.5 The Learned Helplessness Procedure
In Seligman and Maier's study, dogs that could avoid a painful shock would quickly learn to do so. Conversely, dogs that initially learned they could not avoid a shock remained passive when the opportunity to do so was given. The acquired failure to avoid or escape unpleasant circumstances that are perceived as uncontrollable is referred to as learned helplessness.

Working the Scientific Literacy Model

Compensatory Control and Health

The idea of a random world and a lack of personal control can be discomforting. For example, hurricanes and tornados are often referred to as "acts of God," rather than the result of an unfortunate meeting between extreme meteorological activity and populated areas. But does having a sense of control lead to better health?

What do we know about how people cope with seemingly random events?

Some people feel as if they are the victims of random events, while others believe themselves to be the beneficiaries of the whims of life. However, the idea that randomness dictates worldly events can create anxiety in people. Even if a person believes randomness is the rule, he or she can become highly motivated to find meaning in the world and, through this search, a sense that the course of events is determined by the will of individuals or God (Kay et al., 2009). In this way, many people cope with stressful life events through **compensatory control**—*psychological strategies used to preserve a sense of nonrandom order when personal control is compromised* (Kay et al., 2009). For example, people who are skeptical of any divine purpose in the world may change their view in the wake of personal or societal tragedy. Loss of a family member or being the unwitting victim of an economic depression, for example, are types of events known to draw people toward religion. These observations are primarily correlational, but researchers have conducted experiments to determine causal relationships between sense of control and beliefs about randomness versus orderliness.

How can science explain compensatory control?

To study compensatory control, researchers have developed a laboratory task that manipulates people's sense of personal control over a situation (Whitson & Galinsky, 2008). In one study, participants completed a concept identification task in which two symbols were presented on a computer screen, and the participant had to guess which symbol correctly represented the concept that the computer had chosen (e.g., the color of the symbol, its shape). The computer provided feedback on whether the participants chose the correct or incorrect symbol after each trial. Half of the participants received accurate feedback, while the other half received completely random feedback—sometimes their correct answers were recorded as incorrect, and vice versa. Participants receiving random feedback reported feeling a lower sense of control on a self-report measure.

Following the concept identification task, the participants then viewed multiple pictures, such as those shown in Figure 13.6. If you look closely, you will see that one of the pictures has a horse-like figure in it, whereas the other image has no discernible pattern. Participants in both conditions reported seeing faintly drawn figures, such as the horse. However, participants who had a diminished sense of control induced by the random feedback they received on the computer task were more likely to report seeing patterns within completely random images (Whitson & Galinsky, 2008).

It appears that when people feel their sense of control is undermined, they compensate by heightening their search for structure in the world, to the point of calling upon their imagination. This is evident in other domains as well, not just detecting patterns in random, snowy images. People also gain a greater need for structure and become increasingly willing to believe in superstitious rituals and to endorse conspiracy theories when their sense of control is diminished (Figure 13.7; Kay et al., 2009; Whitson & Galinksy, 2008).

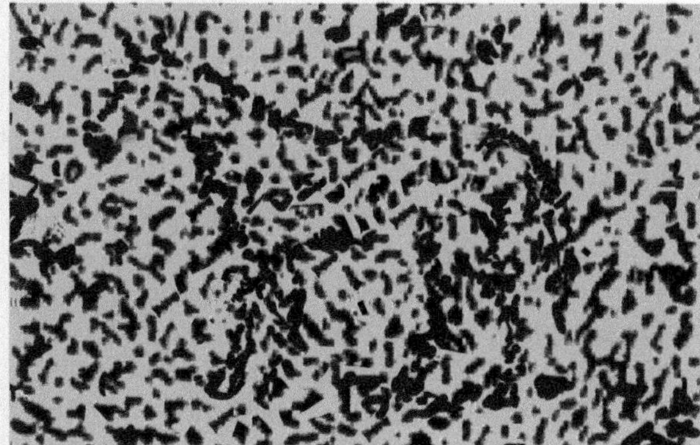

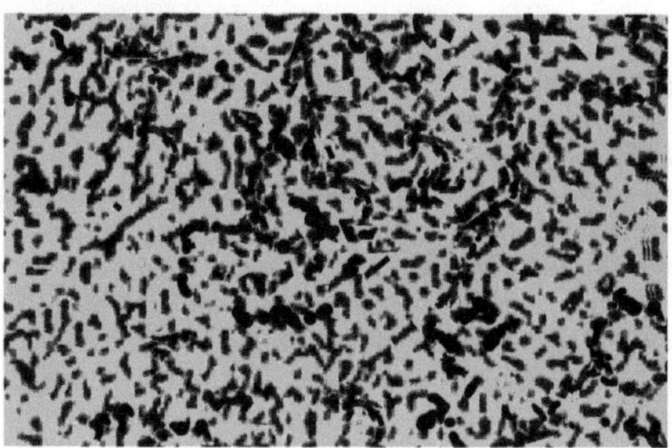

Figure 13.6 Seeing Images Where There Are None
Do you see a figure in the image on the left? You may see a figure resembling a horse. What about on the right? There is no discernible image intended for this image. Psychologists have found that individuals who feel as though they lack control are more likely to detect patterns in the image at right than are people who feel a greater sense of control (Whitson & Galinsky, 2008).

(Continued)

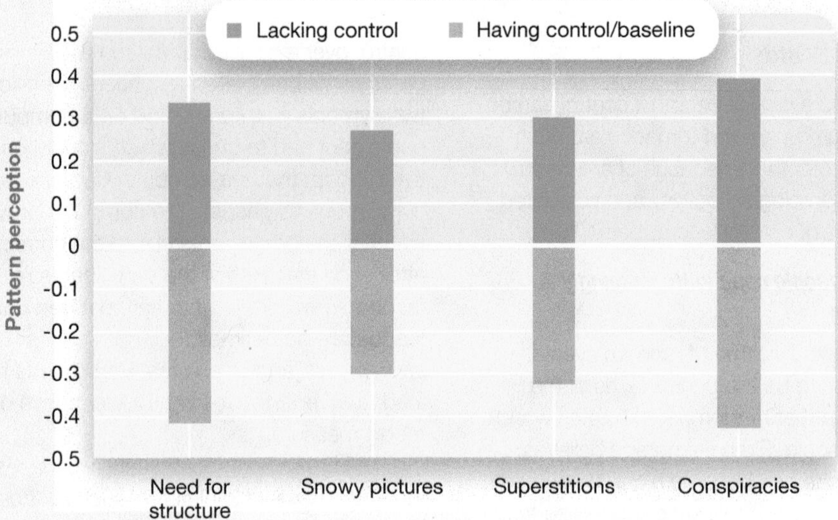

Figure 13.7 Exercising Compensatory Control
When people feel as though they lack control over the world, their need for structure, perceptual order, and beliefs in superstition and conspiracies increases. The orange bars show that participants who perceive that they are in control of events were unlikely to see images in snowy pictures and did not hold superstitious beliefs or endorse conspiracy theories. As the green bars indicate, when the same people perceive that they have lost a sense of control during the experimental procedure, the pattern is completely reversed. The participants report a greater need for structure, perceive images in random arrays, become more superstitious, and endorse conspiracy theories (Kay et al., 2009).

Can we critically evaluate this evidence?

A major advantage of the study described here is that the researchers were able to experimentally induce a perceived lack of control in the participants who received random feedback on their performance on the computerized task. The observation that these participants then perceived images within randomness and showed a heightened belief in superstition and conspiracies may help to explain how people respond to lost control outside of the laboratory. Of course, one limitation is that a real-world lack of control, such as that which occurs in the face of natural disaster or loss of a job, has far greater consequences. Thus, as with any laboratory experiment, there is a limit to the degree to which the results generalize. Also, earlier we commented that belief in a divine force such as God can buffer people from the discomfort produced by the notion that natural and societal events are largely, if not completely, outside of their control. It is important to add that this is not a statement on the existence of God, but rather a description of how perception of events can influence what people believe.

Why is this relevant?

Having a sense of control greatly affects how we think about and interpret the world. In addition, it affects our health. Individuals who believe they can predict and influence present and future events tend to have improved physical and mental well-being compared to people who believe the opposite. For example, patients who are scheduled to undergo medical procedures, such as a colonoscopy, have reduced anxiety for the procedure if they are given clear, informative tutorials about the procedure before it occurs (Luck et al., 1999).

People may also compensate for their lack of control by performing superstitious rituals, which can provide a sense of at least partial control over outcomes. This can be seen in everyday examples, such as among athletes who follow the same steps when preparing for a game, as well as in extreme, maladaptive forms, such as in obsessive–compulsive disorder. Doing nothing is one response, as Seligman and Maier discovered in their studies of learned helplessness. With lost control, people are also more likely to develop beliefs that the world is not random and is controlled and orderly. This perception manifests through beliefs of an intervening God, as well as greater likelihood of defending social and political institutions that offer control of world events (Kay et al., 2009).

NUTRITION AND EXERCISE

"You are what you eat" is a well-worn phrase that was probably around long before scientists confirmed that it holds true. However, we now know that what we eat influences brain physiology and functioning. This being the case, psychologists have begun to investigate how diet affects intellectual ability and performance at work and school.

Nutrition and Cognitive Function

Long-term consumption of fattening and sugary foods can have a negative impact on cognitive functioning. But what about the short-term effects? You have probably heard of the importance of a good breakfast more times than you care to recall. However, breakfast is the most often skipped meal, especially among children and adolescents (Rampersaud et al., 2005). Many people report not having time to eat (or not making time) and a lack of appetite for breakfast foods.

Skipping breakfast may not be a healthy choice for people heading off to school or work. The brain utilizes large amounts of glucose and other nutrients for energy and in the synthesis of neurotransmitters. Overall, research indicates that eating breakfast has a positive effect on academic performance (Adolphus, Lawton, & Dye, 2013). But does this mean eating anything? Would you be better off eating a huge bowl of sugary cereal than eating nothing on the morning of a major exam? Carefully controlled studies on animal subjects and work with humans has shown that being placed on a high-fat nonnutritious diet for just a short period of time results in reduced cognitive performance (Holloway et al., 2011; Murray et al., 2009).

The relationship between diet and cognitive functioning has led some researchers on a quest to isolate specific compounds that are best suited to improving cognition. Certain chemicals found in various plants, called flavanols, appear to improve, or at least help sustain, cognitive functioning (Brickman et al., 2014). It appears that these chemicals protect nerve cells (Reznichenko et al., 2005). Other dietary supplements, such as the omega-3 fatty acids found in fish, can improve brain functioning when combined with exercise (van Praag et al., 2007; Wu et al., 2008).

Exercise

Exercise has considerable physical and psychological benefits, as people ranging from weekend warriors to long-term exercisers can attest. Barring injury, we typically do not hear a committed exerciser express regret about her active lifestyle. So which specific aspects of exercise account for all of its benefits? Obviously, exercise benefits the cardiovascular, muscular, and other physiological systems. How does the nervous system factor in?

Exercise has short-term benefits on mental functioning. For example, researchers in Germany asked college student participants to do all-out sprints, to jog, or to do nothing. The students who sprinted were able to learn 20% more items on a vocabulary list than the students who jogged or were inactive (Winter et al., 2007). Why did this occur? Perhaps the sprinters were more motivated than the others. This explanation sounds plausible, but the researchers randomly assigned healthy participants to the three groups—so there should not be anything inherent to the sprinter group that would lead them to learn more words. It appears that the type of exercise they engaged in led to increased cognitive performance. Which physiological processes might account for the cognitive edge the sprinters gained from their intense physical activity? The researchers discovered that the students who engaged in intense exercising had increased levels of dopamine, epinephrine, and **brain-derived neurotrophic factor (BDNF)**—*a protein in the nervous system that promotes survival, growth, and formation of new synapses*. Cardiovascular exercise also provides immediate benefits in cognitive processing in both grade-school and college-aged students (Hillman et al., 2003, 2014). But these immediate benefits of exercise are not limited to younger people. When sedentary adults between 60 and 85 years of age take up weekly exercise, they show improved brain functioning and cognitive performance (Hillman et al., 2008; Stothart et al., 2014).

One important issue to address is whether these short-term effects translate into lifelong cognitive benefits from exercise. Results from long-term studies indicate that a lifestyle that includes regular exercise helps preserve cognitive function and the brain systems that support it (van Praag, 2009). Researchers have found that older people who are at genetic risk for developing Alzheimer's disease and who show cognitive impairments can slow the rate of memory decline by exercising (Lautenschlager et al., 2008). It appears that levels of brain chemicals such as BDNF are boosted by exercise, which helps explain the changes in the brain that account for the cognitive benefits. Furthermore, exercise supports the development of new nerve cells in the hippocampus, a critical area for memory and cognitive activity (van Praag, 2008).

Journal prompt

Coping with Stress:

Now that you have read about many different coping styles, use terminology from the section to describe how you tend to cope with stress. What positive ways of coping that you learned about (or others you can think of) would you like to use more often?

Summary

Now that you have read this section you should:

KNOW . . .

The key terminology associated with coping and well-being:

biofeedback (p. 413)
brain-derived neurotrophic factor (BDNF) (p. 419)
compensatory control (p. 417)
coping (p. 412)
learned helplessness(p. 416)
negative affectivity (p. 415)
optimism (p. 412)
pessimistic explanatory style (p. 415)
positive psychology (p. 412)
posttraumatic growth (p. 413)
resilience (p. 413)

UNDERSTAND . . .

- ***How control over the environment influences coping and outlook.*** Psychologists have discovered that people (and dogs) become more willing to allow unpleasant events to occur if they learn that their behavior brings no change. Having at least some degree of control helps people with coping and improves their outlook on challenging circumstances. When control is threatened, people use compensatory responses, such as detecting order within random images.
- ***Positive and negative styles of coping.*** Whether someone copes using a positive or negative style is related to personality (e.g., optimism versus pessimism). Positive coping includes the concept of resilience—the ability to recover from adversity, and even benefit from the experience, as is the case with posttraumatic growth. Coping via negative affectivity and pessimism can have both psychological and physiological disadvantages.

APPLY . . .

- ***Your knowledge to better understand your own tendencies when dealing with stressful situations.*** We all fall somewhere on the optimism–pessimism continuum. Completing the How Do You Cope With Stress activity in Table 13.6 provides a sense of where you might fall on it with regard to how you respond to stress. As you read in this section, there are diverse ways of coping with stress, and the strategies we use affect our mental and physical health.

ANALYZE . . .

- ***Whether activities such as relaxation techniques, meditation, and biofeedback actually help people cope with stress and problems.*** Meditation and other relaxation methods have been found to be quite effective in reducing stress. While some training and practice may be necessary, these techniques are by no means inaccessible to those who are motivated to pursue them.

Quick Quiz

KNOW . . .

1. __________ is the tendency to respond to problems with a pattern of anxiety, hostility, anger, guilt, or nervousness.
   a. A coping style
   b. Negative affectivity
   c. Pessimism
   d. An aggression complex

UNDERSTAND . . .

2. A mentally healthy person who is prone to claiming that patterns exist where there are none:
   a. is showing negative affectivity.
   b. is showing signs of posttraumatic growth.
   c. probably feels a lost sense of control over a problem or situation.
   d. has a pessimistic explanatory style.

3. __________ is a positive coping strategy, while __________ is a negative style of coping.
   a. Meditation; resilience
   b. Pessimistic explanatory style; negative affectivity
   c. Meditation; alcohol
   d. Posttraumatic growth; resilience

APPLY . . .

4. If someone experiences a major setback in their physical health, what would be a good step toward helping them cope and possibly recover?
   a. Take care of all of their needs and avoid letting them stress about details of the illness.
   b. Remind them of previous times they experienced luck and that it could happen again.
   c. Load up on alternative, nonmedical options.
   d. Find ways that they can gain a sense of control over their health and ways to overcome the illness.

ANALYZE . . .

5. What is the most accurate conclusion regarding the effects of meditation on stress and well-being?
   a. Mediation helps the individual control his or her physiological responses, thereby decreasing stress and preventing health problems such as cardiovascular disease.
   b. Advanced training in mediation will decrease stress in a manner similar to simple relaxation techniques.
   c. Mediation is the absolute best way to combat stress and protect your body from disease.
   d. Mediation is not a commonly used way of managing stress.

Scientific Literacy Challenge: Forgiveness

Imagine a 50-year-old man with coronary heart disease visits with his physician. After receiving his prescription, he is reminded to eat a healthy diet, exercise, and manage his stress. But what if forgiveness was added to the list? Could this possibly be of any health benefit?

Before you start this activity, take a minute to write your thoughts on forgiveness.

Journal prompt

Write about some ways you think that forgiving someone could have mental and physical health benefits.

What Do We Know About Forgiveness?

Most people know at least *something* about how to live a healthy lifestyle, but forgiveness might not be an obvious choice on the list. In the commentary below, Steve Hanserd, a registered nurse, writes about how his staff is preparing to start a forgiveness intervention for their patients. As you read, remember that it is important to know the boldface key terms and concepts that are covered in Chapter 13.

Forgiveness Leads to a Change of Heart

By Steve Hanserd, RN, President, Association of Cardiac Care Professionals

We have an exciting new project in the works at the CCP medical center: A forgiveness intervention against **heart disease**. Forgiveness has been added to our list of the lifestyle changes we strongly recommend for patients with heart disease. Forgiveness rebuilds relationships and promotes **social resilience**. Social resilience is an important part of psychological health, and research indicates that it may improve physical health as well.

People who choose *not* to forgive, and instead hold onto resentment and anger, suffer numerous health consequences. Anger stimulates the **hypothalamic-pituitary-adrenal (HPA) axis**, our primary stress response system. Sustained activity of the HPA axis leads to negative physical effects, including compromised immune function. The goal of our intervention is to teach, encourage, and facilitate forgiveness. This is not just any forgiveness, but *unconditional* forgiveness. This is the conscious choice to let a transgression go without any conditions or demands; it means the individual is not waiting for an apology or retribution for a wrong that he has suffered.

Mr. Hanserd has stated his position and explained it well. Let's see how well he supported his position with scientific evidence below.

HOW DO SCIENTISTS STUDY FORGIVENESS?

In this section, the author introduces what he has learned about the science of forgiveness. As you read it, try to identify where the article addresses key elements of quality research and then complete the short quiz that follows.

The research supporting the benefits of forgiveness seems pretty clear. Studies published in the *Journal of Behavioral Medicine* showed that people who rarely forgive experience more episodes of anger than others. Anger, in turn, is associated with significantly worse cardiovascular conditions and related risk factors, such as sleep. Of those who do forgive, there are further differences: Individuals who forgive *conditionally* are likely to die earlier than those who forgive unconditionally.

We also know something about how forgiveness works. By decreasing the stress associated with resentment and anger, forgiving can decrease blood pressure, according to research published in the *Journal of Positive Psychology.* Experiments also found that individuals trained with forgiveness techniques showed healthier immune systems, including more disease fighting cells and reduced inflammation responses, which lead to better health.

Finally, the research also shows that forgiveness can be learned and practiced. There is a tendency for some people to be more consistent with forgiveness than others; it is a personality trait of sorts. But there have been several controlled experiments in which adults assigned to a forgiveness-training program improved their ability to consciously let go of an offense better than did controls, which is good evidence that an intervention might be successful.

Hopefully you spotted the references to the important scientific concepts. Test yourself by completing this short quiz, referring back to the article to find the answers.

1. One study showed that people who regularly forgive show lower levels of anger, and that people who experience less anger have better cardiovascular health. From this, we can confidently say that
   a. anger causes cardiovascular problems.
   b. cardiovascular problems cause people to become angry.
   c. forgiveness prevents heart disease.
   d. these variables are correlated with each other.
2. In the research on immunity reported in the *Journal of Positive Psychology*, which of the following was a dependent variable described in the paragraph?
   a. occupation of the participants
   b. presence of a heart condition
   c. inflammation levels
   d. anger
3. What can a scientifically literate individual assume about a study published in a scientific journal (such as the *Journal of Behavioral Medicine*)?
   a. The study was reviewed and published by a credible source.
   b. All the research in it consists exclusively of randomized, placebo-controlled designs.
   c. The editor of the journal hired some psychologists to write about their research.
   d. Claims of health benefits of forgiveness represent psychologists' personal opinions.

Answers: 1. *d* 2. *c* 3. *a*

Next, let's read about how Mr. Hanserd thinks about this program.

HOW SHOULD WE THINK CRITICALLY ABOUT FORGIVENESS?

Remember that critical thinking involves curiosity and reasonable levels of skepticism. Critical thinkers continue to ask questions while evaluating the quality of the answers they find. As you read through the passage below, search for specific statements relevant to critical thinking.

> This is probably the most exciting project I have had the privilege to work on, but I have to remain focused. There is a lot of work left for us to get the program started, which also involves accepting that some research we come across will not necessarily support what we are doing. I continue to remind myself that we don't know yet how helpful our program will be and we will have to collect a substantial amount of data to have strong evidence. Much of the research is correlational in nature so we are not yet 100% sure that forgiveness is what is driving the health benefits we see. I have every reason to be optimistic, however, because there is a growing number of experiments connecting forgiveness to health.

The statements below will help you identify several aspects of critical thinking. Match the following critical thinking statements to the highlighted passages that illustrate them. Note that at least one of these statements is not addressed in Mr. Hanserd's commentary.

1. The author addressed overly emotional thinking.
2. The author addressed the problems of anecdotal evidence.
3. The author appears to tolerate the ambiguity rather than insist on certainty.
4. The author examined the nature and quality of the evidence.

1. Yellow 2. Not addressed 3. Green 4. Blue

Now that you have completed this critical thinking exercise, continue to the next page to think about how this information can be applied.

HOW IS FORGIVENESS RELEVANT?

Mr. Hansard suggests that forgiveness can be studied and applied in a scientific manner to promote physical and mental health. Read how he makes the connection between the research and application in his article, and then consider any newly formed thoughts you may have about the topic in the writing activity that follows.

> Forgiveness is not a cure-all, of course. It is never going to be a substitute for the appropriate medication and healthy lifestyle choices related to diet, exercise, and smoking. However, it is very important to realize that forgiveness can have significant impact on health. Therefore, a combination of education, instruction, and practice should help our patients, especially for those who are inclined to carry a grudge rather than to forgive.

SHARED WRITING

Do you think forgiving might be a useful intervention for cardiovascular patients? If possible, share an instance in your life in which forgiveness seemed to help your overall health.

Quiz

1. What effect does watching food commercials have on the eating habits of viewers?
   - **a.** Food commercials generally have little to no effect on eating habits.
   - **b.** People are more likely to eat the specific product being advertised in the commercial, but not other unrelated foods.
   - **c.** Snacking in general is more likely after viewers watch a food commercial.
   - **d.** The eating habits of adults are influenced more by food commercials than are the eating habits of children.
2. The HPA axis involves which three structures?
   - **a.** Hippocampus, pituitary gland, adrenal glands
   - **b.** Hypothalamus, pineal gland, adenoids
   - **c.** Hippocampus, pineal gland, adrenal glands
   - **d.** Hypothalamus, pituitary gland, adrenal glands
3. A hormone that is associated with enhanced immune responses and social bonding is called __________.
   - **a.** HPA
   - **b.** cortisol
   - **c.** oxytocin
   - **d.** *Helicobacter pylori*
4. Which aspect of Type A personality is most closely correlated with increased risk for heart disease?
   - **a.** Competitiveness
   - **b.** Anger and hostility
   - **c.** Patience
   - **d.** Worrying about time
5. Biofeedback is a therapeutic technique involving:
   - **a.** focusing on a specific thought or sensation, such as an image or a repeated sound.
   - **b.** attending to all thoughts, sensations, and feelings without attempting to judge or control them.
   - **c.** the use of physiological recording instruments to provide feedback that increases awareness of bodily responses.
   - **d.** bodily interaction with thinking and emotion.
6. Gretta is in an abusive relationship with her boyfriend. Although leaving her boyfriend is an obvious way to end the abuse, Gretta has been in this situation for so long that she no longer feels she has any control over it. Gretta's situation illustrates the concept of __________.
   - **a.** compensatory control
   - **b.** posttraumatic growth
   - **c.** resilience
   - **d.** learned helplessness

7. Which of the following statements about how discrimination influences health is most accurate?
   a. Discrimination is unrelated to poor health.
   b. People who experience discrimination are likely to compensate for it by making positive health-related choices.
   c. An immediate increase in heart rate is the biggest problem associated with experiencing discrimination.
   d. Experiencing discrimination stimulates the stress response, which can bring about long-term health problems.
8. In modern times, the leading causes of death in industrialized nations such as the United States are __________.
   a. viral infections
   b. bacterial infections
   c. lifestyle factors
   d. Each of these are equal contributors.
9. What is psychoneuroimmunology?
   a. The study of the relationship between immune system and nervous system functioning
   b. The study of both the positive and negative effects that our behavior and decisions have on health, survival, and well-being
   c. A condition in which plaques form in the blood vessels that supply the heart with blood and oxygen, resulting in restricted blood flow
   d. A hormone secreted by the adrenal gland
10. How does stress affect cancer?
   a. Stress decreases the number of white blood cells in the body, which results in cancer progression.
   b. Hormones from the autonomic nervous system stimulate cells that reside in tumors, which can in turn stimulate growth and proliferation of the tumors.
   c. Stress decreases the growth of cancer cells.
   d. Stress does not affect cancer.
11. People with __________ personality type are patient and easygoing, and have relaxed disposition, whereas __________ personality individuals tend to be impatient and are easily angered, competitive, and highly motivated.
   a. Type A; Type B
   b. stressed; relaxed
   c. Type B; Type A
   d. relaxed; stressed
12. The health risk most likely to be associated with Type A personality is __________.
   a. AIDS
   b. cancer
   c. the cold virus
   d. coronary heart disease
13. What does it mean to say someone is resilient?
   a. The person has the ability to effectively recover from illness or adversity.
   b. The person tends to be calm when challenged or stressed.
   c. The person shows the tendency to have a favorable, constructive view on situations and to expect positive outcomes.
   d. The person uses only positive processes to manage demands, stress, and conflict.
14. __________ is an acquired suppression of avoidance or escape behavior in response to unpleasant, uncontrollable circumstances.
   a. Compensatory control
   b. Learned helplessness
   c. Coping
   d. Resilience
15. People often turn to religion to explain natural disasters. This behavior demonstrates the concept of __________.
   a. compensatory control
   b. learned helplessness
   c. coping
   d. resilience

14

Psychology in the Workplace

BY DOUGLAS A. JOHNSON, PH.D. AND SOPHIE RUBIN, PH.D.

The History of Psychology in the Workplace

Making business decisions based on data can have a dramatic positive impact.

During the late 1940s, the nation of Japan experienced radical changes after the country had been economically crippled in the aftermath of World War II (Leitner, 1999). Business and industry declined due to failed attempts to produce quality goods and as a result their products were not wanted by the world at large or even by Japan's own citizens. The products manufactured by Japan were considered junk by the majority of people. This started to change during the early 1950s, which is the same time that an American statistician named W. Edwards Deming began visiting Japan and lecturing on how to run businesses by using *statistical process control*. Although there were certainly many factors involved in the Japan's resurrection, the application of statistical process control had an enormous impact on the quality of products being sold.

Although the statistical tools used in this process can be complicated, the core idea was a simple lesson in empiricism: *manage your business decisions by data*. Deming recognized that judgments based on intuition or years of experience were poor substitutes for making decisions based on systematic observation, careful measurement, and the application of data analysis tools. In Japan, the application of Deming's principles improved manufacturing standards and business processes, which in turn lead to high quality products being produced at a fast rate (Deming, 1982). In a short period of time, Japanese automobiles and electronics went from bad jokes to favored products worldwide. Japan flourished with this new approach to business and continually grew from the 1960s to 1980s, eventually becoming one of the world's top economic forces. As evidenced by this example, effective business practices can have a dramatic impact on not only the business, but have the potential to change the fate of a nation.

Psychology can help contribute to understanding and improving the time we spend at work.

Business practices can also have a dramatic influence on an individual. Nearly all people will have at least one job during their life and most people will experience many different jobs throughout life. This work will likely consume more of their waking hours than any other activity. Jobs can function as a great source of personal fulfillment that enrich our lives or as a burdensome source of obligation required to pay the bills. How fulfilling your workplace is often has more to do with how you are treated at the job rather than the requirements of the job itself. Managerial interactions with employees, support for workers, career development, and the challenge of the work itself all contribute to the quality of the work environment. These factors have an impact on employee productivity and satisfaction and people are vital to every form of business and industry. Despite how crucial people are to the functioning of every workplace, few people receive comprehensive training on applying psychology in the workplace. People such as Deming demonstrated what could be accomplished by applying empirical methods to business processes. However, Deming lacked a background in psychology and tended to neglect the management of people within those business processes (Daniels & Bailey, 2014; Grote, 2002). For example, how do you get employees and managers to actually implement his guidelines for quality? Deming himself had little to say on this topic beyond general and vague encouragements such "drive out fear" and "remove barriers" (Deming, 1982). In fact, Deming showed a misunderstanding of human psychology when he suggested that people were self-motivated and therefore giving employees incentive pay would not enhance performance (Deming, 1986), a suggestion not supported by psychological research (Abernathy, 1996; Bucklin & Dickinson, 2001).

W. Edwards Deming 1900–1993. *(Source: Courtesy of Catherine Karnow/Corbis Images.)*

Japan made huge gains in the workplace by using data-based decisions to guide quality control, but businesses also have the potential for huge gains by using data-based decisions to guide the performance of people. This is where **industrial/organizational (I/O) psychology** comes in. I/O psychology is the study and application of psychological techniques to improve workplace environments and the individuals employed in these

industrial/organizational psychology
the application of psychological techniques to enhance the functioning of people while at work

Walter Dill Scott 1869-1955. *(Source: Courtesy of Northwestern University Archives.)*

Hugo Münsterberg 1863-1916. *(Source: Courtesy of Newscom.)*

environments. It is a varied discipline covering nearly every aspect of business and therefore relevant to anyone interested in improving work, the activity we invest so much of our lives into. For a better understanding of the roots of I/O psychology, we need to return to both the World Wars and the time preceding those wars.

THE ORIGINS OF INDUSTRIAL/ ORGANIZATIONAL PSYCHOLOGY

I/O psychology is a relatively young application of psychology. Psychology's first foray into the business world can be traced back to the early 1900s, when Walter Dill Scott began investigating psychological applications in advertising (Goodwin, 2008). He published two books on the subject (Scott, 1903; 1908) in which he noted that people were not persuaded by reason and rationality alone in their purchases, but were also heavily influenced by emotional appeals. Psychology's first behaviorist, John B. Watson, later refined these techniques in 1920 through the use of respondent conditioning and applied this science to advertising campaigns (Cohen, 1979). The use of psychology for persuasion in marketing still continues today through the application of social psychology techniques (Goldstein, Martin, & Cialdini, 2008).

However, the first person to begin thinking broadly about psychology's use in the business affairs was Hugo Münsterberg, who is often regarded as the father of industrial/organizational psychology (Hothersall, 2003). Münsterberg was concerned with making psychology more practical and useable to the average person. He published the text *Psychology and Industrial Efficiency* in 1913 (one year before World War I began), in which he dealt with issues such as hiring, increasing employee efficiency, and applications in sales. Unfortunately, much of Münsterberg's work was shunned and ignored when he publicly defended Germany's military actions during World War I. The public harassment and criticism that followed was an intense source of stress for Münsterberg and probably a contributing factor to his death in 1916, when he died in the middle of a lecture, a mere 3 years after his book had been published.

Psychologists Are Called into the War Effort

In 1917, the United States joined the World War I conflict and many of America's psychologists looked for ways to aid in the war effort (Aamodt, 2010; Shiraev, 2011). Their primary

Work equipment can often be re-designed based on an understanding of psychology.

contribution was to evaluate soldiers through various mental tests and make recommendations on where to best place them in the military. Although the military commanders did not act on these suggestions, this experience was enough for psychologists to become more heavily involved in testing following the war's conclusion (Goodwin, 2008). The blossoming field of I/O psychology was becoming a respectable profession, although the adoption of psychological techniques was slow to take place in the business world. Progression became even slower when the economy collapsed during the Great Depression of the early 1930s, which made jobs scarce enough that management could easily find employees who would desperately work hard for very little compensation (Connellan, 1978).

I/O psychology truly cemented its place as a formal and lasting discipline when World War II began in 1939 (Muchinsky, 2011; Schultz & Schultz, 2006). This time the military sought out the help of psychologists to interview soldiers and determine what area of the military they are best suited for. Unlike the previous war, this time the military actually implemented the recommendations regarding selection and placement decisions of soldiers. Furthermore, the war introduced new airplanes, tanks, and other forms of machinery and many of the control panels on these machines were difficult to use and not well-designed (Hunt, 2007). Psychologists were asked to provide advice on how to better design equipment for human-machine interaction, a specialization now known as human factors engineering (more on this later).

Post-War Developments in I/O Psychology

After World War II concluded, the field of I/O psychology exploded and thrived (Beehr, 1996). The field conducted research and broadened its scope beyond the same kinds of services it provided during the previous wars, only this time there was no subsequent economic downturn to slow the growth. Many veterans were returning to work with no prior experiences on their resumes beyond "soldier" and most of the people with the work experience tended to be older (their age had prevented them for serving in the war). As these older managers began approaching retirement age, there was a particularly strong need for immediate training, a service that I/O psychologists were happy to help fulfill. Given these events, it is not surprising that I/O psychology developed a strong emphasis on selection and placement, training, and the design of work equipment during that time period, which is still reflected in much of the research being conducted today. The scope began to expand during the 1960s when the cognitive perspective gained momentum and I/O psychologists began to more frequently explore the role of employee perceptions and other mental processes in the workplace.

The two World Wars were a huge impetus to the growth of I/O psychology.

Around the same time, another approach to the workplace began to develop, one that has roots in applied behavior analysis (Dickinson, 2000). One of the earliest suggestions for this new approach can be traced back to Owen Aldis, who in 1961 suggested that behavioral research had implications for how managers interact with and supervise employees. For example, how and when payments are delivered to employees could potentially have a big impact on their productivity and happiness. Furthermore, many trainers around this time period began to be frustrated when well-developed selection procedures and carefully conducted training still failed to reliably improve day-to-day job performance (Connellan, 1978). Many of the employees *could* perform well after training, but this did not necessarily mean that they *would* perform well.

It began to be recognized that daily management of workplace contingencies (on-the-job antecedents and consequences) was a necessary ingredient to sustain employee motivation, productivity, and safety. This eventually culminated in the creation of organizational behavior management (OBM), the application of behavioral principles in the workplace to develop practical tools for enhancing employee behavior. This was often accomplished through data-oriented techniques such as observing employees, pinpointing and recording the relevant behaviors needed to perform a task, and finally changing the consequences for behavior (Mawhinney, 2011; O'Brien & Dickinson, 1982). OBM also focused less on traditional I/O topics such as selection and placement in favor of topics

Psychology emphasized the need for understanding the mental processes and the work environment of employees.

Training solutions are not useful for problems that could be eliminated if the employee is sufficiently motivated.

such as productivity and quality (Bucklin, Alvero, Dickinson, Austin, & Jackson, 2000), although there is considerable overlap and compatibility between these approaches. Taken all together, I/O psychology includes a variety of applications that are of great importance to the well-being of employed individuals and the organizations they work for. We will begin exploring many of these applications in the subsequent pages, beginning with job analysis.

Analyzing the Requirements to Perform a Job

Before employers can train an individual for a job or even hire an individual, they should know what the job entails. This is the purpose of conducting a **job analysis**, which is the systematic attempt to identify the relevant competencies needed to perform the job, the typical activities that will be performed, and details regarding the work environments including the tools and equipment that will be used for that job (Gatewood, Feild, & Barrick, 2011). Determining the necessary competencies is a critical aspect of this process and these competencies are sometimes called **KSAOs** (Schippmann et al., 2000). KSAO refers to the knowledge, skills, abilities, and other characteristics an individual needs to possess in order to adequately perform the job. Performing a job analysis and developing a list of KSAOs can be done a number of ways, but frequently involves analyzing the necessary job outcomes in detail (i.e., what products or services are created by this job) as well as interviewing both supervisors and the people who currently hold the job. *Subject matter experts* (SME), people who are considered to be experts at their particular job, are particularly useful for interviewing. However, caution is sometimes warranted with SMEs because the skills needed to perform a job often change, therefore experts of the current job may not be experts in the new version of the job. For example, someone who is an expert with a current software program may not necessarily be an expert with future editions of that software. Occasionally, new jobs are invented and therefore no experts are available, especially as the business world continues to change at an accelerated pace (Muchinsky, 2011).

Organizational success depends on finding people with the job-related knowledge, skills, abilities, and other characteristics.

Some psychologists have argued that work analysis is a better term than job analysis. The term work analysis highlights the notion that organizations are placing more emphasis on tasks and skills that are transferable across settings versus the term job analysis which emphasizes a rigid and unchanging job (Schultz & Schultz, 2006). Regardless of the label used, the basic task remains the same: determine what kind of person is best suited for the work tasks by analyzing what is needed for successful performance. This attempt to best match people with the work environment is what makes job analysis an undertaking that is particularly well-suited for psychology (Sanchez & Levine, 2012). A mismatch between the person and their work can be harmful to the business and stressful for the mismatched person.

For example, the *Peter Principle* states that people are sometimes promoted until they become incompetent (Peter & Hull, 1969). If a mechanic was particularly skilled at repairing automobiles, a company may promote that individual to the level of supervisor. Unfortunately, the former mechanic and newly promoted supervisor may be terrible at managing other people. The person's KSAOs (repairing automobiles) did not match the KSAOs needed for the supervisor job (managing others). As a result of this mismatch, the company essentially traded a good mechanic for a bad supervisor.

job analysis
the systematic documentation of the conditions, materials, competencies and activities needed to successfully perform a job

KSAO
a knowledge, skill, ability, or other characteristic that an individual must have in order to perform a job

Legal Considerations in Job Analysis

Having the relevant KSAOs does not automatically mean someone will be a high performer (motivation to perform is necessary too), but it is a critical prerequisite to high performance (Crowell, Hantula, & McArthur, 2011). Job analyses help provide information that can later be used to develop predictors of job performance and criteria for performance appraisals (Sanchez & Levine, 2012). It is critical to do a job analysis carefully, not only because it is the foundation for other organizational tools but also because of legal considerations. An improperly analyzed job potentially leaves an organization open to future discrimination lawsuits. Consider the possibility that an employer requires job applicants to possess a high school diploma and refuses to hire anyone without a diploma. What if it is later discovered that having a diploma wasn't actually relevant for doing the job well? If a certain minority group tended to earn diplomas less often than other groups, the company would have inadvertently discriminated against that minority group since members of that group would rarely be hired (such was the case in the *Griggs v. Duke Power*, 1971 lawsuit). The fact that the company did not intend to discriminate is not a good legal defense; companies are legally obligated to conduct accurate job analyses to determine what personal attributes are truly related to successful job performance (Gatewood, Feild, & Barrick, 2011).

A poor fit between the a person and a job can be stressful for both the individual and organization.

A requirement could even be job related and still result in discrimination if that requirement is exaggerated beyond the real world job demands. For example, a physical test to be a firefighter might require applicants to drag a fire hose across a parking lot for 100 feet. This test may cause most female applicants to be denied the job since men generally tend to be physically stronger. If a job analysis reveals that in actual real world conditions, firefighters would never need to drag a fire hose 100 feet, then that employer has left themselves vulnerable to gender discrimination lawsuits (especially if the women were able to meet the real world requirement). With both of these examples, implementation of the findings from a well-developed job analysis could have protected these organizations. Remember that when I/O psychologists conduct job analyses, they are not measuring every aspect of the person or every attribute they can think of, but are analyzing the fit between the individual and the *necessary* demands of the work.

Job analyses need to reflect real world demands.

Designing the Workplace for Average Human Use

Although every job has demands, some of those demands can be reduced or eliminated, particularly in regards to the tools and equipment being used. Some work equipment is not well designed for use with the average person and therefore adds an unnecessary burden to that person's ability to perform the job well. Imagine if you and a couple of fellow employees were in the control room monitoring safety readings for the functioning of a big industrial plant. Suddenly and without any warning, alarms start going off and the control panel in front of you lights up and flashes like fireworks. This is an incredibly unfamiliar scenario and you have no idea what is going on, but you know it must be bad. Although multiple alarms and lights are going off simultaneously, you figure that some of them have to be more important than others. You spend several minutes trying to figure out what the specific problem is. You notice that a critical yellow light is turned off, which is normally turned on when things are running well (i.e., yellow light off = bad). However, you suddenly remember that if a different orange-colored light is turned on, then the yellow light should actually be off. At least you hope so; your training on those emergency lights was a really long time ago! That orange light is located on the far side of the control panel. It was difficult to see but you notice that orange light is turned on (i.e., yellow light off = good now). Having wasted much time trying to figure out that confusing mess, you finally know that you need to push a green button to fix the situation. It is located

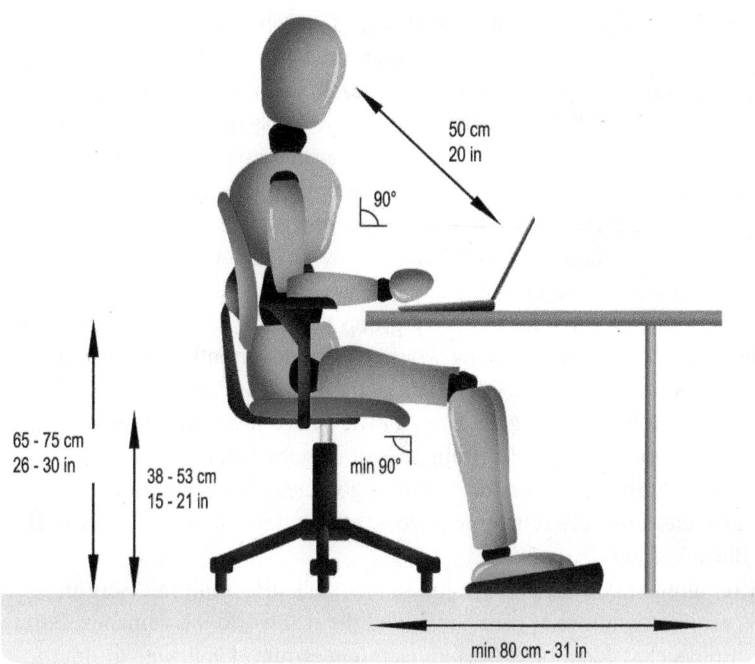

Some psychologists specialize in optimizing the work environment for the average person's capabilities.

on a panel over your head and slightly out of reach. As you reach up and stretch to push the button overhead, you lean on the control panel to brace yourself and hear a *click*. You accidently pushed another button on the control panel and you have no idea which one it was. Hopefully you have not destroyed the plant or surrounding community.

The confusing and possibly deadly mess describe above could have been avoided if the work area had been designed in a more intuitive and easy to use manner. While the specific job or industry was not specified, similar workplace design flaws have confronted many employees working in important work settings such as nuclear power stations, oil drilling rigs, and chemical processing plants (the kind of places where you really don't want an accident). Disastrous accidents have sometimes occurred because employees spent

A confusing work environment can lead to unnecessary and possibly disastrous mistakes.

too long trying to understand multiple alarms, dealing with indicators lights with ambiguous meanings (is the yellow light good or bad?), or environments that are poorly laid out, such as relevant lights being spaced far apart or important switches that are difficult to reach (Meshkati, 2006). Even the best of employees can make errors when surrounded by counterintuitive designs. Many critical industries will place decisions for how to react to such complex environments in the hands of a limited number of people, such as airplane pilots in charge of the cockpits. Despite advances in technology, the decision making process cannot simply be automated away by computer. Somewhere in the process a human being has to be in charge of monitoring the automation system. Furthermore, there are events that are difficult to predict and automated responses by a computer depend on predictable scenarios being pre-programmed. Our tools, machines, and other physical parts of the environment need to be designed with human capabilities and tendencies in mind.

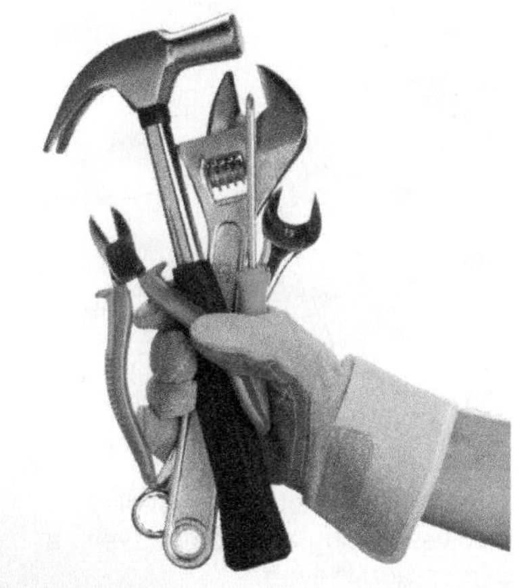

Understanding human strengths and limitations can help in our design of tools.

Given the design flaws seen in numerous workplaces and products, such **human factors engineering** does not come about easily or naturally. It requires a solid understanding of psychology in order to conduct extensive testing and research (Sanders & McCormick, 1993). To design equipment for people, you need to understand physical attributes of the human body, but also the limitations and capabilities of human perception, memory, decision making, and attention. This is not only true for safety concerns, but also for issues such as productivity, satisfaction, comfort, and everyday usage. An example of comfort and satisfaction can be found with the graphical user interfaces (GUI) of computers. These interfaces were designed to allow people to interact with their computer by clicking on-screen images or using a touchscreen. This replaced the older and less intuitive interaction style of only typing text commands. The GUIs of personal computers, cell phones, ATMs, and electronic tablets continue to evolve in an attempt to make the interaction between human and machine as intuitive as possible. This intersection of psychology and technology still has much progress to make, as evidenced by all the times you have failed to get an electronic device to do what you wanted it to do.

By analyzing the amount of time it takes to perform a job in using different motions, psychologists have helped determine the most time efficient ways to work.

As noted earlier, productivity can also be enhanced by redesigning tools and their use. One of the earliest I/O psychology applications were called *time-and-motion studies*, which involved analyzing repetitive tasks and redesigning the workplace to make work more efficient (Schultz & Schultz, 2006). By minimizing distance from tools or ensuring that workers use equipment in a certain way, organizations can save seconds each time the task is completed. That may not sound like much, but when a repetitive tasks is performed thousands of times, those seconds add up quickly.

While you can spend much time analyzing the demands of a job or redesigning equipment to lessen the burden of those demands, at some point you need to find someone to actually do the job. Not everyone will be a perfect fit for a job and some individuals will make better workers than others. Ideally, you want to find someone who will work hard at a job that is well-suited for his or her particular skills and personality. This is where personnel selection and placement comes in.

Creating the Best Fit between the Job and the Person

Part of the success of an organization can be traced to its ability to select and retain the best employees. **Personnel selection** involves collecting the available information about applicants and then evaluating the suitability of that person for that job. In essence, the selection process involves an attempt to identify which applicant is most likely to possess the knowledge, skills, abilities, and other characteristics (KSAOs) relevant for a particular job to make him or her perform more successfully than the other available applicants (Gatewood, Feild, & Barrick, 2011). A well-designed selection process may even help find employees who are more likely to remain at the organization for a long period of time (Barrick & Zimmerman, 2009). A poorly designed selection process can have a severe negative impact on the productivity of a business, possibly even destroying any competitive advantage for that

human factors engineering
the use of psychological knowledge regarding human capabilities, limitations, and tendencies to design tools, machines, and other equipment

personnel selection
the collection and evaluation of information to determine whether to hire an applicant

A major aspect of I/O psychology involves finding a match between a person and the job.

business (Hunter & Schmidt, 1996). As such, this is a serious concern for both small and large organizations, which explains why many I/O psychologists currently specialize in selection and placement. It is also important that psychologists contribute to this aspect of the business world because most managers lack knowledge on the best practices for selecting employees. Further adding to this problem is that fact that many of these managers are overconfident in their ability to select the best candidates despite their lack of knowledge (recall the information on metacognition from Chapter 1).

The selection process may be conducted with internal or external applicants. The goal in selecting from these two groups is essentially the same, but the process differs due to the available information. External applicants are job candidates who are not currently employed by the organization, whereas internal applicants are current employees looking for a promotion or transfer to another part of the organization. Employers have access to much more information when dealing with internal applicants, such as past performance evaluations, job observations, and other forms of employee records. However, this does not mean that selecting internal applicants is an easy task. An employee's success in one part or level of an organization may not necessarily mean he or she will be successful in all parts or levels of an organization (recall the Peter Principle). Furthermore, there are often multiple internal applicants, meaning the employer still has to compare several sources of information to determine the best candidate. If internal and external applicants are being considered at the same time, the employer may need to weigh a known internal applicant against a lesser known but potentially better external applicant. As always, errors in this process can be quite costly.

It is not an easy task to sort through all the potential applicants who might make for good employees.

There are two basic types of errors that can be made in the selection process (Gatewood, Feild, & Barrick, 2011). The first error is a *false negative error*, which occurs when an applicant who would have been the most successful is incorrectly rejected. The company not only runs the risk of having a sub-optimal workforce, but superior applicants who are rejected may end up hired by a rival competitor. Furthermore, a false negative error may violate legal guidelines if it involves a member of a protected minority and the failure to adhere to such guidelines can have severe legal and social repercussions (it is not good for a company's public reputation to be found guilty of discrimination). The second error is a *false positive error*, which occurs when a poor applicant is hired by the organization. Once again, the costs of an error can be

Selection errors can have painful consequences for everyone involved.

The best predictor of future behavior is past behavior.

severe because the organization may be stuck with a low performing employee who may prove difficult to fire after being hired. A poor employee could potentially do much damage to an organization (consider the potential damage from bad customer service or safety protocol violations). Even if the company successfully terminates the employee, there are the increased costs associated with having to repeat the selection process all over again and the productivity impairments that come from being short-staffed. The stakes are high when you consider that these are people's livelihoods (it is a terrible feeling to be rejected from a desired job you were qualified for) and an organization's finances are on the line.

Most applicants get rejected during a review of their biodata.

There are many methods for assessing an applicant's fit for job, including subjective judgments, ratings of applicant responses, statistical analyses of obtained data, or some combination of these. Underlying most assessment procedures is this basic principle: *The best predictor of future behavior is past behavior*. An employee's performance in past jobs or educational settings can tell us much about how he or she will perform in future jobs. Reviews of the research have confirmed that past behavior is an appropriate predictor of the future (Ouellette & Wood, 1998). There are a variety of methods available for an employer to collect such information on past behavior.

Using Biodata for Selection Purposes

One source of information about an applicant is **biodata**. Whenever you have filled in the blanks on a job application, you are providing biodata. Biodata refers to biographical data, which is information collected by questionnaires, applications, or resume submissions and provides details regarding work history, accomplishments, education, opinions, values, and relevant life experiences. The review of biodata is the first step in the selection process and is usually where the largest number of applicants are rejected. Research has shown that biodata can be successfully used to filter out low performing job applicants (Aamodt, 2010).

Job applications are frequent sources of biodata, but it is important that illegal questions regarding demographics such age, gender, or race not be required.

Unfortunately, some employers are careless with biodata because they don't consider it as critical as other selection methods such as interviews. This isn't to say that they ignore biodata, but that they place much higher confidence in their ability to discover valuable information during the interview itself. Given the large number of rejected people, the possibility of false negative errors is considerably high, as is the potential of discriminatory practices. For example, many companies create job applications that require applicants to provide their age, gender, or race. Requiring such information is illegal for nearly all jobs. Some companies have elected to greatly restrict their collection of biodata because of fears regarding discrimination and lawsuits (Barrick & Zimmerman, 2005). However, collecting less information will only increase the possibility of erroneous decisions. An organization should collect as much information as possible, as long as that information can be proven to be relevant for performing well in the job.

Using Work Samples for Selection Purposes

Another way to predict whether an individual will succeed as an employee is to simply have him or her perform the job before being hired. These work simulations by applicants are known as **work samples**. The employer sets up a work station that approximates working conditions and measures how well the applicant handles the various demands (Hunter & Schmidt, 1996). For example, an electrician may be asked to test and repair faulty wiring, a programmer may be asked to debug software, a copywriter may be asked to write an advertisement, etc.

Work samples are advantageous as there are few selection methods that are more realistic for assessing future performance. Even observations as brief as 5 minutes have been shown to produce valuable information about how an employee would act in a given situation (Ambady, Krabbenhoft, & Hogan, 2006). The disadvantage of work samples is that they can only be used for applicants who already know the job and are therefore not

biodata
the biographical information on an applicant that is collected by questionnaires, applications, and resumes

work sample
the performance of work tasks by an applicant that are used to reach a hiring decision

A straightforward method for determining job suitability is to have the applicant simply perform the job.

appropriate for jobs in which new hires will be expected to receive training on basic work tasks (Schmidt & Hunter, 1998).

Using General Mental Ability for Selection Purposes

Psychologists have also used general mental ability to predict employee performance. **General mental ability** is an overall measurement of one's intelligence. It is a single score that summarizes a person's skill on various abilities, such as comprehending written and oral directions, written and oral expression, mathematical fluency, logic and reasoning, memory, conceptual understanding, and problem solving.

For example, the Wonderlic Cognitive Ability Test is a 12-minute pencil and paper test that measures general mental ability through questions on numerical calculations, verbal relations, and spatial understanding (Belcher, 1992). The Wonderlic Cognitive Ability Test is one of the most

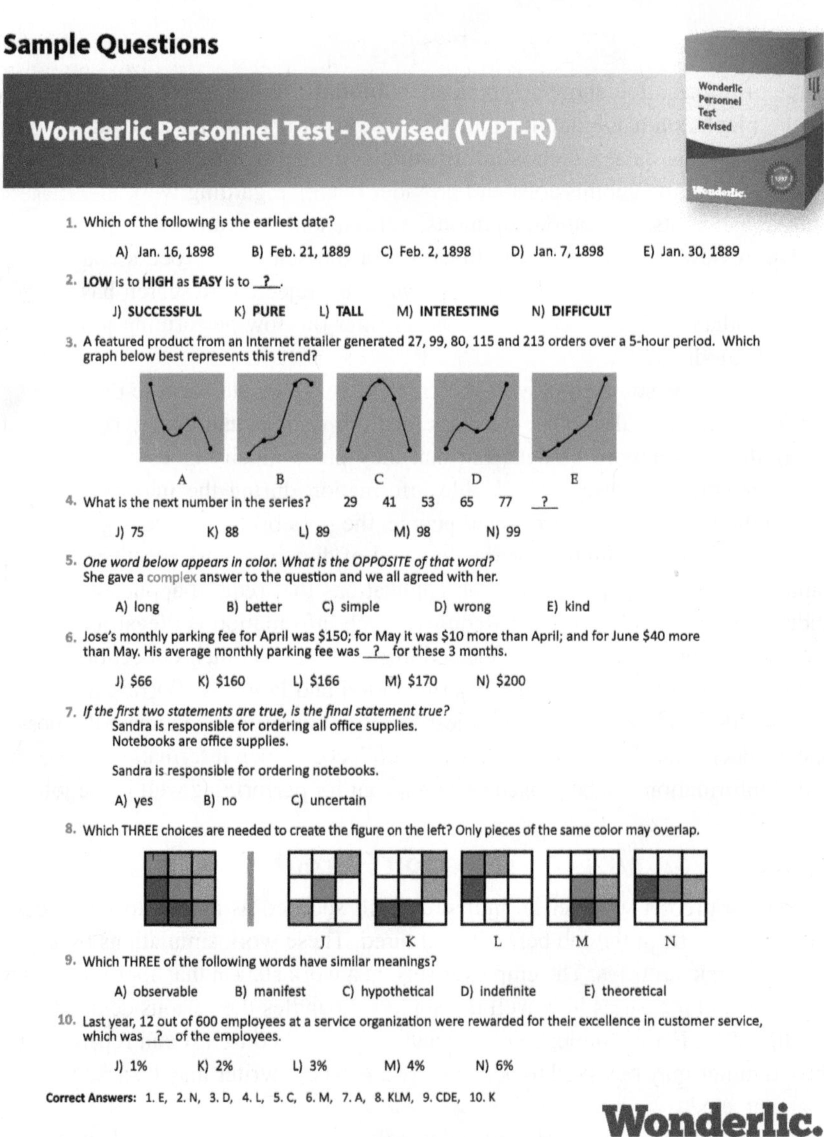

Sample Questions

Wonderlic Personnel Test - Revised (WPT-R)

1. Which of the following is the earliest date?

   A) Jan. 16, 1898 B) Feb. 21, 1889 C) Feb. 2, 1898 D) Jan. 7, 1898 E) Jan. 30, 1889

2. **LOW** is to **HIGH** as **EASY** is to __?__.

   J) **SUCCESSFUL** K) **PURE** L) **TALL** M) **INTERESTING** N) **DIFFICULT**

3. A featured product from an Internet retailer generated 27, 99, 80, 115 and 213 orders over a 5-hour period. Which graph below best represents this trend?

   A B C D E

4. What is the next number in the series? 29 41 53 65 77 __?__

   J) 75 K) 88 L) 89 M) 98 N) 99

5. *One word below appears in color. What is the OPPOSITE of that word?*
   She gave a complex answer to the question and we all agreed with her.

   A) long B) better C) simple D) wrong E) kind

6. Jose's monthly parking fee for April was $150; for May it was $10 more than April; and for June $40 more than May. His average monthly parking fee was __?__ for these 3 months.

   J) $66 K) $160 L) $166 M) $170 N) $200

7. *If the first two statements are true, is the final statement true?*
   Sandra is responsible for ordering all office supplies.
   Notebooks are office supplies.

   Sandra is responsible for ordering notebooks.

   A) yes B) no C) uncertain

8. Which THREE choices are needed to create the figure on the left? Only pieces of the same color may overlap.

   J K L M N

9. Which THREE of the following words have similar meanings?

   A) observable B) manifest C) hypothetical D) indefinite E) theoretical

10. Last year, 12 out of 600 employees at a service organization were rewarded for their excellence in customer service, which was __?__ of the employees.

    J) 1% K) 2% L) 3% M) 4% N) 6%

Correct Answers: 1. E, 2. N, 3. D, 4. L, 5. C, 6. M, 7. A, 8. KLM, 9. CDE, 10. K

Wonderlic.
www.wonderlic.com | 800.323.3742

The Wonderlic measures general cognitive skills using a variety of questions such as "Which of the following words have similar meanings?" and "Which graph best represents the data set?" *(Source: Courtesy of Wonderlic, Inc.)*

general mental ability
an overall measure of how well an individual follows instructions, learns new material, and solves novel problems

popular mental ability tests in business and industry and is even used for the assessment of NFL players during scouting. Other popular general mental ability tests include the Miller Analogies Test, the Quick Test, and the Raven Progressive Matrices (Aamodt, 2010). It is important to note that general mental ability is not an actual concrete thing and should not be treated as such (see the notes on reification from Chapter 2). Keep in mind that the score one receives can only *estimate* past learning and the potential for future learning. Predictions such as these do not guarantee outcomes and an estimate of learning does not summarize all of one's capabilities. However, it can still be a useful predictor of likely future behavior.

General mental ability has successfully predicted future performance across a variety of jobs.

The use of general mental ability to predict future job performance and to make selection decisions remains controversial with the general public (general mental ability is often viewed as being too abstract to be relevant to actual jobs), although most psychologists accept the general mental ability tests are appropriate and justifiable (Murphy, Cronin, & Tam, 2003). General mental ability tests have been shown to predict job performance better than previous job experience, personality, dispositions, or other abilities across nearly all occupations (Schmidt & Hunter, 2004). This includes jobs of various levels of complexity, although it does better predict high complexity jobs (chemist, engineer, accountant, etc.) than low complexity jobs (welder, receptionist, cashier, etc.) (Hunter & Schmidt, 1996). Performance on general mental ability tests closely relates to academic achievement (Gatewood, Feild, & Barrick, 2011). This may be part of the reason many employers will ask for college GPA; how good of a student you were typically predicts how good of an employee you will be. In many ways, general mental ability indirectly assesses a person's ability to learn in formal education settings or training environments. As such, people who rank high in general mental ability are also people who can quickly acquire and apply job knowledge (Hunter & Schmidt, 1996; Schmidt & Hunter, 2004).

Employers can also measure multiple job aptitudes instead of focusing on just an overall mental ability. An **aptitude** is narrower than general mental ability and is defined as the ability to perform a certain kind of work, such as mechanical ability or numerical ability. Intuitively, it makes sense that measuring a job-related aptitude or multiple aptitudes would better predict job performance than the single score of general mental ability. However, psychological research has repeatedly disconfirmed this theory and has shown that general mental ability is a better predictor than any single aptitude or combination of aptitudes.

Some psychologists have suggested the use of aptitudes to predict job performance.

Using Attitudes and Interests for Selection Purposes

Predictions of future job performance could also be assessed by using an individual's attitude or interests in the job. A variety of tests exist for measuring work interests, including

Many psychological assessments have been developed to gauge career interests.

aptitude
the ability to perform a certain kind of work

Personality measures are another type of selection tool used in the workplace.

the popular tests such as the Strong Interest Inventory and Kuder Occupational Interest Survey. Although it appears plausible that an applicant who is confident, motivated, or strongly interested in a job will also perform well in that job after being hired, psychological research does not support this idea (Barrick & Zimmerman, 2009; Gatewood, Feild, & Barrick, 2011, Schmidt & Hunter, 1998). A person's interests may influence the types of jobs he or she applies to; they do not reflect career suitability or KSAOs. Although interest tests are inappropriate for selecting employees, they do have value in counseling individuals on possible careers to consider pursuing. Of course, after identifying a career that is interesting, the individual will then need to obtain the relevant KSAOs through education and training to make them suitable for that career.

Using Personality for Selection Purposes

Some employers have attempted to determine job suitability by assessing the personality of applicants. Research shows that personality measures such as the Five-Factor Model (e.g., people who rate high in conscientiousness tend to be good employees) can be used to predict job performance (Barrick, Mount, & Judge, 2001; Barrick & Zimmerman, 2009). One of the most common personality tests in use is the Myers-Briggs Type Indicator, which places individuals into one of sixteen personality classifications. Despite the popularity of the Myers-Briggs in personnel selection and career counseling, it is a very problematic test when analyzed from a scientific perspective (Anastasi & Urbina, 1997). Applicants taking the test will often obtain very different scores if they take the test just one month apart (this lack of reliability calls into question the ability of the test to measure stable characteristics such as personality) and it does not predict future job performance. As such, it is generally not recommended that organizations use the Myers-Briggs for selection decisions (Boyle, 1995).

Can your handwriting reveal your personality?

Another attempt to evaluate personality for hiring purposes involves the use of graphology. **Graphology** involves the analysis of handwriting characteristics to infer personality traits. For example, you may be an optimist if your handwriting tends to drift upwards, self-centered if you write the letter "I" too large, etc. Although this personality assessment technique isn't in regular use by most businesses, it does periodically gain some popularity by organizations and pop psychology. Research demonstrates that individuals trained in graphology do no better than untrained individuals at guessing personality characteristics. Graphology has consistently shown zero value in predicting job performance, career interests, or personality (Dean, 1992; Klimoski, 1992; Super, 1992). Occasionally graphologists do appear to make successful predictions, but upon closer inspection it appears those successes can be attributed to the content of the writing samples (factors such as grammar skills and written expression), not the handwriting itself (Schmidt & Hunter, 1998).

Using Integrity Tests for Selection Purposes

Employers want to know if you will perform the job well, but also want to make sure you don't engage in undesirable behaviors such as theft or sabotage. This is where **integrity tests** come in, which are intended to detect the likelihood that a job applicant would steal from the organization. A couple of decades ago, employers would use polygraph tests (i.e., the lie detector tests often seen in TV and movies) to assess the honesty of applicants, but the *Employee Polygraph Protection Act of 1988* made the use of polygraphs illegal for workplace hires, with the exception of police and government agencies (Aamodt, 2010).

graphology
the analysis of handwriting to infer traits and characteristics about an individual

integrity tests
tests designed to measure the probability that a job applicant would engage in theft and other counterproductive behaviors

Employers often want to test for an employee's potential to be dishonest.

It is important to remember that tests only predict the likelihood of a behavior, not guarantee that a behavior (such as theft) will occur.

Due to these legal restrictions, pencil and paper tests such as the Hogan Personality Inventory have become more popular (the Hogan Personality Inventory was designed to measure personality, but also includes components for assessing honesty and integrity). Research into attitudes and beliefs of individuals who steal from the workplace shows that such individuals report more temptation to steal, will come up with justifications for their theft, believe that punishment for thieves should be lenient, and are vulnerable to social pressures for stealing (Terris & Jones, 1982). As such, these are the very attitudes and beliefs that integrity tests attempt to measure, such as asking applicants to estimate how common stealing is, if they often feel tempted to steal, how harsh punishments should be, and other opinions correlated with theft. Research reviews have demonstrated that integrity tests can predict not only the probability of employee dishonesty, but can also predict future work performance (Ones, Viswesvaran, & Schmidt, 1993). However, there is some controversy regarding their use, as there is a potential for faking one's responses, as well as the social concerns related to labeling an applicant as a "possible thief" (Anastasi & Urbina, 1997). It is important not to forget that integrity tests measure self-reported behaviors, attitudes, and beliefs associated with theft, not actual theft or intention to steal.

structured employment interview
an interview that is conducted with pre-determined questions and scoring criteria that are used for all applicants

unstructured employment interview
an interview that is conducted without pre-determined questions and scoring criteria or uses a method that is applied inconsistently to applicants

Using Interviews for Selection Purposes

Although many selection tests and techniques exist, by far the most common strategy is the use of an *employment interview*. Regardless of the actual predictive value of interviews, some authors have argued that it is the most important to understand because employers assign so much value to this strategy (Gatewood, Feild, & Barrick, 2011). Furthermore, it is one of the quickest methods for determining an applicant's basic social skills.

There are two basic interviewing formats: structured and unstructured. **Structured employment interviews** will ask the same questions of all applicants and have a standard method for scoring applicant responses, although they may include an unstructured small talk stage for the beginning and end of the interview (Barrick, Swider, & Stewart, 2010). Such questions are preferably based on a job analysis conducted prior to the interview. **Unstructured employment interviews** do the opposite, with the interviewers possessing little to no pre-determined questions or scoring criteria. In essence, the interviewer is just "winging it" during an unstructured format. Many interviewers prefer unstructured formats and have great confidence in their ability to assess job candidates and develop

Interviews are the most common method for selecting employees.

People have a tendency to make snap decisions during interview situations.

useful questions in the moment. However, psychological research has consistently and definitively supported the use of structured over unstructured interviews. Structured interviews select better employees and are less prone to being influenced by irrelevant biases on the part of the interviewer. The standardization of questions and scoring during structured interviews also makes it easier to compare applicants in a meaningful fashion.

Unstructured employment interviews suffer from the fact that interviewers often make snap judgments about applicants that will then bias the remainder of the interview process (Ambady, Krabbenhoft, & Hogan, 2006). Unless there is a structured format to help combat this tendency, such biases often lead to an unfair and inaccurate assessment that will ultimately fail to select the best applicant (Barrick, Shaffer, & DeGrassi, 2009; Barrick, Swider, & Stewart, 2010). There are many factors that influence such snap judgments and increase the probability of being hired, many of which are not job related, but can be powerful nonetheless.

For example, physical appearance has been shown to have a clear influence on whether or not a job offer will be made (sometimes referred to as the "what is beautiful must be good" bias). Research has shown that unattractive applicants are less likely to be hired, even when they are highly qualified and the decision makers tend to report that physical appearance was not a consideration (Boor et al., 1983; Mack & Rainey, 1990). How similar the interviewer is to the applicant (in terms of attitudes, race, and sex) also influences hiring recommendations, despite the fact that similarity has little to do with job performance (Posthuma, Morgeson, & Campoin, 2002). Even an applicant's handshake (a firm one) has been found to reliably predict offers of employment (Stewart, Dustin, Barrick, & Darnold, 2008).

Job interviews can be easily biased by irrelevant factors such as appearance or handshake.

Of course, applicants can take advantage of these factors to increase their chances of being hired, such as enhancing their physical appearance through grooming and dress, expressing opinions they hope are similar to the interviewer's opinions, and looking the other person in the eye while using a firm handshake. This relates to the concept of **impression management**. Impression management involves the use of strategies to create an image that is believed to appeal to the interviewer (Swider, Barrick, Harris, & Stoverink, 2011). This can occur by using forms of self-promotion such as leaving out the negative aspects of past performance, overstating the achievement and value of past accomplishments, downplaying undesirable personality characteristics, focusing solely on desirable qualities, and other forms of exaggeration/omission. Impression management techniques beyond self-promotion exist, such as complimenting the interviewer, expressing frequent agreement with the interviewer, and emotional appeals (Barrick, Shaffer, & DeGrassi, 2009).

People will try to create a good impression during interviews using tactics such as self-promotion, compliments, and imitation.

Even when interviewers ask applicants to be honest, nearly all applicants either consciously or unconsciously use some form of impression management to present themselves as the best person for the job. Any applicant who fails to engage in impression management would be greatly handicapping his or her chances against competing applicants who are likely to ignore interviewer requests to be completely honest (Berry & Sackett, 2009). As such, the interviewer is trying to obtain the most accurate information regarding the applicant, whereas the applicant is trying to present a distorted but favorable impression. These competing agendas between the interviewer and interviewee means there will always be a natural conflict to the interview process.

Despite the inherent conflicts in interviewers and the potential for irrelevant biases to derail to decision making process, there are still steps that can be taken to improve interviews. Here is a list of recommendations grounded in psychological research (adapted from Gatewood, Feild, & Barrick, 2011):

impression management
the application of strategies to make oneself more appealing to an evaluator in a manner that has little relation to actual qualifications

1. Focus the interview on the job relevant KSAOs and restrict it to just the most important 2-3 KSAOs.
2. Conduct interviews using a structured format, developing job-related questions and scoring procedures in advance.

3. Develop multiple questions for each KSAO being assessed during the interview.
4. Minimize the value of any information gained during the unstructured, rapport-building stages of the interview.
5. Utilize multiple interviewers to interview candidates separately.
6. Take the time to train interviewers in advance to ensure the above guidelines are adhered to.

Interviewers and interviewees often have competing agendas.

General Findings on Selection Procedures

To summarize, there are many selection tools available for predicting future work performance. Of all of these, you may be wondering what the best techniques are. Research has reliably shown that general mental ability is the best single predictor of performance for all job types (Schmidt, 2012). Even for jobs that are low in complexity, there are many work tasks to be mastered and applied. The better that one is at learning in general, the more likely they will successfully master and apply those specific work tasks. However, a score from general mental ability test does not represent a person in his or her entirety or reflect everything that would be valued in a job (Murphy, Cronin, & Tam, 2003). As such, it is frequently recommended that employers utilize more than one selection tool. If an employer wishes to select only two tools, research suggests that is best to combine general mental ability tests with work sample tests, although this is restricted to applicants who are already capable of performing the job (Schmidt & Hunter, 1998). The second best pair is a general mental ability test combined with an integrity test and the third best pair involves a general mental ability test and structured interview.

General mental ability tests tend to be the best predictors of job performance.

Note that, despite the value organizations typically assign to interviews, structured interviews rank behind general mental ability, work sample, and integrity tests (recall that unstructured formats are more problematic). This discrepancy between perceived and actual value can be accounted for in a couple of ways. Interviews have the appearance of being less effortful to conduct than assessing for mental ability or requiring a work sample. Additionally, interviews are relatively brief, with the interviewer judging a person's suitability for a job using an observation period that is typically an hour or less and within the context of impression management. Ultimately, the amount of information that can be gleaned from such a situation is limited. Comparatively, general mental ability tests and work samples, despite also being brief, may require an applicant to demonstrate many years of knowledge, skills, and abilities in a manner that is difficult to misrepresent. Yet most interviewers tend to be very confident of their ability to judge the best candidate and trust their intuitions far more than some test. Finally, interviews tend to have more face validity than other forms of selection. That is, interviews *look* like they better measure what they are supposed to be measuring, regardless of whether or not they actually measure it better.

People tend to trust tests less than their own judgment.

Legal and Diversity Considerations in Personnel Selection

As was the case with job analysis, psychologists need to be mindful of legal considerations when conducting or providing recommendations for personnel selection. It is illegal to use selection techniques that *unfairly* discriminate (intentionally or unintentionally) against applicants from protected classes such as race, gender, ethnicity or disability that can be reasonably accommodated. It is legal, however, to use a selection tool that *fairly* discriminates against a protected class. The difference between fair and unfair discrimination is determined by whether or not that selection tool accurately predicts job performance. For

There can be a conflict between selection tools and a desire for diversity.

example, general mental ability will negatively impact the number of hired African-Americans and Hispanics who will be hired, as these groups typically perform worse on such tests (Murphy, Cronin, & Tam, 2003). The reason these minorities perform worse is not inherently due to race, but has more to do with restricted educational opportunities associated with certain demographics. Such discrimination is still considered legal since general mental ability tests do predict future job performance.

However, many organizations value diversity and want to hire minority applicants. Unfortunately, there is no easy solution for resolving the conflicting objectives of wanting to use accurate performance predictors and wanting to create a diverse workforce (Sackett, Borneman, & Connelly, 2008; Wagner, 1997). It is illegal to adjust the test scores of minority applicants and organizations cannot legally ignore the results of a job-related test they dislike in favor of hiring more minorities (even if threatened with a lawsuit from a member of the minority group). After all, ignoring a job-related test means the organization is knowingly hiring the less qualified applicants and thus unfairly discriminating against non-minorities. Solving diversity problems may require solutions broader than personnel selection practices (i.e., changes in social and educational policy).

A good employee is likely to fail when placed against a bad system.

Enhancing Performance through Training Efforts

The type of employee hired is not the only factor in the success of an organization. While employees do bring certain abilities into the workplace, the workplace contingencies can enhance or suppress performance across all types of employees. A good employee is likely to fail when pitted against bad training, conflicting incentives, poorly designed work processes, or other organizational obstacles (Rummler & Brache, 1995). Psychologists not only study who would make the best employees, but what should be done with the employees after being hired. One of the most obvious starting points is employee training.

Psychologists who study training often emphasize a basic point: *simply giving information to an employee is not the same as training* (Molenda & Russell, 2006; Stolovitch & Keeps, 2002). Successful workplace training will require specific objectives and clear expectations of the material to be learned, training content arranged in manageable chunks, multiple opportunities to practice until fluency, and frequent feedback. These criteria are frequently violated by training approaches that just urge employees to do a good job (vague expectation), that simply hand an entire training manual to a new hire, that tell an employee what to do only once, that ask new hires to just follow someone experienced around, or that wait until the employee is actually doing the job before providing corrections.

Training is more than just telling.

We will use **performance-based instruction**, an instructional approach developed for the workplace, to illustrate how training can be successfully implemented (Brethower & Smalley, 1998). Performance-based instruction first begins with *guided observation.* Guided observation involves showing important work tasks to the trainee and explaining how to perform those tasks. During guided observation, trainees are expected to describe the criteria for correct and incorrect workplace behavior and explain why those criteria exist. After a trainee is able to accomplish this, they begin the *guided practice* phase of performance-based instruction. During guided practice, the trainee actually performs the work task while the trainer gives frequent feedback on the accuracy of their performance. The trainer will give progressively less support until the trainee can perform the steps independently. Finally, the trainee enters the *demonstration of mastery* phase. During this phase, the trainee performs the task independently while being observed by the trainer

performance-based instruction
a training approach utilizing the phases of guided observation, guided practice, and demonstration of mastery

During guided observation, trainers explain and show work tasks to the trainee.

Guided practice involves having the trainee perform the task while receiving feedback.

Training concludes with demonstration of mastery, during which trainees fully and independently perform the task.

(who only interrupts if the trainee is about to do something excessively costly or dangerous) and continues until the task can be performed at the level of accuracy, speed, and quality that is expected while on the job. The performance-based instruction process may be repeated for each work task or a complete set of work tasks. It is also better if some or all of the performance-based instruction can take place in the regular work setting or a reasonable simulation.

Instructional designers analyze the best methods for developing training materials.

Training can be facilitated through careful **instructional design**, which is the analysis of the best methods of presenting instructions, selecting examples, and developing appropriate tests (Johnson, 2014). Good instructional design analyzes different types of learning and testing, different skill outcomes (e.g., physical performance, conceptual understanding, application of principles, etc.), and how to teach to fluency using the minimal number of steps (Markle, 1990; Tiemann & Markle, 1990). For example, a sales representative may need training on the difference between good and poor customer service. While one could randomly select examples of customer service to use during training, careful instructional design will suggest the best examples and non-examples to teach customer service in the shortest time while ensuring a complete conceptual understanding for recognizing and then applying such skills.

A popular trend in business is the use of *computer-based training* because of the potential savings in both time and money (Johnson & Dickinson, 2012). However, just as "telling isn't training," "simply putting information on a screen isn't computer-based training." Adequate computer-based training requires more than understanding computer programming; it requires understanding the psychology of learning. Psychological research has demonstrated that computer-based training needs to be interactive enough that learners are required to demonstrate their understanding of the training material during the training process itself (Johnson & Rubin, 2011). Computer-based training should also be very carefully planned in advance and utilize frequent practice, just like good face-to-face training.

It is important that computer-based training be more than fancy bells and whistles.

Managing Daily Performance through Behavioral Science

While good selection and training processes can do much to enhance the functioning of an organization, the benefits of these processes can easily be lost when daily workplace

instructional design
analyzing instructional content in order to develop the best method of presenting instructions, selecting examples, and developing appropriate tests

OBM analyzes the Antecedents, Behaviors, and Consequences in the workplace.

practices oppose them. The specialization of **organizational behavior management** (OBM) has been developed to apply behavioral principles to improve workplace productivity, quality, and safety. This frequently entails the identification of desirable and undesirable work behaviors, the conditions that produce such behaviors, and aligning appropriate consequences for such behaviors.

Psychologists in this specialization would point out that organizations hire people on the basis of desirable behaviors they may produce in service of the organization. Therefore, it is not quite accurate to say that we hire an employee for his or her motivation, attitude, or knowledge because we never actually observe such internal states. In truth, we are hiring someone on the basis of the *behaviors that we take as evidence* for high motivation, good attitude, and relevant knowledge (Daniels, 2001). After the person is hired, we continue observing their behaviors or the results produced by their behaviors. As such, OBM proponents would suggest that psychologists and managers should focus on workplace behaviors when trying to improve the functioning of an organization. Furthermore, such psychologists would suggest that the most important factor in improving organizations is to change the workplace contingencies, not just blaming workers or hoping to hire the "perfect" employee. Not surprisingly, organizational behavior management grew out of the behavioral approach to psychology. There are several common applications within organizational behavior management, which we will detail below (Braksick, 2007; Daniels & Bailey, 2014).

There is limited value in just blaming workers for undesired behavior.

The Importance of Identifying Behavioral Pinpoints and Providing Task Clarification

One of the common starting points in OBM is to identify the desired work outcomes and the behavior needed to produce such outcomes. After these outcomes and the relevant behaviors are identified, it is recommended that a behavioral pinpoint is created. A **behavioral pinpoint** is the specification of the workplace behavior in terms that are observable and capable of being measured. In essence, psychologists are creating an operational definition for the behavior to be examined. Recall that a key aspect of an operational definition is that it is precise enough that two observers can independently agree on whether or not it occurred. All workplace behaviors can be measured, although many employees resist measurement because measurement has historically been associated with punishment (OBM changes this by focusing on the use of measurement to provide reinforcement).

Even valued characteristics such as creativity, trustworthiness, and friendliness can be measured in behavioral terms. The key is to ask oneself, "what behaviors does a creative/trustworthy/friendly person engage in that causes him or her to be labeled as creative/trustworthy/friendly?" Once you have identified the behaviors that produce such

Behavioral pinpoints need to be precise and specific.

Behavioral pinpoints should be under the control of the performer.

organizational behavior management
the analysis and application of behavioral principles to improving functioning within the workplace

behavioral pinpoint
a behavior that is precisely defined in unambiguous and measurable terms

labels, you have identified the relevant behaviors to be pinpointed. It is also important that a selected behavioral pinpoint be under the employee's control. For example, companies commonly hold salespeople accountable for sales. The problem is that a sale isn't always under the salesperson's control. Some customers will not purchase a product regardless of how well done a sales pitch was and some customers will purchase a product no matter how terrible that sales pitch was. Behavioral pinpointing would identify the actual behaviors involved in a good sales pitch and hold the salesperson accountable for doing those behaviors (which is under the employee's control), regardless of whether the sale occurred (which is only partially under the employee's control). Any time the job performance requires the interaction between multiple people, the individual should only be accountable for his or her role in that performance.

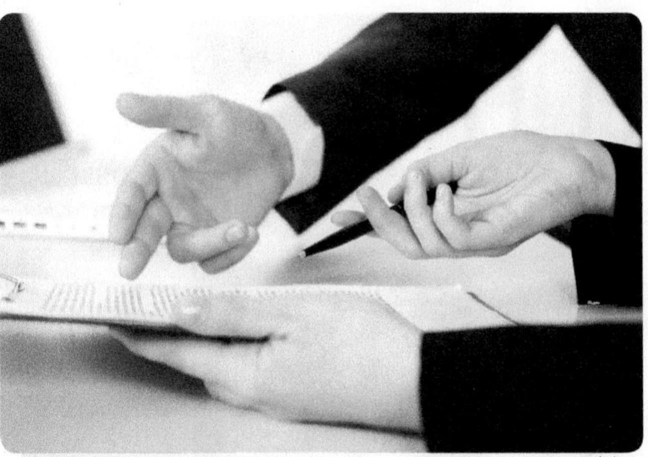

Simply giving clear expectations to an employee can sometimes improve performance.

After the relevant behavioral pinpoints are identified, a common OBM intervention is to simply inform the employees of the behaviors expected of them in a specific and clear manner. This strategy is known as **task clarification** and it is often effective, as demonstrated by the many studies published on its use (Anderson, Crowell, Hantula, & Siroky, 1988; Rose & Ludwig, 2009; Slowiak, Madden, & Mathews, 2005). It may seem surprising that such a simple technique would be effective, but many employees have not been told what is expected of them, at least not in an unambiguous manner. Employees have been frequently told to "work better, harder, or smarter," but have never been told what *specific behaviors* would convince management that they are achieving such goals. As such, many bewildered employees end up working in an ineffective manner or ignore the vague demands of management (after the boss has left the area).

Performance monitoring is key to accurate delivery of consequences.

Monitoring and Measuring Employee Behaviors

Another common OBM strategy is to engage in frequent performance monitoring and measuring of employee behavior. It is not enough to create behavioral pinpoints that are measurable; supervisors also have to actually measure those behaviors and use that data to make evaluation decisions. In fact, research has suggested that *performance monitoring* is the most critical part of good organizational leadership (Komaki, 1986; 1998). Performance monitoring is important because it helps ensure that high performing employees are accurately rewarded and low performing employees receive timely feedback to correct performance deficits or errors. If a supervisor provides rewards or corrections in the absence of performance monitoring, that supervisor may accidently reinforce undesired behavior or punish desired behavior.

Imagine that an employee has spent the past 7 hours working diligently and then decides to pause for a five minute break, failing to notice that her manager is now coming near her workstation. Further imagine that a second employee has spent all day playing solitaire on his computer and then switches to a work task when he notices that the manager is approaching. If this is the only time that day the manager ever comes near the work area, he may end up inappropriately criticizing the hard working employee and complimenting the solitaire playing employee. This is obviously not the lesson the organization wants to teach to its employees and performance monitoring is key to avoiding such a problem. The more frequent monitoring and measuring is, the more likely organizational rewards will be properly aligned.

Setting achievable goals can help motivate employee performance.

When collecting measurement data, it is useful to compare the obtained data against some goal. *Goal setting* is a very common and successful OBM strategy (Amigo, Smith, & Ludwig, 2008; Fellner & Sulzer-Azaroff, 1984; Loewy & Bailey, 2007). However, there important guidelines to follow to ensure goal setting is successful. Goals should be achievable because a goal that is too high is also a goal likely to never be met (Daniels & Bailey, 2014). If this occurs, employees will learn not to bother with efforts to achieve goals again in the future. As such, it is better to err in the direction of setting a goal too easy rather than too hard. After an employee begins reaching the goal regularly (and receiving an effective

task clarification
a clear and precise explanation of the work tasks that the employee is expected to perform

incentive), the goal can be increased gradually over time. This is essentially the application of the shaping principle (see Chapter 7) to workplace behavior.

The Delivery of Feedback and Incentives

OBM also addresses how one should react to the data accumulated while monitoring employee performance. Put differently, another OBM focus is on how to provide consequences. It is critical that the pinpointing, monitoring, and measuring mentioned above is used primarily for the purpose of positive feedback and providing incentives to employees. If pinpointing, monitoring, and measuring is used to primarily punish employees, employees will work to avoid and undermine these OBM techniques. If these techniques are used to find opportunities to reward, then employees will seek out pinpointing, monitoring, and measuring. More importantly, their performance and satisfaction will typically improve. The most effective workplace consequences are ones that are positive in nature, delivered soon after behavior, and reliably follow the appropriate behavior (Braksick, 2007; Daniels & Bailey, 2014). It is also important that a variety of rewards be used so that employees don't tire of a particular consequence.

How workplace consequences are delivered has a significant impact on their effectiveness.

Performance feedback is the provision of information regarding past performance. It is often used as a consequence and can have a powerful impact on increasing desired behavior and correcting undesired behavior (Alvero, Bucklin, & Austin, 2001; Johnson, 2013; Nolan, Jarema, & Austin, 1999). Performance feedback has the added benefits of being relatively inexpensive and easy to administer. It should include some evaluation of the performance, be easy to understand at a quick glance, presented in the form of a graph, and be delivered on an individual basis. While group feedback can be added as well, it is important that each individual receive their own private feedback separate from the group's data (an individual may be performing well despite being in a low performing group). Finally, performance feedback needs to be delivered frequently if it is to influence performance in a meaningful way. This last criterion is often violated by performance appraisals, which are frequently delivered on a quarterly or annual basis. Behavioral principles would suggest that weekly or monthly appraisals would have a greater impact on employee performance.

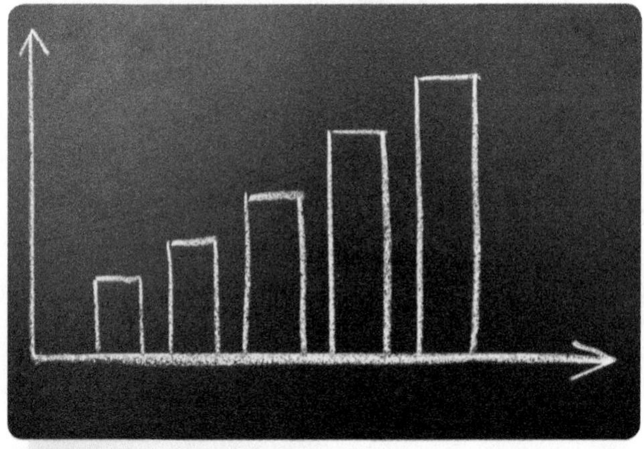

The best feedback is clear, graphic, individualized, and delivered frequently.

Other consequences besides feedback can be used as well, including financial incentives such as **pay for performance**. Pay for performance is the use of bonus pay incentives (beyond standard hourly pay) and is delivered to individuals contingent upon producing desired behaviors (Bucklin & Dickinson, 2001; Bucklin, McGee, & Dickinson, 2003). Note that this is different from profit sharing or annual bonuses, which often deliver extra pay regardless of individual performance. Although pay for performance requires an extra financial investment, such financial incentives do not have to be large to be effective and the gains in productivity can easily offset the costs of extra payments (Frisch & Dickinson, 1990; Johnson, Dickinson, & Huitema, 2008).

Psychologists have spent many years studying the influence of monetary incentives on performance.

In fact, the gains in productivity can be great enough that some companies have eliminated hourly pay in favor of pay for performance only (Handlin, 1992). Some authors have expressed concern over using incentives for motivational purposes for fear that employees will not do work for its

performance feedback
providing information regarding past performance in order to improve future performance

pay for performance
monetary incentives that are provided for meeting individualized performance standards

own sake (Kohn, 1988), but research has shown that any negative effects are short-lived (Cameron & Pierce, 2002; Mawhinney, Dickinson, & Taylor, 1989). Again, the nature of how incentives (monetary and non-monetary incentives) are delivered is the most important determinant of their effectiveness and there is nothing inherently damaging about incentives.

Appropriate delivery of rewards is not going to work if the rewards themselves are not valued by the employee getting the reward. This is why many OBM psychologists have called for the use of **reinforcer preference assessments** (Waldvogel & Dixon, 2008; Wilder, Harris, Casella, Wine, & Postma, 2011). Preference assessments involve presenting employees with a variety of potential rewards and have them rank order their most desired choices. Every person has their own unique interests and preferences, so blindly delivering rewards may have unintended effects on behavior (imagine if someone who takes a bus to work every day was given a special employee parking space as a "reward"). Most supervisors are not very good at guessing employee preferences and a mismatch between preferences and rewards may result in wasted money, loss of potential performance improvements, and incentive systems being prematurely terminated.

One type of reward may not work for all employees.

Let's examine the popular incentive tool known as *employee-of-the-month* to illustrate the importance of ensuring that rewards actually have a reinforcing function. Employee-of-the-month programs are one of the most commonly used incentive tools and are frequently endorsed by various authors as a motivational strategy (Finne & Sivonen, 2009; Godson, 2009; Messmer, 2001). However, various psychologists have pointed out important behavioral flaws in employee-of-the-month programs (Carlaw, Carlaw, Deming, & Friedmann, 2003; Daniels, 2009; Grote, 2002). Among the flaws is the fact that delivery of the reward is not based on behavioral pinpointing or careful measurement. The delivery arrangement restricts the reward to a single employee each month, which inappropriately reduces the number of performers who are recognized for achievements. Furthermore, employees don't seem to greatly value being named employee-of-the-month (they often don't hate the reward, but they rarely work hard for it) and empirical research suggests they do not produce any lasting performance improvements (Johnson & Dickinson, 2010). Just because a supervisor decides that an incentive has been delivered, that doesn't mean the employee will agree.

It is critical to examine the actual effect of rewards, not just assume a nice thing will be motivating.

To illustrate how many of these OBM techniques might be combined to change employee behavior, let's use a study by Tittelbach, DeAngelis, Sturmey, & Alvero (2007) as an example. In this study, the researchers analyzed the customer service behaviors of university advisors. In particular, they examined three behaviors: whether advisors were on time for shifts, how they greeted students, and the posture of advisors while interacting with students. Prior to the OBM intervention, the advisors correctly greeted students only 50% of the time, failed to be on time by an average of 7 minutes, and showed appropriate posture approximately 50% of the time. The researchers then created behavioral pinpoints for each of those three behaviors. These behavioral pinpoints were then used to provide task clarification. For example, correct body posture was defined as "both feet flat on the floor, legs crossed with one foot touching the floor and the other leg resting on top of the leg that touches the floor, both feet resting on the cross legs of the swivel chairs, or one foot resting on the floor with the other resting on one of the legs of the cross legs of the swivel chairs" while "front of one's body facing in the direction of the client." (p. 30). The behavioral pinpoint is so specific that it leaves no room for confusion or misinterpretation. In addition to task clarification, the researchers also set goals for the advisors to meet, observed the advisors while they interacted with students, and provided verbal feedback on their performance. As a result, advisors began to use correct greetings 89% of the time, improved their timeliness by 4 minutes on average, and displayed correct posture 95% of the time.

OBM places a stronger emphasis on reinforcement than any other technique.

In general, OBM techniques tend to downplay the role of punishment procedures for managing employee behavior. This is not to say that punishment procedures are never included in OBM interventions, but rather that the emphasis is on finding opportunities to reinforce desired employee performance. There are several reasons for such an emphasis.

reinforcer preference assessment
a procedure in which an individual selects their most preferred items so that those items can be later be delivered as reinforcers for that individual's behavior

Punishment procedures do not directly teach what an employee should be doing, just what they should not do. There is a tendency to leave things alone when they are going well, but errors and problems have a way of occupying our attention and reactions. Therefore, many managers find punishment of undesired behavior and ignoring of desired behavior to be more familiar to their daily routines and will default to these patterns unless there is an explicit push towards reinforcement-based strategies. Relying too heavily on punishment can have a damaging effect on the relationship between employees and their employers. When this relationship is poor, employees may thwart new programs, produce poor products or services, or simply quit the organization. Reinforcement-based strategies tend to have an opposite effect, creating a better relationship and improving the organization's success.

Psychologists focus on improving a variety of workplace concerns besides productivity, such as quality, satisfaction, and health/safety.

Health Concerns Related to Workplace Performance

When designing measurement and incentive systems to influence employee behavior, it is critical to not just focus on productivity. Outcomes such as quality, employee satisfaction, and safety are important considerations as well. For example, it would not be wise to set extremely high goals that rewarded employees only for the number of items produced. Under that arrangement, items are likely to be of poor quality and the employees may work at such a high rate that they feel "burnt out" and unsatisfied, quit the company, and/or suffer illnesses. In fact, both organizations and psychologists have become increasingly more concerned over the effect of stress in the workplace. Workplace stress can have significant costs related to organizational productivity, employee health, health care insurance, and the overall quality of society (Ivancevich, Mattheson, Freedman, & Phillips, 1990).

Stress management interventions are designed to reduce or offset such workplace stress and some of these solutions involve factors we have already discussed, such as job analyses and selection techniques to make sure an individual is well-suited to the work or redesigning the environment to make it easier to perform work. However, the most common stress management interventions are techniques involving relaxation and meditation (Richarson & Rothstein, 2008). *Meditation interventions* involve training employees to focus attention on a single object or thought without distraction. During *relaxation interventions*, employees learn improved control of their muscle tension so that they can engage in purposeful release of that tension. Relaxation interventions are often combined with deep breathing exercises to produce slow and deep breaths that can counteract stress reactions. Meditation and relaxation training have been shown to successfully reduce workplace stress and have the advantage of being both inexpensive and relatively easy to teach (Bellarosa & Chen, 1997). Furthermore, employees can easily self-implement these techniques whenever they feel the need.

Stress management interventions help employees cope with workplace stressors.

Although meditation and relaxation are the most popular techniques, the most effective stress management interventions are *cognitive-behavioral interventions* (Richardson & Rothstein, 2008). Cognitive-behavioral techniques may involve changing an individual's perception of and reaction to stress (e.g., learning to treat stressors as challenges rather than burdens) and techniques for adaptive coping (e.g., taking action to minimize or eliminate stressors). Unlike meditation and relaxation, cognitive-behavioral interventions teach individuals to directly and actively deal with workplace stressors.

Meditation and relaxation are popular stress management interventions.

Cognitive-behavioral interventions often involve training better ways of navigating job stress.

Although workplace stress poses a serious challenge to health, it is not the only potential threat to the well-being of employees. Accidents and injuries are also a serious concern for all types of businesses and employees. Approximately 3.3% of full-time workers will be injured on the job, with .01% of injuries being severe enough to require at least one day away from work and 0.003% being fatal (Bureau of Labor Statistics, 2012). Although those percentages may seem small, the consequences can be devastating to both the injured employee and company. It has been estimated that approximately 80-90% of accidents are the results of human behavior, so this is another area that is ripe for the contributions of psychology (McSween, 1995). For example, many injuries are caused by employees not using safety equipment, not following safety procedures, or simply overexerting themselves while lifting an object or lowering themselves (musculoskeletal disorders account for approximately 33% of lost-time injuries and require an average of 11 days away from work). The point is not to scapegoat a single employee for behaving badly (these behaviors are often unintentional or involve the behaviors of multiple employees), but to highlight that much needs to be done beyond just writing safety procedures or posting signs reminding employees to be safe.

Employees may work unsafely because it is often easier and faster.

The use of personnel selection (i.e., hiring employees predicted to be safe) is one of the most common but least effective strategies for reducing injuries and accidents (Geller, 2001; Guastello, 1993). Redesigning the work environments through human factors tends to produce better results, as significant strides can often be made in creating equipment that is easier to use in a safe manner. However, human factors engineering cannot eliminate all problems because employees will often override safety features and disregard safety equipment. The reason employees often act in an unsafe manner is because of the consequence associated with doing so. Working unsafe tends to be faster, easier, and feels better (goggles, gloves, and hard hats are often uncomfortable), so people have a natural tendency to take safety shortcuts. As such, **behavior-based safety** interventions are also needed (McSween, 1995; Suzler-Azaroff, 1998).

behavior-based safety
the analysis and application of behavioral principles to promote safe performance and reduce accidents

Behavior-based safety changes the consequences for safe and unsafe performance.

Behavior-based safety uses the standard OBM techniques of pinpointing, measuring, and providing consequences. Once again, the emphasis is on reinforcement, as an overreliance on punishment may result in employees hiding instances of accidents or injuries. Special consideration must be given to the frequency of accidents and injuries. A behavioral pinpoint such as "working without injury" is not a specific enough because injuries are normally very rare events. Rewarding employees for "working without injury" would essentially amount to giving everyone in the organization free gifts, since unsafe behavior does not produce injury most of the time (McSween, 1995).

Instead, safety assessments must be conducted to identify high-risk behaviors involved in most accidents and injuries. Employees tend to engage in high-risk behaviors because they typically remain unharmed by these behaviors. In essence, unsafe performance involves a gamble that pays off most of time, but has severe damages those rare times the gamble doesn't pay off. Behavior-based safety needs to create unnatural rewards for safe behaviors because the natural environment rewards employees for unsafe behaviors (except in those rare but disastrous moments). Implementing behavior-based safety inventions can have powerful influences on the health of employees. For example, Myers, McSween, Medina, Rost, and Alvero (2010) reported a 79% reduction in lost-time injuries and a 97% savings in worker's compensation costs following the implementation of behavior-based safety in a petroleum oil refinery.

LOOKING AT THE BIG PICTURE

It is sometimes necessary to look at the entire organization if interventions are to be successful.

In the process of analyzing or implementing an intervention for a single job, it often becomes apparent that the job is interconnected with other jobs in the organization and how there are communication gaps within the organization (Aamodt, 2010). As such, psychologists working in business settings should be prepared to work with both individual employees and also take a step back to see how the individual fits in with the organizational big picture (Sulzer-Azaroff, 2001). Organizations employ various individuals with various jobs and the amount of complexity in organizations can quickly become massive. An organization is more than just the employees and their individual behaviors; an organization also involves the relationships among employees, departments, and other sources of influence. This may involve thousands of behavioral interactions to fully complete any work process, despite the fact any particular job can look simple from the perspective of a single employee (Brethower, 2006; Malott, 2003). As such, no psychological technique should be blindly implemented as a cure-all for businesses. Instead, attempts to improve the organization will need to be custom tailored for the individual job as well as the broader context in which that job functions.

behavioral systems analysis
an analysis of how different jobs, tasks, and work processes relate to one another for the purpose of developing interventions to benefit the organization as a whole

This notion is the basis of **behavioral systems analysis**, which concerns how individual jobs and departments relate to one another, how work gets done as tasks travel through the entire organization, and how to best align all the individual behaviors of the organization so that each person's position contributes to the overall health of the business. This will require identifying multiple levels of the organization to determine how each part of the organization fits in with the overall purpose, the recipients for every product and service produced, what is required in each job for the employee to operate well, and how to best assess success (Diener, McGee, & Miguel, 2009; Morasky, 1982). This large scale view is often absent in organizations and the importance of cooperation between departments is frequently neglected. Sometimes businesses create organizational maps to show responsibility hierarchies (i.e., who reports to who), but these rarely address how the work actually gets done (i.e., who does what specific behaviors and how do the individual workers cooperate). As a result of this tendency to focus on just reporting up the chain of command, departments might begin viewing each other as competitors for resources rather than allies working toward a common purpose.

Employees may view one another as competitors if the work processes aren't properly aligned.

For example, imagine an automobile company implemented an intervention to improve the behavior of those working in marketing. As part of this intervention, they focus their new marketing campaign on a particular car model. As a result their new and improved sales techniques, sales of that particular model go through the roof. While this intuitively sounds like a good thing since the job of marketing is to increase sales, it is possible that this change may actually hurt the organization overall (Brethower, 1982; Connellan, 1978). If manufacturing wasn't told about the new sales campaign, they may not be able to keep up with the demand. This may result in unsatisfied customers who have to wait an unreasonably long time for their new car to arrive. Marketing may blame manufacturing for failing to keep up. Manufacturing may in turn blame marketing for selling more than can be produced, especially if there are extra quantities of another car model marketing didn't advertise. The real problem is that no-one looked at the big picture to see how the needs and resources of these two departments relate to one another. This illustrates a concept known as the *sub-optimization principle*, which states that sometimes one part of an organization can be improved in a manner that harms other parts of the organization (Brethower, 2006; Malott, 2003). It also illustrates how psychologists need to occasionally take a holistic view and analyze how goals can be integrating across all the departments. Otherwise, behavioral changes at the individual level that are intended to improve the business may actually be damaging and counterproductive.

The application of the psychological principles and empirical data can enhance the well-being of both organizations and employees.

Building Better Business: Why Psychology Is Needed

You are likely to spend a significant portion of your life at work, so it is important that psychology is able to understand and influence employee and employer behaviors. Many of these organizational techniques involved suggestions for better ways to manage employee behavior (with some suggestions for how employees can manage themselves). This is because managers and supervisors are often in a position to enact the greatest changes in the workplace. Organizational psychologists would suggest that these managers need to act like good scientists, actively collecting data and basing business decisions on that data. Although many managers are very data-oriented when it comes to the financial side of business, they often mistakenly leave the human element up to intuition or armchair theories. Considering the world of work touches nearly all our lives and that all businesses involve human behavior, it is critical that psychology continues to play a significant role.

15

Psychological Disorders*

*Taken from *Psychological Science,* Second Edition by Mark Krause and Daniel Corts

Defining and Classifying Psychological Disorders

Scientific knowledge about mental illness and its treatment changed at a blinding speed throughout the 20th century. In 1900, for individuals with serious disorders that we would now call **psychosis,** there was little hope for improvement and they were often thought of as an embarrassment by their families. Therefore, many were locked away in asylums where the public did not have to see them or speak of them. By 2000, there were effective treatments for many disorders that allow individuals who would have once been locked in an "insane asylum" to live in less restrictive settings, often at home. But as the scientific advances allowed people to live more healthy lives, the social changes—the sense of embarrassment people feel about disorders—had not matched that pace. Mental health advocates asked: What good are treatments if people are afraid to seek them out? How are people to adapt to more healthy lives if they constantly cope with stereotypes about their condition? Based on these concerns, mental health advocates have shifted much more attention to fighting stigmatization—a sense of shame or disgrace—about mental health and have made amazing strides. Even 15 years ago, you would not expect openness at a formal, high-profile society event, but at the 2015 Academy Award ceremony, one award winner spoke about his suicide attempt as a teen and another spoke of losing her son to suicide. In 2000, it would have been shocking to have a professional football player speak openly about his experience with mental illness. Yet in 2014, Brandon Marshall of the Chicago Bears did just that, publicizing his personal struggle with borderline personality disorder as part of his efforts to fight stigma. In this section, we will discuss how psychologists understand psychological disorders, and encourage you to think about how friends, relatives, physicians, jurors, and society as a whole understand mental health.

We routinely encounter information about psychological disorders such as depression or autism from many sources, including news, talk shows, and advertisements for prescription drugs. The amount of information floating around about these disorders is vast, and it can be challenging to sift through and critically analyze this enormous volume. To understand psychological disorders, we will apply two complementary models.

Table 15.1 Biological, Psychological, and Sociocultural Factors Influence Both Physical and Mental Disorders

	Diabetes	Major Depression
Biological	Genetic influences on pancreatic function; excessive refined sugars	Genetic influences on neurotransmitter production and function; sleep disruption; lack of positive emotional arousal
Psychological	Poor food choices; sedentary lifestyle; alcohol abuse	Negative self-concept; pessimism; negative life experiences
Sociocultural	Familial and cultural foods and traditions; limited budget for groceries; lack of physical and nutritional education in the schools; lack of role models	Lack of social support; social withdrawal; lack of psychological services; stigma regarding psychological treatments

First is the **medical model**, which means *using our understanding of medical conditions to understand psychological conditions.* Just as diabetes has a set of symptoms, probable causes, and likely outcomes, so do psychological disorders. There are also preventive measures, interventions, and treatments targeted toward psychological disorders, just as there are for conditions such as diabetes or cancer. Today it might seem natural to talk about psychological problems in these terms, but in fact, the medical model has not always been the norm. Throughout history and in various cultures, other explanations have been proposed for what we now call psychological disorders. For example, hallucinations may be symptomatic of a psychological disorder in the United States. However, in another place or time, that same individual might be viewed as possessed by evil spirits, the victim of a curse, or even a prophet.

The second model we adopt includes the multiple perspectives of the *biopsychosocial model* (Table 15.1). For example, one biological factor contributing to depression involves disrupted activity of neurotransmitters such as serotonin. Psychological factors include persistent negative beliefs about the self (e.g., *nothing I do makes any difference in the world*) and feelings of hopelessness. Social factors such as impoverished neighborhoods and stressful family problems contribute to the development of depression as well. As is the case with many physical disorders such as diabetes, psychological disorders can rarely be traced to a single cause, so the biopsychosocial approach helps us develop a comprehensive understanding of psychological disorders.

This chapter focuses on psychological disorders, which, generally speaking, comprise abnormal behavioral and cognitive functioning. Before we go any further, however, we need to identify what is meant by *abnormal* when it comes to human behavior and experience.

Journal prompt

Culture and Mental Illness:

Do you think that the term *abnormal* is relative from one individual to the next, or one cultural group to the next? Explain.

Defining and Diagnosing Abnormal Behavior

Abnormal psychology *is the psychological study of mental illness*, but the term *abnormal* needs some clarification. A person who deliberately cuts or burns himself is behaving abnormally because few people inflict such damage on themselves. Earning a medical degree before the age of 20 is even less typical, statistically speaking, but is not a symptom of mental illness. The difference between these two non-normal activities is that self-injury is a **maladaptive behavior**, *or behavior that hinders a person's ability to function in work, school, relationships, or society.* To distinguish between the abnormal and the unusual, mental health professionals consider three main criteria:

- The behavior causes distress to self or others.
- The behavior impairs the ability to function in day-to-day activities.
- The behavior increases the risk of injury, death, legal problems, or punishment for breaking rules or other detrimental consequences.

At first glance, these criteria may seem to suggest that mental illness is devastating and debilitating to the point where it would be obvious to anyone. However, signs of mental illness can—and often do—go unnoticed by others. It is not uncommon for individuals to keep distressing thoughts and feelings to themselves, or for the signs of mental illness to be more prominent in some contexts than others. To make matters more complicated, some individuals have been wildly successful in a few areas of life while the debilitating aspects of the illness are overlooked. Thus, many individuals who experience mental illness can get by without help, but their quality of life and functioning are impaired nonetheless.

A final point to consider is that psychological disorders can be *dimensional* in nature; they consist of typical experiences, except that they are more severe and longer lasting than usual, and they may occur in inappropriate contexts. We know that everyone experiences sadness, changes in appetite, or a night of sleeplessness, so the challenge of a diagnosis is determining when those characteristics are severe enough to be considered depression. Despite the dimensional nature of most disorders, diagnostic labels such as bipolar disorder or posttraumatic stress disorder (PTSD) can imply that conditions are more clear cut. This *categorical* view is appropriate for a disorder such as Down syndrome because it involves an unusual genetic condition: An individual either has the extra 21st chromosome linked to Down syndrome or does not.

When attempting to diagnose mental illness, psychologists and psychiatrists rely on the *Diagnostic and Statistical Manual for Mental Disorders (DSM-5)* (the 5 reflects the fact that it is currently in its fifth edition). Published by the American Psychiatric Association, the DSM-5 *offers guidelines for diagnosing the presence and severity of all varieties of mental disorder.* For each disorder listed in the *DSM-5*, the guidelines convey several important pieces of information: a set of symptoms that define the condition, how to distinguish it from other disorders that share some of the same symptoms, and the *prognosis*, or how these symptoms will persist or change over time, with or without professional treatment.

The *DSM-5* includes many improvements over the previous edition in that it represents what professionals have learned from latest scientific research and is meant to make diagnosis less complicated. Despite these advantages, the *DSM-5* still has some limitations. Although its guidelines allow for reliable diagnosis of some disorders—multiple professionals will arrive at the same diagnosis for one person—other individuals' cases prove difficult to classify (Regier et al., 2013). Thus, a growing number of psychologists and psychiatrists argue that research should attempt to identify more objective markers of mental disorders such as brain abnormalities (Insel, 2014) or carefully structured interview procedures (Aboraya et al., 2014).

MENTAL HEALTH IN THE PUBLIC SPHERE

Psychological disorders represent a significant health concern. Nearly 20% of adults will experience a disorder within a typical year with about a fifth of those cases classified as severe (National Institutes of Mental Health [NIMH], 2015). Also, serious mental illnesses cut across numerous demographics such as age, gender, and ethnicity (Figure 15.1). Even if you are one of those fortunate individuals who has not personally experienced a psychological disorder, you will benefit from being able to read about and understand mental health issues; if you consider that one in five adults experience a disorder in a given year, it is hard to imagine that you would not live or work with individuals who would benefit from your understanding.

Two major issues about mental health in the public sphere include (1) unjustified stigma about psychological disorders and (2) how the insanity defense factors into criminal cases. We will address both issues in this section.

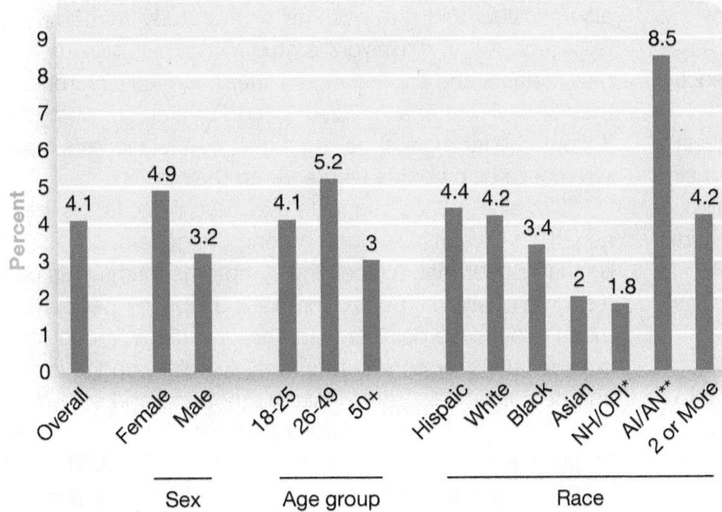

Figure 15.1 Prevalence of Serious Mental Illness Among US, Adults (2012)

The numbers indicate the estimated percentage of the US population diagnosed with a serious mental illness. As you can see, mental illness affects people of all walks of life.

Source: http://www.nimh.nih.gov/health/statistics/prevalence/serious-mental-illness-smi-among-us-adults.shtml

Highly publicized cases involving mental illness often get played out in courtroom proceedings, which can further lead to distorted views of people who are mentally ill. This brings us to the issue of the insanity defense.

Working the Scientific Literacy Model

Labeling, Stigma, and Psychological Disorders

The *DSM-5* provides names or *labels* for psychological disorders, which, in turn, indicate a set of symptoms, probable causes, and potential treatments. However, these diagnostic labels can also have their drawbacks, the worst of which is stigmatization.

What do we know about the stigma of mental disorders?

Stigmas include negative stereotypes about what it means to have a psychological disorder, and stigmatization may lead to discrimination, unjustified fears, and alienation. Attaching such labels can also lead people to misinterpret normal behavior as symptoms of a disorder. Even mental health professionals can be influenced by this practice, as shown by David Rosenhan's classic study from the 1970s. In his investigation, eight normal, healthy individuals volunteered to go to psychiatric hospitals with complaints about auditory hallucinations. All eight were admitted to the hospitals for either schizophrenia or manic depression (bipolar disorder). After their admission, these so-called patients behaved normally, complaining of no psychiatric symptoms whatsoever. Nonetheless, they remained hospitalized for an average of 19 days (Rosenhan, 1973). Apparently, the initial diagnosis led the hospital staff to misinterpret even normal behavior as symptoms of an illness.

How can science explain the personal effects of stigmatization?

Contemporary research is examining the stigma of mental illness from multiple perspectives using self-reports such as surveys and interviews. Perhaps the most important perspective comes from individuals who have been diagnosed. Many people find themselves sensing the stigma in their social interactions; this can lead to feelings of ostracism and isolation. You can imagine how this can compound the experience of depression, a disorder already characterized by feelings of hopelessness and loneliness (Switaj et al., 2014). From another perspective, even

(Continued)

family members of people with mental illness report stigma by association. They often report feeling ostracized and judged as well, almost as if they have caused their loved one to experience the disorder (van der Sanden et al., 2014). More recently, researchers have examined *internalized stigma*—how individuals might come to view themselves more negatively because of their experience with mental illness. Internalized stigma is associated with lower self-esteem and, along with the perceptions of general stigma, a tendency to avoid treatments (Corrigan et al., 2014; Lannin et al., 2015).

Can we critically evaluate this information?

Few people would doubt that stigma can be real and harmful, but some have asked to what degree a diagnostic label itself might be the main source of the problem. If labels can lead professionals to view psychiatric patients differently, as in Rosenhan's study, they may produce the same effect—or an even stronger one—in the general public. However, we should also consider that the "patients" in this study were eventually released with "in remission" status, which also tells us that the psychiatrists and staff caring for them correctly interpreted their behavior after a sufficient period of time observing them. It would be far more shocking if the hospital workers made no attempt to help people who entered their facility.

Not all evidence suggests that psychiatric labels lead to negative views of individuals among the general public. It may be that, rather than a label, the symptoms themselves can be a source of stigma. Schizophrenia is a label for people who might experience delusions and hallucinations, mood disorders provide labels for persistent sadness social withdrawal, and personality disorders include emotional and sometimes aggressive or abrasive behaviors. These symptoms are likely to cause more interpersonal difficulty than a label. Therefore, we would argue that the public, like professionals, should be educated as to the nature of disorders along with the harm that stigma can cause.

Stigma often leads to feelings of isolation. These feelings can, in turn, worsen the negative emotions associated with so many disorders.

Why is this relevant?

Researchers have identified a number of techniques that work in reducing stigmatization, at least for the short term (Stubbs, 2014). For example, research shows that personal contact and knowledge of biopsychosocial explanations of mental illness are associated with lower stigma (Boyd et al., 2010). Student groups at the high school and college levels have had success in reducing the stigma associated with mental illness at their campuses (McKinney, 2009; Murman et al., 2014). Finally, there are also politically oriented groups working to erase stigma through changes in public policy (Carter et al., 2014). Keep these findings in mind as you read the rest of this chapter; as an informed student you will be less likely to judge others and more likely to seek help yourself, or recommend it to others, if it is ever needed (See Table 15.2).

The Insanity Defense

The **insanity defense** *is the legal strategy of claiming that a defendant was unable to differentiate between right and wrong when the criminal act was committed.* Although the insanity defense is always based on testimony from a psychiatrist (and often psychologists), it is important to note that insanity is a legal concept and not a specific disorder or an entry in the *DSM-5*. In fact, it is possible to plead temporary insanity without ever receiving a formal psychological diagnosis or, conversely, to have a psychological disorder—even a rather severe one—without being judged insane.

When successful, this insanity defense can greatly reduce the charges an individual must face, or reduce the duration or severity of a sentence. This was the case for Ebony Wilkerson, who drove her minivan with her three children inside into the Atlantic Ocean at Daytona Beach, Florida. The state's psychiatrist determined that she was

Table 15.2 Attitudes Toward Mental Illness

Complete the following scale to measure your attitude toward mental illness. For each of the items, circle the number that best describes how much you agree or disagree with the statement.

Item	Completely Disagree				Completely Agree
If I had a mentally ill relative, I wouldn't want anyone to know.	1	2	3	4	5
Most of my friends would see me as being weak if they thought that I had a mental illness.	1	2	3	4	5
I would be very embarrassed if I were diagnosed as having a mental illness.	1	2	3	4	5
Mentally ill people scare me.	1	2	3	4	5
I would cross the street if I saw a mentally ill person coming to avoid passing him or her.	1	2	3	4	5
I think that mentally ill people are strange and weird.	1	2	3	4	5
Find your total score by adding up the numbers you circled and dividing by 6.	1	2	3	4	5

Interpretation: This scale measures stigma toward individuals who have a mental illness. Compare your score to a large sample of high school students. Their average on this same scale was 2.13, with higher scores indicating greater levels of stigma. For those with a family member diagnosed with a mental disorder, the mean dropped to 2.05.

Source: Watson, A. C., Miller, F. E., & Lyons, J. S. (2005). Adolescent Attitudes Toward Serious Mental Illness. *Journal of Nervous and Mental Disease, 193*, 769–772.

legally insane, which resulted in lowering the charges from attempted second-degree murder to felony child endangerment; charges for which she was eventually found not guilty. Although this verdict prevented jail time, she was ordered to be treated in a secure, residential mental health center until the professionals there believed she was no longer a threat.

Court decisions like these can bring out strong emotions because some see it as an easy excuse for criminals to escape punishment. In reality, a successful insanity defense is a rare occurrence. Judicial systems do not keep a running count of insanity pleas, so estimating its use is a time-consuming process that few are willing to undertake. In the past 25 years, the best samples of court records and surveys of prosecuting or defense attorneys indicate that the plea is advanced in less than 1% of federal cases. Even then, it has a rather poor success rate—it is successful less than 20% of the time (Melton et al., 2007; Valdes, 2005).

Summary

Now that you have read this section you should:

KNOW . . .

- ***The key terminology associated with defining and classifying psychological disorders:***

abnormal psychology (p. 455)
Diagnostic and Statistical Manual for Mental Disorders (*DSM-5*) (p. 456)
insanity defense (p. 458)
maladaptive behavior (p. 455)
medical model (p. 455)

UNDERSTAND . . .

- ***How disorders are viewed as either dimensional or categorical.*** Disorders are defined and identified according to patterns of symptoms. Some symptoms and disorders are categorical because an individual clearly has the symptoms or does not. However, many, if not most, psychological disorders are dimensional in nature; they vary by degree of severity.
- ***The differences between the concepts of psychological disorders and insanity.*** Many people get their information

(Continued)

about psychological disorders from fiction or sensationalized events in the news, so it is important to make distinctions between the psychological concept of a disorder and the legal concept of insanity. Most people with psychological disorders are not considered insane; in fact, only a small minority of people ever could be. Within the legal system, individuals may be declared insane if they were unable to tell right from wrong when they committed an offense. This designation in no way provides a diagnosis of any specific type of mental disorder.

APPLY . . .

- ***Your knowledge to reduce stigma and misunderstandings about psychological disorders you might encounter.*** We all have misunderstandings about psychological disorders, but we reduce the tendency to stigmatize in at least two ways: Learning the material in this chapter should help, but also examine your own personal thoughts to distinguish what your assumptions are versus what science can tell. The activity in Table 15.2 "Attitudes toward mental illness" is a way to assess your own views on stigma and mental illness.

ANALYZE . . .

- ***Whether the benefits of labeling psychological disorders outweigh the disadvantages.*** To evaluate the importance of the *DSM-5*'s labels, it would be helpful to consider their functions. They organize large amounts of information about symptoms, causes, and outcomes into terminology that mental health professionals can work with. From a practical point of view, this system meets the requirements of the insurance companies that pay for psychological services. One downside to this process is that once the label is applied, people may misinterpret behaviors that are perfectly normal.

Quiz

KNOW . . .

1. The ________ uses an understanding of physical conditions to think about psychological conditions.
   a. biopsychosocial model
   b. dimensional view
   c. categorical view
   d. medical model

UNDERSTAND . . .

2. Viewing a psychological disorder as an extreme case of otherwise normal behavior reflects the ________.
   a. dimensional view
   b. medical model
   c. categorical view
   d. biopsychosocial model

3. As described in this section, insanity:
   a. is itself a psychological disorder.
   b. describes a person with any psychological disorder.
   c. is not recognized by the legal profession or judicial system.
   d. is a legal term meaning that an individual could not distinguish between right and wrong when he or she broke a law.

APPLY . . .

4. Which of the following has been demonstrated an effective way to reduce stigma?
   a. Learning about biopsychosocial explanations for disorders
   b. Understanding that all disorders can be treated as categorical conditions
   c. Avoiding contact with individuals who might exhibit abnormal behaviors
   d. Role-playing by asking to be admitted to a psychiatric hospital

ANALYZE . . .

5. Which statement best describes the effects of labeling someone with a mental disorder?
   a. Labeling always leads to negative perceptions of the individual with the disorder.
   b. Labeling can have either positive or negative effects, depending on factors such as context and expectations.
   c. Knowing that someone has a mental disorder always leads to caring and compassionate responses.
   d. Labeling does not work because the DSM-5 categories are not adequate.

Personality and Dissociative Disorders

Psychopath is one of the most evocative psychological terms out there and it often conjures up images of a ruthless serial killer. Psychologists are more likely to use the term *psychopathy* when describing a collection of traits including self-centeredness, superficial charm, little or no empathy, dominance, and dishonesty. They could be referring to a serial killer, but then again they could also be talking about the men who have served as President of the United States. Psychologists have actually found correlations among psychopathic qualities and presidential performance. Presidents with higher levels of dominance, for example, are more likely to be viewed as world leaders, to start new programs, and demonstrate other measures of success (Lilienfeld et al., 2012). *Psychopath* will not be appearing on any campaign slogans during the next election cycle. Still, this illustrates that personality traits like dominance or empathy can be thought of as dimensions. Some of us regularly show empathy, some rarely, and some do not. As you move down the scale, you will eventually find psychopathy. A combined lack of empathy and ruthlessness can reflect a personality disturbed enough to be classified as a psychological disorder. Psychopathy is associated with antisocial personality disorder, one of several disorders of personality functioning.

In this section, we will begin by examining what happens when individuals experience problems during personality development and the effects it can have on their lives—and on others' lives as well. This discussion will be followed by examination of a different type of disorder known as *dissociative disorders*. Despite their differences, these two categories of disorders are similar in that they are among the most intriguing and challenging to understand.

Defining and Classifying Personality Disorders

Personality disorders *are particularly unusual patterns of behavior for one's culture that are maladaptive, distressing to oneself or others, and resistant to change.* Patterns of behavior in people with a personality disorder might involve an excessive desire to gain attention and approval from others, a dysfunctional style of relating to others, or a lack of empathy and regard for others. Note that these descriptions are dimensional in nature; they could apply to *anyone* at some point, so it is important to remember that the actual disorders represent extreme and persistent cases.

As Table 15.3 shows, the *DSM-5* identifies clusters of personality disorders involving (1) odd or eccentric behavior; (2) dramatic, emotional, and erratic behavior; and (3) anxious, fearful, and inhibited behavior. In this section, we will focus on the disorders that comprise the second category.

Borderline Personality

At the core of personality disorders is emotional dysfunction, and one of the clearest examples of this is borderline personality disorder. **Borderline personality disorder** *is characterized by intense extremes between positive and negative emotions, an unstable sense of self, impulsivity, and difficult social relationships.* Borderline personality disorder is estimated to affect almost 3% of the population in the United States and is highly correlated with anxiety, substance abuse, and mood disorders such as depression (Tomko et al., 2014).

Each of the characteristics of borderline personality disorder seems connected to all-or-none thinking. For example, a person with it may fall in love quickly, professing deep commitment and affection, but just as quickly become disgusted by his partner's perceived imperfections. Friends, family, colleagues, and even public figures can also be idealized and despised in the same way. Thus, the all-or-none thinking associated with borderline personality disorder prevents an individual from rationally dealing with the fact that, in even the best relationship, some expectations are not met and there are bound to be periods of conflict.

Table 15.3 Varieties of Personality Disorders with Brief Descriptions of Each

Cluster	Description
• Odd, eccentric	• **Paranoid Personality Disorder** distrust and suspiciousness such that others' motives are interpreted as malevolent. • **Schizoid Personality Disorder** detachment from social relationships and a restricted range of emotional expression. • **Schizotypal Personality Disorder** acute discomfort in close relationships, cognitive or perceptual distortions, and eccentricities of behavior.
• Dramatic, emotional, erratic	• **Antisocial Personality Disorder** disregard for, and violation of, the rights of others. • **Borderline Personality Disorder** instability in interpersonal relationships, self-image, and affects, and marked impulsivity. • **Histrionic Personality Disorder** excessive emotionality and attention seeking. • **Narcissistic Personality Disorder** grandiosity, need for admiration, and lack of empathy.
• Anxious, fearful, inhibited	• **Avoidant Personality Disorder** social inhibition, feelings of inadequacy, and hypersensitivity to negative evaluation. • **Dependent Personality Disorder** submissive and clinging behavior related to an excessive need to be taken care of. • **Obsessive-Compulsive Personality Disorder** preoccupation with orderliness, perfectionism, and control.
• **Personality Disorder Not Otherwise Specified** is a category provided for two situations: 1) the individual's personality pattern meets the general criteria for a Personality Disorder and traits of several different Personality Disorders are present, but the criteria for any specific Personality Disorder are not met; or 2) the individual's personality pattern meets the general criteria for a Personality Disorder, but the individual is considered to have a Personality Disorder that is not included in the classification (e.g., passive-aggressive personality disorder).	

Source: American Psychiatric Association. (2000). *Diagnostic and statistical manual of mental disorders* (4th ed., text revision). Washington, DC: Author.

As a part of their troubled relationships, people with borderline personality disorder can become paranoid, suspecting that everyone else has similarly unpredictable feelings. Their fear of abandonment is typically intense, and it may drive them to go to extremes to prevent the loss of a relationship. It may also lead to risky sexual behavior as the individual desperately tries to secure relationships. One of the most distinguishing features of borderline personality disorder is the tendency toward *self-injury*, which may involve cutting or burning oneself. Suicide attempts are also quite common among people with this disorder.

According to Greek mythology, Narcissus discovered his image reflecting from the surface of a pool of water. Unable to tear himself away from the beauty of his own face, Narcissus wasted away and died at the water's edge. In modern times, narcissism describes a person who has an inflated sense of self-importance.

Histrionic Personality

Emotional dysfunction can also be seen in **histrionic personality disorder**, *which is characterized by excessive attention seeking and dramatic behavior.* "Histrionic" comes from a Latin word meaning "like an actor or like a theatrical performance"—an apt label for this disorder. People who have histrionic personality disorder are typically successful at drawing people in with flirtatiousness, provocative sexuality, and flattery, but they are simply playing the roles they believe are necessary to be the center of attention. Thus, people with histrionic personality disorder are characterized by extreme shallowness and emotional immaturity.

Narcissistic Personality

Narcissistic personality disorder *is characterized by an inflated sense of self-importance and an intense need for attention and admiration, as well as intense self-doubt and fear of abandonment.* These narcissistic feelings leave little room for empathy. In fact, people with narcissistic personality disorder are known to manipulate and arrange their relationships to make sure their own needs are met, no matter the toll it takes on others. Because of these tendencies, you can see evidence of the disorder in all aspects of behavior. For example, evidence of narcissistic personality disorder may even be found in your classroom: Students with narcissistic tendencies are more likely to engage in academic dishonesty than others, and do so without guilt or remorse (Brunell et al., 2011). Relatedly, another disorder characterized by a lack of guilt or remorse, called *antisocial personality disorder*, has long captured the attention of psychologists, criminologists, and the general public.

Working the Scientific Literacy Model

Antisocial Personality Disorder

Antisocial personality disorder (APD) *refers to a condition marked by a habitual pattern of willingly violating others' personal rights, with little sign of empathy or remorse.* It is a difficult condition to deal with because the actions of people with APD are often distressful and alarming, and the individuals themselves are rarely motivated to change.

What do we know about antisocial personality disorder?

Numerous problematic behaviors characterize APD: People with APD tend to be physically and verbally abusive, destructive, and frequently find themselves in trouble with the law. Symptoms of the disorder typically appear during childhood and adolescence—most often with boys—as patterns of harming or torturing people or animals, destroying property, stealing, and being deceitful (Lynam & Gudonis, 2005). Behind the behaviors, you will usually find the traits of psychopathy that were described in the opening of this section. If you associate *psychopath* with serial killers, you would be equally correct in making that association with APD. However, keep in mind that serial killers represent only a small subset of people with APD or psychopathy. In fact, people who have either antisocial tendencies or full-blown manifestations of APD can be found throughout society. Given their high potential for inflicting physical and psychological harm on others, scientists have sought to understand what is unique about people with APD, and whether this information can be used help treat people who have been diagnosed with it.

(Continued)

How can science explain antisocial personality disorder?

You may have heard stories of people who have snapped under stress and committed horrific acts; this type of situation is different from what would be expected from someone with APD. In contrast, people with APD are *under*-reactive to stress. A flash of light, a loud sound, or the sudden appearance of an angry face will startle most, but individuals with APD show weak startle responses—such as blinking—when exposed to unpleasant stimuli. In one study, researchers recorded the electrical signals of the muscles that control eye blinking while presenting disturbing images to a group of people with APD and a control group without APD. You can see the results in Figure 15.2, in which the strength of the startle response is indicated by the height of the bars. The group of people with APD (the bars on the right side) have much weaker responses than the group without APD (on the left; Levenston et al., 2000).

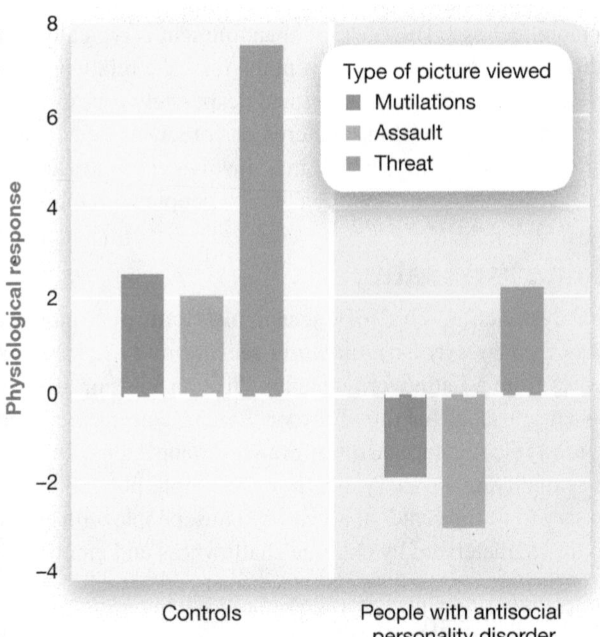

Figure 15.2 Emotional Responses of Individuals with Antisocial Personality Disorder
This graph shows the strength of autonomic response to three types of pictures: mutilations, assault, and threat. Responses are much greater among control subjects (those who do not have APD; the three bars on the left) than among the individuals with antisocial personality disorder (the three bars on the right).

Can we critically evaluate this information?

We must be careful not to assume that all people with APD or psychopathy are violent criminals. Psychopathy can be found in white-collar criminals who cheat and lie for profit. For example, Wall Street power broker Bernard Madoff admitted to stealing billions of dollars from investors who trusted him with their money. Madoff has shown little remorse for ruining the fortunes of many individuals and institutions—including charities. Some have suggested that, although he committed no violent crime, the level of deceit, maliciousness, and egocentrism he exhibited is psychopathic in nature.

Why is this relevant?

Identifying how physiology and brain function differ in people with APD and psychopathy is certainly helpful for psychologists who are trying to treat these disturbing behavioral patterns. People with APD tend to be highly resistant to psychological therapies, so drug treatments that can alter the physiological processes underlying the disorder may be needed. Also, antisocial patterns are often detectable during childhood and adolescence, which are critical periods of brain development. Perhaps therapies will be more highly beneficial if started at an early age, rather than in adulthood.

Journal prompt

Personality Disorders:

About personality—namely "normal" personality traits that we all express to differing degrees (e.g., extraversion, emotional stability). At what point do you think it might be justified, if at all, to diagnose someone with a disordered personality?

The Development of Personality Disorders

Discovering the origins of personality disorders has been challenging, largely because multiple causes are likely at play; they clearly require the biopsychosocial model. The case of APD serves a good example of how researchers understand the development of a personality disorder. The *DSM-5* criteria for APD includes the minimum age of 18 years, but this is not to suggest that traits suddenly appear in early adulthood. Instead, children may be diagnosed with *conduct disorder* when they exhibit severe aggression toward people and often animals, persistent lying or stealing, destructiveness, and a pervasive disregard for rules and authority. Many children with conduct disorder are eventually diagnosed as psychopathic or APD.

During early childhood, most people begin to adapt to social expectations and norms in part by delaying gratification—putting off an immediate reward to later receive a bigger reward or to conform to rules and manners. The biopsychosocial model helps explain why children with conduct disorder fail to adapt to these social expectations. From a social perspective,

Table 15.4 Applying the Biopsychosocial Model to Antisocial Personality Disorder

For antisocial personality disorder and psychopathy:
1. Name one or two biological influences associated with APD and psychopathy.
2. What is at least one psychological factor that distinguishes people with these personality disorders from normal people? (e.g., How does their thinking or emotional processing differ?)
3. What are at least two social or cultural factors associated with APD and psychopathy?

Answers:

1. People with psychopathy show reduced startle reflex and reduced activity in the frontal lobes.
2. Individuals with psychopathy have difficulty learning and following rules. They also lack empathy and show dampened negative emotion to negative events.
3. People who develop psychopathy or APD are more likely to grow up in distressed home environments or neighborhoods where prosocial rules are not easily learned. A history of childhood sexual, physical, or emotional abuse at the hands of adults is also associated with APD and psychopathy.

living in unstable households and neighborhoods is a risk factor (Vaughn et al., 2010). Some children raised in unstable settings might find it adaptive to take advantage of opportunities immediately before they vanish, rather than delay gratification (this can certainly happen in even the most prosperous neighborhoods as well). Interestingly, difficulty in delaying gratification is associated with frontal lobe activity, and brain studies have shown lower levels of frontal lobe function in conduct disorder and APD (Haney-Caron et al., 2014). Also, in these contexts children are often mistreated. Although most children have a reasonably good understanding of how breaking rules might have negative consequences, children with conduct disorder often learn that they will receive negative consequences regardless, and so they develop a disregard for authority figures and simply behave as they wish. Not all children who experience maltreatment develop conduct disorder. In fact, some respond by becoming depressed, and researchers have found specific genetic markers that indicate which trajectory is more likely (Beach et al., 2015). Thus, the research on APD illustrates that psychological, biological, and social factors interact as personality disorders develop (see Table 15.4).

Of course, not all personality disorders are the same, and researchers have been able to uncover clues to the development of their distinctive characteristics. For example, borderline personality disorder (BPD) may stem from profound *invalidation* during childhood, meaning that a child's caregivers did not respond to his or her emotions as if they were real or important (Crowell et al., 2009). As a result, adults with BPD never master the ability to identify and control emotions and tend to react more strongly to everyday life stressors (Glaser et al., 2008).

A final consideration is the high levels of comorbidity among personality disorders. **Comorbidity** *is the presence of two disorders simultaneously or the presence of a second disorder that affects the one being treated.* For example, substance abuse is often comorbid with personality disorders (Goldstein et al., 2007; Gudonis et al., 2009). Their intertwining may actually influence the ongoing development of a personality disorder: It is possible that the personality disorder leads to substance abuse, which, in turn, strengthens the personality problems in a vicious cycle.

Dissociative Identity Disorder

Have you ever been so engaged in driving, reading a book, or playing a game that you were totally unaware of what was going on around you? Psychologists refer to this as a *dissociative experience* because of the separation—or dissociation—between you and your surroundings. Dissociative experiences may arise while you are intensely focused on one activity, or when you drift off while not doing anything in particular, such as daydreaming during a long lecture. People differ in their tendencies to dissociate, but such experiences seem completely normal.

In a few cases, some people have such extreme experiences that they may be diagnosed with a **dissociative disorder**, *a category of mental disorder characterized by a split between conscious awareness from feeling, cognition, memory, and identity*

(Kihlstrom, 2005). Probably the most familiar member of this category is **dissociative identity disorder (DID)** (sometimes referred to as *multiple personality disorder* in popular media), *in which a person claims that his or her identity has split into one or more distinct alter personalities, or alters.* Alters may differ in gender, sexual orientation, personality, memory, and autobiographical sense of self. The dissociation of alter identities can be so strong that one alter may have no memory of events experienced by other alters.

In most cases, dissociative disorders such as DID are thought to be brought on by extreme stress. Some psychologists have hypothesized that, during a traumatic episode (e.g., during a sexual assault), an individual may cope by trying to block out the experience and focus on another time and place. They have further speculated that with repeated experiences, this type of dissociation could become an individual's habitual way of coping with the trauma (van der Kolk, 1994).

Because so few people develop DID, and because even the disorder itself seems implausible to some, many psychologists question the validity of this diagnosis altogether (Gillig, 2009). In contrast to speculation about DID, studies examining more than 10,000 trauma victims found that any forgetting that did occur could be explained by infantile or childhood amnesia (they were simply too young to remember) or just normal forgetting (Pope et al., 2000). The fact is that most trauma victims remember their experiences (Cahill & McGaugh, 1998), and many develop PTSD (described in the next section), which is characterized by the lack of an ability to forget or ignore trauma. Thus, many psychologists find it unlikely that traumatic experiences directly lead to DID.

Although there is little doubt that people regularly have dissociative experiences, a serious condition like DID is difficult to test for given that the symptoms are subjective experiences. However, there are alternative approaches that might be able to detect DID. For example, in one study patients viewed words and pictures and were tested for recall of the stimuli either when they were experiencing the same alter as when they learned, or when they were experiencing a different alter. The results suggested that some types of learning do not transfer between alter identities, thus supporting the diagnosis (Eich et al., 1997). Skeptics, however, might point out that similar results can be produced in the general population simply by instructing volunteers (who do not claim to have DID) to imagine themselves in different contexts (Sahakyan & Kelley, 2002). Moreover, a similar study examining brain recordings (known as event-related potentials) found that the brain activity during recall was similar whether the information was learned in the same state or in another alter (Allen & Movius, 2000). This would suggest that there is no neurological difference between personalities.

Some other observations offer compelling reasons to be skeptical about diagnosing DID. First, 80% of patients diagnosed with DID were unaware of having the disorder before starting therapy (Putnam, 1989). These observations suggest that DID may have its origins in the context of therapy, rather than being a response to trauma. Second, in 1970, there were 79 documented cases of DID (then referred to as multiple personality disorder). In 1986, there were around 6,000; by 1998, the number had risen to more than 40,000 (Lilienfeld & Lynn, 2003). The numbers continue to rise, although compared to other major disorders the prevalence of DID in the population is low. Why did the rate of DID skyrocket from 79 cases to more than 40,000 cases per year in less than three decades? This increased prevalence could simply be a product of awareness: After professionals learned how to identify the disorder, they could begin to diagnose it more effectively. However, it is also possible that the drastic increase seen from 1970 through the 1980s in particular resulted from social and cultural effects, such as the popularization of a film called *Sybil,* which purported to tell the true story of a woman with DID. Diagnoses of DID rose shortly after this film was released. Similarly, the disorder was nonexistent in Japan in 1990 (Takahashi, 1990), but Japanese psychologists began diagnosing patients with DID when the disorder was described by North Americans (An et al., 1998). To many psychologists, these observations point to a predominantly sociocultural phenomenon in which cultural beliefs and therapists determine how the symptoms are manifested (Lilienfeld et al., 1999).

Summary

Now that you have read this section you should:

KNOW . . .

- ***the key terminology associated with personality and dissociative disorders:***

antisocial personality disorder (APD) (p. 463)
borderline personality disorder (p. 462)
comorbidity (p. 465)
dissociative disorder (p. 465)
dissociative identity disorder (DID) (p. 466)
histrionic personality disorder (p. 463)
narcissistic personality disorder (p. 463)
personality disorders (p. 462)

UNDERSTAND . . .

- ***the phenomenon of dissociation and how a dissociative disorder might occur.*** Dissociation can be explained in everyday phenomena such as daydreaming. However, a dissociative disorder may occur when perceptions of mind, body, and surroundings are severely and chronically separated, such as in purported cases of dissociative identity disorder.

APPLY . . .

- ***the biopsychosocial model to understand the causes of personality disorders.*** Take antisocial personality disorder and psychopathy for example: Researchers have been able to study how it develops over the life span, which provides insight into the range of biopsychosocial influences. If you have not done so already, relate your knowledge of the biopsychosocial model to the activity in Table 15.4.

ANALYZE . . .

- ***the status of dissociative identity disorder as a legitimate diagnosis.*** The lack of a physical basis for the disorder and its unusual rate and patterns of diagnosis rightly bring about skepticism. For example, diagnoses of DID increased dramatically after a film depicted a purported case of DID. Ensure that your evaluation (of any condition, not just DID) is not biased by fictional or sensationalized accounts you have seen or read. However, it is also important to remember that many of the mental disorders for which we have a greater understanding were at one time considered mysterious and controversial.

Quiz

KNOW . . .

1. ________ refers to a condition marked by a habitual pattern of willingly violating others' personal rights, with very little sign of empathy or remorse.
   a. Borderline personality disorder
   b. Narcissistic personality disorder
   c. Histrionic personality disorder
   d. Antisocial personality disorder
2. Which of the following individuals demonstrates the definition of comorbidity?
   a. A person who has both borderline personality disorder and a substance abuse disorder
   b. A person who is histrionic who both seeks excessive attention and is emotionally hyper-reactive
   c. A person with borderline personality disorder who is impulsive and tends to be in unstable relationships
   d. A person who experiences a personality disorder that turns out to be fatal

UNDERSTAND . . .

3. What is a defining characteristic of dissociative identity disorder (DID)?
   a. Believe they no longer exist or are real
   b. Lose the sensation of an appendage with no physical or neurological evidence
   c. Emotional distance and callousness
   d. A claim that multiple personalities inhabit one body

APPLY . . .

4. Which of the following biopsychosocial factors is least likely to be related to personality disorders?
   a. Stress reactivity
   b. History of abuse
   c. Decreased activity of the frontal lobes
   d. Enjoyment of pain

ANALYZE . . .

5. Skeptics have argued against the validity of DID in a number of different cases. What is their reasoning?
   a. The disorder appears to be based on cultural expectations.
   b. Most people who experience trauma do not dissociate.
   c. The vast majority of cases come from a very small number of therapists.
   d. Skeptics have cited all of these arguments.

ANXIETY AND MOOD DISORDERS

Waking up with a headache, fever, or sore throat, unpleasant as it is, is not at all unusual. But what about waking up to obsessive–compulsive disorder (OCD)? When it comes to mental disorders, people typically think of signs that something is "not quite right" about a person's behavior, and what follows may be a gradual unfolding of more noticeable personality, behavioral, or emotional problems. Although this is how mental disorders typically develop, sudden onset of OCD—a serious anxiety disorder—has been documented in cases in which young children were infected by bacterial streptococci. Shortly after exposure to the infection, some children rapidly developed symptoms of OCD, including extremely repetitive behaviors and having irrational fears and obsessions (Snider & Swedo, 2004). But why might a relatively common infection result in such rapid behavioral and emotional changes in *some* children? The answer seems to be that when the immune system mounts its reaction to the bacterial infection, it also damages cells in the caudate, a part of the brain related to impulse control, as well as related structures in the same vicinity. As we will see in this section, one theory about OCD is that compulsive, repetitive behaviors (such as hand washing) are ways of dealing with the lost sense of impulse control—a loss that occurs when the caudate is damaged (Huyser et al., 2009). If this theory is correct, then, at least in this case, a psychological disorder can be acquired virtually overnight. This is an exceptional example to two categories of disorder—those involving problems with mood and anxiety—that are among the most prevalent in the world.

Anxiety and mood disorders are among the most common types of psychological disorders. If you have any personal experience with mental illness—maybe you or someone close to you has experienced it—then there is a good chance you will come across a description of the disorder in this section.

ANXIETY DISORDERS

Intense, persistent anxiety can be painful and maladaptive, no matter the source or how it is expressed in an individual's thoughts and behaviors. The *DSM-5* describes three main categories of disorders for which anxiety is a key symptom: Anxiety Disorders, Obsessive–Compulsive Disorders, and Trauma and Stressor-Related Disorders. These are among the most frequently diagnosed disorders, affecting more than 20% of the adult population in the United States (NIMH, 2015).

We all experience anxiety to some degree; it is based on a normal physiological and psychological response to stressful events known as the *fight-or-flight response* (Nesse & Ellsworth, 2009). We experience this response as a racing, pounding heart, increased respiration, knots in the stomach, and sweaty or clammy hands. These physical changes reflect a shift in energy away from non-emergency tasks like digestion and toward fighting or fleeing. The fight-or-flight response seems to be common to all mammals, and it is an adaptive response to threats.

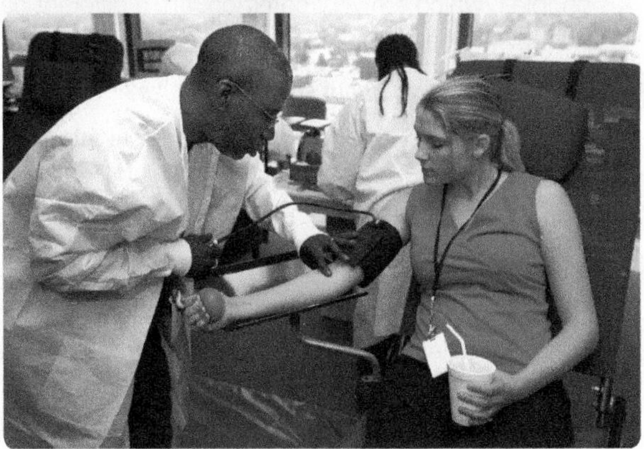

Fight or flight... freeze or faint? In addition to fight-or-flight responses, mammals can also react by freezing—as in the "deer in the headlights" response—or by fainting, as some will do at the sight of blood (Bracha et al., 2004).

If the physiological reactions involved in anxiety are adaptive, then our challenge is to identify symptoms that go beyond typical psychological responses and become maladaptive. The distinction between a typical psychological state and a disorder combines extremes in duration and severity, and a disordered state may be a disproportionate response to real-life events, or it may occur without any precipitating event whatsoever. Anxiety disorders take on a variety of different forms, with bouts of anxiety elicited by highly specific situations or objects, or without any clear reason.

Generalized Anxiety Disorder

Generalized anxiety disorder (GAD) *involves frequently elevated levels of anxiety that are not a response to any particular situation*—the anxiety is *generalized* to just about anything. Additionally, people with GAD often feel irritable and have difficulty sleeping and concentrating, which are not unusual experiences for people with any type of anxiety problem. What makes GAD distinct from other anxiety disorders is that people who have it often struggle to identify the specific reasons for why they are anxious. Moreover, the anxiety that people with GAD experience does not seem to go away, even if a particular problem or issue is resolved. Rather, the anxiety becomes redirected toward some other concern. The onset of GAD can be attributed to a variety of factors, not all of which are clear, but major life changes commonly precede its onset (Newman & Llera, 2011).

Panic Disorder and Agoraphobia

Panic disorder *is an anxiety disorder marked by repeated episodes of sudden, intense fear.* This condition is distinct from GAD because the anxiety occurs in short segments lasting up to 10 minutes, but can be much more severe. The key feature of this disorder is *panic attacks*—moments of extreme anxiety that include a rush of physical activity paired with frightening thoughts. A panic attack escalates when the sudden, intense fear causes increased physical arousal, and the increased physical symptoms feed the frightening thoughts.

For some, a sense of intense fear or a panic response becomes associated with more than one situation. When this fear becomes serious, it may be diagnosed as the distinct, but clearly related disorder **agoraphobia**, *an intense fear of visiting open, public places out of fear of having a panic attack.* As a result of this fear, the individual may begin to avoid public settings so as to avoid the embarrassment and trauma of a panic attack. In its most extreme forms, agoraphobia leads an individual to stay inside his or her home almost permanently.

Working the Scientific Literacy Model

Specific Phobias

In contrast to GAD, where an individual's anxiety occurs in response to many situations, a **phobia** *is a severe, irrational fear of an object or specific situation.* Some of the most common phobias are listed in Table 15.5. The best-known form of phobia is probably **specific phobia**, *which involves an intense fear of an object, activity, or organism.* These include fears of things such as specific animals, heights, thunder, blood, and injections or other medical procedures. (Social phobias, which are very common, are a different category of phobias that are discussed later.)

What do we know about specific phobias?

Phobias develop through unpleasant or frightening experiences—for example, a person who is bitten by a dog might develop a dog phobia. But negative experiences tell only part of the story—not all dog bite victims develop phobias. The overwhelming majority of the triggers for phobias are objects or situations we may *need* to fear, or at least be cautious about. This linkage leads psychologists to believe there is a genetic component to a fear of heights, snakes, and other potential dangers from our evolutionary history (Öhman & Mineka, 2001); in other words, we may be *biologically predisposed* to fear some objects.

How can science explain specific phobias?

If organisms really are biologically prepared to fear certain things, then scientists should be able to find a genetic basis for this tendency. One approach to studying how genes influence fear and anxiety comes from selective breeding techniques. To use this approach, one group of researchers tested a strain of mice for fear conditioning and ranked the mice from least to most easily conditioned. Specifically, they used a classical conditioning technique in which the mice heard a tone followed by an electric shock. Fear was measured by the length of time the mice held still in fear in response to the tone—mice typically show fear by freezing in place (Ponder et al., 2007).

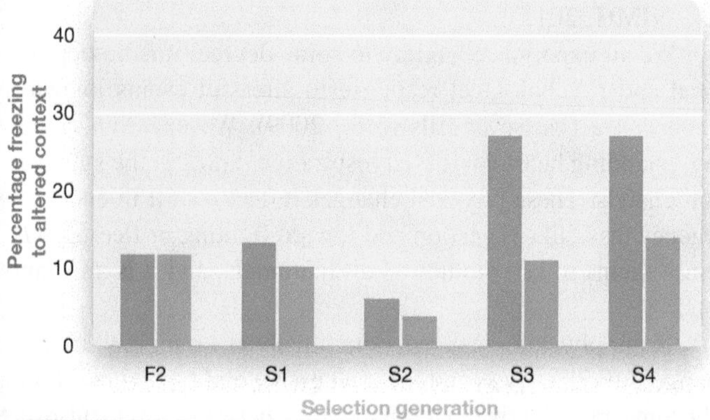

Figure 15.3 Anxiety Levels are Inherited in an Animal Model
Over the course of just a few generations, mice from the highly fearful genetic strain show increasingly strong fear responses as indicated by the height of the red bars.

The most fearful mice were then allowed to breed with each other across four generations. The least fearful animals were also paired up and allowed to breed. As Figure 15.3 shows, across these four generations, fear responses became more and more distinct, with the third and fourth generations being very different from each other; the mice bred from the most fearful families became even more easily conditioned than their great grandparents. Thus, the researchers showed that the disposition to learn certain types of fears can be genetically influenced.

Can we critically evaluate this research?

Fear learning in mice may not *seem* applicable to fear experienced by humans. Although this research informs us that the genes of mice can be selectively bred to increase susceptibility to acquire fear responses, humans are a different species. Though valuable, this particular study does not specify how anxiety and fear are coded in the human genome. Therefore, it is reasonable to look for evidence related specifically to humans. Further, this research might lead you

Table 15.5 What are We Afraid of?

Method	Currently Experiencing the Phobia	Have Experienced the Phobia at One Time
Animals (snakes, birds, or other animals)	4.7%	50.3%
Natural environment (e.g., heights, storms, water)	5.9%	62.7%
Blood or bodily injury (including injections)	4.0%	42.5%
Situations (e.g., dentists, hospitals, crowded places)	5.2%	55.6%
Other specific objects	1.0%	10.6%

Source: "What are We So Afraid Of?" from "The Epidemiology of DSM-IV specific phobia in the USA: Results from the National Epidemiologic Survey on Alcohol and Related Conditions" Adaptation of Table 3 from "The Epidemiology of DSM-IV Specific Phobia in the USA: Results from the National Epidemiologic Survey on Alcohol and Related Conditions" by F. S. Stinson, et al. (2007) *Psychological Medicine, 37,* 1047–1059.

to believe that humans have developed biological tendencies to fear dangerous things in general, but that does not seem to be the case. The objects and events people tend to fear have been a part of human experience for thousands of years—long enough to influence our genetic makeup. This would explain why so many people rapidly develop phobias of snakes or spiders—the threats our ancestors faced—whereas relatively few people develop intense phobias about more modern potential dangers, such as guns.

Why is this relevant?

It is important for mental health professionals to understand that phobias have a genetic component. This relationship suggests that not all fears should be treated equally, nor should all individuals with phobias be treated the same way. By isolating genetic tendencies and determining how they affect the nervous system, researchers will be able to develop more specialized forms of treatment for phobias, and potentially for other anxiety disorders as well.

Social Phobias

Social anxiety disorder *is an irrational fear of being observed, evaluated, or embarrassed in public.* Although each of these are real fears for anyone, someone with social anxiety disorder experiences them to an excessive and unreasonable degree, which leads to avoidance of actual or merely potential social interactions. Consider the day of a college student who has social anxiety:

- This student always shows up to class right as it begins so he does not have to risk awkward conversation with classmates he does not know. Even worse, what if everyone else is having conversations and he has to sit alone without talking to anyone?
- Despite being hungry, the student will not go into the cafeteria because his roommate is not around. He cannot face the prospect of sitting with strangers, especially without his roommate. He finds a quiet spot near the library and gets lunch from a vending machine.
- Walking across a quiet part of campus, he sees his professor approaching. Not knowing if the professor would recognize him, he wonders if he should say hello. Thinking about this issue makes him so tense, he pretends to stop and read a text message to avoid eye contact.

As you can see, the day is a series of unpleasant, tense moments in situations that most people would find completely ordinary. The distress the student feels and the degree to which he shapes his life around his social phobia suggest that he has social anxiety disorder. To make a formal diagnosis of this disorder, a psychologist would need to evaluate the student's full set of symptoms and their duration.

Journal prompt

Fear or Phobia?

The distinction between a phobia and a normal, healthy fear is an important one. What makes the two different and why do psychologists distinguish them?

Obsessive-Compulsive Disorder

The disorder you read about in the introduction to this section is known as **obsessive-compulsive disorder (OCD)**, *which is a disorder characterized by unwanted, inappropriate, and persistent thoughts (obsessions); repetitive stereotyped behaviors (compulsions); or a combination of the two* (see Figure 15.4). We introduced this disorder at the outset by describing how it can occur suddenly in children; however, OCD typically does not set

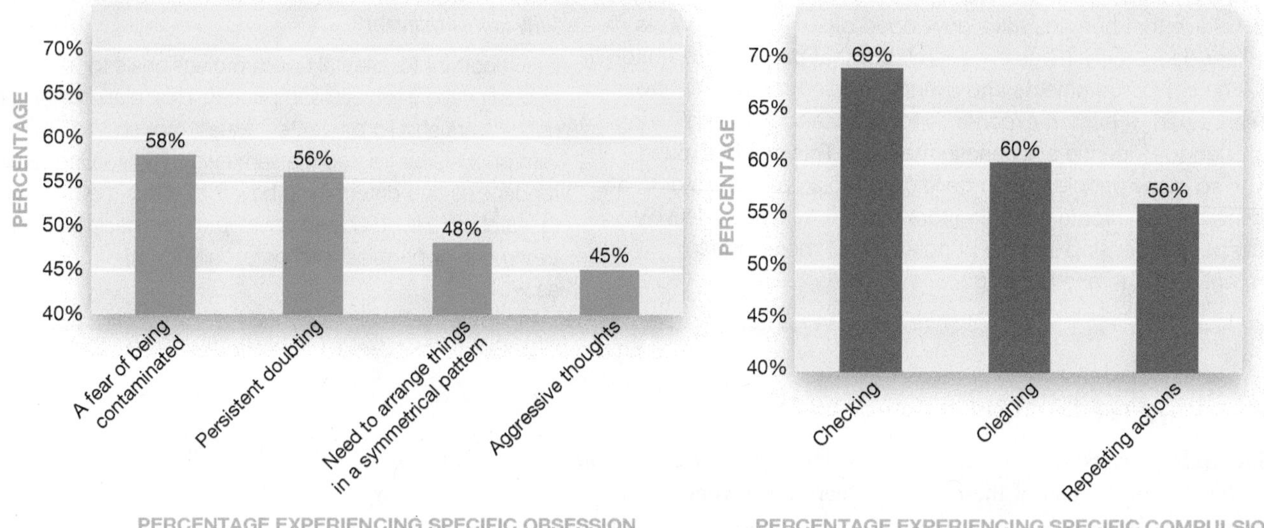

Figure 15.4 Prevalence of Symptoms in People Diagnosed with Obserssive-Compulsive Disorder

in until young adulthood. In addition, it is a dimensional disorder in which normal precautions, such as practicing good hygiene, can develop into extreme, irrational thoughts and behaviors that cannot be ignored. Most of us have had unwanted thoughts such as an annoying song that was stuck in our head, but a person with obsessions about cleanliness might be so worried about picking up germs from everything he touches that he can barely bring himself to do anything at all. As a result of these obsessions, the individual may seek to reduce the anxiety, sometimes in problematic ways such as washing his hands until they become so dried out that he bleeds.

Trauma and Stress-Related Disorders

The *DSM-5* includes a category of disorders that arise from trauma or severe stressors. Within this category, Posttraumatic stress disorder (PTSD) is perhaps the most widely known. PTSD arises from exposure to trauma, which might involve direct experience, witnessing an event, or simply getting prolonged and detailed information about trauma that is excessively graphic or strikes too close to home.

Characteristic symptoms of PTSD include:

- Re-experiencing the event in the form of flashbacks, nightmares, and other vivid, anxiety-provoking thoughts.
- Avoidance occurs when the individual avoids contexts similar to when the trauma or stressor was experienced. Sights, sounds, and smells can all lead to painful re-experiencing symptoms.
- Negative emotions and thoughts repeatedly intrude upon the individual. This may include sadness, anger, guilt, helplessness, or other negative emotions that relate back to the original experience.
- Altered arousal and activity might involve increases in anger, substance abuse, and high-risk behavior. Individuals with PTSD often report that they are always on the lookout for repeated stressors and they are easily startled, even by familiar stimuli.

Although PTSD is probably the best-known disorder from this category, there are other disorders that are quite common, but not always recognized. One example is *adjustment disorder*, which arises from the stress of having to adjust to new situations. Children go through serious stress as parents get divorced, and adults may experience this after being laid off from work. Adjustment disorders do not necessarily arise from a specific traumatic event, but they can have lingering consequences similar to PTSD, including avoidance, negative emotions, and altered arousal and activity.

Notice increased heart rate

Fear of heart problem

Figure 15.5 Vicious Cycle of Panic Attacks

The Vicious Cycle of Anxiety

One of the most difficult aspects of anxiety is that it tends to be self-perpetuating (Figure 15.5). In a sense, having an anxiety disorder today sets you up to have an anxiety disorder next week as well (Hofmann, 2007). For example, think about a young girl who tries to pet a neighbor's cat, but the cat scratches her. The incident did not leave a lasting physical scar, but years later the girl still feels nervous around cats. She is reluctant to even enter a house if the owners have a cat, but if she does, she remains nervous until the cat is taken away to another room or let outside. How might this behavior contribute to a vicious cycle? The sight of a cat triggers an anxiety response. When the cat is removed from the situation, or when the girl avoids the situation altogether, the anxiety fades. This process of reducing the fear, in turn, can actually reinforce the phobia.

Mood Disorders

Mood disorders affect roughly 9.5% of adults in the United States—nearly 21 million people (NIMH, 2015). As a result of a combination of biological, cognitive, and sociocultural differences, rates of depression are twice as high among women as among men, and three times as high among people living in poverty (Hyde et al., 2008). There is also a genetic susceptibility to mood disorders. In this section we discuss the two major types of mood disorders—major depression and bipolar disorder.

Major Depression and Bipolar Disorder

Feelings of sadness and depression are normal aspects of human experience. By comparison, **major depression** *is a disorder marked by prolonged periods of sadness, feelings of worthlessness and hopelessness, social withdrawal, and cognitive and physical sluggishness.* With this definition, it should be clear that depression involves more than just feeling sad for a long period of time—cognition becomes depressed as well. Affected individuals have difficulty concentrating and making decisions. Attention and memory shift toward unpleasant and unhappy events. Physiologically, people with major depression may be lethargic and sleepy, yet experience insomnia. They may experience a change in appetite and the onset of digestive problems such as constipation. People who are feeling sad do not necessarily experience all of these cognitive and biological symptoms, so major depression is clearly a distinct psychological disorder.

Bipolar disorder (formerly referred to as manic depression) *is characterized by extreme highs and lows in mood, motivation, and energy.* It shares many symptoms with major depression—some distinguish the two by referring to major depression as *unipolar*—but it occurs only a third as often as depression (NIMH, 2015). Mania is the polar opposite—a highly energized state that is accompanied by inflated self-confidence and recklessness. Some individuals in this phase talk so fast that their thoughts cannot keep up, others run up credit card bills of thousands of dollars with the idea that somehow they can afford it, and others engage in risky, thrill-seeking behavior with a sense of invincibility. The specific symptoms will vary from person to person as well as the timing. Some people with bipolar disorder experience only a few manic episodes in their lives, whereas others go through mania several times each year. Still others, known as "rapid cyclers," experience abrupt mood swings, sometimes within hours.

Many people have experienced problems with a mood disorder. Those with depression may endure extended periods of sadness and hopelessness that have no apparent cause.

Biopsychosocial Aspects of Depression

Although many mysteries remain, much is known about the biological basis of depression. Twin studies suggest an underlying genetic risk for developing major depression (Figure 15.6). Also, there have been many molecular genetic studies to identify specific strands of DNA associated with physiological factors in depression (Klengel & Binder, 2013). Brain imaging research has identified two primary regions of interest related to depression: (1) the *limbic system*, which is active in emotional responses and processing, and (2) the dorsal (back) of the frontal cortex, which generally plays a role in controlling thoughts and concentrating. As is the case with panic disorder, a vicious cycle appears to occur with depression. The overactive limbic system responds strongly to emotions and sends signals that overwhelm frontal lobe processes (see Figure 15.7), and the decrease in frontal lobe functioning reduces the ability to concentrate and control what one thinks about (Gotlib & Hamilton, 2008). Depression is also linked to impaired *neurogenesis* (the development of new nerve cells) in the hippocampus (Rothenichner et al., 2014).

Abnormally reduced activity of various neurotransmitters of the brain—especially serotonin, dopamine, and norepinephrine—are thought to be associated with depression. The abnormal activity of these neurotransmitters is linked to other physiological systems. The negative emotions of depression co-occur with bodily stress reactions involving the endocrine and immune systems (Fagundes et al., 2013). The result is increased risk for viral illnesses, heart disease, and higher mortality rates in people who are chronically and severely depressed.

Depression is also a disorder of cognition. The cognitive characteristics of depression include rumination (prolonged dwelling over negative thoughts) and a difficulty shifting attention away from negative emotions (Joorman & Vanderlind, 2014). Interestingly, people with depression also report much less detail in autobiographical memories (Sumner et al., 2014). For example, if you ask most people what personal memory comes to mind when they hear "sadness," they will give a specific experience such as when a close friend moved to another city. In contrast, people with depression are more likely to provide a general type of event—such as when they feel ostracized—which is consistent with the fact that sadness is much more pervasive for them. Finally, a characteristic *depressive explanatory style* emerges, in which a depressed individual

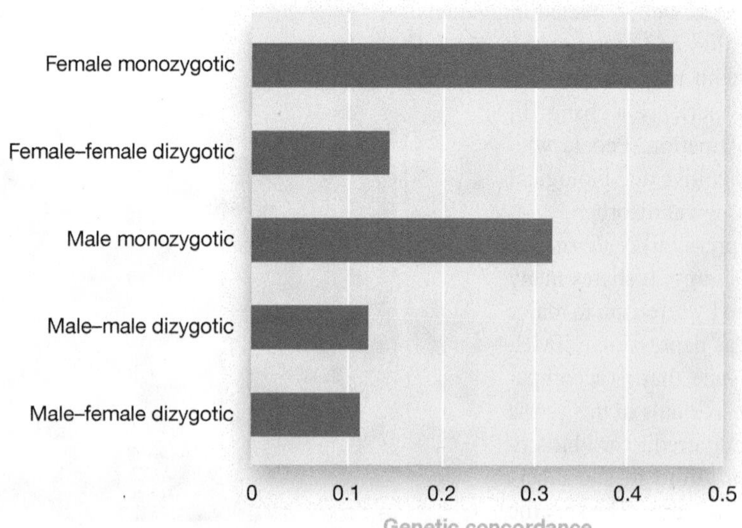

Figure 15.6 Genetic Relatedness and Major Depression
Identical (monozygotic) twins have a greater chance of both developing major depression compared to fraternal (dizygotic) twins. Notice that the genetic correlation is highest for female monozygotic twins.

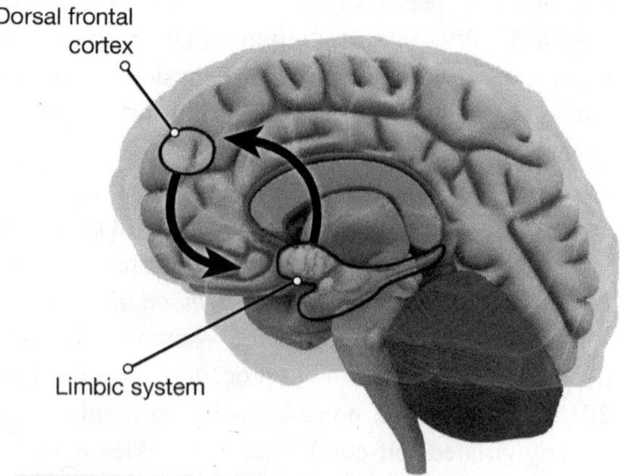

Figure 15.7 Depression and the Brain
Brain imaging research has shown higher than normal levels of activity in the limbic system of people with depression while responding to negative emotional information. This response slows activity in the dorsal frontal cortex, making it more difficult for the individual to control thoughts—especially thoughts that might break the vicious cycle.

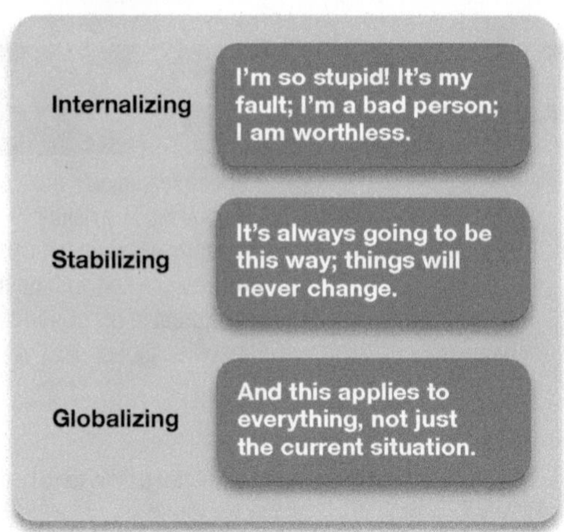

Figure 15.8 Three Elements of the Depressive Explanatory Style
The three elements of the depressive explanatory style are internalizing, stabilizing, and globalizing.

explains life with three qualities: internal, stable, and global (Ledrich & Gana, 2013). Imagine an individual with depression does something as minor as losing his keys, and refer to Figure 15.8 to see the depressive explanatory style at work.

Biological and cognitive components of depression interact with socioeconomic and environmental factors. As Figure 15.9 shows, just living in a specific neighborhood can be a risk factor for three main reasons (Cutrona et al., 2006; Kessler et al., 2014). First, poor neighborhoods are associated with higher daily stress levels because of substandard housing and facilities, increased crime rates, and lack of desirable businesses (e.g., high numbers of adult bookstores and bars, combined with low numbers of revenue-generating family establishments). Second, people living in these neighborhoods are more vulnerable to stressors such as unemployment because they often lack connections, mentors, and job opportunities that professionals have access to in better neighborhoods. Third, disrupted social ties are more prevalent in poor neighborhoods. Low rates of home ownership combined with difficulty making rent can lead to high turnover; people may not know their neighbors well and, therefore, take less interest in one another's well-being.

Suicide

It is difficult to imagine a worse outcome from a mood disorder than suicide. For many people, it is equally difficult to imagine how anyone could reach such a low point. Nonetheless, suicide remains a serious public health concern. Recent statistics from the US Centers for Disease Control indicate just how serious a problem it is:

- Suicide is the 11th most-frequent cause of death in the United States.
- It is the third-leading cause of death among teens.
- Males are four times more likely than females to die by suicide.
- Native American and non-Hispanic White Americans are more than twice as likely to die by suicide than other racial and ethnic groups.
- Despite the most commonly held beliefs, the annual suicide rates among adults 65 years of age and older is typically 70% to 100% higher than the rate for teens.
- Fortunately, research, treatment, and public awareness have significantly reduced the suicide rate among youth since the 1980s (Gould et al., 2003).

Figure 15.9 Social Influences on Depression
Stress and living conditions are linked with increased incidences of depression.

Table 15.6 Warning Signs of Suicide and Helpful Resources

Learn how to recognize the danger signals. Be concerned if someone you know:

- Talks about committing suicide
- Has trouble eating or sleeping
- Exhibits drastic changes in behavior
- Withdraws from friends or social activities
- Loses interest in school, work, or hobbies
- Prepares for death by writing a will and making final arrangements
- Gives away prized possessions
- Has attempted suicide before
- Takes unnecessary risks
- Has recently experienced serious losses
- Seems preoccupied with death and dying
- Loses interest in his or her personal appearance
- Increases alcohol or drug use

Source: American Psychological Association. (2011). Retrieved from http://www.apa.org/topics/suicide/signs.aspx

Thousands of people contact suicide telephone helplines every day. Evidence suggests that the most successful calls provide more than just empathy; they involve problem-solving, referrals, education about treatment, and follow-up calls (Mishara et al., 2007; Mishara & Daigle, 1997). Make sure you can identify sources for help in case you encounter someone who may need it.

In case of an immediate crisis, call 1-800-273-8255. And also consult: http://www.suicidepreventionlifeline.org/

For information about local services or providers, call the National Alliance on Mental Illness (https://www.nami.org/) at 1-800-950-6264.

In addition to NAMI's services, students taking courses on a campus should check to see if there is a counseling service available. Many universities and colleges provide free access to students.

Suicide often comes as a surprise to the family and friends of the victim, although in some cases clear warning signs are evident (Table 15.6). Among people in their teens and early 20s, the most significant risk factors are mood disorders, recent and extremely stressful life events, a family history of mood disorders (with or without suicide), easy access to a lethal means of suicide (most significantly, firearms), and the presence of these factors in conjunction with substance abuse (Gould et al., 2003; Moscicki, 2001). For younger individuals, being the victim of bullying and ostracism is a risk factor, but it is a greater concern when youth are both the victims and the perpetrators of bullying (Klomek et al., 2007). Family and friends have reported that in the weeks before a suicide, individuals have behaved in ways that are now recognized as warning signs. For example, an individual may verbally express despair and hopelessness (*I just want to give up; Nothing matters anymore; They'll be sorry when I'm gone*), give away personal possessions, suddenly withdraw from work or school, have crying spells, or obtain a means of committing the act. Table 15.6 offers information about resources to help people who are experiencing suicidal thoughts.

Summary

Now that you have read this section you should:

KNOW . . .

- ***the key terminology related to anxiety and mood disorders:***

agoraphobia (p. 469)
bipolar disorder (p. 473)
generalized anxiety disorder (GAD) (p. 469)
major depression (p. 473)
obsessive-compulsive disorder (OCD) (p. 471)
panic disorder (p. 469)
phobia (p. 470)
social anxiety disorder (p. 471)
specific phobias (p. 470)

UNDERSTAND . . .

- ***the different types of mood and anxiety disorders.*** Although anxiety disorders share many similarities in symptoms, they differ in terms of what brings about the symptoms and the intensity of the symptoms. The cues that trigger anxiety range widely: In generalized anxiety disorder, just about anything may cause anxiety; in specific phobias, an individual fears only certain objects. Likewise, the intensity can range from near-constant worrying to the brief periods of highly intense anxiety in phobias and panic disorder. There are fewer mood disorders discussed in this section, so it may be simpler to distinguish the two: Although depression and bipolar disorder both involve depressive symptoms (periods of negative mood, social withdrawal, difficulty concentration, and so on), only bipolar includes the elements of mania (periods of high energy, racing thoughts, and excitability).

- ***how anxiety or mood disorders can be self-perpetuating.*** Both depression and anxiety are characterized by a vicious cycle: With anxiety, anxious or fearful thoughts can lead to physiological arousal; physiological arousal can lead to escape and avoidance to get rid of the immediate fear, which in turn reinforces the anxious thoughts. In depression, a similar pattern can occur with depressed thoughts, self-blame, and social withdrawal.

APPLY . . .

- ***your knowledge of anxiety and mood disorders to be alert to people in need.*** It takes years of formal training to diagnose mental disorders. However, you now know some of the most noticeable signs of mood and anxiety disorders, and that there are different ways the disorders manifest. Suicide risk is elevated for people with mental illness. Table 15.6 provided a list of warning signs and resources for helping people at risk for committing suicide. In addition to reviewing this table, take a moment to identify how to contact your college's counseling center (most physical campuses have one). If you are a distance learner or if your school does not provide access to a counseling center, the National Alliance on Mental Illness helps individuals find treatment professionals in their local communities.

ANALYZE . . .

- ***whether maladaptive aspects of psychological disorders might arise from perfectly normal, healthy behaviors.*** To analyze this issue, we need to examine the specific symptoms that occur in someone who has a phobia and is showing an adaptive response (fear, anxiety) but to an inappropriate stimulus or situation. It is perfectly reasonable and healthy to be cautious about heights, for example, in the sense that falls can be dangerous, even life-threatening. This reaction is maladaptive only when the fear response is so intense or out of context that it interferes with daily life. Imagine a house painter who cannot climb a ladder or scaffold; unless she overcomes her fear, she will have to make major adjustments to accommodate her fear.

Quiz

KNOW . . .

1. ________ is characterized by periods of intense depression as well as periods with elevated mood and energy levels.
   a. Major depression
   b. Unipolar depression
   c. Bipolar disorder
   d. Generalized anxiety disorder

UNDERSTAND . . .

2. The difference between obsessions and compulsions is that:
   a. obsessions are repetitive behaviors, whereas compulsions are fears about specific events.
   b. obsessions are repetitive, unwanted thoughts, whereas compulsions are repetitive behaviors.
   c. obsessions are temporary, whereas compulsions are practically permanent.
   d. obsessions and compulsions are the same thing.

3. The idea that anxiety disorders can be self-perpetuating means that:
   a. anxiety in one situation always causes anxiety in another situation, regardless of what is happening in those situations.
   b. the emotions associated with anxiety lead to physiological responses, which in turn lead to more anxious emotions, creating a vicious cycle.
   c. you choose when and what to be anxious about.
   d. anxiety is always limited to one situation or place.

APPLY . . .

4. Sharon feels she is constantly nagged by a strong feeling of tension and worry, no matter what the situation may be. No specific trigger brings these feelings on. This has gone on for months and is so bad that it is hurting her productivity at work and the quality of her home and family life. If you could encourage her to seek treatment, what would a psychologist most likely tell her?
   a. She needs help overcoming her specific phobia.
   b. Panic attacks can be successful treated.
   c. She may have generalized anxiety disorder.
   d. Everyone feels anxiousness, stress, and tension sometimes and so it is not really a sign of a disorder.

ANALYZE . . .

5. If anxiety leads to the onset of so many different disorders, how can it be a beneficial, adaptive process?
   a. It cannot be an adaptive process.
   b. The physiological response underlying anxiety prepares us to fight or flee.
   c. Anxiety is a good way to gain sympathy.
   d. The anxiety response evolved to help attract mates.

SCHIZOPHRENIA

After reading about numerous mental disorders you would not be faulted for thinking the brain is a fragile structure. It certainly can be. However, consider a brain that comprehends unfathomably complex mathematics and creatively disentangles and models natural patterns. Yet, this same brain often struggles to distinguish reality from fiction and spins itself into an entirely confused and chaotic state. Such was the brain of John Nash, a mathematician and Nobel laureate in economics. To academics, Nash was known first for his intellectual ideas. To the general public, he was best recognized as a genius who had schizophrenia. Both are true. By his middle and late twenties Nash was an established giant in the fields of mathematics and economics (he completed his doctorate at 22 years of age). Around this time he also started showing telltale symptoms of schizophrenia, including paranoia and delusional thinking. Among his many unusual experiences, Nash heard voices that were not there and believed there were government conspiracies against him. Despite his mental illness (and, contrary to popular belief, not because of it), Nash was one of the greatest scholars of our time.

Schizophrenia is among the most debilitating of psychological conditions, and it has affected people for at least as long as written history. Writings from early history describe people who seem to have lost touch with reality, who hear voices from within, and who produce bizarre speech and behaviors. These symptoms of schizophrenia can give rise to false beliefs that individuals are possessed by demons or spirits. As we will see, recent scientific findings are providing a different explanation.

Symptoms and Characteristics of Schizophrenia

Schizophrenia *is a mental disorder characterized by chronic and significant breaks from reality, a lack of integration of thoughts and emotions, and serious problems with attention and memory.* One obvious sign of breaking from reality is the experience of **hallucinations,** *which are false perceptions of reality such as hearing internal voices.* Patients may also experience **delusions,** *which are false beliefs about reality.* For example, a person with schizophrenia may have a *delusion of grandeur*, believing that he is Jesus, the Pope, or the president. Consider the following personal account of a man named Kurt Snyder, who wrote a book about his experiences with schizophrenia during college:

Kurt Snyder began experiencing schizophrenia in college. *Me, Myself, and Them* is his personal account of living with schizophrenia.

> I thought about fractals and infinity for many years. I always told myself I was on the verge of discovery, but I simply had to think a little bit harder about it. I just wasn't thinking hard enough. The reality is that the problems I was trying to solve were far beyond my mental abilities, but I didn't recognize this fact. Even though I had no evidence to substantiate my self-image, I knew in my heart that I was just like Einstein, and that someday I would get a flash of inspiration. I didn't recognize the truth—that I am not a genius. I kept most of my mathematical ideas to myself and spoke to very few people about them. I was paranoid that someone else would solve the riddle first if I provided the right clues. (Snyder, 2006, p. 209)

Kurt's experiences, and those of many other individuals diagnosed with schizophrenia, attest to the mind-altering experiences that characterize this disorder.

Schizophrenia occurs throughout the world, and affects an estimated 0.4% to 0.7% of its population (Bhugra, 2005). Men are more likely to have the disorder (7:5 ratio) and tend to develop it earlier in life than women (Aleman et al., 2003). The onset of schizophrenia, in the form of an acute psychotic episode, typically occurs during late adolescence or young adulthood (DeLisi, 1992). More subtle signs, as discussed later in this section, can also appear early—even among toddlers.

Mental health professionals classify symptoms into positive and negative categories. **Positive symptoms** *refer to the presence of unusual behavioral patterns, such as confused and paranoid thinking, and inappropriate emotional reactions.* Positive symptoms involve the presence of maladaptive behavior. In contrast, **negative symptoms** *involve the absence of more typical and adaptive behaviors, such as dampened emotional reactions and lack of speech and motivation.* The *DSM*-5 recognizes that no individual is likely to show every possible symptom of schizophrenia, and notes that any one or combination of the following may warrant a diagnosis:

- Hallucinations or delusions
- Disorganized speech, which consists of sequences of unrelated, incoherent ideas
- Disorganized or catatonic behavior, consisting of behavior and emotional expressions that are poorly integrated and incoherent, and possibly unpredictable. **Catatonia** *is a state of prolonged periods of immobility and muteness.* Repetitive and purposeless movements may also occur.
- Negative symptoms

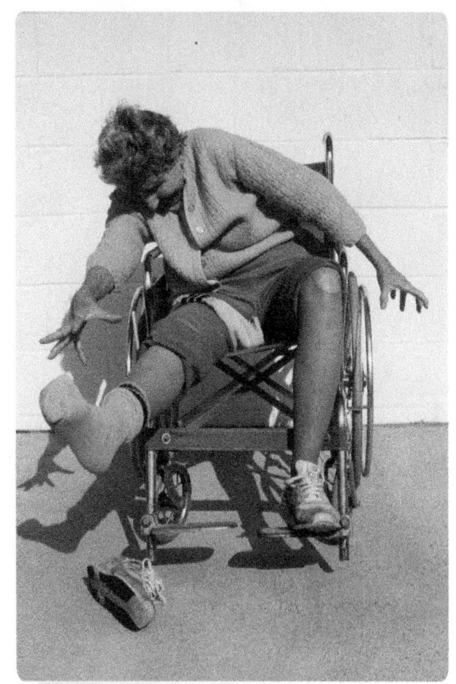

People who experience bouts of catatonia will remain immobile, even if in a bizarre position, for extended periods of time.

Individuals with schizophrenia experience several problems with cognitive functioning. These range from basic startle responses, such as eye blinking (Perry et al., 2002), to the skills involved in standardized achievement tests—test scores tend to drop during adolescence as symptoms of the disorder accelerate (Fuller et al., 2002). Many complex cognitive abilities involve the prefrontal cortex, a brain region showing significant neurological decline in individuals with schizophrenia (Wright et al., 2000). One such ability is working memory, the memory system that allows us to keep track of a train of thought,

Table 15.7 Applying Symptoms of Schizophrenia to Examples

1. Rosalita was helped to a chair and she has sat there, virtually motionless, for about 2 hours.	a. This is not schizophrenia
2. Eyanna refuses to go to the dentist. "Last time I went," she said, "they put a transmitter in my teeth so that the agents can control my thoughts."	b. Delusion
3. Jeff has begun experiencing extreme fear of dogs. He tells himself that few dogs are dangerous, and yet his body seems to tell him otherwise.	c. Catatonia
4. Jinhai hears voices conversing about the pending end of the world, yet he is alone and nobody is nearby.	d. Hallucination

Answers: 1c, 2b, 3a, 4d

organize the sequence of a conversation, and handle multiple memory tasks for a short period of time. Therefore, working memory deficits may partially explain the disorganized thoughts and speech characteristic of schizophrenia (Park et al., 1999).

Social interaction is also difficult for people with schizophrenia. They typically have difficulty reasoning about social situations and show relatively poor social adjustment (Done et al., 1994). In addition, people with schizophrenia may maintain a neutral masklike expression on their faces, and show little response to smiles or other expressions from people around them. (Penn & Combs, 2000). Practice applying the different symptom labels to behavioral examples in the activity on Table 15.7.

Biological Factors of Schizophrenia

Several techniques have been employed to discover the causes and correlates of schizophrenia. As is the case with other types of disorders, no single definitive explanation has emerged, but it seems clear that a complete answer will draw from each facet of the biopsychosocial model.

Myths In Mind

Schizophrenia Is Not a Sign of Violence or Genius

Schizophrenia is a widely recognized term, but it is often misunderstood to mean "split personality." It is an entirely different disorder than multiple personality disorder (now called dissociative identity disorder). Other misconceptions are more difficult to dispel, such as the belief that "madness" goes along with genius, or that schizophrenia makes a person dangerous. These myths persist because of high-profile cases such as those involving Ted Kaczynski and John Nash. Kaczynski, a bright mathematician, became famous as the "Unabomber" after sending mail bombs to prominent researchers at various universities. Nash, who was introduced at the beginning of this section, was another math genius but lived a peaceful, productive life as a researcher at Princeton University; the film *A Beautiful Mind* is based on the story of his life.

Few individuals with schizophrenia commit offenses even approaching the degree of violence brought about by Kaczynski. Moreover, when violence does occur, substance abuse and other factors tend to play a role (Douglas et al., 2009; Fazel et al., 2009). What may be most surprising is that people with mental illness are actually more likely to be *victims* of crime—up to 11 times more likely than nonmentally ill people (Teplin et al., 2005). Perhaps people with schizophrenia should be concerned about the rest of the population.

Also, despite the two well-publicized cases of Kaczynski and Nash, people with schizophrenia typically score slightly below average on IQ tests (Woodberry et al., 2008).

Schizophrenia and the Nervous System

One noticeable neurological characteristic of people with schizophrenia is apparent in the size of the brain ventricles, the fluid-filled spaces occurring within the core of the brain. People with schizophrenia have ventricular spaces that are 20% to 30% larger than the corresponding spaces in people without schizophrenia (see Figure 15.10) (Gottesman & Gould, 2003). The larger ventricular spaces correspond to a loss of brain matter. In fact, the volume of the entire brain is reduced by approximately 2% in individuals with schizophrenia—a small but significant difference. In particular, the reduced volume can be found in structures such as the amygdala, hippocampus, and cerebral cortex (Wright et al., 2000; Roalf et al., 2015). It is important to remember that the anatomical changes associated with schizophrenia may not *cause* the disorder; rather, they might just tend to occur in people who have it.

Brain Volume in One Monozygotic Twin with Schizophrenia and Another without Schizophrenia

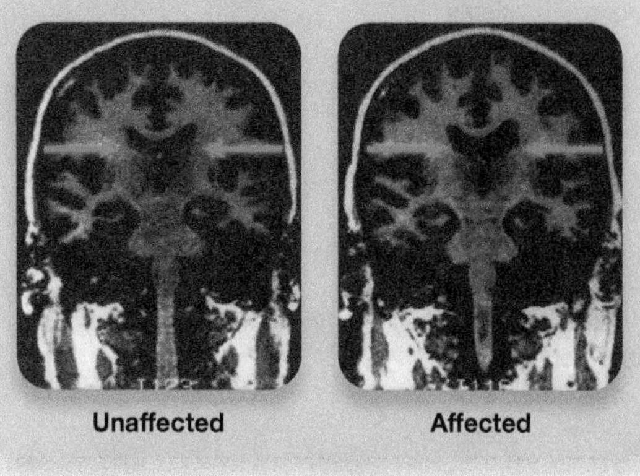

Figure 15.10 Schizophrenia and the Brain
The brains of two genetically identical individuals, one affected with schizophrenia and the other unaffected, are shown here. The arrows point to the spaces created by the ventricles of the brain. Note the significant loss of brain matter in the affected individual.

The brains of people with schizophrenia are not just different in size; they also function differently. Individuals with schizophrenia have been shown to have a lower level of activity in their frontal lobes than those without schizophrenia. In particular, people who have a long history with the disorder show lower levels of activity in their frontal lobes either when they are at a resting state or when their frontal lobes are activated by a cognitive task (Hill et al., 2004). As you just read, these individuals tend to have smaller amygdala and hippocampal regions. These differences also correspond to reduced activity of these structures during cognitive tasks (Hempel et al., 2003).

Imbalances in chemicals coursing through the brain seem to lead to the disordered thinking and emotions associated with schizophrenia. Specifically, individuals with schizophrenia have overactive receptors for the neurotransmitter dopamine (Heinz & Schlagenhauf, 2010). The excess dopamine activity may be involved in producing the outward symptoms of schizophrenia, such as hallucinations and delusions, but not the negative symptoms such as flattened emotion and lack of speech (Andreasen et al., 1995).

Another neurotransmitter, called *glutamate*, appears to be *underactive* in brain regions, including the hippocampus and the frontal cortex, of individuals with schizophrenia. Coincidently, glutamate receptor activity is also inhibited by the drug PCP (angel dust), which in high doses can cause disordered behavior and thinking mirroring that of schizophrenia.

Genetics

Studies using twin, adoption, and family history methods have shown that as genetic relatedness increases, the chance that a relative of a person with schizophrenia will also develop the disorder increases (Modinos et al., 2013; see Figure 15.11). For example, if one identical twin has schizophrenia, the other twin has a 25% to 50% chance of developing it. This rate is significantly higher than the 10% to 17% rate found in dizygotic (fraternal) twin pairs (Gottesman, 1991).

Psychologists have long noted that individuals who are being treated with antipsychotic drugs that block dopamine tend to be heavy smokers. One possible reason is that both the rewarding experiences and the impaired concentration associated with dopamine are reduced by the medication. Heavy nicotine use stimulates the reward and cognitive centers of the brain, thereby helping compensate for the dampening effects the medication has on dopamine (Winterer, 2010).

For decades, behavioral genetic studies have shown that genes contribute to schizophrenia, but they cannot identify the specific genes that contribute to the disorder. However, with the benefit of technological advances in molecular genetics several candidate genes associated with schizophrenia have been discovered. For example, scientists have discovered a distinct pattern of genetic irregularities that is found in 15% of individuals with schizophrenia, compared with only 5% of healthy controls (Walsh et al., 2008). On the one hand, this relationship suggests a possible genetic contribution to schizophrenia. On the other hand, the genetic abnormality was not found in 85% of the individuals. Thus, like most psychological

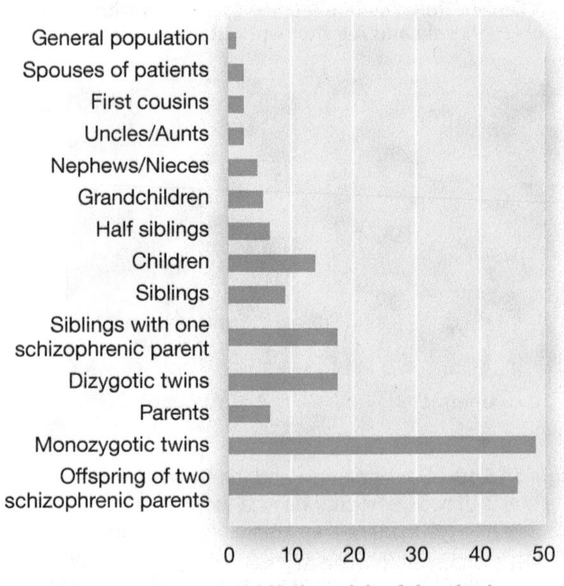

Figure 15.11 Genetic Influences for Schizophrenia
The more genetic similarity an individual has to a person with schizophrenia, the more likely that he or she will also develop the disorder.

disorders, schizophrenia cannot be diagnosed by examining a single gene. Whether an individual develops schizophrenia is probably determined by multiple genetic and molecular switches that are turned on or off in a particular pattern. Critically, the pattern is determined by interactions with the environment (Modinos et al., 2013; EU-GEI, 2014).

Journal prompt

Biology of Schizophrenia:

Reading about biological factors and mental disorders, such as schizophrenia, can lead one to believe that they are the culprits leading to mental illness. Does a biological influence on a mental disorder mean that one is destined to have it eventually, or have it permanently once diagnosed? Why or why not?

Environmental and Cultural Influences on Schizophrenia

Research on the neuroscience of schizophrenia has made inroads toward discovering its causes. But remember a few observations: First, many people who *do not* have mutant versions of the genes involved in schizophrenia may still develop the disorder and, second, an identical twin has roughly a 50% chance of developing schizophrenia if her twin has it. Finally, although approximately 1% of the world population may have the disorder, as much as 10% of the population is at a *genetic risk* for developing schizophrenia (Meehl, 1990). These observations indicate that schizophrenia is not strictly a genetic disorder, and they suggest that we should consider some environmental factors that influence brain development and functioning.

Environmental and Prenatal Factors

When we think about environmental influences, we have to stretch back as far as possible—even before birth. For example, people with schizophrenia are statistically more likely to have been born during winter months (Tochigi et al., 2004). One plausible explanation for this link is that the brain develops a great deal during the second trimester, which would coincide with the onset of flu season for wintertime births. Furthermore, extreme stress such as loss of a spouse and even exposure to war during pregnancy may increase the chances that the infant will subsequently develop schizophrenia. From examples like these, scientists speculate that exposure to viruses or stress hormones may put a person at risk for schizophrenia (Brown & Derkits, 2010; King et al., 2010).

There are a variety of risk factors occurring during childhood and adolescence can increase the chance that schizophrenia will develop. One factor is heavy cannabis use. A small proportion of cannabis users develop psychotic symptoms, possibly because the drug interacts with the genes involved in schizophrenia (Caspi et al., 2005; Radhakrishnan, Wilkinson, & D'Souza, 2014). Head injuries occurring before age 10 also put people who are genetically vulnerable to schizophrenia at greater risk for developing the disorder (AbdelMalik et al., 2003). *Psychosocial stress* is a broad term covering poverty, unemployment, discrimination, divorce, and traumatic events. Being raised in an urban environment, where psychosocial stressors are more abundant, puts individuals who are genetically vulnerable at an even greater risk for developing schizophrenia (van Os et al., 2004; Holtzman et al., 2013).

Cultural Factors

We introduced the topic of cultural perceptions of mental illness. Differing cultural perspectives are evident when it comes to schizophrenia and even influences the types of experiences that individuals report having. In the United States, people with European ancestry tend to focus on the mental experiences of the disorder, such as disorganized thinking and emotions. This is associated with the view that schizophrenia is a mental disorder quite distinct from other types of illness. In contrast, people from Latin America often focus more on how schizophrenia affects the body, such as by producing tension or tiredness. They conceive of the disorder as any other form of illness, rather a unique or distinct type (Weisman et al., 2000).

Another cultural variation is known as *running amok*, which is sometimes used in the United States to describe unusual, energetic, and out-of-control behavior. The term "amok" is actually Indonesian in origin. Psychiatrist Emil Kraepelin concluded that amok is similar to what we call psychosis, albeit with some notable differences. For example, auditory hallucinations—seem to be virtually absent among Indonesian people with schizophrenia. Kraepelin attributed this difference to the low use of speech in this culture (Jilek, 1995).

Beliefs about mental illness are linked to varying cultural views of the world (McGruder, 2004). Many people throughout the world, such as the Swahili of Tanzania, believe that what we call schizophrenia is a sign that spirits have invaded the body. In some cultures, the self is perceived as not wholly separate from an individual, but rather "permeable" to other entities or beings. Spirits, which are thought to overpower humans, can therefore invade the body. When you compare those views with the scientific approach found in the United States, you should see how essential culture is in understanding disorders.

Working the Scientific Literacy Model

The Neurodevelopmental Hypothesis of Schizophrenia

Schizophrenia is obviously a complex disorder, and no one explanation has been able to account for all the variations in symptoms, severity, and duration. A combination of biopsychosocial variables, and the timing in which they occur, may account for the development of the disorder.

Some of the first indicators of schizophrenia are found during infancy and childhood. Children with unusual and unnecessary motor movements, particularly on the left side of the body, may be more likely to develop the disorder.

What do we know about the neurodevelopmental hypothesis?

Factors related to the onset of schizophrenia influence behavior even before birth. The **neurodevelopmental hypothesis (of schizophrenia)** *states that irregular biological and environmental factors interact during prenatal, infant, and child development to produce symptoms of schizophrenia* (Walker et al., 2010). It is important to distinguish this approach from other possibilities, such as a *neurodegenerative hypothesis* proposing that the brain deteriorates to produce schizophrenia. As its name implies, the neurodevelopmental hypothesis posits that the brain grows into a schizophrenic state rather than degenerating into one.

How can science test the neurodevelopmental hypothesis?

The neurodevelopmental hypothesis draws from research on genetics and prenatal events. In addition, the developmental emphasis of the hypothesis gains strength from behavioral evidence collected during childhood and adolescence. For example, when psychologists viewed home movies of infants and children who subsequently developed

(Continued)

schizophrenia, they noted that these children showed some unusual motor patterns, primarily on the left side of the body, such as jerky, repeated, and unnecessary arm movements (Walker et al., 1994). Siblings who did not have schizophrenia did not show these same motor patterns. Similar observations were made in a study of 11- to 13-year-old boys who were considered at risk for schizophrenia. The boys were videotaped eating lunch and observers noted any unusual social behavior and neuromotor (movement) functioning. Kids who showed a combination of these symptoms were more likely to be diagnosed with schizophrenia as adults compared to kids who did not show these behaviors (Schiffman et al., 2004).

In adolescence, psychologists can detect the schizophrenia *prodrome,* a collection of characteristics that resemble mild forms of schizophrenia symptoms. For example, a teenager might become increasingly socially withdrawn and have some difficulty with depression and anxiety. But the most telling—and most perplexing—problems include experiences that resemble hallucinations and delusions, with the exception that the affected individual does not fully believe them. For example, a teen might say, "I seem to keep hearing my mother calling my name before I fall asleep, even when I know she isn't home. It is strange ... " (Walker et al., 2010, p. 206).

Can we critically evaluate this information?

Unusual body movements certainly do not mean a child will develop schizophrenia in early adulthood. Nevertheless, it is at least one irregular developmental pattern that might reflect neurological abnormalities. Its emergence would be consistent with that predicted by the neurodevelopmental hypothesis, which rests on the idea that vulnerability to schizophrenia is present at birth (Walker et al., 2010). Similarly, at some point in adolescence, while most individuals will report at least one of these collections of symptoms, those who report all of them are at increased risk for schizophrenia.

Why is this relevant?

By identifying developmental patterns and catching them early, it may be possible to alter the progression of the disorder, thereby preventing the onset of schizophrenia, or at least controlling its severity. In recent years, a number of attempts to prevent schizophrenia from developing in high-risk populations have been made, but have not proved effective (McGlashan et al., 2006; McGorry et al., 2002). To accomplish this goal, researchers will have to rely on all aspects of the biopsychosocial model: genetics, the function and structure of the brain, neurotransmitters, prenatal influences, and psychosocial factors.

Summary

Now that you have read this section you should:

KNOW . . .

- ***the key terminology associated with schizophrenia:***

catatonia (p. 479)
delusions (p. 479)
hallucinations (p. 479)
negative symptoms (p. 479)
neurodevelopmental hypothesis (of schizophrenia) (p. 483)
positive symptoms (p. 479)
schizophrenia (p. 479)

UNDERSTAND . . .

- ***how different neurotransmitters affect individuals with schizophrenia.*** Abnormal levels of dopamine (too much) and glutamate (too little) are associated with symptoms of schizophrenia.
- ***the genetic and environmental contributions to schizophrenia.*** The neurodevelopmental hypothesis claims that at least some neurological abnormalities are present at birth, although it does not state to what degree these abnormalities are genetic or environmental. Nevertheless, some research suggests that prenatal exposure to the flu or to significant amounts of stress hormones are all risk factors for schizophrenia. Genetics seem to play a role, as twin studies show that if one identical twin has schizophrenia, the other has up to a 50% chance of developing the disorder—a substantial increase over the 1% occurrence rate in the general population.

APPLY . . .

- ***your knowledge to identify symptoms of schizophrenia.*** There are diverse symptoms associated with schizophrenia that include positive and negative varieties. The activity in Table 15.7 provided an opportunity to practice matching symptoms with terminology.

ANALYZE . . .

- ***claims that schizophrenia is related to genius or violent behavior.*** As you have read, some high-profile cases highlight people with schizophrenia who are intellectually brilliant. In reality, however, research tells us that the average intelligence of people with schizophrenia is not much different from those of the general population; in fact, it is a little bit lower than the norm. Similarly, the belief that schizophrenia leads to violence derives from a small group of high-profile examples. In truth, there does not seem to be increased risk of violence associated with schizophrenia alone.

Quiz

KNOW . . .

1. A person with schizophrenia who has become convinced that she is royalty is experiencing a(n) .
   a. delusion
   b. negative symptom
   c. catatonic state
   d. manic state

UNDERSTAND . . .

2. Which of the following statements is most accurate concerning the biochemical basis of schizophrenia?
   a. The neurotransmitter dopamine is overly active.
   b. Dopamine is underactive.
   c. Serotonin levels are too low.
   d. There is too much glutamate activity.
3. The underlying genetic basis for schizophrenia can be described as follows:
   a. A single gene puts people at risk for it, especially if the environment switches it on.
   b. Evidence suggests a minimal role for genetics, with environmental factors playing the strongest role.
   c. If a combination of about 10 genes are inherited, the disorder occurs regardless of environmental triggers.
   d. Multiple genes have been identified as risk factors, and environmental events, especially ones occurring prenatally, further increase the risk of developing the disorder.

APPLY . . .

4. A patient who is nonresponsive and remains still in odd postures is showing what type of symptom of schizophrenia?
   a. Disorganized
   b. Positive
   c. Catatonic
   d. Hallucinogenic

ANALYZE . . .

5. Which of the following statements best summarizes the relationship between schizophrenia and violence?
   a. Generally, people with schizophrenia are no more likely to become violent than nonmentally ill people, and if violence occurs, other factors, such as substance abuse, are likely to contribute to its cause.
   b. People with schizophrenia are twice as likely to be violent as nonmentally ill people.
   c. People with schizophrenia are far more peaceful than nonmentally ill people.
   d. People with schizophrenia cannot differentiate right from wrong, and therefore are prone to violence.

Scientific Literacy Challenge: Bereavement

The editors of the *DSM-5* were challenged by the dimensional nature of many psychological disorders, such as depression. One tough question they struggled with was, at what point does sadness and a lack of energy or motivation become depression? This lack of certainty was particularly difficult when a debate erupted over bereavement. Specifically, mental health professionals argued whether sadness and mourning following the death of a loved one constitutes a diagnosable form of depression. Eventually it was decided that people going through bereavement could be diagnosed with major depressive disorder. The *DSM-5* now recommends a formal diagnosis of depression, even if the loss of a loved one is what triggers the change in mood and emotional functioning. Before you continue on to an article that presents some strong opinions on the matter, consider your own thoughts about the relationship between bereavement and depression.

Journal Prompt

This chapter described what constitutes a psychological disorder. With the concepts of mental illness in mind, do you think it seems appropriate or inappropriate to diagnose an individual who is bereaving with major depression? Please explain.

WHAT DO WE KNOW ABOUT BEREAVEMENT?

In the following column, the president of a regional psychological association argues that the *DSM-5* did the right thing by modifying the requirements for a diagnosis of major depressive episode. As you read the beginning paragraph of his column, make sure you recognize and understand the boldfaced key terms from Chapter 15.

Bereavement belongs in the DSM-5

By Alberto Herrera, President, Tri-State Association for Mental Health

One of the public's key misunderstandings about psychology is what constitutes a psychological disorder. Part of the problem is the difficulty of using **categorical** labels to describe things that are fundamentally **dimensional** in nature. That is definitely the case with bereavement. Prior to the publication of the *DSM-5*, the diagnosis of **Major Depression** included a "bereavement exclusion," indicating that the sadness associated with losing a loved one was somehow different from the sadness associated with traditional depression. In effect, prior to the 2013 publication of the *DSM-5* people could not be diagnosed with major depression if they had recently lost a loved one. Now, individuals who have recently lost a loved one can be diagnosed with major depression, even if they had never experienced depression before. Diagnosing someone with major depression during what seems like a very normal time to feel sad has caused some people to feel uneasy. It is seen as a move to turn a normal process into a pathology. This very type of issue is what makes some members of the public question our discipline's methods. It has been a contentious move in mental health fields as well. However, I argue in favor of this change, and once you look at the evidence, I think you will agree.

Now that we know what the controversy is, read on to find out what kind of evidence Dr. Herrera gathered to support his position.

HOW DO SCIENTISTS STUDY BEREAVEMENT?

Bereavement by itself is not the same thing as major depression, but as you will read here, research shows that it *can* be, and sometimes is. Make sure you pay attention to the scientific terms and concepts, especially in the highlighted sections, and then test yourself with the quiz that follows.

Recently, the journal *Depression and Anxiety* published a review of nine studies that altogether compared over 1,000 individuals experiencing a major depressive episode (MDE) without bereavement to individuals who were diagnosed with a major depressive episode in an extended bereavement period (MDB). The findings are compelling:

- MDE and MDB involve the same frequency and severity of symptoms, as measured by standardized tests for depression.
- MDE and MDB are not different in terms of how long episodes last and how likely they are to reoccur.
- MDE and MDB have similar levels of genetic influence.
- MDE and MDB are equally likely to respond to treatments, and respond to the same type of treatments.

In summary, the most significant difference between MDE and MDB is that one of them follows the loss of a loved one. With the behaviors, treatments, and response to treatments being nearly identical, why should the diagnosis be any different?

Dr. Herrera provided a quick review of the research, but you should be able to spot some important concepts here. Take the quiz below to see which concepts you identified.

1. The review compares two groups of people in multiple studies, but none of them are experiments because
   a. there is no random assignment.
   b. they use convenience sampling.
   c. they do not have a dependent variable.
   d. they do not have reliability.
2. The writer refers to depression scales that were used in the studies, which means that he addressed ________.
   a. the independent variable
   b. whether this is experimental or quasi-experimental
   c. the operational definitions of depression
   d. sample size
3. The scores on the depression scales would constitute a(n) ________.
   a. dependent variable.
   b. confounding variable
   c. generalizing variable
   d. demand characteristics

1. a 2. c 3. a

HOW DO WE THINK CRITICALLY ABOUT BEREAVEMENT?

Remember that critical thinking involves curiosity and reasonable levels of skepticism. As you read the next paragraph of the editorial, actively search for specific statements relevant to critical thinking.

> I have long been convinced that this change to the *DSM* was needed. I don't have anything personal to gain from this and it might not even affect my practice. However, I do think the change will help in the long run. Those who argued to keep the bereavement exclusion predicted that the numbers of Major Depression diagnoses would skyrocket, but that just hasn't happened, according to the article in *Depression and Anxiety*. That is because the mental health profession has been differentiating between MDE and milder forms depression or sadness for years; nothing has changed in that regard.

Did Dr. Herrera apply critical thinking? The statements below will help you identify several aspects of critical thinking. Match the following critical thinking statements to the highlighted passages that illustrate them.

1. The author shows that critical thinking involves considering alternative viewpoints.
2. The author tries to identify sources of bias that might influence how people interpret results.
3. The author adds credibility to the evidence by indicating a reputable source of information.

1. Blue 2. Yellow 3. Green

Dr. Herrera seems to have demonstrated cautious skepticism and a good deal of critical thinking. Next let's see how Dr. Herrera's point of view applies to clinical psychology.

How is Diagnosing Bereavement Relevant?

In closing, Dr. Herrera explains how he thinks removing the bereavement exclusion will help clinical psychologists. Read the following excerpt, then explore any newly formed thoughts you may have about bereavement in the writing activity that follows.

> Dropping the bereavement exclusion does nothing to change how people experience the symptoms of depression. What it does change is very important, however. Identifying depression helps the individual understand that what they are experiencing is a known condition, that they are not alone in those feelings, and that there is a high probability of a successful treatment. These same ideas are communicated to clinicians as well. Therefore, I anticipate the change will shape the way the next generation of professionals thinks about treating people in bereavement.

SHARED WRITING

Do you accept or reject Dr. Herrera's conclusion that people who are bereaving should, if circumstances warrant, be diagnosed with depression and receive treatment for it? How, if at all, did his evidence and critique shape your opinion?

Quiz

1. Psychologists and psychiatrists use the criteria laid out in the most recent edition of the ________ to diagnose psychological disorders.
   a. Dimensional and Categorical Atlas of Mental Health
   b. International Diagnostic Guidelines
   c. Guide to Psychopathology and Abnormal Behavior
   d. Diagnostic and Statistical Manual for Mental Disorders
2. Which of the following is not a psychiatric criterion for mental illness?
   a. Expression of behavior that causes distress to self or others
   b. The condition must be categorical.
   c. Impairment of functioning
   d. Increased risk of lost freedom, pain, or death
3. Aaliyah's few friends complain that she is often melodramatic and emotionally immature. Aaliyah loves attention (especially from men) and is constantly flirting, often inappropriately. If Aaliyah was diagnosed with a psychological disorder, which of the following would be the most likely candidate?
   a. Narcissistic personality disorder
   b. Borderline personality disorder
   c. Histrionic personality disorder
   d. Antisocial personality disorder
4. Which of the following disorders do psychologists believe is *not* a valid diagnosis?
   a. Dissociative identity disorder
   b. Schizophrenia
   c. Histrionic personality disorder
   d. Posttraumatic stress disorder
5. In addition to suffering from panic attacks, people with panic disorder often develop an intense fear of:
   a. having a panic attack when they are alone.
   b. public places.
   c. germs.
   d. leaving the stove on.
6. Huynh washes his hands 100 or more times each day. The constant washing causes the skin on his hands to dry and crack, yet he continues to engage in this behavior. Huynh's behavior is an example of ________.
   a. an obsession
   b. agoraphobia
   c. a compulsion
   d. a negative symptom

7. Allison has an intense fear of flying, so much so that she cannot even bear to close her eyes and imagine that she is on a plane. From this brief description, Allison may be experiencing:
   a. a specific phobia.
   b. a social phobia.
   c. a generalized phobia.
   d. normal levels of anxiety.

8. ________ are false beliefs about reality, whereas ________ are false perceptions of reality such as hearing internal voices.
   a. Positive symptoms; negative symptoms
   b. Negative symptoms; positive symptoms
   c. Hallucinations; delusions
   d. Delusions; hallucinations

9. Suppose a friend described schizophrenia as having a "split personality." How would you respond?
   a. "This is a common misconception caused by people confusing schizophrenia with dissociative identity disorder."
   b. "Only disorganized schizophrenia is characterized by a splitting of personalities."
   c. "That point is controversial; psychologists cannot agree on whether schizophrenia involves a splitting of personality."
   d. "That is an accurate description of schizophrenia."

10. Which of the following statements is true about the average brain of individuals with schizophrenia when they are compared to the brains of individuals who do not have the disorder?
    a. There are no known anatomical differences.
    b. The overall size of the brain is actually larger than normal in people with schizophrenia.
    c. Dopamine activity is lower than normal in people with schizophrenia.
    d. The fluid-filled spaces at the core of the brain are larger in people with schizophrenia.

11. Which of the following is *not* a characteristic of personality disorders?
    a. Traits that are inflexible and maladaptive
    b. Significant functional impairment or subjective distress
    c. Marked deviation from cultural expectations
    d. Typically diagnosed with medical tests

12. ________ involves intense extremes between positive and negative emotions, an unstable sense of self, impulsivity, and difficult social relationships.
    a. Borderline personality disorder
    b. Narcissistic personality disorder
    c. Histrionic personality disorder
    d. Antisocial personality disorder

13. There have been several famous cases of people with superior intellectual abilities as well as schizophrenia. Does this mean that schizophrenia is the cause or the result of genius?
    a. No; in fact, the average IQ of people with schizophrenia may be slightly lower than average.
    b. Yes; in fact, the average IQ of people with schizophrenia is approximately 15% higher than average.
    c. Yes, because people who are that smart are likely to develop schizophrenia simply because they know too much.
    d. No, because schizophrenia is associated with very low IQs.

14. Depression is associated with lower activity in the frontal lobe, which may result in:
    a. lack of appetite.
    b. difficulty concentrating and thinking.
    c. periods of elevated mood and energy.
    d. constipation.

15. Which of the following is not classified as an anxiety disorder?
    a. Panic attack
    b. GAD
    c. Bipolar disorder
    d. Social phobia

16

Psychological and Biological Treatments*

Helping People Change

*Taken from *Psychology from Inquiry to Understanding*, Third Edition by Scott O. Lilienfeld, Steven Jay Lynn, Laura L. Namy, and Nancy J. Woolf

Think About It

- Are more experienced therapists better than inexperienced therapists?
- Do all psychotherapies require people to achieve insight to improve?
- Is Alcoholics Anonymous better than other types of treatment for alcoholism?
- Are some psychotherapies harmful?
- Does electroshock treatment produce long-term brain damage?

Before reading on, picture a typical psychotherapy session. What's the person in therapy—often called the "client" —doing? How about the therapist? What does the room look like? Perhaps your first thought is of the proverbial client on a couch, with the therapist sitting behind him or her, pen and pad in hand, intent on unearthing long-forgotten memories, analyzing dreams, and encouraging the client to vent painful feelings.

If this scenario comes to mind, it's no wonder. From the early days of psychotherapy (often simply called "therapy"), these images have been etched into our cultural consciousness. But we'll discover that this picture doesn't begin to tell the story of the vast array of psychotherapeutic approaches that encompass individual therapy; treatments conducted in groups and with families; and even art, dance, and music therapy. Nor does the scenario capture the powerful biological treatments that have transformed the lives of people with psychological disorders by directly targeting the brain's functioning. In this chapter, we'll examine a broad spectrum of therapies, both psychological and biological, that are designed to alleviate emotional suffering.

Like many concepts in psychology, *psychotherapy* isn't easy to define. Over a half century ago, one pioneer in psychotherapy wrote, half-jokingly, "Psychotherapy is an undefined technique applied to unspecified problems with unpredictable outcomes. For this technique, we recommend rigorous training" (Raimy, 1950, p. 63). Some might contend that things haven't changed much since then. Still, for our purposes, we can define **psychotherapy** as a psychological intervention designed to help people resolve emotional, behavioral, and interpersonal problems and improve the quality of their lives (Engler & Goleman, 1992). Although the popular media often speak of therapy as though it were one thing, there are well over 500 "brands" of psychotherapy (Eisner, 2000), about three times as many as there were in the 1970s. As we'll learn, research demonstrates that many of these therapies are effective, but scores of others haven't been tested. In the pages to come, we'll offer critical thinking tools to help us distinguish scientifically supported psychological and biomedical therapies from therapies that are either ineffective or promising but scientifically unsupported.

Psychotherapy: Clients and Practitioners

16.1 Describe who seeks treatment, who benefits from psychotherapy, and who practices psychotherapy.

16.2 Distinguish between professionals and paraprofessionals and describe what it takes to be an effective therapist.

We'll begin by considering several questions: who seeks and benefits from psychotherapy? How is psychotherapy practiced? What makes a psychotherapist effective?

Popular portrayals of psychotherapy have a long history in the media. (© CartoonBank.com)

Who Seeks and Benefits from Treatment?

The most recent survey of the U.S. public—a 2006 *Newsweek* poll—found that about 20 percent of Americans have received psychological treatment at some point and that about 4 percent are currently in psychotherapy. People grapple with specific problems in psychotherapy, but they also contend frequently with generalized feelings of helplessness, social isolation, and a sense of failure (Garfield, 1978; Lambert, 2003). Still others turn to therapy to expand their self-awareness, learn better ways of relating to others, and consider lifestyle changes.

psychotherapy
psychological intervention designed to help people resolve emotional, behavioral, and interpersonal problems and improve the quality of their lives

The ideal client? A 1964 study (Schofield, 1964) found that many therapists preferred to treat people who were relatively young, attractive, verbal, intelligent, and successful (YAVIS clients). Nevertheless, therapists have recently become more aware of the importance of assisting a broad clientele of all ages and cultural backgrounds.

Gender, Ethnic, and Cultural Differences in Entering Treatment

Some people are more likely to enter psychological treatment than others. Women are more likely to seek treatment than men are (Addis & Mahalik, 2003; DuBrin & Zastowny, 1988), although both sexes benefit equally from psychotherapy (Petry, Tennen, & Affleck, 2000). Members of many racial and ethnic minority groups, particularly Asian Americans and Hispanic Americans, are less likely to seek mental health services than are Caucasian Americans (Sue & Lam, 2002), perhaps because of the lingering stigma surrounding psychotherapy in these groups. Socioeconomic factors also predict who seeks therapy. Therapy can be very costly for those without health insurance or whose health plans don't include mental health coverage (Wang et al., 2008). Nevertheless, when individuals hailing from diverse cultural and ethnic backgrounds obtain psychotherapy, they're likely to benefit from it (Navarro, 1993; Prochaska & Norcross, 2007).

Culturally sensitive psychotherapists maximize their effectiveness by tuning their interventions to clients' cultural values and the difficulties they encounter in adapting to a dominant culture that may differ vastly from their own (Benish et al., 2011; Norcross & Wampold, 2011a; Sue & Sue, 2003). Although ethnic minorities prefer therapists with a similar ethnic background (Coleman, Wampold, & Casali, 1995), there's no consistent evidence that client–therapist ethnic (Shin et al., 2005) or gender (Bowman et al., 2001) matches enhance therapy outcome. Still, when clients are relative newcomers to a culture and not well acquainted with its traditions, therapist–client ethnic match may play a greater role in therapy's effectiveness (Sue, 1998). The good news is that people can be helped by therapists who differ from them in significant ways, including ethnicity and gender (Cardemil, 2010; Whaley & Davis, 2007).

Reaping Benefits from Treatment

The effectiveness of therapy depends on a host of individual differences. Clients who are most likely to improve are better adjusted to begin with, realize they may be contributing to their problems, and are motivated to work on those problems (Prochaska & DiClemente, 1982; Prochaska & Norcross, 2002). Clients who experience some anxiety do better in psychotherapy than do other clients—probably because their distress fuels their motivation to make life changes (Frank, 1974; Miller et al., 1995)—as do clients with temporary or situational problems, such as relationship upheavals (Gasperini et al., 1993; Steinmetz, Lewinsohn, & Antonuccio, 1983).

Who Practices Psychotherapy?

Licensed professionals, especially clinical psychologists, psychiatrists, mental health counselors, and clinical social workers, are the mainstays of the mental health profession (see **TABLE 16.1**) (see Chapter 1). But unlicensed religious, vocational, and rehabilitation counselors, as well as art and music therapists also provide psychological services.

FACtoid

During the first month of treatment, many clients improve considerably. In fact, 40–66 percent of clients report improvement even before attending their first session (Howard et al., 1986). The act of seeking help—doing something about one's problems—apparently inspires hope and breeds confidence (Kirsch, 1990).

Professionals Versus Paraprofessionals

Contrary to the myth that all psychotherapists have advanced degrees in mental health, volunteers and **paraprofessionals**, helpers who have no formal professional training, often provide psychological services in such settings as crisis intervention centers and other social service agencies. In most states, the term *therapist* isn't legally protected, so virtually anyone can hang up a shingle and offer treatment. Many paraprofessionals obtain agency-specific training and attend workshops that enhance their educational backgrounds. They may also be trained to recognize situations that require consultation with professionals with greater expertise. Paraprofessionals help to compensate for the sizable gap between the high demand for and meager supply of licensed practitioners (den Boer et al., 2005).

paraprofessional
person with no professional training who provides mental health services

Again, contrary to popular belief, therapists don't need to be professionally trained or have many years of experience to be effective (Berman & Norton, 1985; Blatt et al.,

Table 16.1 Occupations, Degrees, Roles, and Work Settings of Mental Health Professionals.
Not all therapists are the same: mental health consumers are often unaware of the substantial differences in education, training, and roles of different psychotherapists. This table provides some guidance.

Occupation	Degree/License	Settings/Role
Clinical Psychologist	Ph.D./Psy.D., M.A., M.S.	Private practice, hospitals, schools, community agencies, medical settings, academic, other
Psychiatrist	M.D. or D.O.	Physicians, private practice, hospitals, medical centers, schools, academic, other
Counseling Psychologist	Ph.D., Ed.D., M.A., M.S., M.C.	University clinics, mental health centers; treat people with less severe psychological problems
School Psychologist	Ph.D., Psy.D., Ed.D., Ed.S., M.A., M.S., M.Ed.	In-school interventions, assessment, prevention programs; work with teachers, students, parents
Clinical Social Worker	Training varies widely; B.S.W., M.S.W., D.S.W., L.C.S.W.	Private practice following supervised experience, psychiatric facilities, hospitals/community agencies, schools, case managers; help with social and health problems
Mental Health Counselor	M.S.W., M.S., M.C.	Private practice, community agencies, hospitals, other; career counseling, marriage issues, substance abuse
Psychiatric Nurse	Training varies widely; associate degree, B.S.N., M.S.N., D.N.P., Ph.D.	Hospitals, community health centers, primary care facilities, outpatient mental health clinics; manage medications; with advanced degrees can diagnose, treat mental patients
Pastoral Counselor	Training varies; from bachelor's degree to more advanced degrees	Counseling, support in spiritual context, wellness programs; group, family, and couples therapy

Degree Key: B.S.N., bachelor of science in nursing; B.S.W., bachelor of social work; D.N.P., doctorate nurse practitioner; D.O., doctor of osteopathy; D.S.W., doctor of social work; Ed.D., doctor of education; Ed.S., specialist in education; L.C.S.W., licensed clinical social worker; M.A., master of arts; M.C., master of counseling; M.D., doctor of medicine; M.Ed., master of education; M.S., master of science; M.S.N., master of science in nursing; M.S.W., master of social work; Ph.D., doctor of philosophy; Psy.D., doctor of psychology.

1996; Christensen & Jacobson, 1994). Indeed, most studies reveal few or no differences in effectiveness between more and less experienced therapists (Dawes, 1994; McFall, 2006). Why is this so? As psychiatrist Jerome Frank (1961) noted, regardless of level of professional training, people who fulfill the role of therapist may provide clients with hope, empathy, advice, support, and opportunities for new learning experiences (Frank & Frank, 1991; Lambert & Ogles, 2004).

Even if there are few or no differences in therapy outcome as a function of professional training, there are several clear advantages to consulting with a professional. Professional helpers (1) understand how to operate effectively within the mental health system; (2) appreciate complex ethical, professional, and personal issues; and (3) can select treatments of demonstrated effectiveness (Garske & Anderson, 2003).

What Does it Take to be an Effective Psychotherapist?

Given that training and years of experience aren't critical determinants of what makes a good therapist, what does make a good therapist? Effective therapists are likely to be warm and direct, establish a positive working relationship with clients, and tend not to contradict clients (Friedlander, 1984; Garske & Anderson, 2003; Kazdin, Marciano, & Whitley, 2005; Luborsky et al., 1997; Westerman, Foote, & Winston, 1995). Effective therapists also select important topics on which to focus in sessions (Goldfried, Raue, & Castonguay, 1998), match their treatments to the needs and characteristics of clients (Beutler & Harwood, 2002), and collect feedback from their clients (Norcross & Wampold, 2011b). Still, sizable

? In the HBO television series *In Treatment*, Laura (played by Melissa George) develops sexual feelings for her therapist, Paul (played by Gabriel Byrne). Paul doesn't have a sexual relationship with her, because he experiences a panic attack. A sexual relationship with a client is highly unethical. **Which of the following behaviors is also unethical?** (A) Revealing a client's plan to commit suicide to a family member to prevent the suicide. (B) Revealing a client's plan to assault another person to prevent the assault. (C) Informing a client's elderly father that she harbors hateful feelings toward him. (See answer upside down at bottom of page.)

Answer: (C) With few exceptions, therapists keep all information confidential. However, therapists can share information without the client's written permission when the client is at serious risk for suicide or endangering others.

Table 16.2 What Should I Look for in a Therapist, and What Type of Therapist Should I Avoid?

Tens of thousands of people call themselves therapists, and it's often hard to know what kind of therapist to seek out or avoid. This checklist may help you, your friends, or your loved ones to select a good therapist—and to steer clear of a bad one.

1. I can talk freely and openly with my therapist.
2. My therapist listens carefully to what I say and understands my feelings.
3. My therapist is warm, direct, and provides useful feedback.
4. My therapist explains up front what he or she will be doing and why and is willing to answer questions about his or her qualifications and training, my diagnosis, and our treatment plan.
5. My therapist encourages me to confront challenges and solve problems.
6. My therapist uses scientifically based approaches and discusses the pros and cons of other approaches.
7. My therapist regularly monitors how I'm doing and is willing to change course when treatment isn't going well.

If your answer is yes to one or more of the following statements, the therapist may not be in a good position to help you and even may be harmful.

1. My therapist gets defensive and angry when challenged.
2. My therapist has a "one size fits all" approach to all problems.
3. My therapist spends considerable time each session making "small talk," telling me exactly what to do, and sharing personal anecdotes.
4. My therapist isn't clear about what is expected of me in the treatment plan, and our discussions lack any focus and direction.
5. My therapist doesn't seem willing to discuss the scientific support for what he or she is doing.
6. There are no clear professional boundaries in my relationship with my therapist; for example, my therapist talks a lot about his or her personal life or asks me for personal favors.

differences in therapist characteristics and abilities may overshadow the relatively small differences in the effectiveness of the types of treatments they provide (Ahn & Wampold, 2001; Luborsky et al., 1986). So when it comes to the success of psychotherapy, the choice of *therapist* is every bit as important as the choice of *therapy* (Blow, Sprenkle, & Davis, 2007).

What makes a good therapist from the client's point of view? The composite view of the "good" therapist is that of an expert who's warm, respectful, caring, and engaged (Littauer, Sexton, & Wyan, 2005; Strupp, Fox, & Lessler, 1969). In **TABLE 16.2**, we present some tips for both selecting good therapists and avoiding bad ones.

Assess Your Knowledge FACT OR FICTION?

1. Asian Americans are more likely to seek psychotherapy than are Caucasian Americans. **True / False**
2. Clients who are poorly adjusted to begin with are most likely to improve with therapy. **True / False**
3. All people who practice therapy have advanced degrees in mental health. **True / False**
4. Professional training is necessary to produce good therapy outcomes. **True / False**
5. The choice of a therapist is as important as the choice of therapy. **True / False**

Answers: 1. F (p. 492); **2.** F (p. 492); **3.** F (p. 492); **4.** F (p. 492); **5.** T (p. 493)

Insight Therapies: Acquiring Understanding

16.3 Describe the core beliefs and criticisms of psychodynamic therapies.

16.4 Describe and evaluate the effectiveness of humanistic therapies.

In much of the chapter that lies ahead, we'll examine some of the more prominent therapeutic approaches and evaluate their scientific status. We'll begin with **insight therapies**, which aim to cultivate insight, that is, expanded self-awareness and knowledge. The psychodynamic and humanistic therapies we'll review are two prominent schools of insight therapy.

Psychodynamic therapies are treatments inspired by classical psychoanalysis and influenced by Freud's techniques. Compared with psychoanalysis, which tends to be expensive and lengthy (often lasting years or even decades) and often involves meeting most days of the week, psychodynamic therapy is typically less costly, is briefer—weeks or months or open-ended—and involves meeting only once or twice a week (Shedler, 2010). After we examine Freud's techniques, we'll consider a group of therapists called *neo-Freudians*, who adopted Freud's psychodynamic perspective but modified his approach in distinctive ways.

Under the umbrella of **humanistic therapies**, we can find a variety of approaches rooted in the humanistic perspective on personality. Therapies within this orientation share an emphasis on insight, self-actualization, and the belief that human nature is basically positive (Maslow, 1954; Rogers, 1961; Shlien & Levant, 1984). Humanistic therapists reject the interpretive techniques of psychoanalysis. Instead, they strive to understand clients' inner worlds through empathy and focus on clients' thoughts and feelings in the present moment.

FACtoid

Before Freud developed the technique of free association, he brought forth associations in a very different way. He told his clients to close their eyes and concentrate while he pressed his hand on their forehead. He then suggested that their repressed memories would return to consciousness (Ellenberger, 1970). Today, many therapists would probably regard this procedure as carrying a risk of generating false memories.

The Freudian concept of free association is a bit like a magician pulling kerchiefs out of a hat, with one thought leading to the next, in turn leading to the next, and so on.

Psychoanalytic and Psychodynamic Therapies: Freud's Legacy

Psychodynamic therapists share the following three approaches and beliefs, which form the core of their approach (Blagys & Hilsenroth, 2000; Shedler, 2010:

1. They believe the causes of abnormal behaviors, including unconscious conflicts, wishes, and impulses, stem from traumatic or other adverse childhood experiences.
2. They strive to analyze (a) distressing thoughts and feelings clients avoid, (b) wishes and fantasies, (c) recurring themes and life patterns, (d) significant past events, and (e) the therapeutic relationship.
3. They believe that when clients achieve insight into previously unconscious material, the causes and the significance of symptoms will become evident, often causing symptoms to disappear.

Psychoanalysis: Key Ingredients

Freud's psychoanalysis was one of the first forms of psychotherapy. According to Freud, the goal of psychoanalysis is to decrease guilt and frustration and *make the unconscious conscious* by bringing to awareness previously repressed impulses, conflicts, and memories (Bornstein, 2001; Mellinger & Lynn, 2003). Psychoanalytic therapists, sometimes called "analysts," attempt to fill this tall order using six primary approaches.

1. **Free Association.** As clients lie on a couch in a comfortable position, therapists instruct them to say whatever thoughts come to mind, no matter how meaningless or nonsensical they might seem. This process is called **free association**, because clients are permitted to express themselves without censorship.
2. **Interpretation.** From the client's string of free associations, analysts form hypotheses regarding the origin of the client's difficulties and share them with him or her as the therapeutic relationship evolves. Therapists also formulate

insight therapies
psychotherapies, including psychodynamic, humanistic, and group approaches, with the goal of expanding awareness or insight

humanistic therapies
therapies that emphasize the development of human potential and the belief that human nature is basically positive

free association
technique in which clients express themselves without censorship of any sort

interpretations—explanations—of the unconscious bases of a client's dreams, emotions, and behaviors. They point out the supposedly disguised expression of a repressed idea, impulse, or wish, as in the following interpretation of a client's repeated "accidents" resulting in injury: "Having these accidents perhaps served an unconscious purpose; they assured you of getting the attention you felt you could not get otherwise." As in comedy, timing is everything: if the therapist offers the interpretation before the client is ready to accept it, psychoanalysts maintain, anxiety may derail the flow of new associations.

3. **Dream Analysis.** According to Freud, dreams express unconscious themes that influence the client's conscious life. The therapist's task is to interpret the relation of the dream to the client's waking life and the dream's symbolic significance. Earlier in the text, we discussed the distinction between a dream's manifest (observable) and latent (hidden) content. Thus, the therapist might interpret the appearance of an ogre in a dream—the manifest content—as representing a hated and feared parent—the latent content.
4. **Resistance.** As treatment progresses and people become aware of previously unconscious and often feared aspects of themselves, they often experience **resistance**: they try to avoid further confrontation. Clients express resistance in many ways, including skipping therapy sessions or drawing a blank when the therapist asks a question about painful moments in their past, but all forms of resistance can stall their progress. To minimize resistance, psychoanalysts attempt to make clients aware that they're unconsciously blocking therapeutic efforts and make clear *how* and *what* they're resisting (Anderson & Stewart, 1983).
5. **Transference.** As analysis continues, clients begin to experience **transference**: they project intense, unrealistic feelings and expectations from their past onto the therapist. The ambiguous figure of the analyst supposedly becomes the focus of emotions once directed at significant persons from the client's childhood. In one example, a client brought a gun into treatment and pointed it at the therapist. The therapist replied: "This is what I meant about your murderous feelings toward your father (Laughs). Do you see it now?" (Monroe, 1955). Freud believed that transference provides a vehicle for clients to understand their irrational expectations and demands of others, including the therapist.

   Research suggests that we indeed often react to people in our present life in ways similar to people in our past (Berk & Andersen, 2000; Luborsky, et al., 1985). These findings may suggest that Freud was right about the transference; alternatively, they may mean that our stable personality traits lead us to react to people in similar ways over time. These lingering questions aside, therapists' interpretations of the transference may be helpful for some clients (Ogrodniczuk & Piper, 1999).

ruling out rival hypotheses

HAVE IMPORTANT ALTERNATIVE EXPLANATIONS FOR THE FINDINGS BEEN EXCLUDED?

6. **Working Through.** In the final stage of psychoanalysis, therapists help clients *work through,* or process, their problems. The insight gained in treatment is a helpful starting point, but it's not sufficient. As a consequence, therapists must repeatedly address conflicts and resistance to achieving healthy behavior patterns and help clients confront old and ineffective coping responses as they reemerge in everyday life (Menninger, 1958; Wachtel, 1997).

resistance
attempts to avoid confrontation and anxiety associated with uncovering previously repressed thoughts, emotions, and impulses

transference
act of projecting intense, unrealistic feelings and expectations from the past onto the therapist

interpersonal therapy (IPT)
treatment that strengthens social skills and targets interpersonal problems, conflicts, and life transitions

Developments in Psychoanalysis: The Neo-Freudian Tradition

Freud's ideas spawned new therapeutic approaches in the psychodynamic tradition (Ellis, Abrams, & Abrams, 2008). In contrast to Freudian therapists, neo-Freudian therapists are more concerned with conscious aspects of the client's functioning. For example, according to neo-Freudian Carl Jung, the goal of psychotherapy is *individuation*—the integration of opposing aspects of the personality, like passive versus aggressive tendencies, into a harmonious "whole," namely, the self. To help clients achieve individuation, Jung considered their future goals as well as past experiences. Neo-Freudians also emphasize the impact of cultural and interpersonal influences, such as close friendships and loving relationships, on behavior across the lifespan (Adler, 1938; Mitchell & Black, 1995). Beyond Freud's emphasis on sexuality and aggression, neo-Freudians acknowledge the impact of other needs, including love, dependence, power, and status. They're also more optimistic than was Freud regarding people's prospects for achieving healthy functioning.

The emphasis on interpersonal relationships is the hallmark of Harry Stack Sullivan's *interpersonal psychotherapy*. According to Sullivan (1954), psychotherapy is a collaborative undertaking between client and therapist. Sullivan contended that the analyst's proper role is that of *participant observer*. Through ongoing observations, the analyst discovers and communicates to clients their unrealistic attitudes and behaviors in everyday life.

Sullivan's work influenced the contemporary approach of **interpersonal therapy (IPT)**. Originally a treatment for depression (Klerman et al., 1984; Santor & Kusumakar, 2001), IPT is a short-term intervention (12–16 sessions) designed to strengthen people's social skills and assist them in coping with interpersonal problems, conflicts (such as disputes with family members), and life transitions (such as childbirth and retirement). In addition to effectively treating depression (Klerman et al., 1984; Hinrichsen, 2008), IPT has demonstrated success in treating substance abuse and eating disorders comparable with that of cognitive-behavioral therapies (Klerman & Weissman, 1993; Murphy et al., 2012).

Is Insight Necessary? As we've seen, psychodynamic therapies rely heavily on insight. Many Hollywood films, such as *Good Will Hunting* (1997) and *Analyze This* (1999), reinforce the impression that insight—especially into the childhood origins of problems—is the crucial ingredient in therapeutic change. Yet extensive research demonstrates that understanding our emotional history, however deep and gratifying, isn't required to relieve psychological distress (Weisz et al., 1995). To improve, clients typically need to practice new and more adaptive behaviors in everyday life—that is, to engage in *working through* (Wachtel, 1977).

Some psychodynamic concepts, including therapeutic interpretations, are difficult to falsify. How can we demonstrate that a person's dream of his father scowling at him, for example, points to repressed memories of child abuse, as a therapist might infer? A client might respond, "Aha, that's it!" but this reaction could reflect transference or an attempt to please the therapist. If the client improves, the therapist might conclude that the interpretation is accurate, but the timing could be coincidental rather than causal (Grunbaum, 1984).

The failure to rule out rival hypotheses may lead both therapist and client to mistakenly attribute progress to insight and interpretation when other influences, like placebo effects, are responsible (Meyer, 1981). Research supports this caution. In one long-term study of psychoanalytic treatment (Bachrach et al., 1991), half of 42 clients improved but failed to show insight into their "core conflicts." Yet patients attributed improvement more to the support the therapist provided than to insight.

Are Traumatic Memories Repressed? Although many psychodynamic therapists believe that current difficulties often stem from the repression of traumatic events such as childhood abuse (Frederickson, 1992; Levis, 1995), research doesn't bear out this claim (Lynn et al., 2004; McHugh, 2008). Try this thought experiment. Which event would you be more likely to forget: an instance when your peers ridiculed you and beat you up in third grade for being the class know-it-all or a time when the teacher praised you in class for your participation? Odds are you thought you'd be better able to recall the unsettling event, and you'd be right. Disturbing events are actually *more* memorable and *less* subject to being forgotten than are everyday occurrences (Loftus, 1993; Porter & Peace, 2007. After reviewing the research evidence, Richard McNally (2003) concluded that the scientific support

? This client began crying after her therapist gently suggested that she take more risks in life. "That's exactly what my father used to tell me as a child," she said, and "now I feel criticized by you the same way I felt criticized by my father." According to psychoanalysts, the client is experiencing what phenomenon?

Answer: Transference

FACtoid

One of the strangest psychotherapies of all time is surely "direct analysis," developed by psychiatrist John Rosen as a treatment for schizophrenia. Called direct analysis because Rosen claimed to speak directly to clients' unconscious minds, this method required therapists to yell at clients, call them crazy, and threaten to slice them into pieces. In some cases, Rosen even enlisted psychiatric aides to dress up as FBI agents to question clients about their fantasies. Although once highly influential—Rosen received the 1971 American Academy of Psychotherapy "Man of the Year" award—direct analysis is no longer accepted in the therapeutic community (Dolnick, 1998). The science of psychotherapy, like other domains of science, is self-correcting.

falsifiability

CAN THE CLAIM BE DISPROVED?

ruling out rival hypotheses

HAVE IMPORTANT ALTERNATIVE EXPLANATIONS FOR THE FINDINGS BEEN EXCLUDED?

ruling out rival hypotheses

HAVE IMPORTANT ALTERNATIVE EXPLANATIONS FOR THE FINDINGS BEEN EXCLUDED?

It's always the same dream. I'm in therapy, analyzing my recurring dream.

replicability

CAN THE RESULTS BE DUPLICATED IN OTHER STUDIES?

for repressed memories is weak and that many memories, especially those that stretch to the distant past, are often subject to distortion. Nevertheless, the issue remains controversial (Anderson & Green, 2001; Erdelyi, 2006).

Psychodynamic Therapies Evaluated Scientifically. Valuable as they've been, classical psychodynamic therapies are questionable from a scientific standpoint. Freud and Jung based their therapeutic observations largely on small samples of wealthy, intelligent, and successful people, rendering their external validity unclear. Their clinical sessions weren't observed by others or conducted on a systematic basis that permitted replication by others, as would be the case with rigorously controlled research.

The concerns we've raised aside, research indicates that interpersonal therapies have generally, but not consistently, fared well in comparisons with scientifically supported treatments such as cognitive-behavioral therapy (Luty et al., 2010; Murphy et al., 2012; Vos et al., 2012). Brief versions of psychodynamic therapy are better than no treatment (Leichsenring, Rabung, & Leibing, 2004; Shedler, 2010), although they may be somewhat less effective than or comparable with cognitive-behavioral therapies, which don't emphasize insight (Grawe, Donati, & Bernauer, 1998; Shapiro & Shapiro, 1982; Watzke et al., 2012). Moreover, psychodynamic therapy isn't especially effective for psychotic disorders like schizophrenia, even though some practitioners continue to use it for this purpose (Karon, 1994).

Humanistic Therapies: Achieving Our Potential

Humanistic therapists share a desire to help people overcome the sense of alienation so prevalent in our culture; to develop their sensory and emotional awareness; and to express their creativity and help them become loving, responsible, and authentic. Humanistic therapists stress the importance of assuming responsibility for decisions, not attributing our problems to the past, and living fully and finding meaning in the present.

? According to Rogers, if a father gives his child love only when he receives a good grade, but not when he receives a poor grade, is the father expressing conditional regard or unconditional regard?

Answer: Conditional regard

person-centered therapy
therapy centering on the client's goals and ways of solving problems

Person-Centered Therapy: Attaining Acceptance

No therapist better exemplifies the practice of humanistic therapy than Carl Rogers. Rogers developed a therapy called **person-centered therapy** (formerly called client-centered therapy) in which therapists don't tell clients how to solve their problems and clients can use the therapy hour however they choose (Rogers, 1942). Person-centered therapy is *nondirective* because therapists encourage clients to direct the course of therapy and don't define or diagnose clients' problems or try to get at the root cause of their difficulties. To ensure a positive outcome, the therapist must satisfy three conditions:

1. The therapist must be an authentic, genuine person who reveals his or her own reactions to what the client is communicating.

   Client: I think I'm beyond help.

   Therapist: Huh? Feel as though you're beyond help. I know. You feel just completely hopeless about yourself. I can understand that. I don't feel hopeless, but I realize you do (Meador & Rogers, 1979, p. 157).

2. The therapist must express *unconditional positive regard,* that is, a nonjudgmental acceptance of all feelings the client expresses. Rogers was convinced that unconditional positive regard elicits a more positive self-concept. He maintained that it allows clients to reclaim aspects of their "true selves" that they disowned earlier in life due to others placing conditions of worth on them.

3. The therapist must relate to clients with empathic understanding. In Rogers's words: "To sense the patient's world as if it were our own, but without ever losing the 'as if' quality. This is empathy" (Rogers, 1957, p. 98).

One way to communicate empathy is by way of *reflection,* that is, mirroring back the client's feelings—a technique for which Rogers was famous. Here's an example.

> **Client:** I was small and I envied people who were large. I was—well, I took beatings by boys and I couldn't strike back. . . .
> **Therapist:** You've had plenty of experience in being the underdog. (Rogers, 1942, pp. 145–146)

With increased awareness and heightened self-acceptance, people hopefully come to think more realistically, become more tolerant of others, and engage in more adaptive behaviors (Rogers, 1961). Some researchers have developed computer programs that attempt to simulate Rogers's person-centered therapy, especially Rogers's method of reflection (see **TABLE 16.3**).

Person-centered interviewing techniques, including showing warmth, empathy, and unconditional acceptance; using reflective listening; and avoiding confrontation, lie at the heart of *motivational interviewing* (Miller & Rollnick, 2002; Miller & Rose, 2009). This one- to two-session procedure recognizes that many clients are ambivalent about changing long-standing behaviors and is geared toward clarifying and bringing forth their reasons for changing—and not changing—their lives. Motivational interviewing, initially shown to be helpful in treating alcohol-related problems (Project MATCH Research Group, 1997), has been successful in modifying a variety of health-related behaviors, including exercising, dieting, and complying with medical therapies (Burke, Arkowitz, & Dunn, 2002; Burke, Arkowitz, & Menchola, 2003; Olsen et al., 2012).

Table 16.3 Simulated Conversation between Client and Computer Therapist, Eliza.
Some researchers have developed computer programs that attempt to simulate Rogers's person-centered therapy, especially Rogers's method of reflection. Here, we can read excerpts from a conversation between a client and the computer therapist, Eliza, developed by computer scientist Joseph Weizenbaum. Would Eliza make a good therapist?

Eliza: Hi, I am Eliza.
Client: Hi Eliza.
Eliza: How are you today....What would you like to discuss?
Client: My girlfriend.
Eliza: Tell me more...
Client: I don't know how I feel about her.
Eliza: Why don't you know how you feel about her?
Client: Sometimes she is nice, other times she is not.
Eliza: What does that suggest to you?
Client: She has psychological problems.
Eliza: Come come, elucidate your thoughts.
Client: She changes all the time.
Eliza: I see.
Client: She can be very mean.
Eliza: I see.
Client: But I still love her.
Eliza: I'm not sure I understand you fully.
Client: I don't understand myself.
Eliza: Does that trouble you?

Gestalt Therapy: Becoming Whole

Fritz Perls, the flamboyant founder of **Gestalt therapy**, was trained as a psychodynamic therapist, but imported some concepts from Gestalt psychology into a new brand of therapy. The word *gestalt* (configuration) means an organized whole. Gestalt therapists believe that people with psychological difficulties are "incomplete gestalts" because they've excluded from their awareness experiences and aspects of their personalities that trigger anxiety. As a consequence, Gestalt therapists aim to integrate different and sometimes opposing aspects of clients' personalities into a unified sense of self.

For Gestalt therapists, the key to personal growth is accepting responsibility for one's feelings and maintaining contact with the here and now. Gestalt therapy was the first of many therapies that recognize the importance of awareness, acceptance, and expression of feelings. In the *two-chair technique,* Gestalt therapists ask clients to move from chair to chair, creating a dialogue with two conflicting aspects of their personalities (see **FIGURE 16.1** on page 504). The "good boy" versus the "spoiled brat" may serve as the focal point for such an interchange. Gestalt therapists believe this procedure allows a synthesis of the opposing sides to emerge. For example, the good boy, always eager to please others, may learn from a conversation with the spoiled brat that it's acceptable in certain instances to be assertive, even demanding. Thus, the "good brat" may be more effective and authentic than either personality aspect alone.

falsifiability

CAN THE CLAIM BE DISPROVED?

Humanistic Therapies Evaluated Scientifically

The core concepts of humanistic therapies, such as meaning and self-actualization, are difficult to measure and falsify. For example, at exactly what point can we say a person is self-aware and authentic?

Gestalt therapy
therapy that aims to integrate different and sometimes opposing aspects of personality into a unified sense of self

To his credit, however, Rogers specified three conditions for effective psychotherapy that could be falsified. Research has shown that he was largely on the mark when it comes to the therapeutic relationship. Establishing a strong alliance is helpful to the ultimate success of therapy (Horvath et al., 2011; Wampold, 2001). In fact, the therapeutic relationship is typically a stronger predictor of success in therapy than the use of specific techniques (Bohart et al., 2002). But Rogers was wrong in one key respect: the three core conditions he specified aren't "necessary and sufficient" for improvement (Bohart, 2003; Norcross & Beutler, 1997). Although he overstated their impact, empathy (Bohart, Elliott, & Greenberg, 2002) and positive regard (Farber & Lane, 2002) are modestly related to therapy outcome (Orlinsky & Howard, 1986). Some studies have revealed a positive relation between genuineness and therapeutic outcome, but others haven't (Klein et al., 2002; Orlinsky, Grawe, & Parks, 1994). As we'll learn later, some people can derive considerable benefits from self-help programs that don't even involve therapists (Gould & Clum, 1993), so the therapeutic relationship isn't necessary for improvement. Moreover, research suggests that the causal direction of the relation between the therapeutic alliance and improvement may often be the reverse of what Rogers proposed: clients may first improve and then develop a stronger emotional bond with the therapist as a result (DeRubeis & Feeley, 1990; Kazdin, 2007).

correlation vs. causation

CAN WE BE SURE THAT A CAUSES B?

Figure 16.1 The Two-Chair Technique.
Gestalt therapy's two-chair technique aims to integrate opposing aspects of the client's personality, such as the "good boy" and the "spoiled brat."

Person-centered therapy is more effective than no treatment (Greenberg, Elliot, & Lietaer, 1994). But findings concerning the effectiveness of person-centered therapy are inconsistent, with some suggesting it may not help much more than a placebo treatment such as merely chatting for the same amount of time with a nonprofessional (Smith, Glass, & Miller, 1980). In contrast, other studies suggest that person-centered therapies often result in substantial improvement and may be comparable in effectiveness to the cognitive-behavioral therapies we'll encounter later (Elliott, 2002; Greenberg & Watson, 1998).

Assess Your Knowledge
FACT OR FICTION?

1. The first Freudian analysts were called neo-Freudian therapists. **True / False**
2. Insight is a necesssary and sufficient condition for change to occur in psychotherapy. **True / False**
3. An important criticism of psychoanalytic therapy is that many of its key concepts aren't falsifiable. **True / False**
4. Humanistic psychotherapists place an emphasis on exploring past issues and conflicts. **True / False**
5. Reflection is a central component of person-centered therapy. **True / False**

Answers: **1.** F (p. 495); **2.** F (p. 495); **3.** T (p. 497); **4.** F (p. 498); **5.** T (p. 499)

Group therapy procedures are efficient, time-saving, and less costly than many individual treatment methods.

Group Therapies: The More the Merrier

16.5 **List the advantages of group methods.**

16.6 **Describe the research evidence concerning the effectiveness of Alcoholics Anonymous.**

16.7 **Identify different approaches to treating the dysfunctional family system.**

Since the early 1920s, when Viennese psychiatrist Jacob Moreno introduced the term **group therapy**, helping professionals have appreciated the value of treating more than one person at a time. The popularity of group approaches has paralleled the increased demand for psychological services in the general population. Group therapies, which typically range

group therapy
therapy that treats more than one person at a time

in size from 3 to as many as 20 clients, are efficient, time-saving, and less costly than individual treatments and span all major schools of psychotherapy (Levine, 1979). In a safe group environment, participants can provide and receive support, exchange information and feedback, model effective behaviors and practice new skills, and recognize that they're not alone in struggling with adjustment problems (Yalom, 1985).

Today, psychologists conduct group sessions in a variety of settings, including homes, hospitals, inpatient and residential settings, community agencies, and professional offices. They reach people who are divorced, experiencing marital problems, struggling with gender identity, and experiencing problems with alcoholism and eating disorders, among many other problems in living (Dies, 2003; Lynn & Frauman, 1985). The most recent trend is for self-help groups to form over the Internet, especially for people with problems that may be embarrassing to share in face-to-face encounters (Davison, Pennebaker, & Dickerson, 2000; Golkaramnay et al., 2007). Research suggests that group procedures are effective for a wide range of problems and about as helpful as individual treatments (McEvoy, 2007; Fuhriman & Burlingame, 1994).

Alcoholics Anonymous has been in existence since the 1930s and provides self-help to people of all ages and backgrounds.

Alcoholics Anonymous

Self-help groups are composed of peers who share a similar problem; often they don't include a professional mental illness specialist. Over the past several decades, these groups, of which **Alcoholics Anonymous** (AA) is the best known, have become remarkably popular. AA was founded in 1935 and is now the largest organization for treating people with alcoholism, with more than 2.1 million members and an estimated 114,000 groups worldwide (Galanter, Dermatis, & Santucci, 2012; MacKillop & Gray, in press). At AA meetings, people share their struggles with alcohol, and new members are "sponsored" or mentored by more senior members, who've often achieved years of sobriety.

The program is organized around the famous "Twelve Steps" toward sobriety and is based on the assumptions that alcoholism is a physical disease and "once an alcoholic, always an alcoholic," which require that members never drink another drop after entering treatment. Several of the Twelve Steps ask members to place their trust in a "higher power" and to acknowledge their powerlessness over alcohol. AA also offers a powerful social support network (Vaillant & Milofsky, 1982). Groups based on the Twelve-Step model have been established for drug users (Narcotics Anonymous), gamblers, overeaters, spouses and children of alcoholics, "shopaholics" (compulsive shoppers), sexual addicts, and scores of others experiencing problems with impulse control. Nevertheless, there's virtually no research on the effectiveness of these other Twelve-Step approaches.

Although AA appears to be helpful for some people, many claims regarding its success aren't supported by data. People who attend AA meetings or receive treatment based on the Twelve Steps fare about as well as, but no better than, people who receive other treatments, including cognitive-behavioral therapy (Brandsma, Maultsby, & Welsh, 1980; Ferri, Amoto, & Davoli, 2006; Project MATCH Research Group, 1997). Moreover, AA members who end up in studies are usually the most active participants and have received prior professional help, resulting in an overestimate of how well AA works. Also, as many as 68 percent of participants drop out within three months of joining AA (Emrick, 1987), and those who remain in treatment are probably those who've improved (MacKillop et al., 2003). A study that followed AA members for 16 years found that attendance in the first and third years each predicted abstinence and fewer drinking problems (Moos & Moos, 2006). A key factor in who improves in AA is the ability to participate in an adaptive social network (Kelly et al., 2012). Clearly, for some people with alcoholism, participation in AA may lead to positive outcomes (MacKillop & Gray, in press).

Controlled Drinking and Relapse Prevention

Contrary to the AA philosophy, the behavioral view assumes that excessive drinking is a learned behavior that therapists can modify and control without total abstinence (Marlatt, 1983). There's bitter controversy about whether *controlled drinking,* that is, drinking in

Alcoholics Anonymous
twelve-Step self-help program that provides social support for achieving sobriety

moderation, is even an appropriate treatment goal. Nevertheless, there's considerable evidence that treatment programs that encourage people with alcoholism to set limits, drink moderately, and reinforce their progress can be effective for many clients (MacKillop, et al., 2003; Miller & Hester, 1980; Sobell & Sobell, 1973, 1976). Programs that teach people skills to cope with stressful life circumstances and tolerate negative emotions (Monti, Gulliver, & Myers, 1994) are at least as effective as Twelve-Step programs (Project MATCH Research Group, 1997).

Bucking the popular belief, sometimes repeated in the AA community, of "one drink, one drunk," *relapse prevention* (RP) treatment assumes that many people with alcoholism will at some point experience a lapse, or slip, and resume drinking (Larimer, Palmer, & Marlatt, 1999; Marlatt & Gordon, 1985). RP teaches people not to feel ashamed, guilty, or discouraged when they lapse. Negative feelings about a slip can lead to continued drinking, called the *abstinence violation effect* (Marlatt & Gordon, 1985; Polivy & Herman, 2002). Once someone slips up, he or she figures, "Well, I guess I'm back to drinking again" and goes back to drinking at high levels. RP therapists teach people to rebound after a lapse and avoid situations in which they're tempted to drink. Thus, they learn that a *lapse* doesn't mean a *relapse*. Research suggests that relapse prevention programs are often effective (Irvin et al., 1999). Still, total abstinence is probably the best goal for people with severe dependence on alcohol or for whom controlled drinking has failed (Rosenberg, 1993).

Figure 16.2 Where's the Problem? According to the strategic family therapy approach, families often single out one family member as "the problem" when the problem is actually rooted in the interactional patterns of all family members.

Family Therapies: Treating the Dysfunctional Family System

Family therapists see most psychological problems as rooted in a dysfunctional family system. For them, treatment must focus on the family context out of which conflicts presumably arise. In *family therapy*, the "patient"—the focus of treatment—isn't one person with the most obvious problems, but rather the family unit itself. Family therapists therefore focus on interactions among family members.

In structural family therapy, the therapist immerses himself or herself in the family's everyday activities. Having observed what goes on in the family, the therapist can then advocate for changes in how the family arranges and organizes its interactions.

Strategic Family Therapy

Strategic family interventions are designed to remove barriers to effective communication. According to strategic therapists, including Virginia Satir (1964), Jay Haley (1976), and Paul Watzlawick (Watzlawick, Weakland, & Fisch, 1974), the real source of psychological problems of one or more family members often lies in the dysfunctional ways in which they communicate, solve problems, and relate to one another (see **FIGURE 16.2**).

Strategic therapists invite family members to carry out planned tasks known as *directives,* which shift how family members solve problems and interact. They often involve *paradoxical requests,* which many of us associate with the concept of "reverse psychology." Some researchers (Beutler, Clarkin, & Bongar, 2000) have found that therapists often achieve success when they command their "resistant" or uncooperative clients to intentionally produce the thought, feeling, or behavior that troubled them.

Consider a therapist who "reframed" (cast in a positive light) a couple's arguments by interpreting them as a sign of their emotional closeness. The therapist gave the couple the paradoxical directive to *increase* their arguing to learn more about their love for each other. To show the therapist they were "not in love," they stopped arguing, which was, of course, the therapist's goal in the first place. Once their arguments ceased, their relationship improved (Watzlawick, Beavin, & Jackson, 1967).

strategic family intervention
family therapy approach designed to remove barriers to effective communication

structural family therapy
treatment in which therapists deeply involve themselves in family activities to change how family members arrange and organize interactions

Structural Family Therapy

In **structural family therapy** (Minuchin, 1974), the therapist actively immerses himself or herself in the everyday activities of the family to make changes in how they arrange and organize interactions. Salvatore Minuchin and his colleagues successfully treated a 14-year-old girl named Laura who obtained her father's attention by refusing to eat.

Eventually, Laura could express in words the message that her refusal to eat conveyed indirectly, and she no longer refused to eat to attain affection (Aponte & Hoffman, 1973). Research indicates that family therapy is more effective than no treatment (Hazelrigg, Cooper, & Borduin, 1987; Vetere, 2001) and at least as effective as individual therapy (Foster & Gurman, 1985; Shadish, 1995).

Assess Your Knowledge FACT OR FICTION?

1. Group psychotherapies are generally as effective as individual psychotherapies. **True / False**
2. Self-help groups are often assisted by a professional therapist. **True / False**
3. Alcoholics Anonymous is no more effective than many other alcohol abuse treatments. **True / False**
4. Family therapies focus on the one person in the family with the most problems. **True / False**
5. Planned tasks for family members suggested by strategic family therapists are called directives. **True / False**

Answers: **1.** T (p. 500); **2.** F (p. 501); **3.** T (p. 501); **4.** F (p. 502); **5.** T (p. 502)

Behavioral and Cognitive-Behavioral Approaches: Changing Maladaptive Actions and Thoughts

16.8 **Describe the characteristics of behavior therapy and identify different behavioral approaches.**

16.9 **Describe the features of cognitive-behavioral therapies (CBT) and third wave therapies.**

In sharp contrast to psychotherapists who hold that insight is the key to improvement, **behavior therapists** are so named because they focus on the specific behaviors that lead the client to seek therapy and address the current variables that maintain problematic thoughts, feelings, and behaviors (Antony & Roemer, 2003). Behavior therapists assume that behavior change results from the operation of basic principles of learning, especially classical conditioning, operant conditioning, and observational learning. For example, a client with a dog phobia may reinforce his problematic behaviors by crossing the street whenever he sees a dog. Avoiding the dog helps him obtain negative reinforcement—in this case, escaping anxiety—although he is probably unaware of this function.

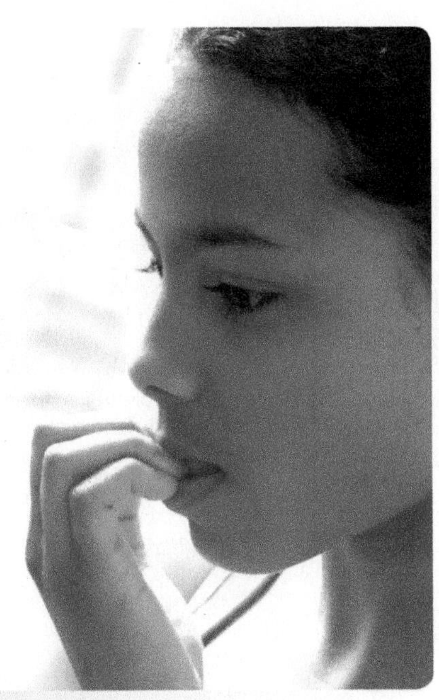

A behavior therapist treating a bad habit, like nail biting, would try to determine the situations in which nail biting occurs, as well as the consequences of nail biting for the person—such as distraction from anxiety.

Behavior therapists use a wide variety of *behavioral assessment* techniques to pinpoint environmental causes of the person's problem, establish specific and measurable treatment goals, and devise therapeutic procedures. Behavior therapists may use direct observations of current and specific behaviors, verbal descriptions of the nature and dimensions of the problem, scores on paper-and-pencil tests, standardized interviews (First et al., 1996), and physiological measures (Yartz & Hawk, 2001) to plan treatment and monitor its progress. A complete assessment considers clients' gender, race, socioeconomic class, culture, sexual orientation, and ethnic factors (Hays, 2009; Ivey, Ivey, & Simek-Morgan, 1993), as well as information about their interpersonal relationships and drug use (Lazarus, 2003). Evaluation of treatment effectiveness is integrated seamlessly into all phases of therapy, and therapists encourage clients to apply their newly acquired coping skills to everyday life. Let's now examine the nuts and bolts of several behavioral approaches.

behavior therapist
therapist who focuses on specific problem behaviors and current variables that maintain problematic thoughts, feelings, and behaviors

Systematic Desensitization and Exposure Therapies: Learning Principles in Action

Systematic desensitization is an excellent example of how behavior therapists apply learning principles to treatment. Psychiatrist Joseph Wolpe developed systematic desensitization (SD) in 1958 to help clients manage phobias. SD gradually exposes clients to anxiety-producing situations through the use of imagined scenes. This technique was the earliest **exposure therapy**, a class of procedures that aims to reduce clients' fears by confronting them directly with the source of their fears.

How Desensitization Works: One Step at a Time

SD is based on the principle of *reciprocal inhibition,* which says that clients can't experience two conflicting responses simultaneously. If a client is relaxed, he or she can't be anxious at the same time. Wolpe described his technique as a form of classical conditioning (see Chapter 6) and called it *counterconditioning.* By pairing an incompatible relaxation response with anxiety, we condition a more adaptive response to anxiety-arousing stimuli.

A therapist begins SD by teaching the client how to relax by alternately tensing and relaxing his or her muscles (Bernstein, Borkovec, & Hazlett-Stevens, 2000; Jacobson, 1938). Next, the therapist helps the client to construct an *anxiety hierarchy*—a "ladder" of situations that climbs from least to most anxiety provoking. We can find a hierarchy used to treat a person with a phobia of dogs in **TABLE 16.4**. The therapy proceeds in a stepwise manner. The therapist asks the client to relax and imagine the first scene, moving to the next, more anxiety-producing scene only after the client reports feeling relaxed while imagining the first scene.

Consider the following example of how a client moves stepwise up the anxiety hierarchy, from the least to most anxiety-producing scene.

> **Therapist:** "Soon I shall ask you to imagine a scene. After you hear a description of the situation, please imagine it as vividly as you can, through your own eyes, as if you were actually there. Try to include all the details in the scene. While you're visualizing the situation, you may continue feeling as relaxed as you are now ... After 5, 10, or 15 seconds, I'll ask you to stop imagining the scene ... and to just relax. But if you begin to feel even the slightest increase in anxiety or tension, please signal this to me by raising your left forefinger ... I'll step in and ask you to stop imagining the situation and then will help you get relaxed once more" (Goldfried & Davison, 1976, pp. 124–125).

If the client reports anxiety at any point, the therapist interrupts the process and helps him or her relax again. Then, the therapist reintroduces the scene that preceded the one that caused anxiety. This process continues until the client can confront the most frightening scenes without anxiety.

FACtoid

Because behavior therapies focus only on observable problems rather than their "root cause," many psychoanalysts once predicted that they would result in *symptom substitution*. That is, following behavior therapy, the client's underlying conflict, such as early aggression toward parents, would merely manifest itself as a different symptom. Yet data show that behavior therapies rarely, if ever, produce symptom substitution (Kazdin & Hersen, 1980; Tryon, 2008). For example, clients whose phobias are eliminated with behavioral therapy don't tend to develop other problems, like depression.

In vivo desensitization: clients gradually approach and handle any fears, as these clients are doing as they overcome their fear of flying.

Table 16.4 A Systematic Desensitization Hierarchy of a Person With a Fear of Dogs.
1. You are looking at pictures of dogs in magazines.
2. You are looking at a video of a dog playing with another dog.
3. You are looking at a video of a dog playing with a person.
4. From 100 feet away, you are watching an Irish Setter playing with the therapist.
5. You are approaching the dog and observing the interaction with the therapist from a distance of 50, 25, 10, and 5 feet in successive trials.
6. You are petting the dog.
7. You are playing with the dog.
8. You are allowing the dog to lick you.

systematic desensitization
clients are taught to relax as they are gradually exposed to what they fear in a stepwise manner

exposure therapy
therapy that confronts clients with what they fear with the goal of reducing the fear

Desensitization can also occur *in vivo,* that is, in "real life." In vivo SD involves gradual exposure to what the client actually fears, rather than imagining the anxiety-provoking situation. SD is effective for a wide range of phobias, insomnia, speech disorders, asthma attacks, nightmares, and some cases of problem drinking (Spiegler & Guevremont, 2003).

The Effectiveness of Systematic Desensitization. Behavior therapists strive to discover not only what works, but also why it works. Researchers can evaluate many therapeutic procedures by isolating the effects of each component and comparing these effects with that of the full treatment package (Wilson & O' Leary, 1980). This approach is called **dismantling**, because it enables researchers to examine the effectiveness of isolated components of a broader treatment. Dismantling helps rule out rival hypotheses about the effective mechanisms of SD and other treatments.

ruling out rival hypotheses

HAVE IMPORTANT ALTERNATIVE EXPLANATIONS FOR THE FINDINGS BEEN EXCLUDED?

Dismantling studies show that no single component of desensitization (relaxation, imagery, an anxiety hierarchy) is essential: we can eliminate each without affecting treatment outcome. Therefore, the door is open to diverse interpretations for the treatment's success (Kazdin & Wilcoxon, 1976; Lohr, DeMaio, & McGlynn, 2003). One possibility is that the credibility of the treatment creates a strong placebo effect; Mineka & Thomas, 1999). Interestingly, desensitization may fare no better than a placebo procedure designed to arouse an equivalent degree of positive expectations (Lick, 1975). Alternatively, when therapists expose clients to what they fear, clients may realize that their fears are irrational, or their fear response may extinguish following repeated uneventful contact with the feared stimulus (see Chapter 6; Casey, Oei, & Newcombe, 2004; Rachman, 1994; Zinbarg, 1993).

ruling out rival hypotheses

HAVE IMPORTANT ALTERNATIVE EXPLANATIONS FOR THE FINDINGS BEEN EXCLUDED?

Flooding And Virtual Reality Exposure

Flooding therapies provide a vivid contrast to SD. Flooding therapists jump right to the top of the anxiety hierarchy and expose clients to images of the stimuli they fear the most for prolonged periods, often for an hour or even several hours. Flooding therapies are based on the idea that fears are maintained by avoidance. For example, because individuals with a height phobia continually avoid high places, they never learn that the disastrous consequences they envision won't occur. Ironically, their avoidance only perpetuates their fears by means of negative reinforcement. The flooding therapist repeatedly provokes anxiety in the absence of actual negative consequences so that extinction of the fear can proceed.

Like SD, flooding can be conducted in vivo. To paraphrase the Nike slogan ("Just do it"): "If you're afraid to do it, do it!" During the first session, a therapist who practices in vivo flooding might accompany a person with a height phobia to the top of a skyscraper and look down for an hour—or however long it takes for anxiety to dissipate. Remarkably, many people with specific phobias—including those who were in psychodynamic therapy for decades with no relief—have been essentially cured of their fears after only a single session (Antony & Barlow, 2002; Williams, Turner, & Peer, 1985). Therapists have successfully used flooding with numerous anxiety disorders, including obsessive-compulsive disorder (OCD), social phobia, posttraumatic stress disorder, and agoraphobia.

Thought Field Therapists claim that touching body parts in a set order can play a role in treating longstanding phobias resistant to treatment by other means.

A crucial component of flooding is **response prevention** (more recently called "ritual prevention" in the case of obsessive-compulsive disorder), in which therapists prevent clients from performing their typical avoidance behaviors (Spiegler, 1983). A therapist may treat a person with a hand-washing compulsion by exposing her to dirt and preventing her from washing her hands (Franklin & Foa, 2002). Research demonstrates that this treatment is effective for OCD and closely related conditions (Chambless & Ollendick, 2001; Gillihan et al., 2012).

Virtual reality exposure therapy is the "new kid on the block" of exposure therapies. With high-tech equipment, which provides a "virtually lifelike" experience of fear-provoking situations, therapists can treat many anxiety-related conditions, including height phobia (Emmelkamp et al., 2001), thunderstorm phobia (Botella et al., 2006), flying phobia (Emmelkamp et al., 2002), and posttraumatic stress disorder (Reger et al., 2011; Rothbaum et al., 2001). Virtual reality exposure not only rivals the effectiveness of

dismantling
research procedure for examining the effectiveness of isolated components of a larger treatment

response prevention
technique in which therapists prevent clients from performing their typical avoidance behaviors

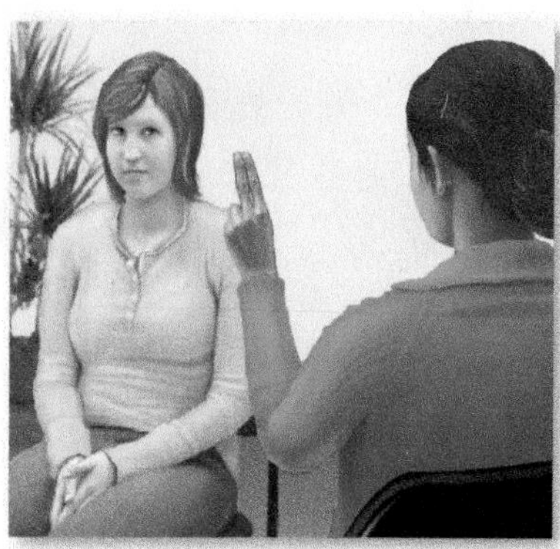

In EMDR, the client focuses on the therapist's fingers as they move back and forth. Nevertheless, studies indicate that such eye movements play no useful role in EMDR's effectiveness.

traditional in vivo exposure, but also provides repeated exposure to situations that often aren't feasible in real life, like flying in airplanes.

In 2005, researchers discovered that the antibiotic D-cycloserine, used for many years to treat tuberculosis, facilitates long-term extinction of fear of heights when administered several hours before people undergo exposure riding in a "virtual glass elevator" (Davis et al., 2005). D-cycloserine works by boosting the functioning of a receptor in the brain that enhances fear-extinction learning in both animals and humans. Today, D-cycloserine is recognized as a promising adjunct to treatments for anxiety-related conditions, including obsessive-compulsive disorder (Norberg, Krystal, & Tolin, 2008) and possibly posttraumatic stress disorder (Kleine et al., 2012). Still, D-cyclocerine does not consistently outperform placebos (Litz et al., 2012), so the verdict regarding its specific effects on various psychological disorders is not settled.

Exposure: Fringe and Fad Techniques

Traditionally, behavior therapists have been careful not to exaggerate claims of the effectiveness of exposure therapies and promote them to the public as cure-alls. We can contrast this cautious approach with that of recent proponents of fringe therapeutic techniques, some of who've made extraordinary claims that don't stack up well against the evidence.

extraordinary claims

IS THE EVIDENCE AS STRONG AS THE CLAIM?

Roger Callahan, who developed *Thought Field Therapy* (TFT), claimed that his procedure could cure phobias in as little as five minutes (Callahan, 1995, 2001) and cure not only human fears, but also fears of horses and dogs. In TFT, the client thinks of a distressing problem while the therapist taps specific points on the client's body in a predetermined order. Meanwhile, the client hums parts of "The Star Spangled Banner," rolls her eyes, or counts (how TFT therapists accomplish these feats with animals is unknown). These decidedly strange procedures supposedly remove invisible "energy blocks" associated with a specific fear. There's no research evidence for the assertion that the technique cures anxiety by manipulating energy fields, which have never been shown to exist, or for the implausible claim of virtually instantaneous cures for the vast majority of phobia sufferers (Lohr et al., 2003; Pignotti & Thyler, 2009). Because the "energy blocks" of TFT aren't measurable, the theoretical claims of TFT are unfalsifiable.

falsifiability

CAN THE CLAIM BE DISPROVED?

Some other exposure-based therapies feature numerous "bells and whistles" that provide them with the superficial veneer of science. Take *eye movement desensitization and reprocessing* (EMDR), which has been marketed widely as a "breakthrough" treatment for anxiety disorders (Shapiro, 1995; Shapiro & Forrest, 1997). As of 2010, more than 80,000 therapists have been trained in EMDR. EMDR proponents claim that clients' lateral eye movements, made while they imagine a past traumatic event, enhance their processing of painful memories. Yet systematic reviews of research demonstrate that the eye movements of EMDR play no role in this treatment's effectiveness. Moreover, EMDR is no more effective than standard exposure treatments (Davidson & Parker, 2001; Lohr, Tolin, & Lilienfeld, 1998; Rubin, 2003). Accordingly, a parsimonious hypothesis is that the active ingredient of EMDR isn't the eye movements for which it's named, but rather the exposure the technique provides.

occam's razor

DOES A SIMPLER EXPLANATION FIT THE DATA JUST AS WELL?

Modeling in Therapy: Learning by Watching

Clients can learn many things by observing therapists model positive behaviors. Modeling is one form of *observational or vicarious learning*. Albert Bandura (1971, 1977) has long advocated **participant modeling**, a technique in which the therapist models a calm encounter with the client's feared object or situation and then guides the client through the steps of the encounter until he or she can cope unassisted.

Assertion Training

Modeling is an important component of assertion and social skills training programs designed to help clients with social anxiety. The primary goals of assertion training are to facilitate the expression of thoughts and feelings in a forthright and socially appropriate manner and to ensure that clients aren't taken advantage of, ignored, or denied their legitimate rights (Alberti & Emmons, 2001). In assertion training, therapists teach clients to avoid extreme reactions to others' unreasonable demands, such as submissiveness, on the one hand, and aggressiveness, on the other. Assertiveness, the middle ground between these extremes, is the goal.

Behavioral Rehearsal

Therapies commonly use behavioral rehearsal in assertion training and other participant modeling techniques. In behavioral rehearsal, the client engages in role-playing with a therapist to learn and practice new skills. The therapist plays the role of a relevant person such as a spouse, parent, or boss. The client reacts to the character enacted by the therapist, and in turn, the therapist offers coaching and feedback. To give the client an opportunity to model assertive behaviors, therapist and client reverse roles, with the therapist playing the client's role. By doing so, the therapist models not only what the client might say, but also how the client might say it.

To transfer what clients learn to everyday life, therapists encourage them to practice their newfound skills outside therapy sessions. Modeling and social skills training can make valuable contributions to treating (although not curing) schizophrenia, autism, depression, attention-deficit/hyperactivity disorder (ADHD), and social anxiety (Antony & Roemer, 2003; Scattone, 2007; Monastra, 2008).

Operant and Classical Conditioning Procedures

Psychologists have used operant conditioning procedures to good effect among children with autism and a host of other childhood disorders. As we'll recall from earlier in the text, operant conditioning is learning in which behavior is modified by its consequences. An example of an operant procedure is the **token economy** widely used in treatment programs in institutional and residential settings, as well as the home. In token economies, certain behaviors, like helping others, are consistently rewarded with tokens that clients can later exchange for more tangible rewards, whereas other behaviors, like screaming at hospital staff, are ignored or punished. In this way, such programs shape, maintain, or alter behaviors by the consistent application of operant conditioning principles (Boerke & Reitman, 2011; Kazdin, 1978). Critics of token economies argue that the benefits don't necessarily generalize to other settings and that they're difficult and impractical to administer (Corrigan, 1995). Nevertheless, token economies have shown some success in the classroom (Boniecki & Moore, 2003), in treating children with ADHD at home and at school (Mueser & Liberman, 1995), and in treating clients with schizophrenia who require long-term hospitalization (Dixon et al., 2010; Paul & Lentz, 1977).

Aversion therapies are based primarily on classical conditioning and pair undesirable behaviors with stimuli that most people experience as painful, unpleasant, or even revolting (see Chapter 6). For example, therapists have used medications such as disulfiram—better known as Antabuse—to make people vomit after drinking alcohol (Brewer, 1992), electric shocks to treat psychologically triggered recurrent sneezing (Kushner, 1968), and verbal descriptions of feeling nauseated while people imagine smoking cigarettes (Cautela, 1971).

Research provides, at best, mixed support for the effectiveness of aversive procedures (Spiegler & Guevremont, 2003). For example, people with alcoholism often simply stop taking Antabuse rather than stop drinking (MacKillop & Gray, in press). In general, therapists attempt minimally unpleasant techniques before moving on to more aversive measures. The decision to implement aversion therapies should be made only after carefully weighing their costs and benefits relative to alternative approaches.

token economy
method in which desirable behaviors are rewarded with tokens that clients can exchange for tangible rewards

aversion therapy
treatment that uses punishment to decrease the frequency of undesirable behaviors

Cognitive-Behavioral and Third Wave Therapies: Learning to Think and Act Differently

Advocates of **cognitive-behavioral therapies** hold that beliefs play the central role in our feelings and behaviors. These therapies share three core assumptions: (1) Cognitions are identifiable and measureable; (2) cognitions are the key players in both healthy and unhealthy psychological functioning; and (3) irrational beliefs or catastrophic thinking such as "I'm worthless and will never succeed at anything" can be replaced with more rational and adaptive cognitions, or viewed in a more accepting light.

The Abcs of Rational Emotive Behavior Therapy

Beginning in the mid-1950s, pioneering therapist Albert Ellis (Ellis, 1958, 1962) advocated *rational emotive therapy* (RET), later renamed *rational emotive behavior therapy* (REBT). In many respects, REBT is a prime example of a cognitive-behavioral approach. It is cognitive in its emphasis on changing how we think (that's the "cognitive" part), but it also focuses on changing how we act (that's the "behavioral" part).

Ellis argued that we respond to an unpleasant activating (internal or external) event (A) with a range of emotional and behavioral consequences (C). As we all know, people often respond very differently to the same objective event; some students respond to a 75 on an exam by celebrating, whereas others respond by berating themselves for not getting a 90 or even a 100. For Ellis, the differences in how we respond to the same event stem largely from differences in (B)—our belief systems (see **FIGURE 16.3**). The ABCs Ellis identified lie at the heart of most, if not all, cognitive-behavior therapies.

Some beliefs are rational: they are flexible, are logical, and promote self-acceptance. In contrast, others are irrational: they're associated with unrealistic demands about the self ("I must be perfect"), others ("I must become worried about other people's problems"), and life conditions ("I must be worried about things I can't control."). Ellis also maintained that psychologically unhealthy people frequently "awfulize," that is, engage in catastrophic thinking about their problems ("If I don't get this job, it would be the worst thing that ever

Figure 16.3 The ABCs of Rational Emotive Behavior Therapy.
How someone feels about an event is determined by his or her beliefs about the event.

cognitive-behavioral therapies
treatments that attempt to replace irrational cognitions and maladaptive behaviors with more rational cognitions and adaptive behaviors

happened to me"). We can find examples of 12 irrational beliefs outlined by Ellis in **TABLE 16.5**. According to Ellis, our vulnerability to psychological disturbance is a product of the frequency and strength of our irrational beliefs (David, Lynn, & Ellis, 2010).

To his ABC scheme, Ellis added a (D) and (E) component to describe how therapists treat clients. REBT therapists encourage clients to actively dispute (D) their irrational beliefs and adopt more effective (E) and rational beliefs to increase adaptive responses. To modify clients' irrational beliefs, the therapist forcefully encourages them to rethink their assumptions and personal philosophy. REBT therapists often assign "homework" designed to falsify clients' maladaptive beliefs. For example, they may give shy clients an assignment to talk to an attractive man or woman to falsify their belief that "If I'm rejected by someone I like, it will be absolutely terrible."

falsifiability

CAN THE CLAIM BE DISPROVED?

Other Cognitive-Behavioral Approaches

Cognitive-behavioral therapists differ in the extent to which they incorporate behavioral methods. Aaron Beck's enormously popular *cognitive therapy*, which many credit as playing an instrumental role in creating the field of cognitive-behavioral therapy (Smith, 2009), emphasizes identifying and modifying distorted thoughts and long-held negative core beliefs ("I'm unlovable") (Beck et al., 1979; J. Beck, 1995). Nevertheless, cognitive therapy places somewhat greater weight on behavioral procedures than does Ellis's REBT (Stricker & Gold, 2003). Researchers have found Beck's approach helpful for people with depression; anxiety disorders; and perhaps even bipolar disorder, schizophrenia, and certain personality disorders such as borderline personality disorder (A. T. Beck, 2005; A.T. Beck & Dozois, 2011; Hollon, Thase, & Markowitz, 2002).

In Donald Meichenbaum's (1985) *stress inoculation training,* therapists teach clients to prepare for and cope with future stressful life events. In this approach, therapists

Two pioneers of cognitive-behavioral therapy, Aaron Beck (*left;* 1921–) and Albert Ellis (1913–2007).

Table 16.5 Irrational Beliefs: "The Dirty Dozen."

Albert Ellis identified 12 irrational ideas ("The Dirty Dozen") that are widespread in our culture. You may find it interesting to see which of these beliefs you've entertained at some point in your life. Because these ideas are so much a part of many people's thinking, don't be surprised if you hold a number of them.

1. You must have nearly constant love and approval from everyone who is important to you.
2. You must prove yourself highly adequate and successful, or at least extremely competent or talented at some valued activity.
3. People who hurt you or treat you poorly are bad, evil, and blameworthy, and deserve to be punished harshly for their actions.
4. When things don't go your way, it's an awful, horrible, or terrible catastrophe.
5. External factors, such as life events, are responsible for your misery; you have little ability to control or eliminate your negative feelings, including sadness and anger.
6. You must become upset and preoccupied with frightening or dangerous situations or people.
7. It's easier to avoid confronting many of life's challenges and responsibilities than it is to become self-disciplined.
8. The past must continue to dominate your feelings and behavior because previous experiences once exerted a strong impact on you.
9. If you can't cope with or resolve everyday hassles quickly, it's terrible; things and relationships should work out better than they do.
10. Being passive with no commitment to accomplish anything other than "enjoying oneself" is a good way to achieve happiness.
11. To feel comfortable, you must be highly organized or certain about how things will turn out.
12. Your worth and acceptance depend on your performance and how others rate you. Rather than evaluate your performance in specific areas of functioning, you should give yourself a global rating ("I'm good," "I'm bad," and so on).

(Based on: Ellis, 1977)

FACtoid

There's some evidence that therapists' theoretical orientation is correlated with their personality traits. Several, although not all, studies suggest that compared with other therapists, psychoanalytic therapists tend to be especially insecure and serious, behavior therapists tend to be especially assertive and self-confident, and cognitive-behavioral therapists tend to be especially rational (Keinan, Almagor, & Ben-Porath, 1989; Walton, 1978).

PERSONAL 110(

About 9 months ago I began to notice a man wearing sunglasses who was watching me from a parking lot across the street. I thought he was suspicious and eventually concluded that he and his colleagues were following me everywhere I went. Even when I went on vacation to California 3000 miles away, I noticed that the same man and his colleagues were not far behind. After several weeks of careful investigation, I decided to leave home and travel to Europe in an attempt to escape him. Even while in Paris, I felt his eyes on me and was quite sure that I even saw him on television one night. I fear he has already contacted my employer and possibly some of my friends, because they all seem more distant from me lately. I want you all to know that everything he says about me is a lie.

?

Each of the three statements below—provided by therapists in response to the person who placed the personal ad—is typical of a different psychotherapy. **Match each statement with the therapy (A. client-centered, B. Freudian, C. REBT) it best represents.** (See answer upside down on bottom of page.)

1. You're being irrational and jumping to conclusions. Even if someone were following you, why conclude that he's contacted your friends just because they're more distant?
2. You've told me that during childhood, your father constantly judged you and that when he stared at you, it brought about tremendous guilt. Perhaps this man you can't escape symbolizes your father?
3. Starting nine months ago, you became suspicious of a man you're now pretty sure will damage relationships you prize. How terrible it must feel to think he's telling lies about you!

Answer: 1-C, 2-B, 3-A

"inoculate" clients against an upcoming stressor by getting them to anticipate it and develop cognitive skills to minimize its harm, much as we receive a vaccine (inoculation) containing a small amount of a virus to ward off illness. Therapists modify clients' *self-statements*, that is, their ongoing mental dialogue (Meichenbaum, 1985). Clients fearful of giving a speech may learn to say things to themselves, like "Even though it's scary, the outcome probably won't be as bad as I fear." Therapists have applied stress inoculation successfully to children and adults facing medical and surgical procedures, public speaking, and exams (Meichenbaum, 1996), as well as to clients with anger problems (Cahill et al., 2003; Novaco, 1994).

Acceptance: The Third Wave of Cognitive-Behavioral Therapy

The past few decades have witnessed a surge of interest in so-called *third wave therapies* that represent a shift from both the first (behavioral) and second (cognitive) waves of the cognitive-behavioral tradition (Hayes, 2004). Instead of trying to change maladaptive behaviors and negative thoughts, third wave therapies embrace a different goal: to assist clients with accepting and being mindful of and attuned to all aspects of their experience, including thoughts, feelings, memories, and physical sensations. Consistent with this goal, research suggests that avoiding and suppressing disturbing experiences, rather than accepting or confronting them, often backfires, creating even greater emotional turmoil (Amir et al., 2001; Teasdale, Segal, & Williams, 2003).

Steven Hayes and colleagues' (Hayes, Follette, & Linehan, 2004; Hayes, Strosahl, & Wilson, 1999) acceptance and commitment therapy (ACT) stands at the vanguard of such approaches. ACT practitioners teach clients that negative thoughts such as "I'm worthless" are merely thoughts, not "facts," while encouraging them to accept and tolerate the full range of their feelings and to act in keeping with their goals and values.

ACT and a growing number of third wave therapies often train clients in mindfulness practices such as meditation, which may involve nothing more than paying attention to the inflow and outflow of the breath while allowing thoughts and feelings to come and go without judgment (Kabat-Zinn, 2003). Mindfulness-based cognitive therapy (Segal, Williams, & Teasdale, 2012), which combines mindfulness with cognitive therapy, produces reductions in the average rate of relapse in depression on the order of 50 percent (Hofmann et al., 2010; Piet & Hougaard, 2011) and substantially reduces anxiety in adults and children (Kim et al., 2010; Semple & Lee, 2011).

Marsha Linehan's (Linehan 1993) dialectical behavior therapy (DBT), another third wave therapy used frequently in the treatment of clients with borderline personality disorder, addresses the *dialectic*—the apparent contradiction between opposing tendencies—of changing problematic behavior and accepting it. Linehan encourages clients to accept their intense emotions while actively attempting to cope with these emotions by making changes in their lives. Research supports the effectiveness of DBT for a number of symptoms of borderline personality disorder, including self-harm behaviors (McMain et al., 2012).

It remains to be seen whether these new techniques are more effective than standard behavioral and cognitive-behavioral therapies. Critics have raised concerns that new wave therapies have been overhyped in the absence of convincing scientific evidence and have questioned whether they represent a significant departure from more traditional cognitive-behavioral therapies (Hofmann & Asmundson, 2008; Ost, 2008). Perhaps a better analogy to these recent developments in psychotherapy is not a wave, but a tree, which represents cognitive-behavioral therapy, with many branches, one of them being third wave approaches (Hofmann, 2010). After all, cognitive-behavioral techniques represent a broad swath of approaches, and asking people to perceive their negative thoughts as nothing more than thoughts, as is done in ACT and mindfulness approaches, can be viewed as yet another way of modifying disturbing cognitions, or at least how one thinks about such cognitions.

Many third wave therapies fall in line with the current trend in psychotherapy for therapists to create individually tailored *eclectic* approaches—treatments that integrate techniques and theories from more than one existing approach (Lazarus, 2006; Stricker & Gold, 2003; Wachtel, 1997). For example, ACT and DBT therapists adopt behavioral techniques and meditation practices from a Buddhist tradition and borrow from humanistic psychology's emphasis on awareness and emotional expression. As we can see in **TABLE 16.6**, the largest percentage of practicing clinical psychologists describe their theoretical orientation as eclectic/integrative (Norcross, 2005; Prochaska & Norcross, 2007).

Only recently have psychologists come to learn which specific therapeutic components contribute to treatment success. For example, *behavioral activation*—getting clients, such as those who are depressed, to participate in reinforcing activities—is a key component of many third wave and cognitive-behavioral approaches and is emerging as a key element of successful psychotherapy (Dimidjian et al., 2006; Hopko, Robertson, & Lejuez, 2006; Ritschel et al., 2011). Intentional or incidental exposure to negative thoughts and feelings is another component of treatment that is probably associated with the success of numerous psychotherapies (Carey, 2011; Kazdin, 2009). Still, the more ingredients that are tossed into the therapeutic mix, the more challenging it becomes to dismantle integrative approaches and evaluate rival hypotheses regarding which ingredients matter.

ruling out rival hypotheses

HAVE IMPORTANT ALTERNATIVE EXPLANATIONS FOR THE FINDINGS BEEN EXCLUDED?

CBT and Third Wave Approaches Evaluated Scientifically

Research allows us to draw the following conclusions about the effectiveness of behavioral and cognitive-behavioral therapies:

1. They're more effective than no treatment or placebo treatment (Bowers & Clum, 1988; Smith, Glass, & Miller, 1980).
2. They're at least as effective (Sloane et al., 1975; Smith & Glass, 1977)—and in some cases more effective—than psychodynamic and person-centered therapies (Grawe, Donati, & Bernauer, 1998).
3. They're at least as effective as drug therapies for depression (Elkin, 1994).
4. In general, CBT and behavioral treatments are about equally effective for most problems (Feske & Chambless, 1995; Jacobson et al., 1996).
5. Third wave approaches have scored successes in treating a variety of disorders, including depression and alcoholism (Marlatt, 2002; Segal, Williams, & Teasdale, 2012), and CBT and ACT achieve comparable outcomes in treating depression and anxiety (Forman et al., 2007).

Table 16.6 Primary Theoretical Orientations of Practicing Clinical Psychologists in the United States. As we can see, the largest proportion of clinical psychologists calls themselves eclectic/integrative.

Orientation	% Clinical Psychologists
Eclectic/Integrative	29
Cognitive	28
Psychodynamic	12
Behavioral	10
Other	7
Interpersonal	4
Psychoanalytic	3
Family Systems	3
Existential-Humanistic	2
Person-Centered	1

(Sources: Prochaska & Norcross, 2007; derived from Bechtold et al., 2001; Norcross, Karpiak, & Santoro, 2005; Norcross, Strausser, & Missar, 1988)

Assess Your Knowledge
FACT OR FICTION?

1. Behavior therapies place a great deal of importance on insight. **True / False**
2. One commonly used assertion training technique is behavioral rehearsal. **True / False**
3. Token economy programs are based on operant conditioning principles. **True / False**
4. According to Albert Ellis, feelings create irrational beliefs. **True / False**
5. Acceptance and commitment therapy borrows techniques from a Buddhist tradition. **True / False**

Answers: 1. F (p. 503); **2.** T (p. 503); **3.** T (p. 507); **4.** F (p. 508); **5.** T (p. 510)

In Lewis Carroll's book *Alice in Wonderland*, the Dodo bird declared after a race, "Everybody has won, and all must have prizes." Psychotherapy researchers use the term *Dodo bird verdict* to refer to the conclusion that all therapies are equivalent in their effects. Not all investigators accept this verdict.

Is Psychotherapy Effective?

16.10 Evaluate the claim that all psychotherapies are equally effective.

16.11 Explain how ineffective therapies can sometimes appear to be effective.

In Lewis Carroll's book *Alice in Wonderland,* the Dodo bird proclaimed after a race, "Everybody has won, and all must have prizes." Seventy years ago, Saul Rosenzweig (1936) delivered the same verdict regarding the effectiveness of different psychotherapies. That is, all appear to be helpful, but are roughly equivalent in their outcomes (see **FIGURE 16.4**).

The Dodo Bird Verdict: Alive or Extinct?

Before the mid-1970s, there was considerable controversy regarding whether psychotherapy was effective at all. Some investigators concluded that it was virtually worthless (Eysenck, 1952), whereas others concluded the opposite.

Beginning in the late 1970s, a scientific consensus emerged that psychotherapy works in alleviating human suffering (Landman & Dawes, 1982; Smith & Glass, 1977)—a consensus that holds to this day. This conclusion derived from studies using a technique called *meta-analysis*. A **meta-analysis**, meaning "analysis of analysis," is a statistical method that helps researchers interpret large bodies of psychological literature. By pooling the results of many studies as though they were one big study, meta-analysis allows researchers to seek patterns across large numbers of studies and to draw general conclusions that hold up across independent laboratories (Hunt, 1997; Rosenthal & DiMatteo, 2001).

Average untreated person
Average psychotherapy client
Number of persons
Poor outcome
Good outcome
80% of treated people have better outcomes than the average untreated person

Figure 16.4 The Effectiveness of Psychotherapy. This graph shows two normal distributions (see Chapter 2) derived from nearly 500 studies of psychotherapy outcomes. The distribution on the left shows people who haven't received psychotherapy, and the distribution on the right shows people who have received psychotherapy. As we can see, across a variety of treatments and samples, 80 percent of people who receive therapy do better than people who don't. (Based on Smith, Glass, & Miller, 1980)

Today, some researchers using meta-analysis have claimed to support the Dodo bird verdict. Their results suggest that a wide range of psychotherapies are about equal in their effects (Duncan, 2010; Wampold et al., 1997, 2002; Wampold, 2010). Studies with experienced therapists who've practiced behavioral, psychodynamic, and person-centered approaches have found that all are more successful in helping clients compared with no treatment, but are no different from each other in their effects (DiLoretto, 1971; Sloane et al., 1975).

Other researchers aren't convinced. They contend that the Dodo bird verdict, like the real Dodo bird, is extinct. Although most forms of psychotherapy work well and many are about equal in their effects, there are notable exceptions (Beutler, 2002; Hunsley & DiGuilio, 2002). For example, behavioral and cognitive-behavioral treatments are clearly more effective compared with other treatments for children and adolescents with behavior problems (Garske & Anderson, 2003; Weisz et al., 1995). Moreover, behavioral and cognitive-behavioral therapies consistently outperform most other therapies for anxiety disorders, including phobias, panic disorder, and obsessive-compulsive disorder (Addis et al., 2004; Chambless & Ollendick, 2001; Tolin, 2010).

Also calling into question the Dodo bird verdict are findings that some psychotherapies can make people worse (Barlow, 2010; Dimidjian & Hollon, 2010; Lilienfeld, 2007). Although we might assume that doing something is always better than doing nothing for psychological distress, research suggests otherwise. A nontrivial proportion of clients, perhaps 5–10 percent, become worse following psychotherapy, and some may become worse *because of* psychotherapy (Castonguay et al., 2010; Rhule, 2005; Strupp, Hadley, & Gomez-Schwartz, 1978). For example, several researchers have found that crisis debriefing can sometimes increase the risk of posttraumatic stress symptoms in people exposed to trauma. The same appears to be true of Scared Straight interventions, which try to "scare away" at-risk adolescents from a life a life of crime by introducing them to actual prisoners (Petrosino, Turpin-Petrosino, & Buehler, 2003). We can see a number of other potentially harmful therapies in **TABLE 16.7** (see page 517).

meta-analysis
statistical method that helps researchers interpret large bodies of psychological literature

Table 16.7 List of Potentially Harmful Therapies.
Research suggests that some psychotherapies are potentially harmful for certain individuals.

Therapy	Intervention	Potential Harm
Facilitated communication	A facilitator holds the hands of children with autism or other developmental disabilities as they type messages on a keyboard (see Chapter 2).	False accusations of child abuse against family members
Scared Straight programs	At-risk adolescents are exposed to the harsh realities of prison life to frighten them away from a life of future crime.	Worsening of conduct problems
Recovered-memory techniques	Therapists use methods to recover memories, including prompting of memories, leading questions, hypnosis, and guided imagery.	Production of false memories of trauma
Dissociative identity disorder (DID)–oriented psychotherapy	Therapists use techniques that imply to clients that they harbor "alter" personalities. Therapists attempt to summon and interact with alters.	Production of alters, creation of serious identity problems
Critical incident stress (crisis) debriefing	Shortly after a traumatic event, therapists urge group members to "process" their negative emotions, describe posttraumatic stress disorder symptoms that members are likely to experience, and discourage members from discontinuing participation.	Heightened risk for posttraumatic stress symptoms
DARE (Drug Abuse and Resistance Education) programs	Police officers teach schoolchildren about the risks of drug use and about social skills to resist peer pressure to try drugs (see Chapter 12).	Increased intake of alcohol and other substances (such as cigarettes)
Coercive restraint therapies	Therapists physically restrain children who have difficulty forming attachments to their parents. These therapies include rebirthing (see Chapter 1) and holding therapy, in which the therapist holds children down until they stop resisting or begin to show eye contact.	Physical injuries, suffocation, death

(Source: Based on data from Lilienfeld, 2007)

? Scared Straight programs expose adolescents to prisoners and prison life in an effort to "scare them" away from criminal careers. Despite the popularity of these programs, research suggests that they are not merely ineffective, but harmful in some cases. **Which principle of learning associated with behavior therapy best explains this finding?**

Answer: Modeling

The bottom line? Many therapies are effective, and many do about equally well. Yet there are clear-cut exceptions to the Dodo bird verdict. Moreover, because at least some therapies are harmful, we shouldn't assume that we'll always be safe randomly picking a therapist out of the telephone book.

How Different Groups of People Respond to Psychotherapy

A void exists in our knowledge of how certain segments of the population respond to psychotherapy (Brown, 2006; Olkin & Taliaferro, 2005; U.S. Surgeon General, 2001). Research suggests that socioeconomic status (SES), gender, race, ethnicity, and age typically have little or no bearing on the outcome of therapy (Beutler, Machado, & Neufeldt, 1994; Cruz et al., 2007; Petry, Tennen, & Affleck, 2000; Rabinowitz & Renert,

FACtoid

David Rubin and Dorthe Bernsten (2009) found that a whopping 61 percent of participants who reported they that would likely seek psychotherapy sometime in the future believed that they might have been victims of childhood sexual abuse they had forgotten. The authors contended that memory recovery techniques could create false memories of abuse in such patients, because they find the idea that they were abused to be plausible (Rubin & Boals, 2010).

FACtoid

Even when placebos are "unmasked" as placebos, they still appear to be effective for some conditions. The expectation of improvement can be so powerful that people with the digestive disorder of irritable bowel syndrome still respond positively to a sugar placebo pill even when a physician informs them it's a placebo (Kaptchuk et al., 2010).

Some therapists claim that contact with dolphins can treat a variety of psychological problems, including autism. However, research does not support the idea that dolphin therapy is effective for any problem or disorder (Marino & Lilienfeld, 1998; 2007).

Positive life events that occur outside therapy sessions, like major job promotions, can help to explain spontaneous remissions of some psychological problems, such as depression. As neo-Freudian theorist Karen Horney observed, "Life itself still remains a very effective therapist" (Horney, 1945, p. 240; see Chapter 14).

1997; Schmidt & Hancey, 1979). Still, we must be tentative in our conclusions because researchers haven't studied these variables in depth. Many controlled studies of psychotherapy don't report participants' race, ethnicity, disability status, or sexual orientation, nor do they analyze whether the effectiveness of psychotherapy depends on these variables (Cardemil, 2010; Sue & Zane, 2006). So we can't be completely confident that therapies effective for Caucasians are equally effective for other populations.

Common Factors

One probable reason many therapies are comparable in effectiveness is that certain *common factors*—those that cut across many or most therapies—are responsible for improvement across diverse treatments. As Jerome Frank (1961) noted in his classic book *Persuasion and Healing*, these common factors include listening with empathy, instilling hope, establishing a strong emotional bond with clients, providing a clear theoretical rationale for treatment, and implementing techniques that offer new ways of thinking, feeling, and behaving (Del Re et al., 2012; Lambert & Ogles, 2004; Miller, Duncan, & Hubble, 2005). Frank observed that these common factors are also shared by many forms of faith healing, religious conversion, and interpersonal persuasion over the centuries and that they extend across most, if not all, cultures. Additional common factors include the therapist assisting the client in making sense of the world, exerting influence and mastery through social means and connecting with others, and developing positive treatment expectancies (Wampold, 2007, 2012). Although we might be tempted to dismiss common factors as "placebos," this would miss the crucial point that they're essential in instilling in clients the motivation to change. Indeed, studies show that common factors typically account for a hefty chunk of improvement in therapy (Cuijpers et al., 2008; Sparks, Duncan, & Miller, 2008).

In contrast, *specific factors* characterize only certain therapies: they include meditating, challenging irrational beliefs, and social skills training. In some cases, specific factors may be key ingredients in psychotherapeutic change; in other cases, they may not enhance treatment effectiveness beyond common factors (Stevens, Hynan, & Allen, 2000). Psychologists are divided about the extent to which common versus specific factors influence the outcome of psychotherapy (Craighead, Sheets, & Bjornsson, 2005; DeRubeis, Brotman, & Gibbons, 2005; Kazdin, 2005), although most agree that both matter.

From Inquiry to Understanding

Why Can Ineffective Therapies Appear to Be Helpful? How We Can Be Fooled

Effective psychotherapy empowers people to contend with the most challenging problems in living. Yet some therapists have successfully marketed a wide variety of interventions that lack research support and rest on questionable premises (Lilienfeld et al., 2003; Norcross, Garofalo, & Koocher, 2006; Singer & Nievod, 2003). They include treatments as seemingly bizarre as dolphin therapy; laughter therapy; primal scream therapy; treatment for the trauma of abduction by aliens (Appelle, Lynn, & Newman, 2000); Neurolinguistic Programming (NLP), in which therapists match clients' nonverbal behaviors such as tone of voice to influence them; and even treatment for resolving problems due to presumed traumas in a past life (Mills & Lynn, 2000).

How might clients and therapists alike come to believe that treatments that are ineffective are helpful? The following five reasons can help us understand why bogus therapies gain a dedicated public following (Arkowitz & Lilienfeld, 2006; Beyerstein, 1997).

1. **Spontaneous remission.** The client's recovery may have nothing at all to do with the treatment. All of us have our "ups and downs." Similarly, many psychological problems are self-limiting or cyclical and improve without intervention. A breakup

with our latest "crush" may depress us for a while, but most of us will improve even without professional help. This phenomenon, known as *spontaneous remission*, occasionally occurs even in serious medical conditions, including cancer (Silverman, 1987).

Spontaneous remission is surprisingly common in psychotherapy. In the first formal review of psychotherapy outcomes, Hans Eysenck (1952) reported the findings of two uncontrolled studies of neurotic (mildly disturbed) clients who received no formal therapy. The rate of spontaneous remission in these studies was a staggering 72 percent! Admittedly, the studies Eysenck selected may have had unusually high rates of spontaneous remission because the individuals he claimed were "untreated" received reassurance and suggestion. Still, there's no question that many people with psychological problems like depression often improve without treatment. Only if people who are treated improve at a rate that exceeds that of untreated people or those on a wait list can we rule out the effects of spontaneous remission.

2. **The placebo effect.** The pesky placebo effect can lead to significant symptom relief. Virtually any credible treatment can be helpful in alleviating our demoralization.
3. **Self-serving biases.** Even when they don't improve, clients who are strongly invested in psychotherapy and have shelled out a lot of money in the pursuit of well-being can persuade themselves they've been helped. Because it would be too troubling to admit to oneself (or others) that it's all been a waste of time, energy, and effort, there's often a strong psychological pull to find value in a treatment (Axsom & Cooper, 1985) while ignoring, downplaying, or explaining away failures as a means of maintaining self-esteem (Beyerstein & Hadaway, 1991).
4. **Retrospective rewriting of the past.** In some cases, we may believe we've improved even when we haven't because we misremember our initial (pretreatment) level of adjustment as worse than it was. We *expect* to change after treatment and may adjust our memories to fit this expectation. In one study, investigators randomly assigned college students either to take a study skills course or serve in a wait-list control group. On objective measures of grades, the course proved worthless. Yet students who took the course thought they'd improved. (Students in the control group did not.) Why? They mistakenly recalled their initial study skills as worse than they actually were (Conway & Ross, 1984). The same phenomenon may sometimes occur in psychotherapy.
5. **Regression to the mean.** It's a statistical fact of life that extreme scores tend to become less extreme on retesting, a phenomenon known as *regression to the mean*. If you receive a zero on your first psychology exam, there's a silver lining to this gray cloud: you'll almost surely do better on your second exam! Conversely, if you receive a 100 on your first exam, odds are also high you won't do as well the second time around. Scores on measures of psychopathology are no different. If a client comes into treatment extremely depressed, the chances are high that he or she will be less depressed in a few weeks. Regression to the mean can fool therapists and clients into believing that a useless treatment is effective. It's an especially tricky problem in evaluating whether psychotherapy is effective, because most clients enter psychotherapy when their symptoms are most extreme.

ruling out rival hypotheses

HAVE IMPORTANT ALTERNATIVE EXPLANATIONS FOR THE FINDINGS BEEN EXCLUDED?

FACtoid

Many "jinxes" probably stem from a failure to consider regression to the mean (Kruger, Savitsky, & Gilovich, 1999). If we've been doing far better than we had expected in a sports tournament and a friend says "Wow, you're doing great," we may fear that our friend has jinxed us. In fact, we *are* likely to do worse after our friend says that, but because of regression to the mean, not because of a jinx. Recall from the post hoc fallacy that because A comes before B doesn't mean that A causes B.

Good psychotherapists keep up with the current state of the research literature, staying informed about which therapies do and don't have strong scientific support.

Empirically Supported Treatments

Because we can be fooled into thinking a therapy is effective when it's not, it may come as a surprise that psychologists are split on the extent to which they should base their treatments on subjective experience and intuition as opposed to carefully controlled research. The *scientist-practitioner gap* (Fox, 1996; Lilienfeld et al., in press b; Tavris, 2003) refers to the sharp cleft between psychologists who view psychotherapy as more an art than a science and those who believe that clinical practice should primarily reflect well-replicated scientific findings (Dawes, 1994; Lilienfeld et al., 2003; Baker, McFall, & Shoham, 2009). Clearly,

replicability

CAN THE RESULTS BE DUPLICATED IN OTHER STUDIES?

FACtoid

Survey data suggest that only a minority of therapists use empirically supported treatments (Baker et al., 2009; Freiheit et al., 2004). For example, a survey of practitioners who treat clients with eating disorders (especially anorexia and bulimia) indicated that most of them don't regularly administer either cognitive-behavioral or interpersonal therapies, the primary interventions found to be helpful for these conditions (Lilienfeld et al., in press a; Pederson et al., 2000).

subjective judgment plays a crucial role in therapy, but such judgment should be informed by scientific evidence. But what kind of evidence should therapists consider? Over the past 15 years or so, researchers have responded to this question by putting forth lists of **empirically supported treatments (ESTs)**, now sometimes called "research supported treatments"—interventions for specific disorders backed by high-quality scientific evidence derived from controlled studies (Chambless et al., 1996; Lebow, 2010).

Behavior therapy and cognitive-behavioral therapy have emerged as ESTs for depression, anxiety disorders, obesity, marital problems, sexual dysfunction, and alcohol problems. Interpersonal therapy has considerable support for depression and bulimia, as do acceptance-based approaches for borderline personality disorder. Still, we shouldn't conclude that a treatment that's not on the EST list isn't effective. The fact that a treatment isn't on the list may mean only that investigators haven't yet conducted research to demonstrate its effectiveness (Arkowitz & Lilienfeld, 2006).

The movement to develop lists of ESTs is controversial. Critics of this movement contend that the research literature isn't sufficiently well developed to conclude that certain treatments are clearly superior to others for certain disorders, so why not base one's treatment on subjective feelings and intuition about "what works" (Levant, 2004; Westen, Novotny, & Thompson-Brenner, 2004)? In response, proponents of this movement argue that the best scientific evidence available should inform clinical practice (Baker et al., 2009). Because current data suggest that at least some treatments are superior to others for some disorders, such as exposure therapy for anxiety disorders, they contend, practitioners have an ethical obligation to rely on ESTs unless there's a compelling reason not to (Chambless & Ollendick, 2001; Crits-Christoph, Wilson, & Hollon, 2005; Hunsley & DiGuilio, 2002). The authors of your text find the latter argument more compelling, because the burden of proof for selecting and administering a treatment should always fall on therapists. Therefore, if there's reasonable evidence that certain treatments are better than others for certain disorders, therapists should be guided by that evidence.

empirically supported treatment (EST)
intervention for specific disorders supported by high-quality scientific evidence

Answers are located at the end of the text.

Evaluating Claims PSYCHOTHERAPIES

There are over 500 different therapies on the market, yet only a small percentage of them are empirically supported. How can you identify which therapies might be helpful, which aren't, and which might even be harmful? Let's evaluate some of these claims, which are modeled after actual advertisements for therapies found online.

"Our breakthrough energy therapy is far superior to any short-term therapy available for anxiety."

What types of control groups would be especially important to include in research evaluating this claim?

"Our debriefing process allows those involved in the incident to process the event and vent their fears and anger associated with it."

What does scientific research tell us about crisis debriefing? Is the "venting" of fears and anger always a good thing?

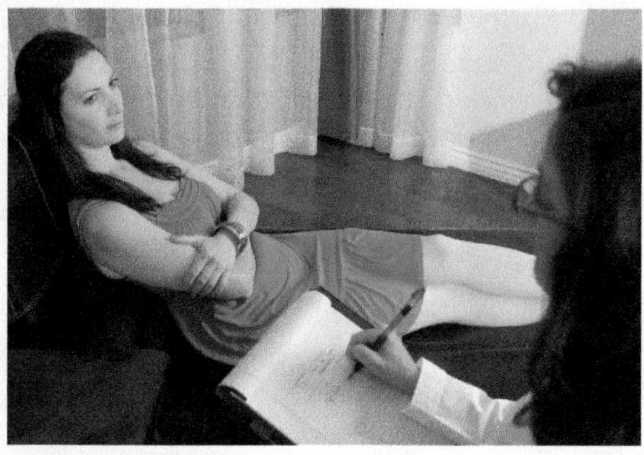

"Cognitive-behavioral therapy may not be effective in all cases, but studies have shown that CBT is equally as effective in the treatment of depression as anti-depressant medication."

This claim avoids exaggerating the benefits of cognitive-behavioral therapy (CBT) by noting that it may not be effective in all cases. The ad notes correctly that CBT is about as effective as antidepressant medication for clinical depression.

Psychomythology

Are Self-Help Books Always Helpful?

Each year Americans can choose from about 3,500 newly published self-help books that promise everything from achieving everlasting bliss and expanded consciousness to freedom from virtually every human failing and foible imaginable. Self-help books are only one piece of the massive quilt of the self-improvement industry that extends to Internet sites; magazines; radio and television shows; CDs; DVDs; lectures; workshops; advice columns; and, most recently, smartphone applications and computerized delivery of evidence-based treatments (Abroms et al., 2011; Craske et al., 2011).

It's no mystery why self-help books are so popular that Americans spend $650 million a year on them, and at least 80 percent of therapists recommend them to their clients (Arkowitz & Lilienfeld, 2007). Researchers have studied the effects of reading self-help books, known in psychology lingo as "bibliotherapy." The relatively small number of studies conducted on self-help books suggests that bibliotherapy and psychotherapy often lead to comparable improvements in depression, anxiety, and other problems (Gould & Clum, 1993).

Still, we should bear in mind three points. First, we can't generalize the limited findings to all of the books on the shelves of our local bookstore, because the overwhelming majority of self-help books are untested (Rosen et al., in press). Second, people who volunteer for research on self-help books may be more motivated to read the entire book and benefit from it compared with the curious person who purchases the book under more casual circumstances. Third, many self-help books address relatively minor problems, like everyday worries and public speaking. When researchers (Menchola, Arkowitz, & Burke, 2007) have examined more serious problems, like major depression and panic disorder, psychotherapy has fared better than bibliotherapy, although both do better than no treatment.

Some people don't respond at all to self-help books (Febbraro et al., 1999), and many self-help books promise far more than they can deliver. Readers who fall short of how the promotional information on the cover assures them they'll respond may feel like failures and be less likely to seek professional help or make changes on their own. Bearing this possibility in mind, Hal Arkowitz and Scott Lilienfeld (2007) offered the following recommendations about selecting self-help books.

- Use books that have research support and are based on valid psychological principles of change (Gambrill, 1992). Make sure the author refers to published research that supports the claims made. Books that have shown positive effects in studies include *Feeling Good* by David Burns, *Mind Over Mood* by Dennis Greenberger and Christine Padesky, and *Coping with Panic* by George Clum.
- Evaluate the author's credentials. Does he or she have the professional training and expertise to write on the topic at hand?
- Be wary of books that make far-fetched promises, such as curing a phobia in five minutes. The 2007 blockbuster best seller *The Secret* (Byrne, 2007), popularized by Oprah Winfrey, informs readers that positive thinking alone can cure cancer, help one become a millionaire, or achieve just about any goal one wants. Yet there's not a shred of research evidence that this kind of wishful thinking is helpful (Smythe, 2007).
- Beware of books that rely on a "one size fits all" approach. A book that tells us to always express anger to our relationship partner fails to take into account the complexity and specifics of the relationship.
- Serious problems like clinical depression, obsessive-compulsive disorder, and schizophrenia warrant professional help rather than self-help alone.

The "secret" to the 2007 best seller *The Secret* by Rhonda Byrne is the so-called *law of attraction*—good thoughts attract good things, and bad thoughts attract bad things. Yet there's no evidence that merely wishing for something good to happen without taking concrete steps to accomplish it is effective. We should be skeptical of self-help books that promise simple answers to complex problems.

Assess Your Knowledge
FACT OR FICTION?

1. Behavioral therapy is inferior to most other therapeutic approaches. **True / False**
2. Doing something about a psychological problem is always better than doing nothing. **True / False**
3. "Common factors" may help to explain why many different therapies are equally effective. **True / False**
4. Spontaneous remission of psychological problems is uncommon. **True / False**
5. Psychotherapists generally shy away from recommending self-help books. **True / False**

Answers: 1. F (p. 512); **2.** F (p. 512); **3.** T (p. 514); **4.** F (p. 514); **5.** F (p. 517)

BIOMEDICAL TREATMENTS: MEDICATIONS, ELECTRICAL STIMULATION, AND SURGERY

16.12 **Recognize different types of drugs and cautions associated with drug treatment.**

16.13 **Outline key considerations in drug treatment.**

16.14 **Identify misconceptions about biomedical treatments.**

Biomedical treatments—including medications, electrical stimulation techniques, and brain surgery—directly alter the brain's chemistry or physiology. Just as the number of psychotherapy approaches has more than tripled since the 1970s, antidepressant prescriptions have quadrupled from 1988–1994 through 2005–2008. Today, antidepressants are the most frequently prescribed medication for adults aged 18–44 years (Pratt et al., 2011). Many people are surprised to learn that about 10 percent of inpatients with major depression still receive electroconvulsive therapy (ECT)—informally called "shock therapy"—which delivers small electric shocks to people's brains to lift their mood (Olfson et al., 1998; Pagnin et al., 2008). By the 1950s, as many as 50,000 patients received psychosurgery, in which the frontal lobes or other brain regions were damaged or removed in an effort to control serious psychological disorders (Tooth & Newton, 1961; Valenstein, 1973). Today, surgeons rarely perform such operations, reflecting the controversies surrounding psychosurgery, and the fact that less risky and more effective treatments are available. As we consider the pros and cons of various biomedical treatments, we'll see that each approach has attracted ardent critics and defenders.

Psychopharmacotherapy: Targeting Brain Chemistry

We'll begin our tour of biomedical treatments with **psychopharmacotherapy**—the use of medications to treat psychological problems. For virtually every psychological disorder treated with psychotherapy, there's an available medication. In 1954, the widespread marketing of the drug Thorazine (chlorpromazine) ushered in the "pharmacological revolution" in the treatment of serious psychological disorders. For the first time, professionals could prescribe powerful medications to ease the symptoms of schizophrenia and related conditions. By 1970, it was unusual for any patient with schizophrenia not to be treated with Thorazine or other "major tranquilizers," as they came to be known.

Pharmaceutical companies soon sensed the promise of medicines to treat a broad spectrum of patients, and their efforts paid off handsomely. Researchers discovered that the emotional storms that torment people with bipolar disorder could be tamed with Lithium, Tegretol, and a new generation of mood stabilizer drugs. Medications are now available for people with more common conditions, ranging from anxiety about public speaking to the harsh realities of stressful circumstances. We can attribute the staggering number of prescriptions for depression largely to the phenomenal popularity of the selective serotonin reuptake inhibitor (SSRI) antidepressants, including Prozac, Zoloft, and Paxil, which boost levels of the neurotransmitter serotonin.

psychopharmacotherapy
use of medications to treat psychological problems

In **TABLE 16.8**, we present commonly used drugs and their presumed mechanisms of action to treat anxiety disorders (anxiolytics or *antianxiety drugs*), depression (*antidepressants*), bipolar disorders (*mood stabilizers*), psychotic conditions (neuroleptics/ *antipsychotics* or major tranquilizers, along with atypical (second generation) antispychotics, with often fewer yet variable side effects), and attention problems (*psychostimulants*, which stimulate the nervous system yet paradoxically treat symptoms of attention-deficit/hyperactivity disorder).

Table 16.8 Commonly Used Medications for Psychological Disorders, Mechanisms of Action, and Other Uses.

	Medication	Examples	Action	Other Uses
Antianxiety Medications	Benzodiazepines	Diazepam (Valium), alprazolam (Xanax), clonazepam (Klonopin), lorazepam (Ativan)	Increase efficiency of GABA binding to receptor sites	Use with antipsychotic medications, treat medication side effects, alcohol detox
	Buspirone (Buspar)		Stabilizes serotonin levels	Depressive and anxiety states; sometimes used with antipsychotics; aggression in people with brain injuries and dementia
	Beta blockers	Atenolol (Tenormin), propranolol (Inderal)	Compete with norepinephrine at receptor sites that control heart and muscle function; reduce rapid heartbeat, muscle tension	Control blood pressure, regulate heartbeat
Antidepressants	Monoamine oxidase (MAO) inhibitors	Isocarboxazid (Marplan), phenelzine (Nardil), tranylcypromine (Parnate)	Inhibit action of enzymes that metabolize norepinephrine and serotonin; inhibit dopamine	Panic and other anxiety disorders
	Cyclic (including tryclic) antidepressants	Amitriptyline (Elavil), imipramine (Tofranil), desipramine (Norpramine), nortriptyline (Pamelor)	Inhibit reuptake of norepinephrine and serotonin	Panic and other anxiety disorders, pain relief
	SSRIs (selective serotonin reuptake inhibitors)	Fluoxetine (Prozac), citalopram (Celexa), sertraline (Zoloft)	Selectively inhibit reuptake of serotonin	Eating disorders (especially bulimia), obsessive-compulsive disorder, social phobia
Mood Stabilizers	Mineral salts	Lithium carbonate (Lithium)	Decrease noradrenaline, increase serotonin	
	Anticonvulsant medications	Carbamazepine (Tegretol), lamotrigine (Lamictal), divalproex sodium (Depakote)	Increase levels of neurotransmitter GABA, inhibit norepinephrine reuptake (Tegretol)	Bipolar disorder
Antipsychotics	First generation antipsychotics	Chlorpromazine (Thorazine), haloperidol (Haldol)	Block postsynaptic dopamine receptors	Tourette syndrome (Haldol), bipolar disorder with the exception of Clozaril
	Serotonin-dopamine antagonists (atypical antipsychotics/ second generation antipsychotics)	Clozapine (Clozaril), risperidone (Risperdal), olanzapine (Zyprexa), ziprasidone (Geodon), quetiapine (Seroquel)	Block activity of serotonin and/or dopamine; also affect norepinephrine, acetylcholine	Schizophrenia, bipolar disorder, sometimes autism off-label
		aripiprazole (Abilify)	Moderates/stabilizes dopamine and serotonin receptors	Schizophrenia, bipolar disorder, clinical depression, and autism
Psychostimulants and Other Medications for Attentional Problems	Psychostimulants	Methylphenidate (Ritalin, Concerta), amphetamine (Adderall), dexmethylphenidate (Focalin) Lisdexamfetamine (Vyvanse)	Release or reuptake of norepinephrine, dopamine, serotonin in frontal regions of the brain, where attention and behavior are regulated	Narcolepsy (Ritalin), Investigated for treatment of major depressive disorder, binge eating disorder, cognitive impairment with schizophrenia, daytime sleepiness (Vyvanse)
	Non-stimulant medications	Atomoxetine (Strattera)	Selectively inhibit reuptake of norepinephrine	Some patients also report reduction in depression

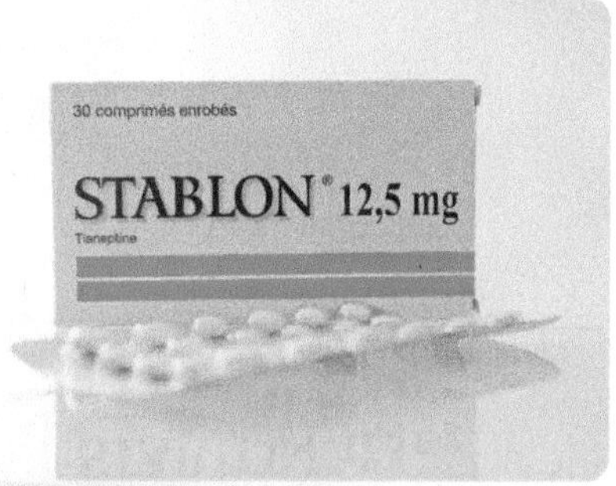

Most modern medications for depression, like fluoxetine (whose brand name is Prozac), appear to work by increasing the amount of serotonin in the brain. Yet this medication for depression, tianeptine (whose brand name is Stablon), appears to work by *decreasing* the amount of serotonin. The fact that medications can treat depression by either raising or lowering serotonin levels suggests that popular "chemical imbalance" theories of depression are oversimplified.

As we can see from the table, many of these medications ease the symptoms of multiple psychological conditions.

Nevertheless, we should bear in mind that we don't know for sure how most of these medications work. Although drug company advertisements, including those we've seen on television, often claim that medications—especially antidepressants—correct a "chemical imbalance" in the brain, this notion is almost surely oversimplified (Kirsch, 2010). For one thing, most medications probably work on multiple neurotransmitter systems. Moreover, there's no scientific evidence for an "optimal" level of serotonin or other neurotransmitters in the brain (Lacasse & Leo, 2005). Finally, many medications, including antidepressants, may exert their effects largely by affecting the sensitivity of neuron receptors rather than the levels of neurotransmitters.

Today, psychologists often refer patients to psychiatrists and other professionals who can prescribe medications and consult with prescribers to plan treatment. Until recently, only psychiatrists and a few other mental health professionals, like psychiatric nurse practitioners, could prescribe medications. But beginning in 1999, psychologists in the U.S. territory of Guam were granted legal permission to prescribe medications followed by two U.S. states (New Mexico in 2002 and Louisiana in 2004). Before being allowed to prescribe, these psychologists must complete a curriculum of course work on physiology, anatomy, and psychopharmacology (the study of medications that affect psychological functioning). Nevertheless, the growing movement to allow psychologists to prescribe medications has been controversial, in part because many critics charge that psychologists don't possess sufficient knowledge of the anatomy and physiology of the human body to adequately evaluate the intended effects and side effects of medications (Fox et al., 2009; Stuart & Heiby, 2007).

Cautions to Consider: Dosage and Side Effects

Psychopharmacotherapy isn't a cure-all. Virtually all medications have side effects that practitioners must weigh against the potential benefits. Most adverse reactions, including nausea, drowsiness, weakness, fatigue, and impaired sexual performance, are reversible when medications are discontinued or when their dosage is lowered. Nevertheless, this isn't the case with *tardive dyskinesia* (TD), a serious side effect of some older antipsychotic medications, those used to treat schizophrenia and other psychoses. The symptoms of TD include grotesque involuntary movements of the facial muscles and mouth and twitching of the neck, arms, and legs. Most often, the disorder begins after several years of high-dosage treatment (*tardive,* like *tardy,* means late-appearing), but it occasionally begins after only a few months of therapy at low dosages (Simpson & Kline, 1976). Newer antipsychotic medicines such as Risperdal, which treat the negative as well as positive symptoms of schizophrenia (see Chapter 15), generally produce fewer serious adverse effects. But they too occasionally produce serious side effects, including sudden cardiac deaths, and the verdict is out regarding whether they're more effective compared with earlier and less costly medications (Correll & Schenk, 2008; Lieberman et al., 2005; Schneeweiss & Avorn, 2009).

One Dose Doesn't "Fit All": Differences in Responses to Medication. People don't all respond equally to the same dose of medication. Weight, age, and even racial differences often affect drug response. African Americans tend to require lower doses of certain antianxiety and antidepressant drugs and have a faster response than do Caucasians, and Asians metabolize (break down) these medications more slowly than do Caucasians (Baker & Bell, 1999; Campinha-Bacote, 2002; Strickland et al., 1997). Because some people become physically and psychologically dependent on medications such as the widely prescribed antianxiety medications Valium and Xanax (known as benzodiazepines), physicians must proceed with caution and determine the lowest dose possible to achieve positive results and minimize unpleasant side effects (Wigal et al., 2006). Discontinuation of certain drugs, such as those for anxiety and depression, should be performed gradually to minimize withdrawal reactions, including anxiety and agitation (Lejoyeux & Ades, 1997).

Medications on Trial: Harmful and Overprescribed? Some psychologists have raised serious questions about the effectiveness of the SSRIs, especially among children and adolescents (Healy, 2004; Kendall, Pilling, & Whittington, 2005). There also are widely publicized indications that SSRIs increase the risk of suicidal thoughts in people younger than 18 years of age, although there's no clear evidence that they increase the risk of *completed* suicide (Goldstein & Ruscio, 2009). For this reason, the U.S. Food and Drug Administration (FDA) now requires drug manufacturers to include warnings on the labels of SSRIs of possible suicide risk. Following these "black box" warnings (so called because they're enclosed in a box with black borders on the medication label), antidepressant prescriptions dropped by nearly 20 percent (Nemeroff et al., 2007; Gibbons et al., 2010).

Parenting a child with attention-deficit/hyperactivity disorder (ADHD) can be challenging and often requires support from teachers and medical professionals.

Scientists don't understand why antidepressants increase suicidal thoughts in some children and adolescents. These drugs sometimes produce agitation, so they may make already depressed people even more distressed and possibly suicidal (Brambilla et al., 2005). Yet the risk of suicide attempts and completions among people prescribed SSRIs remains very low.

Another area of public concern is overprescription. Parents, teachers, and helping professionals have expressed particular alarm that psychostimulants for attention-deficit/hyperactivity disorder (ADHD), such as Ritalin (methylphenidate), are overprescribed and may substitute for teaching effective coping strategies for focusing attention (LeFever, Arcona, & Antonuccio, 2003; Safer, 2000). Since the early 1990s, the number of prescriptions for ADHD has increased fourfold. Although little is known about the long-term safety of Ritalin with children under 6, the number of prescriptions for children ages 2 (!) to 4 nearly tripled between 1991 and 1995 alone (Bentley & Walsh, 2006).

Critics of psychostimulants have pointed to their potential for abuse. Moreover, their adverse effects include decreased appetite, gastrointestinal pain, headache, insomnia, irritability, heart-related complications, and stunted growth (Aagaard & Hansen, 2011). A recent survey indicated that only a fifth of children with ADHD received stimulants for the disorder (Merikangas et al., 2013), suggesting that these medications aren't generally overprescribed. Nevertheless, stimulant overprescription clearly occurs in some cases (Smith & Farah, 2011). Children should be diagnosed with ADHD and placed on stimulants only after they've been evaluated with input from parents and teachers (see Chapter 15). The good news is that 70–80 percent of children with ADHD can be treated effectively with stimulants (Steele et al., 2006), which can sometimes be combined to good advantage with behavior therapy (Jensen et al., 2005). Moreover, more recently developed nonstimulant medications for ADHD, such as Strattera, hold promise for improving concentration and attention.

Polypharmacy—the practice of prescribing multiple medications at the same time—can increase the risk of infrequent yet serious side effects produced by interactions among drugs. The tragic death of actor Heath Ledger in 2008 highlights the possibility of overdose by taking multiple medications that aren't carefully monitored by medical professionals.

Fad treatments and diets are poor alternatives to medications and psychological treatments of ADHD. For example, there's no convincing scientific evidence that reducing the amount of sugar in the diet improves symptoms of ADHD. Other dietary changes, like eliminating artificial food colors or flavors, also have little or no impact on ADHD symptoms (Waschbusch & Hill, 2003).

A final area of concern is *polypharmacy:* prescribing many medications—sometimes five or more—at the same time. This practice can be hazardous if not carefully monitored, because certain medications may interfere with the effects of others or interact with them in dangerous ways. Polypharmacy is a particular problem among the elderly, who tend to be especially susceptible to drug side effects (Fulton & Allen, 2005).

Evaluating Psychopharmacotherapy

To medicate or not to medicate, that is the question. In many instances, psychotherapy, with no added medications, can successfully treat people with many disorders. CBT is at least as effective as antidepressants, even for severe depression, and perhaps more effective than antidepressants are in preventing relapse (DeRubeis, Brotman, & Gibbons, 2005; Hollon, Thase, & Markowitz, 2002). Psychotherapy alone is also effective for a variety of anxiety disorders, mild and moderate depression, bulimia, and insomnia (Otto, Smits, & Reese, 2005; Thase, 2000).

It's a logical error to infer a disorder's cause from its treatment, or vice versa. Headaches can be treated with aspirin, but that doesn't imply that headaches are due to a deficiency of aspirin in the body.

Scientists are finding that when patients benefit from psychotherapy, this change is reflected in the workings of their brain. In some cases, psychotherapy and medication produce similar brain changes, suggesting that different routes to improvement share similar mechanisms (Kumari, 2006) and reminding us that "mind" and "brain" describe the same phenomena at different levels of explanation. Yet although medication and psychotherapy may both normalize brain function, they may also do so in different ways. In a review of 63 studies investigating psychotherapy or pharmacotherapy effects in patients with anxiety and major depressive disorders, medications decreased activity in the limbic system, the seat of emotion and reaction to threat. In contrast, psychotherapy produced changes mostly in the frontal areas of the brain, perhaps reflecting its success at transforming maladaptive to adaptive thoughts (Quidé et al, 2012).

This research cautions us against a widespread logical error, namely, inferring a disorder's optimal treatment from its cause (Ross & Pam, 1995). Many people believe mistakenly that a condition that's largely biological in its causes, like schizophrenia, should be treated with medication and that a condition that's largely environmental in its causes, such as a specific phobia, should be treated with psychotherapy. Yet the research we've reviewed shows that this logic is erroneous, because psychological treatments affect our biology, just as biomedical treatments affect our psychology.

Critics of pharmacotherapy claim that medications are of little value in helping patients learn social skills, modify self-defeating behaviors, or cope with conflict. For example, when patients with anxiety disorders discontinue their medications, half or more may relapse (Marks et. al., 1993). Over the long haul, psychotherapy may be much less expensive than medications, so it often makes sense to try psychotherapy first (Arkowitz & Lilienfeld, 2007).

Still, there are often clear advantages of combining medication with psychotherapy (Thase, 2000). If people's symptoms interfere greatly with their functioning or if psychotherapy alone hasn't worked for a two-month period, adding medication is frequently justified. Generally, research suggests that combining medication with psychotherapy is warranted for schizophrenia, bipolar disorder, long-term major depression, and major depression with psychotic symptoms (Otto, Smits, & Reese, 2005; Thase, 2000). As of 2007, 61 percent of physicians prescribed medications to patients while the patients participated in psychotherapy, reflecting a national trend toward combining medical and psychological treatments (Olfson & Marcus, 2010).

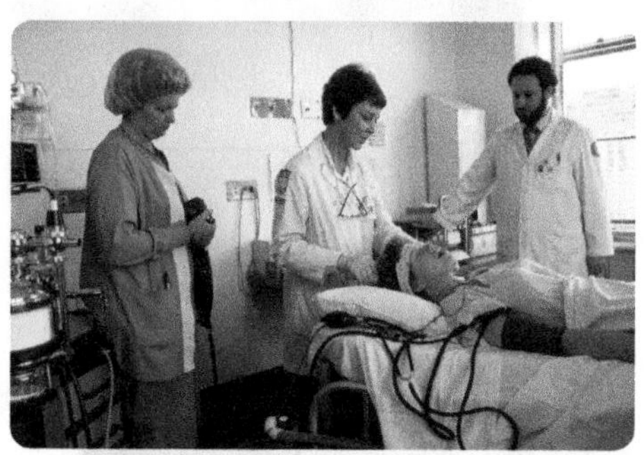

A team of professionals administer electroconvulsive therapy.

Electrical Stimulation: Conceptions and Misconceptions

Consider the following account of **electroconvulsive therapy (ECT)**, which we introduced at the outset of our discussion of biomedical treatments:

> They brought me into the ECT room with the electrodes dangling from the side of a gray machine. The friendly nurse placed them on me and then gave me an injection to "put me out," apparently so I wouldn't be conscious to feel the jolt of electricity. Then suddenly I was awake, but, no matter how hard I tried, I couldn't remember anything. There was a curtain cloaking my memories that I couldn't peer behind, no matter how hard I tried. What exactly happened? How long did it take? Did they do anything to me, after all? But the doctor seemed to be pleased, and the nurse was smiling, so I concluded, it must be over and done with.

Electroconvulsive Therapy: Fact And Fiction

What happened here? As in other cases of modern ECT, medical personnel injected a muscle relaxant and anesthetic and then administered brief electrical pulses to the patient's brain to relieve severe depression that hadn't responded to other treatments. This patient, like others receiving ECT, experienced a full-blown seizure lasting about a minute, much like that experienced by patients with epilepsy. Physicians typically recommend ECT for individuals with serious depression, bipolar disorder, schizophrenia, and severe catatonia and only then as a last resort when all other treatments have failed (see Chapter 15). A typical course of ECT is six to ten treatments, given three times a week.

electroconvulsive therapy (ECT)
treatment for serious psychological problems in which patients receive brief electrical pulses to the brain that produce a seizure

Misconceptions about ECT abound, including the erroneous beliefs that ECT is painful or dangerous and that it invariably produces long-term memory loss, personality changes, and even brain damage (Dowman, Patel, & Rajput, 2005; Malcom, 1989; Santa Maria, Baumeister, & Gouvier, 1999). Media characterizations of ECT, such as in the Academy Award–winning 1975 film *One Flew Over the Cuckoo's Nest,* promote the mistaken idea that ECT is little more than a brutal means of punishment or behavioral control with no redeeming value. Not surprisingly, most Americans hold negative attitudes about ECT (McDonald & Walter, 2004).

Nevertheless, the picture looks quite different when researchers study individuals who've undergone ECT (Chakrabarti, Grover, & Rajagopal, 2010). In one study of 24 patients, 91 percent reported being happy to have received ECT (Goodman et al., 1999). In another study, 98 percent of patients said they'd seek ECT again if their depression returned, and 62 percent said that the treatment was less frightening than a visit to the dentist (Pettinati et al., 1994). More important, researchers report improvement rates as high as 80–90 percent following ECT for severe depression (APA, 2001).

Although harsh public perceptions about ECT may be unwarranted, we should note a few cautions. About 50 percent of people with an initially positive response relapse within six months or so (Bourgon & Kellner, 2000), so ECT isn't a cure-all. In addition, people who experience ECT may be motivated to convince themselves that the treatment helped. Although many patients report feeling better after ECT, they don't always show parallel changes on objective measures of depression and mental functioning (Scovern & Kilmann, 1980). ECT may be helpful because it increases the levels of serotonin in the brain (Rasmussen, Sampson, & Rummans, 2002) and stimulates growth of brain cells in the hippocampus (Bolwig, 2009). A rival hypothesis is that ECT induces strong expectations of improvement and serves as an "electrical placebo." But studies showing that ECT works better than "sham" (fake) ECT render this explanation less likely (Carney et al., 2003).

ruling out rival hypotheses

HAVE IMPORTANT ALTERNATIVE EXPLANATIONS FOR THE FINDINGS BEEN EXCLUDED?

In prescribing ECT, the physician's challenge is to determine whether the therapeutic gains outweigh the potential adverse effects. As the case we read suggests, ECT can create short-term confusion and cloud memory. In most cases, memory loss is restricted to events that occur right before the treatment and generally subsides within a few weeks (Sackeim, 1986). However, memory and attention problems persist in some patients for six months after treatment (Sackeim et al., 2007). When psychiatrists use ECT, it's crucial that patients and their family members understand the procedure, as well as its potential benefits and risks.

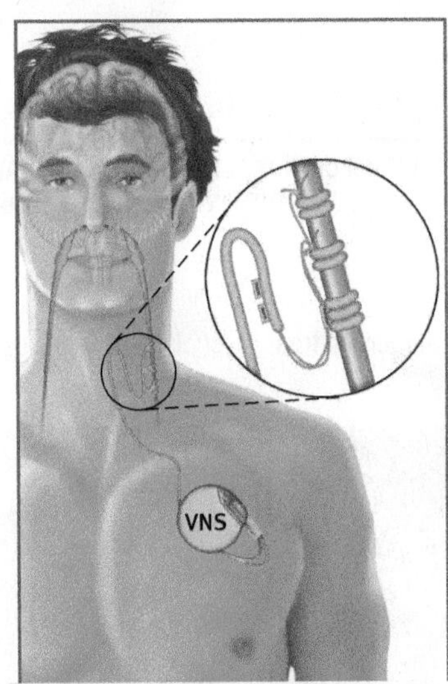

A small vagus nerve stimulator can be implanted under the breastbone in cases of serious treatment-resistant depression.

Vagus Nerve And Transcranial Stimulation

In a recent development, surgeons can implant a small electrical device under the skin near the breastbone to stimulate the vagus nerve to treat severe depression. The vagus nerve projects to many brain areas, and electrical pulses to this nerve may stimulate serotonin and increase brain blood flow (George et al., 2000). The FDA has approved this procedure, as well as repeated transcranial magnetic stimulation (TMS), for depression that hasn't responded to other treatments. Although recent research indicates that repeated TMS is slightly less effective compared with ECT in treating major depression, it produces fewer negative effects on cognition compared with ECT, implying that TMS should be considered as a treatment option (Hansen et al., 2011). Still, well-controlled, large-scale studies on these procedures are mostly lacking. Studies comparing these methods with devices that don't provide any stimulation suggest that improvement may be due to placebo effects (Herwig et al., 2007; Rush et al., 2005).

ruling out rival hypotheses

HAVE IMPORTANT ALTERNATIVE EXPLANATIONS FOR THE FINDINGS BEEN EXCLUDED?

Researchers have recently experimented with deep brain stimulation (DBS) of regions of the frontal cortex and other brain structures with treatment-resistant depressed patients, but it's too early to draw firm conclusions about this procedure's value (Mayberg et al., 2005). A recent study of DBS with treatment-resistant depressed patients followed after three to six years found that at the last follow-up visit, about two-thirds of patients improved, with no adverse events during the follow-up (Kennedy et al., 2011). However,

Before sophisticated surgical techniques were developed, surgeons used tools like these to perform early lobotomies.

two patients died by suicide when their depression relapsed. Clearly, the risks and benefits of each procedure we reviewed must be weighed carefully.

Psychosurgery: An Absolute Last Resort

One reason deep brain stimulation may be a tough sell for patients and physicians is that it conjures up disturbing memories of the dangers of psychosurgery (Johnson, 2009). **Psychosurgery**, or brain surgery to treat psychological disorders, is the most radical and controversial of all biomedical treatments. As is often the case with new treatments, psychosurgery was hailed as a promising innovation not long after it was introduced. Most of the early psychosurgical operations were prefrontal lobotomies. Psychosurgery remained popular until the mid-1950s, when the tide of enthusiasm receded in the face of reports of scores of "dehumanized zombies" and the availability of medicines as alternatives to surgery (Mashour, Walker, & Matura, 2005; Valenstein, 1973). To most critics, the benefits of psychosurgery rarely, if ever, outweighed the costs of impairing memory, diminishing emotion and creativity, and the risks of brain surgery (Neville, 1978).

Critics also noted that the motives for conducting psychosurgery weren't always benign (Valenstein, 1973). Social goals such as the control of behavior of violent sexual criminals, homosexual child abusers, and prison inmates who received lobotomies were occasionally confused with therapeutic goals (Mashour et al., 2005).

In the 1960s, surgeons ushered new forms of psychosurgery to the forefront. Surgeons replaced primitive procedures with ultrasound, electricity, freezing of tissues, and implants of radioactive materials. Automated surgical devices added precision to delicate brain surgery. With the advent of modern psychosurgical techniques, negative physical side effects became less frequent.

Today, surgeons sometimes perform psychosurgery as a last resort for patients with a handful of conditions, such as severe OCD, major depression, and bipolar disorder. There are few well-controlled long-term studies of psychosurgery and an absence of data about which patients respond best. Even when psychosurgery appears successful, we can generate alternative explanations, including placebo effects and self-serving biases, to account for apparent treatment gains (Dawes, 1994).

ruling out rival hypotheses

HAVE IMPORTANT ALTERNATIVE EXPLANATIONS FOR THE FINDINGS BEEN EXCLUDED?

Recognizing the need to protect patient interests, institutional review boards (IRBs; see Chapter 2) in hospitals where surgeons perform psychosurgery must approve each operation. IRBs help ensure that (1) there's a clear rationale for the operation, (2) the patient has received an appropriate preoperative and postoperative evaluation, (3) the patient has consented to the operation, and (4) the surgeon is competent to conduct the procedure (Mashour et al., 2005). Scientific research may one day lead to more effective forms of psychosurgery, but the scientific and ethical debates surrounding such surgery are likely to endure.

psychosurgery
brain surgery to treat psychological problems

Psychosurgery has a long history, as this photo of a 2,000-plus-year-old skull from Peru shows. As we can see, this skull contains a huge hole produced by a procedure called "trephining." Scientists believe that trephining may have been performed in an effort to heal mental disorders or to relieve brain diseases like epilepsy and tumors (Alt et al., 1997).

Assess Your Knowledge FACT OR FICTION?

1. The first major drug for psychological conditions was developed to treat bipolar disorder. **True / False**
2. One serious side effect of antipsychotic medications is tardive dyskinesia. **True / False**
3. People of different races and cultures respond similarly to the same dose of medication. **True / False**
4. Most people experience long-lasting brain damage after a course of ECT. **True / False**
5. Most early psychosurgery operations were prefrontal lobotomies. **True / False**

Answers: **1.** F (p. 518); **2.** T (p. 520); **3.** F (p. 520); **4.** F (p. 522); **5.** T (p. 524)

Your Complete Review System

PSYCHOTHERAPY: CLIENTS AND PRACTITIONERS 491–494

16.1 DESCRIBE WHO SEEKS TREATMENT, WHO BENEFITS FROM PSYCHOTHERAPY, AND WHO PRACTICES PSYCHOTHERAPY.

Therapists treat people of all ages and social, cultural, and ethnic backgrounds. Individuals with anxiety and those with minor and temporary problems are most likely to benefit from therapy. Socioeconomic status, gender, and ethnicity predict who will seek psychotherapy.

1. _________ can be defined as a psychological intervention designed to help people resolve emotional, behavioral, and interpersonal problems and improve the quality of their lives. (p. 491)
2. In general, (women/men) are more likely to seek psychotherapy. (p. 492)
3. Hispanic Americans are (less/more) likely than non–Hispanic Americans to seek mental health services. (p. 492)

4. People (can/can't) be helped by therapists who differ from them in significant ways. (p. 492)
5. Individuals who experience some anxiety or minor temporary problems are (not likely/likely) to benefit from therapy. (p. 492)
6. What was the ideal client like, according to a 1964 study of people in therapy? Has that view changed today? (p. 492)

16.2 DISTINGUISH BETWEEN PROFESSIONALS AND PARAPROFESSIONALS AND DESCRIBE WHAT IT TAKES TO BE AN EFFECTIVE THERAPIST.

Unlicensed paraprofessionals with no formal training, as well as licensed professionals, can be equally effective as trained therapists. Showing warmth, selecting important topics to discuss, not contradicting clients, and establishing a positive relationship are more important determinants of a therapist's effectiveness than is being formally trained or being licensed.

7. A person with no professional training who provides mental health services is called a(n) _________. (p. 492)
8. In most states, the term *therapist* (is/isn't) legally protected. (p. 492)
9. How ethical was the client–therapist relationship in the television drama *In Treatment*? (p. 493)
10. A therapist who talks a lot about his/her personal life is likely to be (effective/ineffective). (p. 493)

INSIGHT THERAPIES: ACQUIRING UNDERSTANDING 495–500

16.3 DESCRIBE THE CORE BELIEFS AND CRITICISMS OF PSYCHODYNAMIC THERAPIES.

The core beliefs of psychodynamic therapies are the importance of (a) analyzing unconscious conflicts, wishes, fantasies, impulses, and life patterns; (b) childhood experiences, including traumatic and adverse life events; (c) the therapeutic relationship; and (d) acquiring insight. Evidence for psychodynamic therapies is based largely on small and highly select patient samples, anecdotal studies, and the questionable curative value of insight, although controlled studies suggest that these therapies may be helpful in some cases.

11. In the technique of _________ _________, clients are allowed to express themselves without censorship of any sort. (p. 495)
12. Neo-Freudians placed (more/less) emphasis on the unconscious than did Freudians. (p. 496)
13. Acccording to Jung, _________ is the integration of opposing aspects of the patient's personality into a harmonious "whole," namely, the self. (p. 497)
14. Critics of psychodynamic therapies assert that understanding our emotional history (is/isn't) required to relieve psychological distress. (p. 498)
15. Psychodynamic therapy (is/isn't) especially effective for psychotic disorders like schizophrenia. (p. 498)

16.4 DESCRIBE AND EVALUATE THE EFFECTIVENESS OF HUMANISTIC THERAPIES.

Humanistic therapies hold that self-actualization is a universal human drive and adopt an experience-based approach in which clients work to fulfill their potential. Research suggests that genuineness, unconditional positive regard, and empathic understanding are related to improvement but not necessary and sufficient conditions for effective psychotherapy.

16. In Rogers's _________ therapy, the therapist uses reflection to communicate empathy to the client. (p. 498)
17. Rogers believed that therapists must express ____ _____ ____, a nonjudgmental acceptance of all feelings, thoughts, and behaviors the client expresses. (p. 498)

(Continued)

18. Explain the two-chair technique used by Gestalt therapists. (p. 499)

19. Research indicates that the therapeutic _______ is often a stronger predictor of success in therapy than the use of specific techniques. (p. 500)
20. Although person-centered therapy is more effective than no treatment, some studies suggest that it may not help much more than a(n) ______ treatment. (p. 500)

GROUP THERAPIES: THE MORE THE MERRIER 500–503

16.5 LIST THE ADVANTAGES OF GROUP METHODS.

Group methods span all schools of psychotherapy and are efficient, time-saving, and less costly than individual methods. Participants learn from others' experiences, benefit from feedback and modeling others, and discover that problems and suffering are widespread.

21. Group therapies are (less helpful than/as helpful as) individual treatments. (p. 500)
22. It is (rare/common) for self-help groups to form on the Internet. (p. 501)

16.6 DESCRIBE THE RESEARCH EVIDENCE CONCERNING THE EFFECTIVENESS OF ALCOHOLICS ANONYMOUS.

AA is helpful for some clients, but it appears to be no more effective than other treatments, including CBT. Research suggests that controlled drinking approaches can be effective with some people with alcoholism.

23. AA's famous "Twelve Steps" is based on the assumption that alcoholism is a ______ that requires members never to drink another drop after entering treatment. (p. 501)
24. People who attend AA meetings or receive treatment based on the Twelve Steps typically fare (better than/no better than) people who receive other treatments. (p. 501)
25. A key factor in who improves in AA is the ability to participate in a(n) ____ ______ ___. (p. 501)
26. The relapse prevention approach teaches people to not feel ashamed or discouraged when they lapse, in an effort to avoid the __________ __________ effect. (p. 502)

16.7 IDENTIFY DIFFERENT APPROACHES TO TREATING THE DYSFUNCTIONAL FAMILY SYSTEM.

Family therapies treat problems in the family system. Strategic family therapists remove barriers to effective communication, whereas structural family therapists plan changes in the way family interactions are structured.

27. Family therapists focus on __________ among family members rather than on the person with the most obvious problems. (p. 502)

28. __________ __________ __________ are designed to remove barriers to effective communication. (p. 502)
29. In __________ family therapy, the therapist is actively involved in the everyday activities of the family to change the structure of their interactions. (p. 502)
30. Research suggests that family therapy is (more effective than/about the same as) no treatment. (p. 502)

BEHAVIORAL AND COGNITIVE-BEHAVIORAL APPROACHES: CHANGING MALADAPTIVE ACTIONS AND THOUGHTS 503–511

16.8 DESCRIBE THE CHARACTERISTICS OF BEHAVIOR THERAPY AND IDENTIFY DIFFERENT BEHAVIORAL APPROACHES.

Behavior therapy is grounded in the scientific method and based on learning principles. Exposure therapies confront people with their fears. Exposure can be gradual and stepwise or start with the most frightening scenes imaginable. Modeling techniques, based on observational learning principles, include behavioral rehearsal and role-playing to foster assertiveness. Token economies and aversion therapies are based on operant conditioning and classical conditioning principles, respectively.

31. A class of procedures that confronts patients with what they fear with the goal of reducing this fear is called __________ __________. (p. 504)
32. During __________ __________, clients are taught to relax as they are gradually exposed to what they fear in a stepwise manner. (p. 504)
33. What is in vivo exposure therapy? How can it help people with a fear of flying? (p. 505)
34. During __________, for prolonged periods, patients are exposed right away to images of stimuli they fear the most. (p. 505)
35. A crucial component of flooding is __________ __________, in which the therapist blocks clients from performing their typical avoidance behaviors. (p. 505)

36. What is EMDR therapy? What role do eye movements play in treatment outcome? (p. 506)

37. During _________ _________, the therapist first models a problematic situation and then guides the client through steps to cope with it. (p. 507)

38. In _________ _________ programs, desirable behaviors are rewarded through the consistent application of operant conditioning principles. (p. 507)

16.9 DESCRIBE THE FEATURES OF COGNITIVE-BEHAVIORAL THERAPIES (CBT) AND THIRD WAVE THERAPIES.

Cognitive-behavioral therapists modify irrational and negative beliefs and distorted thoughts that contribute to unhealthy feelings and behaviors. Ellis's rational emotive behavior therapy, Beck's cognitive therapy, and Meichenbaum's stress inoculation training are influential variations of CBT. So-called third wave CBT approaches include mindfulness and acceptance-based psychotherapies.

39. Ellis's rational emotive-behavior therapy (REBT) emphasizes that our _________ systems play a key role in how we function psychologically. (p. 508)

40. In Meichenbaum's (1985) _________ _________ _________, therapists teach clients to prepare for and cope with future stressful life events. (p. 509)

IS PSYCHOTHERAPY EFFECTIVE? 512–518

16.10 EVALUATE THE CLAIM THAT ALL PSYCHOTHERAPIES ARE EQUALLY EFFECTIVE.

Many therapies are effective. Nevertheless, some therapies, including behavioral and cognitive-behavioral treatments, are more effective than other treatments for specific problems such as anxiety disorders. Still other treatments, like crisis debriefing, appear to be harmful in some cases.

41. The Dodo bird verdict suggests that all types of psychotherapies are equally _________. (p. 512)

42. Among researchers, there is (strong consensus/no consensus) that the Dodo bird verdict is correct. (p. 512)

43. Research shows that behavioral and cognitive behavioral therapies are (more/less) effective than other treatments for children and adolescents with behavioral problems. (p. 512)

44. Most studies show that (20 percent/80 percent) of people who receive psychotherapy do better than the average person who does not receive psychotherapy. (p. 512)

45. What does the research suggest about the effectiveness of Scared Straight programs? (p. 513)

46. What kind of effect can positive life events, like major job promotions, have on psychological problems? (p. 514)

16.11 EXPLAIN HOW INEFFECTIVE THERAPIES CAN SOMETIMES APPEAR TO BE EFFECTIVE.

Ineffective therapies can appear to be helpful because of spontaneous remission, the placebo effect, self-serving biases, regression to the mean, and retrospective rewriting of the past.

47. Even when they don't improve, clients who have invested time, money, and emotional effort in psychotherapy may convince themselves they've been helped, a psychological phenomenon known as the _________ _________. (p. 515)

48. According to the regression to the mean phenomenon, if a client comes into treatment extremely depressed, the chances are (high/low) that he or she will be less depressed in a few weeks. (p. 515)

49. _________ _________ _________ are treatments for specific disorders that are supported by high-quality scientific evidence. (p. 516)

50. Americans spend $650 million a year on _________ _________ that promise self-improvement. (p. 517)

BIOMEDICAL TREATMENTS: MEDICATIONS, ELECTRICAL STIMULATION, AND SURGERY 518–524

16.12 RECOGNIZE DIFFERENT TYPES OF DRUGS AND CAUTIONS ASSOCIATED WITH DRUG TREATMENT.

Medications are available to treat psychotic conditions (neuroleptics/antispsychotics or major tranquilizers), bipolar disorder (mood stabilizers), depression (antidepressants), anxiety (anxiolytics), and attentional problems (psychostimulants).

51. The use of medications to treat psychological problems is called _________. (p. 518)

52. The first major drug for a psychological disorder, Thorazine, was used to treat _________. (p. 518)

53. Prozac and Zoloft are among the best-known _________ _________ _________ inhibitors. (p. 518)

54. There (is/is not) scientific evidence for an "optimal level" of serotonin or other neurotransmitters in the brain. (p. 520)

16.13 OUTLINE KEY CONSIDERATIONS IN DRUG TREATMENT.

People who prescribe drugs must be aware of side effects, must not overprescribe medications, and must carefully monitor the effects of multiple medications (polypharmacy).

55. People of different races and cultures (do/do not) respond equally to the same dose of medication. (p. 520)

56. The safety and effectiveness of SSRIs when prescribed to _________ and _________ have been called into question because of increased risk of suicidal thoughts. (p. 521)

57. The drug Ritalin, used to treat ADHD, is an example of a medication that many believe has been _________ and may substitute for effective coping strategies for focusing attention. (p. 521)

(Continued)

16.14 IDENTIFY MISCONCEPTIONS ABOUT BIOMEDICAL TREATMENTS.

Contrary to popular belief, electroconvulsive therapy (ECT) is not painful or dangerous and doesn't invariably produce memory loss, personality changes, or brain damage. Psychosurgery may be useful as a treatment of absolute last resort.

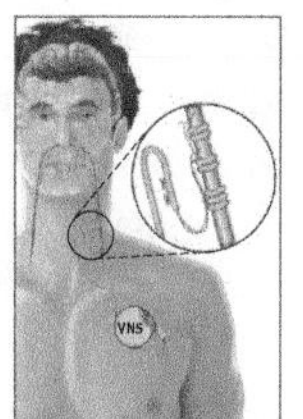

58. During __________ __________, patients receive brief electrical pulses to the brain that produce a seizure to treat serious psychological problems. (p. 522)
59. How does electrical stimulation to the vagus nerve work? Has research shown it to be an effective treatment? (p. 523)
60. Define psychosurgery and explain its potential side effects. (p. 524)

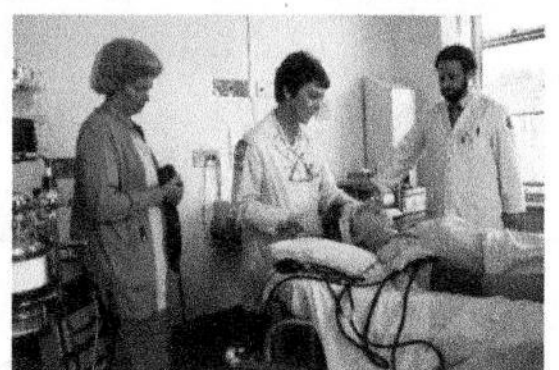

Apply Your Scientific Thinking Skills

Use your scientific thinking skills to answer the following questions, referencing specific scientific thinking principles and common errors in reasoning whenever possible.

1. There's been a lot of media coverage recently on the overprescription of drugs, particularly to younger children with ADHD. Read articles on both sides of this issue and summarize their arguments. What scientific evidence does each side offer? Has each interpreted the research correctly? Explain.
2. Browse through some of the self-help books at your local bookstore or online and select three or four of them (ideally, select books on a wide variety of issues). What scientific research does each book use to support its claims? Do any of the books make extraordinary claims or rely on a "one size fits all" approach to psychological problems? What professional training or expertise, if any, do the authors have?
3. Research one of the potentially harmful therapies in Table 16.7. To what do the proponents of this therapy attribute their success? What, if any, alternative hypotheses have they considered? Do they discuss any of the potentially negative effects of the therapy on their websites or in articles?

Further Your Understanding

EXTEND YOUR KNOWLEDGE WITH THE MYPSYCHLAB VIDEO SERIES

Watch these videos in MyPsychLab. Follow the "Video Series" link.

The Basics: Therapies in Action Learn about the history and application of psychoanalytic, humanistic, behavior, and cognitive behavioral approaches to therapy.

Thinking Like a Psychologist: Assessing Treatment Effectiveness Find out about the incredible advancements in psychological and drug therapies since the Middle Ages, particularly over the last 40 years.

In the Real World: Cognitive Behavioral Therapy Learn how cognitive behavioral therapy works and how it is used to treat patients with anxiety disorders.

What's In It for Me?: Finding a Therapist If You Need One Find out how students can get in touch with a good therapist for very little cost and the four criteria that psychologists consider when deciding whether a person needs professional help.

EXPERIENCE PSYCHOLOGICAL RESEARCH WITH MYPSYCHLAB SIMULATIONS

Access these simulations in MyPsychLab. Follow the "Simulations" link.

How Do You Take Care of Your Mental Health? Participate in a survey to discover how you and others manage personal mental health.

APPLY YOUR CRITICAL THINKING SKILLS WITH MYPSYCHLAB WRITING ASSESSMENTS

Complete these writing assignments in MyPsychLab.

Compare and contrast the following forms of psychotherapy: cognitive, humanistic, and behavioral. Identify the focus of each approach as well as areas in which they are the same and in which they are different.

References

AbdelMalik, P., Husted, J., Chow, E. W., & Bassett, A. S. (2003). Childhood head injury and expression of schizophrenia and multiply affected families. *Archives of General Psychiatry, 60,* 231–236.

Aboraya, A., El-Missiry, A., Barlowe, J., John, C., Ebrahimian, A., Muvvala, S., . . . & Price, E. (2014). The reliability of the Standard for Clinicians' Interview in Psychiatry (SCIP): A clinician-administered tool with categorical, dimensional and numeric output. *Schizophrenia Research, 156*(2–3), 174–183. doi:10.1016/j.schres.2014.04.025

Abrams, David B., & Wilson, G. Terence (1983). Alcohol, sexual arousal, and self-control. *Journal of Personality and Social Psychology, 45,* 188–198.

Acharya, N., & Joshi, S. (2011). Achievement motivation and parental support to adolescents. *Journal of the Indian Academy of Applied Psychology, 37,* 132–139.

Achter, J. A., Lubinski, D., & Benbow, C. P. (1996). Multipotentiality among the intellectually gifted: "It was never there and already it's vanishing." *Journal of Counseling Psychology, 43,* 65–76.

Adam, T. C., & Epel, E. S. (2007). Stress, eating, and the reward system. *Physiology and Behavior, 91*(4), 449–458.

Addis, Donna R.; Wong, Alana T; & Schacter, Daniel L. (2007). Remembering the past and imagining the future: Common and distinct neural substrates during event construction and elaboration. *Neuropsychologia, 45,* 1363–1377.

Addis, M. E., & Mahalik, J. R. (2003). Men, masculinity, and the contexts of help seeking. *American Psychologist, 58,* 5–14.

Addis, M. E., Hatgis, C., Krasnow, A. D., Jacob, K., Bourne, L., & Mansfield, A. (2004). Effectiveness of cognitive-behavioral treatment for panic disorder versus treatment as usual in a managed care setting. *Journal of Consulting and Clinical Psychology, 72,* 625–635.

Adler, A. (1938). *Social interest: A challenge of mankind.* London, England: Faber & Faber.

Adolphs, R. (2006). Perception and emotion. How we recognize facial expressions. *Current Directions in Psychological Science, 15,* 222–226.

Adolphs, R. (2008). Fear, faces, and the human amygdala. *Current Opinion in Neurobiology, 18,* 166–172.

Adolphs, R., & Tranel, D. (2003). Amygdala damage impairs emotion recognition from scenes only when they contain facial expressions. *Neuropsychologia, 41,* 1281–1289.

Adolphs, R., Baron-Cohen, S., & Tranel, D. (2002). Impaired recognition of social emotions following amygdala damage. *Journal of Cognitive Neuroscience, 14,* 1264–1274.

Adolphs, R., Tranel, D., Damasio, H., & Damasio, A. (1994). Impaired recognition of emotion in facial expressions following bilateral damage to the human amygdala. *Nature, 372,* 669–672.

Adolphus, K., Lawton, C., & Dye, L. (2013). The effects of breakfast on behavior and academic performance in children and adolescents. *Frontiers in Human Neuroscience, 7*(425). doi:10.3389/fnhum.2013.00425

Aggarwal, Sunil K.; Carter Gregory T.; Sullivan Mark D.; et al. (2009). Medicinal use of cannabis in the United States: Historical perspectives, current trends, and future directions. *Journal of Opioid Management, 5,* 153–168.

Ahn, H., & Wampold, B. E. (2001). Where oh where are the specific ingredients? A meta-analysis of component studies in counseling and psychotherapy. *Journal of Counseling Psychology, 48,* 251–257.

Alberti, R. E., & Emmons, M. L. (2001). *Your perfect right: Assertiveness and equality in your life and relationships* (8th ed.). New York, NY: Impact.

Alcock, James E. (2011, March/April). Back from the future: Parapsychology and the Bem affair. *Skeptical Inquirer,* 31–39.

Aleman, A., Kahn, R. S., & Selten, J. P. (2003). Sex differences in the risk of schizophrenia. *Archives of General Psychiatry, 60,* 565–571.

Allen, J. B., & Movius, H. I. (2000). The objective assessment of amnesia in dissociative identity disorder using event-related potentials. *International Journal Of Psychophysiology, 38*(1), 21–41. doi:10.1016/S0167-8760(00)00128-8

Alt, K. W., Jeunesse, C., Buitrago-Téllez, C. H., Wächter, R., Boes, E., & Pichler, S. L. (1997). Evidence for Stone Age cranial surgery. *Nature, 387,* 360.

Amar, Mohamed B. (2006). Cannabinoids in medicine: A review of their therapeutic potential. *Journal of Ethnopharmacology, 105,* 1–25.

American Heart Association. (2009). *Overweight in children.* Retrieved from http://www.americanheart.org/presenter.jhtml?identifier=4670

American Psychiatric Association (APA). (2013). *Diagnostic and statistical manual of mental disorders (5th ed.), (DSM-5).* Arlington, VA: Author.

American Psychiatric Association. (2000). *Diagnostic and statistical manual of mental disorders* (4th ed., text revision). Washington, DC: Author.

Amir, N., Coles, M. E., Brigidi, B., & Foa, E. B. (2001). The effect of practice on recall of emotional information in individuals with generalized social phobia. *Journal of Abnormal Psychology, 110,* 76–78.

An, K., Kobayashi, S., Tanaka, K., Kaneda, H., Su-gibayashi, M., & Okazaki, J. (1998). Dissociative identity disorder and childhood trauma in Japan. *Psychiatry and Clinical Neurosciences, 52,* 111–114.

Anderson, C. A., Shibuya, A., Ihori, N., Swing, E. L., Bushman, B. J., Sakamoto, A., . . . Saleem, M. (2010). Violent video game effects on aggression, empathy, and prosocial behavior in Eastern and Western countries: A meta-analytic review. *Psychological Bulletin, 136,* 151–173.

Anderson, C. M., & Stewart, S. (1983). *Mastering resistance.* New York, NY: Guilford Press.

Anderson, John R. (1990). *The adaptive nature of thought.* Hillsdale, NJ: Erlbaum.

Anderson, M. C., & Green, C. (2001). Suppressing unwanted memories by executive control. *Nature, 410,* 366–369.

Andreano, Joseph M., & Cahill, Larry (2006). Glucocorticoid release and memory consolidation in men and women. *Psychological Science, 17,* 466–470.

Andreasen, N. C., Arndt, S., Alliger, R., Miller, D., & Flaum, M. (1995). Symptoms of schizophrenia: Methods, meaning, and mechanisms. *Archives of General Psychiatry, 52,* 341–351.

Ang, R. P., & Woo, A. (2003). Influence of sensation seeking on boys' psychosocial adjustment. *North American Journal of Psychology, 5,* 121–136.

Ano, G. G., & Vasconcelles, E. B. (2005). Religious coping and psychological adjustment to stress: A meta-analysis. *Journal of Clinical Psychology, 61,* 461–480.

Antoni, M. H. (2013). Psychosocial intervention effects on adaptation, disease course and biobehavioral processes in cancer. *Brain, Behavior, and Immunity, 30*(suppl.), S88-S98. doi:10.1016/j.bbi.2012.05.009

Antoni, M., Schneiderman, N., & Penedo, F. (2007). Behavioral interventions and psychoneuroimmunology. In R. Ader, R. Glaser, N. Cohen, & M. Irwin (Eds.), *Psychoneuroimmunology* (4th ed., pp. 615–703). New York: Academic Press.

Antony, M. A., & Barlow, D. H. (2002). Specific phobia. In D. H. Barlow (Ed.), *Anxiety and its disorders: The nature and treatment of anxiety and panic* (2nd ed., pp. 380–417). New York, NY: Guilford Press.

Antony, M. A., & Roemer, L. (2003). Behavior therapy. In A. S. Gurman & S. B. Messer (Eds.), *Essential psychotherapies: Theory and practice* (2nd ed., pp. 182–223). New York, NY: Guilford Press.

Antrobus, John (1991). Dreaming: Cognitive processes during cortical activation and high afferent thresholds. *Psychological Review, 98,* 96–121.

Antrobus, John (2000). How does the dreaming brain explain the dreaming mind? *Behavioral and Brain Sciences, 23,* 904–907.

Aponte, H., & Hoffman, L. (1973). The open door: A structural approach to a family with an anorectic child. *Family Process, 12,* 1–44.

Appelle, S., Lynn, S. J., & Newman, L. (2000). The alien abduction experience: Theoretical and empirical issues. In E. Cardeña, S. J. Lynn, & S. Krippner (Eds.), *The varieties of anomalous experience: Examining the scientific evidence* (pp. 253–283). Washington, DC: American Psychological Association.

Aries, E. (2006). Sex differences in interaction: A reexamination. In K. Dindia & D. J. Canary (Eds.), *Sex differences and similarities in communication* (2nd ed., pp. 21–36). Mahwah, NJ: Erlbaum.

Arkes, H. R. (2013). The consequences of the hindsight bias in medical decision making. *Current Directions in Psychological Science, 22,* 356–360. doi:10.1177/0963721413489988

Arkowitz, H., & Lilienfeld, S. O. (2006). Psychotherapy on trial. *Scientific American Mind, 3,* 42–49.

Arkowitz, H., & Lilienfeld, S. O. (2007). A pill to fix your ills? *Scientific American Mind, 18,* 80–81.

Arsenio, W. F. (2004). The stability of young children's physical aggression: Relations with child care, gender, and aggression subtypes. *Monographs of the Society for Research in Child Development, 69,* 130–143.

Aserinsky, Eugene, & Kleitman, Nathaniel (1955). Two types of ocular motility occurring in sleep. *Journal of Applied Physiology, 8,* 1–10.

Ashkenazi, S., Rosenberg-Lee, M., Tenison, C., & Menon, V. (2012). Weak task-related modulation and stimulus representations during arithmetic problem solving in children with developmental dyscalculia. *Developmental Cognitive Neuroscience, 2,* S152–S166.

Atkinson, Richard C., & Shiffrin, Richard M. (1968). Human memory: A proposed system and its control processes. In K. W. Spence & J. T. Spence (Eds.), *The psychology of learning and motivation: Vol. 2. Advances in research and theory.* New York: Academic Press.

Atkinson, Richard C., & Shiffrin, Richard M. (1971, August). The control of short-term memory. *Scientific American, 225*(2), 82–90.

AuBuchon, Peter G., & Calhoun, Karen S. (1985). Menstrual cycle symptomatology: The role of social expectancy and experimental demand characteristics. *Psychosomatic Medicine, 47,* 35–45.

Axsom, D., & Cooper, J. (1985). Cognitive dissonance and psychotherapy: The role of effort justification in inducing weight loss. *Journal of Experimental Social Psychology, 21,* 149–160.

Bachoo, S., Bhagwanjee, A., & Govender, K. (2013). The influence of anger, impulsivity, sensation seeking and driver attitudes on risky driving behaviour among post-graduate university students in Durban, South Africa. *Accident Analysis and Prevention, 55,* 67–76. doi:10.1016/j.aap.2013.02.021

Bachrach, H., Galatzer-Levy, R., Skolnikoff, A., & Waldron, S. (1991). On the efficacy of psychoanalysis. *Journal of the American Psychoanalytic Association, 39,* 871–916.

Badcock, C. (1991). *Evolution and individual behavior: An introduction to human sociobiology.* Cambridge, MA: Blackwell.

Baddeley, Alan D. (1992). Working memory. *Science, 255,* 556–559.

Baddeley, Alan D. (2007). *Working memory, thought, and action.* New York: Oxford.

Baddeley, R., & Attewell, D. (2009). The relationship between language and the environment: Information theory shows why we have only three lightness terms. *Psychological Science, 20,* 1100–1107.

Baer, J. (2008). Commentary: Divergent thinking tests have problems, but this is not the solution. *Psychology of Aesthetics, Creativity, and the Arts, 2,* 89–92.

Bagemihl, B. (2000). *Biological exuberance: Animal homosexuality and natural diversity.* New York, NY: St. Martin's Press.

Bahcall, O. (2005). Copy number and HIV/AIDS. *Nature Genetics, 37,* 124.

Bahrick, H. P., Bahrick, P. O., & Wittlinger, R. P. (1975). Fifty years of memory for names and faces: A cross-sectional approach. *Journal of Experimental Psychology: General, 104,* 54–75.

Bahrick, Harry P. (1984). Semantic memory content in permastore: Fifty years of memory for Spanish learned in school. *Journal of Experimental Psychology: General, 113,* 1–29.

Bahrick, Harry P.; Bahrick, Phyllis O.; & Wittlinger, Roy P. (1975). Fifty years of memory for names and faces: A cross-sectional approach. *Journal of Experimental Psychology: General, 104,* 54–75.

Baird, B., Smallwood, J., Mrazek, M. D., Kam, J. W. Y., Franklin, M. S., & Schooler, J. W. (2012). Inspired by distraction: Mind wandering facilitates creative incubation. *Psychological Science, 23,* 1117–1122. doi:10.1177/0956797612446024

Baker, F. M., & Bell, C. C. (1999). Issues in the psychiatric treatment of African Americans. *Psychiatry Services, 50,* 362–368.

Baker, T. B., McFall, R. M., & Shoham, V. (2009). Current status and future prospects of clinical psychology toward a scientifically principled approach to mental and behavioral health care. *Perspectives on Psychological Science, 9,* 67–103.

Balfour, M. E. (2004). Sexual behavior causes activation and functional alterations of mesolimbic systems: Neurobiology of motivation and reward. *Dissertation Abstracts International: Section B: The Sciences and Engineering, 64,* 4789.

Balter. M. (2007). Neuroanatomy: Brain evolution studies go micro. *Science, 315,* 1208–1211.

Banaji, M. R., & Hardin, C. D. (1996). Automatic stereotyping. *Psychological Science, 7,* 136–141.

Bandura, A. (1971). *Psychological modeling.* Chicago, IL: Aldine-Atherton.

Bandura, A. (1977). Self-efficacy: Toward a unifying theory of behavioral change. *Psychological Review, 84,* 191–215.

Barash, D. (1982). *Sociobiology and behavior.* London: Hodder and Stoughton.

Bard, K. A., Todd, B. K., Bernier, C., Love, J., & Leavens, D. A. (2006). Self-awareness in human and chimpanzee infants: What is measured and what is meant by the mark and mirror test? *Infancy, 9,* 191–219.

Barlassina, C. D., & Taglietti, M. V. (2003). Genetics of human arterial hypertension. *Journal of Nephrology, 16,* 609–615.

Barlow, D. H. (2010). Negative effects from psychological treatment: A perspective. *American Psychologist, 65,* 13–20.

Barnett, W. S. (1998). Long-term effects on cognitive development and school success. In W. S. Barnett & S. S. Boocock (Eds.), *Early care and education for children in poverty: Promises, programs, and long-term results* (pp. 11–44). Albany: State University of New York Press.

Barrault, S., & Varescon, I. (2013). Impulsive sensation seeking and gambling practice among a sample of online poker players: Comparison between non pathological, problem and pathological gamblers. *Personality and Individual Differences, 55,* 502–507. doi:10.1016/j.paid.2013.04.022

Barron, F. (1963). *Creativity and psychological health.* Princeton, NJ: Van Nostrand.

Barsky, S. H.; Roth, M. D.; Kleerup, E. C.; Simmons, M.; & Tashkin, D. P. (1998). Histopathologic and molecular alterations in bronchial epithelium in habitual smokers of marijuana, cocaine, and/or tobacco. *Journal of the National Cancer Institute, 90,* 1198–1205.

Bartlett, Frederic C. (1932). *Remembering.* Cambridge, England: Cambridge University Press.

Bassetti, C.; Vella, S.; Donati, F.; et al. (2000). SPECT during sleepwalking. *Lancet, 356,* 484–485.

Basson, Rosemary; McInnis, Rosemary; Smith, Mike D.; et al. (2002). Efficacy and safety of sidenafil citrate in women with sexual dysfunction associated with female sexual arousal disorder. *Journal of Women's Health and Gender-Based Medicine, 11,* 367–377.

Bates, T. C., Lewis, G. J., & Weiss, A. (2013). Childhood socioeconomic status amplifies genetic effects on adult intelligence. *Psychological Science, 24,* 2111–2116. Doi:10.1177/ 0956797613488394

Battaglia, Francesco P.; Benchenane, Karim; Sirota, Anton; et al. (2011). The hippocampus: hub of brain network communication for memory. *Trends in Cognitive Sciences, 15,* 310–318.

Bauer, Patricia (2002). Long-term recall memory: Behavioral and neuro-developmental changes in the first 2 years of life. *Current Directions in Psychological Science, 11,* 137–141.

Baum, A., & Valins, S. (1977). *Architecture of social behavior: Psychological studies of social density.* Hillsdale, NJ: Erlbaum.

Baumeister, A. A., & Baumeister, A. A. (2000). Mental retardation: Causes and effects. In M. Hersen & R. T. Ammerman (Eds.), *Advanced abnormal child psychology* (2nd. ed.) (pp. 327–355). Mahwah, NJ: Erlbaum.

Bechtoldt, H., Norcross, J. C., Wyckoff, L. A., Pokrywa, M. L., & Campbell, L. F. (2001). Theoretical orientations and employment settings of clinical and counseling psychologists: A comparative study. *The Clinical Psychologist, 54,* 3–6.

Beck, A. T. (2005). The current state of cognitive therapy: A 40-year retrospective. *Archives of General Psychiatry, 62,* 953–959.

Beck, A. T., Rush, A. J., Shaw, B. F., & Emery, G. (1979). *Cognitive therapy of depression.* New York, NY: Guilford Press.

Beck, J. S. (1995). *Cognitive therapy: Basics and beyond.* New York, NY: Guilford Press.

Beilock, S. L. (2010). *Choke: What the secrets of the brain reveal about getting it right when you have to.* New York: Free Press.

Bem, Daryl (2011). Feeling the future: Experimental evidence for anomalous retroactive influences on cognition and affect. *Journal of Personality and Social Psychology, 100,* 407–425.

Benish, S. G., Quintana, S., & Wampold, B. E. (2011). Culturally adapted psychotherapy and the legitimacy of myth: A direct-comparison meta-analysis. *Journal of Counseling Psychology, 58*(3), 279–289.

Bennett, G. G., Wolin, K. Y., Robinson, E. L., Fowler, S., & Edwards, C. L. (2005). Racial/ethnic harassment and tobacco use among African American young adults. *American Journal of Public Health, 95,* 238–240.

Bennett, K. K., Adams, A. D., & Ricks, J. M. (2012). Pessimistic attributional style and cardiac symptom experiences: Self-efficacy as a mediator. North American *Journal of Psychology, 14*(2), 293–306.

Bentley, K. J., & Walsh, J. (2006). *The social worker and psychotropic medication: Toward effective collaboration with mental health clients, families, and providers* (3rd ed.). Belmont, CA: Thompson.

Benton, D., & Roberts, G. (1988). Effect of vitamin and mineral supplementation on intelligence of a sample of schoolchildren. *Lancet, 1,* 140–143.

Berckmoes, C., & Vingerhoets, G. (2004). Neural foundations of emotional speech processing. *Current Directions in Psychological Science, 13,* 182–185.

Berg, R. C. (2008). Barebacking among MSM Internet users. *AIDS and Behavior, 12,* 822–833.

Berglund, H., Lindström, P., & Savic, I. (2006). Brain response to putative pheromones in lesbian women. *PNAS Proceedings of the National Academy of Sciences of the United States of America, 103,* 8269–8274.

Bergman, O., Hakansson, A., Westberg, l., Nordenstrom, K., Belin, A., Sydow, O., Olson, L., Holmberg, B., Eriksson, E., & Nissbrandt, H. (2010). PITX3 polymorphism is associated with early onset Parkinson's disease. *Neurobiology of Aging, 31,* 114–117.

Berk, M. S., & Andersen, S. M. (2000). The impact of past relationships on interpersonal behavior: Behavioral confirmation in the social-cognitive process of transference. *Journal of Personality and Social Psychology, 79,* 546–562.

Berkowitz, L., & Harmon-Jones, E. (2004). Toward an understanding of the determinants of anger. *Emotion, 4,* 107–130.

Berman, J. S., & Norton, N. C. (1985). Does professional training make a therapist more effective? *Psychological Bulletin, 98,* 401–406.

Bernstein, D. A., Borkovec, T. D., & Hazlett-Stevens, H. (2000). *New directions in progressive relaxation training: A guidebook for helping professionals.* Westport, CT: Praeger.

Bernstein, Daniel M., & Loftus, Elizabeth F. (2009). How to tell if a particular memory is true or false. *Perspectives on Psychological Science, 4,* 370–374.

Berntsen, Dorthe, & Thomsen, Dorthe K. (2005). Personal memories for remote historical events: Accuracy and clarity of flashbulb memories related to World War II. *Journal of Experimental Psychology: General, 134,* 242–257.

Best, Joel (2001). *Damned Lies and Statistics: Untangling numbers from the media, politicians, and activists.* Berkeley and Los Angeles: University of California Press.

Bettencourt, B. A., & Miller, N. (1996). Gender differences in aggression as a function of provocation: A meta-analysis. *Psychological Bulletin, 119,* 422–447.

Beutler, L. E. (2002). The dodo bird is extinct. *Clinical Psychology: Science and Practice, 9,* 30–34.

Beutler, L. E., Clarkin, J. F., & Bongar, B. (2000). *Guidelines for the systematic treatment of the depressed person.* Oxford, England: Oxford University Press.

Beutler, L. E., Machado, P. P., & Neufeldt, S. A. (1994). Therapist variables. In A. E. Bergin & S. L. Garfield (Eds.), *Handbook of psychotherapy and behavior change* (4th ed., pp. 259–260). New York, NY: Wiley.

Beyerstein, B. L. (1997, September/October). Why bogus therapies seem to work. *Skeptical Inquirer, 21,* 29–34.

Beyerstein, B., & Hadaway, P. (1991). On avoiding folly. *Journal of Drug Issues, 20,* 689–700.

Bhatarah, Parveen; Ward, Geoff; & Tan, Lydia (2008). *Examining the relationship between free recall and immediate serial recall: The serial nature of recall and the effect of test expectancy.* Memory & Cognition, 36, 20–34.

Bhattacharya, J., & Bundorf, M. K. (2005). *The incidence of healthcare costs of obesity.* Working Paper #11303. National Bureau of Economic Research.

Bhugra, D. (2005). The global prevalence of schizophrenia. *Plos Medicine, 2,* 372–373.

Bianchi-Demicheli, F., & Ortigue, S. (2007). Toward an understanding of the cerebral substrates of woman's orgasm. *Neuropsychologia, 45,* 2645–2659.

Biesmeijer, J. C., & Seeley, T. D. (2005). The use of waggle dance information by honey bees throughout their foraging careers. *Behavioral Ecology and Sociobiology, 59,* 133–142.

Birmingham, C. L., Su, J., Hlynsky, J. A., Goldner, E. M., & Gao, M. (2005). The mortality rate from anorexia nervosa. *International Journal of Eating Disorders, 38,* 143–146.

Bischof, Matthias, & Bassetti, Claudio L. (2004). Total dream loss: A distinct neuropsychological dysfunction after bilateral PCA stroke. *Annals of Neurology,* published online Sept. 10, 2004. doi: 10.1002/ana.20246.

Biss, Renée K., & Hasher, Lynn (2012). Happy as a lark: Morning-type younger and older adults are higher in positive affect. *Emotion, 12,* 437–441.

Blagrove, Mark (1996). Problems with the cognitive psychological modeling of dreaming. *Journal of Mind and Behavior, 17,* 99–134.

Blagys, M. D., & Hilsenroth, M. J. (2000). Distinctive features of short-term psychodynamic-interpersonal psychotherapy: A review of the comparative psychotherapy process literature. *Clinical Psychology-Science and Practice, 7,* 167–188.

Blatt, S. J., Sanislow, C. A., Zuroff, D. C., & Pilkonis, P. A. (1996). Characteristics of effective therapists: Further analyses of data from the NIMH. TDCRP, *Journal of Consulting and Clinical Psychology, 64,* 1276–1284.

Bliss, T. V., & Collingridge, G. L. (1993). A synaptic model of memory: Long-term potentiation in the hippocampus. *Nature, 361,* 31–39.

Blow, A. J., Sprenkle, D. H., & Davis, S. D. (2007). Is who delivers the treatment more important than the treatment itself? The role of the therapist in common factors. *Journal of Marital and Family Therapy, 33,* 298–317.

Blum, J. M. (1979). *Pseudoscience and mental ability: The origins and fallacies of the IQ controversy.* New York, NY: Monthly Review Press.

Bluming, Avrum, & Tavris, Carol (2009, April 22). Hormone replacement therapy: Real concerns and false alarms. *The Cancer Journal, 15,* 93–104.

Boelte, S., Uhlig, N., & Poustka, F. (2002). *The savant syndrome: A review. Zeitschrift fuer Klinische Psychologie und Psycholtherapie: Forschung und Praxis, 31,* 291–297.

Boerke, K. W., & Reitman, D. (2011). Token Economies. In W. W. Fisher, C .C. Piazza, & H. S. RoAne (Eds.), *Handbook of Applied Behavior Analysis* (pp. 370–381). New York: Guilford Press.

Bogaert, A. F., & Fawcett, C. (2006). Sexual desire issues and problems. In R. D. McAnulty & M. M. Burnette (Eds.), *Sex and sexuality, Vol 2: Sexual function and dysfunction* (pp. 115–134). Westport, CT: Praeger.

Bogen, J. E., & Vogel, P. J. (1963). Treatment of generalized seizures by cerebral commissurotomy. *Surgical Forum, 14,* 431.

Bohart, A. C. (2003). Person-centered psychotherapy and related experiential approaches. In A. S. Gurman & S. B. Messer (Eds.), *Essential psychotherapies: Theory and practice* (2nd ed., pp. 107–148). New York, NY: Guilford Press.

Bohart, A., Elliott, R., Greenberg, L. S., & Watson, J. C. (2002). Empathy redux. In J. Norcross & M. Lambert (Eds.), *Psychotherapy relationships that work* (pp. 89–109). Oxford, England: Oxford University Press.

Bolour, S., & Braunstein, G. (2005). Testosterone therapy in women: A review. *International Journal of Impotence Research, 17,* 399–408.

Bolshakov, Vadim Y., & Siegelbaum, Steven A. (1994). Postsynaptic induction and presynaptic expression of hippocampal long-term depression. *Science, 264,* 1148–1152.

Bolwig, T. (2009). Electroconvulsive therapy: The role of hippocampal neurogenesis. *European Psychiatry, 24,* Supplement 1, S75.

Boniecki, K. A., & Moore, S. (2003). Breaking the silence: Using a token economy to reinforce classroom participation. *Teaching of Psychology, 30,* 224–227.

Bonvillian, J. D., & Patterson, F. G. P. (1997). Sign language acquisition and the development of meaning in a lowland gorilla. In C. Mandell & A. McCabe (Eds.), *The problem of meaning: Behavioral and cognitive perspectives* (pp. 181–219). Amsterdam, Netherlands: North-Holland/Elsevier Science.

Boot, Walter R.; Blakely, Daniel P.; & Simons, Daniel J. (2011, September 13). Do action video games improve perception and cognition? *Frontiers in Psychology, 2,* 226.

Born, Jan, & Wilhelm, Ines (2012). System consolidation of memory during sleep. *Psychological Research, 76,* 192–203.

Bornstein, R. F. (2001). The impending death of psychoanalysis. *Psychoanalytic Psychology, 18,* 3–20.

Borthwick-Duffy, S. A. (2007). Adaptive behavior. In J. W. Jacobson, J. A. Mulick, & J. Rojahn (Eds.), *Handbook of intellectual and developmental disabilities* (pp. 279–293). New York, NY: Springer.

Bosacki, S. L., & Moore, C. (2004). Preschoolers' understanding of simple and complex emotions: Links with gender and language. *Sex Roles, 50,* 659–675.

Botella, C., Banos, R. M., Guerrero, B., Garcia-Palacio, A., Quero, S., & Alcaniz, M. (2006). Using a flexible virtual environment for treating a storm phobia. *PsychNology, 4,* 129–144.

Bouchard, T. J., & McGue, M. (1981). Familial studies of intelligence: A review. *Science, 212,* 1055–1059.

Bouchard, T. J., & Propping, P. (Eds.). (1993). *Twins as a tool of behavior genetics.* Chichester, UK: Wiley.

Boulkroune, N., Wang, L., March, A., Walker, N., & Jacob, T. J. C. (2007). Repetitive olfactory exposure to the biologically significant steroid androstadienone causes a hedonic shift and gender dimorphic changes in olfactory-evoked potentials. *Neuropsychopharmacology, 32,* 1822–1829.

Bourgon, L. N., & Kellner, C. H. (2000). Relapse of depression after ECT: A review. *Journal of ECT, 16,* 19–31.

Bousfield, W. A. (1953). The occurrence of clustering in the recall of randomly arranged associates. *Journal of General Psychology, 49,* 229–240.

Bower, B. (2008, March 22). Road to eureka! Insight may lie at the end of a chain of neural reactions. *Science News, 173*(12), 184–185.

Bower, B. (2013, June 1). Closed thinking. *Science News, 183*(11), 26–29. doi:10.1002/scin.5591831123

Bower, Gordon H., & Forgas, Joseph P. (2000). Affect, memory, and social cognition. In E. Eich et al. (Eds.), *Cognition and emotion.* New York: Oxford University Press.

Bowers, T., & Clum, G. A. (1988). Specific and nonspecific treatment effects in controlled psychotherapy research. *Psychological Bulletin, 103,* 315–323.

Bowman, D., Scogin, F., Floyd, M., & McKendree-Smith, N. (2001). Psychotherapy length of stay and outcome: A meta-analysis of the effect of therapist sex. *Psychotherapy, 38,* 142–150.

Boyd, J. E., Katz, E. P., Link, B. G., & Phelan, J. C. (2010). The relationship of multiple aspects of stigma and personal contact with someone hospitalized for mental illness, in a nationally representative sample. *Social Psychiatry and Psychiatric Epidemiology, 45*(11), 1063–1070.

Boyda, D., & Shevlin, M. (2011). Childhood victimisation as a predictor of muscle dysmorphia in adult male bodybuilders. The Irish *Journal of Psychology, 32(3–4), 105–115. doi:10.1080/03033910.2011.616289*

Boysen, S. T., & Himes, G. T. (1999). Current issues and emerging theories in animal cognition. *Annual Review of Psychology, 50,* 683–705.

Bracha, H., Ralston, T., Matsukawa, J., Williams, A., & Bracha, A. (2004, October). Does "fight or flight" need updating? Psychosomatics: *Journal of Consultation Liaison Psychiatry, 45*(5), 448–449.

Brambilla, P., Cipriani, A., Hotopf, M., & Barbui, C. (2005). Side-effect profile of fluoxetine in comparison with other SSRIs, tricyclic, and newer antidepressants: A meta-analysis of clinical trial data. *Pharmacopsychiatry, 38,* 69–77.

Brand-Miller, Jennie C.; Fatima, Kaniz; Middlemiss, Christopher; et al. (2007). Effect of alcoholic beverages on postprandial glycemia and insulinemia in lean, young, healthy adults. *American Journal of Clinical Nutrition, 85,* 1545–1551.

Brandsma, J. M., Maultsby, M. C., & Welsh, R. J. (1980). Alcoholics Anonymous: An empirical outcome study. *Addictive Behaviors, 5,* 359–370.

Brandt, Allan M. (2007). *The cigarette century: The rise, fall, and deadly persistence of the product that defined America.* New York: Basic.

Brant, A. M., Munakata, Y., Boomsma, D. I., DeFries, J. C., Haworth, C. M. A., Keller, M. C., . . . Hewitt, J. K. (2013). The nature and nurture of high IQ: An extended sensitive period for intellectual development. *Psychological Science, 24,* 1487–1495. doi:10.1177/0956797612473119

Brasic, R., & Kao, A. (2011). *PET scanning in autism spectrum disorder.* Retrieved October 21, 2012, from http://emedicine.medscape.com/article/1155568-overview#a1.

Braun, Kathryn A.; Ellis, Rhiannon; & Loftus, Elizabeth F. (2002). Make my memory: How advertising can change our memories of the past. *Psychology & Marketing, 19,* 1–23.

Brewer, C. (1992). Controlled trials of Antabuse in alcoholism: The importance of supervision and adequate dosage. *Acta Psychiatrica Scandinavica, 86,* 51–58.

Brickman, A. M., Khan, U. A., Provenzano, F. A., Yeung, L. K., Suzuki, W., Schroeter, H., . . . Small, S. A. (2014). Enhancing dentate gyrus function with dietary flavanols improves cognition in older adults. *Nature Neuroscience, 17*(12), 1798–1803. doi:10.1038/nn.3850

Briley, D. A., & Tucker-Drob, E. M. (2013). Explaining the increasing heritability of cognitive ability across development: A meta-analysis of longitudinal twin and adoption studies. *Psychological Science, 24,* 1704–1713. doi:10.1177/0956797613478618

Brissette, I., Scheier, M. F., & Carver, C. S. (2002). The role of optimism and social network development, coping, and psychological adjustment during a life transition. *Journal of Personality and Social Psychology, 82,* 102–111.

Broadway, James M., & Engle, Randall W. (2011). Lapsed attention to elapsed time? Individual differences in working memory capacity and temporal reproduction. *Acta Psychologica, 137,* 115–126.

Brody, L., & Hall, J. (2000). Gender, emotion, and expression. In M. Lewis & J. Haviland-Jones (Eds.), *Handbook of emotions* (2nd ed., pp. 338–349). New York, NY: Guilford Press.

Brondolo, E., Libby, D. J., Denton, E., Thompson, S., Beatty, D. L., Schwartz, J. (2008). Racism and ambulatory blood pressure in a community sample. *Psychosomatic Medicine, 70,* 49–56.

Brooks-Gunn, Jeanne (1986). Differentiating premenstrual symptoms and syndromes. *Psychosomatic Medicine, 48,* 385–387.

Brown, A. S., & Derkits, E. J. (2010). Prenatal infection and schizophrenia: A review of epidemiologic and translational studies. *American Journal of Psychiatry, 167,* 261–280.

Brown, Alan S. (2004). *The déjà vu experience: Essays in cognitive psychology.* New York: Psychology Press.

Brown, Alan S. (2012). *The tip of the tongue state.* New York: Psychology Press.

Brown, D. (2006, November 20). *Some believe "truth serums" will come back.* Washington Post, A08.

Brown, Daniel; Scheflin, Alan W.; & Whitfield, Charles L. (1999). Recovered memories: The current weight of the evidence in science and in the courts. *Journal of Psychiatry and Law, 27,* 5–156.

Brown, I., Buell, M. K., Birkan, R., & Percy, M. (2007). Lifestyles of adults with intellectual and developmental disabilities. In I. Brown & M. Percy (Eds.), *A comprehensive guide to intellectual and developmental disabilities* (pp. 545–560). Baltimore, MD: Paul H Brookes.

Brown, Robert, & Middlefell, Robert (1989). Fifty-five years of cocaine dependence [letter]. British *Journal of Addiction, 84, 946.*

Brown, Roger, & Kulik, James (1977). Flashbulb memories. *Cognition, 5,* 73–99.

Brown, Roger, & McNeill, David (1966). The "tip of the tongue" phenomenon. *Journal of Verbal Learning and Verbal Behavior, 5,* 325–337.

Browne, N. T. (2012). Weight bias, stigmatization, and bullying of obese youth. *Bariatric Nursing and Surgical Patient Care, 7,* 107–115. doi:10.1089/bar.2012.9972

Bruck, Maggie (2003). Effects of suggestion on the reliability and credibility of children's reports. Invited address at the annual meeting of the American Psychological Society, Atlanta.

Brundage, S. (2002). *Preconception health care.* Retrieved November 30, 2006, from http://www.aafp.org/afp/20020615/2507.html

Brunell, A. B., Staats, S., Barden, J., & Hupp, J. M. (2011). Narcissism and academic dishonesty: The exhibitionism dimension and the lack of guilt. *Personality and Individual Differences, 50*(3), 323–328.

Bruno-Petrina, A. (2009). *Motor recovery in stroke.* Retrieved January 15, 2010 from http://emedicine.medscape.com/article/324386-overview.

Buchanan, Tony W. (2007). Retrieval of emotional memories. *Psychological Bulletin, 133,* 761–779.

Buckingham, H. W., Jr., & Kertesz, A. (1974). A linguistic analysis of fluent aphasics. *Brain and Language, 1,* 29–42.

Bühner, M., König, C., Pick, M., & Krumm, S. (2006). Working memory dimensions as differential predictors of the speed and error aspect of multitasking performance. *Human Performance, 19,* 253–275.

Buhrmester, Michael; Kwang, Tracy; & Gosling, Samuel D. (2011). Amazon's Mechanical Turk: A new source of inexpensive, yet high-quality, data? *Perspectives on Psychological Science.* doi: 10.1177/1745691610393980.

Bulik, C. M., Sullivan, P. F., Tozzi, F., Furberg, H., Lichtenstein, P., & Pedersen, N. L. (2006). Prevalence, heritability, and prospective risk factors for anorexia nervosa. *Archives of General Psychiatry, 63,* 305–312.

Buller, D. J. (2005). *Adapting minds: Evolutionary psychology and the persistent quest for human nature.* Cambridge, MA: MIT Press.

Burke, B. L., Arkowitz, H., & Dunn, C. (2002). The efficacy of motivational interviewing. In W. R. Miller & S. Rollnick (Eds.), *Motivational interviewing: Preparing people for change* (2nd ed., pp. 217–250). New York, NY: Guilford Press.

Burke, B. L., Arkowitz, H., & Menchola, M. (2003). The efficacy of motivational interviewing: A meta-analysis of controlled clinical trials. *Journal of Consulting and Clinical Psychology, 71,* 843–861.

Burns, M., & Seligman, M. (1989). Explanatory style across the life span: Evidence for stability over 52 years. *Journal of Personality and Social Psychology, 56*(3), 471–477.

Bushman, B. J. (2002). Does venting anger feed or extinguish the flame? Catharsis rumination, distraction, anger and aggressive responding. *Personality and Social Psychology Bulletin, 28,* 724–731.

Buss, D. (2007). *Evolutionary psychology: The new science of the mind* (3rd ed.). Boston: Allyn & Bacon.

Buss, D. M. (2006). The evolution of love. In R. J. Sternberg & K. Weis (Eds.), *The new psychology of love* (pp. 65–86). New Haven, CT: Yale University Press.

Buss, D. M., Haselton, M. G., Shackelford, T. K., Bleske, A. L., & Wakefield, J. C. (1998). Adaptations, exaptations, and spandrels. *American Psychologist, 53,* 533–548.

Byrne, R. (2007). *The secret.* New York, NY: Atria Books.

Cacioppo, J. T., & Cacioppo, S. (2014). Social relationships and health: The toxic effects of perceived social isolation. *Social and Personality Psychology Compass, 8,* 58–72.

Cacioppo, J. T., Reis, H. T., & Zautra, A. J. (2011). Social resilience. *American Psychologist, 66,* 43–51.

Cahill, L., & McGaugh, J. L. (1998). Mechanisms of emotional arousal and lasting declarative memory. *Trends in Neuroscience, 21,* 294–299.

Cahill, Larry; Prins, Bruce; Weber, Michael; & McGaugh, James L. (1994). ß-adrenergic activation and memory for emotional events. *Nature, 371,* 702–704.

Cahill, S. P., Rauch, S. A. M., Hembree, E. A., & Foa, E. B. (2003). Effectiveness of cognitive behavioral treatments for PTSD on anger. *Journal of Cognitive Psychotherapy, 17*(2), 113–131.

Cahn, B. R., & Polich, J. (2006). Meditation states and traits: EEG, ERP and neuroimaging studies. *Psychological Bulletin, 132,* 180–211.

Calhoun, L. G., & Tedeschi, R. G. (2013) *Posttraumatic growth in clinical practice.* New York: Brunner Routledge.

Callaghan, Glenn M.; Chacon, Cynthia; Coles, Cameron; et al. (2009). An empirical evaluation of the diagnostic criteria for premenstrual dysphoric disorder: Problems with sex specificity and validity. *Women & Therapy, 32,* 1–21.

Callahan, R. J. (1995, August). *A thought field therapy (TFT) algorithm for trauma: A reproducible experiment in psychotherapy.* Paper presented at the 105th Annual Convention of the American Psychological Association, Chicago, IL.

Callahan, R. J. (2001). The impact of thought field therapy on heart rate variability (HRV). *Journal of Clinical Psychology, 57,* 1153–1170.

Campbell, D. T. (1974). Evolutionary epistemology. In P. A. Schlipp (Ed.), *The philosophy of Karl Popper* (Vol. 14–1, pp. 413–463). LaSalle, IL: Open Court Publishing.

Campbell, D. T. (1976). On the conflicts between biological and social evolution and between psychology and moral tradition. *American Psychologist, 30,* 1103–1126.

Camperio-Ciani A., Corna, F., & Capiluppi C. (2004). Evidence for maternally inherited factors favouring male homosexuality and promoting female fecundity. *Proceedings of the Royal Society of London B., 271,* 2217–2221.

Campinha-Bacote, J. (2002). *Resources in transcultural care and mental health* (13th ed.). Cincinnati, OH: Transcultural Care Associated.

Cannon, W. B. (1929). *Bodily changes in pain, hunger, fear and rage* (2nd ed.). New York: Appleton.

Cannon, W. B. (1935). Stresses and strains of homeostasis. *American Journal of Public Health, 189,* 1–14.

Capel, B. (2000). The battle of the sexes. *Mechanisms of Development, 92,* 89–103.

Caporael, L. R. (2001). Evolutionary psychology: Toward a unifying theory and a hybrid science. *Annual Review of Psychology, 52,* 607–628.

Capron, C., & Duyme, M. (1989). Assessment of effects of socioeconomic status on IQ in a full cross-fostering study. *Nature, 340,* 552–554.

Cardemil, E. V. (2010). Cultural adaptations to empirically supported treatments: A research agenda. *Scientific Review of Mental Health Practice, 7*(2), 8–21.

Cardoso, S. H., de Mello, L. C., & Sabbatini, R. M. E. (2000). *How nerve cells work.* Retrieved June 10, 2007 from http://www.cerebromente.org.br/n10/fundamentos/pot2_i.htm.org.br/cm/n09/fundamentos/transmissao/voo_i.htm

Carey, Benedict (2011). You might already know this . . . *The New York Times,* January 11, D1, 3.

Carey, T. A. (2011). Exposure and reorganization: The what and how of effective psychotherapy. *Clinical Psychology Review, 31*(2), 236–248.

Carney, S., Cowen, P., Geddes, J., Goodwin, G., Rogers, R., Dearness, K., . . . Scott, A. (2003). Efficacy and safety of electroconvulsive therapy in depressive disorders: A systematic review and meta-analysis. *Lancet, 361,* 799–808.

Carr, M., Borkowski, J. G., & Maxwell, S. E. (1991). Motivational components of underachievement. *Developmental Psychology, 27,* 108–118.

Carrére, S., Mittmann, A., Woodin, E., Tabares, A., & Yoshimoto, D. (2005). Anger dysregulation, depressive symptoms, and health in married women and men. *Nursing Research, 54,* 184–192.

Carroll, S. B. (2003). Genetics and the making of Homo sapiens. *Nature, 422,* 849–857.

Carter, C. S. (2005). Biological perspectives on social attachment and bonding. In C. S. Carter, L. L. Ahnert, K. E. Grossmann, S. B. Hardy, M. E. Lamb, S. W. Porges, . . . N. N. Sachser (Eds.), *Attachment and bonding: A new synthesis* (pp. 85–100). Cambridge, MA: MIT Press.

Carter, R., Shimkets, R. P., & Bornemann, T. H. (2014). Creating and changing public policy to reduce the stigma of mental illness. *Psychological Science in the Public Interest, 15*(2), 35–36. doi:10.1177/1529100614546119

Cartwright, Rosalind (1977). *Night life: Explorations in dreaming.* Englewood Cliffs, NJ: Prentice-Hall.

Cartwright, Rosalind D. (2010). *The twenty-four hour mind: The role of sleep and dreaming in our emotional lives.* New York: Oxford University Press.

Cartwright, Rosalind D.; Young, Michael A.; Mercer, Patricia; & Bears, Michael (1998). Role of REM sleep and dream variables in the prediction of remission from depression. *Psychiatry Research, 80,* 249–255.

Casey, L. M., Oei, T. P. S., & Newcombe, P. A. (2004). An integrated cognitive model of panic disorder: The role of positive and negative cognitions. *Clinical Psychology Review, 24,* 529–555.

Caspi, A., Moffitt, T. E., Cannon, M., Taylor, A., Craig, I. W., Harrington, H., McClay, J., Mill, J., Martin, J. Braithwaite, A. & Poulton, R. (2005). Moderation of the effect of adolescent-onset cannabis use on adult psychosis by a functional polymorphism in the catechol-O-methyltransferase gene: Longitudinal evidence of a gene X environment interaction. *Biological Psychiatry, 57,* 1117–1127.

Castonguay, L. G., Boswell, J. F., Constantino, M. J., Goldfried, M. R., & Hill, C. E. (2010). Training implications of harmful effects of psychological treatments. *American Psychologist, 65,* 34–49.

Cautela, J. R. (1971). Covert conditioning. In A. Jacobs & L. B. Sachs (Eds.), *The psychology of private events: Perspectives on covert response systems.* New York, NY: Academic Press.

Ceci, S. J., & Williams, W. M. (1997). Schooling, intelligence, and income. *American Psychologist, 52,* 1051–1058.

Ceci, S. J., & Williams, W. M. (2010). Sex differences in math-intensive fields. *Current Directions in Psychological Science, 19,* 275–279.

Ceci, Stephen J., & Bruck, Maggie (1995). *Jeopardy in the courtroom: A scientific analysis of children's testimony.* Washington, DC: American Psychological Association.

Centers for Disease Control and Prevention (CDC). (2009a, April 17). *National Vital Statistics Reports, 57*(14).

Centers for Disease Control and Prevention (CDC). (2010d, September 10). Vital signs: Current cigarette smoking among adults aged ≥ 18 years-United States, 2009. Retrieved July 9, 2011, from http://www.cdc.gov/mmwr/preview/mmwrhtml/mm5935a3.htm

Cermak, Laird S., & Craik, Fergus I. M. (Eds.) (1979). *Levels of processing in human memory.* Hillsdale, NJ: Erlbaum.

Chakrabarti, S., Grover, S., & Rajagopal, R. (2010). Electroconvulsive therapy: A review of knowledge, experience and attitudes of patients concerning the treatment. World *Journal of Biological Psychiatry, 11*(3), 525–537.

Chambless, D. L., & Ollendick, T. H. (2001). Empirically supported psychological interventions: Controversies and evidence. *Annual Review of Psychology, 52,* 685–716.

Chambless, D. L., Sanderson, W. C., Shoham, V., Bennett Johnson, S., Pope, K. S., Crits-Christoph, P., . . . McCurry, S. (1996). An update on empirically validated therapies. *The Clinical Psychologist, 49,* 5–18.

Chamley, C., Carson, P., Randall, D., & Sandwell, M. (2005). *Developmental anatomy and physiology of children.* Edinburgh, Scotland, UK: Elsevier Churchill Livingstone.

Chang, Anne-Marie; Buch, Alison M.; Bradstreet, Dayna S.; et al. (2011). Human diurnal preference and circadian rhythmicity are not associated with the CLOCK 3111C/T gene polymorphism. *Biological Rhythms, 26,* 276–279.

Chaves, J. F. (1989). Hypnotic control of clinical pain. In N. P. Spanos & J. F. Chaves (Eds.), *Hypnosis: The cognitive-behavioral perspective.* Buffalo, NY: Prometheus Books.

Chen, H., & Jackson, T. (2008). Prevalence and sociodemographic correlates of eating disorder endorsements among adolescents and young adults from China. *European Eating Disorders Review, 16,* 375–385.

Chen, J.-Q., Moran, S., & Gardner, H. (Eds.) (2009). *Multiple intelligences around the world.* San Francisco, CA: Jossey-Bass.

Cherniss, C., & Goleman, D. (2001). *The emotionally intelligent workplace: How to select for, measure, and improve emotional intelligence in individuals, groups, and organizations.* San Francisco, CA: Jossey-Bass.

Chilosi, A., Cipriani, P., Bertuccelli, B., Pfanner, L., & Cioni, G. (2001). Early cognitive and communication development in children with focal brain lesions. *Journal of Child Neurology, 16,* 309–316.

Chiu, C., Leung, A. K., & Kwan, L. (2007). Language, cognition, and culture: Beyond the Whorfian hypothesis. In S. Kitayama & D. Cohen (Eds.), *Handbook of cultural psychology* (pp. 668–688). New York, NY: Guilford Press.

Chomsky, N. (1957). *Syntactic structures.* Oxford, England: Mouton.

Chomsky, N., Place, U. T., & Schoneberger, T. (Eds.). (2000). The Chomsky-Place correspondence 1993–1994. *Analysis of Verbal Behavior, 17,* 7–38.

Chrisler, Joan C. (2000). PMS as a culture-bound syndrome. In J. C. Chrisler, C. Golden, & P. D. Rozee (Eds.), *Lectures on the psychology of women* (2nd ed.). New York: McGraw-Hill.

Chrisler, Joan C., & Caplan, Paula (2002). The strange case of Dr. Jekyll and Ms. Hyde: How PMS became a cultural phenomenon and psychiatric disorder. *Annual Review of Sex Research, 13,* 274–306.

Christakis, Dimitri A.; Zimmerman, Frederick J.; DiGiuseppe, David L.; & McCarty, Carolyn A. (2004). Early television exposure and subsequent attentional problems in children. *Pediatrics, 113,* 708–713.

Christakis, N. A., & Fowler, J. H. (2007). The spread of obesity in a large social network over 32 years. *New England Journal of Medicine, 357,* 370–379.

Christakis, N. A., & Fowler, J. H. (2008). The collective dynamics of smoking in a large social network. *New England Journal of Medicine, 358,* 2249–2258.

Christensen, A., & Jacobson, N. S. (1994). Who (or what) can do psychotherapy: The status and challenge of nonprofessional therapies. *Psychological Science, 5,* 8–14.

Cialdini, Robert B. (2009). We have to break up. *Perspectives on Psychological Science, 4,* 5–6.

Clancy, Susan A. (2005). *Abducted: How people come to believe they were kidnapped by aliens.* Cambridge, MA: Harvard University Press.

Clapham, M. M. (2004). The convergent validity of the Torrance Tests of Creative Thinking and Creativity Interest Inventories. *Educational and Psychological Measurement, 64,* 828–841.

Clay, R. A. (2009, February). *Mini-multitaskers. Monitor on Psychology, 40,* 38.

Cleary, Anne M. (2008). Recognition memory, familiarity, and déjà vu experiences. *Current Directions in Psychological Science, 17,* 353–357.

Cloninger, C. Robert (1990). *The genetics and biology of alcoholism.* Cold Springs Harbor, ME: Cold Springs Harbor Press.

Cobos, P., Sánchez, M., Pérez, N., & Vila, J. (2004). Effects of spinal cord injuries on the subjective component of emotions. *Cognition and Emotion, 18,* 281–287.

Cohen, B., Guttmann, D., & Lazar, A. (1998). The willingness to seek help: A cross-national comparison. Cross-Cultural Research: The *Journal of Comparative Social Science, 32,* 342–357.

Cohen, J. (2007a). *Relative differences: The myth of 1%. Science, 316,* 1836.

Cohen, J. (2007b). *Reconstructing the origins of the AIDS epidemic from archived HIV isolates. Science, 318,* 731.

Cohen, N., Mor, N., & Henik, A. (2015). Linking executive control and emotional response: A training procedure to reduce rumination. *Clinical Psychological Science, 3*(1), 15–25.

Cole, Michael, & Scribner, Sylvia (1974). *Culture and thought.* New York: Wiley.

Coleman, H. L. K., Wampold, B. E., & Casali, S. L. (1995). Ethnic minorities' ratings of ethnically similar and European American counselors: A meta-analysis. *Journal of Counseling Psychology, 42,* 55–64.

Coleman, L. J., & Cross, T. L. (2001). *Gifted: Is it a state of being or an application of abilities?* Waco, TX: Prufrock Press.

Collins, Allan M., & Loftus, Elizabeth F. (1975). A spreading-activation theory of semantic processing. *Psychological Review, 82,* 407–428.

Conway, M., & Ross, M. (1984). Getting what you want by revising what you had. *Journal of Personality and Social Psychology, 47,* 783–748.

Cooke, L. J., Chambers, L. C., Añez, E. V., Croker, H. A., Boniface, D., Yeomans, M. R., & Wardle, J. (2011). Eating for pleasure or profit: The effect of incentives on children's enjoyment of vegetables. *Psychological Science, 22,* 190–196.

Cooper, R. M., & Zubek, J. P. (1958). Effects of enriched and restricted early environments on the learning ability of bright and dull rats. *Canadian Journal of Psychology, 12,* 159–164.

Corkin, Suzanne (1984). Lasting consequences of bilateral medial temporal lobectomy: Clinical course and experimental findings in H. M. *Seminars in Neurology, 4,* 249–259.

Corkin, Suzanne; Amaral, David G.; Gonzalez, R. Gilberto; et al. (1997). H. M.'s medial temporal lobe lesion: Findings from magnetic resonance imaging. *Journal of Neuroscience, 17,* 3964–3979.

Cornelius, R. R. (1996). *The science of emotion: Research and tradition in the psychology of emotions.* Upper Saddle River, NJ: Prentice Hall.

Cornell, D. G. (1997). Post hoc explanation is not prediction. Commentary on J. Archer. *American Psychologist, 52,* 1380.

Correll, C. U., & Schenk, E. M. (2008). Tardive dyskinesia and new antipsychotics. *Current Opinion in Psychiatry, 21,* 151–156.

Corrigan, P. W. (1995). Use of a token-economy with seriously mentally-ill patients: Criticisms and misconceptions. *Psychiatric Services, 46,* 1258–1263.

Corrigan, P. W., Druss, B. G., & Perlick, D. A. (2014). The impact of mental illness stigma on seeking and participating in mental health care. *Psychological Science in the Public Interest, 15*(2), 37–70. doi:10.1177/1529100614531398

Council, James R.; Kirsch, Irving; & Grant, D. L. (1996). Imagination, expectancy and hypnotic responding. In R. G. Kunzendorf, N. K. Spanos, & B. J. Wallace (Eds.), *Hypnosis and imagination.* Amityville, NY: Baywood.

Couzin, J. (2008). Crossing the divide. *Science, 319,* 1034–1036.

Coviello, L., Sohn, Y., Kramer, A. D. I., Marlow, C., Franceschetti, M., Christakis, N. A., & Fowler, J. A. (2014). Detecting emotional contagion in massive social networks. *PLoS ONE, 9*(3), e90315. doi:10.1371/journal.pone.0090315

Cowan, Nelson (2001). The magical number 4 in short-term memory: A reconsideration of mental storage capacity. *Behavioral and Brain Sciences, 24,* 87–185.

Cowan, Nelson; Morey, Candice C.; Chen, Zhijian; et al. (2008) Theory and measurement of working memory capacity limits. In B. H. Ross (Ed.), *The psychology of learning and motivation.* San Diego: Elsevier.

Craighead, E., Sheets, E. S., & Bjornsson, A. S. (2005). Specificity and non-specificity in psychotherapy. *Clinical Psychology: Science and Practice, 12,* 189–193.

Craik, Fergus I. M., & Lockhart, Robert (1972). Levels of processing: A framework for memory research. *Journal of Verbal Learning and Verbal Behavior, 11,* 671–684.

Craik, Fergus I. M., & Tulving, Endel (1975). Depth of processing and the retention of words in episodic memory. *Journal of Experimental Psychology: General, 104,* 268–294.

Cramond, B., & Kim, K. H. (2008). The role of creativity tools and measures in assessing potential and growth. In J. L. VanTassel-Baska (Ed.), *Alternative assessments with gifted and talented students* (pp. 203–225). Waco, TX: Prufrock Press.

Crick, F. H, Brenner, S., Klug, A., & Pieczenik, G. (1976). A speculation on the origin of protein synthesis. *Origins of Life, 7,* 389–397.

Crits-Christoph, P., Wilson, G. T., & Hollon, S. D. (2005). Empirically supported psychotherapies: Comment on Westen, Novotny, and Thompson-Brenner (2004). *Psychological Bulletin, 131,* 412–417.

Crosscope-Happel, C. (2005). Male anorexia nervosa: An exploratory study. *Dissertation Abstracts International: Section A: Humanities and Social Sciences, 65,* 4472.

Crowell, S. E., Beauchaine, T. P., & Linehan, M. M. (2009). A biosocial developmental model of borderline personality: Elaborating and extending linehan's theory. *Psychological Bulletin, 135*(3), 495–510. doi:10.1037/a0015616

Crowther, J. H., Kichler, J. C., Shewood, N. E., & Kuhnert, M. E. (2002). The role of familial factors in bulimia nervosa. Eating Disorders: The *Journal of Treatment & Prevention, 10,* 141–151.

Cruz, M., Scott, J., Houck, P., Reynolds, C. F., Frank, E., & Shear, M. K. (2007). Clinical presentation and treatment outcome of African Americans with complicated grief. *Psychiatric Services, 58,* 700–702.

Csikszentmihalyi, M., Rathunde, K. R., Whalen, S., & Wong, M. (1993). *Talented teenagers: The roots of success and failure.* New York, NY: Cambridge University Press.

Cuijpers, P., Vanstraten, A., Warmerdam, L., & Smits, N. (2008). Characteristics of effective psychological treatments of depression: A metaregression analysis. *Psychothreapy Research, 18,* 225–236.

Cumming, Geoff (2012). *Understanding the new statistics: Effect sizes, confidence intervals, and meta-Analysis.* New York: Routledge.

Cumming, Geoff; Fidler, Fiona; Leonard, Martine; et al. (2007). Statistical reform in psychology: Is anything changing? *Psychological Science, 18,* 230–232.

Curtiss, Susan (1977). Genie: A psycholinguistic study of a modern-day "wild child." New York: Academic Press.

Curtiss, Susan (1982). Developmental dissociations of language and cognition. In L. Obler & D. Fein (Eds.), *Exceptional language and linguistics.* New York: Academic Press.

Cutrona, C., Wallace, G., & Wesner, K. (2006). Neighborhood characteristics and depression: An examination of stress processes. *Current Directions in Psychological Science, 15*(4), 188–192.

Daeschler, E. B., Shubin, N. H., & Jenkins, Jr., F. A. (2006). A Devonian tetrapod-like fish and the evolution of the tetrapod body plan. *Nature, 440,* 757.

Dal Cin, S., Gibson, B., Zanna, M. P., Shumate, R., & Fong, G. T. (2007). Smoking in movies, implicit associations of smoking with the self, and intentions to smoke. *Psychological Science, 18,* 559–563.

Danaei, G., Ding, E. L., Mozaffarian, D., Taylor B, & Rehm J. (2009). The preventable causes of death in the United States: Comparative risk assessment of dietary, lifestyle, and metabolic risk factors. *PLoS Med, 6*(4), e1000058. doi:10.1371/journal.pmed.1000058

Darwin, C. (1859). *On the origin of species by means of natural selection.* London: Murray.

Daum, Irene, & Schugens, Markus M. (1996). On the cerebellum and classical conditioning. *Psychological Science, 5,* 58–61.

Davelaar, Eddy J.; Goshen-Gottstein, Yonatan; Ashkenazi, Amir; et al. (2004). The demise of short-term memory revisited: Empirical and computational investigations of recency effects. *Psychological Review, 112,* 3–42.

David, D., Lynn, S. J., & Ellis, A. (2010). *Rational and irrational beliefs.* New York, NY: Oxford University Press.

Davidson, P. R., & Parker, K. C. (2001). Eye movement desensitization and reprocessing (EMDR): A meta-analysis. *Journal of Consulting and Clinical Psychology, 69,* 305–316.

Davidson, R. J. (1992). Emotion and affective style: Hemispheric substrates. *Psychological Science, 3,* 39–43.

Davidson, R. J., Jackson, D. C., & Kalin, N. H. (2000). Emotion, plasticity, context, and regulation: Perspectives from affective neuroscience. *Psychological Bulletin, 126,* 890–909.

Davies, M., Stankov, L., & Roberts, R. D. (1998). Emotional intelligence: In search of an elusive construct. *Journal of Personality and Social Psychology, 75,* 989–1015.

Davis, S. R., Davison, S. L., Donath, S., & Bell, R. J. (2005). Circulating androgen levels and self-reported sexual function in women. *Journal of the American Medical Association, 294,* 91–96.

Davison, K. P., Pennebaker, J. W., & Dickerson, S. S. (2000). Who talks? The social psychology of illness support groups. *American Psychologist, 55,* 205–217.

Dawes, R. M. (1994). *House of cards: Psychology and psychotherapy built on myth.* New York, NY: Free Press.

Dawkins, R. (1996). Climbing mount improbable. New York: W. W. Norton.

de Lacoste, M., Horvath, D., & Woodward, J. (1991). Possible sex differences in the developing human fetal brain. *Journal of Clinical and Experi-mental Neuropsychology, 13, 831.*

Deary, I. J., Johnson, W., & Houlihan, L. (2009). Genetic foundations of human intelligence. *Human Genetics, 126,* 215–232.

Deary, I. J., Pattie, A., & Starr, J. M. (2013). The stability of intelligence from age 11 to age 90 years: The Lothian birth cohort of 1921. *Psychological Science, 24,* 2361–2368. doi:10.1177/0956797613486487

Deary, I. J., Penke, L., & Johnson, W. (2010). The neuroscience of human intelligence differences. *Nature Reviews Neuroscience, 11,* 201–211.

Deci, E. L., & Ryan, R. M. (2008). Facilitating optimal motivation and psychological well-being across life's domains. *Canadian Psychology, 49,* 14–23.

Deci, E. L., Koestner, R., & Ryan, R. M. (2001). Extrinsic rewards and intrinsic motivation in education: Reconsidered once again. *Review of Educational Research, 71,* 1–27.

DeLisi, L. E. (1992). The significance of age of onset for schizophrenia. *Schizophrenia Bulletin, 18,* 209–215.

Dement, William (1978). *Some must watch while some must sleep.* New York: Norton.

Dement, William (1992). *The sleepwatchers.* Stanford, CA: Stanford Alumni Association.

Demuth, J. P., Bie, T. D., Stajich, J.E., Cristianini, N., & Hahn, M. W. (2006) The evolution of mammalian gene families. *PLoS ONE, 1,* e85.

den Boer, P. C. A. M., Wiersma, D., Russo, S., & van den Bosch, R. J. (2005). Paraprofessionals for anxiety and depressive disorders: A meta-analysis. *The Cochrane Database of Systematic Reviews,* Issue 2. Art No: CD004688.

Dennett, D. C. (1995). *Darwin's dangerous idea: Evolution and the meanings of life.* New York: Simon & Schuster.

DeRubeis, R. J., & Feeley, M. (1990). Determinants of change in cognitive therapy for depression. *Cognitive Therapy and Research, 14,* 469–482.

DeRubeis, R. J., Brotman, M. A., & Gibbons, C. J. (2005). A conceptual and methodological analysis of the nonspecifics argument. *Clinical Psychology: Science & Practice, 12,* 174–183.

DeYoung, C., Hirsch, J., Shane, M., Papademetris, X., Rajeevan, N., & Gray, J. (2010). Testing predictions from personality neuroscience: Brain structure and the Big Five. *Psychological Science, 21,* 820–828.

Dienes, Zoltan (2011). Bayesian versus orthodox statistics: Which side are you on? *Perspectives on Psychological Science, 6,* 274–290.

Dies, R. R. (2003). Group psychotherapies. In A. S. Gurman & S. B. Messer (Eds.), *Essential psychotherapies: Theory and practice* (2nd ed., pp. 515–550). New York, NY: Guilford Press.

Dietrich, A., & Kanso, R. (2010). A review of EEG, ERP, and neuroimaging studies of creativity and insight. *Psychological Bulletin, 136,* 822–848.

DiLoretto, A. O. (1971). *Comparative psychotherapy: An experimental analysis.* Chicago, IL: Aldine-Atherton.

Dimidjian, S., & Hollon, S. D. (2010). How would we know if psychotherapy were harmful? *American Psychologist, 65,* 21–33.

Dimidjian, S., Hollon, S. D., Dobson, K. S., Schmaling, K. B., Kohlenberg, R. J., Addis, M. E., . . . Jacobson, N. S. (2006). Randomized trial of behavioral activation, cognitive therapy and antidepressant medication in the acute treatment of adults with mild depression. *Journal of Consulting and Clinical Psychology, 74*(4), 658–670.

Dinges, David F.; Whitehouse, Wayne G.; Orne, Emily C.; et al. (1992). Evaluating hypnotic memory enhancement (hypermnesia and reminiscence) using multitrial forced recall. *Journal of Experimental Psychology: Learning, Memory, and Cognition, 18,* 1139–1147.

Ditzen, B., Schaer, M., Gabriel, B., Bodenmann, G., Ehlert, U., & Heinrichs, M. (2009). Intranasal oxytocin increases positive communication and reduces cortisol levels during couple conflict. *Biological Psychiatry, 65,* 728–731.

Dixon, L. B., Dickerson, F., Bellack, A. S., Bennett, M., Dickinson, D., Goldberg, R. W., . . . Kreyenbuhl, J. (2010). The 2009 Schizophrenia PORT psychosocial treatment recommendations and summary statements. *Schizophrenia Bulletin, 36,* 48–70.

Dobzhansky, T. (1937). *Genetics and the origin of species.* New York: Columbia University Press.

Dolnick, E. (1998). *Madness on the couch: Blaming the victim in the heyday of psychoanalysis.* New York, NY: Simon & Schuster.

Dolnick, Edward (1990, July). What dreams are (really) made of. *The Atlantic Monthly, 226,* 41–45, 48–53, 56–58, 60–61.

Domhoff, G. William (1996). *Finding meaning in dreams: A quantitative approach.* New York: Plenum.

Domhoff, G. William (2003). *The scientific study of dreams: Neural networks, cognitive development, and content analysis.* Washington, DC: American Psychological Association.

Domhoff, G. William (2011). Dreams are embodied simulations that dramatize conceptions and concerns: the continuity hypothesis in empirical, theoretical, historical context. *International Journal of Dream Research, 4,* 50–62.

Donahoe, J. W. (2003). Selectionism. In K. A. Lattal & P. N. Chase (Eds.), *Behavior theory and philosophy* (pp. 103–128). New York: Kluwer Academic/Plenum Publishers.

Done, D. J., Crow, T. J., Johnstone, E. C., & Sacker, A. (1994). Childhood antecedents of schizophrenia and affective illness: Social adjustment at ages 7 and 11. *British Medical Journal, 309,* 699–703.

Donlea, Jeffrey M.; Ramanan, Narendrakumar; & Shaw, Paul J. (2009). Use-dependent plasticity in clock neurons regulates sleep need in Drosophila. *Science, 324,* 105–108.

Doré, R., Wagner, S., Doré, I., & Brunet, J.-P. (2002). From mainstreaming to inclusion: A transformation of service delivery. In R. L. Schalock, P. C. Baker, & M. D. Croser (Eds.), *Embarking on a new century: Mental retardation at the end of the 20th century* (pp. 185–201). Washington, DC: American Association on Mental Retardation.

Douglas, K. S., Guy, L. S., & Hart, S. D. (2009). Psychosis as a risk factor for violence to others: A meta-analysis. *Psychological Bulletin, 135,* 679–706.

Dowman, J., Patel, A., & Rajput, K. (2005). Electroconvulsive therapy: Attitudes and misconceptions. *Journal of ECT, 21,* 84–87.

Drachman, D. (2005). Do we have brain to spare? *Neurology, 64,* 2004–2005.

Driscoll, E. V. (2008, June/July). Bisexual species. *Scientific American Mind, 19*(3), 68–73.

Druskat, V. U., Sala, F., & Mount, G. (2006). *Linking emotional intelligence and performance at work: Current research evidence with individuals and groups.* Mahwah, NJ: Erlbaum.

DuBrin, J. R., & Zastowny, T. R. (1988). Predicting early attrition from psychotherapy: An analysis of a large private practice cohort. *Psychotherapy, 25,* 393–498.

Duffy, Jeanne, F.; Cain, Sean W.; Change, Anne-Marie; et al. (2011). Sex difference in the near-24-hour intrinsic period of the human circadian timing system. *Proceedings of the National Academy of Science, 108,* 15602–15608.

Durex Global Sex Survey (2005). Retrieved from http://www.durex.com/cm/gss2005result.pdf

Eachus, P. (2004). Using the brief sensation seeking scale (BSSS) to predict holiday preferences. *Personality and Individual Differences, 36,* 141–153.

Eagly, A. H., & Steffen, V. J. (1986). Gender and aggressive behavior: A metaanalytic review of the social psychological literature. *Psychological Bulletin, 100,* 309–330.

Earl-Novell, Sarah L., & Jessup, Donna C. (2005). The relationship between perceptions of premenstrual syndrome and degree performance. *Assessment & Evaluation in Higher Education, 30,* 343–352.

Ebbinghaus, Hermann M. (1885/1913). *Memory: A contribution to experimental psychology* (H. A. Ruger & C. E. Bussenius, trans.). New York: Teachers College Press, Columbia University.

Eich, E., Macaulay, D., Lowenstein, R. J., & Dihle, P. H. (1997). Memory, amnesia, and dissociative identity disorder. *Psychological Science, 8,* 417–422.

Eiler, J. M. (2007). Just another rock? *Science, 317,* 1046–1047.

Eisenberg, N., & Lennon, R. (1983). Sex differences in empathy and related capacities. *Psychological Bulletin, 94,* 100–131.

Eisner, D. A. (2000). *The death of psychotherapy: From Freud to alien abductions.* Westport, CT: Praeger.

Ekman, P. (2003). *Emotions revealed: Recognizing faces and feelings to improve communication and emotional life.* New York, NY: Holt.

Ekman, P., & Friesen, W. V. (1971). Constants across cultures in the face and emotion. *Journal of Personality and Social Psychology, 17,* 124–129.

Ekman, P., & Friesen, W. V. (1975). *Unmasking the face.* Englewood Cliffs, NJ: Prentice Hall.

Ekman, P., & O'Sullivan, M. (1991). Who can catch a liar? *American Psychologist, 46,* 913–920.

Ekman, P., Friesen, W. V., & Ellsworth, P. (1972). *Emotion in the human face.* Elmsford, NY: Pergamon.

Ekman, P., Sorenson, E. R., & Friesen, W. V. (1969). Pancultural elements in facial displays of emotion. *Science, 164,* 86–88.

Elena, S. F. & Lenski, R. E. (2003). Evolution experiments with microorganisms: The dynamics and genetic bases of adaptation. *National Review of Genetics, 4,* 457–469.

Elfenbein, H. A., & Ambady, N. (2002). On the universality and cultural specificity of emotion recognition: A meta-analysis. *Psychological Bulletin, 128,* 203–235.

Elfenbein, H. A., & Ambady, N. (2003). Universals and cultural differences in recognizing emotions. *Current Directions in Psychological Science, 12,* 159–164.

Elkin, I. (1994). The NIMH Treatment of Depression Collaborative Research Program: Where we began and where we are now. In A. E. Bergin & S. L. Garfield (Eds.), *Handbook of psychotherapy and behavior change* (4th ed., pp. 114–135). New York, NY: Wiley.

Ellenberger, H. F. (1970). *The discovery of the unconscious: The history and evolution of dynamic psychiatry.* New York, NY: Basic Books.

Elliott, R. (2002). The effectiveness of humanistic therapies: A meta-analysis. In D. J. Cain & J. Seeman (Eds.), *Humanistic psychotherapies: Handbook of research and practice* (pp. 57–81). Washington, DC: American Psychological Association.

Ellis, A. (1958). *Sex without guilt.* New York, NY: Lyle Stuart.

Ellis, A. (1962). *Reason and emotion in psychotherapy.* New York, NY: Lyle Stuart.

Ellis, A. (1977). The basic clinical theory of rational-emotive therapy. In A. Ellis & R. Grieger (Eds.), *Handbook of rational-emotive therapy* (pp. 3–34). New York, NY: Springer.

Ellis, A., Abrams, M., & Abrams, L. D. (2008). *Personality theories: Critical perspectives.* New York, NY: Sage.

Ellis, L., & Coontz, P. D. (1990). Androgens, brain functioning, and criminality: The neurohormonal foundations of antisociality. In L. Ellis & H. Hoffman (Eds.), *Crime in biological, social, and moral contexts* (pp. 36–49). New York, NY: Praeger.

Else-Quest, Nicole M.; Hyde, Janet S.; & Linn, Marcia C. (2010). Cross-national patterns of gender differences in mathematics: A meta-analysis. *Psychological Bulletin, 136,* 103–127.

Emmelkamp, P. M. G., Bruynzeel, M., Drost, L., & van der Mast, C. A. P. G. (2001). Virtual reality treatment in acrophobia: A comparison with exposure in vivo. *CyberPsychology & Behavior, 4,* 335–339.

Emmelkamp, P. M. G., Krijn, M., Hulsbosch, A. M., de Vries, S., Schuemie, M. J., & Van der Mast, C. A. P. G. (2002). Virtual reality treatment versus exposure in vivo: A comparative evaluation in acrophobia. *Behaviour Research and Therapy, 40,* 509–516.

Emrick, C. D. (1987). Alcoholics Anonymous: Affiliation processes and effectiveness as treatment. *Alcoholism: Clinical and Experimental Research, 11,* 416–423.

Enard, W., Przeworski, M., Fisher, S. E., Lai, C. S., Wiebe, V., Kitano, T., Monaco, A. P., & Pääbo, S. (2002). Molecular evolution of FOXP2, a gene involved in speech and language. *Nature, 418,* 869–872.

Engle, Randall W. (2002). Working memory capacity as executive attention. *Current Directions in Psychological Science, 11,* 19–23.

Engler, J., & Goleman, D. (1992). *A consumer's guide to psychotherapy.* New York, NY: Simon & Schuster.

Epstude, K., & Roese, N. J. (2008). The functional theory of counterfactual thinking. *Personality and Social Psychology Review, 12,* 168–192.

Erceg-Hurn, David M., & Miosevich, Vikki M. (2008). Modern robust statistical methods. *American Psychologist, 63,* 591–601.

Erdelyi, M. H. (2006). The unified theory of repression. *Behavioral and Brain Sciences, 29,* 499–551.

Ermer, E., Cosmides, L., & Tooby, J. (2008). Relative status regulates risky decision making about resources in men: Evidence for the co-evolution of motivation and cognition. *Evolution and Human Behavior, 29,* 106–118.

Ersche, K. D., Turton, A. J., Pradhan, S., Bullmore, E. T., & Robbins, T. W. (2010). *Drug addiction endophenotypes: Impulsive versus sensation-seeking personality traits. Biological Psychiatry, 68,* 770–773. doi:10.1016/j.biopsych.2010.06.015

Escera, Carles; Cilveti, Robert; & Grau, Carles (1992). Ultradian rhythms in cognitive operations: Evidence from the P300 component of the event-related potentials. *Medical Science Research, 20,* 137–138.

Etcoff, N., Ekman, P., Magee, J., & Frank, M. (2000). Lie detection and language comprehension. *Nature, 405,* 139.

European Network of National Networks studying Gene-Environment Interactions in Schizophrenia (EU-GEI), van Os, J., Rutten, B. P., Myin-Germeys, I., Delespaul, P., Viechtbauer, W., van Zelst, C., . . . & Mirjanic, J. (2014). Identifying gene-environment interactions in schizophrenia: contemporary challenges for integrated, large-scale investigations. *Schizophrenia Bulletin, 40*(4), 729–736. doi:10.1093/schbul/sbu069

Evans, Christopher (1984). *Landscapes of the night* (edited and completed by Peter Evans). New York: Viking.

Ey, D. (2010). Body dissatisfaction and self-esteem in males: Relationships with muscle dysmorphia. *Dissertation Abstracts International, 71,* 2010. Retrieved from EBSCOhost.

Eysenck, H. J. (1952). The effects of psychotherapy: An evaluation. *Journal of Consulting Psychology, 16,* 319–324.

Fagundes, C. P., Glaser, R., Hwang, B. S., Malarkey, W. B., & Kiecolt-Glaser, J. K. (2013). Depressive symptoms enhance stress-induced inflammatory responses. *Brain, Behavior, and Immunity, 31,* 172–176. doi:10.1016/j.bbi.2012.05.006

Fairburn, C. G., Cooper, Z., Shafran, R., & Wilson, G. T. (2008). Eating disorders: A transdiagnostic protocol. In D. H. Barlow (Ed.), *Clinical handbook of psychological disorders: A step-by-step treatment manual* (4th ed., pp. 578–614). New York, NY: Guilford Press.

Fallon, J., Irvine, D., & Shepherd, R. (2008). Cochlear implants and brain plasticity. *Hearing Research, 238,* 110–117.

Fallon, James H.; Keator, David B.; Mbogori, James; et al. (2004). Hostility differentiates the brain metabolic effects of nicotine. *Cognitive Brain Research, 18,* 142–148.

Fallone, Gahan; Acebo, Christine; Seifer, Ronald; & Carskadon, Mary A. (2005). Experimental restriction of sleep opportunity in children: Effects on teacher ratings. *Sleep, 28,* 1280–1286.

Farber, B. A., & Lane, J. S. (2002). Effective elements of the therapy relationship: Positive regard and support. In J. Norcross (Ed.), *Psychotherapy relationships that work: Therapists' relational contributions to effective psychotherapy* (pp. 175–194). New York, NY: Oxford.

Farde, L. (1996). The advantage of using positron emission tomography in drug research. *Trends in Neurosciences, 19,* 211–214.

Farris, C., Treat, T. A., Viken, R. J., & McFall, R. M. (2008). Perceptual mechanisms that characterize gender differences in decoding women's sexual intent. *Psychological Science, 19,* 348–354.

Fasano, S., D'Antoni, A., Orban, P., Valjent, E., Putigano, E., Vara, H., Pizzorusso, T., Giusetto, M., Yoon, B., Soloway, P., Maldonado, R., Caboche, J., & Brambilla, R. (2009). Ras-guanine nucleotide-releasing factor 1 (Ras-GRF1) controls activation of extracellular signal-regulated kinase (ERK) signaling in the striatum and long-term behavioral responses to cocaine. *Biological Psychiatry, 66,* 758–768.

Faulconbridge, L. H. (2008). Ghrelin and neuropeptide Y: Actions and interactions within the neuroanatomically distributed system for the control of feeding behavior. *Dissertation Abstracts International, 68,* 4294. Retrieved from EBSCOhost.

Fazel, S., Långström, N., Hjern, A., Grann, M., & Lichtenstein, P. (2009). Schizophrenia, substance abuse, and violent crime. *Journal of the American Medical Association, 301,* 2016–2023.

Febbraro, G. A. R., Clum, G. A., Roodman, A. A., & Wright, J. H. (1999). The limits of bibliotherapy: A study of the differential effectiveness of self-administered interventions in individuals with panic attacks. *Behavior Therapy, 30,* 209–222.

Feeney, Brooke C., & Cassidy, Jude (2003). Reconstructive memory related to adolescent-parent conflict interactions. *Journal of Personality and Social Psychology, 85,* 945–955.

Fehr, B. (1994). Prototype-based assessment of laypeople's views of love. *Personal Relationships, 1,* 309–331.

Ferrar, K. & Golley, R. (2015). *Adolescent diet and time use clusters and associations with overweight and obesity and socioeconomic position Health Education and Behavior, 5*(5), 361–369. doi: 10.14336/AD.2014.0500346.

Ferri, M., Amoto, L., & Davoli, M. (2006). Alcoholics Anonymous and other 12-step programmes for alcohol dependence. The Cochrance Review. Art. No: CDOO5032. http://dx.doi.org/10.1002/14651858.CD005032.pub2

Feske, U., & Chambless, D. L. (1995). Cognitive behavioral versus exposure only treatment for social phobia: A meta-analysis. *Behavior Therapy, 26,* 695–720.

Fidler, Fiona, & Loftus, Geoffrey R. (2009). Why figures with error bars should replace p values: Some conceptual arguments and empirical demonstrations. *Journal of Psychology, 217,* 27–37.

Fiedler, K. (2008). Language: A toolbox for sharing and influencing social reality. *Perspectives on Psychological Science, 3,* 36–47.

Finlayson, C., Pacheco, F. G., Rodríguez-Vidal, J., Fa, D. A., Gutierrez López, J. M., Santiago Pérez, A., Finlayson, G., Allue, E., Baena-Preysler, J., Cáceres, I., Carrión, J. S., Fernández-Jalvo, Y., Gleed-Owen, C. P., Jimenez-Es-pejo, F. J., López, P., López-Sáez, J. A., Riquelme- Cantal, J. A., Sánchez-Marco, A., Guzman, F. G., Brown, K., Fuentes, N., Valarino, C. A., Villalpando, A.,

Stringer, C. B., Martinez Ruiz, F., & Sakamoto, T. (2006). Late survival of Neanderthals at the southernmost extreme of Europe. *Nature, 443,* 850–853.

First, M. B., Spitzer, R. L., Gibbon, M., & Williams, J. B. W. (1996). *Structured clinical interview for DSM-IV Axis I disorders-Patient Edition (SCID-I/P, Version 2.0).* New York, NY: Biometrics Research Department, New York State Psychiatric Institute.

Fiscella, K., Tancredi, D., & Franks, P. (2009). Adding socioeconomic status to Framingham scoring to reduce disparities in coronary risk assessment. American Heart *Journal, 157*(6), 988–994.

Fisch, H., Hyun, G., Golden, R., Hensle, T. W, Olsson, C. A, & Liberson, G. L. (2003). The influence of paternal age on Down syndrome. *Journal of Urology, 169,* 2275–2278.

Fischer, A. H., Rodriguez-Mosquera, P. M., van-Vianen, A. E. M., & Manstead, A. S. R. (2004). Gender and culture differences in emotion. *Emotion, 4,* 87–94.

Fitzgerald, Daniel A.; Arnold, Jennifer F.; Becker, Eni S.; et al. (2011). How mood challenges emotional memory formation: An fMRI investigation. *NeuroImage, 56,* 1783–1790.

Fitzgerald, P. J. (2008). A neurotransmitter system theory of sexual orientation. *Journal of Sexual Medicine, 5,* 746–748.

Fivush, Robyn, & Nelson, Katherine (2004). Culture and language in the emergence of autobiographical memory. *Psychological Science, 15,* 573–582.

Fivush, Robyn, & Nelson, Katherine (2005). Parent-child reminiscing locates the self in the past. *British Journal of Developmental Psychology, 24,* 235–251.

Flieller, A. (1999). Comparison of the development of formal thought in adolescent cohorts aged 10–15 years. *Developmental Psychology, 35,* 1048–1058.

Flynn, J. R. (1984). The mean IQ of Americans: Massive gains 1932 to 1978. *Psychological Bulletin, 95,* 29–51.

Flynn, J. R. (1987). Massive IQ gains in 14 nations: What IQ tests really measure. *Psychological Bulletin, 101,* 171–191.

Flynn, J. R. (1999). Searching for justice: The discovery of IQ gains over time. *American Psychologist, 54,* 5–20.

Flynn, J. R. (2012). Are we getting smarter? *Rising IQ in the twenty-first century.* Cambridge University Press.

Folkman, S., & Lazarus, R. S. (1980). An analysis of coping in a middle-aged community sample. *Journal of Health and Social Behavior, 21,* 219–239.

Forman, E. M., Herbert, J. D., Moltra, E., Yeomans, P. D., & Geller, P. A. (2007). A randomized controlled effectiveness trial of acceptance and commitment therapy and cognitive therapy for anxiety and depression. *Behavior Modification, 31,* 772–799.

Foster, Jeffrey L.; Huthwaite, Thomas; Yesberg, Julia A.; et al. (2012). Repetition, not number of sources, increases both susceptibility to misinformation and confidence in the accuracy of eyewitnesses. *Acta Psychologica, 139,* 320–326.

Foster, S., & Gurman, A. (1985). Family therapies. In S. Lynn & J. P. Garske (Eds.), *Contemporary psychotherapies: Models and methods* (pp. 377–418). Columbus, OH: Charles E. Merrill.

Foulkes, David (1962). Dream reports from different states of sleep. *Journal of Abnormal and Social Psychology, 65,* 14–25.

Foulkes, David (1999). *Children's dreaming and the development of consciousness.* Cambridge, MA: Harvard University Press.

Fowler, J. H., & Christakis, N. A. (2008). Dynamic spread of happiness in a large social network: Longitudinal analysis over 20 years in the Framingham Heart Study. British Medical *Journal, 337, a2338.*

Fox, R. E. (1996). Charlatanism, scientism, and psychology's social contract. *American Psychologist, 51,* 777–784.

Francks, C., DeLisi, L., Fisher, S., Laval, S., Rue, J., Stein, J., et al. (2003). Confirmatory evidence for linkage of relative hand skill to 2p12-q11. *American Journal of Human Genetics, 72,* 499–502.

Francks, C., Maegawa, S., Lauren, J., Abrahams, B., Velayos-Baeza, A., Medland, S., Colella, S., Groszer, M., McAuley, E., Caffrey, T., Timmusk, T., Pruunsild, P., Koppel, I., Lind, P., Natsummoto-Itaba, N., Nicok, J., Xiong, L., Joober, R., Enard, W., Krinsky, B., Nanba, E., Richardson, A., Riley, B., Martin, N., Strittmatter, S., Miller, H., Rejuescu, D., St. Clair, D., Muglia, P., Roos, J., Fisher, S., Wade-Martins, R., Rouleau, G., Stain, J., Karayiorgou, M., Geschwind, D., Ragoussis, J., Kendler, K., Airaksinen, M., Oshimura, M., DeLisi, L., & Monaco, A. (2007). LRRTM1 on chromosome 2p12 is a maternally suppressed gene that is associated paternally with handedness and schizophrenia. *Molecular Psychiatry, 12,* 1129–1139.

Frank, J. D. (1961). *Persuasion and healing: A comparative study of psychotherapy* (2nd ed.). Baltimore, MD: Johns Hopkins University Press.

Frank, J. D. (1974). Common features of psychotherapies and their patients. *Psychotherapy and Psychosomatics, 24,* 368–371.

Frank, J. D., & Frank, J. B. (1991). *Persuasion and healing: A comparative study of psychotherapy* (3rd ed.). Baltimore, MD: Johns Hopkins University Press.

Frankl, V. (1959). *Man's search for meaning.* New York: Washington Square Press.

Franklin, M. E., & Foa, E. B. (2002). Cognitive behavioral treatment of obsessive-compulsive disorder. In P. Nathan & J. Gorman (Eds.), *A guide to treatments that work* (2nd ed., pp. 367–386). Oxford, England: Oxford University Press.

Frayling, T. M., Timpson, N. J., Weedon, M. N., Zeggini, E., Freathy, R. M., Lindgren, C. M., . . . McCarthy, M. I. (2007). A common variant in the FTOgene is associated with Body Mass Index and predisposes to childhood and adult obesity. *Science, 316,* 889–894.

Frederickson, R. (1992). *Repressed memories.* New York, NY: Fireside/Parkside.

Freiheit, S. R., Vye, D., Swan, R., & Cady, M. (2004). Cognitive-behavioral therapy for anxiety: Is dissemination working? *The Behavior Therapist, 27,* 25–32.

Freud, Sigmund (1900/1953). The interpretation of dreams. In J. Strachey (Ed.), *The standard edition of the complete psychological works of Sigmund Freud* (Vols. 4 and 5). London: Hogarth Press.

Friderun, A. S., & Cummins, J. M. (1996). Misconceptions about mitochondria and mammalian fertilization: Implications for theories on human evolution. *Proceedings of the National Academy of Science, 93,* 13859–13863.

Friedlander, M. L. (1984). Psychotherapy talk as social control. *Psychotherapy, 21,* 335–341.

Friedman, M., & Rosenman, R. H. (1974). *Type A behavior and your heart.* New York: Knopf.

Frijda, N. H., Markam, S., & Sato, K. (1995). Emotions and emotion words. In J. A. Russell, J.-M. Fernàndez-Dols, A. S. R. Manstead, & J. C. Wellenkamp (Eds.), *Everyday conceptions of emotion: An introduction to the psychology, anthropology and linguistics of emotion* (pp. 121–143). New York, NY: Kluwer Academic/Plenum.

Fuchs, C. S.; Stampfer, M. J.; Colditz, G. A.; et al. (1995, May 11). Alcohol consumption and mortality among women. *New England Journal of Medicine, 332,* 1245–1250.

Fuhriman, A., & Burlingame, G. M. (1994). Group psychotherapy: Research and practice. In A. Fuhriman & G. M. Burlingame (Eds.), *Handbook of group psychother-apy: An empirical and clinical synthesis* (pp. 3–40). New York, NY: Wiley.

Fuller, R., Nopoulos, P., Arndt, S., O'Leary, D., Ho, B. C., & Andreasen, N. C. (2002). Longitudinal assessment of premorbid cognitive functioning in patients with schizophrenia through examination of standardized scholastic test performance. *American Journal of Psychiatry, 159,* 1183–1189.

Fulton, M. M., & Allen, E. R. (2005). Polypharmacy in the elderly: A literature review. *Journal of the American Academy of Nurse Practitioners, 17,* 123–132.

Furnham, A., & Bachtiar, V. (2008). Personality and intelligence as predictors of creativity. *Personality and Individual Differences, 45,* 613–617.

Gadea, M., Martinez-Bisbal, M., Marti-Bonmati, Espert, R., Casanova, B., Coret, F., & Celda, B. (2004). Spectroscopic axonal damage of the right locus coeruleus relates to selective attention impairment in early stage relapsing-remitting multiple sclerosis. *Brain, 127,* 89–98

Gades, N. M., Jacobson, D. J., McGree, M. E., St. Sauver, J. L., Lieber, M. M., Nehra, A., . . . Jacobsen, S. J. (2008). The associations between serum sex hormones, erectile function, and sex drive: The Olmsted County Study of urinary symptoms and health status among men. *Journal of Sexual Medicine, 5,* 2209–2220.

Galanter, M., Dermatis, H., & Santucci, C. (2012). Young people in Alcoholics Anonymous: The role of spiritual orientation and AA member affiliation. *Journal of Addictive Diseases, 31*(2), 173–182.

Gallant, Sheryle J.; Hamilton, Jean A.; Popiel, Debra A.; et al. (1991). Daily moods and symptoms: Effects of awareness of study focus, gender, menstrual-cycle phase, and day of the week. *Health Psychology, 10,* 180–189.

Gallori, E., Biondi, E., & Branciamore, S. (2006). Looking for the primordial genetic honeycomb. *Origins of Life and Evolution of the Bio-sphere, 36,* 493–499.

Gallup, G. G., Jr. (1985). Do minds exist in species other than our own? *Neuroscience and Biobehavioral Reviews, 9,* 631–641.

Gallup, G. G., Jr. (1998). Self-awareness and the evolution of social intelligence. *Behavioural Processes, 42,* 239–247.

Galton, F. (1869). *Hereditary genius: An inquiry into its laws and consequences.* Cleveland, OH: World Publishing.

Galvani, A. P., & Slatkin, M. (2003). Evaluating plague and smallpox as historical selective pressures for the CCR5-delta32 HIV-resistance allele. *Proceedings of the National Academy of Science, 100,* 15276–15279.

Gambrill, E. D. (1992). Self-help books: Pseudoscience in the guise of science? *Skeptical Inquirer, 16*(4), 389–399.

Garavan, H. (2010). Insula and drug cravings. *Brain Structure & Function, 214,* 593–601.

Garber, H., & Heber, R. (1982). Modification of predicted cognitive development in high risk children through early intervention. In D. K. Detterman & R. J. Sternberg (Eds.), *How and how much can intelligence be increased?* (pp. 121–137). Norwood, NJ: Ablex.

Garfield, S. L. (1978). Research on client variables. In S. Garfield & A. Bergin (Eds.), *Handbook of psychotherapy and behavior change* (pp. 191–232). New York, NY: Wiley.

Garner, D. M., & Magana, C. (2006). Cognitive vulnerability to anorexia nervosa. In L. B. Alloy & J. H. Riskind (Eds.), *Cognitive vulnerability to emotional disorders* (pp. 365–403). Mahwah, NJ: Erlbaum.

Garry, Maryanne, & Polaschek, Devon L. L. (2000). Imagination and memory. *Current Directions in Psychological Science, 9,* 6–10.

Garry, Maryanne; Manning, Charles G.; Loftus, Elizabeth F.; & Sherman, Steven J. (1996). Imagination inflation: Imagining a childhood event inflates confidence that it occurred. *Psychonomic Bulletin & Review, 3,* 208–214.

Garske, J. P., & Anderson, T. (2003). Toward a science of psychotherapy research: Present status and evaluation. In S. O. Lilienfeld, S. J. Lynn, & J. M. Lohr (Eds.), *Science and pseudoscience in clinical psychology* (pp. 145–175). New York, NY: Guilford Press.

Garven, Sena; Wood, James M.; Malpass, Roy S.; & Shaw, John S., III (1998). More than suggestion: The effect of interviewing techniques from the McMartin Preschool case. *Journal of Applied Psychology, 83,* 347–359.

Gasperini, M., Scherillo, P., Manfredonia, M. G., Franchini, L., & Smeraldi, E. (1993). A study of relapse in subjects with mood disorder on lithium treatment. *European Neuropsychopharmacology, 3,* 103–110.

Gazzaniga, M. (1970). *The bisected brain.* New York: Appleton- Century-Crofts.

Gazzaniga, M. (1989). Organization of the human brain. *Science, 245,* 947–952.

Gelbard-Sagiv, H.; Mukamel, R.; Harel, M.; et al. (2008, October 3). Internally generated reactivation of single neurons in human hippocampus during free recall. *Science, 322,* 96–101.

George, M. S., Sackeim, H., Rush, A. J., Marangell, L. B., Nahas, Z., Husain, M. M., . . . Ballenger, J. C. (2000). Vagus nerve stimulation: A new tool for treatment-resistant depression. *Biological Psychiatry, 47,* 287–295.

Getzels, J. W., & Jackson, P. (1962). *Creativity and intelligence.* New York, NY: Wiley.

Gevins, A., Leong, H., Smith, M. E., Le, J., & Du, R. (1995). Mapping cognitive brain function with modern high-resolution electroencephalography. *Trends in Neurosciences, 18,* 429–436.

Gibbons, R. D., Amatya, A. K., Brown, C. H., Hur, K., Marcus, S. M., Bhaumik, D. K., & Mann, J. J. (2010). Post-approval drug safety surveillance. *Annual Review of Public Health, 31,* 419–437.

Gibson, G. (2007). Human evolution: Thrifty genes and the dairy queen. *Current Biology, 17,* R295-R296.

Giesbrecht, Timo; Lynn, Steven Jay; Lilienfeld, Scott O.; & Merckelbach, Harald (2008). Cognitive processes in dissociation: An analysis of core theoretical assumptions. *Psychological Bulletin, 134,* 617–647.

Gigerenzer, Gerd; Gaissmaier, Wolfgang; Kurz-Milcke, Elke; et al. (2008) Helping doctors and patients make sense of health statistics. *Psychological Science in the Public Interest, 8,* 53–96.

Gila, A., Castro, J., & Cesena, J. (2005). Anorexia nervosa in male adolescents: Body image, eating attitudes and psychological traits. *Journal of Adolescent Health, 36,* 221–226.

Gilchrist, Amanda L., & Cowan, Nelson (2012). Chunking. In V. Ramachandran (Ed.), *Encyclopedia of human behavior* (Vol. 1). San Diego: Academic Press.

Gilestro, Giorgio F.; Tononi, Giulio; & Cirelli, Chiara (2009). Widespread changes in synaptic markers as a function of sleep and wakefulness in Drosophila. *Science, 324,* 109–112.

Gillig, P. M. (2009). Dissociative identity disorder: A controversial diagnosis. *Psychiatry, 6*(3), 24–29.

Glaser, J. P., Os, J. V., Mengelers, R., & Myin-Germeys, I. (2008). A momentary assessment study of the reputed emotional phenotype associated with borderline personality disorder. *Psychological Medicine, 30,* 1–9.

Gleaves, D. H., Miller, K. J., Williams, T. L., & Summers, S. A. (2000). Eating disorders: An overview. In K. J. Miller & J. S. Mizes (Eds.), *Comparative treatments for eating disorders* (pp. 1–49). New York, NY: Springer.

Gobl, C., & Chasaide, A. N. (2003). The role of voice quality in communicating emotion, mood, and attitude. *Speech Communication, 40,* 189–212.

Golden, Robert M.; Gaynes, Bradley N.; Ekstrom, R. David; et al. (2005). The efficacy of light therapy in the treatment of mood disorders: A review and meta-analysis of the evidence. *American Journal of Psychiatry, 162,* 656–662.

Golder, Scott A., & Macy, Michael W. (2011). Diurnal and seasonal mood vary with work, sleep, and daylength across diverse cultures. *Science, 333,* 1878–1881.

Goldey, K. L., & van Anders, S. M. (2010). Sexy thoughts: Effects of sexual cognitions on testosterone, cortisol, and arousal in women. *Hormones and Behavior, 59,* 754–764. doi:10.1016/j.yhbeh.2010.12.005

Goldfried, M. R., & Davison, G. C. (1976). *Clinical behavior therapy.* New York, NY: Holt, Rinehart, & Winston.

Goldfried, M. R., Raue, P. J., & Castonguay, L. G. (1998). The therapeutic focus in significant sessions of master therapists: A comparison of cognitive-behavioral and psychodynamic-interpersonal interventions. *Journal of Consulting and Clinical Psychology, 66,* 803–810.

Goldman-Rakic, Patricia S. (1996). Opening the mind through neurobiology. Invited address at the annual meeting of the American Psychological Association, Toronto, Canada.

Goldstein, L., & Ruscio, J. (2009). Thinking outside the Black Box: The relative risk of suicide with antidepressant use. *Scientific Review of Mental Health Practice, 7,* 3–16.

Goldstein, R. B., Compton, W. M., Pulay, A. J., Ruan, W. J., Pickering, R. P., Stinson, F. S., & Brant, B. F. (2007). Antisocial behavioral syndromes and DSM-IV drug use disorders in the United States: Results from the National Epidemiologic Survey on Alcohol Related Conditions. *Drug and Alcohol Dependence, 90,* 145–158.

Goleman, D. (1997). *Emotional intelligence.* New York, NY: Bantam.

Golimbet, V. E., Alfimova, M. V., Gritsenko, I. K., & Ebstein, R. P. (2007). Relationship between dopamine system genes and extraversion and novelty seeking. *Neuroscience and Behavioral Physiology, 37,* 601–606.

Golkaramnay, V., Bauer, S., Haug, S., Wolf, M., & Kordy, H. (2007). The exploration of the effectiveness of group therapy through an Internet chat as aftercare: A controlled naturalistic study. *Psychotherapy and Psychosomatics, 76,* 219–225.

Golub, Sharon (1992). *Periods: From menarche to menopause.* Newbury Park, CA: Sage.

Gomà-i-Freixanet, M., Martha, C., & Muro, A. (2012). Does the sensation-seeking trait differ among participants engaged in sports with different levels of physical risk? *Anales De Psicología, 28,* 223–232.

Gomez, P., Gunten, A., & Danuser, B. (2013). Content-specific gender differences in emotion ratings from early to late adulthood. Scandinavian *Journal of Psychology, 54, 451–458. doi:10.1111/sjop.12075*

Gonzales, G. (2014). Same-sex marriage: A prescription for better health. New England *Journal of Medicine, 370, 1373–1376. doi: 10.1056/NEJMp1400254*

Goodman, J. A., Krahn, L. E., Smith, G. G., Rummans, T. A., & Pileggi, T. S. (1999). Patient satisfaction with electroconvulsive therapy. *Mayo Clinic Proceedings, 74,* 967–971.

Gopnik, Alison (2009). *The philosophical baby.* New York: Farrar, Straus and Giroux.

Gorman, J. (2007). *The essential guide to psychiatric drugs* (4th ed.). New York: St. Martin's Press.

Gosling, Samuel D.; Vazire, Simine; Srivatava, Sanjay; & John, Oliver P. (2004). Should we trust web-based studies? A comparative analysis of six preconceptions about Internet questionnaires. *American Psychologist, 59,* 93–104.

Gotlib, I., & Hamilton, J. (2008). Neuroimaging and depression: Current status and unresolved issues. *Current Directions in Psychological Science, 17,* 159–163.

Gottesman, I. (1991). *Schizophrenia genesis.* New York: W. H. Freeman.

Gottesman, I., & Gould, T. D. (2003). The endophenotype concept in psychiatry: Etymology and strategic intentions. *American Journal of Psychiatry, 160,* 636–645.

Gouin, J-P., Carter, C. S., Pournajafi-Nazarloo, H., Glaser, R., Malarkey, W. B., Loving, T. J., Stowell, J., & Kiecolt-Glaser, J. K. (2010). Marital behavior, oxytocin, vasopressin, and wound healing. *Psychoneuroendocrinology, 35,* 1082–1090.

Gouin, J. P., & Kiecolt-Glaser, J. K. (2011). The impact of psychological stress on wound healing: Methods and mechanisms. *Immunology and Allergy Clinics of North America, 31,* 81–93.

Gould, M. S., Greenberg, T., Velting, D. M., & Shaffer, D. (2003). Youth suicide risk and preventive interventions: A review of the past 10 years. *Journal of the American Academy of Child and Adolescent Psychiatry, 42,* 386–405.

Gould, R. A., & Clum, G. A. (1993). A meta-analysis of self-help treatment approaches. *Clinical Psychology Review, 13,* 169–186.

Grant, B. S., & Wiseman, L. L. (2002). Recent history of melanism in American peppered moths. *Journal of Heredity, 93,* 86–90.

Grant, Heidi, & Dweck, Carol S. (2003). Clarifying achievement goals and their impact. *Journal of Personality and Social Psychology, 85,* 541–553.

Grawe, K., Donati, R., & Bernauer, F. (1998). *Psychotherapy in transition.* Seattle, WA: Hogrefe & Huber.

Gray, J. R., Braver, T. S., & Raichle, M. E. (2002). Integration of emotion and cognition in the lateral prefrontal cortex. *PNAS Proceedings of the National Academy of Sciences of the United States of America, 99,* 4115–4120.

Greally, J. M. (2007). Genomics: Encyclopaedia of humble DNA. *Nature, 447,* 782–783.

Green, Joseph P., & Lynn, Steven J. (2010). Hypnotic responsiveness: Expectancy, attitudes, fantasy proneness, absorption, and gender. *Clinical and Experimental Hypnosis, 59,* 103–121.

Greenberg, L. S., & Watson, J. C. (1998). Experiential therapy of depression: Differential effects of client-centered relationship conditions and process experiential interventions. *Psychotherapy Research, 8,* 210–224.

Greenberg, L. S., Elliot, R., & Lietaer, G. (1994). Research on humanistic and experiential psychotherapies. In A. E. Bergin & L. S. Garfield (Eds.), *Handbook of psychotherapy and behavior change* (4th ed., pp. 509–539). New York, NY: Wiley.

Greenfield, P. M. (1998). The cultural evolution of IQ. In U. Neisser (Ed.), *The rising curve: Long-term gains in IQ and related measures* (pp. 81–123). Washington, DC: American Psychological Association.

Greenough, William T. (1984). Structural correlates of information storage in the mammalian brain: A review and hypothesis. *Trends in Neurosciences, 7,* 229–233.

Griffiths, R. R.; Richards, W. A.; Johnson, M. W.; et al. (2008). Mystical-type experiences occasioned by psilocybin mediate the attribution of personal meaning and spiritual significance fourteen months later. *Journal of Psychopharmacology, 22,* 621–632.

Grine, F. E., Bailey, R. M., Harvati, K., Nathan, R. P., Morris, A. G., Henderson, G. M., Ribot, I., & Pike, A. W. G., (2007). Late Pleistocene human skull from Hofmeyr, South Africa, and modern human origins. *Science, 315,* 226–229.

Grinspoon, Lester, & Bakalar, James B. (1993). *Marihuana, the forbidden medicine.* New Haven, CT: Yale University Press.

Grob, Charles S.; Danfroth, Alicia L.; Chopra, Gurpreet S.; et al. (2011). Pilot study of psilocybin treatment for anxiety in patients with advanced-stage cancer. *Archives General Psychiatry, 68,* 71–78.

Gron, G., Wunderlich, A. P., Spitzer, M., Tomczrak, R., & Riepe, M. W. (2000). Brain activation during human navigation: Gender-different neural networks as substrate of performance. *Nature Neuroscience, 3,* 404–408.

Gropper, S. S., Simmons, K. P., Gaines, A., Drawdy, K., Saunders, D., Ulrich, P., & Connell, L. J. (2009). The freshman 15: A closer look. *Journal of American College Health, 58,* 223–231.

Groth-Marnat, G. (2009). *Handbook of Psychological Assessment* (5th ed.). New York, NY: Wiley.

Gruber, H. E., & Wallace, D. B. (2001). Creative work: The case of Charles Darwin. *American Psychologist, 56,* 346–349.

Grunbaum, A. (1984). *The foundations of psychoanalysis: A philosophical critique.* Berkeley, CA: University of California Press.

Gudonis, L. C., Derefinko, K., & Giancola, P. R. (2009). The treatment of substance misuse in psychopathic individuals: Why heterogeneity matters. *Substance Use & Misuse, 44*(9–10), 1415–1433.

Gur, R. C., Turetsky, B., Mastsui, M., Yan, M. Bilker, W., Hughett, P., & Gur, R. E. (1999). Sex differences in brain gray and white matter in healthy young adults: correlations with cognitive performance. *Journal of Neuroscience, 19,* 4067–4072.

Gur, R., Gunning-Dixon, F., Bilker, W., & Gur, R. (2002). Sex differences in temporolimbic and frontal brain volumes of healthy adults. *Cerebral Cortex, 12,* 998–1003.

Gurpegui, M., Jurado, D., Luna, J. D., Fernández-Molina, C., Moreno-Abril, O., & Gálvez, R. (2007). Personality traits associated with caffeine intake and smoking. *Progress in Neuro-Psychopharmacology & Biological Psychiatry, 31,* 997–1005.

Guzman-Marin, Ruben; Suntsova, Natalia; Methippara, Melvi; et al. (2005). Sleep deprivation suppresses neurogenesis in the adult hippocampus of rats. *European Journal of Neuroscience, 22,* 2111–2116.

Gwak, Y., Kang, J., Unabia, G., Hulsebosch, C. (2012). Spatial and temporal activation of spinal glial cells: Role of gliopathy in central neuropathic pain following spinal cord injury in rats. *Experimental Neurology, 234,* 362–372.

Haber, Ralph N. (1970, May). How we remember what we see. *Scientific American, 222,* 104–112.

Haimov, Iris, & Lavie, Peretz (1996). Melatonin-A soporific hormone. *Current Directions in Psychological Science, 5,* 106–111.

Haley, J. (1976). *Problem-solving therapy.* San Francisco, CA: Jossey-Bass.

Hall, Calvin (1953a). A cognitive theory of dreams. *Journal of General Psychology, 49,* 273–282.

Hall, Calvin (1953b). *The meaning of dreams.* New York: McGraw-Hill.

Hall, J. A., & Matsumoto, D. (2004). Gender differences in judgments of multiple emotions from facial expressions. *Emotion, 4,* 201–206.

Hall, J. A., Bernieri, F. J., & Carney, D. R. (2006). Nonverbal behavior and interpersonal sensitivity. In J. A. Harrigan, R. Rosenthal, & K. R. Scherer (Eds.), *The new handbook of methods in nonverbal behavior research* (pp. 237–281). New York, NY: Oxford University Press.

Halpern, D. F. (1992). *Sex differences in cognitive abilities* (2nd ed.). Mahwah, NJ: Erlbaum.

Halpern, D. F., Benbow, C. P., Geary, D. C., Gur, R. C., Hyde, J. S., & Gernsbacher, M. A. (2007). The science of sex differences in science and mathematics. *Psychological Science in the Public Interest, 8,* 1–51.

Hamilton, J. (2008, October 16). Multitasking in the car: Just like drunken driving. *NPR: Morning Edition.* Retrieved from http://www.npr.org/templates/story/story.php?storyId=95702512

Hamilton, W. D. (1964). The genetical evolution of social behaviour: I and II. *Journal of Theoretical Biology, 7,* 1–52.

Hamilton, W. D. (1970). Selfish and spiteful behavior in an evolutionary model. *Nature, 228,* 1218–1220.

Haney-Caron, E., Caprihan, A., & Stevens, M. C. (2014). DTI-measured white matter abnormalities in adolescents with Conduct Disorder. *Journal of Psychiatric Research, 48*(1), 111–120. doi:10.1016/j.jpsychires.2013.09.015

Hansen, P. E. B., Ravnkilde, B., Videbech, P., Clemmensen, K., Sturlason, R., Reiner, M., . . . Vestergaard, P. (2011). Low-frequency repetitive transcranial magnetic stimulation inferior to electroconvulsive therapy in treating depression. *Journal of ECT, 27*(1), 26–32.

Hardie, Elizabeth A. (1997). PMS in the workplace: Dispelling the myth of cyclic function. *Journal of Occupational and Organizational Psychology, 70,* 97–102.

Harlow, H. F. (1958). The nature of love. *American Psychologist, 13,* 673–685.

Harlow, H. F., & Zimmerman, R. R. (1959). Affectional responses in the infant monkey. *Science, 130,* 421–432.

Harlow, J. M. (1848). Passage of an iron rod through the head. *Boston Medical and Surgical Journal, 39,* 389–393.

Harms, W. (2006). *Gender equality leads to better sex lives among people 40 and over.* Retrieved from http://www.eurekalert.org/pub_releases/2006–04/uoc-gel041406.php

Harris, J. L., Bargh, J. A., & Brownell, K. D. (2009). Priming effects of television food advertising on eating behavior. *Health Psychology, 28*(4), 404–413.

Hart, John, Jr.; Berndt, Rita S.; & Caramazza, Alfonso (1985, August 1). Category-specific naming deficit following cerebral infarction. *Nature, 316,* 339–340.

Hatzenbuehler, M. L., O'Cleirigh, C., Grasso, C., Mayer, K., Safren, S., & Bradford, J. (2012). Effect of same-sex marriage laws on health care use and expenditures in sexual minority men: A quasi-natural experiment. *American Journal of Public Health, 102,* 285–291.

Hauser, M. D. (1993). Right hemisphere dominance for the production of facial expression in monkeys. *Science, 261,* 475–477.

Haut, Jennifer S.; Beckwith, Bill E.; Petros, Thomas V.; & Russell, Sue (1989). Gender differences in retrieval from long-term memory following acute intoxication with ethanol. *Physiology and Behavior, 45,* 1161–1165.

Hayes, S. C. (2004). Acceptance and commitment therapy, relational frame theory, and the third wave of behavioral and cognitive therapies. *Behavior Therapy, 35*(4), 639–665.

Hayes, S. C., Strosahl, K., & Wilson, K. G. (1999). *Acceptance and commitment therapy.* New York, NY: Guilford Press.

Hazelrigg, M. D., Cooper, H. M., & Borduin, C. M. (1987). Evaluating the effectiveness of family therapies: An integrative review and analysis. *Psychological Bulletin, 101,* 428–442.

Healy, D. (2004). SSRI and suicide? Reply. *Psychotherapy and Psychosomatics, 73,* 262.

Heatherton, T. F., & Sargent, J. D. (2009). Does watching smoking in movies promote teenage smoking? *Current Directions in Psychological Science, 18,* 63–67.

Hebebrand, J., & Hinney, A. (2009). Environmental and genetic risk factors in obesity. *Child and Adolescent Psychiatric Clinics of North America, 18,* 83–94.

Heber, R., Garber, H., Harrington, S., & Hoffman, C. (1972). *Rehabilitation of families at risk for mental retardation.* Madison: University of Wisconsin, Rehabilitation Research and Training Center in Mental Retardation.

Hébert, Richard (September, 2001). Code overload: Doing a number on memory. *APS Observer, 14,* 1, 7–11.

Hedges, L. B., & Nowell, A. (1995). Sex differences in mental test scores, variability, and numbers of high-scoring individuals. *Science, 269,* 41–45.

Heinz, A., & Schlagenhauf, F. (2010). Dopaminergic dysfunction in schizophrenia: Salience attribution revisited. *Schizophrenia Bulletin, 36,* 472–485.

Helder, S. G., & Collier, D. A. (2011). The genetics of eating disorders. In R. H. Adan & W. H. Kaye (Eds.), *Behavioral neurobiology of eating disorders* (pp. 157–175). New York, NY: Springer-Verlag Publishing.

Hellige, J. B. (1990). Hemispheric asymmetry. *Annual Review of Psychology, 41,* 55–80.

Hempel, A., Hempel, E., Schönknecht, P., Stippich, C., & Schröder, J. (2003). Impairment in basal limbic function in schizophrenia during affect cognition. *Psychiatry Research, 122,* 115–124.

Hendrick, C., & Hendrick, S. S. (2003). Romantic love: Measuring Cupid's arrow. In S. J. Lopez & C. R. Snyder (Eds.), *Positive psychological assessment: A handbook of models and measures* (pp. 235–249). Washington, DC: American Psychological Association.

Henrich, Joseph; Heine, Steven J.; & Norenzayan, Ara (2010, June 15). The weirdest people in the world? *Behavioral and Brain Sciences, 33,* 61–83.

Herman, Judith (1992). *Trauma and recovery.* New York: Basic.

Herman, L. M., Uyeyama, R. K., & Pack, A. A. (2008). Bottlenose dolphins understand relationships between concepts. *Behavioral and Brain Sciences, 31,* 139–140.

Hernandez-Reif, M., Diego, M., & Field, T. (2007). Preterm infants show reduced stress behaviors and activity after 5 days of massage therapy. *Infant Behavior & Development, 30,* 557–561.

Herpertz-Dahlmann, B. (2009). Adolescent eating disorders: Definitions, symptomatology, epidemiology and comorbidity. *Child and Adolescent Psychiatric Clinics of North America, 18,* 31–47.

Herrmann, E., Hernández-Lloreda, M. V., Call, J., Haer, B., & Tomasello, M. (2010). The structure of individual differences in the cognitive abilities of children and chimpanzees. *Psychological Science, 21,* 102–110.

Herwig, U., Fallgatter, A. J., Höppner, J., Eschweiler, G. W., Kron, M., Hajak, G., . . . Schönfeldt-Lecuona, C. (2007). Antidepressant effects of augmentative transcranial magnetic stimulation. A randomized multicenter trial. *British Journal of Psychiatry, 191,* 441–448.

Heschl, A., & Burkart, J. (2006). A new mark test for mirror self-recognition in non-human primates. *Primates, 47,* 187–198.

Hess, U., & Thibault, P. (2009). Darwin and emotional expression. *American Psychologist, 64,* 120–128.

Hilgard, Ernest R. (1977). *Divided consciousness: Multiple controls in human thought and action.* New York: Wiley-Interscience.

Hilgard, Ernest R. (1986). *Divided consciousness: Multiple controls in human thought and action* (2nd ed.). New York: Wiley.

Hill, K. E., Mann, L., Laws, K. R., Stippich, C., & Schröder, J. (2004). Hypofrontality in schizophrenia: A meta-analysis of functional imaging studies. *Acta Psychiatrica Scandinavica, 110,* 243–256.

Hillman, C. H., Snook, E. M., & Jerome, G. J. (2003). Acute cardiovascular exercise and executive control function. International *Journal of Psychophysiology, 48*(3), 307–314.

Hillman, C., Pontifex, M., Castelli, D., Khan, N., Raine, L., Scudder, M., . . . & Kamijo, K. (2014). Effects of the FITKids randomized controlled trial on executive control and brain function. *Pediatrics, 134*(4), E1063-E1071.

Hilts, Philip J. (1995). *Memory's ghost: The strange tale of Mr. M. and the nature of memory.* New York: Simon & Schuster.

Hines, M. (2004). *Brain gender.* New York, NY: Oxford University Press.

Hines, M. (2010). Sex-related variation in human behavior and the brain. *Trends in Cognitive Sciences, 14,* 448–456.

Hinrichsen, G. A. (2008). Interpersonal psychotherapy for late life depression: Current status and new applications. *Journal of Rational-Emotive & Cognitive-Behavior Therapy, 26,* 263–275.

Hobson, J. Allan (1990). Activation, input source, and modulation: A neurocognitive model of the state of the brain mind. In R. R. Bootzin, J. F. Kihlstrom, & D. L. Schacter (Eds.), *Sleep and cognition.* Washington, DC: American Psychological Association.

Hobson, J. Allan (2002). *Dreaming: An introduction to the science of sleep.* New York: Oxford University Press.

Hobson, J. Allan, (1988). *The dreaming brain.* New York: Basic.

Hobson, J. Allan; Pace-Schott, Edward F.; & Stickgold, Robert (2000). Dreaming and the brain: Toward a cognitive neuroscience of consicous states. *Behavioral and Brain Sciences, 23,* 793–842, 904–1018, 1083–1121.

Hobson, J. Allan; Sangsanguan, Suchada; Arantes, Henry; & Kahn, David (2011). Dream logic: The inferential reasoning paradigm. *Dreaming, 21,* 1–15.

Hoffman, E. (2008). Maslow in retrospect: Editorial board member assessments. *Journal of Humanistic Psychology, 48,* 456–457.

Hofmann, S. (2007). Cognitive factors that maintain social anxiety disorder: A comprehensive model and its treatment implications. *Cognitive Behaviour Therapy, 36,* 193–209.

Hofmann, S. G. (2008). Cognitive processes in fear acquisition and extinction in animals and humans: Implications for exposure therapy of anxiety disorders. *Clinical Psychology Review, 28,* 199–210.

Hofmann, S. G., Sawyer, A. T., Witt, A. A., & Oh, D. (2010). The effect of mindfulness-based therapy on anxiety and depression: A meta-analytic review. *Journal of Consulting and Clinical Psychology, 78*(2), 169–183.

Hollon, S. D., Thase, M. E., & Markowitz, J. C. (2002). Treatment and prevention of depression. *Psychological Science in the Public Interest, 3,* 2002.

Holloway, C., Cochlin, L., Emmanuel, Y., Murray, A., Codreanu, I., Edwards, L., . . . Clarke, K. (2011). A high-fat diet impairs cardiac high-energy phosphate metabolism and cognitive function in healthy human subjects. *American Journal of Clinical Nutrition, 93,* 748–755.

Holmes, T. H., & Rahe, R. H. (1967). The Social Readjustment Rating Scale. *Journal of Psychosomatic Research, 11,* 213–218.

Holt-Lunstad, J., Smith, T., Layton, J., & Brayne, C. (2010). Social relationships and mortality risk: A meta-analytic review. *PLoS Medicine, 7*(7), e1000316. doi:10.1371/journal.pmed.1000316

Holtzman, C., Trotman, H., Goulding, S., Ryan, A., Macdonald, A., Shapiro, D., . . . & Walker, E. (2013). Stress and neurodevelopmental processes in the emergence of psychosis. *Neuroscience, 249,* 172–191. doi:10.1016/j.neuroscience.2012.12.017

Hopkins, W., & Cantalupo, C. (2004). Handedness in chimpanzees (Pan troglodytes) is associated with asymmetries of the primary motor cortex but not with homologous language areas. *Behavioral Neuroscience, 118,* 1176–1183.

Hopko, D. R., Robertson, S. M. C., & Lejuez, C. W. (2006). Behavioral activation for anxiety disorders. *The Behavior Analyst Today, 7,* 212–224.

Horney, K. (1945). Our inner conflicts: A constructive theory of neurosis. New York, NY: Summit Books.

Horstmann, G. (2003). What do facial expressions convey: Feeling states, behavioral intentions, or action requests? *Emotion, 3,* 150–166.

Horvath, A. O., Del Re, A. C., Flückiger, C., & Symonds, D. (2011). Alliance in individual psychotherapy. *Psychotherapy, 48*(1), 9.

Howard, A. D., Feighner, S. D., Cully, D. F., Arena, J. P., Liberator, P. A., Rosenblum, C. I., et al. (1996). A receptor in pituitary and hypothalamus that functions in growth hormone release. *Science, 273,* 974–977.

Howard, K. I., Kopta, S. M., Krause, M. S., & Orlinsky, D. E. (1986). The dose-effect relationship in psychotherapy. *American Psychologist, 41,* 159–164.

Howe, Mark L. (2000). *The fate of early memories: Developmental science and the retention of childhood experiences.* Washington, DC: American Psychological Association.

Howe, Mark L.; Courage, Mary L.; & Peterson, Carole (1994). How can I remember when "I" wasn't there? Long-term retention of traumatic experiences and emergence of the cognitive self. *Consciousness and Cognition, 3,* 327–355.

Hu, H.; Real, E.; Takamiya, K.; et al. (2007). Emotion enhances learning via norepinephrine regulation of AMPA-receptor trafficking. *Cell, 131,* 160–173.

Huas, C. C., Caille, A. A., Godart, N. N., Foulon, C. C., Pham-Scottez, A. A., Divac, S. S., . . . Falissard, B. B. (2011). Factors predictive of ten-year mortality in severe anorexia nervosa patients. *Acta Psychiatrica Scandinavica, 123,* 62–70.

Huffman, C. J., Matthews, T. D., & Gagne, P. E. (2001). The role of part-set cuing in the recall of chess positions: Influence of chunking in memory. *North American Journal of Psychology, 3,* 535–542.

Hunsley, J., & DiGuilio, G. (2002). Dodo bird, phoenix, or urban legend? *Scientific Review of Mental Health Practice, 1,* 11–22.

Hunt, E. (2012). What makes nations intelligent? *Perspectives on Psychological Science, 7,* 284–306. doi:10.1177/1745691612442905

Hunt, E. (2013). The intelligence of nations: A rejoinder to commentators. *Perspectives on Psychological Science, 8,* 193–194. doi:10.1177/1745691613476893

Hunt, E., & Carlson, J. (2007). Considerations relating to the study of group differences in intelligence. *Perspectives on Psychological Science, 2,* 194–213.

Hunt, M. (1997). *How science takes stock: The story of meta-analysis.* New York, NY: Russell Sage Foundation.

Huntjens, Rafaële J. C.; Verschuere, Bruno; & McNally, Richard J. (2012). Inter-identity autobiographical amnesia in patients with dissociative identity disorder. *PloS One, 7*(7): e40580.

Huttenlocher, P. (1994). Synaptogenesis, synapse elimination, and neural plasticity in human cerebral cortex. In C. Nelson (Ed.), *The Minnesota symposia on child psychology* (Vol. 27, pp. 35–54). Hillsdale, NJ: Erlbaum.

Huyser, C., Veltman, D. J., de Haan, E., & Boer, F. (2009). Paediatric obsessive-compulsive disorder, a neurodevelopmental disorder? Evidence from neuroimaging. *Neuroscience and Biobehavioral Reviews, 33,* 818–830.

Hyde, J. S. (1984). Children's understanding of sexist language. *Developmental Psychology, 20,* 697–706.

Hyde, J. S. (1986). Gender differences in aggression. In. J. S. Hyde, & M. C. Linn (Eds.), *The psychology of gender differences: Advances through meta-analysis* (pp. 51–66). Baltimore, MD: Johns Hopkins University Press.

Hyde, J. S., & Mezulis, A. H. (2002). Gender difference research: Issues and critique. In J. Worrell (Ed.), *Encyclopedia of women and gender: Sex similarities and differences and the impact of society on gender* (Vol. 1, pp. 551–559). San Diego, CA: Academic Press.

Hyde, J. S., & Oliver, M. B. (2000). Gender differences in sexuality: Results from meta-analysis: Psychology of women. In C. B, Travis & J. W. White (Eds.), *Sexuality, society, and feminism* (pp. 57–77). Washington, DC: American Psychological Association.

Hyde, J., Mezulis, A., & Abramson, L. (2008). The ABCs of depression: Integrating affective, biological, and cognitive models to explain the emergence of the gender difference in depression. *Psychological Review, 115,* 291–313.

Hyman, Ira E., Jr., & Pentland, Joel (1996). The role of mental imagery in the creation of false childhood memories. *Journal of Memory and Language, 35,* 101–117.

Insel, T. R. (2014). The NIHM Research Domain Criteria (RDoC) Project: Precision medicine for psychiatry. The American *Journal of Psychiatry, 171*(4), *395–397. doi:10.1176/appi.ajp.2014.14020138*

Irvin, J. E., Bowers, C. A., Dunn, M. E., & Wang, M. C. (1999). Efficacy of relapse prevention: A meta-analytic review. *Journal of Consulting and Clinical Psychology, 67,* 563–570.

Ivey, A. E., Ivey, M. B., & Simek-Morgan, L. (1993). *Counseling and psychotherapy: A multi-cultural perspective* (3rd ed.). Boston, MA: Allyn & Bacon.

Izard, C. E. (1971). *The face of emotion.* New York, NY: Appleton-Century-Crofts.

Izard, C. E. (1980). Cross-cultural perspectives on emotion and emotion communication. In H. C. Triandis & W. J. Lonner (Eds.), *Handbook of cross-cultural psychology* (Vol. 3, pp. 185–220). Boston, MA: Allyn & Bacon.

Jaakkola, K., Fellner, W., Erb, L., Rodriguez, M., & Guarino, E. (2005). Understanding of the concept of numerically "less" by bottlenose dolphins (Tursiops truncatus). *Journal of Comparative Psychology, 119,* 296–303.

Jack, R. E., Caldara, R., & Schyns, P. G. (2011). Internal representations reveal cultural diversity in expectations of facial expressions of emotion. *Journal of Experimental Psychology: General, 141, 1–7. doi:10.1037/a0023463*

Jacobson, E. (1938). *Progressive relaxation.* Chicago, IL: University of Chicago Press.

Jacobson, N. S., Dobson, K. S., Truax, P. A., Addis, M. E., Koerner, K., Gollan, J. K., . . . Prince, S. E. (1996). A component analysis of cognitive-behavioral treatment for depression. *Journal of Consulting and Clinical Psychology, 64,* 295–304.

James, William (1902/1936). *The varieties of religious experience.* New York: Modern Library.

Jäncke, L., Brunner, B., & Esslen, M. (2008). *Brain activation during fast driving in a driving simulator: The role of the lateral prefrontal cortex. Neuroreport: For Rapid Communication of Neuroscience Research, 19,* 1127–1130.

Janos, P. M., & Robinson, N. M. (1985). Psychosocial development in intellectually gifted children. In F. D. Horowitz & M. O'Brien (Eds.), *Gifted and talented: Developmental perspectives* (pp. 149–195). Washington, DC: American Psychological Association.

Jaynes, J. (1976). *The origin of consciousness and the breakdown of the bicameral mind.* Boston, MA, USA: Houghton Mifflin.

Jehna, M. M., Neuper, C. C., Ischebeck, A. A., Loitfelder, M. M., Ropele, S. S., Langkammer, C. C., . . . Enzinger, C. C. (2011). *The functional correlates of face perception and recognition of emotional facial expressions as evidenced by fmri. Brain Research, 1393,* 73–83. doi:10.1016/j.brainres.2011.04.007

Jenkins, J. J., Jimenez-Pabon, E., Shaw, R. E., & Sefer, J. W. (1975). *Schuell's aphasia in adults: Diagnosis, prognosis, and treatment* (2nd ed.). Hagerstown, MD: Harper & Row.

Jenkins, John G., & Dallenbach, Karl M. (1924). Obliviscence during sleep and waking. *American Journal of Psychology, 35,* 605–612.

Jenkins, L. M., & Andrewes, D. G. (2012). A new set of standardised verbal and nonverbal contemporary film stimuli for the elicitation of emotions. *Brain Impairment, 13,* 212–227. doi:10.1017/BrImp.2012.18

Jensen, P. S., Garcia, J. A., Glied, S., Crow, M., Foster, M., Schlander, M., . . . Wells, K. (2005). Cost-effectiveness of ADHD treatments: Findings from the multi-modal treatment study of children with ADHD. *American Journal of Psychiatry, 162,* 1628–1636.

Jewell, J., & Buehler, B. (2011). *Fragile x syndrome.* Retrieved October 23, 2012 from http://emedicine.medscape.com/article/943776-overview

Jilek, W. G. (1995). Emil Kraepelin and comparative sociocultural psychiatry. *European Archives of Psychiatry and Clinical Neuroscience, 245,* 231–238.

Johnson, Andrew J., & Miles, Christopher (2009). Serial position effects in 2-alternative forced choice recognition: functional equivalence across visual and auditory modalities. *Memory, 17,* 84–91.

Johnson, C. (2002). Obesity, weight management, and self-esteem. In T. A. Wadden & A. J. Stunkard, *Handbook of obesity treatment* (pp. 480–493). New York, NY: Guilford Press.

Johnson, J. (2009). A dark history: Memories of lobotomy in the new era of psychosurgery. *Medicine Studies, 1*(4), 367–378.

Johnson, Marcia K.; Hashtroudi, Shahin; & Lindsay, D. Stephen (1993). Source monitoring. *Psychological Bulletin, 114,* 3–28.

Johnson, Marcia K.; Raye, Carol L.; Mitchell, Karen J.; & Ankudowich, Elizabeth (2011). The cognitive neuroscience of true and false memories. In R. F. Belli (Ed.), *True and false recovered memories: Toward a reconciliation of the debate* (Vol. 58). New York: Springer.

Johnson, W., Turkheimer, E., Gottesman, I., & Bouchard, T. (2009). Beyond heritability: Twin studies in behavioral research. *Current Directions in Psychological Science, 18,* 207–220.

Jones, D., Owens, M., Kumar, M., Cook, R., Weiss, S.M. (2013). The effect of relaxation interventions on cortisol levels in HIV-sero-positive women. *Journal of the International Association of Providers of AIDS Care, 13*(4). *doi:10.1177/2325957413488186*

Jones, J. E., III. (2005). *Kitzmiller v. Dover Area School District* (Case No. 04cv2688). http: //www.pamd.uscourts.gov/kitzmiller/kitzmiller _342.pdf

Joormann, J., & Vanderlind, W. M. (2014). Emotion regulation in depression: The role of biased cognition and reduced cognitive control. *Clinical Psychological Science, 2*(4), 402–421. doi:10.1177/2167702614536163

Joormann, Jutta, & Gotlib, Ian H. (2007). Selective attention to emotional faces following recovery from depression. *Journal of Abnormal Psychology, 116,* 80–85.

Joseph, J. E., Liu, X., Jiang, Y., Lynam, D., & Kelly, T. H. (2009). Neural correlates of emotional reactivity in sensation seeking. *Psychological Science, 20,* 215–223.

Julg, B., & Goebel, F. D. (2005). Susceptibility to HIV/AIDS: An individual characteristic we can measure? *Infection, 33,* 160–162.

Julius, M., Harburg, E., Cottington, E. M., & Johnson, E. H. (1986). Angercoping types, blood pressure, and all-cause mortality: A follow-up in Tecumseh, Michigan (1971–1983). *American Journal of Epidemiology, 124,* 220–233.

Kabat-Zinn, J. (2003). Mindfulness-based interventions in context: Past, present, and future. *Clinical Psychology: Science & Practice, 10,* 144–156.

Kan, K.-J., Wicherts, J. M., Dolan, C. V., & van der Maas, H. L. J. (2013). On the nature and nurture of intelligence and specific cognitive abilities: The more heritable, the more culture dependent. *Psychological Science, 24,* 2420–2428. doi:10.1177/0956797613493292

Kanazawa, S., & Still, M. C. (2001). The emergence of marriage norms: An evolutionary psychological perspective. In M. Hechter (Ed.), *Social norms* (pp. 274–304). New York: Russell Sage Foundation.

Kandel, Eric R. (2001). The molecular biology of memory storage: A dialogue between genes and synapses. *Science, 294,* 1030–1038.

Kandel, Eric R., & Schwartz, James H. (1982). Molecular biology of learning: Modulation of transmitter release. *Science, 218,* 433–443.

Kane, Michael J.; Brown, Leslie H.; McVay, Jennifer C.; et al. (2007). For whom the mind wanders, and when: An experience-sampling study of working memory and executive control in daily life. *Psychological Science, 18,* 614–621.

Karni, Avi; Tanne, David; Rubenstein, Barton S.; et al. (1994). Dependence on REM sleep of overnight improvement of a perceptual skill. *Science, 265,* 679–682.

Karon, B. P. (1994). *Effective psychoanalytic therapy of schizophrenia and other severe disorders* (APA Videotape Series). Washington, DC: American Psychological Association.

Karpicke, Jeffrey D. (2012). Retrieval-based learning: Active retrieval promotes meaningful learning. *Current Directions in Psychological Science, 21,* 157–163.

Karpicke, Jeffrey D., & Roediger, Henry L. III (2008, February 15). The critical importance of retrieval for learning. *Science, 319,* 966–968.

Kaschak, Michael P.; Kutta, Timothy J.; & Jones, John L. (2011). Structural priming as implicit learning: Cumulative priming effects and individual differences. *Psychonomic Bulletin & Review, 18,* 1133–1139.

Kashdan, T. B., & Fincham, F. D. (2002). "Facilitating creativity by regulating curiosity": Comment. *American Psychologist, 57,* 373–374.

Kashdan, T. B., & Silvia, P. J. (2009). Curiosity and interest: The benefits of thriving on novelty and challenge. In S. J. Lopez & C. R. Snyder (Eds.), *Oxford handbook of positive psychology* (2nd ed., pp. 367–374). New York, NY: Oxford University Press.

Kavale, K. A. (2002). Mainstreaming to full inclusion: From orthogenesis to pathogenesis of an idea. International *Journal of Disability, Development and Education, 49,* 201–214.

Kay, A. C., Whitson, J. A., Gaucher, D., & Galinsky, A. D. (2009). Compensatory control: Achieving order through the mind, our institutions, and the heavens. *Current Directions in Psychological Science, 18,* 264–268.

Kazdin, A. E. (1978). The application of operant techniques in treatment, rehabilitation, and education. In S. L. Garfield & A. E. Bergin (Eds.), *Handbook of psychotherapy and behavior change* (2nd ed.). New York, NY: Wiley.

Kazdin, A. E. (2005). Treatment outcomes, common factors, and continued neglect of mechanisms of change. *Clinical Psychology: Science and Practice, 12,* 184–188.

Kazdin, A. E. (2007). Mediators and mechanisms of change in psychotherapy research. *Annual Review of Clinical Psychology, 3,* 1–27.

Kazdin, A. E., & Hersen, M. (1980). The current status of behavior therapy. *Behavior Modification, 4,* 283–302.

Kazdin, A. E., & Wilcoxon, L. A. (1976). Systematic desensitization and non-specific treatment effects: A methodological evaluation. *Psychological Bulletin, 83,* 729–758.

Keel, P. K., Heatherton, T. F., Dorer, D. J., Joiner, T. E., & Zalta, A. K. (2006). Point prevalence of bulimia nervosa in 1982, 1992, and 2002. *Psychological Medicine, 36,* 119–127.

Keinan, G., Almagor, M., & Ben-Porath, Y. S. (1989). A reevaluation of the relationships between psychotherapeutic orientation and perceived personality characteristics. *Psychotherapy, 26,* 218–226.

Kell, H. J., Lubinski, D., & Benbow, C. P. (2013). Who rises to the top? Early indicators. *Psychological Science, 24,* 648–659. doi:10.1177/0956797612457784

Kelly, J. F., Hoeppner, B., Stout, R. L., & Pagano, M. (2012). Determining the relative importance of the mechanisms of behavior change within Alcoholics Anonymous: A multiple mediator analysis. *Addiction, 107*(2), 289–299. http://dx.doi.org/10.1111/j.1360–0443.2011.03593.x

Kendall, T., Pilling, S., & Whittington, C. J. (2005). Are the SSRIs and atypical antidepressants safe and effective for children and adolescents? *Current Opinion in Psychiatry, 18,* 21–25.

Kessler, R. C., Duncan, G. J., Gennetian, L. A., Katz, L. F., Kling, J. R., Sampson, N. A., . . . & Ludwig, J. (2014). Associations of housing mobility interventions for children in high-poverty neighborhoods with subsequent mental disorders during adolescence. JAMA: *Journal of the American Medical Association, 311*(9), 937–947. doi:10.1001/jama.2014.607

Kiecolt-Glaser, J. (1984). Psychosocial modifiers of immunocompetence in medical students. *Psychosomatic Medicine, 46*(1), 7–14.

Kiecolt-Glaser, J. K., & Newton, T. L. (2001). Marriage and health: His and hers. *Psychological Bulletin, 127,* 472–503.

Kihlstrom, J. F. (2005). Dissociative disorders. *Annual Review of Clinical Psychology, 1,* 227–253.

Kihlstrom, John F. (1994). Hypnosis, delayed recall, and the principles of memory. *International Journal of Clinical and Experimental Hypnosis, 40,* 337–345.

Kim, B., Lee, S., Kim, Y. W., Choi, T. K., Yook, K., Suh, S. Y., &Yook, K. (2010). Effectiveness of a mindfulness-based cognitive therapy program as an adjunct to pharmacotherapy in patients with panic disorder. *Journal of Anxiety Disorders, 24*(6), 590–595. http://dx.doi.org/10.1016/j.janxdis.2010.03.019

Kim, E. S., Park, N., Peterson, C (2011). Dispositional optimism protects older adults from stroke: The Health and Retirement Study. *Stroke, 42*(10), 2855–2859. doi:10.1161/STROKEAHA.111.613448

Kim, E. S., Smith, J., Kubzansky, L. D. (2014). Prospective study of the association between dispositional optimism and incident heart failure. *Circulation: Heart Failure, 7*(3), 394–400. doi:10.1161/CIRCHEARTFAILURE.113.000644.

Kim, H. S., Sherman, D. K., & Taylor, S. E. (2008). Culture and social support. *American Psychologist, 63,* 518–526

Kim, L., & Makdissi, A. (2009). Hyperparathyroidism. *Retrieved January 20,* 2010 from http://emedicine.medscape.com/article/ 127351-overview.

King, M. C., & Wilson, A. C. (1975). Evolution at two levels in humans and chimpanzees. *Science, 188,* 107–116.

King, S., St. Hilaire, A., & Heidkamp, D. (2010). Prenatal factors in schizophrenia. *Current Directions in Psychological Science, 19,* 209–213.

Kinney, T. (2008). Task and individual characteristics as predictors of performance in a job-relevant multi-tasking environment. *Dissertation Abstracts International: Section B: The Sciences and Engineering, 68,* 7011.

Kinsey, Alfred C.; Pomeroy, Wardell B.; & Martin, Clyde E. (1948). *Sexual behavior in the human male.* Philadelphia: Saunders.

Kinsey, Alfred C.; Pomeroy, Wardell B.; Martin, Clyde E.; & Gebhard, Paul H. (1953). *Sexual behavior in the human female.* Philadelphia: Saunders.

Kirsch, I. (1990). *Changing expectations: A key to effective psychotherapy.* Pacific Grove, CA: Brooks/Cole.

Kirsch, I. (2010). *The emperor's new drugs.* New York, NY: Basic Books.

Kirsch, Irving (1997). Response expectancy theory and application: A decennial review. *Applied and Preventive Psychology, 6,* 69–70.

Kirsch, Irving, & Lynn, Steven J. (1995). The altered state of hypnosis: Changes in the theoretical landscape. *American Psychologist, 50,* 846–858.

Kirsch, Irving; Silva, Christopher E.; Carone, James E.; et al. (1989). The surreptitious observation design: An experimental paradigm for distinguishing artifact from essence in hypnosis. *Journal of Abnormal Psychology, 98,* 132–136.

Kirshner, H., & Hoffmann, M. (2012). *Aphasia.* Retrieved October 23, 2012, from http://emedicine.medscape.com/article/1135944-clinical#a0217

Kirshner, H., & Jacobs, D. (2008). *Aphasia.* Retrieved February 3, 2009 from *http://emedicine.medscape.com/article/1135944-overview.*

Klar, A. (2003). Human handedness and scalp hair-whorl direction develop from a common genetic mechanism. *Genetics, 165,* 269–276.

Klein, M. H., Kolden, G. G., Michels, J., & Chisholm-Stockard, S. (2002). Effective elements of the therapy relationship: Congruence/genuineness. In J. C. Norcross (Ed.), *Psychotherapy relationships that work: Therapists' relational contributions to effective psychotherapy* (pp. 195–215). London, England: Oxford University Press.

Klein, Raymond, & Armitage, Roseanne (1979). Rhythms in human performance: 1 1/2-hour oscillations in cognitive style. *Science, 204,* 1326–1328.

Klengel, T., & Binder, E. B. (2013). Gene-environment interactions in major depressive disorder. The Canadian *Journal of Psychiatry/La Revue Canadienne de Psychiatrie, 58*(2), 76–83.

Klerman, G. L., & Weissman, M. M. (Eds.). (1993). *New applications of interpersonal psychotherapy.* Washington, DC: American Psychiatric Press.

Klerman, G. L., Weissman, M. M., Rounsaville, B. J., & Chevron, E. S. (1984). *Interpersonal psychotherapy of depression.* New York, NY: Basic Books.

Klimoski, R. (1992). Graphology in personnel selection. In B. L. Beyerstein & D. F. Beyerstein (Eds.), *The write stuff: Evaluations of graphology-The study of handwriting analysis* (pp. 232–268). Buffalo, NY: Prometheus.

Klomek, A., Marrocco, F., Kleinman, M., Schonfeld, I., & Gould, M. (2007). Bullying, depression, and suicidality in adolescents. *Journal of the American Academy of Child & Adolescent Psychiatry, 46,* 40–49.

Kluger, J. (2010, August 16). Inside the minds of animals. Time, 36–43. Knecht, S., Dräger, B., Deppe, M., Bobe, L., Lohmann, H., & Flöel, A., . . . Hennigsen, H. (2000). Handedness and hemispheric language dominance in healthy humans. Brain: A *Journal of Neurology, 123,* 2512–2518.

Knight, G. P., Fabes, R. A., & Higgins, D. A. (1996). Concerns about drawing causal inferences from meta-analyses: An example in the study of gender differences in aggression. *Psychological Bulletin, 119,* 410–421.

Kobayashi, H. (2007). Mimicry as social glue: Spontaneous mimicry in autism spectrum disorder. *Japanese Psychological Review, 50,* 89–95.

Kolata, G. (1998, May 27). *Scientists see a mysterious similarity in a pair of deadly plagues.* New York Times, p. 1.

Kolla, Bhanu, P., & Auger, R. Robert (2011). Jet lag and shift work sleep disorders: How to help reset the internal clock. *Cleveland Clinic Journal of Medicine, 78,* 675–684.

Komiya, N., Good, G. E., & Sherrod, N. B. (2000). Emotional openness as a predictor of college students' attitudes toward seeking psychological help. *Journal of Counseling Psychology, 47,* 138–143.

Koordeman, R., Anschutz, D. J., van Baaren, R. B., & Engels, R. E. (2010). Exposure to soda commercials affects sugar-sweetened soda consumption in young women. An observational experimental study. *Appetite, 54,* 619–622. doi:10.1016/j.appet.2010.03.008

Kornum, Birgitte R.; Faraco, Juliette; & Mignot, Emmanuel (2011). Narcolepsy with hypocretin/orexin deficiency, infections and autoimmunity of the brain. *Current Opinion in Neurobiology, 21,* 897–903.

Kosslyn, Stephen M.; Thompson, William L.; Costantini-Ferrando, Maria F.; et al. (2000). Hypnotic visual illusion alters color processing in the brain. *American Journal of Psychiatry, 157,* 1279–1284.

Kounios, J., Fleck, J. I., Green, D. L., Payne, L., Stevenson, J. L., Bowden, E. M., & Jung-Beeman, M. (2008). The origins of insight in resting-state brain activity. *Neuropsychologia, 46,* 281–291.

Kounios, J., Fleck, J., Green, D., Payne, L., Stevenson, J., Bowden, E., & Jung-Beeman, M. (2008). The origins of insight in resting-state brain activity. *Neuropsychologia, 46,* 281–291.

Kovas, Y., Voronin, I., Kaydalov, A., Malykh, S. B., Dale, P. S., & Plomin, R. (2013). Literacy and numeracy are more heritable than intelligence in primary school. *Psychological Science, 24,* 2048–2056. doi:10.1177/0956797613486982

Kripke, Daniel F. (1974). Ultradian rhythms in sleep and wakefulness. In E. D. Weitzman (Ed.), *Advances in sleep research* (Vol. 1). Flushing, NY: Spectrum.

Kruger, J., & Dunning, D. (1999). Unskilled and unaware of it: How difficulties in recognizing one's own incompetence lead to inflated self-assessments. *Journal of Personality and Social Psychology, 77,* 1121–1134.

Kruk, M., Meelis, W., Halasz, J., & Haller, J. (2004). Fast positive feedback between the adrenocortical stress response and a brain mechanism involved in aggressive behavior. *Behavioral Neuroscience, 118,* 1062–1070.

Kucharska-Pietura, K., & Klimkowski, M. (2002). Perception of facial affect in chronic schizophrenia and right brain damage. *Acta Neurobiologiae Experimentalis, 62,* 33–43.

Kumari, V. (2006). Do psychotherapies produce neurobiological effects? *Acta Neuropsychiatrica, 18,* 61–70.

Kuncel, N. R., Hezlett, S. A., & Ones, D. S. (2004). Academic performance, career potential, creativity, and job performance: Can one construct predict them all? *Journal of Personality and Social Psychology, 86,* 148–161.

Kushner, M. (1968). The operant control of intractable sneezing. In C. D. Spielberger, R. Fox, & B. Masterson (Eds.), *Contributions to general psychology: Selected readings for introductory psychology.* New York, NY: Roland Press.

LaBerge, Stephen, & Levitan, Lynne (1995). Validity established of DreamLight cues for eliciting lucid dreaming. Dreaming: *Journal of the Association for the Study of Dreams, 5,* 159–168.

Lacasse, J. R., & Leo, J. (2005). Serotonin and depression: A disconnect between the advertisements and the scientific literature. *PLoS Medicine, 2,* 101–106.

Lambert, K. G. (2003). The life and career of Paul MacLean: A journey toward social and neurobiological harmony. *Physiology & Behavior, 79,* 373–381.

Lambert, M. J., & Ogles, B. M. (2004). The efficacy and effectiveness of psychotherapy. In M. J. Lambert (Ed.), *Bergin and Garfield's handbook of psychotherapy and behavior change* (5th ed., pp. 139–193). New York, NY: Wiley.

Landman, J. T., & Dawes, R. M. (1982). Psychotherapy outcome: Smith and Glass conclusions stand up under scrutiny. *American Psychologist, 37,* 504–516.

Landrigan, C. P.; Fahrenkopf, A. M.; Lewin, D.; et al. (2008). Effects of the Accreditation Council for Graduate Medical Education duty hour limits on sleep, work hours, and safety. *Pediatrics, 122,* 250–258.

Lang, Ariel J.; Craske, Michelle G.; Brown, Matt; & Ghaneian, Atousa (2001). Fear-related state dependent memory. *Cognition & Emotion, 15,* 695–703.

Langlois, F., Langlois, M., Carpentier, A. C., Brown, C., Lemieux, S., & Hivert, M. (2011). Ghrelin levels are associated with hunger as measured by the Three-Factor Eating Questionnaire in healthy young adults. *Physiology & Behavior, 104,* 373–377. doi:10.1016/j.physbeh.2011.04.013

Lannin, D. G., Vogel, D. L., Brenner, R. E., & Tucker, J. R. (2015). Predicting self-esteem and intentions to seek counseling: The internalized stigma model. *The Counseling Psychologist, 43*(1), 64–93. doi:10.1177/0011000014541550

Lansford, J. E., & Dodge, K. A. (2008). Cultural norms for adult corporal punishment of children and societal rates of endorsement and use of violence. *Parenting: Science and Practice, 8,* 257–270.

Larimer, M. E., Palmer, R. S., & Marlatt, G. A. (1999). Relapse prevention: An overview of Marlatt's cognitive-behavioural model. *Alcohol Research and Health, 23,* 151–160.

Lau, Hiuyan; Alger, Sara E.; & Fishbein, William (2011). Relational memory: A daytime nap facilitates the abstraction of general concepts. *PloS One, 6,* e27139. doi: 10.1371/journal.pone.0027139.

Laumann, E. O., Gagnon, J. H., Michael, R. T, & Michaels, S. (1994). *The social organization of sexuality: Sexual practices in the United States.* Chicago: University of Chicago Press.

Lautenschlager, N. T., Cox, K. L., Flicker, L., Foster, J., van Bockxmeer, F. M., Xiao, J., Greenop, K., & Almeida, O. P. (2008). Effect of physical activity on cognitive function in older adults at risk for Alzheimer disease: A randomized trial. *Journal of the American Medical Association, 300,* 1027–1037.

Lavie, Peretz (1976). Ultradian rhythms in the perception of two apparent motions. *Chronobiologia, 3,* 21–218.

Lavie, Peretz (2001). Sleep-wake as a biological rhythm. *Annual Review of Psychology, 52,* 277–303.

Lawrence, C. J., Lott, I., & Haier, R. J. (2005). Neurobiology of autism, mental retardation, and Down syndrome: What can we learn about intelligence? In C. Stough (Ed.), *Neurobiology of exceptionality* (pp. 125–142). New York, NY: Kluwer/Plenum.

Lazarus, A. A. (2006). *Brief but comprehensive psychotherapy: The multimodal way.* New York, NY: Springer.

Lazarus, R. S. (1991). Cognition and motivation in emotion. *American Psychologist, 46,* 352–367.

Lazarus, R. S. (2003). Does the positive psychology movement have legs? *Psychological Inquiry, 14,* 93–109.

Lebow, J. L. (2010). The effective treatment of personality disorders: Easily within our grasp. *Professional Psychology: Research and Practice, 41,* 73–74.

Leckman, J. F., Hrdy, S. B., Keverne, E. B., & Carter, C. (2006). A biobehavioral model of attachment and bonding. In R. J. Sternberg & K. Weis (Eds.), *The new psychology of love* (pp. 116–145). New Haven, CT: Yale University Press.

LeDoux, J. E. (2000). Emotion circuits in the brain. *Annual Review of Neuroscience, 23,* 155–184.

Ledrich, J., & Gana, K. (2013). Relationship between attributional style, perceived control, self-esteem, and depressive mood in a nonclinical sample: A structural equation-modelling approach. *Psychology and Psychotherapy: Theory, Research and Practice, 86*(4), 413–430. doi:10.1111/j.2044–8341.2012.02067.x

Lee, E. B., & Mattson, M. P. (2013). The neuropathology of obesity: Insights from human disease. *Acta Neuropathologica, 127,* 3–28. doi:10.1007/s00401–013–1190-x

LeFever, G. B., Arcona, A. P., & Antonuccio, D. O. (2003). ADHD among American schoolchildren: Evidence of overdiagnosis and overuse of medication. *Scientific Review of Mental Health Practice, 2,* 49–60.

Leichsenring, F., Rabung, S., & Leibing, E. (2004). The efficacy of short-term psychodynamic psychotherapy in specific psychiatric disorders. *Archives of General Psychiatry, 61,* 1208–1216.

Lejoyeux, M., & Ades, J. (1997). Antidepressant discontinuation: A review of the literature. *Journal of Clinical Psychiatry, 58(Suppl. 7),* 11–15.

Lenz, A., Taylor, R., Fleming, M., & Serman, N. (2014). Effectiveness of dialectical behavior therapy for treating eating disorders. *Journal of Counseling & Development, 92, 26–35. doi:10.1002/j.1556–6676.2014.00127.x*

Leonardo, E., & Hen, R. (2006). Genetics of affective and anxiety disorders. *Annual Review of Psychology, 57,* 117–137.

Leproult, Rachel; Copinschi, Georges; Buxton, Orfeu; & Van Cauter, Eve (1997). Sleep loss results in an elevation of cortisol levels the next evening. *Sleep, 20,* 865–870.

Lerner, C. A., Sundar, I. K., Watson, R. M., Elder, A., Jones, R., Done, D., . . . & Rahman, I. (2015). Environmental health hazards of e-cigarettes and their components: Oxidants and copper in e-cigarette aerosols. *Environmental Pollution, 198,* 100–107. doi:10.1016/j.envpol.2014.12.033

Levant, R. F. (2004). The empirically validated treatments movement: A practitioner/educator perspective. *Clinical Psychology: Science and Practice, 11,* 219–224.

LeVay, S. (1991). A difference in hypothalamic structure between heterosexual and homosexual men. *Science, 253,* 1034–1038.

LeVay, S. (2011). *Gay, straight, and the reason why: The science of sexual orientation.* New York, NY: Oxford University Press.

LeVay, S., & Hamer, D. H. (1994, May). Evidence for a biological influence in male homosexuality. *Scientific American, 270*(5), 44–49.

Levenston, G. K., Patrick, C. J., Bradley, M. M., & Lang, P. J. (2000). The psychopath as observer: Emotion and attention in picture processing. *Journal of Abnormal Psychology, 109*(3), 373–385.

Levin, B. E. (2010). Developmental gene × environment interactions affecting systems regulating energy homeostasis and obesity. *Frontiers in Neuroendocrinology, 31,* 270–283.

Levin, Daniel T. (2000). Race as a visual feature: Using visual search and perceptual discrimination tasks to understand face categories and the cross-race recognition deficit. *Journal of Experimental Psychology: General, 129,* 559–574.

Levine, B. (1979). *Group psychotherapy: Practice and development.* Englewood Cliffs, NJ: Prentice Hall.

Levis, D. J. (1995). Decoding traumatic memory: Implosive theory of psychopathology. In W. O. Donohue & L. Kranser (Eds.), *Theories in behavior therapy* (pp. 173–207). Washington, DC: American Psychological Association.

Levy, J. (1985). Right Brain, Left Brain: Fact and Fiction, *Psychology Today,* May, 43–44.

Levy, J., & Pashler, H. (2008). Task prioritisation in multitasking during driving: Opportunity to abort a concurrent task does not insulate braking responses from dual-task slowing. *Applied Cognitive Psychology, 22,* 507–525.

Levy, J., Pashler, H., & Boer, E. (2006). Central interference in driving: Is there any stopping the psychological refractory period? *Psychological Science, 17,* 228–235.

Lewald, J. (2004). Gender-specific hemispheric asymmetry in auditory space perception. *Cognitive Brain Research, 19,* 92–99.

Lewy, Alfred J.; Ahmed, Saeeduddin; Jackson, Jeanne L.; & Sack, Robert L. (1992). Melatonin shifts human circadian rhythms according to a phase response curve. *Chronobiology International, 9,* 380–392.

Lewy, Alfred J.; Lefler, Bryan J.; Emens, Jonathan S.; & Bauer, Vance K. (2006). The circadian basis of winter depression. *Proceedings of the National Academy of Sciences, 103,* 7414–7419.

Li, J. Z., Absher, D. M., Tang, H., Southwick, A. M., Casto, A. M., Ramachandran, S., Cann, H. M., Barsh, G. S., Feldman, M., Cavalli-Sforza, L. L., & Myers, R. M. (2008). Worldwide human relationships inferred from genome-wide patterns of variation. *Science, 319,* 1100–1104.

Lick, J. (1975). Expectancy, false galvanic skin response feedback, and systematic desensitization in the modification of phobic behavior. *Journal of Consulting and Clinical Psychology, 43,* 557–557.

Lickliter, R., & Honeycutt, H. (2003). Developmental dynamics: Toward a biologically plausible evolutionary psychology. *Psychological Review, 129,* 819–835.

Lieberman, J. A., Stroup, T. S., McEvoy, J. P., Swartz, M. S., Rosenheck, R. A., Perkins, D. O., . . . Hsiao, J. K. (2005). Effectiveness of antipsychotic drugs in patients with chronic schizophrenia. New England *Journal of Medicine, 353(12),* 1209–1223.

Lilienfeld, S. O. (2007). Psychological treatments that cause harm. *Perspectives on Psychological Science, 2*(1), 53–70. http://dx.doi.org/10.1111/j. 1745-6916.2007.00029.x

Lilienfeld, S. O., & Lynn, S. J. (2003). Dissociative identity disorder: Multiple personalities, multiple controversies. In S. O. Lilienfeld, S. J. Lynn, & J. M. Lohr (Eds.), *Science and pseudoscience in clinical psychology* (pp. 109–143). New York, NY: Guilford Press.

Lilienfeld, S. O., & Lynn, S. J. (2003). Dissociative identity disorder: Multiple personality, multiple controversies. In S. O. Lilienfeld, J. M. Lohr, & S. J. Lynn (Eds.), *Science and pseudoscience in clinical psychology* (pp. 109–142). New York: Guilford Press.

Lilienfeld, S. O., Lynn, S. J., Kirsch, I., Chaves, J. F., Sarbin, T. R., Ganaway, G. K., & Powell, R. A. (1999). Dissociative identity disorder and the sociocognitive model: Recalling the lessons of the past. *Psychological Bulletin, 125,* 507–523.

Lilienfeld, S. O., Waldman, I. D., Landfield, K., Watts, A. L., Rubenzer, S., & Faschingbauer, T. R. (2012). Fearless dominance and the U.S. presidency: Implications of psychopathic personality traits for successful and unsuccessful political leadership. *Journal of Personality and Social Psychology, 103*(3), *489–505. doi:10.1037/a0029392*

Lin, L.; Hungs, M.; & Mignot, E. (2001). Narcolepsy and the HLA region. *Journal of Neuroimmunology, 117,* 9–20.

Lindberg, S. M., Hyde, J. S., Petersen, J. L., & Linn, M. C. (2010). New trends in gender and mathematics performance: A meta-analysis. *Psychological Bulletin, 136,* 1123–1135.

Lindsay, D. Stephen, & Read, J. Don (1994). Psychotherapy and memories of childhood sexual abuse: A cognitive perspective. *Applied Cognitive Psychology, 8,* 281–338.

Lindsay, D. Stephen; Hagen, Lisa; Read, J. Don; et al. (2004). True photographs and false memories. *Psychological Science, 15,* 149–154.

Linehan, M. M. (1993). *Cognitive behavioral treatment of borderline personality disorder.* New York, NY: Guilford Press.

Linton, Marigold (1978). Real-world memory after six years: An in vivo study of very long-term memory. In M. M. Gruneberg, P. E. Morris, & R. N. Sykes (Eds.), *Practical aspects of memory.* London: Academic Press.

Lippa, R. R. (2005). *Gender, nature, and nurture* (2nd ed.). Mahwah, NJ: Erlbaum.

Lisman, John; Yasuda, Ryohei; & Raghavachari, Stridhar (2012). Mechanisms of CaMKII action in long-term potentiation. *Nature Reviews Neuroscience, 13,* 169–182.

Littauer, H., Sexton, H., & Wynn, R. (2005). Qualities clients wish for in their therapists. *Scandanavian Journal of Caring Science, 19,* 28–31.

Liu, H., Waite, L. (2014). Bad marriage, broken heart? Age and gender differences in the link between marital quality and cardiovascular risks among older adults. *Journal of Health and Social Behavior, 55*(4), 403–423. doi:10.1177/0022146514556893.

Loehlin, J. (2009). History of behavior genetics. In Kim, Y. (Ed.), *Handbook of behavior genetics* (pp. 3–14). New York: Spring Science + Business Media, LLC.

Loftus, E. F. (1993). The reality of repressed memories. *American Psychologist, 48,* 518–537.

Loftus, Elizabeth F. (2011). Intelligence gathering post-9/11. *American Psychologist, 66,* 532–541.

Loftus, Elizabeth F., & Greene, Edith (1980). Warning: Even memory for faces may be contagious. *Law and Human Behavior, 4,* 323–334.

Loftus, Elizabeth F., & Palmer, John C. (1974). Reconstruction of automobile destruction: An example of the interaction between language and memory. *Journal of Verbal Learning and Verbal Behavior, 13,* 585–589.

Loftus, Elizabeth F., & Pickrell, Jacqueline E. (1995). The formation of false memories. *Psychiatric Annals, 25,* 720–725.

Loftus, Elizabeth F.; Miller, David G.; & Burns, Helen J. (1978). Semantic integration of verbal information into a visual memory. *Journal of Experimental Psychology: Human Learning and Memory, 4,* 19–31.

Loftus, Elizabeth, & Guyer, Melvin J. (2002). Who abused Jane Doe? *Skeptical Inquirer.* Part 1: May/June, 24–32. Part 2: July/August, 37–40.

Logothetis, N. (2008). What we can do and what we cannot do with fMRI. *Nature, 453,* 869–878.

Logue, A. W. (2000). Self-control and health behavior. In W. K. Bickel & R. E. Vuchinich (Eds.), *Reframing health behavior change with behavioral economics* (pp. 167–192). Mahwah, NJ: Erlbaum.

Lohr, J. M., DeMaio, C., & McGlynn, F. D. (2003). Specific and nonspecific treatment factors in the experimental analysis of behavioral treatment efficacy. *Behavior Modification, 27,* 322–368.

Lohr, J. M., Tolin, D. F., & Lilienfeld, S. O. (1998). Efficacy of eye movement desensitization and reprocessing. *Behavior Therapy, 29,* 123–156.

Long, D., & Baynes, K. (2002). Discourse representation in the two cerebral hemispheres. *Journal of Cognitive Neuroscience, 14,* 228–242.

Lonner, Walter J., & Malpass, Roy (Eds.) (1994). *Psychology and culture.* Needham Heights, MA: Allyn & Bacon.

Lorsch, J. R., & Szostak, J. W. (1996). Chance and necessity in the selection of nucleic acid catalysts. *Accounts of Chemical Research, 29,* 103–110.

Luborsky, L., Crits-Christoph, P., McLellan, T., Woody, G., Piper, W., Imber, S., & Liberman, B. (1986). Do therapists vary much in their success? Findings from four outcome studies. *American Journal of Orthopsychiatry, 56,* 501–512.

Luborsky, L., McLellan, A. T., Diguer, L., Woody, G., & Seligman, D. A. (1997). The psychotherapist matters: Comparison of outcomes across twenty-two therapists and seven patient samples. *Clinical Psychology: Science and Practice, 4*(1), 53–65.

Luborsky, L., Mellon, J., van Ravenswaay, P., Childress, A. R., Colen, K., Hole, A., . . . Alexander, K. (1985). A verification of Freud's grandest clinical hypothesis: The transference. *Clinical Psychology Review, 5,* 231–246.

Luck, A., Pearson, S., Maddern, G., & Hewett, P. (1999). Effects of video information on precolonoscopy anxiety and knowledge: A randomised trial. *Lancet, 354,* 2032–2035.

Lugaresi, Elio; Medori, R.; Montagna, P.; et al. (1986, October 16). Fatal familial insomnia and dysautonomia with selective degeneration of thalamic nuclei. *New England Journal of Medicine, 315,* 997–1003.

Luria, Alexander R. (1968). *The mind of a mnemonist* (L. Soltaroff, trans.). New York: Basic.

Lutgendorf, S. K., Costanzo, E., & Siegel, S. (2007). Psychosocial influences in oncology: An expanded model of biobehavioral mechanisms. In R. Ader, R. Glaser, N. Cohen, & M. Irwin (Eds.), *Psychoneuroimmunology* (4th ed., pp. 869–895). New York: Academic Press.

Lutgendorf, S., Slavich, G., Degeest, K., Goodheart, M., Bender, D., Thaker, P., . . . & Sood, A. (2013). Non-cancer life stressors contribute to impaired quality of life in ovarian cancer patients. *Gynecologic Oncology, 131*(3), 667–673. doi:10.1016/j.ygyno.2013.09.025

Luty, S. E., Carter, J. D., McKenzie, J. M., Rae, A. M., Frampton, C., Mulder, R. T., & Joyce, P. R. (2010). Randomised controlled trial of interpersonal psychotherapy and cognitive-behavioural therapy for depression. *Focus, 8*(1), 110.

Lykins, A. D., Meana, M., & Strauss, G. P. (2008). Sex differences in visual attention to erotic and non-erotic stimuli. *Archives of Sexual Behavior, 37,* 219–228.

Lynam, D. R., & Gudonis, L. (2005). The development of psychopathology. *Annual Review of Clinical Psychology, 1,* 381–407.

Lynn, R., & Irwing, P. (2004). Sex differences on the Progressive Matrices: A meta-analysis. *Intelligence, 32,* 481–498.

Lynn, S. J., & Frauman, D. (1985). Group psychotherapy. In S. J. Lynn, & J. P. Garske (Eds.), *Contemporary psychotherapies: Models and methods* (pp. 419–458). Columbus, OH: Charles E. Merrill.

Lynn, Steven Jay, & Green, Joseph P. (2011). The sociocognitive and dissociation theories of hypnosis: Toward a rapprochement. *Clinical and Experimental Hypnosis, 59,* 277–293.

Lynn, Steven Jay; Rhue, Judith W.; & Weekes, John R. (1990). Hypnotic involuntariness: A social cognitive analysis. *Psychological Review, 97,* 69–184.

Lyons, M. J., York, T. P., Franz, C. E., Grant, M. D., Eaves, L. J., Jacobson, K. S., . . .Kremen, W. S. (2009). Genes determine stability and the environment determines change in cognitive ability during 35 years of adulthood. *Psychological Science, 20,* 1146–1152. doi:10.1111/j.1467-9280.2009.02425.x

Ma, W., & Yu, C. (2006). Intramolecular RNA replicase: Possibly the first self-replicating molecule in the RNA world. *Origins of Life and the Evolutionary Biosphere, 36,* 413–420.

Macdonald, K., & Macdonald, T. M. (2010). The peptide that binds: A systematic review of oxytocin and its prosocial effects in humans. *Harvard Review of Psychiatry, 18,* 1–21.

MacKillop, J., Lisman, S. A., Weinstein, A., & Rosenbaum, D. (2003). Controversial treatments for alcoholism. In S. O. Lilienfeld, S. J. Lynn, & J. W. Lohr (Eds.), *Science and pseudoscience in clinical psychology* (pp. 273–306). New York, NY: Guilford Press.

Macleod, John; Oakes, Rachel; Copello, Alex; et al. (2004). Psychological and social sequelae of cannabis and other illicit drug use by young people: A systematic review of longitudinal, general population studies. *The Lancet, 363,* 1568–1569.

MacWhinney, B. (2005). Language evolution and human development. In B. J. Ellis & D. F. Bjorklund (Eds.), *Origins of the social mind: Evolutionary psychology and child development* (pp. 383–410). New York, NY: Guilford Press.

Madsen, Kreesten M.; Hviid, Anders; Vestergaard, Mogens; et al. (2002). A population-based study of measles, mumps, and rubella vaccination and autism. *New England Journal of Medicine, 347,* 1477–1482.

Maes, H. H., Neale, M. C., & Eaves, L. J. (1997). Genetic and environmental factors in relative body weight and human adiposity. *Behavioral Genetics, 27,* 325–351.

Maguire, E. A., Gadian, D. G., Johnsrude, I. S., Good, C. D., Ashburner, J., Frackowiak, R. S. J., & Frith, C. D. (2000). Navigation-related structural change in the hippocampi of taxi drivers. *Proceedings of the National Academy of Science, 97,* 4398–4403.

Maier, S. F., & Watkins, L. R. (1998). Cytokines for psychologists: Implications of bidirectional immune-to-brain communication for understanding behavior, mood, and cognition. *Psychological Review, 105,* 83–107.

Malcom, K. (1989). Patients' perceptions and knowledge of electroconvulsive therapy. *Psychiatric Bulletin, 13,* 161–165.

Maloney, E. A., Sattizahn, J. R., & Beilock, S. L. (2014). Anxiety and cognition. *WIREs Cognitive Science, 5,* 403–411. doi:10.1002/wcs.1299

Malterer, M. B., Glass, S. J., & Newman, J. P. (2008). Psychopathy and trait emotional intelligence. *Personality and Individual Differences, 44,* 735–745.

Mann et al. (2007). Road rage and collision involvement. *American Journal of Health Behavior, 31,* 384–391.

Manning, Carol A.; Hall, J. L.; & Gold, Paul E. (1990). Glucose effects on memory and other neuropsychological tests in elderly humans. *Psychological Science, 1,* 307–311.

Marino, L., & Lilienfeld, S. O. (1998). Dolphin-assisted therapy: Flawed data, flawed conclusions. *Anthrozoos, 11,* 194–200.

Marino, L., & Lilienfeld, S. O. (2007). Dolphin-assisted therapy: More flawed data and more flawed conclusions. *Anthrozoos, 20,* 239–249.

Mark, G., Gudith, D., & Klocke, U. (2008). The cost of interrupted work: More speed and stress. Presented at the Annual Computer Human Interaction (CHI) Conference, Florence, Italy (April 5–10). Retrieved from http://www.ics.uci.edu/~gmark/chi08-mark.pdf

Marks, R. P., Swinson, M., Basoglu, K., & Kuch, H. (1993). Alpraxolam and exposure alone and combined in panic disorder with agoraphobia. *British Journal of Psychiatry, 162,* 788–799.

Marlatt, G. A. (1983). The controlled-drinking controversy: A commentary. *American Psychologist, 10,* 1097–1110.

Marlatt, G. A. (2002). Buddhist philosophy and the treatment of addictive behavior. *Cognitive and Behavioral Practice, 9,* 44–47.

Marlatt, G. A., & Gordon, J. R. (Eds.). (1985). *Relapse prevention: Maintenance strategies in the treatment of addictive behaviors.* New York, NY: Guilford Press.

Marlatt, G. Alan, & Rohsenow, Damaris J. (1980). Cognitive processes in alcohol use: Expectancy and the balanced placebo design. In N. K. Mello (Ed.), *Advances in substance abuse* (Vol. 1). Greenwich, CT: JAI Press.

Marlowe, F., & Wetsman, A. (2001). Preferred waist-to-hip ratio and ecology. *Personality and Individual Differences, 30,* 481–489.

Marsh, A. A., & Blair, R. J. R. (2008). Deficits in facial affect recognition among antisocial populations: A meta-analysis. *Neuroscience & Biobehavioral Reviews, 32,* 454–465.

Marsh, Elizabeth J., & Tversky, Barbara (2004). Spinning the stories of our lives. *Applied Cognitive Psychology, 18,* 491–503.

Martin, Garry, & Pear, Joseph (2011). *Behavior modification: What it is and how to do it* (9th ed.). Upper Saddle River, NJ: Pearson/Prentice Hall.

Maruta, T., Colligan, R. C., Malinchoc, M., & Offord, K. P. (2000). Optimists vs pessimists: Survival rate among medical patients over a 30-year period. *Mayo Clinic Proceedings, 75,* 140–143.

Marvan, M. L.; Diaz-Erosa, M.; & Montesinos, A. (1998). Premenstrual symptoms in Mexican women with different educational levels. *Journal of Psychology, 132,* 517–526.

Mashour, G. A., Walker, E. E., & Martuza, R. L. (2005). Psychosurgery: Past, present, and future. *Brain Research Reviews, 48,* 409–419.

Maslow, A. H. (1954). Motivation and personality. New York, NY: Harper & Row. Mason, M. F., & Morris, M. W. (2010). Culture, attribution and automaticity: A social cognitive neuroscience view. *Social Cognitive and Affective Neuroscience, 5,* 292–306.

Maslow, A. H. (1954). *Motivation and personality.* New York, NY: Harper.

Mason, R., & Just, M. (2004). How the brain processes causal inferences in text: A theoretical account of generation and integration component processes utilizing both cerebral hemispheres. *Psychological Science, 15,* 1–7.

Masters, W. H., & Johnson, V. E. (1966). *Human sexual response.* Boston, MA: Little, Brown.

Mather, G. (2006). *Foundations of perception.* New York, NY, USA: Psychology Press.

Mather, Mara; Shafir, Eldar; & Johnson, Marcia K. (2000). Misremembrance of options past: Source monitoring and choice. *Psychological Science, 11,* 132–138.

Matsumoto, D., Olide, A., Schug, J., Willingham, B., & Callan, M. (2009). Cross-cultural judgments of spontaneous facial expressions of emotion. *Journal of Nonverbal Behavior, 33,* 213–238.

Matsumoto, D., Yoo, S., & Chung, J. (2010). The expression of anger across cultures. In M. Potegal, G. Stemmler, & C. Spielberger (Eds.), *International handbook of anger: Constituent and concomitant biological, psychological, and social processes* (pp. 125–137). New York, NY: Springer.

Matsumoto, David, & Yoo, Seung Hee (2006). Toward a new generation of cross-cultural research. *Perspectives on Psychological Science, 1,* 234–250.

Matthews, K., & Gump, B. B. (2002). Chronic work stress and marital dissolution increase risk of posttrial mortality in men from the Multiple Risk Factor Intervention Trial. *Archives of Internal Medicine, 162,* 309–315.

Mayberg, H. S., Lozano, A. M., Voon, V., McNeely, H. E., Seminowicz, D., Hamani, C., . . . Kennedy, S. H. (2005). Deep brain stimulation for treatment-resistant depression. *Neuron, 45,* 651–660.

Mayr, E. (2000). Darwin's influence on modern thought. *Scientific American, 283,* 79–83.

Mayr, E. (2001). *What evolution is.* New York: Basic Books.

Mazzoni, Giuliana A.; Loftus, Elizabeth F.; Seitz, Aaron; & Lynn, Steven J. (1999). Changing beliefs and memories through dream interpretation. *Applied Cognitive Psychology, 13,* 125–144.

McCall, G. S., & Shields, N. (2008). Examining the evidence from small-scale societies and early prehistory and implications for modern theories of aggression and violence. *Aggression and Violent Behavior, 13,* 1–9.

McClearn, G. E. (1963). The inheritance of behavior. In L. J. Postman (Ed.), *Psychology in the making* (pp. 144–252). New York: Knopf.

McClelland, James L. (1994). The organization of memory: A parallel distributed processing perspective. *Revue Neurologique, 150,* 570–579.

McClelland, James L. (2011). Memory as a constructive process: The parallel-distributed processing approach. In S. Nalbantian, P. Matthews, & J. L. McClelland (Eds.), *The memory process: Neuroscientific and humanistic perspectives.* Cambridge, MA: MIT Press.

McClure, E. B. (2000). A meta-analytic review of sex differences in facial expression processing and their development in infants, children, and adolescents. *Psychological Bulletin, 126,* 424–453.

McCullough, M. E., & Willoughby, B. L. (2009). Religion, self-regulation, and self-control: Associations, explanations, and implications. *Psychological Bulletin, 135,* 69–93.

McCullough, M. E., Hoyt, W. T., Larson, D. B., Koenig, H. G., & Thoresen, C. E. (2000). Religious involvement and mortality: A meta-analytic review. *Health Psychology, 19,* 211–222.

McDonald, A., & Walter, G. (2004). The portrayal of ECT in American movies. *Journal of ECT, 20,* 230–236.

McDonough, Laraine, & Mandler, Jean M. (1994). Very long-term recall in infancy. *Memory, 2,* 339–352.

McEvoy, P. M. (2007). Effectiveness of cognitive behavioural group therapy for social phobia in a community clinic: A benchmarking study. *Behaviour Research and Therapy, 45,* 3030–3040.

McFall, R. M. (2006). Doctoral training in clinical psychology. *Annual Review of Clinical Psychology, 2,* 21–49.

McFarlane, Jessica M., & Williams, Tannis M. (1994). Placing premenstrual syndrome in perspective. *Psychology of Women Quarterly, 18,* 339–373.

McFarlane, Jessica; Martin, Carol L.; & Williams, Tannis M. (1988). Mood fluctuations: Women versus men and menstrual versus other cycles. *Psychology of Women Quarterly, 12,* 201–223.

McGaugh, James L. (1990). Significance and remembrance: The role of neuromodulatory systems. *Psychological Science, 1,* 15–25.

McGeown, William J.; Venneri, Annalena; Kirsch, Irving; et al. (2012). Suggested visual hallucination without hypnosis enhances activity in visual areas of the brain. *Consciousness and Cognition, 21,* 100–116.

McGlashan, T. H., Zipursky, R. B., Perkins, D., Addington, J., Miller, T., & Woods, S. W. (2006). Randomized double-blind clinical trial of olanzapine versus placebo in patients prodromally symptomatic for psychosis. *American Journal of Psychiatry, 163,* 790–799.

McGorry, P. D., Yung, A. R., Phillips, L. J., Yuen, H. P., Francey, S., & Cosgrave, E. M. (2002). Randomized controlled trial of interventions designed to reduce the risk of progression to ?rst-episode psychosis in a clinical sample with subthreshold symptoms. *Archives of General Psychiatry, 59,* 921–928.

McGrayne, Sharon B. (2011). *The theory that would not die: How Bayes' rule cracked the Enigma code, hunted down Russian submarines and emerged triumphant from two centuries of controversy.* New Haven, CT: Yale University Press.

McGregor, Ian, & Holmes, John G. (1999). How storytelling shapes memory and impressions of relationship events over time. *Journal of Personality and Social Psychology, 76,* 403–419.

McGruder, J. (2004). Disease models of mental illness and aftercare patient education: Critical observations from meta-analyses, cross-cultural practice and anthropological study. *British Journal of Occupational Therapy, 67,* 310–318.

McHugh P. R. (2008). *Try to remember: Psychiatry's clash over meaning, memory, and mind.* New York, NY: Dana Press.

McHugh, Paul R.; Lief, Harold I.; Freyd, Pamela P.; & Fetkewicz, Janet M. (2004). From refusal to reconciliation: Family relationships after an accusation based on recovered memories. *Journal of Nervous and Mental Disease, 192,* 525–531.

McIntosh, D. N. (2006). Spontaneous facial mimicry, liking and emotional contagion. *Polish Psychological Bulletin, 37,* 31–42.

McKee, Richard D., & Squire, Larry R. (1992). Equivalent forgetting rates in long-term memory for diencephalic and medial temporal lobe amnesia. *Journal of Neuroscience, 12,* 3765–3772.

McKinney, K. G. (2009). Initial evaluation of Active Minds: A student organization dedicated to reducing the stigma of mental illness. *Journal of College Student Psychotherapy, 23*(4), 281–301.

McMahon, F., Akula, N., Schulze, T., Pierandrea, M., Tozzi, F., Detera-Wadleigh, S., Steele, C., Breuer, R., Strohmaier, J., Wendland, J., Mattheisen, M., Muhleisen, T., Maier, W., Nothen, M., Cichon, S., Farmer, A., Vincent, J., Holsboer, F., Preisig, M., & Reitschel, M. (2010). Meta-analysis of genome-wide association data identifies a risk locus for major mood disorders on 3p21.1. *Nature, 42,* pp. 128–131.

McNally, R. J. (2003). *Remembering trauma.* Cambridge, MA: Belknap Press.

McNally, Richard J. (2003). *Remembering trauma.* Cambridge, MA: Harvard University Press.

McNeil, B. J., Pauker, S. G., Sox, H. C., Jr., & Tversky, A. (1982). On the elicitation of preferences for alternative therapies. *The New England Journal of Medicine, 306,* 1259–1262.

Mcquillan, J. (2007). Predicting achievement for students from low socioeconomic backgrounds using the Wechsler Intelligence Scale for Children-Third Edition and the Universal Nonverbal Intelligence Test. *Dissertation Abstracts International Section A: Humanities and Social Sciences, 67,* 2954.

Mead, C. A. (1989). *Analog VLSI and neural systems.* New York: Addison Wesley.

Meador, B. D. , & Rogers, C. R. (1979). Person centered therapy. In J. R. Corsini (Ed.), *Current psychotherapies.* Itasca, IL: F. E. Peacock.

Medawar, Peter B. (1979). Advice to a young scientist. New York: Harper & Row.

Mednick, S. A. [Sarnoff]. (1962). The associative basis of creativity. *Psychological Review, 69,* 220–232.

Mednick, Sara C.; Cai, Denise J.; Shuman, Tristan; et al. (2011). An opportunistic theory of cellular and systems consolidation. *Trends in Neuroscience, 34,* 504–514.

Mednick, Sara C.; Nakayama, Ken; Cantero, Jose L.; et al. (2002). The restorative effect of naps on perceptual deterioration. *Nature Neuroscience, 5,* 677–681.

Meehl, P. (1990). Toward an integrated theory of schizotaxia, schizotypy, and schizophrenia. *Journal of Personality Disorders, 4,* 1–99.

Mehl, Matthias R.; Vazire, Simine; Ramírez-Esparza, Nairán; & Pennebacker, James W. (2007). Are women really more talkative than men? *Science, 317,* 82.

Meichenbaum, D. (1985). Cognitive-behavioral therapies. In S. J. Lynn, & J. P. Garske (Eds.), *Contemporary psychotherapies: Models and methods* (pp. 261–286). Columbus, OH: Charles E. Merrill.

Meichenbaum, D. (1996). Stress inoculation training for coping with stressors. *The Clinical Psychologist, 49,* 4–10.

Meissner, Christian A., & Brigham, John C. (2001). Thirty years of investigating the own-race bias in memory for faces: A meta-analytic review. *Psychology, Public Policy, & Law, 7,* 3–35.

Mellinger, D. M., & Lynn, S. J. (2003). *The monster in the cave: How to face your fear and anxiety and live your life.* New York, NY: Berkeley.

Melton, G. B., Petrila, J., Poythress, N. G., & Slobogin, C. (2007). *Psychological evaluations for the courts: A handbook for mental health professionals and lawyers* (3rd ed.). New York: Guilford Press.

Menchola, B. L., Arkowitz, H., & Burke, B. L. (2007). Efficacy of self-administered treatments for depression and anxiety: A meta-analysis. *Professional Psychology: Research and Practice, 38,* 421–429.

Menninger, K. (1958). *Theory of psychoanalytic technique.* New York, NY: Basic Books.

Mercer, Jean; Sarner, Larry; and Rosa, Linda (2003). *Attachment therapy on trial.* Westport, CT: Praeger.

Merrick, J., Aspler, S., & Schwarz, G. (2005). Phenylalanine-restricted diet should be life long. A case report on long term follow-up of an adolescent with untreated phenylketonuria. *International Journal of Adolescent Medicine and Health, 15,* 165–168.

Mestre, J. M., Guil, R., Lopes, P. N., Salovey, P., & Gil-Olarte, P. (2006). Emotional intelligence and social and academic adaptation to school. *Psicothema, 18,* 112–117.

Meyer, A. (Ed.). (1981). The Hamburg Short Psychotherapy Comparison Experiment. *Psychotherapy and Psychosomatics, 35,* 81–207.

Meyer, G. J., Finn, S. E., Eyde, L. D., Kay, G. G., Moreland, K. L., Dies, R. R., . . . Read, G. M. (2001). Psychological testing and psychological assessment: A review of evidence and issues. *American Psychologist, 56,* 128–165.

Michael, R. T., Gagnon, J. H., Laumann, E. O., & Kolata, G. (1994). *Sex in America.* Boston, MA: Little, Brown.

Mieda, M., Williams, S. C., Richardson, J. A., Tanaka, K., & Yanagisawa, M. (2006). The dorsomedial hypothalamic nucleus as a putative food-entrainable circadian pacemaker. *PNAS Proceedings of the National Academy of Sciences of the United States of America, 103,* 12150–12155.

Mieda, Michihiro; Willie, Jon T.; Hara, Junko; et al. (2004). Orexin peptides prevent cataplexy and improve wakefulness in an orexin neuron-ablated model of narcolepsy in mice. *Proceedings of the National Academy of Science, 101,* 4649–4654.

Miller, E. R., Pastor-Barriuso, R., Dalal, D., Riemersma, R. A., Appel, L. A., & Guallar, E. (2005). Meta-analysis: High-dosage vitamin E supplementation may increase all-cause mortality. *Annals of Internal Medicine, 142,* 37–46.

Miller, George A. (1956). The magical number seven, plus or minus two: Some limits on our capacity for processing information. *Psychological Review, 63,* 81–97.

Miller, Greg (2011, January 21). ESP paper rekindles discussion about statistics. *Science, 331,* 272–273.

Miller, Gregory E., & Cohen, Sheldon (2001). Psychological interventions and the immune system: A meta-analytic review and critique. *Health Psychology, 20,* 47–63.

Miller, J. D., Scott, E. C., & Okamoto, S. (2006). *Public acceptance of evolution. Science, 313,* 765.

Miller, K. F., Smith, C. M., Zhu, J., & Zhang, H. (1995). Preschool origins of cross-national differences in mathematical competence: The role of number-naming systems. *Psychological Science, 6,* 56–60.

Miller, K. R. (1999). *Finding Darwin's god: A scientist's search for common ground between god and evolution.* New York: Cliff Street Books.

Miller, L. K. (2005). What the savant syndrome can tell us about the nature and nurture of talent. *Journal for the Education of the Gifted, 28,* 361–373.

Miller, W. R., & Hester, R. K. (1980). Treating the problem drinker: Modern approaches. In W. R. Miller (Ed.), *The addictive behaviors: Treatment of alcoholism, drug abuse, smoking, and obesity* (pp. 11–141). Oxford, England: Pergamon Press.

Miller, W. R., & Rollnick, S. (2002). *Motivational interviewing: Preparing people for change.* New York, NY: Guilford Press.

Miller, W. R., & Rose, G. S. (2009). Toward a theory of motivational interviewing. *American Psychologist; American Psychologist, 64*(6), 527–537.

Mills, A., & Lynn, S. J. (2000). Past-life experiences. In E. Cardeña, S. J. Lynn, & S. Krippner (Eds.), *The varieties of anomalous experience.* New York, NY: Guilford Press.

Milner, Brenda (1970). Memory and the temporal regions of the brain. In K. H. Pribram & D. E. Broadbent (Eds.), *Biology of memory.* New York: Academic Press.

Mineka, S., & Thomas, C. (1999). Mechanisms of change in exposure therapy for anxiety disorders. In T. Dalgleish & M. J. Power (Eds.), *Handbook of cognition and emotion* (pp. 747–764). Chichester, England: Wiley.

Minuchin, S. (1974). *Families and family therapy.* Cambridge, MA: Harvard University Press.

Mishara, B. L., & Daigle, M. S. (1997). Effects of different telephone intervention styles with suicidal callers at two suicide prevention centers: An empirical investigation. *American Journal of Community Psychology, 5,* 861–885.

Mishara, B. L., Chagnon, F., Daigle, M., Balan, B., Raymond, S., Marcoux, I., Bardon, C., Campbell, J. K., & Berman, A. (2007). Which helper behaviors and intervention styles are related to better short-term outcomes in telephone crisis intervention? Results from a silent monitoring study of calls to the U.S. 1–800-SUICIDE Network. *Suicide and Life Threatening Behavior, 37,* 308–321.

Mistry, Jayanthi, & Rogoff, Barbara (1994). Remembering in cultural context. In W. J. Lonner & R. Malpass (Eds.), *Psychology and culture.* Needham Heights, MA: Allyn & Bacon.

Mitchell, David B. (2006). Nonconscious priming after 17 years: Invulnerable implicit memory? *Psychological Science, 17,* 925–929.

Mitchell, Karen J., & Johnson, Marcia K. (2009). Source monitoring 15 years later: What have we learned from fMRI about the neural mechanisms of source memory? *Psychological Bulletin, 135,* 638–677.

Mitchell, S. A., & Black, M. J. (1995). *Freud and beyond: A history of modern psychoanalytic thought.* New York, NY: Basic Books.

Mitre, N., Foster, R. C., Lanningham-Foster, L., & Levine, J. A. (2011). The energy expenditure of an activity-promoting video game compared to sedentary video games and TV watching. *Journal of Pediatric Endocrinology and Metabolism, 24(9–10),* 689–695.

Mittelbach, G. G., Schemske, D. W., Cornell, H. V., Allen, A. P., Brown, J. M., Bush, M.B., Harrison, S. P., Hurlbert, A. H., Knowlton, N., Lessios, H. A., McCain, C. M., McCune, A. R., McDade, L. A., McPeek, M. A., Near, T. J., Price, T. D., Ricklefs, R. E., Roy, K., Sax, D. F., Schluter, D., Sobel, J. M., & Turelli. M. (2007). Evolution and the latitudinal diversity gradient: speciation, extinction and biogeography. *Ecology Letters, 10,* 315–331.

Mnookin, Seth (2011). *The panic virus: A true story of medicine, science, and fear.* New York: Simon & Schuster.

Mock T., & Thomas, D. N. (2005). Recent advances in sea-ice microbiology. *Environmental Microbiology, 7,* 605–619.

Modecki, K. (2008). Underlying processes of antisocial decisions: Adolescents versus adults. *Dissertation Abstracts International: Section B: The Sciences and Engineering, 68,* 5635.

Modinos, G., Iyegbe, C., Prata, D., Rivera, M., Kempton, M., Valmaggia, L., . . . & Mcguire, P. (2013). Molecular genetic gene-environment studies using candidate genes in schizophrenia: A systematic review. *Schizophrenia Research, 15*(2–3), 356–365.

Modirrousta, M., & Fellows, L. K. (2008). Medial prefrontal cortex plays a critical and selective role in "feeling of knowing" meta-memory judgments. *Neuropsychologia, 46,* 2958–2965.

Monastra, V. J. (2008). *Unlocking the potential of patients with ADHD.* Washington, DC: American Psychological Association.

Monroe, R. (1955). *Schools of psychoanalytic thought.* New York, NY: Dryden.

Monti, P. M., Gulliver, S. B., & Myers, M. G. (1994). Social skills training for alcoholics: Assessment and treatment. *Alcohol and Alcoholism, 29,* 627–637.

Moore, D. S., & Johnson, S. P. (2008). Mental rotation in human infants. *Psychological Science, 19,* 1063–1066.

Moos, R. H., & Moos, B. S. (2006). Participation in treatment and Alcoholics Anonymous: A 16-year follow-up of initially untreated individuals. *Journal of Clinical Psychology, 62*(6), 735–750. http://dx.doi.org/10.1002/jclp.20259

Morewedge, Carey K., & Norton, Michael I. (2009). When dreaming is believing: The (motivated) interpretation of dreams. *Journal of Personality and Social Psychology, 96,* 249–264.

Morgan, Charles A.; Hazlett, Gary; Baranoski, Madelon; et al. (2007). Accuracy of eyewitness identification is significantly associated with performance on a standardized test of face recognition. *International Journal of Law and Psychiatry, 30,* 213–223.

Morgan, N., Irwin, M.R., Chung, M., & Wang, C. (2014). The effects of mind-body therapies on the immune system: Meta-analysis. *PLoS One, 9,* e100903.

Moscicki, E. K. (2001). Epidemiology of completed and attempted suicide: Toward a framework for prevention. *Clinical Neuroscience Research, 1,* 310–323.

Moser, H. W. (2004). Genetic causes of mental retardation. In S. G. Kaler & O. M. Rennert (Eds.), *Understanding and optimizing human development: From cells to patients to populations* (pp. 44–48). New York, NY: New York Academy of Sciences.

Moss, J., Schunn, C., Schneider, W., McNamara, D., & VanLehn, K. (2011). The neural correlates of strategic reading comprehension: Cognitive control and discourse comprehension. *Neuroimage, 58,* 675–686.

Mueser, K. T., & Liberman, R. P. (1995). Behavior therapy in practice. In B. Bongar & L. E. Beutler (Eds.), *Comprehensive textbook of psychotherapy: Theory and practice* (pp. 84–110). New York, NY: Oxford University Press.

Mukamal, Kenneth J.; Conigrave, Katherine M; Mittleman, Murray A.; et al. (2003). Roles of drinking pattern and type of alcohol consumed in coronary heart disease in men. *New England Journal of Medicine, 348,* 109–118.

Murman, N. M., Buckingham, K. E., Fontilea, P., Villanueva, R., Leventhal, B., & Hinshaw, S. P. (2014). Let's Erase the Stigma (LETS): A quasi-experimental evaluation of adolescent-led school groups intended to reduce mental illness stigma. *Child & Youth Care Forum, 43*(5), 621–637. doi:10.1007/s10566–014–9257-y

Murphy, J. A., & Byrne, G. J. (2012). Prevalence and correlates of the proposed DSM-5 diagnosis of Chronic Depressive Disorder. *Journal of Affective Disorders, 139*(2), 172–180.

Murray, A. J., Knight, N. S., Cochlin, L. W., McAleese, S., Deacon, R. M. J., Rawlins, N. P., & Clarke, K. (2009). Deterioration of physical performance and cognitive function in rats with short-term high-fat feeding. *FASEB Journal, 23,* 4353–4360.

Murray, J. P. (2008). Media violence: The effects are both real and strong. *American Behavioral Scientist, 51,* 1212–1230.

Murray, S. B., Rieger, E., Karlov, L., & Touyz, S. W. (2013). An investigation of the transdiagnostic model of eating disorders in the context of muscle dysmorphia. *European Eating Disorders Review, 21,* 160–164. doi:10.1002/erv.2194

Murty, V., Labar, K., & Adcock, R. (2012). Threat of punishment motivates memory encoding via amygdala, not midbrain, interactions with the medial temporal lobe. *Journal of Neuroscience, 32,* 8969–8976.

Naglieri, J. A., & Kaufman, J. C. (2001). Understanding intelligence, giftedness, and creativity using PASS theory. *Roeper Review, 23,* 151–156.

Nakazawa, K., Sun, L. D., Rondi-Reig, L., Wilson, M. A., & Tanegawa, S. (2003). Hippocampal CA3 NMDA receptors are crucial for memory acquisition of one-time experience. *Neuron, 24,* 147–148.

Nash, Michael R. (1987). What, if anything, is regressed about hypnotic age regression? A review of the empirical literature. *Psychological Bulletin, 102,* 42–52.

Nash, Michael R. (2001, July). The truth and the hype of hypnosis. *Scientific American, 285,* 46–49, 52–55.

Nash, Michael R., & Barnier, Amanda J., (2007). *The Oxford handbook of hypnosis.* Oxford, UK: Oxford University Press.

Nash, Michael R., & Nadon, Robert (1997). Hypnosis. In D. L. Faigman, D. Kaye, M. J. Saks, & J. Sanders (Eds.), *Modern scientific evidence: The law and science of expert testimony.* St. Paul, MN: West.

Nathan, Debbie (2011). *Sybil exposed: The extraordinary story behind the famous multiple personality case.* New York: Free Press.

National Head Start Association. (2008). *Up to 120,000 new jobs in worst-off U.S. communities possible from 4.3 billion boost for Head Start in economic recovery package.* Retrieved from http://www.nhsa.org/press/News_Archived/index_news_010809.htm

National Institute on Alcohol and Addiction (2015). *College Drinking.* Retrieved from http://www.niaaa.nih.gov/alcohol-health/special-populations-co-occurring-disorders/college-drinking.

National Institutes of Mental Health (2015). *Serious Mental Illness (SMI) Among U.S. Adults.* Retrieved from http://www.nimh.nih.gov/health/statistics/prevalence/serious-mental-illness-smi-among-us-adults.shtml

Navarro, A. M. (1993). Effectiveness of psychotherapy with Latinos in the United States: A revised meta-analysis. *Interamerican Journal of Psychology, 27,* 131–146.

Neisser, U. (1998). Introduction: Rising test scores and what they mean. In U. Neisser (Ed.), *The rising curve: Long-term gains in IQ and related measures* (pp. 3–22). Washington, DC: American Psychological Association.

Neisser, Ulric, & Harsch, Nicole (1992). Phantom flashbulbs: False recollections of hearing the news about Challenger. In E. Winograd & U. Neisser (Eds.), *Affect and accuracy in recall: Studies of "flashbulb memories."* New York: Cambridge University Press.

Nemeroff, C. B., Kalali, A., Keller, M. B., Charney, D. S., Lenderts, S. E., Cascade, E. F., . . . Schatzberg, A. F. (2007). Impact of publicity concerning pediatric suicidality data on physician practice patterns in the United States. *Archives of General Psychiatry, 64,* 397.

Nesse, R., & Ellsworth, P. (2009). Evolution, emotions, and emotional disorders. *American Psychologist, 64,* 129–139.

Neville, R. (1978). Psychosurgery. In W. Reich (Ed.), *Encyclopedia of bioethics, Vol. 3* (pp. 1387–1391). New York, NY: Macmillan-Free Press.

Newcombe, Nora S.; Lloyd, Marianne E.; & Balcomb, Frances (2012). Contextualizing the development of recollection: Episodic memory and binding in young children. In S. Ghetti & P. J. Bauer (Eds.), *Origins and development of recollection: Perspectives from psychology and Neuroscience.* New York: Oxford University Press.

Newman, M. G., & Llera, S. J. (2011). A novel theory of experiential avoidance in generalized anxiety disorder: A review and synthesis of research supporting a contrast avoidance model of worry. *Clinical Psychology Review, 31,* 371–382.

Nickerson, Raymond A., & Adams, Marilyn Jager (1979). Long-term memory for a common object. *Cognitive Psychology, 11,* 287–307.

Nisbett, R. E. (2009). *Intelligence and how to get it: Why schools and culture count.* New York, NY: Norton.

Noonan, J. P., Coop, G., Kudaravalli, S., Smith, D., Krause, J., Alessi, J., Chen. F., Platt, D. Pääbo, S., Pritchard, J. K., & Rubin, E. M. (2006). Sequencing and analysis of Neanderthal genomic DNA. *Science, 314,* 1113–1118.

Norcross, J. C. (2005). A primer on psychotherapy integration. In J. C. Norcross & M. R. Goldfried (Eds.), *Handbook of psychotherapy integration* (2nd ed., pp. 3–23). New York, NY: Oxford University Press.

Norcross, J. C., & Beutler, L. (1997). Determining the relationship of choice in brief therapy. In J. N. Butcher (Ed.), *Personality assessment in managed health care* (pp. 42–60). New York, NY: Oxford University Press.

Norcross, J. C., & Wampold, B. E. (2011a). What works for whom: Tailoring psychotherapy to the person. *Journal of Clinical Psychology, 67*(2), 127–132.

Norcross, J. C., & Wampold, B. E. (2011b). *Evidence-based therapy relationships: Research conclusions and clinical practices. Psychotherapy, 48*(1), 98–102.

Norcross, J. C., Garofalo, A., & Koocher, G. (2006). Discredited psychological treatments and tests: A Delphi poll. *Professional Psychology: Research and Practice, 137,* 515–522.

Norcross, J. C., Strausser, D. J., & Missar, C. D. (1988). The process and outcomes of psychotherapists' personal treatment experiences. *Psychotherapy, 25,* 36–43.

Novaco, R. W. (1994). Clinical problems of anger and its assessment and regulation through a stress coping skills approach. In W. O'Donohue & L. Krasner (Eds.), *Handbook of skills training* (pp. 320–338). New York, NY: Pergamon Press.

Nyberg, Lars; Habib, Reza; McIntosh, Anthony R.; & Tulving, Endel (2000). Reactivation of encoding-related brain activity during memory retrieval. *Proceedings of the National Academy of Sciences, 97,* 11120–11124.

O'Neill, Sarah, & Zajac, Rachel (2012). The role of repeated interviewing in children's responses to cross-examination-style questioning. British *Journal of Psychology. doi: 10.1111/j.2044-8295.2011.02096.x.*

Odgers, Candice L.; Caspi, Avshalom; Nagin, Daniel S.; et al. (2008). Is it important to prevent early exposure to drugs and alcohol among adolescents? *Psychological Science, 19,* 1037–1044.

Offit, Paul A. (2008). *Autism's false prophets: Bad science, risky medicine, and the search for a cure.* NY: Columbia University Press.

Ogden, Jenni (2012). *Trouble in mind: Stories from a neuropsychologist's casebook.* New York: Oxford University Press.

Ogden, Jenni A., & Corkin, Suzanne (1991). Memories of H. M. In W. C. Abraham, M. C. Corballis, & K. G. White (Eds.), *Memory mechanisms: A tribute to G. V. Goddard.* Hillsdale, NJ: Erlbaum.

Ogrodniczuk, J. S., & Piper, W. E. (1999). Use of transference interpretations in dynamically oriented individual psychotherapy for patients with personality disorders. *Journal of Personality Disorders, 13,* 297–311.

Öhman, A., & Mineka, S. (2001). Fears, phobias, and preparedness: Toward an evolved module of fear and fear learning. *Psychological Review, 108,* 483–522.

Olfson, M., Marcus, S., Sackheim, H. A., Thompson, J., & Pincus, H. A. (1998). Use of ECT for the inpatient treatment of recurrent major depression. *American Journal of Psychiatry, 155,* 22–29.

Olivardia, R. (2007). Body image and muscularity. In J. E. Grant & M. N. Potenza (Eds.), *Textbook of men's mental health* (pp. 307–324). Arlington, VA: American Psychiatric Publishing.

Olkin, R., & Taliaferro, G. (2005). Evidence-based practices have ignored people with disabilities. In J. C. Norcross, L. E. Beutler, & R. F. Levant (Eds.), *Evidence-based practices in mental health* (pp. 353–358). Washington, DC: American Psychological Association.

Olsen, S., Smith, S. S., Oei, T. P., & Douglas, J. (2012). Motivational interviewing (MINT) improves continuous positive airway pressure (CPAP) acceptance and adherence: A randomized controlled trial. *Journal of Consulting and Clinical Psychology, 80*(1), 151.

Olszewski-Kubilius, P. (2003). Gifted education programs and procedures. In W. M. Reynolds & G. E. Miller (Eds.), *Handbook of psychology: Vol. 7, Educational psychology* (pp. 487–510). New York, NY: Wiley.

Orban, P., Peigneux, P., Lungu, O., Albouy, G., Breton, E., Laberenne, F., Benali, H., Maquet, P., & Doyon, J. (2009). The multifaceted nature of the relationship between performance and brain activity in motor sequence learning. *Neuroimage, 49,* 694–702.

Orlinksy, D. E., & Howard, K. I. (1986). Process and outcome in psychotherapy. In S. L. Garfield & A. E. Bergin (Eds.), *Handbook of psychotherapy and behavior change* (3rd ed., pp. 311–384). New York, NY: Wiley.

Orlinsky, D. E., Grawe, K., & Parks, B. K. (1994). Process and outcome in psychotherapy-Noch einmal. In A. E. Bergin & S. L. Garfield (Eds.), *Handbook of psychotherapy and behavior change* (4th ed., pp. 270–376). New York, NY: Wiley.

Osborne, K. A., Robichon, A., Burgess, E., Butland, S., Shaw, R. A., Coulthard, A., Pereira, H. S., Greenspan, R. H., & Sokolowski, M. B. (1997). Natural behavior polymorphism due to a cGMP-Dependent protein kinase of Drosophila. *Science, 277,* 834–836.

Oshri, A., Tubman, J. G., Morgan-Lopez, A. A., Saavedra, L. M., & Csizmadia, A. (2013). Sexual sensation seeking, co-occurring sex and alcohol use, and sexual risk behavior among adolescents in treatment for substance use problems. *The American Journal On Addictions, 22,* 197–205.

Osland, Teresa M.; Bjorvatn, Bjørn; Steen, Vidar M.; & Pallesen, Ståle (2011). Association study of a variable-number tandem repeat polymorphism in the clock gene PERIOD3 and chronotype in Norwegian university students. *Chronobiology International, 28,* 764–770.

Ost, L. G. (2008). Efficacy of the third wave of behavioral therapies: A systematic review and meta-analysis. *Behaviour Research and Therapy, 46,* 296–321.

Otto, M. W., Smits, J. A. J., & Reese, H. E. (2005). Combined psychotherapy and pharmacotherapy for mood and anxiety disorders in adults: Review and analysis. *Clinical Psychology: Science & Practice, 12,* 72–86.

Ousley, L., Cordero, E. D., & White, S. (2008). Eating disorders and body image of undergraduate men. *Journal of American College Health, 56,* 617–621.

Overeem, Sebastiaan; van Nues, Soffie J.; van der Zande, Wendy L.; et al. (2011). The clinical features of cataplexy: A questionnaire study in narcolepsy patients with and without hypocretin-1 deficiency. *Sleep Medicine, 12,* 12–18.

Pagel, James F. (2003). Non-dreamers. *Sleep Medicine, 4,* 235–241.

Pagnin, D., de Queiroz, V., Pini, S., & Cassano, G. B. (2008, Winter). Efficacy of ECT in depression: A meta-analytic review. *Focus, 6,* 155–162.

Pail, Gerald; Huf, Wolfgang; Pjrek, Edda; et al. (2011). Bright-light therapy in the treatment of mood disorders. *Neuropsychobiology, 64,* 152–162.

Palomares, N. A. (2004). Gender schematicity, gender identity salience, and gender-linked language use. *Human Communication Research, 30,* 556–588.

Panozzo, D. (2013). Advocating for an end to reparative therapy: Methodological grounding and blueprint for change. *Journal of Gay & Lesbian Social Services: The Quarterly Journal of Community & Clinical Practice, 25, 362–377. doi:10.1080/10538720.2013.807214*

Parada, Maria; Corral, Montserrat; Mota, Nayara; et al. (2012). Executive functioning and alcohol binge drinking in university students. *Addictive Behaviors, 37,* 167–172.

Park, S., Püschel, J., Sauter, B. H., Rentsch, M., & Hell, D. (1999). Spatial working memory deficits and clinical symptoms of schizophrenia: A 4-month follow-up study. *Biological Psychiatry, 46,* 392–400.

Parker, Elizabeth S.; Cahill, Larry; & McGaugh, James L. (2006). A case of unusual autobiographical remembering. *Neurocase, 12,* 35–49.

Parks, J. B., & Roberton, M. A. (2004). Explaining age and gender effects on attitudes toward sexist language. *Journal of Language and Social Psychology, 24,* 401–411.

Parlee, Mary B. (1982). Changes in moods and activation levels during the menstrual cycle in experimentally naive subjects. *Psychology of Women Quarterly, 7,* 119–131.

Parlee, Mary B. (1994). The social construction of premenstrual syndrome: A case study of scientific discourse as cultural contestation. In M. G. Winkler & L. B. Cole (Eds.), *The good body: Asceticism in contemporary culture.* New Haven, CT: Yale University Press.

Pastalkova, Eva; Itskov, Vladimir; Amarasingham, Asohan; & Buzsáki, György (2008, September 5). Internally generated cell assembly sequences in the rat hippocampus. *Science, 321,* 1322–1327.

Patterson-Kane, Emily G.; Harper, David; & Hunt, Maree (2001). Cage preferences of laboratory rats. *Laboratory Animals, 35,* 74–79.

Patterson, C. J. (2000). Family relationships of lesbians and gay men. *Journal of Marriage and the Family, 62,* 1052–1069.

Patterson, David R., & Jensen, Mark P. (2003). Hypnosis and clinical pain. *Psychological Bulletin, 129,* 495–521.

Patterson, F. G. (1981). *The education of Koko.* New York, NY: Holt.

Paul, G., & Lentz, R. J. (1977). *Psychosocial treatment of chronic mental patients: Milieu versus social-learning programs.* Cambridge, MA: Harvard University Press.

Payne, Jessica D.; Stickgold, Robert; Swanberg, Kelley; & Kensinger, Elizabeth A. (2008). Sleep preferentially enhances memory for emotional components of scenes. *Psychological Science, 19,* 781–788.

Pedersen, S. L., & McCarthy, D. M. (2008). Person-environment transactions in youth drinking and driving. *Psychology of Addictive Behaviors, 22,* 340–348.

Pederson Mussell, M., Crosby, R. D., Crow, S. J., Knopke, A. J., Peterson, C. B., Wonderlich, S. A., & Mitchell, J. E. (2000). Utilization of empirically supported psychotherapy treatments for individuals with eating disorders: A survey of psychologists. *International Journal of Eating Disorders, 27,* 230–237.

Penn, D. L., & Combs, D. (2000). Modification of affect perception deficits in schizophrenia. *Schizophrenia Research, 46,* 217–229.

Pennisi, E. (2006). Mining the molecules that made our mind. *Science, 313,* 1908–1911.

Pennisi, E. (2007). Ancient DNA: No sex please, we're Neanderthals. *Science, 316,* 967.

Peplau, L. A. (2003). Human sexuality: How do men and women differ? *Current Directions in Psychological Science, 12,* 37–40.

Pepperberg, I. M. (2000). *The Alex studies: Cognitive and communicative abilities of grey parrots.* Cambridge, MA: Harvard University Press.

Pepperberg, I. M. (2007). Grey parrots do not always "parrot": The roles of imitation and phonological awareness in the creation of new labels from existing vocalizations. *Language Sciences, 29,* 1–13.

Perry, W., Feifel, D., Minassian, A., Bhattacharjie, B. S., & Braff, D. L. (2002). Information processing deficits in acutely psychotic schizophrenia patients medicated and unmedicated at the time of admission. *American Journal of Psychiatry, 159,* 1375–1381.

Persky, H. (1978). Plasma testosterone level and sexual behavior of couples. *Archives of Sexual Behavior, 7,* 157–173.

Petersen, J. L., & Hyde, J. (2010). A meta-analytic review of research on gender differences in sexuality, 1993–2007. *Psychological Bulletin, 136,* 21–38.

Petersen, J. L., & Hyde, J. (2011). Gender differences in sexual attitudes and behaviors: A review of meta-analytic results and large datasets. *Journal of Sex Research, 48,* 149–165.

Peterson, Lloyd R., & Peterson, Margaret J. (1959). Short-term retention of individual verbal items. *Journal of Experimental Psychology, 58,* 193–198.

Petrosino. A., Turpin-Petrosino, C., & Buehler, J. (2003, November). "'Scared Straight' and other juvenile awareness programs for preventing juvenile delinquency. Campbell Review Update I." *In The Campbell Collaboration Reviews of Intervention and Policy Evaluations (C2-RIPE).* Philadelphia, PA: Campbell Collaboration. Retrieved from http://web.archive.org/web/20070927013116/http://www.campbellcollaboration.org/doc-pdf/ssrupdt.pdf

Petry, N. M., Tennen, H., & Affleck, G. (2000). Stalking the elusive client variable in psychotherapy research. In C. R. Snyder & R. Ingram (Eds.), *Handbook of psychological change: Psychotherapy processes and practices for the 21st century* (pp. 88–108). New York, NY: Wiley.

Pettinati, H. M., Tamburello, T. A., Ruetsch, C. R., & Kaplan, F. N. (1994). Patient attitudes toward electroconvulsive therapy. *Psychopharmacological Bulletin, 30,* 471–475.

Phelps, C., Bennett, P., & Brain, K. (2008). Understanding emotional responses to breast/ovarian cancer genetic risk assessment: An applied test of a cognitive theory of emotion. *Psychology, Health & Medicine, 13,* 545–558.

Piaget, Jean (1952). *Play, dreams, and imitation in childhood.* New York: W. W. Norton.

Pilley, J. W. (2013). Border collie comprehends sentences containing a prepositional object, verb, and direct object. *Learning and Motivation, 44,* 229–240. doi:10.1016/j.lmot.2013.02.003

Pilley, J. W., & Reid, A. K. (2011). Border collie comprehends object names as verbal referents. *Behavioural Processes, 86,* 184–195. doi:10.1016/j.beproc.2010.11.007

Pinel, J. P. L. (2000). *Biopsychology* (4th ed.). Boston: Allyn & Bacon.

Pinker, S. (2001). Talk of genetics and vice versa. *Nature, 413,* 465–466.

Pinker, S. (2002). *The blank slate: The modern denial of human nature.* New York, NY: Penguin Press.

Pinker, Steven (1994). *The language instinct: How the mind creates language.* New York: Morrow.

Plomin, R. (1997). Identifying genes for cognitive abilities and disabilities. In R. J. Sternberg & E. L. Grigorenko (Eds.), *Intelligence: Heredity and environment* (pp. 89–104). New York, NY: Cambridge University Press.

Plomin, R., & Asbury, K. (2001). Nature and nurture in the family. *Marriage & Family Review, 33*(2–3), 273–281.

Plomin, R., Haworth, C. M. A., Meaburn, E. L., Price, T. S., & Davis, O. S. P. (2013). Common DNA markers can account for more than half of the genetic influence on cognitive abilities. *Psychological Science, 24,* 562–568. doi:10.1177/0956797612457952

Plutchik, R. (1980). *Emotion: A psychoevolutionary synthesis.* New York, NY: Harper & Row.

Pogue, D. (2013, November). Crash text dummies. *Scientific American, 309*(5), 32. doi:10.1038/scientificamerican1113-32

Poldrack, R., & Wagner, A. (2004). What can neuroimaging tell us about the mind? Insights from prefrontal cortex. *Current Directions in Psychological Science, 13,* 177–181.

Polivy, J., & Herman, C. P. (2002). If you first don't succeed. False hopes of self-change. *American Psychologist, 57,* 677–689.

Ponari, M., Conson, M., D'Amico, N., Grossi, D., & Trojano, L. (2012). Mapping correspondence between facial mimicry and emotion recognition in healthy subjects. *Emotion, 12,* 1398–1403. doi:10.1037/a0028588

Ponder, C. A., Kliethermes, C. L., Drew, M. R., Mul-ler, J. J., Das, K. K., Risbrough, V. B., Crabbe, J. C., Gilliam, T.C., & Palmer, A. A. (2007). Selection for contextual fear conditioning affects anxiety-like behaviors and gene expression. *Genes, Brain & Behavior, 6*(8), 736–749.

Poole, Debra A., Lamb, Michael E. (1998). *Investigative interviews of children.* Washington, DC: American Psychological Association.

Pope, C. G., Pope, H. G., & Menard, W. (2005). Clinical features of muscle dysmorphia among males with body dysmorphic disorder. *Body Image, 2,* 395–400.

Pope, H. G., Jr., Oliva, P. S., & Hudson, J. I. (2000). Repressed memories: B. Scientific status. In D. L. Faigman, D. H. Kay, M. J. Saks, & J. Sanders (Eds.), *Modern scientific evidence: The law and science of expert testimony* (pp. 154–195). St. Paul, MN: West.

Porter, S., & Peace, K. A. (2007). The scars of memory: A prospective longitudinal investigation of the consistency of traumatic and positive emotional memories in adulthood. *Psychological Science, 18,* 435–441.

Posner, Michael I., & Rothbart, Mary K. (2011). Brain states and hypnosis research. *Consciousness & Cognition, 20,* 325–327.

Postuma, R. B.; Gagnon, J. F.; Vendette, M.; et al. (2008). Quantifying the risk of neurodegenerative disease in idiopathic REM sleep behavior disorder. *Neurology,* published online December 24, doi:10.1212/01.wnl.0000340980.19702.6e.

Potts, N. L. S., Davidson, J. R. T., & Krishman, K. R. R. (1993). The role of nuclear magnetic resonance imaging in psychiatric research. *Journal of Clinical Psychiatry, 54(12, Suppl.),* 13–18.

Prabhakar, S., Noonan, J. P., Paabo, S., & Rubin, E. M. (2006). *Accelerated evolution on conserved noncoding sequences in humans, Science, 314,* 786.

Preckel, F., Holling, H., & Wiese, M. (2006). Relationship of intelligence and creativity in gifted and non-gifted students: An investigation of threshold theory. *Personality and Individual Differences, 40,* 159–170.

Primack, Brian A.; Silk, Jennifer S.; DeLozier, Christian R.; et al. (2011). Using ecological momentary assessment to determine media use by individuals with and without major depressive disorder. *Archives of Pediatrics & Adolescent Medicine, 165,* 360–365.

Principe, Gabrielle; Kanaya, Tamoe; Ceci, Stephen J.; & Singh, Mona (2006). Believing is seeing: How rumors can engender false memories in preschoolers. *American Psychologist, 17,* 243–248.

Pring, L., Woolf, K., & Tadic, V. (2008). Melody and pitch processing in five musical savants with congenital blindness. *Perception, 37,* 290–307.

Prinz, J. (2008). Embodied emotions. In W. G. Lycan & J. J. Prinz (Eds.), *Mind and cognition: An anthology* (3rd ed., pp. 839–849). Malden, MA: Blackwell Publishing.

Prior, H., Schwarz, A., & Güntürkün, O. (2008). Mirror-induced behavior in the magpie (Pica pica): Evidence of self-recognition. *PLoS Biology, 6:* e202. doi:10.1371/journal.pbio.0060202

Prochaska, J. O., & DiClemente, C. C. (1982). Transtheoretical therapy: Toward a more integrative model of change. *Psychotherapy: Theory, Research, and Practice, 20,* 161–173.

Prochaska, J. O., & Norcross, J. C. (2002). Stages of change. In J. C. Norcross (Ed.), *Psychotherapy relationships that work.* New York, NY: Oxford University Press.

Prochaska, J. O., & Norcross, J. C. (2007). *Systems of psychotherapy: A transtheoretical approach* (6th ed.). Pacific Grove, CA: Brooks/Cole.

Project MATCH Research Group. (1997). Matching alcoholism treatments to client heterogeneity: Project MATCH posttreatment drinking outcomes. *Journal of Studies on Alcohol, 58,* 7–29.

Protzko, J., Aronson, J., & Blair, C. (2013). How to make a young child smarter: Evidence from the Database of Raising Intelligence. *Perspectives on Psychological Science, 8,* 25–40. doi:10.1177/1745691612462585

Pruetz, P., & Bertolani, P. (2007). Savanna chimpanzees, Pan troglodytes verus hunt with tools. *Current Biology, 17,* 412–417.

Prum, R. O. (2003). Palaeontology: Dinosaurs take to the air. *Nature, 421,* 323–324.

Puma, M., Bell, S., Cook, R., & Hyde, C. (2010). *Head Start Impact Study Final Report.* Washington, DC: U.S. Department of Health and Human Services, Administration for Children and Families.

Punamaeki, Raija-Leena, & Joustie, Marja (1998). The role of culture, violence, and personal factors affecting dream content. *Journal of Cross-Cultural Psychology, 29,* 320–342.

Purves, D., Augustine, G., Fitzpatrick, D., Hall, W., LaMantia, A., & White, L. (2011). *Neuroscience 5th ed.* Sinderland, MA: Sinauer Associates, Inc.

Putnam, F.W. (1989). *Diagnosis and treatment of multiple personality disorder.* New York: Guilford Press.

Pynoos, R. S., & Nader, K. (1989). Children's memory and proximity to violence. *Journal of the American Academy of Child and Adolescent Psychiatry, 28,* 236–241.

Qiu, J., Li, H., Jou, J., Wu, Z., & Zhang, Q. (2008). Spatiotemporal cortical activation underlies mental preparation for successful riddle solving: An event-related potential study. *Experimental Brain Research, 186,* 629–634.

Quaid, K., Aschen, S., Smiley, C., Nurnberger, J. (2001). Perceived genetic risks for bipolar disorder in patient population: An exploratory study. *Journal of Genetic Counseling, 10,* 41–51.

Quinn, P. C., & Liben, L. S. (2008). A sex difference in mental rotation in young infants. *Psychological Science, 19,* 1067–1070.

Rabinowitz, J., & Renert, N. (1997). Clinicians' predictions of length of psychotherapy. *Psychiatric Services, 48,* 97–99.

RAC Foundation. (2008). *The effect of text messaging on driver behaviour.* Retrieved from http://www.racfoundation.org/files/textingwhiledrivingreport.pdf

Rachman, S. (1994). Psychological treatment of panic: Mechanisms. In B. E. Wolfe & J. D. Maser (Eds.), *Treatment of panic disorder: A consensus development conference* (pp. 133–148). Washington, DC: American Psychiatric Press.

Radhakrishnan, R., Wilkinson, S. T., & D'Souza, D. C. (2014). Gone to pot-A review of the association between cannabis and psychosis. *Frontiers In Psychiatry, 5.*

Raimy, V. C. (Ed.). (1950). *Training in clinical psychology (Boulder Conference).* New York, NY: Prentice Hall.

Ramadori, G., Lee, C., Bookout, A., Lee, S., Williams, K., Anderson, J., . . . Coppari, R. (2008). Brain SIRT1: Anatomical distribution and regulation by energy availability. *Journal of Neuroscience, 28,* 9989–9996.

Ramey, C. T., & Ramey, S. L. (2007). Early learning and school readiness: Can early intervention make a difference? In G. W. Ladd (Ed.), *Appraising the human developmental sciences: Essays in honor of Merrill-Palmer Quarterly* (pp. 329–350). Detroit, MI: Wayne State University Press.

Ramey, C. T., Ramey, S. L., & Lanzi, R. G. (2001). Intelligence and experience. In R. J. Sternberg & E. L. Grigorenko (Eds.), *Environmental effects on cognitive abilities* (pp. 83–115). Mahwah, NJ: Erlbaum.

Ramey, S. L. (1999). Head Start and preschool education: Toward continued improvement. *American Psychologist, 54,* 344–346.

Rampersaud, G. C., Pereira, M. A., Girard, B. L., Adams, J., & Metzl, J. (2005). Breakfast habits, nutritional status, body weight, and academic performance in children and adolescents. *Journal of the American Diet Association, 105*(5), 743–760.

Randall, David K. (2012). *Dreamland: Adventures in the strange world of sleep.* New York: Norton.

Rasch, Björn; Büchel, Christian; Gais, Steffen; & Born, Jan (2007). Odor cues during slow-wave sleep prompt declarative memory consolidation. *Science, 315,* 1426–1429.

Rasheed, Parveen, & Al-Sowielem, Latifa S. (2003). Prevalence and predictors of premenstrual syndrome among college-aged women in Saudi Arabia. *Annals of Saudi Medicine, 23,* 381–387.

Rasmussen, K., Sampson, S. M., & Rummans, T. A. (2002). Electroconvulsive therapy and newer modalities for the treatment of medication-refractory mental illness. *Mayo Clinic Proceedings, 77,* 552–556.

Rauscher, F. H., & Shaw, G. L. (1998). Key components of the "Mozart effect." *Perceptual and Motor Skills, 86,* 835–841.

Rayner, K., White, S. J., Johnson, R. L., & Liversedge, S. P. (2006). Raeding wrods with jubmled lettres. *Psychological Science, 17,* 192–193.

Raz, Amir; Fan, Jin; & Posner, Michael I. (2005). Hypnotic suggestion reduces conflict in the human brain. *Proceedings of the National Academy of Science, 102,* 9978–9983.

Raz, Amir; Kirsch, Irving; Pollard, Jessica; & Nitkin-Kamer, Yael (2006). Suggestion reduces the Stroop effect. *Psychological Science, 17,* 91–95.

Raz, N., Lindenberger, U., Rodrigue, K., Kennedy, K., Head, D., Williamson, A., Dahle, C., Gerstorf, D., & Acker, J. (2006). Regional brain changes in aging healthy adults: General trends, individual differences and modifiers. *Cerebral Cortex, 15,* 1679–1689.

Razzini, C., Bianchi, F., Leo, R., Fortuna, E., Siracusano, A., & Romeo, F. (2008). Correlations between personality factors and coronary artery disease: From type A behaviour pattern to type D personality. *Journal of Cardiovascular Medicine, 9*(8), 761–768.

Reber, Paul J.; Stark, Craig E. L.; & Squire, Larry R. (1998). Contrasting cortical activity associated with category memory and recognition memory. *Learning & Memory, 5,* 420–428.

Redelmeier, D. A., & Tversky, A. (2004). On the belief that arthritis pain is related to the weather. In E. Shafir (Ed.), *Preference, belief, and similarity: Selected writings by Amos Tversky* (pp. 377–381). Cambridge, MA: MIT Press.

Ree, M. J., & Earles, J. A. (1992). Intelligence is the best predictor of job performance. *Current Directions in Psychological Science, 1,* 86–89.

Reese, Elaine; Jack, Fiona; & White, Naomi (2010). Origins of adolescents' autobiographical memories. *Cognitive Development, 25,* 352–367.

Regier, D. A., Narrow, W. E., Clarke, D. E., Kraemer, H. C., Kuramoto, S. J., Kuhl, E. A., & Kupfer, D. J. (2013). DSM-5 field trials in the United States and Canada, part II: Test-retest reliability of selected categorical diagnoses. The American *Journal of Psychiatry, 170*(1), 59–70. doi:10.1176/appi.ajp.2012.12070999

Reid, R. L. (1991). Premenstrual syndrome. *New England Journal of Medicine, 324,* 1208–1210.

Reiss, S. (2005). Extrinsic and intrinsic motivation at 30: Unresolved scientific issues. *Behavior Analyst, 28,* 1–14.

Renner, M., & Mackin, R. (1998). A life stress instrument for classroom use. *Teaching of Psychology, 25*(1), 46–48.

Revell, Victoria L., & Eastman, Charmane I. (2005). How to fool Mother Nature into letting you fly around or stay up all night. *Journal of Biological Rhythms, 20,* 353–365.

Reynolds, Kristi; Lewis, L. Brian; Nolen, John David L.; et al. (2003). Alcohol consumption and risk of stroke: A meta-analysis. *Journal of the American Medical Association, 289,* 579–588.

Reznichenko. L., Amit, T., Youdim, M.B., & Mandel, S. (2005). Green tea polyphenol (?)-epigallocatechin-3-gallate induces neurorescue of long-term serum-deprived PC12 cells and promotes neurite outgrowth. *Journal of Neurochemistry, 93,* 1157–1167.

Rhule, D. M. (2005). Take care to do no harm: Harmful interventions for youth problem behavior. *Professional Psychology: Research and Practice, 36,* 618–625.

Richards, J., Encel, J., & Shute, R. (2003). The emotional and behavioural adjustment of intellectually gifted adolescents: A multidimensional, multi-informant approach. *High Ability Studies, 14,* 153–164.

Richardson-Klavehn, Alan, & Bjork, Robert A. (1988). Measures of memory. *Annual Review of Psychology, 39,* 475–543.

Richardson, John T. E. (Ed.) (1992). *Cognition and the menstrual cycle.* New York: Springer-Verlag.

Ridley-Johnson, Robyn; Cooper, Harris; & Chance, June (1983). The relation of children's television viewing to school achievement and I.Q. *Journal of Educational Research, 76,* 294–297.

Rischer, C. E., & Easton, T. A. (1992). *Focus on human biology.* New York: HarperCollins.

Roalf, D., Gur, R., Verma, R., Parker, W., Quarmley, M., Ruparel, K., & Gur, R. (2015). White matter microstructure in schizophrenia: Associations to neurocognition and clinical symptomatology. *Schizophrenia Research, 161*(1), 42–49.

Roberts, J., & Bell, M. (2000). Sex differences on a mental rotation task: Variations in electroencephalogram hemispheric activation between children and college students. *Developmental Neuropsychology, 17,* 199–223.

Robinson, A., & Clinkenbeard, P. R. (1998). Giftedness: An exceptionality examined. *Annual Review of Psychology, 49,* 117–139.

Rocha, Beatriz A.; Scearce-Levie, Kimberly; Lucas, Jose J.; et al. (1998). Increased vulnerability to cocaine in mice lacking the serotonin-1B receptor. *Nature, 393,* 175–178.

Roediger, Henry L., III (1990). Implicit memory: Retention without remembering. *American Psychologist, 45,* 1043–1056.

Roediger, Henry L., III, & McDermott, Kathleen B. (1995). Creating false memories: Remembering words not presented in lists. *Journal of Experimental Psychology: Learning, Memory, & Cognition, 21,* 803–814.

Roese, N. J., & Vohs, K. D. (2012). Hindsight bias. *Perspectives on Psychological Science, 7,* 411–426. doi:10.1177/1745691612454303

Rofé, Y. (1984). Stress and affiliation: A utility theory. *Psychological Review, 91,* 251–268.

Rofé, Y., Hoffman, M., & Lewin, I. (1985). Patient affiliation in major illness. *Psychological Medicine, 15,* 895–896.

Rofé, Yacov (2008). Does repression exist? Memory, pathogenic, unconscious and clinical evidence. *Review of General Psychology, 12,* 63–85.

Rogers, C. R. (1942). *Counseling and psychotherapy.* New York, NY: Houghton Mifflin.

Rogers, C. R. (1957). The necessary and sufficient conditions of therapeutic personality change. *Journal of Consulting Psychology, 21,* 95–103.

Rogers, C. R. (1961). *On becoming a person.* Boston, MA: Houghton Mifflin.

Romanczyk, Raymond G.; Arnstein, Laura; Soorya, Latha V.; & Gillis, Jennifer (2003). The myriad of controversial treatments for autism: A critical evaluation of efficacy. In S.O. Lilienfeld, S. J. Lynn, & J. M. Lohr (Eds.), *Science and pseudoscience in clinical psychology.* New York: Guilford.

Ronaldson, A., Molloy, G. J., Wikman, A., Poole, L., Kaski, J. C., Steptoe, A. (2015). Optimism and recovery after acute coronary syndrome: A clinical cohort study [Electronic publication ahead of print]. *Psychosomatic Medicine.*

Roney, J. R. (1999). Distinguishing adaptations from by-products. *American Psychologist, 54,* 435–436.

Rönnqvist, L., & Domellöf, E. (2006). Quantitative assessment of right and left reaching movements in infants: A longitudinal study from 6 to 36 months. *Developmental Psychobiology, 48,* 444–459.

Roozendaal, B., Catello, N., Vedana, G., Barsegyan, A., & McGaugh, J. (2008). Noradrenergic activation of the basolateral amygdala modulates consolidation of object recognition memory. *Neurobiology of Learning and Memory, 90,* 576–579.

Rosch, E. H. (2002). Principles of categorization. In D. J. Levitin (Ed.), *Foundations of Cognitive Psychology: Core Readings* (pp. 251–270). Cambridge, MA: MIT Press.

Rosenberg, H. (1993). Prediction of controlled drinking by alcoholics and problem drinkers. *Psychological Bulletin, 113,* 129–139.

Rosenhan, D. L. (1973). *On being sane in insane places. Science, 179*(4070), 250–258.

Rosenthal, Norman E. (2009). Issues for DSM-V: Seasonal affective disorder and seasonality. *The American Journal of Psychiatry, 166,* 852–853.

Rosenthal, R. (2002). The Pygmalion effect and its mediating mechanisms. In J. Aronson (Ed.), *Improving academic achievement: Impact of psychological factors on education* (pp. 25–36). San Diego, CA: Academic Press.

Rosenthal, R., & DiMatteo, M. R. (2001). Meta-analysis: Recent developments in quantitative methods for literature reviews. *Annual Review of Psychology, 52,* 59–82.

Rosenthal, Robert (1966). *Experimenter effects in behavioral research.* New York: Appleton-Century-Crofts.

Rosenthal, Robert (1994). Interpersonal expectancy effects: A 30-year perspective. *Current Directions in Psychological Science, 3,* 176–179.

Rosenzweig, S. (1936). Some implicit common factors in diverse methods in psychotherapy. *American Journal of Orthopsychiatry, 6,* 412–415.

Rosmand, R. (2005). Role of stress in the pathogenesis of the metabolic syndrome. *Psycho neuroendocrinology, 30,* 1–10.

Ross, C. A., & Pam, A. (1995). *Pseudoscience in biological psychiatry: Blaming the body.* New York, NY: Wiley.

Rothbaum, B. O., Hodges, L., Ready, D., Graap, K., & Alarcon, R. D. (2001). Virtual reality exposure therapy for Vietnam veterans with posttraumatic stress disorder. *Journal of Clinical Psychiatry, 62,* 617–622.

Rothblum, E. D, Brand, P. A., Miller, C. T., & Oetjen, H. A. (1990). The relationship between obesity, employment discrimination, and employment-related victimization. *Journal of Vocational Behavior, 37,* 251–266.

Rovee-Collier, Carolyn (1993). The capacity for long-term memory in infancy. *Current Directions in Psychological Science, 2,* 130–135.

Roy, B., Diez-Roux, A. V., Seeman, T., Ranjit, N., Shea, S., & Cushman, M. (2010). Association of optimism and pessimism with inflammation and hemostasis in the Multi-Ethnic Study of Artherosclerosis (MESA). *Psychosomatic Medicine, 72*(2), 134–140. PsycINFO, EBSCOhost (accessed March 20, 2015).

Rubin, A. (2003). Unanswered questions about the empirical support for EMDR in the treatment of PTSD: A review of research. *Traumatology, 9*(1), 4–30.

Rubinstein, J. S., Meyer, D. E., & Evans, J. E. (2001). Executive control of cognitive processes in task switching. *Journal of Experimental Psychology: Human Perception and Performance, 27,* 763–797.

Rumbaugh, D. M. (1977). *Language learning by a chimpanzee.* New York, NY: Academic Press.

Rumbaugh, D. M., & Savage-Rumbaugh, E. S. (1978). Chimpanzee language research: Status and potential. *Behavior Research Methods and Instrumentation, 10,* 119–131.

Rumelhart, David E.; McClelland, James L.; & the PDP Research Group (1986). *Parallel distributed processing: Explorations in the microstructure of cognition* (Vols. 1 and 2). Cambridge, MA: MIT Press.

Rummel, C., Goodfellow, M., Gast, H., Hauf, M., Amor, F., Stibal, A., Mariani, L., & Schindler, K. (2013). *A systems-level approach to human epileptic seizures. Neuroinformatics, 10, Volume 11*, pp. 159–173.

Runco, M. A. (2008). Commentary: Divergent thinking is not synonymous with creativity. *Psychology of Aesthetics, Creativity, and the Arts, 2,* 93–96.

Rush, A. J., Marangell, L. B., Sackeim, H. A., George, M. S., Brannan, S. K., Davis, S. M., . . . Cooke, R. G. (2005). Vagus nerve stimulation for treatment-resistant depression: A randomized, controlled acute phase trial. *Biological Psychiatry, 58,* 347–354.

Russell, J. A. (1991). Culture and the categorization of emotions. *Psychological Bulletin, 110,* 426–450.

Rust, J. O., & Wallace, M. A. (2004). Adaptive Behavior Assessment System (2nd ed.). *Journal of Psychoeducational Assessment, 22,* 367–373.

Rymer, Russ (1993). *Genie: An abused child's flight from silence.* New York: HarperCollins.

Saban, K. L., Mathews, H. L., DeVon, H. A., & Janusek, L. W. (2014). Epigenetics and social context: implications for disparity in cardiovascular disease. *Aging and Disease, 5*(5), 346–355.

Sabini, J., & Silver, M. (2005). Ekman's basic emotions: Why not love and jealousy? *Cognition & Emotion, 19,* 693–712.

Sacerdote, B. (2001). Peer effects with random assignment: Results for Dartmouth roommates. *Quarterly Journal of Economics, 116,* 681–704.

Sack, Robert L. (2010). Jet lag. *The New England Journal of Medicine, 362,* 440–447.

Sack, Robert L., & Lewy, Alfred J. (1997). Melatonin as a chronobiotic: Treatment of circadian desynchrony in night workers and the blind. *Journal of Biological Rhythms, 12,* 595–603.

Sackeim, H. A. (1986). The efficacy of electroconvulsive therapy. *Annals of the New York Academy of Sciences, 462,* 70–75.

Sackeim, H. A., Prudic, J., Fuller, R., Keilp, J., Lavori, P. W., & Olfson, M. (2007). The cognitive effects of electroconvulsive therapy in community settings. *Neuropsychopharmacology, 32,* 244–254.

Sackett, Paul R.; Borneman, Matthew J.; & Connelly, Brian S. (2008). High-stakes testing in higher education and employment: Appraising the evidence for validity and fairness. *American Psychologist, 63,* 215–227.

Safdar, S., Friedlmeier, W., Matsumoto, D., Yoo, S. H., Kwantes, C. T., Kakai, H., & Shigemasu, E. (2009). Variations of emotional display rules within and across cultures: A comparison between Canada, USA, and Japan. Canadian *Journal of Behavioural Science/Revue canadienne des sciences du comportement, 41,* 1–10.

Safer, D. J. (2000). Are stimulants overprescribed for youths with ADHD? *Annals of Clinical Psychiatry, 12,* 55–62.

Sahakyan, L., & Kelley, C. M. (2002). A contextual change account of the directed forgetting effect. *Journal of Experimental Psychology: Learning, Memory, & Cognition, 28,* 1064–1072.

Salovey, P. (2006). Epilogue: The agenda for future research. In V. U. Druskat, F. Sala, & G. Mount (Eds.), *Linking emotional intelligence and performance at work: Current research evidence with individuals and groups* (pp. 267–272). Mahwah, NJ: Erlbaum.

Sanes, J. N., & Donoghue, J. P. (2000). Plasticity and primary motor cortex. *Annual Review of Neuroscience, 23,* 393–415.

Santa Maria, M. P., Baumeister, A. A., & Gouvier, W. D. (1999). Public knowledge and misconceptions about electroconvulsive therapy: A demographically stratified investigation. *International Journal of Rehabilitation and Health, 4,* 111–116.

Santor, D. A., & Kusumakar, V. (2001). Open trial of interpersonal therapy in adolescents with moderate to severe major depression: Effectiveness of novice IPT therapists. *Journal of the American Academy of Child and Adolescent Psychiatry, 40,* 236–240.

Saper, C., Scammell, T., & Lu, J. (2005). Hypothalamic regulation of sleep and circadian rhythms. *Nature, 437,* 1257–1263.

Saporta, I., & Halpern, J. J. (2002). Being different can hurt: Effects of deviation from physical norms on lawyers' salaries. Industrial Relations: A *Journal of Economy and Society, 41,* 442–466.

Sarbin, Theodore R. (1991). Hypnosis: A fifty-year perspective. *Contemporary Hypnosis, 8,* 1–15.

Sargent, J. D., & Heatherton, T. F. (2009). Comparison of trends for adolescent smoking in movies: 1990–2007. *Journal of the American Medical Association, 301,* 2211–2213.

Satir, V. (1964). *Conjoint family therapy.* New York, NY: Science and Behavior Books.

Sattler, J. M. (1992). *Assessment of children* (3rd ed.). San Diego, CA: Author.

Sattler, J. M. (2005). *Assessment of children: Behavioral and clinical applications* (5th ed.). La Mesa, CA: Author.

Saucier, Deborah M., & Kimura, Doreen (1998). Intrapersonal motor but not extrapersonal targeting skill is enhanced during the midluteal phase of the menstrual cycle. *Developmental Neuropsychology, 14,* 385–398.

Savage-Rumbaugh, E. S., & Lewin, R. (1994). *Kanzi: The ape at the brink of the human mind.* New York, NY: Wiley.

Savic, I., Berglund, H., & Lindström, P. (2007). Brain response to putative pheromones in homosexual men. In G. Einstein (Ed.), *Sex and the brain* (pp. 731–738). Cambridge, MA: MIT Press.

Scattone, D. (2007). Social skills interventions for children with autism. *Psychology in the Schools, 44,* 717–726.

Schachter, S., & Singer, J. E. (1962). Cognitive, social, and physiological determinants of emotional state. *Psychological Review, 69,* 379–399.

Schachter, S., & Singer, J. E. (2001). Cognitive, social, and psychological determinants of emotional state. In. G. W. Parrott (Ed.), *Emotions in social psychology: Essential readings* (pp. 76–93). Philadelphia, PA: Psychology Press.

Schacter, Daniel L. (2001). *The seven sins of memory: How the mind forgets and remembers.* Boston: Houghton-Mifflin.

Schacter, Daniel L. (2012). Constructive memory: Past and future. *Dialogues in Clinical Neuroscience, 14,* 7–18.

Schacter, Daniel L.; Chiu, Chi-yue; & Ochsner, Kevin N. (1993). Implicit memory: A selective review. *Annual Review of Neuroscience, 16,* 159–182.

Schaefer, C. E., & Mattei, D. (2005). Catharsis: Effectiveness in children's aggression. *International Journal of Play Therapy, 14,* 103–109.

Schafe, G. E., & LeDoux, J. E. (2002). Emotional plasticity. In H. Pashler & R. Gallistel (Eds.), *Stevens' handbook of experimental psychology: Vol. 3, Learning, motivation, and emotion* (3rd ed., pp. 535–561). New York, NY: Wiley.

Scheier, M. F., & Carver, C. S. (1985). Optimism, coping, and health: Assessment and implications of generalized outcome expectancies. *Health Psychology, 4*(3), 219–247.

Schenck, Carlos H., & Mahowald, Mark W. (2002). REM sleep behavior disorder: Clinical, developmental, and neuroscience perspectives 16 years after its formal identification in SLEEP. *Sleep, 25,* 120–138.

Scherer, K. R., Schorr, A., & Johnstone, T. (Eds.). (2001). *Appraisal processes in emotion: Theory, methods, research.* New York, NY: Oxford University Press.

Schiller, Daniela, & Phelps, Elizabeth A. (2011). Does reconsolidation occur in humans? *Frontiers in Behavioral Neuroscience, 5,* 1–12.

Schimmack, U., & Crites, S. L., Jr. (2005). The structure of affect. In D. Albarracín, B. T. Johnson, & M. P. Zanna (Eds.), *The handbook of attitudes* (pp. 397–435). Mahwah, NJ: Erlbaum.

Schmid, S. M., Hallschmid, M., Jauch-Chara, K., Born, J., & Schultes, B. (2008). A single night of sleep deprivation increases ghrelin levels and feelings of hunger in normal-weight healthy men. *Journal of Sleep Research, 17,* 331–334.

Schmidt, J. P., & Hancey, R. (1979). Social class and psychiatric treatment: Application of a decision-making model to use patterns in a cost-free clinic. *Journal of Consulting and Clinical Psychology, 47,* 771–772.

Schneeweiss, S., & Avorn, J. (2009). Antipsychotic agents and sudden cardiac death-How should we manage the risk. *New England Journal of Medicine, 360,* 294–296.

Schoenthaler, S. J., Amos, S. P., Eysenck, H. J., Peritz, E., & Yudkin, J. (1991). Controlled trial of vitamin-mineral supplementation: Effects on intelligence and performance. *Personality and Individual Differences, 12,* 251–362.

Schofield, W. (1964). *Psychotherapy: The purchase of friendship.* Englewood Cliffs, NJ: Prentice Hall.

Schooler, C. (1998). Environmental complexity and the Flynn effect. In U. Neisser (Ed.), *The rising curve: Long-term gains in IQ and related measures* (pp. 67–79). Washington, DC: American Psychological Association.

Schultz, W. (2001). Reward signaling by dopamine neurons. *The Neuroscientist, 7,* 293–302.

Scovern, A. W., & Kilmann, P. R. (1980). Status of electroconvulsive therapy: Review of the outcome literature. *Psychological Bulletin, 87,* 260–295.

Searles, L. V. (1949). The organization of hereditary maze brightness and maze dullness. *Genetic Psychology Monographs, 39,* 279–375.

Segal, Z. V., Williams, J. M. G., & Teasdale, J. D. (2012). *Mindfulness-based cognitive therapy for depression.* New York, NY: Guilford Press.

Segerstrom, S. C., & Miller, G. E. (2004). Psychological stress and the immune system: A meta-analytic study of 30 years of inquiry. *Psychological Bulletin, 130,* 601–630.

Seligman, M., & Maier, S. (1967). Failure to escape traumatic shock. *Journal of Experimental Psychology, 74,* 1–9.

Selye, H. (1956). *The stress of life.* New York: McGraw-Hill.

Shackelford, T. K., & Weekes-Shackelford. V. A. (2004). Why don't men pay child support? Insights from evolutionary psychology In C. Crawford, A. Viviana, & C. Salmon (Eds.), *Evolutionary psychology, public policy and personal decisions* (pp. 231–247). Mahwah, NJ: Lawrence Erlbaum.

Shadish, W. R. (1995). The logic of generalization: Five principles common to experiments and ethnographies. *American Journal of Community Psychology, 23,* 419–428.

Shapiro, D. A., & Shapiro, D. (1982). Meta-analysis of comparative therapy outcome studies: A replication and refinement. *Psychological Bulletin, 92,* 581–604.

Shapiro, F. (1995). *Eye movement desensitization and reprocessing: Basic principles, protocols, and procedures.* New York, NY: Guilford Press.

Shapiro, F., & Forrest, M. S. (1997). *EMDR: The breakthrough therapy for overcoming anxiety, stress, and trauma.* New York, NY: Basic Books.

Sharman, Stephanie J.; Manning, Charles G.; & Garry, Maryanne (2005). Explain this: Explaining childhood events inflates confidence for those events. *Applied Cognitive Psychology, 19,* 16–74.

Shaw, P., Bramham, J., Lawrence, E. J., Morris, R., Baron-Cohen, S., & David, A. S. (2005). Differential effects of lesions of the amygdala and prefrontal cortex on recognizing facial expressions of complex emotions. *Journal of Cognitive Neuroscience, 17,* 1410–1419.

Shedler, J. (2010). The efficacy of psychodynamic psychotherapy. *American Psychologist, 65,* 98–109.

Shin, S. M., Chow, C., Camacho-Gonsalves, T., Levy, R. J., Allen, E., & Leff, S. H. (2005). A meta-analytic review of racial-ethnic matching for African American and Caucasian American clients and clinicians. *Journal of Counseling Psychology, 52,* 45–56.

Shlien, J., & Levant, R. (1984). Introduction. In R. Levant & J. Shlien (Eds.), *Client-centered therapy and the person-centered approach: New directions in theory, research and practice* (pp. 1–16). New York, NY: Praeger.

Siegel, J. (2005). Clues to the functions of mammalian sleep. *Nature, 437*(7063), 1264–1271.

Siegel, Ronald K. (1989). *Intoxication: Life in pursuit of artificial paradise.* New York: Dutton.

Siep, N., Roefs, A., Roebroeck, A., Havermans, R., Bonte, M. L., & Jansen, A. (2009). Hunger is the best spice: An fMRI study of the effects of attention, hunger and calorie content on food reward processing in the amygdala and orbitofrontal cortex. *Behavioural Brain Research, 198,* 149–158.

Sikorski, C., Luppa, M., Brähler, E., König, H., & Riedel-Heller, S. G. (2012). Obese children, adults and senior citizens in the eyes of the general public: Results of a representative study on stigma and causation of obesity. *Plos ONE, 7,* doi:10.1371/journal.pone.0046924

Silverman, S. (1987, July). Medical "miracles": Still mysterious despite claims of believers. *Newsletter of the Sacramento Skeptics Society,* Sacramento, CA, pp. 2–7.

Simcock, Gabrielle, & Hayne, Harlene (2002). Breaking the barrier: Children fail to translate their preverbal memories into language. *Psychological Science, 13,* 225–231.

Simpson, G. M., & Kline, N. S. (1976). Tardive dyskinesias: Manifestations, etiology, and treatment. In M. D. Yahr (Ed.), *The basal ganglia* (pp. 167–183). New York, NY: Raven Press.

Singer, M. T., & Nievod, A. (2003). New age therapies. In S. O. Lilienfeld, S. J. Lynn, & J. M. Lohr (Eds.), *Science and pseudoscience in clinical psychology* (pp. 176–204). New York, NY: Guilford Press.

Skaalvik, E. M., & Rankin, R. J. (1994). Gender differences in mathematics and verbal achievement, self-perception and motivation. *British Journal of Educational Psychology, 64,* 419–428.

Skeels, H. M. (1938). Mental development of children in foster homes. *Journal of Consulting Psychology, 2,* 33–43.

Skeels, H. M. (1942). The study of the effects of differential stimulation on mentally retarded children: A follow-up report. *American Journal of Mental Deficiencies, 46,* 340–350.

Skeels, H. M. (1966). Adult status of children with contrasting early life experiences. *Monographs of the Society for Research in Child Development, 31*(3), 1–65.

Skinner, B. F. (1966). The ontogeny and phylogeny of behavior. *Science, 153,* 1203–1213.

Slade, Pauline (1984). Premenstrual emotional changes in normal women: Fact or fiction? *Journal of Psychosomatic Research, 28,* 1–7.

Sligh, A. C., Conners, F. A., & Roskos-Ewoldsen, B. (2005). Relation of creativity to fluid and crystallized intelligence. *Journal of Creative Behavior, 39,* 123–136.

Sloane, R. B., Staples, F., Cristol, A., Yorkston, N., & Whipple, K. (1975). *Psychotherapy versus behavior therapy.* Cambridge, MA: Harvard University Press.

Slof-Op't Landt, M. T., Bartels, M., Middeldorp, C. M., van Beijsterveldt, C. M., Slagboom, P., Boomsma, D. I., . . . Meulenbelt, I. (2013). Genetic variation at the TPH2 gene influences impulsivity in addition to eating disorders. *Behavior Genetics, 43,* 24–33. doi:10.1007/s10519–012–9569–3

Smith, D. B. (2009, August). The doctor is in. *American Scholar.* Retrieved from http://www.theamericanscholar.org/the-doctor-is-in

Smith, M. E., & Farah, M. J. (2011). Are prescription stimulants "smart pills"? The epidemiology and cognitive neuroscience of prescription stimulant use by normal healthy individuals. *Psychological Bulletin, 137,* 717–741.

Smith, M. L. (1980). Teacher expectations. *Evaluation in Education, 4,* 53–55.

Smith, M. L., & Glass, G. V. (1977). Meta-analysis of psychotherapy outcome studies. *American Psychologist, 32,* 752–760.

Smith, T. B., McCullough, M. E., & Poll, J. (2003). Religiousness and depression: Evidence for a main effect and the moderating influence of stressful life events. *Psychological Bulletin, 129,* 614–636.

Smythe, I. H. (2007). The secret behind "The Secret": What is attracting millions to the "Law of Attraction"? *Skeptic, 13*(2), 8–11.

Snider, L. A., & Swedo, S. E. (2004). PANDAS: Current status and directions for research. *Molecular Psychiatry, 9,* 900–907.

Snyder, K. (2006). Kurt Snyder's personal experience with schizophrenia. *Schizophrenia Bulletin, 32,* 209–211.

Sobell, M. B., & Sobell, L. C. (1973). Alcoholics treated by individualized behavior therapy: One year treatment outcome. *Behaviour Research and Therapy, 11,* 599–618.

Sobell, M. B., & Sobell, L. C. (1976). Second year treatment outcome of alcoholics treated by individualized behavior therapy: Results. *Behaviour Research and Therapy, 14,* 195–215.

Sober, E. (1984). *The nature of selection: Evolutionary theory in philosophical focus.* Cambridge, MA: MIT Press.

Soei, E., Koch, B., Schwarz, M., & Daum, I. (2008). Involvement of the human thalamus in relational and non-relational memory. *European Journal of Neuroscience, 28,* 2533–2541.

Solms, Mark (1997). *The neuropsychology of dreams.* Mahwah, NJ: Erlbaum.

Sommer, Robert (1977, January). Toward a psychology of natural behavior. *APA Monitor.* Reprinted in *Readings in psychology* 78/79. Guilford, CT: Dushkin, 1978.

Sommers-Flanagan, R., Sommers-Flanagan, J., & Davis, B. (1993). What's happening on music television? A gender role content analysis. *Sex Roles, 28,* 745–754.

Soussignan, R. (2002). Duchenne smile, emotional experience, and autonomic reactivity: A test of the facial feedback hypothesis. *Emotion, 2,* 52–74.

Spalding, K. L., Arner, E., Westermark, P. O., Bernard, S., Buchholz, B. A., Bergmann, O., . . . Arner, P. (2008). Dynamics of fat cell turnover in humans. *Nature, 453,* 783–787.

Spanos, Nicholas P. (1991). A sociocognitive approach to hypnosis. In S. J. Lynn & J. W. Rhue (Eds.), *Theories of hypnosis: Current models and perspectives.* New York: Guilford Press.

Spanos, Nicholas P. (1996). *Multiple identities and false memories: A sociocognitive perspective.* Washington, DC: American Psychological Association.

Spanos, Nicholas P.; Burgess, Cheryl A.; Roncon, Vera; et al. (1993). Surreptitiously observed hypnotic responding in simulators and in skill-trained and untrained high hypnotizables. *Journal of Personality and Social Psychology, 65,* 391–398.

Spanos, Nicholas P.; Stenstrom, Robert J.; & Johnson, Joseph C. (1988). Hypnosis, placebo, and suggestion in the treatment of warts. *Psychosomatic Medicine, 50,* 245–260.

Sparks, J. A., Duncan, B. L., & Miller, S. D. (2008). Common factors in psychotherapy. In J. L. Lebow (Ed.), *Twenty-first century psychotherapies: Contemporary approaches to theory and practice* (pp. 453–497). Hoboken, NJ: Wiley.

Spencer, R., Zelaznik, H., Diedrichsen, J., & Ivry, R. (2003). Disrupted timing of discontinuous but not continuous movements by cerebellar le-sions. *Science, 300,* 1437–1439.

Spera, S. P., Buhrfeind, E. D., & Pennebaker, J. W. (1994). Expressive writing and coping with job loss. *Academy of Management Journal, 37,* 722–733.

Sperling, George (1960). The information available in brief visual presentations. *Psychological Monographs, 74*(498).

Sperry, R. W. (1964). The great cerebral commissure. *Scientific American, 210,* 42–52.

Sperry, R. W. (1968). Hemisphere deconnection and unity in conscious experience. *American Psychologist, 23,* 723–733.

Spiegler, M. (1983). *Contemporary behavior therapy.* Palo Alto, CA: Mayfield.

Spiegler, M. D., & Guevremont, D. C. (2003). *Contemporary behavior therapy* (4th ed). Belmont, CA: Wadsworth/Thompson Learning.

Spoor, F., Leakey, M. G., Gathogo, P. N., Brown, F. H., Anton, S. C., McDougall, I., Kiarie, C., Manthi, F. K., & Leakey. L. N. (2007). Implications of new early Homo fossils from Ileret, east of Lake Turkana, Kenya. *Nature, 448,* 688–691.

Spreen, O., Risser, A., & Edgell, D. (1995). *Developmental neuropsychology.* New York: Oxford University Press.

Squier, Leslie H., & Domhoff, G. William (1998). The presentation of dreaming and dreams in introductory psychology textbooks: A critical examination with suggestions for textbook authors and course instructors. *Dreaming, 8,* 149–168.

Squire, Larry R., & Zola-Morgan, Stuart (1991). The medial temporal lobe memory system. *Science, 253,* 1380–1386.

Squire, Larry R.; Ojemann, Jeffrey G.; Miezin, Francis M.; et al. (1992). Activation of the hippocampus in normal humans: A functional anatomical study of memory. *Proceedings of the National Academy of Science, 89,* 1837–1841.

Stanovich, Keith (2010). *How to think straight about psychology* (9th ed.). Boston: Allyn & Bacon.

Stanton, Stephen J.; Mullette-Gillman, O'Dhaniel A.; & Huettel, Scott A. (2011). Seasonal variation of salivary testosterone in men, normally cycling women, and women using hormonal contraceptives. *Physiology & Behavior, 104,* 804–808.

Steele, C., & Aronson, J. (1995). Stereotype threat and the intellectual test performance of African Americans. *Journal of Personality & Social Psychology, 69,* 797–811.

Steele, M., Weiss, M., Swanson, J., Wang, J., Prinzo, R., & Binder, C. (2006). A randomized, controlled effectiveness trial of OROS-methylphenidate compared to usual care with immediate release methylphenidate in ADHD. *Canadian Journal of Clinical Pharmacology, 14,* 50–62.

Steffen, P. R., McNeilly, M., Anderson, N., & Sherwood, A. (2003). Effects of perceived racism and anger inhibition on ambulatory blood pressure in African Americans. *Psychosomatic Medicine, 65,* 746–750.

Steffens, Sabine; Veillard, Niels R.; Arnaud Claire; et al. (2005). Low dose oral cannabinoid therapy reduces progression of atherosclerosis in mice. *Nature 434,* 782–786.

Steinmetz, J. L., Lewinsohn, P. M., & Antonuccio, D. O. (1983). Prediction of individual outcome in a group intervention for depression. *Journal of Consulting and Clinical Psychology, 51,* 331–337.

Stel, M., van Dijk, E., & Olivier, E. (2009). You want to know the truth? Then don't mimic! *Psychological Science, 20,* 693–699.

Stelmack, R. M., Knott, V., & Beauchamp, C. M. (2003). Intelligence and neural transmission time: A brain stem auditory evoked potential analysis. *Personality and Individual Differences, 34,* 97–107.

Sternberg, R. J. (2009). Toward a triarchic theory of intelligence. In R. J. Sternberg, J. C. Kaufman, & E. Grigorenko (Ed.), *The essential Sternberg: Essays on intelligence, psychology, and education* (pp. 33–70). New York, NY: Springer.

Sternberg, R. J. (2012). The assessment of creativity: An investment-based approach. Creativity Research *Journal, 24, 3–12. doi:10.1080/10400419.20 12.652925*

Sternson, S. M., Betley, J., & Cao, Z. (2013). Neural circuits and motivational processes for hunger. *Current Opinion in Neurobiology, 23,* 353–360. doi:10.1016/j.conb.2013.04.006

Stessman, J., Rottenberg, Y., Shimshilashvili, I., Ein-Mor, E., Jacobs, J. M. (2014). Loneliness, health, and longevity. The *Journals of Gerontology. Series A, Biological Sciences and Medical Sciences, 69*(6), 744–750. doi:10.1093/gerona/glt147

Stevens, S. E., Hynan, M. T., & Allen, M. (2000). A meta-analysis of common factor and specific treatment effects across the outcome domains of the phase model of psychotherapy. *Clinical Psychology: Science and Practice, 7,* 273–290.

Stevenson, H. W. (1992, December). Learning from Asian schools. *Scientific American, 265*(6), 70–76.

Stevenson, H. W. (1993). Why Asian students still outdistance Americans. *Educational Leadership, 50,* 63–65.

Stevenson, H. W., Lee, S.-Y., & Stigler, J. W. (1986). Mathematics achievment of Chinese, Japanese, and American children. *Science, 231,* 693–697.

Stewart, L. (2008). Do musicians have different brains? *Clinical Medicine, 8,* 304–308.

Stinson, F. S., Dawson, D. A., Chou, P. S., et al. (2007). The epidemiology of DSM-IV specific phobia in the USA: Results from the National Epidemiologic Survey on Alcohol and Related Conditions. *Psychological Medicine, 37,* 1047–1059.

Stokes, P. D. (2006). *Creativity from constraints: The psychology of breakthrough.* New York, NY: Springer.

Stothart, C. R., Simons, D. J., Boot, W. R., & Kramer, A. F. (2014) Is the effect of aerobic exercise on cognition a placebo effect? *PLoS ONE 9*(10), e109557. doi:10.1371/journal.pone.0109557

Strachan, T., & Read, A. P. (1999). *Human molecular genetics.* New York: Wiley.

Strayer, D. L., & Drews, F. A. (2007). Multitasking in the automobile. In A. F. Dramer, D. A. Wiegmann, & A. Kirlik (Eds.), *Attention: From theory to practice* (pp. 121–133). New York, NY: Oxford University Press.

Strayer, D. L., Cooper, J. M., Turrill, J., Coleman, J., Medeiros-Wrad, N., & Biondi, F. (2013). *Measuring cognitive distraction in the automobile.* Washington, DC: AAA Foundation for Traffic Safety. Retrieved from https://www.aaafoundation.org/sites/default/files/MeasuringCognitiveDistractions.pdf.

Strayer, David L.; Drews, Frank A.; & Crouch, Dennis J. (2006). A comparison of the cell phone driver and the drunk driver. *Human Factors, 48,* 381–391.

Stricker, G., & Gold, J. (2003). Integrative approaches to psychotherapy. In A. S. Gurman & S. B. Messer (Eds.), *Essential psychotherapies: Theory and practic* (2nd ed., pp. 317–349). New York, NY: Guilford Press.

Strickland, T. L., Stein, R., Lin, K. M., Risby, E., & Fong, R. (1997). The pharmacologic treatment of anxiety and depression in African Americans: Considerations for the general practitioner. *Archives of Family Medicine, 6,* 371–375.

Strupp, H. H., Fox, R. E., & Lessler, K. (1969). *Patients view their therapy.* Baltimore, MD: Johns Hopkins University Press.

Strupp, H. H., Hadley, S. W., & Gomez-Schwartz, B. (1978). *Psychotherapy for better or worse: An analysis of the problem of negative effects.* New York, NY: Jason Aronson.

Stuart, R. B., & Heiby, E. M. (2007). To prescribe or not prescribe: Eleven exploratory questions. *Scientific Review of Mental Health Practice, 5,* 4–32.

Stubbs, A. (2014). Reducing mental illness stigma in health care students and professionals: A review of the literature. *Australasian Psychiatry, 22*(6), 579–584. doi:10.1177/1039856214556324

Sturm, R., & Hattori, A. (2015). Diet and obesity in Los Angeles County 2007–2012: Is there a measurable effect of the 2008 "fast-food ban"? *Social Science and Medicine, 133,* 205–211.

Subotnik, R. F., & Arnold, K. D. (1994). *Beyond Terman: Contemporary longitudinal studies of giftedness and talent.* Norwood, NJ: Ablex.

Sue, D. W., & Sue, D. (2003). *Counseling the culturally diverse: Theory and practice* (4th ed.). New York, NY: Wiley.

Sue, S. (1998). In search of cultural competence in psychotherapy and counseling. *American Psychologist, 53,* 440–448.

Sue, S., & Lam, A. G. (2002). Cultural and demographic diversity. In J. C. Norcross (Ed.), *Psychotherapy relationships that work* (pp. 401–421). New York, NY: Oxford University Press.

Sue, S., & Zane, N. (2006). Ethnic minority populations have been neglected by evidence-based practices. In J. C. Norcross, L. E. Beutler, & R. F. Levant (Eds.), *Evidence-based practices in mental health* (pp. 329–337). Washington, DC: American Psychological Association.

Sullivan, H. S. (1954). *The psychiatric interview.* New York, NY: Norton.

Sumner, J. A., Mineka, S., Zinbarg, R. E., Craske, M. G., Vrshek-Schallhorn, S., & Epstein, A. (2014). *Examining the long-term stability of overgeneral autobiographical memory. Memory, 22*(3), 163–170. doi:10.1080/09658211.2013.774021

Sundet, J. M., Borren, I., & Tambs, K. (2008). The Flynn effect is partly caused by changing fertility patterns. *Intelligence, 36,* 183–191.

Surguladze, S. A., Young, A. W., Senior, C., Brebion, G., Travis, M. J., & Phillips, M. L. (2004). Recognition accuracy and response bias to happy and sad facial expressions in patients with major depression. *Neuropsychology, 18,* 212–218.

Suzuki, D. T., Griffiths, A. J. F., Miller, J. H., & Lewontin, R. C. (1989). *An introduction to genetic analysis* (4th ed.). New York: Freeman.

Switaj, P., Grygiel, P., Anczewska, M., & Wciórka, J. (2014). Loneliness mediates the relationship between internalized stigma and depression among patients with psychotic disorders. International *Journal of Social Psychiatry, 60*(8), 733–740. doi:10.1177/0020764013513442

Szpunar, Karl K.; Addis, Donna R.; & Schacter, Daniel L. (2012). Memory for emotional simulations: Remembering a rosy future. *Psychological Science, 23,* 24–29.

Takahashi, Y. (1990). Is multiple personality really rare in Japan? *Dissociation, 3,* 57–59.

Taki, Y., Hashizume, H., Sassa, Y., et al. (2012). Correlation among body height, intelligence, and brain gray matter volume in healthy children. *Neuroimage, 16,* 1023–1027.

Talarico, Jennifer M. (2009). Freshman flashbulbs: Memories of unique and first-time evens in starting college. *Memory, 17,* 256–265.

Talarico, Jennifer M., & Rubin, David C. (2003). Confidence, not consistency, characterizes flashbulb memories. *Psychological Science, 14,* 455–461.

Talmi, Deborah; Grady, Cheryl L.; Goshen-Gottstein, Yonatan; & Moscovitch, Morris (2005). Neuroimaging the serial position curve: A test of single-store versus dual-store models. *Psychological Science, 16,* 716–723.

Tang, C. Y., Eaves, E. L., Ng, J. C., Carpenter, D. M., Mai, X., Schroeder, D. H., . . . Haier, R. J. (2010). Brain networks for working memory and factors of intelligence assessed in males and females with fMRI and DTI. *Intelligence, 38,* 293–303.

Tang, Y-Y., Ma, Y., Fan, Y., Feng, H., Wang, J., Feng, S., Lu, Q., Hu, B., Lin, Y., Li, J., Zhang, Y., Wang, Y., Zhou, L., & Fan, M. (2009). Central and autonomic nervous system interaction is altered by short-term meditation. *PNAS: Proceedings of the National Academy of Sciences, 105,* 8865–8870.

Tanner, J. M. (1990). *Fetus into man* (2nd ed.). Cambridge MA: Harvard University Press.

Tavris, C. (2003, September 28). Mind games: Warfare between therapists and scientists. *Chronicle Review, 45*(29), B7.

Tavris, C., & Sadd, S. (1977). The Redbook report on female sexuality. New York: Delacorte Press.

Tavris, Carol, & Aronson, Elliot (2007). *Mistakes were made (but not by me).* Orlando, FL: Houghton Mifflin Harcourt.

Taylor, S. E. (2002). *The tending instinct: How nurturing is essential to who we are and how we live.* New York: Holt.

Taylor, S. E. (2006). Tend and befriend: Biobehavioral bases of affiliation under stress. *Current Directions in Psychological Science, 15,* 273–277.

Teasdale, J. D., Segal, Z. V., & Williams, J. M. G. (2003). Mindfulness training and problem formulation. *Clinical Psychology: Science and Practice, 10,* 157–160.

Teasdale, T. W., & Owen, D. R. (2005). A long-term rise and recent decline in intelligence test performance: The Flynn effect in reverse. *Personality and Individual Differences, 39,* 837–843.

Teplin, L. A., McClelland, G. M., Abram, K. M., & Weiner, D. A. (2005). Crime victimization in adults with severe mental illness: Comparison with the National Crime Victimization Survey. *Archives of General Psychiatry, 62,* 911–921.

Tercyak, K., Johnson, S., Roberts, S., & Cruz, A. (2001). Psychological response to prenatal genetic counseling and amniocentesis. *Patient Education & Counseling, 43,* 73–84.

Terman, L. M. (1925). *Mental and physical traits of a thousand gifted children: Genetic studies of genius* (Vol. 1). Stanford, CA: Stanford University Press.

Terrace, H. S., Son, L. K., & Brannon, E. M. (2003). Serial expertise of rhesus macaques. *Psychological Science, 14,* 66–73.

Thase, M. E. (2000). Psychopharmacology in conjunction with psychotherapy. In C. R. Snyder & R. E. Ingram (Eds.), *Handbook of psychological change* (pp. 474–498). New York, NY: Wiley.

The Genome Sequencing Consortium. (2001). Initial sequencing and analysis of the human genome. *Nature, 409,* 860–921.

Thompson-Cannino, Jennifer; Cottton, Ronald; & Torneo, Erin (2009). *Picking Cotton: Our memoir of injustice and redemption.* New York: St. Martin's Press.

Thompson, Richard F. (1983). Neuronal substrates of simple associative learning: Classical conditioning. *Trends in Neurosciences, 6,* 270–275.

Thompson, Richard F. (1986). The neurobiology of learning and memory. *Science, 233,* 941–947.

Thompson, Richard F., & Kosslyn, Stephen M. (2000). Neural systems activated during visual mental imagery: A review and meta-analyses. In A. W. Toga & J. C. Mazziotta (Eds.), *Brain mapping: The systems.* San Diego, CA: Academic Press.

Thompson, Robin; Emmorey, Karen; & Gollan, Tamar H. (2005). "Tip of the fingers" experiences by deaf signers. *Psychological Science, 16,* 856–860.

Thorpe, S. K., Holder, R. L., & Crompton, R. H. (2007). Origin of human bipedalism as an adaptation for locomotion on flexible branches. *Science, 316,* 1328–1331.

Thurstone, L. L. (1938). Primary mental abilities. *Psychometric Monographs,* 1.

Tinti, Carla; Schmidt, Susanna; Sotgiu, Igor; et al. (2009). The role of importance/consequentiality appraisal in flashbulb memory formation: The case of the death of Pope John Paul III. *Applied Cognitive Psychology, 23,* 236–253.

Tochigi, M., Okazaki, Y., Kato, N., & Sasaki, T. (2004). What causes seasonality of birth in schizophrenia? *Neuroscience Research, 48,* 1–11.

Tomasello, M., & Herrmann, E. (2010). Ape and human cognition: What's the difference? *Current Directions in Psychological Science, 19,* 3–8.

Tomko, R. L., Trull, T. J., Wood, P. K., & Sher, K. J. (2014). Characteristics of borderline personality disorder in a community sample: Comorbidity, treatment utilization, and general functioning. *Journal of Personality Disorders, 28*(5), 734–750.

Tooby, J., & Cosmides, L. (2008). The evolutionary psychology of the emotions and their relationship to internal regulatory variables. In M. Lewis, J. M. Haviland-Jones, & L. F. Barrett (Eds.), *Handbook of emotions* (3rd ed., pp. 114–137). New York, NY: Guilford Press.

Tooth, G. C., & Newton, M. P. (1961). *Leukotomy in England and Wales 1942–1954.* London, Engalnd: Her Majesty's Stationary Office.

Tourangeau, Roger, & Yan, Ting (2007). Sensitive questions in surveys. *Psychological Bulletin, 133,* 859–883.

Tracy, M., Zimmerman, F. J., Galea, S., et al. (2008). What explains the relation between family poverty and childhood depressive symptoms? *Journal of Psychiatric Research, 42(14),* 1163–1175.

Treffert, D. A., & Wallace, G. L. (2002, June). Islands of genius. *Scientific American, 286*(6), 76–85.

Tremblay, J., & Cohen, J. (2005). Spatial configuration and list learning of proximally cued arms by rats in the enclosed four-arm radial maze. *Learning and Behavior, 33,* 78–89.

Trivers, R. L. (1971). The biology of reciprocal altruism. *Quarterly Review of Biology, 46,* 35–57.

Trivers, R. L. (1972). Parental investment and sexual selection. In B. Campbell (Ed.), *Sexual selection and the descent of man.* Chicago: Aldine.

Tryon, R. C. (1940). Genetic differences in maze-learning ability in rats. *Yearbook of the National Society for the Study of Education, 39,* 111–119.

Tryon, W. W. (2008). Whatever happened to symptom substitution? *Clinical Psychology Review, 28,* 963–968.

Tucker-Drob, E. M., Briley, D. A., & Harden, P. (2013). Genetic and environmental influences on cognition across development and context. Psychological Science, 22, 349–355. doi:10.1177/0963721413485087

Tugade, M. M., & Fredrickson, B. L. (2004). Resilient individuals use positive emotions to bounce back from negative emotional experiences. *Journal of Personality and Social Psychology, 86,* 320–333.

Tulving, Endel (1985). How many memory systems are there? *American Psychologist, 40,* 385–398.

Turnbull, S., Ward, A., Treasure, J., Jick, H., & Derby, L. (1996). The demand for eating disorder care. An epidemiological study using the general practice research database. *British Journal of Psychiatry, 169,* 705–712.

Turner, C. F.; Ku, L.; Rogers, S. M.; et al. (1998). Adolescent sexual behavior, drug use, and violence: Increased reporting with computer survey technology. *Science, 280,* 867–873.

Tustin, Karen, & Hayne, Harlene (2010). Defining the boundary: Age-related changes in childhood amnesia. *Developmental Psychology, 46,* 1049–1061.

U.S. Department of Energy. (2009). *Human genome project information.* Retrieved January 17, 2010 from

U.S. Surgeon General. (2001). *Mental health: Culture, race, and ethnicity-A supplement to mental health: A report of the Surgeon General.* Rockville, MD: U.S. Department of Health and Human Services.

United States Census Bureau. (2012). *Statistical abstract of the United States, 2012.* Retrieved January 8, 2013, from http://www.census.gov/compendia/statab/

United States Department of Health and Human Services. (2014). *The health consequences of smoking-50 years of progress: A report of the surgeon general.* Rockville, MD: Author.

Usher, JoNell A., & Neisser, Ulric (1993). Childhood amnesia and the beginnings of memory for four early life events. *Journal of Experimental Psychology: General, 122,* 155–165.

Vaillant, G. E., & Milofsky, E. S. (1982). Natural history of male alcoholism IV: Paths to recovery. *Archives of General Psychiatry, 39,* 127–133.

Valdes, S. G. (2005). Frequency and success: An empirical study of criminal law defenses, federal constitutional evidentiary claims, and plea negotiations. *University of Pennsylvania Law Review, 153,* 1709–1814.

Valenstein, E. S. (1973). *Brain control.* New York, NY: Wiley.

Valentine, Tim, & Mesout, Jan (2009). Eyewitness identification under stress in the London dungeon. *Applied Cognitive Psychology, 23,* 151–161.

Van Boven, Leaf, & Gilovich, Thomas (2003). To do or to have? That is the question. *Journal of Personality and Social Psychology, 85,* 1193–1202.

Van den Bussche, E., Van den Noortgate, W., & Reynvoet, B. (2009). Mechanisms of masked priming: A meta-analysis. *Psychological Bulletin, 135,* 452–477.

van der Kolk, B. A. (1994). The body keeps score: Memory and the evolving psychobiology of posttraumatic stress. *Harvard Review of Psychiatry, 1,* 253–265.

van der Laan, L. N., de Ridder, D. D., Viergever, M. A., & Smeets, P. M. (2011). The first taste is always with the eyes: A meta-analysis on the neural correlates of processing visual food cues. *NeuroImage, 55,* 296–303.

van der Sanden, R. M., Stutterheim, S. E., Pryor, J. B., Kok, G., & Bos, A. R. (2014). Coping with stigma by association and family burden among family members of people with mental illness. *Journal of Nervous and Mental Disease, 202(10), 710–717. doi:10.1097/NMD.0000000000000189*

van Os, J., Pedersen, C. B., & Mortensen, P. B. (2004). Confirmation of synergy between urbanicity and familial liability in the causation of psychosis. *American Journal of Psychiatry, 161,* 2312–2314.

van Praag, H. (2008). Neurogenesis and exercise: Past and future directions. *Neuromolecular Medicine, 10,* 128–140.

van Praag, H., Lucero, M. J., Yeo, G. W., Stecker, K., Heivand, N., Zhao, C., Yip, E., Afanador, M., Schroeter, H., Hammerstone, J., & Gage, F. H. (2007). Plant-derived flavanol (?)epicatechin enhances angiogenesis and retention of spatial memory in mice. *Journal of Neuroscience, 27,* 5869–5878.

Varnum, M. E. W., Grossmann, I., Kitayama, S., & Nisbett, R. E. (2010). The original of cultural differences in cognition: The social orientation hypothesis. *Current Directions in Psychological Science, 19,* 9–13.

Vauclair, J. (1996). *Animal cognition: An introduction to modern comparative psychology.* Cambridge, MA: Harvard University Press.

Vaughn, L. K., Denning, G., Stuhr, K. L., et al. (2010). Endocannabinoid signaling: Has it got rhythm? British *Journal of Pharmacology, 160,* 530–543.

Vedaa, Øystein; West Saxvig, Ingvild; Wilhelmsen-Langeland, Ane; et al. (2012). School start time, sleepiness and functioning in Norwegian adolescents. *Scandinavian Journal of Educational Research, 56,* 55–67.

Verona, E., Joiner, T. E., Johnson, F., & Bender, T. W. (2006). Gender specific gene-environment interactions on laboratory-assessed aggression. *Biological Psychology, 71,* 33–41.

Vetere, A. (2001). Structural family therapy. *Child Psychology and Psychiatry Review, 6,* 133–139.

Vohs, K. D., Redden, J. P., & Rahinel, R. (2013). Physical order produces healthy choices, generosity, and conventionality, whereas disorder produces creativity. *Psychological Science, 24,* 1860–1867. doi:10.1177/0956797613480186

Voight, B. F., Kudaravalli, S., Wen, X., & Pritchard, J. K. (2006). A map of recent positive selection in the human genome. *PLoS Biology, 4,* e72.

Volkow, N., Wang, G., Kollins, S., Wigal, T., Newcorn, J., Telang, F., Fowler, J., Zhu, W., Logan, J., Ma, Y., Pradhan, K., Wong, C., & Swanson, J. (2009). Evaluating dopamine reward pathway in ADHD: Clinical implications. JAMA: *Journal of the American Medical Association, 302,* 1084–1091.

Volkow, Nora D.; Chang, Linda; Wang, Gene-Jack; et al. (2001). Association of dopamine transporter reduction with psychomotor impairment in methamphetamine abusers. *American Journal of Psychiatry, 158,* 377–382.

Volpato, V., Macchiarelli, R., Guatelli-Steinberg, D., et al. (2012). Hand to mouth in a Neandertal: Right-handedness in Regourdou. *PLoS One, 7,* e43949.

von Dawans, B., Fischbacher, U., Kirschbaum, C., Fehr, E., & Heinrichs, M. (2012). *The social dimension of stress reactivity: Acute stress increases prosocial behavior in humans* [Electronic publication ahead of print]. Psychological Science, 1–10. doi:10.1177/0956797611431576

Voorspoels, W., Vanpaemel, W., & Storms, G. (2008). Exemplars and prototypes in natural language concepts: A typicality-based evaluation. *Psychonomic Bulletin & Review, 15,* 630–637.

Vorona, Robert D.; Szklo-Coxe, Mariana; Wu, Andrew; et al. (2011). Dissimilar teen crash rates in two neighboring southeastern Virginia cities with different high school start times. *Journal of Clinical Sleep Medicine, 7, 145.*

Vos, S. P. F., Huibers, M. J. H., Diels, L., & Arntz, A. (2012). A randomized clinical trial of cognitive behavioral therapy and interpersonal psychotherapy for panic disorder with agoraphobia. *Psychological Medicine, 1*(1), 1–12.

Wachtel, P. L. (1977). *Psychoanalysis and behavior therapy: Toward an integration.* New York, NY: Basic Books.

Wachtel, P. L. (1997). Psychoanalysis, behavior therapy, and the relational world. Washington, DC: *American Psychological Association.*

Wagenaar, Willem A. (1986). My memory: A study of autobiographical memory over six years. *Cognitive Psychology, 18,* 225–252.

Wagenmakers, Eric-Jan; Wetzels, Ruud; Borsboom, D.; & van der Maas, H. (2011). Why psychologists must change the way they analyze their data: The case of psi. *Journal of Personality and Social Psychology, 100,* 426–432.

Wagner, Ullrich; Gais, Steffen; Haider, Hilde; et al. (2004). Sleep inspires insight. *Nature, 427,* 352–355.

Wahlstrom, Kyla (2010). School start time and sleepy teens. *Archives of Pediatrics & Adolescent Medicine, 164,* 676–677.

Wai, J., Cacchio, M., Putallaz, M., & Makel, M. C. (2010). Sex differences in the right tail of cognitive abilities: A 30 year examination. *Intelligence, 38,* 412–423.

Waite, L. J., & Joyner, K. (2001). Emotional satisfaction and physical pleasure in sexual unions: Time horizon, sexual behavior, and sexual exclusivity. *Journal of Marriage & the Family, 63,* 247–264.

Walker, Anne (1994). Mood and well-being in consecutive menstrual cycles: Methodological and theoretical implications. *Psychology of Women Quarterly, 18,* 271–290.

Walker, E. G., Savole, T., & Davis, D. (1994). Neuromotor precursors of schizophrenia. *Schizophrenia Bulletin, 20,* 441–451.

Walker, E. G., Shapiro, D., Esterberg, M., & Trotman, H. (2010). Neurodevelopment and schizophrenia: Broadening the focus. *Current Directions in Psychological Science, 19,* 204–208.

Waller, B. M., Parr, L. A., Gothard, K. M., Burrows, A. M., & Fuglevand, A. J. (2008). Mapping the contribution of single muscles to facial movements in the rhesus macaque. *Physiology & Behavior, 95,* 93–100.

Wallner, B., & Machatschke, I. H. (2009). The evolution of violence in men: The function of central cholesterol and serotonin. Progress in Neuro-*Psychopharmacology & Biological Psychiatry, 33,* 391–397.

Wallston, K. A., Wallston, B. S., & DeVellis, R. (1978). Development of the Multidimensional Health Locus of Control (MHLC) scales. *Health Education Monographs, 6,* 160–170.

Walsh, T., McClellan, J. M., McCarthy, S. E., Addington, A. M., Pierce, S. B., et al. (2008). Rare structural variants disrupt multiple genes in neurodevelopmental pathways in schizophrenia. *Science, 320,* 539–543.

Walton, D. E. (1978). An exploratory study: Personality factors and theoretical orientations of therapists. Psychotherapy: Theory, Research, and Practice, 15, 390–395.

Wampold, B. E. (2001). The great psychotherapy debate: Models, methods, and findings. Mahwah, NJ: Erlbaum.

Wampold, B. E. (2010). The research evidence for the common factors models: A historically situated perspective. In B. M. Duncan, S. D. Miller, M. A. Hubble & B. E. Wampold, (Eds). The Heart and Soul of Therapy. (2nd ed., 49–82). Washington, DC: American Psychological Association.

Wampold, B. E. (2012). Humanism as a common factor in psychotherapy. *Psychotherapy Theory Research Practice Training, 49*(4), 445–449.

Wampold, B. E., Minami, T., Baskin, T. W., & Tierney, S. C. (2002). A meta-(re)analysis of the effects of cognitive therapy versus "other therapies" for depression. *Journal of Affective Disorders, 68,* 159–165.

Wampold, B. E., Monding, W., Moody, M., Stich, I., Benson, K., & Ahn, H. (1997). A meta-analysis of outcome studies comparing bona fide psychotherapies: Empirically "all must have prizes." *Psychological Bulletin, 122,* 203–215.

Wang, Alvin Y.; Thomas, Margaret H.; & Ouellette, Judith A. (1992). The keyword mnemonic and retention of second-language vocabulary words. *Journal of Educational Psychology, 84,* 520–528.

Wang, P. S., Gruber, M. J., Powers, R. E., Schoenbaum, M., Speier, A., Wells, K. B., & Kessler, R. C. (2008). Disruption of existing mental health treatments and failure to initiate new treatment after hurricane Katrina. *American Journal of Psychiatry, 165,* 34–41.

Wang, Qi (2008). Being American, being Asian: The bicultural self and autobiographical memory in Asian Americans. *Cognition, 107,* 743–751.

Wang, Y. C. [Claire], Colditz, G. A., & Kuntz, K. M. (2007). Forecasting the obesity epidemic in the aging U.S. population. *Obesity, 15,* 2855–2865.

Ward-Begnoche, W. L., Pasold, T. L., McNeill, V., Peck, K. D., Razzaq, S., Fry, E. M. & Young, K. L. (2009). Childhood obesity treatment literature review. In L. C. James & J. C. Linton (Eds.), *Handbook of obesity intervention for the lifespan* (pp. 1–16). New York, NY: Springer.

Ward, D. M., Ferris, M. J., Nold, S. C., & Bateson, M. M. (1998). A natural view of microbial biodiversity within hot spring cyanobacterial mat communities. *Microbiology and Molecular Biology Reviews, 62,* 1353–1370.

Warren, Gayle H., & Raynes, Anthony E. (1972). Mood changes during three conditions of alcohol intake. *Quarterly Journal of Studies on Alcohol, 33,* 979–989.

Waschbusch, D. A., & Hill, G. P. (2003). Empirically supported, promising, and unsupported treatments for children with attention-deficit/hyperactivity disorder. In S. O. Lilienfeld, S. J. Lynn, & J. M. Lohr (Eds.), *Science and pseudoscience in clinical psychology* (pp. 333–362). New York, NY: Guilford Press.

Washington University School of Medicine. (2003). *Epilepsy surgery* [Online factsheet]. Retrieved September 29, 2003, from *http://neurosurgery.wustl.edu/clinprog/epilepsysurg.htm*

Wasik, B. A., Bond, M. A., & Hindman, A. (2006). The effects of a language and literacy intervention on Head Start children and teachers. *Journal of Educational Psychology, 98,* 63–74.

Waterhouse, L. (2006). Multiple intelligences, the Mozart effect, and emotional intelligence: A critical review. *Educational Psychologist, 41,* 207–225.

Waters, A. J., Gobet, F., & Leyden, G. (2002). Visuospatial abilities of chess players. *British Journal of Psychology, 93,* 557–565.

Watson, A. C., Miller, F. E., & Lyons, J. S. (2005). Adolescent Attitudes Toward Serious Mental Illness. *Journal of Nervous and Mental Disease, 193,* 769–772.

Watve, M. G., & Yajnik, C. S. (2007). Evolutionary origins of insulin resistance: A behavioral switch hypothesis. *BMC Evolutionary Biology, 7,* 1–13.

Watzlawick, P., Beavin, J., & Jackson, D. D. (1967). *Pragmatics of human communication: A study of interactional patterns, pathologies, and paradoxes.* New York, NY: Norton.

Watzlawick, P., Weakland, J. H., & Fisch, R. (1974). *Change: Principles of problem formation and problem resolution.* New York, NY: Norton.

Wegner, Daniel M.; Fuller, Valeria A.; & Sparrlow, Betsy (2003). Clever hands: Uncontrolled intelligence in facilitated communication. *Journal of Personality and Social Psychology, 85,* 5–19.

Wehr, Thomas A.; Duncan, Wallace C.; Sher, Leo; et al. (2001). A circadian signal of change of season in patients with seasonal affective disorder. *Archives of General Psychiatry, 58,* 1108–1114.

Weinberg, M. K., Tronick, E. Z., Cohn, J. F., & Olson, K. L. (1999). Gender differences in emotional expressivity and self-regulation during early infancy. *Developmental Psychology, 35,* 175–188.

Weinsier, R. L., Hunter, G. R., Desmond, R. A., Byrne, N. M., Zuckerman, P. A., & Darnell, B. (2002). Free-living activity expenditure in women successful and unsuccessful at maintaining a normal body weight. *American Journal of Clinical Nutrition, 75,* 499–504.

Weisman, A. G., Lopez, S. R., Ventura, J., Nuechterlein, K. H., Goldstein, M. J., & Hwang, S. (2000). A comparison of psychiatric symptoms between Anglo-Americans and Mexican-Americans with schizophrenia. *Schizophrenia Bulletin, 26,* 817–824.

Weiss, S. J., Wilson, P., & Morrison, D. (2004). Maternal tactile stimulation and the neurodevelopment of low birth weight infants. *Infancy, 5,* 85–107.

Weisz, J. R., Weiss, B., Han, S. S., Granger, D. A., & Morton, T. (1995). Effects of psychotherapy with children and adolescents revisited: A meta-analysis of treatment outcome studies. *Psychological Bulletin, 117,* 450–468.

Wells, Gary L., & Olson, Elisabeth A. (2003). Eyewitness testimony. *Annual Review of Psychology, 54,* 277–295.

Wells, Gary L.; Small, Mark; Penrod, Steven; et al. (1998). Eyewitness identification procedures: Recommendations for lineups and photospreads. *Law and Human Behavior, 22,* 602–647.

Wenzel, Amy (2005). Autobiographical memory tasks in clinical research. In A. Wenzel and D. C. Rubin (Eds.), *Cognitive methods and their application to clinical research.* Washington, DC: American Psychological Association.

West-Eberhard, M. J. (2005). The maintenance of sex as a developmental trap due to sexual selection. *Quarterly Review of Biology, 80,* 47–53.

Westen, D., Novotny, C. M., & Thompson-Brenner, H. (2004). The empirical status of empirically supported psychotherapies: Assumptions, findings, and reporting in controlled clinical trials. *Psychological Bulletin, 130,* 631–663.

Westerman, M. A., Foote, J. P., & Winston, A. (1995). Change in coordination across phases of psychotherapy and outcome: Two mechanisms for the role played by patients' contribution to the alliance. *Journal of Consulting and Clinical Psychology, 63,* 672–675.

Westwell, M. (2007). How too many interruptions is like a "kick in the head." Oxford Research Group. Retrieved from http://www.iii-p.org/research/cxo_reports/Oxford-Interrupt-CxO-April2007.pdf

Wetzels, Ruud; Matzke, Dora; Lee, Michael D.; et al. (2011). Statistical evidence in experimental psychology: An empirical comparison using 855 t tests. *Perspectives on Psychological Science, 6,* 291–298.

Whaley, A. L., & Davis, K. E. (2007). Cultural competence and evidence-based practice in mental health services: A complementary perspective. *American Psychologist, 62,* 563–574.

White, A., Horner, V., & de Waal, F. B. (2005). Conformity to cultural norms of tool use in chimpanzees. *Nature, 437,* 737–740.

Whitlock, Jonathan R.; Heynen, Arnold J.; Shuler, Marshall G.; & Bear, Mark F. (2006, August 25). Learning induces long-term potentiation in the hippocampus. *Science, 313,* 1093–1098.

Whitson, J. A., & Galinsky, A. D. (2008). Lacking control increases illusory pattern perception. *Science, 322,* 115–117.

Whorf, B. L. (1956). *Language, thought, and reality.* New York, NY: MIT Press-Wiley.

Widaman, K. F. (2009). Phenylketonuria in children and mothers. *Current Directions in Psychological Science, 18,* 48–52.

Wiederhold, B., & Wiederhold, M. (2008). Virtual reality with fMRI: A breakthrough cognitive treatment tool. *Virtual Reality, 12,* 259–267.

Wigal, T., Greenhill, L., Chuang, S., McGough, J., Vitiello, B., Skrobala, A., . . . Stehli, A. (2006). Safety and tolerability of methylphenidate in preschool children with ADHD. *Journal of the American Academy of Adolescent Psychiatry, 45, 1294.*

Wilhelm, Ines; Diekelmann, Susanne; Molzow, Ina; et al. (2011). Sleep selectively enhances memory expected to be of future relevance. *The Journal of Neuroscience, 31,* 1563–1569.

Williams, S. L., Turner, S. M., & Peer, D. F. (1985). Guided mastery and performance desensitization treatments for severe acrophobia. *Journal of Consulting and Clinical Psychology, 53,* 234–247.

Wilson, E. O. (1975). *Sociobiology: The new synthesis.* Cambridge, MA: Harvard University Press.

Wilson, G. T., & O'Leary, K. D. (1980). *Principles of behavior therapy.* Englewood Cliffs, NJ: Prentice Hall.

Wilson, G. T., Grilo, C. M., & Vitousek, K. M. (2007). Psychological treatment of eating disorders. *American Psychologist, 62,* 199–216.

Wilson, M. A., & McNaughton, B. L. (1993). Dynamics of the hippocampal ensemble code for space. *Science, 261,* 1055–1058.

Wing, H. (1969). *Conceptual learning and generalization.* Baltimore, MD: Johns Hopkins University Press.

Winner, E. (1998). *Psychological aspects of giftedness.* New York, NY: Basic Books.

Winner, E. (2000). The origins and ends of giftedness. *American Psychologist, 55,* 159–169.

Winter, B., Breitenstein, C., Mooren, F. C., Voelker, K., Fobker, M., Lechtermann, A., Krueger, K., Fromme, A., Korsukewitz, C., Floel, A., & Knecht, S. (2007). High impact running improves learning. *Neurobiology of Learning and Memory, 87,* 597–609.

Winterer, G. (2010). Why do patients with schizophrenia smoke? *Current Opinion in Psychiatry, 23,* 112–119.

Wirth, S., Yanike, M., Frank, L., Smith, A., Brown, E., & Suzuki, W. (2003). Single neurons in the monkey hippocampus and learning of new associations. *Science, 300,* 1578–1581.

Wirz-Justice, A. (2009). From the basic neuroscience of circadian clock function to light therapy for depression: On the emergence of chronotherapeutics. *Journal of Affective Disorders, 116,* 159–160.

Wolke, D., & Sapouna, M. (2008). Big men feeling small: Childhood bullying experience, muscle dysmorphia and other mental health problems in bodybuilders. *Psychology of Sport and Exercise, 9,* 595–604.

Woodberry, K. A., Giuliano, A. J., & Seidman, L. J. (2008). Premorbid IQ in schizophrenia. *American Journal of Psychiatry, 165,* 579–587.

Woodruff, E. J. (2014). Testing a comprehensive model of muscle dysmorphia symptomatology in a nonclinical sample of men. *Dissertation Abstracts International Section A, 74,* 7-A(E).

Woods, S. C., Schwartz, M. W., Baskin, D. G., & Seeley, R. J. (2000). Food intake and the regulation of body weight. *Annual Review of Psychology, 51,* 255–277.

Woody, Erik Z., & Bowers, Kenneth S. (1994). A frontal assault on dissociated control. In S. J. Lynn & J. W. Rhue (Eds.), *Dissociation: Clinical, theoretical and research perspectives.* New York: Guilford.

Woody, Erik Z., & Sadler, Pamela (2012). Dissociation theories of hypnosis. In M. R. Nash, M. Nash, & A. Barnier (Eds.), *The Oxford handbook of hypnosis: Theory, research, and Practice.* New York: Oxford University Press.

Wright, A. A., & Katz, J. S. (2007). Generalization hypothesis of abstract-concept learning: Learning strategies and related issues in Macaca mulatta, Cebus apella, and Columba livia. *Journal of Comparative Psychology, 121,* 387–397.

Wright, I. C., Rabe-Hesketh, S., Woodruff, P. W., David, A. S., Murray, R. M., & Bullmore, E. T. (2000). Meta-analysis of regional brain volumes in schizophrenia. *American Journal of Psychiatry, 157,* 16–25.

Wu, A., Ying, Z., & Gomez-Pinilla, F. (2008). Docosahexaenoic acid dietary supplementation enhances the effects of exercise on synaptic plasticity and cognition. *Neuroscience, 155,* 751–759.

Wubbolding, R. E. (2005). The power of belonging. International *Journal of Reality Therapy, 24, 43–44. 1958–2013. doi:10.1177/0956797613481608*

Yager, C. (2013). An evaluation of the effectiveness of voice-to-text programs at reducing incidences of distracted driving. (Research Report SWUTC/13/600451–00011–1). Retrieved from Texas A&M Transportation Institute website: http://swutc.tamu.edu/publications/technicalreports/600451–00011–1.pdf

Yager, J. (2008). Binge eating disorder: The search for better treatments. *American Journal of Psychiatry, 165,* 4–6.

Yalom, I. (1985). *The theory and practice of group psychotherapy.* New York, NY: Basic Books.

Yamamoto, K., & Chimbidis, M. E. (1966). Achievement, intelligence, and creative thinking in fifth grade children: A correlational study. *Merrill-Palmer Quarterly, 12,* 233–241.

Yang, Q., & Chen, F. (2001). Behavior problems in children with simple obesity. *Chinese Journal of Clinical Psychology, 9,* 273–274.

Yapko, Michael (1994). *Suggestions of abuse: True and false memories of childhood sexual trauma.* New York: Simon & Schuster.

Yartz, A. R., & Hawk, L. W., Jr. (2001). Psychophysiological assessment of anxiety: Tales from the heart. In M. M. Antony, S. M. Orsillo, & L. Roemer (Eds.), *Practitioner's guide to empirically-based measures of anxiety* (pp. 25–30). New York, NY: Kluwer Academic/Plenum.

Yerkes, R., & Dodson, J. (2007). The relation of strength of stimulus to rapidity of habit-formation. In D. Smith & M. Bar-Eli (Eds.), *Essential readings in sport and exercise psychology* (pp. 13–22). Champaign, IL: Human Kinetics. (Reprinted from *Journal of Comparative Neurology and Psychology, 18, 459–482).*

Yoo, S. H., Matsumoto, D., & LeRoux, J. A. (2006). The influence of emotion recognition and emotion regulation on intercultural adjustment. *International Journal of Intercultural Relations, 30,* 345–363.

Yoon, J., Koo, B., Shin, M., Shin, Y., Ko, H., & Shin, Y. (2014). Effect of constraint-induced movement therapy and mirror therapy for patients with subacute stroke. *Annals of Rehabilitation Medicine, 38*(4), 458–466.

Young, G. (2009). Coma. In Schiff, N., & Laureys, S. (Eds.), *Disorders of consciousness. Annals of the New York Academy of Sciences* (pp. 32–47). New York: Wiley-Blackwell.

Young, Larry J., & Francis, Darlene D. (2008). The biochemistry of family commitment and youth competence: Lessons from animal models. In K. Kline (Ed.), *Authoritative communities: The scientific case for nurturing the whole child.* New York: Springer Science + Business Media.

Young, M. C. (1998). *The Guinness book of world records.* New York: Bantam Books.

Young, S. G., & Hugenberg, K. (2010). Mere social categorization modulates identification of facial expressions of emotion. *Journal of Personality and Social Psychology, 99, 964–977. doi:10.1037/a0020400*

Yu, D. W., & Shepard, G. H. (1998). Is beauty in the eye of the beholder? *Nature, 396,* 321–322.

Yu, M.; Zhu, X.; Li, J.; et al. (1996). Perimenstrual symptoms among Chinese women in an urban area of China. *Health Care for Women International, 17,* 161–172.

Yu, Q., & Yuan, D.-H. (2008). The impact of the emotional intelligence of employees and their manager on the job performance of employees. *Acta Psychologica Sinica, 40,* 74–83.

Zajac, Rachel, & Henderson, Nicola (2009). Don't it make my brown eyes blue: Co-witness misinformation about a target's appearance can impair target-absent line-up performance. *Memory, 17,* 266–278.

Zald, D. H., Cowan, R. L., Riccardi, P., Baldwin, R. M., Ansari, M. S., Li, R., . . . Kessler, R. M. (2008). Midbrain dopamine receptor availability is inversely associated with novelty-seeking traits in humans. *The Journal of Neuroscience, 28,* 14372–14378.

Zatorre, R., Belin, P., & Penhune, V. (2002). Structure and function of the auditory cortex: Music and speech. *Trends in Cognitive Sciences, 6,* 37–46.

Zellner, D. A., Loaiza, S., Gonzalez, Z., Pita, J., Morales, J., Pecora, D., & Wolf, A. (2006). Food selection changes under stress. *Physiology and Behavior, 87*(4), 789–793.

Zellner, D. A., Saito, S., & Gonzalez, J. (2007). The effect of stress on men's food selection. *Appetite, 49*(3), 696–699.

Zhai, F. (2008). Effects of Head Start on the outcomes of participants. *Dissertation Abstracts International Section A: Humanities and Social Sciences, 69,* 384.

Zhu, L. X.; Sharma, S.; Stolina, M.; et al. (2000). Delta-9-tetrahydrocannabinol inhibits antitumor immunity by a CB2 receptor-mediated, cytokine-dependent pathway. *Journal of Immunology, 165,* 373–380.

Zigler, E., & Styfco, S. J. (2008). America's head start program: An effort for social justice. In C. Wainryb, J. G. Smetana, & E. Turiel (Eds.), *Social development, social inequalities, and social justice* (pp. 53–80). New York, NY: Taylor & Francis Group/Erlbaum.

Zinbarg, R. (1993). Information processing and classical conditioning: Implications for exposure therapy and the integration of cognitive therapy and behavior therapy. *Journal of Behavior Therapy and Experimental Psychiatry, 24,* 129–139.

Zonnevylle-Bender, M. J. S., van Goozen, S. H. M., Cohen-Kettenis, P. T., van Elburg, A., de Wildt, M., Stevelmans, E., & van Engeland, H. (2004). Emotional functioning in anorexia nervosa patients: Adolescents compared to adults. *Depression and Anxiety, 19,* 35–42.

Zuckerman, M. (2006). Sensation seeking in entertainment. In J. Bryant & P. Vorderer (Eds.), *Psychology of entertainment* (pp. 367–387). Mahwah, NJ: Erlbaum.

Zuckerman, M. (2007a). Sensation seeking. In M. Zuckerman (Ed.), *Sensation seeking and risky behavior* (pp. 3–49). Washington, DC: American Psychological Association.

Zuckerman, M. (2007b). Sensation seeking and risky driving, sports, and vocations. In M. Zuckerman (Ed.), *Sensation seeking and risky behavior* (pp. 73–106). Washington, DC: American Psychological Association.

Credits

TEXT AND ART

CHAPTER 3 **p. 69, Figure 3.4:** (Basson, et al., 2002).

CHAPTER 5 **p. 124, Figure 5.2:** Adapted from Lilienfeld, Lynn, Namy, & Wolf (2009); **p. 129, Figure 5.5:** Lilienfeld, Lynn, Namy, & Woolf (2009); **p. 130, Figure 5.6:** Adapted from Lilienfeld, S., Lynn, S., Namy, L., & Woolf, N. (2009); **p. 135, text:** President John F. Kennedy. **p. 138, Figure 5.11:** Based on Gazzaniga, M. (1983).

CHAPTER 6 **p. 165, Figure 6.1:** Based on Jessica McFarlane, Carol Lynn Martin, and Tannis M. Williams, "Mood changes in men and women," Psychology of Women Quarterly, 12, (1988), pp. 201–223; **p. 171, Figure 6.4:** (Payne et al., 2008).

CHAPTER 9 **p. 247, text:** Chomsky, N. (1957). Syntactic structures. Oxford, England: Mouton; Chomsky, N., Place, U. T., & choneberger, T. (Eds.). (2000). The Chomsky–Place correspondence 1993–1994. Analysis of Verbal Behavior, 17, 7–38; **p. 263, text:** Epstude, K., & Roese, N. J. (2008). The functional theory of counterfactual thinking. Personality and Social Psychology Review, 12, 168–192; **p. 264, text:** Hamilton, J. (2008, October 16). Multitasking in the car: Just like drunken driving. NPR: Morning Edition. Retrieved from http:/www.npr.org/templates/story/story.php?storyId=95702512; **p. 266, text:** Chen, J.-Q., Moran, S., & Gardner, H. (Eds.) (2009). Multiple intelligences around the world. San Francisco, CA: Jossey-Bass; **p. 266, text:** Goleman, D. (1997). Emotional intelligence. New York, NY: Bantam; **p. 268-269, text:** Definition of mental retardation. DSM-IV, APA. Published by the American Psychological Association; **p. 274, text:** Data from Genetics and intelligence: A review; **p. 277, text:** Plomin, R. (1997). Identifying genes for cognitive abilities and disabilities. In R. J. Sternberg & E. L. Grigorenko (Eds.), Intelligence: Heredity and environment (pp. 89–104). New York, NY: Cambridge University Press. (p. 89); **p. 277, text:** Flynn, J. R. (1999). Searching for justice: The discovery of IQ gains over time. American Psychologist, 54, 5–20; **p. 278, text:** Halpern, D. F., Benbow, C. P., Geary, D. C., Gur, R. C., Hyde, J. S., & Gernsbacher, M. A. (2007). The science of sex differences in science and mathematics. Psychological Science in the Public Interest, 8, 1–51. (p. 41); **p. 279, text:** The American Psychiatric Association (2013); **p. 280, text:** Based on APA, DSM5, 2013; **p. 281, text:** P. M., & Robinson, N. M. (1985). Psychosocial development in intellectually gifted children. In F. D. Horowitz & M. O'Brien (Eds.), Gifted and talented: Developmental perspectives (pp. 149–195). Washington, DC: American Psychological Association., (p. 181). Reprinted with permission; **p. 284, text:** Dietrich, A., & Kanso, R. (2010). A review of EEG, ERP, and neuroimaging studies of creativity and insight. Psychological Bulletin, 136, 822–848. (p. 845).

CHAPTER 10 **p. 294, Figure 10.1:** After Hebb, D.O. (1955). Drives and the CNS (conceptual nervous system). Psychological Review, 62, 243–254. Copyright © 1955 American Psychological Association. Reprinted with permission; **p. 299, text:** American Psychiatric Association (APA). (2013). Diagnostic and statistical manual of mental disorders (5th ed.), (DSM-5). Arlington, VA: Author; **p. 301, Figure 10.3:** CDC/National Center for Health Statistics, National Health Education Standards and The National Health and Nutrition Examination Survey (NHANES); **p. 305, Figure 10.4:** Based on http:/www.durex.com/cm/gss2005result.pdf. Used with permission of Durex.com; **p. 305, text:** Michael, R.T., Gagnon, J.H., Laumann, E.O., & Kolata, G. (1994). Sex in America. Boston, MA: Little Brown; 298 Carter, 1998; 325 Elfenben, H.A., & Ambady, N. (2002). On the universality and cultural specificity of emotion recognition: A meta-analysis. Psychological bulletin, 128, 203–235. (p. 228). Copyright © 2002 American Psychological Association. Reprinted with permission.

CHAPTER 11 **p. 354, Figure 11.8:** (a & b) Linton, Marigold (1978), "Real World Memory After Six Years: An In Vivo Study of Very Long Term Memory," in Practical Aspects of Memory, eds., Michael M. Gruneberg, Peter E. Morris and Robert N. Sykes, New York, NY: Academic Press/Elsevier, 77–83. Reprinted by permission of Elsevier.

CHAPTER 13 **p. 392, Table 13.1:** "Estimated Annual Deaths in the United States Due to Behavior-Related Risk Factors" from "The Preventable Causes of Death in the United States: Comparative Risk Assessment of Dietary, Lifestyle, and Metabolic Risk Factors" Derived from data noted in Danaei G, Ding EL, Mozaffarian D, Taylor B, Rehm J, et al. (2009), "The Preventable Causes of Death in the United States: Comparative Risk Assessment of Dietary, Lifestyle, and Metabolic Risk Factors." PLoS Med 6(4): e1000058. doi:10.1371/journal.pmed.1000058; **p. 392, Table 13.2:** "Health Costs of Tobacco Use" http://www.cdc.gov/tobacco/data_statistics/fact_sheets/fast_facts/index.htm. Retrieved June 20, 2011; **p. 393, Figure 13.1:** "Smoking and the Movies" from "Does watching smoking in movies promote teenage smoking?" From "Does Watching Smoking in Movies Promote Teenage Smoking?" by T. F. Heatherton & J. D. Sargent (2009) *Current Directions in Psychological Science*, 18, 63–67. Copyright © 2009 by Sage Publications, Inc. Reprinted by permission of SAGE Publications; **p. 395, Table 13.3:** "The Health Locus of Control Scale" adapted from "Development of the Multidimensional Health Locus of Control (MHLC) Scales" Adapted from "Development of the Multidimensional Health Locus of Control (MHLC) Scales" by K. A. Wallston, B. S. Wallston, & R. DeVellis (1978), *Health Education & Behavior*, 6(1), 160–170. Copyright © 1978 by Sage Publications. Reprinted by permission of SAGE Publications; **p. 401, Figure 13.2:** "Arousal and Performance" (graph depicting difficult task/easy task) From p. 39 in *Psychology*, 3rd ed. by Saundra Ciccarelli and J. Noland White. Copyright © 2012. Printed and electronically reproduced by permission of Pearson Education, Inc., Upper Saddle River, New Jersey; **p. 402, Table 13.4:** "Life-Stress Inventories for the General Adult Population and for College Students" from "A Life-Stress Instrument for Classroom Use" From "A Life-Stress Instrument for Classroom Use" by M. Renner & R. Mackin (1998) *Teaching of Psychology*, 25 (1), 46–48. Copyright © 1998. Reprinted by permission of Taylor & Francis Group. http://www.informaworld.com; **p. 402, Table 13.4:** "Life-Stress Inventories for the General Adult Population and for College Students" from "The Social Readjustment Rating Scale" From "The Social Readjustment Rating Scale" by T. H. Holmes & R. H. Rahe (1967), *Journal of Psychosomatic Research*, 11, 213–218. Copyright © 1967. Reprinted by permission of Elsevier; **p. 417, Figure 13.6:** "Seeing Images Where There are None" from "Lacking Control Increases Illusory Pattern Perception" From "Lacking Control Increases Illusory Pattern Perception" by J. A. Whitson & A. D. Galinsky (2008) *Science*, 322, 115–117. Copyright © 2008. Reprinted with permission from AAAS; **p. 418, Figure 13.7:** "Exercising Compensatory Control" from "Compensatory Control: Achieving Order Through the Mind, Our Institutions, and the Heavens" Figure 1 from "Compensatory Control: Achieving Order Through the Mind, Our Institutions, and the Heavens" by A. C. Kay, J. A. Whitson, D. Gaucher, & A. D. Galinsky (2009) *Current Directions in Psychological Science*, 18(5), 264–268. Copyright © 2009 by Sage Publications. Reprinted by permission of SAGE Publications.

CHAPTER 15 **p. 462, Table 15.3:** "Varieties of Personality Disorders with Brief Descriptions of Each" Reprinted with permission from *The Diagnostic and Statistical Manual of Mental Disorders*, Fourth Edition, Text Revision (Copyright © 2000). American Psychiatric Association; **p. 464, Figure 15.2:** "Emotional Responses of Individuals with Anti-Social Personality Disorder" from "The psychopath as observer: Emotion and attention in picture processing" Adapted from Levenston, G. K., Patrick, C. J., Bradley, M. M., & Lang, P. J. (2000). The psychopath as observer: Emotion and attention in picture processing. *Journal of Abnormal Psychology*, 109 (3), 373–385; **p. 464, Figure 15.2:** "Emotional Responses of Individuals with Antisocial Personality Disorder" American Psychological Association (2011). http://www.apa.org/topics/suicide/signs.aspx; **p. 470, Figure 15.3:** "Anxiety Levels are Inherited in an Animal Model" from "Selection for Contextual Fear Conditioning Affects Anxiety-Like Behaviors and Gene Expression" From "Selection for Contextual Fear Conditioning Affects Anxiety-Like Behaviors and Gene Expression" by C. A. Ponder, C. L. Kliethermes, M. R. Drew, J. Muller, K. Das, V. B. Risbrough, J. C. Crabbe, T. C. Gilliam, & A. A. Palmer (2007) *Genes, Brain & Behavior*, 6(8), 736–749. Copyright © 2007 by John Wiley and Sons. Reprinted by permission of John Wiley and Sons; **p. 470, Table 15.5:** "What are We So Afraid Of?" from "The Epidemiology of DSM-IV Specific Phobia in the USA: Results from the National Epidemiologic Survey on Alcohol and Related Conditions" Adaptation ofTable 3 from "The Epidemiology of DSM-IV Specific Phobia in the USA: Results from the National Epidemiologic Survey on Alcohol and Related Conditions" by F. S. Stinson, et al. (2007) *Psychological Medicine*, 37, 1047–1059. Copyright © 2007 by Cambridge University Press. Reprinted with the permission of Cambridge University Press; **p. 474, Figure 15.7:** "Depression and the Brain" in "Neuroimaging and Depression: Current Status and Unresolved Issues" From "Neuroimaging and Depression: Current Status and Unresolved Issues" by I. Gotlib & J. Hamilton (2008) *Current Directions in Psychological Science*, 17, 159–163. Copyright © 2008 by Sage Publications. Reprinted by permission of SAGE Publications; **p. 475, Figure 15.9:** "Social Influences on Depression" from "Neighborhood Characteristics and Depression: An Examination of Stress Processes" From "Neighborhood Characteristics and Depression: An Examination of Stress Processes" by C. Cutrona, G. Wallace, & K. Wesner (2006) *Current Directions in Psychological Science*, 15 (4), 188–192. Copyright © 2006 by Sage Publications. Reprinted by permission of Sage Publications.

CHAPTER 16 **p. 491, text:** Raimy, V. C. (ed.). (1950). Training in clinical psychology (Boulder Conference). New York: Prentice-Hall; **p. 496, text:** Monroe, R. (1955). Schools of psychoanalytic thought. New York: Dryden; **p. 498, text:** Meador, B. D., & Rogers, C. R.

(1979). Person centered therapy. In J. R. Corsini (ed.), Current psychotherapies. Itasca, IL: F. E. Peacock Publishers; **p. 498, text:** Rogers, C. R. (1957). The necessary and sufficient conditions of therapeutic personality change. Journal of Consulting Psychology, 21, 95–103; **p. 498, text:** Rogers, C. R. (1942). Counseling and psychotherapy. New York: Houghton Mifflin; **p. 504, text:** Goldfried, M. R., & Davison, G. C. (1976). Clinical behavior therapy. New York: Holt, Rinehart, & Winston; **p. 511, Table 16.6:** Prochaska & Norcross, 2007; derived from Bechtold et al., 2001; Norcross, Karpiak, & Santoro, 2005; Norcross, Strausser, & Missar, 1988; **p. 512, Figure 16.4:** Based on Smith, M. L., Glass, G. V., & Miller, T. I. (1980). The benefi ts of psychotherapy. Baltimore: Johns Hopkins University Press; **p. 512, text:** Lewis Carroll, *Alice in Wonderland*; **p. 513, Table 16.7:** Based on data from Lilienfeld, 2007.

PHOTOGRAPHS AND CARTOONS

CHAPTER 3 p. 50: Maridav/Shutterstock; **p. 51:** Tono Balaguer/Age Fotostock; **p. 51 (bottom right):** Alex Segre/Alamy; **p. 56:** S. Harris/www.CartoonStock.com; **p. 57:** Figure from "GENIE: A PSYCHOLINGUISTIC STUDY OF A MODERN DAY "WILD CHILD," by Susan Curtiss, © 1977, Elsevier Science (USA), reproduced by permission of the publisher; **p. 59:** Mira/Alamy; **p. 59:** Michael Lusmore/Alamy; **p. 60:** Roz Chast/The New Yorker Collection/www.cartoonbank.com; **p. 61:** Henry Martin/The New Yorker Collection/www.cartoonbank.com; **p. 65:** Loisjoy Thurstun/Bubbles Photolibrary/Alamy; **p. 65:** Tom Prettyman/PhotoEdit, Inc.; **p. 68:** Peter Mueller/The New Yorker Collection/www.cartoonbank.com; **p. 70:** Morphart Creations inc./Shutterstock; **p. 73:** 1990 and 2011 by Mell Lazarus; **p. 75:** Jim Moulin/Dr. David Strayer; **p. 79:** Mick Stevens/The New Yorker Collection/www.cartoonbank.com; **p. 80:** James Marshall/The Image Works; **p. 80:** Courtesy The Yerkes National Primate Research Center, Emory University.

CHAPTER 4 p. 85: Gilbert Mayers/SuperStock; **p. 86:** Bettmann/Corbis; **p. 87:** North Wind Picture Archives; **p. 93a:** John Reader/Photo Researchers Inc.; **p. 93b:** © 1985 David L. Brill; **p. 93c:** ©Randall White; **p. 100 (left):** CNRI/SPL/Photo Researchers, Inc.; **p. 100 (right):** David Phillips/Photo Researchers, Inc.; **p. 103 (left):** FLPA/Bill Coster/age fotostock; **p. 103 (right):** FLPA/David Hosking/age fotostock; **p. 106:** Will & Deni McIntyre/Photo Researchers, Inc.; **p. 107:** FB-Studio/Alamy; **p. 110:** David Madison/Getty Images.

CHAPTER 5 p. 118, Unfig CO-05: Tom Grill/Corbis; **p. 119:** Barbara Penoyar/Stockbyte/Getty Images; **p. 120:** xpixel/Shutterstock; **p. 120:** Alexander Tsiaras/Science Source/Photo Researchers; **p. 124:** 20th Century Fox/Album/Newscom; **p. 125:** Biophoto Associates/Photo Researchers; **p. 126:** Bill Aron/PhotoEdit, Inc; **p. 131:** Jason Moore/ZUMA Press/Newscom; **p. 137:** Pearson Education; **p. 141:** BSIP/Photo Researchers, Inc.; **p. 148:** Dann Tardif/LWA/Corbis/Bridge/Glow Images.

CHAPTER 6 p. 158: Mehmetcan/Shutterstock; **p. 161:** Thomas Ives; **p. 161:** Jeff Greenberg/PhotoEdit, Inc.; **p. 162:** Sidney Harris/ScienceCartoonsPlus; **p. 163:** Heather Rousseau/MCT/Newscom; **p. 163:** Amy Etra/PhotoEdit, Inc.; **p. 165:** William Haefeli/The New Yorker Collection/www.cartoonbank.com; **p. 168:** Amana Images inc./Alamy; **p. 168:** Vera Kailova/Shutterstock; **p. 169:** amelaxa /Shutterstock; **p. 169:** Earl Roberge/Photo Researchers, Inc.; **p. 170:** Richard Hutchings/PhotoEdit, Inc.; **p. 171:** TheFinalMiracle/Shutterstock; **p. 173:** Dana Fradon/The New Yorker Collection/www.cartoonbank.com, **p. 173:** Betsy Streeter/www.CartoonStock.com; **p. 174:** J. Hobson/Photo Researchers, Inc.; **p. 178:** Bookstaver/AP Images; **p. 179:** Ernest R. Hilgard; **p. 183:** Marc Dozier/Alamy; **p. 183:** Images & Stories/Alamy; **p. 183:** Tibor Hirsch/Photo Researchers, Inc.; **p. 185:** David Pollack/Corbis; **p. 187:** Dana Fradon/The New Yorker Collection/www.cartoonbank.com; **p. 187:** Nemke/Shutterstock; **p. 187:** Jim Commentucci/Syracuse Newspapers/The Image Works; **p. 188:** The Granger Collection, NYC.

CHAPTER 9 p. 245, Opener: James King-Holmes/Science Source; **p. 248:** Sam Gross The New Yorker Collection/The Cartoon Bank; **p. 250:** Simon Cooper/Imagestate Media Partners Limited - Impact Photos/Alamy; **p. 253:** Michael K. Nichols/National Geographic Creative.

CHAPTER 10 p. 291, Opener: Photobac/Shutterstock; **p. 306:** Tim_Booth/Shutterstock; **p. 310:** Catherine Ursillo/Science Source.

CHAPTER 11 p. 326: Ojo Images/Glow Images, Inc.; **p. 327:** Burlington Police Department/HO/AP Images; **p. 329:** Photolibrary/Getty images; **p. 330:** Sidney Harris/ScienceCartoonsPlus; **p. 331:** Moviestore Collection Ltd/Alamy; **p. 332:** Fat Chance Productions/Flirt/Corbis; **p. 333:** Dr. Elizabeth Loftus; **p. 334:** Buddy Norris/Krt/Newscom; **p. 336:** Robert L. May/Modern Curriculum Press/Pearson Education; **p. 340:** Bruce Brander/Photo Researchers, Inc.; **p. 340:** Travis Gering; **p. 341:** Ablestock/Jupiter Images; **p. 342:** Emil Muench/Getty Images; **p. 346:** Humerus Cartoon Syndicate/Jennifer Berman; **p. 347:** "Contrasting Cortical Activity Associated with Category Memory and Recognition Memory" Paul J. Reber, Craig E.L. Stark, Larry R. Squire Learning & Memory. 1998. 5: 420–428. Cold Spring Harbor Press; **p. 350:** Sidney Harris/ScienceCartoonsPlus; **p. 351:** keith morris/Alamy; **p. 354:** Warren Miller/The New Yorker Collection/www.cartoonbank.com; **p. 355:** Karen Preus/The Image Works; **p. 355:** Dr. Elizabeth Loftus; **p. 357:** Mary Evans/Ronald Grant/Everett Collection; **p. 358:** David Sipress/The New Yorker Collection/www.cartoonbank.com; **p. 360:** Carolyn Rovee-Collier; **p. 361:** Jack Ziegler/The New Yorker Collection/www.cartoonbank.com; **p. 363:** Chuck Burton/AP Images.

Chapter 13 p. 390: stock_wales/Alamy; **p. 396:** Visions of America, LLC/Alamy; **p. 398:** James Woodson/Getty Images.; **p. 400:** Imagesource/Glow Images; **p. 401:** Cathy Yeulet/123 RF; **p. 407:** Lightwavemedia/Fotolia; **p. 409:** Photodisc/Getty Images; **p. 411:** John Lund/Stephanie Roeser/Glow Images; **p. 413:** Cindy Charles/PhotoEdit; **p. 414:** Tyler Olson/Shutterstock.

Chapter 15 p. 453: William DeShazer/MCT/Newscom; **p. 458:** Mandy Godbehear/Shutterstock; **p. 461:** UpperCut Images/Getty Images; **p. 463:** Narcissus, c.1597–99 (oil on canvas), Caravaggio, Michelangelo Merisi da (1571–1610)/Palazzo Barberini, Rome, Italy/Bridgeman Art Library; **p. 468:** Matsunaka Takeya/Aflo/Glow Images; **p. 469:** Darren Bridges Photography/Alamy; **p. 469:** David H. Lewis/Getty Images; **p. 473:** Stefanolunardi/Shutterstock; **p. 478:** Handout/Getty Images; **p. 479:** Kurt Snyder; **p. 479:** Grunnitus Studio/Science Source; **p. 481:** ImageBroker/Alamy; **p. 483:** Elaine Walker.

Chapter 16 p. 490, (CO-16a): Masterfile; **p. 490, (CO-16b):** Image Source/Alamy; **p. 491:** Cartoonbank; **p. 492:** Radius/SuperStock; **p. 494:** Claudette Barius/HBO/Courtesy Everett Collection; **p. 497:** Mangostock/Shutterstock; **p. 498 (top):** Mike Baldwin/CartoonStock; **p. 498 (bottom):** Bill Aron/PhotoEdit; **p. 500 (bottom):** Manchan/Digital Vision/Getty Images; **p. 501:** John Van Hasselt/Corbis; **p. 502 (center):** BrandX Pictures/Jupiter Images; **p. 503:** AJPhoto/Science Source; **p. 504 (center left):** Rainer Jensen/DPA/Corbis; **p. 509:** Michael A. Fenichel; **p. 512 (top):** Mary Evans Picture Library/Alamy; **p. 513 (top):** Jeff Greenberg/PhotoEdit; **p. 514 (center):** Miami Herald/MCT/Landov; **p. 514 (bottom):** John Foxx/Stockbyte/Getty Images; **p. 516:** Phase4Photography/Shutterstock; **p. 517:** Robert Pitts/Landov; **p. 520:** BSIP SA/Alamy; **p. 521 (top):** Vstock RV/Alamy; **p. 521 (bottom):** RR3 Wenn Photos/Newscom; **p. 522 (top):** Comstock Images/Th inkstock; **p. 522 (bottom):** Will & Deni McIntyre/Photo Researchers; **p. 524 (top):** Robert Sciarrino/Star Ledger/Corbis News/Corbis; **p. 524 (bottom):** Jim Clare/Nature Picture Library; **p. 525 (center left):** Radius/ SuperStock; **p. 525 (bottom left):** Claudette Barius/HBO/Courtesy Everett Collection; **p. 526 (center left):** Manchan/Digital Vision/Getty Images; **p. 526 (top right):** BrandX Pictures/ Jupiter Images; **p. 527 (center):** Jeff Greenberg/PhotoEdit; **p. 527 (bottom):** John Foxx/ Stockbyte/Getty Images; **p. 528 (right):** Will & Deni McIntyre/Photo Researchers.